MW01009330

GOVERNMENT BY THE PEOPLE

MyPoliSciLab®

AP EDITION
TWENTY-FIFTH EDITION

David B.
MAGLEBY
Brigham Young University

Paul C.
LIGHT
New York University

Christine L.
NEMACHECK
The College of William & Mary

PEARSON

Boston Columbus Indianapolis New York San Francisco
Upper Saddle River Amsterdam Cape Town Dubai London Madrid Milan
Munich Paris Montréal Toronto Delhi Mexico City São Paulo Sydney
Hong Kong Seoul Singapore Taipei Tokyo

Editorial Director: Craig Campanella
Editor-in-Chief: Dickson Musslewhite
Senior Acquisitions Editor: Vikram Mukhija
Assistant Editor: Beverly Fong
Editorial Assistant: Emily Sauerhoff
Editorial Assistant: Isabel Schwab
Director of Development: Sharon Geary
Director of Marketing: Brandy Dawson
Executive Marketing Manager: Wendy Gordon
Marketing Assistant: Zakiyyah Wiley
Senior Managing Editor: Ann Marie McCarthy
Senior Procurement Supervisor: Mary Fischer
Procurement Specialist: Mary Ann Gloriande
Creative Director: Blair Brown
Art Director: John Christiana, Kathryn Foot
Director of Digital Media: Brian Hyland
Senior Digital Media Editor: Paul DeLuca
Digital Media Editor: Alison Lorber
Multimedia Production Manager: Michael Granger
Media Project Manager: Joseph Selby
Full-Service Project Management: GEX Publishing Services
Composition: GEX Publishing Services
Printer/Binder: Courier / Kendallville
Cover Printer: Lehigh-Phoenix Color/Hagerstown
Text Font: Adobe Caslon Pro

Credits and acknowledgments borrowed from other sources and reproduced, with permission, in this textbook appear on appropriate page within text [or on page 632].

Copyright © 2014, 2011, 2009 by Pearson Education, Inc. All rights reserved. Printed in the United States of America. This publication is protected by Copyright, and permission should be obtained from the publisher prior to any prohibited reproduction; storage in a retrieval system; or transmission in any form or by any means, electronic, mechanical, photocopying, recording, or likewise. To obtain permission(s) to use material from this work, please submit a written request to Pearson Education, Inc., Permissions Department, One Lake Street, Upper Saddle River, New Jersey 07458, or you may fax your request to 201-236-3290.

Many of the designations by manufacturers and sellers to distinguish their products are claimed as trademarks. Where those designations appear in this book, and the publisher was aware of a trademark claim, the designations have been printed in initial caps or all caps.

Library of Congress Cataloging-in-Publication Data

Magleby, David B.
Government by the people / Magleby, Light, Nemacheck.—Twenty-fifth edition.
pages cm
Includes bibliographical references and index.
ISBN-13: 978-0-205-86578-9 (alk. paper)
ISBN-10: 0-205-86578-X (alk. paper)
ISBN-13: 978-0-205-93625-0 (alk. paper)
ISBN-10: 0-205-93601-6 (alk. paper)
1. United States—Politics and government—Textbooks. I. Light, Paul Charles.
II. Nemacheck, Christine L. III. Title.
JK276.G68 2014
320.473—dc23

2012040976

AP® is a trademark registered and/or owned by the College Board, which was not involved in the production of, and does not endorse, this product.

10 9 8 7 6 5 4 3 2

PearsonSchool.com/Advanced

Student Edition:
ISBN 10: 0-205-86577-1 (High School Binding)
ISBN 13: 978-0-205-86577-2 (High School Binding)

BRIEF CONTENTS

On MyPoliSciLab

- The Declaration of Independence
- The Constitution of the United States
- Federalist No. 10
- Federalist No. 15
- Federalist No. 51
- Federalist No. 78
- Anti-Federalist No. 17
- *Marbury* v. *Madison*
- *McCulloch* v. *Maryland*
- *Brown* v. *Board of Education*
- The Gettysburg Address
- Washington's Farewell Address

*** The icons listed here and throughout this book lead to learning resources on MyPoliSciLab.**

CONTENTS

*** The icons listed here and throughout this book lead to learning resources on MyPoliSciLab.**

On MyPoliSciLab

- The Declaration of Independence
- The Constitution of the United States
- Federalist No. 10
- Federalist No. 15
- Federalist No. 51
- Federalist No. 78
- Anti-Federalist No. 17
- *Marbury* v. *Madison*
- *McCulloch* v. *Maryland*
- *Brown* v. *Board of Education*
- The Gettysburg Address
- Washington's Farewell Address

TO THE STUDENT

As the title of our book suggests, we view

the idea of government by the people as a defining element of American politics and government. Too often, Americans take their basic rights to life, liberty, and the pursuit of happiness for granted. But these rights were neither guaranteed by those who wrote our Constitution nor by the citizens who have worked, one generation after another, to expand these rights and set our government's course. Rather, government by the people today depends on citizens who are informed and involved in the decisions and processes of our constitutional democracy.

The Framers of our Constitution warned us that we must always safeguard our rights, liberties, and political institutions. But we cannot do so without first understanding the basic rules of the game set by the Constitution. We must see the presidency, Congress, the federal bureaucracy, and the Supreme Court not as a remote "federal government" but as institutions that affect each of us every single day. Government by the people depends on people informing themselves and participating. It is not something that can be outsourced, or that a generation can decide to take a pass on.

This new edition of *Government by the People* will help you embrace the legacy of constitutional government you have inherited, even as it gives you important insights into how you can shape the future direction of our country, guarantee a system that protects minorities and all of our rights and liberties, and defend our government by the people from tyranny. In some ways, you can read this book as an "owner's guide" to American government, and a basic "repair manual" about how you can play a role in making our Constitution work. Whether you act on your own or with others on campus and in your communities, your participation alone will make American government work better. Our constitutional system depends on active engagement—win, lose, or draw. As the old saying goes, politics is a game for people who show up. We want you to get into the game.

Meet Your Authors

 Watch on MyPoliSciLab

DAVID B. MAGLEBY
is a Distinguished Professor of Political Science and Senior Research Fellow at the Center for the Study of Elections and Democracy at Brigham Young University (BYU). He is nationally recognized for his expertise on direct democracy, voting behavior, and campaign finance. Dave is also the recipient of many teaching awards, including the 1990 Utah Professor of the Year Award, the 2001 Rowman & Littlefield Award for Innovative Teaching in Political Science, and several department and university awards.

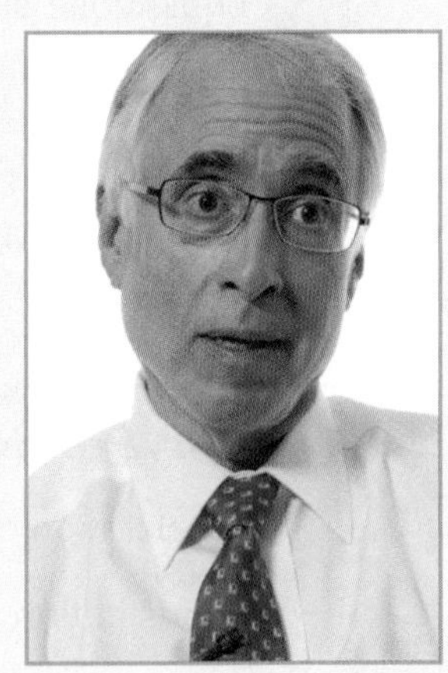

PAUL C. LIGHT
is the Paulette Goddard Professor of Public Service at New York University's Wagner School of Public Service. He has worked on Capitol Hill as a senior committee staffer in the U.S. Senate and as an American Political Science Association Congressional Fellow in the U.S. House of Representatives. Paul is the founding director of the Brookings Institution's Center for Public Service and continues his research on how to invite Americans to serve their communities through public service.

CHRISTINE L. NEMACHECK
is the Alumni Memorial Distinguished Associate Professor of Government at The College of William & Mary. Her research focuses on judicial selection and the role of the courts in a separation-of-powers system. Chris has received a number of awards for her teaching and research activity, including the Alumni Fellowship Award for excellence in teaching at The College of William & Mary.

TO THE TEACHER

The three of us remember well the first time we taught an

American Government class. To pull off our own first class seemed daunting. We also remember our desire for a well-written, carefully researched, well-illustrated, up-to-the-minute book that would help us jump-start student interest in active citizenship.

We also remember our own desire to make a difference through our teaching, and we still care deeply about playing our own role in making American government work. Although we have provided many supplements to this text that will help your students make a difference in their own way, the text itself lays the foundation for leading students forward into political science majors and public service.

These experiences inform our approach, as does the feedback you and your students pass along about what works and what does not. Long after teaching our first American Government classes, we continue to share a common passion for teaching and for the study of American government. Because all of us still teach this course regularly, we recognize the challenges of engaging students and overcoming their cynicism about the subject and doubts about the relevance of the course to their lives. We see American government as a lively subject, and make every effort to provide opportunities for debate and active learning in our own classes using current examples and controversies to help show students the relevance of the topic. We know that students won't learn what they don't read, and we believe we have written a book that gives them every reason to stick with each topic.

This book and the courses we teach are informed by our professional lives and academic research. We are actively engaged in research and publication on courts, campaigns, bureaucracy, the presidency, Congress, public opinion, campaign finance, judicial nominations, and policymaking. Our engagement in studying how government and politics really work has interrupted our teaching careers as we pursued appointments as Congressional Fellows of the American Political Science Association, produced new information for many of the book's figures and charts, and wrote books on the core topics in each of our areas. All of us regularly conduct interviews with leading policymakers in the executive, legislative, and judicial branches, and we study implementation and ongoing controversies through frequent trips to the major centers of government activity across the country. This constant contact with history, theory, and reality buttresses our appreciation for American government, and tempers our interpretations of the many contemporary events we use in this book. We care deeply about the challenges facing American government today, but also rely on history and theory to put those challenges in context.

We are delighted that you are reading the twenty-fifth edition of *Government by the People* AP Edition. First published in the 1950s, the book has reached more than two million students over its sixty-plus years in circulation. Given the distinguished co-authors who came before us, we are always careful about anchoring our writing in the long tradition of careful scholarship embedded in the very fiber of this book. We believe our co-authors were right on point when they decided to title this book *Government by the People* AP Edition. They wanted to emphasize how important people are in our constitutional democracy, and we still make every effort to reinforce the point. Understanding American politics and government must include an understanding of the American people, their similarities and differences, their beliefs and attitudes, as well as their behaviors.

The constitutional democracy we have in the United States is exceedingly hard to achieve, equally hard to sustain, and often hard to understand, especially when contemporary experience seems to frustrate action on the problems we all care about. We know that our democracy has evolved toward a greater and greater role for citizens and voters over the decades since the first edition of *Government by the People* AP Edition was published. Citizens have more rights and political opportunities in 2012 than they had when early editions of this book were published, while social media has made politics available to everyone instantly by providing a deluge of information.

Given the conflicting opinions students often confront in their web browsing, we often remind ourselves of the famous adage that everyone is entitled to their opinions, but not to their facts. That is why we work hard to set the record straight by providing a constitutional anchor for critical thinking, even as we make every effort to keep this book relevant through up-to-the-minute examples, charts, chapter openers, photos, and exercises that challenge the instant analysis that sometimes distorts the real workings of American government.

Like your students, we are sometimes frustrated by the current state of American government and the challenges in solving tough problems, and we are not reluctant to talk about the current level of public cynicism and polarization. But we also know that our work is to educate and activate the next generation of citizens who will take their place in honing the Framer's design to meet the challenges of the future, and we are hopeful that this edition of *Government by the People* AP Edition will help them shape the future, each in his or her own most effective way.

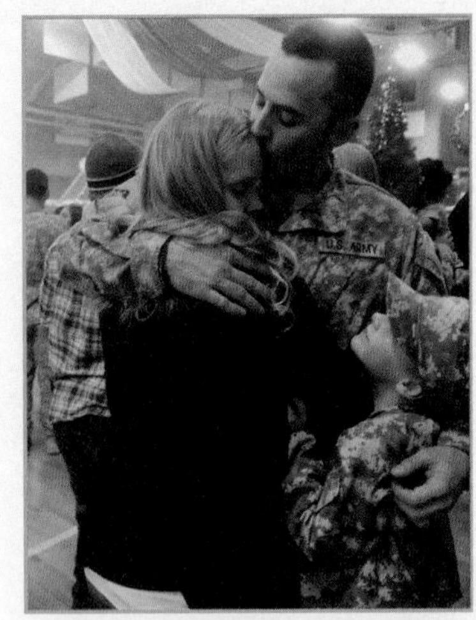

New to This Edition

The new twenty-fifth edition of *Government by the People* AP Edition builds on this book's long reputation for deep, accurate, accessible, and current coverage of the foundations of American government. We have integrated the latest in scholarship on American politics and government, comparisons with countries around the world, and analysis of recent political events, including the 2012 presidential election, legislative controversies over economic, social, and defense and foreign policy, and recent Supreme Court decisions. We also examine emerging constitutional controversies such as campaign finance reform, presidential power, judicial appointments, and rising political polarization. Keeping in mind the current political context as well as the needs of your course, we have made the following the focus of this revision:

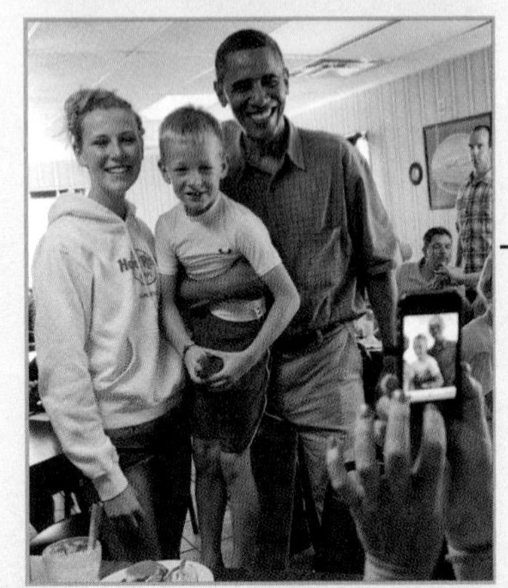

- The book provides a launching pad for discussing all of the major issues that are in the headlines today—the **2012 election results,** the war on terrorism, the Supreme Court's health care decision, the ongoing debt debate, the role of the social media in politics today, the growing polarization of Congress, and the many unresolved questions on the basic performance of government today. Social media is front and center throughout the book, whether in the tools we provide for further analysis through MyPoliSciLab, our analysis of what students can do to make a difference, and our examples, photos, figures, tables, and critical thinking exercises.

- We have combined our past chapters on (1) public opinion, participation, and voting, and (2) political culture and ideology into a single chapter that streamlines the discussion. The new chapter framework allows students to see how each topic builds from start (public opinion) to finish (voting), but we are careful to note that voting is but one of many ways for your students to make a difference in American government and policy.
- We have also combined our past chapters on (1) the federal bureaucracy, and (2) the public policy process into a single chapter that pulls the two highly related topics together. The new framework helps students to understand the close relationship between how government executes policy and where policy comes from. Given the natural time limits in many American government courses, we decided to move the policy process into the main body of the most widely used versions of the book.
- We have streamlined the book to reduce its overall length by 15 percent over the past two editions to make this edition easier to use.

Alongside these major organizational changes, we have also updated the book to make sure your students can see American government as it is today:

- We have reviewed every table and figure in the book to include the most recent information available. We want students to see how public opinion, diversity, campaign finance, congressional action, presidential press conferences and approval, judicial decisions, the federal budget, and even the number of pages in the *Federal Register* have changed in the past two to four years, and how they might change in the future.
- We have also reviewed every photo in the book and replaced almost a third to make sure the art program is relevant to your students. We have not left the iconic photos of the past behind, but have worked both to capture major events from the last few years and to create a visual narrative that enhances rather than repeats the text.

Finally, to create a tighter pedagogical connection between this book and MyPoliSciLab, we integrated several new features that move students from the book to online active learning opportunities.* The icons listed throughout the book lead to learning resources on MyPoliSciLab.

- A new design simplifies the presentation of content to facilitate print and digital reading experiences. It also focuses reading by turning our book's learning objectives into a clear learning path backed by personalized study plans on MyPoliSciLab.
- **Videos** now support the narrative in each chapter. We—the authors—frame each chapter topic, and interviews with political scientists and everyday citizens look at interesting aspects of each topic. The videos are listed at each chapter's start and can be watched on MyPoliSciLab.
- **Infographics** demonstrate how political scientists use data to answer questions like "How Long Did it Take to Ratify the Constitution?" or "What Influences a President's Public Approval?" On MyPoliSciLab, students can use interactive data to further investigate the same question.
- In every chapter, **On MyPoliSciLab** helps students review what they just read. In addition to a chapter summary, key term list, short quiz, and further reading list, there are reminders to use the chapter audio, practice tests, and flashcards on MyPoliSciLab.

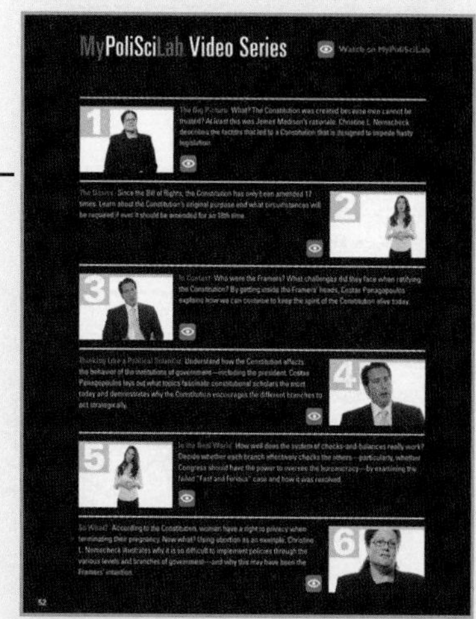

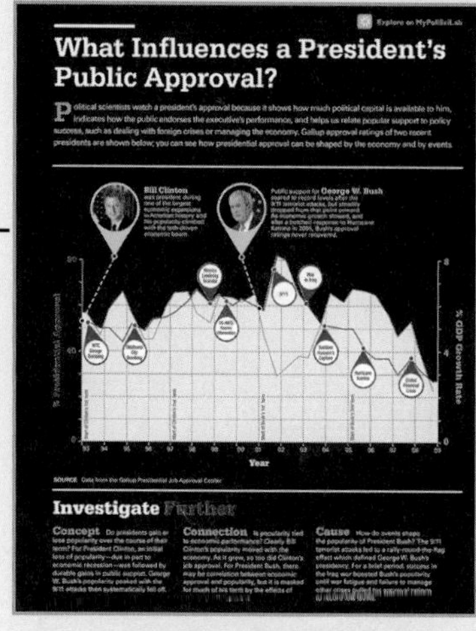

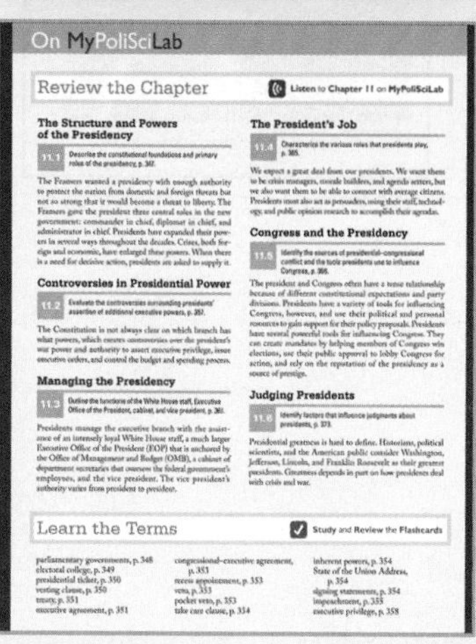

Features

We have not forgotten the long tradition of scholarship that has always made this book credible to the political science community, but have brought new perspectives, stories, and data to make sure every student knows that American government is as relevant to their lives today as it was when our book was first published.

We are obviously proud of what our co-authors produced over the first twenty-four editions. At the same time, we do not rest on the past by merely updating what has come before. We want this book to live on as an exemplar of how to integrate the basic arguments about what the Framers created with what is happening now, and what has changed.

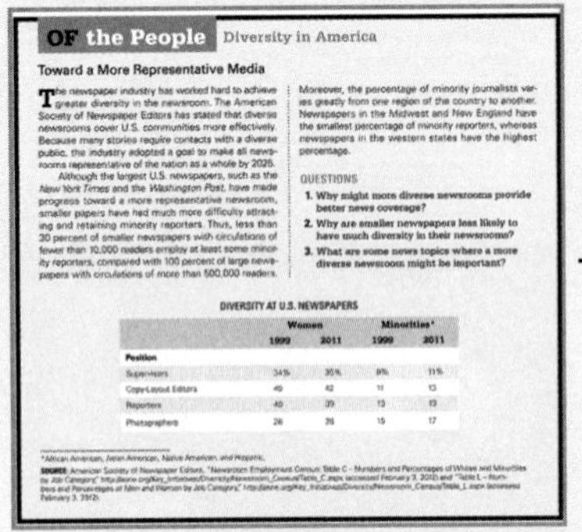

OF the People Diversity in America

Toward a More Representative Media

The newspaper industry has worked hard to achieve greater diversity in the newsroom. The American Society of Newspaper Editors has stated that diverse newsrooms cover U.S. communities more effectively. Because many stories require contacts with a diverse public, the industry adopted a goal to make all newsrooms representative of the nation as a whole by 2025.

Although the largest U.S. newspapers, such as the *New York Times* and the *Washington Post*, have made progress toward a more representative newsroom, smaller papers have had much more difficulty attracting and retaining minority reporters. Thus, less than 30 percent of smaller newspapers with circulations of fewer than 10,000 readers employ at least some minority reporters, compared with 100 percent of large newspapers with circulations of more than 500,000 readers. Moreover, the percentage of minority journalists varies greatly from one region of the country to another. Newspapers in the Midwest and New England have the smallest percentage of minority reporters, whereas newspapers in the western states have the highest percentage.

QUESTIONS

1. **Why might more diverse newsrooms provide better news coverage?**
2. **Why are smaller newspapers less likely to have much diversity in their newsrooms?**
3. **What are some news topics where a more diverse newsroom might be important?**

DIVERSITY AT U.S. NEWSPAPERS

	Women		Minorities*	
	1999	2011	1999	2011
Position				
Supervisors	34%	35%	9%	11%
Copy/Layout Editors	40	42	11	13
Reporters	40	39	13	13
Photographers	26	26	15	17

*African American, Asian American, Native American, and Hispanic.

SOURCE: American Society of Newspaper Editors, "Newsroom Employment Census: Table C - Numbers and Percentages of Whites and Minorities by Job Category," http://asne.org/key_initiatives/DiversityNewsroom_CensusTable_C.aspx (accessed February 3, 2012) and "Table L – Numbers and Percentages of Men and Women by Job Category," http://asne.org/key_initiatives/DiversityNewsroom_CensusTable_L.aspx (accessed February 3, 2012).

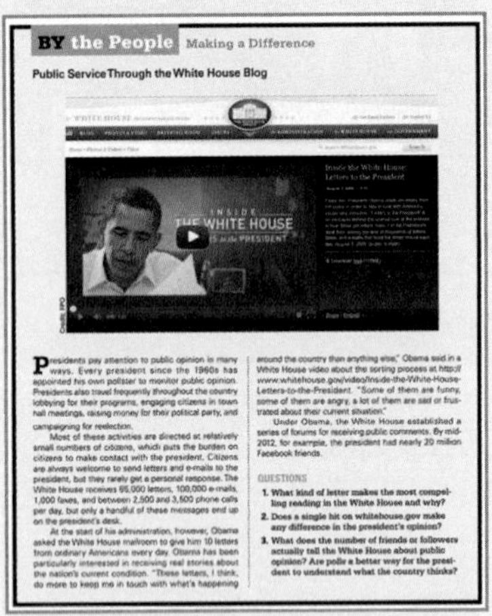

BY the People Making a Difference

Public Service Through the White House Blog

Presidents pay attention to public opinion in many ways. Every president since the 1960s has appointed his own pollster to monitor public opinion. Presidents also travel frequently throughout the country lobbying for their programs, engaging citizens in town hall meetings, raising money for their political party, and campaigning for reelection.

Most of these activities are directed at relatively small numbers of citizens, which puts the burden on citizens to make contact with the president. Citizens are always welcome to send letters and e-mails to the president, but they rarely get a personal response. The White House receives 65,000 letters, 100,000 e-mails, 1,000 faxes, and between 2,500 and 3,500 phone calls per day, but only a handful of these messages end up on the president's desk.

At the start of his administration, however, Obama asked the White House mailroom to give him 10 letters from ordinary Americans every day. Obama has been particularly interested in receiving real stories about the nation's current condition. "These letters, I think, do more to keep me in touch with what's happening around the country than anything else," Obama said in a White House video about the sorting process at http://www.whitehouse.gov/video/Inside-the-White-House-Letters-to-the-President. "Some of them are funny, some of them are angry, a lot of them are sad or frustrated about their current situation."

Under Obama, the White House established a series of forums for receiving public comments. By mid-2012, for example, the president had nearly 20 million Facebook friends.

QUESTIONS

1. **What kind of letter makes the most compelling reading in the White House and why?**
2. **Does a single hit on whitehouse.gov make any difference in the president's opinion?**
3. **What does the number of friends or followers actually tell the White House about public opinion? Are polls a better way for the president to understand what the country thinks?**

FOR the People Government's Greatest Endeavors

Reducing Nuclear Weapons

Presidents have invested enormous amounts of time and energy during the past 30 years to try to control and reduce the number of nuclear weapons throughout the world. Much of that work has involved efforts to stop the "arms race" between the United States and the Soviet Union, which together built enough nuclear weapons to destroy the world many times over.

Presidents negotiated a number of nuclear arms agreements during the long cold war, all of which had to be approved by the U.S. Senate under its treaty-making power. In 1972, for example, the Senate approved a freeze on the development of new weapons by the United States and Soviet Union that lasted through the 1970s. This Strategic Arms Limitation Treaty, negotiated by President Richard Nixon, froze the number of U.S. and Soviet missiles for five years.

In 1988, the Senate also approved a treaty banning the further development of shorter-range nuclear missiles that could be used in Europe and other "hot spots." This treaty, negotiated by President Ronald Reagan, marked the first time that the two nations also agreed to dismantle some of their existing weapons. Although both nations still have large numbers of nuclear weapons and missiles, further negotiations by presidents Bill Clinton and George W. Bush have reduced the numbers of weapons and created a much safer world.

President Obama continued these negotiations into 2012, but he was unable to make progress on his promise to rid the world of nuclear weapons during his first term. To the contrary, worries about the development of nuclear weapons by other nations, such as North Korea, intensified. Iran has also continued work to develop a weapon and test missiles that could reach Israel and Turkey.

QUESTIONS

1. **Why do nations seek nuclear weapons as part of their military strength?**
2. **What can the United States do to reduce the spread of nuclear weapons to other nations?**
3. **What can citizens do to put pressure on the United States and other nations to dismantle their nuclear weapons?**

Toward this goal, we continue to present the book in an accessible tier of increasingly detailed knowledge—we start with a clear introduction telling students what they will read and how we think and pivot to the constitutional foundations and the basic elements of our federalist system. We then provide a deep introduction to the American political landscape to make sure students understand the geographic, demographic (race and ethnicity, religion, gender, sexual orientation, family structure, education, and age), and economic (wealth and income, occupation, social class) factors that shape American government.

The book then turns to core chapters on American political institutions (Congress, the presidency, the bureaucracy and policy process, and the judiciary), follows with chapters on civil rights and liberties, and ends with chapters on economic, social, and defense and foreign policy. The book flows naturally from one section to the other, but we invite you to present these chapters in any order that fits with your own teaching plan.

The AP Edition of *Government by the People* includes a Correlation Guide. This guide lists all of the topics covered in AP Exam and shows how they correlate to this book's coverage. By following this guide, students can comprehensively and successfully study for the AP Exam.

In addition, you will always find five features in each chapter that ask students to think critically about how a government of, by, and for the people operates:

- **Of the People—Diversity in America.** In important ways, the people of the United States today are much more diverse than at any previous time. This feature explores the impact of the ever-increasing level of diversity in the American political landscape, including how race and gender are changing the way the American government works. These unique boxes are designed to reflect the concerns and experiences of ethnic and minority groups in American politics.
- **By the People—Making a Difference.** Citizens have many options for influencing government—for example, combining data sets to create mash-ups that help explain pressing problems such as obesity, telling their stories to news organizations, tracking federal government spending, staying in touch with the White House, following Supreme Court action, lobbying for education policy, tweeting their member of Congress, and becoming involved in campus and community life by building playgrounds, registering voters, and even monitoring college investments.
- **For the People—Government's Greatest Endeavors.** The public has asked government to solve many difficult, important problems in the effort to meet the Constitution's promise of a more perfect union. This feature asks students to explore the benefits and challenges of great endeavors such as reducing disease, fighting discrimination, creating a safe voting

process, reducing crime, building the Internet, providing a strong defense, and fighting campaign corruption.

- **You Will Decide.** Your students face a daunting list of choices about the difficult, important problems ahead. This feature asks students to think through a real decision they will help government decide: Should the United States adopt a national presidential primary? Raise the retirement age? Restrict Senate filibusters against judicial nominees? Ban the death penalty? Promote marriage equality? Send female soldiers into combat? Given the pros and cons of each question, students are asked to make the call.
- **The Global Community.** This feature asks students to examine the opinions of citizens in other countries on many of the big debates today. As your students compare global opinions on everything from freedom of the press to the importance of hard work, fair elections, strong presidents, an independent judiciary, and access to health care, they will gain important insights on how the experiences and opinions of the global communities affect our own system and culture.

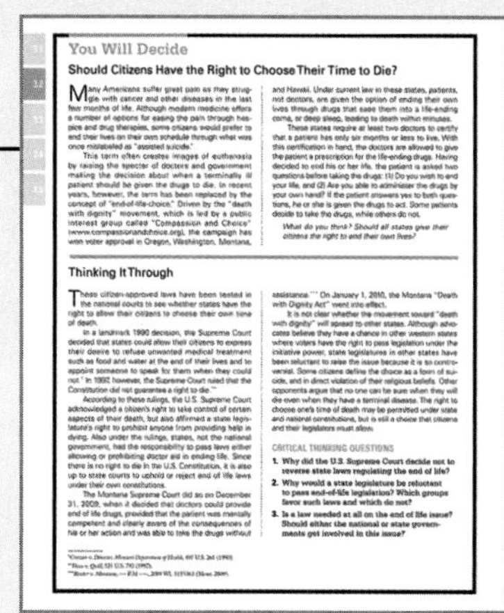
You Will Decide

Should Citizens Have the Right to Choose Their Time to Die?

Thinking It Through

CRITICAL THINKING QUESTIONS

The Global Community

Global Opinion on the Role of Government

CRITICAL THINKING QUESTIONS

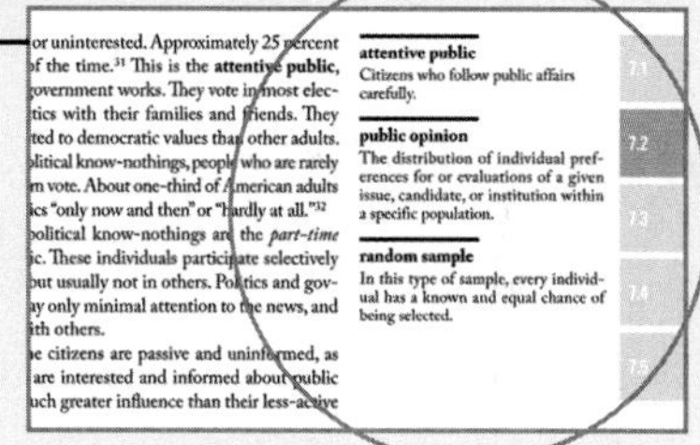
attentive public
Citizens who follow public affairs carefully.

public opinion
The distribution of individual preferences for or evaluations of a given issue, candidate, or institution within a specific population.

random sample
In this type of sample, every individual has a known and equal chance of being selected.

We have placed definitions of key terms in the margins of every chapter to help students define new and important concepts at first encounter. For easy reference, key terms from the **marginal glossary** are repeated at the end of each chapter and in the end-of-book glossary.

These many features, tools, and updates bring the book into the present. Students will never wonder what an example has to do with their reality. They will never ask why the Constitution and history matter to solving big problems and making a difference in our highly divided debate. And they will never ask how American government is being challenged today.

Ultimately, the book draws upon its own past to show students that others have made a difference before, and that they can make their own difference today. We want all of your students to become active participants in our democracy, and have written a book that gives them a broad invitation to engage. This is the enduring commitment of the book, and one that we take very seriously when we sit down every two years to bring American government back into focus through a vibrant emphasis on what they need to know as they accept the call to public service.

AP EDITION PROGRAM COMPONENTS

Pearson is pleased to offer teacher and student program components that will make teaching and learning from the AP Edition of *Government by the People* even more effective and enjoyable.

FOR THE TEACHER

Most of the teacher supplements and resources for this text are also available electronically to qualified adopters on the Instructor's Resource Center (IRC). Upon adoption or to preview, please go to **www.pearsonschool.com/access_request** and select Instructor Resource Center. You will be required to complete a brief one-time registration subject to verification of educator status. Upon verification, access information and instructions will be sent to you via email. Once logged into the IRC, enter ISBN 10: 0-205-86577-1 in the "Search our Catalog" box to locate resources.

- **Instructor's Resource CD.** Includes Instructor's Manual, Test Bank, TestGen, PowerPoints, and Digital Transparency Masters.
- **Instructor's Manual.** Create a comprehensive roadmap for teaching classroom, online, or hybrid courses. Designed for new and experienced instructors, the Instructor's Manual includes a sample syllabus, lecture and discussion suggestions, activities for in or out of class, essays on teaching American Government, and suggestions for using MyPoliSciLab. Available on the Instructor's Resource CD or on the IRC for download.
- **Test Bank.** Evaluate learning at every level. Reviewed for clarity and accuracy, the Test Bank measures this book's learning objectives with multiple-choice, true/false, fill-in-the-blank, short answer, and essay questions. Available on the Instructor's Resource CD or on the IRC for download.
- **Test Gen.** Customize and assign all of the AP-style multiple choice questions from the Test Bank. This fully networkable, user-friendly program enables instructors to view and edit questions and print tests in a variety of formats. Available on the Instructor's Resource CD or on the IRC for download.
- **PowerPoint Presentation.** Make lectures more enriching for students. The PowerPoint Presentation includes a full lecture script, discussion questions, photos and figures from the book, and links to MyPoliSciLab multimedia. Available on the Instructor's Resource CD or on the IRC for download.
- **Digital Transparency Masters.** Features all of the maps, tables, and figures from the text. Available on the Instructor's Resource CD or on the IRC for download.

FOR THE STUDENT

TEST PREP WORKBOOK FOR AP® GOVERNMENT AND POLITICS: UNITED STATES. Contains an overview of the College Board's AP program and the Government and Politics: United States AP Exam, guidelines for mastering multiple-choice and free response questions, practice tests, and more. Available for purchase.

MyPoliSciLab

Media Resources for Teachers and Students

MyPoliSciLab with Pearson eText is an online homework, tutorial, and assessment system that improves results by helping students better master concepts and by providing educators a dynamic set of tools for gauging individual and class performance. Its immersive experiences truly engage students in learning, helping them to understand course material and improve their performance. And MyPoliSciLab comes from Pearson—your partner in providing the best digital learning experiences.

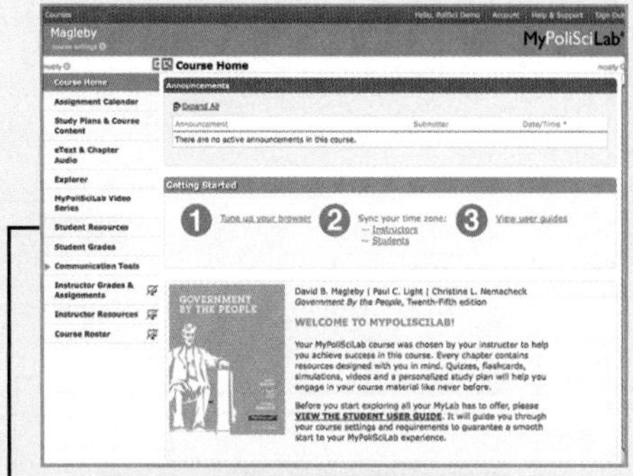

PERSONALIZE LEARNING. Reach every student at each stage of learning, engage them in active rather than passive learning, and measure that learning. Refined after a decade of real-world use, **MyPoliSciLab** can be customized to support each individual student's and educator's success. You can fully control what your students' course looks like; homework, applications, and more can easily be turned on or off. You can also add your own original material.

- The intuitive assignment **calendar** lets educators drag and drop assignments to the desired date and gives students a useful course organizer.
- Automatically graded assessment flows into the **gradebook**, which can be used in MyPoliSciLab or exported.

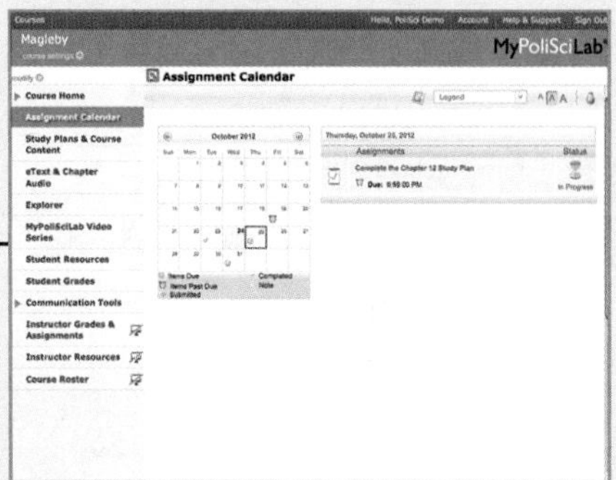

EMPHASIZE OUTCOMES. Keep students focused on what they need to master course concepts.

- **Practice tests** help students achieve this book's learning objectives by creating personalized study plans. Based on a pre-test diagnostic, the study plan suggests reading and multimedia for practice and moves students from comprehension to critical thinking.
- Students can study key terms and concepts with their own personal set of **flashcards**.

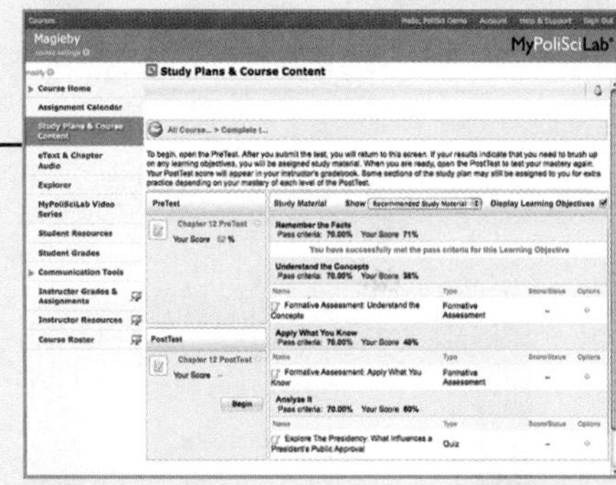

ENGAGE STUDENTS. Students—each one is different. Reach *all* of them with the new **Video Series**, which features this book's authors and top scholars discussing the big ideas in each chapter and applying them to enduring political issues. Each chapter is supported by six videos that help students work through the material and retain its key lessons.

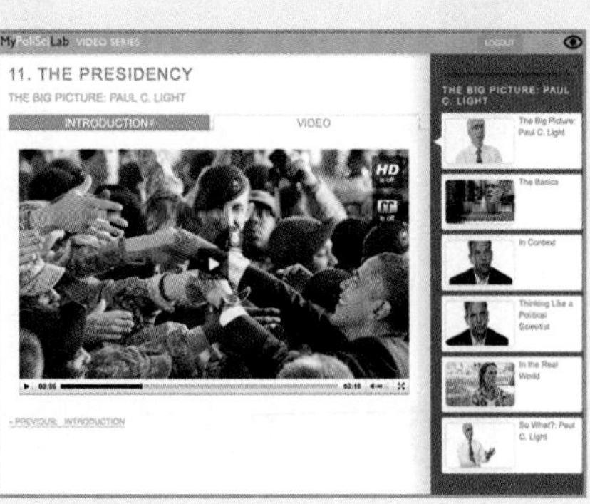

- ***The Big Picture.*** Understand how the topic fits into the American political system.
- ***The Basics.*** Review the topic's core learning objectives.
- ***In Context.*** Examine the historical background of the topic.
- ***Thinking Like a Political Scientist.*** Solve a political puzzle related to the topic.
- ***In the Real World.*** Consider different perspectives on a key issue in American politics.
- ***So What?*** Connect the topic to what is at stake for American democracy.

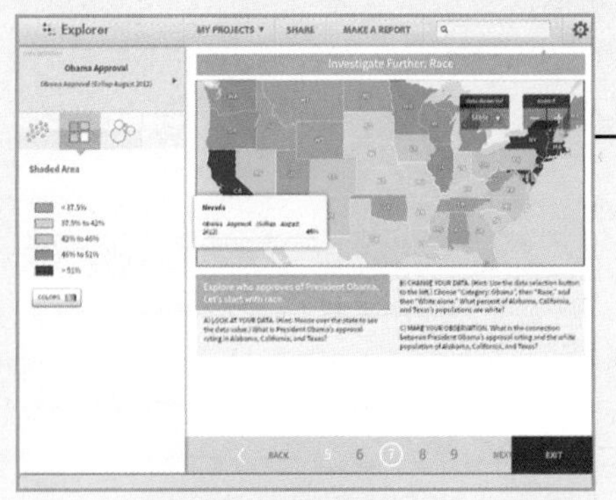

IMPROVE CRITICAL THINKING. Students get a lot of information about politics; your challenge as an educator is to turn them into critical consumers of that information. **Explorer** is a hands-on way to develop quantitative literacy and to move students beyond punditry and opinion. In the book, infographics introduce key questions about politics. On MyPoliSciLab, guided exercises ask students to read the data related to the questions and then find connections among the data to answer the questions. Explorer includes data from the United States Census, General Social Survey, Statistical Abstract of the United States, Gallup, American National Election Studies, and Election Data Services with more data being regularly added.

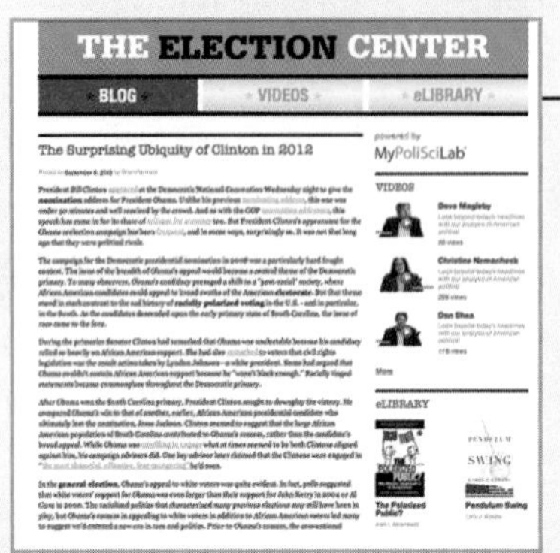

ANALYZE CURRENT EVENTS. Prepare students for a lifetime of following political news. Coverage of the 2012 elections and more keeps politics relevant and models how to analyze developments in the American political system.

- Get up-to-the-minute analysis by top scholars on MyPoliSciLab's **blogs**, take the weekly quiz, and register to vote.
- Or reflect on a theoretical case with the **simulations** in MyPoliSciLab. Easy to assign and complete in a week, each simulation is a game-like opportunity to play the role of a political actor and apply course concepts to make realistic political decisions.

THE PEARSON ETEXT offers a full digital version of the print book and is readable on Apple iPad and Android tablets with the Pearson eText app. Students can highlight relevant passages and add notes. The Pearson eText also includes **primary sources** like the Declaration of Independence, Constitution of the United States, selected Federalist Papers, key Supreme Court decisions, Lincoln's Gettysburg Address, and Washington's Farewell Address.

CHAPTER AUDIO lets students listen to the full text of this book.

Upon textbook purchase, students and teachers are granted access to MyPoliSciLab with Pearson eText. High school teachers can obtain preview or adoption access for MyPoliSciLab in one of the following ways:

Preview Access

Teachers can request preview access online by visiting **www.pearsonschool.com/access_request** and using Option 2. Preview Access information will be sent to the teacher via e-mail.

Adoption Access

- With the purchase of this program, a Pearson Adoption Access Card, with codes and complete instructions, will be delivered with your textbook purchase. (ISBN: 0-13-034391-9)
- Ask your sales representative for an Adoption Access Code Card (ISBN: 0-13-034391-9).

  OR

- Visit PearsonSchool.com/Access_Request, Option 3. Adoption access information will be sent to the teacher via email.

Students, ask your teacher for access.

CORRELATION GUIDE FOR AP GOVERNMENT AND POLITICS: UNITED STATES

GOVERNMENT AND POLITICS: UNITED STATES TOPICS CORRELATED TO *GOVERNMENT BY THE PEOPLE*, 25/E, AP EDITION

AP Topics	***Government by the People*, 25/e, AP Edition**
I. CONSTITUTIONAL UNDERPINNINGS OF UNITED STATES GOVERNMENT	**Chapters 1, 2, 3, 11**
Historical context of the formulation and ratification of the Constitution	pp. 33–36
Underlying ideological and philosophical traditions of the U.S. Constitution	pp. 36–42
The Supreme Court's interpretation of key provisions in the Constitution	pp. 68–69, 87
Theoretical and practical features of federalism	pp. 79–96
Separation of powers	pp. 54–61, 348–349
Checks and balances	pp. 54–61, 348–349
Theories of democratic government	pp. 23–31
II. POLITICAL BELIEFS AND BEHAVIORS	**Chapters 1, 4, 7, 8, 9**
Beliefs about the U.S. government, its leaders, and the political system	pp. 117, 207–211
Formation, evolution, and transmission of political beliefs	pp. 207–211, 215–220
Forms, motivations for, and effects of political participation	pp. 220–227
Causes for differences in political beliefs and behaviors	pp. 127–132
Demographic features of the U.S. population	pp. 114–127
Political participation's influence on the political system	pp. 227–232
III. POLITICAL PARTIES, INTEREST GROUPS, AND MASS MEDIA	**Chapters 2, 5, 6, 7, 8, 9, 13**
Political parties	Chapter 6, pp. 172–203
Evolution of U.S. party system	pp. 182–187
Structure and organization	pp. 187–189
Functions and effects on the political process	pp. 175–178
Ideological and demographic differences between the parties	pp. 215–220, 423–424
Third parties	pp. 153, 181–182
Elections	Chapters 7, 8, 9, 10, 11
Federal and state election laws and systems	pp. 243–247
Party and individual voting behavior	pp. 232–236
Campaign strategies and financing in the electronic age	pp. 249–263, 264–266, 315–320
Role of PACs in elections	pp. 152, 268–270
Interest groups, including political action committees (PACs)	Chapters 2, 5, 8
Political roles of lobbying and interest groups	pp. 139–142, 154–157
Range of interests represented by interest groups	pp. 141–148
Interest group activities	pp. 151–154, 161–164
Effects of interest groups on political process and policy	pp. 59, 165–168, 157–160, 165, 166
Mass media	Chapters 8, 9, 10, 11
The impact of media on public opinion, campaigns and elections, voter perceptions, electoral outcomes, and agenda development	pp. 283–290, 300–306
Media relationship to officials and candidates	pp. 306–308
Media as an industry	pp. 290–299

AP Topics	*Government by the People*, 25/e, AP Edition
IV. INSTITUTIONS OF NATIONAL GOVERNMENT	**Chapters 2, 5, 8, 10, 11, 12, 13**
The major formal and informal institutional arrangements of power	Chapters 2, 10, 11, 12, 13
Congress	pp. 312–343
The presidency	pp. 344–377
The bureaucracy	pp. 378–394
The federal courts	pp. 413–436
Relationships among these four institutions, and varying balances of power	Chapters 5, 6, 9, 10, 11, 12, 13, 14, 15
Linkages between Congress and the following:	
Political parties	pp. 189–191, 337
Interest groups	pp. 152–161
The media	pp. 286, 298, 301–307
Linkages between the presidency and the following:	
Political parties	pp. 368–372
Interest groups	pp. 154–161
The media	pp. 291–298, 301–307
Linkages between the bureaucracy and the following:	
Political parties	pp. 385–386
Interest groups	pp. 165–166
The media	pp. 297–298
State and local governments	pp. 389–390
Linkages between Federal courts and the following:	
Political parties	pp. 419–424
Interest groups	pp. 152, 433
The media	pp. 307–308
State and local governments	pp. 397–400
V. PUBLIC POLICY	**Chapters 7, 8, 12, 16, 17, 18**
Stages in the public policy process	pp. 396–402
Formation of policy agendas	pp. 397–400
Enactment of policies by Congress and the president	pp. 402–403
Implementation and interpretation of policies by the bureaucracy and courts	pp. 403–404, 550–553
Policy networks and issue networks	pp. 400–401
Foreign policy	pp. 519–522, 574–580
Domestic policy	pp. 400–401
Impact on policy processes and policymaking of the following:	
Federalism	pp. 507–509
Interest groups	pp. 215, 403–405
Parties	pp. 517–519 549–551
Elections	p. 276
Major public policies	pp. 539–543, 557–559
VI. CIVIL RIGHTS AND CIVIL LIBERTIES	**Chapters 13, 14, 15**
Development of civil rights and liberties and their impact on citizens	pp. 443–446, 477–478
The workings of the Supreme Court	pp. 425–430
The Supreme Court's most significant decisions on the following:	
Freedom of speech, assembly, and expression	pp. 450–455
Rights of the accused	pp. 458–465
Rights of minority groups and women, and the legal, social, and political effects of the Court's decisions on segregation	pp. 456–458, 479–486, 496–499
The Fourteenth Amendment and the doctrine of selective incorporation	pp. 445–446
Strengths and weaknesses of Supreme Court decisions as tools of social change	pp. 434–436, 499

Upon publication, this text was correlated to the College Board's AP Government and Politics: United States Course Description dated Fall 2010. We continually monitor the College Board's AP Course Description for updates to exam topics. For the most current AP Exam Topic correlation for this textbook, visit **www.pearsonschool.com/advancedcorrelations**.

Acknowledgments

Government by the People AP Edition began in 1948 when two young assistant professors, James MacGregor Burns of Williams College and Jack W. Peltason of Smith College, decided to partner and write an American government text. Their first edition had a publication date of 1952. Their aim was to produce a well-written, accessible, and balanced look at government and politics in the United States. As new authors have become a part of this book, they have embraced that objective. Tom Cronin of Colorado College and David O'Brien of the University of Virginia have been coauthors and made important contributions to the book. As the current authors of *Government by the People* AP Edition, we are grateful for the legacy we have inherited.

Writing the book requires teamwork—first among the coauthors who converse often about the broad themes, features, and focus of the book and who read and rewrite each other's drafts; then with our research assistants, who track down loose ends and give us the perspective of current students; and finally with the editors and other professionals at Pearson. Important to each revision are the detailed reviews by teachers and researchers, who provide concrete suggestions on how to improve the book. We are grateful to all who helped with this edition.

Research assistants for the current edition of *Government by the People* AP Edition are Troy Anderson, Ethan Busby, Olivia Crellin, Rebecca Eaton, Eric Hoyt, and Katie Van Eaton Kleinert of Brigham Young University.

We express appreciation to the superb team at Pearson who has been so supportive and worked so hard to produce this beautiful new edition: political science editor Vikram Mukhija, development editor Jeannine Ciliotta, production editor Joan Foley, Marisa Taylor at GEX Publishing Services for composition and layout, and editorial assistant and photo researcher Emily Sauerhoff.

We also want to thank you, the professors and students who use our book and who send us letters and email messages with suggestions for improving *Government by the People* AP Edition. Please write us in care of Pearson Education or contact us directly:

David B. Magleby Distinguished Professor of Political Science and Dean of FHSS, Brigham Young University, Provo, UT 84602, david_magleby@byu.edu

Paul C. Light Paulette Goddard Professor of Public Service at New York University and Douglas Dillon Senior Fellow at the Brookings Institution, pcl226@nyu.edu

Christine L. Nemacheck Alumni Memorial Distinguished Associate Professor of Government at The College of William & Mary, Williamsburg, VA 23187, clnema@wm.edu

Listen on MyPoliSciLab

Introduction

Government by the People

Mayflower Compact
A governing document created by the members of the *Mayflower* to temporarily establish self-government in the Plymouth Colonies in America.

In 1620, the *Mayflower,* with 102 passengers, including 19 adult women and 33 children, set sail for America. Earlier settlements like Jamestown had not initially included women and children, but the Pilgrim colony at Plymouth would. Before embarking, the Pilgrims sought approval from the Virginia Company to establish a new colony and were granted an area of land, or patent, located south of the 41st parallel, near the Hudson River. Because of poor winds and a near shipwreck on shoals near Cape Cod, they came ashore a good deal north of their planned landing place. There they found an abandoned Native American settlement named Patuxet, whose inhabitants had died in 1617 from illnesses like smallpox and yellow fever, which were attributed to earlier contact with Europeans.

Because the terms of their patent did not apply to the place they decided to establish their settlement, there were concerns that some of the group would leave. An account given by one of the Pilgrims stated: "This day, before we came to harbour, it was thought good there should be an association and agreement, that we should combine together in one body, and to submit to such government and governors as we should by common consent agree to make and choose."[1] On November 11, 1620, 41 of the male passengers on the *Mayflower* signed a document pledging to create a system of self-governance. They stated:

> Having undertaken, for the glory of God, and advancement of the Christian faith and honor of our King and country, a voyage to plant the first colony in the northern parts of Virginia, do by these presents, solemnly and mutually in the presence of God, and one of another, covenant and combine ourselves together into a civil body politic, for our better ordering and preservation and furtherance of the ends aforesaid; and by virtue hereof to enact, constitute and frame such just and equal laws, ordinances, acts, constitutions and offices, from time to time, as shall be thought most meet and convenient and for the general good of the colony; unto which we promise all due submission and obedience.[2]

This document, called the **Mayflower Compact**, is an enduring example of self-government. The compact was intended to unify the group for the arduous tasks of building a settlement, planting and harvesting crops so that they could survive the next winter, and defending themselves against potentially hostile Native Americans.[3] Although some historians view the compact as more about surviving than about self-government,[4] this voluntary action by the Pilgrims became an important model. John Quincy Adams (president from 1825–1829) reflected that the signing was "perhaps the only instance in human history, of that positive, original social compact, which speculative philosophers

MAYFLOWER COMPACT A governing document created and signed by the free men who sailed on the *Mayflower* providing for self-government in Plymouth Colony.

individualism
The moral, political, and ethical philosophy of life that emphasizes individual rights, effort, and independence.

have imagined as the only legitimate source of government. Here was a unanimous and personal assent by all the individuals in a community, to the association by which they became a nation."[5]

Although the debate about what motivated the signers of the Mayflower Compact continues, the document became an important example to later settlers and revolutionaries of self-government, providing what some have called the "seeds" of later American constitutional government.[6] Scholar Louis Hartz described "the concept of a written constitution" as "the end product of a chain of historical experiences that went back to the Mayflower Compact and the Plantation Covenants of the New England towns."[7] American colonists celebrated Forefathers' Day, commemorating the landing of the Pilgrims at Plymouth, which came to be seen, in the words of one scholar, as "part of the repudiation of English Domination and as the inauguration of indigenous American government."[8] In the 1830s and 1840s, the Whig Party praised the Mayflower Compact "as a milestone in the growth of social order and cohesion."[9]

The Idea of America

This book is about the continuing great experiment in self-government launched more than two centuries ago. We will examine the historical context and current practices of the institutions and political processes of American government. As the title signals, this book focuses on the role played by the people in their government. The idea of government by the people was important to the Pilgrims who wrote and signed the Mayflower Compact, committing to a system of democratic government to promote the "general good of the colony."[10] Those who later signed the Declaration of Independence held that government derived its powers from the people, and government violation of that public trust was a legitimate cause for revolution.

In many respects, the early experience of the Pilgrims mirrors a set of enduring elements that form what we might call the idea of America. These elements include individualism, a desire for self-government, the pursuit of opportunity, and a commitment to equality of opportunity, to freedom of religion, and the importance of economic liberty. A list like this was identified by Alexis de Tocqueville, the French aristocrat who visited the United States in the 1820s and whose book *Democracy in America* (written for French readers and published in 1835) remains insightful. More recently, other writers have identified a similar set of ideas as enduring elements of the American political tradition.[11] We will focus here on five core values: individualism, popular sovereignty, equality of opportunity, freedom of religion, and economic liberty. We discuss these briefly here and then return to them again in the chapter "Constitutional Democracy."

☐ Individualism

Although the term **individualism** was first used by de Tocqueville to describe the American focus on the importance of the individual in comparison to a focus on a group, society, or nation, the concept of individualism is much older. Individualism emphasizes the importance of individual rights, worth, freedom, and well-being. The idea of individualism is central to democracy, with the idea that each person has one vote, and to economic liberty, with the idea that individuals may own property. In the United States, individual economic freedoms are protected, as are political freedoms. The rhetoric of contemporary political campaigns and the arguments politicians make often center on the value of individualism.

Popular Sovereignty

As illustrated by the examples of the Mayflower Compact, the Declaration of Independence, and the Constitution, central to the American view of politics is the idea that the ultimate political authority rests with the people and that the people can create, alter, or abolish government. This idea is sometimes called **popular sovereignty**. On some occasions, as with the Mayflower Compact and Declaration of Independence, popular sovereignty is exercised directly. More often, it is exercised through representative institutions, such as Congress or local decision-making bodies with popularly elected members. But self-government is practiced whenever people write, amend, or revise local, state, or federal constitutions or laws. Popular sovereignty is a political extension of individualism. The notion that individuals have rights, including most fundamentally political and economic rights, undergirds popular sovereignty.

Implicit in the idea of popular sovereignty is the idea of individual responsibility for self-government. If individuals in a constitutional democracy will not exercise that responsibility through participation in the governing process, the system ceases to function. Also important in American political thought is the enduring suspicion of political power, especially concentrated political power—a suspicion that should motivate but sometimes hinders civic involvement. As we frequently explore in this book, government by the people is both a right and a responsibility. As we will also show, Americans value popular rule while being critical of government.

popular sovereignty
The belief that the authority and legitimacy of government is based in the consent and authority of the individuals living within its boundaries.

equality of opportunity
All individuals, regardless of race, gender, or circumstance, have the opportunity to participate in politics, self-government, and the economy.

freedom of religion
The belief that individuals living in a society should be free to exercise their personal religious convictions without government restrictions.

Equality of Opportunity

In the lexicon of core American values, equality is important, but its meaning has changed dramatically over time and means different things to different people. In the early twenty-first century, political scientist Jack Citrin wrote: "If liberty is the most basic American political value, equality is a close second."[12] Yet the signers of the Mayflower Compact, Declaration of Independence, and Constitution did not include any women or persons of color—a contradiction of modern ideas about equality. And in what aspects can all persons be considered "equal," when individuals differ widely in such things as aptitude, motivation, and inheritance? A more functional objective for American government is **equality of opportunity**: all individuals, regardless of race, gender, or circumstance, have the same opportunity to participate in politics, self-government, and the economy.

Freedom of Religion

The Framers understood the importance of freedom of conscience and freedom of worship to a free society. **Freedom of religion** has always been important to a large proportion of Americans. Indeed, as one author has noted, "American political culture celebrates freedom of religion, not freedom from religion."[13] Of course, freedom of religion does not extend to religious practice that is contrary to public peace or morality, or that causes harm to others. Central to the view of the Framers was the importance of a separation of church and state. It requires, in part, that there be no religious test for public office, meaning that an individual need not belong to a particular church, or any at all, in order to hold office and, at least since passage of the Constitution, that there be no national church. The example of the *Mayflower* Pilgrims is informative, as the Separatists were Puritans who had fled England rather than accept King James's official state church. They favored a return to the church found in the New Testament. About half of the Pilgrims were Separatists. Those who did not hold to the same theology were called Strangers.[14] The New World afforded both groups the opportunity to practice their religion.

economic liberty
The belief that individuals should be allowed to pursue their economic self-interest without government restrictions.

government
The processes and institutions through which binding decisions are made for a society.

politics
The process by which decisions are made and carried out within and among nations, groups, and individuals.

politician
An individual who participates in politics and government, often in the service of a group or political community.

political science
An academic discipline that studies the theory and practice of politics and government. It is one of the social sciences that use data and methods that overlap with anthropology, economics, geography, history, psychology, and sociology.

☐ Economic Liberty

The economic application of the idea of individualism is **economic liberty**. A driving force for much of the immigration to the United States from the Mayflower Pilgrims to the present day has been the pursuit of economic opportunity and the idea that, in this new world, individuals can shape their own destinies. Given the remnants of feudalism still existing in sixteenth- and seventeenth-century Europe, the possibility of owning property in the new world meant individual freedom and wealth. Property rights were also important to America's founders, as was protecting the functioning of a free market. To them, economic liberty came as a reaction to tariffs as well as trade and production restrictions imposed by governments under a system called mercantilism. The American Revolution was a reaction against these practices in favor of economic liberty for individuals and a view that government should have limited involvement in regulating the economy.

Economic liberty has been possible in the United States in part because of our initiative but also because of our resource advantages. As Benjamin Freedman has written, "There are many countries with abundant natural resources, and other physical advantages, but among large nations, only in America have they been used to produce such a consistently high level of income, and with consistent economic growth over time."[15] Today, government plays a larger role in economic affairs, but the idea that individuals are free to pursue their own self-interests and be rewarded for their innovations remains central.

Although the ideals of individualism, self-government, equality of opportunity, freedom of religion, and economic liberty were articulated early in our nation's history and have endured, the extent to which they have been put into practice has varied over time. Take the concept of equality, for example, which was one of the "self-evident" truths listed by Thomas Jefferson in the Declaration of Independence. The actual practice of Jefferson and other founders in owning slaves was contrary to equality. Even after slavery was abolished, state-sanctioned discrimination against blacks continued and was clearly not egalitarian.[16] Although our constitutional democracy is imperfect, Americans were path breakers in their effort to move toward full expression of these values. As we examine American government in practice over time and especially today, we will demonstrate that these values remain important to government and politics in the United States.

A Distinctive Constitutional Democracy

Before moving ahead, we need to define some of the basic terms we will use throughout this book. **Government** refers to the procedures and institutions (such as elections, courts, and legislatures) by which a people govern and rule themselves. **Politics**, at least in our system of government, is the process by which people decide who shall govern and what policies shall be adopted. Such processes invariably require discussions, debates, and compromises about tactics and goals. **Politicians** are the people who fulfill the tasks of overseeing and directing a government. Some politicians—legislators, mayors, and presidents—come to office through election. Nonelected politicians may be political party officials or aides, advisers, or consultants to elected officials. **Political science** is the study of the principles, procedures, and structures of government and the analysis of political ideas, institutions, behaviors, and practices.

social contract
An agreement whereby individuals voluntarily commit to establish a government that will protect the common interests of all.

As we demonstrate throughout the book, an understanding of history is important to putting government and politics in context. That was also the case with the establishment of our Constitutional structure. Many of those who led the American Revolution and wrote the U.S. Constitution were familiar with the writings of thinkers like Locke, Hobbes, Hume, and Rousseau, who had written in the century or so before the 1770s, as well as with philosophers who wrote centuries earlier, like Aristotle.[17] These influential thinkers, like the Framers themselves, relied on their understanding and reading of history, their observation of human behavior, and what they called "right reason," which essentially meant that an argument or idea seemed sensible.[18]

Out of this intellectual tradition emerged a view that people have inherent rights. John Locke, the English philosopher, wrote that people were once free, living in what he called the "state of nature."[19] In this condition, according to Locke, they enjoyed rights to life, liberty, and property, and they could freely enter into what he called a "social contract" to govern themselves.[20] Nearly a half-century ago, Louis Hartz explained the appeal of Locke in the new world: "In America, one not only found a society sufficiently fluid to give a touch of meaning to the individualist norms of Locke, but one also found letter-perfect replicas of the very image he used. There was a frontier that was a veritable state of nature. There were agreements, such as the Mayflower Compact, that were veritable social contracts."[21] Indeed, Locke's ideas about inherent rights and the necessity of popular consent to government are echoed in Jefferson's words in the Declaration of Independence.[22]

The philosophical debate over human tendencies as either virtuous or evil was also important to the thinking of our republic's founders. Predisposition to do evil included such vices as pride, greed, superstition, injustice, bigotry, betrayal, and overweening self-interest. David Hume, the Scottish philosopher, warned that people following their self-interest could infringe on the rights and liberties of others. But Hume did not always see self-interest as a danger. Guided by law, self-interest could motivate work and innovation.[23] Designing a government that would not fall prey to humans' worst tendencies and might direct these tendencies to productive ends was thus a major aim of the Constitution. The founders were also influenced by philosophers like Jean-Jacques Rousseau, who saw people as not inherently inclined to evil and as possessing a drive for public service. For Rousseau, citizen involvement was essential. He wrote, "As soon as any man says of the affairs of the State, 'What does it matter to me?' the State may be given up for lost."[24]

Unlike the governing systems in Europe, which grew out of centuries of feudalism, government's development in America was based on the idea that individuals have rights distinct from those granted by any government. Following Locke, the writers of the Constitution believed that government derived its powers from the consent of the governed; in other words, individuals can agree to form a government with powers specified by those individuals. These **social contracts** had appeared in informal contexts throughout the world for centuries, especially in ancient Rome. At the same time, the American Revolution, the Constitution, and early governing conditions were something new in world history. As Peter Shuck and James Wilson have noted, "nobody then knew what it meant to live in a country where equality of condition was so widespread and where the common people actually ruled themselves."[25] A central and recurrent element of the idea of America then is that government by the people is preferred to other forms of government.

James Madison can be thought of as the architect of the constitution. He was its principal author and one of its strongest supporters as a contributing author of the *Federalist Papers*.

Understanding and applying lessons from history were important to those who signed the Declaration of Independence in 1776 and designed our distinctive Constitution in 1787. They were aware of the Mayflower Compact. They knew of the successes and failures of past experiments with self-government, most notably Greece and Rome.[26] They were well versed in political ideas. In today's world, as our generation works to sustain constitutional democracy, an understanding of history and politics is also critical.

The founders shared a common perspective on the rule of law through courts and an idea of representation based on their background as Englishmen. The lack of responsiveness of Parliament and the King to their frequent petitions reinforced their sense that they needed to "throw off such Government, and to provide new Guards for their future security."[27] What the Framers prescribed as *the structure of government* was written into the Constitution, and the *protections from government* became the Bill of Rights. The need for both structure and protection was reinforced by their common experience with monarchy under King George III and with ineffective governments under the Articles of Confederation, the limited governing structure established by the states to wage the revolutionary war and provide for a minimal national government.

The designers of our constitution were at least as unified in what they did *not* want to include in government as in what they did want to include. They did not want to have a monarchy, they did not want to create a government so strong that it could threaten rights, and they did not want to establish a state religion. Nor did they wish to foster mob rule by providing too great a provision for democracy.

For James Madison and others who participated in creating our constitutional democracy, there were predictable patterns to human history and human nature. Taking into account these regularities was something Madison described as political science. But shouldn't science apply to things like gravity, motion, and molecules, and not to something like politics? You may be asked this question if you decide to major in political science.

Educated men of the period considered science, as well as politics and economics, within their sphere of knowledge. Influenced by Isaac Newton's discoveries, they were fascinated by machinery that operated by balancing forces one against another. The Framers thought the Constitution should embody the principles of such machines, with each part of government exerting force upon the others. Newton's success in describing physical laws reinforced the Framers' belief that they could identify, understand, and harness forces in human nature.

In a famous essay now known as *The Federalist*, No. 10, Madison claims it is possible and important to understand human nature, because out of that understanding come ways to limit people's negative tendencies. Madison identified the following aspects of human nature that need to be considered in designing a government: "zeal for different opinions,...attachment to different leaders,...[and the] propensity of mankind to fall into mutual animosities most commonly concerning the unequal distribution of property."[28] Madison, borrowing from Locke, connected understanding of human nature to constitutional structure, as follows: "If men were angels, no government would be necessary. If angels were to govern men, neither external nor internal controls on government would be necessary."[29] In other words, human nature as Madison understood it required some type of government to regulate citizens' behavior and some type of control over that government to regulate citizen-politicians' behavior, as well.

Madison's idea of harnessing the human capacity for evil found its fullest expression in the constitutional provisions for dividing powers among the branches. The president cannot sit in the legislature; a senator cannot also be in the House. The president shares in legislation with the power to sign and veto bills. Congress shares in the executive power by providing all the money, but the spending is done by the executive branch. The president has the power to conduct foreign relations and wage war, but Congress must ratify treaties and provide declarations of war. Most appointments are made by the president, but Congress must ratify these candidates. The judiciary can check both of the other branches by determining if executive or legislative actions are consistent with the Constitution. The executive has the power to appoint federal court judges, and the Senate must consent to these appointments. Each branch thus is given ways to check the others. For Madison, the science of politics included understanding human nature and designing constitutional mechanisms to channel power to good, and not bad, ends.

□ American Government Today

As important as the study of government and politics was to the Framers, it is just as relevant today. Government and politics matter. Consider such areas as the economy, educational opportunity, and public health. One of the lessons from the government's poor response to Hurricane Katrina in 2005 is that in such times we all greatly depend on government to provide safety and security. The government's response to the British Petroleum (BP) oil spill in 2010 has also been criticized for minimizing the scale of the spill and as a result undermining public confidence in government.[30] In contrast, the government appeared to have learned lessons in how to prepare people for a major hurricane in the way it handled Hurricane Irene in 2011.[31] In all of these examples we can see that we rely on the government to provide accurate information and security. Without that security, we face a world of anarchy. Even though government can fail, as it did in its response to Katrina, it can also succeed, as it did when polio was largely eradicated, or the public was given adequate notice of Hurricane Irene. We title this book *Government by the People* because we want to emphasize the important role people play in our constitutional democracy. Understanding American politics and government must include an appreciation of the people, their similarities and differences, their beliefs and attitudes, and their behaviors. Examining such aspects of our population as race, ethnicity, gender, age, religion, income, and region helps us see how the diversity of our country is important politically.

Constitutional democracy—the kind we have in the United States—is extremely hard to achieve, equally hard to sustain, and often hard to understand. Our political history has been an evolution toward an enlarged role for citizens and voters. Citizens have more rights and political opportunities in 2011 and 2012 than they had in 1800 or 1900. The Framers of our Constitution warned that we must be vigilant in safeguarding our rights, liberties, and political institutions. But to do this, we must understand these institutions and the forces that have shaped them.

Government Of, By, and For the People

Our emphasis on the important role people play in our constitutional democracy extends not only through the text but also through the features. The features—titled *Of*, *By*, and *For the People*—are intended to help you understand how the theory of self-government is put into practice and see the important role that you play as a citizen in this country's present and future.

The title of this book and these features are drawn from President Abraham Lincoln's famous Gettysburg Address in 1863. In his brief but powerful speech, Lincoln reminded Americans of their heritage of self-government. He began by referring to the Declaration of Independence and the enduring commitment to the principle of human equality. Lincoln then closed with the admonition that those who had died, giving "the last full measure of devotion" to preserve the United States, should lead the living to resolve "that government of the people, by the people, for the people, shall not perish from the earth." We use these three important ways in which Lincoln defined American government as grounded in "the people" to focus our features.

☐ Of the People: Diversity in America

One interpretation of the phrase "of the people" is that our nation by design does not have a monarchy. The phrase answers the question "Who governs?" with the answer, "The people do." Political leaders in the United States are not born into positions of power, as political leaders have been for much of history. Moreover, as we explore in this book, "the people" have changed throughout the course of U.S. history and have come to be a more inclusive group. In each chapter, we explore the implications of the

OF the People Diversity in America

From the *Mayflower* to Today

Understanding how the American population has changed is examined in boxes in each chapter, which we have titled *Of the People: Diversity in America*. From the initial landing of the *Mayflower* to today, the people who make up America have changed, and these changes have affected government and society in the United States.

Of the 102 Pilgrims who started the Plymouth settlement, 52 were male, and in other early settlements like Jamestown the settlers were all male. Yet by the time the first census of the United States was conducted in 1790, the population was nearly equally divided between men and women, and has remained so since.

All of those on the *Mayflower* were European Caucasian, but the population where they settled was largely native peoples. As many as 72,000 native people occupied New England in 1610, but by the time the Pilgrims arrived in 1621 that number had been reduced by epidemics.[*] The population of what became the United States grew more racially diverse with the arrival of African slaves in Jamestown in 1619. The number of slaves of African descent increased to more than 1.2 million in the 1810 census, two years after Congress banned the practice of importing slaves in 1808.[†]

The average age of the *Mayflower* settlers was 32. In the 1800 census of the United States, the median age was 16. Over time the median age rose to 22.9 in 1900 and 35.8 in 2000. The rise in median age over the course of U.S. history is due to advances in medical care, hygiene, and nutrition.

Throughout the book we will examine how the changing population in the United States has affected our politics and government. It is important to understand the changing characteristics of the people in a government by the people.

QUESTIONS

1. Why might the age, race or gender of people be important to a study of government?
2. What are some of the implications of an increasingly older population?
3. What are the implications of America becoming more diverse?

[*]Sherburne F. Cook, "The Indian Population of New England in the Seventeenth Century," *Publications in Anthropology,* 12 (1976):84.
[†]James A. McMillon. T*he Final Victims: Foreign Slave Trade to North America, 1783–1910.* University of South Carolina Press. (Columbia: South Carolina 2004), 56.

changing face of America for our experiment in self-government through the feature *Of the People: Diversity in America* (see the box).

☐ By the People: Making a Difference

The phrase "government by the people" communicates that people are engaged in their self-government. Throughout the course of U.S. history, the people have become more and more involved in their own government. For example, U.S. senators, once elected by state legislatures, are now elected by the people. The right to vote has been dramatically expanded over time. The 2008 and 2012 elections demonstrated the power of the Internet as a means to participate in politics. In addition to being active citizens, individuals can and do make a difference in their communities in addressing important problems. Seemingly small acts by individuals, many of them young people, have the potential to make real progress toward solving problems. In each chapter of the book, we include an example of how people are making a difference through involvement in government or public service. As you review this *By the People: Making a Difference* feature (see the box, next page) in each chapter, consider ways you can make a difference.

☐ For the People: What Government Can Do

Abraham Lincoln's final way of linking the people to their government implies that government exists for the people—and that what is good for the people should guide the government's aims. In the case of the United States, the Constitution's preamble spells out the government's assignments: to achieve justice, domestic tranquility, security ("common defense"), and general welfare. But how these lofty aims get translated into policies that make them more a reality is a challenge that endures and will be part of your experience as a citizen. Throughout the country's history, the government has achieved remarkable goals in the service of the people, such as building an interstate highway system, promoting space exploration, fighting discrimination in public spaces and the workplace, and reducing the crime rate. Although there have been achievements in each of these areas, these endeavors are, of necessity, ongoing. In each chapter, we explore the important accomplishments of government in the service of its citizens as well as the related unresolved policy questions for today through the feature *For the People: Government's Greatest Endeavors* (see the box).

☐ The Global Community

Although the subject of this book is government and politics in the United States of America, the country does not exist in a vacuum. It is part of a larger global community and there are important lessons to be learned from how other societies are governed. Given our emphasis on the role of people in government, each chapter also includes a comparison of how people in different countries and cultures view the same question or challenge through the feature *The Global Community* (see the box). All of the Pew survey information used in the Global Community boxes in this book comes from the Pew Research Center's Global Attitudes Survey. The year of the survey is noted in the text of each of the Global Community boxes throughout this book. The Pew Research Center bears no responsibility for the analyses or interpretations of the data presented in any outside publication.

BY the People Making a Difference

Geoffrey Canada and the Harlem Children's Zone

Having found a way out of the cycle of poverty in his own life through education at Bowdoin College (BA in sociology and psychology) and Harvard University (Ed.M. in education), Geoffrey Canada has done pioneering work helping children and families in Harlem, New York. Canada's vision of education reform includes making sure children and their families have access to a comprehensive range of services including early-childhood education, after school arts and music programs, health and psychological services and access to good nutrition. The stated goal of Canada and his organization is "to create a 'tipping point' in the neighborhood so that children are surrounded by an enriching environment of college-oriented peers and supportive adults, a counterweight to 'the street.'"[1]

The challenge of educating at-risk students where expectations and performance have been chronically low did not deter Geoffrey Canada. His Harlem Children's Zone (HCZ) has achieved extraordinary success. One study of his program done by two Harvard economists found that the HCZ found that the typical sixth grade student entering Canada's charter middle school, Promise Academy, scored in the 39th percentile among New York City students in math. Two years later these same students had test scores in math in the 74th percentile.[2] Canada's schools and the HCZ participants are committed to a "no excuses" approach, with a recognition that students and families need to invest time in education. Promise Academy students who are performing below grade level spend twice as much time in school as other New York City students while those performing at grade level spend 50 percent more time in school.[3] The investment of time and the commitment to raising expectations while also focusing on positive social skills appears to be paying off. Canada started small, with just a single city block in Harlem, but now his HCZ encompasses one hundred city blocks. President Obama has praised the HCZ model and set a goal to replicate the model in what Obama has called the "Promise Neighborhoods" program.[4]

Geoffrey Canada's commitment to finding a solution to chronic poverty through educational opportunity and reinforced by social services for disadvantaged children and their families is an example of a person making a difference. Throughout the book we showcase individuals like Canada who have made a difference. Just as coming to America on the Mayflower offered freedom and economic opportunity for those who came, programs like the HCZ give people today a chance to pursue economic opportunity. To learn more about Geoffrey Canada and the HCZ you can go to **http://topics.nytimes.com/topics/reference/timestopics/people/c/geoffrey_canada/index.html**

QUESTIONS

1. What is different about the approach Geoffrey Canada is taking to education and why might it be making a difference in educational attainment?
2. How does Geoffrey Canada demonstrate the possibility that individuals can make a difference?
3. Why is education a way to break the cycle of poverty?

[1]Harlem Children's Zone, "The HCZ Project," http://www.hcz.org/about-us/the-hcz-project (accessed October 27, 2011).

[2]Will Dobbie and Roland G. Fryer, Jr., "Are High-Quality Schools Enough to Increase Achievement Among the Poor? Evidence from the Harlem Children's Zone," American Journal of Applied Economics 3 (July 2011): 158-87. Some question the impact of the community services in the overall HCZ. See, Grover J. Whitehurst and Michelle Croft, "The Harlem Children's Zone, Promise Neighborhoods, and the Broader, Bolder Approach to Education." (Washington, D.C.: Brown Center on Education Policy, Brookings Institution, July 20, 1010. http://www.brookings.edu/opinions/2010/0728_hcz_whitehurst.aspx

[3]David Brooks, "The Harlem Miracle," New York Times, May 7, 2009

[4]Justin Hamilton, "U.S. Department of Education Opens Competition for Promise Neighborhoods," U.S. Department of Education, April 30, 2010. http://www2.ed.gov/news/pressreleases/2010/04/04302010b.html (Accessed October 27, 2011).

FOR the People Government's Greatest Endeavors

Making Government by the People more of a Reality

Moving from the idea that the people could govern themselves—as expressed by the Pilgrims and the early colonists in North America—to actually accomplishing that ambition in the form of a government is a theme we will return to again and again in this book. Take the simple act of voting, for example. Owning property was commonly required of those who voted in the early years of the United States. By the election of Andrew Jackson in 1828, the right to vote had been extended to white males, without regard to owning property, at least in federal elections.

Later, as a result of the Civil War and the Fifteenth Amendment (1870), the Constitution was amended to say states could not deny the right to vote "on account of race, color, or previous condition of servitude." A half-century later, the Nineteenth Amendment (1920) was adopted granting the right to vote to women. More recently, the Constitution has been amended to prohibit poll taxes (Twenty-Fourth Amendment in 1964) and to lower the voting age to 18 (Twenty-Sixth Amendment, 1971). There was resistance to each of these changes, and yet, 200 years after the signing of the Declaration of Independence, our notions of who may and who may not participate in elections have changed dramatically.

However, barriers to full participation still remain. The United States, in most states, retains a system of voter registration that requires people to complete a process of registering with local or state officials well in advance of the election. As recent elections taught us, the ballots or voting machines we use to cast our ballots are far from perfect. An enduring debate centers on whether a goal of government should be to make voting easier. But when examined over the broad sweep of U.S. history, one of government's greatest successes is the expansion of voting to more and more people.

Over the past few years, legislatures in several states have enacted laws requiring people who are registered to vote and want to vote to show a government issued identification card or utility bill confirming residency. Not everyone has such identification and others may not know of the new requirement, meaning that to vote they may have to go to the polls twice. The justification for the laws is the possibility of fraudulent voting, something which occurs infrequently in the United States.* These new requirements are likely to lower turnout.

QUESTIONS

1. What have been the benefits to our democracy of extending the right to vote to more people?
2. Should the right to vote be extended to persons age 16 and older? Why or why not?
3. How does requiring people to register to vote before election day and register again each time they move discourage participation?

*Public Radio International, "Voter ID Laws a Contentious Issue as Election Seasons Heats Up," January 10, 2012, http://www.pri.org/stories/politics-society/voter-id-laws-a-contentious-issue-as-election-season-heats-up-7880.html; R. Michael Alvarez, Thad Edward Hall, and Susan D. Hyde, *Election Fraud: Detecting and Deterring Electoral Manipulation* (Brookings Institution Press 2008).

☐ You Will Decide

The study of government and politics should invite you to critically evaluate the subject. These skills are enhanced with practice, and to assist you with this critical learning we have provided a box in each chapter called *You Will Decide*. This feature asks a question that you as a citizen will decide. After reading the description of the question and the issues related to it, we invite you to think about how you would answer the question. We also provide an opportunity for you to compare your thinking with other ways to think through the question. There is no right or wrong answer—what is important is that you have considered multiple ways to answer the question and how you would go about answering it. The *You Will Decide* feature appears in all the numbered chapters.

The Global Community

Opinion of the United States

As Americans, we assume the world has a high regard for our country and what it stands for. Our history of freedom and our sustained constitutional democracy stand out in world history. But how do the people in other countries actually view the United States? The Pew Global Attitudes survey included a question that asked respondents the following: "Please tell me if you have a very favorable, somewhat favorable, somewhat unfavorable, or very unfavorable opinion of the United States."

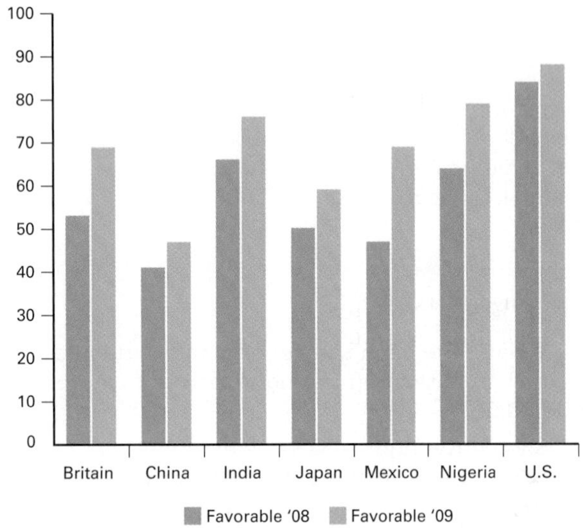

SOURCE: Pew Research Center's Spring 2008 and Spring 2009 Global Attitudes Surveys.

In the year following the election of Barack Obama, people's views toward the United States became more favorable in all of the countries in our sample. The most dramatic change in views toward the United States occurred in Mexico, which had a 22 percentage point rise in the proportion seeing the United States very or somewhat favorably in 2009 as compared to 2008. In the United States, the increase was insignificant, indicating that who currently occupies the White House matters less to Americans' views of their own country than to those in other countries.

During 2011, the world watched as pro-democracy movements spread from one Arab country to another. Protesters took to the streets and in Libya the protests became essentially a civil war until the death of Moammar Gadhafi. The United States and NATO allies, especially France and Britain, supported those seeking to overthrow Gadhafi, and urged the longstanding dictators in Tunisia, Egypt, Syria, and Yemen to step down. Early indications are that this has not helped the image of the United States in the region. Public opinion towards the United States in Turkey, Jordan, and Lebanon declined in 2011 compared to 2009 or 2010. In Egypt, the proportion having a favorable view of the United States rose slightly in 2011 over 2010 but not to the level of 2009, the year Obama made his speech in Cairo.* Less clearly a positive for the United States was the outcome of the wars in Iraq and Afghanistan. While some allies fought with the United States in these conflicts, they were for the most part American wars.

CRITICAL THINKING QUESTIONS

1. Why is it important how the people in other countries view the United States?
2. Why do you think residents of China have the least favorable views toward the United States of our sample countries?
3. What about the election of Barack Obama in 2008 may explain why people in the nations presented here viewed the United States more favorably?

*http://www.pewglobal.org/files/2011/07/Pew-Global-Attitudes-Balance-of-Power-U.S.-Image-Report-FINAL-July-13-2011-pdf. Date accessed, November 18, 2011.

Learning Objectives

We hope the thematic "Of, By, and For the People" approach as well as boxes in each chapter that compare the United States to other countries and a box inviting you to think critically about a question you will decide shows you the important role people like you play in our constitutional democracy. We also employ a Learning Objectives framework to help you use this book to succeed in the course. Using the Chapter Objectives can help you to systematically build your understanding of the fundamentals and develop the skills necessary to analyze, evaluate, and engage in the study of political science.

What are Learning Objectives? Your professor, the department, and the college faculty will often have identified key learning objectives as the important concepts, skills, motivation, and knowledge you should have acquired through completion of the course, major, or in your undergraduate education. Some examples of Learning Objectives for the Introduction to American Government course include understanding the historical foundations and development of American government, being able to identify and discuss the governmental and political institutions, and being able to think critically and analytically about important issues.

To understand these big picture concepts, you'll first need to understand the basics, so at the chapter level, there are **Chapter Learning Objectives.** These are the specific concepts you should understand after studying each chapter. For example, in the chapter on the Constitution, you'll see the objectives include such goals as being able to describe the basic structure of the Constitution and the Bill of Rights, analyzing how the Constitution limits and separates power between the branches, and explaining how we make changes to the Constitution. These Chapter Learning Objectives appear as a list at the beginning of each chapter and also appear in the chapter where the concept is discussed. Refer to these Chapter Learning Objectives as you read through the chapters to make sure you understand the key concepts. We recap the objectives in a **Review the Chapter section** at the end of the chapter, and we provide a set of review questions in **Test Yourself** to help you assess your progress in meeting the Chapter Learning Objectives and so that you know where to focus your studying.

The Chapter Learning Objectives can help guide you in your reading and studying of the course material, but asking your own questions as you read will also help you understand and apply the material. One way to prepare for exams is to turn chapter titles or major headings into possible essay questions. The chapter title "Making Economic Policy," for example, can be turned into a question like, "Explain how economic policy is made in the United States, and assess the strengths and weaknesses of that process in light of the recession of 2008–2010, and the high unemployment rate through 2012."

If you approach the book with questions in mind, you will often have better recall of the content and you will develop a capacity in critical thinking, which is one of the intellectual skills that can come from a college education. You can use the Chapter Learning Objectives as a good jumping off point and a model for this method of organization and study.

Conclusion

A text like *Government by the People* is intended to assist you in your study of American government. As authors of the book, we find the subject fascinating. As teachers of this course, we realize there is a great deal of material to learn. Our aim is to organize the subject matter and current research in a thorough, balanced, and engaging way. *Government by the People* provides a foundation for your course but also for other courses that will follow.[32] As we introduce you to American government at a college level, we are also introducing you to political science as an academic discipline, a way of thinking about the world in a systematic and rigorous way. Yale Law School Dean Robert Post defined a discipline as "not merely a body of knowledge but also a set of practices by which that knowledge is acquired, confirmed, implemented, preserved, and reproduced."[33]

We want you to come away from reading this book with a richer understanding of American politics, government, the job of politicians, and the important role you, as a citizen, play in this country's present and future. We hope you will participate actively in making this constitutional democracy more vital and responsive to the urgent problems of the twenty-first century.

Finally, as you begin your American government course, and perhaps your study of the political science discipline, keep in mind the wisdom of early education reformer Horace Mann. Regarding Americans' quest for equality, he said, "Education, then, beyond all other devices of human origin, is the great equalizer of the conditions of men—the balance-wheel of the social machinery."[34]

On MyPoliSciLab

Learn the Terms

Study and **Review** the **Flashcards**

Mayflower Compact, p. 2
individualism, p. 4
popular sovereignty, p. 5
equality of opportunity, p. 5
freedom of religion, p. 5
economic liberty, p. 6
government, p. 6
politics, p. 6
politician, p. 6
political science, p. 6
social contract, p. 7

Explore Further

IN THE LIBRARY

Alexis De Tocqueville, *Democracy in America*, 2 vols. (1835).

Robert A. Dahl, *On Democracy* (Yale University Press, 1998).

Louis Hartz, *The Liberal Tradition in America* (Harcourt, 1955).

Pauline Maier, *American Scripture: Making the Declaration of Independence* (Vintage Books, 1997, Paw Prints, 2008).

Pippa Norris, ed., *Critical Citizens: Global Support for Democratic Institutions* (Oxford University Press, 1999).

Robert Putnam, *Making Democracy Work* (Princeton University Press, 1993, 2004).

Michael J. Sandel, *Democracy's Discontent: America in Search of a Public Philosophy* (Belknap Press, 1996).

Peter H. Schuck And James Q. Wilson, *Understanding America: The Anatomy of an Exceptional Nation* (Public Affairs, 2008).

Cass R. Sunstein, *Designing Democracy: What Constitutions Do* (Oxford University Press, 2001).

Paul Tough, *Whatever it Takes: Geoffrey Canada's Quest to Change Harlem and America* (Houghton Mifflin Harcourt, 2008).

Garry Wills, *A Necessary Evil: A History of American Distrust of Government* (Simon & Schuster, 1999, Paw Prints 2008).

ON THE WEB

loc.gov
The Library of Congress's Web site contains historical information on America's founding documents as well as general history information.

tocqueville.org
This site explains the life and works of Alexis de Tocqueville.

Liberty Fund (libertyfund.org)
Publishes books and materials and sponsors conferences related to freedom and personal responsibility.

Mayflower Society (themayflowersociety.com)
The Mayflower Society has as one of its primary purposes furthering the understanding of the Mayflower Compact.

Philosophy Pages (philosophypages.com/ph/index.htm)
This site provides information on a wide range of political philosophers.

bc.edu/centers/cloughcenter/
Located at Boston College, the Clough Center for the Study of Constitutional Democracy seeks to foster self-government and reflection on constitutional government.

Listen to Chapter 1 on MyPoliSciLab

1

Constitutional Democracy

In 2011, the world watched as the people in Tunisia, Egypt, Libya, and other Middle Eastern countries defied their governments by taking to the streets, protesting the entrenched leadership in their countries. Tunisian President Zine El Abidine Ben Ali, who during his 23 years in power had been criticized for violating human rights, restricting the press, and generally suppressing criticism of the government, was forced to flee the country.[1] Only days later, protests erupted in Egypt, where President Hosni Mubarak had held power for 29 years. Hundreds of thousands gathered in Tahrir Square, and hundreds were wounded and at least seven died in the bloodiest day of clashes.[2] Less than a month after Ben Ali fled Tunisia, Mubarak relinquished power to the military. Within days, what started as widespread protests in Libya soon became an armed insurrection against dictator Muammar al-Gaddafi. Gaddafi had imposed authoritarian rule in Libya in 1969 and had remained in power ever since. In Libya the anti-Gaddafi forces benefited from air strikes against Libyan forces by the North Atlantic Treaty Organization (NATO). Most of the bombing was carried out by French and British aircraft along with some U.S. involvement (though the United States typically used drones). A few months later, when Gaddafi was forced to flee his compound, he was killed by the rebels.[3]

In Tunisia, Ben Ali had repeatedly won elections by large margins, although some disputed the validity of these elections.[4] Mubarak had also been elected in Egypt, but the balloting was often limited to a referendum on his selection by Parliament, with no other option given to voters.[5] Only in 2005, after an amendment to the Egyptian Constitution, did Mubarak run in an election with more than one candidate. In an election seen by some as unfair, Mubarak won with 88 percent of the vote.[6] In Libya, some forms of democracy existed formally, but Gaddafi kept control of even local politics through groups sometimes called "revolutionary councils."[7]

Before the protests of 2011, none of the three leaders had shown signs of giving up power, and in the case of Mubarak and Gaddafi, their likely successors were presumed to be family members. All three had tremendous power at their disposal and used it against the protesters. The response of Gaddafi's forces was especially harsh; they showed no hesitation to use deadly

1.1

Use the concept of constitutional democracy to explain U.S. government and politics.
p. 21

1.2

Differentiate democracy from other forms of government, and identify conditions conducive to a successful democracy.
p. 23

1.3

Show how politics before 1787 shaped the Constitution.
p. 33

1.4

Assess the important compromises reached by the delegates to the Constitutional Convention of 1787.
p. 36

1.5

Evaluate the arguments for and against the ratification of the Constitution.
p. 42

Barack Obama and George Bush in the White House as a new president (Obama) takes over from his predecessor, George W. Bush.

MyPoliSciLab Video Series

The Big Picture How could one of the world's most powerful democracies ever consider an African American to be 3/5 of a person? Using slavery and the Equal Rights Amendment for women as examples, author David B. Magleby illustrates why politics and Constitution-writing is an ongoing process.

The Basics What function does government serve? In this video, you will analyze this question and explore the core values that shape our political system and how the growing diversity of our population is changing—and reaffirming—the definition of what it means to be American.

In Context Where did the basic principles of American government come from? Boston University political scientist Neta C. Crawford uncovers the Greek, Roman, and Iroquois roots of our political system. She also traces the expansion of the concept of accountability since the birth of the nation.

Thinking Like a Political Scientist Find out how and why research on American politics has shifted. Boston University political scientist Neta C. Crawford discusses how scholars who once focused on voters and institutions are now looking at deliberation as the primary indicator of the health of a democratic system.

In the Real World What is the government's function in everyday life? Real people share their opinions on how involved the federal government should be in education by evaluating the effectiveness of the No Child Left Behind Act, which encourages standardized testing.

So What? Tyranny, revolution, self-government, chaos, tyranny, etc.—most nations have experienced this cycle in some form throughout their history. Author David B. Magleby explains how the U.S. Constitution has safeguarded America from this pattern and allowed us to become one of the most powerful democracies in the world.

force. And yet, in each of these three countries, the leader stepped down or was forced into hiding, leaving behind uncertainty about how to govern the country. These experiences demonstrate the difficulty of establishing a democratic process that consistently results in a peaceful transfer of power.

In the United States, citizens take the peaceful transfer of power following elections for granted. Many people view elections with disdain, saying things like, "Voting does not matter," "Nothing ever changes," or "It's just all politics." But in fact, U.S. elections are remarkable and consequential. They conclude with a rare event in human history: the peaceful transfer of political power. What is unusual is what is *not* happening. In many nations, those in power got there because they were born to the right family or because they killed or jailed their opponents. During most of history, no one, especially not an opposition political party, could openly criticize the government, and a political opponent was an enemy. England's King George III reportedly said that George Washington would be "the greatest man alive in the world" if he were to voluntarily step down as president after two terms.[8]

This remarkably smooth transition of power was demonstrated again in the 2000 presidential election. Democrat Al Gore won the popular vote only to see George W. Bush declared the winner by the Electoral College, after the Supreme Court effectively ruled 5 to 4 that Bush's slim Florida plurality should stand. Even in a highly contested election, Gore graciously conceded defeat: "I say to President-elect Bush that what remains of partisan rancor must now be put aside, and may God bless his stewardship of this country. Neither he nor I anticipated this long and difficult road. Certainly neither of us wanted it to happen. Yet it came, and now it has ended, resolved, as it must be resolved, through the honored institutions of our democracy."[9] The Democrats thus turned over the keys to the White House to George W. Bush and the Republicans. In many countries, the irregularities of the voting process in Florida and other states would have been sufficient excuse for the party in power to declare that a new election needed to be held.

After the 2008 election outcome appeared certain, John McCain graciously conceded defeat to Barack Obama and the process of organizing a new administration began. Outgoing presidents do not attempt to prolong their time in office by calling on the military to keep the other party from taking power. Supporters of the losing candidate do not take up arms or leave the country or go underground to plan a revolution. Instead, they almost immediately began planning how to win the next election. Nor do the victors seriously think about punishing their opponents once they gain power. The winners want to throw the opposition out of office, not in jail. In all these ways, the election of 2008 was a routine transfer—a constitutional democracy at work. With the reelection of Barack Obama in 2012, party control of the presidency did not change. But the concession speech by Mitt Romney on election night was conciliatory, as is generally the case for defeated candidates in both parties.

The peaceful transfer of power is only one example of the successful functioning of our political system. In this chapter, we begin our exploration of the U.S. experiment with government by the people by taking a closer look at the meaning of democracy and the historical events that created the constitutional democracy of the United States.

U.S. Government and Politicians in Context

1.1 Use the concept of constitutional democracy to explain U.S. government and politics.

As the oldest constitutional democracy in the world, the United States of America has survived for more than two centuries, yet it is still a work in progress. We think of it as an enduring, strong government, but our political system is built on a fragile foundation. The U.S. Constitution and Bill

Thomas Jefferson, author of the Declaration of Independence, third president of the United States, and founder of the University of Virginia.

of Rights survive, not because we still have the parchment they were written on, but because each generation of U.S. citizens has respected and worked to understand the principles and values found in these documents. Each generation has faced different challenges in preserving, protecting, and defending our way of government.

The U.S. constitutional democracy has shown resilience and adaptability. We have held 113 presidential and midterm elections (including the 2012 election), and we have witnessed the peaceful transfer of power from one party to another on dozens of occasions. The United States has succeeded largely because its citizens love their country, revere the Constitution, and respect the free enterprise system. We also believe that debate, compromise, and free elections are the best ways to reconcile our differences. From an early age, we practice democracy in elementary school elections, and even though we may be critical of elected leaders, we recognize the need for political leadership. We also know there are deep divisions and unsolved problems in the United States. Many people are concerned about the persistence of racism, about religious bigotry, and about the gap in economic opportunities between rich and poor. And we want our government, in addition to defending us against terrorism and foreign enemies, to address domestic problems like basic health care, education, and unemployment.

But what is this government of which we expect so much? The reality is that "government by the people" is built on the foundation of hundreds of thousands of our fellow citizens: the people we elect and the people they appoint to promote the general welfare, provide for domestic tranquility, and secure the blessings of liberty for us.

More than any other form of government, the kind of democracy that has emerged under the U.S. Constitution requires active participation and a balance between faith and skepticism. Government by the people does not, however, mean that *everyone* must be involved in politics and policy making or that those who are involved need to do so through traditional avenues such as campaigning for a political candidate or interning in a representative's office. Some individuals run for office seeking to represent the voters, many of whom will always be too busy doing other things, and some of whom will always be apathetic about government and politics. Moreover, the public must be sufficiently attentive, interested, involved, informed, and willing, when necessary, to criticize and change the direction of government.

Thomas Jefferson, author of the Declaration of Independence and a champion of constitutional democracy, believed in the common sense of the people and in the possibilities of the human spirit. Jefferson warned that every government degenerates when it is left solely in the hands of the rulers. The people themselves, Jefferson wrote, are the only safe repositories of government. He believed in popular control, representative processes, and accountable leadership. But he was no believer in the simple participatory democracy of ancient Greece, where all eligible citizens were directly involved in decision making in the political process. Even the power of the people, Jefferson believed, must be restrained from time to time.

Government by the people requires faith in our common human enterprise, a belief that the people can be trusted with their own self-government, and an optimism that when things begin to go wrong, the people can be relied on to set them right. But we also need a healthy skepticism. Democracy requires us to question our leaders and never entrust a group or institution with too much power. And even though constitutional advocates prize majority rule, they must think critically about whether the majority is always right.

Constitutional democracy requires constant attention to protecting the rights and opinions of others, to ensure that our democratic processes serve the principles of liberty, equality, and justice. A peculiar blend of faith and caution is warranted when dealing with the will of the people.

Constitutional democracy means government by representative politicians. A central feature of democracy is that those who hold power do so only by winning a free and fair election. In our political system, the fragmentation of powers requires elected officials to mediate among factions, build coalitions, and work out compromises among and within the branches of our government to produce policy and action. We expect our politicians to operate within the rules of democracy and to be honest, humble, patriotic, compassionate, well informed, self-confident, and inspirational. We want politicians, in other words, to be perfect, to have all the answers, and to have all the "correct" values (as we perceive them). We want them to solve our problems, yet we also make them scapegoats for the things we dislike about government: taxes, regulations, hard times, and limits on our freedom. Many of these ideals are unrealistic, and no one could live up to all of them. Like all people, politicians live in a world in which perfection may be the goal, but compromise, ambition, fund raising, and self-promotion are necessary.

U.S. citizens will never be satisfied with their political candidates and politicians. The ideal politician is a myth. Politicians become "ideal" only when they are dead. Politicians and candidates, as well as the people they represent, all have different ideas about what is best for the nation. Indeed, liberty invites disagreements about ideology and values. That is why we have politics, candidates, opposition parties, heated political debates, and elections.

Defining Democracy

1.2 Differentiate democracy from other forms of government, and identify conditions conducive to a successful democracy.

The distinguishing feature of democracy is that government derives its authority from its citizens. In fact, the word comes from two Greek words: *demos,* "the people," and *kratos,* "authority" or "power." Thus **democracy** means *government by the people,* not government by one person (a monarch, dictator, or priest) or government by the few (an oligarchy or aristocracy).

The word "democracy" is nowhere to be found in the Declaration of Independence or in the U.S. Constitution, nor was it a term the founders used. Ancient Athens, a few other Greek city-states, and the Roman Republic had a **direct democracy** in which citizens assembled to discuss and pass laws and select their officials. Most of these Greek city-states and the Roman Republic degenerated into mob rule and then resorted to dictators or rule by aristocrats. When this nation was founded, *democracy* was used to describe unruly groups or mobs, and a system that encouraged leaders to gain power by appealing to the emotions and prejudices of the people. In 1787, James Madison, in *The Federalist,* No. 10, reflected the view of many of the Framers of the U.S. Constitution when he wrote, "Such democracies [as the Greek and Roman]... have ever been found incompatible with personal security, or the rights of property; and have in general been as short in their lives, as they have been violent in their deaths." Madison feared that empowering citizens to decide policy directly would be dangerous to freedom, minorities, and property and would result in violence by one group against another.

Over time, our democracy has increasingly combined representative and direct democracy. The most important examples of direct democracy were added roughly a century ago and include the **direct primary**, in which voters, rather than party leaders or other elected officials, select who may run for office; the **initiative** and **referendum**, which allow citizens to vote on state laws or constitutional amendments; and the **recall**, which lets voters remove state and local elected officials from office between elections. Initiatives and referendums are not permitted in all states, but where they are available and used, they have been important. For example, in 2008, California's Proposition 8 divided the state on the issue of gay marriage. Proposition 8 was an initiative stating that "only marriage between a man and a woman is valid or recognized in California." Overall, $73.4 million was spent by the two sides in an intensely fought campaign. The measure was passed with 52 percent of the vote and was deemed constitutional by the California Supreme Court in 2009.[10] Since then it has been declared unconstitutional by the federal courts.[11] This is not the first vote of the people to be overturned by the courts. In the 1960s the

democracy
Government by the people, both directly or indirectly, with free and frequent elections.

direct democracy
Government in which citizens vote on laws and select officials directly.

direct primary
An election in which voters choose party nominees.

initiative
A procedure whereby a certain number of voters may, by petition, propose a law or constitutional amendment and have it submitted to the voters.

referendum
procedure for submitting to popular vote measures passed by the legislature or proposed amendments to a state constitution.

recall
A procedure for submitting to popular vote the removal of officials from office before the end of their term.

You Will Decide

Should the United States Adopt a National Initiative Process?

Even though more than half the states have some form of initiative or popular referendum in which voters can petition to vote directly on policy issues, the national government does not provide for such a process. Those who wrote our Constitution were not supporters of direct democracy, which is why it is not part of their document. They favored more indirect means of public involvement in making policy. Voters in many other democracies directly ratify constitutional changes like our constitutional amendments in a national election.

Proposals for a national initiative or referendum process have been put forward for more than a century. What might voters decide using a process for national petitions? They could, for example, petition to change the Senate so that instead of two senators, each state have a minimum of one and the remainder be apportioned by population. Others might petition to institute mandatory school prayer or to legalize medicinal marijuana as a guaranteed constitutional right. Do the possibilities for what might be decided by referendum affect your opinion on whether it should be used?

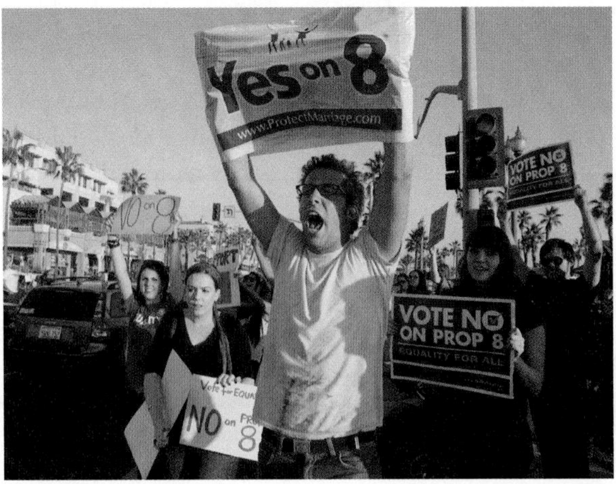

What do you think? Should the United States adopt a national initiative process? What are some of the arguments for or against this?

Thinking It Through

Involving voters directly in the process of deciding public policy is appealing and consistent with the move toward direct democracy the United States has experienced during the past century. Such votes may help legitimate major constitutional changes by demonstrating voter approval of them, and if a petition process were permitted, citizens could directly put before their fellow voters whatever constitutional changes they wanted. But as in the examples above, should some issues be out of bounds? If so, who decides? In most of the United States, these kinds of issues are decided by courts, but that puts courts in a politically charged position. Is that a good idea?

Although letting voters decide policy questions is an extension of direct democracy, in practice, the initiative and referendum may actually impede representative democracy. Congress and the president may evade tough issues by waiting for someone to put them to a vote of the people. An initiative also forces a "yes" or "no" vote, and compromise is not possible. Who decides how the question will be worded? How many signatures would be required to place a measure on the ballot? How many initiatives or referendums can we put before the voters in any single election?

When it comes to implementing a successful initiative or referendum, does that vote supersede the Constitution itself? Could the Supreme Court declare a national initiative unconstitutional, or is the vote of the people the final word on a matter? How would Congress and the president allocate tax money for implementing an initiative? The authors of our Constitution clearly preferred a more representative and deliberative form of democracy to the initiative. What were their reservations about direct democracy, and were they correct?

CRITICAL THINKING QUESTIONS

1. **Who should word the question put to voters in a referendum, and what effect does the way a question is worded have on the process?**
2. **Could a majority group vote to limit the rights of a minority in a referendum?**
3. **How is voters deciding a referendum different from legislators deciding legislation?**

U.S. Supreme Court reversed a ballot initiative enacted by California voters sanctioning racial discrimination in the sale of housing, sometimes called the *open housing initiative.*[12]

Today, it is no longer possible, even if it were desirable, to assemble the citizens of any but the smallest towns to make their laws or select their officials directly.

Rather, we have invented a system of representation. Democracy today means **representative democracy**, or a *republic,* in which those who have governmental authority get and retain that power directly or indirectly by winning free elections in which all adult citizens are allowed to participate. These elected officials are the people who determine budgets, pass laws, and are responsible for the performance of government. The Framers used the term "republic" to avoid any confusion between direct democracy, which they disliked, and representative democracy, which they liked and thought secured all the advantages of a direct democracy while curing its weaknesses.

representative democracy
Government in which the people elect those who govern and pass laws; also called a *republic.*

constitutional democracy
Government that enforces recognized limits on those who govern and allows the voice of the people to be heard through free, fair, and relatively frequent elections.

Many of the ideas that came to be part of the Constitution can be traced to philosophers' writings—in some cases, centuries before the American Revolution and the constitutional convention. Among those philosophers the Framers would have read and been influenced by were Aristotle, Hobbes, Locke, and Montesquieu. Aristotle, a Greek philosopher writing in the fourth century BC, had provided important ideas on a political unit called a state but also on the idea of a constitution and on various forms of governing.[13] John Locke, an English philosopher, also profoundly influenced the authors of the Declaration of Independence and Constitution. Locke rejected the idea that kings had a divine right to rule, advocated a constitutional democracy, and provided a philosophic justification for revolution.[14] Locke, like his fellow Englishman Thomas Hobbes, asserted that there was a social contract whereby people formed governments for security and to avoid what he called the state of nature, where chaos existed and where "everyone was against everyone."[15]

In defining democracy, we need to clarify other terms. **Constitutional democracy** refers to a government in which individuals exercise governmental power as the result of winning free and relatively frequent elections. It is a government in which there are recognized, enforced limits on the powers of all governmental officials. Generally, it also includes a written set of governmental rules and procedures—a constitution. The idea that constitutional provisions can limit power by having another part of the government balance or check it is one more good example of how the Framers applied ideas from earlier thinkers—in this case, the French philosopher Charles de Montesquieu.[16]

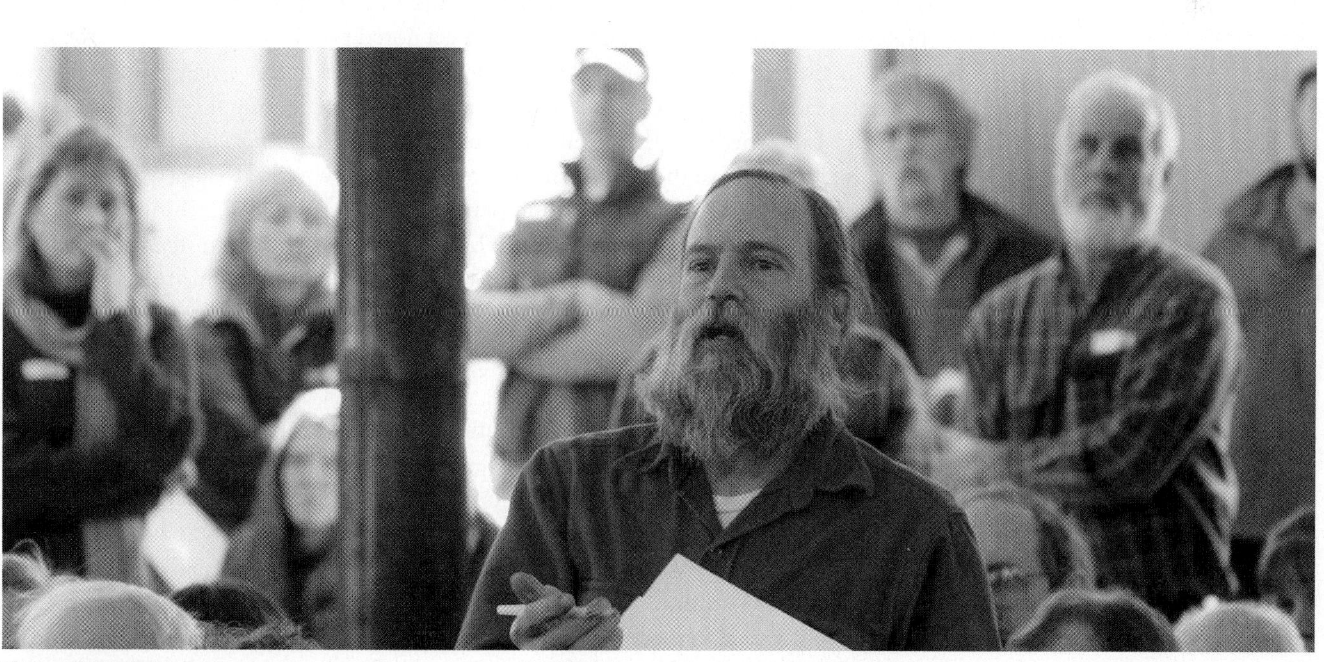

Steve Marx stands up to speak at the Strafford Meeting Hall in Strafford, Vt., during a town meeting. Since colonial times, many local governments in New England have held meetings at which all community members are invited to discuss issues with public officials.

constitutionalism
The set of arrangements, including checks and balances, federalism, separation of powers, rule of law, due process, and a bill of rights, that requires our leaders to listen, think, bargain, and explain before they act or make laws. We then hold them politically and legally accountable for how they exercise their powers.

natural rights
The rights of all people to dignity and worth.

political culture
The widely shared beliefs, values, and norms citizens hold about their relationship to government and to one another.

Constitutionalism is a term we apply to arrangements—checks and balances, federalism, separation of powers, rule of law, due process, and a bill of rights—that require our leaders to listen, think, bargain, and explain before they make laws; this prevents politicians from abusing their power. We then hold them politically and legally accountable for the way they exercise their powers.

Like most political concepts, democracy encompasses many ideas and has many meanings. It is a way of life, a form of government, a way of governing, a type of nation, a state of mind, and a variety of processes. We can divide these many meanings of democracy into three broad categories: a system of interacting values, a system of interrelated political processes, and a system of interdependent political structures.

☐ Democracy as a System of Interacting Values

A constitutional democracy is strengthened by an educated and prosperous public that has confidence in its ability to work out differences through the political process. The founders of our nation claimed that individuals have certain **natural rights**—the rights of all people to dignity and worth—and that government must be limited and controlled because it was a threat to those rights. A set of interacting values provides a foundation for that public confidence. Personal and economic liberty, individualism, equality of opportunity, and popular sovereignty are at the core of democratic values.

Political scientists use the term **political culture** to refer to the widely shared beliefs, values, and norms citizens hold about their relationship to government and to one another. We can discover the specifics of a nation's political culture not only by studying what its people believe and say, but also by observing how they behave. That behavior includes such fundamental decisions as who may participate in political decisions, what rights and liberties citizens have, how political decisions are made, and what people think about politicians and government generally.

PERSONAL LIBERTY No value in the American political culture is more revered than liberty. "We have always been a nation obsessed with liberty. Liberty over authority, freedom over responsibility, rights over duties—these are our historic preferences," wrote the late Clinton Rossiter, a noted political scientist. "Not the good man but the free man has been the measure of all things in this sweet 'land of liberty'; not national glory but individual liberty has been the object of political authority and the test of its worth."[17] The essence of liberty is *self-determination,* meaning that all individuals must have the opportunity to realize their own goals. Liberty is not simply the absence of external restraint on a person (freedom *from* something); it is also a person's freedom and capacity to reach his or her goals (freedom *to do* something). Not all students of U.S. political thought accept this emphasis on freedom and individualism over virtue and the public good, and in reality both sets of values are important.[18]

INDIVIDUALISM Popular rule in a democracy flows from a belief that every person has the potential for common sense, rationality, and fairness. Individuals have important rights; collectively, those rights are the source of all legitimate governmental authority and power. These concepts pervade democratic thought, and constitutional democracies make the *individual*—rich or poor, black or white, male or female—the central measure of value. As Peter Shuck and James Q. Wilson have written, "This belief in individualism causes Americans to place an unparalleled emphasis on the notion of individual rights in every area of social life and, correspondingly, to be suspicious of group rights."[19] Policies that limit individual choice generate intense political conflict. The debates over legalized abortion and universal health care are often framed in terms of our ability to exercise choices. Although American citizens support individual rights and freedoms, they also understand that their rights can conflict with another person's or with the government's need to maintain order or promote the general welfare.

Not all political systems put the individual first. Some promote **statism**, a form of government based on centralized authority and control, especially over the economy. China, Vietnam, and Cuba, for example, take this approach. In a modern democracy, the nation, or even the community, is less important than the individuals who compose it.

statism
The idea that the rights of the nation are supreme over the rights of the individuals who make up the nation.

American dream
A complex set of ideas that holds that the United States is a land of opportunity where individual initiative and hard work can bring economic success.

EQUALITY Thomas Jefferson's famous words in the Declaration of Independence express the strength of our views of equality: "We hold these truths to be self-evident, that all men are created equal, that they are endowed by their Creator with certain unalienable rights, that among these are life, liberty, and the pursuit of happiness." In contrast to Europeans, our nation shunned aristocracy, and our Constitution explicitly prohibits governments from granting titles of nobility. Although our rhetoric about equality was not always matched by our policy—slavery, racial segregation in schools—the value of social equality is now deeply rooted.

American citizens also believe in *political equality,* the idea that every individual has a right to equal protection under the law and equal voting power. Although political equality has always been a goal, it has not always been a reality. In the past, African Americans, Native Americans, Asian Americans, and women were denied rights extended to white males.

Equality encompasses the idea of *equal opportunity,* especially with regard to improving our economic status. American adults believe social background should not limit our opportunity to achieve to the best of our ability, nor should race, gender, or religion. The nation's commitment to public education programs such as Head Start for disadvantaged preschool children, state support for public colleges and universities, and federal financial aid for higher education reflects this belief in equal opportunity.

OPPORTUNITY AND THE AMERICAN DREAM Many of our political values come together in the **American dream**, a complex set of ideas that holds that the United States is a land of opportunity where individual initiative and hard work can bring

People wave flags to celebrate Revolution Day on July 26 in Santiago de Cuba. In Cuba, government is based on centralized control and loyalty to the state.

The Global Community

Importance of Freedoms

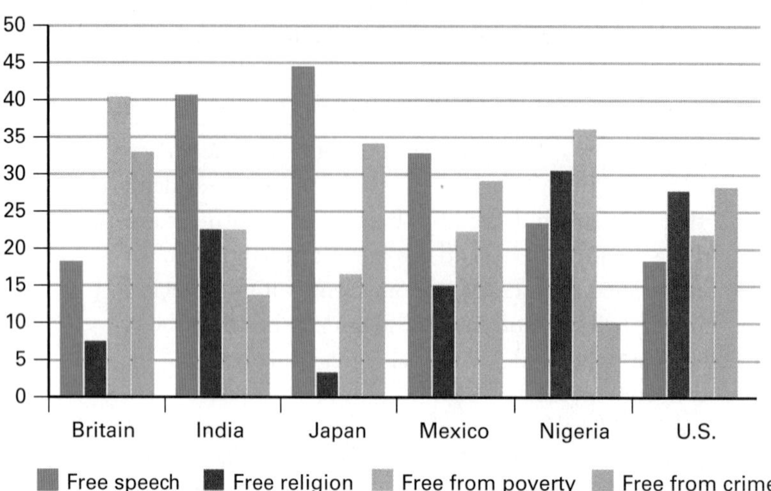

SOURCE: Pew Research Center, Global Views on Life Satisfaction, National Conditions, and the Global Economy: Highlights from the 2007 Pew Global Attitudes 47-Nation Survey (Pew Research Center, 2007).

The United States has been known as a place where people value freedom. In today's world, what value do the people of the United States place on different freedoms, and how do they compare to the rest of the world? The respondents in the Pew Global survey were asked: "Thinking about your own personal life, which of these is MOST important to you: Being free to say whatever you want in public, Being free to practice your religion, Being free from hunger and poverty, Being free from crime and violence?"

In Britain and Nigeria the most frequent response given was freedom from poverty, with 40 percent choosing this in Britain and 36 percent choosing this in Nigeria. In the United States, respondents are more evenly divided across the four competing values than in any other country.

In Japan, India, and Mexico, freedom to say whatever a person wanted to in public was the most frequently given response. Given the poverty in India and Mexico, this is a surprising answer. Both of these countries are relatively new democracies, so perhaps freedom of speech is more frequently cited there than in countries where it may be taken for granted. In Japan, this may be a reflection of the fact that the Japanese lost freedom of speech protections in the late nineteenth century and did not regain them until they were reinstated in the post–World War II constitution.

Being free to practice religion was most important to only 3 percent in Japan and 7 percent in Britain. In contrast, it was most important to 28 percent in the United States, where this value nearly tied for first place with being free from crime. The very clear differences among countries in what freedom they most valued is striking. Industrialized or wealthy countries do not always value the same things, nor do developing or less wealthy countries.

CRITICAL THINKING QUESTIONS

1. Why do many Americans say that they personally value freedom of religion as the most important value? What are the implications of this for American politics?
2. How can we account for the vast difference in what the people in these different countries most highly value?

capitalism
An economic system based on private property, competitive markets, economic incentives, and limited government involvement in the production, pricing, and distribution of goods and services.

economic success. Whether fulfilled or not, this dream speaks to our most deeply held hopes and goals. Its essence is expressed in our enthusiasm for **capitalism**, an economic system based on private property, competitive markets, economic incentives, and limited government involvement in the production, pricing, and distribution of goods and services.[20]

The concept of *private property* enjoys extraordinary popularity in the United States. Most cherish the dream of acquiring property and believe that the owners of property have the right to decide how to use it. And yet the unequal distribution of property, observed by James Madison and still an issue today, is an enduring cause of faction or political division.[21] The conflict in values between a *competitive economy*, in which individuals reap large rewards for their initiative and hard work, and an *egalitarian society*, in which everyone earns a decent living, carries over into politics. How the public resolves this tension changes over time and from issue to issue.

The right to private property is just one of the economic incentives that cement our support for capitalism and fuel the American dream. Although it is difficult to compare social mobility across countries, especially because of differences in rates of immigration, the American dream is more attainable for middle-income persons in the United States than in Europe. But the bottom fifth of the economic distribution in the United States appears to be less upwardly mobile than in Europe.[22]

What explains these differences? We assume that people who have more ability or who work hard will get ahead, earn more, and enjoy economic rewards. We also believe that people should be able to pass most of the wealth they have accumulated along to their children and relatives. Even the poorest generally oppose high inheritance taxes or limits on how much someone can earn. American adults believe that the free market system gives almost everyone a fair chance, that capitalism is necessary, and that freedom depends on capitalism. We reject communism and socialism—a rejection fortified in recent decades as most communist nations shifted toward capitalism. In the United States, individuals and corporations have acquired wealth and, at the same time, exercised political clout. Their power has in turn been widely criticized.

As important as the American dream is as an aspiration, it remains unfulfilled. The gap between rich and poor has grown in recent years, and a sharp income difference between whites and blacks remains tenacious.[23] For more people than we want to admit, chances for success still depend on the family they were born into, the neighborhood they grew up in, or the college they attended. An underclass persists in the form of impoverished families, malnourished and poorly educated children, and the homeless.[24] Many cities are actually two cities, where some residents live in luxury, others in squalor.

Most people today support a semi-regulated or mixed free enterprise system that checks the worst tendencies of capitalism, but they reject excessive government intervention. Much of American politics centers on how to achieve this balance. Currently, most people agree that some governmental intervention is necessary to assist those who fall short in the competition for education and economic prosperity and to encourage ventures that, though they have substantial public benefit, might not be undertaken without government assistance.

POPULAR SOVEREIGNTY The animating principle of the American Revolution, the Declaration of Independence, and the resulting new nation was popular sovereignty—the idea that ultimate political authority rests with the people. This means that a just government must derive its powers from the consent of the people it governs, or **popular consent**. A commitment to democracy thus means that a community must be willing to participate and make decisions in government. These principles sound unobjectionable, but in practice, they mean that candidates and their supporters must be willing to accept defeat when more people vote the other way

popular consent
The idea that a just government must derive its powers from the consent of the people it governs.

☐ Democracy as a System of Interrelated Political Processes

In addition to meeting a few key conditions and having a consensus of core democratic values, a successful, democratic government requires a well-defined political process as well as a stable governmental structure. To make democratic values a reality, a nation must incorporate such ideas into its political process, in the form of free and fair elections, majority rule, freedom of expression, and the right of its citizens to peaceably assemble and protest.

FREE AND FAIR ELECTIONS Democratic government is based on free and fair elections held at intervals frequent enough to make them relevant to policy choices.

1.1

1.2

1.3

1.4

1.5

majority rule
Governance according to the expressed preferences of the majority.

majority
The candidate or party that wins more than half the votes cast in an election.

plurality
The candidate or party with the most votes cast in an election, not necessarily more than half.

Elections are one of the most important devices for keeping officials and representatives accountable to the voters.

Crucial to modern-day definitions of democracy is the idea that opposition political parties can exist, can run candidates in elections, and have a chance to replace those who currently hold public office. Thus *political competition and choice* are crucial to the existence of democracy. Although free and fair elections do not imply that everyone will have equal political *influence*, they do have equal voting power, and each citizen—president or plumber, corporate CEO or college student—casts only one vote.

MAJORITY AND PLURALITY RULE Governance according to the expressed preferences of the majority, or **majority rule**, is a basic rule of democracy. The **majority** candidate or party is the one that receives *more than half* the votes and so wins the election and takes charge of the government until the next election. In practice, however, democracies often function by **plurality** rule. Here, the candidate or party with the *most* votes wins the election, even though the candidate or party may not have received more than half the votes because votes were divided among three or more candidates or parties.

Should the side with the most votes always prevail? American citizens answer this question in various ways. Some insist that majority views should be enacted into laws and regulations. However, an effective representative democracy requires far more than simply counting individual preferences and implementing the will of most of the people. In a constitutional democracy, the will of a majority may run counter to the rights of individuals.

The Framers of the U.S. Constitution wanted to guard society against oppression of any one faction of the people by any other faction. The Constitution reflects their fear of tyranny by majorities, especially momentary majorities that spring from temporary passions. They insulated certain rights (such as freedom of speech) and institutions (such as the Supreme Court and, until the Constitution was changed in 1913, even the Senate) from popular choice. Effective representation of the people, the Framers insisted, should not be based solely on parochial interests or the shifting breezes of opinion.

FREEDOM OF EXPRESSION Free and fair elections depend on voters having access to facts, competing ideas, and the views of candidates. This means that competing, nongovernment-owned newspapers, radio stations, and television stations must be allowed to flourish. If the government controls what is said and how it is said, elections cannot be free and fair, and there is no democracy. We examine free expression in greater detail in a later chapter on civil liberties.

THE RIGHT TO ASSEMBLE AND PROTEST Citizens must be free to organize for political purposes. Obviously, individuals can be more effective if they join with others in a party, a pressure group, a protest movement, or a demonstration. The right to oppose the government, to form opposition parties, and to have a chance to defeat incumbents is a defining characteristic of a democracy.

JUSTICE AND THE RULE OF LAW Inscribed over the entrance to the U.S. Supreme Court are the words "Equal Justice Under Law." The *rule of law* means government is based on a body of laws applied equally and by just procedures, as opposed to arbitrary rule by an elite group whose whims decides policy or resolve disputes. In 1803, Chief Justice John Marshall summarized this principle: "The government of the United States has been emphatically termed a government of laws, not of men."[25] Americans believe strongly in fairness: everyone is entitled to the same legal rights and protections.

To adhere to the rule of law, government should follow these five rules:

1. *Generality:* Laws should be stated generally and not single out any group or individual.

2. *Prospectivity:* Laws should apply to the present and the future, not punish something someone did in the past.
3. *Publicity:* Laws cannot be kept secret and then enforced.
4. *Authority:* Valid laws are made by those with legitimate power, and the people legitimate that power through some form of popular consent.
5. *Due process:* Laws must be enforced impartially with fair processes.

☐ Democracy as a System of Interdependent Political Structures

Democracy is, of course, more than the values and processes we have discussed so far. Its third characteristic is political structures that safeguard these values and processes. The Constitution and its first ten amendments—the Bill of Rights—set up an ingenious structure that both grants and checks government power. A system of political parties, interest groups, media, and other institutions that intercede between the electorate and those who govern reinforces this constitutional structure and thus helps maintain democratic stability. For example, the president, justices of the Supreme Court, and members of Congress all swear to uphold the Constitution. Moreover, individuals, groups, and the media also play a role in the functioning of the Constitution. Individuals, including elected officials, do not always secure their desired outcome in a particular matter, but by working within the constitutional framework they reinforce it.

The U.S. constitutional system has five distinctive elements: *federalism,* the division of powers between the national and state governments; *separation of powers* among the executive, judicial, and legislative branches; *bicameralism,* the division of legislative power between the House of Representatives and the Senate; *checks and balances* in which each branch is given the constitutional means, the political independence, and the motives to check the powers of the other branches so that a relative balance of power between the branches endures; and a judicially enforceable, written, explicit *Bill of Rights* that provides a guarantee of individual liberties and due process before the law. We will discuss all of these in more detail in the chapter on the Constitution.

☐ Conditions Favorable for Constitutional Democracy

Although it is hard to specify the precise conditions that consistently establish and preserve a democracy, we can identify some patterns that foster its growth.

EDUCATIONAL CONDITIONS The exercise of voting privileges requires an educated citizenry. But a high level of education (measured by the number of high school diplomas and university degrees granted) does not guarantee democratic government. Still, voting makes little sense unless many of the voters can read and write and express their interests and opinions. The poorly educated and illiterate often get left out in a democracy. Direct democracy puts a further premium on education.[26]

ECONOMIC CONDITIONS A relatively prosperous nation, with an equitable distribution of wealth, provides the best context for democracy. Starving people are more interested in food than in voting. Where economic power is concentrated, political power is also likely to be concentrated; thus, well-to-do nations have a better chance of sustaining democratic governments than do those with widespread poverty. As a result, the prospects for an enduring democracy are greater in Canada or France than in Zimbabwe or Egypt.

Private ownership of property and a market economy are also related to the creation and maintenance of democratic institutions. Freedom to make economic choices is linked to other freedoms, like freedom of religion and the right to vote. Democracies can range from heavily regulated economies with public ownership of many enterprises, such as Sweden, to those in which there is little government regulation of the marketplace, such as the United States. But there are no democracies with a highly centralized,

1.1

1.2

1.3

1.4

1.5

democratic consensus
A condition for democracy is that the people widely share a set of attitudes and beliefs about governmental procedures, institutions, core documents and fundamental values.

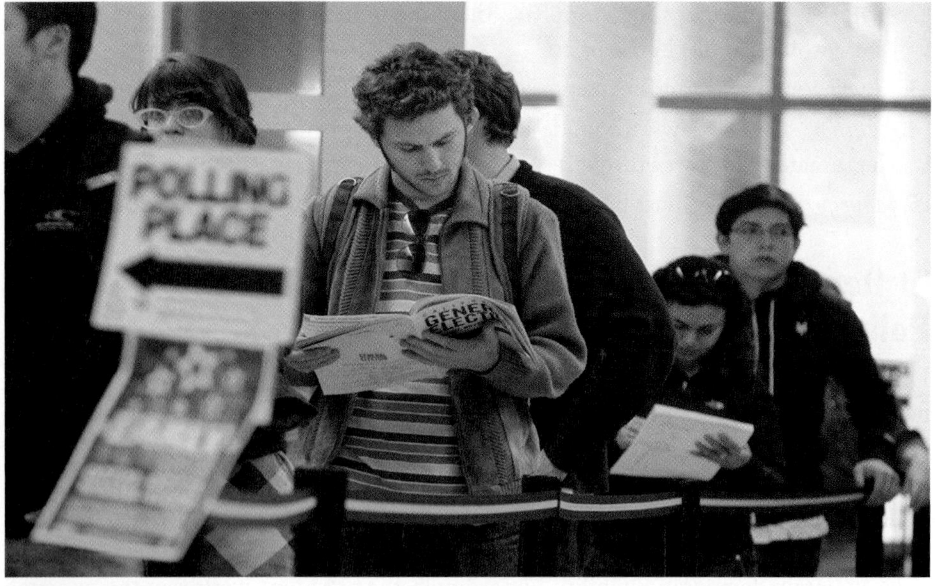

Clay De Long, center, a student at the University of California, Davis, studies a voters guide as he waits to vote early at a campus polling site in Davis, California.

government-run economy and little private ownership of property. When we examine experiments with democracy in other countries, we can find examples of democracies that struggled in settings in which conditions were not favorable. Economic challenges during the Weimar Republic in Germany (1919–1933) undermined that short-lived experiment in self-rule, for example.[27]

SOCIAL CONDITIONS Economic development generally makes democracy possible, but proper social conditions are necessary to make it real.[28] In a society fragmented into warring groups that fiercely disagree on fundamental issues, government by discussion and compromise is difficult, as we have seen in Afghanistan and Iraq. When ideologically separated groups consider the issues at stake to be vital, they may prefer to fight rather than accept the verdict of the ballot box, as happened in the United States in 1861 with the outbreak of the Civil War.

In a society that consists of many overlapping associations and groupings, however, individuals are less likely to identify completely with a single group and give their allegiance to it. For example, Joe Smith is a Baptist, an African American, a southerner, a Democrat, an electrician, and a member of the National Rifle Association (NRA), and he makes $50,000 a year. On some issues, Joe thinks as a Baptist, on others as a member of the NRA, and on still others as an African American. Joe and his fellow Americans may differ on some issues and agree on others, but they share an overriding common interest in maintaining a democracy.[29]

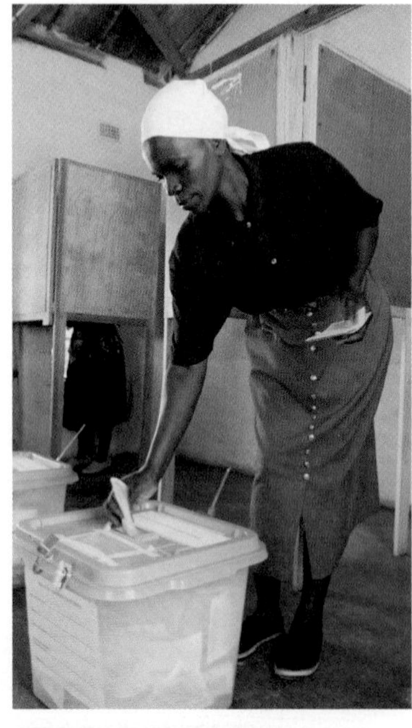

A woman casts her vote in Harare, Zimbabwe, where long lines formed at the polling stations hours before they opened.

IDEOLOGICAL CONDITIONS American adults have basic beliefs about power, government, and political practices—beliefs that arise from the educational, economic, and social conditions of their individual experience. From these conditions must also develop a general acceptance of the ideals of democracy and a willingness of a substantial number of people to agree to proceed democratically. This acceptance is sometimes called the **democratic consensus,** a set of widely shared attitudes and beliefs about government and its values, procedures, documents, and institutions. Without such a consensus, attempts at democracy will not succeed. For example, China has made major strides in improving its educational and economic circumstances in recent years, but it lacks a democratic consensus or the institutions and liberties vital to a democracy.

TABLE 1.1 CONDITIONS FOR DEMOCRATIC STABILITY

These countries vary dramatically in many aspects. For example, note the extremely young population of Nigeria compared to the generally older population of Japan. *What are the implications of this difference for both governments?* Notice that the U.S. population is less than one-fourth that of China. *How might population size affect some of these factors?* Compare the differences in literacy between men and women in India, Nigeria, and China. *What do you think accounts for these differences?*

	World	Britain	China	India	Japan	Mexico	Nigeria	United States
Population (millions; July 2011 est.)	6,928.20	62.70	1,336.72	1,189.17	126.48	113.72	155.22	313.23
Median Age (years)	28.4	40	35.5	26.2	44.8	27.1	19.2	36.9
Life Expectancy (years)	67.07	80.05	74.68	66.8	82.25	76.47	47.56	78.37
Literacy:								
Male	88.3%	99	96	73.4	99	86.9	75.7	99
Female	79.2%	99	88.5	47.8	99	85.3	60.6	99
Government Type		Constitutional monarchy	Communist state	Federal republic	Constitutional monarchy	Federal republic	Federal republic	Federal republic
GDP (purchasing power parity)*	74.54 (trillion)	2.173	10.09	4.06	4.31	1.567	0.378	14.66
Freedom House**		Free	Not Free	Free	Free	Partly Free	Partly free	Free

NOTES: *Calculated based on the country's official exchange rate in trillions of USD; **For more on Freedom House's Freedom Index, see www.freedomhouse.org/template.cfm?page=351&ana_page=333&year=2011.

SOURCE: Central Intelligence Agency, *The World Factbook*, at https://www.cia.gov/library/publications/the-world-factbook/geos/us.html; and Freedom House, *Freedom in the World 2011: The Annual Survey of Political Rights and Civil Liberties*, at www.freedomhouse.org/template.cfm?page=363&year=2011.

STABILITY Political scientists have long tried to determine what factors contribute to stability in a democracy. Comparative studies have often linked factors such as national prosperity, education, and literacy to democratic success. Table 1.1 lists several different dimensions for the countries that we will be comparing to the United States throughout the book.

The basic values of democracy do not always coexist happily. Individualism may conflict with the collective welfare or the public good. Self-determination may conflict with equal opportunity. A media outlet's freedom to publish classified documents about foreign or defense policy may conflict with the government's constitutional requirement to "provide for the common defense."

Much of our political debate revolves around how to strike a balance among democratic values. How, for example, do we protect the Declaration of Independence's unalienable rights of life, liberty, and the pursuit of happiness, while trying to "promote the general Welfare" as the Constitution proclaims?

We have discussed the values, political processes, and political structures that help foster viable constitutional democracy, as well as the conditions conducive to it. These provide a foundation on which we can assess governments throughout the world, as well as the extraordinary story of the founding and enlargement of constitutional democracy in the United States, to which we turn next.

The Roots of the American Constitutional Experiment

1.3 Show how politics before 1787 shaped the Constitution.

Most of us probably consider having a democracy and a constitution as part of the natural order of history. Although we have essentially inherited a functioning system—the work of others, generations ago—we take pride in our ability to make it work. Our job is not only to keep it going but to

1.1
1.2
1.3
1.4
1.5

theocracy
Government by religious leaders, who claim divine guidance.

Articles of Confederation
The first governing document of the confederated states, drafted in 1777, ratified in 1781, and replaced by the present Constitution in 1789.

improve and adapt it to the challenges of our times. To do so, however, we must first understand it by recalling our democratic and constitutional roots.

☐ The Colonial Beginnings

Our democratic experiment might well have failed. The 13 original states (formerly colonies) were independent and could have gone their separate ways. Differences between them, based on social and economic conditions, especially the southern states' dependence on slavery, were an obvious challenge to unity. Given these potential problems, how did democracy survive? The Framers of the Constitution had experience to guide them. For nearly two centuries, Europeans had been sailing to the New World in search of liberty—especially religious liberty—as well as land and work. The experience of settling a new land, overcoming obstacles, and enjoying the fruits of their labors was also important to the spirit of independence in the colonies.[30]

But freedom in the colonies was limited. Ironically, given their concern for religious liberty, the Puritans in Massachusetts established a **theocracy**, a system of government in which religious leaders claimed divine guidance and in which other sects were denied religious liberty. Later, as that system was challenged, the Puritans continued to worry "about what would maintain order in a society lacking an established church, an attachment to place, and the uncontested leadership of men of merit."[31] Nine of the 13 colonies eventually set up a state church. Throughout the 1700s, Puritans in Massachusetts barred certain men from voting on the basis of church membership. Women, slaves, and Native Americans could not vote at all.

By the 1700s, editors in the colonies found they could speak freely in their newspapers, dissenters could distribute leaflets, and agitators could protest in taverns or in the streets. And yet dissenters were occasionally exiled, imprisoned, and even executed, and some printers were beaten and had their shops closed. In short, the colonists struggled with the balance between unity and diversity, stability and dissent, order and liberty.

☐ The Rise of Revolutionary Fervor

As resentment against British rule mounted during the 1770s, the colonists became determined to fight the British to win their rights and liberties. In 1776, a year after the fighting broke out in Massachusetts, the Declaration of Independence proclaimed, in ringing tones, that all men are created equal, endowed by their Creator with certain unalienable rights; that among them are "life, liberty, and the pursuit of happiness"; that to secure those rights, governments are instituted among men; and that whenever a government becomes destructive of those ends, it is the right of the people to alter or abolish it. (Read the full text of the Declaration of Independence.)

We have heard these great ideals so often that we take them for granted. Revolutionary leaders did not. They were deadly serious about these rights and willing to fight and pledge their lives, fortunes, and sacred honor for them. Indeed, by signing the Declaration of Independence, they were effectively signing their own death warrants if the Revolution failed.[32] In most cases, state constitutions guaranteed the underlying rights referred to in the Declaration: free speech, freedom of religion, and the natural rights to life, liberty, and property. All their constitutions spelled out the rights of persons accused of crime, such as knowing the nature of the accusation, confronting their accusers, and receiving a timely and public trial by jury.[33] Moreover, these guarantees were set out *in writing*, in sharp contrast to the unwritten British constitution.

☐ Toward Unity and Order

As the war against the British widened to include all 13 colonies, the need arose for a stronger central government to unite them. In 1777, Congress established a new national government, the Confederation, under a written document called the **Articles of Confederation**.[34] The Articles were not approved by all the state legislatures until 1781, after Washington's troops had been fighting for six years.

FOR the People Government's Greatest Endeavors

Creating a Lasting Government

The wars in Afghanistan and Iraq were fought not only to limit al Qaeda (Afghanistan and Iraq), capture or kill Osama bin Laden (Afghanistan), and remove weapons of mass destruction (Iraq), but also to create stable and lasting governments that protect minorities and provide rights to women. Creating stable and lasting governments that respect basic human rights is sometimes called *nation building*. To create a government that protects basic liberties while incorporating popular sovereignty is a challenging task. Those who designed the U.S. Constitution in Philadelphia in 1787 could and did draw on the lessons learned in the drafting of the constitutions of the former colonies as they became states in 1776. From those experiences as well as other historical documents and political theory, the Framers developed the fundamental values and principles of our government.

For example, the Framers drew much inspiration on how to create the structures of their new government from the constitution of Virginia. The 1776 Virginia Constitution declared Virginia to be separate from Great Britain, and accused England's King George III of "detestable and insupportable tyranny."* To ensure a future executive could not wield such unilateral power, the structure of the new government included a separation of powers between the executive (Governor) and a two-house legislature (General Assembly). James Madison had participated in designing Virginia's Constitution, and he used those experiences to later incorporate separation of powers and a bicameral legislature into the federal constitution.

The Bill of Rights, essential for protecting the rights and liberties of the people, also benefited from the Framers' use of a number of historical documents and experiences. George Mason, a statesman from Virginia, drew from the Magna Carta and the English Bill of Rights to write the "Virginia Declaration of Rights." This document guaranteed freedom of the press, civilian control of the military, and trial by jury; required search warrants; and prohibited cruel and unusual punishments. Mason went on to become a delegate from Virginia to the U.S. Constitutional Convention, and his document served as a model for other states and for the Bill of Rights for the U.S. Constitution.

Drawing from the lessons of history, the founders created a government that has endured drastic social, demographic, and economic change and that has served and protected the rights of the people for more than 200 years. The challenge of establishing governments that aspire to these same values when they have not been part of the collective experience of the people as in Afghanistan and Iraq is very difficult. Factionalism, distrust, ethnic and religious differences, and longstanding grievances obstruct the building of a stable constitutional democracy and make the American experiment with self-government all the more noteworthy.

QUESTIONS

1. **What criteria would you use to assess whether a constitution is successful or not?**
2. **Why did Mason, Madison, and the other Virginians rely on documents like the Magna Carta when they designed their state's founding documents?**
3. **What are some of the things the Virginia Constitution appears to have been designed to avoid?**

The Constitution of Virginia, June 29, 1776, http://www.nhinet.org/ccs/docs/va-1776.htm (accessed March 2, 2010).

The Confederation was more like a fragile league of friendship than a national government. There was no national executive, judiciary, or national currency. Congress had to work through the states and had no direct authority over citizens. It could not levy taxes, regulate trade between the states or with other nations, or prevent the states from taxing each other's goods or issuing their own currencies. The lack of a judicial system meant that the national government had to rely on state courts to enforce national laws and settle disputes between the states. In practice, state courts could overturn national laws. Moreover, with the end of the Revolutionary War in 1783, the sense of urgency that had produced unity among the states began to fade. Conflicts between states and between creditors and debtors within the various states grew intense. Foreign threats continued; territories ruled by England and Spain surrounded the weak new nation. As pressures on the Confederation mounted, many leaders became convinced that a more powerful central government was needed to create a union strong enough to deal with internal diversity and factionalism and to resist external threats.

Annapolis Convention
A convention held in September 1786 to consider problems of trade and navigation, attended by five states and important because it issued the call to Congress and the states for what became the Constitutional Convention.

In September 1786, under the leadership of Alexander Hamilton, supporters of a truly national government took advantage of the **Annapolis Convention**—a meeting in Annapolis, Maryland, on problems of trade and navigation attended by delegates

1.1

1.2

1.3

1.4

1.5

Constitutional Convention
The convention in Philadelphia, from May 25 to September 17, 1787, that debated and agreed on the Constitution of the United States.

Shays' Rebellion
A rebellion led by Daniel Shays of farmers in western Massachusetts in 1786–1787 protesting mortgage foreclosures. It highlighted the need for a strong national government just as the call for the Constitutional Convention went out.

from five states—to issue a call for a convention to consider basic amendments to the Articles of Confederation. The delegates were to meet in Philadelphia on the second Monday of May 1787 "to devise such further provisions as shall appear to them necessary to render the Constitution of the Federal Government adequate to the exigencies of the Union."[35] This meeting became the **Constitutional Convention**.

For a short time, all was quiet. Then, late in 1786, messengers rode into George Washington's plantation at Mount Vernon in Virginia with the kind of news he and other leaders had dreaded. Farmers in western Massachusetts, crushed by debts and taxes, were rebelling against foreclosures, forcing judges out of their courtrooms, and freeing debtors from jails. These actions came to be known as **Shays' Rebellion**, named for Daniel Shays, the leader of the insurrection. As a patriot and a wealthy landowner, Washington was appalled. "What, gracious God, is man?" he exclaimed.

Not all reacted as Washington did. When Abigail Adams, the politically knowledgeable wife of John Adams, the Revolutionary statesman from Massachusetts, sent news of the rebellion to Thomas Jefferson, the Virginian replied, "I like a little rebellion now and then." He noted that the "tree of liberty must be refreshed from time to time with the blood of patriots and tyrants. It is its natural manure."[36] But the rebellion highlighted the lack of a mechanism to enforce contractual obligations in the absence of a strong central government.

Some, like historian Charles A. Beard, have argued that the primary motive of the authors of the U.S. Constitution was the protection of their economic interests more than a concern for other values.[37] Beard's views have been challenged.[38] Most agree that even though the early leaders of the United States were protecting their own economic interests, that was not their only motive.

Shays' Rebellion petered out after the farmers attacked an arsenal and were cut down by cannon fire. The uprising had threatened prosperity, the established order, and the rule of law, and it reinforced the view that a stronger national government was needed. Congress issued a cautiously worded call to all the state legislatures to appoint delegates for the "sole and express purpose of revising the Articles of Confederation."[39] The call for a convention specified that no recommendation would be effective unless approved by Congress and confirmed by all the state legislatures, as provided by the Articles.

The Constitutional Convention of 1787

1.4 Assess the important compromises reached by the delegates to the Constitutional Convention of 1787.

Explore on MyPoliSciLab Simulation: You Are a Candidate for Congress

The delegates who assembled in Philadelphia in May 1787 had to establish a national government powerful enough to prevent the young nation from dissolving but not so powerful that it would crush individual liberty. What these men did continues to have a major impact on how we are governed. It also provides an outstanding lesson in political science for the world.

The Delegates

The various states appointed 74 delegates, but only 55 arrived in Philadelphia. Of these, approximately 40 actually took part in the work of the convention. It was a distinguished gathering. Many of the most important men of the nation were there: successful merchants, planters, bankers, lawyers, and former and present governors and congressional representatives (39 of the delegates had served in Congress). Most had read the classics of political thought. Most had experience constructing local governments. Many had also worked hard to create and direct the national confederation of the states. And the Constitutional Convention also included eight of the 56 signers of the Declaration of Independence.

The convention was as representative as most political gatherings were at the time: the participants were all white male landowners. These well-read, well-fed, well-bred, and often well-wed delegates were mainly state or national leaders, for in the 1780s; ordinary people were not likely to participate in politics. (Even today, farm laborers, factory workers, and truck drivers are seldom found in Congress—although a haberdasher, a peanut farmer, and a movie actor have made their way to the White House.)

Although active in the movement to revise the Articles of Confederation, George Washington had been reluctant to attend the convention and accepted only when persuaded that his prestige was needed for its success. He was selected unanimously to preside over the meetings. According to the records, he spoke only twice during the deliberations, but his influence was felt in the informal gatherings as well as during the sessions. Everyone understood that Washington favored a more powerful central government led by a president. In fact, the general expectation that he would be the first president played a crucial role in the creation of the presidency. "No one feared that he would misuse power.... His genuine hesitancy, his reluctance to assume the position, only served to reinforce the almost universal desire that he do so."[40]

To encourage everyone to speak freely and allow delegates to change their minds after debate and discussion, the proceedings of the convention were kept secret and delegates were forbidden to discuss them with outsiders. The delegates also knew that if word of the inevitable disagreements got out, it would provide ammunition for the enemies of the convention.

OF the People Diversity in America

The Constitutional Convention

If the Constitutional Convention were convened today, how would the delegates compare to the all-white, all-male, property-owning delegates who drafted the Constitution in Philadelphia in 1787? One likely similarity is that they would be successful and generally well-educated individuals willing to engage in public service.

Many of those who drafted the Constitution had served in state legislatures. If the Constitutional Convention were held today and included state legislators, it would be much more diverse. Nearly 25 percent of state legislators are now female, including at least a third in Maryland, Delaware, Arizona, Colorado, Kansas, Nevada, and Vermont. At the same time, state legislatures remain almost entirely white—only 9 percent were African American in 2009, and only 3 percent were Hispanic.*

Many of those who drafted the Constitution were also lawyers and successful business managers. If the Constitutional Convention were held today and included these professions, the proportion of women participating would be between 35 and 40 percent, and 15 percent of the delegates would not be white.† Although these proportions show a growing diversity among the delegates who might be called to Philadelphia today, they do not yet reflect the diversity of the population at large.

QUESTIONS

1. How would the recent changes in U.S. demographics translate into changes in the content of any constitution produced by a Constitutional Convention held today?
2. Why are lawyers disproportionately represented in politics, both today and at the Constitutional Convention? What difference does having so many lawyers as constitution makers have on the process and on the document they produce?

*Conference of State Legislators, "2009 African American Legislators," http://www.ncsl.org/Default.aspx?TabId=14767 (accessed February 16, 2010).

†U.S. Equal Employment Opportunity Commission, "Diversity in Law Firms," 2003, http://www.eeoc.gov/eeoc/statistics/reports/diversitylaw/lawfirms.pdf.

Representing different constituencies and different ideologies, the Constitutional Convention devised a totally new form of government that provided for a central government strong enough to rule but still responsible to its citizens and to the member states.

☐ Consensus

Critical to the success of the Constitutional Convention were its three famous compromises: the compromise between large and small states over representation in Congress, the compromise between North and South over the regulation and taxation of foreign commerce, and the compromise between North and South over how to count slaves for the purposes of taxation and representation. There were other important compromises. But on many significant issues, most of the delegates were in agreement.

All the delegates publicly supported a republican form of government based on elected representatives of the people. This was the only form the convention seriously considered and the only form acceptable to the nation. Equally important, all the delegates opposed arbitrary and unrestrained government.

Most of the delegates were in favor of *balanced government* in which no single interest would dominate and in which the national government would be strong enough to protect property and business from outbreaks like Shays' Rebellion.

Benjamin Franklin, the 81-year-old delegate from Pennsylvania, favored extending the right to vote to all white males, but most of the delegates believed landowners were the best guardians of liberty. James Madison feared that if given the right to vote, those without property might combine to deprive property owners of their rights. Delegates agreed in principle on limited voting rights but differed on the kind and amount of property owned as a prerequisite to vote. The Framers recognized that they would jeopardize approval of the Constitution if they made the qualifications to vote in federal elections more restrictive than those of the states. As a result, each state was left to determine its own qualifications for electing members of the House of Representatives, the only branch of the national government that was to be elected directly by the voters.

Within five days of its opening, the convention voted—with only the Connecticut delegates dissenting—that "a national government ought to be established consisting of a supreme legislative, executive, and judiciary." This decision profoundly changed the nature of the union, from a loose confederation of states to a true nation.

Few dissented from proposals to give the new Congress all the powers of the old Congress, plus all other powers necessary to ensure that state legislation would not challenge the integrity of the United States. After the delegates agreed on the extensive powers of the legislative branch and the close connection between its lower house and the people, they also agreed that a strong executive, which the Articles of Confederation had lacked, was necessary to provide energy, direction, and a check on the legislature. They also accepted an independent judiciary without much debate. Other issues, however, sparked conflict.

Conflict and Compromise

Serious differences among the various delegates, especially between those from the large and small states, predated the Constitutional Convention. With the success of the War of Independence, the United States gained the formerly British land west of the colonial borders. States with large western borders, such as Virginia, claimed that their borders should simply be extended, as depicted in Figure 1.1. Colonies without open western borders, such as New Jersey and Connecticut, took exception to these claims, reinforcing the tension between the colonies. The matter was resolved in the Land Ordinance of 1785 and the Northwest Ordinance of 1787, when all states agreed to cede the western lands to the national government and permit them to eventually become part of new states rather than expand the borders of existing states. But the rivalries between the former colonies remained sharp at the convention in Philadelphia in 1787. For example, the large states also favored a strong national government (which they expected to dominate), while delegates from small states were anxious to avoid being dominated.

This tension surfaced in the first discussions of representation in Congress. Franklin favored a single-house national legislature, but most states had had two-chamber legislatures since colonial times, and the delegates were used to this system. **Bicameralism**—the principle of the two-house legislature—reflected delegates' belief in the need for balanced government. The Senate, the smaller chamber, would represent the states, and to some extent the wealthier classes, and it would offset the larger, more democratic House of Representatives.

THE VIRGINIA PLAN The Virginia delegation, and especially James Madison, took the initiative. They presented 15 resolutions known as the **Virginia Plan**. This called for a strong central government with a legislature composed of two chambers. The voters were to elect the members of the more representative chamber, which would choose the members of the smaller chamber from nominees submitted by the state legislatures. Representation in both houses would be based on either wealth or population. Wealth was based on a 1783 law where "general expenses were apportioned on the basis of land values with their improvements." The more wealthy states were also the more populous ones—Massachusetts, Pennsylvania, and Virginia—which gave them a majority in the national legislature.

The Congress that the Virginia Plan would have created was to have all the legislative power of its predecessor under the Articles of Confederation, as well as the power "to legislate in all cases in which the separate States are incompetent" which is understood to mean areas that concerned the states collectively,[41] to veto state legislation that conflicted with the proposed constitution, and to choose a national executive with extensive jurisdiction. A national Supreme Court, along with the executive, would have a qualified veto over acts of Congress. In sum, the Virginia Plan would have created a strong national government with disproportionate power to the more populous states.

THE NEW JERSEY PLAN The Virginia Plan dominated the discussion for the first few weeks. That changed when delegates from the small states put forward their plan. William Paterson of New Jersey presented a series of resolutions known as the **New Jersey Plan**. Paterson did not question the need for a strengthened central government, but he was concerned about how this strength might be used. The New Jersey Plan would give Congress the right to tax and regulate commerce and

bicameralism
The principle of a two-house legislature.

Virginia Plan
The initial proposal at the Constitutional Convention made by the Virginia delegation for a strong central government with a bicameral legislature dominated by the big states.

New Jersey Plan
The proposal at the Constitutional Convention made by William Paterson of New Jersey for a central government with a single-house legislature in which each state would be represented equally.

Connecticut Compromise

The compromise agreement by states at the Constitutional Convention for a bicameral legislature with a lower house in which representation would be based on population and an upper house in which each state would have two senators.

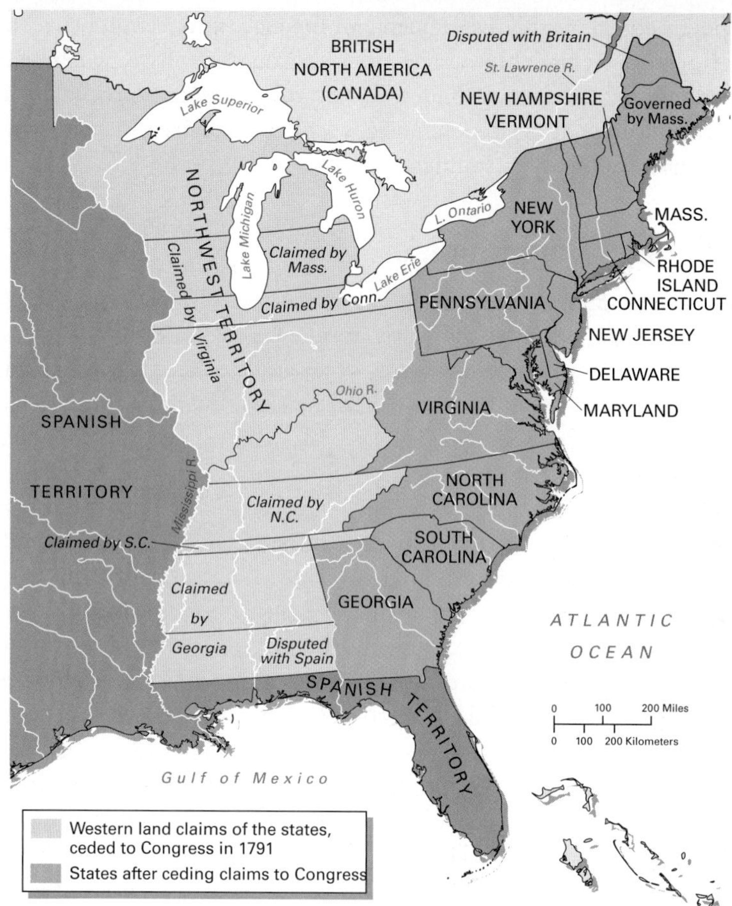

FIGURE 1.1 WESTERN EXPANSION, 1791

Tension between small states and large states was intensified by the dispute over claims to Western land acquired after the Revolutionary War.

■ *Why might the size of a state be important in a federal system of government?*

to coerce states, and it would retain the single-house or unicameral legislature (as under the Articles of Confederation) in which each state, regardless of size, would have the same vote.

The New Jersey Plan contained the germ of what eventually came to be a key provision of our Constitution: the *supremacy clause.* The national Supreme Court was to hear appeals from state judges, and the supremacy clause would require all judges—state and national—to treat laws of the national government and the treaties of the United States as superior to the constitutions and laws of each of the states.

For a time, the convention was deadlocked. The small states believed that all states should be represented equally in Congress, especially in the smaller "upper house" if there were to be two chambers. The large states insisted that representation in both houses be based on population or wealth, and that voters, not state legislatures, should elect national legislators. Finally, the so-called Committee of Eleven, a committee of 11 men, one from each of the member states, was elected to devise a compromise.[42] On July 5, it presented its proposals, including what came to be known as the great or Connecticut Compromise.

THE CONNECTICUT COMPROMISE The **Connecticut Compromise** (so labeled because of the prominent role the Connecticut delegation played in constructing it) called for one house in which each state would have an equal vote, and a second house in which representation would be based on population and in which all bills for raising or appropriating money—a key function of government—would originate. This proposal was a setback for the large states, which agreed to it only when the smaller states made it clear this was their price for union. After the delegates accepted equality of state representation in the Senate, most objections to a strong national government dissolved. (Table 1.2 outlines the key features of the Virginia Plan, the New Jersey Plan, and the Connecticut Compromise.)

NORTH–SOUTH COMPROMISES Other issues split the delegates from the North and South. Southerners were afraid that a northern majority in Congress might discriminate against southern trade. They had some basis for this concern. John Jay, a New Yorker who was secretary of foreign affairs for the Confederation, had proposed a treaty with Great Britain that would have given advantages to northern merchants at the expense of southern exporters of agricultural products such as tobacco and cotton. To protect themselves, the southern delegates insisted that a two-thirds majority in the Senate be required to ratify a treaty.

One subject that appears not to have been open for resolution was slavery. The view widely shared among historians is that the states with a greater reliance on slaves would have left the convention if the document had reduced or eliminated the practice. The issue did arise on whether to count slaves for the purpose of apportioning seats in the House of Representatives. To gain more representatives, the South wanted to count slaves; the North resisted. After heated debate, the delegates agreed on the **three-fifths compromise**. Three of every five slaves would be counted for purposes of apportionment in the House and of direct taxation. This three-fifths fraction was chosen because it maintained a balance of power between the North and the South. The compromise also included a provision to eliminate the importation of slaves in 20 years, and Congress did so in 1808. The issue of balance between North and South would recur in the early history of our nation as territorial governments were established and territories that applied for statehood decided whether to permit or ban slavery.

OTHER ISSUES Delegates also argued about other issues. Should the national government have lower courts, or would one federal Supreme Court be enough? This issue was left to Congress to resolve. The Constitution states that there shall be one Supreme Court and that Congress may establish lower courts.

How should the president be selected? For a long time, the convention favored allowing Congress to pick the president, but some delegates feared that Congress would then dominate the president, or vice versa. The convention also rejected election by the state legislatures because the delegates distrusted the state legislatures. The delegates finally settled on election of the president by the **Electoral College**,

three-fifths compromise
The compromise between northern and southern states at the Constitutional Convention that three-fifths of the slave population would be counted for determining direct taxation and representation in the House of Representatives.

Electoral College
The electoral system used in electing the president and vice president, in which voters vote for electors pledged to cast their ballots for a particular party's candidates.

TABLE 1.2 THE CONSTITUTIONAL CONVENTION: CONFLICT AND COMPROMISE

Virginia Plan	New Jersey Plan	Connecticut Compromise
Legitimacy derived from citizens, based on popular representation	Derived from states, based on equal votes for each state	Derived from citizens and the states
Bicameral legislature, representation in both houses determined by population	Unicameral legislature, representation equal by state	Bicameral legislature with seats in the Senate apportioned by states and seats in the House apportioned by population
Executive size undetermined, elected and removable by Congress	More than one person, removable by state majority	Single executive elected by electoral college, not removable by state majority
Judicial life tenure, able to veto state legislation	No federal judicial power over states	Judicial life tenure, able to veto state legislation in violation of constitution
Legislature can override state laws	Government can compel obedience to national laws	
Ratification by citizens	Ratification by states	Ratification by states, with process open to citizen ratification

1.1

1.2

1.3

1.4

1.5

Federalists
Supporters of ratification of the Constitution and of a strong central government.

Antifederalists
Opponents of ratification of the Constitution and of a strong central government generally.

a group of individuals equal in number to the U.S. senators and representatives. Originally, it was thought electors would exercise their own judgment in selecting the president. But the college quickly came to reflect partisanship, and today, for most states, electors cast ballots for the candidate who wins the popular vote of that state. (We discuss the Electoral College in greater detail in the chapter on campaigns and elections.) This was perhaps the delegates' most novel contribution as well as the most contrived, and it has long been one of the most criticized provisions in the Constitution.[43] (See Article II, Section 1 of the Constitution.)

After three months, the delegates stopped debating. On September 17, 1787, all but three of those still present signed the document they were recommending to the nation. Others who opposed the general drift of the convention had already left. Their work well done, the delegates adjourned to the nearby City Tavern to celebrate.

According to an old story, a woman confronted Benjamin Franklin as he left the last session of the convention.

"What kind of government have you given us, Dr. Franklin?" she asked. "A republic or a monarchy?"

"A republic, Madam," he answered, "if you can keep it."

To Adopt or Not to Adopt?

1.5 Evaluate the arguments for and against the ratification of the Constitution.

The delegates had gone far. Indeed, they had disregarded Congress's instruction to do no more than revise the Articles of Confederation. In particular, they had ignored Article XIII, which declared the Union to be perpetual and prohibited any alteration of the Articles unless Congress and *every one of the state legislatures* agreed—a provision that had made it impossible to amend the Articles. The convention delegates, however, boldly declared that their newly proposed Constitution should go into effect when ratified by popularly elected conventions in nine states.

They turned to this method of ratification for practical considerations as well as to secure legitimacy for their proposed government. Not only were the delegates aware that there was little chance of winning approval of the new Constitution in all state legislatures, but many also believed that a constitution approved *by the people* would have higher legal and moral status than one approved only by a legislature. The Articles of Confederation had been a compact of state governments, but the Constitution was based on the will of the people (recall its opening words: "We the People..."). Still, even this method of ratification would not be easy.

Federalists Versus Antifederalists

Supporters of the new government, by cleverly appropriating the name **Federalists**, forced their opponents to be known as the **Antifederalists** and pointed out the negative character of the arguments opposing ratification. While advocating a strong national government but also retaining state prerogatives, the Federalists took some of the sting out of charges that they were trying to destroy the states and establish an all-powerful central government.

The split was in part geographic. Seaboard and city regions tended to be Federalist strongholds; backcountry regions from Maine (then part of Massachusetts) through Georgia, inhabited by farmers and other relatively poor people, were generally Antifederalist. The underlying regional and economic differences led to fears by those opposing the new form of government that it would not protect individual rights, and reinforced the "Antifederalist charge that the Constitution was an aristocratic document."[44] But as in most political contests, no single factor completely accounted for the division between Federalists and Antifederalists. Thus, in Virginia, the leaders of both sides came from the same general social and economic class. New York City and Philadelphia strongly supported the Constitution, yet so did predominantly rural New Jersey and Connecticut.

The great debate was conducted through pamphlets, newspapers, letters to editors, and speeches. It provides an outstanding example of a free people publicly discussing the nature of their fundamental laws. Out of the debate came a series of essays known as ***The Federalist***, written under the pseudonym Publius by Alexander Hamilton, James Madison, and John Jay to persuade the voters of New York to ratify the Constitution. *The Federalist* is still "widely regarded as the most profound single treatise on the Constitution ever written and as among the few masterly works in political science produced in all the centuries of history."[45]

The Federalist
Essays promoting ratification of the Constitution, published anonymously by Alexander Hamilton, John Jay, and James Madison in 1787 and 1788.

Antifederalists opposed the creation of a strong central government. They worried that, under the Constitution, Congress would "impose barriers against commerce," and they were concerned that the Constitution did not do enough to ensure "frequent rotation of office," worrying that elected officials would not be recalled through elections and over time would become less concerned with their constituents.[46]

The Antifederalists' most telling criticism of the proposed Constitution was its failure to include a bill of rights.[47] The Federalists believed a bill of rights was unnecessary because the proposed national government had *only* the specific powers that the states and the people delegated to it. Thus, there was no need to specify that Congress could not, for example, abridge freedom of the press because the states and the people had not given the national government power to regulate the press in the first

BY the People Making a Difference

Becoming an American Citizen

Many Americans take their government for granted and have not thought much about the importance of their citizenship in this country. That is not the case for those who have gone through the process of securing U.S. citizenship. The process involves a detailed application, a criminal records search, information about your family, and an interview that includes an assessment of proficiency in English and knowledge of the U.S. government and Constitution. You can view samples of these civics questions by clicking on the "Naturalization Test" at http://www.uscis.gov/portal/site/uscis and then under the "Citizenship" heading follow the link to "the naturalization test." How would you do on the oral exam? One current sample question, for example, asks applicants: "The idea of self-government is in the first three words of the Constitution. What are these three words?" The correct answer is "We the people." To pass the test, an applicant must answer six of the ten questions correctly.*

For many people wanting to become U.S. citizens, the application process, interview, and examination are intimidating. The U.S. Committee for Refugees and Immigrants (USCRI) makes a difference in helping people attain U.S. Citizenship. The USCRI is the nation's oldest (founded in 1911) and largest network of nonprofit organizations serving foreign-born people. The USCRI has resettled a quarter million refugees in the past two decades. It has a "Partnership for Citizenship Program" that helps individuals prepare to become citizens. Some of those seeking citizenship are refugees who also need assistance in such basics as writing resumes and preparing for job interviews, as well as information on where they can go for food, clothing, and housing.

You can make a difference by volunteering at an agency assisting refugees and others in your community. Some universities, like Harvard University, have programs where undergraduates tutor individuals to prepare them for the citizenship exam. If your institution does not have such a program, you might organize one. Given your study of American government, you will be prepared to assist in the English and Civics preparation for the citizenship screening interview.

QUESTIONS

1. Would all Americans take citizenship more seriously if they had to apply for citizenship and pass an oral exam on U.S. government?
2. How restrictive should the government be in extending citizenship?

*U.S. Citizenship and Immigration Services, "The Naturalization Test," http://www.uscis.gov/portal/site/uscis/menuitem (accessed April 27, 2010).

Patrick Henry's famous cry of "Give me liberty or give me death!" helped rally support for the revolution against Britain. Later, he was an outspoken opponent of ratification of the Constitution and was instrumental in forcing adoption of the Bill of Rights.

place. Moreover, the Federalists argued, to guarantee some rights might be dangerous, because rights not listed could be assumed to be denied. The Constitution itself already protected some important rights—the requirement of trial by jury in federal criminal cases, provided for in Article III, for example. Hamilton and others also insisted that paper guarantees were feeble protection against governmental tyranny.

The Antifederalists were unconvinced. If some rights were protected, what could be the objection to providing constitutional protection for others? Without a bill of rights, what was to prevent Congress from using one of its delegated powers to abridge free speech? If bills of rights were needed in state constitutions to limit state governments, why did the national constitution not include a bill of rights to limit the national government? This was a government further from the people, they contended, with a greater tendency to subvert natural rights than was true of state governments.

□ The Politics of Ratification

The absence of a bill of rights in the proposed Constitution dominated the struggle over its adoption. In taverns, churches, and newspaper offices, people were muttering, "No bill of rights—no Constitution!" This feeling was so strong that some Antifederalists, though they were far more concerned with states' rights than individual rights, joined forces with those wanting a bill of rights in order to defeat the proposed Constitution.

The Federalists began the debate over the Constitution as soon as the delegates left Philadelphia in mid-September 1787. Their tactic was to secure ratification in as many states as possible before the opposition had time to organize. The Antifederalists were handicapped because most newspapers supported ratification. Moreover, Antifederalist strength was concentrated in rural areas, which were underrepresented in some state legislatures and in which it was more difficult to arouse the people to political action. The Antifederalists needed time to organize, while the Federalists moved in a hurry.

Most of the small states, now satisfied by getting equal Senate representation, ratified the Constitution without difficulty. Delaware was the first, and by early 1788, Pennsylvania, New Jersey, Georgia, and Connecticut had also ratified (see Table 1.3). In Massachusetts, however, opposition was growing. Key leaders, such as John Hancock and Samuel Adams, were doubtful or opposed. The debate in Boston raged for most of January 1788 and into February. But in the end, the Massachusetts Convention narrowly ratified the Constitution in that state, 187 to 168.

TABLE 1.3 RATIFICATION OF THE U.S. CONSTITUTION

State	Date
Delaware	December 7, 1787
Pennsylvania	December 12, 1787
New Jersey	December 18, 1787
Georgia	January 2, 1788
Connecticut	January 9, 1788
Massachusetts	February 6, 1788
Maryland	April 28, 1788
South Carolina	May 23, 1788
New Hampshire	June 21, 1788
Virginia	June 25, 1788
New York	July 26, 1788
North Carolina	November 21, 1789
Rhode Island	May 29, 1790

■ *By what date did the Constitution have enough state support to go into effect? Why was it still important for the remaining states to ratify the Constitution?*

Explore on MyPoliSciLab

How Long Did It Take to Ratify the Constitution?

Americans today overwhelmingly support the principles of the Constitution, but after the Framers adjourned on September 17, 1787, three years passed before all thirteen states approved the document. The ensuing ratification debate was an inherently political game of multiple moves, in which the Constitution was kept alive by relatively narrow majorities, particularly in two strategically located states.

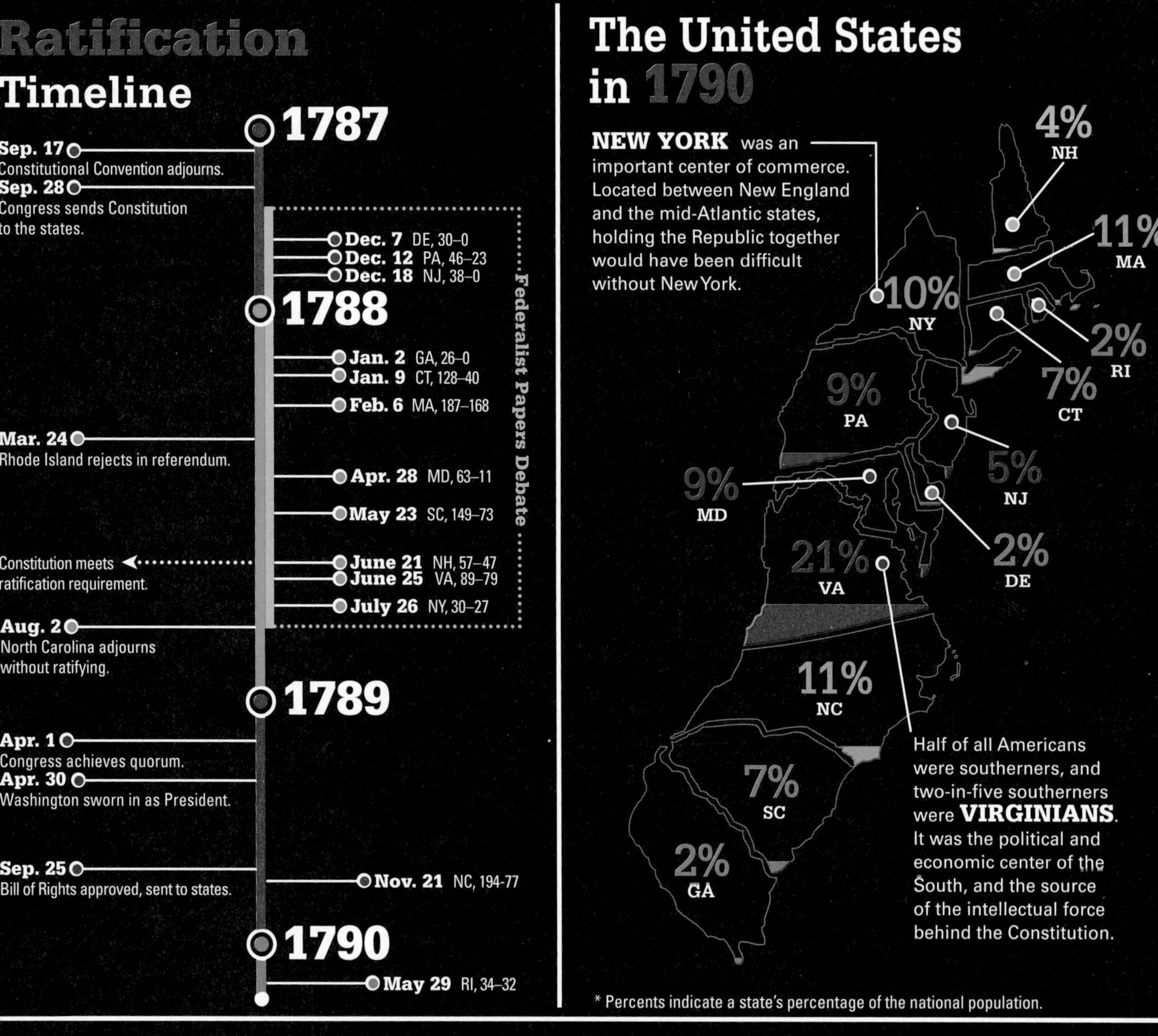

Investigate Further

Concept Why did it take three years to ratify the Constitution? The first states to ratify the Constitution did so with a strong majority of support for the document. But as those states signed on, opposition in remaining states grew, and the ratification debate intensified.

Connection Which states were most closely divided on ratification? The debate intensified in two strategic states: New York and Virginia. Ratification in those two holdout states was necessary in order to lend legitimacy to the new government.

Cause What were the issues of the debate? Written in support of the new government, *The Federalist Papers* addressed New Yorkers' concerns about federal power. For Virginians, the sticking point was a Bill of Rights, which James Madison promised to introduce in the new Congress.

By June 21, 1788, Maryland, South Carolina, and New Hampshire had also ratified, giving the Constitution the nine states required for it to go into effect. But two big hurdles remained: Virginia and New York. It would be impossible to begin the new government without the consent of these two major states. Virginia, as the most populous state and the home of Washington, Jefferson, and Madison, was a link between North and South. The Virginia ratifying convention rivaled the Constitutional Convention in the caliber of its delegates. Madison, who had only recently switched to favoring a bill of rights after saying earlier that it was unnecessary, captained the Federalist forces. The fiery Patrick Henry led the opposition. In an epic debate, Henry cried that liberty was the issue: "Liberty, the greatest of earthly possessions...that precious jewel!" But Madison promised that a bill of rights embracing the freedoms of religion, speech, and assembly would be added to the Constitution as soon as the new government was established. Washington tipped the balance with a letter urging ratification. News of the Virginia vote, 89 for the Constitution and 79 opposed, was rushed to New York.[48]

The great landowners along New York's Hudson River, unlike the southern planters, opposed the Constitution. They feared federal taxation of their holdings, and they did not want to abolish the profitable tax New York had been levying on trade and commerce with other states. When the convention assembled, the Federalists were greatly outnumbered, but they were aided by Alexander Hamilton's strategy and skill, and by word of Virginia's ratification. New York approved by a margin of three votes. Although North Carolina and Rhode Island still remained outside the Union (the former ratified in November 1789, the latter six months later), the new nation was created. In New York, a few members of the old Congress assembled to issue the call for elections under the new Constitution. Then they adjourned without setting a date for reconvening.

While the ratified Constitution had limitations and shortcomings, it remains to this day an extraordinary governing document. It allowed the states to unite, it provided a workable structure, and it protected fundamental rights and liberties. Over the centuries since it was ratified it has been amended and interpreted by succeeding generations to meet changing needs and circumstances.

On MyPoliSciLab

Review the Chapter

Listen to **Chapter 1** on **MyPoliSciLab**

U.S. Government and Politicians in Context

1.1 Use the concept of constitutional democracy to explain U.S. government and politics, p. 21.

The United States operates under a constitutional democracy. In our system, the Constitution lays out the basic rules of the game under which politicians act to accomplish their different agendas. "Politics" is a broad term that can be used to describe what happens between these politicians in pursuit of their goals. "Government" is another broad term that encompasses the many different institutions enumerated by the Constitution in which the politicians function. Political science studies the interaction among politics, politicians, the government, and, within the American context, our constitutional democracy.

Defining Democracy

1.2 Differentiate democracy from other forms of government, and identify conditions conducive to a successful democracy, p. 23.

In the United States, we often use the term "democracy" to describe our form of government. This is true to an extent, but a more accurate term would be "representative democracy" or "republic." The politicians in our system are elected representatives meant to stand up for the interests of their constituents. Representative democracy differs from direct democracy in the level of citizen participation.

Scholars have identified several conditions that may help democratic governments form and consolidate. Among these, educational, economic, social, and ideological conditions are the most important. These conditions further democratic values such as a belief in personal liberty, respect for the individual, equality of opportunity, and popular consent. Our representative democracy functions through political structures including courts, legislatures, the executive, administrative agencies, federalism, and the principle of limited government. Also important to our tradition is the rule of law and freedom of expression.

The Roots of the American Constitutional Experiment

1.3 Show how politics before 1787 shaped the Constitution, p. 33.

In the formative years of American democracy, several competing factions worked, sometimes at cross purposes, to develop the Constitution. Some of the most divisive issues that the Framers had to address were the challenges presented by a federal system. Small states had real concerns about their role in a democratic system. There were also issues that had more to do with geography and economics. The divide between the North and the South on slavery was also important at the convention.

The Constitutional Convention of 1787

1.4 Assess the important compromises reached by the delegates to the Constitutional Convention of 1787, p. 36.

The Framers came up with some brilliant compromises to address these issues, such as the Connecticut Compromise that led to our current bicameral legislative branch. Other issues were put on hold. For example, the Framers postponed dealing with slavery and compromised on counting slaves as three-fifths of a person for purposes of apportionment.

To Adopt or Not to Adopt?

1.5 Evaluate the arguments for and against the ratification of the Constitution, p. 42.

Some of the same themes that dominated the debate over ratification can still be heard today. Federalists argued for a central government that would be strong enough to make the newly united states capable of standing up to the great powers of the time. Antifederalists worried about what might come of a strong central government and were particularly concerned about the lack of any bill of rights in the document.

Learn the Terms

Study and **Review** the **Flashcards**

democracy, p. 23
direct democracy, p. 23
direct primary, p. 23
initiative, p. 23
referendum, p. 23
recall, p. 23
representative democracy, p. 25
constitutional democracy, p. 25
constitutionalism, p. 25
natural rights, p. 25
political culture, p. 26
statism, p. 27
American dream, p. 27
capitalism, p. 28
popular consent, p. 29

majority rule, p. 30
majority, p. 30
plurality, p. 30
democratic consensus, p. 32
theocracy, p. 34
Articles of Confederation, p. 34
Annapolis Convention, p. 35
Constitutional Convention, p. 36
Shays' Rebellion, p. 36
bicameralism, p. 39
Virginia Plan, p. 39
New Jersey Plan, p. 39
Connecticut Compromise, p. 40
three-fifths compromise, p. 41
Electoral College, p. 41
Federalists, p. 42
Antifederalists, p. 42
The Federalist, p. 43

Test Yourself

Study and **Review** the **Practice Tests**

MULTIPLE CHOICE QUESTIONS

1.1 Use the concept of constitutional democracy to explain U.S. government and politics.

In a constitutional democracy elected officials
- **a.** build coalitions.
- **b.** mediate among factions.
- **c.** are expected to embody many positive attributes.
- **d.** are made scapegoats.
- **e.** all of the above

1.2 Differentiate democracy from other forms of government, and identify conditions conducive to a successful democracy.

Specific values have contributed to the relative longevity of democracy in the United States. Which values seem most important to U.S. citizens?
- **a.** Constitutional democracy
- **b.** Federalism
- **c.** Republic
- **d.** Statism
- **e.** Direct democracy

1.3 Show how politics before 1787 shaped the Constitution.

Which of the following resulted in a federal system with a strong central government?
- **a.** The Articles of Confederation
- **b.** Revolutionary War
- **c.** The Declaration of Independence
- **d.** The Constitutional Convention
- **e.** Shays' Rebellion

1.4 Assess the important compromises reached by the delegates to the Constitutional Convention of 1787.

Which state was the compromise that led to a bicameral legislature named after?
- **a.** Rhode Island
- **b.** Connecticut
- **c.** New Hampshire
- **d.** Maine
- **e.** New York

1.5 Evaluate the arguments for and against the ratification of the Constitution.

Identify arguments that impeded ratification of the Constitution.
- **a.** opposition to a strong central government
- **b.** lack of a Bill of Rights
- **c.** equal representation in Congress for large and small states
- **d.** barriers to free commerce
- **e.** all of the above

ESSAY QUESTION

What are some of the important differences between the Articles of Confederation and the Constitution? How would the United States be different today if the Constitution were never drafted and the government instead relied on the Articles of Confederation?

Explore Further

IN THE LIBRARY

Bernard Bailyn, ed., *The Debate on the Constitution: Federalist and Antifederalist Speeches, Articles, and Letters During the Struggle over Ratification*, 2 vols. (Library of America, 1993).

Lance Banning, *The Sacred Fire of Liberty: James Madison and the Founding of the Federal Republic* (Cornell University Press, 1995).

Ron Chernow, *Washington: A Life* (Penguin Press, 2010).

Robert A. Dahl, *How Democratic Is the American Constitution*, 2nd ed. (Yale University Press, 2003).

Stanley Elkins and Eric Mckitrick, *The Age of Federalism: The Early American Republic, 1788–1800* (Oxford University Press, 1994).

Alan Gibson, *Understanding the Founding: Crucial Questions* (University Press of Kansas, 2007).

Alexander Hamilton, James Madison, and John Jay, *The Federalist Papers*, ed. Clinton Rossiter (New American Library, 1961). Also in several other editions.

Philip B. Kurland and Ralph Lerner, *The Founders' Constitution*, 5 vols. (University of Chicago Press, 1987).

Sanford Levinson, *Our Undemocratic Constitution* (Oxford University Press, 2006).

Arend Lijphart, *Patterns of Democracy: Government Forms and Performance in Thirty-Six Countries* (Yale University Press, 1999).

Jack N. Rakove, *Original Meanings: Politics and Ideas in the Making of the Constitution* (Vintage Books, 1997).

Michael Schudson, *The Good Citizen: A History of American Civic Life* (Harvard University Press, 1998).

Gordon S. Wood, *The Radicalism of the American Revolution* (Knopf, 1992). See also the *Journal of Democracy* (Johns Hopkins University Press).

ON THE WEB

www.usa.gov/Agencies/federal.shtml
This site provides a variety of information on the government and its agencies.

www.constitutionfacts.com/
This site provides quotes, facts, and quizzes about the Constitution.

www.archives.gov/
This site provides information on America's key historical documents.

www.teachingamericanhistory.org/
This site is all about American history.

www.people.brandeis.edu/~teuber/polphil.html
This site provides resources for exploring the political philosophies important to the founders.

2

Listen to Chapter 2 on MyPoliSciLab

Constitutional Foundations

The United States Constitution is the oldest written constitution in the world; it is also one of the shortest. The original Constitution contains only 4,543 words. In comparison, India's constitution is 117,000 words, and the longest state constitution—that of Alabama—is over 350,000 words. The Framers had long deliberations over the appropriate wording of the document, and in the end, it was not ratified until an initial ten amendments, the Bill of Rights, was added. The Constitution established an enduring system of government that has been altered only seventeen more times in over 225 years. But that stability masks a great deal of debate over its meaning, debate that continues today.

One current debate over the Constitution's meaning concerns the Second Amendment's protection of the right to bear arms. What does the Amendment mean? Does each person have such a right? Or, based on the opening clause of the Amendment, does the right extend only to members of state militias? After 70 years of silence on the issue, the U.S. Supreme Court addressed it in June 2008. By a 5-to-4 vote, the Court decided the amendment means that individual citizens, apart from any association with a state militia, have a constitutional right to own a gun (*District of Columbia* v. *Heller* [2008]).[1] The Court's interpretation of the Second Amendment invalidated the District of Columbia's ban on registering (and thus owning) handguns. Two years later, the Court weighed in again on the Second Amendment—this time to determine whether it also prohibits states from restricting handgun ownership. In *McDonald* v. *Chicago* (2010),[2] the Court ruled that it does. For the first time, the Court found that states are barred from encroaching on citizens' Second Amendment rights.

Even after the Court's decisions in these two landmark cases, the debate over the degree to which guns can be restricted continues. One of the more recent questions of state action and litigation is whether handguns can be banned from college campuses. In March 2012, the Colorado Supreme Court struck down the University of Colorado's ban on concealed weapons on the system's campuses.[3] In doing so, Colorado joined Oregon and Utah in allowing those with permits to carry concealed weapons anywhere on college campuses.[4] Several other states, including Mississippi and Wisconsin, have passed similar legislation and others are currently considering it. Given outbursts of violence on college campuses, such as the tragedy at Virginia Tech in April 2007, where 33 people were killed, the debate is unlikely to end soon.

2.1 Describe the basic structure of the Constitution and its Bill of Rights, p. 53.

2.2 Analyze how the Constitution grants, limits, separates, and balances governmental power, p. 54.

2.3 Explain how the use of judicial review strengthens the courts in a separation of powers system, p. 62.

2.4 Assess how the Constitution has evolved through changes in the informal, unwritten Constitution, p. 65.

2.5 Describe the processes by which formal changes to the Constitution can be made, p. 68.

Adrienne O'Reilly is the Oklahoma director of Students for Concealed Carry on Campus. O'Reilly and other students in favor of allowing concealed weapons on college campuses wore empty holsters at Oklahoma State University to show support for legislation that would permit it.

The Big Picture What? The Constitution was created because men cannot be trusted? At least this was James Madison's rationale. Christine L. Nemacheck describes the factors that led to a Constitution that is designed to impede hasty legislation.

The Basics What is the purpose of a Constitution? In this video, you will discover the reasons why the Framers wrote the Constitution and how the Constitution sets up checks and balances, the protection of liberties, and the framework we need for a functioning democracy.

In Context Why is it unusual that the United States Constitution has governed so long in its present form? Fordham University political scientist Costas Panagopolos explains why the Constitution is such a rarity and how it has succeeded in an evolving American society.

Thinking Like a Political Scientist How do the institutions created by the U.S. Constitution operate and how has their role changed over time? Fordham University political scientist Costas Panagopolos examines this and other emerging issues in the research and in the study of the Constitution.

In the Real World How well does the system of checks and balances in the United States work, and is it actually fair? Real people voice their opinions on whether or not they believe it is constitutional for Congress to check the power of the president—and vice versa.

So What? According to the Constitution, women have a right to privacy when terminating their pregnancy. Now what? Using abortion as an example, Christine L. Nemacheck illustrates why it is so difficult to implement policies through the various levels and branches of government—and why this may have been the Framers' intention.

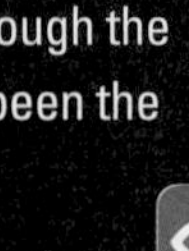

Disagreement over the Second Amendment's meaning highlights both the genius of and a flaw in the Constitution—its lack of specificity. In composing the Constitution, the Framers were conscious that they were writing a document that needed to withstand the test of time. By not specifying what is meant by the right to "keep and bear arms," they designed a document that others could apply to changing circumstances. However, this generality also results in continuing debates, which have included the appropriate authority of the governing branches and the extent of national government authority over the states. The power of the courts to determine what exactly the Constitution means has also led to scrutiny of the ways by which it reaches those decisions.

In this chapter, we discuss our constitutionally arranged system of separation of powers and checks and balances, as well as how special-interest groups and political parties try to circumvent these protections. We will see how the judiciary came to be widely accepted as the final interpreter of constitutional meaning and the way both the executive and the legislature have used the Constitution to pursue their own ends. Finally, we examine the difficult process through which citizens can amend the Constitution. As the Framers intended, it is no small feat, and one that is an important factor in the stability of our Constitution.

natural law
God's or nature's law that defines right from wrong and is higher than human law.

Views of the Constitution

2.1 Describe the basic structure of the Constitution and its Bill of Rights.

The Constitution's basic structure is straightforward. Article I establishes a bicameral Congress, with a House of Representatives and a Senate, and empowers it to enact legislation, for example, governing foreign and interstate commerce. Article II vests the executive power in the president, and Article III vests the judicial power in the Supreme Court and other federal courts that Congress may establish. Article IV guarantees the privileges and immunities of citizens and specifies the conditions for admitting new states. Article V provides for the methods of amending the Constitution, and Article VI specifies that the Constitution and all laws made under it are the supreme law of the land. Finally, Article VII provides that the Constitution had to be ratified by 9 of the original 13 states to go into effect. In 1791, the first 10 amendments, the Bill of Rights, were added, and another 17 amendments have been added since.

Despite its brevity, the Constitution firmly established the Framers' experiment in free-government-in-the-making that each generation reinterprets and renews. That is why after more than 225 years we have not had another written Constitution—let alone two, three, or more, like other countries around the world. Part of the reason is the public's widespread acceptance of the Constitution. But the Constitution has also endured because it is a brilliant structure for limited government and one that the Framers designed to be adaptable and flexible.

As the Constitution won the support of citizens in the early years of the Republic, it took on the aura of **natural law**—law that defines right from wrong, which is higher than human law. Like the Crown in Great Britain, the Constitution became a symbol of national unity and loyalty, evoking both emotional and intellectual support from Americans, regardless of their differences. The Framers' work became part of U.S. culture.[5] The Constitution stands for liberty, equality before the law, limited or expanded government—indeed, it stands for just about anything anyone wants to read into it.

Even today, U.S. citizens generally revere the Constitution, although many do not know what is in it. A poll by the National Constitution Center found that nine of ten U.S. adults are proud of the Constitution and feel it is important to them. However, a third mistakenly believe the Constitution establishes English as the country's official language. One in six believes it establishes the United States as a Christian nation. Only one in four could name a single First Amendment right. Although two in three knew the Constitution created three branches of the national government, only one in three could name all three branches.[6]

Citizens can view the original U.S. Constitution at the National Archives in Washington, D.C.

2.1

2.2

2.3

2.4

2.5

BY the People Making a Difference

Celebrating Constitution Day

On September 17, 1787, the Framers of the United States Constitution met to sign their names to the document. Almost 220 years later, in 2005, Congress declared September 17 to be Constitution Day and mandated that educational institutions commemorate the day. The purpose of the law was to provide instruction to American citizens about their rights and responsibilities under the Constitution.

Across the United States, students from elementary schools through colleges celebrate Constitution Day. In many cases, administrators plan events where a professor or outside guest gives a talk on the importance of our constitutional protections. But, in other cases, college students have celebrated Constitution Day by exercising their constitutional rights. At Jackson Community College in Jackson, Michigan, students organized a Constitution Day voter registration drive and held discussions on a documentary addressing failures of the US educational system.*

At Purdue University, students from a variety of campus organizations teamed up to test their knowledge of the Constitution in a college bowl competition. Representatives of Purdue's student government also held sessions to inform students about internship opportunities in their state government.†

At the University of Texas at San Antonio, students from the group Young Americans for Liberty created a 17 foot Constitution that students signed to pledge their support for understanding the document according to the Framers' original intent. The students also handed out pocket copies of the Constitution and encouraged discussion of its proper interpretation.††

None of these celebrations required more time or effort to organize than most campus activities and they served to inform students about our founding document. What kind of Constitution Day activity can you organize or take part in on your campus?

QUESTIONS

1. **Why might Congress have thought it important to establish a "Constitution Day?"**
2. **What constitutional protections might be especially important for college students?**

*http://www.mlive.com/news/jackson/index.ssf/2011/09/jackson_community_college_to_c_1.html
†http://www.purdue.edu/constitution-day/
††http://studentsforliberty.org/upcoming-events/student-movement-update-an-xxl-constitution-day/

James Madison was the fourth president of the United States (1809–1817) and an author of *The Federalist Papers*. Madison's view on a separated system of government in which each branch checks the power of other branches shapes our governmental structure.

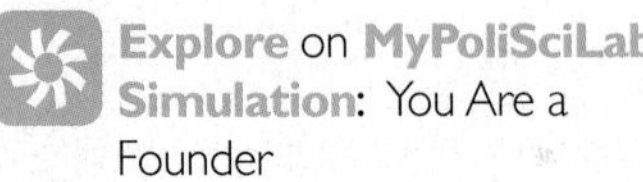

Explore on MyPoliSciLab Simulation: You Are a Founder

The Constitution is more than a symbol, however. It is the supreme and binding law that both grants and limits powers. "In framing a government which is to be administered by men over men," wrote James Madison in *The Federalist*, No. 51, "the great difficulty lies in this: You must first enable the government to control the governed; and in the next place oblige it to control itself." The Constitution is both a positive instrument of government, which enables the governors to control the governed, and a restraint on government, which enables the ruled to check their government and its leaders.

This chapter examines a number of questions that are still being asked long after the Framers completed their work. How does the Constitution limit the power of the government? How does it create governmental power? How has it managed to serve as a great symbol of national unity and, at the same time, as an adaptable instrument of government? The secret is an ingenious separation of powers and a system of checks and balances that limits power with power.

Checking Power with Power

2.2 Analyze how the Constitution grants, limits, separates, and balances governmental power.

"If men were angels," James Madison argued in *The Federalist,* No. 51, "no government would be necessary. If angels were to govern men, neither external nor internal controls on government would be necessary."[7] But the Framers knew well that men were not angels, and thus, to create a successful government, they would need to create a government of *limited* authority. How? Within the government, competing interests would check each other, and externally, the governed would check the government through elections, petitions, protests, and amendments.

Explore on MyPoliSciLab

How Do You Measure Freedom?

How did the threat of terrorism affect Americans' perceptions of freedom? Most Americans do not believe authorities should randomly frisk people, but more than half support tapping potential terrorists phones or indefinitely detaining them. And less than half of respondents in 2010 supported free speech protections for radical Muslim clerics.

Support for Free Speech Strengthens

Between 1980 and 2010, more Americans support free speech for more groups. The exceptions are racists and radical Muslims.

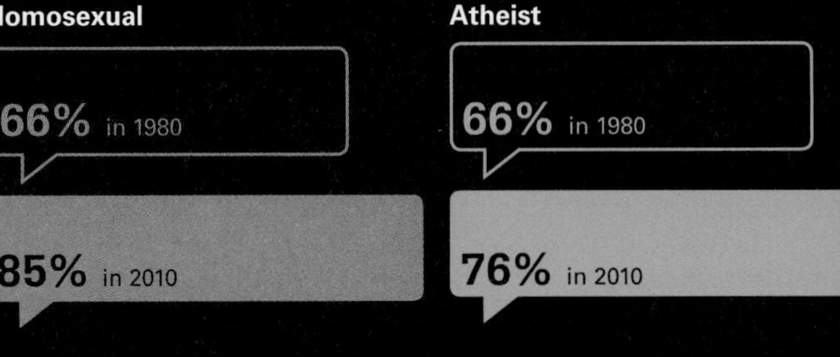

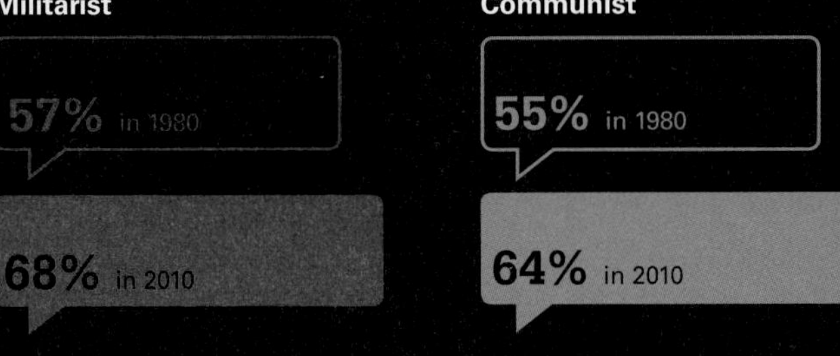

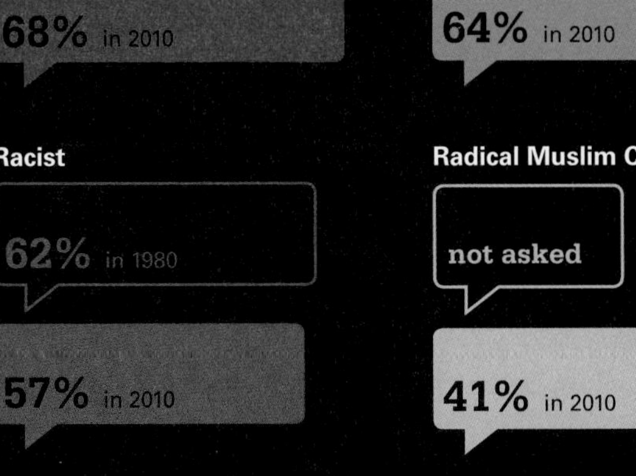

Support for Privacy Weakens

If the government suspects that a terrorist act is about to happen, do you think the authorities should have the right to ...

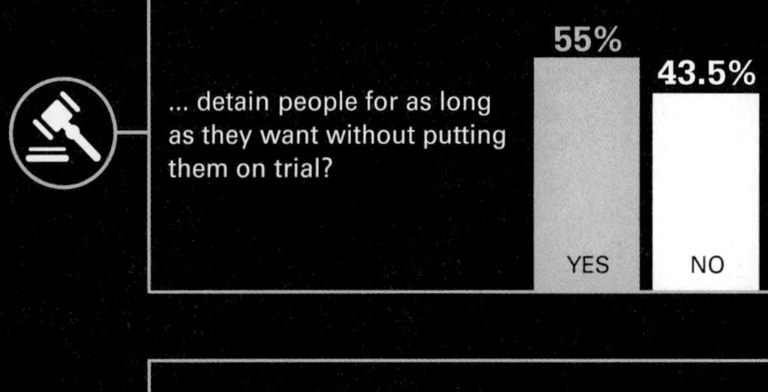

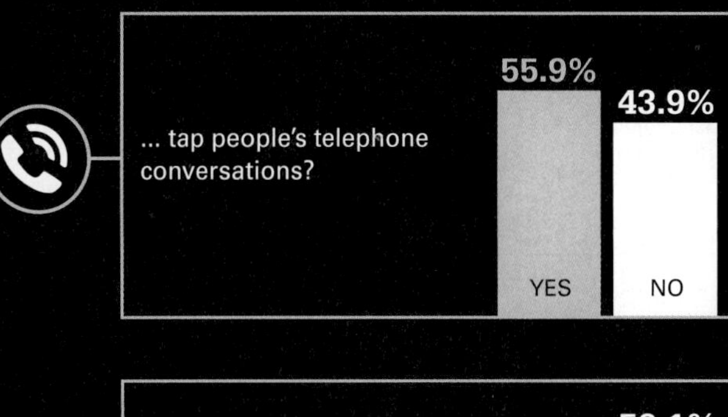

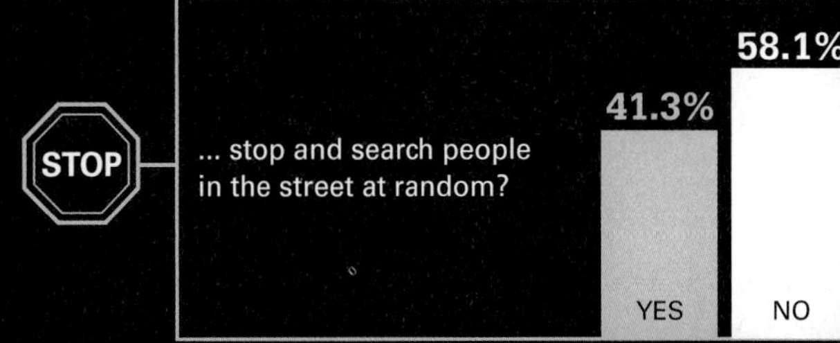

SOURCE: Data from General Social Survey, 1980, 2006, and 2010

Investigate Further

Concept How does support for free speech and individual privacy measure freedom? Protecting free speech ensures that all ideas can be expressed and debated, even if they are unpopular. Likewise, protecting the privacy rights of everyone, even those who appear to be threatening, ensures equal treatment for all.

Connection How has Americans' support for free speech changed between 1980 and 2010? Overall, Americans are more tolerant of speech from "controversial" groups. More Americans support free speech for people who were previously marginalized, particularly atheists and homosexuals. Fewer are willing to tolerate racist speech.

Cause How did the threat of terrorism change freedom in America? Most Americans will still not tolerate random public frisks of people who might not be suspects. But after 9/11, Americans don't support speech by radical Muslim clerics and they are willing to detain potential terrorists indefinitely and wire-tap suspects' phones.

2.1
2.2
2.3
2.4
2.5

The Global Community

Increasing Concern over Government Control

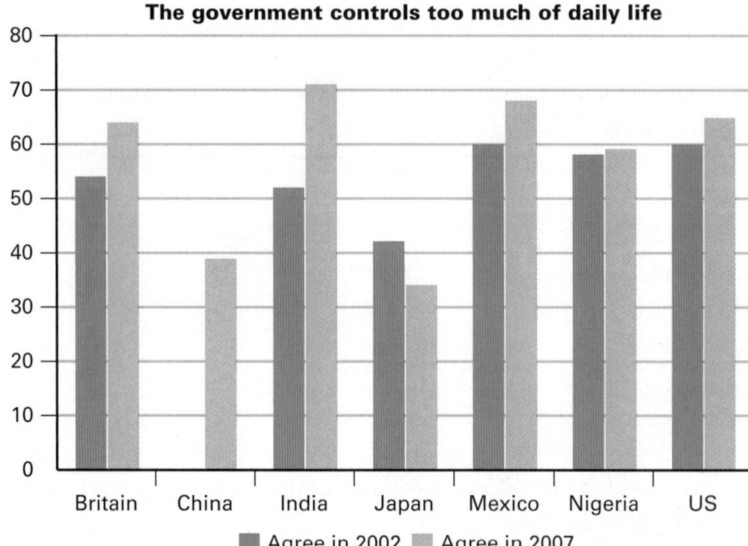

SOURCE: Pew Research Center, *Global Views on Life Satisfaction, National Conditions, and the Global Economy: Highlights from the 2007 Pew Global Attitudes 47-Nation Survey* (Pew Research Center, 2007).

Although our Constitution places limits on the reach of our federal government, citizens in the United States, as elsewhere in the world, show concern over government assuming too much control. According to the Pew Research Center's Global Attitudes surveys, majorities in most countries surveyed in 2007 agreed that their governments have too much control over their daily lives. Respondents were asked how much they agreed with the statement, "The (state or national government) controls too much of our daily lives." Another Pew survey in 2002 asked the same question and allows us to compare the shift in concern between 2002 and 2007.

In the United States, for example, the percentage of respondents indicating that our government had too much control over our daily lives increased from 60 to 65 percent from 2002 to 2007. This trend was even more pronounced in Great Britain, where the percentage of respondents agreeing with that statement increased 10 percentage points from 54 to 64 percent. These changes may not be surprising given the kind of increased security measures governments have instituted since the September 11, 2001, attacks in New York and Washington, D.C.

These concerns are not confined to Western countries involved in the fight against terrorism. We also see an increase in India and Nigeria. In Japan, however, the percentage of survey respondents who are concerned about the government having too much control over their daily lives decreased between 2002 and 2007 (from 42 to 34 percent). Given that our Constitution sets limits on the reach of government, citizens' perceptions that government has too much control over their daily lives might indicate an inconsistency between the theory and practice of constitutional government.

CRITICAL THINKING QUESTIONS

1. What factors might contribute to respondents' views that their governments have too much control over their lives?
2. How might a government's effort to become more open increase its citizens' views that it is too controlling?
3. In what ways does your federal government have control over your day-to-day life?

The Framers wanted a stronger and more effective national government than they had under the Articles of Confederation. But they were keenly aware that the people would not accept too much central control. Efficiency and order were important, but liberty was more important. The Framers wanted to ensure domestic tranquility and prevent future rebellions; they also wanted to prevent the emergence of a homegrown King George III. Accordingly, they allotted certain powers to the national government and reserved the rest for the states, thus establishing a system whose nature and problems we discuss in the chapter on American Federalism. But even this was not enough. The Framers believed additional restraints were needed to limit the national government.

The most important means they devised to make public officials observe the constitutional limits on their powers was *free and fair elections,* through which voters could throw out of office anyone who abused power. Yet the Framers did not fully trust the people's judgment. "Free government is founded on jealousy, and not in confidence," said Thomas Jefferson. "In questions of power, then, let no more be heard of confidence in man, but bind him down from mischief by the chains of the Constitution."[8]

No less important, the Framers feared a majority might deprive minorities of their rights. This risk was certainly real at the time of the framing, as it is today. As *District of Columbia* v. *Heller* shows, even if there were sufficient public support for the District's legislation restricting gun ownership when it was enacted in 1976, the Second Amendment protects citizens' right to own guns for their own self-protection. "A dependence on the people is, no doubt, the primary control on the government," Madison contended in *The Federalist,* No. 51, "but experience has taught mankind the necessity of auxiliary precautions."[9] What were these "auxiliary precautions" against popular tyranny?

separation of powers
Constitutional division of powers among the legislative, executive, and judicial branches, with the legislative branch making law, the executive applying and enforcing the law, and the judiciary interpreting the law.

checks and balances
A constitutional grant of powers that enables each of the three branches of government to check some acts of the others and therefore ensures that no branch can dominate.

☐ Separation of Powers

The first step against potential tyranny of the majority was the **separation of powers**, the distribution of constitutional authority among the three branches of the national government. In *The Federalist,* No. 47, Madison wrote: "No political truth is certainly of greater intrinsic value, or is stamped with the authority of more enlightened patrons of liberty, than that...the accumulation of all powers, legislative, executive, and judiciary, in the same hands...may justly be pronounced the very definition of tyranny."[10] Chief among the "enlightened patrons of liberty" to whose authority Madison was appealing were the eighteenth-century philosophers John Locke and Montesquieu, whose works most educated citizens knew well.

The intrinsic value of the dispersion of power, however, is not the only reason the Framers included it in the Constitution. It had already been the general practice in the colonies for more than 100 years. Only during the Revolutionary period did some of the states concentrate authority in the hands of the legislature, and that unhappy experience as well as that under the Articles of Confederation confirmed the Framers' belief in the merits of the separation of powers. Many attributed the evils of state government and lack of energy in the central government to the lack of a strong executive who would check legislative abuses and give energy and direction to administration.

Still, separating power by itself was not enough to protect the people from tyranny. It might not prevent the branches of the government and officials from pooling their authority and acting together, or from responding alike to the same pressures—from the demand of a majority to restrict handgun ownership, for example, or to impose confiscatory taxes on the rich. What else could be done?

☐ Checks and Balances: Ambition to Counteract Ambition

The Framers' answer was a system of **checks and balances** (see Table 2.1). Madison's idea to avoid concentration of power was to give each branch the constitutional power to check the others. "Ambition must be made to counteract ambition."[11] Each branch therefore has a role in the actions of the others (see Figure 2.1).

TABLE 2.1 THE EXERCISE OF CHECKS AND BALANCES, 1789–2012

Vetoes Presidents have vetoed more than 2,500 acts of Congress. Congress has overridden presidential vetoes more than 100 times.

Judicial Review The Supreme Court has ruled more than 175 congressional acts or parts thereof unconstitutional.

Impeachment The House of Representatives has impeached two presidents, one senator, one secretary of war, and 16 federal judges; the Senate has convicted seven of the judges but neither president.

Confirmation The Senate has refused to confirm nine cabinet nominations. Many other cabinet and subcabinet appointments were withdrawn because the Senate seemed likely to reject them.

SOURCE: The American Presidency Project, University of California, Santa Barbara, http://www.presidency.ucsb.edu/data/vetoes.php. For additional resources on the Constitution, go to www.archives.gov/exhibits/charters/constitution.html.

■ *Does the relative infrequency of veto overrides surprise you? Why or why not? Are there other checks Congress can use against the president?*

Congress enacts legislation, which the president must sign into law or veto. The Supreme Court can declare laws passed by Congress and signed by the president unconstitutional, but the president appoints the justices and all the other federal judges, with the Senate's approval. The president administers the laws, but Congress provides the money to run the government. Moreover, the Senate and the House of Representatives have absolute veto power over each other because both houses must approve bills before they can become law.

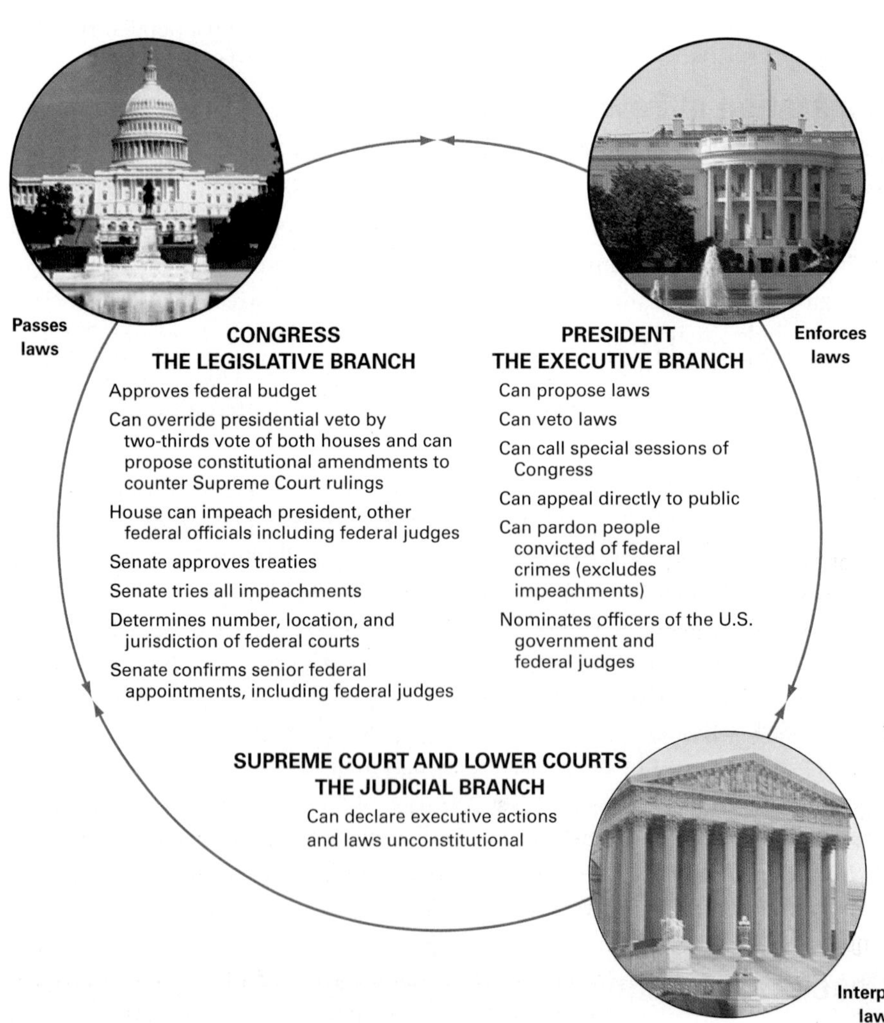

FIGURE 2.1 THE SEPARATION OF POWERS AND CHECKS AND BALANCES

■ *Does the fact that the judiciary has the fewest number of checks make it the least powerful?*

Not only does each branch have some authority over the others, but each is also politically independent of the others. Voters in each local district choose members of the House; voters in each state choose senators; the president is elected by the voters in all the states, through the Electoral College. With the consent of the Senate, the president appoints federal judges, who remain in office until they retire or are impeached.

The Framers also ensured that a majority of the voters could win control over only part of the government at one time. In an off-year (nonpresidential) election where a new majority might take control of the House of Representatives, the president still has at least two more years, and senators hold office for six years. Finally, there are independent federal courts, which exercise their own powerful checks.

Distrustful of both the elites and the masses, the Framers deliberately built into our political system mechanisms to make changing the system difficult. They designed the decision-making process so that the national government can act decisively only when there is a consensus among most groups and after all sides have had their say. "The doctrine of the separation of powers was adopted by the convention of 1787," in the words of Justice Louis D. Brandeis, "not to promote efficiency but to preclude the exercise of arbitrary power. The purpose was not to avoid friction, but, by means of the inevitable friction incident to the distribution of the governmental powers among three departments, to save the people from **autocracy**"[12]—a system in which one person has control over the populace. Still, even though the fragmentation of political power written into the Constitution remains, constitutional silences, or topics the Constitution does not address, and subsequent developments have modified the way the system of checks and balances works.

autocracy
A type of government in which one person with unlimited power rules.

partisanship
Strong allegiance to one's own political party, often leading to unwillingness to compromise with members of the opposing party.

divided government
Governance divided between the parties, especially when one holds the presidency and the other controls one or both houses of Congress.

unified government
Governance in which one party controls both the White House and both houses of Congress.

2.1
2.2
2.3
2.4
2.5

☐ National Political Parties and Interest Groups

Political parties—the Republican and Democratic parties being the largest—can serve as unifying factors, at times drawing the president, senators, representatives, and sometimes even judges together behind common programs. When parties do this, they help bridge the separation of powers. Yet they can be splintered and weakened by having to work through a system of fragmented governmental power, and by the increasing influence of special-interest groups, so that they never become so strong or cohesive that they threaten liberty.

When one party controls Congress or one of its chambers and the other party controls the White House, **partisanship** is intensified, and Congress is inclined to more closely monitor the executive branch. Because his party controlled Congress during much of his presidency, President George W. Bush was remarkably free from congressional investigations of his administration. However, when Democrats regained control in both the Senate and the House of Representatives in 2006, they quickly began congressional investigations into the use of intelligence leading up to the war in Iraq and the firing of U.S. Attorneys by the U.S. Justice Department. More conflict is certainly to be expected during divided government, but even when one party controls both branches, the pressures of competing interest groups may make cooperation among legislators difficult.

Because of this competition between the legislative and executive branches, each is prone to encroaching on the power of the other when given the opportunity.[13] Thus we have battles over the budget and angry confirmation hearings for the appointment of Supreme Court justices, lower federal court judges, and members of the executive branch; as a result, some might suspect that less would be accomplished during periods of divided government. The division of powers also makes it difficult for the voters to hold anyone or any party accountable. "Presidents blame Congress...while members of Congress attack the president.... Citizens genuinely cannot tell who is to blame."[14]

Yet when all the shouting dies down, political scientist David Mayhew concludes, there is just as much important legislation passed when one party controls Congress and another controls the presidency (**divided government**) as when the same party controls both branches (**unified government**.)[15] New research on the government's most significant investigations since World War II by our co-author Paul Light is consistent with Mayhew's conclusion—divided government actually produces more

Electoral College
The electoral system used in electing the president and vice president, in which voters vote for electors pledged to cast their ballots for a particular party's candidates.

significant investigations and greater impetus toward improving government performance than does unified government.[16] And Charles Jones, a noted authority on Congress and the presidency, adds that divided government is precisely what the voters appear to have wanted through much of our history.[17] As we discuss in detail in the chapter on Congress, divided government frequently occurs when the president's party loses congressional seats in the midterm elections.

☐ Expansion of the Electorate and the Move Toward More Direct Democracy

The **Electoral College** was another provision of the Constitution meant to provide a buffer against the "whims of the masses" (see *The Federalist,* No. 10). The Framers wanted the Electoral College—wise, independent citizens free of popular passions and hero worship—to choose the president rather than leave the job to ordinary citizens. Almost from the beginning, though, the Electoral College did not work this way.[18] Rather, voters actually do select the president because the presidential electors that the voters choose pledge in advance to cast their electoral votes for their party's candidates for president and vice president. Nevertheless, presidential candidates may occasionally win the national popular vote but lose the vote in the Electoral College, as happened when Al Gore won the popular vote in the 2000 presidential election but lost the Electoral College with 266 votes to George W. Bush's 271.

The kind of people allowed to vote has expanded from free, white, property-owning males to include all citizens over the age of 18. In addition, during the past century, U.S. states have expanded the role of the electorate through such means as direct primaries, initiatives, referendums and recalls. And since the ratification of the Seventeenth Amendment in 1913, senators are no longer elected by state legislatures but are chosen directly by the people.

☐ Changes in Technology

Because of new technologies, today's system of checks and balances operates differently from the way it did in 1789. There were no televised congressional committee hearings in 1789, no electronic communications; no *The Daily Show* with Jon Stewart; no

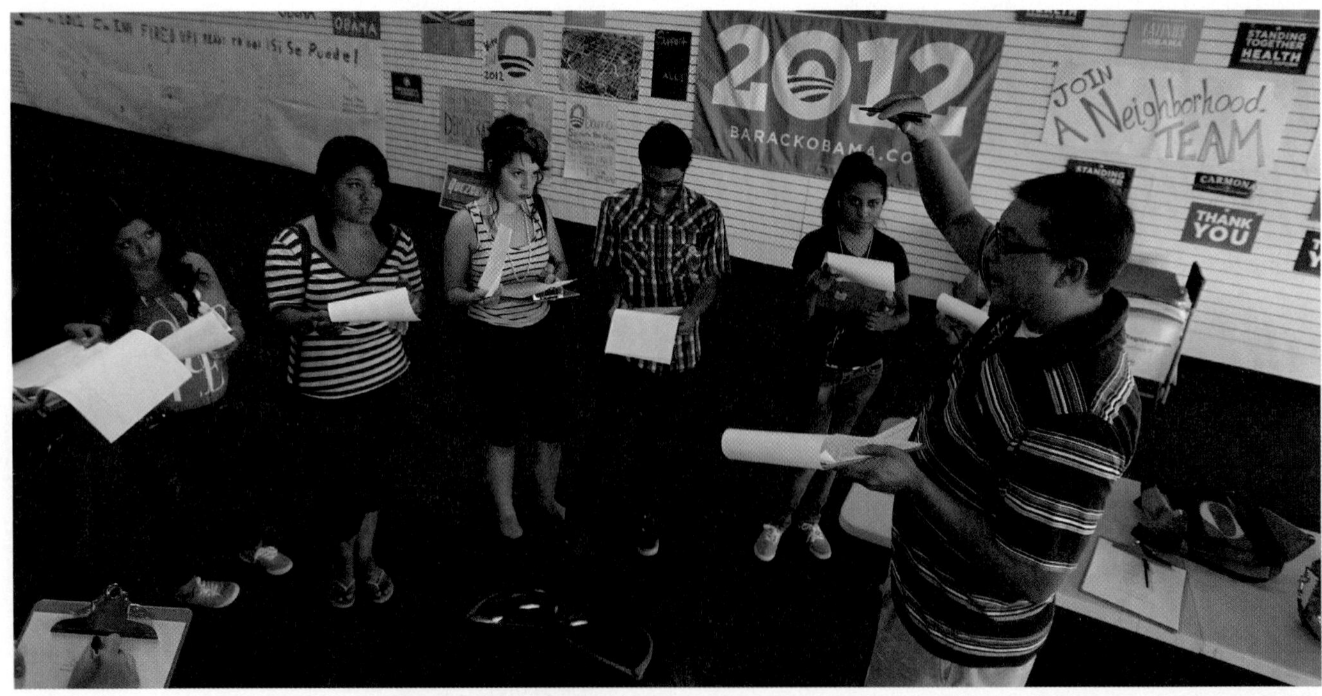

Although overall voter turnout remained largely unchanged in the 2004 and 2008 presidential elections, turnout among voters 18–24 years of age increased, as did the numbers of black, Hispanic, and Asian voters. Here volunteers for President Obama's 2012 reelection campaign prepare to register new voters in heavily Latino neighborhoods in Phoenix, Arizona.

Linda McMahon, 2012 Republican candidate for an open Senate seat in Connecticut and former CEO of World Wrestling Entertainment, used her personal fortune to outspend her primary challenger at a rate of nearly 12 to 1.

New York Times, USA Today, CNN, Fox News, or C-SPAN; no Internet; no nightly news programs with national audiences; no presidential press conferences; no Facebook or Twitter, and no live coverage of wars and of U.S. soldiers fighting in foreign lands. Nuclear bombs, television, computers, cell phones, Smartphones, and iPads—these and other innovations create conditions today that are unimaginably different from those of two centuries ago. We live in a time of instant communication and polls that tell us what people are thinking about public issues almost from one day to the next.

In some ways, these new technologies have added to the powers of presidents by permitting them to appeal directly to millions of people and giving them immediate access to public opinion. In turn, they have enabled interest groups to target thousands of letters, e-mails, and calls at members of Congress; to orchestrate campaigns to write letters to editors; and to organize and mobilize on the Internet. New technologies have also given greater independence and influence to nongovernmental institutions such as special-interest groups and the press. They have made it possible for rich people to bypass political parties and carry their message directly to the electorate, as Meg Whitman, the billionaire former chief of eBay did, spending some $144 million of her own money on her failed 2010 gubernatorial bid in California.[19]

☐ The Growth of Presidential Power

Today, problems elsewhere in the world—Afghanistan, Israel, Pakistan, Iran, North Korea—often create crises for the United States. The need to deal with perpetual emergencies has concentrated power in the hands of the chief executive and the presidential staff. As a result, the president of the United States has emerged as the most significant player on the world stage, and media coverage of summit conferences with foreign leaders enhances the president's status. Headline-generating events give the president a visibility no congressional leader can achieve. The office of the president has on occasion modified the system of checks and balances, especially between the executive branch and Congress, and provided a measure of national unity. Drawing on constitutional, political, and emergency powers, the president can sometimes overcome the restraints the Constitution imposes on the exercise of governmental power—to the applause of some and the alarm of others. The Obama administration argued strongly

judicial review
The power of a court to review laws or governmental regulations to determine whether they are consistent with the U.S. Constitution, or in a state court, the state constitution.

Federalists
A group that argued for ratification of the Constitution, including a stronger national government at the expense of states' power. They controlled the new federal government until Thomas Jefferson's election in 1800.

for recognizing the authority of the executive, particularly given national security concerns. Obama was following the lead of his predecessors, including President George W. Bush, who asserted that he had authority to use wiretaps to monitor communications of U.S. citizens without court-approved search warrants.[20]

Judicial Review and the "Guardians of the Constitution"

2.3 Explain how the use of judicial review strengthens the courts in a separation of powers system.

The judiciary has become so important in our system of checks and balances that it deserves special attention. Judges did not claim the power of **judicial review**—the power to review a law or government regulation and strike it down if the judges believe it conflicts with the Constitution—until some years after the Constitution had been adopted. However, many understood that judges would provide an important check on the other branches. Alexander Hamilton, for example, emphasized the importance of judicial independence for protection "against the occasional ill humors in the society."[21]

Judicial review is a major contribution of the United States to the art of government, one that many other nations have adopted. In Canada, Germany, France, Italy, and Spain, constitutional courts have the power to review laws referred to them. However, the degree to which the courts utilize this power, and the point in the legislative process at which it occurs, varies across countries.[22]

Origins of Judicial Review

The Constitution says nothing about who should have the final word in disputes that may arise over its meaning. Today, most scholars agree that the Framers intended the Supreme Court to have the power to declare acts of the legislative and executive branches unconstitutional. But in the years following ratification, the scope of the Court's power remained uncertain.

The **Federalists**—who urged ratification of the Constitution and controlled the national government until 1801—generally supported a strong role for federal courts and thus favored judicial review. Their opponents, the Jeffersonian Republicans (called *Democrats* after 1832), were less enthusiastic. In the Kentucky and Virginia Resolutions of 1798 and 1799, respectively, Jefferson and Madison (who by this time had left the Federalist camp) came close to arguing that state legislatures—and not the Supreme Court—had the ultimate power to interpret the Constitution. These resolutions seemed to question whether the Supreme Court even had final authority to review *state* legislation, a point about which there had been little doubt.

When the Jeffersonians defeated the Federalists in the election of 1800, the question of whether the Supreme Court would actually exercise the power of judicial review was still undecided. Then in 1803 came *Marbury* v. *Madison,* the most path-breaking Supreme Court decision of all time.[23]

Marbury v. *Madison*

President John Adams and fellow Federalists did not take their 1800 defeat by Thomas Jefferson easily. Not only did they lose control of the executive office, they also lost both houses of Congress. That left the judiciary as the last remaining Federalist stronghold.

Chief Justice John Marshall (1755–1835) is our most influential Supreme Court justice. Appointed in 1801, Marshall served until 1835. Earlier he had been a staunch defender of the U.S. Constitution at the Virginia ratifying convention, a member of Congress, and a secretary of state. He was one of those rare people who served in all three branches of government.

writ of mandamus
A court order directing an official to perform an official duty.

2.1 2.2 2.3 2.4 2.5

To further shore up the federal judiciary, the outgoing Federalist Congress created dozens of new judgeships. By March 3, 1801, the day before Jefferson was due to become president, Adams had appointed, and the Senate had confirmed, loyal Federalists to all of these new positions. Although the commissions were signed and sealed, a few, for the newly appointed justices of the peace for the District of Columbia, were not delivered. John Marshall, the outgoing secretary of state and newly confirmed chief justice of the Supreme Court, left the delivery of these commissions for his successor as secretary of state, James Madison.

This "packing" of the judiciary angered Jefferson, now inaugurated as president. When he discovered that some of the commissions were still lying on a table in the Department of State, he instructed a clerk not to deliver them. Jefferson could see no reason why the District needed so many justices of the peace, especially Federalist justices.[24]

William Marbury never received his commission and decided to seek action from the courts. Section 13 of the Judiciary Act of 1789 authorized the Supreme Court "to issue **writs of mandamus**," orders directing an official, such as the secretary of state, to perform a duty, such as delivering a commission. Marbury went directly to the Supreme Court and, citing Section 13, made his request.

Marbury's request presented Chief Justice John Marshall and the Supreme Court with a difficult dilemma. On the one hand, if the Court issued the writ, Jefferson and Madison would probably ignore it. The Court would be powerless, and its prestige, already low, might suffer a fatal blow. On the other hand, by refusing to issue the writ, the judges would appear to support the Jeffersonian Republicans' claim that the Court had no authority to interfere with the executive. Would Marshall issue the writ? Most people thought he would; angry Republicans even threatened impeachment if he did so.

On February 24, 1803, the Supreme Court delivered what is still considered a brilliantly written and politically savvy decision. First, Marshall, writing for a unanimous Court, took Jefferson and Madison to task. Marbury was entitled to his commission, and Madison should have delivered it to him. Moreover, the proper court could issue a writ of mandamus, even against so high an officer as the secretary of state.

However, Marshall concluded that Section 13 of the Judiciary Act, giving the Supreme Court original jurisdiction to issue writs of mandamus, was in error. It impermissibly expanded the Court's original jurisdiction, which is detailed in Article III of the Constitution. Marshall concluded that the grant of original jurisdiction in Article III was meant to be limited to those cases explicitly mentioned: when an ambassador, foreign minister, or a state is a party. Because none of these was at issue in Marbury's request for the writ of mandamus, the Court deemed Section 13 of the Judiciary Act contrary to the Constitution. Given that Article VI provided that the Constitution is the "supreme Law of the Land," and judges took an oath to uphold the Constitution, any law in conflict with it could not withstand the Court's review.

Although the Federalists suffered a political loss in not seating all their "midnight judges" on the bench, Marshall and the Court gained a much more important power: to declare laws passed by Congress unconstitutional. Subsequent generations might have interpreted *Marbury* v. *Madison* in a limited way, such as that the Supreme Court had the right to determine the scope of its own powers under Article III, but Congress and the president had the authority to interpret their powers under Articles I and II. But throughout the decades, building on Marshall's precedent, the Court has taken the commanding position as the authoritative interpreter of the Constitution.

Once we accept Marshall's argument that judges are the official interpreters of the Constitution, several important consequences follow. The most important is that people can challenge laws enacted by Congress and approved by the president, as did a variety of states and parties in challenging health care reform. Simply by bringing a lawsuit, those who lack the clout to get a bill through Congress can often secure a judicial hearing. And organized interest groups often find they can achieve goals through litigation that they could not attain through legislation. For example, as discussed at the

Following the Supreme Court's 2008 decision affirming individual citizens' right to own handguns and thus making it more difficult to restrict gun ownership, Laurence Tansel shopped for his first handgun.

beginning of this chapter, gun rights activists were able to achieve success in the courts through cases like *District of Columbia* v. *Heller* (2008) and *McDonald* v. *Chicago* (2010) that they were not able to achieve by rolling back restrictions on handguns legislatively. Litigation thus supplements, and at times even takes precedence over, legislation as a way to make public policy.[25]

Informal Change: The Unwritten Constitution

2.4 Assess how the Constitution has evolved through changes in the informal, unwritten Constitution.

As careful as the Constitution's Framers were to limit the powers they gave the national government, the main reason they assembled in Philadelphia was to create a stronger national government. Having learned that a weak central government was a danger to liberty, they wished to establish a national government with enough authority to meet the country's needs. They made general grants of power, leaving it to succeeding generations to fill in the details and organize the structure of government in accordance with experience.

Hence our formal, written Constitution is only a skeleton. It is filled out in numerous ways that we must consider part of our constitutional system in a larger sense. In fact, our system is kept up to date primarily through changes in the informal, unwritten Constitution. These changes exist in certain basic statutes and historical practices of Congress, presidential actions, and court decisions.

For the People — Government's Greatest Endeavors

Establishing a Durable Constitution

The Constitution of the United States is the world's oldest written constitution. Some 235 other countries have written constitutions; more than 50 new constitutions have been enacted as recently as 2000. Seven countries have no written constitution, including Oman, New Zealand, and the United Kingdom.*

Debate was critical in getting the signers' agreement to the U.S. Constitution in 1787. Since then, the ambiguity and brevity of many constitutional provisions have spurred a great deal of additional debate, although there has not been a serious effort to alter our basic system of government since the Constitution went into effect in 1789. Indeed, the potential to alter the Constitution through the amendment process has created a remarkable democratic system of government capable of withstanding a civil war, two world wars, and internal and external security threats, all the while providing individual protections for an increasingly diverse population.

Our governing document provides for a unique balance between our national and state governments. This allows us to take advantage of nation-wide policies that provide for equity across the states, while also meeting the specific needs of localities through protections on state power. The Constitution also protects our most closely held liberties, including our right to express our views, to due process of the law, and to worship (or not) as we each see fit.

The Framers of the Constitution provided American citizens with the tools of self-government; indeed for a *Government by the People*. As Benjamin Franklin is reported to have said to a woman as he was leaving the Constitutional Convention, the Framers gave us "a republic, if [we] can keep it."†

QUESTIONS

1. **What features have led to the durability of the United States Constitution?**
2. **In what situations might it be important to have consistency in law across the United States?**

*The World Factbook Online, Central Intelligence Agency. Accessed 12.19.11 https://www.cia.gov/library/publications/the-world-factbook/fields/2063.html#; online edition updated weekly.

†Miner, Margaret and Hugh Rawson. 2005. *The Oxford Dictionary of American Quotations*. 2nd Edition. Oxford: Oxford University Press, 21.

2.1

2.2

2.3

2.4

2.5

congressional elaboration
Congressional legislation that gives further meaning to the Constitution based on sometimes vague constitutional authority, such as the necessary and proper clause.

impeachment
A formal accusation by the lower house of a legislature against a public official; the first step in removal from office.

executive order
A directive issued by a president or governor that has the force of law.

executive privilege
The power to keep executive communications confidential, especially if they relate to national security.

impoundment
Presidential refusal to allow an agency to spend funds that Congress authorized and appropriated.

Congressional Elaboration

Because the Framers gave Congress authority to provide for the structural details of the national government, it is not necessary to amend the Constitution every time a change is needed. Rather, Congress can create legislation to meet the need with what we refer to as **congressional elaboration.** The Judiciary Act of 1789, for example, laid the foundations for our national judicial system, just as other laws established the organization and functions of all federal executive officials subordinate to the president and enacted the rules of procedure, internal organization, and practices of Congress.

Another example of this congressional elaboration of our constitutional system is the use of the impeachment and removal power. An **impeachment** is a formal accusation against a public official and the first step in removing him or her from office. Constitutional language defining the grounds for impeachment is sparse. In fact, the last time the House of Representatives formally accused a president of an impeachable offense, President Bill Clinton in 1998, House members had nearly 20 scholars testify before them as to the clause's meaning, and they still did not find consensus on it. Although the Constitution provides for the basic procedural structure of impeachments, it leaves up to Congress to determine when a president's actions amount to an impeachable offense.

A more recent example involves the debate over health care reform and whether Congress has the power to mandate that American citizens purchase health insurance. Part of that debate centers on congressional authority under the commerce clause (Article I Section 8). Although the Constitution is clear that Congress has the authority to regulate "commerce… among the several States," just what "commerce" is, and how far congressional authority to regulate it extends, is something on which many experts disagree. In arguments before the U.S. Supreme Court, the U.S. government contended that Congress has the authority to regulate health insurance, which accounts for 17% of the U.S. economy. Opponents of the reform argued that Congress cannot require American citizens to buy health insurance based only on the fact that they are citizens of the United States.[26] In its decision, the Court ruled that Congress had unconstitutionally exceeded its authority under the commerce clause when it enacted the Patient Protection and Affordable Care Act, but it upheld the Act based on Congress's taxing authority.[27]

Presidential Practices

Although the formal constitutional powers of the president have not changed, the office is dramatically more important and more central today than it was in 1789. Vigorous presidents—George Washington, Thomas Jefferson, Andrew Jackson, Abraham Lincoln, Theodore Roosevelt, Woodrow Wilson, Franklin Roosevelt, Harry Truman, Lyndon Johnson, Bill Clinton, and George W. Bush—have boldly exercised their political and constitutional powers, especially during times of national crisis such as the war against international terrorism and the 2008 economic crisis. Their presidential practices have established important precedent, building the power and influence of the office.

A major practice is the use of **executive orders**, which carry the full force of law but do not require congressional approval, though they are subject to legal challenge. Executive orders direct the executive branch to take some action, such as President Franklin Roosevelt's 1942 order to intern Japanese Americans during World War II or President Truman's order to integrate the armed forces in 1948. Not all executive orders are as path-breaking as these two examples, but even so they are a tool for the executive. For example, President Obama has issued executive orders to stimulate the U.S. economy, such as an order establishing the SelectUSA Initiative aimed at improving opportunities for investment in the United States.[28] Presidents have long used these orders to achieve goals that may lack congressional support. Other practices include **executive privilege**, the right to confidentiality of executive communications, especially those that relate to national security; **impoundment** by a president of funds previously appropriated by Congress; the power to send armed forces into hostilities; and the authority to propose legislation and work actively to secure its passage by Congress.

Foreign and economic crises as well as nuclear-age realities and the war against international terrorism have expanded the president's role: "When it comes to action risking nuclear war, technology has modified the Constitution: the President, perforce, becomes the only such man in the system capable of exercising judgment under the extraordinary limits now imposed by secrecy, complexity, and time."[29] The presidency has also become the pivotal office for regulating the economy and promoting the general welfare through an expanded federal bureaucracy. In addition, the president has become a leader in sponsoring legislation as well as the nation's chief executive.

originalist approach
An approach to constitutional interpretation that envisions the document as having a fixed meaning that might be determined by a strict reading of the text or the Framers' intent.

adaptive approach
A method used to interpret the Constitution that understands the document to be flexible and responsive to the changing needs of the times.

You Will Decide

Should We Interpret the Constitution According to Original Intent or Today's Needs?

Debate about how to interpret the Constitution began almost immediately, and, as we have seen, it continues to this day, with very important practical implications for citizens.

One kind of constitutional interpretation is the **originalist approach**. Originalists believe that the Constitution should be understood according to the Framers' intent. If the exact wording of the document does not provide a conclusive answer, most originalists consider the context of the times in which it was written and interpret it in light of that history. Especially important are writings or speeches by the Framers themselves or by proponents of subsequent amendments.

A second approach to interpreting the Constitution sees it as a changing and evolving document that provides a basic framework for government but that allows, and even encourages, new generations to interpret ideas such as "equal justice" and "due process" in light of the needs of their time. This **adaptive approach** may mean that subsequent generations will interpret the same document differently from prior generations.

The adaptive approach makes the Supreme Court a more powerful institution in U.S. government. The originalist approach forces people and institutions to adopt amendments if they want constitutional change.

What do you think? Should we interpret the Constitution according to the Framers' original intent, or should it be considered in light of the needs of today's society? What are some of the arguments for or against each approach?

Thinking It Through

Differences between the adaptive and the originalist views do not necessarily align with political labels such as *conservative* or *liberal,* although they may in particular cases. For example, Justice Antonin Scalia, who tends to be originalist in his approach, voted in *District of Columbia* v. *Heller* to strike down the District's prohibition on registering handguns through a close reading of the original, literal meaning of the Second Amendment. Because the Amendment indicates that "the right of the people to keep and bear Arms, shall not be infringed," Justice Scalia, writing for the majority of the Court, determined that individual citizens had a constitutionally protected right to own handguns.

Justice Stephen Breyer typically favors a more adaptive approach. In his dissent to the Court's majority opinion, Justice Breyer argued that the Court must consider the District of Columbia's restriction on handguns in light of present day conditions, such as the public safety concerns raised by gun violence. Justice Breyer weighed an individual's right to own a handgun against the District's responsibility to protect its citizenry, and sided with the District of Columbia.

If the Constitution is indeed open to changing interpretations, are any constitutional principles absolute and *not* open to new interpretation? This danger in the adaptive approach worries some because the selection of judges is only indirectly democratic; due to lifetime appointments, judges could lose the people's confidence yet retain their power. There are problems with the originalist approach as well. A global economy, electronic and mass media, and the need to respond immediately to national security threats are only some examples of circumstances the Framers could not consider or address in the Constitution. In other instances, such as with privacy, for example, the original wording of the Constitution implies an interpretation but does not explicitly say it.

CRITICAL THINKING QUESTIONS

1. How do you think we should interpret the Constitution? What are the best arguments of both sides of this question?
2. Why does it matter whether we take an originalist or an adaptive approach to interpreting the Constitution?

2.1

2.2

2.3

2.4

2.5

☐ Judicial Interpretation

In its decision in *Marbury* v. *Madison* (1803),[30] the Supreme Court established that it was the judiciary's responsibility to interpret the Constitution. The courts have made far-reaching decisions that have settled, at least for a time, what some of the vague clauses of the document mean. For example, the Supreme Court ruled that segregation by race, even when equal facilities were provided, violated the requirements of the equal protection clause (*Brown* v. *Board of Education* [1954]),[31] and that Americans have a constitutionally protected right to privacy, even though the word "privacy" appears nowhere in the Constitution (*Griswold* v. *Connecticut* [1965]).[32] In both of these cases and a myriad of others, the Court's definition of what the Constitution meant led to changes in our political system without any amendment to the document itself. Although there is relatively little current debate over the judiciary's authority to interpret the Constitution, there is substantial disagreement over *how* it should be read.

Changing the Letter of the Constitution

2.5 Describe the processes by which formal changes to the Constitution can be made.

The idea of a constantly changing system disturbs many people. How, they contend, can you have a constitutional government when the Constitution is constantly being twisted by interpretation and changed by informal methods? This view fails to distinguish between two aspects of the Constitution. As an expression of *basic and timeless personal liberties,* the Constitution does not and should not change. For example, a government cannot destroy free speech and still remain a constitutional government. In this sense, the Constitution is unchanging. But when we consider the Constitution as an *instrument of government* and a positive grant of power, we realize that if it did not grow with the nation it serves, it would soon be irrelevant and ignored.

The Framers could never have conceived of the problems facing the government of a large, powerful, and wealthy nation of approximately 300 million people at the beginning of the twenty-first century. Although the general purposes of government remain the same—to establish liberty, promote justice, ensure domestic tranquility, and provide for the common defense—the powers of government that were adequate to accomplish these purposes in 1787 are simply insufficient more than 225 years later. The Framers knew that future experiences would call for changes in the text of the Constitution and that it would need to be formally amended. In Article V, they gave responsibility for amending the Constitution to Congress and to the states. The president has no formal authority over constitutional amendments; presidential veto power does not extend to them, although presidential influence is often crucial in getting amendments proposed and ratified.

Outside the 1984 Republican National Convention, Gregory Johnson burned an American flag to protest the Reagan administration's policies. The U.S. Supreme Court upheld his right to do so as a protected form of expression under the First Amendment.

☐ Proposing Amendments

The first method for proposing amendments—and the only one used so far—is by *a two-thirds vote of both houses of Congress.* Dozens of resolutions proposing amendments are introduced in every session, but Congress has proposed only 31 amendments, of which 27 have been ratified (see Figure 2.2).

Why is introducing amendments to the Constitution so popular? In part because the nation needs to make government more responsive to changing times. In part

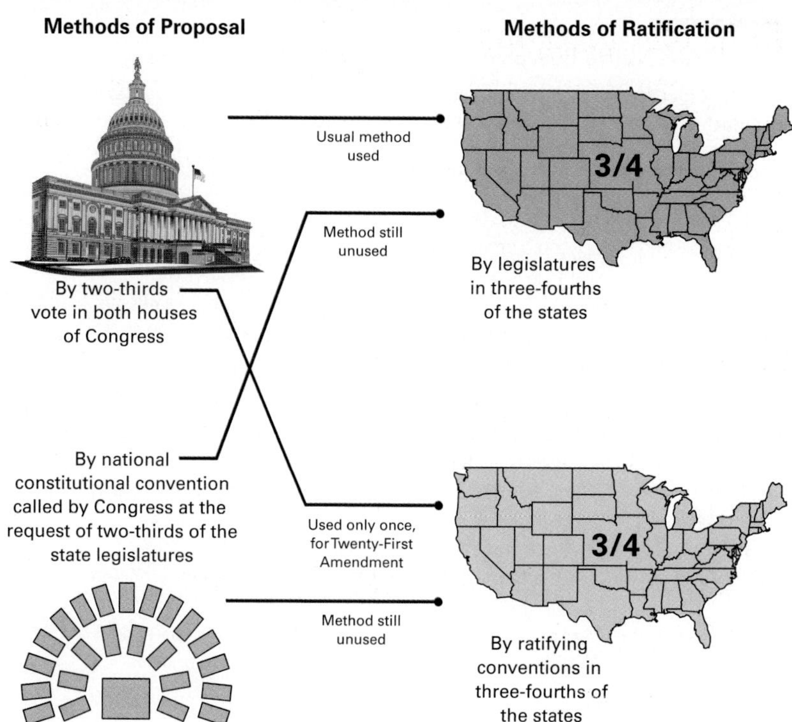

FIGURE 2.2 FOUR METHODS OF AMENDING THE CONSTITUTION

Why do you think Congress has been reluctant to call for a national constitutional convention?

because groups frustrated by their inability to get things done in Congress hope to bypass it. In part because Congress, the president, interest groups, or the public may want to overturn unpopular Supreme Court decisions. All of these participants were involved in an effort to overturn the Supreme Court's decision to strike down a Texas law barring flag burning (*Texas* v. *Johnson* [1989]).[33] Though Congress attempted to bypass the decision with the Federal Flag Protection Act of 1989, which prohibited intentionally burning or defiling the flag, the Court struck down that law as well (*United States* v. *Eichman* [1990]).[34] In doing so, the Court ruled that the First Amendment protects burning the flag as a form of political speech.

Following its failure to overturn the decision through new laws, Congress has made repeated efforts to send a constitutional amendment banning flag burning to the states.[35] The House of Representatives has voted seven times since the early 1990s on an amendment prohibiting the "physical desecration of the flag of the United States," but the Senate has been unable to garner the necessary two-thirds vote. It came close to succeeding in June 2006, but the vote fell one short of the number required to send the amendment to the states for ratification.[36] See Table 2.2 on how the amending power has been used.

The second method for proposing amendments—*a convention called by Congress* at the request of the legislatures in two-thirds of the states—has never been used. Under Article V of the Constitution, Congress could call for such a convention without the concurrence of the president. This method presents difficult questions including whether state legislatures must apply for a convention to propose specific amendments on one topic, or a convention with full powers to revise the entire Constitution.[37] Under most proposals Congress has considered clarifying the process: each state would have as many delegates to the convention as it has representatives and senators in Congress and a constitutional convention would be limited to considering only the subject specified in the state legislative petitions and described in the congressional call for the convention. Scholars are divided, however, on whether Congress has the authority to limit what a constitutional convention might propose[38] and to date, Congress has not passed any legislation on the topic.

2.1

2.2

2.3

2.4

2.5

TABLE 2.2 THE AMENDING POWER AND HOW IT HAS BEEN USED

Leaving aside the first ten amendments (the Bill of Rights), the power of constitutional amendment has served a number of purposes:

To Increase or Decrease the Power of the National Government

The Eleventh took some jurisdiction away from the national courts.
The Thirteenth abolished slavery and authorized Congress to legislate against it.
The Sixteenth enabled Congress to levy an income tax.
The Eighteenth authorized Congress to prohibit the manufacture, sale, or transportation of liquor.
The Twenty-First repealed the Eighteenth and gave states the authority to regulate liquor sales.
The Twenty-Seventh limited the power of Congress to set members' salaries.

To Expand the Electorate and Its Power

The Fifteenth extended suffrage to all male African Americans over the age of 21.
The Seventeenth took the right to elect U.S. senators away from state legislatures and gave it to the voters in each state.
The Nineteenth extended suffrage to women over the age of 21.
The Twenty-Third gave voters of the District of Columbia the right to vote for president and vice president.
The Twenty-Fourth outlawed the poll tax, thereby prohibiting states from taxing the right to vote.
The Twenty-Sixth extended suffrage to otherwise qualified persons aged 18 or older.

To Reduce the Electorate's Power

The Twenty-Second took away from the electorate the right to elect a person to the office of president for more than two full terms.

To Limit State Government Power

The Thirteenth abolished slavery.
The Fourteenth granted national citizenship and prohibited states from abridging privileges of national citizenship; from denying persons life, liberty, and property without due process; and from denying persons equal protection of the laws. This amendment has come to be interpreted as imposing restraints on state powers in every area of public life.

To Make Structural Changes in Government

The Twelfth corrected deficiencies in the operation of the Electoral College that the development of a two-party national system had revealed.
The Twentieth altered the calendar for congressional sessions and shortened the time between the election of presidents and their assumption of office.
The Twenty-Fifth provided procedures for filling vacancies in the vice presidency and for determining whether presidents are unable to perform their duties.

■ *Overall, have constitutional amendments resulted in a stronger or weaker federal government than was established in the Constitution?*

□ Ratifying Amendments

After Congress has proposed an amendment, the states must ratify it before it takes effect. Again, the Constitution provides two methods, and Congress may choose: approval by the legislatures in three-fourths of the states or approval by special ratifying conventions in three-fourths of the states. Congress has submitted all amendments except one—the Twenty-First (to repeal the Eighteenth, the Prohibition Amendment)—to the state legislatures for ratification.

Seven state constitutions specify that their state legislatures must ratify a proposed amendment to the U.S. Constitution by majorities of three-fifths or two-thirds of each chamber. Although a state legislature may change its mind and ratify an amendment after it has voted against ratification, the weight of opinion is that once a state has ratified an amendment, it cannot "unratify" it.[39]

The Supreme Court has said that ratification must take place within a "reasonable time" so that it is "sufficiently contemporaneous to reflect the will of the people."[40] However, when Congress approved ratification of the Twenty-Seventh Amendment, it had been before the nation for nearly 203 years, so there seems to be no limit on what it considers a "reasonable time" (see Figure 2.3). In fact, ratification ordinarily takes place rather quickly—one-third of all amendments were ratified within about one year, and 80 percent were ratified within

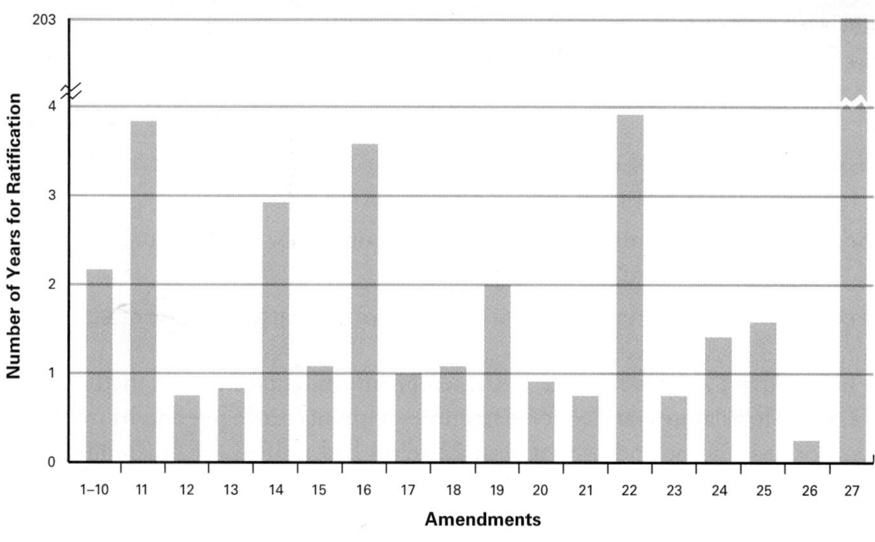

FIGURE 2.3 THE TIME FOR RATIFICATION OF THE 27 AMENDMENTS TO THE CONSTITUTION

■ *What is an appropriate time for ratification of a proposed amendment? In thinking about your answer, should the length of elected legislators' terms play a role in your decision?*

about two years. Congress will probably continue to stipulate that ratification must occur within seven years of the date it submits an amendment to the states.

□ Ratification Politics

The failure of the Equal Rights Amendment (ERA) to be ratified provides a vivid example of the pitfalls of ratification. First introduced in 1923, the ERA did not get much support until the 1960s. By the 1970s, the ERA had overwhelming support in both houses of Congress and in both national party platforms. Every president from

OF the People Diversity in America

Women in the Workforce Forty Years After Failure to Ratify the ERA

As mentioned in the text, although the Equal Rights Amendment had substantial support, it failed to get the necessary votes to be ratified. Many who were opposed to the amendment suggested that women would be subject to the military draft and that full-time housewives and mothers would be forced to work outside the home.

Even without the Equal Rights Amendment, the role of women in American society has changed greatly since the amendment was first passed by Congress and submitted to the states. In 1973, for example, approximately 76 percent of all men were employed in the civilian labor force compared to only 42 percent of all women. And, unemployment figures for women seeking work during that year was 50 percent higher than for their male counterparts.

In contrast, by 2010 nearly 54 percent of all women were employed in the civilian labor force compared to 64 percent of men. Although unemployment figures for both men and women were higher due to the troubled economic conditions of the day, a smaller percent of women who were actively seeking work were unable to get it (8.6 percent) as compared to men (10.5 percent).*

Even though women are more greatly represented in the workforce today than they were when Congress passed the ERA, one of proponents' primary goals, removing income equality, has remained elusive. According to the Department of Labor, women on average received lower wages than men. For every dollar the average male worker makes, the average female worker makes only 81 cents, even after controlling for the type of employment. For example, in 2010, the median weekly salary for male financial managers was $1,546 compared to only $1,022 for their female counterparts.**

QUESTIONS

1. Why might income inequality persist even though men and women serve in more equal numbers today in the work force?
2. What effect would ratifying the ERA have had on women's representation in the 1970s work force?

*Department of Labor Statistics, 2011 Employment & Earnings Online. http://bls.gov/opub/ee/2011/cps/annavg2_2010.pdf
**Department of Labor Statistics, 2011 Employment & Earnings Online. http://bls.gov/opub/ee/2011/cps/annavg39_2010.pdf

Harry Truman to Ronald Reagan, and many of their wives, endorsed the amendment. More than 450 organizations with a total membership of more than 50 million were on record in support of the ERA.[41] The ERA provided for the following:

> **Section 1.** Equality of rights under the law shall not be denied or abridged by the United States or by any State on account of sex.
>
> **Section 2.** The Congress shall have power to enforce, by appropriate legislation, the provisions of this article.
>
> **Section 3.** This amendment shall take effect two years after the date of ratification.[42]

Soon after Congress passed the amendment and submitted it to the states in 1972, many legislatures ratified it—sometimes without hearings—and by overwhelming majorities. By the end of that year, 22 states had ratified the amendment, and it appeared that the ERA would soon become part of the Constitution. But because of opposition organized under the leadership of Phyllis Schlafly, a prominent spokesperson for conservative causes, the ERA became controversial.

Opponents argued that "women would not only be subject to the military draft but also assigned to combat duty. Full-time housewives and mothers would be forced to join the labor force. Further, women would no longer enjoy existing advantages under state domestic relations codes and under labor law."[43] Opposition to ratification arose chiefly in the same cluster of southern states that had opposed ratification of the Nineteenth Amendment, which gave women the right to vote. In the end, despite extensions on the deadline to ratify the ERA, the amendment fell three states short of the 38 needed for ratification.

The Framers intended that amending the Constitution should be difficult, and the ERA ratification battle demonstrates how well they planned. Through interpretation, practices, usages, and judicial decisions, the Constitution has proved a remarkably enduring and adaptable governing document and one that is frequently used as a model for emerging democracies. But it is essential for citizens, individually and together, to keep watch that constitutional provisions are enforced and that change comes when necessary. Not all efforts for constitutional change are successful, but even failed drives for constitutional amendments can achieve a degree of success through the legislative process, influence on the executive, or calls for action by the judiciary.

Although the Equal Rights Amendment failed to be ratified by the 1982 deadline, men and women continue to lobby for equal rights.

On MyPoliSciLab

Review the Chapter

Listen to **Chapter 2** on **MyPoliSciLab**

Views of the Constitution

2.1 Describe the basic structure of the Constitution and its Bill of Rights, p. 53.

The U.S. Constitution's first three articles establish the legislature, the executive, and the judiciary. The Bill of Rights, the first ten amendments to the Constitution, was added in 1791 and provides protections from federal government infringement on individual liberties.

Checking Power with Power

2.2 Analyze how the Constitution grants, limits, separates, and balances governmental power, p. 54.

The U.S. Constitution separates power vested in the legislature, which has the power to create law; the executive, with the power to enforce the law; and the judiciary, which interprets the law. None of the branches depends on the others for its authority, and each branch has the power to limit the others through the system of checks and balances.

Competing interests within this structure check and balance one another. Political parties may sometimes overcome the separation of powers, especially if the same party controls both houses of Congress and the presidency. Typically, this is not the case, however, and a divided government intensifies checks and balances. Presidential power, which has increased over time, has sometimes overcome restraints the Constitution imposes on it.

Judicial Review and the "Guardians of the Constitution"

2.3 Explain how the use of judicial review strengthens the courts in a separation of powers system, p. 62.

Judicial review is the power of the courts to review acts of Congress, the executive branch, and the states and, if necessary, strike them down as unconstitutional. This authority provides the judiciary a powerful check on the other branches of government. In deciding that it lacked the jurisdiction to order a judicial commission be delivered, the Supreme Court, in *Marbury* v. *Madison,* established its authority to rule an act of the federal legislature unconstitutional. The Court's decision was politically savvy and greatly enhanced the role of the judiciary in a separation of powers system.

Informal Change: The Unwritten Constitution

2.4 Assess how the Constitution has evolved through changes in the informal, unwritten Constitution, p. 65.

The Constitution is the framework of our governmental system. The constitutional system has been modified over time, adapting to new conditions through congressional elaboration, presidential practices, and judicial interpretation.

Some jurists believe the Constitution is a static document with a set meaning, and they tend to interpret the Constitution according to a close reading of the text or according to what they think the Framers intended. Others consider the document's meaning to evolve with time and changing circumstances.

Changing the Letter of the Constitution

2.5 Describe the processes by which formal changes to the Constitution can be made, p. 68.

Although adaptable, the Constitution itself needs to be altered from time to time, and the Framers provided a formal procedure for its amendment. An amendment must be both proposed and ratified: proposed by either a two-thirds vote in each chamber of Congress or by a national convention called by Congress on petition of the legislatures in two-thirds of the states; ratified either by the legislatures in three-fourths of the states or by special ratifying conventions in three-fourths of the states.

Learn the Terms

Study and **Review** the **Flashcards**

natural law, p. 53
separation of powers, p. 57
checks and balances, p. 57
autocracy, p. 59
unified government, p. 59
divided government, p. 59
partisanship, p. 59
Electoral College, p. 60
judicial review, p. 62
Federalists, p. 62
writ of mandamus, p. 63
congressional elaboration, p. 66
impeachment, p. 66
executive order, p. 66
executive privilege, p. 66
impoundment, p. 66
originalist approach, p. 67
adaptive approach, p. 67

Test Yourself

MULTIPLE CHOICE QUESTIONS

2.1 Describe the basic structure of the Constitution and its Bill of Rights.

The Constitution reflects the Framers' respect for ________ law, which implies a universal sense of right and wrong.

- **a.** natural
- **b.** formal
- **c.** federal
- **d.** corporal
- **e.** civil

2.2 Analyze how the Constitution grants, limits, separates, and balances governmental power.

The Constitutional provision that the Senate must confirm the president's nominees to the federal courts represents the

- **a.** principle of separation of powers.
- **b.** limited authority of the national government.
- **c.** system of checks and balances.
- **d.** system of federalism.
- **e.** principle of judicial review.

2.3 Explain how the use of judicial review strengthens the courts in a separation of powers system.

Which of the following is an example of judicial review?

- **a.** Congressional review of federal court nominees
- **b.** Presidential appointment of federal court judges
- **c.** The federal courts agreeing to review one's detention
- **d.** The federal courts' determination that a law is consistent with the Constitution
- **e.** The federal courts agreeing to review a case from lower courts

2.4 Assess how the Constitution has evolved through changes in the informal, unwritten Constitution.

The Supreme Court's determination that the necessary and proper clause permitted the establishment of a national bank illustrates the concept of

- **a.** congressional elaboration.
- **b.** judicial interpretation.
- **c.** executive privilege.
- **d.** reserve powers.
- **e.** substantive due process.

2.5 Describe the processes by which formal changes to the Constitution can be made.

One of the reasons that the Constitution has never been altered through the convention process includes which of the following?

- **a.** All states are required to agree to the convention
- **b.** Amendment petitions must be agreed to by three-fifths of the states
- **c.** Uncertainty over what could and could not be considered at a convention
- **d.** The president's willingness to alter the Constitution as necessary
- **e.** Congressional authority to unilaterally amend the Constitution.

ESSAY QUESTION

Madison's understanding of human nature greatly affected his views on government. Explain how the system of separation of powers and checks and balances reflect Madison's views. Has the Constitution been successful in addressing Madison's concerns? Why or why not?

Explore Further

IN THE LIBRARY

Akhil Reed Amar, *America's Constitution: A Biography* (Random House, 2005).

Carol Berkin, *A Brilliant Solution: Inventing the American Constitution* (Harcourt, 2002).

Joan Biskupic, *American Original: The Life and Constitution of Supreme Court Justice Antonin Scalia* (Farrar, Straus and Giroux, 2009).

Stephen Breyer, *Active Liberty: Interpreting Our Democratic Constitution* (Knopf, 2005).

James Macgregor Burns, *The Vineyard of Liberty* (Knopf, 1982).

Ken I. Kersch, *Constructing Civil Liberties: Discontinuities in the Development of American Constitutional Law* (Cambridge University Press, 2004).

Library Of Congress, Congressional Research Service, Jonny Killian, ed., *The Constitution of the United States of America: Analysis and Interpretation* (U.S. Government Printing Office, 2006).

Antonin Scalia, *A Matter of Interpretation: Federal Courts and the Law* (Princeton University Press, 1997).

Cass Sunstein, *Designing Democracy: What Constitutions Do* (Oxford University Press, 2001).

John R. Vile, ed., *Encyclopedia of Constitutional Amendments, Proposed Amendments, and Amending Issues, 1789–2002* (ABC-Clio, 2003).

Keith E. Whittington, *Political Foundations of Judicial Supremacy: The Presidency, the Supreme Court, and Constitutional Leadership in U.S. History* (Princeton University Press, 2007).

ON THE WEB

www.constitutioncenter.org/
The National Constitution Center's Web site includes information on the Constitution and its Framers as well as an interactive constitution, online exhibits, and news updates.

www.memory.loc.gov/ammem/amlaw/lawhome.html
This Library of Congress Web site is devoted to the Continental Congress and the Constitutional Convention. There are links to online documents contained in the Library's collection.

www.archives.gov/
The National Archives' Web site includes links to many online collections and historical documents.

Listen to Chapter 3 on MyPoliSciLab

3 American Federalism

The relationship of the national government to the states has been the subject of intense debate since the founding.[1] In 1787, members of what would become the Federalist Party defended the creation of a strong national government. Their rivals, the Anti-Federalists, warned that a strong national government would overshadow the states. The debate over which level of government best represents the people continues to this day.

State governments often complain that the national government is either taking over responsibilities that belong to them under the Constitution's Tenth Amendment, which reserves to them all powers not given to the national government, or controlling too much of what they do. Yet, in policy areas such as civil rights, educational opportunities for people with disabilities, and handgun control, the states have been slow to respond, and the national government has taken steps to deal with these issues.

At the same time, states retain enormous authority under the Constitution to regulate life within their borders. Working with the local governments they create, states police the streets, fight fires, impose their own taxes, create most of the laws that govern their citizens, define the meaning of marriage, set the rules for elections and register voters, run the public schools, and administer most of the programs to help the poor, even when the money for those programs comes from the national government. This broad scope begs the question, where does the national government end and state government begin?

This question involves a host of questions that involve how far states can go in drafting their own laws and how aggressive they should be in enforcing national laws. Under Article I, for example, the Founders gave Congress the power to set the rules regarding naturalization, which is the process by which immigrants are given U.S. citizenship and the rights that go with it.

3.1 Interpret the definitions of federalism, and analyze the advantages and disadvantages of the American system of federalism, p. 79.

3.2 Differentiate the powers the Constitution provides to national and state governments, p. 86.

3.3 Assess the role of the national courts in defining the relationship between the national and state governments, and evaluate the positions of decentralists and centralists, p. 92.

3.4 Evaluate the budget as a tool of federalism, and its impact on state and local governments, p. 96.

3.5 Describe the relationship between the national and state governments and the challenges for federalism, p. 101.

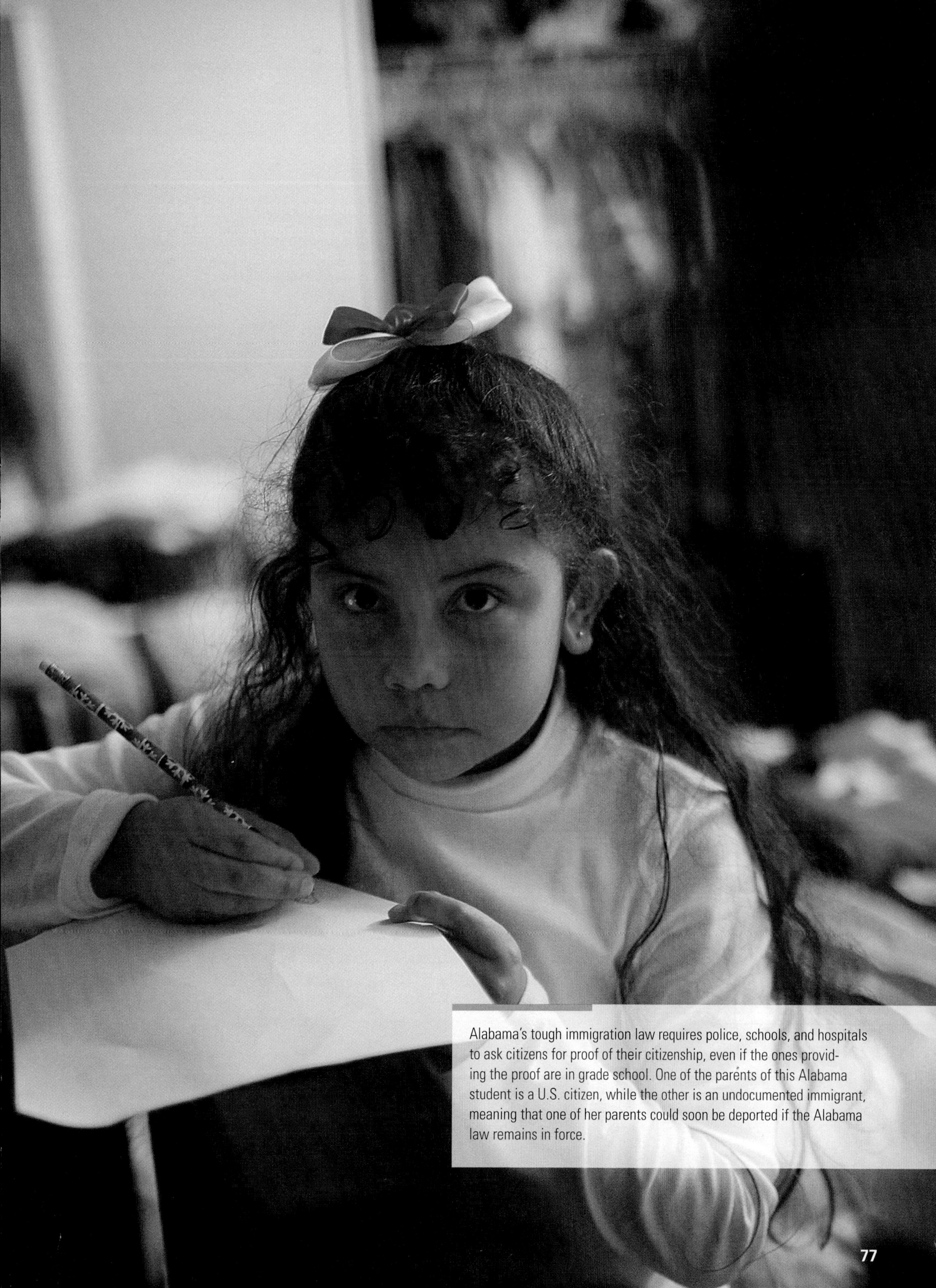

Alabama's tough immigration law requires police, schools, and hospitals to ask citizens for proof of their citizenship, even if the ones providing the proof are in grade school. One of the parents of this Alabama student is a U.S. citizen, while the other is an undocumented immigrant, meaning that one of her parents could soon be deported if the Alabama law remains in force.

MyPoliSciLab Video Series

Watch on MyPoliSciLab

The Big Picture Is the national government the same thing as the federal government? Not quite. Author Paul C. Light explains the difference, as well as the types of government that make up America's federal system—from national to local and from executive to judicial.

The Basics Are you a states-right advocate? This video will help you understand how powers and responsibilities are divided between the national and state governments. You'll also discover how the powers of the national government have expanded and consider whether this is in the best interests of the people.

In Context What is the primary mechanism for federalism in the United States? In this video, Barnard College political scientist Scott L. Minkoff explains how the national government tries to force state governments to adopt its policies and how state governments respond.

Thinking Like a Political Scientist Find answers to the most current questions that scholars of federalism are raising in the areas of welfare reform and state rights. Barnard College political scientist Scott L. Minkoff explores the challenges faced by state-rights advocates once they are elected to Congress.

In the Real World Should the federal government be allowed to mandate health care reform or should that power belong to the states? Hear supporters and detractors of Obamacare explain their opinions, and learn about the recent Supreme Court decision that handed this power to the federal government.

So What? If American government was a type of cake, what cake would it be? Using marble cake as a metaphor, author Paul C. Light explains the importance of understanding America's "blended" government so that students can determine which level or branch can best address their concerns.

In recent years, however, many states have passed laws that challenge the national government's supremacy in setting rules covering undocumented immigrants who reside in the U.S. illegally. With the nation and most states suffering from high unemployment starting in 2008 and continuing to this day, some states have argued that undocumented immigrants are taking jobs that would go to U.S. citizens. They have passed laws that put tight restrictions on state benefits such as public education and college tuition benefits for the children of illegal immigrants. Although some of these laws have been declared unconstitutional by the national courts, states continue to try new ways of reducing illegal immigration. In 2006, 84 immigration bills were enacted by state legislatures and signed into law; by 2010, the number had climbed to 364, with further increases in 2011.[2]

In June 2011, for example, Alabama enacted one of the most restrictive immigration laws in the nation. Under the law, illegal immigrants are considered state criminals who are subject to arrest and possible imprisonment. Most significantly, the law requires that public schools must check the immigration status of all their students. Under the provision, school children were required to reveal the immigration status of their parents.

In revealing their own immigration status, students had little choice but to tell school administrators whether their parents were in the United States legally. Although any child born in the United States is automatically deemed a citizen under national law and the Constitution, some Alabama school children were born to illegal immigrants. As a result, many parents kept their children home on October 1 when the law took effect, and some fled the state to avoid the law.[3] The same law also contained a provision that required residents of mobile homes to prove their legal status before renewing their annual home registration tags.

Even as the Alabama law was going into effect, an equally tough Arizona law was moving toward the Supreme Court. After hearing arguments in April, a 5 to 3 majority declared that the national government, not the states, had the "broad, undoubted power over the subject of immigration and the status of aliens." The national laws were supreme to any state laws,rendering most of Arizona's law unconstitutional. At the same time, the Court did permit Arizona to implement its "show me your papers" provision, which gives police the authority to ask drivers for their citizenship papers when stopped for other reasons. The Court ruled that the provision was a constitutional exercise of state powers. It is still not clear how much of Alabama's law will survive further tests based on the Court's decision. For now, Alabama says it is still in force.[4]

In this chapter, we first define federalism and its advantages and disadvantages. We then look at the constitutional basis for our federal system and how court decisions and political developments have shaped, and continue to shape, federalism in the United States. Throughout, you should think about how you influence the issues you care about, even in your local city council or mayor's office. The Constitution clearly encourages, and even depends on, you to express your view at all levels of government, which is why action in a single state can start a process that spreads to other states or the national government.

federalism

A constitutional arrangement in which power is distributed between a central government and states, which are sometimes called provinces in other nations. The national and states exercise direct authority over individuals.

3.1 3.2 3.3 3.4 3.5

Defining Federalism

3.1 Interpret the definitions of federalism, and assess the advantages and disadvantages of the American system of federalism.

Wars have been fought over what federalism means in part because the term itself is laden with ideological interpretation.[5]

Federalism, as we define it in nonpartisan terms, is a form of government in which a constitution distributes authority and powers between a central government and smaller regional governments—usually called states or provinces—giving to both the national and the state governments substantial responsibilities and powers, including the power to collect taxes and to pass and enforce laws regulating the conduct of individuals. When we use the term "federalism" or "federal system," we are referring to this system of national and state governments; when we use the term "federal government" in all other chapters of this book, we are referring to the Congress, presidency, and judiciary created under the U.S. Constitution.

The mere existence of both national and state governments does not make a system federal. What is important is that a *constitution divides governmental powers between the national government and state governments,* giving clearly defined functions to each. Neither the central nor the regional government receives its powers from the other; both derive them from a common source—the Constitution. No ordinary act of legislation at either the national or the state level can change this constitutional distribution of powers. Both levels of government operate through their own agents and exercise power directly over individuals.

Constitutionally, the federal system of the United States consists of only the national government and the 50 states. "Cities are not," the Supreme Court reminded us, "sovereign entities."[6] This does not make for a tidy, efficient, easy-to-understand system; yet, as we shall see, it has its virtues.

There are several different ways that power can be shared in a federal system, and political scientists have devised terms to explain these various, sometimes overlapping, kinds of federalism. At different times in the United States' history, our system of federalism has shared power based on each of these interpretations:

- *Dual or "layer-cake" federalism* is defined as a strict separation of powers between the national and state governments in which each layer of has its own responsibilities, and reigns supreme within its constitutional realm. Dual federalism was dominant from the 1790s until the 1930s.
- *Cooperative or "marble-cake" federalism* is defined as a flexible relationship between the national and state government in which both work together on a variety of issues and programs.[7] Cooperative federalism was dominant from the 1930s through the 1970s.
- *Competitive federalism* is defined as a way to improve government performance by encouraging state and local governments to compete against each other for residents, businesses, investment, and national funding.[8] Competitive federalism has coexisted with other definitions of federalism since the 1980s.

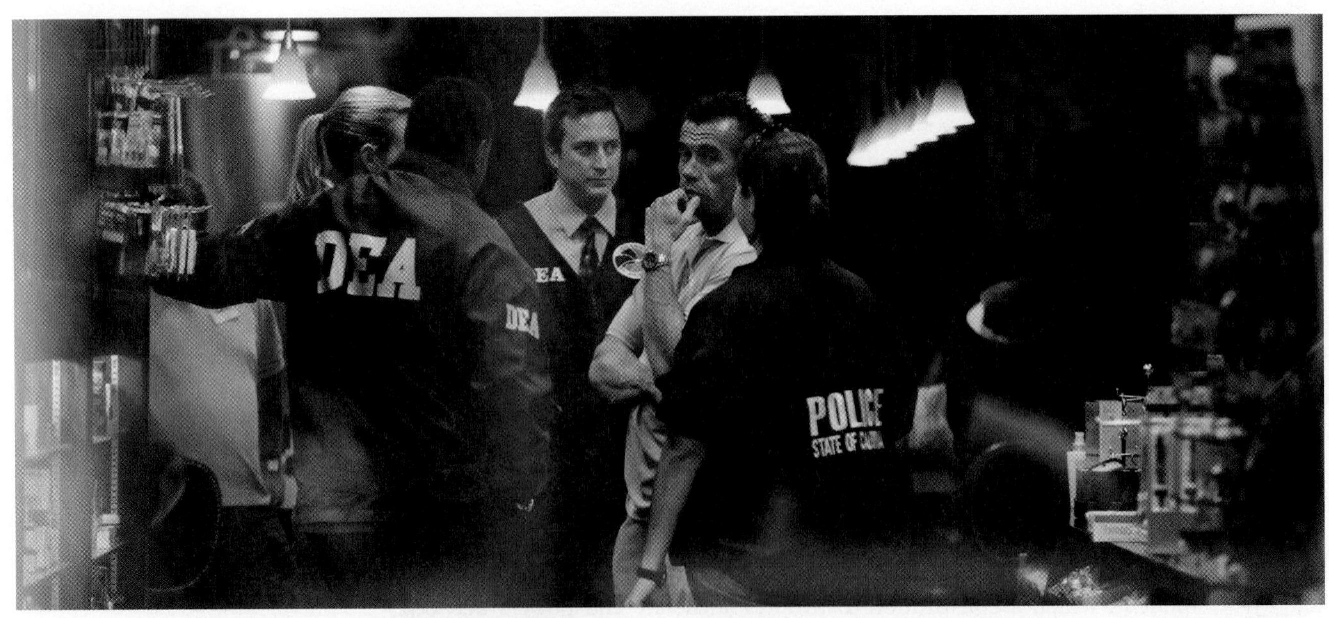

State and local governments are responsible for policing the streets but not for enforcing federal laws. Still, they often work with national agencies such as the Federal Bureau of Investigation and the Drug Enforcement Administration. This kind of joint action is an example of cooperative federalism.

- *Permissive federalism* is defined as a strong national government that only allows, or permits the states to act when it decides to do so. Although federalism generally assumes that the national and state governments will share power, permissive federalism argues that the power to share belongs to the national government, and national government alone.[9] Permissive federalism has been dominant on specific issues such as civil rights since the 1960s.
- *Coercive federalism* is also defined as a strong national government that exerts tight control of the states through orders or mandates—typically without accompanying financial resources. If states want federal grants, they must follow the mandates. Coercive federalism is sometimes called centralized federalism, which focuses on the national government's strong voice in shaping what states do. Coercive federalism has also been dominant on specific issues such as public education and the environment since the 1960s.
- *New federalism* is defined as a recent effort to reduce the national government's power by returning, or devolving responsibilities to the states. It is sometimes characterized as part of the *devolution revolution* discussed later in this chapter. The new federalism has been seen as a modern form of dual federalism based on the Tenth Amendment, and was first introduced by President Richard Nixon in 1969.

unitary system
A constitutional arrangement that concentrates power in a central government.

confederation
A constitutional arrangement in which sovereign nations or states, by compact, create a central government but carefully limit its power and do not give it direct authority over individuals.

☐ Alternatives to Federalism

Among the alternatives to federalism are **unitary systems** of government, in which a constitution vests all governmental power in the central government. The central government, if it so chooses, may delegate authority to constituent units, but what it delegates, it may take away. China, France, the Scandinavian countries, and Israel have unitary governments. In the United States, state constitutions usually create this kind of relationship between the state and its local governments.

At the other extreme from unitary governments are **confederations**, in which sovereign nations, through a constitutional compact, create a central government but carefully limit its authority and do not give it the power to regulate the conduct of individuals directly. The central government makes regulations for the constituent governments, but it exists and operates only at their direction. The 13 states under the Articles of Confederation operated in this manner, as did the southern Confederacy during the Civil War. The closest current example of an operating confederacy in the world is the European Union (EU), which is composed of 27 nations. Although the EU does bind its members to a common currency called the Euro, and does have a European Parliament and European Court of Justice and European Commission, members such as France, Germany, Italy, and Spain retain their own laws and authority. The EU may look like a confederation, but it acts more like a traditional alliance such as the United Nations, or the North Atlantic Treaty Organization.[10]

Even among all the nations that call themselves federations, there is no single model for dividing authority between the national and state governments. Some countries have no federal system at all, whereas others have different variations of power sharing between the national and state governments. Indeed, even the United States has varied greatly over time in its balance of national–state power.

Britain's government, for example, is divided into three tiers: national, county, and district governments. County and district governments deliver roughly one-fifth of all government services, including education, housing, and police and fire protection. As a rule, most power is reserved for the central government on the theory that there should be "territorial justice," which means that all citizens should be governed by the same laws and standards. In recent years, however, Great Britain has devolved substantial authority to Scotland, Wales, and Northern Ireland.

The Global Community

Global Opinion on the Role of Government

State and local governments are on the front lines of most programs for helping the needy. They provide much of the money and/or administration for unemployment insurance for the jobless, health care clinics and hospitals for the poor, school lunch programs for hungry children, and homeless shelters. Although many U.S. citizens see poverty firsthand as volunteers for local charities such as food pantries, some have doubts about how much government should do to help poor people who cannot take care of themselves. According to the Pew Research Center's Spring 2007 Global Attitudes Survey, citizens of other nations vary greatly on the question of whether "It is the responsibility of the (state or government) to take care of very poor people who can't take care of themselves."

These opinions reflect very different social and economic conditions in each country. Japan has a culture of self-reliance that puts the burden on individuals to help themselves, while Nigeria continues to suffer from some of the highest poverty rates in the world. In this regard, U.S. citizens tend to mirror the Japanese—they want government to help the less fortunate but also want the less fortunate to help themselves. As a general conclusion, citizens of wealthier nations think poor people should take advantage of the opportunities that already exist in their economies, whereas citizens of poor nations believe that government should be more aggressive in providing support.

This does not mean wealthier nations are uncaring toward citizens in need, but it does suggest that they sometimes view poverty as the fault of the poor. In the United States, these opinions reflect the importance of equality of opportunity as a basic social value, meaning that all individuals regardless of race, gender, or circumstance have the same opportunity to participate in politics, self-government, and the economy. Most Americans want to help the less fortunate, but only when they are truly needy, not when they fail because they will not help themselves.

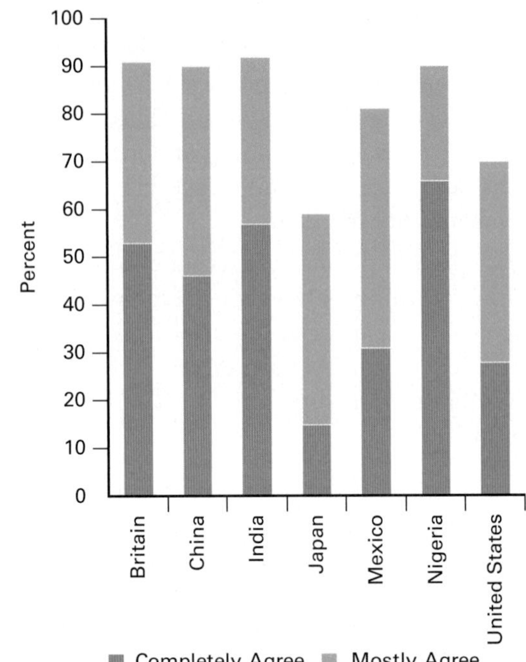

SOURCE: Pew Research Center, *Global Views on Life Satisfaction, National Conditions, and the Global Economy: Highlights from the 2007 Pew Global Attitudes 47-Nation Survey* (Pew Research Center, 2007).

CRITICAL THINKING QUESTIONS

1. What are the advantages and disadvantages of having the government provide services for the poor?
2. Why might more wealthy nations be more likely to believe that individuals ought to take care of themselves and not rely on the state?
3. Which level of government might be most effective in providing services to the poor?

☐ Advantages of Federalism

In 1787, federalism was a compromise between centrists, who supported a strong national government, and those who favored decentralization. Confederation had proved unsuccessful. A unitary system was out of the question because most people were too deeply attached to their state governments to permit subordination to central rule. Many scholars think that federalism is ideally suited to the needs of a diverse people spread throughout a large continent, suspicious of concentrated power, and desiring unity but not uniformity. Yet, even though federalism offers a number of advantages over other forms of government, no system is perfect. Federalism offered, and still offers, both advantages and disadvantages.

FEDERALISM CHECKS THE GROWTH OF TYRANNY Federalism has not always prevented tyranny, even in the United States, when Southern states seceded from the Union rather than end slavery. Today, however, U.S. citizens tend to associate federalism with freedom.[11] When one political party loses control of the national government, it is still likely to hold office in a number of states and can continue to challenge the party in power at the national level. To the Framers, who feared that a single interest group might capture the national government and suppress the interests of others, this diffusion of power was an advantage. There are now nearly 90,000 governments in the United States, including one national government, 50 state governments, and thousands of county, city, and town governments, as well as school boards and special districts that provide specific functions from managing hospitals or parks to mosquito control.[12] (See Figure 3.1 for the number of governments in the United States.)

FEDERALISM ALLOWS UNITY WITHOUT UNIFORMITY National politicians and parties do not have to iron out every difference on every issue that divides us, whether the issue is abortion, same-sex marriage, gun control, capital punishment, welfare financing, or assisted suicide. Instead, these issues are debated in state legislatures, county courthouses, and city halls. Information about state action spreads quickly from government to government, especially during periods when the national government is relatively slow to respond to pressing issues.

FEDERALISM ENCOURAGES EXPERIMENTATION As Justice Louis Brandeis once argued, states can be laboratories of democracy.[13] If they adopt programs that fail, the negative effects are limited; if programs succeed, they can be adopted by other states and by the national government. Georgia, for example, was the first state to permit 18-year-olds to vote; Wisconsin was a leader in requiring welfare recipients to work; California moved early on global warming; and Massachusetts created one of the first state programs to provide health insurance to all its citizens.

FEDERALISM PROVIDES TRAINING AND CREATES OPPORTUNITIES FOR FUTURE NATIONAL LEADERS Federalism provides a training ground for state

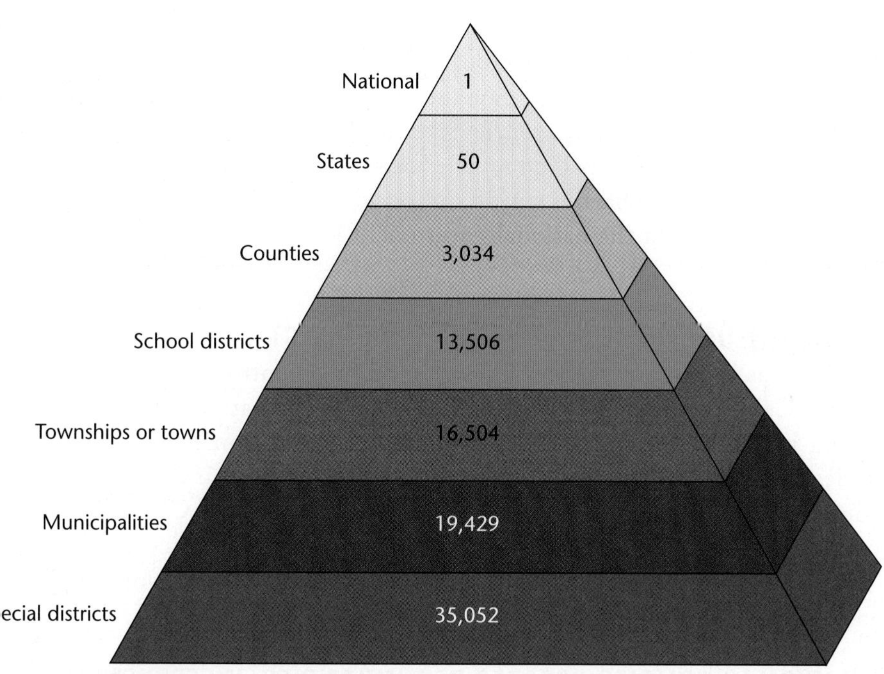

FIGURE 3.1 NUMBER OF SEPARATE GOVERNMENTS IN THE FEDERAL SYSTEM

How do the levels and numbers of governments in the United States help to prevent tyranny?

SOURCE: U.S. Census Bureau, *2012 Statistical Abstract of the United States,* www.census.gov/prod/2012/tables/12s428.pdf.

3.1
3.2
3.3
3.4
3.5

and local politicians to gain experience before moving to the national stage. Presidents Jimmy Carter, Ronald Reagan, Bill Clinton, and George W. Bush previously served as governor of the respective states of Georgia, California, Arkansas, and Texas. All totaled, 20 of the nation's 44 presidents served as governor at some points before winning the presidency. In addition, three former governors (Jon Huntsman, Rick Perry, and Mitt Romney) ran for the Republican Party nomination for president in 2012, and several were heavily recruited for the campaign but declined.

FEDERALISM KEEPS GOVERNMENT CLOSER TO THE PEOPLE By providing numerous arenas for decision making, federalism provides many opportunities for Americans to participate in the process of government and helps keep government closer to the people. Every day, thousands of U.S. adults serve on city councils, school boards, neighborhood associations, and planning commissions. Federalism also builds on the public's greater trust in government at the state and local levels. The closer the specific level of government is to the people, the more citizens trust the government.

☐ Disadvantages of Federalism

DIVIDING POWER MAKES IT MUCH MORE DIFFICULT FOR GOVERNMENT TO RESPOND QUICKLY TO NATIONAL PROBLEMS There was a great demand for stronger and more effective homeland security after the September 11, 2001, terrorist attacks, and the national government created a new Department of Homeland Security in response. However, the department quickly discovered that there would be great difficulty coordinating its efforts with 50 state governments and thousands of local governments already providing fire, police, transportation, immigration, and other governmental services.

THE DIVISION OF POWER MAKES IT DIFFICULT FOR VOTERS TO HOLD ELECTED OFFICIALS ACCOUNTABLE When something goes well, who should voters reward? When something goes wrong, who should they punish? When Hurricane Katrina hit New Orleans and the surrounding areas in late August 2005 (and Rita less than a month later near Houston), many thousands of people lost their homes and billions of dollars in damage was done. Who was responsible? Did the national government and agencies like the Federal Emergency Management Agency (FEMA) drop the ball on relief efforts, or was it the state or local government's responsibility? Did the mayor and/or governor fail to plan adequately for such a crisis, or should the national government have had more supplies on hand in advance?

THE LACK OF UNIFORMITY CAN LEAD TO CONFLICT States often disagree on issues such as health care, school reform, and crime control. In January 2008, for example, California joined 15 other states in suing the national government over a ruling issued by the national Environmental Protection Agency (EPA). For decades, the EPA had allowed California to enact tougher air quality restrictions through higher mileage standards than required by the national Clean Air Act (first enacted in 1970). The Bush administration rejected a similar request for permission to raise mileage standards in 2008, only to be reversed by the Obama administration in 2009.

VARIATION IN POLICIES CREATES REDUNDANCIES, INEFFICIENCIES, AND INEQUALITIES Labor laws, teacher certification rules, gun ownership laws, and even the licensing requirements for optometrists vary throughout the 50 states, and this is on top of many national regulations. Companies seeking to do business across state

OF the People Diversity in America

Where Americans Come From and Where They Live

The United States is a nation of immigrants who have arrived from many parts of the world. Throughout the decades, the portrait of immigrants has been changing from mostly white to mostly minority. In 2009, for example, 38.5 million Americans, or 12.5 percent, were foreign born, consisting of 16.8 million naturalized citizens, 10 million long-term visitors, and less than 11 million undocumented immigrants. The number of unauthorized, or illegal, immigrants has fallen somewhat in recent years due to the economic recession, which has depressed employment opportunities.

Many foreign-born residents live in the nation's largest cities. The New York City-area population includes more than 3 million foreign-born residents, while Los Angeles includes another 1.5 million; Miami, slightly more than 2 million; Chicago, just under 600,000, and San Francisco, 275,000. Although inner cities host a majority of foreign-born residents, there has been recent movement of immigrants to the suburbs and some movement toward certain areas of the country such as the southwest.

The changing face of America brings great diversity in all aspects of life, from schools to farm fields and small businesses. It also enriches the quality of life through the mix of old and new cultures, and can often be a source of innovation in how the economy operates.

However, this diversity also provokes complaints about undocumented immigrants. Some groups complain that undocumented immigrants take jobs that should go to U.S. citizens, whereas others worry about the costs associated with high poverty rates.

Governments at all levels must reconcile these pros and cons with our history of welcoming immigrants from all around the world.

QUESTIONS

1. How are foreign-born citizens from different regions of the world different from each other?
2. Why do you think foreign-born citizens tend to live in our nation's largest cities?
3. How do foreign-born citizens contribute to the nation's quality of life?

The Statue of Liberty symbolizes America's long tradition of welcoming immigrants to its shores.

lines must learn and abide by many different sets of laws, while individuals in licensed professions must consider whether they face recertification if they choose to relocate to another state. Where national laws do not exist, it is tempting for each state to try to undercut others' regulations to get a competitive advantage in such areas as attracting new industry, regulating environmental concerns, or setting basic eligibility standards for welfare or health benefits.

The Constitutional Structure of American Federalism

3.2 Differentiate the powers the Constitution provides to national and state governments.

delegated (express) powers
Powers given explicitly to the national government and listed in the Constitution.

implied powers
Powers inferred from the express powers that allow Congress to carry out its functions.

necessary and proper clause
The clause in the Constitution (Article I, Section 8, Clause 3) setting forth the implied powers of Congress. It states that Congress, in addition to its express powers, has the right to make all laws necessary and proper to carry out all powers the Constitution vests in the national government.

inherent powers
The powers of the national government in foreign affairs that the Supreme Court has declared do not depend on constitutional grants but rather grow out of the national government's obligation to protect the nation from domestic and foreign threats.

The division of powers and responsibilities between the national and state governments has resulted in thousands of court decisions, as well as hundreds of books and endless speeches to explain them—and even then the division lacks precise definition. Nonetheless, it is helpful to have a basic understanding of how the Constitution divides these powers and responsibilities and what obligations it imposes on each level of government.

The constitutional framework of our federal system is relatively simple:

1. The national government has only those powers delegated to it by the Constitution (with the important exception of the inherent power over foreign affairs).
2. Within the scope of its operations, the national government is supreme.
3. The state governments have all of the powers not delegated to the central government except those denied to them by the Constitution and their state constitutions.
4. Some powers are specifically denied to both the national and state governments; others are specifically denied only to the states or to the national government.

Powers of the National Government

The Constitution explicitly gives legislative, executive, and judicial powers to the national government. In addition to these **delegated or expressed powers**, such as the power to regulate interstate commerce and to appropriate funds, the national government has assumed constitutionally **implied powers**, such as the power to create banks, which are inferred from delegated powers. The constitutional basis for the implied powers of Congress is the **necessary and proper clause** (Article I, Section 8, Clause 3). This clause gives Congress the right "to make all Laws which shall be necessary and proper for carrying into Execution the foregoing Powers, and all other Powers vested ... in the Government of the United States." (Powers specifically listed in the Constitution are also called **express powers** because they are listed expressly.)

In foreign affairs, the national government has **inherent powers**. The national government has the same authority to deal with other nations as if it were the central government in a unitary system. Such inherent powers do not depend on specific constitutional provisions but exist because of the creation of the national government itself. For example, the government of the United States may acquire territory by purchase or by discovery and occupation, even though no specific clause in the Constitution allows such acquisition.

The national and state governments may have their own lists of powers, but the national government relies on four constitutional pillars for its ultimate authority over the states: (1) the *supremacy clause,* (2) the *war power,* (3) the *commerce clause,* and especially (4) the *power to tax and spend* for the general welfare. All four of these pillars are discussed individually below.

Together, however, they have permitted a steady expansion of the national government's functions to the point where some states complain they have lost the power to regulate their own actions. Despite the Supreme Court's recent declaration that some national laws exceed Congress's constitutional powers, the national government has, in effect, almost full power to enact any legislation that Congress deems necessary, so long as it does not conflict with provisions of the Constitution designed to protect individual rights and the powers of the states. In addition, Section 5 of the Fourteenth Amendment, ratified in 1868, gives Congress the power to enact legislation to remedy constitutional violations and the denial of due process or equal protection of the laws.

THE SUPREMACY CLAUSE The **supremacy clause** may be the most important pillar of U.S. federalism. Found in Article VI of the Constitution, the clause is simple and direct: "This Constitution, and the Laws of the United States which shall be made in Pursuance thereof; and all Treaties made...under the Authority of the United States, shall be the supreme Law of the Land; and the Judges in every State shall be bound thereby; any Thing in the Constitution or Laws of any State to the Contrary notwithstanding." Under the clause, state and local governments may not ignore or create their own substitutes for national laws and regulations. Because national laws and regulations of national agencies are supreme, conflicting state and local regulations are unenforceable. States must abide by the national government's minimum wage laws, for example, but are allowed to set the minimum wage higher if they wish.

supremacy clause
Contained in Article IV of the Constitution, the clause gives national laws the absolute power even when states have enacted a competing law.

commerce clause
The clause in the Constitution (Article I, Section 8, Clause 1) that gives Congress the power to regulate all business activities that cross state lines or affect more than one state or other nations.

THE WAR POWER The national government is responsible for protecting the nation from external aggression, whether from other nations or from international terrorism. The government's power to maintain national security includes the power to wage war. In today's world, military strength depends not only on the presence of troops in the field, but also on the ability to mobilize the nation's industrial might and apply scientific and technological knowledge to the tasks of defense. As Charles Evans Hughes, who became chief justice in 1930, observed: "The power to wage war is the power to wage war successfully."[14] The national government is free to create "no-fly" zones only for its military aircraft both within and across state borders, for example, and may use any airports it needs during times of war or peace.

THE POWER TO REGULATE INTERSTATE AND FOREIGN COMMERCE Congressional authority extends to all commerce that affects more than one state. Commerce includes the production, buying, selling, renting, and transporting of goods, services, and properties. The **commerce clause** (Article I, Section 8, Clause 1) packs a tremendous constitutional punch; it gives Congress the power "to regulate Commerce with foreign Nations, and among the several States, and with the Indian Tribes." In these few words, the national government has found constitutional justification for regulating a wide range of human activity because few aspects of our economy today affect commerce in only one state, the requirement that would render the activity outside the scope of the national government's constitutional authority.

The landmark ruling of *Gibbons* v. *Ogden* in 1824, affirmed the broad authority of Congress over interstate commerce.[15] The case involved a New York state license that gave Aaron Ogden the exclusive right to operate steamboats between New York and New Jersey. Using the license, Ogden asked the New York state courts to stop Thomas Gibbons from running a competing ferry. Although Gibbons countered that his boats were licensed under a 1793 act of Congress governing vessels "in the coasting trade and fisheries," the New York courts sided with Ogden. Just as the national government and states both have the power to tax, the New York courts said they both had the power to regulate commerce.

Gibbons appealed to the Supreme Court and asked a simple question: Which government had the ultimate power to regulate interstate commerce? The Supreme Court gave an equally simple answer: The national government's laws were supreme.

Gibbons v. *Ogden* was immediately heralded for promoting a national economic common market, in holding that states may not discriminate against interstate transportation and out-of-state commerce. The Supreme Court's brilliant definition of "commerce" as *intercourse among the states* provided the basis for national regulation of "things in commerce"[16] and an expanding range of economic activities, including the sale of lottery tickets,[17] prostitution,[18] radio and television broadcasts,[19] and telecommunications and the Internet.

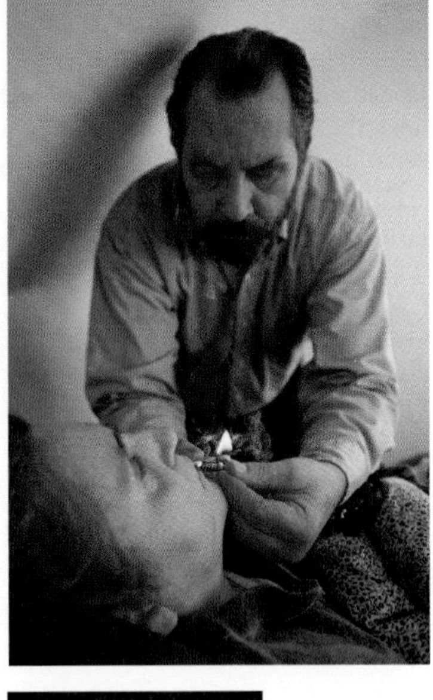

Though many states allow the use of medicinal marijuana, the Supreme Court decided that the national government could regulate its use in the states as a form of interstate commerce.

federal mandate

A requirement the national government imposes as a condition for receiving federal funds.

reserve powers

All powers not specifically delegated to the national government by the Constitution. The reserve power can be found in the Tenth Amendment to the Constitution.

concurrent powers

Powers that the Constitution gives to both the national and state governments, such as the power to levy taxes.

THE POWER TO TAX AND SPEND Congress lacks constitutional authority to pass laws solely on the grounds that they will promote the general welfare, but it may raise taxes and spend money for this purpose. For example, even when the national government lacks the power to regulate education or agriculture directly, it still has the power to appropriate money to support education or to pay farm subsidies. By attaching conditions to its grants of money, the national government creates incentives that affect state action. If states want the money, they must accept the conditions.

When the national government provides the money, it can determine how the money will be spent. By withholding or threatening to withhold funds, the national government can influence or control state operations and regulate individual conduct. For example, the national government has stipulated that national funds should be withdrawn from any program in which any person is denied benefits because of race, color, national origin, sex, or physical handicap. The national government also used its "power of the purse" to force states to raise the drinking age to 21 by tying such a condition to national dollars for building and maintaining highways.

Congress frequently requires states to provide specific programs—for example, services to indigent mothers, and clean air and water. These requirements are called **federal mandates**. Often the national government does not supply the funds required to carry out "unfunded mandates" (discussed later in the chapter). Its failure to do so has become an important issue as states face growing expenditures with limited resources.

☐ Powers of the States

The Constitution *reserves for the states all powers not granted to the national government,* subject only to the limitations of the Constitution. Only the states have the **reserve powers** to create schools and local governments, for example. Both are powers not given exclusively to the national government by the Constitution or judicial interpretation, so that states can exercise these powers as long as they do not conflict with national law.

The national and state governments also share powers. These **concurrent powers** with the national government include the power to levy taxes and regulate commerce internal to each state.

In general, states may levy taxes on the same items the national government taxes, such as incomes, alcohol, and gasoline, but a state cannot, by a tax, "unduly burden" commerce among the states, interfere with a function of the national government, complicate the operation of a national law, or abridge the terms of a treaty of the United States. However, where the national government has not asserted its supremacy, states may regulate interstate businesses, provided these regulations do not cover matters requiring uniform national treatment or unduly burden interstate commerce.

(See Table 3.1 for the constitutional division of powers.)

Who decides which matters require "uniform national treatment" or what actions might place an "undue burden" on interstate commerce? Congress does, subject to the president's signature and final review by the Supreme Court. When Congress is silent or does not clearly state its intent, the courts—ultimately, the Supreme Court—decide whether there is a conflict with the national Constitution or whether a state law or regulation has preempted the national government's authority.

☐ Constitutional Limits and Obligations

To ensure that federalism works, the Constitution imposes restraints on both the national and the state governments. States are prohibited from doing the following:

1. Making treaties with foreign governments
2. Authorizing private citizens or organizations to interfere with the shipping and commerce of other nations
3. Coining money, issuing bills of credit, or making anything but gold and silver coins legal tender in payment of debts

TABLE 3.1 THE CONSTITUTIONAL DIVISION OF NATIONAL AND STATE POWERS

Examples of Powers Delegated to the National Government
Regulate trade and interstate commerce
Declare war
Create post offices
Coin money
Examples of Powers Reserved for State Governments
Create local governments
Police citizens
Oversee primary and elementary education
Examples of Concurrent Powers Shared by the National and State Governments
Impose and collect taxes and fees
Borrow and spend money
Establish courts at their level of government
Enact and enforce laws
Protect civil rights
Conduct elections
Protect health and welfare

4. Taxing imports or exports
5. Taxing foreign ships
6. Keeping troops or ships of war in time of peace (except for the state militia, now called the National Guard)
7. Engaging in war

In turn, the Constitution requires the national government to refrain from exercising its powers, especially its powers to tax and to regulate interstate commerce, in such a way as to interfere substantially with the states' abilities to perform their responsibilities. But politicians, judges, and scholars disagree about whether the national political process—specifically the executive and the legislature—or the courts should ultimately define the boundaries between the powers of the national government and the states. Some argue that the states' protection from intrusions by the national government comes primarily from the political process because senators

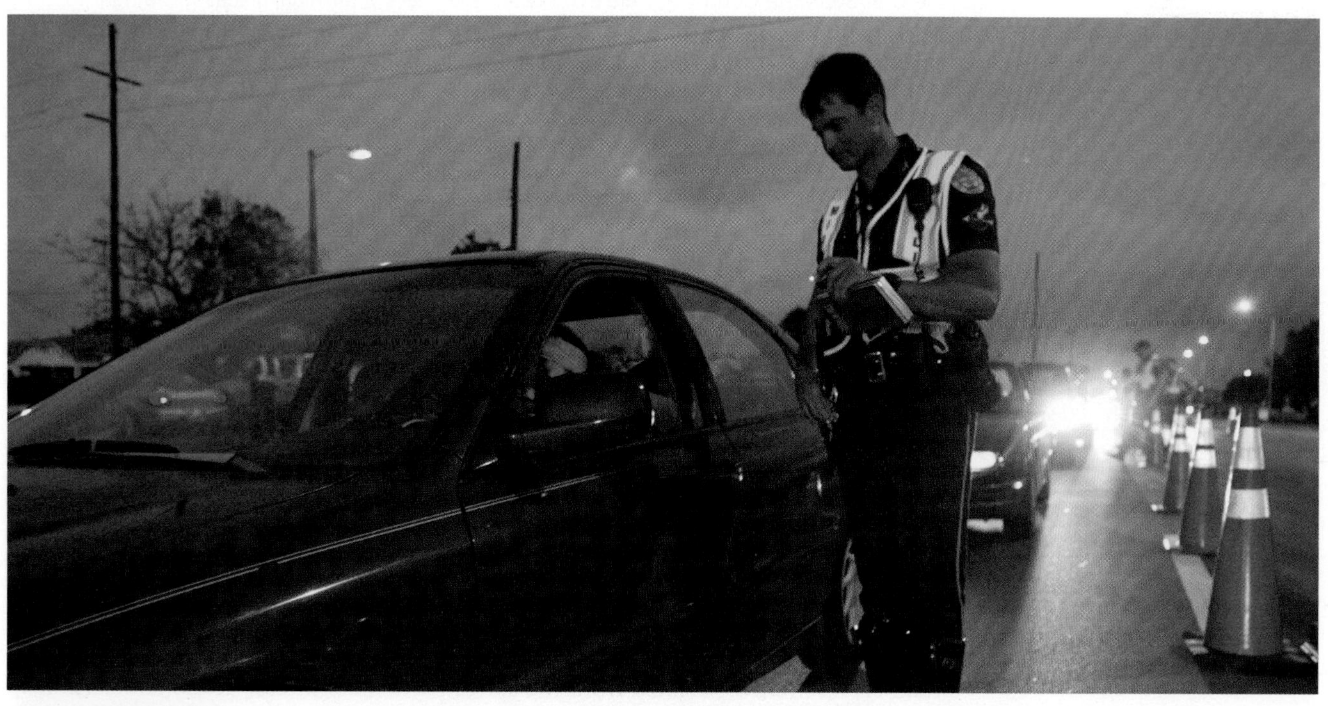

Under national pressure and the threat that they will lose national funding if they do not act, states have raised the drinking age to 21. States are also under pressure to monitor drunk driving more aggressively. When states operate these checkpoints because they will lose national funding, the action reflects coercive federalism.

3.1

3.2

3.3

3.4

3.5

You Will Decide

Should Citizens Have the Right to Choose Their Time to Die?

Many Americans suffer great pain as they struggle with cancer and other diseases in the last few months of life. Although modern medicine offers a number of options for easing the pain through hospice and drug therapies, some citizens would prefer to end their lives on their own schedule through what was once mislabeled as "assisted suicide."

This term often creates images of euthanasia by raising the specter of doctors and government making the decision about when a terminally ill patient should be given the drugs to die. In recent years, however, the term has been replaced by the concept of "end-of-life-choice." Driven by the "death with dignity" movement, which is led by a public interest group called "Compassion and Choice" (www.compassionandchoice.org), the campaign has won voter approval in Oregon, Washington, Montana, and Hawaii. Under current law in these states, patients, not doctors, are given the option of ending their own lives through drugs that ease them into a life-ending coma, or deep sleep, leading to death within minutes.

These states require at least two doctors to certify that a patient has only six months or less to live. With this certification in hand, the doctors are allowed to give the patient a prescription for the life-ending drugs. Having decided to end his or her life, the patient is asked two questions before taking the drugs: (1) Do you wish to end your life, and (2) Are you able to administer the drugs by your own hand? If the patient answers yes to both questions, he or she is given the drugs to act. Some patients decide to take the drugs, while others do not.

What do you think? Should all states give their citizens the right to end their own lives?

Thinking It Through

These citizen-approved laws have been tested in the national courts to see whether states have the right to allow their citizens to choose their own time of death.

In a landmark 1990 decision, the Supreme Court decided that states could allow their citizens to express their desire to refuse unwanted medical treatment such as food and water at the end of their lives and to appoint someone to speak for them when they could not.* In 1997, however, the Supreme Court ruled that the Constitution did not guarantee a right to die.**

According to these rulings, the U.S. Supreme Court acknowledged a citizen's right to take control of certain aspects of their death, but also affirmed a state legislature's right to prohibit anyone from providing help in dying. Also under the rulings, states, not the national government, had the responsibility to pass laws either allowing or prohibiting doctor aid in ending life. Since there is no right to die in the U.S. Constitution, it is also up to state courts to uphold or reject end of life laws under their own constitutions.

The Montana Supreme Court did so on December 31, 2009, when it decided that doctors could provide end of life drugs, provided that the patient was mentally competent and clearly aware of the consequences of his or her action and was able to take the drugs without assistance.*** On January 1, 2010, the Montana "Death with Dignity Act" went into effect.

It is not clear whether the movement toward "death with dignity" will spread to other states. Although advocates believe they have a chance in other western states where voters have the right to pass legislation under the initiative power, state legislatures in other states have been reluctant to raise the issue because it is so controversial. Some citizens define the choice as a form of suicide, and in direct violation of their religious beliefs. Other opponents argue that no one can be sure when they will die even when they have a terminal disease. The right to choose one's time of death may be permitted under state and national constitutions, but is still a choice that citizens and their legislators must allow.

CRITICAL THINKING QUESTIONS

1. **Why did the U.S. Supreme Court decide not to reverse state laws regulating the end of life?**
2. **Why would a state legislature be reluctant to pass end-of-life legislation? Which groups favor such laws and which do not?**
3. **Is a law needed at all on the end of life issue? Should either the national or state governments get involved in this issue?**

**Cruzan v. Director, Missouri Department of Health*, 497 U.S. 261 (1990).

***Vacco v. Quill*, 521 U.S. 793 (1997).

****Baxter v. Montana*, --- P.3d ----, 2009 WL 5155363 (Mont. 2009).

and representatives elected from the states participate in congressional decisions.[20] Others maintain that the Supreme Court should limit the national government's power and defend the states.[21]

On a case-by-case basis, the Court has held that the national government may not command states to enact laws to comply with or order state employees to enforce national laws. In *Printz* v. *United States,* the Court held that states were not required to conduct instant national background checks prior to selling a handgun.[22] Referring broadly to the concept of dual federalism discussed earlier in this chapter, the Supreme Court said that the national government could not "draft" local police to do its bidding. But as previously discussed, even if the national government cannot force states to enforce certain national laws, it can threaten to withhold its funding if states do not comply with national policies, such as lowering the minimum drinking age or speed limit.

The Constitution also obliges the national government to protect states against *domestic insurrection.* Congress has delegated to the president the authority to dispatch troops to put down such insurrections when the proper state authorities request them.

☐ Interstate Relationships

Three clauses in the Constitution, taken from the Articles of Confederation, require states to give full faith and credit to each other's public acts, records, and judicial proceedings; to extend to each other's citizens the privileges and immunities of their own citizens; and to return persons who are fleeing from justice.

FULL FAITH AND CREDIT The **full faith and credit clause** (Article IV, Section 1), one of the more technical provisions of the Constitution, requires state courts to enforce the civil judgments of the courts of other states and accept their public records and acts as valid.[23] It does not require states to enforce the criminal laws or legislation and administrative acts of other states; in most cases, for one state to enforce the criminal laws of another would raise constitutional issues. The clause applies primarily to enforcing judicial settlements and court awards.

INTERSTATE PRIVILEGES AND IMMUNITIES Under Article IV, Section 2, individual states must give citizens of all other states the privileges and immunities they grant to their own citizens, including the protection of the laws, the right to engage in peaceful occupations, access to the courts, and freedom from discriminatory taxes. Because of this clause, states may not impose unreasonable residency requirements, that is, withhold rights to American citizens who have recently moved to the state and thereby have become citizens of that state.

EXTRADITION In Article IV, Section 2, the Constitution asserts that, when individuals charged with crimes have fled from one state to another, the state to which they have fled is to deliver them to the proper officials on demand of the executive authority of the state from which they fled. This process is called **extradition.** "The obvious objective of the Extradition Clause," the courts have claimed, "is that no State should become a safe haven for the fugitives from a sister State's criminal justice system."[24] Congress has supplemented this constitutional provision by making the governor of the state to which fugitives have fled responsible for returning them.

INTERSTATE COMPACTS The Constitution also requires states to settle disputes with one another without the use of force. States may carry their legal disputes to the Supreme Court, or they may negotiate **interstate compacts.** Interstate compacts often establish interstate agencies to handle problems affecting an entire region. Before most interstate compacts become effective, Congress has to approve them. Then the compact becomes binding on all states that sign it, and the national judiciary can enforce its terms. A typical state may belong to 20 compacts dealing with such subjects as environmental protection, crime control, water rights, and higher education exchanges.[25]

full faith and credit clause
The clause in the Constitution (Article IV, Section 1) requiring each state to recognize the civil judgments rendered by the courts of the other states and to accept their public records and acts as valid.

extradition
The legal process whereby an alleged criminal offender is surrendered by the officials of one state to officials of the state in which the crime is alleged to have been committed.

interstate compact
An agreement among two or more states. Congress must approve most such agreements.

national supremacy
A constitutional doctrine that whenever conflict occurs between the constitutionally authorized actions of the national government and those of a state or local government, the actions of the national government prevail.

Explore on MyPoliSciLab Simulation: You Are a Federal Judge

The National Courts and Federalism

3.3 Assess the role of the national courts in defining the relationship between the national and state governments, and evaluate the positions of decentralists and centralists.

Although the political process ultimately decides how power will be divided between the national and the state governments, the national court system is often called on to umpire the ongoing debate about which level of government should do what, for whom, and to whom. The nation's highest court claimed this role in the celebrated case of *McCulloch* v. *Maryland.*

McCulloch v. *Maryland*

In *McCulloch* v. *Maryland* (1819), the Supreme Court had the first of many chances to define the division of power between the national and state governments.[26] Congress had established the Bank of the United States, but Maryland opposed any national bank and levied a $10,000 tax on any bank not incorporated in the state. James William McCulloch, the cashier of the bank, refused to pay on the grounds that a state could not tax an instrument of the national government.

Maryland was represented before the Court by some of the country's most distinguished lawyers, including Luther Martin, who had been a delegate to the Constitutional Convention. Martin said the Constitution did not expressly delegate to the national government the power to create a bank. Martin maintained that the necessary and proper clause gives Congress only the power to choose those means and to pass those laws absolutely essential to the execution of its expressly granted powers. Because a bank is not absolutely necessary to the exercise of its delegated powers, Martin argued, Congress had no authority to establish it.

The national government was represented by equally distinguished lawyers, most notably, Daniel Webster. Webster conceded that the power to create a bank was not one of the express powers of the national government. However, the power to pass laws necessary and proper to carry out Congress's express powers is specifically delegated to Congress. Webster argued that the Constitution leaves no room for doubt which level of government has the final authority. When national and state laws conflict, Webster argued, the national law must be obeyed.

Speaking for a unanimous Court, Chief Justice John Marshall rejected every one of Maryland's contentions. He summarized his views on the powers of the national government in these now-famous words: "Let the end be legitimate, let it be within the scope of the Constitution, and all means which are appropriate, which are plainly adapted to that end, which are not prohibited, but consistent with the letter and spirit of the constitution, are constitutional."

Having established the presence of *implied national powers,* Marshall then outlined the concept of **national supremacy.** No state, he said, can use its taxing powers to tax a national instrument. "The power to tax involves the power to destroy.... If the right of the States to tax the means employed by the general government be conceded, the declaration that the Constitution, and the laws made in pursuance thereof, shall be the supreme law of the land, is empty and unmeaning declamation." Marshall's ruling was based on the Constitution's supremacy clause.

It is difficult to overstate the long-range significance of *McCulloch* v. *Maryland* in providing support for the developing forces of nationalism and a unified economy. If the contrary arguments in favor of the states had been accepted, they would have strapped the national government in a constitutional straitjacket and denied it powers needed to deal with the problems of an expanding nation.

National Courts and the Relationship with the States

The authority of national judges to review the activities of state and local governments has expanded dramatically in recent decades because of modern judicial interpretations of the Fourteenth Amendment, which forbids states to deprive any person of life, liberty, or property without *due process of the law.* States may not deny any person the *equal protection of the laws,* including congressional legislation enacted to implement the Fourteenth Amendment. Almost every action by state and local officials is now subject to challenge before a national judge as a violation of the Constitution or of national law.

preemption
The right of a national law or regulation to preclude enforcement of a state or local law or regulation.

Preemption occurs when a national law or regulation takes precedence over a state or local law or regulation. State and local laws are preempted not only when they conflict directly with national laws and regulations, but also when they touch on a field in which the "federal interest is so dominant that the federal system will be assumed to preclude enforcement of state laws on the same subject."[27] Examples of national preemption include laws regulating hazardous substances, water quality, clean air standards, and many civil rights acts, especially the Civil Rights Act of 1964 and the Voting Rights Act of 1965.

Throughout the years, national judges, under the leadership of the Supreme Court, have generally favored the powers of the national government over those of the states. Despite the Supreme Court's recent bias in favor of state over national authority, few would deny the Supreme Court the power to review and set aside state actions. As Justice Oliver Wendell Holmes of the Supreme Court once remarked, "I do not think the United States would come to an end if we lost our power to declare an Act of Congress void. I do think the Union would be imperiled if we could not make that declaration as to the laws of the several States."[28]

☐ The Supreme Court and the Role of Congress

From 1937 until the 1990s, the Supreme Court essentially removed national courts from what had been their role of protecting states from acts of Congress. The Supreme Court broadly interpreted the commerce clause to allow Congress to do

States are responsible for registering voters, but the national government is responsible for assuring that state registration rules are constitutional.

3.1

3.2

3.3

3.4

3.5

centralists
People who favor national action over action at the state and local levels.

decentralists
People who favor state or local action rather than national action.

whatever Congress thought necessary and proper to promote the common good, even if national laws and regulations infringed on the activities of state and local governments.

In the past 15 years, however, the Supreme Court has signaled that national courts should be more active in resolving federalism issues.[29] The Court declared that a state could not impose term limits on its members of Congress, but it did so by only a 5-to-4 vote. Justice John Paul Stevens, writing for the majority, built his argument on the concept of the federal union as espoused by the great Chief Justice John Marshall, as a compact among the people, with the national government serving as the people's agent.

The Supreme Court also declared that Congress had the power to regulate commerce between states and Native Indian tribes, but not the power to allow national courts to resolve conflicts between the two.[30] Unless states consent to such suits, they enjoy "sovereign immunity" under the Eleventh Amendment. The effect of this decision goes beyond Indian tribes. As a result—except to enforce rights stemming from the Fourteenth Amendment, which the Court explicitly acknowledged to be within Congress's power—Congress may no longer authorize individuals to bring legal actions against states to force their compliance with national law in either national or state courts.[31]

Building on those rulings, the Court continues to press ahead with its "constitutional counterrevolution"[32] and return to an older vision of federalism from the 1930s. Among other recent rulings, in *United States* v. *Morrison,* the Court struck down portions of the Violence Against Women Act, which had given women who are victims of violence the right to sue their attackers for damages.[33] Congress had found that violence against women annually costs the national economy $3 billion, but a bare majority of the Court held that gender-motivated crimes did not have a substantial impact on interstate commerce and that Congress had thus exceeded its powers in enacting the law and intruded on the powers of the states.

These Supreme Court decisions—most of which split the Court 5 to 4 along ideological lines, with the conservative justices favoring states' rights—have signaled a shift in the Court's interpretation of the constitutional nature of our federal system. It is a shift that has been reinforced with the most recent Supreme Court appointments made by Presidents Bush and Obama. Chief Justice John Roberts and Justice Samuel Alito, each appointed by President George W. Bush, tend to favor the states, while justices Sonia Sotomayor and Elena Kagan, Obama appointees, tend to side with the national government.

□ The Continuing Debate Between Centralists and Decentralists

From the beginning of the Republic, there has been an ongoing debate about the "proper" distribution of powers, functions, and responsibilities between the national government and the states. Did the national government have the authority to outlaw slavery in the territories? Did the states have the authority to operate racially segregated schools? Could Congress regulate labor relations? Does Congress have the power to regulate the sale and use of firearms? Does Congress have the right to tell states how to clean up air and water pollution?

Today, the debate continues between **centralists,** who favor national action on issues such as environmental protection and gun control, and **decentralists,** who defend the powers of the states and favor action at the state and local levels on these issues.

THE CENTRALIST POSITION The centralist position has been supported by presidents, Congress, and the Supreme Court. Presidents Abraham Lincoln, Theodore Roosevelt, Franklin Roosevelt, and Lyndon Johnson were particularly strong supporters, and the Supreme Court has generally ruled in favor of the centralist position.

Centralists reject the idea of the Constitution as an interstate compact. They view it as a supreme law established by the people. The national government is an agent of the people, not of the states, because it was the people who drew up the Constitution and created the national government. They intended that the national political process should define the central government's powers and that the national government be denied authority only when the Constitution clearly prohibits it from acting.

Centralists argue that the national government is a government of all the people, whereas each state speaks for only some of the people. Although the Tenth Amendment clearly reserves powers for the states, it does not deny the national government the authority to exercise all of its powers to the fullest extent. Moreover, the supremacy of the national government restricts the states because governments representing part of the people cannot be allowed to interfere with a government representing all of them.

states' rights
Powers expressly or implicitly reserved to the states.

THE DECENTRALIST POSITION Among those favoring the decentralist or **states' rights** interpretation were the Anti-Federalists, Thomas Jefferson, the pre–Civil War statesman from South Carolina John C. Calhoun, the Supreme Court from the 1920s to 1937, and, more recently, Presidents Ronald Reagan and George H. W. Bush, the Republican leaders of Congress, former Chief Justice William H. Rehnquist, and current Justices Antonin Scalia and Clarence Thomas.

Most decentralists contend that the Constitution is basically a compact among sovereign states that created the central government and gave it limited authority. Thus the national government is little more than an agent of the states, and every one of its powers should be narrowly defined. Any question about whether the states have given a

States have the power to prohibit texting while driving for their citizens, while the federal government has the power to prohibit texting while driving for truck and bus drivers engaged in interstate commerce.

devolution revolution
The effort to slow the growth of the national government by returning many functions to the states.

particular function to the central government or have reserved it for themselves should be resolved in favor of the states.

Decentralists believe that the national government should not interfere with activities reserved for the states. Their argument is based on the Tenth Amendment, which states: "The powers not delegated to the United States by the Constitution, nor prohibited by it to the States, are reserved to the States respectively, or to the people." Decentralists insist that state governments are closer to the people and reflect the people's wishes more accurately than the national government does.

Decentralists have been particularly supportive of the **devolution revolution,** which argues for returning responsibilities to the states.[34] In the 1990s, the Republican-controlled Congress gave states more authority over some programs such as welfare, and President Clinton also proclaimed, "The era of big government is over." However, he tempered his comments by adding, "But we cannot go back to the time when our citizens were left to fend for themselves," and despite its dramatic name, the revolution has fallen short of the hoped-for results.

The national government has continued to enact laws regulating the states. Following the September 11 terrorist attacks, for example, Congress passed a long list of laws giving states specific responsibilities for defending homeland security, including the implementation of national criteria for issuing driver's licenses. It has also ordered states not to sell any citizen's personal information to private companies, ended state regulation of mutual funds, nullified state laws that restrict telecommunication competition, and given the national judiciary the power to prosecute a number of state and local crimes, including carjacking and acts of terrorism.

The National Budget as a Tool of Federalism

3.4 Analyze the budget as a tool of federalism, and evaluate its impact on state and local governments.

Congress authorizes programs, establishes general rules for how the programs will operate, and decides whether room should be left for state or local discretion and how much. Most important, Congress appropriates the funds for these programs and generally has deeper pockets than even the richest states. National grants are one of Congress's most potent tools for influencing policy at the state and local levels.

National grants serve four purposes, the most important of which is the fourth:

1. To supply state and local governments with revenue
2. To establish minimum national standards for such things as highways and clean air
3. To equalize resources among the states by taking money from people with high incomes through national taxes and spending it, through grants, in states where the poor live
4. To attack national problems but minimize the growth of national agencies

Types of National Government Grants

National, or federal, grants can be classified on two separate dimensions: (1) how much discretion the national government uses in making the grant decision and, (2) what kinds of requirements the national government puts on how the funding can be spent. There are four types of national grants to the states: (1) *project grants, (2) formula grants,* (3) *categorical grants,* and (4) *block grants* (sometimes called *flexible grants*). According to the national government's 2011 tracking reports, states received about $25 billion in project grants that year, $485 billion in formula grants, $682 billion in categorical grants, and $9 billion in block grants.[35] (As we shall see below, these grant totals often contain a mix of different kinds of grants—for example, categorical grants often contain formula grants. Thus, the total of all grants to the states in 2010 was $600 billion. By 2016, the president's budget office estimates that the total will rise by another $100 billion.[36])

PROJECT GRANTS The national government supports states through project grants for specific activities, such as scientific research, homeland security, and some education programs. Most project grants are awarded through a competitive process following an application process. Project grants are generally restricted to a fixed amount of time and can only be spent within tight guidelines. Many university-based medical schools rely on project grants to support their efforts to cure life-threatening diseases such as cancer and heart disease. In order for a state or local government to receive funding through a project grant, the state or local government must apply for the funding. This gives the grantor the discretion to approve some applications and reject others based typically on the technical requirements of the individual grant program.

FORMULA GRANTS Formula grants are distributed to the states based on procedures set out in the granting legislation. The simplest formula is population—each recipient government receives a certain number of dollars for each person who lives in the jurisdiction. More complex formulas might define the target population—for example, the number of people below the poverty line or above the age of 65. Other formulas do not involve people at all, but specific measures of a problem such as the number of boarded-up houses in a state. Early rounds of homeland security funding were based largely on a population formula, while the most recent rounds have taken both population and the risk of a terrorist attack into consideration in granting funds to state and local governments.

CATEGORICAL GRANTS Categorical grants are made for specific purposes; hence, the term "categorical." Categorical grants for specific purposes, such as Medicaid health care for the poor, are tightly monitored to ensure that the money is spent exactly as directed. Categorical grants have the most strings attached—state and local governments need to conform to all aspects of the funding legislation in order to receive the national funds. Although states have leeway in deciding how some categorical grants can be spent for programs such as highway construction, the national government often attaches strings to the overall category. Categorical grants involve the largest amount of federal support, but often require the states to match some percentage of each national dollar.

BLOCK GRANTS Block grants are made for more generalized governmental functions such as public assistance, health services, child care, or community development. By definition, these blocks of funding are provided with very few requirements attached. States have great flexibility in deciding how to spend block grant dollars, but unlike programs such as national unemployment insurance that are guaranteed for everyone who qualifies for them, block grants are limited to specific amounts set by the national government.

These four types of grants are occasionally combined within a single program area. Some categorical grants contain formulas, for example, while block grants are generally restricted to a broad issue such as education and assistance to the poor. As the following examples demonstrate, the national government often mixes and matches the grant types to accomplish its goals:

- The National School Lunch Program is both a categorical and formula grant—school districts receive funding for each meal served to a qualified student. To receive the funding the school district must guarantee that the lunches meet U.S. Department of Agriculture nutrition standards.

3.1

3.2

3.3

3.4

3.5

FOR the People Government's Greatest Endeavors

Helping States Educate Their Citizens

At first glance, the national government provides only limited assistance to states and localities to support public schools and universities. National grants for education programs such as the No Child Left Behind Act enacted in the George W. Bush administration and still in effect is relatively small compared to total state and local spending, and they often come with significant unfunded mandates.

However, much of the national government's support for state and local education is hidden from view. In the 1940s and 1950s, for example, the national government gave returning World War II veterans the tuition to earn college degrees through the GI Bill. These tuition grants, not loans, helped thousands of veterans get better jobs, purchase homes, and rebuild the economy, which was suffering from a post-war slump.

Out of 15 million eligible veterans, 8 million went to college or training programs. In 1947 alone, veterans accounted for nearly half of all college enrollment. According to past research by Congress, every dollar invested over the life of the program generated between $5 and $12.50 in tax revenues from veterans whose college education gave them better jobs and higher salaries than they otherwise would have had.*

The GI Bill exists to this day, and covers college tuition for veterans of all recent wars, including the wars in Iraq and Afghanistan.

The national government also provides significant support to help rebuild public schools, encourage educational innovations such as charter schools, and support college students as they work toward their degrees. In 2001, for example, Congress passed the "No Child Left Behind Act," which set national math and reading standards tied to national funding for public schools. The act remains in effect even though many states have raised objections to the strict standards.

More recently, the Obama administration launched a $4.5 billion national competition called "Race to the Top" to encourage innovative school programs through an annual competition for billions of dollars in federal funds. Of the 48 states that entered the competition, 15 states made the first cut, and Delaware, the District of Columbia, Florida, Georgia, Hawaii, Maryland, Massachusetts, New York, North Carolina, Rhode Island, and Tennessee won grants from $75 million to $700 million.**

The GI Bill, No Child Left Behind Act, and Race to the Top show how federalism can help all levels of government accomplish broad national goals from homeland security to disaster relief and educational reform. Sometimes the national grants can be very large as in Race to the Top, but even the relatively small amount of funding that actually reach an individual public school can motivate significant changes within our federal system.

QUESTIONS

1. What are some of the advantages of national and local governments working collectively on problems like education? What are the disadvantages?
2. Why might state and local governments want to enter competitions such as Race to the Top even when the amount of funding at stake is so small in comparison to what they spend?
3. What kind of federalism is the GI Bill tuition program? What kind of federalism is Race to the Top?

President Obama congratulates graduates after delivering the commencement address for Kalamazoo Central High School, winner of the 2010 Race to the Top High School Commencement Challenge, June 7, 2010.

*Cited by the United States Commission on National Security/21st Century, *Road Map for National Security: Imperative for Change: The Phase III Report*, (Government Printing Office, 2001), footnote 145.

**Information on the competition is available at http://www2.ed.gov/programs/racetothetop

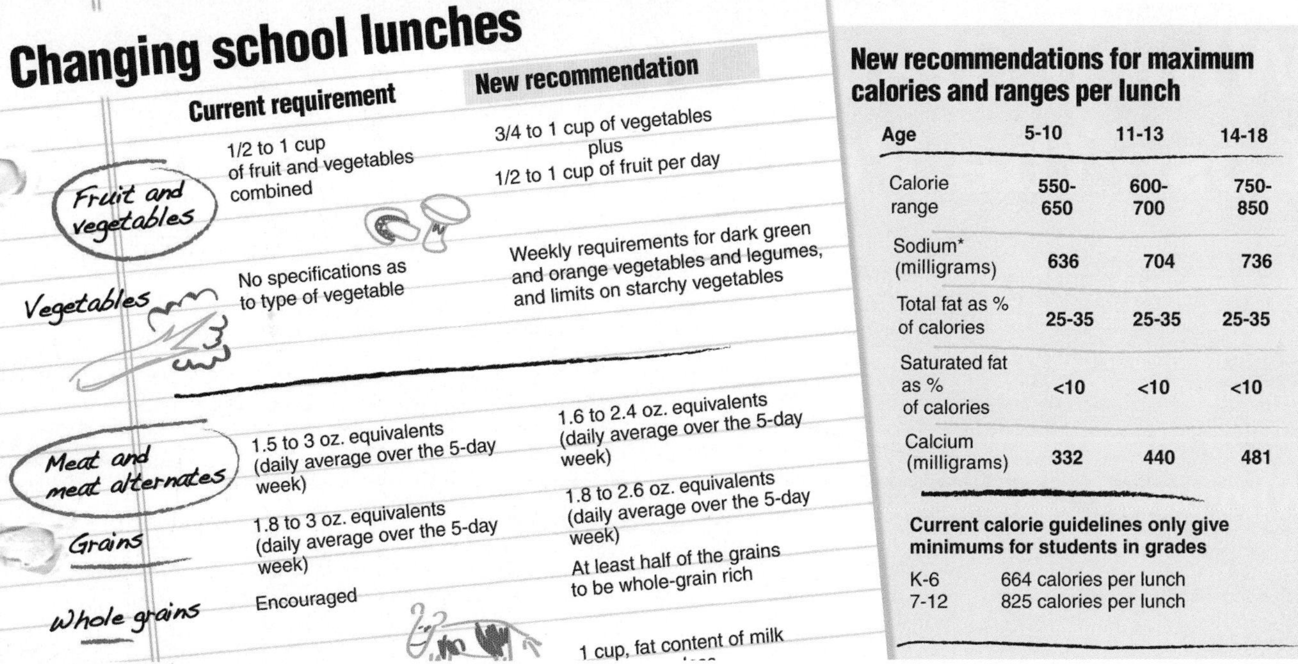

Changing school lunches

	Current requirement	New recommendation
Fruit and vegetables	1/2 to 1 cup of fruit and vegetables combined	3/4 to 1 cup of vegetables plus 1/2 to 1 cup of fruit per day
Vegetables	No specifications as to type of vegetable	Weekly requirements for dark green and orange vegetables and legumes, and limits on starchy vegetables
Meat and meat alternates	1.5 to 3 oz. equivalents (daily average over the 5-day week)	1.6 to 2.4 oz. equivalents (daily average over the 5-day week)
Grains	1.8 to 3 oz. equivalents (daily average over the 5-day week)	1.8 to 2.6 oz. equivalents (daily average over the 5-day week)
Whole grains	Encouraged	At least half of the grains to be whole-grain rich
		1 cup, fat content of milk

New recommendations for maximum calories and ranges per lunch

Age	5-10	11-13	14-18
Calorie range	550-650	600-700	750-850
Sodium* (milligrams)	636	704	736
Total fat as % of calories	25-35	25-35	25-35
Saturated fat as % of calories	<10	<10	<10
Calcium (milligrams)	332	440	481

Current calorie guidelines only give minimums for students in grades

K-6	664 calories per lunch
7-12	825 calories per lunch

The national government's school lunch program provides basic support for undernourished children, and is administered by local public school districts under state guidelines. The program is an example of cooperative federalism.

- The Community Development Block Grant (CDBG) program is both a block and formula grant—states receive funding from the national government based on a formula that includes a number of need-based variables.
- National research grants from agencies such as the National Institutes of Health or National Science Foundation are both project and categorical in nature with strict formulas for allocating the money in making final decisions.
- The Federal Aviation Administration's (FAA) Airport Improvement Program is both a block and project grant. The FAA takes applications and issues grants for the broad purpose of planning and developing airports in the United States.

The Politics of National Grants

Republicans "have consistently favored fewer strings, less national supervision, and the delegation of spending discretion to the state and local governments."[37] Democrats have generally been less supportive of broad discretionary block grants, instead favoring more detailed, federally supervised spending. The Republican-controlled Congress in the 1990s gave high priority to creating block grants, but it ran into trouble when it tried to lump together welfare, school lunch and breakfast programs, prenatal nutrition programs, and child protection programs in one block grant.

The battle over national versus state control of spending tends to be cyclical. As one scholar of federalism explains, "Complaints about excessive federal control tend to be followed by proposals to shift more power to state and local governments. Then, when problems arise in state and local administration—and problems inevitably arise when any organization tries to administer anything—demands for closer federal supervision and tighter federal controls follow."[38]

The Battle for Grants

With so much funding at stake, it is not surprising that state and local government might engage in aggressive lobbying to win their fair share, especially in setting the formulas that dictate funding within many grants. Whether by using their connections

Explore on MyPoliSciLab

Which States Win and Lose the Federal Aid Game?

The national government collects taxes from everyone, but it doesn't always spend money in the state where it gets it. Instead, the federal government transfers wealth from state to state. Recipient states pay less in federal taxes than they receive, while donor states pay more in taxes than they receive back. In 2007, there were 19 donor states and 31 recipient states. The political explanation for who were donor and recipient states is surprising.

Who pays? DELAWARE, MINNESOTA, NEW JERSEY, and CONNECTICUT

all paid at least $6,000 more in federal taxes per person than they received in federal aid. 15 other states were net donors.

Net Donor: Over $5,000 Per Person				
	Connecticut $6,241	New Jersey $6,644	Minnesota $7,431	Delaware $12,285

Net Donor: Between $1 and $5,000 per person				
	Ohio $49	North Carolina $1,108	Massachusetts $2,133	Rhode Island $2,732
	Georgia $434	California $1,466	Colorado $2,176	Illinois $3,640
	Washington $773	Nevada $1,616	Nebraska $2,850	New York $4,502
	Wisconsin $1,000	Arkansas $1,723	Texas $2,243	

Who receives? ALASKA took in twice the federal money in 2007 that it paid in taxes.

31 states are recipient states. Of the top six recipient states, four are southern.

Net Recipient: Over $5,000 Per Person						
	Alaska –$7,448	New Mexico –$7,143	Mississippi –$6,765	Virginia –$6,239	West Virginia –$5,820	Alabama –$5,130

Net Recipient: Between $1 and $5,000 per person					
	Hawaii –$4983	South Carolina –$3,756	Arizona –$1,976	Utah –$792	Pennsylvania –$385
	North Dakota –$4,856	Kentucky –$3,012	Idaho –$1,281	Indiana –$723	Oklahoma –$376
	South Dakota –$4,414	Maryland –$3,010	Wyoming –$1,205	Tennessee –$603	New Hampshire –$349
	Maine –$4,221	Vermont –$2,854	Missouri –$1,190	Florida –$581	Michigan –$171
	Montana –$4,149	Louisiana –$2,180	Iowa –$1,075	Oregon –$474	Kansas –$154

SOURCE: Data from United States Internal Revenue Service; *Statistical Abstract of the United States 2012;* and *U.S. Census of Population and Housing, 2010.*

Who are the Recipient States?

Recipient states by party

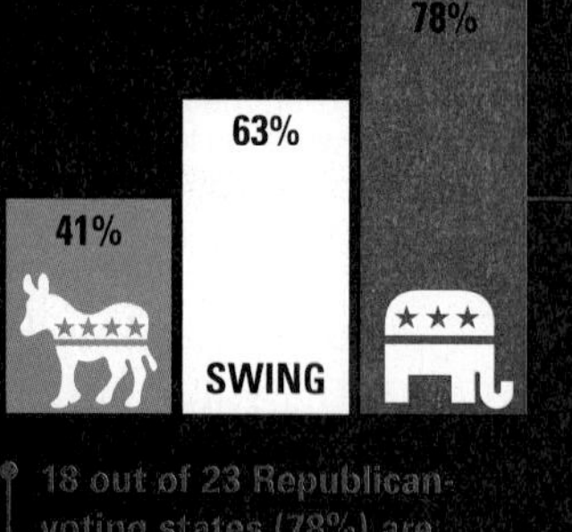

18 out of 23 Republican-voting states (78%) are recipient states compared to 8 out of the 19 Democratic-voting states (42%).

Recipient states by poverty level

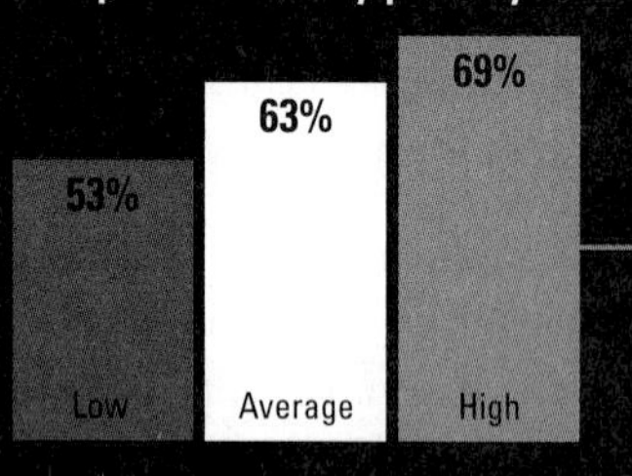

9 of 13 states with high poverty levels are recipient states (69%), while only 9 of 17 states with low poverty levels are recipient states (53%).

Investigate Further

Concept How do we determine donor and recipient states? Per person, we subtract the federal aid dollars sent to a state from the federal tax dollars paid in a state. If the result is positive, a state is a donor state, otherwise it's a recipient state.

Connection What relationship exists between politics and whether a state is a recipient or donor? Recipient states are most often Republican in national politics, while donor states tend to be more Democratic in national politics.

Cause Is there a policy explanation for which states are recipient states? The federal government fights poverty by moving money around the country. Recipient states usually have higher poverty levels and lower average incomes. Therefore, they tend to pay less federal tax

with members of Congress or the president, or by direct lobbying through their state offices in Washington or their national trade associations, state and local governments often intervene at several points in the funding process.

First, the specific instructions Congress develops in allocating formula grants involves often-intricate negotiation. Small changes in the terms—or the weight that the terms carry—in a given formula can advantage some states and disadvantage others. It is now a simple matter for states to analyze various proposed formulas in new legislation and to calculate how well they will do using each of those the rival formulas. Second, when a grant program is project-oriented, state and local governments often employ professional grant writers who know the inside workings of the national grant-making process and so know how to orient grant applications to make them more attractive to the officials who review the proposals. And third, state officials generally prefer (and lobby Congress for) block grants that have fewer restrictions on how the states can spend the funding to categorical grants that have more restrictions. In tough financial times when the competition for national grants increases, lobbying becomes increasingly more common.

☐ Unfunded Mandates

Fewer national dollars do not necessarily mean fewer national controls. On the contrary, the national government has imposed mandates on states and local governments, often without providing national funds. State and local officials complained about this, and their protests were effective. The Unfunded Mandates Reform Act of 1995 was championed by then-House Republican Speaker Newt Gingrich as part of the GOP's Contract with America. The act was considered part of what commentators called the "Newt Federalism."

The law requires Congress to evaluate the impact of unfunded mandates and imposes mild constraints on Congress itself. A congressional committee that approves any legislation containing a national mandate must draw attention to the mandate in its report and describe its cost to state and local governments. If the committee intends any mandate to be partially unfunded, it must explain why it is appropriate for state and local governments to pay for it.

At least during its first 15 years, the Unfunded Mandates Reform Act has been mostly successful in restraining mandates.[39] According to the National Conference of State Legislatures, the national government has enacted only 11 laws since 1995 that impose unfunded mandates. Three of these unfunded mandates involved increases in the minimum wage that apply to all state and local employees.[40]

The Politics of Federalism

3.5 Evaluate the current relationship between the national and state governments and the future challenges for federalism.

The formal structures of our federal system have not changed much since 1787, but the political realities, especially during the past half-century, have greatly altered the way federalism works. To understand these changes, we need to look at some of the trends that continue to fuel the debate about the meaning of federalism.

☐ The Growth of National Government

Throughout the past two centuries, power has accrued to the national government. As the Advisory Commission on Intergovernmental Relations observed in a 1981 report, "No one planned the growth, but everyone played a part in it."[41]

BY the People Making a Difference

Do a Data Mash-up on Your State

Governments and other organizations produce enormous amounts of information every year on how states raise and spend money, where people live, and even how they travel, eat, and spend their free time.

However, as the amount of information has expanded rapidly over the decade, new organizations have become engaged in helping citizens "mash-up" the data to reveal trends, ratings, and rankings in how their own states compare with other states. Using what some experts call "data-scraping" computer programs, these organizations allow citizens to track the issues and problems that matter most to them, while exploring possible causes and effects along the way. In doing so, they can keep track of what their governments are doing to encourage or discourage particular behaviors and make informed judgments about how to solve public problems.

Datamasher.org is one of the new Web sites dedicated to helping advance citizen knowledge. With hundreds of information sources to work with, you are free to search for patterns in topics like the number of fast-food restaurants and the level of obesity in your state. The question in this specific mash-up is whether the number of these restaurants somehow relates to obesity.

In some states such as Colorado, the ratio of restaurants to obesity is relatively low, compared with much higher levels in other states such as Kansas. Recognizing that correlation is not causation, the mash-up does not prove that higher obesity leads to more fast-food restaurants, or vice versa. But, mash-up provides an interesting way of thinking about whether some trends are related to each other in your state and suggests questions deserving more rigorous investigation. Simply asked, are there some conditions that lead to a stronger relationship between the two measures in Kansas than its next-door neighbor Colorado?

Datamasher.org also allows you to create your own mash-ups built on specific questions you might have. What is the relationship between the divorce rate and high school graduation rate? What is the relationship between smoking and cancer? What is the relationship between a high SAT score and having a solar panel on your house? These mash-ups produce maps and tables that show what is happening in your state, and suggest many ideas for moving your state up or down the rankings.

QUESTIONS

1. **How could keeping track of statistics about your state be a way to hold government accountable for what it does?**
2. **Is there too much information now available on what governments do and how problems relate to each other? Are rankings of states a good way to improve the way governments operate and make decisions?**
3. **What are the risks of using data mash-ups to make a case for government action?**

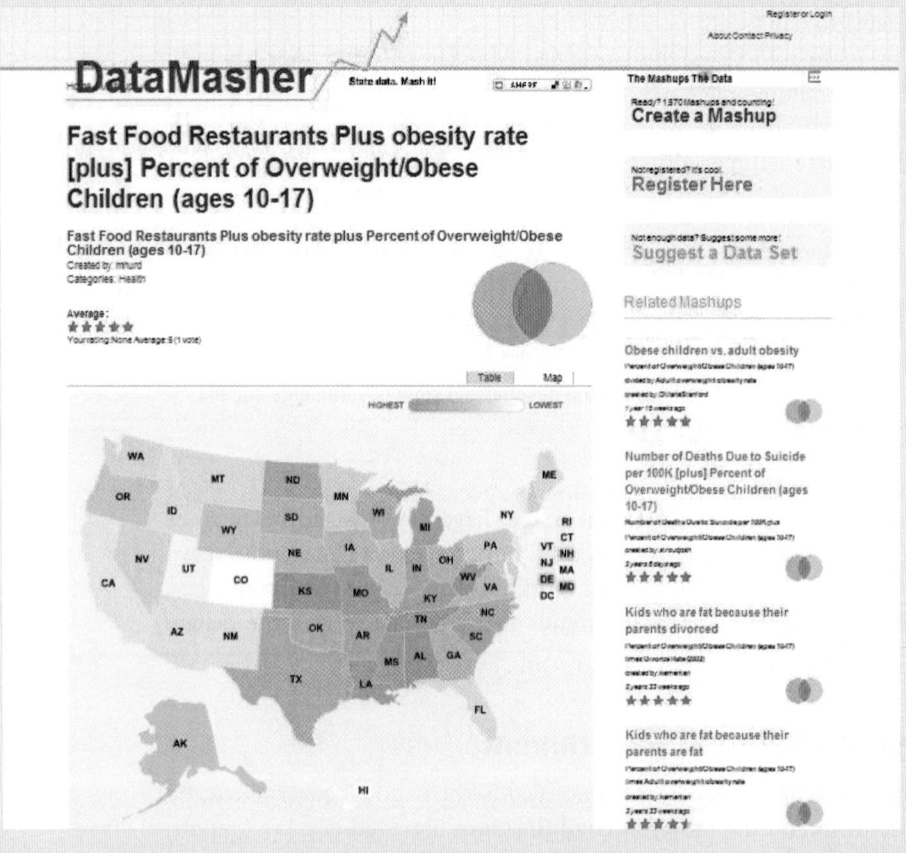

This shift occurred for a variety of reasons. One is that many of our problems have become national in scope. Much that was local in 1789, in 1860, or in 1930 is now national, even global. State governments could supervise the relationships between small merchants and their few employees, for instance, but only the national government can supervise relationships between multinational corporations and their thousands of worldwide employees, many of whom are organized in national unions.

As the economy grew rapidly during the early nineteenth century, powerful interests made demands on the national government. Business groups called on the government for aid in the form of tariffs, a national banking system, subsidies to railroads and the merchant marine, and uniform rules on the environment. And companies such as automobile makers that sell their products in all states typically prefer one national set of regulations rather than a different set in every state. Farmers learned that the national government could give more aid than the states, and they too began to demand help. By the beginning of the twentieth century, urban groups in general and organized labor in particular were pressing their claims. Big business, big agriculture, and big labor all added up to big government.

The growth of the national economy and the creation of national transportation and communications networks altered people's attitudes toward the national government. Before the Civil War, citizens saw the national government as a distant, even foreign, entity. Today, in part because of television and the Internet, most people know more about Washington than they know about their state capitals, and they know more about the president and their national legislators than about their governor, their state legislators, or even the local officials who run their cities and schools. Voter turnout in local elections is generally lower than in state elections and lower in state elections than in presidential elections.

The Great Depression of the 1930s stimulated extensive national action on welfare, unemployment, and farm surpluses. World War II brought federal regulation of wages, prices, and employment, as well as national efforts to allocate resources, train personnel, and support engineering and inventions. After the war, the national government helped veterans obtain college degrees and inaugurated a vast system of support for university research. The United States became the most powerful leader of the free world, maintaining substantial military forces even in times of peace.

Although economic and social conditions created many of the pressures for expanding the national government, so did political claims. Once established, federal programs generate groups with vested interests in promoting, defending, and expanding them. Associations are formed and alliances are made. "In a word, the growth of government has created a constituency of, by, and for government."[42] The national budget can become a negative issue for Congress and the president if it grows too large, however. In 2011–2012, for example, Congress and the president adopted deep cuts in federal aid to the states in an effort to reduce the federal deficit. The cuts were needed to reassure financial markets that the United States was making progress to reduce its rapidly increasing debt.

The politics of federalism are changing, and Congress is being pressured to reduce the size and scope of national programs, while dealing with the demands for homeland security. Meanwhile, the cost of entitlement programs such as Social Security and Medicare is rising because there are more older people with chronic health conditions, and they are living longer. These programs have widespread public support: to cut them is politically risky. "With all other options disappearing, it is politically tempting to finance tax cuts by turning over to the states many of the social programs...that have become the responsibility of the national government."[43]

☐ The Future of Federalism

During recent decades, state governments have undergone a major transformation. Most have improved their governmental structures, taken on greater roles in funding education and welfare, launched programs to help distressed cities, expanded their tax

3.1

3.2

3.3

3.4

3.5

bases by allowing citizens to deduct their state and local taxes from the national income tax, and assumed greater roles in maintaining homeland security and in fighting corporate corruption.

After the civil rights revolution of the 1960s, segregationists feared that national officials would work for racial integration. Thus, they praised local government, emphasized the dangers of centralization, and argued that the protection of civil rights was not a proper function of the national government. As one political scientist observed, "Federalism has a dark history to overcome. For nearly 200 years, states' rights have been asserted to protect slavery, segregation, and discrimination."[44]

Today, the politics of federalism, even with respect to civil rights, is more complicated than in the past. The national government is not necessarily more sympathetic to the claims of minorities than state or city governments are. Rulings on same-sex marriages and "civil unions" by state courts interpreting their state constitutions have extended more protection for these rights than has the Supreme Court's interpretation of the U.S. Constitution. Other states, however, are passing legislation that would eliminate such protections, and opponents are pressing for a constitutional amendment to bar same-sex marriages.

The national government is not likely to retreat to a more passive role. Indeed, international terrorism, the wars in Afghanistan and Iraq, and rising deficits have substantially altered the underlying economic and social conditions that generated the demand for federal action. In addition to such traditional challenges as helping people find jobs and preventing inflation and depressions—which still require national action—combating terrorism and surviving in a global economy based on the information explosion, e-commerce, and advancing technologies have added countless new issues to the national agenda.

Most American citizens have strong attachments to the Constitution's federal system measured broadly to mean all levels of government. However, they remain highly critical of the politicians who run government and are often angry at the stalemates in their national, state, and local legislatures. Although Americans still trust their state and local governments more than the national government in Washington, D.C., they are increasingly reluctant to give their states and localities a ringing endorsement.

Federalism can be a source of great reward for the nation, especially when it allows states to lead the nation in creating new programs to address problems such as poverty, global warming, and health care access. If the people cannot move the national government toward action, they can always push their state and local governments. By giving them different leverage points to make a difference, the Constitution guarantees that government *is* by the people.

Federalism can also be a source of enormous frustration, especially when national and state governments disagree on basic issues such as civil rights and liberties. This is when the people need to step forward not as citizens of their states but as citizens of the nation as a whole. Even as they influence their state and local governments, the people must understand they have a national voice that often needs to be heard.

Review the Chapter

Listen to Chapter 3 on MyPoliSciLab

Defining Federalism

3.1 Interpret the definitions of federalism, and assess the advantages and disadvantages of the American system of federalism, p. 76.

A federal system is one in which the constitution divides powers between the central government and lower-level governments such as states or provinces. But, over time, there has been support for different balances between state and government power such as the shift from dual federalism to marble cake federalism. The federal system in the United States does protect us from tyranny, permit local variation in policy, and encourage experimentation, but it comes at the cost of greater complexity, conflict, and difficulty in determining exactly which level of government is responsible for providing which goods and services that citizens might demand.

The Constitutional Structure of American Federalism

3.2 Differentiate the powers the Constitution provides to national and state governments, p. 86.

The Constitution gives three types of powers to the national and state governments: delegated powers to the national government, reserve powers for the states, and concurrent powers that the national and state governments share. Beyond delegated powers, the national government also has implied powers under the necessary and proper clause and inherent powers during periods of war and national crisis.

The national government's power over the states stems primarily from several constitutional pillars: the national supremacy clause, the war powers, its powers to regulate commerce among the states to tax and spend, and its power to do what Congress thinks is necessary and proper to promote the general welfare and to provide for the common defense. These constitutional pillars have permitted tremendous expansion of the functions of the national government.

The National Courts and Federalism

3.3 Assess the role of the national courts in defining the relationship between the national and state governments, and evaluate the positions of decentralists and centralists, p. 92.

The national courts umpire the division of power between the national and state governments. The Marshall Court, in decisions such as *Gibbons* v. *Ogden* and *McCulloch* v. *Maryland*, asserted the power of the national government over the states and promoted a national economic common market. These decisions also reinforced the supremacy of the national government over the states.

Today, debates about federalism are less often about its constitutional structure than about whether action should come from the national or the state and local levels. Recent Supreme Court decisions favor a decentralist position and signal shifts in the Court's interpretation of the constitutional nature of our federal system.

The National Budget as a Tool of Federalism

3.4 Analyze the budget as a tool of federalism, and evaluate its impact on state and local governments, p. 96.

The major instruments of national intervention in state programs have been various kinds of financial grants-in-aid, of which the most prominent are categorical grants, formula grants, project grants, and block grants. The national government also imposes federal mandates and controls activities of state and local governments by other means.

The Politics of Federalism

3.5 Evaluate the current relationship between the national and state governments and the future challenges for federalism, p. 101.

The national government has grown dramatically throughout the past 200 years. Its budget dwarfs many state budgets combined. As it has grown, the national government has asked states to do more on its behalf. States have pressed back against the national government, however, and continue to fight for their authority to use powers that are reserved for them under the Constitution.

Learn the Terms

 **Study** and **Review** the **Flashcards**

federalism, p. 79
unitary system, p. 81
confederation, p. 81
delegated (express) powers, p. 86
implied powers, p. 86
necessary and proper clause, p. 86
inherent powers, p. 86
supremacy clause, p. 87
commerce clause, p. 87
federal mandate, p. 88
reserve powers, p. 88
concurrent powers, p. 88
full faith and credit clause, p. 91
extradition, p. 91
interstate compact, p. 91
national supremacy, p. 91
preemption, p. 93
centralists, p. 94
decentralists, p. 94
states' rights, p. 95
devolution revolution, p. 96

Test Yourself

 **Study** and **Review** the **Practice Tests**

MULTIPLE CHOICE QUESTIONS

3.1 Interpret the definitions of federalism, and assess the advantages and disadvantages of the American system of federalism.

Canada has a central government in Ottawa, the nation's capital, along with ten provinces and three territories, each of which has its own government. According to Canada's constitution, both the provinces and the central government have powers to tax and regulate individual citizens. Which type of government best describes Canada?

a. A unitary state
b. A cooperative federalist state
c. A confederation
d. A territorial union
e. A competitive federalist state

3.2 Differentiate the powers the Constitution provides to national and state governments.

Determine whether the following powers are delegated to the national government, reserved for the states, or shared by both:

a. Power to establish courts
b. Power to tax citizens and businesses
c. Power to regulate interstate commerce
d. Power to oversee primary and elementary education
e. Power to make war

3.3 Assess the role of the national courts in defining the relationship between the national and state governments, and evaluate the positions of decentralists and centralists.

Which of the following arguments support the decentralist case?

a. The Constitution is a compact among sovereign states.
b. The national government is an agent of the states.
c. The national government should not interfere with activities reserved to the states.
d. State governments reflect the people's wishes more accurately than the national government.
e. All of the above

3.4 Analyze the budget as a tool of federalism, and evaluate its impact on state and local governments.

Which of the following are examples of a *federal mandate*:

a. The New York state legislature passes a law requiring all New York school teachers to spend ten hours a year learning new teaching techniques.
b. Congress passes a law requiring all coal plants in the United States to reduce their carbon emissions by 30 percent by 2015.
c. The Supreme Court upholds a law requiring teenage women to get parental permission before having an abortion.
d. The Federal Emergency Management Agency sends funds from the national government to help clean up after a tornado.
e. Congress passes an increase in the minimum wage that applies to all state and local employees.

3.5 Evaluate the current relationship between the national and state governments and the future challenges for federalism.

What is a likely future for federalism?

a. Congress may reduce the size of national programs.
b. Homeland security will be turned over to the states.
c. There will be many new issues on the national agenda.
d. The national government will become more passive.
e. The decentralist position will prevail.

ESSAY QUESTION

In a few sentences, discuss the "constitutional counterrevolution" instigated by Chief Justice William Rehnquist and continued by Chief Justice John Roberts. Why is preemption such a powerful tool for influencing state governments? Use this answer to write an essay appraising whether the balance of governmental power should lean more toward either the national government or the states.

Explore Further

IN THE LIBRARY

Samuel H. Beer, *To Make a Nation: The Rediscovery of American Federalism* (Harvard University Press, 1993).

Michael Burgess, *Comparative Federalism Theory and Practice* (Routledge, 2006).

Center For The Study Of Federalism, *The Federalism Report* (published quarterly by Temple University; this publication notes research, books and articles, and scholarly conferences).

Center For The Study Of Federalism, *Publius: The Journal of Federalism* (published quarterly by Temple University; one issue each year is an "Annual Review of the State of American Federalism"; Web site is www.lafayette.edu/˜publius).

Timothy J. Conlan, *From New Federalism to Devolution: Twenty-Five Years of Intergovernmental Reforms* (Brookings Institution Press, 1998).

Daniel J. Elazar and John Kincaid, eds., *The Covenant Connection: From Federal Theology to Modern Federalism* (Lexington Books, 2000).

Allison L. Lacroix *The Ideological Origins of American Federalism* (Harvard University Press, 2010).

John D. Nugent *Safeguarding Federalism: How States Protect Their Interests in National Policymaking* (University of Oklahoma Press, 2009).

Pietro Nivola, *Tense Commandments: Federal Prescriptions and City Problems* (Brookings Institution Press, 2002).

John T. Noonan, *Narrowing the Nation's Power: The Supreme Court Sides with the States* (University of California Press, 2002).

William H. Riker, *The Development of American Federalism* (Academic Press, 1987).

Denise Scheberle, *Federalism and Environmental Policy: Trust and the Politics of Implementation* (Georgetown University Press, 2004).

Kevin Smith, ed., *State and Local Government, 2008–2009* (CQ Press, 2008).

Carl Van Horn, ed., *The State of the States*, 4th ed. (CQ Press, 2008).

ON THE WEB

www.ncsl.org
The top source of information on pending legislative action and policy controversy in the states.

www.nga.org
The primary Web site for the state governors.

www.USASpending.gov
The national government's summary of all spending activity. Includes charts and graphs on overall spending trends and amounts of funding dedicated to state governments.

www.governing.com
The Web site for the major national magazine on state and local governments.

4

Listen to Chapter 4 on MyPoliSciLab

The American Political Landscape

A major focus of politics in 2011 and 2012 was the growing gap in income and wealth between the top 1 percent of Americans and the remaining 99 percent. During the 1950s and 1960s the United States had a relatively flat income distribution that fostered a large middle class. Over the past three decades, income has risen for most families but not nearly as much as it did for the three decades after World War II. In the three most recent decades, income for the top 1 percent of earners (those earning nearly $350,000 a year in 2007) rose 275 percent while for the 60 percent in the middle income group (those earning between just under $15,000 and $70,578), income rose by 40 percent.[1]

This disparity in income and wealth was a central focus of the Occupy Wall Street and other "Occupy" protests, and became part of the 2012 presidential election campaign. Republican Mitt Romney characterized efforts to reduce inequality as advocating an "entitlement society" in which he argued "everyone receives the same or similar rewards, regardless of education, effort, and willingness to take risk. That which is earned by some is redistributed to the others. And the only people who truly enjoy any real rewards are those who do the redistributing—the government. The truth is that everyone may get the same rewards, but virtually everyone will be worse off."[2] The Democrats, and especially President Obama, countered by arguing, "When middle-class families can no longer afford to buy the goods and services that businesses are selling, it drags down the entire economy, from top to bottom." Obama's view is that "inequality also distorts our democracy, it gives an outsized voice to the few who can afford high-priced lobbyists and unlimited campaign contributions, and runs the risk of selling out our democracy to the highest bidder."[3]

For several years, scholars have been describing the growing economic inequality in the United States. Political Scientist Larry Bartels attributes the persistent and growing inequality to

4.1 Understand the origins and impacts of American exceptionalism, p. 111.

4.2 Assess the role of geography in building a national identity, p. 112.

4.3 Evaluate the importance of where we live on American politics, p. 114.

4.4 Analyze how such social and demographic factors as race and ethnicity, religion, gender, family structures, education, and age affect American politics, p. 117.

4.5 Describe the importance of income, wealth, occupation, and social class in American politics, p. 127.

4.6 Evaluate the degree to which America has achieved a measure of unity in a land of diversity, p. 132.

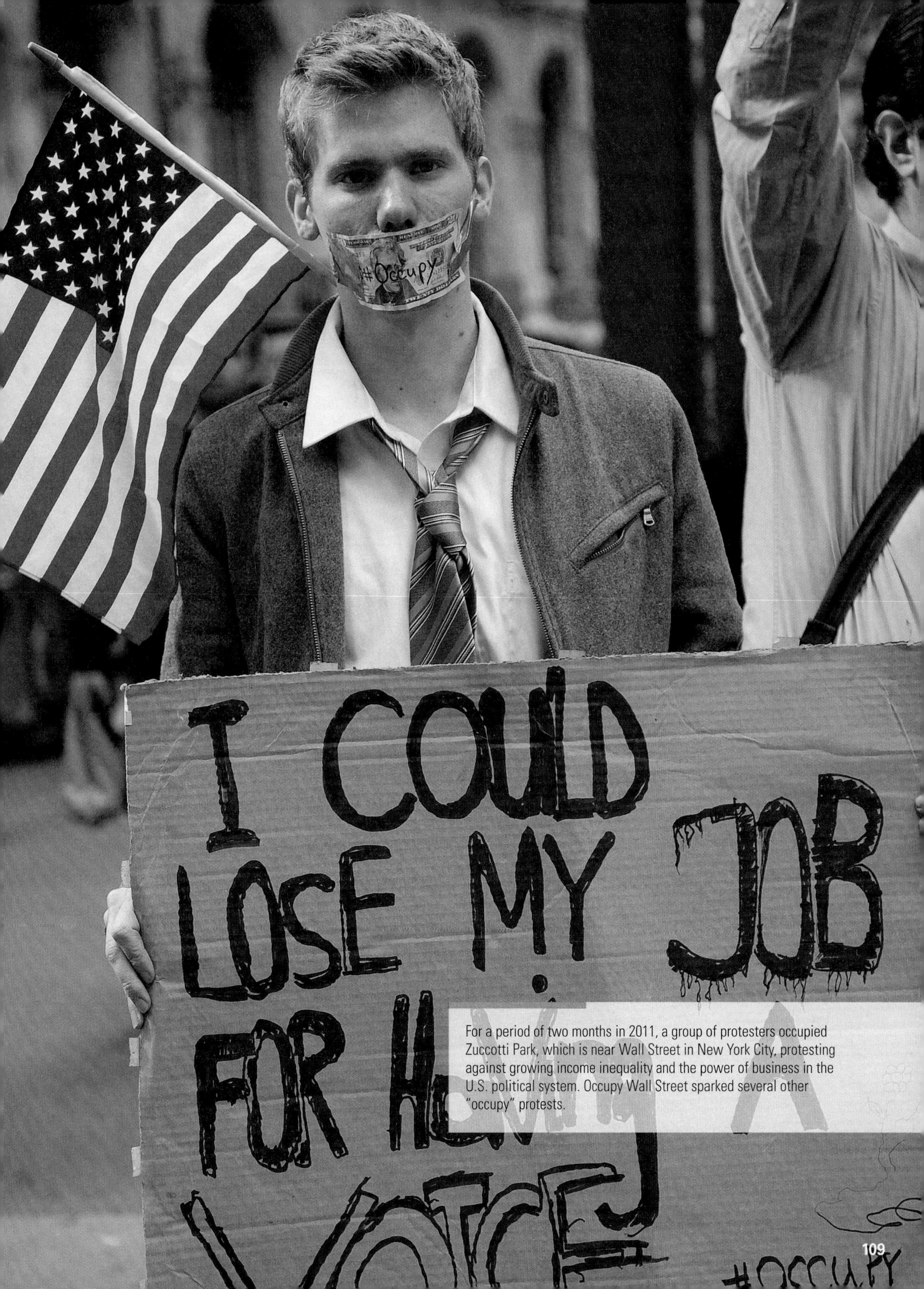

For a period of two months in 2011, a group of protesters occupied Zuccotti Park, which is near Wall Street in New York City, protesting against growing income inequality and the power of business in the U.S. political system. Occupy Wall Street sparked several other "occupy" protests.

MyPoliSciLab Video Series

Watch on MyPoliSciLab

The Big Picture Age, education, income, occupation, race, gender, sexuality—how do all of these things impact a person's political affiliations? Author David B. Magleby considers what it means to be a "Government by the People" with such a diverse national population.

The Basics What is political culture and how is it formed? In this video, you will hear how some people describe American political culture. In the process, you will discover what core political values Americans share, how they are formed, and what major ideologies American embrace.

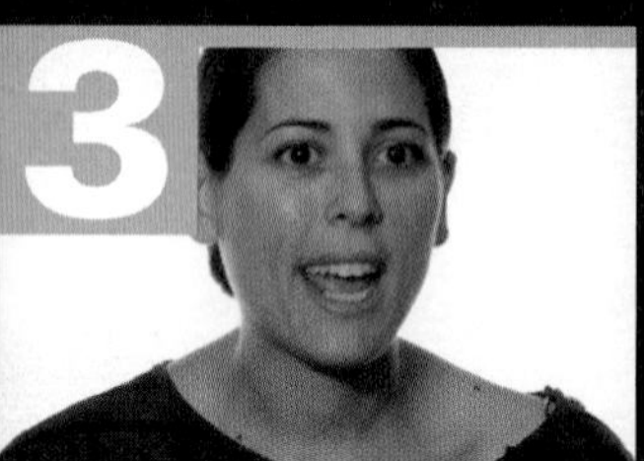

In Context Discuss the importance of American exceptionalism in American political culture. In this video, University of Oklahoma political scientist Allyson Shortle examines the core values that make up American political culture. She also discusses how these values gave rise to the American Dream.

Thinking Like a Political Scientist Find out what questions political scientists are investigating in the field of political culture. Southern Methodist University political scientist James Matthew Wilson assesses the impact of globalization and the emergence of ethnic and religious subcultures in the United States.

In the Real World Should the government correct the gap between the rich and the poor in the United States? This segment examines two opposing social movements—the Occupy movement and the Tea Party movement—and it considers the differences between their expectations for government.

So What? Why is it that some people support same-sex marriage while others oppose it? Author David B. Magleby encourages students to take advantage of diversity on campus and consider the variables that shape their peers' opinions on hot-button issues, like this one.

"the policies and priorities of Republican presidents."[4] Bartels also argues that inequality may have "deleterious social implications in the realms of family and community life, health and education."[5] Some others who have studied inequality have come to different conclusions. They see economic inequality as a natural consequence of a free market that rewards initiative, creativity, and hard work, and that may lead to big gaps between rich and poor. This view holds that for government, as a matter of policy, to try to close those gaps will likely result in less economic growth, potentially hurting everybody.[6]

Central to the debate is the role that government plays in the distribution of wealth and income through tax and other policies. We discuss those policies in more detail elsewhere in the book. Here we focus on how the distribution of income and wealth influence how people see candidates, parties, and politics generally. When candidates talk about taxing the wealthy more, they are often accused of "class warfare." Implicit in this charge is the view that people should not perceive themselves in terms of social class. While American politics is not primarily focused on issues relating to social class, social and economic differences clearly still matter a great deal. They have long been part of the broader landscape of American politics, along with race, age, region, gender, ethnicity, religion, and sexual orientation.

In the United States we celebrate our diversity and our immigrant past and proudly recite the words of Emma Lazarus, inscribed at the base of the Statue of Liberty: "Give me your tired, your poor, your huddled masses yearning to breathe free." Albert Einstein, who himself immigrated to the United States from Germany in the 1930s, once said that most people are incapable of expressing opinions that differ much from the prejudices of their social upbringing.[7] This **ethnocentrism**—selective perception based on our background, attitudes, and biases—is not uncommon. People often assume that others share their economic opportunities, social attitudes, sense of civic responsibility, and self-confidence, so in this chapter we consider how our social and economic environment explains, or at least shapes, our opinions and prejudices.

This chapter explores how differences in race, ethnicity, gender, family structure, religion, wealth and income, occupation, and social class influence opinions and voting choices; the effects of regional or state identity on political perspectives; and the relationship between age, education, and political participation. People's personal characteristics or attributes are important to understanding attitudes and behavior, political parties; public opinion, participation, and voting behavior, all of which are covered in subsequent chapters. Social scientists use the term **demography** to describe the study of such population characteristics. When social and economic differences reinforce each other, social scientists call them **reinforcing cleavages**; they can make political conflict more intense and society more polarized. Nations can also have **cross-cutting cleavages**, when, instead of reinforcing each other, differences pull people in different directions. American diversity has generally been more of the cross-cutting than the reinforcing type. This chapter lays the foundation for how different aspects of who we are as people influence how we behave politically.

ethnocentrism
Belief in the superiority of one's nation or ethnic group.

demography
The study of the characteristics of populations.

reinforcing cleavages
Divisions within society that reinforce one another, making groups more homogeneous or similar.

cross-cutting cleavages
Divisions within society that cut across demographic categories to produce groups that are more heterogeneous or different.

American exceptionalism
The view that due to circumstances of history, the Constitution, and liberty, the United States is different from other nations.

An Exceptional America

4.1 Understand the origins and effects of American exceptionalism.

Most nations consist of groups of people who have lived together for centuries and who speak the same language, embrace the same religious beliefs, and share a common history. Most Japanese citizens are Japanese in the fullest sense of the word, and this sense of shared identity is generally as strong in Sweden, Saudi Arabia, and China. The United States is different. We have attracted the poor and oppressed, the adventurous, and the talented from all over the world, and we have been more open to accepting strangers than many other nations.

Our isolation, relative wealth, prosperity, and sense of destiny have fostered a view that the United States is different from the world. This **American exceptionalism**, a

4.1

4.2

4.3

4.4

4.5

4.6

manifest destiny
A notion held by nineteenth-century Americans that the United States was destined to rule the continent, from the Atlantic to the Pacific.

term first used by de Tocqueville in 1831, has historically been defined as "the perception that the United States differs qualitatively from other developed nations, because of its unique origins, national credo, historical evolution, and distinctive political and religious institutions."[8]

The term has long been used to describe not only the distinctive elements of the United States, but the sense that the United States is a just and moral country. Exceptionalism can thus convey a sense of moral superiority or power that is not well received outside the United States, especially when the United States is seen to be acting in ways that other nations find objectionable or hypocritical. In the 2012 presidential election several Republican candidates explicitly referred to American exceptionalism. During the battle for the GOP nomination, Texas governor Rick Perry's Web site promised to "restore confidence in the American Dream and American Exceptionalism."[9] Mitt Romney was equally explicit in his rhetoric. For example, in his book published just before the campaign he wrote: "I believe in American exceptionalism. I am convinced that we can act together to strengthen the nation, to preserve our global leadership, and to protect freedom where it exists and promote it where it does not."[10] Democrats also see the United States as exceptonal. In a speech at the U.S. Airforce Academy, President Barack Obama said, "Never bet against the United States…the United States has been, and will always be, the one indispensable nation in world affairs. This is one of the many examples of why America is exceptional…I see an American century because of the character of our country—the spirit that has always made us exceptional."[11]

Geography and National Identity

4.2 Assess the role of geography in building a national identity.

The United States is a geographically large and historically isolated country. In the 1830s, French commentator Alexis de Tocqueville observed that the country had no major political or economic powers on its borders "and consequently no great wars, financial crises, invasions, or conquests to fear."[12] Geographic isolation from the major powers of the world during our government's formative period helps explain American politics.[13] The Atlantic Ocean served as a barrier to European meddling, giving us time to establish our political tradition and develop our economy.

Remarkably few foreign enemies have successfully struck within U.S. continental borders: most notably, England in the War of 1812 and terrorists in the World Trade Center bombing in 1993 and the attacks of September 11, 2001.[14] Although geographic location may have previously provided a substantial buffer from foreign attack, technological advances make that less the case today. The ability of terrorists to harm the United States and other countries, especially if they are willing to die along with their victims, means that national defense and homeland security pose new and difficult challenges.

Size also confers an advantage. The Western frontier gave the expanding population of the United States room to spread out. This defused some of the political conflicts arising from religion, social class, and national origin because groups could isolate themselves from one another. Moreover, plentiful and accessible land helped foster the perspective that the United States had a **manifest destiny** to be a continental nation reaching from the Atlantic to the Pacific Ocean. Early settlers used this notion to justify taking land from Native Americans, Canadians, and Mexicans, especially the huge territory acquired after victory in the Mexican–American War (1846–1848).

The United States is also a land of abundant natural resources. We have rich farmland, which not only feeds our population but also makes us the largest exporter of food in the world.[15] We are rich in such natural resources as coal, iron, uranium, oil, and precious metals. All of these resources enhance economic growth, provide jobs, and stabilize government.

The Global Community

Restricting Immigration

Immigration is an issue in many countries, not just the United States. The Pew Global Attitudes Project asked individuals: "Please tell me whether you completely agree, mostly agree, mostly disagree, or completely disagree with this statement: We should restrict and control entry of people into our country more than we do now." In the figure below we have combined those who completely and mostly agree into one category and those who mostly and completely disagree into another.

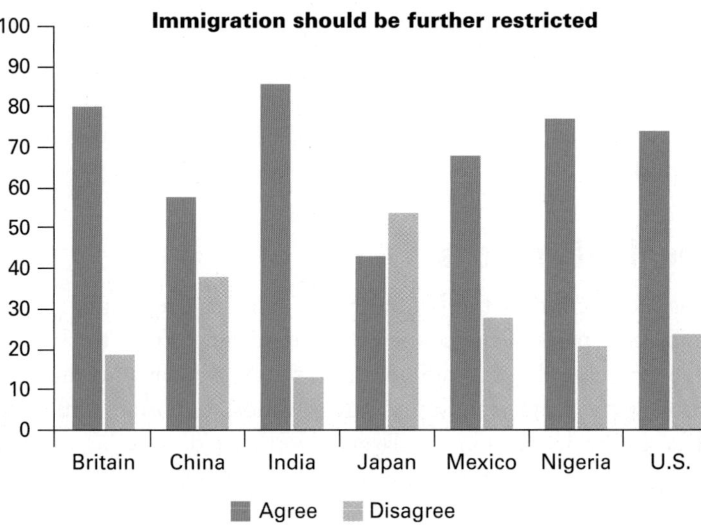

SOURCE: Pew Research Center, *2009 Spring Survey of Global Attitudes Project* (Pew Research Center, 2009).

The country with the most distinctive views on immigration is Japan, where more people disagree (53 percent) than agree (44 percent) with making immigration more restrictive. One possible explanation for this is that as a matter of policy, Japan has historically had low levels of immigration. In China, a country that has also had very little immigration, a greater percentage of respondents favor further restrictions (58 percent) than in Japan, but that percentage is significantly lower than in other countries in our sample of nations.

Nearly three-quarters of Americans favor further restrictions on immigration. But people in Nigeria, Britain, and India are even more uniformly of this view. A striking 86 percent of people in India favor more restrictions on immigration. This attitude may be a result of the perceived problems in India arising from immigrants from Bangladesh. Most illegal immigrants in the United States today come from Mexico, and yet within Mexico, 69 percent favor further restrictions on immigration. This may be explained in part by the presence of illegal immigrants in Mexico from other central and South American countries.

CRITICAL THINKING QUESTIONS

1. Why are people outside of Japan generally inclined to want to further restrict immigration?
2. Why would so many people in Mexico favor further restrictions on immigration in their country?
3. On many questions we examine, as many as 10 percent or more don't know their views. That is not the case with immigration, where no more than 4 percent report not knowing their views. Why is this the case?

Where We Live

4.3 Evaluate the importance of where we live on American politics.

Geography also helps explain our diversity. Parts of the United States are wonderfully suited to agriculture, others to mining or ranching, and still others to shipping and manufacturing. These differences produce diverse regional economic concerns, which in turn influence politics. For instance, a person from the agricultural heartland may see foreign trade differently from the way an automobile worker in Detroit sees it. But unlike the case in many other countries, geography in the United States does *not* define an ethnic or religious division. All the Serbians in the United States do not live in one place, nor do all French-speaking Catholics or Hispanic immigrants reside in others. Sectional, or regional, differences in the United States are primarily geographic, not ethnic or religious.

☐ Regional Differences

The most distinct section of the United States remains the South, although its differences from other parts of the country are diminishing. From the beginning of the Republic, the agricultural South differed from the North, where commerce, and later, manufacturing, were more significant. But the most important difference between the regions was the institution of slavery. Northern opposition to slavery, which grew increasingly intense by the 1850s, reinforced sectional economic interests. The 11 Confederate states, by deciding to secede from the Union, reinforced a common political identity. After the Civil War, Reconstruction and the problems of race relations reinforced regional differences. The Civil War made the Democratic Party the party of the South, and the Republican Party (the party of Lincoln), the party of the North. The Democratic "solid South" remained a fixture of American politics for more than a century.

Today the South is becoming less distinct. In addition to undergoing tremendous economic change, the large number of people moving to the South from other regions has diminished the sense of regional identity. The civil rights revolution of the 1960s eliminated legal and social barriers that prevented African Americans from voting, ended legal segregation, opened up new educational opportunities, and helped integrate the South into the national economy.

Starting in the mid-1960s, the South has become more reliably Republican. In 1992 and 1996, even with two southerners on the ticket—Bill Clinton and Al Gore—Democrats won only 4 of the 11 former Confederate states. In 2000 and 2004, Republican George W. Bush carried all 11 southern states, including Al Gore's home state of Tennessee in 2000 and vice presidential candidate John Edwards's home state of North Carolina in 2004. In 2008, Barack Obama made some inroads by winning in Florida, Virginia, and North Carolina, but in both North Carolina and Florida the margins were close. The partisan shift in the South can also be seen in the rising percentage of U.S. Representatives who are Republicans, which grew from about 10 percent in the 1960s to nearly 60 percent in 2012.[16]

Although Republican success in the South came first at the presidential level, gains in Congress and state legislatures have followed. The Republican share of Southern legislators in the House and Senate rose from 5 percent and 4 percent in 1960 to 48 percent and 50 percent, respectively, in 2012. In 2012, Republicans also controlled 9 of the 11 governorships in the former Confederate states. In the state legislatures, remnants of the old Democratic "solid South" remain, but Republicans have made major inroads, and politics in the region are becoming more predictably

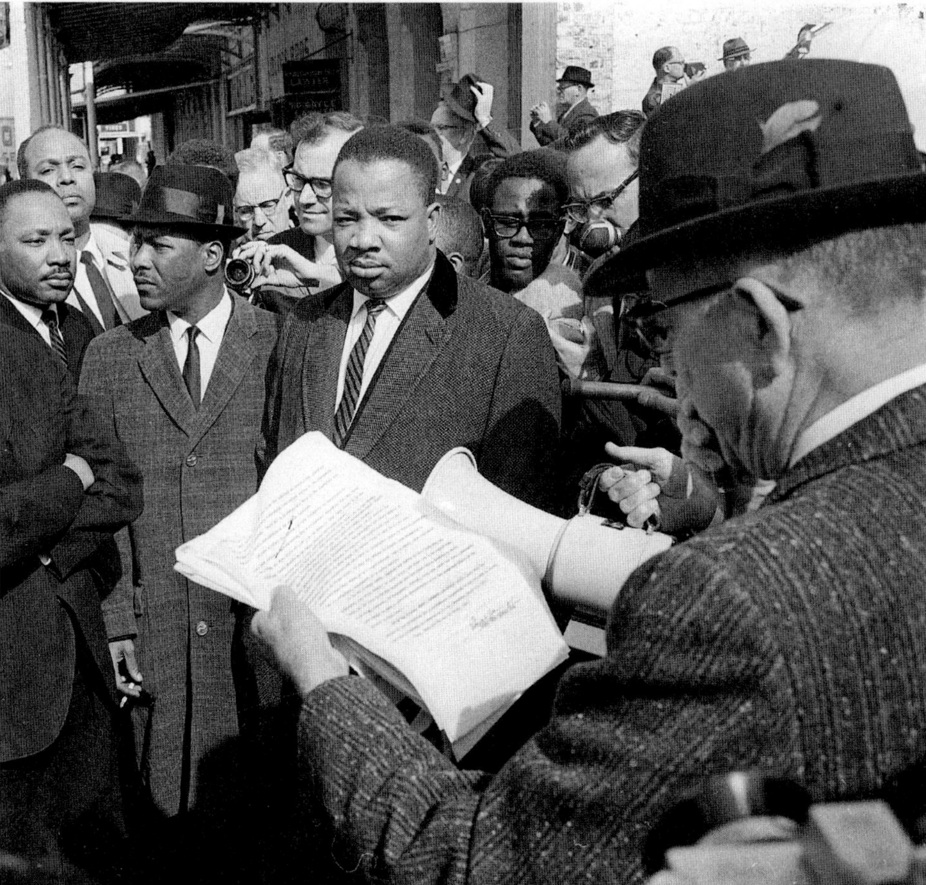

On March 7, 1965, police officers used clubs and tear gas against a group of civil rights demonstrators led by the Reverend Martin Luther King, Jr. as they protested the denial of voting rights in Alabama. This attack occurred as protesters attempted to cross the Edmund Pettus Bridge in Selma, Alabama. News reports of the police attack helped galvanize support for the 1965 Voting Rights Act.

Sun Belt

The region of the United States in the South and Southwest that has seen population growth relative to the rest of the country and which, because of its climate, has attracted retirees.

Bible Belt

The region of states in the South and states bordering the South with a large number of strongly committed Protestants who see a public role for religion.

Rust Belt

States in the Midwest once known for their industrial output, which have seen factories close and have experienced relatively high unemployment.

Republican. Another sectional division is the **Sun Belt**—the 11 former Confederate states plus New Mexico, Arizona, Nevada, and the southern half of California. Sun Belt states are growing much more rapidly than the rest of the country (see Figure 4.1). Reapportionment has shifted seats in the House of Representatives to the Sun Belt, which has tended to help the Republican Party. Some of the states in the Sun Belt are also part of the **Bible Belt**, a region long known for having more committed Protestants as measured by church attendance and a greater role for public religion.[17] The Bible Belt includes the former Confederate States plus nearby states like Kentucky, Oklahoma, and West Virginia.

Other sectional groupings of states include the **Rust Belt** of states in the Midwest where industrial production and jobs have left the region, leaving rusting factories vacant. States in the Rust Belt include Ohio, Pennsylvania, Michigan, and parts of Indiana and New York. The interior western states are another section with economic and political similarities. Much of the land in the West is owned by the federal government, which provides tension between state and local governments and the federal government.

□ State and Local Identity

Within the regions discussed above, states also have distinctive political cultures that affect public opinion and policies. Individuals often have a sense of identification with their state.[18] Part of the reason for enduring state identities is that we elect members of Congress and the president at the state level. States such as Iowa and New Hampshire play important roles in narrowing the field of presidential candidates

urban

A densely settled territory that is often the central part of a city of metropolitan area.

suburban

An area that typically surrounds the central city, is often residential, and is not as densely populated.

rural

Sparsely populated territory and small towns, often associated with farming.

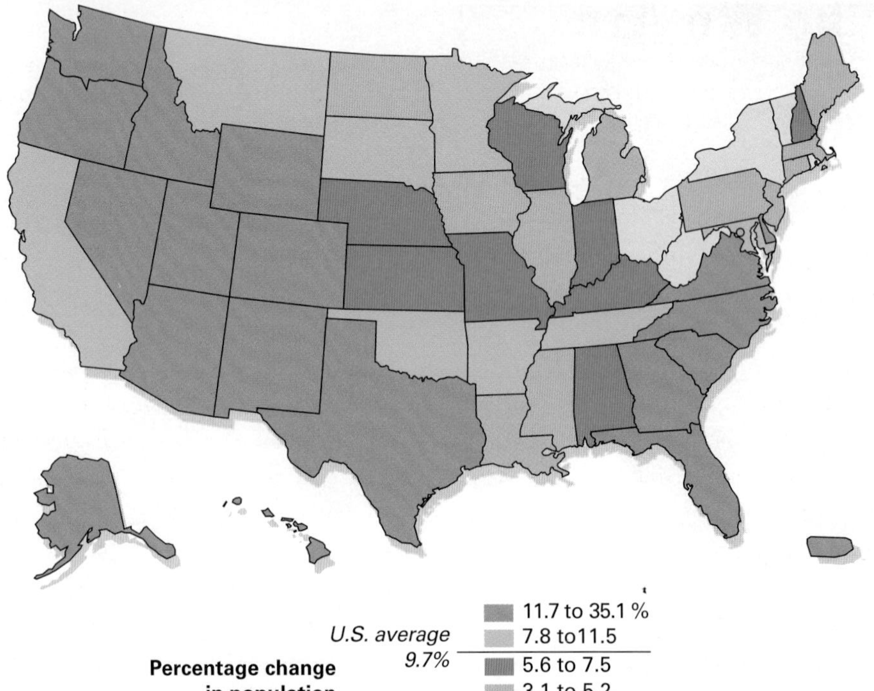

FIGURE 4.1 PERCENTAGE CHANGE IN RESIDENT POPULATION, 2000–2010

Which states saw the greatest shifts in population, and how might you account for some of the changes?

SOURCE: U.S. Census Bureau, *Statistical Abstract of the United States: 2012*, p. 19.

seeking their party's nomination. Differences in state laws relating to driving, drinking, gambling, and taxes reinforce the relevance of state identity. Colleges and universities may have the same effect while reinforcing competition between different states. California also stands out in American politics today, if only because nearly one of eight U.S. citizens lives in the state.[19] In economic and political importance, California is in a league by itself.

□ Urban and Rural Populations

Where we live can be categorized as one of three types of areas: **urban**, which is defined by the Census Bureau as "densely settled territory," often also the central part of a city; **suburban**, which is typically less densely settled and surrounds the central city; and **rural**, which is more sparsely populated and where farmers often reside. Four of five people in the United States now live in urban areas.[20] During the early twentieth century, the movement of population was from rural areas to central cities, which we call *urbanization,* but the movement since the 1950s has been from the central cities to their suburbs. Today the most urban states are California and New Jersey (both have 94 percent of their population living in cities or suburbs). Vermont is the least urban, with only 38 percent living in cities or suburbs.[21] Regionally, the West and Northeast are the most urban, and the South and Midwest the most rural.

People move from cities to the suburbs for many reasons—better housing, new transportation systems that make it easier to get to work, a lower cost of living, the desire for cleaner air and safer streets. Another reason is "white flight," the movement of white people away from the central cities so children can avoid being bused for racial balance and attend generally better schools. White, middle-class migration to the suburbs has made American cities increasingly poor, African American, and Democratic.

Who We Are

4.4 Analyze how such social and demographic factors as race and ethnicity, religion, gender, family structures, education, and age affect American politics.

race
A grouping of human beings with distinctive characteristics determined by genetic inheritance.

ethnicity
A social division based on national origin, religion, language, and often race.

Geography does less to distinguish one American from another than it did a century or even a half-century ago. Today we are more likely to define ourselves by a number of other characteristics, each of which may influence how we vote or think about candidates, issues, or policies. In recent elections, both parties have developed the ability to target individual voters based on computer models they have developed from historic patterns of the relationships between particular individual characteristics and political behaviors, as well as large sample-size polls that assess attitudes towards issues and candidates in a particular election environment. Individuals fitting a certain profile in their age, gender, religion, and race may be targeted for particular communications, a process known as "microtargeting." Other variables like education, sexual orientation, partisanship, ideology, and even the kind of car people own or what types of magazines they read may also be predictive of attitudes and behaviors. The ability of computers to store large amounts of data on people has made it possible for our politics to increasingly focus campaign appeals and messages to particular individuals.

Race and Ethnicity

Racial and ethnic differences have always had political significance. By **race**, social scientists may mean classifications of human beings with distinctive physical characteristics determined by genetic inheritance,[22] while others see it as more culturally determined.[23] The Census Bureau defines race "as a social definition... recognized in this country and not an attempt to define race biologically, anthropologically or genetically."[24] **Ethnicity** is a social division based on national origin, religion, and language, often within the same race, and includes a sense of attachment to that group. Many retain an identity with the land of their ancestors, even after three or four generations. Families, churches, and other close-knit ethnic groups foster these ties. Examples of ethnic groups with enduring relevance to American politics include Italian Americans, Irish Americans, Polish Americans, and Korean Americans, though most race and ethnicity issues in the United States today focus primarily on African Americans, Asian Americans, Native Americans, and Hispanics.

There are more than 39 million African Americans in the United States, nearly 13 percent of the population. Asian Americans constitute less than 5 percent of the population, and Native Americans comprise about 0.2 percent.[25] Most American Hispanics classify themselves as white, although Hispanics can be of any race. At more than 48 million, Hispanics are the fastest-growing U.S. ethnic group, constituting nearly 16 percent of the population.[26] Because of differences in immigration and birthrates, non-Hispanic whites will decrease to about 50 percent of the population by 2050.[27]

NATIVE AMERICANS The original inhabitants of what became the United States have played an important role in its history and continue to be important to the politics of states like South Dakota, New Mexico, Alaska, and Oklahoma. More than half the names of states and hundreds of the names of cities, rivers, and mountains in the United States are Native American. In United States Senate elections in South Dakota and Alaska, the Native American vote has been important.[28] One-third of Native Americans and Alaskan Natives have incomes below the federal poverty level. This percent is higher than those for African Americans and Hispanics.[29] Many Native Americans still live on reservations, areas of land managed by a Native American tribe. Some tribes have developed casinos on their reservations and secured added revenues, but many reservations have high infant mortality, low life expectancy, and greater poverty than the state as a whole in which the reservation is located.[30]

4.1

4.2

4.3

4.4

4.5

4.6

OF the People Diversity in America

A More Diverse Population

The United States has become much more diverse over the past 60 years and will become even more so over the next half-century. In 1950, nearly 9 of every 10 persons in the United States were white, and Hispanics were not a category the U.S. Census Bureau reported. By 2008, just fewer than four in five persons in the United States were white, but that fraction included Hispanic whites. Non-Hispanic whites are now about two-thirds of the U.S. population. Groups projected to have the most growth between 2008 and 2050 are Asians, Pacific Islanders, and Hispanics. In the aggregate, about one in every four persons in the United States in 2025 will be Asian, Pacific Islander, or Hispanic. Although regional differences matter less to American politics than they once did, the emergence of "majority minority" communities and legislative districts, in which a majority of the population are from racial minorities, ensures that race will have a greater influence in some areas of the country than others.

The changing face of U.S. politics is increasingly diverse. Despite the surge in Hispanic population, there has not been a similar surge in political participation or representation. Researchers cite many reasons for this, including redistricting, low rates of citizenship and motivations for voting, and a lack of common party commitment.

QUESTIONS

1. **What does it say about our conceptions of race and ethnicity that Hispanic was not a category on the 1950 census?**
2. **How will U.S. politics be different in 2050 when 49.1 percent of the population will be non-Hispanic whites?**

CHANGING RACIAL COMPOSITION OF THE U.S. POLITY, 1950–2050

	1950	1990	2010	2025	2050
White	89.5%	83.9%	72.4%	77.3%	74.0%
Non-Hispanic White	—	75.7	63.7	59.7	49.1
African American	10.0	12.2	12.6	13.0	13.0
Native American, Inuit, Aleut	0.2	0.8	0.9	1.1	1.3
Asian and Pacific Islander	0.2	3.0	5.0	6.1	8.11
Hispanic	—	9.0	16.3	20.8	29.6

NOTE: Percentages do not equal 100 because Hispanics can be of any race. Figures for 2025 and 2050 are projections. Categories from the 1950 census are different from those used in the last several decades. For example, the 1950 census did not provide a classification for Hispanic, Native Americans were classified as "Indian," and Asians were separated into Japanese and Chinese.

SOURCE: 1950 figures from U.S. Bureau of the Census, *Census of Population: 1950, Volume II Part I* (U.S. Government Printing Office, 1950), p. 106. 1990 figures from U.S. Bureau of the Census, *Statistical Abstract of the United States, 2001* (U.S. Government Printing Office, 2001), pp. 16–17. 2010 figures from U.S. Census Bureau, "Overview of Race and Hispanic Origin: 2010," March 2011, http://www.census.gov/prod/cen2010/briefs/c2010br-02.pdf, p. 4 (accessed June 11, 2012). All other figures from U.S. Bureau of the Census, "Projections of the Population by Sex, Race, and Hispanic Origin for the United States: 2010 to 2050," *National Population Projections Released 2008 (Based on Census 2000)*, August 13, 2008, http://www.census.gov/population/www/projections/summarytables.html

AFRICAN AMERICANS Most immigrants chose to come to this country in search of freedom and opportunity. In contrast, most African Americans came against their will as slaves. Although the Emancipation Proclamation and Thirteenth Amendment ended slavery in the 1860s, racial divisions still affect American politics. Until 1900, more than 90 percent of all African Americans lived in the South; a century later, that figure was 55 percent.[31] Many African Americans left the South hoping to improve their lives by settling in the large cities of the Northeast, Midwest, and West. But what many of them found was urban poverty. More recently, African Americans have been returning to the South, especially to states like Mississippi, Florida, Georgia, Texas, Virginia, and North Carolina.[32]

Most African Americans are more vulnerable economically than most whites. Income is strongly related to education. Among recent high school graduates, 71 percent of white Americans go on to college, and 70 percent of African Americans do.[33] The difference is in graduation rates: 31 percent of whites graduate from college, whereas only about 18 percent of African Americans do.[34] African American median family income is under \$39,000, compared to over \$62,000 for whites.[35] About 23 percent of

African American families live below the poverty level, compared to about 9 percent of white families.[36] However, African Americans have been doing better in recent years; 33 percent of African American households earned more than $50,000 in 2009 (compared to 50 percent of white households).[37] Some African Americans, like basketball player LeBron James and syndicated talk show host and corporate chief executive Oprah Winfrey, have risen to the top of their professions in terms of earnings.

The African American population is much younger than the white population; the median age for whites in 2010 was 38.4 years, compared to 31.7 for African Americans.[38] The combination of a younger African American population, a lower level of education, and their concentration in economically depressed urban areas has resulted in a much higher unemployment rate for young African Americans. In 2010, the average unemployment rate for African Americans was 16 percent compared with just under 9 percent for whites. Unemployment can in turn contribute to social problems such as crime, drug and alcohol abuse, and family dissolution.

African Americans had little political power until after World War II. Owing their freedom from slavery to the "party of Lincoln," most African Americans initially identified with the Republicans, but this loyalty started to change in the 1930s and 1940s under President Franklin D. Roosevelt, who insisted on equal treatment for African Americans in his New Deal programs.[39] After World War II, African Americans came to see the Democrats as the party of civil rights. The 1964 Republican platform position on civil rights espoused *states' rights*—at the time, the creed of southern segregationists—in what appeared to be an effort to win the support of southern white voters. Virtually all African Americans voted for Lyndon Johnson in 1964, and in presidential elections between 1984 and 2012, their Democratic vote averaged nearly 89 percent.[40]

In 2008, with an African American running for president, 95 percent of blacks voted for Obama and in 2012 the proportion was 93 percent.[41] In both years, African Americans were 13 percent of all voters. Exit polls found Obama also did substantially better among Latinos in both 2008 and 2012, getting 71 percent of the Latino vote in 2012. Evidence of growing African American political power is the dramatic increase in the number of African American state legislators, which rose from 168 in 1970 to 623 in 2008.[42] Georgia has 54 African American state legislators, the most of any state. Alabama, Maryland, Mississippi, New York, and South Carolina all have more than 30.[43]

HISPANICS Hispanic Americans are not a monolithic group, and although they share a common linguistic heritage in Spanish, they often differ from one another depending on the country from which they or their forebears emigrated. Cuban Americans, for instance, tend to be Republicans, while Mexican Americans and Puerto Ricans living on the mainland are disproportionately Democrats.[44] Hispanics are politically important in a growing number of states. Nearly two-thirds of Cuban Americans live in Florida, especially in greater Miami. Mainland Puerto Ricans are concentrated in and around New York City; many Mexican Americans live in the Southwest and California. More than 13 million Hispanics live in California.[45]

Because Hispanics are not politically homogeneous, they are not a united voting bloc. The many noncitizen Hispanics and the relative youth of the Hispanic population also diminish the group's political power. For example, 13.9 million foreign-born Hispanics are not citizens,[46] and of the estimated 10.8 million unauthorized immigrants, three-fifths are from Mexico.[47] This group cannot vote, nor can those under age 18, who make up a greater percentage of the Hispanic population than in other ethnic groups. The median age of Hispanics in 2010 was 27.5 years, more than 10 years younger than whites (38.4 years), and younger than blacks (31.7 years).[48] Language problems also reduce Hispanic citizens' voter registration and turnout.

Both major parties are aggressively cultivating Hispanic candidates. Several Hispanics have been cabinet members. Ken Salazar, a Hispanic Democrat, was also elected to the Senate in 2004 from Colorado, and became Secretary of Interior in the Obama administration. Bob Menendez, a Democrat, was appointed to the Senate from New Jersey and then elected in 2006 and reelected in 2012. Republican U.S.

In 2009, Sonia Sotomayor became the first Hispanic and the third woman to serve on the U.S. Supreme Court. She was born in New York and is of Puerto Rican descent. She is seen here in her Bronx neighborhood after her Senate confirmation.

Senator Marco Rubio, a Tea Party favorite and son of Cuban immigrants, was elected in Florida in 2010. In 2009, President Obama appointed and the Senate confirmed Sonia Sotomayor to the U.S. Supreme Court. Sotomayor became the first Hispanic U.S. Supreme Court Justice. In 2012 Republican Ted Cruz, whose father was a Cuban immigrant, won election to the U.S. Senate from Texas.

ASIAN AMERICANS The U.S. Census Bureau classifies Asian Americans together for statistical purposes, but like Hispanics, they show significant differences in culture, language, and political experience in the United States. Asian Americans include, among others, persons of Chinese, Japanese, Indian, Korean, Vietnamese, Filipino, and Thai origin, as well as persons from the Pacific Islands. As with Hispanics, there are differences among these subgroups.[49] For example, Japanese Americans were more likely to register as Democrats than Korean Americans or other Asian Americans. Japanese Americans also were somewhat more likely to vote than other Asian ethnic groups.[50]

Many Asian Americans have done well economically and educationally. Their income is well above the national median, and 52.5 percent have graduated from college, compared to 30.4 percent of whites and 19.5 percent of African Americans.[51]

THE TIES OF ETHNICITY Except for Native Americans and the descendants of slaves, all U.S. citizens have immigrant ancestors who chose to come to the American continent. There have been two large waves of new immigrants to the United States. The first wave came between 1900 and 1924, when 17.3 million people immigrated primarily from Southern and Eastern Europe. The second large wave is now underway. From 1991 to 2009, nearly 18.6 million immigrants, primarily from the Caribbean, Mexico, and Asian countries such as the Philippines, Vietnam, and China, have obtained permanent resident status in the U.S. In addition to this group of legal immigrants, since 1980, an estimated 10.8 million came into the country illegally.[52]

Large numbers of immigrants can pose challenges to any political and social system. Immigrants are often a source of social conflict as they compete with more established groups for jobs, rights, political power, and influence.

☐ Religion

In many parts of the world, religious differences, especially when combined with disputes over territory or sovereignty, are a source of violence. The conflict between

4.1

4.2

4.3

4.4

4.5

4.6

You Will Decide

Who Should the Census Count, and How Should They Be Counted?

As established in the Constitution, every 10 years the government conducts a count of all persons in the United States. For the 2000 census, the Census Bureau proposed using random sampling rather than attempting to count all households. The proposed sample approach would have contacted 90 percent of the households in a census tract consisting of roughly 1,700 individuals. The bureau would then check the accuracy of the sample by surveying 750,000 households throughout the nation and adjusting the final total accordingly. The sampling approach responded to complaints about the flawed 1990 census, which cost $2.6 billion (a 400 percent increase over the cost of the 1980 census) and failed to account for 10 million people while double-counting 6 million others, according to a study by the National Academy of Sciences.*

The 2010 census did not employ statistical sampling. In addition, while the census has always counted all individuals, citizens and noncitizens alike, it has not always asked about citizenship. Some members of Congress introduced legislation to require that citizenship be a question on the 2010 census, and that illegal immigrants be excluded from the census count.

What do you think? As we assess the success of the 2010 census and look to the future censuses, who should the census count, and how should they be counted? What arguments would you make for and against the use of sampling or questions about citizenship?

Thinking It Through

Both questions are really less about *how* to count as *whom* to count. The proposed sampling method would have produced a more accurate count of inner-city Hispanics and African Americans—the most difficult to count. Hispanics and African Americans are more likely to be homeless or living in poverty in urban areas. Using a sampling method would arrive at a more accurate count of these groups and would likely have resulted in a greater representation for Hispanics and African Americans in state legislatures and the U.S. House of Representatives. A more complete count of minorities could also mean that the Republican Party would lose a few seats in the House to Democrats, which is one reason Republicans generally opposed the sampling approach while Democrats favored it.

The constitutionality of sampling is disputed, as the Constitution calls for an "actual enumeration" of the people. Democrats are quick to point out that under three presidents—Jimmy Carter, George Bush, and Bill Clinton—the Justice Department concluded that sampling is legal. Sampling as a method of determining population for congressional apportionment is not allowed under current law,** while methods similar to sampling in order to fill in data missing from the "actual enumeration" has been upheld in the Supreme Court.†

Citizenship has been a question asked in the past in the census (1820–1960) but noncitizens have always been counted. Slaves counted as three-fifths of a person in the Constitution for apportionment purposes, and the Fourteenth Amendment refers to the "whole number of persons" being counted without regards to citizenship. But counting illegal immigrants runs counter to our notions of political representation and is understandably unpopular. If illegal immigrants were excluded it could take away seats from states like California, Arizona, and Texas.

CRITICAL THINKING QUESTIONS

1. **Why do you think sampling may result in higher counts of minorities?**
2. **Do you think it is possible to decide questions about representation without considering partisan politics?**
3. **Should illegal immigrants and persons under age 18 be counted for purposes of apportioning seats in Congress or for counts of persons for distribution of federal monies to state and local governments?**

*Duane L. Steffey and Norman M. Bradburn (eds.), Counting People in the Information Age (Panel to Evaluate Alternative Census Methods, National Research Council, Washington DC: National academy Press, 1994).

***Department of Commerce et al.* v. *U.S. House of Representatives et al.*, 119 S.Ct. 765 (1999).

†*Utah* v. *Evans*, 122 S.Ct. 2191 (2002).

Israelis and Palestinians has motivated suicide bombers who kill Israeli civilians along with themselves, and Israelis who attack Palestinian settlements and leaders. The war between India and Pakistan over Kashmir is largely a religious battle between Muslims and Hindus, and the Shi'ite–Sunni conflict among different branches of Islam threatens the stability of the new government in Iraq.

4.1

4.2

4.3

4.4

4.5

4.6

fundamentalists
Conservative Christians who, as a group, have become more active in politics in the last two decades and were especially influential in the 2000 and 2004 presidential elections.

Jews have often been the target of religious discrimination and persecution (anti-Semitism), which reached its greatest intensity in the Holocaust of the 1940s, during which the Nazis murdered an estimated 6 million Jews.[53] The United States has not been immune from such hatred, despite its principle of religious freedom. In 1838, Governor Lilburn W. Boggs of Missouri issued an extermination order that made legal the killing of any Mormons in the state.[54]

Our government is founded on the premise that religious liberty flourishes when there is no predominant or official faith, which is why the framers of the Constitution did not sanction a national church. The absence of an official church does not mean that religion is unimportant in American politics; indeed, there were established churches in individual states in this country until the 1830s. At one time, people thought voters' religious preferences could prevent a Catholic from being elected president. John F. Kennedy's election in 1960 resolved that question. Nevertheless, a candidate's religion may still become an issue today if the candidate's religious convictions on sensitive issues such as abortion threaten to conflict with public obligations.

Religion has also been an important catalyst for political change. The Catholic Church helped overthrow communism in parts of Eastern Europe.[55] Black churches provided many of the leaders in the American civil rights movement. More recently, political activity among fundamentalist Christians has increased. Led by ministers such as Pat Robertson and Focus on the Family founder James Dobson, evangelicals, sometimes called **fundamentalists**, are an important force in the Republican Party and in some local governments.[56] Their agenda includes the return of school prayer, the outlawing of abortion, restrictions on homosexuals, opposition to gun control, and opposition to the teaching of evolution and sex education in public schools.

Many American adults take their religious beliefs seriously, more than do citizens of other democracies. [57] Thirty-seven percent attend houses of worship at least once a week, 16 percent once or twice a month, and 18 percent at least several times a year.[58] Religion, like ethnicity, is a *shared identity.* People identify themselves as Baptist, Catholic, Jewish, Buddhist, or no religion at all. Sometimes religious attendance or nonattendance rather than belonging to a particular religion or denomination determines attitudes toward issues.

The United States houses a tremendous variety of religious denominations. Approximately half the people in the United States describe themselves as Protestant (see Figure 4.2). Because Protestants are divided among so many different churches, Catholics have the largest single membership in the United States, constituting just under a quarter of the population.[59] Jews represent less than 2 percent of the population.[60] Muslims number more than 1.3 million, which is approximately one-half of 1 percent of the U.S. population.[61]

Religion is important in American politics in part because people of particular religions are concentrated in a few states. Catholics number over half the population of Rhode Island.[62] Baptists represent 16 percent of the American population, yet they account for roughly a third of the population of Mississippi and Alabama.[63] Mormons represent less than 2 percent of the American population but three-fifths of the population of Utah. [64] The state of New York has the highest percentage of Jews with 8.5 percent; the New York City metro area is 10.7 percent Jewish.[65]

Religious groups vary in their rates of political participation. In recent elections Jews have the highest rate of reported voter turnout, more than 90 percent in 2000 and 2004, while those who claim no religious affiliation have the lowest, an average of roughly 60 percent in 2000, 2004, and 2008.[66] In recent presidential elections, most Protestants voted Republican, while most Catholics and Jews voted Democratic.[67] In 2012, Romney got 57 percent of the Protestant vote. Obama did better among Protestants in 2008 than Kerry in 2004 and received a majority of the Catholic vote in both 2008 and 2012.[68] In 2012 Romney argued that the Obama administration had not been as supportive of Israel. Obama's share of the Jewish vote declined from 78 percent in 2008 to 69 percent in 2012; the Catholic vote also dropped from 54 to 50 percent.

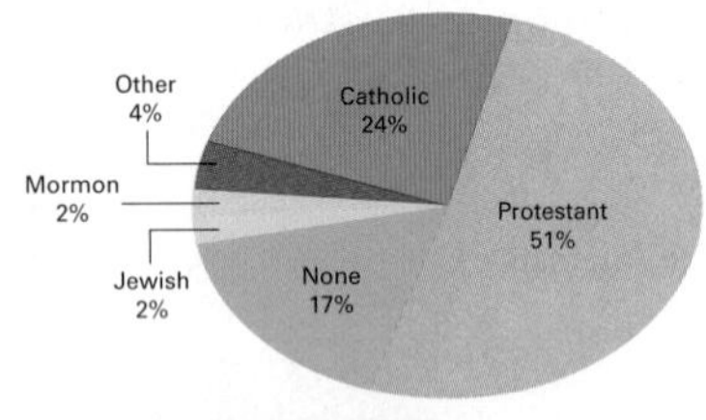

FIGURE 4.2 RELIGIOUS GROUPS IN THE UNITED STATES

Three-fourths of Americans describe themselves as Christian.

- *In what areas of public policy do we see this playing a role? How important should religion be as a factor in making political decisions?*

SOURCE: U.S. Religious Landscape Survey, Pew Forum on Religion & Public Life, http://religions.pewforum.org. Copyright 2008 Pew Research Center.

□ Gender

gender gap
The difference between the political opinions or political behavior of men and of women.

For most of U.S. history, politics and government were men's business. Women first gained the right to vote primarily in the western territories, beginning with Wyoming in 1869 and Utah in 1870, and then in Colorado and Idaho before 1900.[69] The right was not extended nationally to women until 1920 with passage of the Nineteenth Amendment.

For a half-century after gaining the right to vote, American women voted at a lower rate than women in other Western democracies.[70] In 2008, as in the prior three presidential elections, slightly more women than men voted in the presidential elections, and the same has been the case in recent midterm elections.[71] Women have chosen to work within the existing political parties and do not overwhelmingly support female candidates, especially if they must cross party lines to do so.[72] Polls found a majority of women saying Sarah Palin was not qualified to be president and men more likely to support Palin.[73] The number of women in Congress reached new highs in the 1990s. At the beginning of 2012, there were 6 female governors, 17 women serving in the Senate, and 72 women in the House.[74] The proportion of women serving in the House of Representatives is about the same as in the Senate: about 17 percent. In contrast, some state legislative chambers like those in Colorado, Vermont, and New Hampshire are nearly 40 percent female.[75]

Is there a **gender gap**, or a persistent difference between men and women in voting and in attitudes on important issues? In recent elections, women have been more likely than men to vote for Democratic presidential candidates (see Figure 4.3). In 2000, Al Gore's share of the vote among women was 12 percent higher than among men.[76] In 2004, women preferred Kerry over Bush by 3 percent.[77] The gender gap was even wider in 2008, with women voting for Obama at 56 percent and McCain at 43 percent.[78] Men also gave Obama more votes than McCain, with 49 percent of men voting for Obama and 48 percent for McCain. In 2012 the gender gap narrowed to a 10 percent difference, with 55 percent of women and 45 percent of men voting for Obama. In 2008, 56 percent of women voted for him, and 49 percent of men.

The women's movement in American politics seeks equal opportunity, education, jobs, skills, and respect in what has long been a male-dominated system.[79] Women are more likely than men to oppose violence in any form, and are more likely to favor government-provided health insurance and family services. They also identify work and family issues such as day care, maternity leave, and equal treatment in the workplace as important.[80] Other gender issues, some of them focal points in recent elections, include reproductive rights and restrictions on pornography, gun control, and sexual harassment.[81]

There are serious income inequalities between men and women. Nearly twice as many women as men have an annual income of less than $15,000, and nearly three times as many men as women make more than $75,000 a year.[82] Because an increasing number of women today are the sole breadwinners for their families, the implications of this low income level are significant. Women earn on average less than men for the same work. After controlling for characteristics such as job experience, education, occupation, and other measures of productivity, a U.S. Census Bureau study shows that wage discrimination between the genders is 77 cents on every dollar.[83]

Unemployment in the economic recession of 2008–2010 affected more men than women. Four out of the five jobs lost in the recession were jobs held by men in such industries as manufacturing and construction.[84] The result of this unequal impact of the recession is that for the first time the number of women working could surpass men, though this may be a temporary change as the recession ends and men again find jobs.[85]

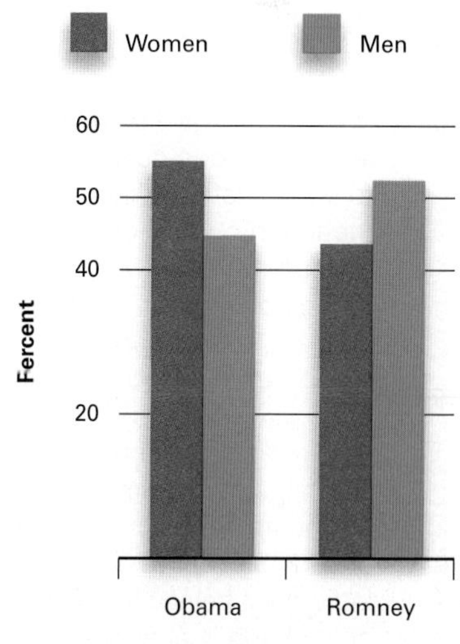

FIGURE 4.3 GENDER AND THE VOTE FOR PRESIDENT

- *What are some of the issues raised in the 2012 election that may have led women to vote disproportionately Democratic?*

SOURCE: www.washingtonpost.com/wp-srv/special/politics/2012-exit-polls/table.html.

□ Sexual Orientation

The modern movement for expanded rights for gays and lesbians traces its roots to 1969, when New York City police raided the Stonewall Inn, a bar in Greenwich Village, and a riot ensued.[86] Since then gays and lesbians have become more active and visible in pushing for legal rights and protections.

The precise number of homosexuals in the United States is unclear. Estimates range from 2 to 10 percent of the U.S. population.[87] Whatever its overall size, the gay

4.1

4.2

4.3

4.4

4.5

4.6

Annise Parker became the mayor of Houston, Texas, in 2010. She is the first openly gay mayor of a city with more than 1 million people, as well as Houston's second female mayor.

and lesbian community has become important politically in several cities, notably San Francisco. Its lobbying power has increased noticeably in many states as well, and being gay or lesbian is no longer a barrier to election in many places.

The political agenda for gay and lesbian advocacy groups includes fighting discrimination, such as laws barring same-sex marriage and the military's "don't ask, don't tell" policy. On some fronts, the groups have been successful. For example, in 2010, President Obama signed legislation overturning the "don't ask, don't tell" policy, allowing gays and lesbians to serve in the military without having to hide their sexual orientation.[88] In 2012, President Obama, who previously said his views on same-sex marriage were evolving, announced that he favored allowing gays and lesbians to marry.[89]

Many local governments and private employers now grant health care and other benefits for same-sex domestic partners. Some states have legalized same-sex marriage, including Massachusetts, Connecticut, New Hampshire, Vermont, Iowa, and New York, as well as the District of Columbia, and a number of others provide for some types of civil unions for same-sex couples.

□ Family Structure

Throughout the past half-century, the typical American family (mother and father married, with children in the home) has become anything but typical. The traditional family had several key characteristics: it married early, had children, and stayed together through thick and thin. However, the number of American adults who live with someone of the opposite sex without being married increased to 5.7 percent of households in 2009.[90] Marriage also used to occur earlier in life, but people now marry later: the average age for first marriage for men is 28; for women it is 26.[91]

Children were also essential to the traditional families, but birthrates have been falling for decades. Birthrates in the United States dropped in the late 1960s and 1970s. In the early 1960s, a woman statistically averaged about 3.5 children. By 2011 that number was at 2.06 children, just below the 2.1 needed to replace the population.[92] In other words, if the current trend continues, the native-born population will actually decrease over time.[93]

BY the People Making a Difference

Improving Literacy

In an extensive study released in 1993, between one-fifth and one-quarter of adult Americans were found to be illiterate, defined as being unable to "locate information in a text" or "make low-level inferences using printed material." A follow-up study released in 2006 found no significant improvement in U.S. adult literacy. Illiteracy, or the inability to use printed and written information effectively, is a significant problem for the illiterate individuals and for society as a whole. Most jobs require minimal literacy, as do daily activities like reading contracts or instructions on medications. Filling out governmental forms, including voter registration forms, and engaging in active citizenship in other ways is based on individuals being literate. Those not able to read often do not engage in active citizenship, and exhibit a lack confidence in dealing with other people and institutions.

You can make a difference in helping children and adults learn literacy. Some college students have organized programs at their institutions to enhance literacy in their own communities. Baylor University, for example, has "Camp Success," which is a four-week language and literacy therapy camp for area children. Begun in 2003, the camp has had over 500 children participate. Professor Michaela Ritter, who directs the camp, indicates that "most kids make from one to three years' progress" during the camp.*

You don't have to find an organized program to make a difference in enhancing literacy. One-on-one reading with a child is something you can readily arrange in your local community. Most public schools are very eager for volunteers to read with struggling students, and local libraries often have such programs as well.

QUESTIONS

1. Does it surprise you that 20–25% of Americans are illiterate? Why or why not?
2. Why is literacy a condition of active citizenship?
3. Why do you think having a caring college student read with a younger person has such positive results?

*Tim Woods, "Baylor University Reading Program for Children May be Taken Statewide," *Waco Tribune-Herald*, July 3, 2009.

Finally, the traditional family stayed together, but the divorce rate has nearly doubled since 1950.[94] Today it is estimated that about half of all marriages will end in divorce.[95] Divorce is one reason why the number of households headed by women has risen.

☐ Education

Differences in education affect not only economic well-being but political participation and involvement as well. Thomas Jefferson wrote of education, "Enlighten the people generally, and tyranny and oppressions of body and mind will vanish like evil spirits at the dawn of day."[96] Most American students are educated in public schools. Nine of every ten students in kindergarten through high school attend public schools, and nearly three of four college students are in public institutions.[97]

In 1992, for the first time the number of American college graduates surpassed the number of persons who did not graduate from high school.[98] Just over half of all U.S. adults have not gone to college, though many college students assume that almost everyone goes to college. Approximately 30 percent of whites are college graduates, compared to 20 percent of African Americans and 14 percent of Hispanics; roughly 16 percent of African Americans and 37 percent of all Hispanics left school before completing high school (see Figure 4.4).[99]

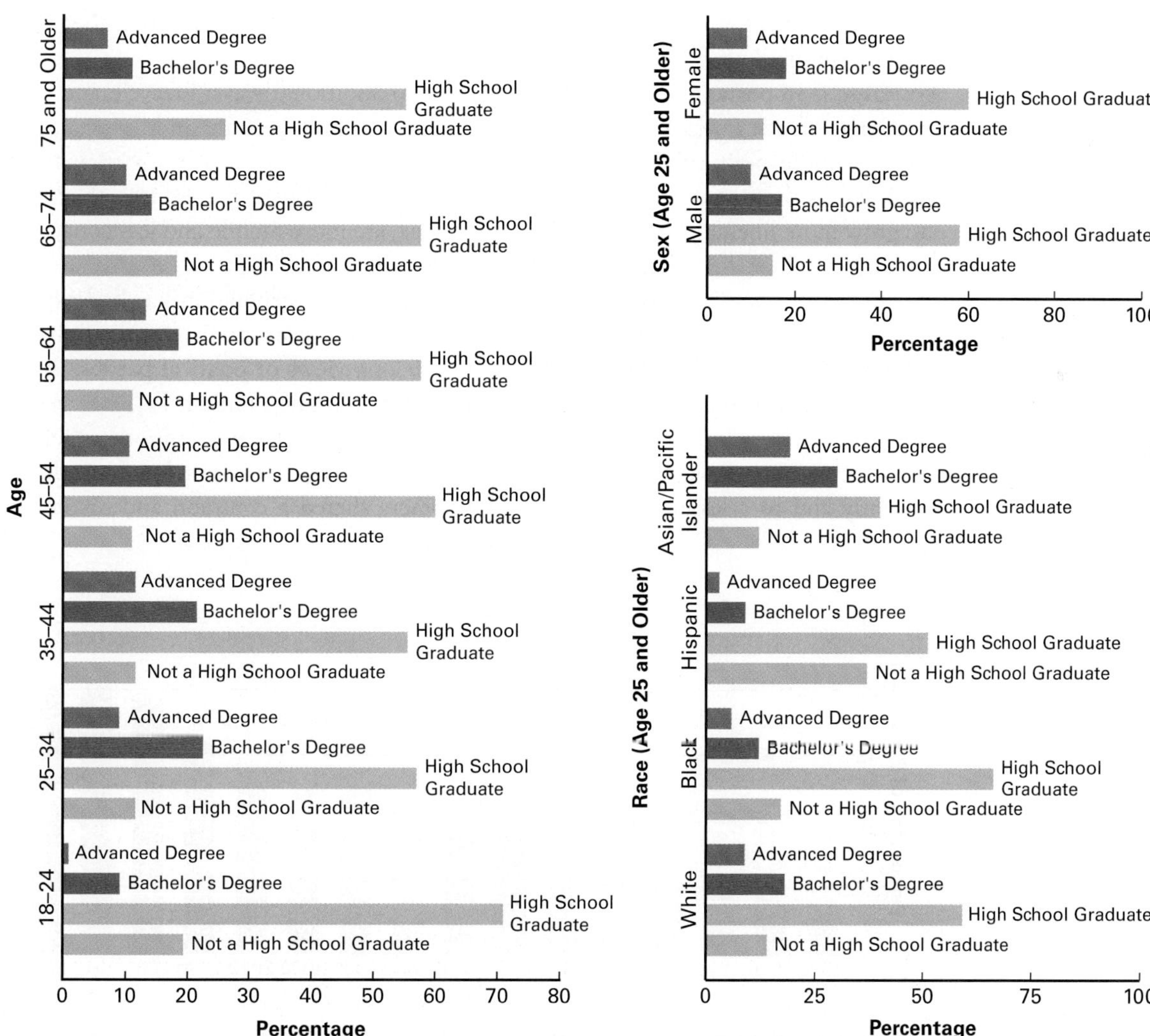

FIGURE 4.4 EDUCATIONAL ATTAINMENT IN THE UNITED STATES

■ *Based on the percentages of Americans who are high school graduates in each age bracket, what assumptions might you make about how the educational system and culture in America has changed?*

SOURCE: U.S. Census Bureau, *Educational Attainment in the United States: 2009*, www.census.gov/population/www/socdemo/education/cps2009.html.

Education is one of the most important variables in predicting political participation, confidence in dealing with government, and awareness of issues. Education is also related to the acquisition of democratic values. People who have failed to learn the prevailing norms of American society are far more likely to express opposition to democratic and capitalist ideals than those who are well educated and politically knowledgeable.[100]

☐ Age

We are living longer, a phenomenon that has been dubbed the "graying of America" (Figure 4.5).[101] This demographic change has increased the proportion of the population over age 65 and increased the demand for medical care, retirement benefits, and a host of other age-related services.[102] Persons over age 65 constitute less than 13 percent of the population yet account for more than 36 percent of the total medical expenditures.[103] With the decreasing birthrate discussed earlier, the graying of America has given rise to concern about maintaining an adequate workforce in the future.

Older adults are more politically aware and vote more often than younger ones, making them a potent political force. Their vote is especially important in western states and in Florida, the state with the largest proportion of people over age 65. Several groups made registering younger voters and getting them to the polls a high priority. An estimated 3.4 million more 18–29-year-olds voted in 2008.[104] In 2012 they were 19 percent of all voters, compared to 18 percent in 2008.

Age is important in terms of politics in two additional ways: lifecycle and generational effects. *Lifecycle effects* have shown that as people become middle-aged, they become more politically conservative, less mobile, and more likely to participate in politics. As they age further and rely more on the government for services, they tend to grow more liberal.[105] Young people, in contrast, are more mobile and less concerned about the delivery of government services.

Generational effects in politics arise when a particular generation has had experiences that make it politically distinct. For example, for those who lived through it, the Great Depression of the 1930s shaped their lifelong views of political parties, issues, and political leaders. Some members of this generation saw Franklin D. Roosevelt as the leader who saved the country by pulling it out of the Depression; others felt he sold the country down the river by launching too many government programs. More recently and to a lesser extent, the baby boomers shared a common and distinctive

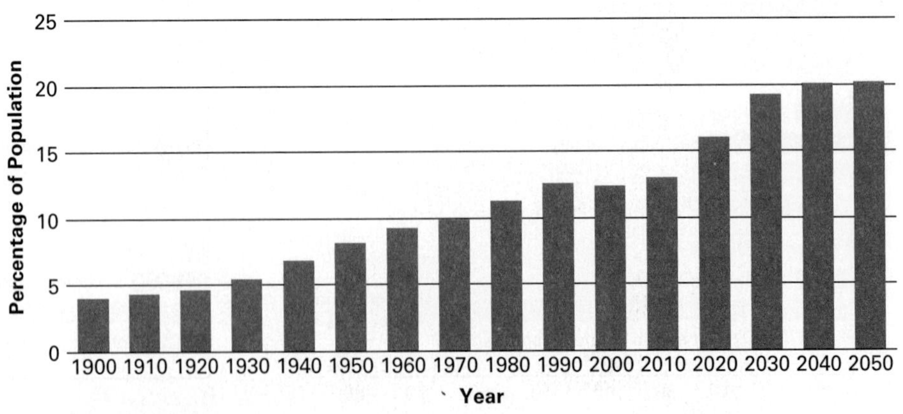

FIGURE 4.5 PERCENTAGE OF POPULATION OVER THE AGE OF 65, 1900–2050

■ *How will the population 30 years from now compare to that of today? In what areas of politics and society might that difference have an impact?*

SOURCE: U.S. Census Bureau, *Statistical Abstract of the United States: 2012*, Table 9, http://www.census.gov/prod/2011pubs/12statab/pop.pdf

political experience. It is too soon to know if any events of the last 10 to 15 years will shape the political outlook of those now under 30 years of age. It is possible that the recession of 2008–2011 may leave a lasting impact on people's attitudes towards the economy and government, and it is also possible that the terrorist attacks of 2001 and the subsequent war on terror may have generational effects.

How Much We Own

4.5 Describe the importance of income, wealth, occupation, and social class in American politics.

The extent to which a society is divided along economic lines and whether people feel they and their children can improve their economic standing are important to democratic stability. The United States has long been known as a land of economic opportunity. This, along with freedom more generally, is a reason so many immigrants came to America. Also woven into the fabric of our nation is the idea that hard work and initiative can lead to success, an aspiration sometimes called the American Dream. Much of the political debate in 2012 was about the economy and the extent to which people at different income levels were hurt or advantaged by government policies. To put this important debate in context we need to understand how social scientists measure the economic standing of individuals.

Wealth and Income

The United States is a wealthy nation. Indeed, to some knowledgeable observers, "the most striking thing about the United States has been its phenomenal wealth."[106] Most American

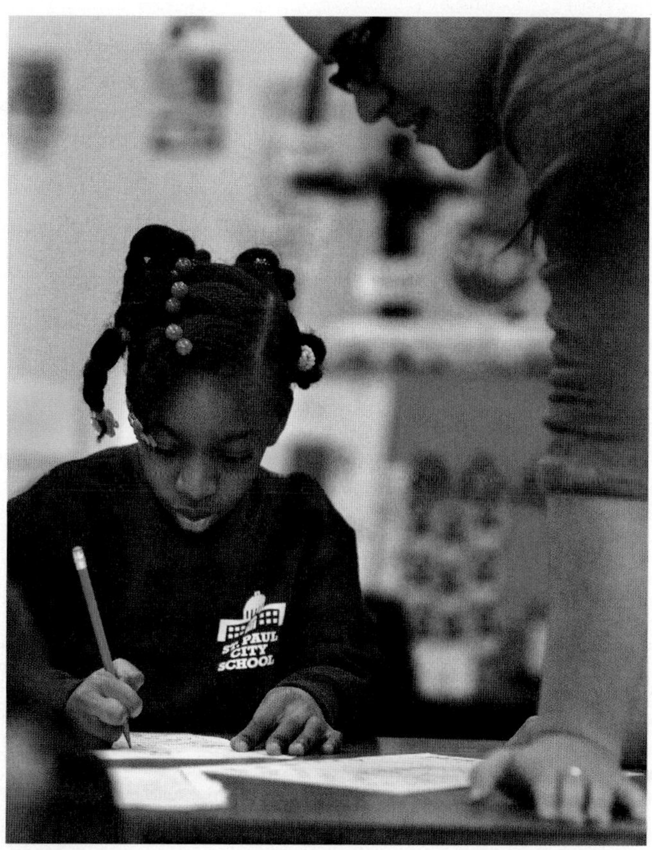

A child is tutored by a student through the America Reads program, a program designed to help disadvantaged children.

4.1

4.2

4.3

4.4

4.5

4.6

citizens lead comfortable lives. They eat and live well and have first-class medical care. But the unequal distribution of wealth and income results in political divisions and conflicts.

Wealth, the total value of someone's possessions, is more concentrated than income (annual earnings). The wealthiest families hold most of the property and other forms of wealth such as stocks and savings. Historically, concentrated wealth fosters an aristocracy. The framers of the Constitution recognized the dangers of an unequal concentration of wealth. "The most common and durable source of factions has been the various and unequal distribution of property," wrote James Madison in *The Federalist*, No. 10. Economic differences often lead to conflict, and we remain divided politically along economic lines. Aside from race, income may be the single most important factor in explaining views on issues, partisanship, and ideology. Most rich people are Republicans, most poor people are Democrats, and this has been true since at least the Great Depression of the 1930s.

Between the 1950s and the 1970s, inflation-adjusted income doubled, but since then it has fluctuated, with no substantial change over time.[107] As of 2009, 14.3 percent of the population fell below the poverty line and had the lowest per capita incomes, after factoring in family size.[108] In 2011 the official poverty level for a family of four with two children was an income below $23,018.[109] Families headed by a single female are more than two times as likely to fall below the poverty line than families headed by a single male, with 29.9 percent of all households headed by females falling below the poverty line.[110] Nearly 21 percent of the poor are children under age 18, and many appear to be trapped in a cycle of poverty where children raised in poverty are more likely to be poor as adults (see Figure 4.6).[111] African American and Hispanic children are more than twice as likely to be poor as white children.[112] The poor are a minority who lack political power. They vote less than wealthier people and are less confident and organized in dealing with politics and government.

As discussed in the beginning of this chapter, the growth in income for most Americans leveled off after the period of rapid growth in the 1950s and 1960s. That period produced a relatively flat income distribution.[113] In the period since 1979 and up to 2007

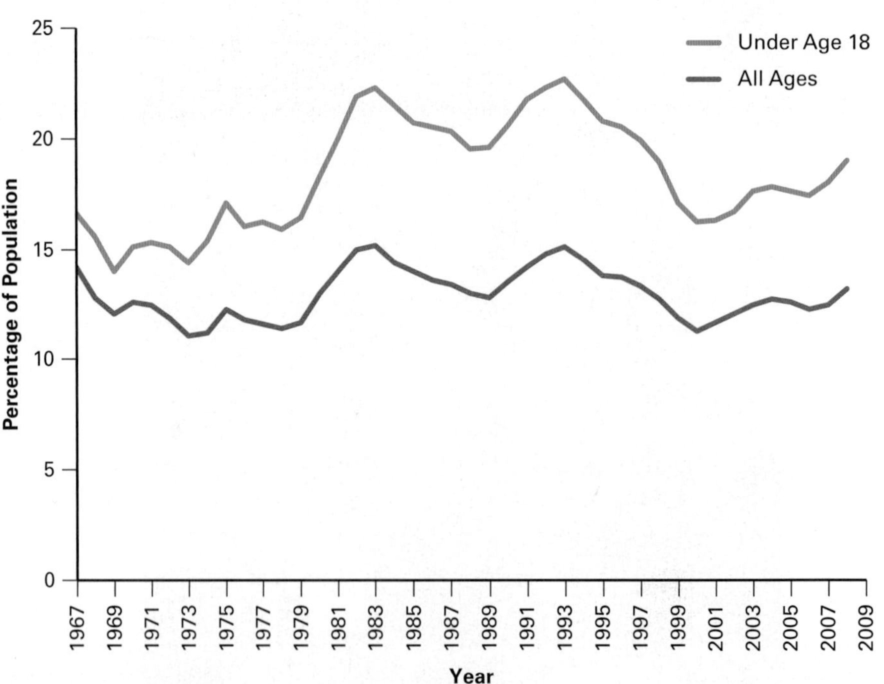

FIGURE 4.6 PERCENTAGE OF AMERICANS LIVING IN POVERTY, BY AGE, 1967–2010

What other factors could influence the percentage of Americans classified as living in poverty at any given time?

SOURCE: U.S. Census Bureau, "Table 3—Poverty Status, by Age, Race, and Hispanic Origin," http://www.census.gov/hhes/www/poverty/data/historical/people.html (accessed June 7, 2012).

Can You Get Ahead in America?

Whether or not the American Dream is still attainable is a question that goes to the core of American national identity. In 1994 and 2010, survey researchers asked Americans "Do you think your own standard of living is better than that of your parents?" In both years, the majority believe the Dream exists, but there are distinct differences across generations caused by economic factors such as the unemployment rate.

Generational Differences

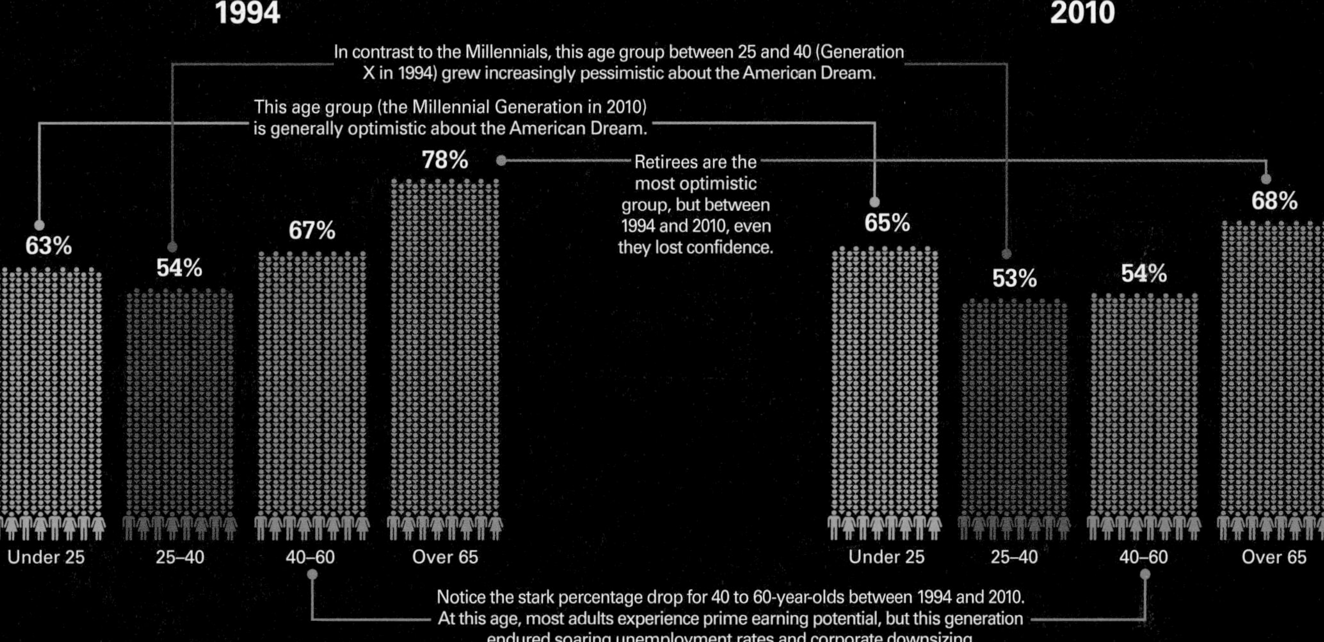

Unemployment in the United States

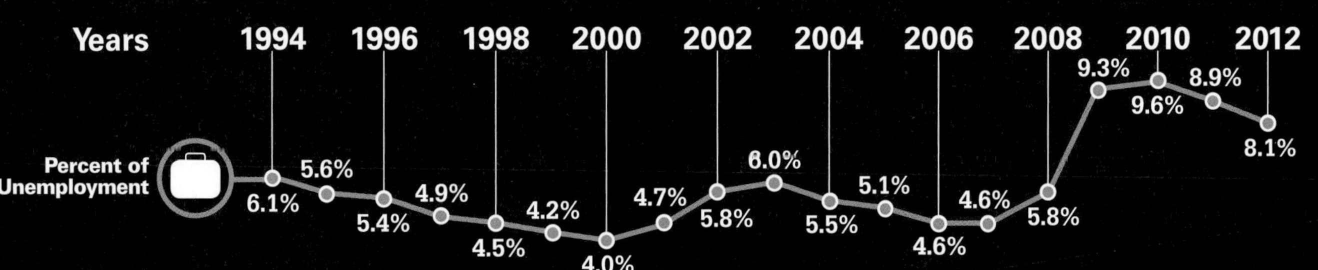

SOURCE: Data from General Social Survey, 1994 and 2010; and the U.S. Bureau of Labor Statistics.

Investigate Further

Concept What is the American Dream? The American Dream is the belief that the next generation will do better than the one before it. It is measured by asking people if they think they are doing better than their parents at the same stage of life.

Connection How do the generations differ when it comes to the American Dream? Millennials face high unemployment, but they are more likely to believe in the dream than 25 to 40-year-olds in 2010. Generation X, now middle aged, was increasingly less likely to believe in the Dream from 1994 to 2010.

Cause Why is Generation X less likely to believe in the Dream? Initial and prime earning years for this age group were accompanied by recessions in 1990, 2000, and 2009, and by spikes in unemployment that affect both them and their children's generation.

gross domestic product (GDP) The total output of all economic activity in the nation, including goods and services.

for the 1 percent of the population with the highest income, average real after-tax household income grew by 275 percent. For the 60 percent of the population in the middle of the income scale (21st through 80th percentiles), the growth in average real after-tax household income was just under 40 percent.[114] This large difference in who benefited economically in the 1980s and since was frequently debated during the 2012 election.

A gap in income and wealth is not new. Writing in the early 1980s, political scientist Robert Dahl observed: "it is a striking fact that the presence of vast disparities in wealth and income, and so in political resources, has never become a highly salient issue in American politics or, certainly, a persistent one."[115] For 30 years after Dahl wrote these words, his description of the limited attention given to the income and wealth gaps remained true; but in 2011–2012 that changed.

This gap led one commentator to state that "income inequality, by many measures, is now greater than it has been since the 1920s."[116] Economists and political candidates alike have debated the causes of the growing income and wealth gap. Some economists point out that market forces like increased trade and technological advances have allowed well-educated and highly skilled individuals to demand more pay. The argument is that today's marketplace rewards creative people with technical skills. Many of those skills are gained in undergraduate and graduate education, so colleges and universities are not only pathways to higher pay, but a screening mechanism that helps identify talented people.[117]

Others argue that deregulation, tax policy and the decline of unions have allowed the better off to become even more well-off. Political Scientist Larry Bartels's research finds evidence that public policy matters in the level of income inequality. He writes, "partisan differences in macroeconomic priorities and performance have clearly had a very significant impact on the economic fortunes of American families over the past half-century, and that impact has been especially marked at the point in the electoral cycle when presidents are most politically influential."[118] The partisan differences he finds are that "under Democratic presidents, poor families did slightly better than richer families (at least in proportional terms), producing a modest net decrease in income inequality; under Republican presidents, rich families did vastly better than poorer families, producing a considerable increase in income inequality."[119]

The 2012 elections had as a centerpiece a debate over which segments of society should be advantaged by public policy. President Obama and the Democrats sought to roll back the tax cuts enacted during the George W. Bush administration and to pay for broad based tax relief with higher taxes on individuals earning $250,000 or more. Republicans countered, sometimes criticizing the Democrats for "class warfare," arguing the better-off are the people who create jobs and we should not tax job creators when the country has such high unemployment. Others made more general arguments about not raising taxes generally or in a time of economic difficulty.

The distribution of income in a society can have important consequences for democratic stability. If enough people believe that only the few at the top of the economic ladder can hope to earn enough for an adequate standard of living, domestic unrest and even revolution may follow.

☐ Occupation

In Jefferson's day and for several generations after, most people in the United States worked primarily on farms, but by 1900, the United States had become the world's leading industrial nation. As workers moved from farms to cities to find better-paying jobs, the cities grew rapidly. Labor conditions, including child labor, the length of the workweek, and safety conditions in mines and factories, became important political issues. New technology, combined with abundant natural and human resources, meant that the American **gross domestic product (GDP)** rose, after adjusting for inflation, by more than 370 percent from 1960 to 2011.[120] Gross domestic product is one measure of the size of a country's economy. It is the total market value of goods and services produced in that country in a specified period of time.

The United States has entered what Daniel Bell, a noted sociologist, labeled the "postindustrial" phase of its development: "A postindustrial society, being primarily a technical society, awards less on the basis of inheritance or property ... than on education and skill."[121] *Knowledge* is the organizing device of the postindustrial era. Postindustrial societies have greater affluence and a class structure less defined along traditional labor-versus-management lines. Figure 4.7, which shows the percentage of American workers in various occupations, demonstrates the changing dynamics of the country's labor force.

The white-collar sector of our economy has grown tremendously throughout the past 50 years. This sector includes managers, accountants, and lawyers, as well as professionals and technicians in such rapid-growth areas as computers, communications, finance, insurance, and research. A dramatic decline in the number of people engaged in agriculture and a more modest decline in the number of people in manufacturing (which together make up the blue-collar sector) has accompanied this shift. Today agriculture employs 2 percent of working adults, and manufacturing employs 10 percent.[122] Federal, state, and local governments employ 5 percent of jobholders, while government expenditures account for slightly less than 19 percent of our gross domestic product.[123]

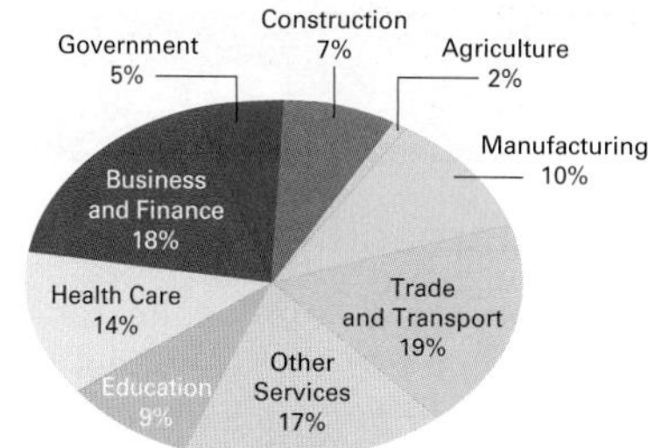

FIGURE 4.7 EMPLOYMENT BY OCCUPATIONAL GROUPS, 2010

During the 2012 campaign, the decline in the American manufacturing sector relative to other sectors was an issue. What other sectors in this graph exceed manufacturing? What is the largest sector? Why was the decline in manufacturing jobs an issue?

SOURCE: http://www.census.gov/compendia/statab/2012/tables/12s0620.0df

□ Social Class

Why do U.S. citizens not divide themselves into social classes as Europeans do? American workers have not formed their own political party, nor does class seem to dominate our political life. Karl Marx's categories of *proletariat* (those who sell their labor) and *bourgeoisie* (those who own or control the means of production) are far less important here than they have been in Europe. Still, we do have social classes and what social scientists call **socioeconomic status (SES)**—a division of the population based on occupation, income, and education.

socioeconomic status (SES)
A division of population based on occupation, income, and education.

Conventionally the terms used to describe social class are "upper class," "middle class," and "lower class." Most American adults say they are middle class. Few see themselves as lower class or upper class. In many other industrial democracies, large proportions of the population think of themselves as "working class" rather than middle class.[124]

While plumbers may lack the social status and years of formal training of school teachers, they are often better paid. Like many blue-collar occupations, plumbers tend to be male. Here, plumber Jarrod Taylor repairs a natural gas pipe in Washington DC.

4.1

4.2

4.3

4.4

4.5

4.6

FOR the People Government's Greatest Endeavors

Increasing Access for the Disabled

People today take for granted that Americans restricted to a wheel chair have access to public transportation and buildings, that hearing-impaired persons can use telecommunications, and that persons with disabilities are not subject to discrimination. But this was not always the case.

Prior to 1990, when President George H.W. Bush signed into law the Americans with Disabilities Act, discrimination and physical barriers greatly restricted disabled persons. For example, one of those who fought hard for the Americans with Disabilities Act was Justin W. Dart, Jr. Born into affluence, Dart contracted polio at age 18, shortly before entering the University of Houston. That institution denied him a teaching certificate because of his disability. After a career in business, Dart became an advocate for the rights of people with disabilities.

Because the law established requirements for buildings and public transportation, persons with disabilities now are able to travel and enjoy going to a restaurant, hotel, or theater. While many changes still need to be made, the improvements have made it much easier for persons with disabilities to participate in daily activities. Similarly, employment regulations have helped prevent discrimination and allowed these individuals to participate more fully in society. As you consider your college campus and community, imagine how different it would be if persons with disabilities were denied access to public transportation, buildings, and employment.

QUESTIONS

1. How does the Americans with Disabilities Act foster equality of opportunity?
2. What are the advantages to society of making public transportation, accommodations and buildings, and employment more accessible to persons with disabilities?
3. What arguments could you make against legislation like the ADA?

What constitutes the middle class in the United States is highly subjective. For instance, some individuals perform working-class tasks (such as plumbing), but their income places them in the middle class or even the upper-middle class. A schoolteacher's income is below that of many working-class jobs, but in terms of status, teaching ranks among middle-class jobs.

Unity in a Land of Diversity

4.6 Evaluate the degree to which America has achieved a measure of unity in a land of diversity.

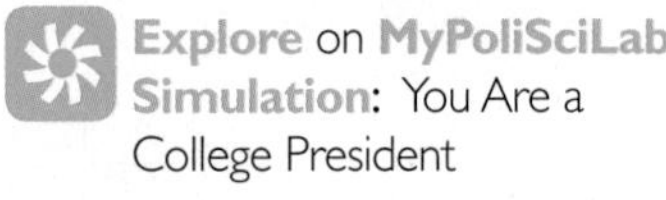

As remarkable as American diversity is, the existence of a strong and widely shared sense of national unity and identity may be even more remarkable. Economic and social mobility have unified much of the U.S. population. Education has been an important part of this, as was the nationalizing influence of World War II. We are united by our shared commitment to democratic values, economic opportunity, work ethic, and the American dream. Social scientists used to speak of the "melting pot," meaning that as various ethnic groups associate with other groups, they are assimilated into U.S. society and come to share democratic values such as majority rule, individualism, and the ideal of the United States as a land of opportunity. Critics have argued that the melting pot idea assumes there is something wrong with differences between groups, and that these distinctions should be discouraged. In its place, they propose the concept of the "salad bowl," in which every ingredient enriches the whole.

As this chapter has demonstrated, regional, social, and economic differences have important political consequences. They influence public opinion, participation, voting, interest groups, and political parties. At the same time, our country has achieved a sense of unity despite our remarkable diversity.

Review the Chapter

 **Listen** to **Chapter 4** on **MyPoliSciLab**

An Exceptional America

4.1 Understand the origins and effects of American exceptionalism, p. 111.

Differences between people can foster a vibrant, open society or they can lead to discrimination, division, and even civil war. Citizens of the United States represent a remarkable diversity that has been a defining characteristic of our polity. Our differences have more often been cross-cutting than reinforcing, which has helped to reduce conflict. At the same time our geographic, regional, social, and economic differences have been part of what has divided our country. The continuing controversy over illegal immigration in the United States is an example of such a conflict.

Geography and National Identity

4.2 Assess the role of geography in building a national identity, p. 112.

The United States is a continental nation, which has provided ample land for population growth and access to both the Atlantic and Pacific Oceans. Our people have benefited from abundant natural resources. These characteristics help explain American politics and traditions, including the notions of manifest destiny, ethnocentrism, and isolationism. Social and economic differences can foster conflict and violence.

Where We Live

4.3 Evaluate the importance of where we live on American politics, p. 114.

For much of U.S. history, the South has been a distinct region in the United States, in large part because of its agricultural base and its history of slavery and troubled race relations. Today, the region is Republican and conservative. Other regional clusterings that have political relevance include the upper-Midwest states, which once had a strong manufacturing economy but more recently have been in decline, and the West, with large open spaces and with much of the land under the control of the federal government. People also live in communities that are classified as urban, suburban, and rural. These differences have political significance as these living environments foster different kinds of issues and concerns and different styles of politics. Recently, the most significant migration in the United States has been from cities to suburbs. Today, many large U.S. cities are increasingly poor, African American, and Democratic, surrounded by suburbs that are primarily middle class, white, and Republican.

Who We Are

4.4 Analyze how such social and demographic factors as race and ethnicity, religion, gender, family structures, education, and age affect American politics, p. 117.

Race has been and remains among the most important of the differences in our political landscape. Although we fought a civil war over freedom for African Americans, racial equality was largely postponed until the latter half of the twentieth century. Ethnicity, including the rising numbers of Hispanics, continues to be a factor in politics. The United States has many religious denominations, and these differences, including between those who are religious and those who are not, help explain public opinion and political behavior. Gender, sexual orientation, and family structures have become more important in politics. Age and education are also important to understanding political participation.

How Much We Own

4.5 Describe the importance of income, wealth, occupation, and social class in American politics, p. 127.

Throughout U.S. history one of the most important sources of political division has been the unequal distribution of income and wealth. Although some people in America continue to achieve great wealth and there remains a large middle class, the gap between the most affluent and the remainder of society has grown in recent decades. It has become the source of protest and conflict in the Occupy Wall Street movement. At the same time and in part due to the recession of the 2008–2010 period, poverty has grown, especially among African Americans, Native Americans, Hispanics, and single-parent households. Women as a group continue to earn less than men, even in the same occupations.

Unity in a Land of Diversity

4.6 Evaluate the degree to which America has achieved a measure of unity in a land of diversity, p. 132.

Even though social, economic, and other differences abound, there is also a shared commitment to the ideals of constitutional democracy in the United States. The American dream continues to exist and reinforces this unity. Some events serve to reinforce this sense of unity, like the terrorist attacks of September 11, 2001.

Learn the Terms

 **Study** and **Review** the **Flashcards**

ethnocentrism, p. 111
demography, p. 111
reinforcing cleavages, p. 111
cross-cutting cleavages, p. 111
American exceptionalism, p. 111
manifest destiny, p. 112
Sun Belt, p. 115
Bible Belt, p. 115
Rust Belt, p. 115
urban, p. 116
suburban, p. 116
rural, p. 116
race, p. 117
ethnicity, p. 117
fundamentalists, p. 122
gender gap, p. 123
gross domestic product (GDP), p. 130
socioeconomic status (SES), p. 131

Test Yourself

 **Study** and **Review** the **Practice Tests**

MULTIPLE CHOICE QUESTIONS

4.1 Understand the origins and effects of American exceptionalism.

Who first used the phrase "American exceptionalism" to describe the uniqueness of the United States?

a. James Madison
b. Alexis de Tocqueville
c. Rick Perry
d. Marquis de Lafayette
e. Frederick Jackson Turner

4.2 Assess the role of geography in building a national identity.

Which of these are advantages of the size and location of the United States?

a. buffered from foreign attack
b. room for population to grow and expand
c. abundant resources
d. abundant opportunities for jobs
e. all of the above

4.3 Evaluate the importance of where we live on American politics.

Which of the following is not true of regional trends in the United States?

a. Southern states today vote more heavily Republican than 100 years ago.
b. Since the 1950s, more Americans have relocated to rural settings.
c. Urban areas tend to vote Democratic.
d. The Rust Belt includes states like Ohio and Michigan.
e. The region with the most distinctive politics remains the South.

4.4 Analyze how demographic factors as race and ethnicity, religion, gender, family structures, education, class, and age affect American politics.

About what percent of African Americans have voted Democratic for president since 1964?

a. 40 percent
b. 60 percent
c. 70 percent
d. 80 percent
e. more than 85 percent

4.5 Describe the importance of income, wealth, occupation, and social class in American politics.

Which is not considered a factor in the growing income gap?

a. deregulation
b. tax policy
c. decline of unions
d. rewards based on individual talents
e. agricultural subsidies

4.6 Evaluate the degree to which America has achieved a measure of unity in a land of diversity.

Americans are united by

a. shared democratic values.
b. economic opportunity.
c. work ethic.
d. shared outlook on immigration.
e. the American dream.

ESSAY QUESTION

Analyze how demographic factors—including race and ethnicity, religion, gender, family structures, education, income, class, and age—affect American politics. Provide specific examples.

Explore Further

IN THE LIBRARY

Earl Black and Merle Black, *The Rise of Southern Republicans* (Belknap Press, 2002).

David T. Canon, *Race, Redistricting, and Representation: The Unintended Consequences of Black Majority Districts* (University of Chicago Press, 1999).

Maureen Dezell, *Irish America: Coming into Clover* (Anchor Books, 2000).

Julie Anne Dolan, Melissa M. Deckman, and Michelle L. Swers, *Women and Politics: Paths to Power and Political Influence* (Longman, 2010).

Lois Duke Whitaker, ed., *Women in Politics: Outsiders or Insiders?* 5th ed. (Longman, 2011).

F. Chris Garcia, and Gabriel R. Sanchez, *Hispanics and the U.S. Political System* (Pearson, 2008).

Donald R. Kinder and Lynn M. Sanders, *Divided by Color: Racial Politics and Democratic Ideals* (University of Chicago Press, 1996).

Taeku Lee, S. Karthick Ramakrishnan, and Ricardo Ramirez, *Transforming Politics, Transforming America: The Political and Civic Incorporation of Immigrants in the United States (Race, Ethnicity, and Politics)* (University Press of Virginia, 2006).

Jan E. Leighley, *Strength in Numbers? The Political Mobilization of Racial and Ethnic Minorities* (Princeton University Press, 2001).

Andrew Aoki and Okiyoshi Takeda, *Asian American Politics* (Polity, 2009).

Jeremy D. Mayer, *Running on Race: Racial Politics in Presidential Campaigns, 1960–2000* (Random House, 2002).

Nancy E. McGlen, Karen O'Connor, Laura Van Assendelft, and Wendy Gunther-Canada, *Women, Politics, and American Society*, 5th ed. (Longman, 2011).

S. Karthick Ramakrishnan, *Democracy in Immigrant America: Changing Demographics and Political Participation* (Stanford University Press, 2005).

Mark Robert Rank, *One Nation, Underprivileged: Why American Poverty Affects Us All* (Oxford University Press, 2004).

Michelle M. Taylor-Robinson, *Do the Poor Count? Democratic Institutions and Accountability in a Context of Poverty* (Pennsylvania State University Press, 2010).

Kenneth D. Wald, *Religion and Politics in the United States*, 6th ed. (Rowman & Littlefield, 2010).

Janelle Wong, *Democracy's Promise: Immigrants and American Civic Institutions (The Politics of Race and Ethnicity)* (University of Michigan Press, 2006).

Garry Wills, *A Necessary Evil: A History of American Distrust of Government* (Simon & Schuster, 1999).

ON THE WEB

www.census.gov
The census provides demographic statistics for the country as a whole and for all 50 states.

www.usa.gov/Citizen/Topics/History_Culture.shtml
USA.gov provides information on a variety of subjects, including detailed information on America's cultural history.

www.pewforum.org
The Pew Forum provides detailed information on the religious makeup of America.

www.pbs.org/peoplelikeus/
This PBS site gives stats, stories, and other information about class in America.

www.conginst.org
A Web site that provides up-to-date survey data on the American political culture.

www.loc.gov
The Library of Congress Web site; provides access to more than 70 million historical and contemporary U.S. documents.

5

Listen to Chapter 5 on MyPoliSciLab

Interest Groups

The Politics of Influence

Starting in 1962, federal government employees were allowed to join unions.[1] Today roughly 600,000 public employees at the federal level are represented by the American Federation of Government Employees,[2] and most state and local government employees are represented by the American Federation of State, County and Municipal Employees (AFSCME) union, which in 2011 had over 1.6 million members.[3] One of the primary reasons to join a union is to benefit from **collective bargaining,** the process where the union represents a group of employees in negotiations with management about wages, benefits, and workplace safety.

Wisconsin was the first state to allow public employees to bargain collectively, passing legislation to this effect in 1959. Decades earlier in 1911, Wisconsin was also the first state to enact a workers' compensation law, which is an insurance program that provides cash benefits and medical care to workers injured on the job. It was first as well to provide unemployment compensation (1936), a program that provides funds for a limited time to unemployed workers meeting specified criteria.[4]

But following the 2010 election, Wisconsin became a battleground for efforts to roll back public employee bargaining rights and benefits. In 2010, voters elected Republican Scott Walker governor and gave the Republicans majorities in both houses of the state legislature.[5] Soon after taking office, Walker and the state legislature set about to enact some of his campaign promises. With the state budget deficit rising quickly during the economic downturn, Walker wanted public employees to pay more towards their pension and health care benefits. He also wanted to limit public employee union rights as a way to reduce salaries negotiated through collective bargaining agreements in which all employee salaries went up together (police and fire unions were not part of the proposed change).[6]

Protestors demonstrate in the capitol rotunda on February 25, 2011, in Madison, Wisconsin. They have occupied the building for the past 11 days protesting the governor's attempt to push through a bill that would restrict collective bargaining for most government workers.

The Big Picture If you belonged to an interest group, would you rather it be as as big as the AARP or as wealthy as the American Petroleum Institute? In this video, author David B. Magleby talks about what characteristics determine an interest group's political leverage.

The Basics What are interest groups and what role do they play in our democracy? Listen to real people tackle these and other questions. Learn what types of interest groups exist in our country, what tactics they use to achieve their goals, and why interest groups matter.

In Context Examine the emergence of interest groups in American politics. In this video, Boston College political scientist Kay Schlozman traces the roots of interest group involvement in American politics and why they are an important part of the political process today.

Thinking Like a Political Scientist Do interest groups have an impact on policy? Boston College political scientist Kay Schlozman explains why this is not an easy question to answer. She also discusses how scholars determine which groups are represented and which groups are not.

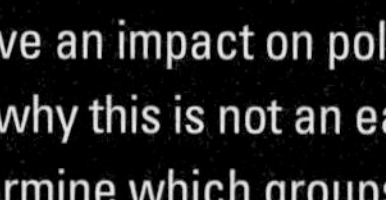

In the Real World Is pizza a vegetable? This video illustrates the difference between elitist and populist theories of interest groups by examining real people's reactions to the recent debate over whether school cafeterias should count pizza sauce as a full serving of vegetables.

So What? Have interest groups in American politics become too powerful? Author David B. Magleby looks at the recent events that dramatically deregulated these groups, and he considers the possibility of a new constitutional amendment to counter this trend.

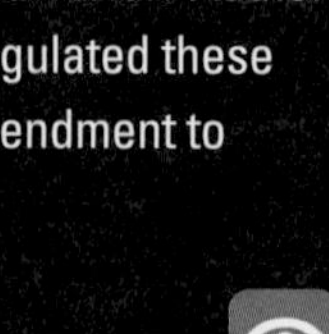

In response, the public employee unions and allied groups organized protests, shut down some public services, and a group of 14 Democratic state senators left the state, denying the Republicans the necessary number of senators present to enact the changes. Governor Walker and the Republican legislative majorities prevailed and enacted their changes. The unions then filed lawsuits against the new law, successfully recalled two Republican state senators, and launched a successful **recall** drive against Governor Walker that gave voters the option to remove Walker from office prior to the normal end of his term.

After a hotly contested election contest in which national figures like former president Bill Clinton campaigned for Democrat Tom Barrett and Republicans like South Carolina governor Nikki Haley campaigned for Walker, Walker won with 53 percent of the vote. Even though the race was seen as having national implications, President Obama did not campaign in the state for Barrett. Walker and the Republicans interpreted his victory as a vindication of his policies.[7]

Wisconsin is not the only state trying to abolish public employee unions' right to collective bargaining. Ohio passed legislation similar to Wisconsin's, but that legislation was later resoundingly rejected in a referendum, with 61 percent voting to repeal the ban on collective bargaining. Ohio Republican Governor John Kasich, who, like Walker, was elected in 2010, said after the election, "It's clear that the people have spoken. Part of leading is listening to and hearing what people have to say to you."[8]

The political battles over public unions are only one example of the interplay between interest groups and the government, or among interest groups themselves. For example, during the 2012 election, substantial attention was given to efforts by the federal government to assist the auto industry in 2008 and 2009 and whether these "bailouts" had been good public policy. Attention was also directed to new regulations of the banking industry enacted in 2010.[9] Banks, auto companies, and public employee unions are all examples of interest groups. Like other interest groups, they use a variety of strategies, from local citizens spontaneously organizing for some political purpose to more organized, election-focused political action committees (PACs). In 2010 and 2012, individuals and groups could give unlimited amounts to "independent expenditure only committees" or "Super PACs."

Interest groups like these have long been important in electing and defeating candidates, in providing information to officeholders, and in setting the agenda of American politics. Similarly, U.S. citizens have been concerned about the power of "special interests" and the groups' focus on their self-interest at the expense of less well-organized groups or the general public. Restraining the negative tendencies of interest groups while protecting their liberty is not easy. In this chapter, we examine the full range of interest group activities as well as efforts to limit their potentially negative influences, including reforming campaign finance regulations.

collective bargaining, p. 136
The process in which a union represents a group of employees in negotiations with the employer about wages, benefits, and workplace safety.

recall
A procedure for submitting to popular vote the removal of officials from office before the end of their term.

faction
A term the founders used to refer to political parties and special interests or interest groups.

Interest Groups Past and Present: The "Mischiefs of Faction"

5.1 Explain the role of interest groups and social movements in American politics.

The founders of the Republic were very worried about groups with common interests, which they called **factions.** (They also thought of political parties as factions.) For the framers of the Constitution, the daunting problem was how to establish a stable and orderly constitutional system that would both respect the liberty of free citizens and prevent the tyranny of the majority or of a single dominant interest.

5.1

5.2

5.3

5.4

5.5

5.6

pluralism
A theory of government that holds that open, multiple, and competing groups can check the asserted power by any one group.

interest group
A collection of people who share a common interest or attitude and seek to influence government for specific ends. Interest groups usually work within the framework of government and try to achieve their goals through tactics such as lobbying.

social movement
A large body of people interested in a common issue, idea, or concern that is of continuing significance and who are willing to take action. Movements seek to change attitudes or institutions, not just policies.

As a talented practical politician and a brilliant theorist, James Madison offered both a diagnosis and a solution in *The Federalist*, No. 10. He began with a basic proposition: "The latent causes of faction are...sown in the nature of man." All individuals pursue their self-interest, seeking advantage or power over others. Acknowledging that we live in a maze of group interests, Madison argued that the "most common and durable source of factions has been the various and unequal distribution of property." Madison defined a faction as "a number of citizens, whether amounting to a majority or minority of the whole, who are united and actuated by some common impulse of passion, or of interest, adverse to the rights of other citizens, or to the permanent and aggregate interests of the community." For Madison, "the *causes* of faction cannot be removed, and...relief is only to be sought in the means of controlling its *effects*."[10]

James Madison played a critical role in drafting and enacting the Constitution, and many of its provisions are aimed at limiting the "mischiefs of faction." Separation of powers and checks and balances make it hard for a faction to dominate government. Staggered terms of office make it necessary for a faction to endure. But rather than trying to encourage one or another faction, the Constitution encourages competition between them. Indeed, checks and balances arguably function best when factions within the branches work to counter one another. The Constitution envisions a plurality of groups competing with each other, an idea that has been called **pluralism.**

How well pluralism has worked in practice is debated.[11] We will see that over time, government has sought to regulate factions as a response to the power some groups such as corporations, unions, and wealthy individuals have had in American government. The debate about how to check their power without damaging their liberty is an enduring one.

☐ A Nation of Interests

Some U.S. citizens identify with groups distinguished by race, gender, ethnic background, age, occupation, religion, or sexual orientation. Others form voluntary groups based on their opinions about issues such as gun control or tax reduction. When such associations seek to influence government, they are called **interest groups.**

Interest groups are also sometimes called "special interests." Politicians and the media often use this term in a pejorative way. What makes an interest group a "special" one? The answer is highly subjective. One person's *special* interest is another's *public* interest. However, so-called public interest groups such as Common Cause or the League of Women Voters support policies that not everyone agrees with. Politics is best seen as a clash among interests, with differing concepts of what is in the public interest, rather than as a battle between the special interests on one side and "the people" or the public interest on the other.

In fact, the term "special interest" conveys a selfish or narrow view, one that may lack credibility. For this reason, we use the neutral term "interest groups." An interest group simply speaks for some, but not all, of us. A democracy includes many interests and many organized interest groups. The democratic process exists to decide among them. Part of the politics of interest groups is thus to persuade the general public that the interest their group represents is more important than others.

☐ Social Movements

Interest groups sometimes begin as social movements. A **social movement** consists of many people interested in a significant issue, idea, or concern who are willing to take action to support or oppose it. Examples include the civil rights, environmental, anti-tax, animal rights, women's rights, Christian Right, gay rights, anti-immigration, and antiwar movements. In some respects, the Tea Party groups

The mass protests that were part of the Arab Spring in 2011, like this one in Tahrir Square in Cairo, helped bring down the Mubarak government. The movement was made up of several groups united by opposition to Mubarak but not on what to do once he was deposed. The protests were often violent, and on the day seen in this photo, six people were killed and more than 800 injured.

that formed in 2009 and 2010 and remained active through the 2012 election are examples of social movements. The Tea Party began in early 2009, not long after Barack Obama took office; groups started forming to protest the $787 billion economic stimulus package, officially known as the American Recovery and Reinvestment Act of 2009. These groups adopted the name Tea Party, a reference to the Boston Tea Party of 1773 when colonists rebelled against what they thought to be unfair British taxes on tea. The group's general concerns are about increasing government spending and growing government power. While exhibiting many characteristics of a social movement, the Tea Party has also become part of the Republican Party.

The Bill of Rights protects movements, popular or unpopular, by supporting free assembly, free speech, and due process. Consequently, those who disagree with government policies do not have to engage in violence or other extreme activities in the United States, as they do in some countries, and they need not fear prosecution for demonstrating peacefully. In a democratic system that restricts the power of government, movements have considerable room to operate *within* the constitutional system.

Types of Interest Groups

5.2 Categorize American interest groups into types.

Some interest groups are formal associations or organizations like the National Rifle Association (NRA); others have no formal organization. Some are organized primarily to persuade public officials on issues of concern to the group such as reducing greenhouse gases; others conduct research, or influence public opinion with published reports and mass mailings.

We can categorize interest groups into several broad types: (1) economic, including both business and labor; (2) ideological or single-issue; (3) public interest; (4) foreign policy; and (5) government itself. Obviously, these categories are not mutually exclusive. Most American adults are represented by a number of interest groups, even if they don't know it. For instance, people aged 50 and older may not know that AARP (which began as the American Association of Retired Persons) claims to represent *all* older citizens, not only those who are actually members. Similarly, the American Automobile Association (AAA) claims to represent all motorists, not only those who join. The varied and overlapping nature of interest groups in the United States has been described as *interest group pluralism*, meaning that competition among open, responsive, and diverse groups helps preserve democratic values and limits the concentration of power in any single group. We look at each category of interest group next.

□ Economic Interest Groups

There are thousands of economic interests: agriculture, consumers, plumbers, the airplane industry, landlords, truckers, bondholders, property owners, and more. Economic interests pursue what benefits them both financially and politically.

BUSINESS The most familiar business institution is the large corporation. Corporations range from one-person enterprises to vast multinational entities. General Motors, AT&T, Microsoft, Coca-Cola, McDonald's, Wal-Mart, Wall Street banks and investment firms, and other large companies exercise considerable political influence, as do hundreds of smaller corporations. For example, as Microsoft and Wal-Mart came under heightened government and public scrutiny, their political contributions expanded.[12] Corporate power and a changing American and global economy make business practices important political issues.

Cooperation between groups can increase their effectiveness, giving even small business an important voice in public policy. The Commerce Department, for example, includes a Small Business Administration. Small businesses are also organized into groups such as the National Federation of Independent Business (NFIB) that help elect pro-business candidates and persuade the national government on behalf of its members.

TRADE AND OTHER ASSOCIATIONS Businesses with similar interests join together as *trade associations*, as diverse as the products and services they provide. Businesses of all types are also organized into large nationwide associations such as the National Association of Realtors and smaller ones like the American Wind Energy Association.

The broadest business trade association is the Chamber of Commerce of the United States. Organized in 1912, the Chamber is a federation of thousands of local Chambers of Commerce representing millions of businesses. Loosely allied with the Chamber on most issues is the National Association of Manufacturers, which, since 1893, has tended to speak for the more conservative elements of American business.

LABOR Workers' associations have a range of interests, including professional standards and wages and working conditions. Labor unions are one of the most important groups representing workers, yet the American workforce is among the least unionized of any industrial democracy.[13] (See Figure 5.1.) Two areas where unions have seen growth in recent years are service employees and public employees.[14] As discussed earlier in this chapter, public sector unions have become the focus of controversy in recent years. The level of unionization has policy consequences. For example, a nation's minimum wage rates increase with unionization.

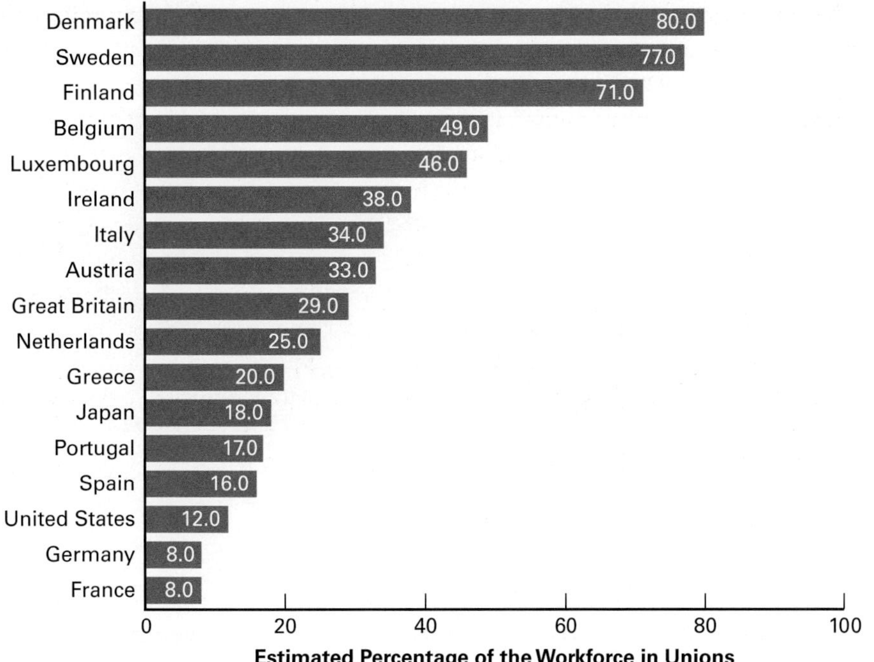

FIGURE 5.1 UNION MEMBERSHIP IN THE UNITED STATES COMPARED TO OTHER COUNTRIES

How might aspects of American culture and ideology help explain the relatively low unionization of the American workforce?

SOURCE: http://www.oecd.org/dataoecd/37/2/35695665.pdf. Data obtained from the Online OECD Employment database, http://www.oecd.org/document/34/0,3746,en_2649_33927_40917154_1_1_1_1,00.html.

open shop
A company with a labor agreement under which union membership cannot be required as a condition of employment.

closed shop
A company with a labor agreement under which union membership can be a condition of employment.

Throughout the nineteenth century, American workers organized political parties and local unions. Their most ambitious effort at national organization, the Knights of Labor, registered 700,000 members in the 1890s. But by approximately 1900, the American Federation of Labor (AFL), a confederation of strong and independent-minded national unions mainly representing craft workers, was the dominant organization. During the 1930s, unions more responsive to industrial workers broke away from the AFL and formed a rival national organization of industry groups, the Congress of Industrial Organizations (CIO). In 1955, the AFL and CIO reunited. In 2005, more than a third of AFL-CIO members (4.5 of 13 million members), affiliated with the Service Employees International Union (SEIU), the International Brotherhood of Teamsters, and two other unions, split off from the AFL-CIO, forming a new group named the Change to Win Federation.[15] Unions today are thus less unified, but by 2007, dues paid to the AFL-CIO exceeded levels before the division.[16]

The AFL CIO speaks for approximately three-fourths of unionized labor,[17] and unions represent about 13 percent of the nation's workforce (see Figure 5.2).[18] The proportion of the U.S. workforce belonging to all unions has fallen, in part because of the shift from an industrial to a service and information economy. Dwindling membership limits organized labor's influence. In Wisconsin after the change in public sector collective bargaining in 2011 the number of union members fell sharply.[19] Recently, however, some service sector unions have begun to expand, and even some doctors have unionized. Membership in SEIU rose from 1.58 million in 2006, a membership number little changed from 2003, to 2.1 million in 2012.[20]

Union membership is optional in states whose laws permit the **open shop,** in which workers cannot be required to join a union as a condition of employment. In states with the **closed shop,** workers may be required to join a union to be hired at a particular company if most employees at that company vote to unionize. In both cases,

5.1
5.2
5.3
5.4
5.5
5.6

free rider
An individual who does not join a group representing his or her interests yet receives the benefit of the group's influence.

professional associations
Groups of individuals who share a common profession and are often organized for common political purposes related to that profession.

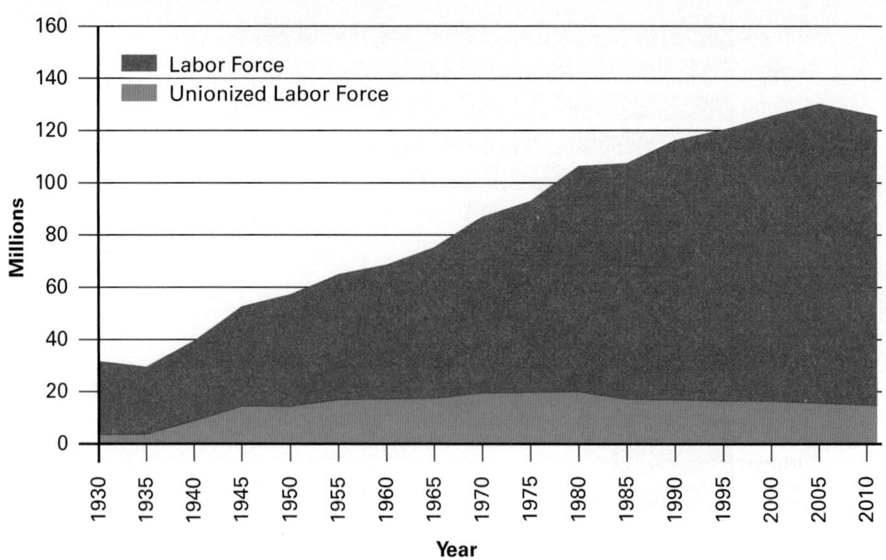

FIGURE 5.2 LABOR FORCE AND UNION MEMBERSHIP, 1930–2011

■ *How can you explain the steady upward growth of the labor force without a comparable growth in the unionized labor force?*

SOURCE: Barry Hirsch, Georgia State University, and David Macpherson, Florida State University, 1973–2011, "Union Membership, Coverage, Density, and Employment Among All Wage and Salary Workers, 1973–2011," http://www.unionstats.com.

the unions negotiate with management, and all workers share the benefits the unions gain. In open-shop states, many workers may choose not to affiliate with a union because they can secure the same benefits that unionized workers enjoy without incurring the costs of joining the union. When a person benefits from the work or service of an organization like a union (or even a public TV or radio station) without joining or contributing to it, this condition is referred to as the **free rider** problem, which is an issue discussed later in the chapter.

Since 1998, in political campaigns, unions have emphasized direct contact with members and their families through mail, e-mail, on the phone, and in person. They have organized get-out-the-vote drives and paid for television advertising. Unlike the case in 2000, when unions were important to securing Al Gore's nomination,[21] in the 2004 and 2008 Democratic presidential primaries they were divided. In 2008, some unions such as SEIU and the Change to Win Federation supported Senator Barack Obama, whereas the United Steel Workers supported John Edwards, and the American Federation of State, County, and Municipal Employees supported Senator Hillary Clinton. In the 2012 general election, unions were unified in backing Obama. Unions experienced mixed results in state level elections in 2011 and 2012. As noted, a ballot measure in Ohio passed reversing legislation that would have limited public employee collective bargaining,[22] but the 2012 Wisconsin recall election was widely seen as a defeat for public sector unions.[23]

Traditionally identified with the Democratic Party, unions have not enjoyed a close relationship with Republican legislatures or executives. Given labor's limited resources, one option for unions is to form temporary coalitions with consumer, public interest, liberal, and sometimes even industry groups, especially on issues related to foreign imports. Labor has been unsuccessful in blocking free trade agreements like the North American Free Trade Agreement (NAFTA).[24]

PROFESSIONAL ASSOCIATIONS Professional people join **professional associations** such as the American Medical Association (AMA) and the American Bar Association (ABA), which serve some of the same functions as unions. Other

Barack Obama meets with labor union members over breakfast while campaigning for the Democratic nomination for the presidency in 2008.

professions are divided into many subgroups. Teachers and professors, for example, belong to the National Education Association, the American Federation of Teachers, and the American Association of University Professors, and also to subgroups based on specialties, such as the Modern Language Association and the American Political Science Association.

Government, especially at the state level, regulates many professions. Lawyers are licensed by states, which, often as a result of pressure from lawyers themselves, set standards of admission to the state bar. Professional associations also use the courts to pursue their agendas. In the area of medical malpractice, for example, doctors lobby hard for limited-liability laws, while trial lawyers resist them. Teachers, hairstylists, and marriage therapists are licensed by states and work for or against legislation that concerns them. It is not surprising, then, that groups representing professional associations such as the AMA and the National Association of Home Builders are among the largest donors to political campaigns.

☐ Ideological or Single-Issue Interest Groups

Ideological groups focus on issues—often a single issue. Members generally share a common view and a desire for government to pursue policies consistent with it. Such *single-issue* groups are often unwilling to compromise. Right-to-life and pro-choice groups on abortion fit this description, as do the National Rifle Association (NRA) and anti-immigration groups.

Countless groups have organized around other specific issues, such as civil liberties, environmental protection, nuclear energy, and nuclear disarmament.[25] Such associations are not new. The Anti-Saloon League of the 1890s was devoted solely to barring the sale and manufacture of alcoholic beverages, and it did not care whether legislators were drunk or sober as long as they voted dry. One of the best-known single-issue groups today is the NRA, with almost 4 million members committed to protecting the right to bear arms.[26] Other single-issue groups include the Club for Growth, a generally libertarian and anti-tax group.

Nongovernmental organization (NGO)

A nonprofit association or group operating outside government that advocates and pursues policy objectives.

☐ Public Interest Groups

Out of the political ferment of the 1960s came groups that claim to promote "the public interest." For example, Common Cause campaigns for electoral reform, for making the political process more open and participatory, and to stem media consolidation. Its Washington staff raises money through direct-mail campaigns, oversees state chapters of the group, publishes research reports and press releases on current issues, and lobbies Congress and government departments.

After uncovering design flaws in the Ford Pinto in 1977 resulting in 180 deaths, consumer activists like Ralph Nader charged Ford "with sacrificing human lives for profit."[27] Ralph Nader was instrumental in forming organizations to investigate and report on governmental and corporate action—or inaction—relating to consumer interests. Public interest research groups (PIRGs), as these groups are called, today seek to influence policy on Capitol Hill and in several state legislatures on environmental issues, safe energy, and consumer protection.

☐ Foreign Policy Interest Groups

Interest groups also organize to promote or oppose foreign policies. Among the most prestigious is the Council on Foreign Relations in New York City. Other groups pressure Congress and the president to enact specific policies. For example, interest groups have been trying to influence American policy on China's refusal to grant independence for Tibet. Other groups support or oppose free trade. Foreign policy groups should not be confused with foreign governments and interest groups in other nations, which are banned from making campaign contributions but often seek to influence policy through lobbying firms.

One of the most influential foreign policy groups is the American Israel Political Action Committee (AIPAC), with more than 100,000 members.[28] Because AIPAC's primary focus is influencing government directly, not distributing campaign funds, it is not required to disclose where its money comes from or goes. AIPAC's successes include enactment of aid packages to Israel, passage of the 1985 United States–Israel Free Trade Agreement, and emergency assistance to Israel in the wake of the 1992 Gulf War. Its counterpart, the Arab American Institute, lobbies to support Arab causes. Efforts to secure a negotiated settlement between the Palestinians and Israel have kept U.S. interest groups on both sides visible and important.

Nongovernmental organizations (NGOs), nonprofit groups that operate outside the institutions of government but often pursue public policy objectives and lobby governments, are another type of foreign policy interest group. The most common are social, cultural, or environmental groups such as Greenpeace, Amnesty International, and the Humane Society of the United States.

☐ Public Sector Interest Groups

Governments are themselves important interest groups. Many cities and most states retain Washington lobbyists, individuals who advocate on behalf of the city or state before Congress and with the executive branch of the federal government. Governors are organized through the National Governors Association, cities through the National League of Cities, and counties through the National Association of Counties. Other officials—lieutenant governors, secretaries of state, mayors—have their own national associations.

Government employees form a large and well-organized group. The National Education Association (NEA), for example, has 3.2 million members.[29] The NEA

The Global Community

Global Climate Change

Much of the debate over global warming has been about the accuracy of the scientific claims about changes in the Earth's climate. Interest groups on both sides of the debate have cited studies supporting their point of view and a wide range of interest groups have a stake in what, if anything, governments should do.

Examples of such interests include oil companies, automobile manufacturers, and environmental groups like the Natural Resources Defense Council, the Environmental Defense Fund, and the Union of Concerned Scientists. Public opinion on whether global warming is a serious problem was part of the Pew Global Attitudes Survey. Respondents were asked, "In your view, is global climate change a very serious problem, somewhat serious, not too serious, or not a problem?" The graph plots responses from our sample countries to this question.

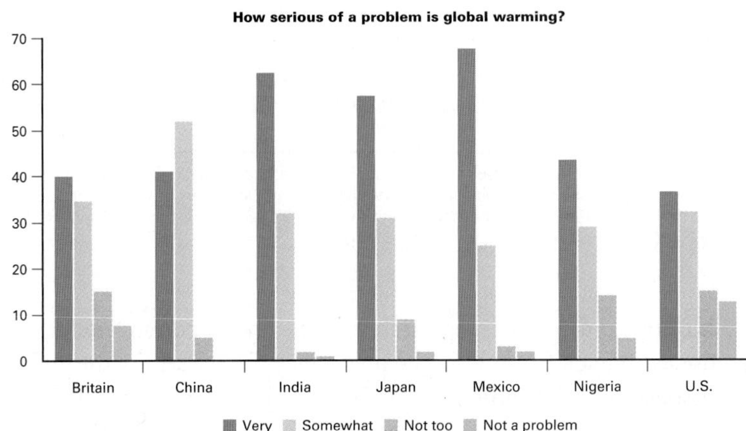

In your view, is global climate change a very serious problem, somewhat serious, not too serious, or not a problem?

SOURCE: Pew Research Center, *2010 Spring Survey of the Global Attitudes Project* (Pew Research Center, 2010).

On this question, the United States stands apart in that fewer Americans think global warming is a very or somewhat serious problem. Between 72 and 94 percent of people surveyed in our sample of countries outside the United States saw global warming as a very serious or somewhat serious problem. In the United States, the proportion was 70 percent. When we look only at those with the more strongly held view that global warming is a "very serious" problem, the United States is again lower than all other countries in the percent having that view. In contrast, roughly three-fifths to two-thirds of people in Mexico, Japan, and India think global warming is a very serious problem. In China, 41 percent think global warming is a very serious problem.

CRITICAL THINKING QUESTIONS

1. Why does public opinion on the severity of global warming differ between the United States and other countries?
2. Why would people in China be the least likely to respond that global warming is a very serious problem?
3. Do you think attitudes on this question are related to whether people would be willing to accept limitations in lifestyle to reduce the threat of global warming?

5.1

5.2

5.3

5.4

5.5

5.6

TABLE 5.1 ENVIRONMENTAL GROUPS' RESOURCES AND STRATEGIES

Group	Membership	Issues	Activities
Sierra Club	1,400,000	Wilderness, pollution, global warming, human rights, population, suburban sprawl	Grassroots action; litigation; news releases
Natural Resources Defense Council	1,300,000	Resources, energy, global warming, pollution, nuclear weapons	Lobbying; litigation; watchdog; its scientists compete with experts from agencies and industry
Defenders of Wildlife	1,110,000	Imperiled wildlife and habitat, public lands, climate change impacts, international wildlife trade	Grassroots advocacy; litigation; hands-on conservation; lobbying
Greenpeace USA	250,000	Forests, global warming, genetically engineered foods, oceans, persistent organic pollutants, nuclear weapons	Media events; mass mailings; grassroots activity; does not lobby government
Wilderness Society	500,000	Wilderness areas, public lands, energy development	Scientific studies; analysis; advocacy group

SOURCE: Greenpeace USA, www.greenpeaceusa.org; Natural Resources Defense Council, www.nrdc.org; Sierra Club, www.sierraclub.org; and Wilderness Society, www.wilderness.org; Defenders of Wildlife, Inga Sedlovsky, Executive Assistant to the President, e-mail message to author, June 27, 2012. Greenpeace worldwide membership is 2.86 million.

endorses politicians from both parties but more typically supports Democrats. In 2008, the NEA endorsed Barack Obama for the presidency. The NEA fits the definition of a professional association, labor union, and public sector interest group. Public employees are increasingly important to organized labor because they constitute the fastest-growing unions.

☐ Other Interest Groups

American adults are often emotionally and financially engaged by a wide variety of groups: veterans' groups, nationality groups, and religious organizations, among others. Individuals join groups because of a common interest, because of a shared identification, or because of an issue or concern. The American Legion or Veterans of Foreign Wars not only provide opportunities for military veterans to meet other veterans, but the groups provide an important advocacy function for veterans as they deal with Congress or the Veterans' Administration bureaucracy.

Women's organizations have long been important in advocating for equal rights, most notably for the right to vote. Among the best-known group in the area of political rights for women is the League of Women Voters, formed in 1920 and with chapters in all 50 states. Interest groups with a focus on reproductive rights include NARAL Pro-Choice America or Planned Parenthood. More broadly focused is the National Organization of Women (NOW).

Environmental groups are increasingly active (see Table 5.1). Among the best known of these groups is the Sierra Club. Founded in 1892, the Sierra Club is the oldest and largest environmental organization. The Sierra Club is active in environmental protection efforts in states and local communities, and it has a lobbying presence in Washington, D.C. Another group known for its efforts to elect pro-environment candidates is the League of Conservation Voters (LCV). The Defenders of Wildlife and the Wilderness Society have members and paid staff committed to protecting wildlife and securing preserving and protecting wilderness.

Characteristics and Power of Interest Groups

5.3 Analyze sources of interest group power.

Political scientists, sociologists, and economists have described the differing ways groups form and organize to pursue their goals or objectives. Securing the participation of individuals in groups—what economist Mancur Olson labeled **collective action,**[30] and others describe as **public choice**[31]—is challenging because often the benefits from the group efforts are shared with everyone, including those who do not participate in the work of securing the benefit. This creates the *free rider* problem. For example, unions that achieve wage concessions from management do so for all workers in and out of the union. This results in little incentive to join the union or support it financially. Groups sometimes attempt to sanction or punish free riders, which is why unions prefer that only union workers be employed in a given firm or industry. When this is not possible, group leaders try to reduce the free rider problem through persuasion or group pressure.

Explore on MyPoliSciLab Simulation: You Are a Lobbyist

collective action
How groups form and organize to pursue their goals or objectives, including how to get individuals and groups to participate and cooperate. The term has many applications in the various social sciences such as political science, sociology, and economics.

public choice
Synonymous with "collective action," specifically studies how government officials, politicians, and voters respond to positive and negative incentives.

Groups vary in their goals, methods, and power. Among their most important characteristics are size, incentives to participate, resources, cohesiveness, leadership, and techniques. As we will demonstrate, these different resources and objectives help us understand the power of interest groups.

Size and Resources

Obviously, size is important to political power; an organization representing 5 million voters has more influence than one speaking for 5,000. Perhaps even more important is the number of members who are active and willing to fight for policy objectives. Interest groups often provide tangible incentives to join, such as exclusive magazines, travel benefits, professional meetings and job opportunities, and discounts on insurance, merchandise, and admission to cultural institutions. Some are "compelling enough to attract the potential free rider."

Many government programs provide services that benefit everyone such as clean air, national defense, and street lights. One solution to the free rider problem is to pay for these widely shared benefits through taxes. Nongovernment service providers can require a number of people to pay for the service before providing it. It is then in everyone's interest to pay for the service or face the prospect that no one will have it. For example, during the recession of 2010 and 2011, scores of cities and towns cancelled their local July 4th fireworks because private and public sources were no longer able to provide the funding. Groups rarely overcome the risk of free riders, but unless we offer some compensation for providing easily shared goods and services, they are not likely to be produced.

Although the size of an interest group is important to its success, so is its *spread*—the extent to which membership is concentrated or dispersed. Because automobile manufacturing is concentrated in Michigan and a few other states, the auto industry's influence does not have the same spread as the American Medical Association, which has an active chapter in virtually every congressional district. Concentration of membership in a key battleground state, however, such as Cuban Americans in Florida or ethanol producers in Iowa, enhances that group's influence.

Finally, groups differ in the extent of their *resources*—money, volunteers, expertise, and reputation. Some groups can influence many centers of power—both houses of Congress, the White House, federal agencies, the courts, and state and local

Actor Dennis Quaid is seen here on the cover of the AARP Magazine, which featured an article about medical errors that nearly cost the lives of his twin children. Quaid, like any person over fifty years of age, can join the AARP (American Association of Retired Persons). The AARP is active on issues of concern to older Americans.

governments—whereas others cannot. The U.S. Chamber of Commerce has a broad reach, with active "chambers" at the local, state, and national levels. An even larger group, the American Association of Retired Persons (AARP) touts its larger and national membership in policy debates. Particular industries, like citrus growers, have a spread that includes only a few states.

☐ Cohesiveness

Most mass-membership organizations include three types of members: (1) a relatively small number of formal leaders who may hold full-time, paid positions or devote much time, effort, and money to the group's activities; (2) a few hundred people intensely involved in the group who identify with its aims, attend meetings, pay dues, and do much of the legwork; and (3) thousands of people who are members in name only and cannot be depended on to vote in elections or act as the leadership wants. When these groups share common views on the aims of the organization, the group is more cohesive; single-issue groups typically enjoy strong cohesion among their members. An example of a cohesive group with strong organizational structures is Planned Parenthood, which operates offices all over the country and has a clear purpose that is well understood by its supporters. In 2012, when one underwriter announced it was no longer contributing to Planned Parenthood, the reaction was swift and strong and the sponsor reversed itself and resumed funding the organization.

☐ Leadership

In a group that embraces many attitudes and interests, leaders may either weld the various elements together or sharpen their disunity. The leader of a national business association, for example, must tread cautiously between big business and small business, between exporters and importers, between chain stores and corner grocery stores, and between the producers and the sellers of competing products.

The group leader is in the same position as a president or a member of Congress; he or she must know when to lead and when to follow. An example of an effective group leader is Thomas J. Donohue, the president of the U.S. Chamber of Commerce.

Under Donohue's leadership, the Chamber has grown in size and influence. He has also met with President Obama, even though the Chamber and the president are often on opposing sides.

lobbying
Engaging in activities aimed at influencing public officials, especially legislators, and the policies they enact.

Federal Register
An official document, published every weekday, that lists the new and proposed regulations of executive departments and regulatory agencies.

☐ Techniques for Exerting Influence

Our separation-of-powers system provides many access points for any group attempting to influence government. They can present their case to Congress, the White House staff, state and local governments, and federal agencies and departments. They can also challenge actions in court. Efforts by individuals or groups to inform and influence public officials are called **lobbying.** Groups also become involved in litigation, protests, and election activities and even establish their own political parties. Groups vary in the extent to which they have widespread support that comes from the people (grassroots) vs. activity that is orchestrated or initiated centrally but looks to be grassroots (astroturf).

PUBLICITY, MASS MEDIA, AND THE INTERNET One way to attempt to influence policy makers is through the public. Interest groups use the media—television, radio, the Internet including Web sites, newspapers, leaflets, signs, direct mail, and word of mouth—to influence voters during elections and motivate them to contact their representatives between elections. Businesses enjoy a special advantage because, as large-scale advertisers, they know how to deliver their message effectively or can find an advertising agency to do it for them. But organized labor is also effective in communicating with its membership through shop stewards, mail, phone calls, and personal contact.

Mobilization increasingly occurs through the Internet, especially through social media such as Facebook and Twitter. Business organizations like the Business and Industrial Political Action Committee (BIPAC) have used the Internet to communicate with members and employees of affiliated businesses. BIPAC's Web site provides downloadable forms to request absentee ballots and the roll call votes of legislators on issues of interest to their businesses.[32] Some groups, such as MoveOn.org, operate almost exclusively online, while massive forums such as DailyKos.com and Townhall.com act as a clearinghouse for left- and right-wing causes. As one scholar noted, much of what modern interest groups do "could not work without the Internet."[33]

The Internet helps interest groups in two ways. First, it allows citizens to easily organize themselves for rallies, marches, letter-writing drives, and other kinds of civic participation. Second, the Internet opens new, exclusively online forms of political action, such as sending mass e-mails, posting videos, joining Facebook groups, donating money online, commenting on articles, and blogging. We discuss these developments in greater detail in the media chapter.

MASS MAILING/E-MAILING One means of communication that has increased the reach and effectiveness of interest groups is computerized and targeted mass mailing.[34] Before computers, interest groups could either cull lists of people to contact from telephone directories and other sources or send mailings indiscriminately. Today's computerized communication technology can target personalized letters and e-mails to specific groups and individuals. Environmental groups make extensive use of targeted mail and e-mail. The Obama campaign had a list of over 13 million e-mail addresses after the 2008 campaign,[35] which it used to communicate messages during Obama's first term and which provided the foundation for the e-mail list for the 2012 reelection campaign.

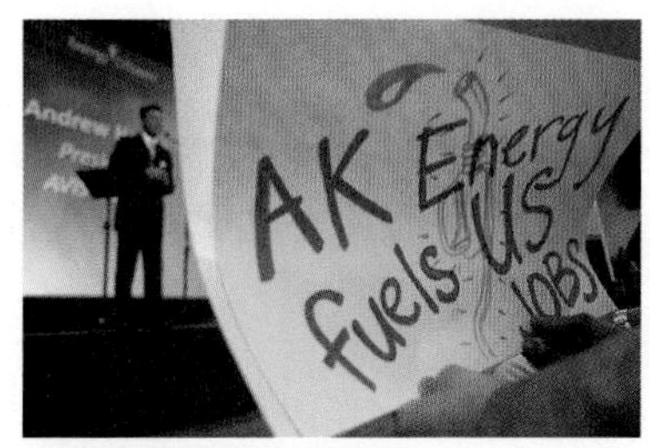

Vote 4 Energy, a group backed by the American Petroleum Institute, advertised widely in 2012 on the theme that energy resources are important and people should vote with energy in mind.

DIRECT CONTACT WITH GOVERNMENT Organized groups have ready access to the executive and regulatory agencies that write the rules implementing laws passed by Congress. Government agencies publish proposed regulations in the ***Federal Register*** and invite responses from all interested persons before the rules are finalized—in the "notice and comments period."[36] Well-staffed associations and corporations use the *Register* to obtain the specific language and deadlines for pending regulations. Lobbyists prepare written responses to the proposed rules, draft alternative rules, and make their case at the hearings.

LITIGATION When groups find the political channels closed to them, they may turn to the courts.[37] The Legal Defense and Educational Fund of the National Association for the Advancement of Colored People (NAACP), for example, initiated and won numerous court cases in its efforts to end racial segregation and protect the right to vote for African Americans. Urban interest groups, feeling underrepresented in state and national legislatures, turned to the courts to press for one-person, one-vote rulings to overcome the disproportionate power rural interest groups had in legislatures and to otherwise influence the political process.[38] Individuals and groups opposed to campaign finance reform have challenged federal, state, and local laws in this area and in recent years been able to overturn laws and regulations.[39]

In addition to initiating lawsuits, associations can gain a forum for their views in the courts by filing ***amicus curiae* briefs** (literally, "friend of the court" briefs), presenting arguments in cases in which they are not direct parties. It is not unusual for courts to cite such briefs in their opinions. *Amicus* briefs have been found to influence decisions on whether to review cases.[40] In some cases, like the review of the constitutionality of health care reform, the number of briefs was more than were submitted in the prior two record-holder affirmative action cases: The Supreme Court received 136 *amicus* briefs on the health care case.[41]

***amicus curiae* brief**
Literally, a "friend of the court" brief, filed by an individual or organization urging the Supreme Court to hear a case (or discouraging it from doing so) or, at the merits stage, to present arguments in addition to those presented by the immediate parties to a case.

Super PACs
Independent expenditure-only PACs are known as Super PACs because they may accept donations of any size and can endorse candidates. Their contributions and expenditures must be periodically reported to the FEC.

PROTEST To generate interest and broaden support for their cause, movements and groups often use protest demonstrations. For example, after the House of Representatives passed new laws on illegal immigration in 2006, pro-immigrant groups mounted protests in cities such as Phoenix and Washington, D.C., with more than 1 million participants.[42] Two months later, more than 600,000 protesters gathered in Los Angeles and 400,000 in Chicago to focus greater media attention on the important role immigrants play in the economy. (The legislation died when differences between the Senate and House versions of the bill could not be reconciled.)

More recently, individuals have come together to protest the unequal distribution of income and the greater power the rich have influencing government. The group called itself "Occupy Wall Street" and occupied a small park in New York City, near Wall Street. Other "occupy" groups emerged, most notably in Oakland, California, where protests turned to violence.[43] The Occupy groups achieved one of their aims as the 2012 election focused more on income and wealth distribution than had the elections of 2008 or 2010. Other movements or groups that have used protest include the civil rights movement and antiwar, environmental, and anti-globalization groups.[44]

CONTRIBUTIONS TO CAMPAIGNS Interest groups also form political action committees (PACs), which are the legal mechanism for them to contribute money to candidates, political party committees, and other political committees. One of the oldest PACs is the Committee on Political Education (COPE) of the AFL-CIO, but business groups and others have long existed to direct money to favored candidates. PACs also encourage other PACs to contribute to favored candidates, occasionally hosting joint fund-raisers for candidates. In 2012 a new type of PAC, a **Super PAC**, was allowed to form. A Super PAC can spend money supporting or opposing candidates with no limitations as to the amount of money individuals, corporations, or unions could contribute. These groups played a critical role in the Republican presidential nomination contest and in the presidential general election, and also in several congressional election campaigns.

Individuals clearly associated with an interest group also contribute to campaigns as individuals in ways that make clear to the candidate the interest of the donor. Often one party gathers contributions from several individuals and then gives the checks made out to the candidate's campaign in a bundle, a process called **bundling.** This can also be done via the computer. In 2012 Super PACs had individual donors who contributed in excess of $5 million, and Las Vegas casino owner Sheldon Adelson and his wife Miriam Adelson together gave $20 million to "Winning Our Future," the Super PAC supporting Newt Gingrich. Overall the Adelsons gave a reported $53 million to Republican Super PACs; another individual, Harold Simmons, gave nearly $27 million.[45]

bundling
A tactic in which PACs collect contributions from like-minded individuals (each limited to $2,000) and present them to a candidate or political party as a "bundle," thus increasing the PAC's influence.

CANDIDATE SUPPORT/OPPOSITION Most large organizations are politically engaged in some way, though they may be, or try to be, *nonpartisan.* Most organized interest groups try to work through *both* parties and want to be friendly with the winners, which often means they contribute to incumbents. But as competition for control of both houses of Congress has intensified and with presidential contests also hotly contested, many interest groups invest mostly in one party or the other.

Many interest groups also publicly endorse candidates for office. Ideological groups like Americans for Democratic Action and the American Conservative Union publish ratings of the voting records of members of Congress on liberal and conservative issues. Other interest groups, such as the U.S. Chamber of Commerce and the League of Conservation Voters, create scorecards of key legislative votes and report to their members how their representative voted on those issues.

NEW POLITICAL PARTIES Another interest group strategy is to form a political party, not so much to win elections as to publicize a cause. Success in such cases may occur when a major party co-opts the interest group's issue. The Free Soil Party was formed in the mid-1840s to work against the spread of slavery into the territories, and the Prohibition Party was organized two decades later to ban the sale of liquor. Farmers have formed a variety of such parties. More often, however, interest groups prefer to work through existing parties. This is also true for factions like the Tea Party, which is closely identified with the Republican Party.

Today, environmental groups and voters for whom the environment is a central issue must choose between supporting the Green Party, which has yet to elect a candidate to federal office, an Independent candidate such as Ralph Nader in 2008, or one of the two major parties. Sometimes minor-party candidates can spoil the chances of a major-party candidate. In a New Mexico congressional special election in 1997, the Green Party candidate won 17 percent of the vote, taking some votes from the Democrat and thereby helping to elect a Republican to what had been a Democratic seat. The Tea Party Movement became a rallying cry for some candidates in 2010. However, although more closely identified with Republicans than Democrats, the Tea Party movement is not currently a party.

COOPERATIVE LOBBYING Like-minded groups often form cooperative groups. In 1987, the Leadership Conference on Civil Rights and People for the American Way brought together many groups to defeat the nomination of outspoken federal judge Robert Bork to the U.S. Supreme Court.[46] Different types of environmentalists work together, as do consumer and ideological groups on the right and on the left. For example, although a large variety of groups that reflect diverse interests represent women, the larger the coalition, the greater the chance that members may divide over such issues as abortion, or opposition to the War in Afghanistan, and no longer be able to pursue cooperative lobbying.

Since 2004, a group of pro-Democratic interest groups, under pressure from some major donors, have come together to share information and campaign support plans with each other on an ongoing basis during the campaign. The coordinating group

5.1 **lobbyist**
A person who is employed by and acts for an organized interest group or corporation to try to influence policy decisions and positions in the executive and legislative branches.

5.2

revolving door
5.3 An employment cycle in which individuals who work for government agencies that regulate interests eventually end up working for interest groups
5.4 or businesses with the same policy concern.

issue network
5.5 Relationships among interest groups, congressional committees and subcommittees, and the government agencies that share a common policy
5.6 concern.

is named America Votes and those who coordinate with each other include Planned Parenthood, EMILY's List, Sierra Club, League of Conservation Voters, several unions, Move-On, and other groups.[47] Another example of a cooperative group is the Business Roundtable, an association of chief executive officers of the 200 largest American corporations, which promotes policies that help large businesses, such as free trade and less government regulation.

The Influence of Lobbyists

5.4 Describe lobbyists and the activities through which they seek to influence policy.

Individuals who try to influence policy decisions and positions, often representing groups, are called **lobbyists**. The term "lobbying" was not generally used until around the mid-nineteenth century in the United States. These words refer to the lobby or hallway outside the House and Senate chambers in the U.S. Capitol and to those who hung around the lobby of the old Willard Hotel in Washington, D.C., when presidents dined there. The noun "lobby" is now used as a verb.

Despite their negative public image, lobbyists perform useful functions for government. They provide information for decision makers in all three branches of government, help educate and mobilize public opinion, help prepare legislation and testify before legislative hearings, and contribute a large share of the costs of campaigns. But many people fear that lobbyists have too much influence on government and add to legislative gridlock by stopping action on pressing problems.

☐ Who Are the Lobbyists?

The typical image of policy making is of powerful, hard-nosed lobbyists who use a combination of knowledge, persuasiveness, personal influence, charm, and money to influence legislators and bureaucrats. Often former public servants themselves, lobbyists are experienced in government and often go to work for one of the interests they dealt with while in government, or for a lobbying firm.

Moving from a government job to a job with an interest group—or vice versa—is so common that this career path is called the **revolving door**. Although it is illegal for former national government employees to directly lobby the agency from which they came, their contacts made during government service are helpful to interest groups. Many former members of Congress use their congressional experience as full-time lobbyists. Of those who left Congress or lost seats in the 2010 election and have found new employment, 33% are employed by lobbying firms and 20% are employed by lobbying clients.[48]

In 2007, Congress passed the Honest Leadership and Open Government Act, which requires more disclosure of employment history of lobbyists, sets stricter limits on lobbyist activities, requires senators to wait two years before lobbying, and requires staff to wait one year before lobbying any Senate office. The Obama Administration used this lobbying list to prohibit any registered lobbyists from serving in any White House or executive branch jobs.

Many lobbyists participate in **issue networks** or relationships among interest groups, congressional committees and subcommittees, and government agencies that share a common policy concern. Personal relationships among members of these groups can sometimes allow these networks to become so strong and mutually beneficial that they almost form a separate branch of government.

Legal and political skills, along with specialized knowledge, are so crucial in executive and legislative policy-making that they have become a form of power in and of themselves. Elected representatives increasingly depend on their staffs for

OF the People Diversity in America

Breaking into a Male-Dominated Profession

Relatively few women and even fewer minorities are lobbyists. The first woman to own a lobbying firm was Anne Wexler, who started her own firm after leaving the Carter administration in 1981. Wexler observed that when she started, "there were very few women in lobbying. It was completely male dominated."[*] More women head lobbying firms today. For example, April Burke, who was trained as a lawyer and spent time both on Capitol Hill and in the not-for-profit sector, heads Lewis-Burke Associates LLC. She has represented clients with interests in technology transfer, health policy, higher education, science, and energy sectors.

Women have begun to make inroads into the lobbying profession, especially in areas such as health care, reproductive rights, and education. Because the number of women serving in senior congressional and White House staffs has grown, the pool of women that would likely become lobbyists has similarly grown. Today, more than one-third of lobbyists in Washington are women, according to research by Denise Benoit Scott, the author of *The Best Kept Secret: Women Corporate Lobbyists, Policy & Power in the United States,*[**] and a similar proportion of lobbyists at the state level are female.[†] While the new hires have boosted the ranks of minority lobbyists, they remain a small group. There are more than 30,000 registered lobbyists in Washington. Among them, there are about 200 blacks, according to the Washington Government Relations Group, a black lobbying organization. The newly founded Hispanic Lobbyists Association counts 60 members in its group.[‡]

QUESTIONS

1. Why have so few women become lobbyists?
2. Why are so few racial minorities lobbyists?

[*]Jeffrey H. Birnbaum, "Women, Minorities Make Up New Generation of Lobbyists," *Washington Post* (May 1, 2006), p. D1.

[**]Denise Benoit Scott, The Best-Kept Secret: Women Corporate Lobbyists, Politics and Power in the United States. (New Brunswick, NJ: Rutgers University Press, 2007).

[†]Michael G. Bath, Jennifer Gayvert-Owen, and Anthony J. Nownes, "Women Lobbyists: The Gender Gap and Interest Representation," *Politics and Policy*, 33 (March 2005), pp. 136–152.

[‡]Jeanne Cummings, "Minority Lobbyists Gain Ground," *Politico*, May 7, 2007, http://www.politico.com/news/stories/0507/3858.html (accessed June 19, 2012).

guidance, and these issue specialists know more about "Section 504" or "Title IX" or "the 2012 amendments"—and who wrote them and why—than most political and administrative leaders, who are usually generalists.[49] New laws often need specific rules and applications spelled out in detail by the agencies charged to administer them. In this rule-making activity, interest groups and issue networks assume even more significance.

5.1

5.2

5.3

5.4

5.5

5.6

FOR the People Government's Greatest Endeavors

Disclosure of Lobbyist Activity

Obtaining meaningful and timely disclosure of interest group and lobbyist activities is an important way to protect the political process from the undue influence of interest groups. During the last few decades, the government has been engaged in reform efforts seeking to achieve more meaningful disclosure.

One of the problems of prior efforts at disclosing lobbying activities was an imprecise definition of lobbying. The Lobbying Disclosure Act of 1995 (LDA) requires all lobbyists to register with the Clerk of the House of Representatives or the Secretary of the Senate and provides a more detailed definition of exactly what is considered lobbying and who is considered a lobbyist. Lobbyists must file quarterly reports about their lobbying activity, the compensation they received, the time they spent, and the expenses they incurred.

Congress and the president went a step further in 2007 with passage of amendments to the 1995 law known as the Honest Leadership and Open Government Act of 2007 (HLOGA). This law made the lobbyist registration and their reports publicly available online and permits the House clerk and Senate secretary to review the reports for accuracy. The HLOGA includes further restrictions on gifts and privately funded travel for members of Congress, and also requires lobbyists who bundle contributions from individual donors to disclose that activity.*

Although some progress has been made in achieving greater disclosure of lobbying activity, substantial gaps remain. A 2008 study found that approximately two-thirds of the details in lobbyists reports could not be verified and the level of detail in the reports was sometimes lacking.† In addition, disclosure laws do not apply to people who only indirectly try to influence policy or legislation through activities such as organizing *others* to write letters or call decision makers. Newt Gingrich, who received more than $1.6 million from one entity after leaving Congress, claimed he only offered "strategic advice," and therefore did not have to file as a lobbyist.‡

QUESTIONS

1. **Why is disclosure assumed to limit abuses by lobbyists?**
2. **Why is there resistance to full and complete disclosure by lobbyists and legislators?**

*Anthony Corrado, "The Regulatory Environment," in David B. Magleby and Anthony Corrado, eds., *Financing the 2008 Election* (Washington, D.C.: Brookings Institution Press, forthcoming).

†United States Government Accountability Office, "2008 Lobbying Disclosure: Observations on Lobbyists' Compliance with Disclosure Requirements," April 2009.

‡Eric Lichtblau, "Gingrich's Deep Ties to Fannie Mae and Freddie Mac," *New York Times*, February 3, 2012, http://www.nytimes.com/2012/02/04/us/politics/gingrichs-deep-ties-to-fannie-mae-and-freddie-mac.html?_r=1&pagewanted=all (accessed May 3, 2012).

□ What Do Lobbyists Do?

Thousands of lobbyists are active in Washington, but few are as glamorous or as unscrupulous as the media suggest. Nor are they necessarily influential. One limit on their power is the competition among interest groups. As we have seen, rarely does any one group have a policy area all to itself.

To members of Congress, the single most important thing lobbyists provide is money for their next reelection campaign. "Reelection underlies everything else," writes political scientist David Mayhew.[50] Money from interest groups is the most important source funding this driving need among incumbents. Interest groups also provide volunteers for campaign activity. In addition, their failure to support the opposition can enhance an incumbent's chances of being reelected.

Beyond their central role in campaigns and elections, interest groups provide information of two important types, political and substantive. *Political information* includes such matters as who supports or opposes legislation, including the executive branch, and how strongly they feel about it.[51] *Substantive information,* such as the impact of proposed laws, may not be available from any other source. Lobbyists often provide technical assistance for drafting bills and amendments, identifying persons to testify at legislative hearings, and formulating questions to ask administration officials at oversight hearings.[52] An example of a group that not only lobbied for legislation but has drafted laws that were introduced as written in four states is named the American

Legislative Exchange Council (ALEC). The group is funded by oil companies and other corporations.

Interest groups sometimes attempt to influence legislators and regulators by going directly to the people and urging them to contact public officials. They sometimes do this through television advertising, but also through mail, e-mail, and banner ads on the Internet. During the protracted debate over health care reform in 2009–2010, multiple groups took their message directly to the people, not only to influence public opinion on possible legislation, but also as a way to try to pressure Congress. In 2010, an estimated $200 million was spent in TV advertising on health care.[53]

political action committee (PAC)
The political arm of an interest group that is legally entitled to raise funds on a voluntary basis from members, stockholders, or employees to contribute funds to candidates or political parties.

Money and Politics

5.5 Identify ways interest groups use money in elections and assess efforts to regulate this spending.

Interest groups also seek to influence politics and public policy by spending money on elections. They can do this in several ways. One way is by contributing money to candidates for their election campaigns; another is by contributing to political parties that assist candidates seeking office, especially in contested races. They can also contribute money to other interest groups; communicate to the members of their group, including employees; and spend money independently of the parties and candidates.

Helping to elect candidates creates a relationship between the interest group and the elected official that a group may later exploit. At a minimum, substantial involvement in the election process helps provide access to policy makers.[54] We discuss the dynamics of campaign finance and efforts to reform or regulate it in a later chapter. Here, we discuss the most important ways interest groups organize and participate in funding campaigns and elections.

Political Action Committees (PACs)

A **political action committee (PAC)** is the political arm of an interest group legally entitled to raise limited and disclosed funds on a voluntary basis from members, stockholders, or employees in order to contribute funds to favored candidates or political parties. PACs link two vital techniques of influence—giving money and other political aid to politicians and persuading officeholders to act or vote "the right way" on issues. Thus, PACs are one important means by which interest groups seek to influence which legislators are elected and what they do once they take office.[55] We categorize PACs according to the type of interest they represent: corporations, trade and health organizations, labor unions, ideological organizations, and so on.

PACs grew in number and importance in the 1970s, in part because of campaign finance reform legislation enacted in that decade. The number of PACs registered rose from 608 in 1974 to 4,611 today.[56] Corporations and trade associations contributed most to this growth; today, their PACs constitute the majority of all PACs. Labor PACs, by contrast, represent less than 6 percent of all PACs.[57] But the increase in the number of PACs is less important than the intensity of PAC participation in elections and lobbying (see Figure 5.3).

Surprisingly, considering that the growth in numbers of PACs has occurred mainly in the business world, organized labor invented this device. In the 1930s, John L. Lewis, president of the United Mine Workers, set up the Non-Partisan Political League as the political arm of the newly formed Congress of Industrial Organizations (CIO). When the CIO merged with the American Federation of Labor (AFL), the new labor group established the Committee on Political Education (COPE), a model

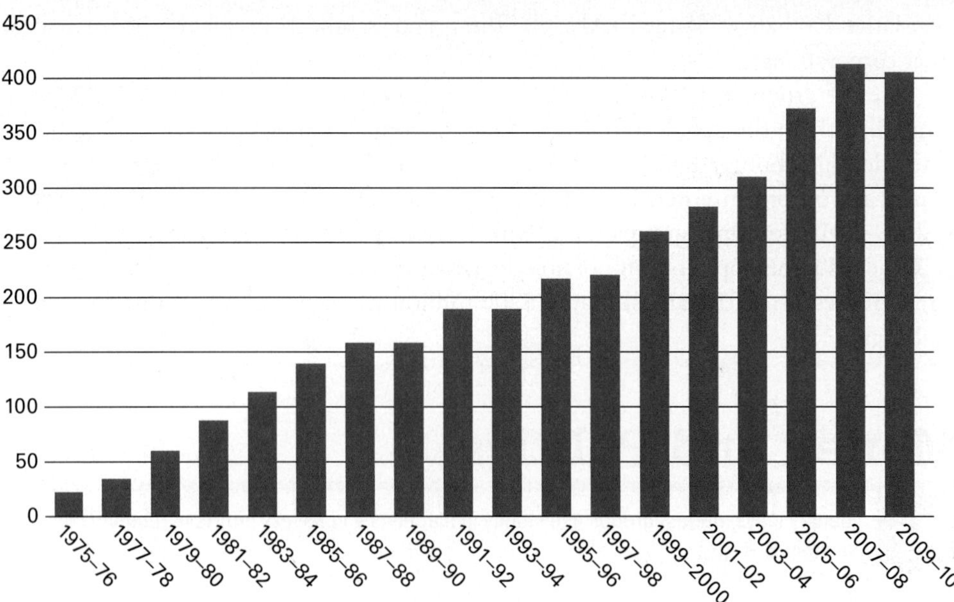

FIGURE 5.3 TOTAL PAC CONTRIBUTIONS TO CANDIDATES FOR U.S. CONGRESS, 1975–2010 (IN MILLIONS).

SOURCE: Harold W. Stanley and Richard G. Niemi, *Vital Statistics on American Politics 2005–2006* (CQ Press), p. 103; and Federal Election Commission, "PAC Activity Continues to Climb in 2006," Press Release, October 5, 2007, www.fec.gov/press/press2007/20071009pac/20071009pac.shtml.

for PACs. Some years later, manufacturers formed the Business and Industry Political Action Committee (BIPAC), but the most active business PAC today is the one affiliated with the National Association of Realtors.[58] Table 5.2 lists the most active PACs in elections since 2000.

The 2012 elections saw growth in a new type of PAC—Super PACs, which could spend unlimited amounts of money in support of or opposition to federal candidates. Super PACs came into existence in 2010 after the U.S. Supreme Court declared limits on corporations' or unions' spending from their general funds on campaign communications unconstitutional in the *Citizens United* v. *FEC*.[59] In the 2010 election cycle, Super PACs spent over $60 million,[60] a training exercise for some of them in anticipation of even more spending and activity in 2012. For years, corporations and unions

TABLE 5.2 PACs THAT GAVE THE MOST TO FEDERAL CANDIDATES, CUMULATIVELY, 2000–2010 (MILLIONS OF DOLLARS)

What kinds of interests do the most active PACs support? What responsibility do candidates who receive funds have to those PACs?

PAC	2000	2002	2004	2006	2008	2010	Total
1. National Association of Realtors	$3.42	$3.65	$3.77	$3.75	$4.01	$3.79	$18.61
2. National Auto Dealers Association	$2.50	$2.58	$2.58	$2.82	$2.86	$2.98	$13.35
3. International Brotherhood of Electrical Workers	$2.46	$2.21	$2.30	$2.78	$3.33	$2.48	$13.09
4. National Beer Wholesalers Association	$1.87	$2.07	$2.29	$2.95	$2.87	$3.30	$12.04
5. National Association of Home Builders	$1.82	$1.92	$2.22	$2.90	$2.48	$2.13	$11.35
6. International Brotherhood of Teamsters	$2.49	$2.33	$1.89	$2.07	$2.20	$2.31	$10.99
7. American Federation of State, County, and Municipal Employees	$2.59	$2.42	$1.64	$2.05	$2.11	$2.31	$10.81
8. United Auto Workers	$2.16	$2.34	$2.07	$2.22	$1.99	$1.64	$10.77
9. Laborers Union	$1.79	$2.25	$2.25	$2.32	$2.05	$1.73	$10.66
10. International Association of Machinists and Aerospace Workers	$2.18	$2.20	$1.91	$1.76	$2.33	$2.01	$10.37

SOURCE: Federal Election Commission, "Top 50 PACs by Contributions to Candidates," includes activity through 12/31/10, www.fec.gov/press/2010_Full_summary_Data.shtml.

Explore on MyPoliSciLab

Can Interest Groups Buy Public Policy?

Interest groups such as banks and labor unions work to influence legislation their members care about, such as tax policy or social benefits. They form political action committees (PACs) that contribute to campaigns. Incumbents receive the most support, especially those on congressional committees that might affect the group sponsoring the PAC. Both labor unions and banks donate to candidates, but they have different contribution strategies.

Banks and Labor Unions Have Similar Campaign Funding

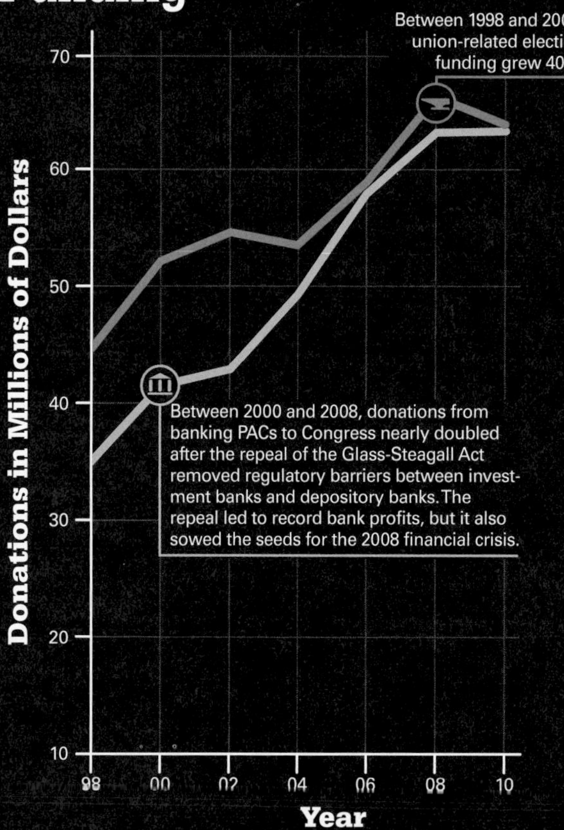

SOURCE: Data from the Federal Election Commission, www.fec.gov.

Banks and Labor Unions Have Different Party Priorities

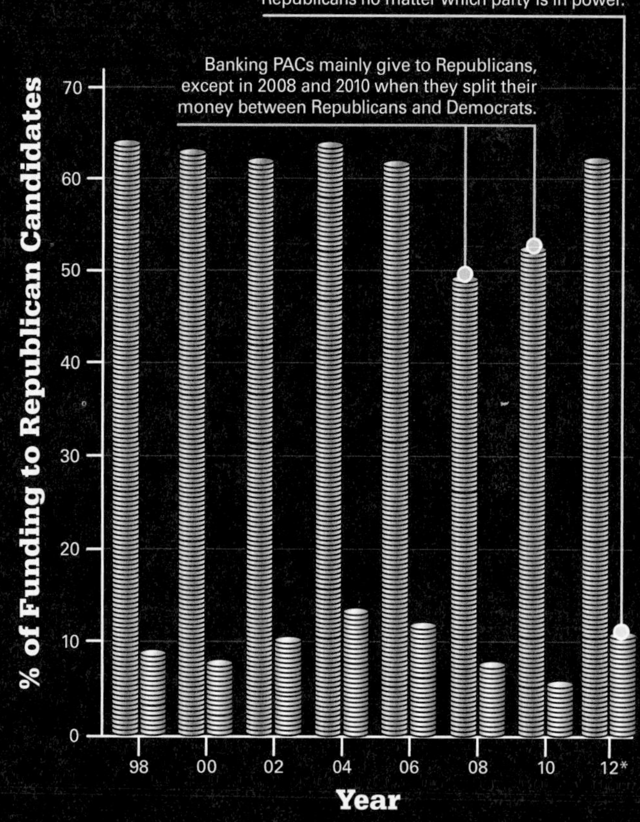

Investigate Further

Concept Are banks or labor unions giving more money to politicians through their PACs? They are giving roughly similar amounts of money. In fact, labor PACs donate more money than banking PACs.

Connection How are labor unions' donation strategies different from those of banks? Labor PACs consistently give the majority of their PAC money to Democrats even when Republicans control Congress. Banking PACs give more strategically. During most years, they focus their money on Republicans, but when Democrats are in power they split their donations between both parties.

Cause How do interest groups buy policy? Interest groups use PACs and campaign financing to reinforce political friendships with legislators. Labor PACs use their donations to support Democrats who share their ideological values, while banking PACs change their donation strategy depending on which party is in power.

5.1

5.2

5.3

5.4

5.5

5.6

leadership PAC
A PAC formed by an officeholder that collects contributions from individuals and other PACs and then makes contributions to other candidates and political parties.

Bipartisan Campaign Reform Act (BCRA)
Largely banned party soft money, restored long-standing prohibition on corporations and labor unions use of general treasury funds for electoral purposes, and narrowed the definition of issue advocacy.

TABLE 5.3 CANDIDATE SUPPORTIVE SUPER PACS AND MONEY THEY SPENT IN 2011–2012

Newt Gingrich	Winning Our Future	$17,007,762
Mitt Romney	Restore Our Future	$142,655,220
Rick Santorum	Red, White and Blue	$7,529,554
Ron Paul	Endorse Liberty	$4,321,935
Rick Perry	Make Us Great Again	$3,959,824
Barack Obama	Priorities USA Action	$67,496,077

SOURCE: Federal Election Commission. Data updated daily as reported by the *New York Times*, www.elections.nytimes.com/2012/campaign-finance/independent-expenditures/totals. Updated through 2012 election, www.opensecrets.org/pacs/superpacs/php.

had PACs that made limited contributions, but they had not been able use their profits or general funds to influence elections. It is important to note that corporations and unions are still prohibited from contributing money to candidate's campaigns from their profits or general funds. After the *Citizens United* decision, a subsequent U.S. District Court ruling involving a group named Speech Now prompted the Federal Election Commission to create PACs that are "independent expenditure only committees."[61] In the 2011-12 presidential election these Super PACs provided substantial support to candidates like Newt Gingrich, Mitt Romney, Rick Santorum, and Barack Obama. See Table 5.3 for the amounts of money the candidates spent out of their campaign funds through August 2012 (money raised with contribution limits) and how much the Super PACs spent on the candidates' behalf.

Elected officials also form their own PACs to collect contributions from individuals and other PACs and then make contributions to candidates and political parties. These committees, called **leadership PACs**, were initially a tool of aspiring congressional leaders to curry favor with candidates in their political party. For example, Republican Speaker John Boehner's PAC spent $4.5 million in the 2010 cycle and expended even more in 2012.[62]

☐ How PACs Invest Their Money

PACs are important not only because they contribute such a large share of the money congressional candidates raise for their campaigns, but also because they contribute so disproportionately to incumbents, committee chairs, and party leadership. PACs often give not only to the majority party, but to key incumbents in the minority. In the 2010 cycle, House incumbents seeking reelection raised 42 percent of the funds for their campaigns from PACs, compared to only 9 percent for the challengers opposing them. In total, House incumbents raised more than nine PAC dollars for every one PAC dollar going to a challenger.[63] Senate incumbents raise proportionately more from individuals but also enjoy a fundraising advantage among PACs compared to Senate challengers (see Figure 5.4). One reason members of Congress become entrenched in their seats is that PACs fund them.

The law limits the amount of money that PACs, like individuals, can contribute to any single candidate in an election cycle. But raising money from PACs was for many years more efficient for a candidate than raising it from individuals. Since the 1970s, PAC contributions to any federal candidate have been limited to $10,000 per election cycle (primary and general elections), whereas until 2004 individuals were limited to $2,000 per candidate per election cycle. The **Bipartisan Campaign Reform Act (BCRA)** doubled individual contribution limits and mandated that they increase with inflation while leaving PAC contribution limits unchanged. The contribution limit for 2011–2012 was $5,000 (primary and general elections combined). This means two individuals giving the maximum allowable can now equal the maximum allowable PAC contribution. This probably reflected the view of the legislators that actual corruption or the appearance of it is more likely to come from organized interests such as unions, trade associations, and businesses than from individuals.

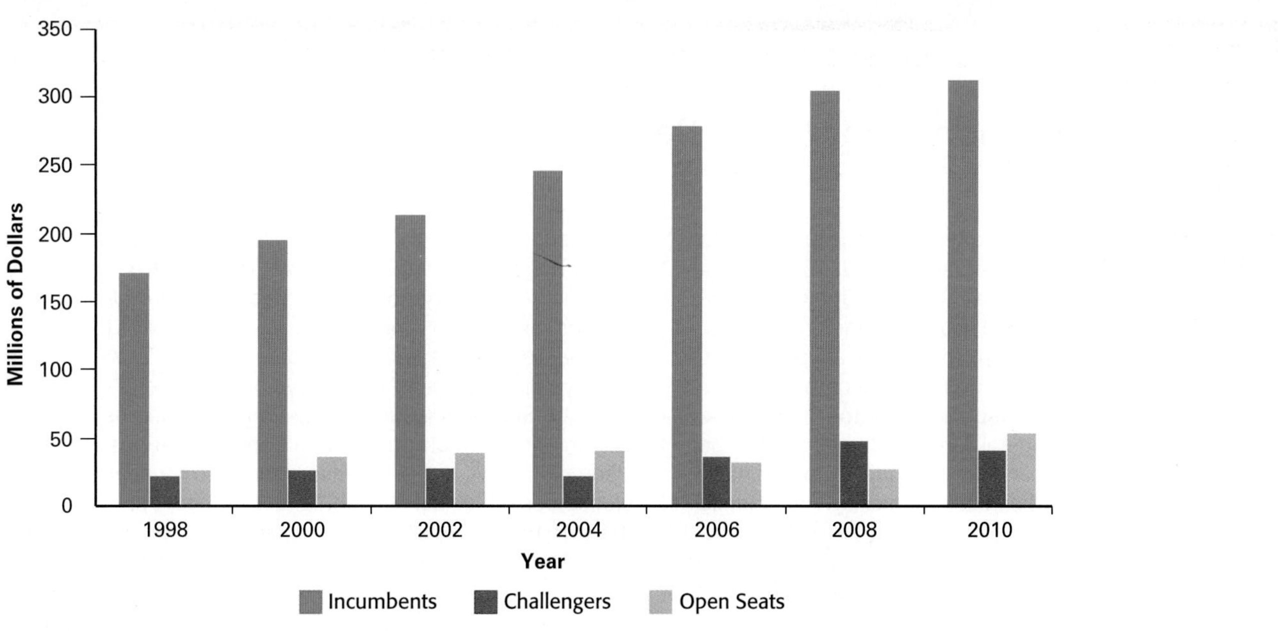

FIGURE 5.4 PAC CONTRIBUTIONS TO CONGRESSIONAL CANDIDATES, 1998–2010

■ *Over time, how has the distribution of PAC money changed? Why do PACs contribute so disproportionately to incumbents?*

SOURCE: Compiled from Federal Election Commission data, "Candidate Financial Summaries," www.fec.gov/finance/disclosure/ftpsum.shtml.

PAC contributions are especially made to committee chairs and party leaders. To reinforce this relationship, the Republicans developed a strategy, the "K Street Project," to do even better in getting PAC contributions. (K Street in Washington, D.C., houses many of the lobbying and law firms that represent trade associations and corporations that make contributions.)

After the Democratic Party took control of Congress in 2007, some PACs changed loyalties. In the House, approximately 60 percent of PAC money went to Democrats and 40 percent to Republicans.[64] Before Congress changed hands, just the opposite was true—approximately 60 percent of PAC money went to Republicans. In the Senate, Republicans once received more PAC money than Democrats, but in recent elections there has been near parity in PAC giving to the two parties.[65]

soft money
Money raised in unlimited amounts by political parties for party-building purposes. Now largely illegal except for limited contributions to state or local parties for voter registration and get-out-the-vote efforts.

☐ Mobilizing Employees and Members

Another way interest groups can influence the outcome of elections is by persuading their employees, members, or stockholders to vote in a way consistent with the interests of the group or corporation. They accomplish this mobilization through targeted communications at the workplace, through the mail, on the telephone, or on the Internet. As we discuss elsewhere in this chapter, labor unions have been especially effective in member communications. Corporations and business associations have been following labor's lead. Membership organizations such as the NRA have also been able to mobilize their members, as well as allied individuals and groups.[66]

☐ Other Modes of Electioneering

Until the 2004 election cycle, interest groups and individuals could avoid the contribution limitation to political parties by contributing so-called **soft money** to political parties. Originally justified as an exception to contribution limits to help the political parties by funding get-out-the-vote drives or party appeals that are not specific, soft money came to be used for candidate-specific electioneering.[67] We discuss party soft money in greater detail in the next chapter and the Bipartisan Campaign Reform Act in a later chapter.

You Will Decide

Should Corporations and Unions Be Unlimited in Running Campaign Ads?

Does limiting the ability of corporations or unions to use their general or "treasury" funds for election-related expenditures violate the constitutional guarantee of freedom of speech? Corporations and unions, like other groups, are free to form political action committees to make contributions to candidates and parties. What has been at dispute is whether they could take their profits or general funds and spend those on electing or defeating candidates or in support of party efforts. For more than a century, federal law had banned unions and corporations from spending general or treasury funds on electoral politics.

These rules changed in 1979 when the Federal Election Commission allowed unions and corporations to give unlimited general treasury funds or profits to help political parties generally. This was called soft money. In 1996, unions and later corporations began spending unlimited and undisclosed amounts of money on "issue ads," which were really campaign commercials. The Bipartisan Campaign Reform Act banned soft money contributions to parties and more clearly defined election communications as television or radio ads that refer to a specific candidate and that air within 30 days of the primary or 60 days of the general election. The Supreme Court initially upheld both bans but later reversed itself on election communications and also now allows general treasury funds to be spent on election-specific ads. Given this reversal, opponents of the soft money ban are likely to again challenge this provision in court.

What do you think? Should corporations and unions be unlimited in funding parties and in running issue ads? What are some arguments for or against this?

Thinking It Through

The Supreme Court in *McConnell* v. *FEC* cited a long list of precedents in upholding the limitation on unions and corporations using their general funds to influence elections.[*] The economic power of corporations such as Microsoft or major unions could, if unconstrained, drown out the voices of other participants and corrupt the electoral process.

But unions and corporations argue that constraints on them are unfair when compared with the ability of wealthy individuals to spend unlimited amounts of their own money on politics via independent expenditures, which the Court allowed in its prior landmark decision, *Buckley* v. *Valeo*.[**] They would agree with Justice Scalia's dissent in *McConnell* v. *FEC* that restricting how much a group "can spend to broadcast [its] political views is a direct restriction on speech."[†]

With respect to electioneering or issue ads, in 2007, the reconstituted Supreme Court in *FEC* v. *Wisconsin Right to Life, Inc.* said the BCRA language was too broad in defining electioneering and that unions and corporations had a right to communicate with voters about political topics in the days and weeks before primary and general elections.[‡] Chief Justice Roberts substituted a new, more open definition of electioneering communication. In the past, language like that used by Chief Justice Roberts provided media consultants with enough latitude to craft election communications, arguing that they were about issues and not candidates. In 2010, the Supreme Court further broadened the opportunity for corporations and unions to engage in electioneering for or against candidates by reversing a long-standing ban on the use of corporate or union general funds, including profits.[§] This means that future elections could have substantial electioneering by unions and corporations on the eve of elections that is not subject to the other limitations of the law.

CRITICAL THINKING QUESTIONS

1. **What are the implications for voters of unlimited spending by corporations and unions in campaigns?**
2. **If in an election there is an imbalance in the spending by groups supporting the two sides in an election, is that a cause for concern?**

[*] *McConnell* v. *FEC*, 124 S. Ct. 533 (2003).

[**] *Buckley* v. *Valeo*, 96 S. Ct. 760 (1976).

[†] Justice Antonin Scalia, dissenting in *McConnell* v. *FEC*, 124 S. Ct. 618 (2003).

[‡] *Federal Election Commission* v. *Wisconsin Right to Life Inc.*, 466 F. Supp. 2d 195 (2007).

[§] *Citizens United* v. *Federal Election Commission*, 130 S. Ct. 876 (2010).

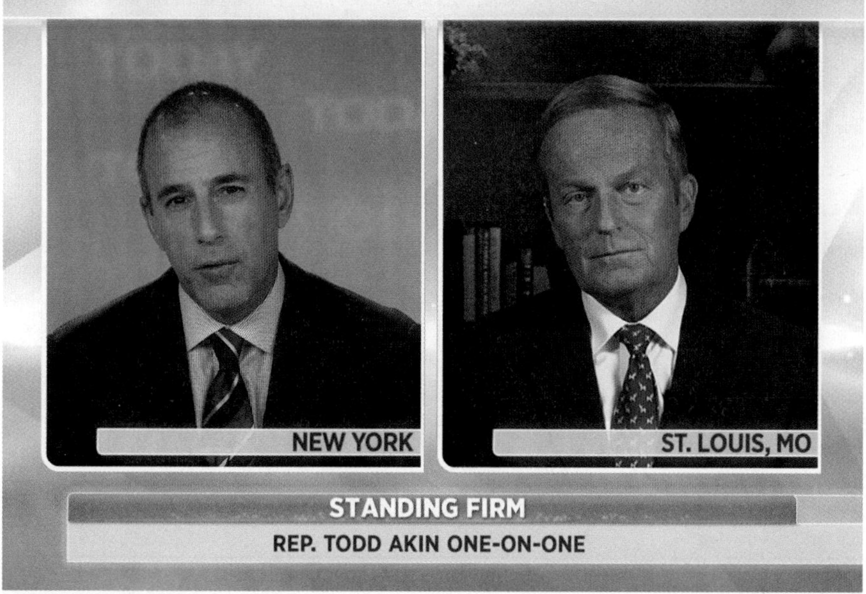

Missouri Republican Congressman and 2012 Senate candidate Todd Akin is seen here being interviewed by Matt Lauer of the *NBC Today Show*. Akin had stated in a televised interview that women who are victims of "legitimate rape" rarely get pregnant. Later he described his opponent, Senator Claire McCaskill, as a "wildcat" in her debate performance. After negative publicity, groups planning to spend money supporting Akin announced they would not. Akin lost the election.

independent expenditures

The Supreme Court has ruled that individuals, groups, and parties can spend unlimited amounts in campaigns for or against candidates as long as they operate independently from the candidates. When an individual, group, or party does so, they are making an independent expenditure.

Between 1996 and 2002, interest groups could also help fund so-called issue ads supporting or opposing candidates as long as the ads did not use certain words. The Supreme Court in 2007 declared parts of BCRA relating to these kinds of ads unconstitutional, allowing corporations and unions to again spend their general funds on ads that advocate a point of view on political issues, which may affect elections.[68] Their 5-to-4 decision in *Citizens United* v. *FEC* in 2010, discussed above, allowed corporations and unions to use unlimited general funds for election-specific ads and has resulted in much greater spending by corporations and unions in this mode of electioneering in competitive federal election contests.[69] Interest groups can avoid disclosure if they communicate with voters through the mail, in newspaper ads, on billboards, on the phone, and by e-mail.

Not all interest groups typically make the presidential campaign their highest priority. Some groups, such as the League of Conservation Voters (LCV), in the past had invested some of their resources in presidential races, especially in 2004, but have generally made House and Senate races higher priorities. The major groups representing business and labor invest heavily in both presidential and congressional elections.

☐ Independent Expenditures

The Supreme Court in 1976 declared that limits on independent expenditures were unconstitutional when the contributions or expenditures were truly independent of a party or candidate. Hence, groups, like individuals, can campaign for or against a candidate, independent of a party or candidate committee and in addition to making contributions to candidates and party committees from their PAC. These **independent expenditures** are unlimited but must be disclosed to the Federal Election Commission (FEC). Interest-group independent expenditures fall well below PAC contributions to candidates and parties. Groups that have made heavy use of independent expenditures include MoveOn PAC, NRA, EMILY's List, several unions, National Right to Life PAC, the Club for Growth, and the National Association of Realtors. (See Table 5.4 on page 164.)

Independent expenditures enable groups to direct unlimited amounts of money to a particular race. In 2010, for example, Crossroads Grassroots Policy Strategies was

5.1

5.2

5.3

5.4

5.5

5.6

issue advocacy
Unlimited and undisclosed spending by an individual or group on communications that do not use words like "vote for" or "vote against," although much of this activity is actually about electing or defeating candidates.

527 organization
A political group organized under section 527 of the IRS Code that may accept and spend unlimited amounts of money on election activities so long as they are not spent on broadcast ads run in the last 30 days before a primary or 60 days before a general election in which a clearly identified candidate is referred to and a relevant electorate is targeted.

TABLE 5.4 INDEPENDENT EXPENDITURES BY TOP INTEREST GROUPS, 2004–2010

Interest Group	Expenditure
New Data:	
Service Employees International Union	$119,281,405
America Coming Together	$85,038,718
Joint Victory Campaign 2004	$72,588,053
Media Fund	$59,679,624
America Votes	$53,485,149
Progress for America	$52,294,819
American Solutions Winning	$51,434,217
College Republican National Committee	$43,680,636
EMILY's List	$42,578,601
Club for Growth	$26,031,363

NOTE: Expenditures for all national affiliates of an organization are combined, but expenditures for state affiliates are excluded.

SOURCE: Center for Responsive Politics, "Top 50 Federally Focused Organizations," www.opensecrets.org/527s/527cmtes.php?level=C&cycle=2010 (accessed May 4, 2012).

active in several key races. They spent nearly $4.5 million in independent expenditures in the Illinois Senate race on television ads attacking the Democratic candidate.[70] American Crossroads was another group involved in making independent expenditures in competitive races across the country. They spent nearly $6 million in the Colorado Senate race on various media and other advertising expenditures attacking the Democratic candidate and supporting the Republican.[71]

This spending dwarfs what groups can do through PAC contributions. Groups making independent expenditures receive credit with their members for their activity because the source of independent expenditures is clearly communicated.

□ Campaigning Through Other Groups

For more than a century, reformers had sought disclosure of money in politics. In campaigns and elections, disclosure was often incomplete, and groups quickly found ways to avoid it. Then, the disclosure provisions of the Federal Election Campaign Act of 1971, amended in 1974, were defined by the Supreme Court as applying to communications that used words such as "vote for" or "vote against" and made them subject to disclosure and spending limits.[72]

For a time, citizens, journalists, and scholars had a complete picture of who was giving what to whom, and who was spending money and in what ways, to influence elections. That changed in 1994 and 1996, when interest groups found a way to circumvent disclosure and contribution limits through **issue advocacy.** They simply made election ads without words like "vote for" or "vote against," and then they spent millions attacking or promoting particular candidates. Labor unions were the first to exploit this tactic in a major way, spending an estimated $35 million in 1996, mostly against Republican candidates.[73] Corporations and ideological groups quickly followed labor's lead, spending millions on issue ads in 1996–2002, before they were limited by the 2002 Bipartisan Campaign Reform Act (BCRA).[74]

In the post–campaign reform elections of 2004 through 2012, interest groups continued to mount their own campaigns against or for candidates in ways similar to the old issue advocacy. For example, some Vietnam War veterans formed a group they named Swift Boat Veterans for Truth and ran ads attacking Senator John Kerry's Vietnam War record.[75] Groups like Swift Boat Veterans for Truth are called **527 organizations** or groups because they are tax-exempt groups organized

An important part of campaigns is registering new voters and canvassing them about their views on issues. In this photo, a volunteer from an interest group focusing on get-out-the-vote efforts uses a hand-held device to record survey responses from a Minnesota family.

under section 527 of the Internal Revenue Service Code. They can run ads against or for candidates but under somewhat more restrictive conditions than existed before 2004.

How Much Do Interest Groups Influence Elections and Legislation?

5.6 Evaluate the effectiveness of interest groups in influencing elections and legislation.

We have said that because PACs give more money to incumbents, challengers have difficulty funding their campaigns and have to rely more on individual contributors. Even with the larger individual contribution limits allowed in 2004 and since, most challengers still had much less money than their incumbent opponents.

How much does interest group money influence election outcomes, legislation, and representation? Former U.S. senator Alan Simpson (R-WY) said that "too often, members' first thought is not what is right or what they believe, but how it will affect fundraising. Who, after all, can seriously contend that a $100,000 donation does not alter the way one thinks about—and quite possibly votes on—an issue?"[76] Another former senator, Warren Rudman (R-NH) says, "You can't swim in the ocean without getting wet; you can't be part of this system without getting dirty."[77] In this area, as in others, money obviously talks. But it is easy to exaggerate its influence. Although a candidate may receive a great amount of interest group money, only a fraction of that

5.1

5.2

5.3

5.4

5.5

5.6

BY the People Making a Difference

Lobbying for Education Policy

Lobbying on education policy has important implications for college students. Numerous policies and laws enacted by Congress directly affect students and universities, and so it is important for students and universities to try to influence these policies for their own best interests.

For example, approximately two-thirds of college students graduating in 2008 with a bachelor's degree had some debt, with the average amount more than $22,000.* Approximately 8 million students received a Federal Pell Grant in 2009–2010.† Congress recently enacted changes in student loans and Pell grants through two pieces of legislation—the College Cost Reduction and Access Act and the American Recovery and Reinvestment Act. Under these acts, the maximum Pell Grant scholarship for the 2009–2010 school year will be $5,350—more than $600 higher than in 2008–2009. Among the groups active in lobbying Congress on this matter were Sallie Mae, the nation's largest student lender, but also the Consumer Bankers Association and the National Direct Student Loan Coalition.

Most universities and colleges retain a lobbyist to help them secure the support of government, either at the state level, the federal level, or both. Public institutions rely more on the state legislature than do private institutions. You can search online to learn about whether your institution has a lobbyist and how much the institution spent lobbying last year. Find a site on lobbyists in your state—such as http://cal-access.sos.ca.gov/lobbying/ for California or www.ethics.state.tx.us/main/search.htm for Texas—to get information on how your school lobbies the state government.

QUESTIONS

1. Why do you think your university or college hires lobbyists?
2. On matters like changes in the laws relating to student loans, do you think students' perspectives are adequately represented before Congress and the bureaucracy?
3. Is the money your school spent on lobbyists well spent? Why or why not?

*FinAid Page, "Student Loans," FinAid Page, LLC, 2010, www.finaid.org/loans/ (accessed March 15, 2010).

†David Leonhardt, "Behind the Rise in Pell Grants," *New York Times*, May 24, 2011, http://economix.blogs.nytimes.com/2011/05/24/behind-the-rise-in-pell-grants/ (accessed June 15, 2012).

total comes from any single group. It is also debatable how much campaign contributions affect elections, and there is no guarantee that money produces a payoff in legislation. What the substantial spending by Super PACs showed in 2012, however, is that allowing an individual to spend unlimited amounts through a Super PAC in support of a candidate can allow that candidate to continue to stay in the race. Without Super PAC support, it is doubtful that Gingrich or Santorum would have been able to stay in the race as long as they did.

Numerous groups seek to mobilize their membership in elections. They create Web sites for members to obtain information about their view of candidates and provide voter registration materials and absentee ballot request forms. How effective is electioneering by interest groups? In general, mass-membership organizations fail to mobilize their full membership in elections, although they can effectively mobilize when their interests are directly attacked.[78] More typically, too many cross-pressures operate in the pluralistic politics of the United States for any one group to assume a commanding role. Some groups reach their maximum influence only by allying themselves closely with one of the two major parties. They may place their members on local, state, and national party committees and help send them to party conventions as delegates, but forming such alliances means losing some independence.

☐ Curing the Mischiefs of Faction—Two Centuries Later

If James Madison were to return today, neither the existence of interest groups nor their variety would surprise him. However, the varied weapons of group influence, the deep investment of interest groups in the electoral process, and the vast number of lobbyists in Washington and the state capitals might come as a surprise. And doubtless, Madison would still be concerned about the power of interest groups and possible "mischiefs of faction," especially their tendency to foster instability and injustice.

Concern about the evils of interest groups has been a recurrent theme throughout U.S. history. President Dwight Eisenhower used his Farewell Address to warn against the "military-industrial complex," the alliance of defense industries and the U.S. military formed to pursue more spending on weapons. President Ronald Reagan in his Farewell Address warned of the power of "special interests."[79]

Single-issue interest groups organized for or against particular policies—abortion, handgun control, tobacco subsidies, animal rights—have aroused increasing concern in recent years. "It is said that citizen groups organizing in ever greater numbers to push single issues ruin the careers of otherwise fine politicians who disagree with them on one emotional issue, paralyze the traditional process of governmental compromise, and ignore the common good in their selfish insistence on getting their own way."[80] But which single issues reflect narrow interests? Women's rights—even a specific issue such as sexual harassment or abortion—are hardly "narrow," women's rights leaders contend, because women represent more than half the population. These issues may seem different from those related to subsidies for dairy farmers, for example.

One of the main arguments against interest groups is that they do not represent people equally. For example, fewer interest groups represent young or low-income people than represent senior citizens or corporations. Further, some groups are better organized and better financed, allowing them a decided advantage over more general groups. And the existence of a multiplicity of interests often leads to incoherent policies, inefficiency, and delay as lawmakers try to appease conflicting interests. In addition, the propensity of interest groups to support incumbents in elections increases the advantages of incumbency, which is often seen as undesirable.

What—if anything—should we do about factions? For decades, American citizens have tried to find ways to keep interest groups in check. They have agreed with James Madison that the "remedy" of outlawing factions would be worse than the disease. It would be absurd to abolish liberty simply because it nourished faction. And the Constitution solidly protects the existence and activity of interest groups and lobbies. Moreover, interest groups provide important services. They supply needed and accurate information to government officials. But by safeguarding the value of liberty, have we allowed interest groups to threaten equality, the second great value in our national heritage? The question remains: How can we regulate interest groups in a way that does not threaten our constitutional liberties? Should we?

The United States has generally responded to this question by seeking to regulate lobbying in general and political money in particular. Concern over the use of money—especially corporate funds—to influence politicians goes back more than a century, to the administration of Ulysses S. Grant in the 1870s, when members of Congress promoted the Crédit Mobilier construction company in exchange for the right to make huge profits by buying its stock below market value. In the Progressive Era during the first two decades of the twentieth century, Congress legislated against corporate contributions in federal elections and required disclosure of the use of the money (Tillman Act, 1907 and Federal Corrupt Practices Act, 1925).[81] But federal legislation was not very effective and was loosely enforced. Many candidates filed incomplete reports or none at all. The reform mood of the 1960s and the Watergate scandal of 1972 brought basic changes. The outcome was the Federal Election Campaign Act of 1971 (FECA), amended in 1974. We discuss FECA and the more recent Bipartisan Campaign Reform Act in greater detail in the chapter on campaigns and elections.

During President Bill Clinton's first term, and after the Republicans won control of Congress in 1994, Congress passed the first major overhaul of lobbying laws since 1946. Under the Lobbying Disclosure Act of 1995, the definition of a lobbyist was expanded to include part-time lobbyists, those who deal with congressional staff or executive branch agencies, and those who represent foreign-owned companies and foreign entities. The number of registered "clients" nearly doubled eight years after

5.1

5.2

5.3

5.4

5.5

5.6

enactment of the act,[82] and more recent estimates show additional growth in numbers. The act also included specific disclosure and information requirements.

But as the 2012 election highlighted, disclosure was still incomplete or came after key election contests. For example, a group led by Republican political professionals, Crossroads GPS, spent in excess of $20 million in anti-Obama ads in 2012 without having to disclose their donors because the group ostensibly was not supporting any specific candidate.[83] The disclosure of Super PAC donors did not come in most cases until January 31, 2012, which was after the Iowa Caucuses and New Hampshire and South Carolina primaries. Participants in those contests did not know who was funding the multimillion-dollar advertising campaigns being run in their states.

More broadly, interest groups provide important opportunities for individuals to work together to pursue common objectives. Sometimes, this means that individuals join existing groups; at other times, they form new ones. Interest groups not only foster healthy competition in our politics, but they also teach important lessons about self-government. While the potential for abuse by interest groups is real, they serve critical functions in American government.

Review the Chapter

 **Listen** to **Chapter 5** on **MyPoliSciLab**

Interest Groups Past and President: The "Mischiefs of Faction"

5.1 Explain the role of interest groups and social movements in American politics, p. 139.

Interest groups form when a collection of people share similar political goals and organize to achieve them. Sometimes, these groups are based on a shared group identity, such as race, ethnicity, gender, or sexual orientation. Others are based on specific policy issues, such as reducing taxes or combating global warming. Still others claim to operate in the public interest on broad issues, such as educating voters or reducing the federal deficit. Interest groups sometimes begin as social movements, which consist of many people at the grassroots level who are interested in a significant issue, idea, or concern and take action to support or oppose it.

Types of Interest Groups

5.2 Categorize American interest groups into types, p. 141.

Interest groups can be categorized as economic, ideological or single-issue, public interest, foreign policy, and government itself. Economic groups include corporations, labor unions, and professional and trade associations; they lobby officials and campaign for candidates whose trade, tax, and regulation policies favor their perspective. Ideological groups typically pursue a single policy goal through many means; for example, the ACLU pursues civil liberties cases. Public interest groups are presumably more broadly based, including watchdog groups and charities. Foreign policy groups work to influence some area of the United States' international affairs. Finally, government groups include public sector unions and other government entities.

Characteristics and Power of Interest Groups

5.3 Analyze sources of interest group power, p. 149.

Size, resources, cohesiveness, leadership, and techniques, especially the ability to contribute to candidates and political parties and to fund lobbyists, affect interest group power. But the actual power of an interest group stems from how these elements relate to the political and governmental environment in which the interest group operates. Interest groups typically include people with many other cross-cutting interests, which both reduces and stabilizes their influence.

The Influence of Lobbyists

5.4 Describe lobbyists and the activities through which they seek to influence policy, p. 154.

Lobbyists represent organized interests before government. Lobbying involves communicating with legislators and executive-branch officials, making campaign contributions, and assisting in election activity, especially through political action committees (PACs). Interest groups also communicate their message directly to the public through mass mailings, advertising, and online media.

Money and Politics

5.5 Identify ways interest groups use money in elections and assess efforts to regulate this spending, p. 157.

Interest groups spend money to lobby government officials and to support or defeat candidates, especially through the expanded use of PACs. Groups that lack money typically struggle to get their message out to the public and fail to influence public officials.

Congress has enacted laws to regulate and reform excesses of interest groups in electoral democracy. The Federal Election Campaign Act (FECA) was passed in the 1970s in response to the Watergate scandal, and the Bipartisan Campaign Reform Act (BCRA) was passed in 2002 in response to soft money and other abuses by political parties and interest groups. Court decisions like *Citizens United* v. *FEC* have removed some of the restrictions on interest group activities during elections.

How Much Do Interest Groups Influence Elections and Legislation?

5.6 Evaluate the effectiveness of interest groups in influencing elections and legislation, p. 165.

Interest groups can be important in influencing elections. In 2004, groups helped George W. Bush by attacking John Kerry's heroism and patriotism and by promoting Bush's leadership. In more recent elections, groups were important in competitive contests and in reinforcing the electorate's tendency to reelect incumbents. The influence of groups in the legislative process is greatest when there is an absence of strong groups on the other side of the issue and when members of Congress do not have a strong constituency interest.

Learn the Terms

Study and **Review** the **Flashcards**

collective bargaining, p. 139
recall, p. 139
faction, p. 139
pluralism, p. 140
interest group, p. 140
social movement, p. 140
open shop, p. 142
closed shop, p. 142
free rider, p. 144
professional associations, p. 144
nongovernmental organization (NGO), p. 146
collective action, p. 149
public choice, p. 149
lobbying, p. 151
Federal Register, p. 151
amicus curiae brief, p. 152
Super PAC, p. 152
bundling, p. 153
lobbyist, p. 154
revolving door, p. 154
issue network, p. 154
political action committee (PAC), p. 157
leadership PAC, p. 160
Bipartisan Campaign Reform Act (BCRA), p. 160
soft money, p. 161
independent expenditures, p. 163
issue advocacy, p. 164
527 organization, p. 164

Test Yourself

Study and **Review** the **Practice Tests**

MULTIPLE CHOICE QUESTIONS

5.1 Explain the role of interest groups and social movements in American politics.

The Bill of Rights protects social movements by supporting all of the following rights, except

a. freedom of assembly.
b. free speech.
c. freedom of religion.
d. due process of law.
e. the right to bear arms.

5.2 Categorize American interest groups into types.

A firm lobbying for fewer regulations on airplane travel would be an example of a/an

a. public interest group.
b. trade association.
c. economic interest group.
d. local government group.
e. foreign policy group.

5.3 Analyze sources of interest group power.

Though single-issue groups might have fewer members than more general public interest groups, they do benefit from

a. superior leadership.
b. larger geographic spread.
c. greater monetary contributions.
d. group cohesion.
e. greater variation in membership.

5.4 Describe lobbyists and the activities through which they seek to influence policy.

PACs that collect contributions from a number of individuals and present them as a single package to a candidate engage in the practice of

a. targeting.
b. bundling.
c. giving soft money.
d. influence peddling.
e. influencing legislation.

5.5 Identify ways interest groups use money in elections and assess efforts to regulate this spending.

According to the U.S. Supreme Court's decision in *Citizens United* v. *FEC*, regulations on spending from unions' and corporations' general treasuries violated

a. the organizations' freedom of speech.
b. soft money rules.
c. the doctrine of independent expenditures.
d. bundling rules.
e. the organizations' right to use general funds for election-specific ads.

5.6 Evaluate the effectiveness of interest groups in influencing elections and legislation.

According to James Madison, ending the role of interest groups in U.S. government would require

a. strict spending limits.
b. removing liberty.
c. ending independent expenditures.
d. regular contribution disclosures.
e. outlawing factions.

ESSAY QUESTION

In a short essay, compare and contrast the three sources of interest group power: size, cohesiveness, and leadership. In your answer, provide an example of at least one group that exhibits each of the three sources and assess how and why it uses that power to influence national policy.

Explore Further

IN THE LIBRARY

Frank R. Baumgartner, *Lobbying and Policy Change: Who wins, Who Loses, and Why* (University of Chicago Press, 2009).

Jeffrey H. Birnbaum, *The Money Men: The Real Story of Fund-Raising's Influence on Political Power in America* (Crown, 2000).

Allan J. Cigler and Burdett A. Loomis, eds., *Interest Group Politics*, 8th ed. (CQ Press, 2011).

Martha A. Derthick, *Up in Smoke*, 3rd ed. (CQ Press, 2011).

Kenneth M. Goldstein, *Interest Groups, Lobbying, and Participation in America* (Cambridge University Press, 1999).

Gene Grossman and Elhanan Helpman, *Special Interest Politics* (MIT Press, 2001).

Paul S. Herrnson, Ronald G. Shaiko, and Clyde Wilcox, *The Interest Group Connection: Electioneering, Lobbying, and Policymaking in Washington*, 2nd ed. revised (CQ Press, 2005).

Kevin W. Hula, *Lobbying Together: Interest Group Coalitions in Legislative Politics* (Georgetown University Press, 1999).

David B. Magleby, *The Change Election* (Temple University Press, 2010).

David B. Magleby and Anthony D. Corrado, eds., *Financing the 2008 Election* (Brookings Institution Press).

Anthony J. Nownes, *Total Lobbying: What Lobbyists Want (and How They Try to Get It)* (Cambridge University Press, 2006).

Mancur Olson, *The Logic of Collective Action* (Harvard University Press, 1965).

Mark J. Rozell, Clyde Wilcox, and Michael M. Franz, eds., *Interest Groups in American Campaigns: The New Face of Electioneering*, 3rd ed. revised (Oxford University Press, 2011).

David Vogel, *Kindred Strangers: The Uneasy Relationship Between Politics and Business in America* (Princeton University Press, 1996).

Jack L. Walker, Jr., *Mobilizing Interest Groups in America: Patrons, Professions, and Social Movements* (University of Michigan Press, 1991).

ON THE WEB

www.fec.gov

The Federal Election Commission site provides information on elections, campaign finance, parties, voting, and PACs.

www.pirg.org

This is the Web site of the Public Interest Research Group (PIRG); this group has chapters on many college campuses. PIRG provides state-by-state policy and other information.

www.townhall.com

This Web site of the American Conservative Union (ACU) provides policy and political information.

www.adaction.org

The Web site of the American for Democratic Action provides information and ratings on members of Congress.

Listen to Chapter 6 on MyPoliSciLab

6

Political Parties

Essential to Democracy

Some years ago, a community college district in Los Angeles held a nonpartisan election for its trustees in which any registered voter could run if he or she paid the $50 filing fee and gathered 500 valid signatures on a petition. Each voter could cast up to seven votes. Political parties were not allowed to nominate candidates, and party labels did not appear on the ballot. In addition, because the community college district was newly created, none of the candidates was incumbents. As a result, incumbency—another frequently used voting cue—was also absent. A total of 133 candidates ran, and they were listed alphabetically.

So how do people vote in an election without parties? Party labels typically help voters get a sense for the candidates; without knowing anything about the individual candidate, voters can make reliable assumptions about the candidate's stance on issues based on his or her political party. Based on the results of the election, having a Mexican American surname seemed to be an advantage. Those whose names began with the letters A to F did better than those later in the alphabet. Having a well-known name also helped. One of the winners, E. G. "Jerry" Brown Jr., was the son of a former governor. Winning this election launched his political career; later he was elected California governor in 1975 and then again in 2010. Endorsements by the *Los Angeles Times* also influenced the outcome, as did campaigning by a conservative group.

Clearly, parties play an important role in facilitating voting by organizing elections and simplifying choices. Rarely are American voters asked to choose from among 133 candidates. E. E. Schattschneider, a noted political scientist, once said, "The political parties created democracy, and modern democracy is unthinkable save in terms of the parties."[1] This view that parties are essential to democracy runs counter to a long-standing and deeply seated distrust of parties. But without parties, voters would face the daunting challenge of choosing between scores of candidates for each office, as happened in Los Angeles. They would need to research the policy positions of each individual candidate in order to make an educated choice.

6.1

Identify the primary functions of parties in democracies and distinguish the U.S. party system from those in European democracies, p. 175.

6.2

Describe changes in American political parties and identify four realigning elections, p. 182.

6.3

Evaluate the functions of parties as institutions, parties in government, and parties in the electorate, p. 187.

6.4

Explain party fund-raising and expenditures, and assess their regulation, p. 196.

6.5

Assess the effects of recent party reforms and the long-term prospects for the current party system, p. 197.

Republican presidential candidate Mitt Romney, right, and his vice presidential running mate Representative Paul Ryan, R-Wis., left, campaigning down to the wire on Sunday, Oct. 28, 2012, in hard-fought Ohio.

The Big Picture Find out why the saying, "Americans vote for the person, not the party" is simply not true. Author David B. Magleby explains the organizing role that partisanship plays in American government, as well as its ability to simplify campaign messages and political processes for citizens.

The Basics Why do we have political parties in America? In this video, you will learn about the rise of political parties in the United States, the reasons why the two-party system continues to dominate American politics, and how the major parties differ from one another.

In Context Trace the development of political parties in the United States from the time of the ratification of the Constitution. Oklahoma State University political scientist Jeanette M. Mendez explains why political parties emerged and what role they play in our democratic system.

Thinking Like a Political Scientist How can we tell that Americans are increasingly polarized and what are the implications of this trend? In this video, Oklahoma State University political scientist Jeanette M. Mendez reveals how scholars measure party polarization at the elite and mass level and who is behind this phenomenon.

In the Real World Why do Americans only have two party choices—Democrats and Republicans? Real people evaluate the effectiveness of the "winner takes all" electoral system in the United States, and they weigh in on whether third parties—such as the Libertarians and the Green Party—should have more representation in national elections.

So What? How permeable are America's political parties? Using the examples of young Democrats in the 2008 election and The Tea Party, author David B. Magleby emphasizes the power that party members have to change their organization's values and priorities.

Parties are both a consequence of democracy and an instrument of it. They serve many functions, including narrowing the choices for voters and making national and state elections work.[2] American voters take for granted the peaceful transfer of power from one elected official to another and from one party to another, yet in new democracies where holding power may be more important than democratic principles, the peaceful transfer of power after an election is often a problem. Well-established parties help stabilize democracy.

This chapter begins by examining why parties are so vital to the functioning of democracy. We then examine the evolution of American political parties. Although U.S. political parties have changed over time, they remain important in three different settings: as institutions, in government, and in the electorate. We will look at the way parties facilitate democracy in all three. Finally, we discuss the strength of parties today and the prospects for party reform and renewal.

political party
An organization that seeks political power by electing people to office so that its positions and philosophy become public policy.

nonpartisan election
An election in which candidates are not selected or endorsed by political parties, and party affiliation is not listed on ballots.

What Parties Do for Democracy

6.1 Identify the primary functions of parties in democracies and distinguish the U.S. party system from those in European democracies.

merican political parties serve a variety of political and social functions, some well and others not so well. The way they perform them differs across time and place.

☐ Party Functions

Political parties play an important role in organizing elections, simplifying choices for voters, and helping elect people who will help their party's positions and philosophy become public policy.

ORGANIZE THE COMPETITION Parties exist primarily as an organizing mechanism to win elections and thus win control of government. They recruit and nominate candidates for office; register and activate voters; and help candidates by training them, raising money for them, providing them with research and voter lists, and enlisting volunteers to work for them.[3]

However, not all elections allow candidates to identify their party. Most local and judicial elections are **nonpartisan elections**, which gives parties little opportunity to influence the outcome. Advocates of nonpartisan elections contend that partisanship is not relevant to being a good judge, mayor, or school board member. Lacking a party cue as a simplifying device, voters turn to name familiarity of candidates or other simplifying devices like incumbency. These local elections are also often held at times other than when state or federal elections are held. As a result, fewer voters tend to turn out for nonpartisan elections than for standard partisan elections.[4]

UNIFY THE ELECTORATE Parties are often accused of creating conflict, but they actually help unify the electorate and moderate conflict, at least within the party. Parties have a strong incentive to resolve their internal differences and come together to take on the opposition. Moreover, to win elections, parties need to reach out to voters outside their party and gain their support. This action also helps unify the electorate, at least into the two large national political parties in the American system.

Parties have great difficulty building coalitions on controversial issues such as birth control, abortion, or gun control. Not surprisingly, candidates and parties generally try to avoid defining themselves or the election in single-issue terms. Rather, they hope that if voters disagree with the party's stand on one issue, they will still support it because they agree on other issues.

6.1

6.2

6.3

6.4

6.5

patronage
The dispensing of government jobs to persons who belong to the winning political party.

Political parties help inform and motivate voters. Here, a senior and political science major at Western Kentucky University makes calls from the local Republican Party headquarters urging voters to support GOP candidates.

ORGANIZE THE GOVERNMENT Political parties in the United States are important when it comes to organizing state and national governments. Congress is organized along party lines: the party with the most votes in each chamber elects the officers of that chamber, selects committee chairs, and has a majority on all the committees. State legislatures, except Nebraska, are also organized along party lines. The 2010 election returned the Republicans to a majority in the House; the Democrats retained a slim 3-seat majority in the Senate. Before the 2012 election it was expected that the Democrats would lose Senate seats because of the large number of Democrats up for reelection and retirements on both sides. But two Republicans' widely publicized statements about rape hurt their campaigns. Democrats gained two seats, bringing their Senate majority to 55 to 45. There was little change in the House; here Republicans retained their majority.

The party that controls the White House, the governor's mansion, or city hall gets **patronage**, which means its leaders can select party members as public officials or judges. Such appointments are limited only by civil service regulations that restrict patronage typically to the top posts, but these posts, which number approximately 3,000 in the federal government (not including ambassadors, U.S. Marshals, and U.S. Attorneys), are also numerous at the state and local levels. Patronage provides an incentive for people to become engaged in politics and gives party leaders and elected politicians loyal partisans in key positions to help them achieve their policy objectives. Patronage, sometimes called the *spoils system*, has declined dramatically in importance due to civil service reform, which we discuss later in this chapter and in the chapter on the bureaucracy and policy.

MAKE POLICY One of the great strengths of our democracy is that even the party that wins an election usually has to moderate what it does to win reelection. Public policy seldom changes dramatically after elections. Nonetheless, the party that wins the election has a chance to enact its policies and campaign promises.

American parties have had only limited success in setting the course of national policy, especially compared to countries with strong parties. The European model of party government, which has been called a *responsible party system*, assumes that parties discipline their members through their control over nominations and campaigns. Officeholders in such party-centered systems are expected to act according to party wishes and vote along party lines—or they will not be allowed to run again under the party label, generally preventing their reelection. Candidates also run on fairly specific party platforms and are expected to implement them if they win control in the election.

Because American parties do not control nominations, they are less able to discipline members who express views contrary to those of the party.[5] The American system is largely *candidate centered*; politicians are nominated largely on the basis of their qualifications and personal appeal, not party loyalty. In fact, it is more correct to say that in most contests, we have *candidate* politics rather than *party* politics. As a consequence, party leaders cannot guarantee passage of their program, even if they are in the majority.

PROVIDE LOYAL OPPOSITION The party out of power closely monitors and comments on the actions of the party in power, providing accountability. When national security is at issue or the country is under attack, parties restrain their criticism, as the Democrats in Congress did for some time after September 11, 2001. There is usually a polite interval following an election—known as the **honeymoon**—after which the opposition party begins to criticize the party that controls the White House, especially when the opposition controls one or both houses of Congress.[6] The length of the honeymoon depends, in part, on how close the vote was in the election, on how contentious the agenda of the new administration is, and on the leadership skills of the new president. Honeymoons have grown shorter throughout the past few decades as candidates from the president's own party and the opposition party get ready for the next presidential election. This puts pressure on the new president to move quickly to set the legislative agenda. Early success in enacting policy can prolong the honeymoon; mistakes or controversies can shorten it.

honeymoon
The period at the beginning of a new president's term during which the president enjoys generally positive relations with the press and Congress, usually lasting about six months.

caucus
A meeting of local party members to choose party officials or candidates for public office and to decide the platform.

party convention
A meeting of party delegates to vote on matters of policy and, in some cases, to select party candidates for public office.

direct primary
An election in which voters choose party nominees.

☐ The Nomination of Candidates

From the beginning, parties have been the mechanism by which candidates for public office are chosen, although parties have used various means to choose candidates.

THE CAUCUS The **caucus** played an important part in pre-Revolutionary politics and continued to be important in our early history as elected officials organized themselves into groups or parties and together selected candidates to run for higher office, including the presidency. This method of nomination operated for several decades after the United States was established.

As early as the 1820s, however, critics were making charges of "secret deals." Moreover, the caucus was not representative of people from areas where a party was in a minority or nonexistent, as only officeholders took part in it. The *mixed caucus* was an effort to make the caucus more representative of rank-and-file party members. It brought in delegates from districts in which the party had no elected legislators.

THE PARTY CONVENTION During the 1830s and 1840s, a system of **party conventions** was instituted. Delegates, usually chosen directly by party members in towns and cities, selected the party candidates, debated and adopted a platform, and built party spirit by celebrating noisily. But the convention method soon was criticized as being controlled by the party bosses and their machines. To draw more voters and reduce the power of the bosses, states adopted the **direct primary**, in which people could vote for the party's nominees for office. As a result, delegates have little freedom to change their votes during the convention, especially at the national level.

THE DIRECT PRIMARY Primaries spread rapidly after Wisconsin adopted them in 1905—in the North, as a Progressive Era reform, and in the South, as a way to bring democracy to a region that had seen no meaningful general elections since the end of Reconstruction in the 1870s because of one-party Democratic rule. By 1920, direct primaries were the norm for some offices in nearly all states.

Today, the direct primary is the typical method of picking party candidates. Primaries vary significantly from state to state. They differ in terms of (1) who may run in a primary and how he or she qualifies for the ballot; (2) whether the party

6.1

6.2

6.3

6.4

6.5

open primary
A primary election in which any voter, regardless of party, may vote.

crossover voting
Voting by a member of one party for a candidate of another party.

closed primary
A primary election in which only persons registered in the party holding the primary may vote.

organization can or does endorse candidates before the primary; (3) who may vote in a party's primary—that is, whether a voter must register with a party to vote in that party's primary; and (4) how many votes are needed for nomination—the most votes (a plurality), more than 50 percent (a majority), or some other number determined by party rule or state law. The differences among primaries are not trivial; they have an important impact on the role played by party organizations and on the strategy used by candidates.

In states with **open primaries**, any voter, regardless of party, can participate in the primary of whichever party he or she chooses. This kind of primary permits **crossover voting**—Republicans and Independents helping to determine whom the Democratic nominee will be, and vice versa. Other states use **closed primaries**, in which only persons already registered in that party may participate. Some states, such as Washington and California, experimented with *blanket primaries*, in which all voters could vote for any candidate, regardless of party. They could vote for a candidate of one party for one office and for a candidate from another party for another office, something not permitted under either closed or open primaries. But, in 2000, upon challenge from the California Democratic Party, the Supreme Court held that the blanket primary violated its members' free association rights.[7] In 2010 and 2012 California voters invented another new form of primary voting when they overwhelmingly passed an initiative to allow voters to cast their primary ballot for a candidate from any party, with the top two vote getters then running in the general election. Proponents of the "top two vote getter" primary see it as fostering more moderate politics.[8]

Along with modern communications and fund-raising techniques, direct primaries have diminished the influence of leaders of political parties. Many critics believe this change has had some undesirable consequences. Party leaders now have less influence over who gets to be the party's candidate, and candidates are less accountable to the party both during and after the election.

LOCAL CAUCUSES Direct primaries nominate most party candidates for most offices. Yet in some states, local caucuses choose delegates to attend regional meetings, which in turn select delegates to state and national conventions where they nominate party candidates for offices. In 2012, more than a dozen states used caucuses to determine delegates for the presidential nominations.[9] The Iowa and Maine GOP presidential caucuses had

Iowa's Democratic caucus is an unwieldy and complex process. Here, a precinct captain takes a head count to determine support for various candidates.

6.1

6.2

6.3

6.4

6.5

The Global Community

A Competitive Two-Party System

Having a competitive two-party system is something that citizens of the United States take for granted, but not all countries place the same level of importance on it. In the Pew Research Center's 2002 Spring Global Attitudes Survey respondents were asked, "How important is it to you to live in a country where honest elections are held regularly with a choice of at least two political parties?"

Respondents from the United States were most likely to say that being able to choose from at least two political parties was very important, with 84 percent giving this response. In contrast, only 43 percent of respondents from Korea gave this answer, and nearly two-thirds in India thought a choice of at least two political parties is very important. Mexico, a country governed by one party for many years, also had two-thirds of respondents thinking a choice between two parties is very important.

Germany, like many countries in Europe, has a strong party system and more than two competitive parties and had a similar pattern of opinion to the United States on the importance of a two-party system.

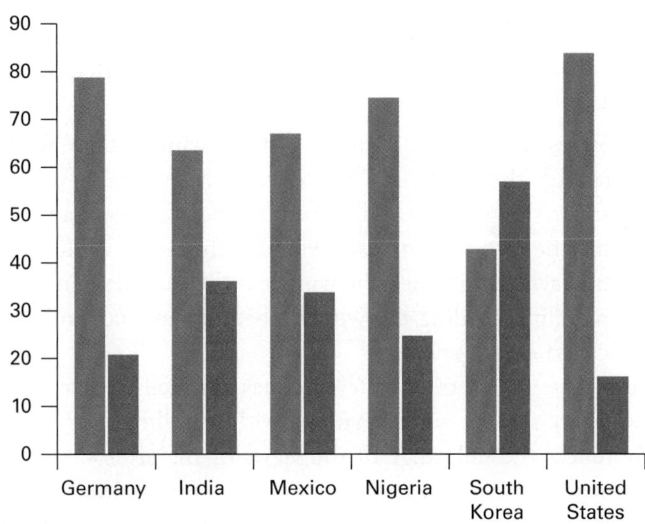

SOURCE: Data for Germany, South Korea, and the United States came from the Pew Research Center's 2002 Spring Global Attitudes Survey. Data for India, Mexico, and Nigeria came from the Pew Research Center's 2008 Global Attitudes Survey. Because not all countries were included in the 2009 survey, we have included responses from the most recent survey for that country.

CRITICAL THINKING QUESTIONS

1. What factors do you think explain people's belief that having a choice between at least two political parties is important?
2. When Hitler rose to power in Germany, the German two-party system was replaced with a dominant single party. To what extent do you think that experience influences the attitudes of Germans toward a competitive two-party system today?
3. South Korea is a neighbor to North Korea, one of the few remaining single-party states. Given this, why do you think South Koreans are not more inclined to see a competitive two-party system as very important?

6.1

6.2

6.3

6.4

6.5

minor party
A small political party that persists over time that is often composed of ideologies on the right or left, or centered on a charismatic candidate. Such a party is also called a *third party*.

proportional representation
An election system in which each party running receives the proportion of legislative seats corresponding to its proportion of the vote.

winner-take-all system
An election system in which the candidate with the most votes wins.

higher turnout in 2012 than in 2008. Democratic participation in primaries and caucuses was down in 2012 compared to 2008, in large part because President Obama ran unopposed. Republican participation in some states was also lower in 2012.[10]

☐ Party Systems

Although the United States has had several **minor parties**, only the two major parties have much of a chance to win elections. Multiparty systems are almost always found in countries that have a parliamentary government, in contrast to our presidential system.

Parliamentary systems usually have a *head of state*, often called the president, but they also have a *head of the government*, often called the prime minister or chancellor, who is the leader of one of the large parties in the legislature.

Parliamentary democracies often operate with multiparty systems. These systems often have fierce competition among many parties for even small numbers of seats, because winners are determined through **proportional representation**, in which the parties receive a proportion of the legislators corresponding to their share of the vote. Even small percentages of votes can produce enough seats to give a party bargaining power in forming a coalition to run government. Minor parties can gain concessions—positions in a cabinet or support of policies they want implemented—in return for joining a coalition. Major parties need the minor parties and are therefore willing to bargain. Thus, the multiparty system favors the existence of minor parties by giving them incentives to persevere and disproportionate power if they will help form a government.

The United States has a single-member district, **winner-take-all system**, where only the candidate with the most votes in a district or state takes office.[11] Because a party does not gain anything by finishing second, minor parties in a two-party system can rarely overcome the assumption that a vote for them is a wasted vote.[12] For this reason, in an election system in which the winner is the candidate in a single-member district with the plurality deciding the winner, there is tendency to have two parties. This regularity is called *Duverger's law*.[13]

In multiparty systems, parties at the extremes are likely to have more influence than in our two-party system, and in nations with a multiparty system, legislatures more accurately reflect the full range of the views of the electorate. In contrast, our two-party system tends to create *centrist* parties that appeal to moderate elements and suppress the views of extremists in the electorate. Moreover, once elected, our parties do not form as cohesive a voting bloc as ideological parties do in multiparty systems.

German Chancellor Angela Merkel is from the Christian Democratic Union (CDU) Party, which has a majority in the Bundestag (Parliament) thanks to an alliance with two other parties. Merkel has been under pressure domestically not to go too far in assisting the European Union's struggling economies and under international pressure to be as supportive of them as possible.

Multiparty parliamentary systems often make governments unstable as coalitions form and collapse. In addition, swings in policy when party control changes can be dramatic. In contrast, two-party systems produce governments that tend to be stable and centrist, and as a result, policy changes occur incrementally.

☐ Minor Parties: Persistence and Frustration

Although we have a two-party system in the United States, we also have minor parties, sometimes called *third parties.* Candidate-based parties that arise around a candidate usually disappear when the charismatic personality does. In most states, candidates can get their names on the ballot as an Independent or minor-party candidate by securing the required number of signatures on a nomination petition. This is hard to do.

Minor parties that are organized around an ideology usually persist over a longer time than those built around a particular leader. Communist, Prohibition, Libertarian, Right to Life, and Green parties are of the ideological type. Minor parties of both types come and go, and several minor parties usually run in any given election. Some parties arise around a single issue, like the Right to Life Party active in some states like New York. The Green Party is another example of an ideological third party. Although they are occasionally visible, minor parties have never won the presidency (see Table 6.1) or more than a handful of congressional seats.[14] They have done only somewhat better in gubernatorial elections.[15] They have never shaped national policy from *inside* the government, and their influence on national policy and on the platforms of the two major parties has been limited.[16] Minor parties operating in recent elections include the Libertarian, Green, and Reform parties.

TABLE 6.1 MINOR PARTIES IN THE UNITED STATES

Year	Party	Presidential Candidate	Percentage of Popular Vote Received	Electoral Votes
1832	Anti-Masonic	William Wirt	8	7
1856	American (Know-Nothing)	Millard Fillmore	22	8
1860	Democratic (Secessionist)	John C. Breckinridge	18	72
1860	Constitutional Union	John Bell	13	39
1892	People's (Populist)	James B. Weaver	9	22
1912	Bull Moose	Theodore Roosevelt	27	88
1912	Socialist	Eugene V. Debs	6	0
1924	Progressive	Robert M. La Follette	17	13
1948	States' Rights (Dixiecrat)	Strom Thurmond	2	39
1948	Progressive	Henry A. Wallace	2	0
1968	American Independent	George C. Wallace	14	46
1980	National Unity	John Anderson	7	0
1992	Independent	Ross Perot	19	0
1996	Reform	Ross Perot	8	0
2000	Reform	Pat Buchanan	0	0
2000	Green	Ralph Nader	3	0
2004	Reform	Ralph Nader	0	0
2008	Independent	Ralph Nader	0	0
2012	Libertarian	Gary Johnson	1	0

NOTE: Only includes parties that received electoral votes at least once, or more than 3 percent of the popular vote at least once.

■ *How does the percentage of popular vote received compare to the electoral votes received? How can you explain the difference in these numbers?*

SOURCE: C.Q. Press Voting and Elections Collection, 2010, http://library.cqpress.com/elections/search.php.

You Will Decide

Is a Vote for a Third-Party Candidate with Little Chance of Winning a Wasted Vote?

In several close elections, including the 2000 presidential election, the vote cast for one or another minor party, if cast for the likely second choice of those voters, would have changed the outcome of the election. Ralph Nader, for example, received 92,241 votes in Florida; if 537 of them had been cast for Al Gore and none for George Bush, Gore would have won the election. This may have also been true in the 2009 special election in New York's 23rd Congressional District, where the Conservative candidate Douglas Hoffman and Republican Dede Scozzafava together got more than 52 percent of the vote, but neither candidate could match the 48 percent of the vote the Democrat, Bill Owens, received. In such a situation, should voters care more about influencing who wins an election or more about casting a vote for a candidate whose views are closest to their own, even if that candidate has little chance of winning?

What do you think? Should voters ever cast votes for third-party candidates who have little chance of winning? What arguments would you make for or against your position?

Thinking It Through

How you answer this question depends on what you want to accomplish with your vote. Those who see the vote as a largely symbolic exercise will likely vote for a minor party candidate with little chance of winning. The problem is that the more electable candidate who is clearly preferred over the other more competitive alternative may not win office at all if a voter does not consider electability. The winner-take-all system makes this trade-off more consequential. In a system in which proportional representation is possible, a voter is more likely to be able to translate policy preferences into a vote for representatives. But in our system, voters must often vote for their second choice in order to avoid letting their third choice win office. Interest groups, like environmental groups, often find themselves not endorsing a minor party candidate who may be closer to their views because they want to avoid helping to elect a competitive alternative candidate whose views they abhor.

One way to lessen the influence of these candidates is to require a runoff election of the top two vote getters if no candidate receives a majority. Although this would force another election in some instances, it would also force people who vote to decide among the more viable options. A counterargument is that many people who support minor party candidates would opt out of an election without this chance to express their preferences, and so such a runoff is already accomplished with the plurality-winner system we now have.

CRITICAL THINKING QUESTIONS

1. Was a vote for someone other than Bush or Gore in 2000 a wasted vote? Why or why not?
2. What are some issues a minor party might push that would affect the major parties, even if the minor party does not win an election?
3. What are the obstacles minor parties' face that major parties do not?

A Brief History of American Political Parties

6.2 Describe changes in American political parties and identify four realigning elections.

To the founders of the young Republic, parties meant bigger, better-organized, and fiercer factions, which they did not want. Benjamin Franklin worried about the "infinite mutual abuse of parties, tearing to pieces the best of characters." In his Farewell Address, George Washington warned against the "baneful effects of the Spirit of Party." And Thomas Jefferson said, "If I could not go to heaven but with a party, I would not go there at all."[17]

How, then, did parties start?

☐ The Nation's First Parties

Political parties emerged largely out of practical necessity. The same early leaders who so frequently stated their opposition to them also recognized the need to organize officeholders who shared their views so that government could act. In 1787, parties began to form as citizens debated ratifying the U.S. Constitution. To get Congress to pass its measures, the Washington administration had to fashion a coalition among factions. This job fell to Treasury secretary Alexander Hamilton, who built an informal Federalist party, while Washington stayed "above politics."

Secretary of State Jefferson and other officials, many of whom despised Hamilton and his aristocratic ways as much as they opposed the policies he favored, were uncertain about how to deal with these political differences. Their overriding concern was the success of the new government; personal loyalty to Washington was a close second. Despite his opposition to Washington's policies, Jefferson stayed in the cabinet through most of the first term. When he left the cabinet at the end of 1793, many who joined him in opposition to the administration's economic policies remained in Congress, forming a group of legislators opposed to Federalist fiscal policies and eventually to Federalist foreign policy, which appeared "soft on Britain." This party was later known as Republicans, then as Democratic-Republicans, and finally as Democrats.[18]

realigning election
An election during periods of expanded suffrage and change in the economy and society that proves to be a turning point, redefining the agenda of politics and the alignment of voters within parties.

☐ Realigning Elections

American political parties have evolved and changed over time, but some underlying characteristics have been constant. Historically, we have had a two-party system with minor parties. Our parties are moderate and accommodative, meaning they are open to people with diverse outlooks. Political scientist V. O. Key and others have argued that our party system has been shaped in large part by **realigning elections**. Also called *critical elections*, these turning points define the agenda of politics and the alignment of voters within parties during periods of historic change in the economy and society.

Realigning elections are characterized by intense voter involvement, disruptions of traditional voting patterns, changes in the relationships of power within the broader political community, and the formation of new and durable electoral groupings. They have occurred cyclically, about every 32 years, and tend to coincide with expansions of suffrage or changes in the rate of voting.[19] Political scientists generally agree that there have been four realigning elections in American party history: 1824, 1860, 1896, and 1932. Although some argued that the United States was due for another in the 1970s and 1980s,[20] there is little evidence that such an election occurred or is likely in the immediate future.

1824: ANDREW JACKSON AND THE DEMOCRATS Party politics was invigorated following the election of 1824, in which the leader in the popular vote—the hero of the battle of New Orleans in the War of 1812, Democrat Andrew Jackson—failed to achieve the necessary majority of the electoral college and was defeated by John Quincy Adams in the runoff election in the House of Representatives. Jackson, brilliantly aided by Martin Van Buren, a veteran party builder in New York State, later knitted together a winning combination of regions, interest groups, and political doctrines to win the presidency in 1828. The Whigs succeeded the Federalists as the opposition party. By the time Van Buren, another Democrat, followed Jackson in the White House in 1837, the Democrats had become a large, nationwide movement with national and state leadership, a clear party doctrine, and a grassroots organization. The Whigs were nearly as strong: in 1840, they put their own man, General William Henry Harrison ("Old Tippecanoe"), into the White House. A two-party system had been born.

1860: THE CIVIL WAR AND THE RISE OF THE REPUBLICANS Out of the crisis over slavery evolved the second Republican Party—the first being the National Republican Party that existed for barely a decade in the 1820s. The second Republican Party ultimately adopted the nickname "Grand Old Party" (GOP).[21] Abraham Lincoln was elected in 1860 with the support not only of financiers, industrialists, and merchants but also of many workers and farmers. For 50 years after 1860, the Republican coalition won every presidential race except for Grover Cleveland's victories in 1884 and 1892. The Democratic Party survived with its durable white-male base in the South.

1896: A PARTY IN TRANSITION Economic changes, including industrialization and hard times for farmers, led to changes in the Republican Party in the late 1800s.[22] Some Republicans insisted on maintaining their Reconstruction policies into the 1890s until it became obvious it would jeopardize their electoral base.[23] A combination of western and southern farmers and mining interests sought an alliance with workers in the East and Midwest to "recapturing America from the foreign moneyed interests responsible for industrialization. The crisis of industrialization squarely placed an agrarian-fundamentalist view of life against an industrial-progressive view...."[24] William Jennings Bryan, the Democratic candidate for president in 1896, was a talented orator but lost the race to William McKinley.[25] The 1896 realignment differs from the others, however, in that the party in power did not change hands. In that sense, it was a *converting realignment* because it reinforced the Republican majority status that had been in place since 1860.[26]

The Progressive Era, the first two decades of the twentieth century, produced a wave of political reform led by the Progressive wing of the Republican Party. Much of the agenda of the Progressives focused on the corrupt political parties. Civil service reforms shifted some of the patronage out of the hands of party officials. The direct primary election took control of nominations from party leaders and gave it to the rank-and-file. In addition, a number of cities instituted nonpartisan governments, totally eliminating the role of a party.

Equally important, the progressive era produced major changes in political power. In 1913, voters won the right to choose their senators through popular vote under the Seventeenth Amendment to the Constitution; in 1920, women won the right to vote under the Nineteenth Amendment. Thus, in a short time, the electorate changed, the rules changed, and even the stakes of the game changed. Democrats were unable to build a durable winning coalition during this time and remained the minority party until the early 1930s, when the Great Depression overwhelmed the Republican Hoover administration.[27]

1932: FRANKLIN ROOSEVELT AND THE NEW DEAL ALIGNMENT The 1932 election was a turning point in U.S. politics. In the 1930s, the United States faced a devastating economic collapse. Between 1929 and 1932, the gross national product fell more than 10 percent per year, and unemployment rose from 1.5 million to more than 12 million, with millions more working only part time.[28]

With the economic crisis deepening, Franklin D. Roosevelt and the Democrats were swept into office in 1932 on a tide of anti-Hoover and anti-Republican sentiment. Roosevelt promised that his response to the Depression would be a "New Deal for America." After a century of sporadic government action, the New Dealers fundamentally altered the relationship between government and society by providing government jobs for the unemployed and using government expenditures to stimulate economic growth.

The dividing line between Republicans and Democrats was the role of government in the economy. Roosevelt Democrats argued that the government had to act to pull the country out of the Depression. Republicans objected to enlarging the scope of government and intruding into the economy. This basic disagreement about whether

The 1932 election is seen as a "critical election" resulting in an enduring realignment. Franklin Roosevelt and the Democrats enlarged the role of government in response to the Great Depression. Roosevelt is seen here greeting farmers in Georgia in October 1932 as he campaigned for the presidency.

the national government should play an active role in regulating and promoting our economy remains one of the most important divisions between the Democratic and Republican parties today, although with time, the country and both parties accepted many of the New Deal programs.

divided government
Governance divided between the parties, as when one holds the presidency and the other controls one or both houses of Congress.

☐ The Last Half Century

Major shifts in party demographics have occurred in recent decades. The once "Solid South" that Democrats could count on to bolster their legislative majorities and help win the White House has now become the "Republican South" in presidential elections and increasingly in congressional elections as well. Republican congressional leaders have often been from southern states that once rarely elected Republicans. This shift is explained by the movement of large numbers of white people out of the Democratic Party, in part because of the party's position on civil rights but also because of national Democrats' stand on abortion and other social issues. The rise of the Republican South reinforced the shift to conservatism in the GOP. This shift, combined with the diminished ranks of conservative southern Democrats, made the Democratic Party, especially the congressional Democrats, more unified and more liberal than in the days when more of its congressional members had "safe" southern seats.[29]

Since 1953, **divided government**, with one party controlling Congress and the other the White House, has been in effect twice as long as united government, in which one party controls both legislative and executive branches. At other times, Congress has had divided control with one party having a majority in the House and the other in the Senate. Although there have been significant periods of unified party control of government during the past half century, they have been more volatile and short-lived than earlier realignments.

The current system of party identification is built on a foundation of the New Deal and the critical election of 1932, events that took place more than three-quarters of a century ago. How can events so removed from the present still shape our party system?

6.1

6.2

6.3

6.4

6.5

FOR the People Government's Greatest Endeavors

Secret Ballots

The means by which people vote matters. We take for granted that voters cast their ballots in secret with no one seeing or knowing how we voted, but this has not always been the case. For most of the first century of U.S. history, ballots were not provided by the government, but printed by the parties on different colored paper or distributed in partisan newspapers. In this system, voters turned in their ballots and observers knew how they voted, making it possible for parties to reward or punish individuals based on how they voted. Other voting systems in our early history included voting orally or casting a pebble or bean into a hat.*

Australia was the first country to adopt secret ballots in 1857; the trend later spread to other English-speaking countries and was first proposed in the United States in 1882. An article by Henry George, a writer and politician, published in the *North American Review*, argued that the secret ballot would prevent the bribery or intimidation of voters fostered by the party ballot system. Opponents of the reform contended that state printed ballots distributed at voting places would take too long, resulting in long lines, and would cost the taxpayers too much money.† Massachusetts was the first state to adopt the system in 1888 and by 1896, all but six states were using secret ballots.

Different states adopted different formats for their ballots. Some organized the ballots by party, others by office. The organization of the ballot can be important in fostering more or less partisan voting. Later, some states permitted voters to vote via machines and today, many states use electronic voting machines. How people vote in other types of elections, like whether or not to unionize, has generated controversy in recent years. But providing, at state expense, voting systems that protect the privacy of the act of voting is now taken for granted.

QUESTIONS

1. **Why might parties have been opposed to using the Australian ballot system in the United States?**
2. **What are the advantages and disadvantages of paper and electronic ballots?**
3. **How can ballot organization affect outcomes?**

*Jill Lepore, "Rock, Paper, Scissors: How We Used to Vote," *The New Yorker*, October 13, 2008, http://www.newyorker.com/reporting/2008/10/13/ 081013fa_fact_lepore (accessed March 29, 2010).

†Ibid.

When will there be another realignment—an election that dramatically changes the voters' partisan identification? Or has such a realignment already occurred? The question is frequently debated. Most scholars believe that we have not experienced a major realignment since 1932.[30]

Elections during the past few decades have seen power change hands many times without any long-term shifts in the population in party allegiance. There has been some sorting, with Southern whites now more consistently Republican, African Americans more consistently Democratic, and Hispanics increasingly Democratic. But the fundamental party divide has remained remarkably stable. Could 2008 have been the long-awaited realigning election or at least the beginning of a realigning era? The answer is not yet clear. On the one hand, the number of registered voters expanded steadily during the 2008 election, suggesting high levels of voter interest. In addition, participation in the primary elections also grew dramatically as more than 1-in-10 voters in 2008 were first-time voters. On the other hand, the 2008 election produced an immediate backlash among conservative voters that later became known as the Tea Party Movement. Although most Tea Party activists were also Republicans,[31] they were particularly concerned about growing deficits, health care reform, illegal immigration, protecting gun rights, and big government.[32] Compared to other Republicans, they see Barack Obama even more unfavorably, are in favor of reducing the deficit more than creating jobs, and watch Fox News.[33] Tea Party supporters were seen as part of the coalition that elected Scott Brown to the U.S. Senate in the Massachusetts Special Election in January 2010, and they were active in denying renomination to Senator Bob Bennett in Utah.[34] The Tea Party was seen as helping the GOP secure a majority in the House of Representatives in 2010, but impeding the party in its hope of winning a majority in the U.S. Senate. Tea Party–supported candidates lost in Senate races in Nevada, Delaware, and Colorado.[35]

In 2012, Tea Party Republicans had two Senate candidates. In Indiana Richard Mourdock defeated six-term senator Richard Lugar for the nomination. Todd Akin was the candidate in Missouri. But in August, Akin defended his opposition to abortion even in cases of rape: "If it's a legitimate rape, the female body has ways to try to shut that whole thing down." Weeks later Mourdock said a pregnancy resulting from rape "... is something that God intended to happen." Both were defeated.

national party convention
A national meeting of delegates elected in primaries, caucuses, or state conventions who assemble once every four years to nominate candidates for president and vice president, ratify the party platform, elect officers, and adopt rules.

American Parties Today

6.3 Evaluate the functions of parties as institutions, parties in government, and parties in the electorate.

Explore on MyPoliSciLab Simulation: You Are a Voter

merican adults typically take political parties for granted.[36] If anything, most people are critical or distrustful of them. Some see parties as corrupt institutions, interested only in the spoils of politics. Critics charge that parties evade the issues, fail to deliver on their promises, have no new ideas, follow public opinion rather than lead it, or are just one more special interest.

Still, most people understand that parties are necessary. They want party labels kept on the ballot, at least for congressional, presidential, and statewide elections. Most voters think of themselves as Democrats or Republicans and typically vote for candidates from their party. They collectively contribute millions of dollars to the two major parties.[37] Thus, they appreciate, at least vaguely, that you cannot run a big democracy without parties.

Both the Democratic and Republican national parties and most state parties are moderate in their policies and leadership.[38] Successful party leaders must be diplomatic; to win presidential elections and congressional majorities, they must find a middle ground among competing and sometimes hostile groups. Members of the House of Representatives, to be elected and reelected, have to appeal to a majority of the voters from their own district. As more districts have become "safe" for incumbents, the House has had fewer moderates and is prone to more partisan ideological clashes than the Senate.

Parties as Institutions

Like other institutions of government—Congress, the presidency, and the courts—political parties have rules, procedures, and organizational structure. What are the institutional characteristics of political parties?

NATIONAL PARTY LEADERSHIP The supreme authority in both major parties is the **national party convention**, which meets every four years for four days to nominate candidates for president and vice president, to ratify the party platform, and to adopt rules.

In charge of the national party, when it is not assembled in convention, is the *national committee*. In recent years, both parties have strengthened the role of the national committee and enhanced the influence of individual committee members. The committees are now more representative of the party rank-and-file. But in neither party is the national committee the center of party leadership.

Each major party has a *national chair* as its top official. The national committee formally elects the chair, but in reality, this official is the choice of the presidential nominee. For the party that controls the White House, the chair actually serves at the pleasure of the president and does the president's bidding. Party chairs often change after elections. The Republican National Committee (RNC) was chaired in 2011–2012 by Reince Priebus who had been successful in leading the Wisconsin GOP in 2010 and was seen as a leader who could work effectively with the Tea Party. During 2011–2012,

6.1

6.2

6.3

6.4

6.5

platform
Every four years the political parties draft a document stating the policy positions of the party. This party platform details general party-wide issue stances. The process sometimes engenders disputes among fellow partisans but is rarely an election issue and often is written to avoid controversy.

the Democratic National Committee (DNC) was chaired by Florida Congresswoman Debbie Wasserman Schultz. She emerged as a party leader due in part to her successful fundraising efforts for other House Democrats.

She is the third woman to head the Democratic National Committee and the first sitting congresswoman to do so. Her party responsibilities, especially with the presidential campaign, led to criticism from the media and some opponents. But during the nomination period when the focus was on the Republicans because President Obama ran uncontested, Wasserman Schultz became a principal spokesperson for the President and Democratic party.

National party organizations are often agents of an incumbent president in securing his renomination. When there is no incumbent president seeking reelection, the national party committee is generally neutral until the nominee has been selected. National committees play an important role for the Republicans in organizing and coordinating the party get-out-the-vote (GOTV) efforts and were significant in 2004 and to a lesser extent in 2008.[39] Much of the voter mobilization in 2012 was done by the two candidate campaigns along with allied party and interest group partners. The Romney/Ryan campaign relied on a set of joint "victory" campaign organizations in battleground states funded by the presidential campaign and the RNC. The 2012 Obama camplaign built a voter operation in many ways similar to its 2008 operation, with roughly twice as many field offices, more staff, and more volunteers compared to the Romney/RNC effort. Both sides targeted individuals based on past behavior and used sophisticated computer models to predict which individuals would be most likely to vote. Democrats continue to rely heavily on allied groups like unions, environmentalists, and pro-choice groups to get the vote out.

In addition to the national party committees, there are national congressional and senatorial campaign committees. These committees work to recruit candidates, train them, make limited contributions to them, and spend independently in some of the most competitive contests.[40] The National Republican Senatorial Committee (NRSC) and Democratic Senatorial Campaign Committee (DSCC) are led by senators elected to two-year terms by their fellow party members in the Senate. The National Republican Campaign Committee (NRCC) and Democratic Congressional Campaign Committee (DCCC) have leaders chosen in the same manner by fellow partisans in the House. Chairs of campaign committees are nominated by their party leadership and typically ratified by their party caucus.

PARTY PLATFORMS Although national party committees exist primarily to win elections and gain control of government, policy goals are also important. Every four years, each party adopts a platform at the national nominating convention. The typical party **platform**—the official statement of party policy that hardly anyone reads—is often a vague and ponderous document, the result of many meetings and compromises between groups and individuals. Platforms are ambiguous by design, giving voters few obvious reasons to vote against the party (see Figure 6.1).[41]

Many politicians contend that platforms rarely help elect anyone, but platform positions can hurt a presidential candidate. Because the nominee does not always control the platform-writing process, presidential candidates can disagree with their own party platform. But the platform-drafting process gives partisans, and generally the nominee through people he or she appoints, an opportunity to express their views. It spells out the most important values and principles on which the parties are based. Once elected, politicians are rarely reminded of their platform position on a given issue. Even so, the winning party actually seeks to enact much of its party platform.[42] One major exception was former president George H. W. Bush's memorable promise not to raise taxes if elected in 1988, "Read my lips—no new taxes." He was forced to eat those words when taxes were raised in 1990.[43]

Republican National Committee Chair Reince Priebus at the 2012 GOP Convention with House Speaker John Boehner (R-OH).

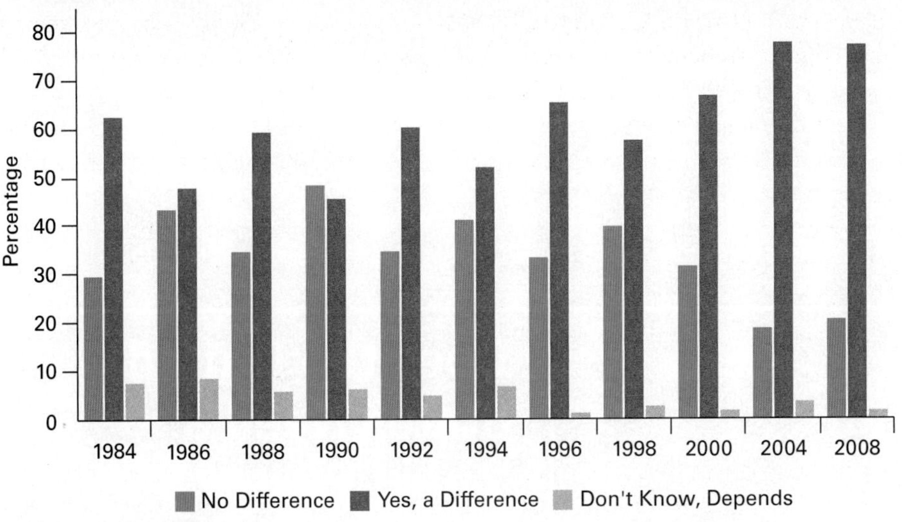

FIGURE 6.1 DIFFERENCE IN PERCEPTION OF WHAT THE PARTIES STAND FOR, 1984–2008

A National Election survey tracks responses to the question, "Do you think there are any important differences in what the Republicans and Democrats stand for?"

Why would people be more likely to see differences between parties in presidential election years than in midterm election years?

SOURCE: *2004 National Election Study,* "Important Difference in What Democratic and Republican Parties Stand For, 1952–2004" (Center for Political Studies, University of Michigan, 2004); and *2008 National Election Study* (Center for Political Studies, University of Michigan, 2008).

PARTIES AT THE STATE AND LOCAL LEVELS The two major parties are decentralized. They have organizations for each level of government—national, state, and local—and organize for elections at each level. The state and local levels are structured much like the national level. Each state has a *state committee* headed by a *state chair.* State law determines the composition of the state committees and regulates them. Members of state committees are usually elected from local areas.

Despite much state-to-state variation, the trend is toward stronger state organizations, with Republicans typically being much better funded.[44] Some states have significant third and fourth parties. New York, for instance, has a Conservative Party in addition to the Democratic and Republican parties. The role that minor parties play in statewide elections can be important, even though they rarely win office themselves.

Below the state committees are *county committees,* which vary widely in function and power. These committees recruit candidates for such offices as county commissioner, sheriff, and treasurer. Often this means finding a candidate for the office, not deciding among competing contenders. For a party that rarely wins an election, the county committee has to struggle to find someone willing to run. When the chance of winning is greater, primaries, not the party leaders, usually decide the winner.[45] Many county organizations are active, distributing campaign literature, organizing telephone campaigns, putting up posters and lawn signs, and canvassing door-to-door. Other county committees do not function at all, and many party leaders are just figureheads.

☐ Parties in Government

Political parties are central to the operation of our government. They help bridge the separation of powers and facilitate coordination between levels of government in a federal system.

IN THE LEGISLATIVE BRANCH Members of Congress take their partisanship seriously, at least while in Washington. Their power and influence are determined by whether their party is in control of the House or Senate; they also have a stake in which party controls the White House. The chairs of all standing committees in Congress come from the majority party, as do the presiding officials of both chambers. Members of both

Which Party Governs Better?

When asked which party governs better, Americans are influenced by partisanship—Democrats and Republicans each think government runs better when their party is in charge. Even so, general dissatisfaction with both major parties is substantial. Nearly half of Americans believe that a third party option is needed in the United States.

Your Level of Trust Depends on Your Party

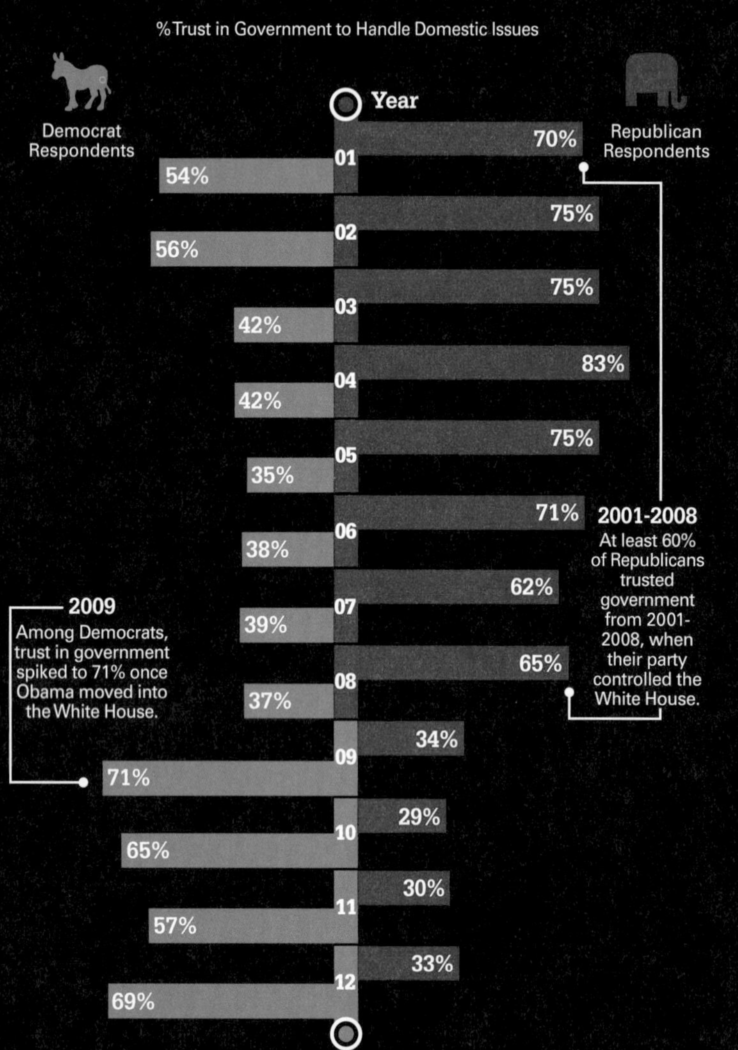

SOURCE: Data from Gallup.

Does the United States Need a Third Party?

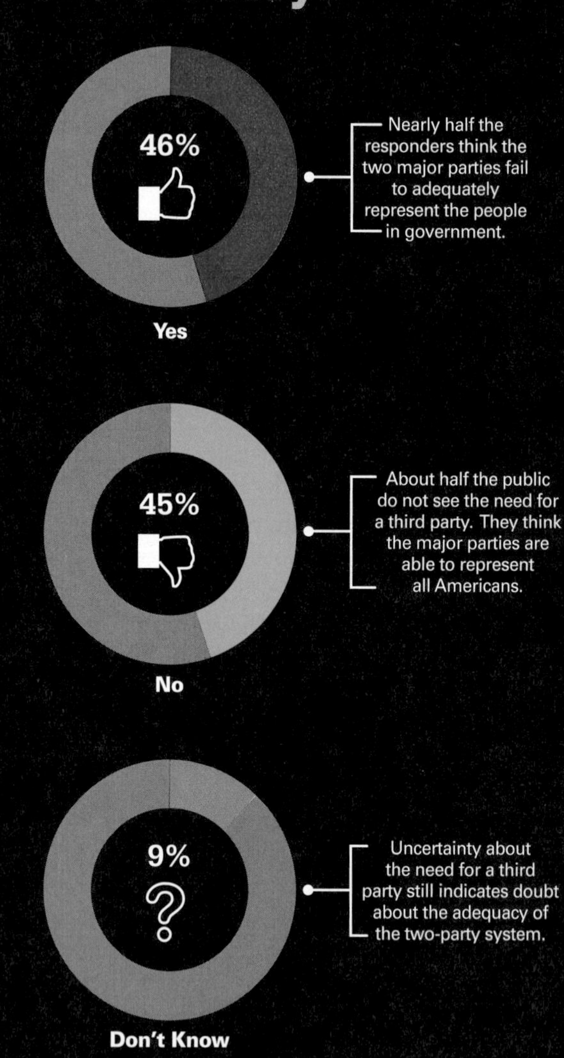

Investigate Further

Concept How do we measure which party governs better? Survey research allows us to track public opinion on party performance on certain issues. Historically, when it comes to trusting government, partisans trust their party to govern, but not the other. Partisanship is a lens through which voters evaluate and determine trust of parties and government.

Connection Which party do Americans think governs better? Voters think *their* party governs better. Democrats think we are governed better when Democrats rule. Republicans think the same when Republicans rule. The parties represent different governing philosophies, so each party has a different definition of what it means to "govern better."

Cause Why are third parties rarely viable? Third parties are rarely viable because while many people express dissatisfaction with the two major parties, they continue to vote for them and do not want to risk wasting their vote by supporting a third party with little chance of winning.

houses sit together on the floor and in committee. (We discuss the role of parties in Congress in greater detail in the chapter on Congress.) Political parties help bridge the separation of powers between the legislative and executive branches by creating partisan incentives to cooperate. Partisanship can also help unify the two houses of Congress.

Congressional staffs are also partisan. Members of Congress expect their staff—from the volunteer intern to the senior staffer—to be loyal, first to them and then to their party. Should you decide to go to work for a representative or senator, you would be expected to identify yourself with that person's party, and you would have difficulty finding a job with the other party later. Employees of the House and Senate—elevator operators, Capitol Hill police, and even the chaplain—hold patronage jobs. With few exceptions, such jobs go to persons from the party that has a majority in the House or the Senate.

party registration
The act of declaring party affiliation; required by some states when one registers to vote.

IN THE EXECUTIVE BRANCH Presidents select nearly all senior White House staff and cabinet members from their own party. In addition, presidents typically surround themselves with advisers who have campaigned with them and proved their party loyalty. Partisanship is also important in presidential appointments to the highest levels of the federal workforce. Party commitment, including making campaign contributions, is expected of those who seek these positions. However, presidents usually fill at least one or two senior posts with members of the opposition party. It is a time-honored way to emphasize bipartisanship.

IN THE JUDICIAL BRANCH The judicial branch of the national government, with its lifetime tenure and political independence, is designed to operate in an expressly nonpartisan manner. Judges, unlike Congress, do not sit together by party. But the appointment process for judges has always been partisan. The landmark case establishing the principle of judicial review, *Marbury* v. *Madison* (1803), concerned Federalists' efforts to stack the judiciary with fellow partisans before leaving office.[46] Today, party identification remains an important consideration when nominating federal judges.

AT THE STATE AND LOCAL LEVELS The importance of party in the operation of local government varies among states and localities. In some states, such as New York and Illinois, local parties play an even stronger role than they do at the national level. In others, such as Nebraska, parties play almost no role. In Nebraska, the state legislature is expressly nonpartisan, although factions perform like parties and still play a role. Parties are likewise unimportant in the government of most city councils. But in most states and many cities, parties are important to the operation of the legislature, governorship, or mayoralty. Judicial selection in most states is also a partisan matter. The 2000 Bush campaign made much of the fact that six of the seven Florida Supreme Court justices deciding the 2000 ballot-counting case in favor of former Vice President Gore were Democrats. Similarly, Democrats noted that the five U.S. Supreme Court justices whose decision ended the Florida recount and led to Bush's election were nominated by Republican presidents.

Parties in the Electorate

Political parties would be of little significance if they did not have meaning to the electorate. Adherents of the two parties are drawn to them by a combination of factors, including their stand on the issues; personal or party history; religious, racial, or social peer grouping; and the appeal of their candidates. The emphases among these factors change over time, but they are remarkably consistent with those that political scientists identified more than 40 years ago.[47]

PARTY REGISTRATION For citizens in most states, "party" has a particular legal meaning—**party registration**. When voters register to vote in these states, they are asked to state their party preference. They then become registered members of one of the two major parties or a third party, although they can change their party registration. The purpose of party registration is to limit the participants in primary elections to members of that party and to make it easier for parties to contact people who might vote for their party.

Texas Republican U.S. Senate candidate Ted Cruz in 2012 on the night of his primary election victory, when he defeated a more established candidate. A favorite of the Tea Party and the son of a Cuban immigrant, Cruz went on to win the general election.

party identification
An affiliation with a political party that most people acquire in childhood. The best predictor of voting behavior in partisan candidate elections.

PARTY ACTIVISTS People who invest time and effort in political parties are often called party activists. They tend to fall into three broad categories: party regulars, candidate activists, and issue activists. *Party regulars* place the party first. They value winning elections and understand that compromise and moderation may be necessary to reach that objective. They also realize that it is important to keep the party together because a fractured party only helps the opposition.

Candidate activists are followers of a particular candidate who see the party as the means to elect their candidate. Candidate activists are often not concerned with the other operations of the party—with nominees for other offices or with raising money for the party. Candidate activists may have a strong ideological orientation, which means they take a strong interest in the party platform debates and the issue positions of the eventual nominees. For example, many people who supported Ron Paul in his unsuccessful run for the presidency as a Republican in 2008 and 2012 were candidate activists. Paul, a Libertarian Republican congressman from Texas, had previously run for the presidency as a Libertarian.

Issue activists wish to push the parties in a particular direction on a single issue or a narrow range of issues: the wars in Iraq and Afghanistan, abortion, taxes, school prayer, the environment, or civil rights, among others. To issue activists, the party platform is an important battleground because they want the party to endorse their position. Issue activists are also often candidate activists if they can find a candidate willing to embrace their position. Some candidates like Ron Paul attract both candidate and issue activists.

☐ Party Identification

Party registration and party activists are important, but many voters are not registered with a political party. Most American adults lack the partisan commitment and interest needed for active involvement. This is not to say that they find parties irrelevant or unimportant. For them, partisanship is what political scientists call **party identification**—a psychological attachment to a political party that most people acquire in childhood

OF the People Diversity in America

Portrait of the Electorate

Throughout the 44-year period from 1964–2008, the demographic composition of the two major political parties has undergone some changes, while at the same time retaining some important similarities. Consistent with the Republican Party's having become stronger, there were slightly more Republicans than Democrats among men in 2008. In 1964, men were twice as likely to be Democrats as Republicans. Women were disproportionately Democratic in 2008, as they were in 1964. Lower-income voters have consistently been more Democratic, and higher-income voters more Republican. Younger voters in both 1964 and 2008 were more likely to be Democrats. In 1964, Democrats enjoyed strong support from Protestants, Catholics, and Jews. By 2008, Protestants were disproportionately Republican, and the Democratic margin among Catholics had dropped significantly. Jewish voters remained heavily Democratic. In 1964, 59 percent of whites were Democrats; by 2008, the white population was more Republican than Democratic. Blacks were heavily Democratic in both 1964 and 2008. The changing face of party composition has implications for electoral competition and campaign strategy.

QUESTIONS

1. Why have more white men become Republicans while white women have remained Democrats?
2. What might explain the shift to the GOP among Protestants and Catholics but not Jews?
3. How does the changing demographics of the two parties affect campaigns?

	1964			2008		
	Republican	**Democrat**	**Independent**	**Republican**	**Democrat**	**Independent**
Sex						
Male	30%	61%	8%	40%	46%	12%
Female	30	61	7	35	55	9
Race						
White	33	59	8	45	43	10
Black	8	82	6	6	85	8
Hispanic	—	—	—	22	63	14
Age						
18–34	26	64	9	30	56	12
35–45	32	59	8	41	47	10
46–55	26	65	8	41	49	9
56–64	28	66	6	35	54	11
65+	43	49	6	44	48	7
Religion						
Protestant	34	58	7	54	39	7
Catholic	22	70	9	39	51	10
Jewish	11	76	13	19	81	0
Other	28	55	16	28	58	13
Region						
Northeast	36	54	10	34	54	11
North-Central	36	55	8	36	51	11
South	20	71	7	42	46	11
West	30	63	7	32	60	7
Total	30	61	8	37	51	10

NOTE: Numbers may not add to 100 because of rounding. Independents that lean toward a party are classified with the party toward which they lean. Race is defined by the first race with which a respondent identifies. Income is classified as the respondent's household income.

SOURCE: *1964 National Election Study* (Center for Political Studies, University of Michigan, 1964); and *2008 National Election Study* (Center for Political Studies, University of Michigan, 2008).

from their parents.[48] This type of voter may sometimes vote for a candidate from the other party, but without a compelling reason to do otherwise, most will vote according to their party identification. Peers and early political experiences reinforce party identification as part of the political socialization process (see the chapter on public opinion).

Political scientists and pollsters use the answers to the following questions to measure party identification: "Generally speaking, in politics, do you usually think of yourself as a Republican, a Democrat, an Independent, or what?" Persons who answer Republican or Democrat are then asked, "Would you call yourself a strong or a not very strong Republican/Democrat?" Persons who answer Independent are asked, "Do you think of yourself as closer to the Republican or the Democratic Party?" Persons who do not indicate Democrat, Republican, or Independent to the first question rarely exceed 2 percent of the electorate and include those who are apolitical or who identify with one of the minor political parties.

When these questions are combined in a single measure, there are seven categories of partisan identification: (1) strong Democrats, (2) weak Democrats, (3) Independent-leaning Democrats, (4) pure Independents, (5) Independent-leaning Republicans, (6) weak Republicans, and (7) strong Republicans. During the more than 50-year period in which political scientists have been conducting such surveys, partisan preferences of the public as a whole have remained remarkably stable, even though new voters have been added to the electorate—minorities and 18- to 21-year-olds (see Table 6.2). For some sub-populations like Protestants and Catholics, partisan allegiances have changed over time (see *Of the People: Diversity in America* box).

Party identification is the single best predictor of how people will vote.[49] Unlike candidates and issues, which come and go, party identification is a long-term element in voting choice. The strength of party identification is also important in predicting participation and political interest. Strong Republicans and strong Democrats participate more actively in politics than any other group, are generally better informed about political issues, and most predictably partisan in their voting behavior. Pure Independents are just the opposite; they vote at the lowest rates and have the lowest levels of interest and awareness of any of the categories of party identification. This evidence runs counter to the notions that persons who are strong partisans are unthinking party adherents and that Independents are informed and ideal citizens.[50] However, Independents who acknowledge party leanings tend to vote for the party toward which they lean. Weak partisans are less reliably partisan and vote at lower rates than strong partisans or some Independents with partisan leanings.

☐ Partisan Dealignment?

As we noted, partisan identification has been stable for more than four decades, despite such changes to the electorate as adding minorities and 18- to 21-year-olds. In addition, as Figure 6.2 suggests, Americans have shown no consistent preference for one party

TABLE 6.2 COMBINED PARTY IDENTIFICATION BY DECADES, 1950s–2000s

Decade	Strong Democrat	Weak Democrat	Independent-Leaning Democrat	Independent	Independent-Leaning Republican	Weak Republican	Strong Republican	Other
1950*	23%	23%	8%	7%	7%	15%	13%	4%
1960	22	25	8	10	7	15	12	2
1970	17	24	12	14	10	14	9	2
1980	18	26	11	12	11	14	11	2
1990	18	19	13	10	12	15	13	1
2000†	18	16	16	10	12	13	14	2

*1950s percentages based on years 1952, 1956, and 1958.

†2000s percentages based on years 2000, 2002, 2004, and 2008.

NOTE: Data may not sum to 100 percent because of averaging. *How has the strength of party identification changed over time?*

SOURCE: *National Election Study* (Center for Political Studies, University of Michigan, 2004).

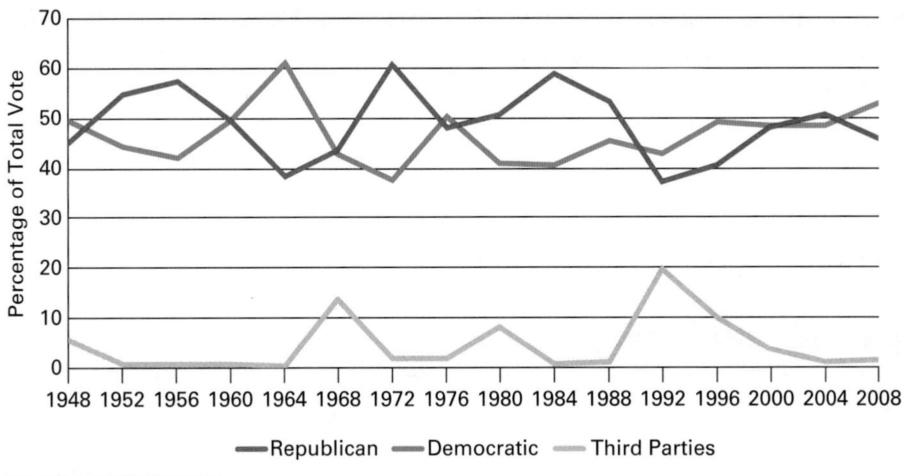

FIGURE 6.2 PRESIDENTIAL VOTE BY PARTY

Based on this graph, what share of the vote do third parties generally get? How many elections since 1952 have been exceptions to this?

SOURCE: Stanley and Niemi, *Vital Statistics on American Politics 2011–2012*, pp. 20–21.

dealignment
Weakening of partisan preferences that point to a rejection of both major parties and a rise in the number of Independents.

over the other in their votes in presidential elections. In a time of electoral volatility, the basics of politics determine the winners and losers: who attracts positive voter attention, who strikes themes that motivate voters to participate, and who communicates better with voters.

However, some experts argue that Independents are increasing in number, suggesting that the party system may be in a period of **dealignment**, in which partisan preferences are weakening and there is a rise in the number of Independents. Indeed, the number of self-classified Independents has increased from 22 percent in the 1950s to approach 40 percent in 2010s. However, two-thirds of all self-identified Independents are really partisans in their voting behavior and attitudes. Table 6.3 summarizes voting behavior in recent contests for president and the House of Representatives. One-third of those who claim to

TABLE 6.3 VOTING BEHAVIOR OF PARTISANS AND INDEPENDENTS, 1992–2008

Percent Voting for Democratic Presidential Candidate					
	1992	**1996**	**2000**	**2004**	**2008**
Strong Democrats	94%	96%	97%	98%	95%
Weak Democrats	69	84	85	85	86
Independent-Leaning Democrats	70	74	78	88	91
Pure Independents	41	39	45	58	55
Independent-Leaning Republicans	11	23	14	15	18
Weak Republicans	14	21	16	11	12
Strong Republicans	3	4	2	3	4

Percent Voting for Democratic House Candidate							
	1994	**1996**	**1998**	**2000**	**2002**	**2004**	**2008**
Strong Democrats	90%	88%	83%	89%	92%	91%	92%
Weak Democrats	72	72	63	73	69	86	84
Independent-Leaning Democrats	66	72	65	73	68	80	83
Pure Independents	51	42	46	52	38	57	43
Independent-Leaning Republicans	25	20	25	26	28	34	21
Weak Republicans	22	20	27	17	27	17	22
Strong Republicans	8	3	8	12	8	10	7

In years that were good for Democrats in congressional elections, like 2004 and 2008, what support did they have that they didn't in weaker elections, like 1994 and 1998?

SOURCE: National Election Study Cumulative File (Center for Political Studies, University of Michigan, 2005); and 2008 National Election Study (Center for Political Studies, University of Michigan, 2008).

soft money
Money raised in unlimited amounts by political parties for party-building purposes. Now largely illegal except for limited contributions to state or local parties for voter registration and get-out-the-vote efforts.

party-independent expenditures
Spending by political party committees that is independent of the candidate. The spending occurs in relatively few competitive contests and is often substantial.

hard money
Political contributions given to a party, candidate, or interest group that are limited in amount and fully disclosed. Raising such limited funds was harder than raising unlimited soft money, hence the term *hard money*.

be Independents lean toward the Democratic Party and vote Democratic in election after election. Another third lean toward Republicans and just as predictably vote Republican. The remaining third, who appear to be genuine Independents, do not vote consistently and appear to have little interest in politics. Thus, despite the reported growth in numbers, pure Independents make up approximately the same proportion of voters today as in 1956.

How Parties Raise and Spend Money

6.4 Explain party fund-raising and expenditures, and assess their regulation.

lthough parties cannot exert tight control over candidates, their ability to raise and spend money has had a significant influence. Political parties, like candidates, rely on contributions from individuals and interest groups to fund their activities. Because of the close connection political parties have with officeholders, the courts have long permitted regulation of the source and amount of money people and groups can contribute to parties, as well as the amount parties can spend with or contribute to candidates.

Under the reforms enacted after President Richard Nixon resigned from office following the Watergate scandal, contributions to the parties from individuals were limited to $20,000, whereas the limit for political action committees (PACs) was $15,000.[51] As we discuss in the chapter on interest groups, PACs are more inclined to give to candidates than party committees.

After the 1976 election, both parties pressed for further amendments to FECA, claiming that campaign finance reforms resulted in insufficient money for generic party activities such as billboard advertising and get-out-the-vote drives. The 1979 amendments to FECA and the interpretations of this legislation by the Federal Election Commission (FEC) permitted unlimited **soft money** contributions to the parties by individuals and PACs for these party-building purposes. Unions and corporations were also allowed to give parties unlimited amounts of soft money. Two decades later, in 1996, candidates and parties found ways to spend this soft money to promote the election or defeat of specific candidates. By the elections of 2000, all party committees combined raised $500 million in soft money, a feat they repeated in 2002. This money was spent in large amounts in the most competitive races.

After repeated defeats in one or both houses of Congress for 15 years, Congress regulated this unrestricted soft money under the Bipartisan Campaign Reform Act (BCRA) in 2002. Soft money was almost entirely banned under the Act, whereas the limits on individual contributions to candidates and party committees were roughly doubled and indexed to inflation, and a more realistic definition of what constituted election communications by groups was enacted.

Party Expenditures

Party committees are permitted to make contributions to candidates and can also spend a limited amount of money in what are called "coordinated expenditures." In the last several election cycles, the party committees have concentrated their contributions and coordinated expenditures in the most competitive contests.

Parties, like individuals and groups, can now also spend unlimited amounts for and against candidates as long as the expenditures were independent of the candidate or a party committee.[52] Unlike soft money, **party-independent expenditures** had to use money raised with normal **hard money** contribution limits. As long as the party committees could use soft money, independent expenditures were of lesser importance, but with the BCRA ban on soft money, there has been a surge in party-independent expenditure activity.

Aside from the Democratic National Committee, all other party committees continued to spend heavily in independent expenditures in 2008. This money in 2008 and 2010 was again spent in only a few competitive races. But where parties invest, they do so in substantial amounts. Spending by the congressional campaign committees was about the same for the Democrats in 2010 as in the last midterm in 2006. Independent spending by Republicans in congressional races was up slightly in the Senate but down substantially in the House when compared to 2006. Democrats spent overall about $34 million more in independent expenditures in 2010.

During the debate over BCRA, and in the court case on its constitutionality, some such as political scientist Sidney Milkis speculated that BCRA's soft money ban would weaken political parties.[53] The surge in individual contributions has demonstrated the opposite; the DNC and RNC could and did find an alternative to unregulated money. It remains unclear whether the four congressional party committees can make up for the loss of soft money, but the surge in individual contributions to them is promising. The independent expenditure option allows parties to continue to direct money well in excess of the normal limits to races they thought were more competitive.

Compared to other countries, the United States has less public funding of political parties and candidates. Holding the United States aside, wealthier countries (by GDP per capita) have broader regulations than do less-wealthy countries. Britain and Japan, for example, both have limits on the sources of money allowed, disclosure, free television time to parties, and limits on paid television advertising.[54] In contrast, Nigeria only requires disclosure of donors, which could account for the overwhelming role that money plays in Nigerian elections.[55]

Are the Political Parties Dying?

6.5 Assess the effects of recent party reforms and the long-term prospects for the current party system.

Critics of the U.S. party system typically make four allegations against it: (1) parties do not take meaningful and contrasting positions on most issues, (2) party membership is essentially meaningless, (3) parties are so concerned with accommodating the middle of the ideological spectrum that they are incapable of serving as an avenue for social progress, or (4) others argue that extremes have captured both parties and that this polarization results in deadlock in Congress and between Congress and the president. Are these statements accurate? And if they are accurate, are they important?

Some analysts fear that parties are in severe decline or even mortally ill. They point first to the long-run adverse impact on political parties of the Progressive movement reforms early in this century, reforms that robbed party organizations of their control of the nomination process by allowing masses of Independent and "uninformed" voters to enter the primaries and nominate candidates who might not be acceptable to party leaders. They also point to the spread of nonpartisan elections in cities and towns and to the staggering of national, state, and local elections that made it harder for parties to influence the election process.

Legislation limiting the viability and functions of parties was bad enough, say the party pessimists, but parties suffer from additional ills. The rise of television and electronic technology and the parallel increase in the number of campaign, media, and direct-mail consultants have made parties less relevant in educating, mobilizing, and organizing the electorate. Television, radio, the Internet, telephones, and social

6.1

6.2

6.3

6.4

6.5

media have strengthened the role of candidates and lessened the importance of parties. (See the chapter on the media for a fuller discussion.) Advocates of strong parties counter that there are signs of party revival, or at least the persistence of party. The national party organizations own permanent, modern buildings in Washington, D.C., located a few blocks from the U.S. Capitol, and remain capable of providing assistance to candidates in competitive races and to state and local party organizations.

☐ Reform Among the Democrats

In Chicago in 1968, the Democratic National Convention saw disputes inside the hall and riots outside, largely because of protests against the country's policy in Vietnam. Responding to the disarray and to disputes about the fairness of delegate selection procedures, members of the party agreed to a number of reforms. They established a process that led to greater use of direct primaries for the selection of delegates to the national convention and greater representation of younger voters, women, and minorities as elected delegates. Another reform was the abolition of the winner-take-all rule (the *unit rule*) that gave all delegates to the primary or convention winner. This rule was replaced by a system of *proportionality* in which candidates won delegates in rough proportion to the votes they received in the primary election or convention in each state. These rule changes became important in 2008 as proportionality rules meant that neither Hillary Clinton nor Barack Obama could benefit from the "winner-take-all" rules that helped propel John McCain to the Republican Party's nomination.

The reforms following 1968 achieved greater diversity of representation among delegates and, as noted, meant that more states adopted primaries. But the new process also meant that elected officials who wanted a voice in determining presidential candidates had to run for delegate to the national convention. Some elected officials feared losing in their own party process, and others wanted to delay endorsing a candidate.

BY the People Making a Difference

Party Politics on Campus

Citizens gain a stronger voice in American politics by becoming involved in a political party. For all of the reasons discussed in this chapter, parties are vital to the functioning of democracy. Moreover, parties are highly permeable institutions, meaning they are open to influence by individuals like you. As with most Americans, you likely have a party preference or party identification, even if you are an Independent who leans toward one or the other of the political parties.

If your preference is with the Republican Party, you might become involved with the local affiliate of the College Republican National Committee (CRNC). This organization has been in existence for more than a century and has more than a quarter of a million members on more than 1,500 campuses. College Republicans pursue a variety of activities intended to help elect Republicans. You can learn more about the organization at www.cnrc.org. One well-known CRNC alum is Karl Rove, who served as executive director of the organization from 1971–1973.

If you identify more with Democrats, there is likely also a chapter of the College Democrats on your campus. College Democrats was founded in 1932 to help with FDR's campaign. CDA seeks to foster participation by college students in politics, often making use of Twitter, blogs, Facebook, and other social networking sites to recruit other students. The national organization maintains an active Web site at www.collegedems.com.

Some students in both parties also become directly involved in campaigns of candidates they like. But as exciting as working for a candidate can be, becoming involved in making a political party stronger will serve many candidates. Groups like these help young voters get involved and learn how to make a difference.

QUESTIONS

1. Why do both parties invest in college student organizations?
2. What functions of a political party most interest you?
3. How could college students' participation in party politics affect the party system?

Responding to this criticism, the party created "superdelegate" positions for elected officials and party leaders who were not required to run for election as delegates. Initially in 2008, most superdelegates favored Clinton, but by late May 2008, a majority of them supported Obama. They were decisive in determining the nominee, as neither Hillary Clinton nor Barack Obama had enough delegates selected in primaries or caucuses to win the nomination. In 2012, as the incumbent, there was little doubt Democratic superdelegates would support Obama. In the contested Republican primary, less than one-third had committed to support one of the candidates in March as Romney was emerging as the likely nominee with Romney having a two-to-one advantage over all the other candidates combined.[56]

☐ Reform Among the Republicans

Republicans have not been immune to criticism that their conventions and procedures were keeping out the rank-and-file. They did not make changes as drastic as those made by the Democrats, but they did give the national committee more control over presidential campaigns, and state parties were urged to encourage broader participation by all groups, including women, minorities, youth, and the poor.

The Republican Party has long been better organized than the Democrats. In the 1970s, the GOP emphasized grassroots organization and membership recruitment. Seminars taught Republican candidates how to make speeches and hold press conferences, and weekend conferences were organized for training young party

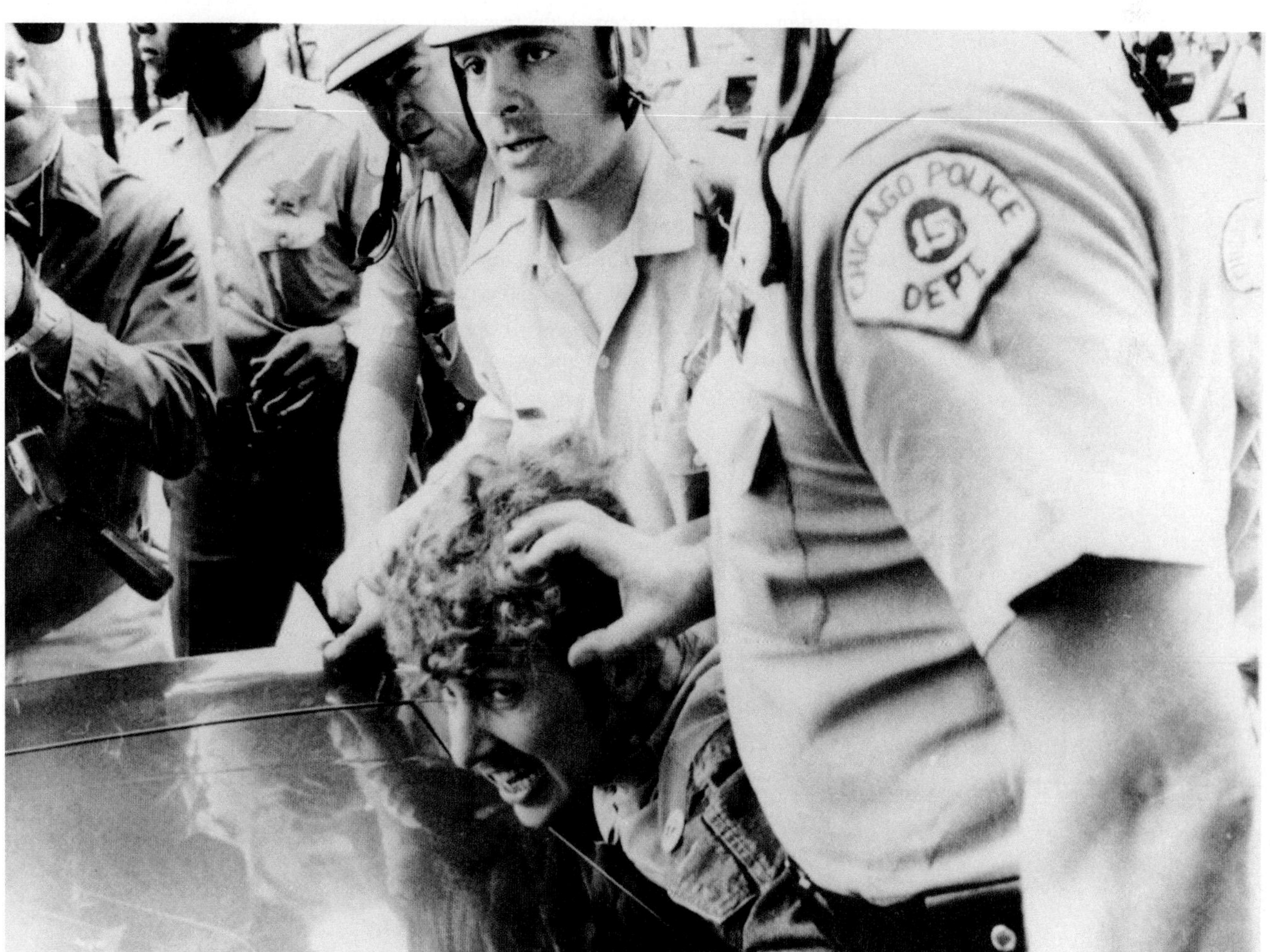

Chicago police officers push a protestor's head against the hood of a car as they restrain him after he climbed onto a wooden barricade near the headquarters of the 1968 Democratic National Convention and waved a Vietcong flag during anti-Vietnam War demonstrations, August 1968.

professionals. The Democrats have become better organized and more professional than they were previously.[57] Until 2004, Republicans had cultivated a larger donor base and were less reliant on the large-donor soft money contributions that became so controversial between 1996 and 2002. In 2006, however, the Democratic committees closed the donor gap, with 45 percent of their money raised from small donors, compared to 46 percent from small donors among the Republican committees. The trend toward small donors continued in 2008, especially in the Obama campaign, which set new records not only for total contributions but also for the number of individuals contributing to the campaign. Many of these donors were new donors making contributions that did not exceed $200.

In the 2010 election cycle, the Democratic Party committees all raised and spent more than the Republican Party committees, a gap that was filled in part by interest groups, which were more active on the Republican side. In 2010, all party committees raised substantial amounts ($29–$107 million) from donors giving in the aggregate $200 or less to a committee. Such small donors continue to give a larger proportion to the RNC than small donors give the DNC, but the DNC raised more from donors giving under $200 than donors giving more than $200. Small donors were important to Tea Party insurgent candidates like Rand Paul, who was elected to the U.S. Senate from Kentucky.

□ Continued Importance of Parties

As we have demonstrated in this chapter, political parties are vital to the functioning of democracy. They organize electoral competition, unify large portions of the electorate, simplify democracy for voters, help transform individual preferences into policy, and provide a mechanism for opposition.

Parties are just as important in organizing the government. They help straddle the separation of powers as party members cooperate between the executive and legislative branches or between the House and Senate. Senior government appointees get their jobs in part because of party loyalty.

Parties also provide an important way for citizens to influence government. Because they are the means by which politicians secure office, participation in the parties can help determine the course of American government. Parties also provide opportunities to learn about how other people see issues and to learn to compromise. Rather than being an impediment to democracy, they make government by the people possible.

Review the Chapter

 **Listen** to **Chapter 6** on **MyPoliSciLab**

What Parties Do for Democracy

6.1 Identify the primary functions of parties in democracies and distinguish the U.S. party system from those in European democracies, p. 175.

Political parties are essential to democracy. They simplify voting choices, organize electoral competition, unify the electorate, help organize government by bridging the separation of powers and fostering cooperation among branches of government, translate public preferences into policy, and provide loyal opposition.

A Brief History of American Political Parties

6.2 Describe changes in American political parties and identify four realigning elections, p. 182.

Despite their reservations about political parties, the founders became early leaders of a two-party system. Since then, American parties have experienced critical elections and realignments. Most political scientists agree that the last realignment occurred in 1932. During the last half-century, the two parties have been fairly evenly matched, with both parties able to win elections and with divided government more common than unified government. Party identification has remained the best predictor of voting choice and most Americans have a party preference, especially if Independent leaners are included with partisans.

American Parties Today

6.3 Evaluate the functions of parties as institutions, parties in government, and parties in the electorate, p. 187.

Parties play many different roles. As institutions, they are governed by their national and state committees, which are led by the party chairs, and they recruit and elect candidates, promote their party's principles, and keep the party organized. In government, Congress is organized around parties, and judicial and many executive branch appointments are based in large part on partisanship. In the electorate, parties actively seek to organize elections, simplify voting choices, and strengthen individuals' party identification. In recent years, there has been an increase in the number of persons who call themselves Independents. This trend is sometimes called dealignment, but most Independents are closet partisans who vote fairly consistently for the party toward which they lean.

How Parties Raise and Spend Money

6.4 Explain party fund-raising and expenditures, and assess their regulation, p. 196.

With the rise of soft money in the 1990s and early 2000s, parties had more resources to spend on politics. In 2002, Congress passed the Bipartisan Campaign Reform Act (BCRA), which banned soft money except for some narrowly defined and limited activities. The parties adapted to BCRA by building a larger individual donor base. Donors wanting to spend more than the BCRA limits did so in 2008 through a range of interest groups, many of which ran parallel campaigns with the candidates and parties.

Are the Political Parties Dying?

6.5 Assess the effects of recent party reforms and the long-term prospects for the current party system, p. 197.

Frequent efforts have been made to reform our parties. The Progressive movement saw parties, as then organized, as an impediment to democracy and pushed direct primaries as a means to reform them. Following the 1968 election, the Democratic Party took the lead in pushing primaries and stressing greater diversity among the individuals elected as delegates. Republicans have also encouraged broader participation, and they have improved their party structure and finances. There has been some party renewal in recent years as party competition has grown in the South and the parties themselves have initiated reforms.

Learn the Terms

 **Study** and **Review** the **Flashcards**

political party, p. 175
nonpartisan election, p. 175
patronage, p. 176
honeymoon, p. 177
caucus, p. 177
party convention, p. 177
direct primary, p. 177
open primary, p. 178
crossover voting, p. 178
closed primary, p. 178
minor party, p. 180
proportional representation, p. 180
winner-take-all system, p. 180
realigning election, p. 183
divided government, p. 185
national party convention, p. 187
platform, p. 188
party registration, p. 191
party identification, p. 194
dealignment, p. 195
soft money, p. 196
party-independent expenditures, p. 196
hard money, p. 196

Test Yourself

 **Study** and **Review** the **Practice Tests**

MULTIPLE CHOICE QUESTIONS

6.1 Identify the primary functions of parties in democracies and distinguish the U.S. party system from those in European democracies.

Each of the following is a major function of a political party EXCEPT

- **a.** linking the separate branches of the federal government.
- **b.** connecting the national government with state and local governments.
- **c.** unifying the electorate.
- **d.** coordinating expenditures with interest groups.
- **e.** making policy.

6.2 Describe changes in American political parties and identify four realigning elections.

The partisan realignment in 1932 resulted in

- **a.** Republican control of the House and Senate, but not the executive.
- **b.** Unified Democratic control of both the presidency and the Congress.
- **c.** Democratic control of the House and Senate, but not the executive.
- **d.** Unified Republican control of the presidency and the Congress.
- **e.** Federalist control of the executive and both houses of Congress.

6.3 Evaluate the functions of parties as institutions, parties in government, and parties in the electorate.

Which is true of American political parties today?

- **a.** Party platforms are ultimately decided by the candidate running for president.
- **b.** Just as at the national level, each state has a strong two-party system.
- **c.** Presidential candidates become the leaders of their respective parties for the next four years.
- **d.** Most declared Independent voters are actually partisan in their voting patterns.
- **e.** Political party is rarely a consideration when appointing judges or hiring staff.

6.4 Explain party fund-raising and expenditures, and assess their regulation.

From where do the national party committees get most of their money today?

- **a.** soft money
- **b.** individual donors
- **c.** the general funds of unions and corporations
- **d.** their parties' candidates
- **e.** foreign nationals

6.5 Assess the effects of recent party reforms and the long-term prospects for the current party system.

As a result of changes made to the Democratic Party's nominating system

- **a.** party candidates for the general election will be determined earlier in the primary election cycle.
- **b.** republican candidates are at a unique disadvantage.
- **c.** democratic candidates win delegates in proportion to the votes they receive in the primary election.
- **d.** democratic candidates no longer participate in states in which caucuses are held.
- **e.** republicans are more likely to win general elections.

ESSAY QUESTION

Identify the primary functions of parties in democracies and distinguish the U.S. party system from those in European democracies.

Explore Further

IN THE LIBRARY

John H. Aldrich, *Why Parties? The Origin and Transformation of Party Politics in America* (University of Chicago Press, 1995).

David Boaz, *Libertarianism: A Primer* (Free Press, 1998).

Bruce E. Cain and Elisabeth R. Gerber, eds., *Voting at the Political Fault Line: California's Experiment with the Blanket Primary* (University of California Press, 2002).

Donald T. Critchlow, *The Conservative Ascendancy: How the GOP Right Made Political History* (Harvard University Press, 2007).

Leon Epstein, *Political Parties in the American Mold* (University of Wisconsin Press, 1986).

John C. Green and Daniel J. Coffey, eds., *The State of the Parties: The Changing Role of Contemporary American Parties*, 6th ed. (Rowman & Littlefield, 2010).

Marjorie Randon Hershey, *Party Politics in America*, 15th ed. (Longman, 2013).

Bruce E. Keith, David B. Magleby, Candice J. Nelson, Elizabeth Orr, Mark C. Westlye, and Raymond E. Wolfinger, *The Myth of the Independent Voter* (University of California Press, 1992).

Michael S. Lewis-Beck, Helmut Norpoth, William G. Jacoby, and Herbert F. Weisberg, *The American Voter Revisited* (University of Michigan Press, 2008).

David B. Magleby and Anthony D. Corrado, eds., *Financing the 2008 Election* (Brookings Institution Press, 2011).

David B. Magleby, ed., *The Change Election: Money, Mobilization, and Persuasion in the 2008 Federal Elections* (Temple University Press, 2011).

L. Sandy Maisel and Mark D. Brewer, *Parties and Elections in America: The Electoral Process*, 6th ed. (Rowman & Littlefield, 2012).

Kelly D. Patterson, *Political Parties and the Maintenance of Liberal Democracy* (Columbia University Press, 1996).

Steven J. Rosenstone, Roy L. Behr, and Edward H. Lazarus, *Third Parties in America: Citizen Response to Major Party Failure*, 2nd ed. (Princeton University Press, 1996).

James Sundquist, *Dynamics of the Party System: Alignment and Realignment of Political Parties in the United States*, rev. ed. (Brookings Institution Press, 1983).

ON THE WEB

www.GOP.com; *www.democrats.org*
These are the main Web sites of the Republican National Committee and Democratic National Committee, respectively. These sites have information about each party's national party convention and platform as well as party history and information about how to volunteer for party activities.

www.nrsc.org; *www.dscc.org*
These are the Web sites for the National Republican Senatorial Committee and Democratic Senatorial Campaign Committee, respectively. These committees focus on helping their party's candidates win election to the United States Senate. Individuals can volunteer for and contribute to candidates on each site.

www.nrcc.org; *www.dccc.org*
These are the Web sites for the National Republican Congressional Committee and Democratic Congressional Campaign Committee, respectively. These committees focus on helping their party's candidates win election to the United States House of Representatives. Individuals can volunteer for and contribute to candidates on each site.

www.gp.org
The Web site for the Green Party of the United States. The site has information about the party's platform, party history, and how to volunteer for party activists and contribute financially.

www.opensecrets.org/parties/index.php
The Center for Responsive Politics maintains this Web site with a large amount of information about how parties raise money.

7

Listen to Chapter 7 on MyPoliSciLab

Public Opinion, Ideology, Participation, and Voting

Unlike in many countries, citizens in the United States do not have a state-issued national identification card. When asked to present identification, most people display their driver's license or, in some situations, a passport. But not everyone has a passport or driver's license. By some estimates, as much as 11 percent of the population does not have a state-issued form of voter identification.[1] Voter identification requirements pose a challenge for this group. Since 2002, 17 states have enacted some form of voter identification requirement.[2] One of the most stringent voter identification laws took effect in Indiana in 2006; in order to vote in Indiana, a citizen must present an identifying document issued by the state or federal government with a photo, an expiration date, and the same name as appears on the voter registration list. Indiana provides a state ID card at no cost, but a citizen must go to the county motor vehicle bureau with documents like a birth certificate, certificate of citizenship, military ID, or passport. The citizen must also provide proof of a Social Security number and Indiana residency.[3]

Provisions for voter identification requirements vary somewhat. Some allow citizens to bring a paycheck or utility bill showing the same address as on the voter registration list, while others require a photo ID. The Indiana law, which requires a photo, was challenged, and the U.S. Supreme Court ultimately upheld Indiana's law in *Crawford* v. *Marion County Election Board*.[4] The Court ruled that slight burden on voters did not outweigh the state's legitimate interest in preventing voter fraud.

Lawmakers justify voter ID requirements as a way to combat voter fraud. Senator John Cornyn, Republican of Texas, supports voter photo identification because "of allegations of voter fraud throughout the United States." Cornyn lists

7.1 Identify the forces that create and shape individuals' political attitudes, p. 207.

7.2 Describe the key dimensions of public opinion, how public opinion is measured, and the relationship between public opinion and public policy, p. 211.

7.3 Compare and contrast political ideologies and evaluate the critiques of each ideology, p. 215.

7.4 Identify forms of political participation, and assess the effect on voter turnout of demographic, legal, and electioneering factors, p. 220.

7.5 Analyze why people vote the way they do in elections, p. 232.

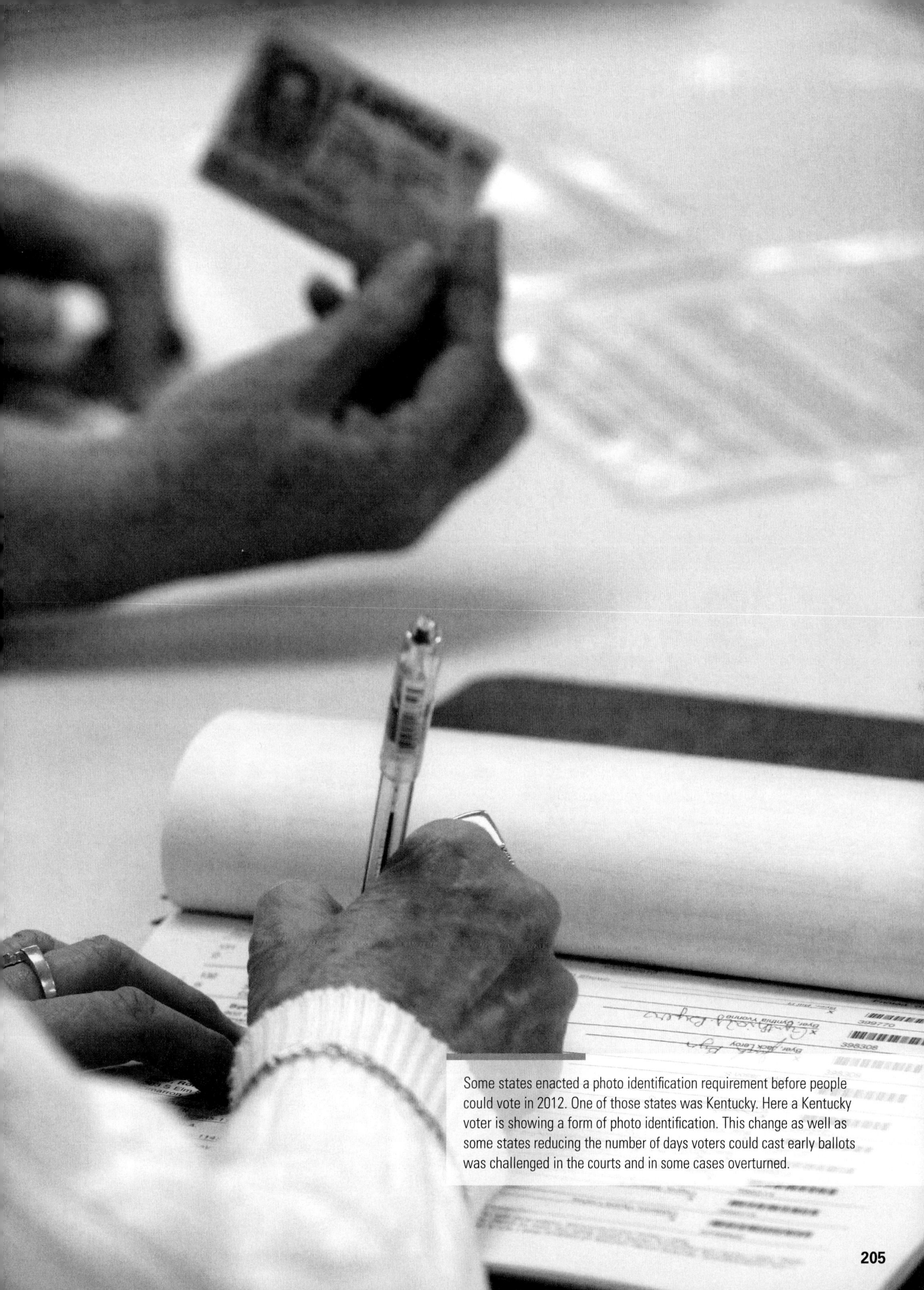

Some states enacted a photo identification requirement before people could vote in 2012. One of those states was Kentucky. Here a Kentucky voter is showing a form of photo identification. This change as well as some states reducing the number of days voters could cast early ballots was challenged in the courts and in some cases overturned.

The Big Picture Americans vote more often and for more offices than do the citizens of any other democracy. Author David B. Magleby explains some of the factors that citizens take with them into the voting booth, including partisanship, candidate appeal, opinions on hot-button issues, and reference groups.

The Basics How do people form opinions? In this video, we examine how we know what opinions the public holds, and how they come by those opinions. As we go along, you'll discover that Americans aren't always well-informed about government and policies, but that they share core values.

In Context How was political involvement unique to the United States during the nineteenth century? In this video, Tufts University political scientist Peter Levine examines the historical trends of political participation and the role of parties in organizing this participation.

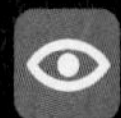

Thinking Like a Political Scientist Why has the United States experienced a surge in voter turnout? Columbia University political scientist Donald P. Green analyzes voter turnout trends, and takes a look at how research conducted by political scientists on this subject has contributed to increased voter turnout.

In the Real World Should politicians listen more to their constituents (who may not be educated about all of the issues), or to their own sense of what is right and wrong? Hear real people weigh in on this question, and learn how presidents have dealt with it in the past.

So What? Want to get more involved in politics, but not sure where to begin? By using the mother who founded Mothers Against Drunk Driving (MADD) as a model, author David B. Magleby encourages students to think about the issues they are passionate about and become informed and active participants in related organizations and movements.

examples of voter registration fraud in Nevada and Minnesota, some happening in the 2008 election.[5] Support for voter ID requirements is found mostly among Republican legislators; new laws were passed in six states in 2011, with an additional four states toughening their identification provisions to require photo identification.[6] Speaking about a proposed law in Virginia, former Virginia Governor and current U.S. Senator Mark Warner commented on his state's voter identification law, "I've been involved in elections for a long time in Virginia. I've never heard Democrats or Republicans complain about this [issue] prior to this bill coming to the floor."[7]

Credible studies of possible fraud have found that "the best available evidence shows that voter fraud is a minor issue in American elections. There is little hard evidence that it occurs, even less evidence that it is widespread, and almost no indication that it has altered election outcomes."[8] The absence of evidence of widespread fraud has not deterred states from imposing the identification requirements.

Voter identification laws are highly controversial. These new rules disproportionately affect citizens who lack a driver's license or passport, and these citizens tend to be poorer, less educated, and from minority populations. The new rules also give poll workers substantial power to determine whether people get to vote—one study found the poll workers in New Mexico applied voter identification rules inconsistently.[9] Despite the Court's ruling in *Crawford* v. *Marion County Election Board,* the U.S. Department of Justice in its review of Texas voter ID provisions determined that it failed to protect voting rights.[10]

The right to vote is among our most fundamental rights. Who exercises this right and why people vote as they do is the subject of this chapter. We also explore public opinion, how it is measured, and what factors affect the formation of opinions. We begin by looking at how we get our political opinions and values.

political socialization
The process—most notably in families and schools—by which we develop our political attitudes, values, and beliefs.

Forming Political Opinions and Values

7.1 Identify the forces that create and shape individuals' political attitudes.

No one is born with political views. Rather, they are learned and acquired through experience and association with other people. **Political socialization**—the way in which we come to see society and ourselves and learn to interact with other individuals and in groups—provides the foundation for political beliefs, values, ideology, and partisanship. It is a process that continues throughout our lives. How people come to see the political world can change, but our core values and beliefs seldom do. More transitory opinions, say, on banking regulation, tend to be volatile, whereas core values on such things as liberty or freedom tend to remain more stable. This difference is important for understanding the varied levels on which people think about politics.

Political Socialization

We develop our political attitudes from many mentors and teachers through a process that starts in childhood, and families and schools are usually our two most important political teachers. We learn about our culture in childhood and adolescence, but we reshape our opinions as we mature.[11] A common element of political socialization in most cultures is *nationalism*, a consciousness of the nation-state and of belonging to it.

The pluralistic political culture of the United States makes the sources of our views immensely varied. Political attitudes may stem from religious, racial, gender, or ethnic backgrounds, or economic beliefs and values. But we can safely make at least one generalization: We form our attitudes through participation in *groups*. Close-knit groups such as the family are especially influential. At an early age, children in the United States adopt common values that provide continuity with the past and that legitimate the U.S. political system. Young children know what country they live in, and they quickly develop national loyalty. Although the details of our political system may elude them, most young citizens

7.1

7.2

7.3

7.4

7.5

attitudes
An individual's propensity to perceive, interpret, or act toward a particular object in a particular way.

acquire a respect for the Constitution and for the concept of participatory democracy, as well as an initially positive view of the most visible figure in our democracy, the president.[12]

FAMILY Most social psychologists agree that family is the most powerful socializing agent.[13] What we first learn in the family is not so much specific political opinions as basic **attitudes**, broad or general, that shape our opinions about our neighbors, political parties, other classes or types of people, particular leaders (especially presidents), and society in general. Attitudes are understood to be "a propensity in an individual to perceive, interpret, and act toward a particular object in particular ways."[14] Attitudes are often seen as positive or negative toward the object, person, or idea.

American children typically show political interest by age 10, and by the early teens, their awareness may be fairly high. Studies of high school students indicate a strong correlation between their partisan identification and their parents' political party that continues throughout life. In other words, people tend to belong to the same political party as their parents. Does the direct influence of parents create the correspondence? Or does living in the same social environment—neighborhood, church, and socioeconomic group—influence parents and children? The answer is *both*. One influence often strengthens the other.

SCHOOLS Schools also mold young citizens' political attitudes. U.S. schools see part of their purpose as preparing students to be citizens and active participants in governing their communities and the nation. Especially important in fostering later political involvement are extracurricular activities such as student government and debate.[15]

From kindergarten through college, students generally develop political values consistent with the democratic process and supportive of the U.S. political system. In their study of U.S. history, they are introduced to our nation's heroes and heroines, important events, and the ideals of U.S. society. Other aspects of their experience, such as the daily Pledge of Allegiance and school programs or assemblies, reinforce respect for country. Children also gain practical experience in the way democracy works through elections for student government. In many states, high school and even college students are required by law to take courses in U.S. history or government to graduate.

Do school courses and activities give young people the skills needed to participate in elections and democratic institutions? A study of 18- to 24-year-olds commissioned by the National Association of Secretaries of State found that young people "lack any real understanding of citizenship…information and understanding about the democratic process… and information about candidates and political parties."[16] Furthermore, the Secretaries of State report noted that "most young people do not seek out political information and that they are not very likely to do so in the future."[17] You and your classmates are not a representative sample, in part because you have more interest and knowledge than most people. Others have argued that such findings simply follow a centuries-old tradition of blaming social problems on younger generations, and that young people today are more politically engaged than previous generations—even if they do not conform to traditional measures of political activism. The advent of the Internet and social media is changing the nature of politics today, and the younger generation is deeply involved in this new activism.[18]

PEERS AND FRIENDS People of all ages learn from peers and friends, but for younger people they are especially important. For example, friends help with adaptation to school, including college. The influence of friends and peers stems from the human desire to be like people around us.[19] Peer groups not only define fashion and social norms, they reinforce or may challenge what has been experienced in families. One study suggests that college students are more likely than non-college students of the same age to be knowledgeable about politics, more in favor of free speech, and more likely to talk and read about politics.[20]

Technology has expanded the ways we interact with peers through Facebook or other social media. Some scholars have found that users of social networking sites "are no more knowledgeable about politics (in general and about the field of presidential candidates) than are their counterparts and, in fact, seem to be less so. Their political participation, as such, seems to be limited to Internet activity, and they do not seem to be more likely to

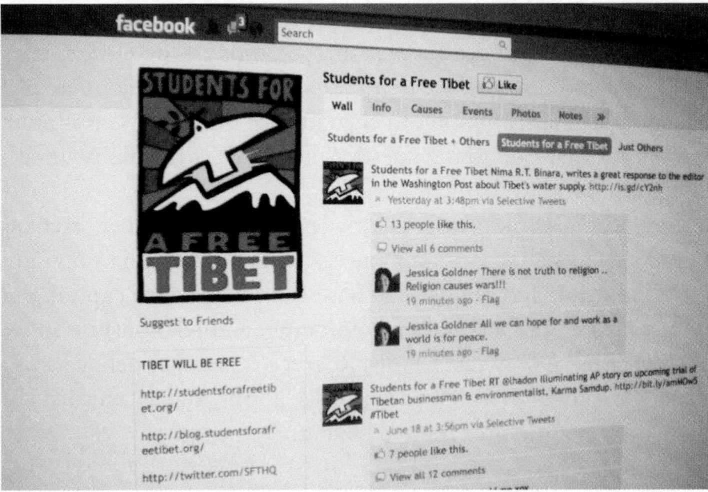

Facebook groups like Students for a Free Tibet allow peers to share their political interests and rally friends to their cause, all without leaving their dorm rooms.

selective exposure
Individuals choosing to access media with which they agree or avoiding media with which they disagree.

vote."[21] Other research has found that "young adults who spend more time on Facebook are better at showing 'virtual empathy' to their online friends" and that "social networking can provide tools for teaching in compelling ways that engage young students."[22]

MASS MEDIA Like everyone else, young people are exposed to a wide range of media—school newspapers, national and local newspapers, the Internet, movies, radio, and television—all of which influence what they think, and like everyone else, they often pick and choose the media with which they agree, a process called **selective exposure**. The mass media also serve as agents of political socialization by exposing individuals to the values and behavior of others. Media influence is greater on attitudes about issues and individual politicians than on underlying values.[23]

OTHER INFLUENCES Religious, ethnic, and racial backgrounds as well as the workplace can also shape opinions, both within and outside the family. Some scholars have found, for example, that the religious composition of a community has a direct impact on knowledge, discussion, and self-confidence among students in dealing with politics.[24] However, even though generalizations about how people vote are useful, we have to be careful about stereotyping. For example, not all African Americans vote Democratic, and many Catholics disagree with their church's opposition to abortion. It is a mistake to assume that because we know a person's religious affiliation or racial background, we know his or her political opinions.

☐ Stability and Change

Adults are not simply the sum of their early experiences, but adults' opinions do tend to remain stable. Even if the world around us changes rapidly, we are slow to shift our loyalties or to change our minds about things that matter to us. In general, people who remain in the same place, in the same occupation, and in the same income group throughout their lives tend to have stable opinions. People often carry their attitudes with them, and families who move from cities to suburbs often retain their big-city attitudes after they have moved, at least for a time. Political analysts are becoming more interested in how adults modify their views. A harsh experience—a war, an economic depression, or an event like the terrorist attacks of September 11, 2001—may be a catalyst that changes attitudes and opinions. Political scientist Robert D. Putnam studied the public's greater confidence in political leaders and higher levels of community interaction following the terrorist attacks. Putnam has found that, for those aged 18 to 25, the post-2001 increase in civic engagement continues.[25]

Because they are part of our core values, views on abortion, the death penalty, and doctor-assisted suicide, for example, tend to remain stable over time. On issues less central to our values, such as how a president is performing, opinions can change

7.1
7.2
7.3
7.4
7.5

deliberation
The idea of people coming together, listening to each other, exchanging ideas, learning to appreciate each other's differences, and defending their opinions.

social capital
The value of social contacts, associations, and networks individuals form which can foster trust, coordination, and cooperation.

substantially. Figure 7.1 contrasts the public's opinion toward President George W. Bush with its views on abortion over time. Although the electorate's opinion of President Bush changed noticeably over time, opinions on abortion remained remarkably stable. On many issues, opinion can change once the public learns more about the issue or perceives another side to the question. These are the issues politicians can help shape by calling attention to them and leading the debate.

The idea of people coming together, listening to each other, exchanging ideas, learning to appreciate each other's differences, and defending their opinions is sometimes called **deliberation** and builds what has been called **social capital**. Such interaction is thought to foster and strengthen community and relationships in ways that do not happen when citizens only cast ballots. Robert Putnam has defined social capital as "features of social organization such as networks, norms, and social trust that facilitate coordination and cooperation for mutual benefit."[26]

☐ Awareness and Interest

Many people find politics complicated and difficult to understand. And they should because democracy is complicated and difficult to understand. The mechanics and structures of our government, such as how the government operates, how the Electoral College works, how Congress is set up, and the length of terms for the president and for members of the Senate and House of Representatives are examples of such complexity that are important to our constitutional democracy.

Younger adults who remember learning the details in school typically know most about how the government works. In general, however, adults fare poorly when quizzed about their elected officials.[27] Slightly more than 15 percent know the names of the congressional candidates from their district.[28] With so few voters knowing the candidates, it is not surprising that "on even hotly debated issues before Congress, few people know where their Congress member stands."[29] In 2010, only 28 percent could identify John Roberts as the chief justice of the U.S. Supreme Court.[30] The public knows even less about important public policy issues.

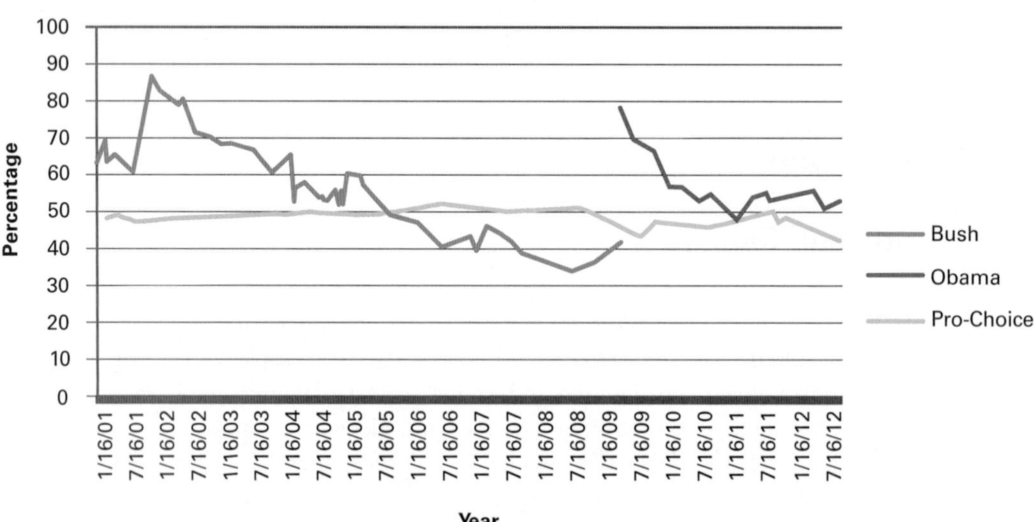

FIGURE 7.1 COMPARISON OF OPINION OF PRESIDENT GEORGE W. BUSH AND BARACK OBAMA WITH ATTITUDE ON ABORTION OVER TIME

■ *Why is attitude on abortion so consistent in comparison to the fluctuation in opinions of Presidents Bush and Obama over time?*

SOURCE: Gallup and Gallup/USA Today polls, compiled by Polling Report, Public Opinion: Taking the Pulse of the People www.pollingreport.com/abortion.htm, www.pollingreport.com/BushJob1.htm, and http://www.pollingreport.com/obama.htm.

Fortunately, not everyone is uninformed or uninterested. Approximately 25 percent of the public is interested in politics most of the time.[31] This is the **attentive public**, people who know and understand how the government works. They vote in most elections, read a daily newspaper, and talk politics with their families and friends. They tend to be better educated and more committed to democratic values than other adults.

At the opposite end of the spectrum are political know-nothings, people who are rarely interested in politics or public affairs and seldom vote. About one-third of American adults have indicated that they are interested in politics "only now and then" or "hardly at all."[32]

Between the attentive public and the political know-nothings are the *part-time citizens,* roughly 40 percent of the U.S. public. These individuals participate selectively in elections, voting in presidential elections but usually not in others. Politics and government do not greatly interest them, they pay only minimal attention to the news, and they rarely discuss candidates or elections with others.

Democracy can survive even when some citizens are passive and uninformed, as long as others serve as opinion leaders and are interested and informed about public affairs. Obviously, these activists will have much greater influence than their less-active fellow citizens.

attentive public
Citizens who follow public affairs carefully.

public opinion
The distribution of individual preferences for or evaluations of a given issue, candidate, or institution within a specific population.

random sample
In this type of sample, every individual has a known and equal chance of being selected.

Public Opinion: Taking the Pulse of the People

7.2 Describe the key dimensions of public opinion, how public opinion is measured, and the relationship between public opinion and public policy.

All governments in all nations must be concerned with public opinion. Even in nondemocratic nations, unrest and protest can topple those in power. We saw this in 2011 as mass protests brought down the long-standing autocratic regimes in Egypt and Tunisia. The long-term impact of the move to democracy in the Middle East is uncertain, but in 2012 Egypt had contested elections. In a constitutional democracy, citizens can express opinions in a variety of ways, including through demonstrations, in conversations, by writing to their elected representatives and to newspapers, through the use of social media like Twitter and YouTube, and by voting in free and regularly scheduled elections. In short, democracy and public opinion go hand in hand.

What Is Public Opinion?

Politicians frequently talk about what "the people" think or want. But social scientists use the term "public opinion" more precisely: **public opinion** is the distribution of individual preferences for or evaluations of a given issue, candidate, or institution within a specific population as measured by public opinion surveys. *Distribution* means the proportion of the population that holds a particular opinion, compared to people who have opposing opinions or no opinion at all. The most accurate way to study public opinion is through systematic measurement in polls or surveys. For instance, final preelection polls in 2012 by the Gallup Poll found that, among likely voters and removing those with no opinion, 48 percent said they were voting for Barack Obama, 49 percent said they were voting for Mitt Romney and 1 percent said they were voting for someone else.[33] The actual vote was Obama, 50 percent; Romney, 48 percent; and 2 percent voted for all others.

In addition to polls conducted by Gallup, Pew, and other such organizations, newspapers and TV networks conduct polls on election preferences and numerous other subjects.

Measuring Public Opinion

In a public opinion poll, a relatively small number of people can accurately represent the opinions of a larger population if the researchers use *random sampling.* In a **random sample**, every individual in the group has a known and equal chance of being selected.

7.1

7.2

7.3

7.4

7.5

margin of error
The range of percentage points in which the sample accurately reflects the population.

For instance, a survey of 18- to 24-year-olds should not consist solely of college students because nearly half of this age group does not attend college.[34] If only college students are selected, everyone in this age group does not have an equal chance of being included. A more reliable way to draw a sample today is with random-digit dialing, in which a computer generates phone numbers at random, allowing the researcher to reach unlisted numbers and cell phones as well as home phones. Exit polls, when properly administered, interview voters at random as they leave the polls at a randomly selected set of precincts.

Even with proper sampling, surveys have a **margin of error**, meaning the sample accurately reflects the population within a certain range—usually plus or minus 3 percent for a sample of at least 1,000 individuals. If, for example, a preelection poll had one candidate getting 50 percent of the vote and another 48 percent, and the margin of error was plus or minus 3 percent, the first candidate's share could be as high as 53 percent or as low as 47 percent, and the second candidate's could be as high as 51percent or as low as 45 percent. In such a race, the result would be within the margin of error and too close to say who was ahead. If the sample is sufficiently large and randomly selected, these margins of error would apply in about 95 of 100 cases. The final preelection survey results in 2008 were within this margin of error for the actual vote.

The *art of asking questions* is also important to scientific polling. Questions can measure respondents' factual knowledge, their opinions, the intensity of their opinions, or their views on hypothetical situations. The type of questions asked should be determined by the kind of information desired by the researcher. The way questions are worded and the order in which they are asked can influence respondents' answers. (See Table 7.1.) Researchers should pretest their questions to be sure they are as clear and as specific

TABLE 7.1 THE WAY YOU ASK THE QUESTION MATTERS

The way you ask a polling question can make a lot of difference in the way people answer it. In 2012, President Barack Obama stated that he believed same-sex couples should be allowed to marry. Following the controversial statement, several sources collected information on public opinion of gay marriage and President Obama's statement. However, different sources asked slightly different questions, which led to different interpretations of public opinion of gay marriage. Consider the following questions about gay marriage, each of which was asked between March and May, 2012. Read each question and consider how you would have responded if asked by an interviewer.

1. Do you think it should be legal or illegal for gay and lesbian couples to get married? Do you feel that way strongly or somewhat?

Legal			Illegal		
Strongly—36%	Somewhat—17%	Total—52%	Strongly—36%	Somewhat—7%	Total—43%

No opinion— 5%*

2. Do you believe gays and lesbians should be allowed to get legally married, allowed a legal partnership similar to but not called marriage, or should there be no legal recognition given to gay and lesbian relationships?

Legally married—37% Legal partnership—33% No legal recognition—25% Unsure—5%**

3. Which comes closest to your view? Gay couples should be allowed to legally marry. OR, Gay couples should be allowed to form civil unions but not legally marry. OR, There should be no legal recognition of a gay couple's relationship:

Legal marriage—38% Civil unions—24% No legal recognition—33% Unsure—5%†

4. If you had to decide, do you think it should be legal or not legal for same-sex couples to marry?

Legal—42% Not legal—51% Unsure—7%†

5. Do you think marriages between same-sex couples should or should not be recognized by the law as valid, with the same rights as traditional marriages?

Should be valid—50% Should not be valid—48%‡

■ *What about the question's wording might explain the very different results in these polls? Which of the questions do you think led to the most accurate measure of opinion? Why?*

* *Washington Post*-ABC News (March 2012).
**Fox News (May 2012).
†CBS News/New York Times (May 2012).
‡Gallup (May 2012).

as possible. Professional interviewers should read the questions exactly as written and without any bias in their voices.

Open-ended questions permit respondents to answer in their own words rather than by choosing responses from set categories. These questions are harder to record and compare, but they allow respondents to express their views more clearly and may provide deeper insight into their thinking.

Scientific polls also require thorough *analysis and reporting of the results.* Such polls must specify the sample size, the margin of error, and when and where the poll was conducted. Moreover, because public opinion can change from day to day and even from hour to hour, polls are really only snapshots of opinion at a particular point in time. One way to track opinion *change* is to interview the same sample more than once. Such surveys are called *panel surveys.* Although they can be informative, it can also be difficult and expensive to contact respondents for a second or third set of interviews, and the fact that those in the sample know they will be interviewed again may influence their responses.

Defining public opinion as the distribution of *individual preferences* emphasizes that the unit of measurement is *individuals*—not groups. The **universe** or *population* is the group of people whose preferences the researcher wants to measure. The sample of whom we ask the questions in the survey should be representative of this universe. When a substantial percentage of a sample agrees on an issue—say, that we should honor the U.S. flag—there is a *consensus.* But on most issues, opinions are divided. When two opposing sides feel intensely about an issue and the difference between the major alternatives is wide, the public is said to be *polarized.* On such issues, it can be difficult to compromise or find a middle ground. The Vietnam War in the 1960s and 1970s was a polarizing issue. A more recent example is gay marriage. Neither those who favor legalizing gay marriage nor those who unequivocally oppose it see much room for compromise. Somewhere in the middle are those who oppose gay marriage but favor giving gay couples legal rights through "civil unions." (See Table 7.2.)

INTENSITY The degree to which people feel strongly about their opinions, or **intensity**, produces the brightest and deepest hues in the fabric of public opinion. For example, some individuals mildly favor gun control legislation, others mildly oppose it; some people are emphatically for or against it; and some have no interest in gun control at all. Others may not have even heard of it. People who lost their jobs or retirement savings because of corporate scandals are likely to feel more intensely about enhanced regulation of corporations and financial institutions than those not directly affected. We typically measure intensity by asking people how strongly they feel about an issue or about a politician. Such a question is sometimes called a *scale.*

LATENCY When people hold political opinions but do not fully express them, the opinions are described as **latent**. These opinions may not have crystallized, yet they are still important, because they can be aroused by leaders or events and thereby motivate people to support them. Latent opinions set rough boundaries for leaders who know that, if they take certain actions, they will trigger either opposition or support from millions of people. If leaders understand people's unexpressed wants, needs, and hopes, they will know how to mobilize people and draw them to the polls on Election Day. A recent example of a latent opinion is the concern for security from foreign enemies, which had not been an issue in the United States before the terrorist attacks of September 11, 2001. The need for homeland security has now become a **manifest opinion**, a widely shared and consciously held view.

SALIENCE Issues that people believe are important to them are **salient**. Most people are more concerned about personal issues such as paying their bills and keeping their jobs than about national issues, but if national issues somehow threaten their security or safety, their salience rises sharply. Salience and intensity, though different, are often correlated on the same issue.

The salience of issues may change over time. During the Great Depression of the 1930s, people were concerned mainly about jobs, wages, and economic security. By the 1940s, with the onset of World War II, foreign affairs came to the forefront.

universe
The group of people whose preferences we try to measure by taking a sample; also called population.

intensity
A measure of how strongly an individual holds a particular opinion.

latency
Political opinions that are held but not yet expressed.

manifest opinion
A widely shared and consciously held view, such as support for abortion rights or for homeland security.

salience
An individual's belief that an issue is important or relevant to him or her.

7.1

7.2

7.3

7.4

7.5

TABLE 7.2 DIFFERING OPINIONS ON GAY MARRIAGE

	Gay Marriage Should Not Be Allowed	Gay Marriage Should Not Be Allowed, but Civil Unions Should Be Allowed (volunteered response)	Gay Marriage Should Be Allowed
Total Gender	**35%**	**26%**	**39%**
Men	37	27	36
Women	33	25	42
Region			
Northeast	24	28	49
Midwest	42	26	32
South	42	25	33
West	22	27	52
Age			
18–29	22	18	61
30–44	26	27	47
45–64	40	30	30
65+	53	28	19
Church Attendance			
Every week	59	26	15
Almost every week	44	24	32
Once or twice a month	34	31	36
A few times a year	21	28	51
Never	24	24	52
Race			
White	34	27	39
African American	47	20	33
Hispanic	31	22	47
Other	29	24	47
Party			
Republican	45	33	23
Democrat	27	22	51
Independent	36	22	42
Other	25	17	58
Political Philosophy			
Conservative	53	31	16
Moderate	27	29	44
Liberal	15	20	65
Do not know/Have not thought about it	35	22	43
Marital Status			
Married	39	30	31
Widowed	48	21	30
Divorced	35	28	37
Separated	33	18	50
Single, never married	23	19	58
Partnered, not married	18	33	49
Education			
High school or less	43	22	35
Some college	31	27	42
College degree or more	27	31	42

NOTE: Numbers may not add to 100 because of rounding. Independents that lean toward a party are classified with the party toward which they lean. Race is defined by the first race with which a respondent identifies.

SOURCE: *2008 National Election Study* (Center for Political Studies, University of Michigan, 2008).

■ *Why do you suppose more women than men support gay marriage? What might help explain the lack of support for gay marriage among African Americans, another disadvantaged group?*

In the 1960s, problems of race and poverty were important to many. In the 1970s, Vietnam and then the Watergate scandals became the focus of attention.

political ideology
A constant pattern of ideas or beliefs about political values and the role of government, including how it should work and how it actually does work.

liberalism
A belief that government can bring about justice and equality of opportunity.

☐ Public Opinion and Public Policy

For much of human history, public opinion has been difficult to measure. "What I want," Abraham Lincoln once said, "is to get done what the people desire to be done, and the question for me is how to find that out exactly."[35] Politicians today do not face such uncertainty about public opinion—far from it.[36] Polling informs them about public opinion on all major policy issues. Politicians can commission polls themselves, or they can turn to public or media polls. All national and some local newspapers and television stations conduct or commission their own polls.[37]

Many examples from history show how public opinion can shape policy and, in turn, how policies shape opinion. On May 3, 2003, the day after President Bush announced "Mission Accomplished" in the Iraq War, 72 percent of American adults approved of the way he had handled the situation in Iraq. About one year later, after revelations of torture by U.S. soldiers in the Abu Ghraib prison and repeated attacks on U.S. forces in Iraq, Bush's approval rating had fallen to 34 percent,[38] and in 2008, it fell to less than 30 percent.[39] Obama began his presidency with a 69 percent approval rating, only to see that drop to 49 percent in 2010, not long after Congress enacted health care reform, and fall further to 38 percent in 2011.[40] In October 2012, Obama had an approval rating of about 50 percent, which was similar to positive ratings between 48 percent and 52 percent, which George Bush had in October 2004 as he sought reelection.[41]

Typically, elected officials focus on issues of importance to the public.[42] In a sense, they follow public opinion by using polls to learn how to talk about issues in ways that resonate with the public. Members of Congress want to win reelection by showing greater attention to public opinion as Election Day looms.[43] Candidates use polls to determine where, how, and even whether to campaign. The decision in 2012 about which states and districts the two parties and allied interest groups most contested in the presidential and congressional races was driven by the polls. Even less populous states such as New Hampshire and Nevada received substantial attention. Larger states such as New York, California, Illinois, and Texas were taken for granted because one side or the other was so far ahead in them and gaining a plurality in the national popular vote was a secondary objective to securing 270 electoral votes.

Polls are no substitute for elections. With a choice between candidates before them, voters must now translate their opinions into concrete decisions and decide what is important and what is not. Democracy is more than the expression of views, a simple mirror of opinion. It is the thoughtful participation of people in the political process. Elections are the critical link between the many opinions "We the People" hold and how we select our leaders.

Political Ideology and Attitudes Toward Government

7.3 Compare and contrast political ideologies and evaluate the critiques of each ideology.

One central component of public opinion is ideology. **Political ideology** refers to a consistent pattern of ideas or beliefs about political values and the role of government, including how it should work and how it actually does work.

Two major schools of political ideology dominate American politics: *liberalism* and *conservatism*. Two less popular schools of thought—*socialism* and *libertarianism*—also help define the spectrum of ideology. We measure ideology by asking people a question like, "When it comes to politics do you usually think of yourself

7.1

7.2

7.3

7.4

7.5

as extremely liberal, liberal, slightly liberal, moderate or middle of the road, slightly conservative, conservative, extremely conservative, or haven't you thought much about this?"[44] People rather consistently self-classify themselves as liberal or conservative and are also willing to report the strength of their views (e.g. extremely conservative, slightly liberal, etc.). At the same time a large group of people respond to the question by saying they are "moderate" or "have not thought much about this." (See Table 7.3.)

□ Liberalism

In the eighteenth and nineteenth centuries, classical liberals favored *limited government* and sought to protect people from governmental harassment in their political and economic lives. Over time, the liberal emphasis on individualism has remained constant, but the perception of the need for government changed.

CONTEMPORARY LIBERALS In its current U.S. usage, **liberalism** refers to a belief that government can bring about justice and equality of opportunity. Modern-day liberals wish to preserve the rights of the individual and the right to own private property, yet they believe that some government intervention in the economy is

TABLE 7.3 DIFFERENCES IN POLITICAL IDEOLOGY

	Conservative	Moderate	Liberal	Don't Know/Haven't Thought About It
Sex				
Male	39%	23%	20%	18%
Female	31	24	22	23
Race				
White	39	24	21	17
Black	18	21	22	39
Asian	20	26	36	18
Hispanic	22	25	20	32
Age				
18–34	26	24	28	23
35–45	36	26	17	20
46–55	37	23	19	20
56–64	38	21	26	15
Religion				
Protestant	45	18	16	15
Catholic	31	28	18	23
Jewish	26	12	63	0
Education				
Less than high school	25	20	14	42
High school diploma	29	27	11	33
Some college	38	25	22	15
Bachelor's degree	42	21	32	5
Advanced degree	45	14	39	3
Party				
Democrat	13	27	37	23
Independent	14	35	11	40
Republican	70	15	5	11

This table displays how ideology is correlated to sex, race, age, religion, education, and political party.

■ *In which factors do you see the strongest and weakest correlations, and how might you account for that?*

SOURCE: Center for Political Studies, University of Michigan, *2008 American National Election Study Guide to Public Opinion and Electoral Behavior.*

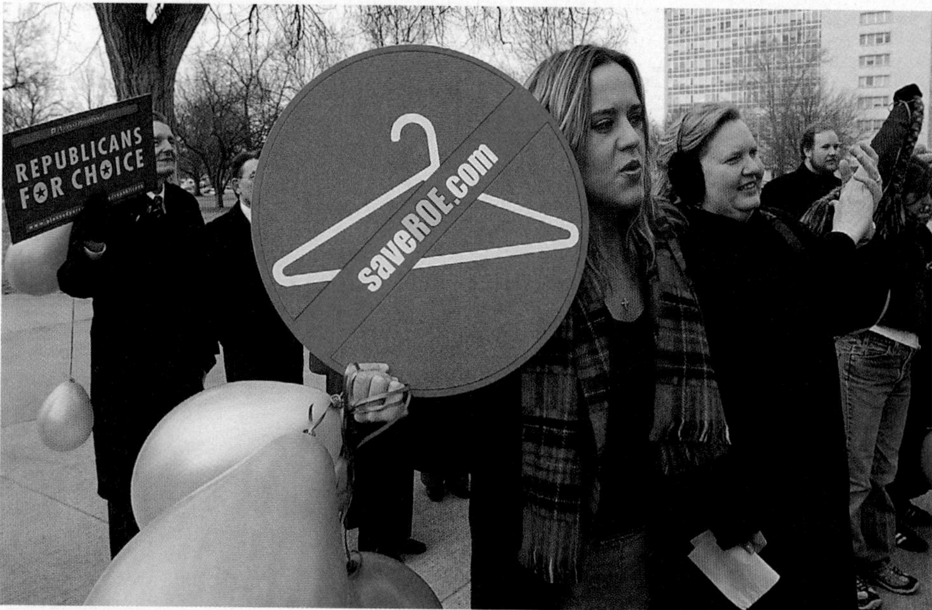

Liberals favor individual choice for women. Pro-abortion advocate Robin Clarke, of Overland Park, Kansas, participates in a rally on the anniversary of the Roe v. Wade decision in the state capital, Topeka.

conservatism
A belief in private property rights and free enterprise.

7.1
7.2
7.3
7.4
7.5

necessary to remedy the shortcomings of capitalism. Liberals advocate equal access to health care, housing, and education for all citizens. They generally believe in affirmative action programs, protections for workers' health and safety, tax rates that rise with a person's income, and unions' rights to organize and strike. Liberals are generally more inclined to favor greater environmental protection and individual choice in such matters as same-sex marriage and abortion.

Liberals generally believe that the future will be better than the past or the present—that obstacles can be overcome and the government can be trusted to, and should, play a role in that progress. Liberals led in expanding civil rights in the 1960s and 1970s and favor affirmative action today. Most favor a certain minimum level of income for all. Rather than placing a cap on wealth, they want to build a floor beneath the poor. If necessary, they favor raising taxes to achieve these goals. In the recent health care reform debate, liberals favored a public insurance plan providing something like Medicare for all citizens.

CRITICISMS OF LIBERALISM Critics say liberals rely too much on government, higher taxes, and bureaucracy to solve the nation's problems. They argue that liberals have forgotten that government has to be limited if it is to serve our best interests. Too much dependence on government can corrupt the spirit, undermine self-reliance, and make people forget those personal freedoms and property rights the Republic was founded to secure and protect. In short, critics of modern liberalism contend that the welfare and regulatory state liberals advocate will ultimately destroy individual initiative, the entrepreneurial spirit, and the very engine of economic growth that might lead to true equality of economic opportunity. Since the late 1960s, Republicans have made liberalism a villain while claiming that their own presidential candidates represent the mainstream.

☐ Conservatism

Belief in private property rights and free enterprise are cardinal attributes of contemporary **conservatism**. In contrast to liberals, conservatives want to enhance individual liberty by keeping government small, especially the national government, although they support a strong national defense. Conservatives take a more pessimistic view of

One of President Bush's priorities was the "No Child Left Behind" legislation. He is seen here signing the law early in his presidency (2001). Motivated by a desire to improve educational performance, the law set standards for educational attainment based on standardized tests. The law has drawn criticism from both sides of the political spectrum. Conservatives attack the act for its interference with local control of education, and liberals criticize the implementation of the act and its inadequate funding.

SOURCE: http://standardizedtests.procon.org/view.resource.php?resourceID=4343

social conservatives
Focus less on economics and more on morality and lifestyle.

human nature than liberals do. Given that a primary task of government is to ensure order, they maintain that people need strong leadership, firm laws, and strict moral codes. Conservatives also believe that people are the architects of their own success or failure.

TRADITIONAL CONSERVATIVES Conservatives are emphatically pro-business. They favor tax cuts and resist all but the minimum antitrust, trade, and environmental regulations on corporations. They believe that the sole functions of government should be to protect the nation from foreign enemies, preserve law and order, enforce private contracts, encourage economic growth by fostering competitive markets and free and fair trade, and promote family values. Traditional conservatives favor dispersing power throughout the political and social systems to avoid an overly powerful national government; they believe that the market, not the government, should provide services. These views were tested by the Bush administration's advocacy of a massive government bailout of financial institutions in 2008 and more broadly by concerns about government spending and budget deficits during the Bush administration.

Conservatives opposed the New Deal programs of the 1930s, the War on Poverty in the 1960s, many civil rights and affirmative action programs, and the Obama administration's push for a larger government role in health care. Families and private charities, they say, can and should take care of human needs and social and economic problems. Government social activism, they say, has been expensive and counterproductive. State and local government should address those social problems that need a government response. Conservatives, especially those in office, do, however, selectively advocate government activism, often expressing a desire for a more effective and efficient government.

SOCIAL CONSERVATIVES Some conservatives focus less on economics and more on morality and lifestyle. **Social conservatives** favor strong governmental action to protect children from pornography and drugs. They want to overturn or repeal judicial rulings and laws that permit abortion, same-sex marriage, and affirmative action programs. This brand of conservatism—sometimes called the New Right—emerged in the 1980s. Social conservatives share with traditional conservatives a love of freedom and support an aggressive effort to defend American interests abroad.

A defining characteristic of social conservatism is a strong desire to impose *social controls*. Christian conservatives, who are disproportionately evangelical, seek to preserve traditional values and protect the institution of the family. In 2012, the connection between Christian conservatives and the GOP was further reinforced by the candidacy of former Pennsylvania Senator Rick Santorum, who emphasized his religion and Christian religious values in his campaign.[45]

socialism
A governmental system where some of the means of production are controlled by the state and where the state provides key human welfare services like health care and old age assistance. Allows for free markets in other activities.

communism
A belief that the state owns property in common for all people and a single political party that represents the working classes controls the government.

CRITICISMS OF CONSERVATISM Not everyone agreed with Ronald Reagan's statement that "government is the problem." Indeed, critics point out that conservatives themselves urge more government when it serves their purposes—to regulate pornography and abortion, for example—but are opposed to government when it serves somebody else's. Conservatives may also have fewer objections to big government when individuals have a choice in determining how government will affect them. Vouchers for schools, choices in prescription-drug benefit plans, and options to manage Social Security savings are examples of such choices.[46]

Conservatives' great faith in the market economy often puts them at odds with labor unions and consumer activists and in close alliance with businesspeople, particularly large corporations. Hostility to regulation and a belief in competition lead conservatives to push for deregulation. This approach has not always had positive results, as illustrated by the collapse of many savings and loan companies in the 1980s[47] and the 2008 financial crisis, brought about by troubled subprime mortgages and other risky lending practices.[48] Conservatives counter that overall it is still best to rely on the free market.

The policy of lowering taxes is consistent with the conservative hostility to big government. Many conservatives embrace the idea that if the rich pay fewer taxes, they will spend and invest more, and the benefits of this increased economic activity will "trickle down" to others including the poor. But Democrats and liberals argue that most of the growth in income and wealth that followed 1980s tax cuts was largely concentrated among the well-to-do and that reduced taxes and increased government spending, especially for defense, tripled the deficit during the 1980s, when conservatives were in control.[49] The temporary tax cuts pushed by President George W. Bush during his first term have been extended three times.[50] Republicans and conservatives favor making the cuts permanent and all of the 2012 Republican presidential candidates favored even more extensive tax cuts.

Liberals counter that the Bush tax cuts should be repealed because they further benefit the rich while hurting everyone else and have proposed increasing taxes for those making more than $1 million, a reform sometimes called "the Buffett Rule," named after billionaire Warren Buffett, who endorsed higher taxes for the wealthy.[51] Who should pay what in taxes was a central issue in the 2012 elections and shows the enduring ideological divide over taxing and government spending.

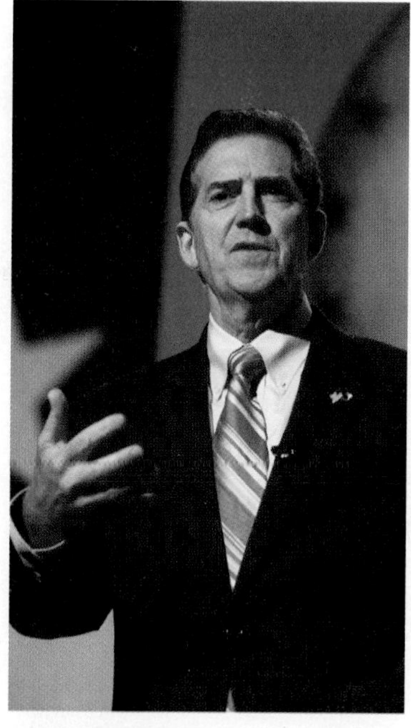

Senator Jim DeMint (R-SC) is both a fiscal and social conservative. He is closely identified with the Tea Party movement and founded of the Senate Conservative Fund, a PAC that supports conservative Republican U.S. Senate candidates. In 2012, he also started a Super PAC to help elect conservative Senators.

☐ Socialism and Communism

Socialism is an economic and governmental system based on public ownership of some of the means of production and exchange and a wider role for government in providing social programs meeting such needs as health care and old-age assistance. Socialism allows for capitalism in many economic sectors, but favors more government regulation. The nineteenth-century German philosopher Karl Marx once described socialism as a transitional stage of society between capitalism and communism. In a capitalist system, the means of production and most property are privately owned; under **communism** the state owns property in common for all the people, and a single political party that represents the working classes controls the government.

Senate Assistant Majority Leader Richard Durbin, D-Ill., one of the most liberal senators, seen here meeting with reporters to introduce a bipartisan marketplace fairness bill.

In communist countries such as Cuba and China, the Communist Party allows no opposition. Some countries, such as Sweden, have combined limited government ownership and operation of business with democracy. Most western European countries and Canada have various forms of socialized or government-run medical systems and sometimes telecommunications networks, while keeping most economic sectors private.

American socialists—of whom there are only a few prominent examples, including one United States senator, Vermont's Bernie Sanders—favor a greatly expanded role for the government, but argue that such a system is compatible with democracy. They would nationalize certain industries, institute a public jobs program so that all who want to work could work, tax the wealthy much more heavily, and drastically cut defense spending.[52] Canada and most of the democracies of Western Europe are more influenced by socialist ideas than we are in the United States, but they remain, like the United States, largely market economies. Debate will continue about the proper role of government and what the market can do better than government can.[53]

□ Libertarianism

libertarianism
Would limit government to such vital activities as national defense while fostering individual liberty. Unlike conservatives, libertarians oppose all government regulation, even of personal morality.

Libertarianism is a political ideology that cherishes individual liberty and insists on sharply limited government. Libertarians oppose nearly all government programs. They favor massive cuts in government spending and an end to the Federal Bureau of Investigation (FBI), the Central Intelligence Agency (CIA), the Internal Revenue Service (IRS), and most regulatory commissions. They oppose American participation in the United Nations and favor armed forces that would defend the United States only if directly attacked. They oppose *all* government regulation, including, for example, mandatory seat-belt and helmet laws, in part because they believe individuals will all benefit more from an undistorted free market, and more generally because they embrace the attitude "live and let live." Unlike conservatives, libertarians would repeal laws that regulate personal morality, including abortion, pornography, prostitution, and illicit drugs. The Libertarian Party has gained a following among people who share this perspective. Ron Paul, who ran as a Libertarian for president in 1988, continued to espouse many of the positions identified with Libertarians in his 2008 and 2012 bids to become the Republican nominee for president.[54]

Despite the twists and turns of American politics, the distribution of ideology in the nation has been remarkably consistent (see Figure 7.2). Conservatives outnumber liberals, but the proportion of conservatives did not increase substantially with the decisive Republican presidential victories of the 1980s or the congressional victories of the 1990s. Moreover, in the United States most people are moderates. In recent years only 2–3 percent of Americans viewed themselves as extreme liberal, while extreme conservatives ranged from 2 to 4 percent.

Participation: Translating Opinions into Action

7.4 Identify forms of political participation, and assess the effect on voter turnout of demographic, legal, and electioneering factors.

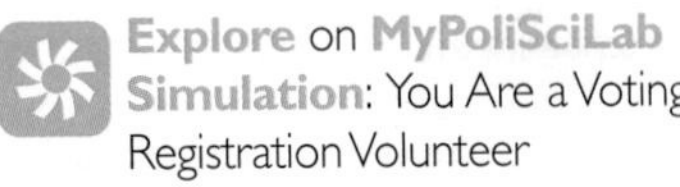

Explore on MyPoliSciLab Simulation: You Are a Voting Registration Volunteer

U.S. citizens influence their government's actions in several ways, many of which the Constitution protects. In addition to voting in elections, they participate in Internet political blogs, join interest groups, go to political party meetings, ring doorbells, urge friends to vote for issues or candidates, sign petitions, write letters to newspapers, and call radio talk shows. This kind of "citizen-to-citizen" participation can be important and may become more so as more people use the Internet and its social capital-building applications, such as social networking sites.[55]

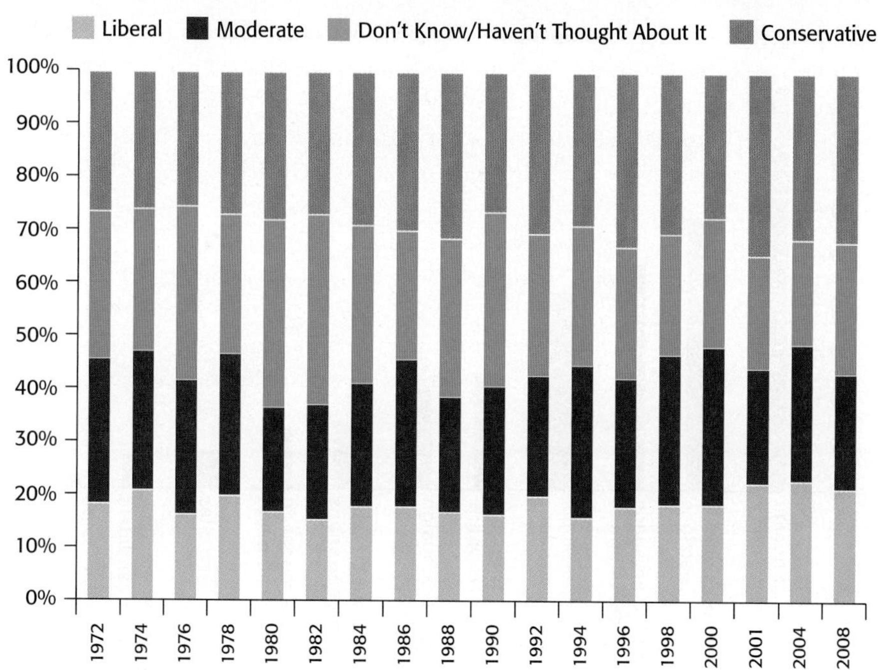

FIGURE 7.2 IDEOLOGY OVER TIME

What factors might account for the stability in Americans' ideology over time?

SOURCE: Center for Political Studies, University of Michigan, *2008 American National Election Study.*

Protest is also a form of political participation. Our political system is remarkably tolerant of protest that is not destructive or violent. Boycotts, picketing, sit-ins, and marches are all legally protected. Rosa Parks and Martin Luther King Jr. used nonviolent protest to call attention to unfair laws. Relative to voting, few people participate in protests, but the actions of those who do can substantially shape public opinion, as the Tea Party activities demonstrated in 2010 and 2012, and the Occupy Wall Street protesters demonstrated in 2011 and 2012. In extreme cases, people may feel so strongly about an issue that they would rather fight than accept the verdict of an election. The classic example is the American Civil War.

For most people, politics is a private activity. Some still consider it impolite to discuss politics at dinner parties. To say that politics is private does not mean that people do not have opinions or will not discuss them when asked by others, including pollsters. But many people avoid discussing politics with neighbors, co-workers, or even friends and family because it is too divisive or upsetting. Typically, fewer than one person in four attempts to influence how another person votes in an election,[56] although that number rose in 2008,[57] and even fewer people contribute financially to a candidate.[58] Fewer still write letters to elected officials or to newspapers for publication or participate in protest groups or activities. Yet, despite the small number of people who engage in these activities, they can make a difference in politics and government. An individual or small group can generate media interest in an issue and thereby expand the issue's impact.

Levels of political participation rose during the 2008 presidential election, in part because of increased use of the Internet to persuade and mobilize voters (see Figure 7.3). Candidates' Web sites allowed individuals to register with the campaign and be connected with other politically active individuals in their area. They also provided calling lists for volunteers to call from their own phones. Local campaign leaders in turn used the Internet to contact individuals in the area who had expressed an interest in working with the campaign. The Internet helped campaigns organize more effectively and made it easier for interested people to participate. Supporters of some candidates in 2008 created their own music videos and Web political advertisements,

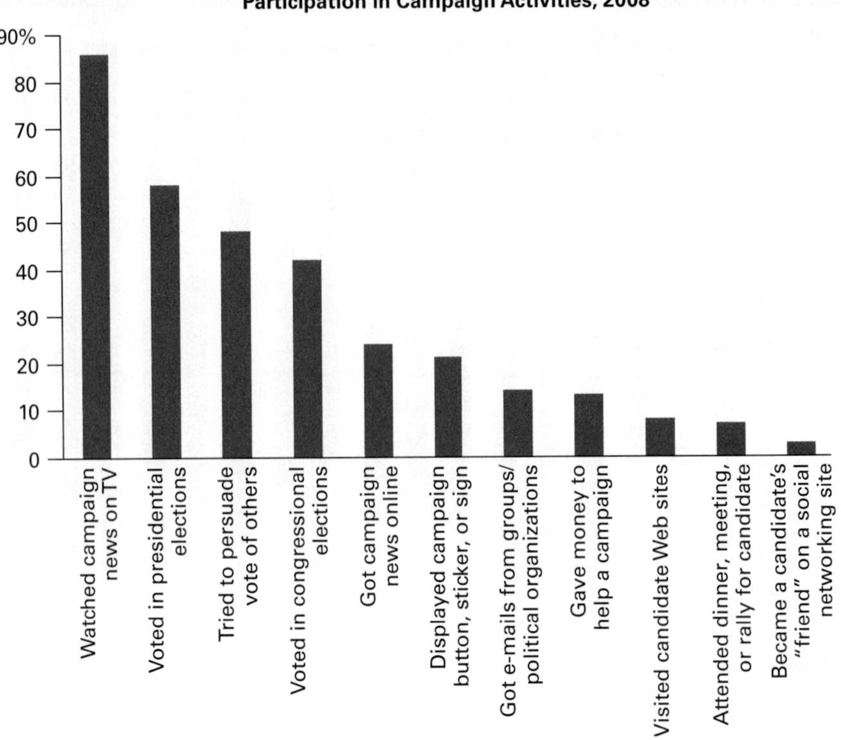

FIGURE 7.3 POLITICAL PARTICIPATION AND AWARENESS IN THE UNITED STATES

■ *Ten years from now, which of these activities would you expect to become more prevalent, and which less so?*

SOURCE: U.S. Census Bureau, *Statistical Abstract of the United States: 2006* (U.S. Government Printing Office, 2006), p. 263; *2008 National Election Study*, Center for Political Studies, University of Michigan; NES Guide to Public Opinion and Electoral Behavior, http://www.electionstudies.org/studypages/2008prepost/2008prepost.htm; and Pew Research Center, "Social Networking and Online Videos Take Off," January 11, 2008, http://www.pewinternet.org/Reports/2008/The-Internet-Gains-in-Politics/Summary-of-Findings.aspx (accessed June 29, 2012).

which they uploaded to YouTube and other video-hosting Web sites. Candidates and groups used the Internet for communications and mobilization in 2010 and 2012.

Candidates' Web sites made it easy for individuals to donate and to invite their friends to donate through e-mail, Facebook, MySpace, and other social-networking Web sites. The Obama campaign was especially innovative in its use of the Internet in 2008 and ActBlue, a liberal political action committee, has used the Internet to make it much easier for people to donate to the Democratic candidates of their choice, while Slatecard has tried to achieve the same for Republicans.

□ Voting

For most people politics and elections are of secondary importance and if they become involved at all, they do so by voting. The United States is a constitutional democracy with more than 200 years of free and frequent elections. Elections have consequences resulting in the peaceful transfer of power scores of times between competing groups and parties. But who may vote and what we vote for has changed over time. Our ideas about suffrage, the right to vote, have changed from a belief that only property-owning white men should be allowed to vote to a conviction that all adults, excluding felons in some states, should have the right; as an example see the women's suffrage timeline (Table 7.4). The role of voters has also expanded. Citizens now may vote in party primaries to select nominees for office instead of having nominees chosen by party leaders.

Originally, the Constitution left it to the individual states to determine who could vote, and qualifications for voting differed considerably from state to state. All states except New Jersey barred women from voting, most did not permit African Americans or Native Americans to vote, and until the 1830s, property ownership was often a requirement. By the time of the Civil War (1861–1865), however, every state had

TABLE 7.4 WOMEN'S SUFFRAGE TIMELINE*

Timeline	Change
1821	Emma Willard founds the Troy Female Seminary, the first school to offer girls classical and scientific studies on a collegiate level.
1833	Oberlin College is founded as the first coeducational institution of higher learning.
1837	Mount Holyoke, the first college for women, is founded by Mary Lyon in South Hadley, MA.
1839	Mississippi becomes the first state to grant women the right to hold property in their own name.**
1848	The first woman's rights convention is held in Seneca Falls, New York. State Legislature passes a law that gives women the right to retain possession of property they owned prior to their marriage.
1869	National Woman Suffrage Association is founded with Elizabeth Cady Stanton as president. Wyoming Territory grants suffrage to women.
1890	Wyoming joins the union as the first state with voting rights for women.
1912	Suffrage referendums are passed in Arizona, Kansas, and Oregon.
1916	Jeannette Rankin, a Republican from Montana, is elected to the House of Representatives and becomes the first woman to serve in Congress.
1920	The Nineteenth Amendment to the U.S. Constitution granting women the right to vote is adopted.
1936	Federal court rules birth control legal for its own sake, rather than solely for prevention of disease.
1960	FDA approves birth control pills.
1964	Civil Rights Act prohibits job discrimination on the basis of race or sex and establishes Equal Employment Opportunity Commission to address discrimination claims.
1972	After nearly 50 years, Equal Rights Amendment passes both houses and is signed by President Richard Nixon. Title IX prohibits sex discrimination in educational programs and activities.†
1973	In *Roe* v. *Wade*, U.S. Supreme Court affirms women's right to first trimester abortions without state intervention.
1981	Sandra Day O'Connor is appointed first woman U.S. Supreme Court justice.
1993	The Family and Medical Leave Act requires employers to provide up to 12 weeks of unpaid leave within one year of the birth of a child.‡

*Unless otherwise indicated, drawn from Susan B. Anthony Timeline," Anthony Center for Women's Leadership at the University of Rochester. www.rochester.edu/sba/suffragetimeline.html. All rights reserved.
**http://www.wearewoman.us/p/us-womens-rights-history.html
†Title IX is a portion of the Education Amendments of 1972, Public Law No. 92-318, 86 Stat. 235 (June 23, 1972), codified at 20 U.S.C. sections 1681 through 1688nces.ed.gov/fastfacts/display.asp?id=93
‡www.dol.gov/whd/fmla/

extended the franchise to white male citizens. Since that time, eligibility standards for voting have been expanded seven times by congressional legislation and constitutional amendments (see Table 7.5).

TABLE 7.5 CHANGES IN VOTING ELIGIBILITY STANDARDS SINCE 1870

Timeline	Change
1870	Fifteenth Amendment forbade states from denying the right to vote because of "race, color, or previous condition of servitude."
1920	Nineteenth Amendment gave women the right to vote.
1924	Congress granted Native Americans citizenship and voting rights.
1961	Twenty-Third Amendment permitted District of Columbia residents to vote in federal elections.
1964	Twenty-Fourth Amendment prohibited the use of poll taxes in federal elections.
1965	Voting Rights Act removed restrictions that kept African Americans from voting.
1971	Twenty-Sixth Amendment extended the vote to citizens age 18 and older.

■ *How have "the people" included in our government by the people changed since the founding of the country?*

voter registration
A system designed to reduce voter fraud by limiting voting to those who have established eligibility to vote by submitting the proper documents, including proof of residency.

The civil rights movement in the 1960s made voting rights a central issue. In 1964, President Lyndon Johnson pushed for passage of the Twenty-Fourth Amendment, which banned poll taxes, and in 1965, for passage of the National Voting Rights Act, which outlawed the use of literacy tests as a requirement for voting. Anticipating that some state or local governments would change election rules to foster discrimination, the Act also required that any changes to voting practices, requirements, or procedures must be cleared in advance with the Department of Justice or the U.S. District Court for the District of Columbia. The ban on the poll tax and the provisions of the Voting Rights Act resulted in a dramatic expansion of registration and voting by African Americans. Once African Americans were permitted to register to vote, "the focus of voting discrimination shifted… to preventing them from winning elections."[59] In southern legislative districts where African Americans are in the majority, however, there has been a "dramatic increase in the proportion of African American legislators elected.[60] The number of African Americans in the U.S. House of Representatives from all states hit a new high of 42 following the 2010 election, plus two delegates who are also African American.[61]

REGISTRATION One legal requirement—**voter registration**—arose as a response to concerns about voting abuses, but it also discourages voting.[62] It requires voters to take an extra step—usually filling out a form at the county courthouse, when renewing a driver's license, or with a roving registrar—days or weeks before the election and every time they move to a new address. Average turnout in the United States is more than 30 percentage points lower than in countries such as Denmark, Germany, and Israel where voter registration is not required.[63] This was not always the case. In fact, in the 1800s, turnout in the United States was much like that of these countries today. It began to drop significantly around 1900, in part as a result of election reforms (see Figure 7.4).

Laws vary by state, but every state except North Dakota requires registration, usually in advance. Idaho, Maine, Minnesota, New Hampshire, Wisconsin, and Wyoming permit Election-Day registration. The most important provision regarding voter registration may be the closing date. Until the early 1970s, closing dates in many states were six months before the election. Now, federal law prevents a state from closing registration more than 30 days before a federal election.[64] Other important provisions include places and hours of registration and, as discussed at the beginning of the chapter, some states require that voters show photo identification before voting.[65]

MOTOR VOTER In 1993, the burdens of voter registration were eased a bit with the National Voter Registration Act—called the "Motor Voter" bill—which allows people to register to vote while applying for or renewing a driver's license. Offices that provide welfare and disability assistance can also facilitate voter registration. States may use public schools, libraries, and city and county clerks' offices as registration sites. The law requires states to allow registration by mail using a standardized form. To purge the voting rolls of those who may have died or changed residence, states must mail a questionnaire to

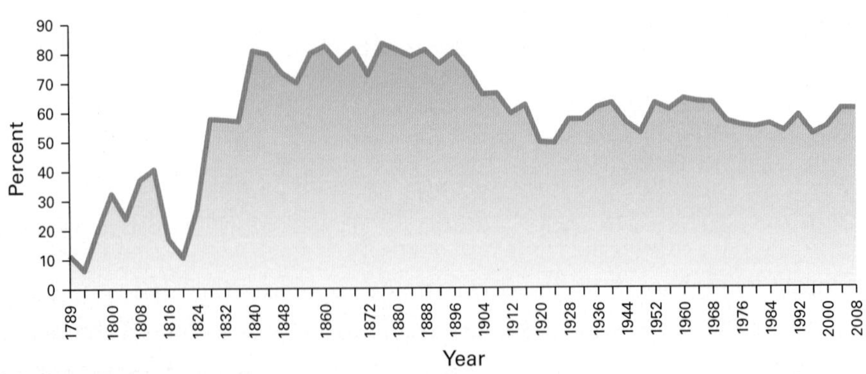

FIGURE 7.4 VOTER TURNOUT IN PRESIDENTIAL ELECTIONS, 1789–2008

SOURCE: Curtis Gans, Howard W. Stanley, and Richard G. Niemi, *Vital Statistics on American Politics, 2011–2012* (CQ Press, 2011), pp. 4–5.

voters every four years. But Motor Voter forbids states from purging the rolls for any other reason, such as because a person has not voted in multiple previous elections.

As a result of this law, more new voters have registered.[66] Data on the impact of Motor Voter suggest that neither Democrats nor Republicans are the primary beneficiaries because most new voters who have registered claim to be Independent.[67] Yet Motor Voter alone does not appear to have increased turnout. Instead, when states actively invite citizens to register at the time they renew their driver's license, there is a boost in turnout of 4 percent.[68]

ABSENTEE AND EARLY VOTING Growing numbers of people choose not to vote in person at their local voting places on Election Day. Instead they use *absentee voting* to vote early by mail. Absentee voting has been used since the Civil War[69] and has recently become more popular. Three in ten voters in 2008 cast their vote away from a traditional, Election-Day polling location, the most in the history of the United States.[70] In 1998, Oregon was the first state to switch to statewide elections done through the mail, an experiment that was widely seen as a success in that state. Election officials like vote-by-mail because it lowers cost and is easier to administer than an in-person voting process held on only one day. Vote-by-mail has been found to increase turnout, at least in the initial period after adoption,[71] and in Oregon, it continues to foster greater turnout in presidential general elections.[72] Opponents of vote-by-mail worry about potential abuses of the process, where people might fraudulently cast the ballot of another person or bribe a person to vote a certain way and then mail in that person's ballot. Some see value in casting a ballot in public with other voters on a designated day. More fundamentally, some question the value of making it easier for people to vote, which voting by mail does. This viewpoint is based on the perceived importance of citizens being willing to invest time and effort, which in-person voting requires. To date, Oregon is the only state to have switched to vote-by-mail as its means to conduct elections.

FOR the People Government's Greatest Endeavors

Helping America Vote

The exceedingly close Florida vote in the 2000 presidential election called attention to multiple problems with the voting process not only in that state but in many states. Among the problems were poorly maintained and outdated voting machines, confusing ballot designs, inconsistent rules for counting absentee ballots, and the need for more and better trained poll workers. In response to these and other problems, Congress enacted in 2002 the Help America Vote Act (HAVA).

HAVA for the first time established accessibility standards for voting systems in the United States. The Americans with Disabilities Act of 1990 required that voting places be accessible to persons with disabilities, but prior to HAVA, individuals with disabilities in some states could only vote with the assistance of a poll worker, which compromised the privacy of their vote. HAVA required that states provide voting machines for persons with disabilities, including the visually impaired, that allow these voters the same level of privacy as any other voter.

The system of voter registration in the United States is largely administered at the county level, and as such, there was widespread variability in the way counties maintained the list of registered voters. HAVA mandated the creation of statewide, computerized voter registration lists. The Act also mandated the creation of a toll-free phone number that individuals could use to learn about their registration status.

Poll workers are critical to the administration of elections. HAVA provides federal grants to help train poll workers and to involve college and high school students in assisting at the polls on Election Day (see *By the People: Be a Poll Worker* box in this chapter). HAVA created the Election Assistance Commission to assist states with election administration and ensure that minimum federal standards in such areas as accessibility are met. Although problems remain in making elections work well, HAVA has helped state and local governments make substantial strides.

QUESTIONS

1. Why is the privacy of the voting act important to voters?
2. How would a common statewide list of registered voters enhance participation?
3. What are some other ways in which the voting process could be improved?

7.1
7.2
7.3
7.4
7.5

general election
Election in which voters elect officeholders.

primary election
Election in which voters determine party nominees.

presidential election
Election held in year when the president is on the ballot.

midterm election
Election held midway between presidential elections.

turnout
The proportion of the voting-age public that votes, sometimes defined as the number of registered voters that vote.

Another innovation designed to make voting easier is allowing people to vote early but at a polling location. This change was in part the result of concerns about having insufficient voting machines for Election Day. In 2012, 26 states allowed early voting, either through the mail or in person at polling locations, without needing to claim travel, work, or other reasons to vote early,[73] but eight states reduced their early voting time periods for the 2012 election.[74]

□ Turnout

The United States holds more elections for more offices than any other democracy. That may be why U.S. voters tend to be selective about the elections in which they vote. We elect officeholders in **general elections**, determine party nominees in **primary elections**, and replace members of the House of Representatives who have died or left office in *special elections*.

Elections held in years when the president is on the ballot are called **presidential elections**; elections held midway between presidential elections are called **midterm elections**, and elections held in odd-numbered calendar years are called *off-year elections*. Midterm elections (such as the ones in 2006 and 2010) elect one-third of the U.S. Senate, all members of the House of Representatives, and many governors, other statewide officeholders, and state legislators. Many local elections for city council members and mayors are held in the spring of odd-numbered years.

Turnout—the proportion of the voting-age public that votes—is higher in general elections than in primary elections, and higher in primary elections than in special elections. It is also higher in presidential general elections than in midterm general elections, and higher in presidential primary elections than in midterm primary elections (see Figure 7.5).[75] Presidential elections attract greater interest and awareness. Turnout is also higher in elections in which candidates for federal office are on the ballot (U.S. senator, member of the House of Representatives, and president) than in state elections in years when there are no federal contests. Some states—for example, New Jersey, Virginia, and Kentucky—elect their governor and other state officials in odd-numbered years in part to separate state from national politics. The result is generally lower turnout. Finally, local or municipal elections have lower turnout than state elections, and municipal primaries generally have the lowest rates of participation.

Turnout reached more than 65 percent of those eligible to vote in the presidential election of 1960, but it declined to slightly more than 60 percent in 2004, and rose to 61.7 percent in 2008.[76] In midterm elections, turnout was 41.6 percent nationally in 2010, up slightly from 2006 and 2002. More competitive elections generate more interest among the public and more spending by the candidates, which in turn stimulate participation. However, more than 80 million eligible citizens failed to vote in the 2004 presidential election, and even more did not vote in midterm, state, and local elections.[77] In some democracies, like Brazil, Greece, and the Philippines, voting

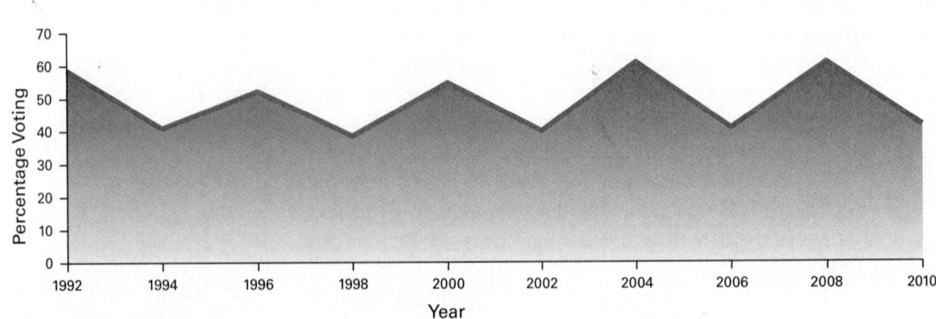

FIGURE 7.5 VOTER TURNOUT IN PRESIDENTIAL AND MIDTERM ELECTIONS, 1992–2010

■ *How can you explain the consistent pattern of voting demonstrated in the accompanying graph?*

SOURCE: Curtis Gans, Howard W. Stanley, and Richard G. Niemi, *Vital Statistics on American Politics, 2011–2012* (CQ Press, 2011), pp. 4–5.

BY the People Making a Difference

Be a Poll Worker

The people who staff voting places on Election Day are unsung heroes in our democracy. In most states, these individuals work long hours, often starting two hours before the polls open at around 7:00 a.m. and not completing their work until two or more hours after the polls close at 7 or 8 p.m. Although they are paid modest stipends, most poll workers report that they participate in this activity out of a deep sense of duty.

Studies of poll workers have found that 40 percent or more are 65 or older.* As we have moved to the use of computers and technology at the voting place, election officials believe that they have a need for poll workers with more confidence dealing with technology. Your ability to use computers means you have a lot to offer as a poll worker. When poll workers are courteous and competent, voters report more confidence in the voting process and more satisfaction with the voting experience. Even though some training is required, what is really needed is a willingness to help make democracy function well on Election Day.

To watch democracy in action and help make it function more smoothly, contact your county election official to find out how you can become a poll worker. At some colleges like Muhlenberg College in Pennsylvania, there is an established partnership between the college and local election administrators. At Muhlenberg, participating students serve as poll workers or Spanish-language interpreters. You might inquire of faculty at your institution if they would be willing to create a college poll worker program and apply for funding from the U.S. Election Assistance Commission. For more information, go to http://www.eac.gov/payments_and_grants/help_america_vote_college_program.aspx.

Although an organized program at your campus would help facilitate the process, volunteering as a poll worker is something you can do yourself. You will find that you can truly make a difference and enjoy observing the inner-workings of democracy.

QUESTIONS

1. **With computers more important in voting, why would having people like college students more involved as poll workers be important?**
2. **What are some things you might learn in a day working as a poll worker?**
3. **Why do studies show that poll workers can have a positive impact on how people feel about the voting experience?**

*Stephen T. Mockabee, J. Quin Monson, and Kelly D. Patterson, "Evaluating Online Training," Center for the Study of Elections and Democracy, December 21, 2009, http://csed.byu.edu/Assets/OnlineFinalReport2.pdf (accessed April 29, 2010); and Kelly D. Patterson, J. Quin Monson, and David B. Magleby, "Evaluating the Quality of the Voting Experience," Center for the Study of Elections and Democracy, August 31, 2008, http://csed.byu.edu/Assets/Evaluating%20the%20Quality%20of%20the%20Voting%20Experience.pdf (accessed April 29, 2010).

is mandatory,[78] while in the U.S. it is voluntary and requires more effort on the part of voters in keeping their voter registration current.

Who Votes?

The extent of voting varies widely among different groups. Level of education is an important predictor in whether people will vote; as education increases, so does the propensity to vote. According to one study, education gives people the ability to understand complicated topics like politics, and an understanding of the meaning of civic responsibility. Education also gives students experience with bureaucracy and large organizations—they learn to meet deadlines, fill out forms, fulfill requirements, and go to interviews.[79]

Race and ethnic background are linked with different levels of voting, largely because they correlate with education. In other words, racial and ethnic minorities with college degrees vote at approximately the same rate as white people with college degrees. As a group, African Americans vote at lower rates than Caucasians, although this is beginning to change.[80] In 2010, African Americans were 10 percent of the vote, a 2 percent decrease from 2008.[81]

In recent elections, both parties mounted major efforts to register and mobilize Hispanic voters, as Hispanics have become the largest minority group in the United States. Despite these efforts, the proportion of Hispanics voting in 2008 was up

This poster, published by the League of Women Voters, urged women to use the vote the Nineteenth Amendment had given them.

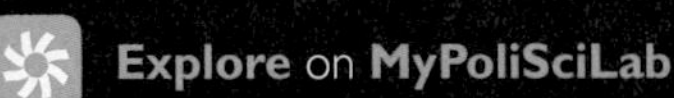

How Are People Involved in Politics?

There are a lot of ways to participate in politics. According to the 2008 American National Election Study, most Americans have attended a city council meeting, participated in a school board meeting, or signed a paper petition. But many have not protested, given money to political organizations, or distributed political information. How people engage in politics—and how often—is in part a function of efficacy, or whether or not individuals believe they have a say in government.

Political Activity

Signed a paper petition

Attended a city council or school board meeting

Gave money to a social/political organization

Attended meeting on a political or social issue

Distributed social/political group information

Joined a protest rally or march

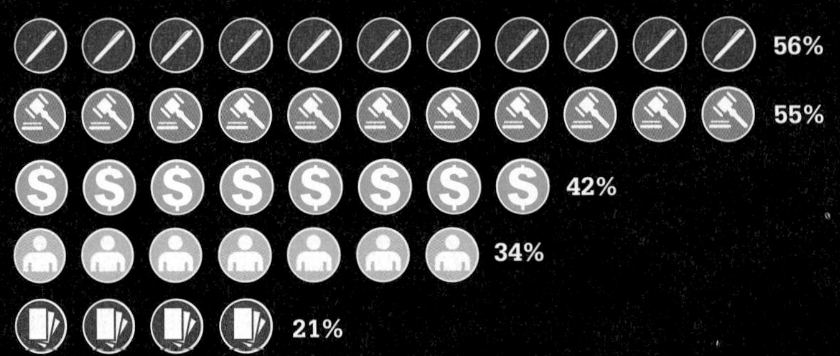

Do You Have a Say in Government?

I HAVE A SAY

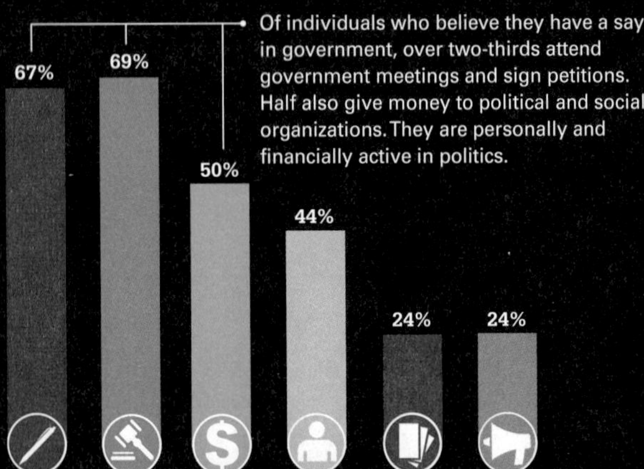

I DON'T HAVE A SAY

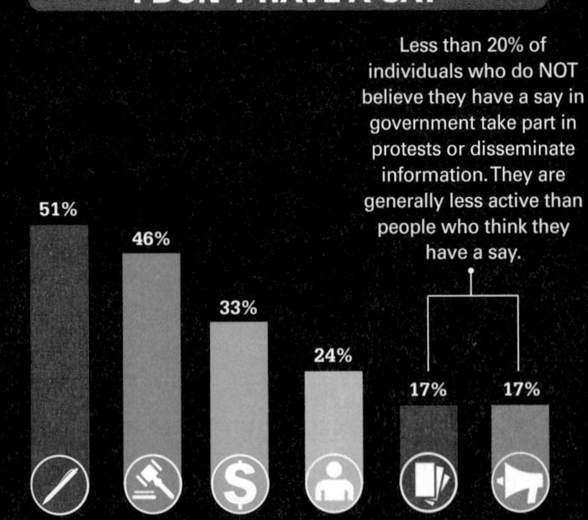

SOURCE: Data from The American National Election Study, 2008 Time Series Study, post-election interview responses only.

Investigate Further

Concept What are the most frequent forms of participation? Americans most frequently participate by attending local government meetings and signing paper petitions. Attending protests and rallies and distributing political information are less common.

Connection How are city council and school board meetings different from protests and petitions? Council and board meetings can make policy for government. Protests and petitions are ways of communicating information about issues to people with authority to make policy.

Cause How is participation related to efficacy? Those who believe they don't have a say in government are generally less active, while those who do think they have a say are more likely to engage in all forms of political activity. Regardless of their perceived influence, people are more likely to engage in activities that interact with institutions than to protest or disseminate information.

only slightly over 2004, 49.9 percent as compared to 47.2 percent.[82] As the illegal immigrant issue took center stage in 2006, Democrats, Republicans, and allied groups again sought to expand the number of Hispanic voters. Exit polls found that 9 percent of voters in 2008 were Latinos, with two-thirds of them voting for Obama.[83] The Hispanic share of the vote in 2010 was 8 percent.[84]

Women, another historically underrepresented group, have voted in greater numbers than men since 1984.[85] That was true again in 2008 and 2010.[86] Women's higher turnout is generally attributed to increasing levels of education and employment. Interest groups, including prominent pro-choice groups, have sought to mobilize female supporters of their agenda in recent elections.

Age is also highly correlated with the propensity to vote. As age increases, so does the proportion of persons voting. Older people, health permitting, are more likely to vote than younger people. The greater propensity of older persons to vote will amplify the importance of this group as baby boomers age and retire.

Young voters volunteered in large numbers for candidates in 2008, especially for the Obama campaign. Based on exit polls, their share of the vote also rose slightly. In 2004, 17 percent of all voters were 18 to 29 years of age. In 2008, they were 18 percent of all voters.[87] But because turnout was higher generally, the number of young people voting was up substantially.[88] In 2008, there were 3.4 million more voters under the age of 30 than had voted in 2004.[89] In 2010, the Democrats again did better among young voters than other voters, but turnout in this group declined by 7 percent compared to 2008.

In 2012 nearly one in five voters (19 percent) was under the age of 29, and they voted heavily for Obama (60 percent). Latino voters also voted more in 2012. Racial minorities, younger voters, and women were important to Obama's winning coalition. In battleground states, these voters stood in long lines both on election day and at early voting sites.[90]

☐ Mobilization

In a nation as evenly divided politically as the United States is now, candidates must also mobilize their most loyal supporters, or their "base." To do this, they reaffirm their support for issues or groups that matter to the base. In 2012, Mitt Romney and the Republicans did this by calling for tax cuts, fewer regulations on business and opposition to same-sex marriage and abortion. On the Democratic side, Barack Obama and the Democrats argued for tax increases on those making more than $250,000, the implementation of healthcare reform and support for abortion rights, same-sex marriage, and immigration reform.

In the 2012 "battleground" states where polls showed the race to be close, postcards urging residents to vote and phone calls reminding them it was Election Day bombarded voters. In addition, the candidates and parties mobilized their supporters to vote early in states where it was possible. This effort, sometimes called "banking the vote," reduced the list of people the campaigns needed to mobilize on Election Day, when poll watchers would track those who had not yet voted and would urge those who had pledged support to vote.

Campaigners learn which issues matter to potential voters and which candidates these voters prefer by conducting interviews on the telephone or in person, a process called a *canvass*. Individuals who are undecided and probable voters in competitive races are likely to receive communications designed to persuade them to vote for a particular candidate. Interest groups, including in 2012 the Super PACs and political parties, may also conduct a canvass, followed by mail and phone calls that often reinforce the same themes the candidates themselves express.

Undecided or "swing voters" are a major focus of mobilization efforts, and they received a lot of attention in competitive states in recent elections. Both sides intensely courted these voters through numerous person-to-person contacts, mailings, telephone calls, and efforts to register new voters. Candidates, groups, and parties are all part

7.1

7.2

7.3

7.4

7.5

of this "ground war." The volume of communication in competitive contests and battleground states in recent elections has been extraordinary.[91]

☐ How Serious Is Nonvoting?

Although voters can hardly avoid reading or hearing about political campaigns, especially during an election as intensely fought as recent presidential elections, about 40 percent of all eligible citizens fail to vote. This amounts to approximately 80 million people.[92] Who are they? Why don't they vote? Is the fact that so many people choose not to vote a cause for alarm? If so, what can we do about it?

There is considerable disagreement about how to interpret low voter turnout. The simplest explanation is that people are lazy and voting takes effort, but there is more to it than that. Of course, some people are apathetic, but most are not. Paradoxically, we compare favorably with other nations in political interest and awareness, but for a variety of institutional and political reasons, we fail to convert this interest in politics into voting (see Table 7.6).

In the United States, voting is more difficult and takes more time and effort than in other democracies. In our system, as we have seen, people must first register to vote and then decide how to vote, not only for many different offices but also often for referendums on public policy or constitutional amendments. As we discussed earlier in this chapter, voting was made more difficult for some Americans by the addition of voter identification requirements. The United States also holds elections on weekdays, when people are at work, rather than on holidays or weekends as other countries often do. Another factor in the percentage decline of voter turnout since the 1960s is, paradoxically, the Twenty-Sixth Amendment, which increased the number of eligible voters by lowering the voting age to 18. Young people are the least likely to vote, and after the amendment was ratified in 1971, turnout in the presidential election fell from 62 percent in 1968 to 57 percent in 1972.[93]

Some political scientists argue that nonvoting does not change the outcome, as nonvoters closely resemble voters in policy views.[94] "Nonvoting is not a social disease," wrote Austin Ranney, a noted political scientist. He pointed out that legal and extralegal denial of the vote to African Americans, women, Hispanics, persons over the age of 18, and other groups has been outlawed, so nonvoting is voluntary. The late Senator Sam

TABLE 7.6 WHY PEOPLE DO NOT VOTE

Reason	Percent
Too busy, conflicting schedule	17.5%
Illness or disability	14.9%
Other reason	11.3%
Not interested	13.4%
Did not like candidates or campaign issues	12.9%
Out of town	8.8%
Do not know or refused	7.0%
Registration problems	6.0%
Forgot to vote	2.6%
Inconvenient polling place	2.7%
Transportation problems	2.6%
Bad weather conditions	0.2%

■ *What reforms could you suggest to help negate the most often citing reason for not voting?*

SOURCE: U.S. Census Bureau, "Table 12, Reasons for Not Voting, by Selected Characteristics: November 2008,." http://www.census.gov/hhes/www/socdemo/voting/publications/p20/2008/tables.html.

OF the People Diversity in America

Voter Turnout by Demographic Factors

Throughout the course of U.S. history, the right to vote has been extended and protected for women and racial minorities. Groups that did not have the franchise, or that had been effectively barred or discouraged from using it, have become as active in their rates of voting as white men.

In the following table, note that women have voted in higher percentages than men in each election since 1992. It took decades for women to reach this milestone and dismiss the old adage that "politics is men's business." The rate of voting among African Americans was about 10 percentage points below white persons in 1992 and 1994, but more recently has lagged by only approximately 4 percentage points. Hispanics are not yet participating at rates similar to those of women and African Americans. History suggests that over time this will change.

QUESTIONS

1. **Why might the rate of voting for women have increased over time?**
2. **How do presidential elections influence rates of voting? Why?**
3. **What factors might explain the change in the rate of voting among African Americans?**

PERCENTAGE OF PEOPLE IN DIFFERENT GROUPS WHO VOTED

	1992	1994	1996	1998	2000	2002	2004	2006	2008	2010
Sex										
Men	60%	44%	53%	41%	53%	41%	56%	42%	56%	41%
Women	62	45	56	42	56	43	60	45	60	43%
Race										
White	64	47	56	43	56	44	60	46	60	43%
Black	54	37	51	40	54	40	56	39	61	41%
Hispanic	29	19	27	20	28	19	28	19	32	21%

SOURCE: U.S. Census Bureau, *Statistical Abstract of the United States: 2012*, Washington D.C., 2011; http://www.census.gov/compendia/statab/, p. 246.

Ervin of North Carolina provided a rationale for registration when he said, "I don't believe in making it easy for apathetic, lazy people to vote."[95]

Those who argue that nonvoting is a serious problem cite the "class bias" of those who do vote. The social makeup and attitudes of nonvoters differ significantly from those of voters and hence distort the representative system. "The very poor… have about two-thirds the representation among voters than their numbers would suggest." Thus, the people who need the most help from the government lack their share of electoral power to obtain it.[96] Some may contend that younger voters, the poor, and minority citizens do not vote because politicians pay less attention to them. But politicians understandably cater to people who vote more than to people who do not.

How might increased voter turnout affect national elections? It might make a difference because there are partisan differences between different demographic groups, and poorer persons are more likely to be Democrats. Candidates would have to adjust to the demands of this expanded electorate. A noted political scientist, while acknowledging that no political system could achieve 100 percent participation, pointed out that if the large nonvoter population decided to vote, it could overturn the balance of power in the political system.[97] Others contend that the difference may not be that pronounced because, on many issues, nonvoters have much the same attitudes as voters. Nor are nonvoters more egalitarian. They are, however, more inclined to favor additional spending on welfare programs.[98] Finally, for better or worse, low voter turnout may indicate approval of the status quo, whereas high voter turnout may signify disapproval and widespread desire for change.

7.1

7.2

7.3

7.4

7.5

party identification
An informal and subjective affiliation with a political party that most people acquire in childhood.

candidate appeal
How voters feel about a candidate's background, personality, leadership ability, and other personal qualities.

Voting Choices

7.5 Analyze why people vote the way they do in elections.

Why do people vote the way they do? Political scientists have identified three main elements of the voting choice: party identification, candidate appeal, and issues. These elements often overlap.

Voting on the Basis of Party

Party identification is our sense of identification or affiliation with a political party; it often predicts a person's stand on issues. It is part of our national mythology that we vote for the person and not the party. But, in fact, we vote most often for a person *from the party we prefer.*

The number of self-declared Independents since the mid-1970s has increased dramatically, and today, Independents outnumber Republicans and Democrats. But two-thirds of all Independents are, in fact, partisans in their voting behavior. There are three distinct types of Independents: Independent-leaning Democrats, Independent-leaning Republicans, and Pure Independents. Independent-leaning Democrats are predictably Democratic in their voting behavior, and Independent-leaning Republicans vote heavily Republican. Independent "leaners" are thus different from each other and from Pure Independents. Pure Independents have the lowest rate of turnout, but most of them generally side with the winner in presidential elections. Independent leaners vote at about the same rate as partisans and more than Pure Independents. Independent leaners vote for the party toward which they lean at approximately the same rate, or even more so, than weak partisans do. This data on Independents only reinforces the importance of partisanship in explaining voting choice. When we consider Independent-leaning Democrats and Independent-leaning Republicans as Democrats and Republicans respectively, only 10 percent of the population was Pure Independents in 2004.[99] In 2008, that number had risen slightly to 11 percent.[100] This proportion is consistent with earlier election years. In short, there are few genuinely Independent voters.

Although party identification has fluctuated in the past 40 years, it remains more stable than attitudes about issues or political ideology. Fluctuations in party identification appear to come in response to economic conditions and political performance, especially of the president. The more information voters have about their choices, the more likely they are to defect from their party and vote for a candidate from the other party.

Voting on the Basis of Candidates

Although long-term party identification is important, it is clearly not the only factor in voting choices. Otherwise, the Democrats would have won every presidential election since the last major realignment in partisanship, which occurred during the Great Depression in the election of Franklin Roosevelt in 1932. In fact, since 1952, there have been five Democratic presidents elected and the same number of Republicans.[101] The reason is largely found in a second major explanation of voting choice—**candidate appeal**.

Candidate-centered politics means that rather than relying on parties or groups to build a coalition of supporters for a candidate, the candidates make their case directly to the voters. In many races, the parties and groups also make the candidate the major focus of attention, minimizing partisanship or group identification.[102] The fact that we vote for officials separately—president/vice president, senator, governor, state attorney general, and so on—means voters are asked repeatedly to choose from among competing candidates. Although the party of the candidates is an important clue to voters, in most contested races, voters also look to candidate-specific information.

The Global Community

Corruption Among Political Leaders

In a free society where public opinion can be translated into action through elections and other means, there should in theory be less political corruption. In every country, there are corrupt individuals, but the ability to remove those people from office is enhanced through the expression of public opinion and the accountability afforded by elections. In 2007, for example, the Pew Research Center Global Attitudes Survey asked its respondents the following question on corruption: "I am going to read you a list of things that may be problems in our country. As I read each one, please tell me if you think it is a very big problem, a moderately big problem, a small problem, or not a problem at all: corrupt political leaders."

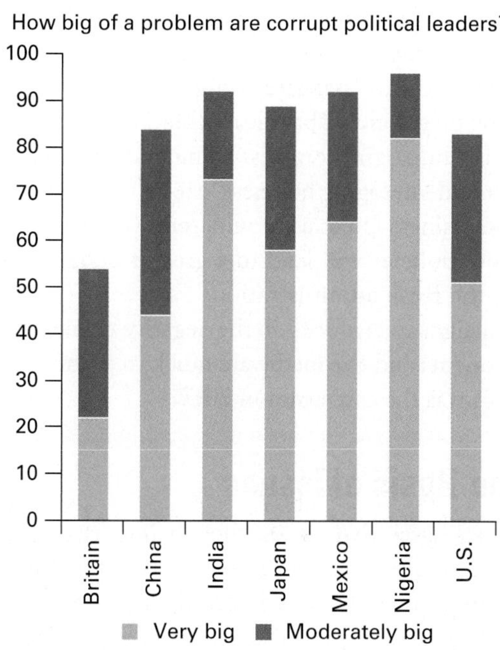

Source: Pew Research Center, 2007 Spring Survey of the Global Attitudes Project. (Pew Research Center, 2007).

Corruption is seen as a very big problem for most people in India (73 percent) and Nigeria (82 percent) with Mexico not far behind (64 percent). Even though studies have found similar levels of corruption in the United States and Britain, people in Britain are much less likely to say it is a very big problem in their country. In China, which does not allow the free expression of public opinion nor does it have free elections, 44 percent say corruption is a very big problem and 40 percent saying it is a moderately big problem. Unlike democratic countries, individuals in China lack an electoral way to punish a corrupt government.

CRITICAL THINKING QUESTIONS

1. Why are people in the United States twice as likely to think corruption is a very big problem than people in Britain?
2. Is it possible that corruption may be such a part of the political culture that it is not seen as something elections or public opinion can do much about?
3. What checks are there on corruption in a country like China when the government acts as if there is no corruption?

7.1

7.2

7.3

7.4

7.5

prospective issue voting
Voting based on what a candidate pledges to do in the future about an issue if elected.

retrospective issue voting
Holding incumbents, usually the president's party, responsible for their records on issues, such as the economy or foreign policy.

Candidate appeal often includes an assessment of a candidate's character. Is the candidate honest? Consistent? Dedicated to "family values"? Does the candidate have religious or spiritual commitments? In recent elections, the press has sometimes played the role of "character cop," asking questions about candidates' private lives and lifestyles. The press asks these questions because voters are interested in a political leader's background—perhaps even more interested in personal character than in a candidate's political position on hard-to-understand health care or regulatory policy issues.

Candidate appeal, or the lack of it—in terms of leadership, experience, good judgment, integrity, competence, strength, and energy—is sometimes more important than party or issues. Many voters saw Bill Clinton in 1992 and 1996 as a regular working-class person who had risen against the odds. Dwight Eisenhower, who was elected president in 1952 and reelected in 1956, had great candidate appeal. He was a five-star general, a legendary hero of the Allied effort in World War II. His unmilitary manner, his moderation, his personal charm, and his appearance of seeming to rise above partisanship appealed across the ideological spectrum. In 2012, Republicans attempted to define Barack Obama as a failed leader who presided over an economy with persistent high unemployment and little growth, who raided Medicare to pay for Obamacare, his healthcare reform law, and who failed to live up to his campaign promises. Democrats, in turn, attempted to define Mitt Romney as an out-of-touch business executive who supports tax cuts for the rich, whose pro-business policies would remove banking and environmental regulations, and whose policies will lead to a greater budget deficit and a return to the failed policies of the Bush administration.

Increasingly, campaigns today focus on the negative elements of candidates' history and personality. Opponents and the media are quick to point out a candidate's limitations or problems. This was the case again in 2012.

☐ Voting on the Basis of Issues

Most political scientists agree that issues, though important, have less influence on how people vote than party identification and candidate appeal do.[103] This occurs partly because candidates often intentionally obscure their positions on issues—an understandable strategy.[104] When he was running for president in 1968, Richard Nixon said he had a plan to end the Vietnam War, which was clearly the most important issue that year, but he would not reveal the specifics. By not detailing his plan, he stood to gain votes both from those who wanted a more aggressive war effort and those who wanted a cease-fire. In 2008, Obama and the Democrats emphasized change from the Bush administration, a general theme that exploited public sentiment.

For issue voting to become important, a substantial number of voters must find the issue itself important, opposing candidates must take opposite stands on the issues, and voters must know these positions and vote accordingly. Rarely do candidates focus on only one issue. Voters often agree with one candidate on one issue and with the opposing candidate on another. In such cases, issues will probably not determine how people vote. But voters' lack of interest in issues does not mean candidates can take any position they please.[105]

Political parties and candidates often look for issues that motivate particular segments of the electorate to vote and on which the opposing candidate or party has a less popular position. These issues are sometimes called *wedge issues.* In recent elections, wedge issues have been gay marriage, the minimum wage, and abortion. One way to exploit a wedge issue is to place on the ballot an initiative to decide a proposed law or amendment on the issue. Both parties and allied groups are expanding their use of ballot initiatives in this way.

More likely than **prospective issue voting**, or voting based on what a candidate pledges to do about an issue if elected, is **retrospective issue voting**, or holding incumbents, usually the president's party, responsible for past performance on issues, such as the economy or foreign policy.[106] In times of peace and prosperity, voters will reward the incumbent. If the nation falls short on either, voters are more likely to elect the opposition.

But good economic times do not always guarantee that an incumbent party will be reelected, as Vice President Al Gore learned in 2000 when he was the Democratic candidate for president.[107] His inability to effectively claim credit for the good economic times hurt him, especially when Republicans contended that the American people, not the government under President Bill Clinton, had produced the strong economy. Neither do bad economic times guarantee defeat for an incumbent. In 2012 President Obama overcame slow economic growth and chronically high unemployment to win a second term.

You Will Decide

Should We Allow Voting on the Internet?

During the past two centuries of constitutional government, this nation has gradually adopted a more expansive view of popular participation. It seems logical that the next step in our democratic progress is permitting voters to cast ballots via the Internet. Not only would such a reform make voting easier, but it would permit us to have more elections. For example, when a city council wants voters to decide whether to build a new football stadium or when there is need for a special election to fill the term of a member of Congress who has died or resigned, election officials could announce via e-mail and other means that voting via the Internet will commence and close on specified dates. The technology exists to have voting via the Internet. Should we allow Internet voting?

What do you think? Should we move toward replacing the ballot box with the computer? What arguments would you make for and against Internet voting?

Thinking It Through

Allowing voting via the Internet could encourage more frequent elections and longer ballots. One of the problems with making elections more frequent is that voters will tire. Americans already vote more frequently and for more offices than citizens of any other democracy. Asking them to make voting choices even more frequently could result in lower turnout and less rational consideration. Many voters may be unaware that an election is going on. Yet the advantage of Internet voting likely would be an increase in turnout, at least initially. What political scientists dispute is whether such increases in participation will continue when the novelty wears off.

Some critics of electronic democracy worry about fraud. Voting by computer also has the possibility of allowing people to pressure or harass voters. Another concern is late returns. Concerns about electronic voting have been reinforced by claims that the computer software is not secure and that some electronic voting fails to count all the votes.*

Another criticism is that electronic voting could be skewed toward participation by better-educated and higher-income voters, who routinely pay their bills online, make purchases on their computer, and own a personal computer with Internet access. Advocates of these new voting procedures contend that voters who do not own computers can drop off their ballots in some public building and that eventually computers will be available widely enough that access will not be a problem.†

If the integrity of the vote can be protected and the new ways of voting become widely accessible, such changes are probably inevitable. With more people having access to computers and confidence using them for important transactions, the Internet is likely to be used for voting in the future. Electronic voting has been tested for military personnel overseas,‡ and states like Michigan and Washington have experimented with new applications of computer voting.

CRITICAL THINKING QUESTIONS

1. **What advantages do you see in allowing people to vote via the Internet?**
2. **What would be the disadvantages of allowing Internet voting?**
3. **If we move to voting by Internet, how often do you think voters would be likely to participate in an election?**

*E. J. Dionne, Jr., "Election Dangers to Be Avoided," *The Washington Post*, May 25, 2004.
†Adam J. Berinsky, Nancy Burns, and Michael W. Traugott, "Who Votes By Mail? A Dynamic Model of the Individual-Level Consequences of Voting-by-Mail Systems," *Public Opinion Quarterly* 65 (Summer 2001), pp. 178–197.
‡http://www.servesecurityreport.org/DoDMay2007.pdf.

The state of the economy is often the central issue in both midterm and presidential elections. Studies have found that the better the economy seems to be doing, the more congressional seats the "in" party retains or gains. The reverse is also true. The worse the economy seems to be doing, the more seats the "out" party gains.[108] Political scientists have been able to locate the sources of this effect in the way individual voters decide to vote. Voters tend to vote against the party in power if they perceive that their personal financial situations have declined or stagnated.[109] Anxiety over the economy and high unemployment were important to the vote in 2010, and the Democrats, as the party in power, were punished at the polls. Republicans also exploited fears about health care reform and growing federal budget deficits.

One aspect of the 2012 election that political scientists will long debate is how Obama won with unemployment at or above 8 percent for most of his term. He did this by linking his opponent to the policies of the Bush administration and by portraying Romney as concerned only with affluent Americans. In a speech at a Boca Raton fundraiser (which he did not know was being recorded), Romney labeled 47 percent of the population as "dependent on government" and supporters of President Obama "no matter what." In key auto-producing states like Michigan and Ohio, Romney's initial recommendation to let the auto industry go bankrupt reinforced the theme that he did not care about working families. Neither the auto bailout nor the "47 percent" comment changed the underlying economic concerns of many Americans, but Romney's missteps may have influenced enough voters for Obama to win reelection.

☐ The Impact of Campaigns

Candidates and campaigns are important to the voting choice. Given the frequency of elections in the United States and the number of offices people vote for, it is not surprising that voters look for simplifying devices such as partisanship to help them decide how to vote. Effective campaigns give them reasons to vote for their candidate and reasons to vote against the opposition.

Campaigns are a team sport, with the political parties and interest groups also important to the process of persuading and motivating voters.[110] Groups and parties are heavily engaged in all aspects of campaigns, and their efforts are often indistinguishable from the candidates' campaigns.

Although having enough money is necessary to run a competitive campaign, spending more money does not guarantee that a candidate will win. Effective campaigners find ways to communicate with voters that are memorable and persuasive.

Campaigns are not for the faint of heart. Electoral politics is intensely competitive, and campaigns are often negative and personal. Campaigns give voters a sense of how politicians react to adversity because most competitive races involve adversity. Skills learned in the campaign environment, in some respects at least, carry over into the skill set needed to govern.

Who votes and how they do so has changed dramatically throughout the course of U.S. history. Our process has become more democratic, and citizens today have a wider array of candidate contests and ballot questions to decide than ever before. Although there has been progress in making voting easier, challenges remain. It is important that every vote be counted and counted accurately. That goal has not yet been achieved.

Government by the people is most frequently exercised by voting. This is why, when younger persons do not vote, they leave to others decisions about important parts of their lives. Government, directly or indirectly, has a bearing on educational opportunity, taxes, and the environment, to name only a few examples. Elected officials are most attuned to the will of those who vote, and so when people fail to vote, they lessen their impact and enlarge the voice of those who do register and vote.

Review the Chapter

 **Listen** to **Chapter 7** on **MyPoliSciLab**

Forming Political Opinions and Values

7.1 Identify the forces that create and shape individuals' political attitudes, p. 207.

People's political attitudes form early in life, mainly through the influence of family. Schools, the media, social groups, and changing personal and national circumstances can cause attitudes to change, although most of our political opinions remain constant throughout life. Most people do not follow politics and government closely and have little knowledge of political issues.

Public Opinion: Taking the Pulse of the People

7.2 Describe the key dimensions of public opinion, how public opinion is measured, and the relationship between public opinion and public policy, p. 211.

Public opinion is the distribution across the population of a complex combination of views and attitudes that individuals hold, and we measure it through careful, unbiased, random-selection surveys. Public opinion takes on qualities of intensity, latency, consensus, and polarization—each of which is affected by people's feelings about the salience of issues.

Sometimes, politicians follow prevailing public opinion on policy questions; in other cases, they attempt to lead public opinion toward a different policy option. Major events, such as economic crises and wars, affect both public opinion and government policy. Citizens who wish to affect opinion, policy, or both, can take action by voting or engaging in other forms of political participation.

Political Ideology and Attitudes Toward Government

7.3 Compare and contrast political ideologies and evaluate the critiques of each ideology, p. 215.

The two most important ideologies in American politics are liberalism, a belief that government can and should help achieve justice and equality of opportunity, and conservatism, a belief in limited government to ensure order, competitive markets, and personal opportunity while relying on free markets and individual initiative to solve social and economic problems. Critics of liberalism contend that liberals, by favoring government solutions to problems, limit the capacity of markets to function well and create large and unmanageable bureaucracies. Critics of conservatism contend that some problems require government to become part of the solution and that too much faith in the market to solve the problem is misplaced. Socialism, which favors public ownership of the means of production, and libertarianism, which puts a premium on individual liberty and limited government, attract only modest followings in the United States.

Participation: Translating Opinions into Action

7.4 Identify forms of political participation, and assess the effect on voter turnout of demographic, legal, and electioneering factors, p. 220.

One of the hallmarks of democracy is that citizens can participate in politics in a variety of ways. Citizens who are dissatisfied with government can protest. Individual citizens participate by writing letters to elected officials, calling radio talk shows, serving as jurors, voting, or donating time and money to political campaigns. The Internet has allowed individuals to volunteer for campaigns in a wider variety of ways, to donate money more easily, and to produce content that can be uploaded onto the Internet and viewed by any interested people.

Better-educated, more affluent, older people, and those who are involved with parties and interest groups tend to vote more. The young vote the least. Voter turnout is usually higher in national elections than in state and local elections, higher in presidential elections than in midterm elections, and higher in general elections than in primary elections. Close elections generate interest and efforts to mobilize voters and thus have higher turnout than uncompetitive elections.

Voting Choices

7.5 Analyze why people vote the way they do in elections, p. 232.

Party identification remains the most important element in determining how most people vote. It represents a long-term attachment and is a "lens" through which voters view candidates and issues as they make their voting choices. Candidate appeal, including character and record, is another key factor in voter choice. Less frequently, voters decide on the basis of issues.

Learn the Terms

 **Study** and **Review** the **Flashcards**

political socialization, p. 207
attitudes, p. 208
selective exposure, p. 209
deliberation, p. 210
social capital, p. 210
attentive public, p. 211
public opinion, p. 211
random sample, p. 211
margin of error, p. 212
universe, p. 213
intensity, p. 214
latency, p. 214
manifest opinion, p. 214
salience, p. 214
political ideology, p. 215
liberalism, p. 215
conservatism, p. 217
social conservative, p. 218
socialism, p. 219
communism, p. 219
libertarianism, p. 220
voter registration, p. 224
general election, p. 226
primary election, p. 226
presidential election, p. 226
midterm election, p. 226
turnout, p. 226
party identification, p. 232
candidate appeal, p. 232
prospective issue voting, p. 234
retrospective issue voting, p. 234

Test Yourself

 **Study** and **Review** the **Practice Tests**

MULTIPLE CHOICE QUESTIONS

7.1 Identify the forces that create and shape individuals' political attitudes.

Which of the following statements is true?

a. Most people never change their political opinions.
b. Most people change their political opinions quite often.
c. Many people change their political opinions only when they meet new people.
d. Many people change their political opinions after major experiences such as a war.
e. Many people change their political opinions on issues on which they have much knowledge.

7.2 Outline the key dimensions of public opinion, how public opinion is measured, and the relationship between public opinion and public policy.

What word describes opinions people may hold but have not fully expressed?

a. Interest
b. Salience
c. Latency
d. Intensity
e. Projection

7.3 Compare and contrast political ideologies and evaluate the critiques of each ideology.

Identify which of the following is a major tenet of libertarianism:

a. Public ownership of business
b. Opposition to all government regulation
c. Government provision of universal health care
d. Use of government regulation only for moral issues such as abortion
e. Unregulated markets

7.4 Identify forms of political participation, and assess the effect on voter turnout of demographic, legal, and electioneering factors.

Which of the following is *not* a way individuals have used the Internet to participate in recent campaigns?

a. Participate in local caucuses online.
b. Create campaign-centered music videos to upload to YouTube.
c. Call other individuals using calling lists provided on a candidate's Web site.
d. Invite other individuals to donate to campaigns through Facebook and MySpace.
e. Donate money to candidates' campaigns.

7.5 Analyze why people vote the way they do in elections.

Which of the following is an example of retrospective voting?

a. A citizen makes her voting decision based on a candidate's promised actions if elected to office.
b. A voter casts his vote for the Republican candidate because his parents were Republicans.
c. A citizen votes for the incumbent because of her success in reinvigorating the economy.
d. A voter casts her vote based on the candidate's gender.
e. A voter casts his vote based on the groups that support a particular candidate.

ESSAY QUESTION

Think of the three main elements of vote choice—party identification, candidate appeal, and issues. Briefly define each and explain why they were important in the 2008 and 2012 presidential elections. Of the three elements which is most important and why?

Explore Further

IN THE LIBRARY

R. Michael Alvarez and John Brehm, *Hard Choices, Easy Answers: Values, Information, and American Public Opinion* (Princeton University Press, 2002).

Herbert Asher, *Polling and the Public: What Every Citizen Should Know,* 8th ed. (CQ Press, 2011).

Barbara A. Bardes and Robert W. Oldendick, *Public Opinion: Measuring the American Mind,* 4th ed. (Rowman & Littlefield, 2012).

M. Margaret Conway, *Political Participation in the United States,* 3rd ed. (CQ Press, 2000).

Robert M. Eisinger, *The Evolution of Presidential Polling* (Cambridge University Press, 2003).

Robert S. Erikson and Kent L. Tedin, *American Public Opinion: Its Origins, Content, and Impact,* updated 8th ed. (Longman, 2011).

William H. Flanigan and Nancy H. Zingale, *Political Behavior of the American Electorate,* updated 12th ed. (CQ Press, 2011).

Donald P. Green and Alan S. Gerber, *Get Out the Vote!: How to Increase Voter Turnout,* 2nd ed. (Brookings Institution Press, 2008).

Diane J. Heath, *Polling to Govern: Public Opinion and Presidential Leadership* (Stanford University Press, 2004).

Bruce E. Keith, David B. Magleby, Candice J. Nelson, Elizabeth Orr, Mark C. Westlye, and Raymond E. Wolfinger, *The Myth of the Independent Voter* (University of California Press, 1992).

V. O. Key, Jr., *Public Opinion and American Democracy* (Knopf, 1961).

Richard G. Niemi and Herbert F. Weisberg, eds., *Classics in Voting Behavior* (CQ Press, 1993).

Richard G. Niemi and Herbert F. Weisberg, eds., *Controversies in Voting Behavior,* 4th ed. (CQ Press, 2001).

Frank R. Parker, *Black Votes Count: Political Empowerment in Mississippi After 1965* (University of North Carolina Press, 1990).

James A. Thurber And Candice J. Nelson, eds., *Campaigns and Elections American Style,* 3rd ed. (Westview Press, 2010).

Michael W. Traugott and Paul J. Lavrakas, *The Voter's Guide to Election Polls,* 4th ed. (Rowman & Littlefield, 2008).

Martin P. Wattenberg, *Is Voting for Young People?,* 3rd ed. (Longman, 2011).

John Zaller, *The Nature and Origins of Mass Opinion* (Cambridge University Press, 1992). See also *Public Opinion Quarterly, The American Journal of Political Science,* and *American Political Science Review.*

ON THE WEB

www.votesmart.org
This is the Web site for Project Vote Smart. The site lists extensive nonpartisan information about candidates for both federal and state elections throughout the United States, including voting records and candidate positions.

http://www.longdistancevoter.org
A collection of information and forms for individuals who would like to vote absentee in any state. The site includes explanations of the different registration policies in each state. Although individual states have different registration requirements, you only need to follow the link for your home state in order to access the materials you will need to vote absentee in the next election.

www.rockthevote.org
The home page for Rock the Vote, an organization that focuses on helping young people register to vote and participate in politics in general. The site includes voter registration materials, information on how to vote absentee, and information about other policy issues that young people may care about.

www.aapor.org
As the home page of the American Association for Public Opinion Research, this site contains resources for both creators and users of polls and polling data. The site has information about how to accurately conduct a poll, how to understand polling data, and how to identify fake or poorly constructed polls.

Listen to Chapter 8 on MyPoliSciLab

8 Campaigns and Elections

Democracy in Action

Foster Friess was among the supporters who stood directly behind Rick Santorum as he gave his victory speech on the night he won the 2012 Missouri Republican primary. Friess was not just an ordinary supporter, however. He was a wealthy Wyoming investment banker who had given more than $1.6 million to the "Red, White, and Blue" campaign group that backed Santorum's campaign.[1] The PAC, technically known as an "independent expenditure only committee," but more commonly called a Super PAC, was something most presidential candidates had supporting them in 2011 and 2012.[2] Because Super PACs operate in ways independent of the candidate, the Federal Election Commission, following court rulings in *Citizens United* v. *FEC*[3] and *SpeechNow.org* v. *FEC*[4] allowed the formation of these committees late in the 2010 campaign season.

But was Red, White, and Blue really independent of the candidate if its major donor traveled with the candidate and was center stage behind the candidate at his victory speech? The Super PAC associated with Rick Santorum was not alone in raising money in million-dollar increments and larger. During the nomination phase of the 2012 presidential race, Sheldon and Miriam Adelson gave $20 million to "Winning Our Future," which supported Newt Gingrich; Bob Perry gave $4 million to "Restore Our Future, Inc." supporting Mitt Romney; and Jeff Katzenberg and Bill Mahr gave $2 million and $1 million, respectively, to "Priorities USA Action," which supported Barack Obama.[5] Most of the money supporting these Super PACs came from donors giving a million dollars or more; Gingrich's Super PAC alone drew 85 percent of its funds from such large donors.[6]

At earlier times in U.S. history, wealthy individuals had played a large role in financing campaigns, but that trend declined after Congress reformed campaign finance rules following the

8.1 Assess the implications of election rules in the United States, p. 243.

8.2 Identify problems associated with administering elections and evaluate proposed solutions to those problems, p. 247.

8.3 Explain how congressional elections work and why they are generally not competitive, p. 249.

8.4 Describe the stages in U.S. presidential elections and the differences in campaigning at each stage, p. 255.

8.5 Evaluate the influence of money in American elections and the main approaches to campaign finance reform, p. 264.

8.6 Assess concerns regarding presidential elections and reforms that have been proposed, p. 271.

President Barack Obama, reelected to a second term, walks out on the stage with his wife Michelle and daughters Sasha and Malia at his election night party in Chicago.

The Big Picture Where are the battle states? Which matters more — the popular vote or the electoral vote? Where is a candidate's funding coming from? Author David B. Magleby explains three of the most important rules to consider when devising a campaign strategy.

The Basics Do you have trouble figuring out when all the elections are and who you should vote for? If you do, you are not alone. This video will help you understand why the United States has so many types of elections, what purposes they serve, and whether money and campaign staff is vital to campaign victories.

In Context Discover why voting and elections are essential to a democracy. In this video, Fordham University political scientist Costas Panagopolos discusses why voting is important in the United States. He also explains how electoral reforms have expanded the voting population throughout the years.

Thinking Like a Political Scientist Discover how scholars respond when voter turnout—even in presidential elections—declines, as it did during the last half of the twentieth century. Fordham University political scientist Costas Panagopolos explorers the research behind this issue, recent trends, and factors that may explain these outcomes.

In the Real World In its controversial Citizen's United decision, the Supreme Court ruled that money is speech and thus the courts cannot put a limit on the amount of money an individual—or a corporation—spends on an election. Real people decide whether or not they agree with that decision, and they consider some of its long-term implications.

So What? In many ways, politics is a team sport…it's not just the candidates. Author David B. Magleby identifies the other players in campaigns and elections and the importance of knowing which team you are most comfortable joining.

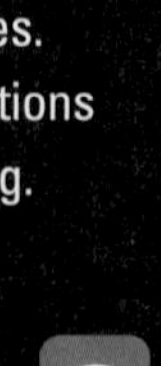

Watergate scandal in 1972. Individuals have long been able to spend unlimited amounts independently, but it was unclear in 2012 if Super PACs were really independent entities. Another concern with Super PACs was the strongly negative tone of the ads they ran. In one analysis of ads in the 2012 Republican primaries, nearly three-quarters of Super PAC ads were negative.[7]

Money spent on elections is only one marker of their importance. Time devoted to campaigns by candidates, political parties, interest groups, and individuals is also substantial. Our system of federalism means we hold elections at the national, state and local levels of government. In the United States, citizens vote more often and for more offices than citizens of any other democracy. We hold thousands of elections for everything from community college directors to county sheriffs. Approximately half a million persons hold elected state and local offices.[8] In 2012, we elected the president and vice president, 33 U.S. senators,[9] all 435 members of the U.S. House of Representatives, 14 state governors, and, in many states, treasurers, secretaries of state, and judges.

In addition to electing people, voters in 27 states are allowed to vote on laws or constitutional amendments proposed by initiative petitions or on popular referendums put on the ballot by petition. In every state except Delaware, voters must approve all changes to the state constitution.

In this chapter, we explore our election rules. We note four important problems: the lack of competition for some offices, the complexities of nominating presidential candidates, the distortions of the Electoral College, and the influence of money. We also discuss proposed reforms in each of these areas.

Elections: The Rules of the Game

8.1 Assess the implications of election rules in the United States.

he rules of the game—the electoral game—make a difference. Although the Constitution sets certain conditions and requirements, state law determines most electoral rules. Our focus in this chapter is on presidential and congressional elections, although much of the discussion is also relevant to state and local elections.

Regularly Scheduled Elections

In our system, elections are held at fixed intervals that the party in power cannot change. It does not make any difference if the nation is at war, as we were during the Civil War, or in the midst of a crisis, as in the Great Depression; when the calendar calls for an election, the election is held. Elections for members of Congress occur on the first Tuesday after the first Monday in November of even-numbered years. Although there are exceptions (for special elections or peculiar state provisions), participants know *in advance* just when the next election will be. In most parliamentary democracies, such as Great Britain and Canada, the party in power can call elections at a time of its choosing. The predetermined timing of elections is one of the defining characteristics of democracy in the United States.

Fixed, Staggered, and Sometimes Limited Terms

Our electoral system is based on *fixed terms,* meaning the length of a term in office is specified, not indefinite. The Constitution sets the term of office for the U.S. House of Representatives at two years, the Senate at six years, and the presidency at four years.

Our system also has *staggered terms* for some offices; not all offices are up for election at the same time. All House members are up for election every two years, but only

8.1
8.2
8.3
8.4
8.5
8.6

winner-take-all system
An election system in which the candidate with the most votes wins.

single-member district
An electoral district in which voters choose one representative or official.

proportional representation
An election system in which each party running receives the proportion of legislative seats corresponding to its proportion of the vote.

one-third of senators are up for election at the same time. Because presidential elections can occur two or four years into a senator's six-year term, senators can often run for the presidency without fear of losing their seat, as John Kerry did in 2004 and John McCain, Barack Obama, Hillary Clinton, and Joe Biden (for the vice presidency) did in 2008.

But if their Senate term expires the same year as the presidential election, the laws of many states require them to give up their Senate seat to run for president, vice president, or any other position. An example of a state that permits a candidate to run for election to two offices is Connecticut, where Joseph Lieberman was reelected to the U.S. Senate in 2000 while being narrowly defeated in his race for vice president. Had he been victorious in both campaigns, he would have resigned his Senate seat.

☐ Term Limits

The Twenty-Second Amendment to the Constitution, adopted in 1951, limits presidents to two terms. Knowing that a president cannot run again changes the way members of Congress, the voters, and the press regard the chief executive. A politician who cannot, or has announced he or she will not, run again is called a *lame duck.* Lame ducks are often seen as less influential because other politicians know that these officials' ability to bestow or withhold favors is coming to an end. Efforts to limit the terms of other offices have become a major issue in several states. The most frequent targets have been state legislators. One consequence of term limits is more lame ducks.

Term limits at the state level were largely adopted during the 1990s. Currently, 15 states have term limits for state legislatures. Six states have rescinded term limits either through legislation or state court rulings. South Dakota voters were given the option of repealing term limits, and they overwhelmingly voted to keep them.[10] Despite their popularity at the state level, proposals for term limits on federal legislators have repeatedly been defeated when they have come to a vote in Congress. The Supreme Court, by a vote of 5-to-4, declared that a state does not have the constitutional power to impose limits on the number of terms for which its members of the U.S. Congress are eligible, either by amendment to its own constitution or by state law.[11] Congress has refused to propose a constitutional amendment to impose a limit on congressional terms.

☐ Winner Take All

An important feature of our electoral process is the **winner-take-all system**, sometimes referred to as "first past the post" in other countries.[12] In most U.S. electoral settings, the candidate with the most votes wins. The winner does not need to have a *majority* (more than half the votes cast); in a multicandidate race, the winner may have only a *plurality* (the largest number of votes). An example is the 2009 special election held in New York's 23rd Congressional District. In a three-candidate race, Democrat Bill Owens won with 48 percent of the vote, a plurality, not a majority. The Conservative party candidate Doug Hoffman received 46 percent of the vote, and the Republican Dierdre Scozzafava received less than 6 percent.[13] Winner-take-all electoral systems tend to reinforce moderate and centrist candidates because they are more likely to secure a plurality or a majority. Candidates in a winner-take-all system often stress that a vote for a minor party candidate is a "wasted vote" that may actually help elect the voter's least desired candidate.

Most U.S. electoral districts are **single-member districts**, meaning that in any district for any given election—senator, governor, U.S. House, and state legislative seat—the voters choose *one* representative or official.[14] When the single-member district and winner-take-all systems are combined, minor parties find it especially hard to win and a two-party political system is virtually guaranteed. For example, even if a third party gets 25 percent of the vote in several districts, it still gets no seats. The single-member districts and winner-take-all system are different from a **proportional representation** system, in which political parties secure legislative seats and power in proportion to the number of votes they receive in the election. Countries that practice some form of proportional representation include Germany, Israel, Italy, and Japan.

Proportional representation more accurately reveals the division of voter preferences and gives those who do not vote with the plurality some influence as a result of their vote. For this reason, proportional representation may encourage greater turnout for people who identify with parties that rarely win elections, such as Democrats in Utah or Republicans in Massachusetts. Proportional representation may also encourage issue-oriented campaigns and enhance the representation of women and minorities.

But proportional representation can cause problems. It may make it harder to have a clear winner, especially if minor parties are likely to win seats. As a result, it may encourage the proliferation of minor parties. Opponents of proportional representation worry that it can contribute to political instability and ideological extremism.

Electoral College
The electoral system used in electing the president and vice president, in which voters vote for electors pledged to cast their ballots for a particular party's candidates.

☐ The Electoral College

We elect our president and vice president not by a national vote but by an indirect device known as the **Electoral College**. The Framers of the U.S. Constitution devised this system because they did not trust the choice of president to a direct vote of the people. Under this system, each state has as many electors as it has representatives and senators. California therefore has 55 electoral votes (53 House seats and 2 Senate seats), whereas 7 states and the District of Columbia have 3 electoral votes each.

Each state legislature is free to determine how it selects its electors. Each party nominates a slate of electors, usually longtime party workers. They are expected to cast their electoral votes for the party's candidates for president and vice president if their party's candidates get a plurality of the vote in their state. In our entire history, no "faithless elector"—an elector who does not vote for his or her state's popular vote winner—has ever cast the deciding vote, and the incidence of a faithless elector is rare.[15]

Candidates who win a plurality of the popular vote in a state secure all of that state's electoral votes, except in Nebraska and Maine, which allocate electoral votes to the winner in each congressional district plus two electoral votes for the winner of the state as a whole. Winning electors go to their state capital on the first Monday after the second Wednesday in December to cast their ballots. These ballots are then sent to Congress, and early in January, Congress formally counts the ballots and declares who won the election for president and vice president.

In two of the four elections in which winners of the popular vote did not become president, the electoral college did not decide the winner. The 1824 election was decided by the U.S. House of Representatives. In the controversial 1876 presidential election between Rutherford B. Hayes and Samuel Tilden, the electoral vote in four states was disputed, resulting in the appointment of an electoral commission to decide how those votes should be counted. The Electoral Commission of 1877, depicted in the drawing, met in secret session, and after many contested votes, Hayes was elected.

8.1

8.2

8.3

8.4

8.5

8.6

It takes a majority of the electoral votes to win. If no candidate gets a majority of the electoral votes for president, the House chooses among the top three candidates, with each state delegation having one vote. If no candidate gets a majority of the electoral votes for vice president, the Senate chooses between the top two candidates, with each senator casting one vote.

When there are only two major candidates for the presidency, the chances of an election being thrown into the House are remote. But twice in our history, the House has had to act: in 1800, the House had to choose in a tie vote between Thomas Jefferson and Aaron Burr; and in 1824, the House picked John Quincy Adams over Andrew Jackson. The 1800 election prompted the Twelfth Amendment, ratified in 1804, requiring that electors in the Electoral College vote for one person as president and for another as vice president.

As we were reminded in 2000, our Electoral College system makes it possible for a presidential candidate to receive the most popular votes, as Al Gore did, and yet not get enough electoral votes to be elected president. Gore lost the Electoral College vote 271 to 266, and George Bush became president.[16] This also happened in 1824, when Andrew Jackson won 12 percent more of the vote than John Quincy Adams; in 1876, when Samuel Tilden received more popular votes than Rutherford B. Hayes; and in 1888, when Grover Cleveland received more popular votes than Benjamin Harrison. It almost happened in 1916, 1960, and 1976, when the shift of a few votes in a few key states could have resulted in the election of a president without a popular majority.

Questions about the Electoral College arise every time a serious third-party candidate runs for president. If no candidate receives a majority in the Electoral College and the decision is left to Congress, which Congress casts the vote, the one serving during the election, or the newly elected one? The answer is the newly elected one, the one elected in November and taking office the first week in January. Because

TABLE 8.1 2004, 2008, AND 2012 BATTLEGROUND STATES

As the table shows, many of the 2004 battleground states swung strongly in Obama's favor in 2008. That lead lessened in 2012, but Obama still maintained the lead and won reelection.

State	Electoral Votes in 2012	Percent Difference in 2004 Popular Vote	Percent Difference in 2008 Popular Vote	Percent Difference in 2012 Popular Vote
Wisconsin	10	0.38 Kerry	13.91 Obama	6.7 Obama
New Mexico	5	0.79 Bush	15.13 Obama	9.9 Obama
Iowa	6	0.67 Bush	9.54 Obama	5.6 Obama
New Hampshire	4	1.37 Kerry	9.61 Obama	5.8 Obama
Pennsylvania	20	2.50 Kerry	10.32 Obama	5.2 Obama
Ohio	18	2.10 Bush	4.59 Obama	1.9 Obama
Nevada	6	2.59 Bush	12.50 Obama	6.6 Obama
Michigan	16	3.42 Kerry	16.47 Obama	8.5 Obama
Oregon	7	4.16 Kerry	16.35 Obama	11.7 Obama
Florida	29	5.01 Bush	2.81 Obama	0.6 Obama
Missouri	10	7.20 Bush	0.14 McCain	9.6 Romney
Virginia	13	8.20 Bush	6.30 Obama	1.0 Obama
North Carolina	15	12.44 Bush	0.32 Obama	2.2 Romney
Indiana	11	20.68 Bush	1.04 Obama	10.5 Romney

Which states had the largest change in vote share to the two parties between 2004 and 2008? What do these states have in common?

SOURCE: Federal Election Commission, "Election Results," http://www.fec.gov/pubrec/electionresults.shtml (accessed March 23, 2010); "President Map" *New York Times,* November 8, 2012 (accessed November 8, 2012). http://elections.nytimes.com/2012/results/president.

each state has one vote in the House, what happens if a state delegation's vote is tied? The answer: its vote does not count. Would it be possible to have a president of one party and a vice president of another? Yes, if the election were thrown into the House and Senate, and a different party controlled each chamber.

The Electoral College sharply influences presidential politics. To win a presidential election, a candidate must appeal successfully to voters in populous states such as California, Texas, Ohio, Illinois, Florida, and New York. California's electoral vote of 55 in 2008 exceeded the combined electoral votes of the 14 least populous states plus the District of Columbia. Sparsely populated states such as Wyoming and Vermont also have disproportionate representation in the Electoral College because each has one representative, regardless of population. When the contest is close, as it was in recent elections, every state's electoral votes are crucial to the outcome, and so greater emphasis is given to states in which the contest is close (see Table 8.1).[17]

Counting Votes

8.2 Identify problems associated with administering elections and evaluate proposed solutions to those problems.

Until the 2000 election, most citizens assumed they could cast a vote and have it count as long as they played by the rules. They registered to vote, showed up at their local polling place ready to decide, waited in line to be given a ballot, cast their secret ballot, and assumed it would be counted. They did not expect to be challenged for special identification, or questioned about how they had registered to vote. And they certainly did not expect their ballot to be lost or miscounted.

Votes are counted in the United States according to state law as administered by local officials. The technology used in voting varies greatly from state to state and in different parts of the same state. In Florida in 2000, some counties used paper ballots, others voting machines, and others punch-card ballots, and at least one county used ballots that a computer could scan. More recently, states have moved from touchscreen computerized voting systems to paper ballots that can be optically scanned. Reasons for this include lower costs for optical scan machines and a paper ballot making recounts easier.

As we discuss in the chapter on public opinion, voter identification requirements and heightened scrutiny over the voter registration process has become more common since the 2010 election. In 2012 there was also controversy over the move in some battleground states to reduce the number of early voting days. The trust voters had in how ballots are counted changed after the 2000 election when the nation waited for weeks to find out whether George W. Bush or Al Gore would be president. The outcome hinged on a few damaged ballots that were cast and counted or not counted in Florida. Not only did the dispute raise important questions about how votes are counted, it also opened a broad debate about how votes are cast.

Another lesson the recent ballot-counting controversies have reinforced is that in every election, in every jurisdiction, and with every technology, voting is imperfect. Touchscreen software can be manipulated; people can miscount paper ballots; punch cards may not always be completely perforated; and so on. The goal in election administration is to minimize errors and eliminate as much bias and outright fraud as possible.

But counting votes is more complicated than the means by which we vote. Election officials have to make judgment calls about incomplete or flawed ballots. Decisions about which ballots to count and which ones not to count matter in an election decided by only 537 votes, as Florida's presidential election was in 2000. With the growth in absentee voting, and with military personnel and civilians living abroad voting by mail, a close election may not be decided until days after the polls officially close.

8.1

8.2

8.3

8.4

8.5

8.6

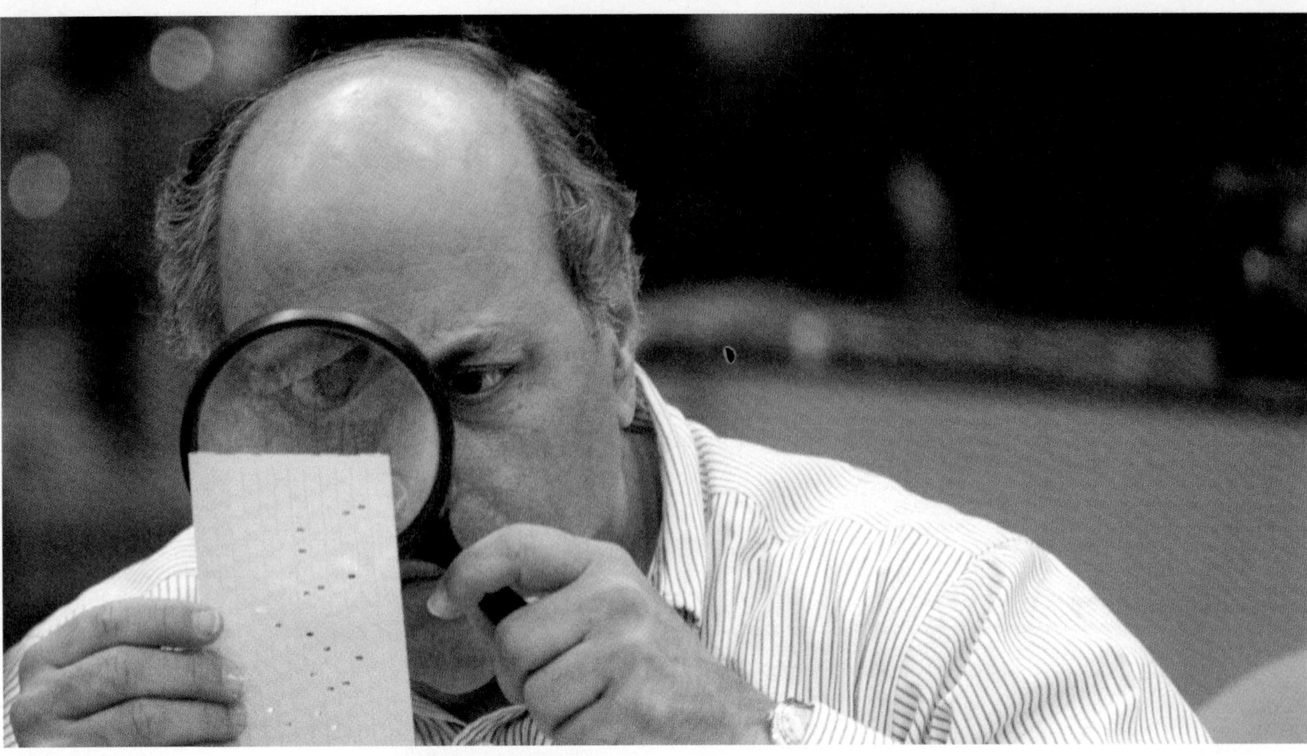

Judge Robert Rosenberg of the Broward County Canvassing Board uses a magnifying glass to examine a dimpled chad on a punch card ballot, November 24, 2000, during a vote recount. The presidential election in 2000 in Florida was plagued with vote counting and ballot problems. For example, several counties used punch cards, and some voters failed to make their vote clear by successfully punching out the "chad" for the choice selected. This led to discussion of "dangling chads" and "dimpled chads." In other counties, the format of the ballot itself was confusing. The Florida problems led to passage of the Help America Vote Act.

When voters appear in person to vote at one of the nation's thousands of voting places, or *polls*, they are greeted and given a ballot by citizens from their own neighborhood. These volunteer poll workers arrive at the polls hours before voting starts to set up equipment and ensure that the voter lists, ballots, and voting equipment are ready to go. Recent research has found that poll workers can greatly influence the security, efficiency, and overall environment of polling locations. Those who receive high-quality training and are confident in both their expertise and the accuracy of the polling location create an overall environment that makes voters feel more confident.[18]

Who is and who is not allowed to vote on Election Day is also a source of controversy. In most states, persons must be registered voters in order to vote. Voters are expected to vote in designated voting places. In 2012, as a result of the 2010 redistricting, some voting places and precincts in parts of the country changed, which confused some voters who went to the wrong place to vote. The law permits voters who think they should be allowed to vote but who are not on the rolls to cast what are called provisional ballots. These ballots are counted only if the voter is, in fact, registered to vote.

Following the 2000 and 2004 elections, federal and state governments invested billions of dollars in new voting technology, established new rules on provisional ballots, and modernized voting methods. Interest groups, political parties, and candidates have made the integrity of the voting process a high priority. In 2012, with some states adding photo identification requirements in order to vote and some more actively purging their voter lists of presumed illegal immigrants, more attention was given to who may and may not vote. Groups established toll-free hotlines for voters to call if they felt they were not being treated fairly, and in key jurisdictions, lawyers were on call to file immediate challenges when a person's right to vote was contested.

FOR the People Government's Greatest Endeavors

Expanding the Electorate

Central to government by the people is the right to vote. But which people have been granted this right has changed dramatically over the course of U.S. history. In the early years of our republic suffrage was generally only a right for white, male property owners over the age of 21. Such an exclusive granting of the right to vote was consistent with the granting of other rights at the time. For example, until 1900, married women were often not allowed to own property in their own name nor keep their own earnings.

Gradually barriers to voting rights were removed, with North Carolina the last state to remove property ownership as a requirement in 1856. Extending the right to vote to women came gradually. Due to vague constitutional language, New Jersey women could vote between 1776 and 1807,* and Wyoming extended the right to vote to women in 1869. It took another half century for all adult women to have the right.

Blacks were extended the right to vote in five states before the Civil War, and after the war many African Americans assumed they were full citizens with voting rights. But the former Confederate states effectively barred Blacks and many poor whites from voting through barriers like poll taxes, literacy tests, and threats of physical violence. It took a constitutional amendment and passage of the Voting Rights Act to break down this barrier.

During the 1970s, young people argued that it was not right that 18- and 19-year-olds were drafted to fight in Vietnam but did not have the right to vote. As with gender and race, it took another constitutional amendment to extend the right to vote to persons 18–21 years of age.

Expanding the electorate has been an important endeavor for our government. It has made government by the people a more accurate description of our system of government than was the case when Lincoln uttered the phrase in 1863.

QUESTIONS

1. In the early years of our republic why was property ownership seen as relevant to who could vote?
2. Have we gone too far in extending the right to vote? Should voters need to pass a mental competency test? Should they be required to be literate?
3. What arguments can you give for or against granting the right to vote to 16–18-year-olds?

*Judith Apter Klinghoffer and Lois Elkis. 'The Petticoat Electors': Women's Suffrage in New Jersey, 1776––1807. Journal of the Early Republic, Vol. 12, No. 2 (Summer 1992), pp. 159–193.

Running for Congress

8.3 Explain how congressional elections work and why they are generally not competitive.

How candidates run for Congress differs depending on the nature of their district or state, on whether candidates are incumbents or challengers, on the strength of their personal organization, on how well known they are, and on how much money they have to spend on their campaign. There are both similarities and differences between House and Senate elections.

Explore on MyPoliSciLab Simulation: You Are a Campaign Strategist

safe seat
An elected office that is predictably won by one party or the other, so the success of that party's candidate is almost taken for granted.

coattail effect
The boost that candidates may get in an election because of the popularity of candidates above them on the ballot, especially the president.

First, most House elections are not close (see Figure 8.1). In districts where most people belong to one party or where incumbents are popular and enjoy fundraising and other campaign advantages, there is often little competition.[19] Districts are typically drawn in ways that enhance party control and incumbent reelection, a process called *partisan gerrymandering*. Those who believe that competition is essential to constitutional democracy are concerned that so many officeholders have **safe seats**. Some contend that when officeholders do not have to fight to retain their seats, elections are not performing their proper role.[20]

Competition is more likely when both candidates have adequate funding, which is not often the case in U.S. House elections. Elections for governor and for the U.S. Senate are more seriously contested and more adequately financed than those for the U.S. House.

Presidential popularity affects both House and Senate races during both presidential and midterm elections. The boost candidates get from running along with a popular presidential candidate from their party is known as the **coattail effect**. But winning presidential candidates do not always provide such a boost. The Republicans

8.1
8.2
8.3
8.4
8.5
8.6

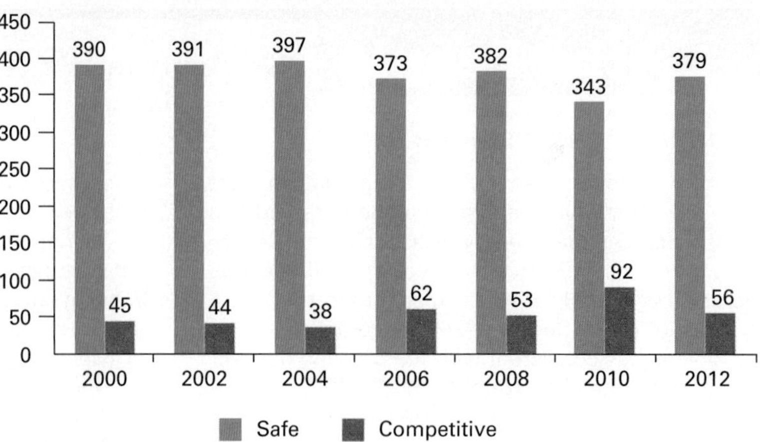

FIGURE 8.1 SAFE AND COMPETITIVE HOUSE SEATS, 2000–2010

SOURCE: Charlie Cook, "National Overview," *Cook Political Report*, October 16, 2008, p. 6; and Charlie Cook, "Competitive House Race Chart," *Cook Political Report*, http://cookpolitical.com/house/archive/chart/house/race-ratings/2010-10-11_15-22-53; Charlie Cook, "2012 House race ratings for October 11, 2012," *The Cook Political Report*, October 11, 2012, accessed Oct. 15, 2012, http://cookpolitical.com/house/charts/race-ratings.

Note: Competitive seats include both tossup, lean Republican, and lean Democrat.

suffered a net loss of six House seats in 1988, even though George H. W. Bush won the presidency, and the Democrats suffered a net loss of ten House seats in 1992 when Bill Clinton won the presidential election. On the coattails of Barack Obama's convincing presidential win in 2008, the Democrats saw a net gain of 21 House seats and 8 Senate seats. Overall, "measurable coattail effects continue to appear," according to congressional elections scholar Gary Jacobson, but their impact is "erratic and usually modest."[21]

In midterm elections, presidential popularity and economic conditions have long been associated with the number of House seats a president's party loses.[22] These same factors are associated with how well the president's party does in Senate races, but the association is less strong.[23] Figure 8.2 shows the number of seats in the House of Representatives and U.S. Senate gained or lost by the party controlling the White House in midterm elections since 1954. In all of the midterm elections between 1934 and 1998, the party controlling the White House lost seats in the House. But in 1998 and 2002, the long-standing pattern of the president's party losing seats in a midterm election did not hold. In 2006, however, that pattern reemerged, with the Republicans losing 30 House seats and 6 Senate seats.[24] The net result of the Democrats success in 2006 and 2008 was that they had won many of the most competitive districts, making them vulnerable to the GOP in 2010.

In 2010, Republicans won a net gain of 6 U.S. Senate seats and 64 House seats. Putting this victory in historical perspective, this was the greatest number of House seats gained by a party since 1938 when the GOP had a net gain of 72 seats, and it surpassed the 54 seats the Democrats lost in 1994 and 1946. Republicans did especially well in defeating centrist Democrats, sometimes called Blue Dog Democrats. More than half of this group in the House were defeated or retired in 2010.

□ The House of Representatives

Every two years, as many as 1,000 candidates—including approximately 400 incumbents—campaign for Congress. Incumbents are rarely challenged for renomination from within their own party. In the 1990s, for example, on average only two House incumbents were denied renomination in each election. In 2010, four House incumbents were denied renomination, and 29 ran unopposed.[25] Challengers from other parties running against incumbents rarely encounter opposition in their own party.[26] In 2010, Tea Party-supported candidates defeated the party leader's preferred Senate candidates in Kentucky, Nevada, and Delaware, something that also happened in Indiana and Texas in 2012.

MOUNTING A PRIMARY CAMPAIGN The first step for would-be challengers is to raise hundreds of thousands of dollars (or even more) to mount a serious campaign.

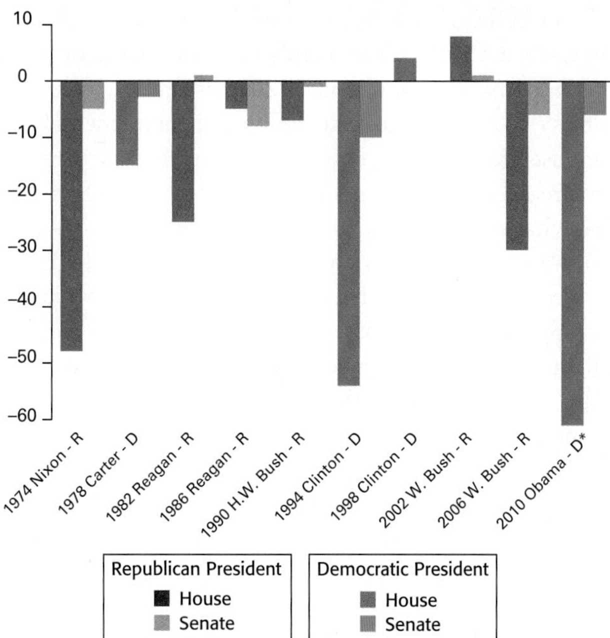

FIGURE 8.2 SEATS GAINED OR LOST BY THE PRESIDENT'S PARTY IN MIDTERM ELECTIONS, 1974–2010

Based on past midterm elections, how does 2010 compare in terms of the seats lost by the President's party?

SOURCE: Harold W. Stanley and Richard G. Niemi, *Vital Statistics on American Politics 2011–2012* (CQ Press, 2011), p. 63.

candidate appeal

The tendency in elections to focus on the personal attributes of a candidate, such as his or her strengths, weaknesses, background, experience, and visibility.

national tide

The inclination to focus on national issues, rather than local issues, in an election campaign. The impact of a national tide can be reduced by the nature of the candidates on the ballot who may have differentiated themselves from their party or its leader if the tide is negative, as well as competition in the election.

This requires asking friends and acquaintances as well as interest groups for money. Candidates need money to hire campaign managers and technicians, buy television and other advertising, conduct polls, and pay for a variety of activities. Parties can sometimes help, but they shy away from giving money in primary contests. The party organization usually stays neutral until the nomination is decided.

Another early step is to build a *personal organization.* A congressional candidate can build an organization while holding another office, such as a seat in the state legislature, by serving in civic causes, helping other candidates, and being conspicuous without being controversial.

A candidate's main hurdle is gaining visibility. Candidates work hard to be mentioned by the media. In large cities with many simultaneous campaigns, congressional candidates are frequently overlooked, and in all areas, television is devoting less time to political news.[27] Candidates rely on personal contacts, on hand shaking and door-to-door campaigning, and on identifying likely supporters and courting their favor—the same techniques used in campaigns for lesser offices. Despite these efforts, the turnout in primaries tends to be low, except in campaigns in which large sums of money are spent on advertising.

CAMPAIGNING FOR THE GENERAL ELECTION The electorate in a general election is different from that in a primary election. Many more voters turn out in general elections, especially the less-committed partisans and Independents. Partisanship is more important in a general election, as many voters use party as a simplifying device to select from among candidates in the many races they decide. Not surprisingly, candidates in districts where their party is strong make their partisanship clear, and candidates from a minority party deemphasize it. General elections also focus on **candidate appeal**, the strengths and weaknesses of the candidates and their background, experience, and visibility.

Issues can also be important in general elections, but they are often more local than national issues. Occasionally, a major national issue can help or hurt one party. Candidates who have differentiated themselves from their party or its leader can reduce the impact of such a **national tide** if it is negative. Some elections for Congress or the state legislature are in part referendums on the president or governor, but public opinion concerning the president or governor is rarely the only factor in play.

name recognition
Incumbents have an advantage over challengers in election campaigns because voters are more familiar with them, and incumbents are more recognizable.

As mentioned, most incumbent members of Congress win reelection.[28] Since 1970, nearly 94 percent of incumbent House members seeking reelection have won, but the percentage hit a low point for this period in 2010, when 86 percent were reelected.[29] This lends credibility to the charge that we have a "permanent Congress." Why is reelection to a House seat so much easier than defeating an incumbent or winning an open seat? One reason is incumbents have a host of advantages. They are generally better known than challengers, something called **name recognition**, and benefit from years of media coverage of their generally positive efforts on behalf of the district.

Incumbents also win so often because they are able to outspend challengers in campaigns by approximately 3 to 1 in the House and more than 2 to 1 in the Senate, although in 2010 the differences were not as large.[30] Most challengers run campaigns that are much less visible than incumbents, contact fewer voters, and lose badly. Many potential challengers are scared away by the prospect of having to raise more than $1 million in campaign funds, and some do not want to face the media scrutiny that comes with a serious race for Congress. Nonetheless, in each election, a few challengers mount serious campaigns because of the incumbent's perceived vulnerability, the challengers' own wealth, party or political action committee efforts, or other factors.

In those competitive House races, the party committees and outside groups often spend as much as the candidates on mostly attack advertising.[31] Super PACs and other interest groups also spend heavily on these contests. One new group, Campaign for Primary Accountability, spent more than $3 million against both Republican and Democratic incumbents in primaries; four of the group's targets lost.[32]

In addition, incumbents generally win because their district boundaries have been drawn to be made up of voters who favor their party. Retirements and redistricting create *open seats,* which can result in more competitive elections. If, however, the district is heavily partisan, the predominant party is likely to retain the seat, and once elected, the incumbent then reaps the other incumbency advantages as well. In these cases, the contest for the nomination in the predominant party effectively determines who will be the new representative.

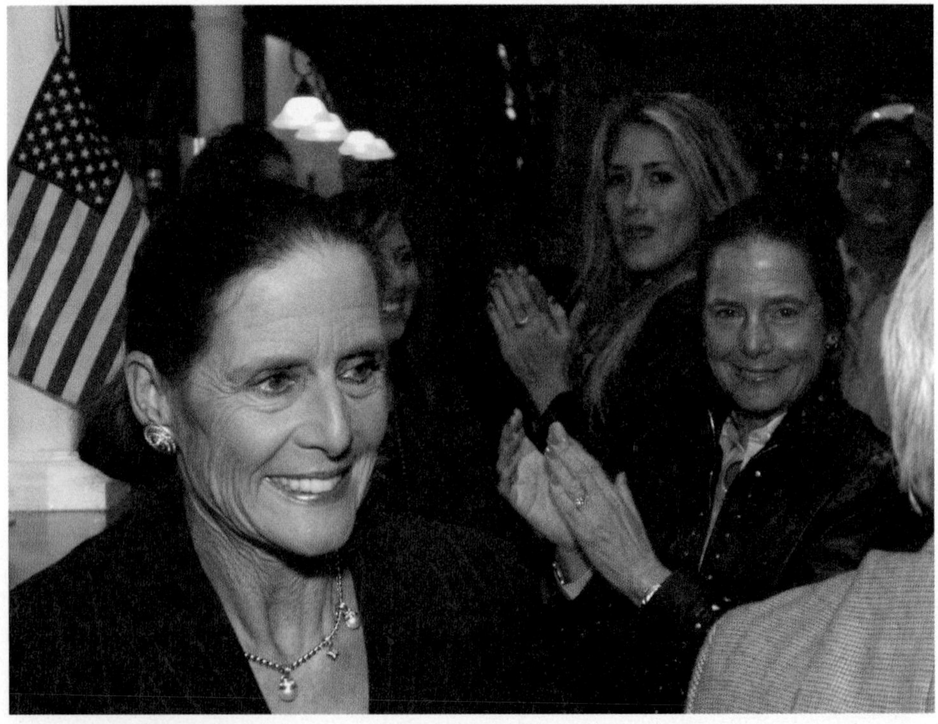

One representative who was defeated in her bid for renomination in 2012 was Ohio congresswoman Jean Schmidt. Her district boundaries had been redrawn as a result of redistricting and an outside group, the Campaign for Primary Accountability, ran radio ads against her before the primary.

The Senate

Running for the Senate is generally more high-profile than running for the House. The six-year term, the fact that there are only two senators per state, and the national exposure many senators enjoy make a Senate seat a glittering prize. Individual Senate campaigns cost more than individual House races and are more likely to be seriously contested; though in the aggregate, because there are so many more House races, overall spending on House races surpasses overall spending on Senate races (see Figure 8.3).[33] The essential tactics are to raise large amounts of money, hire a professional and experienced campaign staff, make as many personal contacts as possible (especially in states with smaller populations), avoid giving the opposition any positive publicity, and have a clear and consistent campaign theme. Incumbency is an advantage for senators, although not as much as it is for representatives.[34] Incumbent senators are widely known, but often so are their opponents, who generally raise and spend significant amounts of money.[35]

When one party controls the Senate by only a few seats, as has been the case in recent years, both parties and the White House become more involved in recruiting competitive candidates. Sometimes, the party leadership attempts to "clear the field" for a preferred candidate by discouraging other candidates from running while endorsing a candidate it considers more competitive. In 2012, Democratic Senator and Majority Leader Harry Reid successfully courted former U.S. Senator Bob Kerry to run for an open senate seat in Nebraska.[36]

The cost of Senate campaigns can vary greatly. California has nearly 70 times the number of potential voters as Wyoming; not surprisingly, running for a seat from Wyoming is much cheaper than running for a seat from California. As a result, interest groups and parties direct more money to competitive races in small states where their campaign dollars have a greater potential impact.[37]

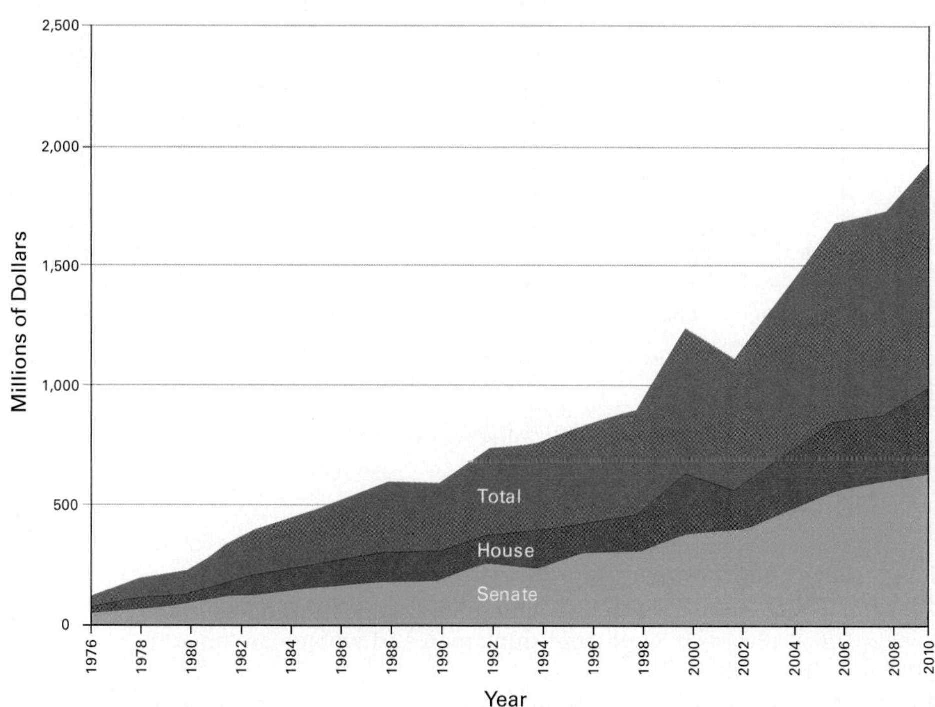

FIGURE 8.3 RISING CAMPAIGN COSTS IN CONGRESSIONAL GENERAL ELECTIONS

What are some of the ways in which the rising cost of campaigns might impact who runs for office, how campaigns are funded, and the priorities of candidates?

SOURCE: 1976—1998: Harold W. Stanley and Richard G. Niemi, Vital Statistics on American Politics 2007–2008 (CQ Press, 2008), p. 101; 2000–2010: Center for Responsive Politics, "Price of Admission: Winners," www.opensecrets.org/bigpicture/stats.php?cycle=2008&display=T&Type=W (accessed 9 April 2012).

8.1

8.2

8.3

8.4

8.5

8.6

The Global Community

Who Makes a Better Political Leader?

Voters in the United States have increasingly had the opportunity to vote for women for governor, president, vice president, senator, representative, and other offices. How do people feel about women versus men serving in these offices? The Pew Global Attitudes survey asked respondents the following question: "Which of the following statements comes closest to your opinion about men and women as political leaders: Men generally make better political leaders than women, women generally make better political leaders than men, or, in general, women and men make equally good political leaders."

Holding aside Nigeria, the most common response in all countries in our sample is that men and women are equally qualified to be political leaders. In Britain, this response is given by 83 percent, perhaps a reflection of the fact that the position of prime minister in Britain has been held by a woman. Japan, Mexico, and the United States all have high proportions of respondents saying both genders make equally good leaders. However, in Nigeria, there is a preference for male leaders, with 48 percent saying they make better leaders. This likely stems from the political culture of Nigeria where women are often marginalized for social and religious reasons.*

Another way to look at these data is to compare the views of those who do not think men and women make equally good leaders. Of this group, people in India, Britain, and Mexico are about equally divided with all favoring men. In the other countries men are preferred as leaders over women by 2.5 to 1 or more. Again, this is only among people who do not see the two genders as equally well qualified.

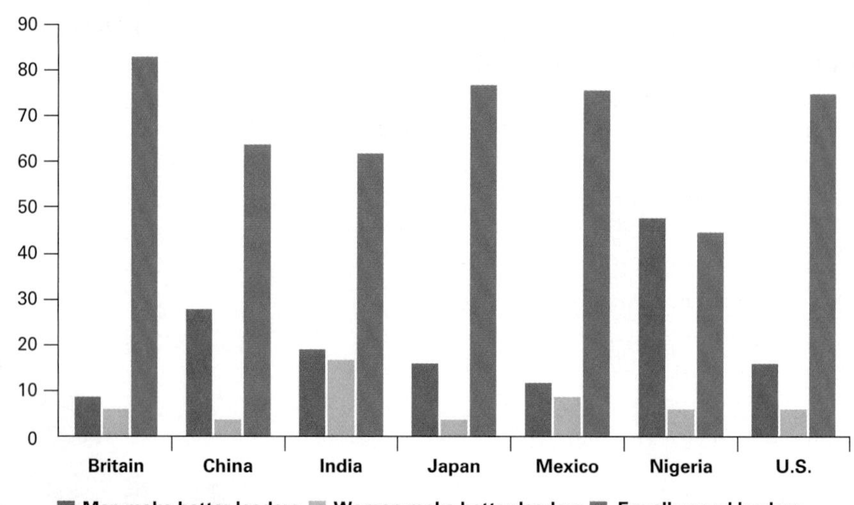

SOURCE: Pew Research Center, *Global Views on life Satisfaction, National Conditions, and the Global Economy: Highlights from the 2007 Pew Global Attitudes 47-Nation Survey* (Pew Research Center, 2007).

CRITICAL THINKING QUESTIONS

1. What do you think the answer to this survey question would have been 100 years ago, 50 years ago, 20 years ago?
2. Why do we not see more women holding political office in the United States if 75 percent think men and women are equally well qualified?
3. How would you expect men and women political leaders to be different?

*Muhammad Mustapha, "In the Shadows of Men: Women's Political Marginalization," *Inter Press Service*, March 12, 2010, http://ipsnews.net/news.asp?idnews=50648 (accessed May 6, 2010).

Running for President

8.4 Describe the stages in U.S. presidential elections and the differences in campaigning at each stage.

residential elections are major media events, with candidates seeking as much positive television coverage as possible and trying to avoid negative coverage. The formal campaign has three stages: winning the nomination, campaigning at the convention, and mobilizing support in the general election.

☐ Stage 1: The Nomination

Presidential hopefuls must make a series of critical tactical decisions. The first is when to start campaigning. For the presidential election of 2012, some candidates began soon after the 2008 presidential election.[38] Mitt Romney's nomination opponents often quipped that he had been running for president for more than six years. Romney was not alone in building on a 2008 run in his 2012 race; Ron Paul had run in the Republican contest in 2008 and as the Libertarian candidate in 1988. Candidates generally formally announce their candidacy in March or April, and most had announced by June 2011. Republican Rick Perry delayed his entry until August, a decision that lessened his time to campaign and compete in fundraising, but that does not explain his poor performance in the debates.[39]

Early decisions are increasingly necessary for candidates to raise money and assemble an organization. Campaigning begins well before any actual declaration of candidacy, as candidates try to line up supporters to win caucuses or primaries in key states and to raise money for their nomination effort. This period in the campaign has been called the "invisible primary."[40]

One of the hardest jobs for candidates and their strategists is calculating how to deal with the complex maze of presidential primaries and caucuses that constitutes the delegate selection system. The system for electing delegates to the national party convention varies from state to state and often from one party to the other in the same state. In some parties in some states, for example, candidates must provide lists of delegates who support them months before the primary.

In 2012, for example, both Rick Santorum and Newt Gingrich failed to secure sufficient petition signatures to qualify for the Virginia primary.[41] Santorum's campaign also lost delegates to Romney he would otherwise have won in Ohio because he failed to file a full slate of delegates.[42] Another decision candidates must make is whether to participate in partial public financing of their primary campaigns. The presidential campaign finance system provides funds to match small individual contributions during the nomination phase for candidates who agree to remain within spending limitations. However, not all candidates accept the funding, which limits the total amount they can raise from other sources.

For example, George W. Bush declined federal funds in the 2000 and 2004 nomination phase, as did Democrats John Kerry and Howard Dean in 2004. In 2008, Barack Obama, Hillary Clinton, Mitt Romney, Rudy Giuliani, Ron Paul, Mike Huckabee, and Fred Thompson all turned down matching funds. John McCain at one point said he would accept them and then later declined them. In 2012, only Charles "Buddy" Roemer III, a largely invisible candidate who unsuccessfully sought the "Americans Elect" nomination, was eligible for and received matching funds.[43] Forgoing the public matching funds allows greater flexibility in spending campaign money and removes the overall limit for this phase of the process. Today, most serious contenders for the White House are likely to decline federal matching funds.

PRESIDENTIAL PRIMARIES State presidential primaries, unknown before 1900, have become the main method of choosing delegates to the national convention. A delegate is a person chosen by local partisans to represent them in selecting nominees, party leaders, and party positions. Today, more than three-fourths of the states use

8.1

8.2

8.3

8.4

8.5

8.6

caucus
A meeting of local party members to choose party officials or candidates for public office and to decide the platform.

presidential primaries. In 2012, 81 percent of the Democratic delegates and 74 percent of the Republican delegates were chosen in primaries.[44] The rest of the delegates were chosen by state party caucuses or conventions or were party leaders who served as "superdelegates," a term describing delegates not typically elected through the primaries or caucuses but who are delegates due to their holding an elective office or party position.

The states have different means of determining delegates, and state primaries allocate delegates using the following systems:[45]

- *Proportional representation:* Delegates to the national convention are allocated on the basis of the percentage of votes candidates win in the primary. This system has been used in most of the states, including several of the largest ones. The Democrats mandate proportional representation for all their primaries, with three-quarters of the states' delegates elected in primaries determined by the proportional vote in congressional districts.[46] Republicans largely followed suit in 2012 when more than half (52%) of Republican delegates were determined proportionally, including those in 27 states plus American Samoa and Puerto Rico.[47]
- *Winner take all:* Whoever gets the most votes wins all that state's delegates or the share of delegates from each congressional district. Republicans still used the winner-take-all system at the state level in ten states and the District of Columbia in 2012.[48] California was the largest state to use a winner-take-all primary in 2012. To win all the delegates of a big state such as California is an enormous bonus to a candidate.
- *Superdelegates and delegate selection without a commitment to a candidate:* Following the 1972 election, when some elected officials and party leaders were not elected delegates, there was an effort to give more influence in the selection of the presidential candidate to party leaders and elected officials. This led to the creation of superdelegates. In 2012, as many as seven states had ten unbound at-large delegates.[49] In 2008, a lot of attention was paid to Democratic superdelegates. Superdelegates cast the deciding vote for Obama in 2008 because no candidate secured a majority of all delegates through the primary and caucus process.
- *Delegate selection and separate presidential poll:* In several states, voters decide twice: once to indicate their choice for president and again to choose delegates pledged, or at least favorable, to a presidential candidate. In 2012, eight states had contests like this.

Voters in states such as Iowa and New Hampshire, which are the first states to pick delegates, bask in media attention for weeks and even months before they cast the first ballots in the presidential sweepstakes. Because these early contests have had the effect of limiting the choices of voters in states that come later in the process, states have tended to move their primaries up in a process called "front loading." California, which traditionally held its primary in June, moved it to March in 2000 and 2004 so that its voters would play a more important role in selecting the nominee. In a cost-saving move, California returned to June as the date again in 2012.[50]

As states have competed more aggressively for early positioning in shaping primary contests, the parties have sought to prevent too much front loading. In 2008, when Florida and Michigan moved their primaries up to January 29 and January 15 (respectively), ahead of what party rules allowed, the Democratic National Committee (DNC) voted that delegates so selected would not be seated.[51] The controversy was resolved by giving each Florida and Michigan delegate a half vote, but at the convention, the Party relented and each delegate was given a full vote. In 2012, Florida moved up its GOP primary and the national party took away half of the state's delegates as a punishment.[52] The Republican nomination contest in 2012 was not as protracted as the Democratic contest of 2008, but lasted longer than the 2008 GOP contest, with four candidates—Mitt Romney, Newt Gingrich, Rick Santorum, and Ron Paul—all remaining in the contest into April, before Mitt Romney emerged as the presumptive nominee.

CAUCUSES AND CONVENTIONS A meeting of party members and supporters of various candidates who may elect state or national convention delegates, who in turn vote for the presidential nominee, is called a **caucus**. In about 13 states (or 19 states and territories), one or both parties use a caucus or convention system (or both) to choose delegates.[53] Each state's parties and legislature regulate the methods used.[54] The caucus or convention is the oldest method of choosing delegates, and unlike the primary system, it centers on staffing local party positions such as voting district chair, and often includes party discussions of issues and candidates in addition to a vote on delegates to the county or state convention, who in turn vote on delegates to the national convention where the nominee is selected.

The best-known example of a caucus is in Iowa, because Iowa has held the earliest caucuses in the most recent presidential nominating contests. In January in a presidential election year, Iowans have the opportunity to attend Republican and Democratic precinct meetings or caucuses.[55] In 2008, Barack Obama outperformed Hillary Clinton in the Democratic caucuses.[56] In the Republican 2012 contest, Romney did well in both caucuses and primaries, winning about two-thirds of both types of contests during the period that the race was contested. Rick Santorum did better in caucuses than in primaries.

STRATEGIES Presidential hopefuls face a dilemma: to get the Republican nomination, a candidate has to appeal to the more intensely conservative Republican partisans. Those who vote in caucuses and primaries and actively support campaigns were different from the general population in 2012 in that they were more likely to be male

You Will Decide

Should We Establish a National Presidential Primary?

States that have their caucuses or conventions early in the presidential selection process get more attention and have generally had a greater say in selecting the presidential candidates. For several election cycles prior to 2008, many states held presidential primaries after the nominee had effectively been selected. Continuing a trend from past election cycles, several states moved up their primary or caucus dates in 2008. The ordering of the states, with Iowa and New Hampshire first, has been disputed by other states that have proposed either a national primary or a set of regional primaries.

Another criticism of the current system is that the states asserting a claim to going first are not representative of their party or the country. Yet another problem is the threat of one party's voters participating in another's primary in hopes of nominating a weak candidate or prolonging the primary contest, such as when Rush Limbaugh urged Republicans, through his "Operation Chaos," to vote for Hillary Clinton to draw out the 2008 Democratic race for as long as possible. A national primary would give all U.S. voters an equal say as to their party nominee.

What do you think? Should we establish a national presidential primary? What are some of the arguments for or against it?

Thinking It Through

Our current system of state primaries or caucuses grows out of federalism and the rights of the states to govern elections. Mandating a national primary, though likely constitutional, would be a departure from federalism, and some may object to it as a step toward the federal government's controlling voter registration, voting technology, and other aspects of election administration that were long the province of the states. A national primary could force states that prefer the caucus system to adopt primaries. Because states sometimes combine the presidential primary with their primary for other offices, it may mean adding another election to the calendar.

A national primary would have the advantage of giving every voter an equal say in determining the nominee. It would also take away the kind of dispute that clouded the 2008 Democratic contest, in which Florida and Michigan voted earlier than the national party rules allowed.

A national primary would substantially change the nature of the campaign. Our current system means candidates with less money can spend more time meeting the voters of Iowa and New Hampshire and prove themselves in order to move on in the process. A national primary would help candidates with more money and greater name recognition because there would be little person-to-person campaigning.

CRITICAL THINKING QUESTIONS

1. Do you think it is fair that Iowa and New Hampshire are always first in the nominating process?
2. What are the strengths and weaknesses of the current system?
3. When should a national primary be held, and why?

Presidential primaries include debates among candidates. In this one, Mitt Romney (R) extends his hand and bets $10,000 that Texas Governor. Rick Perry (L) is wrong about what Romney had written about a national health care mandate during the ABC News GOP Presidential debate in Des Moines, Iowa.

(52 percent), white (95 percent), hold a college degree (49 percent), and make more than $100,000 (31 percent). Most said they supported the Tea Party (61 percent) and about half were Evangelical Christians.[57] Democratic hopefuls have to appeal to the liberal wing of their party as well as to minorities, union members, and environmental activists. But to win the general election, candidates have to win support from moderate and pragmatic voters, many of whom do not vote in the primaries. If candidates position themselves too far from the moderates in their nomination campaign, they risk being labeled extreme in the general election and losing these votes to their opponents. In 2012, for example, Mitt Romney's position on illegal immigration was more conservative than some of his primary opponents like Governor Rick Perry of Texas or former House Speaker Newt Gingrich. Later, during the general election campaign, Obama and his allies used Romney's earlier statements to portray Romney as extreme in his views and unsympathetic to Hispanics.

Strategies for securing the nomination have changed throughout the years. Some candidates think it wise to skip some of the earlier contests and enter first in states where their strength lies. John McCain pursued such a strategy in 2000 and again in 2008, ignoring Iowa and concentrating on New Hampshire. Former Utah governor Jon Huntsman bypassed Iowa in 2012, and Mitt Romney did not invest as much time or money there in 2012 as he did in 2008. With polls showing a close race, Romney became more active in Iowa as the caucuses drew nearer. In an unusual turn of events, Romney was declared the winner by 8 votes (out of over 120,000 votes cast) only to have Santorum declared the winner by 34 votes more than two weeks later, after party officials found inaccuracies in the vote count in 131 precincts, with all ballots missing from 8 precincts.[58] Most candidates choose to run hard in Iowa and New Hampshire, hoping that early showings in these states, which receive a great deal of media attention, will move them into the spotlight for later contests.

During this early phase, the ability of candidates to generate momentum by managing the media's expectations of their performance is especially important. Winning in the primaries thus centers on a game of expectations, and candidates may intentionally seek to lower expectations so that "doing better than expected" will generate momentum for their campaign. The media and pollsters generally set these expectations in their coverage of candidates. For example, in 2012 the Michigan primary was presumed to be one Romney would easily win. He was born in the state, his father had been governor of Michigan in the 1960s, and he won the state against John McCain in 2008. But

Rick Santorum had surprising wins in Colorado, Minnesota, and Missouri three weeks before Michigan voted, and then climbed into the lead in polls in Michigan. Romney intensified his efforts and won Michigan by 3 percent, regaining the momentum.

national party convention
A national meeting of delegates elected in primaries, caucuses, or state conventions who assemble once every four years to nominate candidates for president and vice president, ratify the party platform, elect officers, and adopt rules.

□ Stage 2: The National Party Convention

The delegates elected in primaries, caucuses, or state conventions assemble at their **national party convention** in the summer before the election to pick the party's presidential and vice presidential candidates. Conventions follow standard rules, routines, and rituals. Usually, the first day is devoted to a keynote address and other speeches touting the party and denouncing the opposition; the second day, to committee reports, including party and convention rules and the party platform; the third day, to presidential and vice presidential balloting; and the fourth day, to the presidential candidate's acceptance speech.

National party conventions used to be events of high excitement because there was no clear nominee before the convention. In the past, delegates also arrived at national nominating conventions with differing degrees of commitment to presidential candidates; some delegates were pledged to no candidate at all, others to a specific candidate for one or two ballots, and others firmly to one candidate only. Because of reforms encouraging delegates to stick with the person to whom they are pledged, there has been less room to maneuver at conventions. For a half century, conventions have ratified a candidate who has already been selected in the primaries and caucuses.

Despite the lack of suspense about whom the nominee will be, conventions continue to be major media events. As recently as 1988, the major networks gave the Democratic and Republican national conventions gavel-to-gavel coverage, meaning that television covered the conventions from the beginning of the first night to the end of the fourth night. Now, the major networks leave comprehensive coverage to C-SPAN. The long-term decline in viewership and the reduced hours of coverage have altered the parties' strategies. The parties feature their most important speakers and highlight their most important messages in the limited time the networks give them. In 2008, coverage and viewership of the conventions increased; this was especially the case for the Obama, Palin, and McCain acceptance speeches. An estimated 40 million people viewed the McCain speech, slightly higher than the number who saw Obama's acceptance speech.[59] In 2012, an estimated 35.7 million people watched Obama's acceptance speech at the Democratic convention, compared to 30.3 million who watched Romney's acceptance speech at the Republican convention.[60]

Senator Marco Rubio, R-Fl, a rising Republican star and Tea Party favorite, was surrounded by reporters on the night he spoke at the Republican National Convention just before Mitt Romney delivered his acceptance speech.

Acceptance speeches provide the nominees with an opportunity to define themselves and their candidacy. An example of an acceptance speech that worked more to the benefit of the opposition was Barry Goldwater's speech to the Republican convention in 1964 when he said, "Extremism in the defense of liberty is no vice."[61] This only helped to define Goldwater as "dangerous" and "extreme," themes his opponent, Lyndon Johnson, exploited. Democrats hoped Ronald Reagan would also self-destruct in 1980. Instead, Reagan came off as warm and confident. At two places in his acceptance speech, he quoted Franklin D. Roosevelt, once by name. Candidates of one party rarely quote a president of the other party in favorable terms as Reagan did.[62] This was clearly an effort to reach out to Democrats.

THE PARTY PLATFORM Delegates to the national party conventions decide on the *platform,* a statement of party perspectives on public policy. Why does anyone care what is in the party platform? Critics have long pointed out that the party platform is binding on no one and is more likely to hurt than to help a candidate by advocating positions unpopular to moderate or Independent voters, whose support the candidate may need to win in the general election. But presidential candidates, as well as delegates, take the platform seriously because it defines the direction a party wants to take. Also, despite the charge that the platform is ignored, most presidents try to implement much of it.[63]

THE VICE PRESIDENTIAL NOMINEE The choice of the vice presidential nominee garners widespread attention. Rarely does a person actually "run" for the vice presidential nomination because only the presidential nominee's vote counts. However, there is a good deal of maneuvering to capture that one vote. Sometimes, the choice of a running mate is made at the convention—not a time conducive to careful and deliberate thought. But usually, it is made before, and the announcement is timed to enhance media coverage and momentum going into the convention. The last time a presidential candidate left the choice of vice president to the delegates was the Democratic convention in 1956.

In 2008 and 2012, Barack Obama selected Delaware Senator Joe Biden to be his running mate. Biden, who himself had twice been a candidate for the presidency including a bid in 2008, was seen as adding extensive foreign policy experience to the ticket. Biden was also expected to assist in winning working class and Catholic support in his native Pennsylvania and other battleground states. John McCain's selection in 2008 of Alaska Governor Sarah Palin surprised many but quickly helped energize the Republican Party base. Later in the campaign, Palin became a liability: her media interviews were seen as showing a lack of knowledge and experience. Exit polls found that 60 percent of voters thought Palin was not qualified to be president, if necessary, compared with 31 percent having that view of Biden.[64] Mitt Romney's selection of Paul Ryan as his running mate in 2012 added youth and energy to the ticket and Ryan, a favorite of conservatives, helped motivate the Republican Party's base to turn out.

THE VALUE OF CONVENTIONS Why do the parties continue to have conventions if the nominee is known in advance and the vice presidential nominee is the choice of one person? What role do conventions play in our system? For the parties, they are a time of "coming together" to endorse a party program and to build unity and enthusiasm for the fall campaign. For candidates, as well as other party leaders, conventions are a chance to capture the national spotlight and further their political ambitions. For nominees, they are an opportunity to define themselves in positive ways. The potential exists to heal wounds festering from the primary campaign and move into the general election united, but it is not always realized. Conventions can be potentially divisive, as the Republicans learned in 1964 when conservative Goldwater delegates loudly booed New York governor Nelson Rockefeller, and as the Democrats learned in 1968 in Chicago when the convention spotlighted divisions within the party over Vietnam, as well as ugly battles between police and protesters near the convention hotels.

NOMINATION BY PETITION There is a way to run for president of the United States that avoids the grueling process of primary elections and conventions—if you are rich enough or well-known enough to use it. Third-party and Independent candidates can qualify for the ballot by meeting each state's ballot access requirements. This takes time, organization, and money. In 2012, the petition process was as simple as submitting the signatures of 1,000 registered voters in Washington State[65] or by paying $500 or securing petition signatures in Colorado or Louisiana,[66] and as difficult as getting the signatures of currently registered voters equal to 2 percent of total votes cast in the last election in North Carolina (69,734 signatures).[67]

In 2012, a new group formed to nominate an independent candidate and place that candidate on the ballot of all states. The group was named "Americans Elect" and was backed by anonymous funders. Enthusiasts of the "Americans Elect" effort saw it as innovative: using technology to supplant the traditional nomination system just as technology has supplanted traditional methods for selling books, music, and prescription drugs. The only problem is that the market for candidates may not be anything like the market for books, music, and drugs. The group promised the "first online convention" but was unable to find a candidate meeting their criteria for nomination.[68]

☐ Stage 3: The General Election

The national party convention adjourns immediately after the presidential and vice presidential candidates deliver their acceptance speeches to the delegates and the national television audience. Traditionally, the weeks between the conventions and Labor Day were a time for resting, for binding up wounds from the fight for the nomination, for gearing up for action, and for planning campaign strategy. In recent elections, however, the candidates have not paused after the convention but launched directly into all-out campaigning. In 2012, especially in battleground states, the two candidates and their allies advertised heavily. Romney also cultivated key constituencies and aggressively pursued fundraising during the period between when he became the presumptive nominee and the convention. Obama, who did not face competition for renomination, also made fund raising a high priority and attempted to define Romney through ads and speeches months before the traditional start of the general campaign.

OF the People Diversity in America

Diversity Among National Party Nomination Convention Delegates

One of the criticisms of the Democratic and Republican Parties in the contentious 1968 election was that the delegates to the national party nominating conventions were not representative of their parties as a whole. A commission was formed in the Democratic Party to reform the process of delegate selection. One result was a rise in the number of states holding presidential primaries rather than caucuses. Another consequence was a much more diverse group of delegates in nominating conventions.

In 1968, delegates were mostly older white males. By 1972, in response to the recommendations of the Democratic Party Reform Commission, the proportion of males had dropped from nearly 90 to 60 percent, the proportion of black delegates tripled, and the proportion of younger delegates rose from 4 to 21 percent. In all cases except young delegates, the 2008 Democratic delegates approximated the composition of the 1972 Democratic delegates.

Republicans have not become as diverse in their delegate composition. In 2008, one-third of GOP delegates were women, compared with 49 percent for Democrats. There were fewer minority and young delegates at the 2008 Republican convention than at the 2008 Democratic convention. Only 2 percent of GOP delegates were black compared with 23 percent for Democrats. Ninety-three percent of Republican delegates were white compared with 65 percent of Democratic delegates. In 2008, only 3 percent of Republican delegates were under 30 years of age compared with 7 percent for Democrats. But both parties are sensitive to the symbolism of diversity and showcase delegates and others who can help the party connect to different demographic groups. Similar information on the 2012 conventions will not be available until 2013, but all indications suggest a continuation of the trend toward more diversity in the Democratic Party, and only slight increases in the Republican Party.

QUESTIONS

1. Why have Republican delegates remained less diverse than Democratic delegates?
2. What kind of changes in a party delegation might you expect as a result of a shift from caucuses to primary elections?
3. Why might the percentage of younger delegates in 2008 have differed from 1972?

PRESIDENTIAL DEBATES Televised presidential debates are a major feature of presidential elections. The Republican contest for the nomination in 2012 had a series of 27 televised debates, which generally lasted two hours each, with opportunities for some candidates to shine and others to stumble.[69] Former House speaker Newt Gingrich benefitted from his debate performances, often using the occasion to attack the elite media and the network hosts. The debates had the added benefit to Gingrich and former Pennsylvania Senator Rick Santorum of providing free visibility to counter in part Mitt Romney's superior fundraising. Presidential debates in the general election have come to be more of a joint appearance with opening and closing statements than a debate in which the candidates interact much with each other.

Since 1988, the nonpartisan Commission on Presidential Debates has sponsored and produced the presidential and vice presidential general election debates. The commission includes representatives from such neutral groups as the League of Women Voters. Before the commission became involved, there was often a protracted discussion about the format, the timing, and even whether to have debates. No detail seemed too small to the candidates' managers—whether the candidates would sit or stand, whether they would be able to ask each other questions, whether they would be allowed to bring notes, and whether a single journalist, a panel of reporters, or a group of citizens would ask the questions. By negotiating in advance many of the contentious details and arranging for debate locations, the commission now facilitates the presidential and vice presidential debates. The format of the 2012 presidential debates had two presidential debates with a standard format and one with a town hall format, and one vice-presidential debate with a standard format.

Minor party candidates often charge that those organizing debates are biased in favor of the two major parties. To be included in presidential debates, such candidates must have an average of 15 percent or higher in the five major polls the commission uses for this purpose.[70] Candidates must also be legally eligible and on the ballot in enough states to be able to win at least 270 electoral votes.[71] In recent elections, no minor party candidate has participated in the debates. Including or excluding minor party candidates remains a contentious issue. Including them takes time away from the major party candidates, especially if two or more minor party candidates are invited. It may also reduce the likelihood of both major parties' candidates' participating. But excluding them raises issues of fairness and free speech.

Although some critics are quick to express their dissatisfaction with presidential candidates for being so concerned with makeup and rehearsed answers, and although the debates have not significantly affected the outcomes of elections, they have provided important opportunities for candidates to distinguish themselves and for the public to weigh their qualifications. Candidates who do well in these debates are at a great advantage. They have to be quick on their feet, seem knowledgeable but not overly rehearsed, and project a positive image. Most presidential candidates are adept at these skills.

TELEVISION AND RADIO ADVERTISING Presidential candidates communicate with voters in a general election and in many primary elections through the media: broadcast television, radio, cable television, and satellite radio. Approximately 630,000 commercials were run across the country during the 2004 presidential election,[72] and in 2008 the number rose to 782,782.[73] Spending on television has risen from $623 million in 2000 to $1.2 billion in 2004 to $1.6 billion in 2008.[74]

As with campaign activity generally, the competitive or battleground states see much more activity—candidate visits and mail or phone calls about the candidates. Candidates and their consultants believe that advertising on television and radio helps motivate people to vote and persuade voters to vote for them—or against their opponent. With the growth in cable television, candidates can target ads to particular audiences—people who watch the Golf Channel or Fox News, for instance. Political party committees and interest groups also run television and radio ads for and against candidates.

THE OUTCOME Though each election is unique, politicians, pollsters, and political scientists have collected enough information to agree broadly on a number of basic factors they believe affect outcomes. The state of the economy probably has the most to do with who wins a presidential election, but as we have noted, most voters vote primarily on the basis of party and candidate appeal.[75] Who wins thus also depends on voter turnout, and here the strength of party organization and allied groups is important. The Democrats' long-standing advantage in the number of people who identify themselves as Democrats has declined in recent years and is mitigated by generally higher voter turnout among Republicans. Republican candidates also usually have better access to money, which means they can run more television ads in more places, more often, and can spend more money on get-out-the-vote efforts.

In the presidential election of 2008, the tables were turned. In 2012, President Obama's reelection campaign again outraised the competition, but money from outside groups let Mitt Romney catch up. Both sides spent about $1 billion on the presidential election. Obama's ability to get funds from donors directly to his campaign allowed him to benefit from the more favorable advertising rates given to candidates, but not party committees or outside groups.

After the votes are cast, they must be counted. And the way they are counted can be critical in close races. This came into sharp focus in 2000 with the count and recount of ballots in Florida and with the outcome of the contest between George Bush and Al Gore ultimately determined by the U.S. Supreme Court. Even before the votes were counted in 2004, 2008, and 2012, both parties had deployed thousands of lawyers to observe the voting and ballot counting and to launch legal challenges if necessary. In 2012, Democrats and allied groups challenged in courts the new voter identification laws in several states, as well as cutbacks on the number of early voting days in some of these same states. Ultimately the votes are counted and we see the peaceful transfer of power from one individual or party to another. This, especially after contested elections, is an important and culminating event in electoral democracy.

This June 24, 2011, image shows a pen pointing to a Romney for President Website advertisement. "Obama Isn't Working" read the mocked-up campaign poster, in tribute to the Conservative Party's devastating "Labour Isn't Working" ad, which helped Margaret Thatcher sweep to power in 1979. The Romney version, apart from a slogan adapted to Obama, features the same picture of a snaking line of workers outside an unemployment office used by the original ad.

Federal Election Commission (FEC)

A commission created by the 1974 amendments to the Federal Election Campaign Act to administer election reform laws. It consists of six commissioners appointed by the president and confirmed by the Senate. Its duties include overseeing disclosure of campaign finance information, public funding of presidential elections, and enforcing contribution limits.

Money in U.S. Elections

8.5 Evaluate the influence of money in American elections and the main approaches to campaign finance reform.

Election campaigns cost money, and the methods of obtaining that money have long been controversial. Campaign money can come from a candidate's own wealth, political parties, supportive individuals, or interest groups. Money is contributed to candidates for a variety of reasons, including ideology, group identification and support, and self-interest. Concern about campaign finance stems from the possibility that candidates or parties, in their pursuit of campaign funds, will decide it is more important to represent the will of their financial contributors rather than that of their own conscience or the voters. The potential corruption resulting from politicians' dependence on interested money concerns many observers of U.S. politics.

Scandals involving the influence of money on policy are not new. In 1925, for example, a cabinet member was convicted of accepting bribes in 1922 for arranging for the lease of federal land in Wyoming and California for private oil developments.[76] Responding to what then became known as the Teapot Dome scandal, Congress passed the Corrupt Practices Act, which required disclosure of campaign funds but was "written in such a way as to exempt virtually all [members of Congress] from its provisions."[77]

Similarly, the 1972 Watergate scandal—in which persons associated with the Nixon campaign broke into the Democratic Party headquarters to steal campaign documents and plant listening devices—led to media scrutiny and congressional investigations which discovered that large amounts of money from corporations and individuals had been deposited into secret bank accounts outside the country for political and campaign purposes. The public outcry from these discoveries prompted Congress to enact the body of reforms that still largely regulate the financing of federal elections.[78]

☐ Efforts at Reform

Reformers have tried three basic strategies to prevent abuse in political contributions: (1) imposing limits on giving, receiving, and spending political money; (2) requiring public disclosure of the sources and uses of political money; and (3) giving governmental subsidies to presidential candidates, campaigns, and parties to reduce their reliance on campaign contributors. By 2012, all three of these strategies had been limited by court and administrative decisions and by changing campaign dynamics. Of the three, disclosure remains the primary strategy still in place.

THE FEDERAL ELECTION CAMPAIGN ACT In 1971, Congress passed the Federal Election Campaign Act (FECA), which limited amounts that candidates for federal office could spend on advertising and required disclosure of the sources of campaign funds and how they are spent. It also required political action committees to register with the government and report all major contributions and expenditures.

In 1974, the Watergate scandal helped push Congress to amend FECA in the most sweeping campaign reform measure in U.S. history. These amendments established more realistic limits on contributions and spending by candidates and party committees, strengthened disclosure laws, created the **Federal Election Commission (FEC)** to administer the new laws, and provided for partial public funding for presidential primaries and a grant to major party presidential general election candidates. The money to fund the presidential candidates comes from taxpayers who choose to allocate $3 of their income taxes by checking a box on their tax returns.

The 1974 law was extensively amended after the Supreme Court's 1976 *Buckley v. Valeo* decision, which overturned several of its provisions on grounds that they violated the First Amendment free speech protection.[79] The *Buckley* decision still allowed limitations on contributions and full and open disclosure of fundraising and campaign spending by candidates for federal office, as well as the system of public financing for presidential elections.[80] The FEC, which has six commissioners, three from each party, is often deadlocked along partisan lines.

However, the Supreme Court made a distinction between campaign spending and campaign contributions, holding that the First Amendment protects spending; therefore, although Congress may limit how much people contribute to somebody else's campaign, legislatures may not limit how much of their own money people spend on their own campaigns or that they spend independent of a candidate or political party.

Bipartisan Campaign Reform Act (BCRA)
Largely banned party soft money, restored a long-standing prohibition on corporations and labor unions for using general treasury funds for electoral purposes, and narrowed the definition of issue advocacy.

One of the success stories of FECA was that for 20 years presidential candidates of both parties chose to accept the limitations on fundraising and campaign spending that were part of the public financing provisions. During the nomination phase, candidates receive federal matching funds for campaign contributions up to $250. Accepting the federal matching funds means candidates accept state-by-state spending limits for the caucuses and the primaries. Until 2000, presidential candidates (except a few wealthy, self-financed candidates) accepted the voluntary limitations that come with partial public financing of presidential nomination campaigns. In 2012, the number of candidates in both parties who turned down the matching funds in the primaries increased and included Obama, Romney, Santorum, Paul, Gingrich, Pawlenty, Bachmann, Perry, and Cain. Why the change between 1996 and 2012? Starting with George W. Bush in 2000 and expanding to more and more candidates subsequently, there is a view that the spending limits associated with matching funds are too limiting. Rather than focusing on the small (under $250) matchable contribution, candidates should focus on the max-out donors who gave four times that amount in 2000 and eight or more times that amount since.

Public funding in the presidential general election is a grant that, if accepted, requires candidates to end fundraising for their own campaign. However, if candidates accept public funding, they can continue to raise money for the national party. In 2008, Obama was the first major party candidate since the system was created to reject taxpayers' money for the general election; he ultimately had access to much greater funds than did his opponent, John McCain. In 2012, both Obama and Romney turned down the public grant and both led the pack in money raised in the early stages of the 2012 campaign (see Figure 8.4).

THE BIPARTISAN CAMPAIGN REFORM ACT (BCRA) After years of legislative debate, Senate filibusters, and even a presidential veto, Congress passed and President Bush signed into law the **Bipartisan Campaign Reform Act (BCRA)** in 2002.

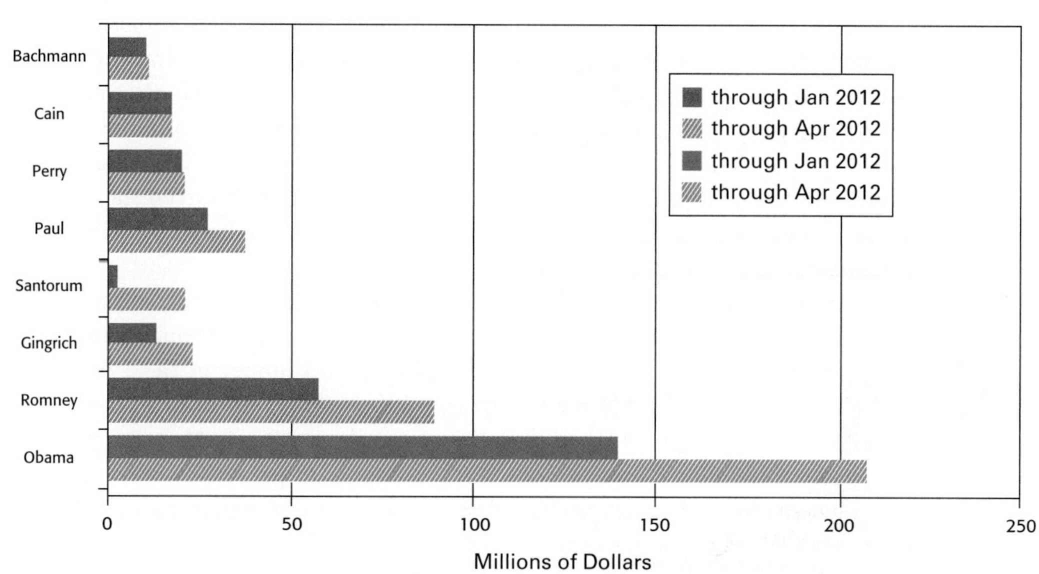

FIGURE 8.4 PRESIDENTIAL PRIMARY CUMULATIVE RECEIPTS, 2011–2012 (MILLIONS OF DOLLARS)

What are some of the benefits for a candidate of raising more money than a competitor?

SOURCE: FEC reports from each campaign at www.fec.gov,http://fec.gov/finance/disclosure/efile_search.shtml.

8.1

8.2

8.3

8.4

8.5

8.6

soft money
Money raised in unlimited amounts by political parties for party-building purposes. Now largely illegal except for limited contributions to state or local parties for voter registration and get-out-the-vote efforts.

hard money
Political contributions given to a party, candidate, or interest group that are limited in amount and fully disclosed. Raising such limited funds is harder than raising unlimited funds, hence the term "hard money."

This legislation, often known as the McCain–Feingold bill after its two chief sponsors in the Senate, was written with the understanding that it would immediately be challenged in court—and it was. The Supreme Court upheld most of the provisions of BCRA in *McConnell* v. *FEC*.[81]

BCRA is best understood as incremental change. It continued the public financing of presidential campaigns with funds from the income tax check off. It left unchanged the limits on spending by candidates for presidential nominations (on a state-by-state basis and in total) and in the presidential general elections for those candidates who accept public funding. Although recognizing that individuals are free to spend unlimited amounts on their own campaigns, BCRA provided increased contribution limits for candidates running against an opponent who was spending substantial amounts of his or her own money, a provision later declared unconstitutional by the Supreme Court.[82] Finally, it left unchanged the limits on the amounts the national parties can spend on presidential campaigns and on individual congressional and senatorial campaigns.

The limits under BCRA for 2011–2012 for individuals giving to candidates were $2,500 for each primary, general, or runoff election. Runoffs are rare in the United States, so for most individuals the total contribution limit to a candidate in 2011–2012 was $5,000. Individuals also have an aggregate two-year election cycle limit of $117,000. In 2011–2012, they could give up to $46,200 to federal candidates, up to $70,800 total to national party committees, federal PACs, and state party federal accounts, and up to $30,800 to a single party committee. Within this aggregate limit, individuals can give up to $10,000 per cycle to any single political action committee (PAC) or federal or state party committee. Individuals who want to give the maximum total of $117,000 in the 2011–2012 election cycle must thus allocate money to candidates, party committees, and PACs under the constraints noted.[83] BCRA gave party committees an opportunity to appeal to "max out" donors, something both parties pursued. Individuals could also contribute unlimited amounts to independent expenditure-only PACs (Super PACs) and some gave several million dollars, calling into question the contribution limits to candidates, party committees, and conventional PACs.

SOFT MONEY BCRA also has a major impact on stopping novel ways to evade the campaign finance laws. One particularly effective tool involved party efforts to register voters and run generic party ads, for what were called "party building purposes."[84] This money came to be defined as **soft money**,[85] in contrast to the limited and more-difficult-to-raise **hard money** contributions to candidates and party committees that are committed to candidate-specific electoral activity. Over time, soft money became more important. The 1996 election saw aggressive soft money fundraising by the Clinton–Gore campaign, including opportunities for donors to have meetings with the president, to fly with him on Air Force One, and to spend the night in the Lincoln Bedroom at the White House. A congressional investigation into these and related concerns about campaign finance in the 1996 election cycle reinforced the case for reform.[86] From the perspective of the voter, the advertising purchased by soft money was indistinguishable from other campaign expenditures.[87]

After 1996, both parties continued to make raising and spending soft money a major priority, and soft money spending rose dramatically. All national party committees combined raised more than $509 million of soft money in the 1999–2000 election cycle, and nearly that much again in 2001–2002,[88] up from $110 million adjusted for inflation in 1991–1992.[89] Banning soft money became the primary objective of reformers and was one of the more important provisions in the BCRA. Soft money enabled large donors to be major players in campaign finance. It also strengthened the power of the national party committees, which allocated the money to state parties and indirectly to candidates. To the Supreme Court, which upheld the BCRA soft money ban, one of the major problems with soft money was that it purchased access to elected officials, and with that access can come influence and the possibility or appearance of corruption.[90]

☐ Resisting Reform

Despite the Supreme Court's decisions to uphold much of FECA and BCRA, the fight to reverse campaign finance reform has continued for almost three decades. Opponents have fought the limits in the courts, Congress, and the Federal Election Commission, hoping to weaken the rules.

ISSUE ADVOCACY Much of the fight against campaign finance reform has tried to exploit the Supreme Court's 1976 ruling in *Buckley* v. *Valeo*, which challenged restrictions on campaign advertisements that were about issues and not candidate campaigns. The Supreme Court agreed with this challenge and decided that groups were free to run advertisements during the campaign season as long as the ads did not use such words as "vote for" or "vote against" a specific candidate. The Supreme Court's 1976 *Buckley* v. *Valeo* decision defined election communication as "communications containing express words of advocacy of election or defeat, such as 'vote for,' 'elect,' 'support,' 'cast your ballot for,' 'Smith for Congress,' 'vote against,' 'defeat,' and 'reject.'"[91] Communications that did not use these "magic words" were defined as issue ads, presumably because they deal with issues not candidates, and thus are not subject to disclosure required by FECA restrictions. Not surprisingly, interest groups and media consultants found a way to form groups that avoid disclosure or to communicate an electioneering message without using the magic words.

The 1996 election saw a surge in candidate-specific **issue advocacy**. Issue ad spending in some U.S. House races exceeded $1 million. A prominent example of issue advocacy against a candidate was the ad campaign by Republicans for Clean Air, formed by two Texans attacking John McCain in some 2000 presidential primaries.[92] Legislation to limit groups doing electioneering through the guise of issue ads was struck down by the courts so that today we again have groups able to spend money against or for a candidate masking their identity behind some obscure name like Citizens for Freedom.

Like soft money ads, issue advertisements sponsored by interest groups are largely indistinguishable from candidate-run advertisements.[93] In some competitive contests, interest groups and parties spent more money than the candidates themselves. Typically, these party and group ads are even more negative than the ads run by candidates. Many candidates disavowed ads intended to help them and hurt their opponent, but one of the problems with non-candidate ads in an election context is determining who is accountable for the content of the ads. In 2012, businesses, labor unions, health care organizations, environmental groups, energy groups, pro- and antigun groups, pro- and antiabortion groups, and the pharmaceutical industry all ran issue ads.

INDEPENDENT EXPENDITURES The Supreme Court made clear in its ruling on FECA in 1976 that individuals and groups have the right to spend as much money as they wish for or against candidates as long as they are truly independent of the candidate and the money is not corporate or union treasury money. BCRA does not constrain **independent expenditures** by groups, political parties, or individuals, as long as the expenditures by those individuals, parties, or groups are independent of the candidate and fully disclosed to the FEC. Some groups such as the American Medical Association, the National Education Association, and the National Rifle Association have long tried to influence elections independently rather than through a party committee or a candidate's campaign. The Supreme Court, in 1996, extended to political parties the same rights to make independent expenditures afforded to groups and individuals.[94]

In recent election cycles, independent expenditures by the party committee were important in several competitive contests. For example, in the 2008 North Carolina U.S. Senate race, Democratic challenger Kay Hagan received $8.1 million from the Democratic Senatorial Campaign Committee, which helped her defeat Republican incumbent Elizabeth Dole, who only received $3.5 million from the National Republican Senatorial Committee.[95] In 2010, Republicans and Democrats received roughly equal amounts of independent expenditures in U.S. House races, while the Democrats received

issue advocacy
Promoting a particular position or an issue paid for by interest groups or individuals but not candidates. Much issue advocacy is often electioneering for or against a candidate, avoiding words like "vote for," and until 2004 had not been subject to any regulation.

independent expenditures
Money spent by individuals or groups not associated with candidates to elect or defeat candidates for office.

8.1

8.2

8.3

8.4

8.5

8.6

Super PACs
An independent expenditure only committee first allowed in 2010 after court decisions allowing unlimited contributions to such PACs. Super PACs were important in the 2010 and 2012 elections.

substantially more in U.S. Senate races than did the Republicans.[96] In 2012, both parties benefitted from similar amounts of outside spending.

Individuals have also made large independent expenditures. Michael Goland, a California entrepreneur, spent $1.1 million against Senator Charles Percy (R-Ill.) in the 1984 election because he considered Percy unfriendly to Israel. In the 2000 presidential election, Stephen Adams, owner of an outdoor advertising firm, spent $2 million to support George W. Bush.[97] In 2004, billionaire George Soros, who gave millions to organizations opposing the reelection of Bush, also spent $2.3 million in independent expenditures against the president. As discussed at the beginning of the chapter, in 2012 individuals wanting to invest large amounts through independent expenditures did so through Super PACs, the "independent expenditure only" committee that became possible because of the court rulings in 2010.

SUPER PACS The biggest victory against campaign finance reform came when the electioneering of one group, Citizens United, led to a major legal shift in campaign finance. In 2010, the Supreme Court, in a 5-to-4 decision in *Citizens United* v. *FEC,* rejected the longstanding ban on unions and corporations using their general funds on ads about the election or defeat of a candidate.[98] The application of this decision and a subsequent decision in *SpeechNow, Inc.* v. *FEC* opened the door to **Super PACs**, a type of organization that can receive unlimited money from individuals, unions, and even corporations. These Super PACs proved instrumental in 2012 (see Figure 8.5).

Unlike 2004 and 2006, when Democratic groups were more visible and spent more money, Republican groups played an important role in making more contests competitive in both 2010 and 2012 and in helping elect Republicans. Former Bush political strategist Karl Rove and others organized American Crossroads and Crossroads Grassroots Policy Strategies, while other prominent Republicans organized American Action Network and other groups. Moreover, these groups coordinated their spending with other GOP allied groups like the Chamber of Commerce, Club for Growth and the National Rifle Association. Some groups organized under sections of the law that allowed them to avoid disclosing their donors, and all groups tapped corporation and union general treasury funds for the first time in decades. The threat of secret outside money was frequently cited by President Obama in his 2010 and 2012 campaign appearances as "a threat to our democracy."[99]

☐ Continuing Problems with Campaign Finance

The continuing problems with federal election fundraising are easy to identify: dramatically escalating costs, dependence on PAC money for congressional candidates, decreasing visibility and competitiveness of challengers (especially for the House), and the advantage wealthy individuals have in funding their own campaigns. BCRA reduced the danger of large contributions influencing lawmakers directly or indirectly through

Name of SuperPAC and Candidate Supported	Total Funds (Millions)	Number of Million Dollar Donors	Percent of Million Dollar Donors
Priorities USA (Obama)	$ 6.5	3	62%
Restore Our Future (Romney)	$ 43.2	10	31%
Red White and Blue Fund (Santorum)	$ 5.8	3	71%
Winning Our Future (Gingrich)	$ 18.9	3	85%
Endorse Liberty (Paul)	$ 3.7	1	71%

FIGURE 8.5 SUPER PACs AND MILLION DOLLAR DONORS IN 2012 PRESIDENTIAL ELECTION CAMPAIGN

political parties. But large contributions can still influence the outcome of elections, as Super PACs have demonstrated. Supreme Court decisions have made campaign finance an increasingly deregulated activity. Interest groups like corporations and unions have been given much greater latitude to attempt to influence the outcome of elections.

RISING COSTS OF CAMPAIGNS The U.S. ideal that anyone—even a person of modest or little wealth—can run for public office and hope to win has become more of a myth than a reality.[100] Serious candidates in the future are likely to bypass public funding and instead try to replicate the kind of fundraising success Barack Obama had in 2007–2008. Rising costs also mean that incumbents spend more time raising funds and therefore less time legislating and representing their districts. Since FECA became law in 1972, total expenditures by candidates for the House of Representatives have more than doubled after controlling for inflation, and they have risen even more in Senate elections (see Table 8.2). A major reason for escalating costs is television advertising. Organizing and running a campaign is expensive

TABLE 8.2 AVERAGE CAMPAIGN EXPENDITURES OF CANDIDATES FOR THE HOUSE OF REPRESENTATIVES, 1988–2010 GENERAL ELECTION (IN THOUSANDS OF DOLLARS)

	Incumbents	Challengers	Open Seats
Democrats			
2010	$1,734,398	$322,950	$986,757
2008	$1,252,446	$612,883	$1,637,500
2006	$971,735	$549,227	$1,387,429
2004	$926,321	$287,966	$955,455
2002	$812,176	$323,975	$1,038,043
2000	$735,631	$358,483	$1,048,438
1998	$562,268	$243,519	$748,235
1996	$571,520	$296,351	$628,113
1994	$606,106	$161,923	$581,702
1992	$604,789	$160,786	$482,162
1990	$401,928	$110,458	$535,484
1988	$358,266	$143,766	$447,037
Republicans			
2010	$1,316,474	$783,900	$1,364,595
2008	$1,456,176	$375,779	$1,380,571
2006	$1,518,436	$245,817	$1,355,588
2004	$1,086,143	$249,325	$1,260,833
2002	[illegible]	$193,333	$1,187,391
2000	$876,396	$251,600	$1,240,313
1998	$697,488	$260,336	$810,938
1996	$738,169	$211,379	$629,020
1994	$460,382	$243,134	$641,277
1992	$549,130	$188,796	$364,429
1990	$398,113	$110,780	$453,448
1988	$409,207	$100,412	$484,615

SOURCE: Federal Election Commission, "FEC Reports on Congressional Financial Activity for 2000," press release, May 15, 2001; Federal Election Commission, "Financial Activity of General Election Congressional Candidates—1992–2010," includes activity through 12/31/10, www.fec.gov/press/2010_Full_summary_Data.shtml.

NOTE: *General election candidates only.*

■ *What are the patterns of spending for incumbents, challengers, and open seat candidate, across both parties?*

and effectively limits the field of challengers to those who have their own resources or are willing to spend more than a year raising money from interest groups and individuals.

DECLINING COMPETITION Unless something is done to help finance challengers, incumbents will continue to have the advantage in seeking reelection. Nothing in BCRA addressed this problem. Challengers in both parties are typically underfunded. House Republican challengers averaged just under $250,000 in spending in 2004 and House Democratic challengers $288,000,[101] whereas incumbents in both parties spent an average of about $1 million each in 2004.[102] In today's expensive campaigns, candidates are generally invisible if they have less than $400,000 to spend.

The high cost of campaigns dampens competition by discouraging individuals from running for office. Potential challengers look at the fundraising advantages incumbents enjoy—at incumbents' campaign war chests carried over from previous campaigns that can reach $1 million or more and at the time it will take them to raise enough money to launch a minimal campaign—and they decide not to run. Moreover, unlike incumbents, whose salaries are being paid while they are campaigning and raising money, most challengers have to support themselves and their families throughout the campaign, which for a seat in Congress often lasts more than one year.

DEPENDENCE ON PACs FOR CONGRESSIONAL INCUMBENTS For most House incumbents, much of their campaign money comes from political action committees (PACs). In recent years, nearly two out of five incumbents seeking reelection raised more money from PACs than from individuals (see Figure 8.6).[103] Senators get a smaller percentage of their campaign funds from PACs, but because they spend so much more, they need to raise even more money from PACs than House incumbents do. PACs are pragmatic, giving largely to incumbents. Challengers receive little because PACs do not want to offend politicians in power. BCRA left intact the cap for PAC contributions at $10,000 for the primary and general election combined. Incumbents will continue to rely on PACs because relatively few individuals have the means to give $5,000 to a campaign, as they could have in 2011–2012. It also often takes less time to raise money from PACs than from individuals.

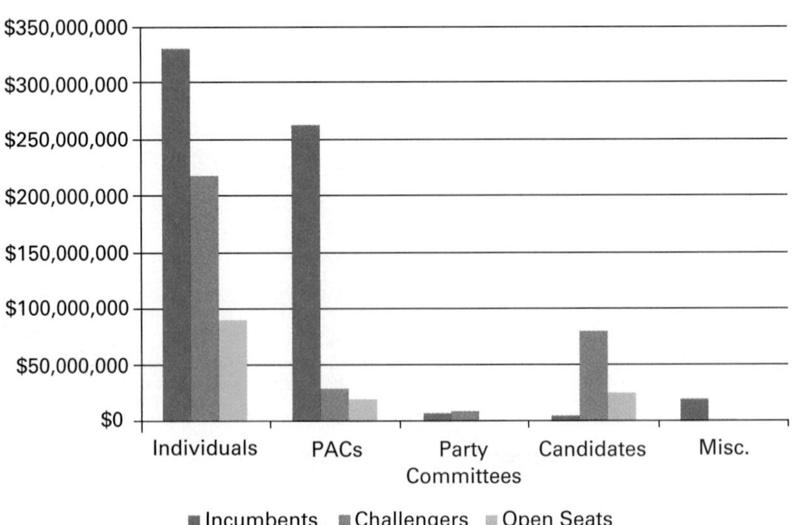

FIGURE 8.6 HOW PACs AND OTHERS ALLOCATED CAMPAIGN CONTRIBUTIONS TO HOUSE CANDIDATES, 2009–2010

Why might PACs be more apt than individuals or party committees to skew their funding so heavily to incumbents?

SOURCE: Federal Election Commission, "2009–2010 Financial Activity of All Senate and House Campaigns," includes activity through 12/31/10, www.fec.gov/press/2010_Full_summary_Data.shtml.

To be sure, PACs and individuals spend money on campaigns for many reasons. Most of them want certain laws to be passed or repealed, certain funds to be appropriated, or certain administrative decisions to be rendered. At a minimum, they want access to officeholders and a chance to talk with members before key votes.

Defenders of PACs point out that there is no demonstrable relationship between contributions and legislators' votes. But influence in the legislative process depends on access to staff and members of Congress, and most analysts agree that campaign contributions give donors extraordinary access. PACs influence the legislative process in other ways as well. Their access helps them structure the legislative agenda with friendly legislators and influence the drafting of legislation or amendments to existing bills.

CANDIDATES' PERSONAL WEALTH Campaign finance legislation cannot constitutionally restrict rich candidates—the Rockefellers, the Kennedys, the Perots, the Clintons, the Romneys—from spending heavily on their own campaigns. Big money can make a big difference, and wealthy candidates can afford to spend big money. In presidential politics, this advantage can be most meaningful before the primaries begin. The personal wealth advantage also applies to congressional and gubernatorial races. Investment banker Jon Corzine spent $133.5 million in one decade on his own gubernatorial and U.S. Senate campaigns, winning two of the three races.[104] Meg Whitman, the unsuccessful Republican candidate for governor of California in 2010, spent over $140 million of her own money on her campaign, breaking the previous record held by New York Mayor Michael Bloomberg ($109 million).

GROWTH IN INDIVIDUAL CONTRIBUTIONS AND USE OF THE INTERNET TO FUND CAMPAIGNS BCRA made individuals more important as sources of money to candidates because it increased the amount they could give and indexed those limits to inflation. In the election cycles since BCRA took effect, there has been substantial growth in individual contributions, especially to the Democrats, who once were more reliant on soft money.

Another development that has made individual donors more important is the Internet. Starting in 2000 with the McCain presidential campaign and then expanding with Howard Dean's campaign for president in 2004, individuals started giving to candidates via the Internet. But it was the Obama campaign in 2008 that demonstrated the extraordinary power of the Internet as a means to reach donors and a way for people to contribute to a candidate.[105] As former senator Tom Daschle said, the Internet "is an evolution away from Washington's control, away from the power that big money and big donors used to have a monopoly on."[106] It is clear that the Internet has the potential to change the way campaigns are funded.

Improving Elections

8.6 Assess concerns regarding presidential elections and reforms that have been proposed.

A combination of party rules and state laws determines how we choose nominees for president. Reformers agree that the current process is flawed but disagree about which aspects should be changed. Concern over how we choose presidents now centers on three issues: how we fund presidential elections; the number, timing, and representativeness of presidential primaries and caucuses; and the role of the Electoral College, including the possibility that a presidential election may be thrown into the House of Representatives.

8.1

8.2

8.3

8.4

8.5

8.6

☐ Reforming Campaign Finance

The incremental reforms of BCRA and the subsequent Supreme Court decisions have not resolved the issues of campaign finance. Among the unresolved issues are how presidential campaigns will be financed, the role of Super PACs, the adequacy of disclosure, and the long-term strength and viability of the political parties. More broadly, the FEC's inability to reach decisions because of its partisan deadlock, as demonstrated by its inaction on Super PACs, has generated growing pressure to reform the agency.

The 2004 election cycle, with its substantial interest group activity, was seen by those who favor deregulation of campaign finance as another example of the impossibility of limiting money in elections. The surge in individual donors in 2008 is used by some as further evidence that public financing is unnecessary. This school of thought will continue to push for disclosure as the sole regulatory aim of government in this area.

Another group of reformers presses for more aggressive reforms than those found in BCRA. Included in this agenda will be reining in the Super PACs, restructuring the public financing of presidential elections, providing incentives for individuals to contribute to candidates and parties, and denying foreign corporations and those doing business with the government the ability to spend money on federal elections. While there is near consensus on the importance of disclosure of donors and the timing and amounts of contributions, there remain ways for individuals and groups to avoid disclosure. Enhanced disclosure, including electronic filings of campaign contributions by campaigns on a more frequent basis, is a first step for reformers. Both sides are likely to agree that the FEC needs to be changed, but will not agree on how to change it.

BY the People Making a Difference

Volunteering for a Campaign

You can make a difference in your community, state, or country by volunteering for a campaign. Campaigns are dependent on individuals like you to help make democracy happen. It is also a great way to learn about public opinion, representation, and the political process. If you decide to get involved, you may participate in a wide range of activities, including contacting voters in person, on the telephone, or through the Internet; helping with fundraising; or assisting in organizing events. Be sure to let the campaign know in what areas you have experience or expertise, such as database management or graphic design.

To have a good experience, it is important to understand that campaigns are hectic and intense. The election day cannot be postponed, and winning is the objective. But there is also an excitement and energy to campaigns that you will not forget. Because of the number and frequency of elections in the United States, there is likely a candidate or ballot measure campaign of some sort happening in your area that would welcome your assistance. Call, e-mail, or drop by the campaign office and inform the campaign manager of the kinds of things you would like to do and how you can assist.

You might also check on your campus to see if there is a possibility to do an internship with a campaign or if there is a clearing house for such opportunities. Occidental College, for example, had an internship program, "Campaign Semester," in which a student could get a full semester's worth of college credit (16 credits) for volunteering full time with a presidential or U.S. Senate campaign.

QUESTIONS

1. **Why do many political leaders get their start in government or politics by volunteering in a campaign?**
2. **What aspect of campaigns most interests you?**
3. **If we judge a potential leader by the quality of his or her campaign, what are the markers of a good campaign?**

*Peter Dreier and Caroline Heldman, "Campaign Semester Fall 2008," http://departments.oxy.edu/politics/campaignsemester.htm (accessed May 3, 2010).

☐ Reforming the Nominating Process

In 2008 and 2012, the importance of voters in early primary or caucus states such as Iowa and New Hampshire again generated controversy, as these early states are not broadly representative of the country or of their respective parties. Voters in primaries and caucuses also tend to be more ideological than voters generally, a further bias in the current nominating process. The 2008 contest pushed to the forefront controversy over whether the Democrats' proportionality rule made it more difficult to have a winner emerge from the process, and the adoption by the GOP of similar rules in many states for 2012 also had the effect of prolonging their party's battle for the nomination. Between 2008 and 2012, Republican parties in many states changed their delegate selection rules from winner-take-all to proportionality allocation. A few states, like Florida, Arizona, Delaware, and Utah, retained their winner-take-all rules in the 2012 GOP contest. Finally, the role of superdelegates in determining the 2008 Democratic nominee raised concerns about their role compared to delegates selected through a democratic process.

What would the critics substitute for state presidential primaries (see Figure 8.7)? Some argue in favor of a *national presidential primary* that would take the form of a single nationwide election, probably held in May or September, or separate state primaries held in all the states on the same day.[107] Supporters contend that a one-shot national presidential primary (though a runoff might be necessary) would be simple, direct, and representative. It would cut down the wear-and-tear on candidates and the media coverage would attract a large turnout. Opponents argue that such a reform would worsen the present system by enhancing the role of showmanship and gamesmanship and hurting the chances of candidates who lack strong financial backing due to its enormous expense.

A more modest proposal is to hold *regional primaries,* possibly at two- or three-week intervals across the country. Regional primaries might bring more coherence to the process and encourage more emphasis on issues of regional concern. But such

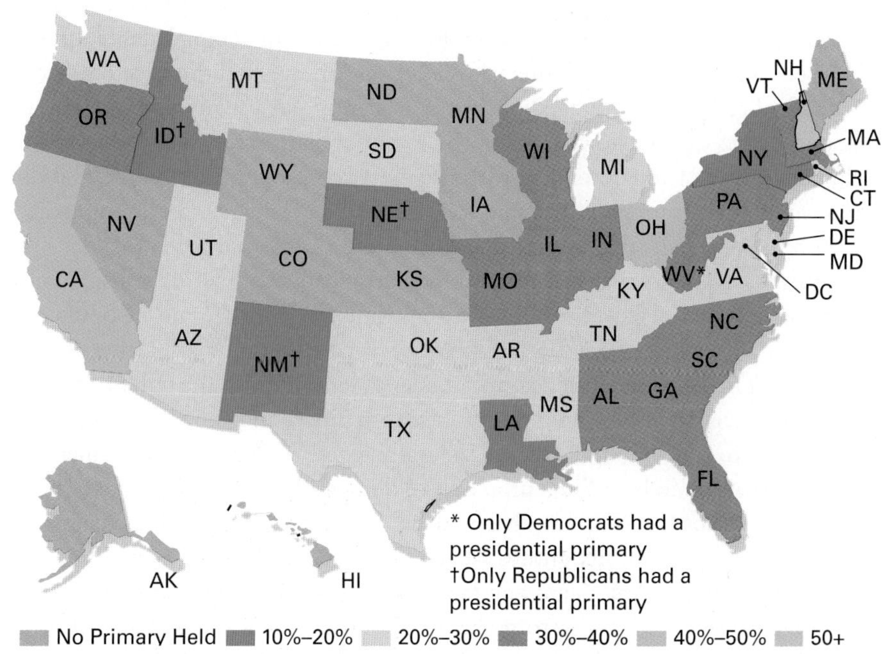

FIGURE 8.7 VOTER TURNOUT IN THE 2008 PRESIDENTIAL PRIMARIES

■ *What aspect of the presidential nomination process likely influenced the high voter turnout in New Hampshire compared to Delaware—a state of similar size and political leaning? What can help explain the higher turnout in California and Ohio?*

SOURCE: Michael McDonald, "2008 Presidential Primary Turnout Rates," United States Election Project at George Mason University, elections.gmu.edu/Voter_Turnout_2008_ primaries.htm.

8.1

8.2

8.3

8.4

8.5

8.6

primaries would retain most of the disadvantages of the present system—especially the emphasis on money and media. Clearly, they would give an advantage to candidates from whatever region held the first primary, encouraging regional candidates and increasing polarization among sections of the country.

A different proposal is to drastically reduce the number of presidential primaries and make more use of the caucus system. The turnout of voters in Democratic caucuses in 2008 shows that participation can be high, although that was not the case in the Republican caucuses in 2012,[108] and the time participants spent discussing candidates and issues shows that such participation can be thoughtful and informed. However, 2008 was unusual in its highly competitive prolonged competition. If more states adopted caucuses, their turnout would not likely be as high as in 2008 because they would lack the media and candidate attention that came that year. In caucus states, candidates are more dependent on convincing political activists, who will show up for a political meeting. By relying on party meetings to select delegates, the caucus system would also, some say, enhance the role of the party.[109]

Given the problems with the current nomination process, why has it not been reformed? Part of the answer is strong resistance from the states that benefit from the current system. In our federal system, imposing a national or regional primary means those states would lose power.

Does the present nominating process help or hurt candidates and parties? News coverage of candidates in nomination contests allows voters to evaluate the candidates' political qualities and their abilities to organize campaigns; communicate through the media; stand up under pressure; avoid making mistakes (or recover when mistakes are made); adjust their appeals to shifting events and to different regions of the country; control and utilize their staffs; and be decisive, articulate, resilient, humorous, informed, and ultimately successful in winning votes. In short, supporters of the current system claim that primaries test candidates on the very qualities they must exhibit in the presidency.[110]

☐ Reforming the Electoral College

The Florida recount after the 2000 election, and the fact that the winner of the popular vote did not become president, renewed a national debate on the Electoral College. The most frequently proposed reform is *direct popular election* of the president. Presidents would be elected directly by the voters, just as governors are, and the Electoral College and individual electors would be abolished. Such proposals usually provide that, if no candidate receives at least 40 percent of the total popular vote, a *runoff election* would be held between the two contenders with the most votes. Supporters argue that direct election would give every voter the same weight in the presidential balloting in accordance with the one-person, one-vote doctrine.

Opponents contend that the plan would further undermine federalism, encourage unrestrained majority rule, political extremism, and hurt the most populous and competitive states, which would lose some of their present influence. Others fear that the plan would make presidential campaigns more remote from the voters; candidates might stress television and give up their forays into diners and shopping centers.[111]

From time to time, Congress considers proposals for a constitutional amendment to elect presidents directly.[112] Such proposals seldom get far, however, because of strong opposition from those who believe they may be disadvantaged by such a change, especially small states and minority groups whose role is enlarged by the Electoral College. Groups such as African Americans and farmers, for example, fear they might lose their swing vote power—their ability to make a difference in key states that may tip the Electoral College balance.

Another alternative to the Electoral College is sometimes called the National Bonus Plan. This plan would add another 102 Electoral College members to the current 538. These 102 members would be awarded on a winner-take-all basis to the candidate with the most votes, so long as that candidate received more than 40 percent of the popular vote. This system would avoid elections being thrown into the House of

Explore on MyPoliSciLab

Is the Electoral College Democratic?

In 2000, George W. Bush won the presidency despite the fact that over 500,000 more Americans voted for Al Gore. The result set off a renewed debate about the Electoral College's role in presidential elections. In the Electoral College, each state is assigned a number of "electors" equal to the total number of U.S. Senators and U.S. Representatives in the state. In all but two states, the winner of the state's popular vote takes all of the electoral votes. The candidate with a majority (270) of *electoral votes* becomes president. In 2000, the presidential election came down to the state of Florida which Bush won by 537 popular votes.

The Electoral College Across the United States in 2000

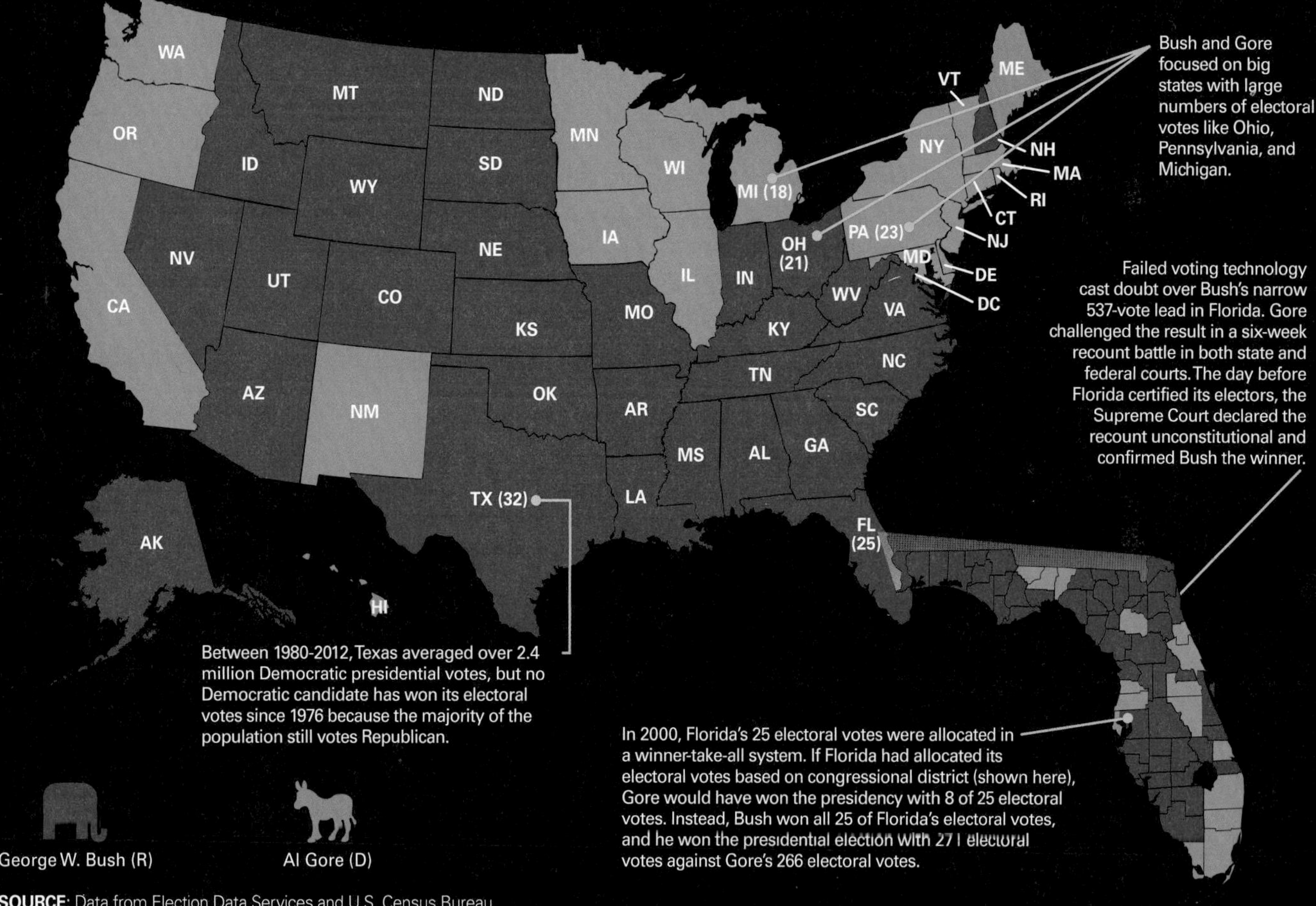

SOURCE: Data from Election Data Services and U.S. Census Bureau.

Investigate Further

Concept What is the difference between the popular vote and the Electoral College vote? The popular vote winner is the candidate who got the most votes, either as a plurality or a majority. The Electoral College determines the winner on the basis of who wins enough states to amass a majority of electors (270). The Electoral College is thus a form of indirect democracy.

Connection How do electoral votes lead to controversy? Using the Electoral College in winner-take-all elections makes candidates focus on competitive states, especially populous ones. Winner-take-all allocations can also result in millions of individual votes having no direct impact on the election outcome. People who vote for candidates who do not win their state do not have their choice represented in the Electoral College.

Cause How might the Electoral College be more democratic? The winner-take-all way electoral votes are allocated does not provide for representation of those who did not get the most votes in nearly all states. If more states were to allocate electoral votes on the basis of who wins each congressional district in the state, political minorities would have a greater impact on the presidential race. In states like Florida, where hundreds of thousands of voters get no chance to contribute to their candidate's potential success, district voting would allow them some influence on the election.

8.1

8.2

8.3

8.4

8.5

8.6

Representatives and would help ensure that the candidate who won the popular vote became president. The most serious liabilities of the plan are that it is complicated and that it requires a runoff election if there is no winner.

Finally, two states, Maine and Nebraska, have already adopted a district system in which the candidate who carries each congressional district gets that electoral vote and the candidate who carries the state gets the state's two additional electoral votes. This quasi-proportional representation system has the advantage of not shutting out a candidate who is strong in some areas of a state and not others, but otherwise it does not address the larger concerns with the Electoral College.

The failure of attempts to change the system points to an important conclusion about procedural reform: U.S. voters normally do not focus on procedures. Even after the intense controversy on the outcome of the 2000 election, including the role of the Electoral College, reform was not seriously considered.

□ The Importance of Elections

We have seen that elections matter in a constitutional democracy. They determine who holds office and what policies the government adopts. Elections are complex, and the rules of the game affect how it is played. Our winner-take-all system is an example of a rule that has influenced the nature of our party system, the strategy of candidates, and the stability of our institutions. Over time, the rules of the electoral game have been changed. Today, party nominees are largely selected by voters in primaries, whereas early in our nation's history, candidates were selected by party caucuses. Over time, our system has expanded the role of citizens and voters, as illustrated by the predominance of primaries.

Central to the functioning of a constitutional democracy, like that in the United States, is a system of fair elections that is well administered, so the outcome has legitimacy. Voter trust and confidence in elections centers on the kinds of issues we have examined in this chapter. Over time, we have learned ways to make elections better, including the secret ballot, the disclosure and limitation of campaign contributions, and the expansion of the role of citizens through primaries. As important as these structural and institutional changes are, without the participation of people in politics, the system will not function well.

Individual citizens can make a difference in elections in many ways. They do this through voting, being active in selecting candidates, working for political parties, making financial contributions, and organizing groups around common interests. Because candidates, parties, and groups need money and volunteers to operate, donating money and time are also important ways in which people invest in elections. People also influence the votes of friends and neighbors, as voters are more likely to respond positively to a personal request to vote for a candidate or ballot proposition than they are to requests from other sources. New technologies like mobile payment apps on smartphones could change the way people participating in helping fund elections. It is also likely that in the future people will be able to vote via the Internet, another change that could alter the way individuals make a difference.

Review the Chapter

 **Listen** to **Chapter 8** on **MyPoliSciLab**

Elections: The Rules of the Game

8.1 Assess the implications of election rules in the United States, p. 243.

The U.S. electoral system is based on winner-take-all rules, typically with single-member districts. These rules encourage a moderate, two-party system. Fixed and staggered terms of office add predictability to our electoral system. Although term limits have been popular with the public, Congress has not introduced any term limits to its members.

The Electoral College is the means by which presidents are elected. To win a state's electoral votes, a candidate must have a plurality of votes in that state. Except in two states, the winner takes all. Thus, candidates cannot afford to lose the popular vote in the most populous states. The Electoral College also gives disproportionate power to the largest states, especially if they are competitive. It has the potential to defeat the national popular vote winner.

Counting Votes

8.2 Identify problems associated with administering elections and evaluate proposed solutions to those problems, p. 247.

Ballot-counting irregularities, equipment shortages and problems, and voter registration challenges have been problems in recent elections. Standardizing election administration; replacing old voting machines with computers, the Internet, and vote-by-mail elections; and reforming registration procedures are all potential solutions to election problems.

Running for Congress

8.3 Explain how congressional elections work and why they are generally not competitive, p. 249.

Candidates for Congress must raise money, develop a personal organization, and increase visibility in order to be nominated for the election. Incumbents have significant advantages over their challengers, with House incumbents having stronger advantages than their Senate counterparts, whose challengers often have strong name recognition and more easily raise money. The cost of elections and incumbency advantages make congressional elections widely noncompetitive.

Running for President

8.4 Describe the stages in U.S. presidential elections and the differences in campaigning at each stage, p. 255.

The three stages in a presidential election are winning enough delegate support in presidential primaries and caucuses to secure the nomination, campaigning at the national party convention, and mobilizing voters in enough states to get the most votes in the Electoral College. The nomination phase is dominated by more partisan and often more ideological voters. Early contests are often important, which means candidates start early. The connection phase is important in defining candidates for less engaged voters. The general election concentrates candidate time and money in a relatively few contested states.

Money in U.S. Elections

8.5 Evaluate the influence of money in American elections and the main approaches to campaign finance reform, p. 264.

The rising costs of campaigns have led to declining competition for congressional seats and increasing dependence on PACs and wealthy donors. Because large campaign contributors are suspected of improperly influencing public officials, Congress has long sought to regulate political contributions. The main approaches to reform have been (1) imposing limitations on giving, receiving, and spending political money; (2) requiring public disclosure of the sources and uses of political money; and (3) giving governmental subsidies to presidential candidates, campaigns, and parties, including incentive arrangements. Present regulation includes all three approaches.

Improving Elections

8.6 Assess concerns regarding presidential elections and reforms that have been proposed, p. 271.

The present presidential selection system is under criticism because of its length and expense, because of uncertainties and biases in the Electoral College, and because it seems to test candidates for media skills less needed in the White House than the ability to govern, including the capacity to form coalitions and make hard decisions. Reform efforts center on presidential primaries, the Electoral College, and campaign finance.

Learn the Terms

 Study and Review the Flashcards

winner-take-all system, p. 244
single-member district, p. 244
proportional representation, p. 244
Electoral College, p. 245
safe seat, p. 249
coattail effect, p. 249
candidate appeal, p. 251
national tide, p. 251
name recognition, p. 252
caucus, p. 256
national party convention, p. 259
Federal Election Commission (FEC), p. 264
Bipartisan Campaign Reform Act (BCRA), p. 265
soft money, p. 266
hard money, p. 266
issue advocacy, p. 267
independent expenditures, p. 267
Super PAC, p. 268

Test Yourself

 Study and Review the Practice Tests

MULTIPLE CHOICE QUESTIONS

8.1 Assess the implications of election rules in the United States.

Which system allows political parties to secure legislative seats and power in proportion to the number of votes they receive in the election?

a. cumulative voting
b. winner-take-all system
c. single-member districts
d. proportional representation
e. retrospective voting

8.2 Identify problems associated with administering elections and evaluate proposed solutions to those problems.

If a person thinks he or she should be allowed to vote on Election Day, but is not on the list of registered voters, he or she

a. must register at the Department of Motor Vehicles before voting.
b. may submit a provisional ballot.
c. may not vote.
d. may not submit an absentee ballot.
e. must present identification to the polling official.

8.3 Explain how congressional elections work and why they are generally not competitive.

The boost candidates from the president's party get from running along with a popular presidential candidate is known as the ______ .

a. safe effect
b. wave effect
c. coattail effect
d. proportional effect
e. incumbent effect

8.4 Describe the stages in U.S. presidential elections and the differences in campaigning at each stage.

Which of the following is not one of the ways delegates are selected to attend the national party conventions?

a. They are voted for by the state legislature.
b. They are selected in state caucuses.
c. They are "super delegates," or state party leaders not bound by popular vote.
d. They are awarded based on results in state primary elections.
e. They are elected by the state's voters.

8.5 Evaluate the influence of money in American elections and the main approaches to campaign finance reform.

Which of the following is NOT true of BCRA?

a. It does not constrain independent expenditures that are reported to the FEC.
b. It is also called the McCain—Feingold bill.
c. Its most important provision was to create Super PACs, a new type of independent organization.
d. It banned soft money contributions to parties.
e. It was mostly upheld in the Supreme Court decision *McConnell* v. *FEC*.

8.6 Assess concerns regarding presidential elections and reforms that have been proposed.

Which of the following arguments is frequently given in opposition to reforming the Electoral College system?

a. The Electoral College allows candidates to win the presidency even if they lose the national popular vote.
b. The Electoral College system makes candidates travel throughout the country meeting voters instead of merely running a remote television campaign.
c. A national direct popular election could include a runoff election if no candidate receives more than 40% of the vote.
d. The Electoral College guarantees that all citizens' votes are equally weighted.
e. The Electoral College ensures that each state has an equal say in who becomes president.

ESSAY QUESTION

Identify three reasons why congressional elections are often not very competitive and explain why these reasons have come to be important. Finally, what are some ways congressional elections could be made more competitive?

Explore Further

IN THE LIBRARY

R. Michael Alvarez, *Information and Elections* (University of Michigan Press, 1998).

R. Michael Alvarez and Thad E. Hall, *Electronic Elections: The Perils and Promises of Digital Democracy* (Princeton University Press, 2008).

Larry M. Bartels, *Presidential Primaries and the Dynamics of Public Choice* (Princeton University Press, 1988).

Earl Black and Merle Black, *The Vital South: How Presidents Are Elected* paperback ed. (Harvard University Press, 2002).

Bruce Buchanan, *Presidential Campaign Quality: Incentives and Reform* (Pearson, 2004).

Ann N. Crigler, Marion R. Just, and Edward J. Mccaffery, eds., *Rethinking the Vote: The Politics and Prospects of American Election Reform* (Oxford University Press, 2004).

Ronald Keith Gaddie, *Born to Run: Origins of the Political Career* (Rowman & Littlefield, 2004).

Roderick P. Hart, *Campaign Talk* (Princeton University Press, 2000).

Paul S. Herrnson, *Congressional Elections: Campaigning at Home and in Washington*, 6th ed. (CQ Press, 2011).

Gary C. Jacobson, *The Politics of Congressional Elections*, 8th ed. (Longman, 2013).

Kim F. Kahn and Patrick J. Kenney, *The Spectacle of U.S. Senate Campaigns* (Princeton University Press, 1999).

Donald R. Kinder and Allison Dale-Riddle, *The End of Race: Obama, 2008, and Racial Politics in America* (Yale University Press, 2012).

David B. Magleby and Anthony Corrado, eds., *Financing the 2008 Election* (Brookings Institution Press, forthcoming).

David B. Magleby, ed., *The Change Election: Money, Mobilization, and Persuasion in the 2008 Federal Elections* (Temple University Press, 2011).

L. Sandy Maisel and Mark D. Brewer, *Parties and Elections in America: The Electoral Process,* updated 6th ed. (Rowman & Littlefield, 2011).

William G. Mayer and Andrew E. Busch, *The Front-Loading Problem in Presidential Nominations* (Brookings Institution Press, 2004).

Stephen K. Medvic, *Political Consultants in U.S. Congressional Elections* (Ohio State University Press, 2001).

Samuel L. Popkin, *The Reasoning Voter: Communication and Persuasion in Presidential Campaigns*, 2d ed. (University of Chicago Press, 1994).

Stephen J. Wayne, *The Road to the White House 2008* 9th ed. (Wadsworth, 2012). See also *Public Opinion Quarterly, The American Journal of Politics*, and *American Political Science Review*.

ON THE WEB

www.fec.gov
The Web site of the Federal Election Commission. This site contains information on elections, voting, parties, PACs, and campaign finance.

elections.gmu.edu/voter_turnout.htm
The Web site of the United States Elections Project. This site contains voter turnout and registration data in primary and general elections.

www.politico.com
This Web site focuses on political news and elections.

www.eac.gov
The Web site of the United States Election Assistance Commission. This site contains information on voter registration, elections and election regulations, and other forms of election participation.

www.archives.gov/federal-register/electoral-college/calculator.html
An Electoral College calculator that lets you tally different predictions for the electoral vote; a fun way to get a good understanding of how the Electoral College works.

9

Listen to Chapter 9 on MyPoliSciLab

The Media and U.S. Politics

Just as television revolutionized American politics in the 1950s and 1960s, the Internet is bringing major changes to American politics today. Television meant large numbers of people could see in their own homes such events as the 1960 presidential campaign debate between John Kennedy and Richard Nixon, the protests and riots at the 1968 Democratic National Convention, and the last U.S. troops leaving the Vietnam War. Much of American politics became centered on television in the decades after the 1950s, and television remains central to how Americans receive their news. But in 2008 and since, we have seen another dramatic change in how many people get their news and interact with each other about politics. The Internet has meant people can access multiple news sources instantly, including the ability to watch political videos on YouTube. The Internet also allows people to communicate with friends about politics via Facebook, Twitter, and other social networking sites. By early in the 2012 campaign, for example, there were 100 million active Twitter users, a tenfold increase over 2008. Campaigns not only sent messages out via Twitter but used it as "an early warning signal" of what reporters and the public were tweeting about. The Romney campaign, for example, monitored the Twitter stream from reporters covering the campaign to anticipate questions that might be asked of the candidate, but also to communicate the campaign's view of events.[1]

More than any other campaign before it, the Obama campaign in 2008 used these new media tools to engage supporters in a wide range of activities, including making campaign contributions, volunteering for the candidate, communicating with Facebook friends, and encouraging people to vote. Obama's 2008 campaign manager David Plouffe wrote after the election that "technology was core to our campaign from Day One."[2] Obama built on the experience of unknown candidates like Howard Dean in 2004 and new campaign groups like MoveOn, which had both used the Internet to engage and mobilize people.

Since 2008, the Internet and social media have also been used by conservative candidates, by groups like the Tea Party, and in support of candidates like Scott Brown in his campaign in the

9.1 Describe changes in the nature and extent of the political influence of the various news media, p. 283.

9.2 Trace the evolution of the news media over the course of U.S. history, p. 290.

9.3 Evaluate the media's influence on public opinion and attention, p. 296.

9.4 Describe the media's role in elections and the associated problems and benefits, p. 301.

9.5 Assess the media's relationship to governance in the United States, p. 306.

A supporter of the Republican presidential candidate, former Massachusetts Governor Mitt Romney, uses a cell phone to take a picture during a campaign rally in Toledo, Ohio.

MyPoliSciLab Video Series

Watch on MyPoliSciLab

The Big Picture Did the government do all they could to aid Hurricane Katrina victims? Was it clear that there were weapons of mass-destruction in Iraq? Does a certain candidate really favor big businesses? By tracing the history of news media over the last 100 years, author David B. Magleby illustrates its impact on public opinion and why it is important for readers to ask hard questions.

The Basics How do the media help support our democratic institutions? In this video, you will find out how a free press functions not just as a source of knowledge, but also as a public forum and a government watchdog. You'll also analyze how private ownership and partisanship impact the ability of the media to do its job.

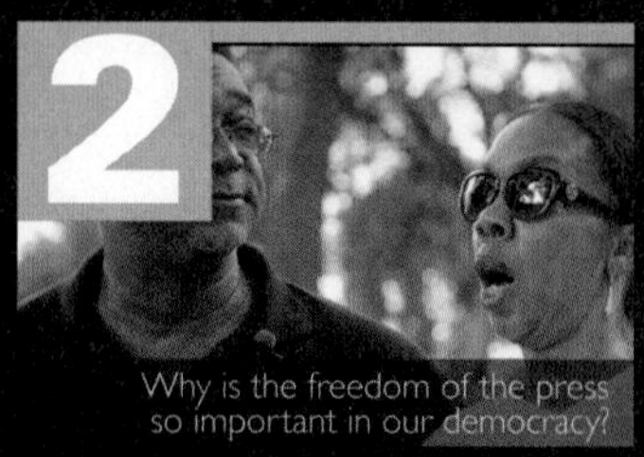

In Context Trace the evolution of media outlets from newspapers to the new media that exists today. In this video, University of Oklahoma political scientist Tyler Johnson examines the history of media outlets and the effect of both traditional and new media on the political information and messages that reach the public.

Thinking Like a Political Scientist How does the media shape public opinion? In this video, University of Oklahoma political scientist Tyler Johnson discusses how media framing works and what market factors are influencing this process.

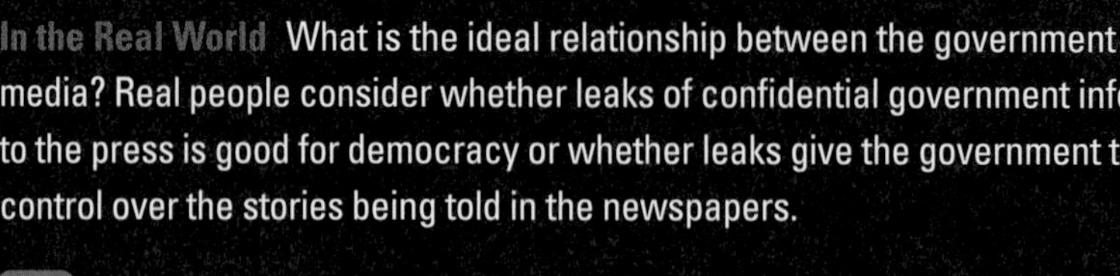

In the Real World What is the ideal relationship between the government and the media? Real people consider whether leaks of confidential government information to the press is good for democracy or whether leaks give the government too much control over the stories being told in the newspapers.

So What? How many sources do you consult regularly for news coverage? Author David B. Magleby warns against the dangers of relying solely on partisan news providers, such as Fox News and MSNBC, and he gives advice on how to avoid bias in the media.

2010 Massachusetts special election for the U.S. Senate. The former Republican vice presidential candidate Sarah Palin has retained a substantial Internet presence, routinely posting notes to her nearly 3 million followers on Facebook in order to bypass what she calls the 'lamestream' media."[3]

Use of the Internet and social media grew in 2008 and remained at these higher levels in 2010. In 2008, nearly half (46 percent) of all voters went online for information about the election or to communicate with others about the campaigns.[4] In 2010, the voters who used social media rose to 54 percent.[5] Elected officials have learned that tweets and YouTube postings can reach large audiences. For example, after budget talks with the Republicans broke down in 2011, California governor Jerry Brown posted a video with his views on the impasse on YouTube. Barack Obama announced his candidacy for the 2012 presidential election with online videos.[6]

As important as the new media have become, Americans continue to make use of a wide array of traditional news media as well, especially television, radio, and newspapers. In this chapter, we explore the role of the media; its influence on public opinion, elections, institutions, and policy; and how it has changed over time.

mass media
Means of communication that reach the public, including newspapers and magazines, radio, television (broadcast, cable, and satellite), films, recordings, books, and electronic communication.

news media
Media that emphasize the news.

The Influence of the Media on Politics

9.1 Describe changes in the nature and extent of the political influence of the various news media.

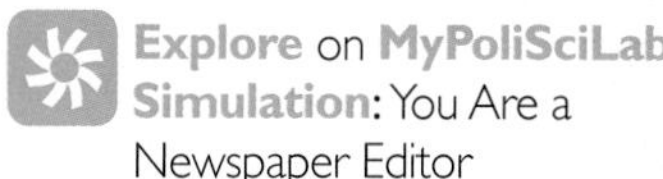

The media, in particular the print media, have been called the "fourth estate" and the "fourth branch of government."[7] Evidence that the media influence our culture and politics is plentiful. In one form or another, the **mass media**—newspapers and magazines, radio, television (broadcast, cable, and satellite), the Internet, films, recordings, books, and electronic communication—reach nearly everyone in the United States.[8] The **news media** are the parts of the mass media that tell the public what is going on in the country and the world, although the distinctions between entertainment and news have become increasingly blurred. News programs often have entertainment value, and entertainment programs often convey news. Programs in this latter category include TV newsmagazines such as *60 Minutes* and *Dateline*; talk shows with hosts such as Piers Morgan and Sean Hannity; Jon Stewart's parody of the news, *The Daily Show;* and *The Colbert Report.*

By definition, and to make money, the mass media disseminate messages to a large and often heterogeneous audience. Because they must have broad appeal, their messages are often simplified, stereotyped, and predictable. But how much political clout do the media have? Two factors are important in answering this question: the media's pervasiveness, and their role as a link between politicians and government officials and the public.

The Internet has become a more important source of news in the United States, taking its place alongside print, radio, and television. The number of people who go online for news has grown dramatically and promises to become even more politically important as organizations and campaigns increasingly use the Internet to reach the public.[9] The Internet enables people to obtain information on any subject and from multiple sources—some of which may be unreliable—at any time of the day or night. The Internet also allows people to communicate and organize rapidly in response to political events. The Internet and social media have also become important means of communication and coordination by protest groups around the world. During the Arab Spring protests in 2011 and 2012, "anti-government protesters in Tunisia and Egypt used Twitter, Facebook and other platforms to run rings around attempts at censorship and organize demonstrations."[10]

Why have the Internet and social media become so much more important in American politics? Part of the reason is these tools have become much more accessible. In 2009 nearly two-thirds (64 percent) of households used a high-speed Internet connection, up from 4 percent in 2000.[11] Not only can people go to news sources like CNN.com, ABC.com, or the Drudge report, but they can read blogs, watch videos on YouTube, and communicate with friends through Facebook and on Twitter. Another reason is the Internet and social media allow people immediate access to the information they want. These media tools also make communication with friends, family, and colleagues easier. Included in this is communicating with elected officials at all levels of government. Constituents now routinely e-mail questions to members of Congress or the White House, and office holders seek to activate supporters via these new media as well. For example, during the 2011 showdown over the federal debt ceiling, both sides used online communications to push their side. President Obama, for example, tweeted on his campaign account asking millions of Americans to tweet Congress about a compromise. The tweet said, "The time for putting party first is over. If you want to see a bipartisan #compromise, let Congress know. Call. Email. Tweet. –BO"[12]

A majority of individuals who use the Internet to learn about politics and to engage with others about current events acknowledge that they are sometimes skeptical about the quality of information on the Web. A majority also feels that the Internet increases the influence of those with extreme political views. And government officials have also come to understand the role the Internet and social media can play in policy discussions.

☐ The Pervasiveness of Television

Television has changed U.S. politics more than any other invention. With its immediacy, visual imagery, and drama, television has an emotional impact that print media can rarely match.[13] It cuts across age groups, educational levels, social classes, and races. In contrast, newspapers provide more detail about the news and often contain opposing points of view, at least on the editorial pages.

People in Times Square watch events at the World Trade Center live on large screen televisions in New York the day after 9/11.

Where Do You Get Your Political News?

Politically-interested people get their news from four news outlets—television, the Internet, print, and radio. Among these media sources, TV is used the most (93 percent) with Internet, Print and Radio all used by about three quarters of respondents. There are partisan differences, Republicans more often go to Fox News, while more Democrats go to NPR's "All Things Considered".

Americans Go To These News Sources

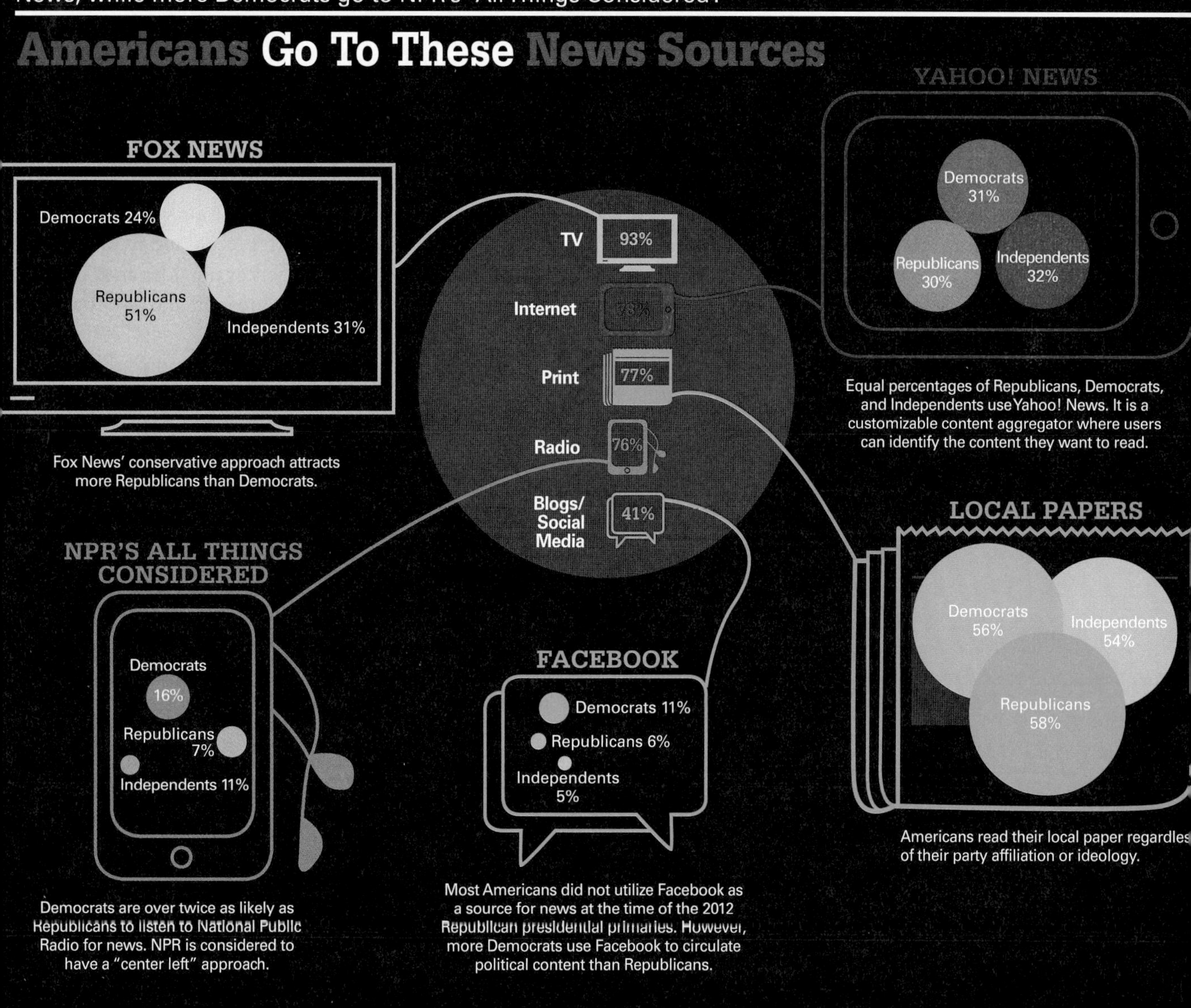

Fox News' conservative approach attracts more Republicans than Democrats.

Equal percentages of Republicans, Democrats, and Independents use Yahoo! News. It is a customizable content aggregator where users can identify the content they want to read.

Democrats are over twice as likely as Republicans to listen to National Public Radio for news. NPR is considered to have a "center left" approach.

Most Americans did not utilize Facebook as a source for news at the time of the 2012 Republican presidential primaries. However, more Democrats use Facebook to circulate political content than Republicans.

Americans read their local paper regardles of their party affiliation or ideology.

SOURCE: Data from American National Election Study, "Evaluations of Government and Society Study," Release Wave 4, February 2012.

Investigate Further

Concept Where are people getting their political news? Politically-interested Americans go to several types of outlets for political news. Television is still the most popular news source, but the Internet, print, and radio are frequently used. Despite widespread popularity among youth, social media—like Facebook—is not yet a dominant source for political news.

Connection How is politics related to media choices? In general, Americans tend to seek information that reinforces their politics. The rise of cable television and Internet sources compartmentalized information. Many people can't read or watch all the news, so they choose a few "comfortable" content providers who reinforce their opinions and beliefs.

Cause Do the partisans exhibit particular media consumption habits? For example, Republicans rely more on Fox News while Democrats tend toward NPR's "All Things Considered". However, party crossover in media use does exist, particularly for Internet and social media sources. There are few partisan differences in use of local papers.

9.1

9.2

9.3

9.4

9.5

24/7 news cycle
News is now constantly updated and presented via Internet sites like the *New York Times* or *Wall Street Journal* and cable news sources like CNN, Fox News, and MSNBC.

The average American watches more than four and one-half hours of television a day, and most homes have more than two television sets.[14] Television provides instant access to news from around the country and the globe, permitting citizens and leaders alike to observe events firsthand.

The growth of the **24/7 news cycle**, around-the-clock cable news and information shows, is one of the most important developments in recent years. Until the late 1980s, the network news programs on CBS, NBC, and ABC captured more than 90 percent of the audience for television news in the morning and early evening. Although the "big three" networks have seen their audiences decline by about one million viewers a year since then, they still hold the majority of viewers. In 2011, the networks attracted on average approximately 21.6 million evening news viewers,[15] whereas the cable news networks CNN, Fox News, and MSNBC had average audiences of about 3.2 million evening viewers.[16]

There are substantial differences in where people of different ages go for news. For example, when asked where they went for news of the presidential campaign, the most common response among persons ages 18–29 was the Internet (42 percent) followed by cable news networks (35 percent). Persons over fifty years of age relied more on television local news (50 percent) and cable news networks or nightly network news (40–41 percent).[17] News organizations of all types now communicate via Twitter; all of the major networks and most major newspapers have Twitter feeds, and in many cases news anchors and reporters have their own feeds as well. Twitter provides an additional means for news organizations to communicate and build followings, and also to receive feedback from their publics.[18]

Satellites, cable television, Internet search engines such as Google, blogs, and podcasts make vast amounts of political information available 24 hours a day. These technologies eliminate the obstacles of time and distance and increase the volume of information viewers can store, retrieve, and watch. They have also reduced the impact of single sources of broadcast or cable news. Competition from cable stations has put pressure on broadcast networks to remain profitable, which has both reduced budgets for broadcast news coverage and created the need to boost its entertainment value. For example, more viewers watched Barack Obama's and Mitt Romney's 2012 acceptance speeches at the party conventions on cable stations than on ABC, CBS, or NBC. CNN had the most viewers.[19]

The way television influences American politics has changed over time. Television stations now devote less time to reporting on elections. But at the same time, television commercials have become more important as a source of information about candidates and issues.[20] The Supreme Court's recent decisions in campaign finance cases will likely foster more political advertising by groups running their own ads for and against candidates.[21] Successful candidates must be able to communicate with voters through this medium, and attempt to define their opponent as well as themselves. To get their message across to television audiences, politicians rely on media advisers. The amount of local television news devoted to politics has also been declining and now constitutes less than one minute per half-hour broadcast.[22]

In large urban areas, viewers rarely see stories about their member of Congress, in part because those media markets usually contain several congressional districts. Newspapers do a better job of covering politics and devote more attention to it than television stations do, but the declining number of newspapers means there is less overall coverage of local politics and government. The decline in news coverage of elections and voting, especially on television, has only increased the impact of political advertising on television, through the mail, and over the telephone.

☐ The Persistence of Radio

Television and the Internet have not displaced radio. On the contrary, radio continues to reach more U.S. households than television does. Only 1 household in 100 does not have a radio,[23] compared with 3 in 100 without a television.[24] More than 8 in 10 people

The Global Community

Popular Sources for News

Do people in different countries turn to one medium more than another for news? This question is answered by the following question from the 2009 Pew Research Center's Global Attitudes Survey: "Where do you most often turn to get news about national and international issues—television, newspapers, radio, magazines, or the Internet?"

There are substantial differences across countries in where the people "turn to get news about national and international issues." Television clearly dominates all other media around the world, but particularly in China, with 86 percent reporting they turn to television for news. More than 70 percent of people in China, India, and Mexico also rely more on television for news. The United States stands out from other countries in the 22 percent who turn to the Internet for news. This proportion is more than double that found in any other country. Another distinctive country is Nigeria, where 34 percent turn to radio, roughly double the share of the world sample that use radio for news. In Britain and India, fewer than one in five turn to newspapers for the news, and in Japan, a similar proportion rely on newspapers.

The reasons for these differences are probably based on what is most readily available to a population. Fewer people in Nigeria have access to television and newspapers, so radio is more important. Britain has a long history with newspapers, which helps explain the continued importance of newspapers in Britain, and the historic influence of the British on India may be part of the relatively greater popularity of newspapers in India. Given its leadership in developing the Internet, it is not surprising that people in the United States use the Web more than people in any other country.

CRITICAL THINKING QUESTIONS

1. Does it make a difference where people turn to get their news?
2. In five or ten years, how do you think this question would be answered in the United States?
3. Is there an advantage to having competing sources of news—radio, television, newspaper, and the Internet?

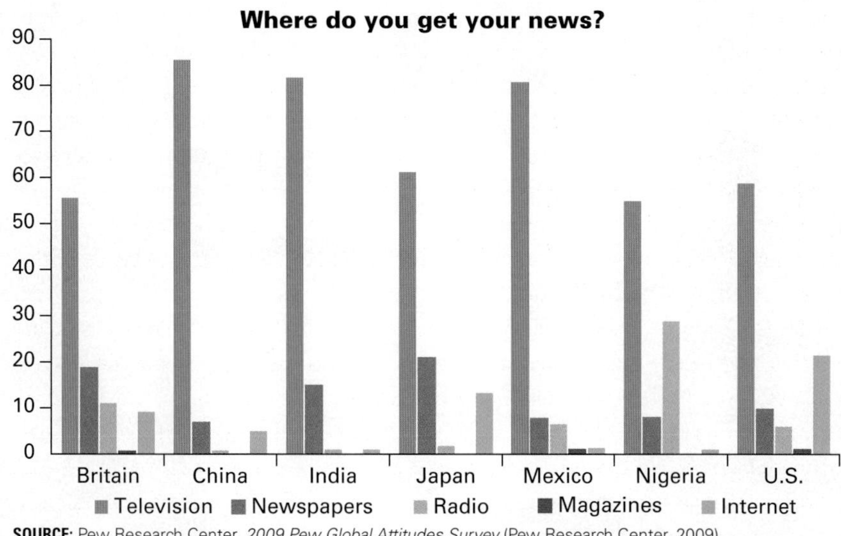

SOURCE: Pew Research Center, *2009 Pew Global Attitudes Survey* (Pew Research Center, 2009).

listen to the radio every week,[25] and nearly 7 in 10 do so every day. Many consider the radio an essential companion when driving. Certainly American adults get more than "the facts" from radio; they also get analysis and opinion from commentators and talk show hosts.

Political campaigns continue to use radio to communicate with particular types of voters. Because radio audiences are distinctive, campaigns can target younger or older voters, women, Hispanics, and so on. Many candidates in 2008 used radio to "micro-target" particular audiences in this way.[26] One particularly important source of news on the radio is National Public Radio (NPR). An estimated audience of 13 million listens to programs such as *Morning Edition*.[27] NPR rivals conservative radio commentator Rush Limbaugh for size of audience.[28]

☐ The Declining Importance of Newspapers and Newsmagazines

Despite vigorous competition from radio and television, newspapers remain important. Daily newspaper circulation has been declining for the past 20 years from more than 62 million in 1990 to less than 46 million nationwide currently—or less than one copy for every six people.[29] The circulation figures for newspapers reflect a troubling decline in readership among younger persons: the percentage of young people who read newspapers on a regular basis declined by more than half between 1967 and 2008.[30]

People still get news from newspapers, but not always on paper. Here, someone reads the *New York Times* on an Apple iPad tablet computer.

9.1

9.2

9.3

9.4

9.5

Newspapers have become less profitable because of declining circulation, in part because the Internet provides instantly available information for free.[31] The Internet has also hurt newspapers' bottom lines most by providing an alternative medium for retail advertisers, and particularly for classified ads via sites such as Craigslist. One estimate is that advertising revenue for "help wanted" ads in newspapers fell by more than 90 percent in the past decade.[32] Newspapers once earned about 40 percent of their revenue from classifieds; today, they receive only 20 percent.[33]

In addition to metropolitan and local newspapers, Americans now have at least three national newspapers, *USA Today,* the *Wall Street Journal,* and the *New York Times.* With a circulation of nearly 2.1 million, the *Wall Street Journal* has replaced *USA Today* as the top-circulating U.S. newspaper.[34] Newsmagazines, like newspapers, have also undergone major changes in recent years. Magazines such as *Time, Newsweek,* and *U.S. News and World Report* have experienced substantial declines in circulation and become less profitable. *Newsweek* was sold in 2010 for $1, with the buyer agreeing to take on an estimated $70 million in debt owed by the publication.[35] Declines in advertising revenue hurt the newsweeklies, as these magazines are called, just as it had hurt newspapers.[36]

The Growing Popularity of the Internet

From its humble beginnings as a Pentagon research project in the 1960s,[37] the Internet has blossomed into a global phenomenon. There are now more than one trillion unique URLs on the Web,[38] and more than 117 million active domains have been registered worldwide.[39]

FOR the People Government's Greatest Endeavors

Creating the Internet

The development of the Internet began in the 1950s with the U.S. Air Force funding researchers at the RAND Corporation to develop technology for a communications network that could survive nuclear attack. To avoid the problems that would result from an attack on what was a centralized communications system, researchers created a system that could function even if parts were destroyed, called *distributed communications.* Under the Defense Advanced Research Projects Agency (DARPA), government-funded researchers at the University of California, Los Angeles (UCLA), gave the concept its first large-scale test in 1969. The early system was intended for researchers and the military to be able to transmit information and share use of computers by granting remote access.

For decades, the government did not make access to the new technology generally available. Some entities like the National Science Foundation (NSF) developed NSFNET, linking much of the academic and research community. In 1993, Congress passed legislation allowing NSF to open NSFNET to commercial use, and by the mid-1990s, several commercial networks were in existence.[*] Today, there are thousands of Internet service providers (ISPs) connecting an estimated 676 million computers worldwide to the Internet. More than half of these connected computers are in the United States, although China leads the world in estimated numbers of Internet users.[†]

Access to the Internet does not necessarily mean unlimited access. In repressive regimes like China, Iran, and Russia, communications on the Internet are monitored by the government, with some sites blocked and some communications censored. At the same time, in Tunisia, Egypt, and Syria the Internet and social media were frequently used by protesters to communicate with each other and the outside world during the uprisings in 2011 that came to be known as the Arab Spring. So the high-speed electronic communications network that started as a government research endeavor, you use for everything from e-mail to shopping to reading the latest news releases, while people in repressive regimes have used it as a tool for greater self-government.

QUESTIONS

1. How has the Internet changed your life?
2. What other inventions can be traced to government-funded research?
3. Does the Internet enhance national defense, the reason for its creation?[*]

[*]CNN.com, "Transcript: Vice President Gore on CNN's 'Late Edition,'" March 9, 1999 http://www.cnn.com/ALLPOLITICS/stories/1999/03/09/president.2000/transcript.gore/index.html (accessed June 8, 2010).

[†]CIA, "The World Factbook," https://www.cia.gov/library/publications/the-world-factbook/geos/ch.html (accessed June 30, 2012).

The Internet opens up resources in dramatic ways. One study found that nearly half of Internet users go online to search for news on a particular topic; somewhat smaller proportions go online for updates on stock quotes and sports scores. Among Americans ages 18–39 and for the nearly four-fifths of Americans who are online, the Internet ranks as a top source of information for local subjects like education, entertainment, and restaurants.[40] For approximately 37 percent of Internet users, the Internet is a primary source of news.[41] As noted, Internet users can also interact with politicians or other people about politics through e-mail, social networking sites, and blogs. Younger people, including teenagers, use the Internet extensively for schoolwork, and nearly three in four of them prefer it to the library.[42] A remarkable 63 percent of teenagers get news online, and the same proportion of teenagers use the Internet every day.[43]

The Internet provides an inexpensive way for candidates and campaigns to communicate with volunteers, contributors, and voters, and promises to become an even larger component of future campaigns. Candidates' Web sites offer not only extensive information about the candidates themselves and their stands on issues, but also tools for meeting fellow supporters, for receiving news and materials from the campaign, for volunteering, and for setting up personalized home pages, such as at my.barackobama.com. This is in addition to candidates' YouTube channels, social networking profiles, and affiliated blogs. Although much is still unknown about the impact of the Internet, it has at least the potential to fragment the influence of other media.[44]

During the past decade, there has been a dramatic increase in the use of social networking computer sites, and these have come to be important in American politics. Social networking sites allow individuals to create profiles and connect via the Web to other individuals via the site. Early sites had targeted populations like African Americans (BlackPlanet) or Asian Americans (AsianAvenue), but with the advent of Facebook, MySpace, and Twitter, social networking became a more generalized phenomenon. Since Facebook became available to more than only Harvard University students, the number of people with a Facebook profile has risen to more than half of all Americans over the age of 12,[45] and worldwide, there are nearly 500 million Facebook users.[46] Twitter has also experienced substantial growth.[47] Candidates, political movements, and even law enforcement have all used social networking in recent years.[48] However, it is important to note that social networking has its dangers, not the least of which is the viral nature of damaging messages. Almost everything candidates and officials say is instantly posted and can never be withdrawn.

The Changing Role of the U.S. News Media

9.2 Trace the evolution of the news media over the course of U.S. history.

American adults spend on average 70 minutes per day consuming news, and the older they are, the more time they spend.[49] Yet media bashing has become a national pastime. We blame the media for phenomena as varied as increased tension between the races, biased attacks on public officials, sleaze and sensationalism, increased violence in our society, and the elevation of the profit motive over the job of conveying information. Many in the media agree with these charges and think the media are headed in the wrong direction.[50]

But complaints may simply be a case of criticizing the messenger to avoid dealing with the message.

9.1

9.2

9.3

9.4

9.5

☐ A Political Tool

The news media have changed dramatically throughout the course of U.S. history. When the Constitution was being ratified, newspapers consisted of a single sheet, often published irregularly by merchants to hawk their services or goods. Delinquent subscribers and high costs meant that newspapers rarely stayed in business more than a year.[51] But the Framers understood the importance of the press as a watchdog of politicians and government, and the Bill of Rights guaranteed freedom of the press.

The new nation's political leaders, including Alexander Hamilton and Thomas Jefferson, recognized the need to keep voters informed. Political parties as we know them did not exist, but the support the press had given to the Revolution had fostered a growing awareness of the political potential of newspapers. Hamilton recruited staunch Federalist John Fenno to edit and publish a newspaper in the new national capital of Philadelphia. Jefferson responded by attracting Philip Freneau, a talented writer and editor and a loyal Republican, to do the same for the Republicans. (Jefferson's Republicans later became the Democratic Party.)

The two papers became the nucleus of a network of competing partisan newspapers throughout the nation. Although they competed in Philadelphia for only a few years, they became a model for future partisan papers. The early U.S. press served as a mouthpiece for political leaders. Its close connection with politicians and political parties offered the opportunity for financial stability—but at the cost of journalistic independence.

☐ Financial Independence

During the Jacksonian era of the late 1820s and 1830s, the right to vote was extended to all free white adult males through the elimination of property qualifications. The press began to shift its appeal away from elite readers and toward the mass of less-educated and less-politically interested readers. Thus, increased political participation by the common people—along with the rise of literacy—began to alter the relationship between politicians and the press.

Some newspaper publishers began to experiment with a new way to finance their newspapers. They charged a penny a paper, paid on delivery, instead of the traditional annual subscription fee of $8 to $10, which most readers could not afford. The "penny press," as it was called, expanded circulation and increased advertising, enabling newspapers to become financially independent of the political parties.

The changing finances of newspapers also affected the definition of news. Before the penny press, all news was political—speeches, documents, and editorials—directed at politically interested readers.[52] The penny press reshaped the definition of news as it sought to appeal to less politically aware readers with human interest stories and reports on sports, crime, trials, fashion, and social activities.

☐ "Objective Journalism"

By the early twentieth century, many journalists began to argue that the press should be independent of the political parties. *New York Tribune* editor Whitelaw Reid eloquently expressed this sentiment: "Independent journalism! That is the watchword of the future in the profession. An end of concealments because it would hurt the party; an end of one-sided expositions...; an end of assaults that are not believed fully just but must be made because the exigency of party warfare demands them."[53] Objective journalism was also a reaction to exaggeration and sensationalism in the news media, something called *yellow journalism* at the time.

863,956 WORLDS CIRCULATED YESTERDAY

The World.

863,956 WORLDS CIRCULATED YESTERDAY

"Circulation Books Open to All."

NEW YORK, THURSDAY, FEBRUARY 17, 1898.

MAINE EXPLOSION CAUSED BY BOMB OR TORPEDO?

Capt. Sigsbee and Consul-General Lee Are in Doubt---The World Has Sent a Special Tug, With Submarine Divers, to Havana to Find Out---Lee Asks for an Immediate Court of Inquiry---Capt. Sigsbee's Suspicions.

CAPT. SIGSBEE, IN A SUPPRESSED DESPATCH TO THE STATE DEPARTMENT, SAYS THE ACCIDENT WAS MADE POSSIBLE BY AN ENEMY.

Dr. E. C. Pendleton, Just Arrived from Havana, Says He Overheard Talk There of a Plot to Blow Up the Ship---Capt Zalinski, the Dynamite Expert, and Other Experts Report to The World that the Wreck Was Not Accidental---Washington Officials Ready for Vigorous Action if Spanish Responsibility Can Be Shown---Divers to Be Sent Down to Make Careful Examinations.

The New York World a day after

By the late nineteenth century, more and more people were literate and got their news from newspapers. This was the front page of the *New York World* on February 17, 1898. and the illustration depicted the explosion of the battleship *Maine* in Havana harbor, one of the causes for the Spanish-American War.

Journalists began to view their work as a profession, and they established professional associations with journals and codes of ethics. This professionalization reinforced the notion that journalists should be independent of partisan politics. Further strengthening the trend toward objectivity was the rise of the wire services, such as the Associated Press and Reuters, which remained politically neutral to attract more customers.

□ The Impact of Broadcasting

Radio and television nationalized and personalized the news. People could now follow events as they were happening and not have to wait for the publication of a newspaper. From the 1920s, when radio networks were formed, radio carried political speeches, campaign advertising, and coverage of political events such as national party conventions.[54] Politicians could now speak directly to listeners, bypassing the screening of editors and reporters. Radio also increased interest in national and international news because it enabled its audience to follow faraway events as if they were actually there.

Beginning in 1933, President Franklin Roosevelt used radio with remarkable effectiveness. Before then, most radio speeches were formal orations, but Roosevelt spoke to his audience on a personal level, seemingly in one-on-one conversations. These "fireside chats," as he called them, established a standard that politicians still follow today. When Roosevelt began speaking over the microphone, he would visualize a tiny group of average citizens in front of him. He "would smile and light up," observers said, "as though he were actually sitting on the front porch or in the parlor with them."[55]

Television added a dramatic visual dimension, which increased audience interest in national events and allowed viewers to witness lunar landings and the aftermath of political assassinations, as well as more mundane events. By 1963, the two largest networks at the time, CBS and NBC, had expanded their evening news programs from 15 to 30 minutes. Today, news broadcasting has expanded to the point that many local stations provide 90 minutes of local news every evening as well as a half-hour in the morning and at noon. Programs such as *20/20* and other newsmagazine shows are among the most popular in the prime-time evening hours.

Cable television created the round-the-clock, 24/7 news cycle. With the advent of CNN, Fox News, and MSNBC, cable viewers have access to news twenty-four hours a day, seven days a week. Providing this much original news content is challenging and often leads to the same stories being repeated over and over again. It also means that some like FOX and MSNBC have chosen to emphasize a particular ideological perspective in programs that combine news and commentary.[56] Many other news sources, like the *New York Times* or CNN, now provide 24/7 news coverage on the Internet. No longer must people wait for the morning paper to learn about current events: they can immediately turn to Internet news sources or cable TV. During the Clinton impeachment hearings in 1998, the 2000 Florida ballot-counting controversy, the "shock and awe" bombing of Iraq in March 2003, and news that U.S. forces had found and killed Osama bin Laden in May 2011, audiences around the world watched U.S. cable news for its instantaneous coverage. C-SPAN now provides uninterrupted coverage of congressional deliberations and presidential nominating conventions.

Franklin D. Roosevelt was the first president to recognize the effectiveness of radio to reach the public. His "fireside chats" were the model for later presidents.

☐ Investigatory Journalism

News reporters today do more than convey the news; they investigate it, and their investigations often have political consequences. An investigative team at *60 Minutes* of CBS News broke the story of torture of Iraqi prisoners held by U.S. soldiers at Abu Ghraib in 2004,[57] and in 2005 Dana Priest of the *Washington Post* revealed the existence of secret CIA prisons that were being used to hold and interrogate suspected terrorists.[58] One highly publicized release of secret documents came in 2010 by WikiLeaks. This Web-based news source released 250,000 diplomatic communications, 11,000 of which were marked secret. The documents were global in scope, including such sensitive international "hot spots" as North Korea, Iran, Iraq, and Afghanistan, as well as some regarding the base in Guantanamo Bay, Cuba, where the U.S. held suspected terrorists.[59]

In many ways, the best example of the power of investigatory journalism is in the role the media played in the Watergate scandal.[60] Without persistent reporting by columnist Jack Anderson and two young *Washington Post* reporters, Robert Woodward and Carl Bernstein, the story would probably have been limited to a report of a failed burglary of the headquarters of the Democratic National Committee at the Watergate building.[61] The news reporting, coupled with congressional investigations, put a spotlight on the inner workings of the Nixon White House and the Nixon reelection committee, which had funded the attempted burglary and other political dirty tricks. Critical to the reporting on the broadening scandal, which ultimately brought down the president, was a confidential source, nicknamed Deep Throat by Woodward and Bernstein.[62] (In 2005, more than 30 years after these events, the former deputy director of the FBI, W. Mark Felt, identified himself as Deep Throat.)

☐ Media Consolidation

Local firms used to own regional newspapers, radio, and television stations. As in other sectors of the economy, media companies have merged and created large conglomerates of many newspapers and broadcasting stations. Some of these conglomerates are multinational. Rupert Murdoch, an Australian-born U.S. citizen and founder of the FOX Network, owns 35 television stations in the United States, DirecTV, 20th Century Fox, HarperCollins Publishers, and MySpace.com. His acquisition of the *Wall Street Journal* gave him one of the few national newspapers in the United States.[63] Murdoch also owns nine newspapers abroad and five television networks around the world.[64] Until 2012, Murdoch had combined his newspapers with his entertainment enterprises all

9.1

9.2

9.3

9.4

9.5

OF the People Diversity in America

Toward a More Representative Media

The newspaper industry has worked hard to achieve greater diversity in the newsroom. The American Society of Newspaper Editors has stated that diverse newsrooms cover U.S. communities more effectively. Because many stories require contacts with a diverse public, the industry adopted a goal to make all newsrooms representative of the nation as a whole by 2025.

Although the largest U.S. newspapers, such as the *New York Times* and the *Washington Post,* have made progress toward a more representative newsroom, smaller papers have had much more difficulty attracting and retaining minority reporters. Thus, less than 30 percent of smaller newspapers with circulations of fewer than 10,000 readers employ at least some minority reporters, compared with 100 percent of large newspapers with circulations of more than 500,000 readers. Moreover, the percentage of minority journalists varies greatly from one region of the country to another. Newspapers in the Midwest and New England have the smallest percentage of minority reporters, whereas newspapers in the western states have the highest percentage.

QUESTIONS

1. Why might more diverse newsrooms provide better news coverage?
2. Why are smaller newspapers less likely to have much diversity in their newsrooms?
3. What are some news topics where a more diverse newsroom might be important?

DIVERSITY AT U.S. NEWSPAPERS

	Women		Minorities*	
	1999	2011	1999	2011
Position				
Supervisors	34%	35%	9%	11%
Copy-Layout Editors	40	42	11	13
Reporters	40	39	13	13
Photographers	26	26	15	17

*African American, Asian American, Native American, and Hispanic.

SOURCE: American Society of Newspaper Editors, "Newsroom Employment Census: Table C – Numbers and Percentages of Whites and Minorities by Job Category," http://asne.org/Key_Initiatives/Diversity/Newsroom_Census/Table_C.aspx (accessed February 3, 2012) and "Table L – Numbers and Percentages of Men and Women by Job Category," http://asne.org/Key_Initiatives/Diversity/Newsroom_Census/Table_L.aspx (accessed February 3, 2012).

under one conglomerate. But in 2012 he separated the newspapers from the other enterprises because "they had become a drag on the stock" of the other businesses.[65] Some of Murdoch's international holdings have generated controversy. Murdoch, his son James Murdoch, and editors and reporters at Murdoch's British newspaper, *News of the World,* were called before a parliamentary committee because of telephone wiretaps or "hacking" done by reporters at the newspaper.[66] In response, Murdoch ceased publication of the newspaper, issued an apology to the victims of the hacking, and paid damages to them of $23.4 million.[67]

When television was in its infancy, radio networks and newspapers were among the first to purchase television stations. These mergers established cross-ownership patterns that persist today. The Gannett Company, for example, owns 100 daily newspapers in the United States and United Kingdom and 23 television stations and cable television systems—assets that provide news coverage to more than 21 million households in the United States.[68] The Tribune Company, parent of the *Chicago Tribune,* purchased Times-Mirror, publisher of the *Los Angeles Times,* in 2000 and now has combined assets of nine newspapers, 24 television stations, one radio station, superstation WGN, and a growing online business.[69] In such acquisitions, some newspapers are subsequently sold to other conglomerates.

Sean Hannity reaches substantial audiences through his cable news show, radio program, books, and his Web site for political news and opinion. Hannity is seen here signing copies of his book *Deliver Us From Evil.*

At the same time, on the national level, the cable networks—CNN, Fox News, and others such as C-SPAN—have expanded the number of news sources available to the 91.5 percent of households receiving TV cable or satellite service.[70] The courts and the Federal Communications Commission (FCC)—an independent regulatory commission charged with licensing stations—are reinforcing the trend toward media conglomeration by relaxing and striking down regulations that limit cable and television network ownership by the same company.[71]

Will greater concentration of media ownership limit or restrict the free flow of information to the public? This concern is most evident in cities that once had two or more competing daily papers and now have only one newspaper.[72] Although the number of local broadcast stations has not declined to the same extent, conglomerates without ties to the community now own more of these stations. The nationalization of media extends to some media personalities who have a large presence on television, radio, and through their books.

☐ Regulation of the Media

The government has regulated the broadcast media in some form since their inception. Because of the limited number of television and radio frequencies, the national government oversees their licensing, financing, and even regulates content through the FCC. For example, the FCC fined CBS for broadcasting as part of its 2004 Super Bowl half-time show an incident in which Justin Timberlake removed part of Janet Jackson's costume, exposing her right breast.[73] However, the FCC's regulatory power has been challenged by the broadcast media who contend that, due to technological advancements in the availability of broadcast media outlets, the First Amendment no longer permits such content restrictions. In 2012, the Supreme Court declined for the second time to deal with that question directly and instead ruled against the FCC on the grounds that they had not properly alerted broadcasters of a change in policy that led to large fines levied against several television networks and their affiliates.[74]

The Media and Public Opinion

9.3 Evaluate the media's influence on public opinion and attention.

When dramatic events such as the terrorist attacks on September 11, 2001, occur, we realize television's power to bring world events into our lives. Osama bin Laden, the mastermind behind those attacks, also understood the power of the media both inside and outside the United States, as evidenced by his release of videotapes of himself after the attacks.

The pervasiveness of newspapers, magazines, radio, and television confers enormous influence on the individuals who determine what we read, hear, and see because they can reach so many people so quickly. The news media have also assumed the role of speaking for the people. Journalists report what "the people" want and think, and then they tell the people what politicians and policy makers are doing about it. Politicians know they depend on the media to reach voters, and they are well aware that a hostile press can hurt or even destroy them. That explains why today's politicians spend so much time developing good relationships with the press.

Television's ability to present images and communicate events has influenced U.S. public opinion. Footage of the violence done to black and white protesters during the civil rights revolution of the 1950s and 1960s made the issue more real and immediate. News coverage of the war in Vietnam galvanized the antiwar movement in the United States because of the gruesome images news shows brought into people's homes. The testimony of White House staff before the Senate about Watergate and later House Judiciary committees further weakened confidence in the Nixon administration. Television coverage of the terrorist attacks on the World Trade Center and the Pentagon, the devastation left by Hurricane Katrina on the Gulf Coast, the earthquake in Haiti, and the tsunami in Japan made indelible impressions on all who watched.

A wave approaches Miyako City in Japan's Iwate Prefecture after a magnitude 8.9 earthquake struck the area on March 11, 2011. Natural disasters in a distant part of the world become part of global news coverage, as with the 2011 tsunami in Japan.

For a long time, analysts argued that political leaders wielded more influence in U.S. politics than the media did. Franklin D. Roosevelt's fireside chats symbolized the power of the politician over that of the news editor. Roosevelt spoke directly to his listeners over the radio in a way and at a time of his own choosing, and no network official could block or influence that direct connection. President John Kennedy's use of the televised press conference established similar direct contact with the public. President Ronald Reagan was nicknamed "the Great Communicator" because of his ability to talk with the people persuasively and often passionately about public policy issues through television.

Now the media are more aggressive in news gathering. Controversy over the justification for going to war with Iraq became a major focus of the media in George W. Bush's second term and helped explain the declining public assessment of his performance. In addition, the media can exert significant influence on public opinion through *agenda setting* and *issue framing*.

☐ Agenda Setting

By calling public attention to certain issues, the media helps determine what topics will become subjects of public debate and legislation.[75] However, the media do not have absolute power to set the public agenda. The audience and the nature of any particular issue limit it.[76] According to former vice president Walter Mondale (1976–1980): "If I had to give up… the opportunity to get on the evening news or the veto power,…I'd throw the veto power away. [Television news] is the president's most indispensable power."[77]

BY the People Making a Difference

Citizen Media

Newspapers have long published feedback from readers in the form of "letters to the editor." Other media also have long shared some form of public feedback and commentary. The published "letters" are often short, and out of necessity the media outlet can share only a small fraction of what has been submitted.

In the Internet age there are more opportunities for citizens to communicate broadly on a wide range of topics. Some of these web-based tools are run by the media. An example is the CNN iReport, which is a CNN-run Web site that allows people to post articles and videos. CNN is quick to make clear that stories posted at CNN iReport "are not edited, fact-checked, or screened before they post." Some of the postings at CNN iReport are verified by CNN and occasionally they become a part of CNN news coverage. A prominent example of this is Virginia Tech graduate student Jamal Albarghouti, who captured dramatic video of the Virginia Tech shooting in 2007, which became part of CNN's coverage of the tragic incident.*

Citizens also use the Web to post blogs, which if well written and relevant can generate a substantial audience. The "Drudge Report" and the "Huffington Post" have gone from relative obscurity to being what some have described as two of the most powerful blogs in the world.† YouTube adds a sound and video component to citizen reporting. The power of timely and newsworthy video clips first posted on YouTube to influence public discourse is now clear.

The same can be said for citizens using Twitter. The media have relied on tweets to report on natural disasters like the earthquakes in Mexico, the post-election revolts in Iran, and shootings in U.S. cities. The impact of citizen reporting through tweets, blogs, or YouTube-like postings is also substantial at the local level or on your college campus. If you observe an event that the media should cover you can pass it along. Expressing your views online is another way you can attempt to influence government.

QUESTIONS

1. How does citizen journalism broaden the reach of the media?
2. What are the advantages and disadvantages of using blogs as your primary news source?
3. In what ways might the use of Twitter change the way government functions?

*"CNN Celebrates Second Anniversary of iReport, More than 175,000 Contributions," TimeWarner, August 20, 2008, available at http://www.timewarner.com/corp/newsroom/pr/0,20812,1834490,00.html.

†Jessica Aldred, Amanda Astell, Rafael Behr, Lauren Cochrane, John Hind, Anna Pickard, Laura Potter, Alice Wignall, and Eva Wiseman, "The World's 50 Most Powerful Blogs," *The Observer*, March 9, 2008, available at http://www.guardian.co.uk/technology/2008/mar/09/blogs.

9.1
9.2
9.3
9.4
9.5

Communicating through the media works, especially when the communication is—or at least appears to be—natural and unscripted. When President Bush first visited the scene of the destruction of the World Trade Center in New York City in September 2001, he took a bullhorn and said, "I can hear you. The rest of the world hears you, and the people who knocked these buildings down will hear all of us soon."[78] This action projected presidential leadership and reassured a nation that was still shocked by the attacks.

☐ Issue Framing

Politicians, like everyone else, try to frame issues to win support, and they try to influence the "spin" the media will give to their actions or issues. The media provide the means. Opponents of U.S. intervention in Bosnia in the 1990s tried to portray it as another Vietnam. Objectors to normal trade relations with China frame that relationship as a human rights travesty. People who favor the right to have an abortion define the issue as one of freedom of choice; those who oppose it define it as murder. Health care reform was debated in the 2008 presidential campaign and as Congress considered and passed reform in 2010. It remained a contentious issue in the 2012 election. Both parties strategized about how to best frame the issue for their side of the debate. Republican pollster Frank Luntz in his analysis is reported to have said, "If the dynamic becomes 'President Obama is on the side of reform and Republicans are against it,' then the battle is lost and every word in this document is useless." How the two parties sought to be seen as the real reformers while also showing concern for other key elements of the debate including cost is a good example of issue framing.[79] In referendum campaigns, the side that wins the battle of defining what the referendum is about, wins.[80]

☐ The Question of Media Bias

We tend to blame the media for being either too conservative or too liberal. Conservatives often complain that the media are too liberal. Radio talk show host Rush Limbaugh observed that "back in the day before we existed, they [the liberals] owned it [the media], they had a monopoly."[81] Some liberal critics contend that the media reflect a conservative bias not only in what they report, but also in what they choose to ignore. They point to Fox News as an example of conservative cable television.

In fact, most U.S. news media are committed to being unbiased. Newspapers and television management go to some lengths to insulate reporters from their advertising and business operations, in part to reduce criticism about favorable editorial treatment of large advertisers or the corporate owners. In 2007, when the management of the *Los Angeles Times* attempted to foster closer relationships between the business and news divisions, they were criticized out of a concern that advertisers would influence news coverage.[82]

Some commentators have suggested that a possible bias flows from the fact that reporters and editors become too friendly with the people and organizations they write about. David Broder, a highly regarded *Washington Post* reporter and columnist, opposed the idea of journalists becoming government officials and vice versa.[83] Others argue that journalists with previous government service have close working relationships with politicians and can give us a valuable perspective on government without losing their professional neutrality.

The media's alleged political bias is also a frequent target of criticism, in part because the journalists tend to be more liberal than the rest of the public (see Table 9.1). Their worldview, some contend, may govern their choice of issues to cover and the way they cover them.[84] Critics counter that conservative forces in the media, such as corporate ownership, lead to disproportionate time and influence given to conservative pundits. The question of whether there is an ideological bias in the media has not been

TABLE 9.1 PARTISANSHIP AND IDEOLOGY OF JOURNALISTS, POLICY MAKERS, AND THE PUBLIC

	Journalists	Policy Makers	Public
Party Identification			
Democrat	27%	43%	34%
Republican	4	24	28
Independent	55	26	21
Other	5	5	12
Do Not Know/Refused	9	2	4
Self-Described Ideology			
Liberal	25%	25%	21%
Moderate	59	52	37
Conservative	6	18	35
Do Not Know/Refused	11	5	7

■ *Why do you think journalists identify as Independent in a far greater percentage than policy makers or the public?*

SOURCE: The Kaiser Foundation, *The Role of Polls in Policy Making,* Combined Topline Results, June 2001, p. 27, www.kff.org/kaiserpolls/loader.cfm?url=/commonspot/security/getfile.cfm&PageID=13842.

political socialization
The process by which we develop our political attitudes, values, and beliefs.

selective exposure
The process by which individuals screen out messages that do not conform to their own biases.

selective perception
The process by which individuals perceive what they want in media messages.

authoritatively answered. A further question is whether bias, if it exists and whatever its direction, seeps into the content of the news. Here too, the answer remains unclear. One source that seeks to inform media consumers about detecting media bias is a group named Fairness and Accuracy in Reporting (FAIR).[85]

One bias that does not have a partisan or ideological slant is the bias toward sensationalism. Scandals happen to liberals and conservatives, Republicans and Democrats. Once the province of tabloids like the *National Enquirer,* stories about sex, drugs, or other scandals involving celebrities and politicians have become commonplace in the mainstream media.

□ Factors That Limit Media Influence

Despite the varied means the media has for influencing public opinion, people are not just empty vessels into which politicians and journalists pour information and ideas. The way we interpret political messages depends on a variety of factors: political socialization, selectivity, needs, and our ability to recall and comprehend the message.

POLITICAL SOCIALIZATION We develop our political attitudes, values, and beliefs through an education process social scientists call **political socialization**.[86] Although they are not as important as family in influencing our values and attitudes,[87] the media are a socializing force and help shape public perceptions and knowledge. Party identification is also a filter through which people view the media. Face-to-face contacts with friends and business associates (*peer pressure*) often have far more impact than the information or views we get from an impersonal television program or newspaper article. Strong identification with a party also acts as a powerful filter.[88] A conservative Republican from Arizona may watch the "liberal eastern networks" and complain about their biased news coverage while sticking to her own opinions. A liberal from New York will often complain about right-wing talk radio, even if he listens to it occasionally (see Figures 9.1 and 9.2).

SELECTIVITY We all practice **selective exposure**—screening out messages that do not conform to our own biases. We subscribe to newspapers or magazines or turn to television and cable news outlets that support our views.[89] We also practice **selective perception**—perceiving what we want to in media messages.[90]

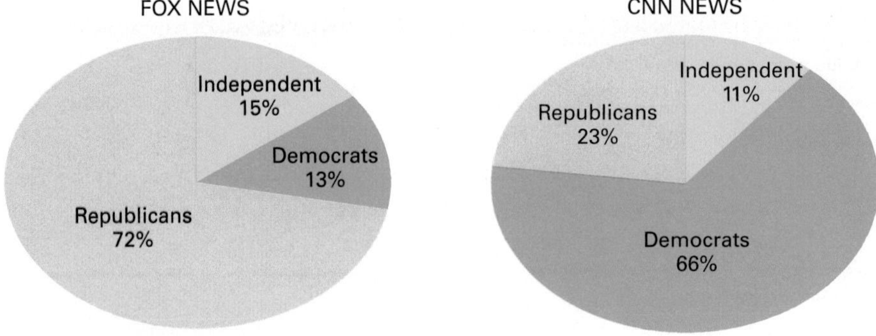

FIGURE 9.1 PARTISANSHIP AND PREFERRED NEWS SOURCE

■ *What do these figures imply about the practice of selective exposure?*

SOURCE: Pew Research Center for the People & the Press, "July 2009 Political-Media Survey" dataset, http://www.people-press.org/2009/07/30/july-2009-political-media-survey/

NEEDS People read newspapers, listen to the radio, or watch television for different reasons.[91] Media affect people differently depending on whether they are seeking information about politics or want to be entertained. Members of the broader audience are also more likely to pay attention to news that directly affects their lives, such as interest rate changes or the price of gasoline.[92]

AUDIENCE FRAGMENTATION The growth of cable television and new media such as the Internet have reduced the dominance of broadcast media and newspapers in transmitting information. Because people are scattered across more press outlets and these outlets cover politics in varied ways, the impact of the press has become more diffuse. Fragmentation of the media audience has tended to counteract the impact of media conglomeration. But as media giants acquire both cable and broadcast stations and outlets and promote their own online sites, the importance of media conglomerates such as NBC, CNBC, and MSNBC will increase.

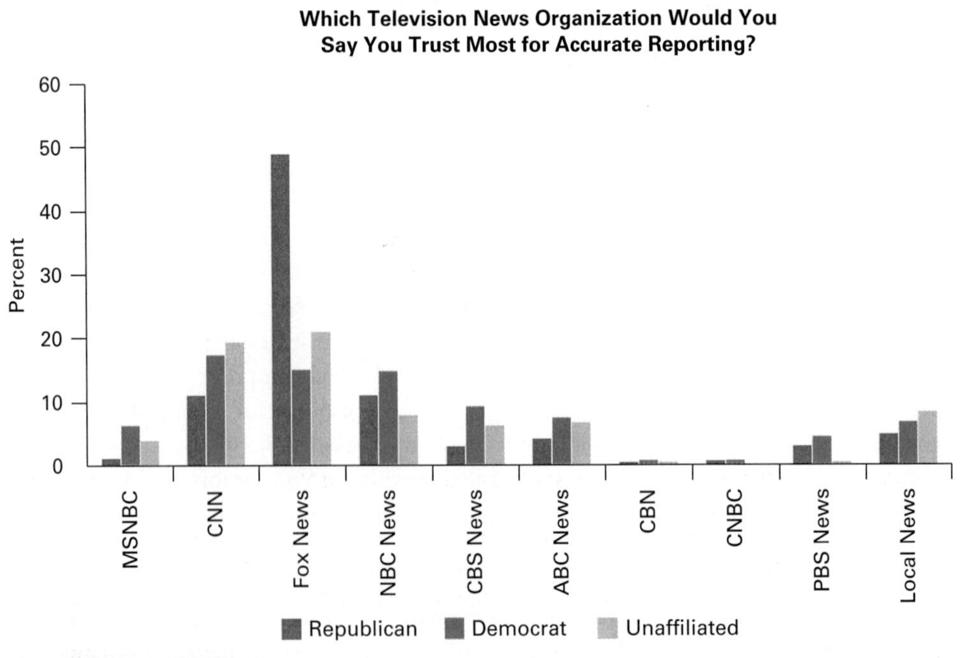

FIGURE 9.2 PARTISANSHIP AND NEWS SOURCE CREDIBILITY

SOURCE: Sacred Heart University poll on media and politics, November 2007; data compiled by Jerry Lindsay, April 30, 2008.

The Media and Elections

9.4 Describe the media's role in elections and the associated problems and benefits.

News coverage of campaigns and elections is greatest in presidential contests, less in statewide races for governor and U.S. senator, and least for other state and local races. Generally, the more news attention given the campaign, the less likely voters are to be swayed by any one source. Hence, news coverage is likely to be more influential in a city council contest than in an election for president or the Senate. For most city elections, there are only one or two sources of information about what candidates say and stand for; there are many sources for statewide and national contests.

Diversification also lessens the ability of any one medium to influence the outcome of elections. Newspaper publishers who were once seen as key figures in state and local

You Will Decide

Should the Internet Be Regulated?

People all around the world increasingly use the Internet to purchase music, movies, software from their computers, and apps for their smart phones. People generally pay for these items electronically using debit or credit cards. But some people get the items for a fraction of the cost others pay because they are purchasing pirated copies. This Internet piracy lead to a debate in 2012 about how to effectively protect those whose creative talent produced the item, something that is called intellectual property and is often protected by copyrights or patents. Industry groups estimate that Internet content theft costs U.S. workers and companies $5.5 billion annually. The pharmaceutical industry loses billions more to Internet sellers of drugs illegally produced, falsely advertised, and possibly harmful.*

Well-known Internet giants like Google, Facebook, and Twitter strongly opposed the proposed Internet piracy legislation because it and similar regulations would stifle creativity, and force Internet search engines and social media to become "police officers for the Justice Department."** The act could affect third parties like Paypal that would be barred from supporting transactions involving illegal sellers. Content providers like Wikipedia also objected to the regulations because they saw them as limiting the free flow of information on the Internet.

What do you think? Should the government more aggressively enforce copyright and intellectual property rights on Internet pirates?

Thinking It Through

Opponents of Internet regulation fear that even well-intended laws to protect against Internet piracy might lead to censorship of the Internet or a desire to limit or regulate it in other ways. This new medium, they contend, has flourished with the freedom it has experienced and to regulate it now may well limit its future breakthroughs. Concerns about censorship also have to be taken seriously not only in countries that already suppress dissent but also in countries like England and the U.S., where some have suggested limiting e-mail or Facebook during riots or potentially violent protests. Regulation could dampen the "watchdog" role the Internet has played in bringing to light abuses of power and allowing the public to view public officials on YouTube in unscripted settings.

But to do nothing in the face of widespread theft of intellectual property sets a dangerous precedent. People who invented and developed computer software deserve to be paid for their inventions and those who made movies, wrote books or recorded music should not have their creative work and intellectual property stolen and sold. Since much of the Internet piracy is done outside the U.S. it can be argued that any U.S. law is likely to not stop the activity. Proponents of the law counter that if we do nothing we cannot exert pressure on other countries to enforce international patent and copyright agreements.

*http://www.suntimes.com/business/10089668-420/understanding-the-internet-piracy-bills-sopa-and-pipa.html

**http://www.nytimes.com/2012/01/21/technology/senate-postpones-piracy-vote.html?_r=2

politics are now less important because politicians and their media advisers are no longer so dependent on newspapers to communicate their messages. Candidates can use ads on radio and television, direct mail, phone, the Web, and cable television to reach voters. In local contests, or even in larger settings such as the Iowa caucuses or the New Hampshire primary, personal contact can also be important.

□ Choice of Candidates

The extensive use of television has made looking and sounding good on television much more important. It has also led to the growth of the political consulting industry and made *visibility* the watchword in politics. Television strongly influences the public's idea of what traits are important in a candidate. A century ago, successful candidates needed a strong pair of lungs; today, they need a telegenic appearance, a pleasing voice, and no obvious physical impairments.

Although the media insist that they pay attention to all candidates who have a chance to win, they also influence who gets such a chance. Consequently, candidates have to come up with creative ways to attract media attention. The late Paul Wellstone, in his 1990 campaign for the Senate in Minnesota, said in his advertisements that he did not have much money to pay for ads, so he would have to talk fast to cram what he had to say into fewer commercials. His witty commercial became a news event itself—it got Wellstone additional coverage.

Sometimes, a limited ad buy can generate funding for a much larger one. This was the case with the group that attacked the credibility and heroism of John Kerry in the 2004 presidential election; the Swift Boat Veterans for Truth turned a relatively small $550,000 ad buy into millions of dollars in contributions, which funded the airing of additional ads.[93] Critical to this expanded campaign was the widespread news coverage generated by the controversy the first ad set off.[94]

□ Campaign Events

Candidates schedule events—press conferences, interviews, and "photo ops"—in settings that reinforce their verbal messages and public image. Barack Obama skillfully used a backdrop of young and diverse voters for his rallies and post-primary speeches. In contrast, other candidates were often surrounded by older and less diverse political leaders from the state or community. Many campaign events fail to receive attention from reporters because others are more newsworthy stories or the media may sense that they have been staged to generate news coverage.

The parties' national conventions used to capture national attention. However, because party primaries now select candidates, the conventions no longer provide much suspense or make news, except perhaps over who will be the vice presidential nominee. This is one reason the networks have cut back their coverage of presidential nominating conventions. In 1952, the average television set was tuned to the political conventions for 26 hours, or an average of more than three hours a night for the eight nights of convention coverage.[95]

During the last decade, by contrast, the major networks provided only one or two hours of prime-time coverage each evening. But cable channels now carry extensive coverage of the proceedings.

□ Technology

Although the expense associated with television advertising has contributed to the skyrocketing costs of campaigning, it has also made politics more accessible to more people. Now with satellites, candidates can conduct local television interviews without having to travel to local studios. They can target specific voter groups through cable television or low-power television stations that reach homogeneous neighborhoods and small towns. DVDs, Facebook postings, and Twitter tweets with messages

The presidential campaign, 2012: President Obama poses with patrons at the Kozy Corner restaurant in Oak Harbor, Ohio, on July 5, 2012, where he made an unannounced visit to speak with supporters while on a bus tour of Ohio and Pennsylvania.

from the candidates further extend the campaign's reach.[96] All serious candidates for Congress and governor now make themselves and their positions available through a Web page on the Internet.

Campaigns have primarily used the Internet and e-mail to reinforce voter preferences or help answer questions, more than to reach and persuade more passive citizens. But citizens can now interact with each other online on a wide range of political topics. In this sense, the Internet is like a town meeting, but one that people can attend without leaving their homes or offices. In recent elections, people have made greater use of blogs as sources of information, and campaigns have often created their own blogs.

Of growing importance are political communications posted on YouTube or Facebook, as illustrated by the examples cited at the beginning of this chapter. The

In 2012, Republican presidential candidate Mitt Romney signs autographs and greets supporters after holding a campaign rally at Harmon's Tree Farm in Gilbert, South Carolina, before the primary in that state.

widespread availability of cameras and phones that can capture politicians' embarrassing statements, as happened to 2012 Republican presidential candidate Mitt Romney when he was recorded on video at a private fund raiser characterizing 47 percent of the public as "dependent on government" and unwilling to "take personal responsibility." The video garnered significant media attention, eventually requiring a Romney apology.[97] Similarly, as New York Congressman Anthony Weiner learned in 2011, e-mailing photos of himself in his underwear could result in those images being widely circulated and force his resignation.

☐ Image Making and Media Consultants

Consistent with the media's focus on personality is its highlighting of mistakes and gaffes by candidates and officeholders. Long before Jon Stewart and *The Daily Show*, print and broadcast media devoted considerable attention to such things as Gerald Ford mistakenly classifying Poland as a free country in the 1976 presidential debates.[98] More recently, Texas governor and presidential hopeful Rick Perry had a memory lapse in a Republican presidential candidate debate when he said there were three agencies in Washington, D.C. he would close if elected but then could only name two of them.[99]

This ability of television and the Internet to reach a mass audience and the power of the visual image on television has contributed to the rise of new players in campaign politics, most notably *media consultants*—campaign professionals who provide candidates with advice and services on media relations, advertising strategy, and opinion polling.[100] A primary responsibility of a campaign media consultant is to present a positive image of the candidate and to reinforce negative images of the opponent. Both parties have scores of media consultants who have handled congressional, gubernatorial, and referendum campaigns. These consultants have also been blamed for the negative tone and tactics of recent campaigns.

Today, consultants coach candidates about how to act and behave on television and what to discuss on the air. Consultants report the results of *focus groups* (small sample groups of people who are asked questions about candidates and issues in a discussion setting) and *public opinion polls,* which in turn determine what the candidate says and does. Some critics allege that political consultants have become a new "political elite" that can virtually choose candidates by determining in advance which men and women have the right images, or at least images that the consultants can restyle for the widest popularity.[101] But political consultants who specialize in media advertising and image making know their own limitations in packaging candidates. As one media consultant put it, "It is a very hard job to turn a turkey into a movie star; you try instead to make people like the turkey."[102]

horse race
A close contest; by extension, any contest in which the focus is on who is ahead and by how much rather than on substantive differences between the candidates.

☐ Impact on Voter Choice

As television and the Internet have become increasingly important to politics—and reforms such as primary elections have weakened the political parties and made news coverage of candidates more important—the question arises, what difference does the media make?

PERSONALITY OVER SUBSTANCE Some critics think reporters pay too much attention to candidates' personality and background and not enough attention to issues and policy. Others say character and personality are among the most important characteristics for readers and viewers to know about. The public appetite for stories on candidates' personal strengths and weaknesses is not new and is likely to continue.

The influence of the media on the public varies by level of sophistication of the voters. Better-informed and more-educated voters are more sophisticated and therefore less swayed by new information from the media.[103] But for the public generally, other scholars contend that "television news is news that matters."[104]

THE HORSE RACE A common tendency in the media is to comment less on a candidate's position on issues than on a candidate's position in the polls compared with other candidates—what is sometimes called the **horse race**.[105] "Many stories focus on who is ahead, who is behind, who is going to win, and who is going to lose, rather than examining how and why the race is as it is."[106] Reporters focus on the tactics and strategy of campaigns because they think such coverage interests the public.[107] The media's propensity to focus on the "game" of campaigns displaces coverage of issues.

NEGATIVE ADVERTISING Paid political advertising, much of it negative in tone, is another source of information for voters. Political advertising has always attacked opponents, but recent campaigns have taken on an increasingly negative tone. A rule of thumb used to be to ignore the opposition's charges and thus avoid giving them, or the opposition, importance or standing. More recently, media advisers recommend responding quickly and aggressively to attacks.

Voters say the attack style of politics turns them off, but most campaign consultants believe that negative campaigning works. This seeming inconsistency may be explained by evidence suggesting that negative advertising may discourage some voters who would be inclined to support a candidate (a phenomenon known as *vote suppression*) while making supporters more likely to vote.[108] Other research suggests that negative advertising is more informative than positive advertising and does not discourage voter turnout, but it does alienate people from government.[109] Finally, in some contexts at least, negative ads may stimulate individuals to contribute to both the candidate attacked by the ad as well as the candidate running, while positive ads that include partisan content increase donations to the candidate running the ad.[110]

MAKING A DECISION Newspapers, television, and the Internet seem to have more influence in determining the outcome of primaries than of general elections,[111] probably because voters in a primary are less likely to know about the candidates and have fewer clues about how they stand. By the time of the November general election, however, party affiliation, incumbency, and other factors diminish the impact of media messages. The mass media are more likely to influence undecided voters, who, in a close election, can determine who wins and who loses.

ELECTION NIGHT REPORTING Does television coverage on election night affect the outcome of elections? Election returns from the East Coast come in three hours before the polls close on the West Coast. Because major networks often project the presidential winner well before polls close in western states, it can affect western voters. When one candidate appears to be winning by a large margin, it may make voters believe their vote is meaningless and dampen voter turnout. In a close presidential election, however, such early reporting may stimulate turnout because voters know their vote could determine the outcome.

Controversy over exit polls grew after the 2000 election when television networks projected that Al Gore had won Florida, only to later retract that prediction. Hours later, Fox News projected Bush winning Florida. The truth was that the vote in Florida was by every measure too close to judge. In 2004, leaks of early exit polls in the media showed John Kerry winning Ohio,[112] a state carried by Bush. Despite these problems, exit polls are generally accurate and inform the public about who voted and why people voted the way they did. Exit polls are one source of data used in this book, for example.

The Media and Governance

9.5 Assess the media's relationship to governance in the United States.

When policies are being formulated and implemented, decision makers are at their most impressionable.[113] Yet by that time, the press has moved on to another issue.

Lack of press attention to the way policies are implemented explains in part why we know less about how government officials go about their business than we do about heated legislative debates or policy deadlocks between congress and the president. Only in the case of a policy scandal, such as the lax security surrounding nuclear secrets at Los Alamos National Laboratory for more than a decade between 1999 and 2010, does the press take notice of how policies are implemented.

Some critics contend that the media pressure on policy makers to provide immediate answers forces them to make hasty decisions, a particular danger in foreign policy: If an ominous foreign event is featured on television news, the president and his advisers feel pressured to respond almost as soon as the crisis happens, because thanks to the 24-hour news cycle, citizens expect instantaneous leadership, just as they have become accustomed to on-the-spot reporting. The longer the president delays, the easier it is for opponents to attack him for indecisiveness, while portraying themselves as capable and unflappable in a crisis.[114]

□ Political Institutions and the News Media

Presidents have become the stars of the media, particularly television, and have made the media their forum for setting the public agenda and achieving their legislative aims. Presidential news conferences command attention (see Table 9.2). Every public activity a president engages in, both professional and personal, is potentially newsworthy; a presidential illness can become front-page news, as can the president's vacations and pets.

A president attempts to manipulate news coverage to his benefit, as in the Bush administration's decision to embed reporters with U.S. forces during the early stages of the Iraq War. Presidents or their staff also selectively leak news to reporters. Presidents

TABLE 9.2 PRESIDENTIAL PRESS CONFERENCES: JOINT* AND SOLO SESSIONS, 1913–2012

President	Total	Solo	Joint	Joint as Percentage of Total	Months in Office
Wilson	159	159	0	0	96
Harding		No Transcripts Available			29
Coolidge	521	521	0	0	67
Hoover	268	267	1	0.4	48
Roosevelt	1020	984	33	3.2	145.5
Truman	324	311	13	4.0	94.5
Eisenhower	193	192	1	0.5	96
Kennedy	65	65	0	0	34
Johnson	135	118	16	11.9	62
Nixon	39	39	0	0	66
Ford	40	39	1	2.5	30
Carter	59	59	0	0	48
Reagan	46	46	0	0	96
G. H. W. Bush	143	84	59	41.3	48
Clinton	193	62	131	67.9	96
G. W. Bush	208	50	158	76.0	96
Obama	74	33	41	55.4	45

*In a joint press conference, the president answers questions along with someone else, most often a foreign leader. In a solo session, only the president answers questions. There are three missing transcripts for Roosevelt and one for Johnson, which makes it impossible to determine whether those sessions were solo or joint ones.

■ *How does President Obama's use of press conferences compare to his recent predecessors?*

SOURCE: Martha Joynt Kumar, e-mail correspondence September 2012.

use speeches to set the national agenda or spur congressional action. Presidential travel to foreign countries usually boosts popular support at home, due to largely favorable news coverage.

Members of Congress have long sought to cultivate positive relationships with news reporters in their states and districts. They typically have a press relations staffer who informs local media of newsworthy events, produces press releases, and generally tries to promote the senator or representative.[115] Congress also provides recording studios for taping of news segments, and both parties have recording studios near the Capitol explicitly for electoral ads. Finally, politicians often appear on talk radio, which they can readily do from their offices in Washington. But the focus of this media cultivation is on the individual member and not on the institution of Congress as a whole.

Congress is more likely to get negative coverage than either the White House or the Supreme Court. Unlike the executive branch, it lacks an ultimate spokesperson, a single person who can speak for the whole institution.[116] Congress does not make it easy for the press to cover it. Whereas the White House attentively cares for and feeds the press corps, Congress does not arrange its schedule to accommodate the media; floor debates, for example, often compete with committee hearings and press conferences.[117] Singularly dramatic actions rarely occur in Congress; the press therefore turns to the president to describe the activity of the federal government on a day-to-day basis and treats Congress largely as a foil to the president. Most coverage of Congress is about how it acts on pressing matters, with some focus on legislative process, especially when there are conflicts between Congress and the president.[118]

The federal judiciary is least dependent on the press. The Supreme Court does not rely on public communication for political support. Rather, it depends indirectly on public opinion for continued deference to or compliance with its decisions.[119] The

Court does not allow television cameras to cover oral arguments, controls the release of audiotape, and bars reporters as well as anyone other than the justices when it meets to discuss cases. It has strong incentives to avoid being seen as manipulating the press, so it retains an image of aloofness from politics and public opinion. The justices' manipulation of press coverage is far more subtle and complex than that of the other two institutions.[120] For example, the complexity of the Supreme Court's decision in the 2000 Florida presidential vote recount case, with multiple dissents and concurrences and no press release or executive summary, made broadcast reporting on the decision difficult.

Not all who think the media are powerful agree that power is harmful. After all, they argue, the media perform a vital educational function. Nearly three-quarters (74 percent) of the public thinks the press is a watchdog that keeps government leaders from doing bad things.[121] At the least, the media have the power to mold the public agenda; at most, in the words of the late Theodore White, they have the power to "determine what people will talk and think about—an authority that in other nations is reserved for tyrants, priests, parties, and mandarins."[122]

Review the Chapter

Listen to **Chapter 9** on **MyPoliSciLab**

The Influence of the Media on Politics

9.1 Describe changes in the nature and extent of the political influence of the various news media, p. 283.

The news media include newspapers, magazines, radio, television, films, recordings, books, and electronic communications in all their forms. These means of communication have been called the "fourth branch of government," for they are a pervasive feature of U.S. politics. The media provide and carry information among political actors, the government, and the public.

The Changing Role of the U.S. News Media

9.2 Trace the evolution of the news media over the course of U.S. history, p. 290.

Our modern news media emerged from a more partisan and less professional past. Journalists today strive for objectivity and also engage in investigatory journalism. Corporate ownership and consolidation of media outlets raise questions about media competition and orientation. Radio and television broadcasting have changed the news media, and these are the sources from which most people get their news. The Internet has emerged as a new source of both information and political participation.

The Media and Public Opinion

9.3 Evaluate the media's influence on public opinion and attention, p. 296.

The mass media's influence over public opinion is significant but not overwhelming. People may not pay much attention to the media or may not believe everything they read, see, or hear. People tend to filter the news through their political socialization, selectivity, needs, and ability to recall or comprehend the news. Although conservatives charge that the media are too liberal and liberals charge that the media are captive to business interests, little evidence exists of actual, deliberate bias in news reporting. The media's influence is most strongly felt in their ability to determine what problems and events will come to the public's attention and how those issues are framed.

The Media and Elections

9.4 Describe the media's role in elections and the associated problems and benefits, p. 301.

Media coverage dominates presidential campaigns, and candidates depend on media exposure to build name recognition, a positive image, and thereby votes. Because of the way the media cover elections, most people seem more interested in the contest as a game or "horse race" than as a serious discussion of issues and candidates. Another effect of media influence has been the rise of image making and the media consultant.

The Media and Governance

9.5 Assess the media's relationship to governance in the United States, p. 306.

The press serves as both observer and participant in politics and as a watchdog, agenda setter, and check on the abuse of power, but it rarely gives much attention to the implementation or administration phases of the policy process. Exceptions include major mistakes such as the government's response to Hurricane Katrina.

Learn the Terms

Study and **Review** the **Flashcards**

mass media, p. 283
news media, p. 283
24/7 news cycle, p. 286
political socialization, p. 299
selective exposure, p. 299
selective perception, p. 299
horse race, p. 305

Test Yourself

Study and Review the Practice Tests

MULTIPLE CHOICE QUESTIONS

9.1 Describe changes in the nature and extent of the political influence of the various news media.

Programs like television's *Dateline* are examples of
- **a.** the mass media.
- **b.** the news media.
- **c.** sensationalism.
- **d.** the political media.
- **e.** conservative reporting.

9.2 Trace the evolution of the news media over the course of U.S. history.

One of the primary effects of FCC regulations has been
- **a.** a relaxation of rules regarding obscenity.
- **b.** the government imposed rating of cable television shows.
- **c.** media consolidation.
- **d.** fewer cable stations.
- **e.** less horse-race journalism.

9.3 Evaluate the media's influence on public opinion and attention.

The process by which individuals perceive what they want to in media messages is
- **a.** selective exposure.
- **b.** political alienation.
- **c.** selective perception.
- **d.** political socialization.
- **e.** media socialization.

9.4 Describe the media's role in elections and the associated problems and benefits.

As a result of increasing media coverage of presidential elections,
- **a.** voter turnout has greatly increased since 1960.
- **b.** candidate personality is more important to voters.
- **c.** political parties are much more important to presidential candidates.
- **d.** issues receive far more attention than poll results.
- **e.** newspapers have become American's primary source of news.

9.5 Assess the media's relationship to governance in the United States.

The media are more likely to portray Congress in a negative light than either the president or the courts because
- **a.** the Supreme Court is very accommodating to television news coverage.
- **b.** members of Congress are reluctant to grant interviews.
- **c.** it is more difficult to cover than either the president or the courts.
- **d.** all floor proceedings are secret.
- **e.** the committee structure forbids anyone other than chairs from communicating with the media.

ESSAY QUESTION

Trace the evolution of the news media over the course of U.S. history. How have changes in the nature and use of media influenced U.S. politics?

Explore Further

IN THE LIBRARY

Stephen Ansolabehere and Shanto Iyengar, *Going Negative: How Attack Ads Shrink and Polarize the Electorate* (Free Press, 1996).

R. Douglas Arnold, *Congress, The Press, and Political* Accountability (Princeton University Press, 2005).

Matthew Baum and Tim J. Groeling, *War Stories: The Causes and Consequences of Public Views of War* (Princeton University Press, 2010).

Keith Bybee, *Bench Press: The Collision of Courts, Politics, and the Media* (Stanford Law and Politics Press, 2007).

Andrew Chadwick and Philip N. Howard, eds. *Routledge Handbook of Internet Politics*, eds. (Routledge, 2009).

Jeffrey E. Cohen, *The Presidency in the Era of 24-Hour News* (Princeton University Press, 2008).

Richard Davis, *Typing Politics: The Role of Blogs in American Politics* (Oxford University Press, 2009).

Bob Franklin, ed., *Local Journalism and the Local Media: Making the Local News* (Routledge, 2006).

John G. Geer, *In Defense of Negativity: Attack Ads in Presidential Campaigns* (University of Chicago Press, 2006).

Doris A. Graber, *Mass Media and American Politics,* 8th ed. (CQ Press, 2009).

Tim Groseclose, *Left Turn: How Liberal Media Bias Distorts the American Mind* (St. Martins, 2011).

Roderick P. Hart, *Campaign Talk: Why Elections Are Good for Us* (Princeton University Press, 2002).

Matthew S. Hindman, *The Myth of Digital Democracy* (Princeton University Press, 2009).

Thomas A. Hollihan, *Uncivil Wars: Political Campaigns in a Media Age* (Bedford/St. Martin's, 2009).

Kathleen H. Jamison, *The Press Effect: Politicians, Journalists, and the Stories That Shape the Political World* (Oxford University Press, 2003).

Kathleen H. Jamison and Joseph N. Cappella, *Echo Chamber: Rush Limbaugh and the Conservative Media Establishment* (Oxford University Press, 2008).
David D. Perlmutter, *Blog Wars: The New Political Battleground* (Oxford University Press, 2008).
Donald A. Ritchie, *Reporting from Washington: The History of the Washington Press Corps* (Oxford University Press, 2006).
Cass Sunstein, *Republic.com 2.0* (Princeton University Press, 2007).
Darrell M. West, *Air Wars: Television Advertising in Election Campaigns, 1952–2008,* 5th ed. (CQ Press, 2009).

ON THE WEB

www.sunshineingovernment.org/
The Web site for the Sunshine in Government Initiative, which is a coalition of media groups that focus on ensuring open and accountable government.

www.mrc.org/public/default.aspx
The Web site for the Media Research Center, which calls itself "America's Media Watchdog." It is an attempt to try and balance news media, originally trying to correct a "liberal bias."

mediamatters.org/p/about_us/
The Web site for Media Matters for America, which tries to correct "conservative misinformation in the U.S. media."

www.prwatch.org/cmd/index.html
The Center for Media and Democracy Web site, which tries to investigate issues and inform the public as well as promote transparency and promote "open content" media.

www.spj.org/mission.asp
The website for the Society for Professional Journalists (SPJ) provides information on the mission of SPJ to foster a free and responsible press.

10

Listen to Chapter 10 on MyPoliSciLab

Congress
The People's Branch

The Framers created the legislative branch in the first section of the Constitution to make sure voters, which at the time meant only white males who owned property, had a strong voice in making the laws. The Framers also gave the legislative branch an extensive list of responsibilities for national policies, including the power to borrow money when the federal government does not have enough revenue to cover its spending. Although many states require their legislatures to produce a balanced budget every year, the federal government is allowed to run deficits paid through the sale of bonds called "Treasury notes," which are sometimes called "T-notes." Buyers of this federal debt are guaranteed a small interest rate in return for their purchases, which create federal "IOUs" that have to be repaid sooner or later.

As the federal budget grew beyond its revenues during the 2000s because of tax cuts and the cost of the wars in Iraq and Afghanistan, the federal debt grew dramatically. In 2001, the total federal debt was $5.6 trillion; by 2011, the total had more than doubled to nearly $14.3 trillion.[1] Again because only Congress has the power to borrow money, it was responsible for raising the debt ceiling, which is the total amount that the federal government is allowed to borrow. With the economic downturn still cutting into revenues, Congress was forced to decide how much more money to borrow to keep the federal government solvent.

The decision to raise the ceiling was extremely controversial. Congressional Democrats wanted a "clean" debt ceiling proposal without any spending cuts, while Republicans wanted deep budget cuts as part of the deal. The result was a desperate fight to allow more borrowing in time to keep the federal government from shutting down due to a lack of money.

The debate began early in 2011 when President Barack Obama asked Congress to raise the ceiling to more than $15 trillion, which was only enough to cover federal borrowing through early 2013. But with conservative Republicans in charge of the House, even a short-term increase in the debt ceiling was anything but certain. Republicans pledged not to approve any increase in borrowing without a package of cuts.

10.1 Describe the congressional election process and the advantages it gives incumbents, p. 315.

10.2 Differentiate the powers of Congress, and compare and contrast the structure and powers of the House and Senate, p. 320.

10.3 Compare and contrast the leadership systems used in the House and Senate, and explain how work is done through congressional committees, p. 322.

10.4 Identify the steps by which a bill becomes a law and the ways a bill can be stopped at each step, p. 329.

10.5 Characterize the two ways legislators represent their constituents, and identify the various influences on their votes, p. 333.

10.6 Evaluate the influence of citizens on the legislative process, p. 339.

On August 2, 2011, the Dow Jones went up on the New York Stock Exchange at the news of a deal to raise the debt ceiling.

The Big Picture Why is Congress' approval rating at an all-time low? Author Paul C. Light describes the phenomenon of polarization in American politics, which has made it increasingly difficult for Congress to accomplish anything, and he reveals why the Framers actually intended for Congress to slow things down.

The Basics Why do we have two houses of Congress? This video reveals the answer to this question and explores the differences are between the two houses in their organization and procedures. You will also learn how a bill becomes a law, how Congress is organized, and how members of Congress represent you.

In Context Discover the role that the Framers expected Congress to serve in the U.S. government. Columbia University political scientist Greg Wawro discusses how Congress has become more expansive in its powers. Listen as Greg Wawro also delves into the process of creating coalitions in Congress to achieve policy results.

Thinking Like a Political Scientist Why has the United States become more polarized in the last decade? Columbia University political scientist Greg Wawro examines this central question and explains why polarization may be correlated to the income gap between the wealthy and the poor. He also explores recent research on the Senate as a super-majoritarian institution.

In the Real World Congress today is the most divided it has been since the end of WWII. It is also the least effective. Is compromise the answer? Real people consider the benefits and the dangers of compromise, and they discuss issues—like abortion—where compromise seems impossible.

So What? What are the odds that a bill introduced in Congress will pass? Not very good. Author Paul C. Light examines the complex process a bill undergoes before it is brought to the president, and he gives answers on why politicians even bother proposing them in the first place.

Democrats and Republicans negotiated for months to find some common ground that would avoid a damaging default on Treasury notes. Some Republicans favored using the threat of a default as a way to force the president and his party to reduce federal spending. However, with the mid-summer deadline rapidly approaching, Democrats and Republicans began serious negotiations over the increase.

The impasse was resolved one day before the existing ceiling on federal borrowing would have forced a crippling default in paying the government's bills for programs such as Social Security, health care, medical research, and defense. Under the final agreement, the federal government had to cut spending by $1 trillion, with another $1 trillion to be generated by a newly created "Super Committee" composed of six members of Congress—three senators and three members of the House, equally divided by party.[2] Exercising his constitutional authority to sign into law or veto, President Obama signed the bill on August 2 at 2:00 p.m.

The Super Committee failed to reach an agreement on how to cut the deficit by the one trillion dollars mandated by its November 23 deadline. The stalemate triggered $1.2 trillion automatic cuts in both domestic and defense spending to be implemented by 2013, after the 2012 presidential election. Although Americans were angered by the bitter debate, Congress was actually performing just as the Framers intended—absent a national consensus on how to address complaints about big government and the sluggish economy, the Framers preferred stalemate to action.

In this chapter, we examine how the Framers designed the legislative branch to protect the nation against tyranny and how it actually works today. We will also explore the role of interest groups, colleagues, committees, leadership, congressional staff, the two parties, and the president in shaping decisions; discuss how a bill becomes a law; and explore the ethics issue in more detail.

Before turning to these questions, however, we will look at how members of Congress reach office in the first place. The way we elect members of the House and Senate has a great deal to do with how they behave once in office, and it influences everything from committee assignments to legislative interests. We will also ask why individual members of Congress win reelection so easily.

Readers should also note that the word "Congress" is used two ways in this book. When we put a number before the word "Congress," we are referring to the two years of congressional activity that begin on January 3rd of every odd-numbered year and end two years later after the next election when a new Congress convenes. Thus the 112th Congress was gaveled into session in 2011, exactly 226 years after the First Congress, and was followed by the 113th on January 3, 2013. When we use the word "Congress" without a number, however, we are referring to the legislative branch as a whole.

constituents
The residents of a congressional district or state.

Congressional Elections

10.1 Describe the congressional election process and the advantages it gives incumbents.

The Constitution created one Congress, but two very different chambers that check each other even as the institution as a whole checks the president and judiciary.

The most important difference between the House and Senate involves the term of office. Whereas all 435 House members serve for two years and stand for election at the same time, all 100 senators serve for six years and only a third stand for election at the same time. The Framers set these very different calendars to make House members more responsive to their **constituents** back home, while giving senators more insulation from factions.

House members and senators also run for their first elections under different age and residency rules. House members must be 25 years old at the time they take office and must have been citizens for seven years, whereas senators must be 30 years old and have

10.1

10.2

10.3

10.4

10.5

10.6

reapportionment
The assigning by Congress of congressional seats after each census. State legislatures reapportion state legislative districts.

redistricting
The redrawing of congressional and other legislative district lines following the census to accommodate population shifts and keep districts as equal as possible in population.

gerrymandering
The drawing of legislative district boundaries to benefit a party, group, or incumbent. There are two types of gerrymandering—*cracking*, which the majority party uses to break a strong minority party district into pieces to be merged with other districts, thereby reducing the minority party's strength in that one district, and *packing*, which merges pieces of the majority party in its weak districts into a single, strong district.

safe seat
An elected office that is predictably won by one party or the other, so the success of that party's candidate is almost taken for granted.

incumbent
The current holder of elected office.

been citizens for nine years. House and Senate candidates must be residents of the states from which they are elected, but House members do not need to reside in their district.

The Framers hoped that by setting the Senate's requirements higher, they would shape the Senate as a check against what they saw as the less predictable House. Concerned about the "fickleness and passion" of the House of Representatives, James Madison in particular saw the Senate as "a necessary fence against this danger."[3] This is why the Framers decided that senators would be selected by their state legislatures. Although the Constitution was amended in 1913 to require the direct election of all senators, governors appoint new senators to fill vacant seats, while special elections are used to fill vacant House seats.

☐ Drawing District Lines

The Framers of the Constitution set the Senate and the House apart in terms of the populations they serve. Every state has two senators, each of whom represents the entire state. Members of the House of Representatives, on the other hand, serve districts within their states. A state's population determines the number of districts—hence, states with more citizens have more districts, and big states clearly have more influence in the House.

The exact number of districts assigned to each state is determined by a national census of the population taken every 10 years, which is also specified in the Constitution. When the population changes, so does the potential number of districts or seats in each state. This process of changing the number of seats allotted to each state is called **reapportionment**. The Constitution gives the House responsibility for setting the number of seats in the chamber, which was originally set at 59 in 1789 and was eventually capped under the Seventeenth Amendment at 435 in 1913. Every census produces at least some change in the number of House seats assigned to the states as populations rise and fall. New York and Ohio each lost two seats after the 2010 census, eight states lost one, six states gained one, Florida gained two, Texas gained four, and the rest of the states held steady. These changes took effect in 2012. Small states such as South Dakota are guaranteed at least one House seat and two Senate seats, which gives every state at least three.

The Constitution gives states, not Congress, the power to draw House district lines for the number of seats within their borders. This process of converting the number of seats into districts is called **redistricting**.[4] Under the Constitution, state governments are responsible for determining the time, place, and manner of elections, which includes drawing district maps.

District lines can be drawn several ways to favor one party—a district can be "packed" with a large number of party voters, thereby diluting that party's strength in the districts next door, or a party stronghold can be spread over several districts, thereby possibly weakening that opposition party's strength in several districts. In extreme cases, this process is known as **gerrymandering**, a term dating to the early 1800s when Massachusetts governor Elbridge Gerry won passage of a redistricting plan that created a salamander-shaped district drawn to help his party win another seat.

☐ Advantages of Incumbency

It only takes one defeat to end a House or Senate career, which is why so many House members and senators work so hard to create safe seats. A **safe seat** is almost certain to be won by the current officeholder, or **incumbent**. It usually occurs in a district where one party has a clear majority of voters, virtually ensuring the election of the candidate from the dominant party. However, even safe seats can become competitive as happened in Massachusetts when a seat that had been held by Democratic Senator Ted Kennedy went to Republican Scott Brown in a special election after Kennedy's death in 2009.

Although there are still competitive seats in the House, most are considered invulnerable to challenge. Of 435 seats up for election in 2012, roughly 115 were considered competitive, while more than 300 were considered safe. In general, the vast majority of members who decide to run for reelection win handily. Even in the dramatic 2010 elections (see Figure 10.1), which returned the House to Republican control,

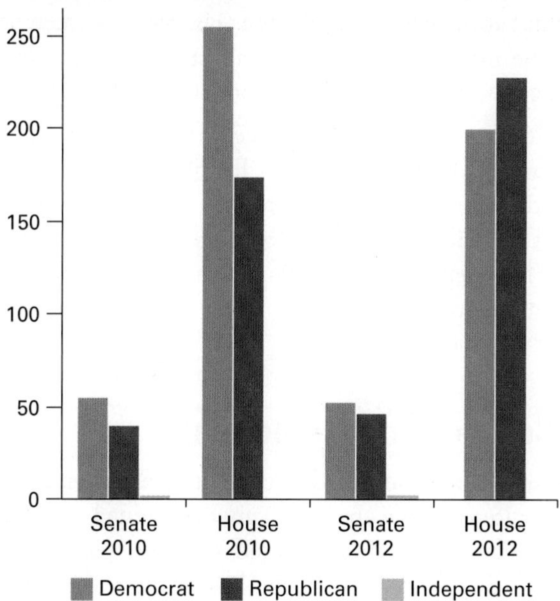

FIGURE 10.1 CONGRESSIONAL ELECTION RESULTS, 2010 AND 2012

How did the party balance of Congress change after the 2012 elections, and what effect, if any, will that have on how Congress functions?

NOTE: *House 2012 figure includes 7 Democrats and 2 Republicans who were leading their races as of November 8, but had not yet been declared winners.*

86 percent of incumbents won reelection, down from 94 percent in both 2008 and 2006. Although the incumbency advantage was only slightly below the average dating back to the 1960s, 52 of the 54 incumbents who lost were Democrats. Add in the number of competitive seats that went Republican, and the lower reelection rate was more than enough to elect 63 new Republicans to the House.

Conventional wisdom suggests that senators are more vulnerable to defeat than are their colleagues in the House. Where House incumbents often outspend their opponents by wide margins, Senate candidates are more evenly matched, in part because Senate elections are so visible nationally. With only one-third of the Senate up for reelection at any one time, the public can pay closer attention to campaign issues and advertisements, and the two parties can invest more money in their candidates.[5] But even senators are often reelected. Of the 33 Senate seats up for reelection in 2012, only 13 were generally considered competitive, leaving the other 20 safe.

Members of Congress seek reelection for many reasons, not the least of which is a relatively high salary compared to most Americans, generous health benefits, and retirement packages tied to length of service.[6] In addition, incumbents have a number of advantages that make them very hard to defeat.

- Incumbents help their constituents get their benefits from agencies such as the Social Security Administration, nominate students to West Point and the other military academies, provide internships to college students, and give constituents American flags that have been flown over the Capitol Building.
- Incumbents also maintain a visible presence back home through emails, letters, press releases, radio and television appearances, and active use of social media. Every member also has at least one district office to provide face-to-face contact, and does not pay any postage on mailings to constituents.
- Incumbents often use their committee and subcommittee positions to influence legislation to help their districts create jobs, build federal office buildings, build and repair roads and bridges, and support local businesses through federal loans. Most have greater "free media" access through newspapers and television than their opponents, especially on local or state issues, which produce very high name recognition in their districts.

earmarks
Special spending projects that are set aside on behalf of individual members of Congress for their constituents.

- Incumbents tend to be skilled candidates, having won many campaigns during their careers. The more elections they win, the better they are known, the more experienced they become, and the more connections they build.
- Incumbents also have substantial influence on federal spending for their districts through **earmarks**. Although Congress banned formal earmarks in late 2010, members can still urge federal agencies to spend money on special projects in their districts.[7] Most agencies are reluctant to ignore these suggestions, in part because future funding may depend on following what they see as the "will of Congress." Opponents of the earmark ban justify this practice as a legitimate way to give taxpayers a fair return on their taxes.[8]

☐ The 2012 Congressional Elections

The 2012 congressional elections produced plenty of excitement and several tight Senate races, but resulted in little change. Democrats added two seats to their Senate majority, Republicans lost seven. If the two independents caucus with the Democrats, the party has a 55–45 Senate majority in the 113th Congress, while Republicans have a 235–200 House margin.

At first glance, the congressional elections merely reinforced the status quo—Congress will remain divided against itself, and President Obama will face the same constellation of opposition from the House. Although Republicans clearly lost the election, they will still retain considerable power to frustrate the president's agenda, and block legislation in the House and Senate as the nation enters a desperate debate to prevent already scheduled tax increases and budget cuts in 2013. There were early expressions of bipartisan support for compromise on the continuing debt battles described at the start of the chapter, but the elements for partisan conflict over budget cuts and tax increases remained in place as the nation approached a "fiscal cliff."

If there was any absolute winner in the 2012 races, it was incumbency. By most counts, there were only 120 competitive House races for the 435 House seats. The Senate had more competitive races, but most incumbents coasted to easy victories. Most state legislatures used the redistricting process that began after the 2010 census to shore up safe seats for their parties, which limited the size of the battlegrounds across the country.

Money was also a winner in most cases. House incumbents who faced a challenger spent almost $6 for every $1 spent by their opponents, which clearly increased

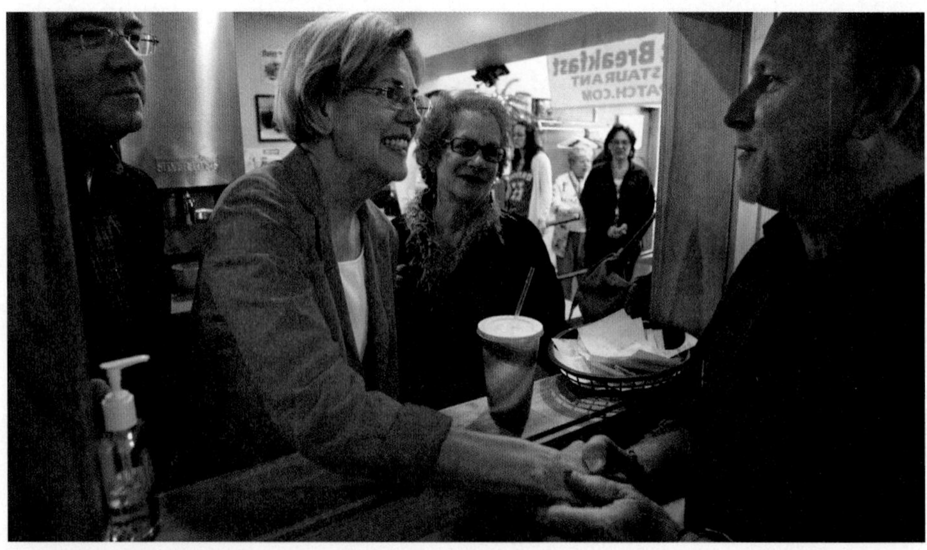

Democratic candidate for U.S. Senate Elizabeth Warren, center, greets Bruce Trotto, of Shrewsbury, Mass., during a campaign stop in 2012. Warren defeated incumbent Republican Senator Scott Brown by 8 percentage points.

OF the People Diversity in America

Members of the 112th Congress, 2011–2013

Although the Constitution does not mention race, gender, or wealth among the qualifications for office, the Framers expected members of Congress to be white male property owners. After all, women, slaves, and freed slaves could not vote, let alone hold office.

The Framers would therefore be surprised at the face of Congress today. Recent Congresses have had record numbers of women and minorities.

These numbers would not have increased without the rise of a new generation of women and minority candidates. Although voting participation by women and minority groups has increased dramatically throughout the past half-century, it took time for women and minority candidates to gain the experience to increase the odds of their winning office.

Although Congress is becoming more diverse by race and gender, it still remains very different from the rest of the United States in income and occupation. Nearly one-third of the senators who served in the 112th Congress are millionaires, and more than half hold law degrees. At the current rate of change in the number of women, for example, it will take another 400 years before women constitute a majority in the House. The demographic figures presented below do not reflect changes in the 2012 election, which were too fresh for analysis in this book.

QUESTIONS

1. How does increasing diversity change the issues that Congress works on? Should Congress reflect the levels of diversity in the U.S. population in order to best represent our citizenry?
2. Does increasing diversity help strengthen public approval of Congress?
3. Did the election of Nancy Pelosi as Speaker of the House make any difference in the power of the office or the overall performance of Congress?

Religion

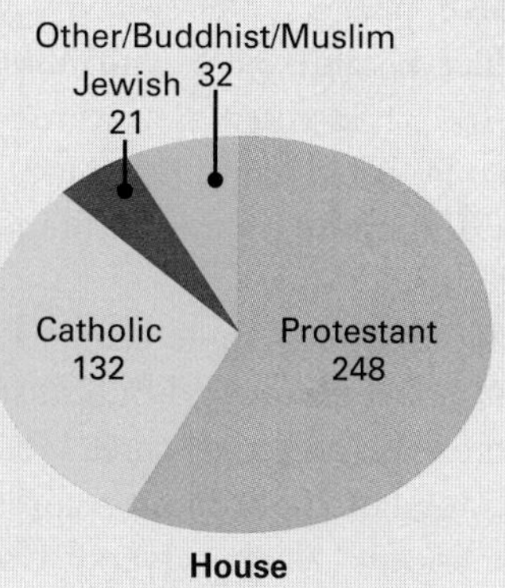

House

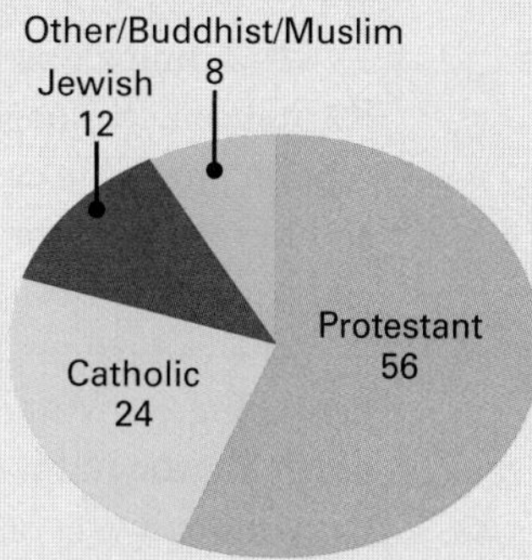

Senate

Race

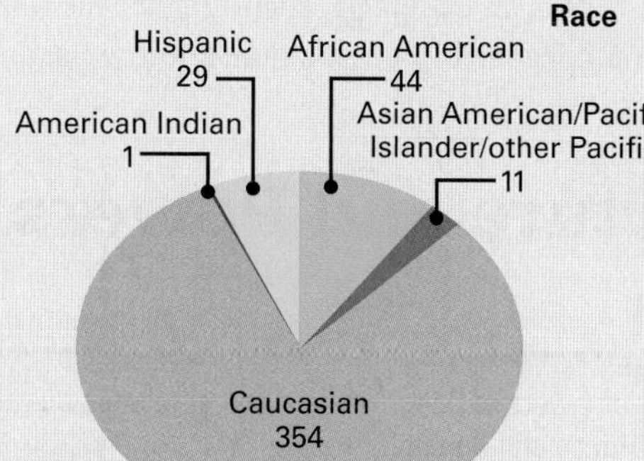

House

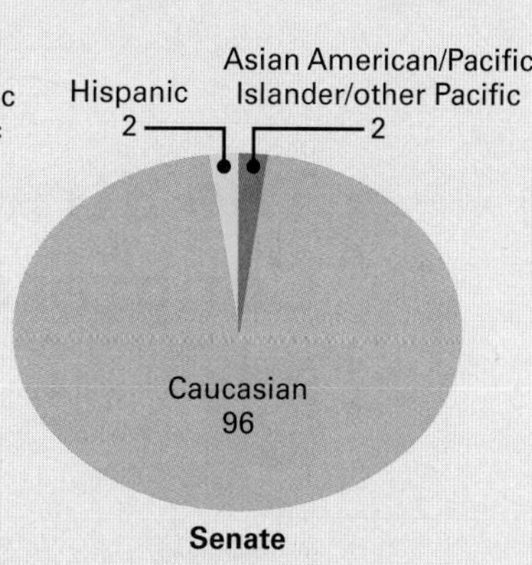

Senate

Gender

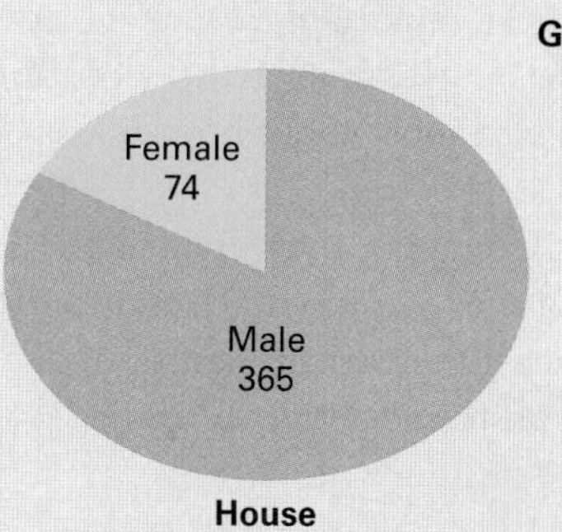

House

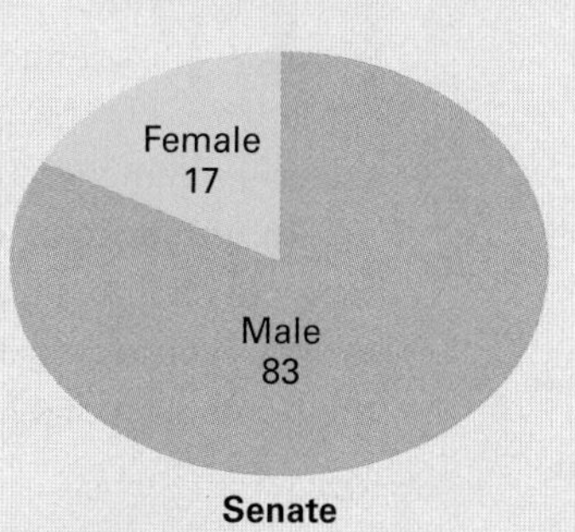

Senate

(continued)

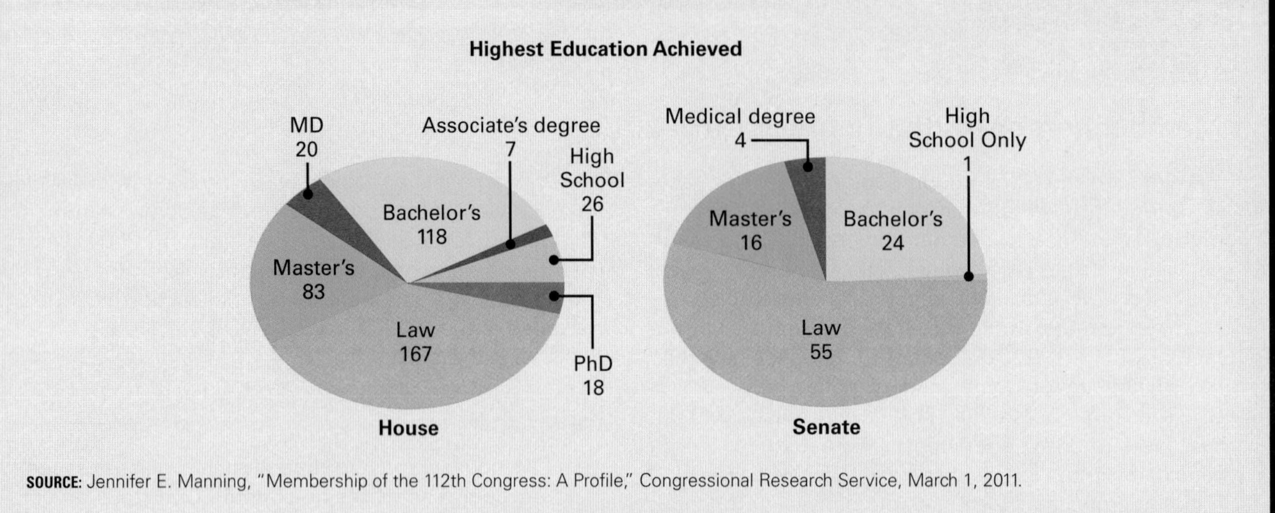

SOURCE: Jennifer E. Manning, "Membership of the 112th Congress: A Profile," Congressional Research Service, March 1, 2011.

the incumbency advantage. Money was no guarantee of success in the Senate, where the bigger spenders lost in 7 of the 10 most expensive races. Connecticut Republican challenger and former World Wrestling Federation chief Linda McMahon spent $40 million of her own money, yet still lost to Democrat Christopher Murphy, who did not spend a penny out of his own pocket.

The campaigns did produce notable gaffes and misstatements. Missouri Senate Republican challenger Todd Akin told voters that women could shut down the conception process in cases of what he called "legitimate rape," while Wisconsin challenger and former Governor Tommy Thompson promised voters that he would kill Medicare and Medicaid. Both candidates lost.

The campaigns also produced at least some changes in the demographics of the new Congress. Voters elected the first Hindu and Buddhist members of Congress, both of whom won in Hawaii. Women also picked up three House seats for a total of 79, and three more in the Senate for a total of 20. Both set records. Hispanics picked up three House seats, while African Americans lost one. Overall, Congress became slightly more diverse, and welcomed the first gay Senator, Wisconsin Democrat Tammy Baldwin. Despite more than $1 billion in campaign spending, it was a status quo election that left the House and Senate leadership unchanged, and the partisanship in place.

The Structure and Powers of Congress

10.2 Differentiate the powers of Congress, and compare and contrast the structure and powers of the House and Senate.

The Framers expected that Congress, not the president or the judiciary, would be the most important branch of government, which is why it is defined in the first article of the Constitution, Article I, Section 1. Hence, they worried most about how to keep Congress from dominating the other branches.

In an effort to control Congress, they divided the legislative branch into two separate chambers, the House of Representatives and the Senate, which would "be as little connected with each other as the nature of their common functions and their common dependence on the society will admit."[9]

A Divided Branch

bicameralism
The principle of a two-house legislature.

enumerated powers
The powers explicitly given to Congress in the Constitution.

Bicameralism, or a two-house legislature, remains the most important organizational feature of the U.S. Congress. Each chamber meets in its own wing of the Capitol Building; each has offices for its members on separate sides of Capitol Street; each has its own committee structure, its own rules for considering legislation, and its own record of proceedings (even though the records are published together as the *Congressional Record*); and each sets the rules governing its own members.[10] As James Madison explained in *The Federalist,* No. 51, "In order to control the legislative authority, you must divide it."

The Powers of Congress

The Framers gave Congress a long list of express or **enumerated powers**. Because the Revolutionary War had been sparked by unfair taxation, the power "to lay and collect Taxes" was the very first of these powers. Another 17 express powers of Congress fall into five basic categories:

1. **The Power to Raise, Make, and Borrow Money.** Congress has the power to tax, borrow money, issue currency, and coin money.
2. **The Power to Regulate Commerce.** Congress has the power to regulate commerce between the United States and other nations, as well as between the states. It can also set standards for determining the value of products through weights and measures, establish uniform bankruptcy laws that govern private businesses, and promote the arts and sciences by granting copyright protection to authors and patents to inventors.
3. **The Power to Unify and Expand the Country.** Congress has the power to create post offices and postal roads, which link the states together; to determine the rules for becoming a citizen; and to acquire, manage, and dispose of federal land.
4. **The Power to Prepare and Declare War.** Alongside the power to declare war, Congress can raise, support, and regulate armies and a navy; provide for organizing, arming, disciplining, and calling on the state militia (now called the National Guard); execute laws suppressing civil unrest; and repel foreign invasions.
5. **The Power to Create the Federal Judiciary.** Congress is responsible for creating all "inferior" courts below the Supreme Court and for determining their jurisdiction, as well as the appellate jurisdiction of the Supreme Court (discussed in the chapter on the judiciary).

Many of these powers are limited in some way, however. Congress has the power to collect taxes only for the common defense and general welfare of the nation, for example, and may not tax exports to other nations. Similarly, it may declare war, but only the president has the power to command the military.

The Framers also gave Congress implied powers such as the power to "make all Laws which shall be necessary and proper for carrying into Execution the foregoing Powers, and all other Powers vested by this Constitution in the Government of the United States, or in any Department or Officer thereof."

Finally, the Constitution gave Congress important checks on government, including the power to remove the president and judges from office through the impeachment process. The House has the authority to charge, or impeach, a president or judge for committing "high crimes and misdemeanors," but the Senate has the responsibility to conduct the trial to determine guilt or innocence. Impeachment requires a majority vote in the House, but conviction requires a two-thirds vote of the Senate.

The Constitution gives different duties to each chamber (see Table 10.1). The Senate has the power to give its advice and consent in confirming or rejecting the president's

Alcee Hastings was one of only seven federal judges ever impeached and removed from office by Congress. He was impeached for corruption by the House in 1988 and removed by the Senate in 1989. Hastings was elected to the House in Florida's 23rd district in 1992, and had served ten terms by 2012.

TABLE 10.1 DIFFERENCES BETWEEN THE HOUSE OF REPRESENTATIVES AND THE SENATE

House	Senate
Size	**Size**
435 members	100 Members
Elections	**Elections**
Two-year term	Six-year term
All seats are open for election every two years	One-third of seats are open for each election every two years
Elected in districts	Elected by states as a whole
Leadership	**Leadership**
Strong leadership controls action by individual members	Weaker leadership provides more freedom to individual members
More powerful committee leaders	More equal distribution of power among committee members
Legislation	**Legislation**
Decision to consider legislation made by majority; final decisions require a "rule" or ticket to the floor from the House Rules Committee	Decision to consider legislation made by unanimous consent of all members; one senator can stop action
Responsible for moving first on raising revenues	Responsible for giving advice and consent on presidential appointees and treaties
All amendments to legislation must be approved for consideration in advance of legislative action	Amendments are generally allowed
Debate	**Debate**
Strict limits on debate	Flexible limits on debate approved by unanimous consent
Single member or group of members cannot stop debate once the bill is approved for action by the Rules Committee	Single member can stop action through the filibuster

How are the rules for debate in the House and Senate related to their relative sizes and traditions?

nominees for senior executive branch positions and for the federal courts. The Senate also has the power to give its advice and consent in approving or rejecting treaties made by the president. All treaties must be ratified by a two-thirds vote in the Senate.

The House has its own responsibilities, too, most notably the power to author "all bills for raising revenues." But these powers are less significant than those given to the Senate, in part because the Framers worried that House members would be too close to the people and therefore more likely to act in haste. Although all revenue bills must originate in the House, for example, the Constitution invites the Senate to propose amendments to revenue bills, sometimes to the point of changing every sentence except the title.

Congressional Leadership and Committees

10.3 Compare and contrast the leadership systems used in the House and Senate, and explain how work is done through congressional committees.

Given the differences between the chambers that are summarized in Table 10.1, we should not be surprised that the House and Senate have different kinds of leadership and rules. Whereas the House holds tight control over its large number of members, the Senate has much looser controls. This makes legislation easier to pass in the House and much more difficult in the Senate.

FOR the People Government's Greatest Endeavors

Building a Strong Defense

The United States spends more money on defense than any other nation in the world. In 2013 alone, the nation will spend more than $500 billion on defense. The Department of Defense, which houses all the military services, has invested heavily in sophisticated technologies that make the nation almost impossible to defeat in a traditional war. It is not clear, however, that these technologies assure that the nation can win a war against the kind of deeply committed insurgents that fought the United States in Iraq and Afghanistan.

Presidents support a strong national defense, but Congress is responsible for authorizing the spending. Defense spending is spread across most of the states, and many congressional districts and congressional incumbents eagerly seek spending in their districts. The interests of the nation and individual members of Congress can merge, as they did in 2011 when members agreed to cut defense spending during the debt ceiling debate discussed at the beginning of this chapter. Defense spending remains difficult to cut, however, in part because so many members of Congress represent districts that house defense industries.

Even with further cuts, however, Congress continues to fund a long list of programs that may make soldiers safer on the battlefield. The Defense Department is increasingly using unmanned drone aircraft to launch long-range attacks against targets, and it has designed a variety of high-technology tools to survey the battlefield. Nevertheless, the military has been highly susceptible to the unsophisticated improvised explosive devices that were used in Iraq and Afghanistan, suggesting that strengthening our defense for new kinds of war still needs to be a top priority.

QUESTIONS

1. **Why do many members of Congress support high levels of defense spending?**
2. **Does the military buy the right equipment or the equipment that is right for political support?**
3. **How does U.S. defense spending affect global views of our nation?**

☐ Leading the House of Representatives

The House of Representatives has a more powerful leadership system the Senate, in large part because it has so many more members with much shorter terms of office. It is arguably easier to guide 100 senators who serve six-year terms and enter office one-third at a time than 435 House members who serve two-year terms and enter office at the same time. As a result, House leaders have more power to control the actions of their members than do Senate leaders.

Speaker
The presiding officer in the House of Representatives, formally elected by the House but selected by the majority party.

THE SPEAKER OF THE HOUSE The **Speaker** of the House is generally viewed as the single most important member of Congress. Selected by the majority party and ratified by the House as a whole, the Speaker has enormous power to reward and punish individual members, set the legislative agenda, influence congressional campaigns, and control the flow of particularly controversial floor debates. Members of both parties are free to challenge the Speaker's decisions, but do so at their own electoral peril. The Speaker is also the next in line for the presidency in the event that both the president and vice president are unable to fulfill their constitutional duties.[11]

It is important to note, however, that the Speaker is more powerful when the majority party is unified, which Speaker John Boehner (R-OH) quickly discovered when he tried to lead his new Republican majority after the 2010 elections. In theory, the party's large majority should have given Boehner significant power. In reality, his Tea Party members were unwilling to compromise with him on the debt ceiling increase. In turn, he was unable to compromise with the Democrats and the president, and was widely viewed as a Speaker without a following.

THE PARTY CAUCUS The House makes many of its most important decisions when Democrats and Republicans meet, or caucus separately. Candidates who are elected as independents must decide whether to caucus with the Democrats or Republicans, thereby declaring their allegiance, if not absolute loyalty, to one or the other.

10.1

party caucus
A meeting of the members of a party in a legislative chamber to select party leaders and to develop party policy.

10.2

majority leader
The legislative leader selected by the majority party who helps plan party strategy, confers with other party leaders, and tries to keep members of the party in line.

10.3

minority leader
The legislative leader selected by the minority party as spokesperson for the opposition.

10.4

10.5

whip
The party leader who is the liaison between the leadership and the rank-and-file in the legislature.

10.6

The Global Community

How the World Views the Need for Strong Leaders

Citizens around the globe are often frustrated by the democratic barriers to fast decisions on threats to their future whether coming from inside or outside their countries. These frustrations are particularly intense during times of great economic stress and war. Angry at the political stalemates they often see in their legislatures, many citizens come to believe that they need stronger leaders even at the price of less democracy. Although democracies can move fast in the face of danger, they are also capable of deadlock as different factions fight over ways to solve problems.

The desire for democracy can also increase during periods of great domestic turmoil of the kind the world witnessed during the "Arab Spring," which began in late 2010 with riots in Tunisia, Egypt, Libya, Yemen, and Syria.

The proportion of the public in these countries that favored democracy over a strong leader grew dramatically between 2007 and 2011 according to the Pew Research Center's Spring 2011 Global Attitudes Survey. Anger over the lack of democratic rights and the actions of oppressive leaders motivated many citizens to demand new and more democratic governments.

In the Palestinian Territories created after the 1967 war between Israel and its Arab neighbors, the percentage of citizens who favor democratic government jumped from just 36 percent before citizen pressure for independence and the Arab Spring to 56 percent. In Egypt, where the riots took place in 2010–2011, the number increased from 50 percent to 64 percent.*

These preferences for democracy have been more stable in other nations, however. According to the Pew Research Center's 2010 survey of a limited number of countries, most global citizens reject the preference for strong leaders. These attitudes are strongest in Western Nations especially in Europe where 82 percent of the French, 79 percent of Germans, 78 percent of Spaniards, and 81 percent of citizens in the Czech Republican preferred democratic government. In contrast, only 29 percent of Russians felt the same.**

CRITICAL THINKING QUESTIONS

1. **Why might democratic governments be slower in reacting to economic difficulties than other systems of government?**
2. **What factors might affect a nation's preferences for strong political leaders?**

*Pew Research Center, *Obama's Challenge in the Muslim World: Arab Spring Fails to Improve U.S. Image*, (May 17, 2011), p. 65.

**Unfortunately, the Pew Research Center had not released similar information on the rest of the world by the time this book went to press.

Each **party caucus** plays its most important role when it selects the party's leaders at the start of a two-year Congress. However, each caucus also exerts significant influence when controversial legislation reaches the floor. The majority party caucus wields more power because it selects the Speaker, approves the basic organization of its chamber, approves the committee list, and sets the number of majority and minority members on each committee. The minority party caucus can be almost as influential if it can enforce the party line on key votes.

OTHER HOUSE LEADERS The majority party also selects the **majority leader**, who helps plan party strategy, confers with other party leaders, and tries to keep members of the party in line. The minority party elects the **minority leader**, who usually becomes Speaker when his or her party gains a majority in the House. Both parties also select **whips** who help "whip up" votes for or against specific legislation. The majority and minority whips are generally given a list of members to keep in line on particularly controversial votes.

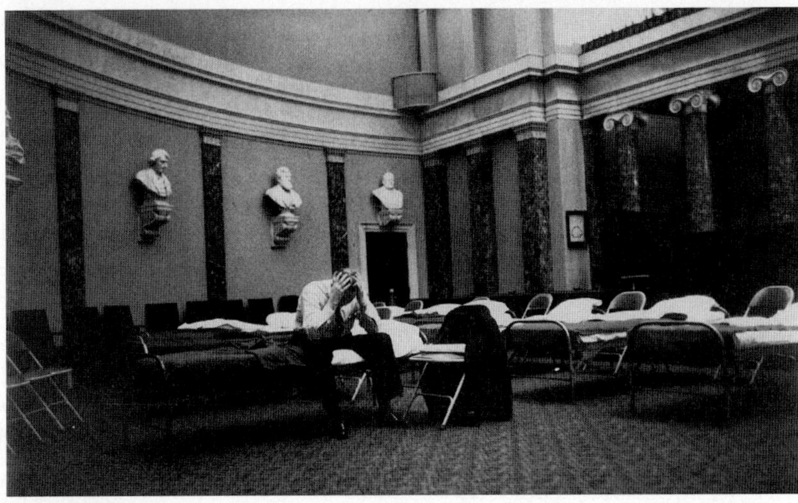

Old-fashioned filibusters went through the night. Here, a senator sits on his cot awaiting action to break a filibuster on the Civil Rights Act in March 1964. Today, the threat alone of a filibuster can require that legislation has a supermajority in order to pass.

closed rule
A procedural rule in the House of Representatives that prohibits any amendments to bills or provides that only members of the committee reporting the bill may offer amendments.

open rule
A procedural rule in the House of Representatives that permits floor amendments within the overall time allocated to the bill.

president pro tempore
An officer of the Senate selected by the majority party to act as chair in the absence of the vice president.

THE HOUSE RULES COMMITTEE The House Rules Committee is almost certainly the most powerful committee in either chamber. Under the much tighter rules that govern the larger House, the Rules Committee decides the rules governing the length of the floor debate on any legislative issue and sets limits on the number and kinds of floor amendments that will be allowed. By refusing to grant a *rule,* which is a ticket to the floor, the Rules Committee can delay consideration of a bill. A **closed rule** prohibits amendments altogether or provides that only members of the committee reporting the bill may offer amendments; closed rules are usually reserved for tax and spending bills. An **open rule** permits debate within the overall time allocated to the bill.

Leading the Senate

The Senate has the same basic committee structure, elected party leadership, and committee-based power as the House, but because the Senate is a smaller body, its procedures are more informal, and it permits more time for debate. It is a more open, fluid, and decentralized body now than it was a generation or two ago. Indeed, it is often said that the Senate has 100 separate power centers and is so splintered that party leaders have difficulty arranging the day-to-day schedule.[12]

The Senate is led by the Senate majority leader, who is elected by the majority party. When the majority leader is from the president's party, the president becomes the party's most visible leader on Capitol Hill and in the nation as a whole. However, when the majority leader and the president are from different parties, the Senate majority leader is considered his or her party's national spokesperson. Senator Harry Reid (D-NV) was elected as Senate majority leader in 2007 after Democrats persuaded the two Independents to help create a majority. Although that majority grew to 60 votes in 2009, it dropped to just a handful of seats after the 2010 midterm elections. Reid barely retained his seat after a tough reelection campaign against a well-financed opponent.

Although the majority leader has great authority, a Senate floor debate is actually led by a **president pro tempore**, usually the most senior member of the majority party. Presiding over the Senate on most occasions is a thankless chore, so the president pro tempore regularly delegates this responsibility to junior members of the chamber's majority party. The vice president is responsible for breaking tie votes and controlling debate in those situations.

Party machinery in the Senate is similar to that in the House. Each Senate party meets in caucus at the start of a new Congress, each selects its own leadership, and each

10.1

10.2

10.3

10.4

10.5

10.6

filibuster

A procedural practice in the Senate whereby a senator refuses to relinquish the floor and thereby delays proceedings and prevents a vote on a controversial issue.

cloture

A procedure for terminating debate, especially filibusters, in the Senate.

standing committee

A permanent committee established in a legislature, usually focusing on a policy area.

special or select committee

A congressional committee created for a specific purpose, sometimes to conduct an investigation.

joint committee

A committee composed of members of both the House of Representatives and the Senate; such committees oversee the Library of Congress and conduct investigations.

has a policy committee that helps set the legislative agenda. In the Senate, the party policy committees help the leadership monitor legislation and provide policy expertise. Moreover, the Senate's rules allow individual senators to offer amendments on virtually any topic to a pending bill, occasionally allowing them to delay passage of a bill long enough to prevent passage.[13]

Individual senators also have the power to engage in unlimited debate, known as the **filibuster**, which was invented in the 1830s. A filibuster allows any individual senator to delay Senate proceedings by holding the floor continuously, thereby preventing action. Filibusters often begin with an individual senator issuing a legislative hold, putting a stop to all action. At one time, the filibuster was a favorite weapon of southern senators for blocking civil rights legislation.

Cloture is the Senate's only formal method for ending a filibuster. Once a motion to end debate is approved by 60 senators, cloture imposes a strict limit on further debate and prohibits any senator from speaking for more than an hour.

Despite the Senate's tradition of long debates, the number of successful cloture votes has actually increased in recent decades as the chamber has confronted a surge in filibuster threats on seemingly trivial issues. There were just four successful cloture votes during the 1960s, for example, but 174 between 2001 and September 2012.[14]

☐ Congressional Committees

Committees are where much of the work is done in Congress. They draft legislation, review nominees, conduct investigations of executive branch departments and agencies, and are usually responsible for ironing out differences between House and Senate versions of the same legislation.

TYPES OF COMMITTEES In theory, all congressional committees are created anew in each new Congress. But most continue with little change from Congress to Congress. **Standing committees** are the most durable and are the sources of most bills and are sometimes called full committees, whereas **special or select committees** come together to address both short-term and long-term issues such as investigating the September 11th terrorist attacks, but they rarely author legislation. **Joint committees** have members from both the House and the Senate and exist either to study an issue of interest to the entire Congress or to oversee congressional support agencies such as the Governmental Accountability Office.

Of the various types of committees, standing committees are the most important for making laws and representing constituents, and they fall into six types: (1) rules and administration, (2) budget, (3) authorizing, (4) appropriations, (5) revenue, and (6) oversight. (See Table 10.2.)

1. ***Rules and Administration Committees*** Rules committees in both chambers determine the basic operations of their chamber—for example, how many staffers individual members get and what the ratio of majority to minority members and staff will be. The House Rules Committee has more power than its Senate counterpart largely because it controls the only path to the floor. The House cannot vote on any bill unless it comes to the floor with a rule, while the Senate has a much more flexible process.
2. ***Budget Committees*** The House and Senate have one budget committee each. Budget committees were created as permanent standing committees in 1974 to give each chamber greater information and discipline on the overall federal budget. They set broad targets for spending and taxes at the start of each session of Congress and push authorizing and appropriations committees to follow those guidelines as they work on legislation.
3. ***Authorizing Committees*** Authorizing committees pass the laws that tell government what to do. The House and Senate education and labor committees, for example, are

TABLE 10.2 CONGRESSIONAL STANDING COMMITTEES, 2011–2013

House	Senate
Rules Committees	**Rules Committee**
House Administration	Rules and Administration
Rules	
Budget Committees	**Budget Committees**
Budget	Budget
Authorizing Committees	**Authorizing Committees**
Agriculture	Agriculture, Nutrition, and Forestry
Armed Services	Armed Services
Education and the Workforce	Banking, Housing, and Urban Affairs
Energy and Commerce	Commerce, Science, and Transportation
Financial Services	Energy and Natural Resources
Foreign Affairs	Environment and Public Works
Homeland Security	Foreign Relations
Judiciary	Health, Education, Labor, and Pensions
Natural Resources	Indian Affairs
Science, Space, and Technology	Judiciary
Small Business	Small Business and Entrepreneurship
Transportation and Infrastructure	Veterans' Affairs
Veterans' Affairs	
Appropriations Committees	**Appropriations Committees**
Appropriations	Appropriations
Revenue Committees	**Revenue Committees**
Ways and Means	Finance
Oversight Committees	**Oversight Committees**
Oversight and Government Reform	Homeland Security and Governmental Affairs

responsible for setting rules governing the federal government's student loan programs, including who can apply, how much they can get, where the loans come from, what the interest rate will be, and how defaults are handled. Authorizing committees are also responsible for reviewing past programs that are about to expire. In the Senate, they also hold confirmation hearings for the president's political appointees.

4. ***Appropriations Committees*** Appropriations committees make decisions about how much money government can spend on authorized programs. Although there is only one appropriations committee in each chamber, each appropriations committee has one subcommittee for each of the 13 appropriations bills that must be enacted each year to keep government running. Even if an authorizing committee sets a large amount of money for a specific program, the appropriations committee actually decides the final amount, which is sometimes less.
5. ***Revenue Committees*** Revenue and budget committees deal with raising the money appropriating committees spend. Because it exists to raise revenues through taxes, the House Ways and Means Committee is one of the most powerful committees in Congress, for it both raises and authorizes spending. Although the appropriations committee determines how much is spent on specific programs, the Ways and Means Committee is the only committee in either chamber that can originate tax and revenue legislation. It is also responsible for making basic decisions on the huge Social Security and Medicare programs.
6. ***General Oversight Committees*** There are two major oversight committees in Congress: the House Oversight and Government Reform Committee and the Senate Homeland Security and Governmental Affairs Committee. Both committees have wide latitude to investigate the performance of government. They are also free to authorize programs for fixing government-wide management problems.

10.1

10.2

10.3

10.4

10.5

10.6

seniority rule
A legislative practice that assigns the chair of a committee or subcommittee to the member of the majority party with the longest continuous service on the committee.

conference committee
A committee appointed by the presiding officers of each chamber to adjust differences on a particular bill passed by each in different form.

Ohio Republican John Boehner became Speaker of the House in 2011 following the Republican takeover of the House in the 2010 midterm elections. Boehner was known as a moderate for most of his career, but soon found himself under great pressure from conservative Republicans who wanted deep cuts in government spending.

CHOOSING COMMITTEE MEMBERS Each political party controls the selection of standing committee members. Because some committees are more prestigious than others, the debate over committee assignments can be intense. These committees control more important programs or more money and give their members important advantages in helping their home districts.

Each party in each chamber is responsible for selecting its committee members. House Republicans use their Committee on Committees to make the selections, House Democrats use their Steering and Policy Committee, Senate Republicans use their Steering Committee, while Senate Democrats use their Steering Committee. The selections may take place in different committees, but they are all based on what the party needs and what its members want. The majority party selects the chair of each committee, while the minority party selects the ranking member.

Most committee chairs are selected on the basis of the **seniority rule**; the member of the majority party with the longest continuous service on the committee becomes chair on the retirement of the current chair or a change in the party in control of Congress. The seniority rule lessens the influence of states or districts where the two parties are more evenly matched and where there is more turnover.[15]

THE SPECIAL ROLE OF CONFERENCE COMMITTEES Given the differences between the House and the Senate, it is not surprising that the version of a bill passed by one chamber may differ substantially from the version passed by the other. Only if both houses pass an absolutely identical measure can it become law. Most of the time, one house accepts the language of the other, but approximately 10–12 percent of all bills passed, usually major ones, must be referred to a **conference committee**—a special committee of members from each chamber that settles the differences between versions.[16] Both parties are represented on conference committees, but the majority party is given more slots to fill. The two party leaders make the final choice of their separate slates of committee members.

MEMBER CAUCUSES In contrast to the party caucuses that Congress uses to select its leaders, member caucuses are informal groups of senators and/or House members that come together to promote shared legislative interests such as the arts, arthritis, children, defense, immigration, tax reform, women's rights, veterans, and a host of industries such corn, lumber, rice, shellfish, and steel.

Officially called *Congressional Member Organizations*, member caucuses do not have any authority to review legislation or make legislative decisions, but they do provide an opportunity for members to show their support for specific ideas. As of April 2012, there were almost 300 member caucuses in Congress, many of which were bipartisan.[17]

10.1
10.2
10.3
10.4
10.5
10.6

Members of the Black Caucus often meet to decide what its members should do on particular issues. From left, Maxine Waters, Emanuel Cleaver, and John Conyers, members of the Congressional Black Caucus. The most visible member caucuses in Congress are built around race and ethnicity.

How a Bill Becomes a Law

10.4 Identify the steps by which a bill becomes a law and the ways a bill can be stopped at each step.

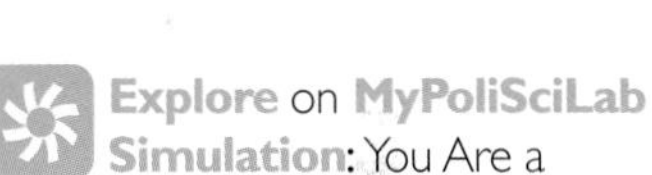

Explore on MyPoliSciLab Simulation: You Are a Consumer Advocate

Congress operates under a system of multiple vetoes. The Framers intentionally dispersed powers so that no would-be tyrant or majority could accumulate enough authority to oppress the nation. Follow a bill through the legislative process, and there are dozens of ways it can be killed. Only approximately 1 out of 10 bills even receives minimal attention. By election day in 2012, members of the House and Senate had introduced 4,700 bills, but passed only 83.[18]

How Ideas Become Bills

Most members come to Washington to make a difference for their party and country. Members of Congress clearly care about national issues such as education, energy, the economy, and foreign policy. In choosing ideas for legislation, they often secure long-standing reputations as leading thinkers far into the future. Fifteen years after leaving the Senate, Wyoming Republican Alan Simpson remains an active and highly visible advocate of reducing the national deficit, joining many other former members of the House and Senate in providing a strong voice in national policy.

How Bills Become Laws

A bill must win many small contests on the way to final passage, and most die well before they reach the floor of either chamber. According to the "resume" of action published each year by Congress, members of the House and Senate only considered 413 of the bills and resolutions that were sent to the House or Senate in the second session of the 112th Congress. Although every last one was sent to a committee for review, only 415 were reported by committees to the House or Senate as a whole, of which

Former Republican Senator Alan Simpson joined a small group of former members of Congress who continue to influence major decisions long after they leave office. Called "elder statesmen" by some, they often work together across party lines to build compromises that office-holders cannot.

just 558 were passed, and, again, only 83 were signed into law by the president.[19] The odds against passage have increased dramatically over the decades largely because of increasing party conflict in Congress.

A bill must survive many tests to reach the president's desk for final signature: (1) introduction, which means putting a formal proposal before the House or the Senate, (2) referral to a committee for further review, (3) committee and subcommittee review, (4) committee and subcommittee "mark up" of the bill before it goes to the floor, (5) floor debate and passage, which means getting on the legislative calendar, passing once in each chamber, surviving a conference to iron out any differences between the House and Senate versions, and passing in each chamber, and (6) presidential approval. These steps are summarized in Figure 10.2.

INTRODUCING A BILL House members introduce a bill by placing it into a mahogany box (called the *hopper*) on a desk at the front of the House chamber; senators introduce a bill by either handing it to the clerk of the Senate or by presenting it to their colleagues in a floor speech. In the more informal Senate, members sometimes short-circuit the formalities by offering a bill as an amendment to pending legislation. A bill that comes from the House is always designated H.R. (House of Representatives) followed by its number, and a bill from the Senate is always designated S. (Senate) followed by its number. Presidents have no authority to introduce legislation, although they recommend many proposals that are in turn introduced as possible legislation by legislators.

THE REFERRAL DECISION Once a bill has been introduced in either chamber, it is read into the daily congressional record as a formal proposal and referred by the House or Senate parliamentarian to a specific committee—tax bills to Ways and Means or Finance; farm bills to Agriculture; technology bills to Science, Space, and Technology; small business to Small Business; and so forth. The committee often refers the bill to a specific subcommittee.

COMMITTEE AND SUBCOMMITTEE REVIEW Most bills go to committees and are never heard from again. However, at least some are subject to committee and subcommittee hearings, and eventual passage. In general, committees pass these proposals down to highly specialized subcommittees, which make the first move toward passage. Once finished with their review, subcommittees send their bills back up to the full committee for another round of hearings and review. This step is the most likely point at which bills are killed—hearings are only held on the most important legislation. Committees and subcommittees only have so much time to review bills, and must choose which ones to consider.

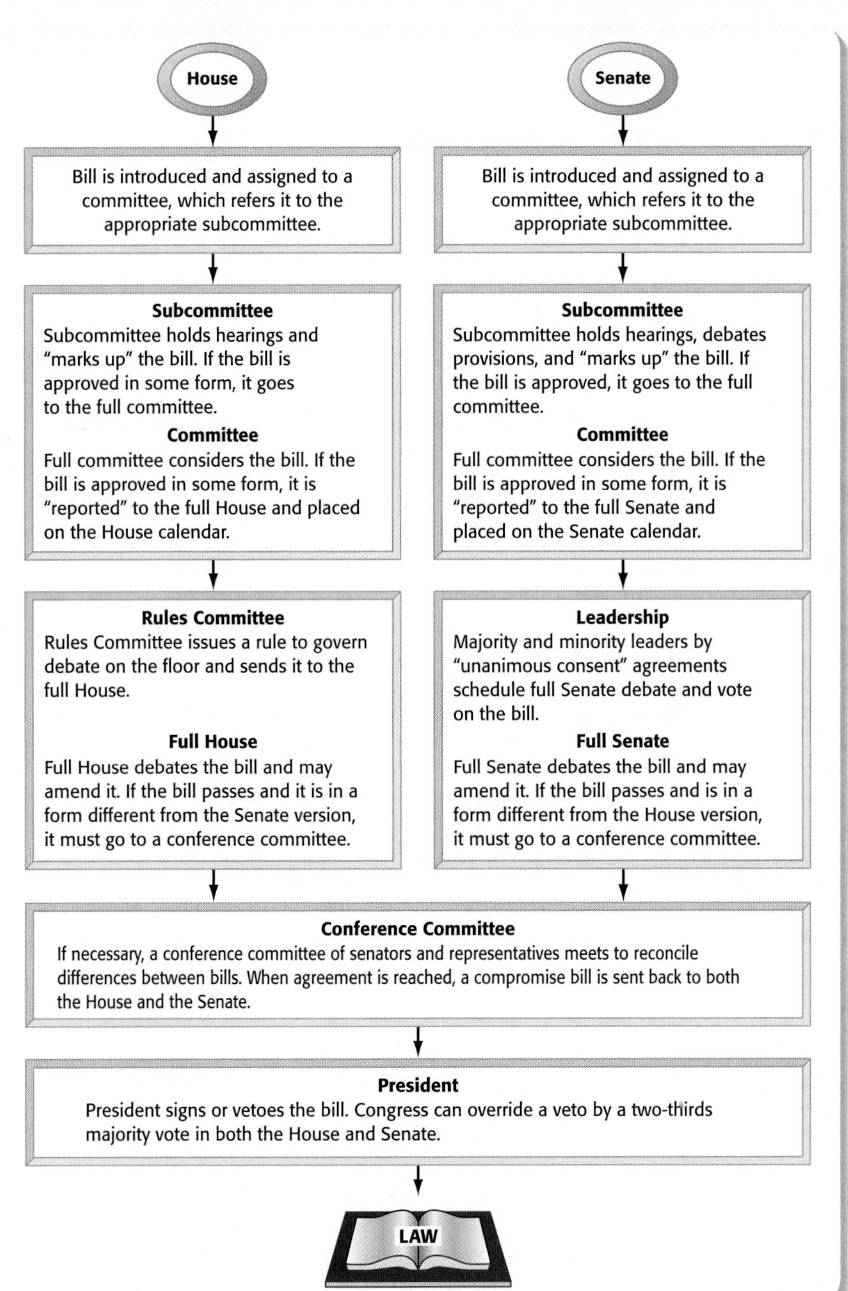

FIGURE 10.2 HOW A BILL BECOMES A LAW

Analyzing this legislative process, why is it so much easier for a bill to be killed than passed?

MARKUP Once a committee or subcommittee decides to pass the bill, it "marks it up" to modify or amend its version of the bill. The term *markup* refers to the pencil marks that members literally make on the final version of the bill before it is typed into the text.

Once markup is over, the bill must be passed by the committee or subcommittee and forwarded to the next step in the process. If it is passed by a subcommittee, for example, it is forwarded to the full committee; if it is passed by a full committee in the House, it is then forwarded to the House Rules Committee for a rule that will govern debate on the floor; if it is passed by a full committee in the Senate, it is forwarded to the full chamber.

DISCHARGE Most bills die in committee without a hearing or further review, largely because the majority party simply does not favor action. However, a bill can be forced to the floor of the House through a **discharge petition** signed by a majority of

10.1

10.2

10.3

10.4

10.5

10.6

You Will Decide

Should Congress Create a College Football Playoff?

The 112th Congress had many issues on its agenda in 2012, including unemployment, the debt ceiling, health care reform, and ending the wars in Iraq and Afghanistan. But as with other congresses in history, it also had time for less important bills. In December 2009, Representative Joe Barton (R-TX) introduced a bill to require the National Collegiate Athletic Conference to create a national football playoff.

Barton was incensed that the undefeated Texas Christian University football team, champion of the Mountain West Conference, had been excluded from the Bowl Championship Series (BCS) championship game in 2009. He was supported by members of the Western Athletic Conference, who were also outraged that the undefeated Boise State team from their conference had been excluded as well.

Barton's bill was quite simple. It prohibited any person to promote, market, or advertise a post-season NCAA Division I football bowl game as a championship or national championship game unless it was the final game of a single elimination post-season playoff system for which *all* NCAA Division I schools are eligible.

Under his "College Football Playoff Act," Baron asked Congress to find that college football games involve and affect interstate commerce, and therefore Congress had the constitutional power to act on the issue, and the economic reasons to protect non-BCS schools.

The bill was referred to the House Committee on Energy and Commerce, which referred it down to the Subcommittee on Commerce, Trade, and Consumer Protection. Although the bill was marked up for full committee consideration, it died at the end of the 111th Congress.

The idea was far from dead, however. Only days after the BCS picked undefeated Louisiana State University the University of Alabama for the 2012 national championship game, Barton reintroduced his bill with Tennessee Democrat Steve Cohen as a cosponsor. At the same moment, a group of supporters launched the "We Want a Playoff Now" campaign to provide lobbying muscle. Although the bill is highly unlikely to pass, Barton's legislation put pressure on college football to act on its own. It did so in 2012 by creating a new playoff system involving four teams selected through the BCS ranking system.

What do you think? Should Congress create a college football playoff? What are the arguments for and against this?

Thinking It Through

Barton was clearly serious about the legislation, as was a newly created political action committee called Playoff PAC, which funded an advertisement supporting a national playoff that aired during halftime of the TCU–Boise State game on Monday, January 4, 2010. (The commercial can be viewed at www.youtube.com/user/Playoff PAC.) Moreover, the public was sympathetic to the proposal. According to a December 2009 Quinnipiac University Poll, 63 percent of Americans approved of a new playoff system.

However, many members of Congress objected to using scarce legislative time for such a seemingly trivial issue. "With all due respect," Representative John Barrow (D-GA) told Barton, "I really think we have more important things to spend our time on." As for the public, despite support for a national playoff, nearly half also said that they did not think Congress should resolve the issue.

The case for reform was well made—most pundits and members of Congress wanted a BCS playoff involving four or eight teams. So did President Obama, who endorsed the idea only weeks after he won the 2008 election.

Furthermore, Congress can handle multiple issues, big and small, at the same time, especially because most bills pass with minimal debate or controversy. As Representative Bobby Rush (D-IL) said, "We can walk and chew gum at the same time."

CRITICAL THINKING QUESTIONS

1. **Should Congress take on issues such a national college playoff game?**
2. **Does the playoff bill help or hurt Congress's reputation among the American public?**
3. **Should the president have made any comments on the bill? Did his support help or hurt the bill given that Barton was a Republican member of Congress?**

*Hatch was quoted by realclearsports.com on February 8, 2011.

SOURCE: ESPN.com, (December 9, 2009). "Subcommittee OKs college playoff bill." From http://sports.espn.go.com/espn/print?id=4727426&type=story.

the membership. Because most members share a strong sense of reciprocity, or mutual respect toward other committees, House discharge petitions are rarely successful. The Senate does not use discharge petitions.

FLOOR DEBATE AND PASSAGE Once reported to the full chamber directly from committee in the Senate or through the Rules Committee in the House, a bill would usually be scheduled for floor action or dropped entirely. Having come this far, most bills are passed into law.

Final passage sometimes comes at a very high price, however, especially for spending bills. Although House members must accept the terms of debate set by the House Rules Committee, senators often attach **riders**, or unrelated amendments, to a bill, either to win concessions from the sponsors or to reduce the odds of passage. Sponsors can also use riders to sweeten a bill and improve the odds of passage.

PRESIDENTIAL APPROVAL Once a bill has passed both houses in identical form, it is inscribed on parchment paper and hand-delivered to the president, who may *sign* it into law or *veto* it. If Congress is in session and the president waits ten days (not counting Sundays), the bill becomes law *without* his signature. If Congress has adjourned and the president waits ten days without signing the bill, it is defeated by what is known as a **pocket veto**. After a pocket veto, the bill is dead. Otherwise, when a bill is vetoed, it is returned to the chamber of its origin by the president with a message explaining the reasons for the veto. Congress can **override** the veto by a two-thirds vote in each chamber, but assembling such an extraordinary majority is often difficult.

discharge petition
A petition that, if signed by a majority of the members of the House of Representatives, will pry a bill from committee and bring it to the floor for consideration.

rider
A provision attached to a bill—to which it may or may not be related—in order to secure its passage or defeat.

pocket veto
A veto exercised by the president after Congress has adjourned; if the president takes no action for ten days, the bill does not become law and is not returned to Congress for a possible override.

override
An action taken by Congress to reverse a presidential veto, requiring a two-thirds majority in each chamber.

10.1 10.2 10.3 10.4 10.5 10.6

The Job of the Legislator

10.5 Characterize the two ways legislators represent their constituents, and identify the various influences on their votes.

Membership in Congress was once a part-time job. Senators and Representatives came to Washington for a few terms, averaged less than five years of continuous service, and returned to private life. Pay was low, and Washington was no farther than a carriage ride from home.[20]

Congress started to meet more frequently in the late 1800s, pay increased, and being a member became increasingly attractive.[21] In the 1850s, roughly half of all House members retired or were defeated at each election; by 1900, the number who left at the end of each term had fallen to roughly one-quarter; by the 1970s, it was barely a tenth. Even in the 1994 congressional elections, when Republicans won the House majority for the first time in 40 years, 90 percent of House incumbents who ran for reelection won.[22]

As members of Congress became attached to their careers, they began to abandon many of the norms, or informal rules, that once guided their behavior in office.[23] The old norms were simple. Members were supposed to specialize in a small number of issues (the norm of specialization), defer to members with longer tenure in office (the norm of seniority), never criticize anyone personally (the norm of courtesy), and wait their turn to speak and introduce legislation (the norm of apprenticeship). As longtime House Speaker Sam Rayburn once said, new members were to go along in order to get along, and to be seen and not heard.

☐ Legislators as Representatives

Congress has a split personality. On the one hand, it is a *lawmaking institution* that writes laws and makes policy for the entire nation. In this capacity, all the members are expected to set aside their personal ambitions and perhaps even the concerns of their own constituencies.

Explore on MyPoliSciLab

Can Congress Get Anything Done?

A government cannot operate without a budget, revenue, or appropriations. But over the past thirty years, members of Congress have grown so polarized that they cannot agree on a budget or much of anything else. Polarization occurs when members of both parties move away from the moderate middle and share increasingly less common ground. Since 2001, Congress failed to pass a budget eight times, succeeding only in approving temporary budgets to keep government running. As the parties grow more polarized, Congress is less able to pass a permanent budget and the national debt increases.

Party Polarization

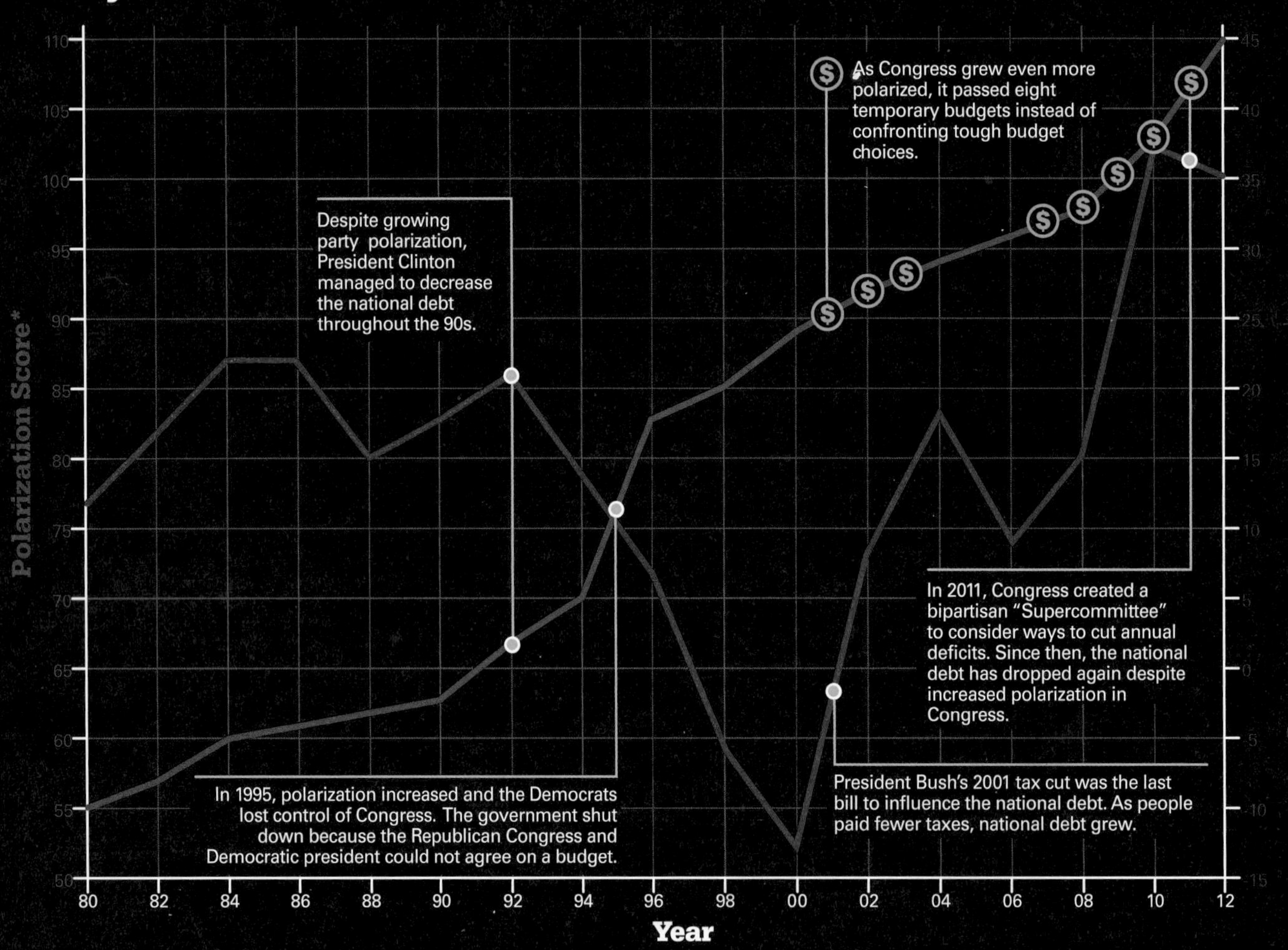

*** Polarization is measured as the distance between the two parties' ideological scores as computed from data at Voteview.com.**
SOURCE: Data from Voteview and the U.S. Government Accountability Office.

Investigate Further

Concept What is political polarization? Polarization occurs when members of both political parties consistently vote along ideological lines. Political scientists track polarization because it has nearly doubled in the past thirty years, and it tends to impede the government's ability to function.

Connection Is polarization related to greater annual debt? On a yearly basis, polarization is largely independent of the debt incurred by the United States—notice, for example, during the Clinton presidency how polarization grew even as debt decreased. However, as a long-term trend, both national debt and polarization in Congress do increase together.

Cause Does polarization impede Congress's ability to create annual budgets? Yes. The more polarized Congress becomes, the more likely the disagreements over permanent budget solutions lead to temporary resolutions that barely stave off government shutdown.

Individual members of Congress perceive their roles differently. Some believe they should serve as **delegates** from their districts, finding out what "the folks back home" want and acting accordingly. The word "delegate" refers to a member who tries to do what constituents want. Other members see themselves as **trustees** to act and vote based on what they think is best for their district, state, and country, even if their constituents oppose that position.

Most legislators shift back and forth between the delegate and trustee roles, depending on their perception of the public interest, their standing in the last and next elections, and the pressures of the moment. Most also view themselves more as free agents than as instructed delegates for their districts. And recent research suggests they often *are* free to vote as they please. Although approximately half of citizens do not know how their representatives voted on major legislation, most still believe their representative voted with the district or state. Moreover, members of Congress spend a great deal of time helping their constituency, reaching out to swing voters, and worrying about how a vote on a controversial issue will "play" back home.[24] However, members of Congress are often very different from their constituents—at least in recent years, they have been more educated than most Americans and are much more likely to be white males. They have also been more likely to be former bankers and lawyers, and almost half came to Congress with experience as state legislators, mayors, congressional staffers, government appointees, or campaign aides.

delegate
An official who is expected to represent the views of his or her constituents even when personally holding different views; one interpretation of the role of the legislator.

trustee
An official who is expected to vote independently based on his or her judgment of the circumstances; one interpretation of the role of the legislator.

logrolling
Mutual aid and vote trading among legislators.

attentive public
Citizens who follow public affairs closely.

□ Making Legislative Choices

As noted, thousands of bills are introduced in the House and Senate during a two-year congress, but only a small fraction receives committee or subcommittee consideration. Although House members and senators cast 1,000 votes each year, most are voice votes on noncontroversial matters.[25] Because members pay attention to different factors depending on the bill at hand, they vote on the basis of a long list of varying influences that are presented in alphabetical order next.

COLLEAGUES Their busy schedules and the great number of votes force legislators to depend on the advice of like-minded colleagues and close friends in Congress. In particular, they look to respected members of the committee who worked on a bill.[26]

A member may also vote with a colleague in the expectation that the colleague will later vote for a measure about which the member is concerned—a practice called **logrolling**, meaning that members trade among themselves to get the legislation (log) moving. Some vote trading takes place to build coalitions so that members can "bring home the bacon" to their constituents. Other vote trading reflects reciprocity in congressional relations or deference to colleagues' superior information or expertise.

CONGRESSIONAL STAFF The complexity of the issues and increasingly demanding schedules created a demand for additional congressional staff. Because both chambers have roughly equal amounts of money for staff, the 100 senators and their committees have much larger staffs than their 435 House counterparts. Many congressional staffers work in district and state offices back home, one of the advantages incumbents enjoy over challengers.

CONSTITUENTS Members of Congress rarely vote against the strong wishes of most of their constituents, but they often think their constituents are more interested in a particular issue than they really are.[27] Representatives mostly hear from the **attentive public**—meaning citizens who follow public affairs closely—rather than the general public. Members of Congress are generally concerned about how they will explain their votes, especially as election day approaches. Even if only a few voters are aware of their stand on a given issue, this group may make the difference between victory and defeat.

polarization
The extent to which liberals and conservatives occupy the more extreme positions on the liberal–conservative ideological spectrum.

IDEOLOGY Members of Congress are influenced by their own experiences and attitudes about the role of government.[28] Ideology is closely related to a member's party as a predictor of congressional voting, but political party is not a perfect predictor of ideology.

In 1994, for example, moderate and conservative Democrats created the "Blue Dog Coalition" to work for budget cuts and increased defense spending. Members called themselves "blue dogs" because they felt they had been "choked blue" by liberals in their party. By 2012, the coalition had 25 members, including some of the most senior members in the House. The coalition also had enough votes to force major compromises on a long list of legislative proposals, including the economic stimulus package and health care reform.

Ideology can also be measured by studies of actual votes that calculate the percentages of liberals and conservatives in both chambers. Although both chambers of Congress have become slightly more conservative over the past two decades, the House has moved further to the right. The House was more liberal when Democrats were in control during the 1980s and early 1990s, but became much more conservative after Republicans took control in the 1994 midterm elections, and even more conservative after Republicans took control again in the 2010 election.

This conservative shift is part of a general movement toward more **polarization** in Congress, which is the extent to which liberals and conservatives disagree with each other. Polarization is partially driven by the reapportionment process discussed earlier in this chapter. Safe seats in Congress tend to produce more ideological battles during the primary process, which tend to give party activists more say in who runs for office. Because these activists tend to be more ideological than voters in general elections, their candidates also tend to be more extreme. Moderate members of Congress face more opposition in the primaries, and are therefore less likely to be elected. As a result, the gulf between the two parties in Congress has widened.

INTEREST GROUPS Interest groups influence the legislative process in many ways. They make contributions to congressional campaigns, testify before committees, provide information to legislative staff, and build public pressure for or against their cause. Congressional lobbying has existed since the early 1800s and is a perfectly legal exercise of the First Amendment right to petition government.

Interest groups often cancel each other out by taking opposing positions on issues, thereby killing a bill. Some of this maneuvering occurs at the subcommittee level and is almost invisible to the public. But it is always visible to the interest groups themselves

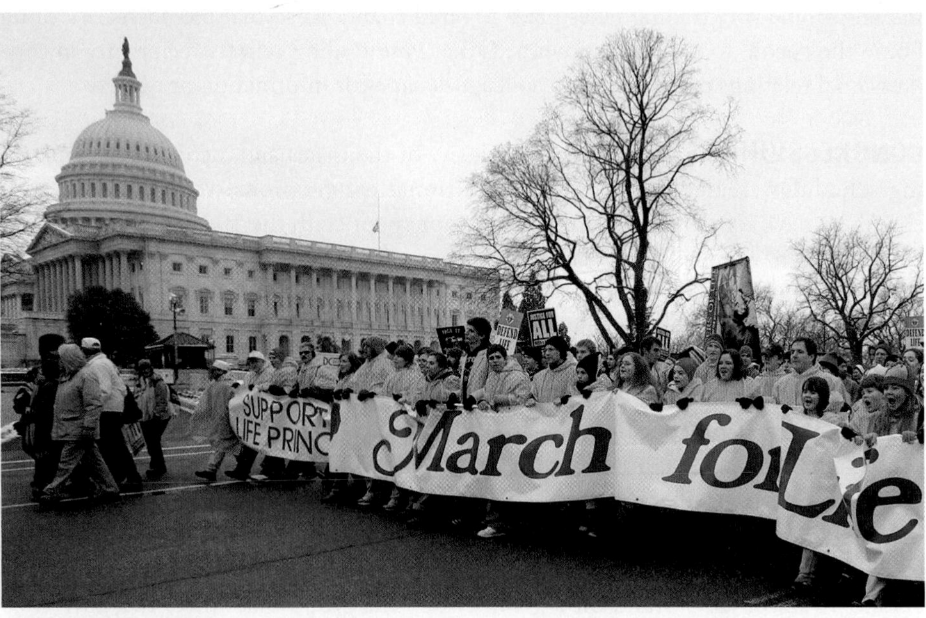

Constituents and interest groups often put pressure on Congress in person. Every January, opponents of abortion march on Washington.

and to Congress. "The result," Senator Joe Lieberman (I-CT) said before he retired in 2012, "is that everyone on Capitol Hill is keeping a close eye on everyone else, creating a self-adjusting system of checks and balances."[29]

PARTY Members generally vote with their party. Whether as a result of party pressure or natural affinity, on major bills, most Democrats tend to be arrayed against most Republicans. Partisan voting increased in the House after the early 1970s and intensified even more since the 1994 elections. Indeed, party-line voting has been greater in recent years than at any time in recent decades, in part because each party has become more liberal or more conservative. Since 2000, nearly 90 percent of congressional Democrats and Republicans have voted with their party on key votes, compared with less than 70 percent on average during the 1970s, and less than 80 percent in the 1980s.[30]

THE PRESIDENT Presidents wield a variety of tools for influencing Congress, not least of which is the ability to distribute government resources to their friends. Presidents also help set the legislative agenda through their annual State of the Union Address, the budget, and assorted legislative messages, and they lobby Congress on particularly important issues.

When asked why they vote one way or the other, members of Congress tend to deny the president's influence. Presidents work hard to influence public opinion, and they have a long list of incentives to encourage congressional support, not the least of which are invitations to special White House dinners and federal grants to support key projects back home.

☐ Congressional Ethics

Under the Constitution, Congress is responsible for disciplining its own members. Although individual members are subject to federal prosecution for bribery and other criminal acts, the House and Senate set the more general rules for ethical conduct and investigate all complaints of misbehavior.

Members of Congress have never been under greater scrutiny regarding their conduct, in part because recent years have witnessed a parade of members accused and even convicted of trading their votes for cash and other gifts. "Super-lobbyist" Jack Abramoff admitted in 2006 that he had given several members of Congress free golfing trips, meals, and concert tickets in direct violation of congressional ethics rules.

Under new rules enacted in September 2007, members of Congress may not accept any gifts or meals from any lobbyist. Although they can accept free admission at large meetings, conventions, discussions, and events where admission is free to other members, they may not accept free travel from any lobbyist.[31]

In addition, members may not accept any payment for making a speech, attending an event, or writing an article. Although they may accept free travel and expenses for making speeches and attending events, such travel must be related to their official duties as a member of Congress and publicly reported. These rules also apply to lobbyists, who may not offer gifts, free attendance, or travel.

Finally, under the Stock Act of 2012, members of Congress may not make any stock trades in their portfolios after learning about changes in the state of the economy or new federal action before the public knows. According to an analysis of stock portfolios, several leaders of Congress and chairmen of key financial committees made 166 stock trades in response to early warnings of either good or bad news from key administration officials and the Federal Reserve Board.[32]

The House and Senate enforce the rules through separate ethics committees (the House Committee on Standards of Official Conduct and the Senate Ethics Committee). Because the seats on both committees are equally divided between Democrats and Republicans (four on each side in the House, and three on each side in the Senate), and are filled through the normal committee selection process, members are under tremendous pressure not to hurt their own party.

10.1
10.2
10.3
10.4
10.5
10.6

BY the People Making a Difference

Staying in Touch with Congress

There are many ways that citizens can stay connected to Congress and their members, not the least of which are traditional means such as attending town hall meetings, sending letters, and voting.

More recently, however, members have started to use social networks such as Facebook to cultivate support and raise money. Some have even set up Twitter sites to keep their constituents informed on their work. As of January 2010, 19 members of the Senate and 51 members of the House were tweeting regularly with a mix of big and small news. They seem to accept TweetCongress.org's new version of the preamble to the Constitution:

> We the Tweeple of the United States, in order to form a more perfect government, establish communication, and promote transparency do hereby tweet the Congress of the United States of America.

Congressional staffers are paying attention. They keep track of hits for their boss, summarize tweets, and provide advice on how to reach out more effectively to the kinds of people who tweet or use Facebook.

Citizens can make a difference through social media on Facebook, too. Roughly two-thirds of Senators and members of the House now have Facebook pages that are loaded with photos, statements, YouTube videos, and links to their committee work. Search as you might, however, you will not find the typical lists of friends and will only rarely find friend activity posts. You will not find too many likes either, though almost all congressional Facebook walls have Twitter feeds.

Much deeper Facebook information can be found on the Congress page as a whole. Most government agencies have Facebook pages, and the politics page leads to a news stream on elections and links to a long list of resources.

The best available information suggests that these sources of information for following Congress and policy issues make a difference. According to one recent count, 36 percent of social-media users have changed their opinions of someone based on political content posted to Facebook or Twitter.* The effects are difficult to measure in terms of votes, but the social media are a force in politics, which is why members of Congress are paying attention.

QUESTIONS

1. **Is social networking a new form of political participation? How might it affect congressional elections?**
2. **Is tweeting an effective platform for sharing political ideas? What about Facebook?**
3. **What is the quality of information you have found on Twitter and Facebook? What makes it so influential, and what are the dangers of that influence?**

Rep. Brad Miller, D-N.C., checks his Facebook page in his office in the Longworth House Office Building.

*These figures come from http://mashable.com/2011/11/21/social-media-politics/

Citizens can play an important role in monitoring congressional ethics, starting with careful monitoring of lobbying expenditures and campaign contributions. One of the best ways to get this information is from the Center for Responsive Politics, which operates a Web site at opensecrets.org. The Web site contains detailed information on what individual members of Congress spent on their campaigns, where the money came from, and how much they received from political action committees. The site also provides information on how much lobbyists spend each year trying to influence Congress. According to the Center, corporations, interest groups, and even universities and colleges spent $2.5 billion on lobbying in 2011, up from $1.4 billion in 1996. The U.S. Chamber of Commerce was the top spender from 1996-2011 at $414 million, followed by General Electric at $103 million. To find out what your college or university spent on lobbying, visit the Web site at http://www.opensecrets.org/lobby/top.php?indexType=s and type in your college or university's name under client.

An Assessment of Congress

10.6 Evaluate the influence of citizens in the legislative process.

More than two centuries after its creation, Congress is a larger and very different kind of institution from the one the Framers envisioned. It has become much more complex, more polarized, and much more active. Although most incumbents are easily reelected, most campaign constantly to stay in office, creating what some observers have called the "permanent campaign."[33] Members appear driven by their desire to win reelection, so that much of what takes

The FBI found $90,000 in bribes mixed in with the frozen food in Louisiana Rep. William Jefferson's freezer. He was indicted for corruption, convicted, and sentenced to 13 years in federal prison in 2011 in what the prosecutor called "the most extensive and pervasive pattern of corruption in the history of Congress."

place in Congress seems mainly designed to promote reelection. These efforts usually pay off: we have seen that those who seek reelection almost always win.

This *permanent campaign* also affects legislative progress. In an institution in which most members act as individual entrepreneurs, the task of providing institutional leadership is increasingly difficult. With limited resources, and only sometimes aided by the president, congressional leaders are asked to bring together a diverse, fragmented, and independent institution. The congressional system acts only when majorities can be achieved. The Framers clearly accomplished their original objective in creating a legislature that would rarely move quickly.

Citizens often complain about the lack of action, which is one reason why public approval of Congress is low. But citizens can play a role in speeding Congress up by demanding action from their own members. As discussed above, even incumbents worry about losing elections. Indeed, as of August 2012, only 10 percent of Americans approved of the way Congress was handling its job (See Figure 10.3 for the recent trend in public approval for Congress as measured by the Gallup Poll over the past two decades).

Much of the public's recent discomfort with Congress involves the intense conflict surrounding major legislation such as health care reform and the debt ceiling. But the public is also angry that Congress has been unable to fix the economy. Americans are more favorable toward both Congress and the president when the economy is running smoothly, but they become frustrated when their political leaders cannot reach agreement during national crises. However, much of the frustration reflects the Framers' design. Congress was designed not to work efficiently, and has been doing so very well. The question remains whether Congress has become so polarized that it is failing to do its job in addressing domestic and international threats. Many Americans undoubtedly believe the answer is yes, especially if they have lost their job or are having trouble paying their bills.

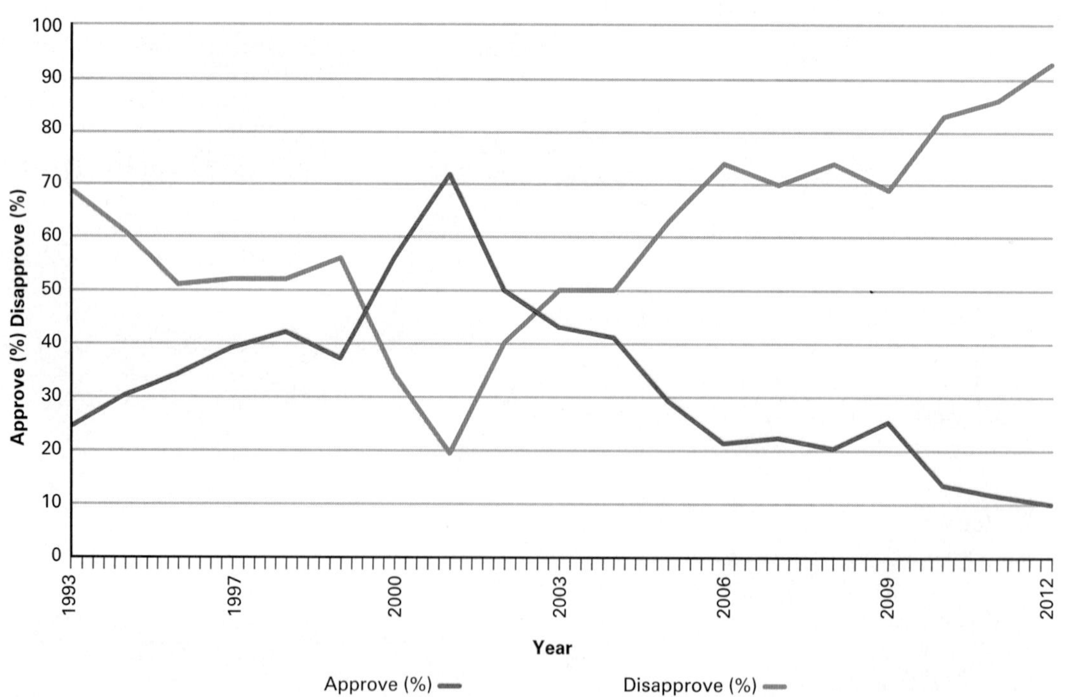

FIGURE 10.3 PUBLIC APPROVAL OF CONGRESS, 1997–2010

When were some of the highest and lowest points in Congressional approval? What reasons can you think of to explain these levels?

SOURCE: Gallup polls summarized by pollingreport.com at http://pollingreport.com

On MyPoliSciLab

Review the Chapter

 **Listen** to **Chapter 10** on **MyPoliSciLab**

Congressional Elections

10.1 Describe the congressional election process and the advantages it gives incumbents, p. 315.

The congressional election process requires decisions about who can run for office, when they run, and how long they serve. Most House elections concern local issues, whereas Senate elections are more likely to be about national concerns. Incumbents enjoy a variety of protections, including name visibility and the ability to send mail and other messages back home free of charge, to help constituents, and to raise money.

The Structure and Powers of Congress

10.2 Differentiate the powers of Congress, and compare and contrast the structure and powers of the House and Senate, p. 320.

Congress has express powers, implied powers, and checks and balances. The most important powers are the power to borrow and make money, regulate commerce, unify the country, declare and fund war, and create the inferior federal courts.

The most distinctive feature of Congress is its bicameralism, which the Framers intended as a moderating influence on partisanship and possible error. The House has the power to propose legislation to raise revenue, whereas the Senate has the power to confirm presidential appointees (by a majority vote) and ratify treaties (by a two-thirds vote).

Congressional Leadership and Committees

10.3 Compare and contrast the leadership systems used in the House and Senate, and explain how work is done through congressional committees, p. 322.

The House is led by the Speaker, a majority and a minority leader, and whips in each party, whereas the Senate is led by a majority and a minority leader. The Senate is more difficult to lead because of its greater individualism, sometimes expressed through the use of holds and filibusters to control the legislative process.

Most of the work in Congress is done in committees and subcommittees, which are classified into six types: (1) rules and administration, (2) budget, (3) appropriations, (4) authorizing, (5) revenue, and (6) oversight. Authorizing committees author all legislation, whereas appropriations committees spend the money needed to implement the legislation.

How a Bill Becomes a Law

10.4 Identify the steps by which a bill becomes a law and the ways a bill can be stopped at each step, p. 329.

A bill moves through a difficult process to become a law, if ever it becomes a law at all—an idea must first be converted into a proposal, then be introduced and referred to a committee, receive a hearing and markup, and move to the floor. Although all formal bills are referred to committees for consideration, very few receive a hearing, even fewer are marked up and sent to the floor, and fewer still are enacted by both chambers and signed into law by the president. In addition, the legislative obstacle course sometimes includes filibusters, riders, holds, and the occasional override of a presidential veto.

The Job of the Legislator

10.5 Characterize the two ways legislators represent their constituents, and identify the various influences on their votes, p. 333.

Legislators must balance the needs of their constituents against the national good. In addressing constituent needs, they often act as representatives of public opinion in their home districts. In addressing national issues, they often act as trustees of the greater good. Members must balance these two roles.

Members of Congress vote on the basis of a long list of varying influences that include their colleagues, constituents, staff, ideology, their party, and the president. These influences vary in strength from issue to issue.

An Assessment of Congress

10.6 Evaluate the influence of citizens on the legislative process, p. 339.

Citizens can influence Congress in many ways, not the least of which is voting in midterm elections. They can also use a variety of methods to express their opinions, including Facebook and Twitter. And they register their concerns about the lack of progress on big issues such as health care through public opinion surveys and their level of congressional approval.

Learn the Terms

 **Study** and **Review** the **Flashcards**

constituents, p. 315
reapportionment, p. 316
redistricting, p. 316
gerrymandering, p. 316
safe seat, p. 316
incumbent, p. 316
earmarks, p. 318
bicameralism, p. 321
enumerated powers, p. 321
Speaker, p. 323
party caucus, p. 324
majority leader, p. 324
minority leader, p. 324
whip, p. 324
closed rule, p. 325
open rule, p. 325
president pro tempore, p. 325
filibuster, p. 326
cloture, p. 326
standing committee, p. 326
special or select committee, p. 326
joint committee, p. 326
seniority rule, p. 328
conference committee, p. 328
discharge petition, p. 333
rider, p. 333
pocket veto, p. 333
override, p. 333
delegate, p. 335
trustee, p. 335
logrolling, p. 335
attentive public, p. 335
polarization, p. 336

Test Yourself

 **Study** and **Review** the **Practice Tests**

MULTIPLE CHOICE QUESTIONS

10.1 Describe the congressional election process and the advantages it gives incumbents.

Which of the following are not incumbency advantages?
- **a.** Helping constituents receive government benefits.
- **b.** Maintaining high public approval by visiting the district often.
- **c.** Issuing press releases on recent accomplishments for the district.
- **d.** Attending special events hosted by the president at the White House.
- **e.** Helping constituents with personal problems.

10.2 Differentiate the powers of Congress, and compare and contrast the structure and powers of the House and Senate.

The following powers were given to Congress under the Constitution
- **a.** the power to manage executive departments and agencies.
- **b.** the power to declare war.
- **c.** the power to negotiate foreign treaties.
- **d.** the power to confirm the president's nominees for ambassadorships.
- **e.** the power to convene a special session of Congress.

10.3 Compare and contrast the leadership systems used in the House and Senate, and explain how work is done through congressional committees.

The most powerful leader on Capitol Hill is
- **a.** the president.
- **b.** the Speaker of the House.
- **c.** the Senate majority leader.
- **d.** the president pro tempore.
- **e.** the party whip.

10.4 Identify the steps by which a bill becomes a law, and the most important way a bill can be stopped.

The best time to kill a bill is
- **a.** when a bill is referred to committee.
- **b.** when a committee reviews the bill for further consideration by the House or Senate as a whole.
- **c.** when a bill is presented for final passage.
- **d.** when the president decides to sign or veto the bill.
- **e.** when the bill is marked up.

10.5 Characterize the ways that legislators make decisions about bills.

The major influences on final legislative passage do not include
- **a.** ideology.
- **b.** interest groups.
- **c.** the president.
- **d.** constituents.
- **e.** friends and family.

10.6 Evaluate the influence of citizens on the legislative process.

Americans are disappointed with the performance of Congress because of
- **a.** stalemates in solving important problems.
- **b.** the poor performance of the economy.
- **c.** the lack of congressional responsiveness to constituents.
- **d.** the permanent campaign for reelection.
- **e.** all of the above.

ESSAY QUESTION

Identify the steps by which a bill becomes a law and the ways a bill can be stopped at each step. Then write a short essay showing the two ways legislators represent their constituents.

Explore Further

IN THE LIBRARY

E. Scott Adler, *Why Congressional Reforms Fail: Reelection and the House Committee System* (University of Chicago Press, 2002).

Sarah A. Binder, *Stalemate: Causes and Consequences of Legislative Gridlock* (Brookings Institution Press, 2003).

Roger H. Davidson, Walter J. Oleszek, and Frances E. Lee, *Congress and Its Members,* 13th ed. (CQ Press, 2011).

Richard F. Fenno, Jr., *Senators on the Campaign Trail: The Politics of Representation* (University of Oklahoma Press, 1996).

Morris P. Fiorina, *Congress: Keystone of the Washington Establishment,* 2nd ed. (Yale University Press, 1989).

Paul Herrnson, *Congressional Elections*, 6th ed. (CQ Press, 2011).

Godfrey Hodgson, *The Gentleman from New York: Daniel Patrick Moynihan* (Houghton Mifflin, 2000).

Gary Jacobson, *Politics of Congressional Elections,* 7th ed. (Longman, 2008).

Linda Killian, *The Freshmen: What Happened to the Republican Revolution?* (Westview Press, 1998).

Thomas Mann And Norm Ornstein, *The Broken Branch: How Congress Is Failing America and How to Get It Back on Track* (Oxford University Press, 2006).

Thomas Mann and Norm Ornstein, *It's Even Worse Than It Looks: How the American Constitutional System Collided With the New Politics of Extremism*(Basic Books, 2012)

David R. Mayhew, *America's Congress: Actions in the Public Sphere, James Madison Through Newt Gingrich* (Yale University Press, 2002).

Walter J. Oleszek, *Congressional Procedures and the Policy Process,* 6th ed. (CQ Press, 2004).

Ronald M. Peters, Jr., ed., *The Speaker: Leadership in the U.S. House of Representatives* (CQ Press, 1995).

Steven S. Smith, Jason M. Roberts, And Ryan J. Vander Wielen, *The American Congress* (Cambridge University Press, 2011).

Barbara Sinclair, *Unorthodox Lawmaking: New Legislative Processes in the U.S. Congress,* 2nd ed. (CQ Press, 2000).

ON THE WEB

www.opencongress.org
An easily accessible inventory of congressional activities and work, including lists of bills, members, committees, votes, issues, and campaign contributions.

www.GAO.gov
The Web site for the Government Accountability Office, which provides studies on issues facing Congress.

www.CBO.gov
The Web site for the Congressional Budget Office, which analyzes every bill for its costs and tracks key economic trends.

www.senate.gov
The Senate's Web site. Pay particular notion to the historian's office and the oral histories section.

www.house.gov
The House's Web site. Links to all committees.

http://thomas.loc.gov
The Library of Congress Web site for tracking all legislation.

11

Listen to Chapter 11 on MyPoliSciLab

The Presidency

President Barack Obama entered office with an extensive list of first-year priorities. Within months of his inauguration on January 20, 2009, he sent Congress three major proposals, including an $800 billion economic stimulus package, a massive health insurance package that came to be known as Obamacare, and an expansion in the federal government's Americorps volunteer action program.

As commander in chief, Obama also promised to find and kill Osama bin Laden, the mastermind of the terrorist attacks that had killed 3,000 Americans the morning of September 11, 2001. President George W. Bush also told the nation the U.S. would catch bin Laden "dead or alive," but the leader of the terrorist organization al Qaeda was still alive a decade later, hiding somewhere in Afghanistan or Pakistan.

Bush and Obama both used their broad authority as commander in chief to hunt for bin Laden. Although the Constitution gives Congress the power to declare war and appropriate money for troops and weapons, presidents are given wide latitude to defend the nation and wage war. Presidents have occasionally stretched this power to move quickly without congressional approval through military interventions.

After years of searching, the Central Intelligence Agency finally found bin Laden living in the small Pakistani city of Abbottabad. Having followed the trail to a heavily protected house for years, the Central Intelligence Agency was convinced that bin Laden was home on April 31, 2011.[1] Given all of the available intelligence, Obama ordered commandos into place on that day, and then gathered his national security team in the White House Situation Room for a go or no-go decision to launch the mission. According to Vice President Joe Biden, Obama asked each of the president's national security advisers for his or her opinion on the raid. "He went around the table with all the senior people, including the chiefs of staff, and he said, "I have to make a decision. What is your opinion?'" Biden said the president stood up and simply said "Go."[2]

OBAMA AND HIS TEAM WATCH THE BIN LADEN RAID Obama's national security advisers gathered in the White House Situation Room to monitor the dangerous operation.

The Big Picture What makes a president great? Author Paul C. Light discusses some of the characteristics and circumstances that America's favorite presidents have had in common. And he reveals why current and future presidents are going to have a harder time earning the same praise.

The Basics What do presidents do? The simple answer is "an awful lot." In this video, you'll hear what ordinary people think about what presidents should do. In the process, you'll discover why there is often a gap between what we expect and what we get.

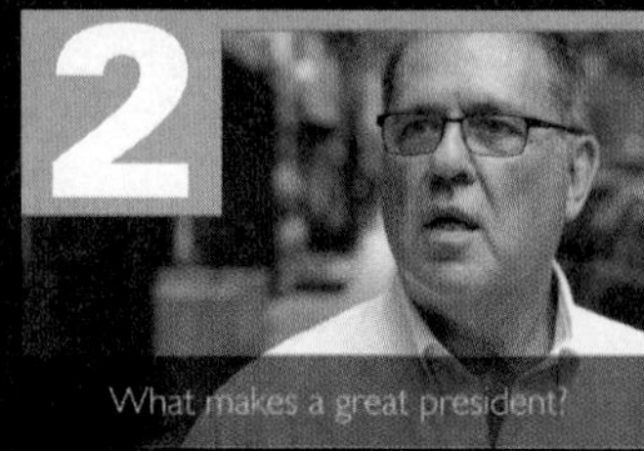

In Context Uncover the historical context that led the Framers to fear a strong executive. In this video University of Oklahoma political scientist Glen Krutz not only reveals the reason behind the Framers' apprehension, but also explores how this fear still restricts presidents today as they struggle to create new policies.

Thinking Like a Political Scientist Why do presidents try to persuade you to support their policies? In this video, University of Oklahoma political scientist Glen Krutz discloses why persuasion is vital to a president's success and how technology has created obstacles and opportunities for presidents.

In the Real World Should President Obama have used an executive order to change immigration policy? The president bypassed Congress to implement his own agenda. Find out why some people believe the president abused his powers and others think he was entirely justified.

So What? Find out the difference between Thomas Jefferson's honeymoon period and Barack Obama's. Author Paul C. Light compares the office of the president today with how it was originally conceived by the founders, and shares what it really means to be a "lame duck" president.

Being president is one of the most influential jobs in the world. Here, President Barack Obama meets with the four living ex-presidents to discuss general issues of governing the nation from the White House.

11.1 11.2 11.3 11.4 11.5 11.6

U.S. Navy Seals led the raid just after midnight on May 1. Ferried into combat by specially muffled "stealth" Black Hawk helicopters designed to evade radar and detection, the Seals moved quickly to find bin Laden. Despite his prominence as a leader of the most dangerous global terrorist organization, bin Laden had only a handful of guards to protect him. They were killed within seconds as the Seals advanced quickly to bin Laden's house. Given authority to kill bin Laden if he offered any resistance, the Seals eventually worked their way up to his bedroom, where he was shot twice. Bin Laden was buried at sea.

Obama and his advisers followed the raid through night-vision images forwarded to the Situation Room from commando helmet cameras, while listening to radio traffic between the 79 troops on the mission. Although it is still not clear that they saw the fatal shots that killed bin Laden, Obama responded with the simple words, "We got him."

The Framers of the Constitution embraced the need for a strong president who would protect the nation from threats such as bin Laden. At the same time, they also created many checks and balances to protect against presidential tyranny. This chapter will examine the Framers' intent in designing the presidency, review the president's powers, and then turn to the continuing controversies surrounding the exercise of these powers. We will also explore the many jobs of the president and ask how Congress and the president work together and against each other in making the laws. We conclude with a discussion of how history judges presidents.

The Structure and Powers of the Presidency

11.1 Describe the constitutional foundations and primary roles of the presidency.

Explore on **MyPoliSciLab**: You Are a First-Term President

The Framers wanted the president to act with "dispatch" against international and domestic threats, but they also worried that the president could become too powerful. Although they gave the president the power to run the executive branch, which now includes the White House and all departments and agencies, they limited the president's other powers to a relatively short list, including the power to wage wars declared by Congress, report to the nation from

parliamentary government
A form of government in which the chief executive is the leader of the majority party in the legislature.

Young citizens massed at the Lincoln Memorial on May Day, 1970, vowing to shut down the federal government to protest the Vietnam War.

time to time on the State of the Union, nominate judges and executive appointees for Senate confirmation, and negotiate treaties. They wanted a presidential office that would steer clear of parties and factions, enforce the laws passed by Congress, handle communications with foreign governments, and help states put down disorders. They wanted a presidency strong enough to match Congress but not so strong that it would overpower Congress.

The Framers believed the "jarrings of parties" in Congress were perfectly appropriate in making the laws but not in fighting wars and running the executive branch. They did not believe the president should have unlimited freedom to act, however. Having given a much longer list of powers to Congress, they saw the president as a powerful check on legislative action and essential to the administration of government. As Alexander Hamilton argued in *The Federalist*, No. 70, "A feeble executive implies a feeble execution of the government. A feeble execution is but another phrase for a bad execution: And a government ill executed, whatever it may be in theory, must be in practice a bad government."[3]

☐ The Presidency and the Separation of Powers

The president's power to act as commander in chief is part of the Constitution's separation of powers. Even though Congress often gives the president the freedom to take action on foreign policy, it does retain the authority to cut off funding for foreign involvement, and the Senate is required to ratify all treaties with other nations. Nevertheless, merely having three branches of a national government—legislative, executive, and judicial—does not by itself create a pure system of separated powers.

Unlike the United States, which has a separate path to the presidency, **parliamentary governments** elect their prime ministers from the parliament itself. In theory, this system makes the prime minister more influential—he or she controls both the executive and legislative branches. Great Britain is the oldest parliamentary government in the world, and its prime minister is possibly the most powerful. Becoming the prime minister is hardly easy—prime ministers must be members of Parliament, elected as their party's leader, and be able to lead their parties to a majority in a national election. Once in office, the prime minister has many of the same roles as the U.S. president.

In the United States, however, the legislative, executive, and judicial branches are independent of one another. Although the legislative and executive branch are unlike the United States, which has a complicated path to the presidency, parliamentary governments are automatically led by the head of the majority party in parliament itself. Voters select the majority party, the majority party selects its top leader, and the top leader automatically becomes prime minister. Also unlike the United States, where the transition from election day to inauguration lasts more than three months, the prime minister moves into Number 10 Downing Street (the British equivalent of the White House) the day after the votes are counted.

Because prime ministers across the world represent parliament, their programs have automatic support from the majority. Once in office, prime ministers have many of the same duties as the U.S. president, but have much greater influence over the other branches of government.

The United States is one of the few world powers that is neither a parliamentary democracy nor a wholly executive-dominated government. Our Constitution plainly invites both Congress and the president to set policy and govern the nation. Leadership and policy change are likely only when Congress and the president, and sometimes the courts along with them, agree that new directions are desirable.

Electoral College
The electoral system used in electing the president and vice president, in which voters vote for electors pledged to cast their ballots for a particular party's candidates.

☐ The Framers and the Presidency

The Framers' most important decision about the presidency was also their first. Meeting on June 1, 1787, the Constitutional Convention decided there would be a single "unitary" executive. Despite worries that a single president might lay the groundwork for a future monarchy, the Framers also believed the new government needed energy in the executive. Instead of a council of three chief executives, they chose just one.

Once past this first decision, the Framers had to decide just how independent that executive would be from the rest of the national government. This meant finding an appropriate method of selection or election. Had they wanted Congress to select the president from among its members, the Framers would have created a parliamentary system that would look more like the European governments. The delegates were initially divided on how the president would be selected. A small number favored direct election by the people, which Pennsylvania's James Wilson thought would ensure that the president was completely independent of Congress. The delegates rejected direct election in favor of the **Electoral College**: voters would cast their ballots for competing slates of electors, who would in turn cast their electoral votes for president.

The Framers also gave the executive a four-year term of office, further balancing the House with its two-year terms and the Senate with its six-year terms. Although the Constitution allowed presidents to serve as many terms as they wished, to run for reelection as long as they wished, the Twenty-Second Amendment to the Constitution limits presidents to two terms in office.

The Framers then created the position of vice president just in case the president left office before the end of the term. With little debate, they decided to give the vice president the power to break tie votes in the Senate. Otherwise, the vice president has no constitutional duties but to wait for the president to be incapacitated or otherwise unable to discharge the powers and duties of the presidency. In recent years, however, presidents have given their vice presidents greater responsibilities.[4] Moreover, the vice presidency is a well-recognized stepping-stone to the presidency. Fourteen of the 44 U.S. presidents were vice presidents before they became president—nine moved into the post after their president died or resigned in office, another four were elected immediately after their president left office at the end of a term, and one was elected eight years after leaving office.

The Framers also established three simple qualifications for both offices. Under the Constitution, the president and vice president must be (1) at least 35 years old on inauguration day; (2) natural-born citizens of the United States, as opposed to immigrants who become citizens by applying to the U.S. government for naturalization; and (3) residents of the United States for the previous 14 years. The citizenship and

11.1

11.2

11.3

11.4

11.5

11.6

presidential ticket
The joint listing of the presidential and vice presidential candidates on the same ballot, as required by the Twelfth Amendment.

vesting clause
The president's constitutional authority to control most executive functions.

residency requirements were designed to prevent a popular foreign-born citizen from capturing the office.

With this basic structure in place, the Framers had to decide how the vice president would be selected. Once again, they created a remarkable electoral arrangement: The candidate who received the most Electoral College votes would become president, and the candidate who came in second would become vice president. Any tie votes in the Electoral College were to be broken by a majority vote in the House of Representatives.

It did not take long for the Framers to discover the problem with this runner-up rule. The 1796 election produced Federalist President John Adams and Republican Vice President Thomas Jefferson. Because the two disagreed so sharply about the future of the country, Jefferson was rendered virtually irrelevant to government.

After a constitutional crisis in 1800, Congress decided to change the rule through a Constitutional Amendment. Under the Twelfth Amendment, ratified in 1804, electors were allowed to cast separate votes for the president and vice president. This new practice encouraged candidates to run together as members of a **presidential ticket** that lists the presidential and vice presidential candidates first and second.

□ Presidential Powers

Article II of the Constitution begins: "The executive Power shall be vested in a President of the United States of America." Presidents often use this **vesting clause** to argue that they control everything that happens in the executive branch after a bill becomes a law.[5] However, the Supreme Court has cast doubt on this breadth of the authority in a variety of past cases—presidents may control the executive branch, but they do not have unlimited command. The Supreme Court has also ruled that Congress cannot delegate powers to the president that the Constitution reserves for the legislative branch under Article I.

Although short, Article II does address foreign threats and the day-to-day operations of government, establishing the president's authority to play three central

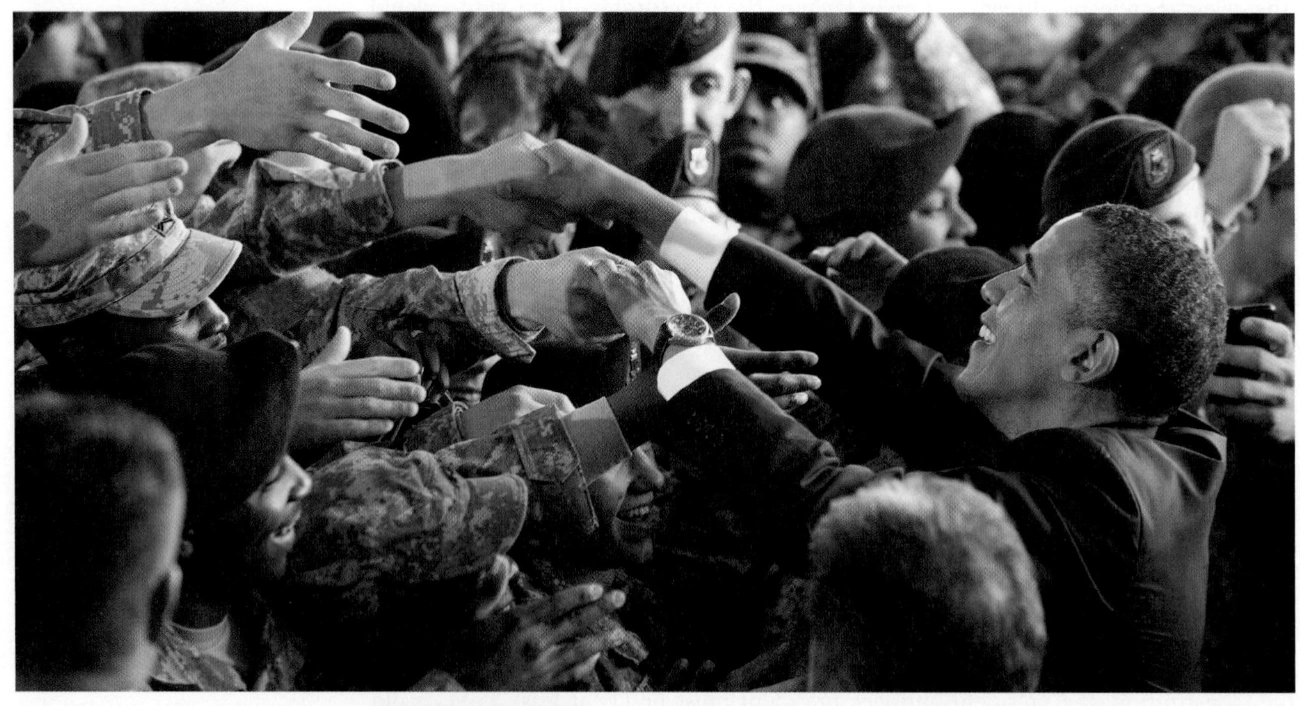

President Obama shakes hands with U.S. Army troops in North Carolina on December 14, 2011, the day that the United States formally ended the war in Iraq. In doing so, he performed his role as morale-builder in chief by thanking the troops for their service.

roles in the new government: (1) commander in chief, (2) diplomat in chief, and (3) administrator in chief.

It is important to note that the Framers designed the presidency fully expecting that George Washington would take the post. Washington commanded the public's trust and respect, and he was unanimously elected the first president of the new Republic. He understood that the people needed to have confidence in their fledgling government, a sense of continuity with the past, and a time of calm and stability free of emergencies and crises. He also knew that the new nation faced both domestic and foreign threats to its future.

As president, Washington set important precedents for the future. He not only established the legitimacy and basic authority of the office but negotiated the new government's first treaty, appointed its first judges and department heads, received its first foreign ambassadors, vetoed its first legislation, and signed its first laws, thereby demonstrating just how future presidents should execute and influence the laws.

Washington's most important precedent may have been his retirement after serving two terms. Although he would have been easily reelected to a third term, Washington believed two terms were enough and returned to his Mount Vernon estate in 1796. It was a precedent that held until Franklin Roosevelt ran for a third term in 1940 and then a fourth term in 1944. Roosevelt's long service prompted the two-term limit created under the Twenty-Second Amendment to the Constitution in 1951.

treaty
A formal, public agreement between the United States and one or more nations that must be approved by two-thirds of the Senate.

executive agreement
A formal agreement between the U.S. president and the leaders of other nations that does not require Senate approval.

COMMANDER IN CHIEF The Constitution explicitly states that the president is to be commander in chief of the army and navy, but the Framers were divided over which branch would both declare and make war.[6]

The Framers initially agreed that Congress would make war, raise armies, build and equip fleets, enforce treaties, and suppress and repel invasions, but they eventually changed the phrase "make war" to "declare war." At the same time, the Framers limited the presidential war power by giving Congress the power to appropriate money for the purchase of arms and military pay and by giving the Senate the power to approve military promotions. Although Congress has the sole authority to declare war, presidents have used their power as commander in chief to order U.S. troops into battle without formal declarations dozens of times throughout the past century, including the recent wars in Afghanistan and Iraq. Presidents have often interpreted the war power even more broadly, as the George W. Bush administration did in authorizing the domestic eavesdropping program in the midst of the War on Terror.[7] In 2012, the nation learned that Obama used the war power to create "kill lists" of terrorists without congressional approval. As with bin Laden, Obama made the decision to strike without congressional approval.

DIPLOMAT IN CHIEF Article II also makes the president negotiator in chief of treaties with foreign nations, which must be approved by the Senate by a two-thirds vote. A **treaty** is a binding and public agreement between the United States and one or more nations that requires mutual action toward a common goal. The United States has signed hundreds of treaties throughout the past 200 years, including limits on the number of nuclear, biological, and chemical weapons a nation can possess. Although presidents cannot make treaties without Senate approval, past presidents have argued that they have the power to terminate treaties without Senate consent.

Presidents are also free to make **executive agreements** with other nations. Unlike treaties, executive agreements are negotiated without Senate participation. In 2003, for example, the Bush administration negotiated a 22-item executive agreement with Mexico to create a "smart border" that would limit the movement of illegal aliens into the United States, while improving the flow of goods between the two nations. Although some executive orders are secret, most are made public.

FOR the People Government's Greatest Endeavors

Reducing Nuclear Weapons

Presidents have invested enormous amounts of time and energy during the past 30 years to try to control and reduce the number of nuclear weapons throughout the world. Much of that work has involved efforts to stop the "arms race" between the United States and the Soviet Union, which together built enough nuclear weapons to destroy the world many times over.

Presidents negotiated a number of nuclear arms agreements during the long cold war, all of which had to be approved by the U.S. Senate under its treaty-making power. In 1972, for example, the Senate approved a freeze on the development of new weapons by the United States and Soviet Union that lasted through the 1970s. This Strategic Arms Limitation Treaty, negotiated by President Richard Nixon, froze the number of U.S. and Soviet missiles for five years.

In 1988, the Senate also approved a treaty banning the further development of shorter-range nuclear missiles that could be used in Europe and other "hot spots." This treaty, negotiated by President Ronald Reagan, marked the first time that the two nations also agreed to dismantle some of their existing weapons. Although both nations still have large numbers of nuclear weapons and missiles, further negotiations by presidents Bill Clinton and George W. Bush have reduced the numbers of weapons and created a much safer world.

President Obama continued these negotiations into 2012, but he was unable to make progress on his promise to rid the world of nuclear weapons during his first term. To the contrary, worries about the development of nuclear weapons by other nations, such as North Korea, intensified. Iran has also continued work to develop a weapon and test missiles that could reach Israel and Turkey.

QUESTIONS

1. Why do nations seek nuclear weapons as part of their military strength?
2. What can the United States do to reduce the spread of nuclear weapons to other nations?
3. What can citizens do to put pressure on the United States and other nations to dismantle their nuclear weapons?

North Korea has been working steadily to create nuclear weapons over many years despite international pressures to stop. North Korea claims that its nuclear program is peaceful, and has offered proof through inspections of its facilities, including the ones that house spent fuel rods. However, the nation has not allowed international inspectors to review its more advanced plants.

Finally, presidents are also free to make **congressional–executive agreements** with other nations. Like treaties, congressional–executive agreements require mutual action toward a common goal. Unlike treaties, they require approval by both houses of Congress by a simple majority vote.

congressional–executive agreement
A formal agreement between the U.S. president and the leaders of other nations that requires approval by both houses of Congress.

ADMINISTRATOR IN CHIEF By giving the president the power to require the opinion of the principal officer in each of the executive departments "upon any subject relating to the duties of their respective offices," the Constitution puts the president in charge of the day-to-day operations of the federal departments and agencies.

recess appointment
Presidential appointment made without Senate confirmation during Senate recess.

ADDITIONAL EXECUTIVE POWERS The Constitution also gives the president five additional powers to lead government: (1) the power to nominate judges and the top officers of government; (2) the power to veto legislation; (3) the power to grant pardons to individuals convicted of federal crimes; (4) the power to take care that the laws are faithfully executed; and (5) the power convene Congress.

veto
A formal decision to reject a bill passed by Congress.

pocket veto
A formal decision to reject a bill passed by Congress after it adjourns—if Congress adjourns during the ten days that the president is allowed to sign or veto a law, the president can reject the law by taking no action at all.

1. *The Appointment Power.* The Constitution gives the president authority to nominate judges, ambassadors, and other officers of the executive branch subject to confirmation by a majority vote of the Senate.

   Because the Senate almost always gives its favorable "advice and consent" to the president's nominees, this power gives presidents the ability to control what happens inside departments and agencies during their terms and to shape the federal judiciary far into the future. Presidents choose executive branch appointees on the basis of party loyalty, interest group pressure, and management ability. The Senate has failed to confirm only eight cabinet secretaries between 1789 and 2012, and only 36 of 159 nominations to the Supreme Court.

   Presidents also have the power to make **recess appointments** when Congress takes a formal recess, or break, during its two-year term. Although the power was originally intended to be used only when a vacancy occurs during the break, presidents now use recess appointments regularly to appoint particularly controversial nominees to office without Senate confirmation. These appointments end at the start of the Congress that is elected after the appointment is made.[8] George W. Bush made 171 recess appointments during his first and second terms, while Obama made more than 30 recess appointments from 2009 to 2012.

2. *The Veto Power.* The Constitution requires that bills passed by the U.S. House of Representatives and Senate "shall be presented to the President of the United States," and the president can then approve the measure or issue a **veto**. If a bill is vetoed by a president, it can be enacted only if the veto is overridden, which requires a two-thirds vote in each chamber of Congress.

   A variation of the veto is the **pocket veto**. In the ordinary course of events, if a president does not sign or veto a bill within ten days after receiving it (not counting Sundays), the bill becomes law without the president's signature. But if Congress adjourns within the ten days, the president, by taking no action, can kill the bill with a pocket veto.

   The power of a veto lies in the difficulty of overriding a president's decision. Recall that two-thirds of both houses must vote to overturn a veto. This requirement is a vital bargaining chip in the legislative process, in which the mere threat of a veto can strengthen a president's hand. Historically, Congress has voted to override less than 10 percent of presidents' regular vetoes.

   This veto threat is credible, however, only if the president is actually willing to use it. Whereas Ronald Reagan vetoed 78 bills in his two terms from 1981–1988, George H. W. Bush vetoed 44, and Bill Clinton vetoed 37, George W. Bush vetoed only 11 bills during his two terms, and Obama issued just 2 from 2009 to 2012.

   Once his Republican Party lost control of the House and Senate in 2007, however, Bush began using his veto power to stop Democratic legislation. In July 2007, for example, he vetoed legislation to allow federal funding of stem cell

11.1
11.2
11.3
11.4
11.5
11.6

take care clause
The constitutional requirement (in Article II, Section 3) that presidents take care that the laws are faithfully executed, even if they disagree with the purpose of those laws.

inherent powers
Powers that grow out of the very existence of government.

State of the Union Address
The president's annual statement to Congress and the nation.

signing statements
A formal document that explains why a president is signing a particular bill into law. These statements may contain objections to the bill and promises not to implement key sections.

research. Obama's order to fund the research was overturned by a federal district court in 2009, but was affirmed as constitutional in May 2001. The decision is still under fire in Congress, but no legislation had passed before the end of his first term.[9] Obama had fewer opportunities to use the veto because Congress passed so few bills during the period.

3. *The Pardon Power.* The pardon power can be traced directly to the royal authority of the king of England, and it is probably the most delicate power presidents exercise. Presidents can shorten prison sentences, correct judicial errors, and protect citizens from future prosecution. The power can also create controversy. President Bush pardoned White House aid "Scooter Libby" in July 2007. Libby had been sentenced to 30 months in federal prison for leaking the name of a Central Intelligence Agency secret operative. But Bush ended his administration with the fewest pardons of any recent president.[10]
4. *The Take Care Power.* Located near the end of Article II is the simple statement that the president "shall take Care that the Laws be faithfully executed." This **take care clause** makes the president responsible for implementing the laws Congress enacts, even through the override of a presidential veto.

   Presidents sometimes use the take care clause to claim **inherent powers**, meaning powers they believe are essential to protecting the nation. Jefferson drew on this broad notion in making the Louisiana Purchase in 1803. Abraham Lincoln extended the concept early in the Civil War to suspend the rights of prisoners to seek judicial review of their detention, to impose a blockade of Confederate shipping, and to expand the size of the army beyond authorized ceilings, all without prior congressional approval as required under the Constitution's lawmaking power.

5. *The Power to Inform and Convene Congress.* Under Article II, presidents are required "from time to time to give to the Congress Information of the State of the Union, and recommend to their Consideration such Measures as he shall judge necessary." Throughout the years, the phrase "from time to time" has evolved to mean a constant stream of presidential messages, as well as the annual **State of the Union Address** in late January or early February. This power gives presidents a significant platform for presenting their legislative agenda to both Congress and the people.

   The president also has the power to convene Congress in extraordinary circumstances and recommend "such Measures as he shall judge necessary and expedient." In August 2010, for example, Obama convened Congress to push for health care reform. Some presidents have used this power to convene Congress for lame duck sessions that occur after the election and before the next session of Congress begins.

Past presidents have also argued that they have unilateral powers that are not subject to traditional checks and balances, including the power to act during national emergencies. Presidents have argued that they have considerable freedom to interpret the often-unclear laws that Congress passes. In recent decades, presidents have used **signing statements** to signal their intent not to implement a specific provision in a law. These signing statements are issued when the president signs a particular bill into law. Hence, the term "signing statements."[11]

The rise and fall in the number of signing statements over the past 100 years reflects both the number of bills passed by Congress, which has declined, and the drift toward larger bills that contain "riders" or unrelated provisions buried in the text. Reagan issued 250 signing statements during his administration, compared with 228 by George H.W. Bush, 381 by Clinton, 161 by George W. Bush, and fewer than 20 by Obama from 2009 to 2013, again in part because Congress passed fewer bills that provided an opportunity for presidential objections..[12]

On April 11, 2011, for example, Obama signed a Defense Department funding bill that contained a provision limiting the number of senior White House policy advisers, or what some in Congress called "policy czars." Even though Obama exercised his Constitutional authority to sign the bill into law, he argued that the provision violated the "Take Care" clause and was therefore unconstitutional: "Legislative efforts that significantly impede the President's ability to exercise his supervisory and coordinating authorities or to obtain the views of the appropriate senior advisers violate the separation of powers by undermining the President's ability to exercise his constitutional responsibilities and take care that the laws be faithfully executed."[13]

impeachment
A formal accusation against the president or another public official; the first step in removal from office.

11.1 11.2 11.3 11.4 11.5 11.6

□ Presidential Removal and Succession

The Framers also gave Congress the power to remove the president through **impeachment**. Under this constitutional check, the House of Representatives is responsible for drafting the articles of impeachment that charge the president with treason, bribery, or other high crimes and misdemeanors. If the articles are approved by a majority vote in the House, the chief justice of the Supreme Court oversees a

You Will Decide

Should the Two-Term Limit Be Repealed?

The Twenty-Second Amendment was ratified in 1951 to limit the president's time in office to two terms. The amendment also restricts vice presidents to ten years of service in total if they become president after their president dies, resigns, or is declared incapable of fulfilling the duties of the presidency or resign. Under this restriction, vice presidents are thereby allowed to finish the term they inherit and stand for reelection twice. The president can serve the two terms either consecutively or by returning to office after a resignation or defeat.

President Obama is now operating under the two-term limit and must leave office in 2017.

All of the presidents who have been elected since 1951 have supported repeal of the Twenty-second Amendment. They argue that the amendment effectively renders them *lame ducks* in their second terms. Because they cannot stand for reelection, Congress and the public tend to ignore them as thoughts turn to who will be the president after them. Nor can they be held accountable in the voting booth for their second-term decisions.

What do you think? Should the two-term limit be repealed? What arguments would you make for or against such an idea?

Thinking It Through

The Framers clearly believed that elections serve to discipline presidents for their actions, while the four-year term provides enough time to achieve policy results. They believed that steadiness in administration would help the country survive its early years, while giving the president a reason to create policies that would help the nation long into the future. Presidents are arguably more effective if their allies and opponents assume they may be running for another term. Otherwise, they become "lame ducks" early in their second terms, meaning that they have little influence.

Much as they may have applauded Washington's two-term precedent, the Framers did not support the idea of a formal term limit—such a limit would have weakened the public's voice in keeping the president honest. Instead of starting a second term knowing they could not serve again, presidents would be able to keep Congress and the public guessing, thereby retaining influence until the last possible minute.

Repealing the two-term limit would have negative consequences, too. Even if they fail in their first two terms, presidents could use their substantial public visibility to stay in office for third term or more. Although they would still have to be reelected, they would have more power to pursue unpopular policies. Repeal would also reverse the Framers' ideal of rotation in office.

CRITICAL THINKING QUESTIONS

1. Are presidents so popular that they could win reelection to a third term?
2. Does the two-term limit weaken the president's ability to influence the course of the nation in the second term?
3. What checks and balances ensure that presidents can be held accountable even if they are lame ducks?

Vice President Lyndon Baines Johnson takes the oath of office on Air Force One to become president on November 22, 1963, following the assassination of John F. Kennedy. In the wake of these events, the Twenty-fifth Amendment was adopted to provide for replacing the vice president or removing a president from office for reasons of illness or disability. First Lady Jacqueline Kennedy was standing at his side.

trial before the Senate. If two-thirds of the Senate votes to convict, the president is removed immediately from office.

Impeachment charges have been filed against nine presidents in history, but the House has voted to impeach the president only twice: in 1868 against Andrew Johnson, and in 1998 against Bill Clinton. In each case, the Senate trials resulted in acquittals and the two presidents remained in office. However, both presidencies were stained by the controversy.

Although the Framers did not limit the number of terms a president could serve, the nation eventually ratified the Twenty-Second Amendment, limits presidents to two terms, or ten years in total. This restriction does not require the president to serve the two terms back to back. A president can be defeated after serving one term, and still return for a second term after a future election. The amendment is discussed in the "You Will Decide" box. The ratification effort was led by Republicans who wanted to prevent a repeat of Franklin Roosevelt's four consecutive terms in office, which concentrated power in the White House and led to the great expansion of federal government power under the New Deal.

In 1967, the nation ratified the Twenty-Fifth Amendment, which allows for the temporary removal of the president due to illness or disability. The president can only be removed temporarily if (1) the vice president and (2) a majority of either Congress or the president's own department secretaries declare the president to be unable to discharge the powers and duties of office. During the temporary removal of the president, the vice president becomes the acting president. If the president dies or resigns, the vice president becomes the president and must nominate a new vice president. The new president's choice for vice president must be confirmed by majority votes in both the House and Senate.

The amendment has been triggered six times since ratification in 1967: (1) when Gerald Ford became vice president after his predecessor Spiro Agnew resigned in disgrace in 1973, (2) when Ford then became president after Richard Nixon also resigned in disgrace in 1974, (3) when Nelson Rockefeller then became vice president after Ford became president, (4) when vice president George H. W. Bush became acting president when Ronald Reagan had surgery to remove a polyp from his colon in 1985, and (5) and (6) when George W. Bush had a simple colon screen under a light anesthetic in both 2002 and 2007.

War Power Resolution
A resolution passed in 1973 requiring the president to give advance warning of a military attack or ask Congress for a declaration of war or specific legislation.

Controversies in Presidential Power

11.2 Evaluate the controversies surrounding presidents' assertion of additional executive powers.

he president, today more visible than ever as a national and international leader, is still constrained by constitutional checks and balances. These do not stop presidents from asserting powers the Framers intended for Congress or the judiciary, however.

The War Power

Article I of the Constitution gives Congress the power to declare war, but Article II gives the president the power to wage war as commander in chief. The Framers recognized that declaring war was both one of the most important powers of government and one of the most easily abused.[14]

During the past half-century, U.S. presidents have ordered troops into battle in Korea, Vietnam, Grenada, Panama, Iraq (once in 1990 and again in 2003), Kosovo, and Afghanistan, all without asking Congress for a formal declaration of war. When they have asked for congressional approval, presidents have usually sought broad resolutions of support. In 2002, for example, Bush merely asked Congress to give him the authority to deploy U.S. forces as he determines to be "necessary and appropriate" to defend national security against the threat posed by Iraq. Although the request was eventually approved by wide margins in the House and Senate, White House lawyers also argued that the president already had the authority to act with or without congressional approval.[15]

Legal scholars and political scientists blame Congress for abdicating its constitutional authority to the presidency. Constitutional scholar Louis Fisher holds that Congress has repeatedly given up its fundamental war powers to the president. The Framers knew what monarchy looked like and rejected it, writes Fisher. "Yet, especially in matters of the war power, the United States is re-creating a system of monarchy while it professes to champion democracy and the rule of law abroad."[16]

Congress tried to reassert its role and authority in the use of military force at the end of the Vietnam War. In 1973, for example, Congress enacted the **War Powers Resolution** over Nixon's veto. The law, still in place, declares that a president can commit the armed forces only (1) after a declaration of war by Congress, (2) by specific statutory authorization, or (3) in a national emergency created by an attack on the United States or its armed forces. After committing the armed forces under the third circumstance, the president is required to report to Congress within 48 hours. Unless Congress declares war, the troop commitment must be ended within 60 days.

This resolution signaled a new determination by Congress to take its prerogatives seriously, but presidents have generally ignored it. And many leading scholars now believe that this earnest and well-intentioned effort by Congress to reclaim its proper role actually gave presidents even more freedom to act without congressional action. Because presidents can declare a national emergency under almost any circumstances and often act under broad legislation that authorizes the use of force in ambiguous situations, the War Powers Resolution is almost always ignored

executive privilege
The right to keep executive communications confidential, especially if they relate to national security.

The Bush administration refused to release information on its use of "enhanced interrogation" techniques such as sleep deprivation at the Guantanamo interrogation facility. The decision was eventually reversed by the Obama administration, which released the Bush administration's "torture memos" in 2009.

for what presidents often see as emergency action, such as the missile strike on al Qaeda training bases in Afghanistan immediately after the September 11, 2001, terrorist attacks.

□ The Power to Invoke Executive Privilege

The courts have recognized that presidents have the power, or **executive privilege**, to keep secrets, especially if doing so is essential to protect national security or confidential White House conversations about public policy.

Some experts argue that executive privilege has no constitutional basis.[17] Yet presidents have withheld documents from Congress at least as far back as 1792, when President George Washington temporarily refused to share sensitive documents with a House committee studying an Indian massacre of federal troops. Thomas Jefferson and the primary author of the Constitution, James Madison, also withheld information during their presidencies.

Most scholars, the courts, and even members of Congress agree that a president has the implicit, if not constitutionally explicit, right to withhold information that could harm national security. Presidents must keep secrets, and they often fight hard to do so. However, they cannot assert executive privilege in either congressional or judicial proceedings when it means refusing to cooperate in investigations of personal wrongdoing.

Nixon created enormous and continuing controversy over the term "executive privilege."[18] In an effort to hide his own role in the Watergate scandal, which involved a failed burglary of the Democratic National Committee offices during the 1972 election, Nixon refused to release the secret tapes of the White House meetings that led to a cover-up of the attempt. Nixon and his lawyers went so far as to claim that the decision to invoke executive privilege was not subject to review by Congress or the federal courts.

Ruling in April 1974, a unanimous Supreme Court acknowledged for the first time that presidents do indeed have the power to claim executive privilege if the release of certain information would be damaging to the nation's security interests. But the Court held that such claims are not exempt from review by the courts. More importantly for Nixon's future, the Court also held that national security was not threatened by the public release of the Watergate tapes. The Court ordered Nixon to yield his tapes, effectively dooming his presidency.[19]

The Bush administration formally invoked executive privilege four times between 2001 and 2007, and in late 2007, to prevent congressional testimony by two White House aides in a Justice Department scandal. Obama invoked executive privilege in 2012 in an effort to shield the Justice Department and Attorney General Eric Holder from a congressional investigation of a failed gun-tracking program. Congress cited Holder for contempt of Congress, which triggered further action to remove him from office through the judicial process.

☐ The Power to Issue Executive Orders

Presidents execute the laws and direct the federal departments and agencies in part through **executive orders**, formal directives that are just as strong as laws and can be challenged in the courts. According to past Supreme Court decisions, executive orders are generally accepted as the law of the land unless they conflict with the Constitution or a federal law. Executive orders are numbered dating back to President George Washington's first order three months after his inauguration. Executive orders can be reversed by future presidents, however, which make them less enduring than formal laws.

Beginning with George Washington, presidents have issued nearly 14,000 executive orders. Presidents have used executive orders to implement a variety of decisions, including a declaration of U.S. neutrality in the war between France and England (1793). President George W. Bush issued 270 executive orders during his eight-year term, while Obama issued more than 130 from 2009 to 2013. (See Figure 11.1 for a comparison of the number of executive orders issued, by president.) Obama's first executive order, issued the day after his inauguration, required all presidential appointees to sign a tough ethics pledge.[20]

Presidents also have the authority to issue **executive memoranda** that guide executive branch decisions. These memoranda are based on the Constitution's Take Care clause, and direct specific actions by government as a whole or individual departments and agencies. On November 28, 2011, for example, Obama ordered the executive branch as a whole to accelerate efforts to make information available to the public. Like executive orders, presidential memoranda are not subject to congressional passage or review. Presidential memoranda are not recorded in any numbered count, and are usually only available on the president's Web site or in press releases.[21] Like executive orders, executive memoranda can be overturned by future presidents.

executive orders

Formal orders to government or an agency or agencies as a whole that carry the force of law issued by the president to direct action by the federal bureaucracy.

executive memorandum

A less powerful formal order to an agency or agencies, that does not carry the force of law, to undertake a particular course of action.

11.1
11.2
11.3
11.4
11.5
11.6

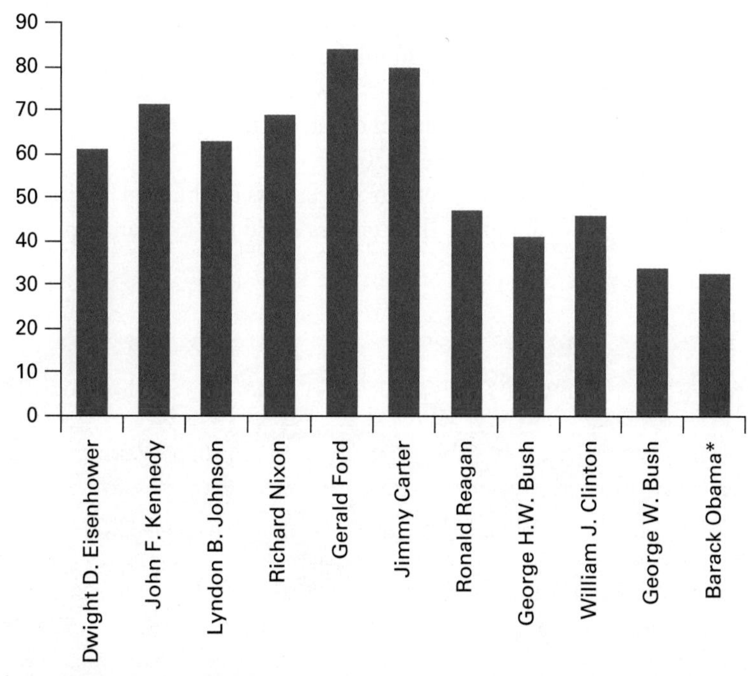

FIGURE 11.1 AVERAGE NUMBER OF EXECUTIVE ORDERS ISSUED PER YEAR DURING EACH PRESIDENTIAL ADMINISTRATION

■ *Why has the average number of executive orders issued declined so much over the past six decades? What other tools might presidents now be using to influence policies and government?*

SOURCE: U.S. National Archives, Executive Orders Disposition Tables, available at http://www.archives.gov/federal-register/executive-orders/disposition.html

11.1
11.2
11.3
11.4
11.5
11.6

impoundment
A decision by the president not to spend money appropriated by Congress, now prohibited under federal law.

line item veto
Presidential power to strike, or remove, specific items from a spending bill without vetoing the entire package; declared unconstitutional by the Supreme Court.

The Power to Submit a Budget to Congress

The Constitution explicitly gives Congress the power to appropriate money, but presidents are responsible for actually spending it. Presidents are also responsible for providing a budget proposal to Congress at the start of the budgeting process.

This authority was contained in the Budget and Accounting Act of 1921. The act required the president to submit annual budgets to Congress. It also created the president's Bureau of the Budget, which in 1970 became the Office of Management and Budget. Although the 1921 act also created the General Accounting Office as an auditing and oversight arm of Congress, presidents have played an increasingly powerful role in shaping the federal budget.[22]

In 1974, Congress approved the Congressional Budget and Impoundment Control Act, which sharply curtailed the president's use of **impoundment**, or refusal to spend appropriations that had been passed into law. Enacted over Nixon's veto, the law gave Congress new powers to control its own budget process, created the Congressional Budget Office (CBO) to give the institution its own sources of economic and spending forecasts, and required the president to submit detailed requests to Congress for any proposed *rescission* (cancellation) of congressional appropriations.

In an effort to control its own tendency to overspend, Congress in 1996 voted to give the president greater budget power through the **line item veto**, which would have allowed presidents to strike out specific sections of an appropriations bill while signing the rest into law. In essence, the line item veto is a legal form of impoundment. Although many governors have the line item veto, the Supreme Court decided the law disturbed the "finely wrought" procedure for making the laws and declared it unconstitutional in a 6-to-3 vote in 1998. If Congress wanted a new procedure for making the laws, Justice John Paul Stevens wrote for the majority, it would have to pursue a constitutional amendment.[23]

The Evolution of Presidential Power

The history of presidential power is one of steady growth. Of the individuals who have filled the office, approximately one-third have enlarged its powers. Andrew Jackson, Abraham Lincoln, Theodore Roosevelt, Franklin Delano Roosevelt, and Harry Truman all redefined the institution and many of its powers by the way they set priorities and responded to crises. Much of this expansion occurred during wartime or national crises such as the economic depression of the 1930s.

Nevertheless, today's presidency reflects precedents established by the nation's first chief executive, George Washington. The Framers could not have anticipated the kinds

Franklin Roosevelt's Depression-era Works Progress Administration (WPA) put millions of people to work on public projects, as depicted in this mural by Marvin Beerbohm, displayed at the Detroit Post Office.

of foreign and domestic threats that now preoccupy the office, but they did recognize the importance of the presidency in protecting the nation in times of trouble.

Today's presidency also reflects the steady expansion that began during the Civil War when President Abraham Lincoln exercised extraordinary powers to win the war, and accelerated dramatically during Franklin Delano Roosevelt's four terms in office. Roosevelt expanded the role in every area. Inaugurated during the Great Depression, Roosevelt took command, and his first 100 days in office in 1933 still stand as the most significant moment of presidential leadership in modern history. Most of his New Deal agenda for helping workers and the poor is still law today.

Roosevelt's impact extends well beyond the legislative agenda, however. He also exploited the powers of the presidency to build a highly personal relationship with the U.S. public, using his "fireside chats" on radio to calm the public during the darkest days of the economic depression, while calling the nation to action during the early days of World War II. Starting each broadcast with the simple phrase "My friends," he became the nation's communicator in chief.

Managing the Presidency

11.3 Outline the functions of the White House staff, Executive Office of the President, cabinet, and vice president.

residents cannot do their job without help. Although some of that help comes from their *inner circle,* composed of their closest advisers, including the first lady, presidents rely on a vast array of support that extends well beyond the White House to the executive branch as a whole.

☐ The White House Staff

The president's most important advisers work inside the cramped confines of the West Wing of the White House.[24] Whereas presidents often view their cabinet secretaries as advocates of their departments, they view their White House staff as intensely loyal and responsive to the president, and the president alone.

Generally, the closer a staff member is to the president's Oval Office, the more power he or she has. However, power is also dependent on how the president organizes the staff for making decisions. Among modern presidents, Franklin Roosevelt and Lyndon Johnson both used the *competitive* approach for managing the White House staff, a "survival of the fittest" situation in which the president allows aides to fight each other for access to the Oval Office. Johnson sometimes gave different staffers the same assignment, hoping the competition would produce a better final decision.

In contrast, John Kennedy, Jimmy Carter, and Bill Clinton all used the *collegial* approach, encouraging aides to work together toward a common position. It is a friendlier way to work but may have the serious drawback of producing *groupthink,* the tendency of small groups to stifle dissent in the search for common ground.[25] Obama used the collegial approach, but also created a long list of "policy czars" within the White House to coordinate executive branch decisions on health care, energy, and education. Republicans criticized the czars as an unconstitutional expansion of presidential authority, but were unable to change Obama's appointments.

Finally, Dwight Eisenhower, Richard Nixon, Ronald Reagan, and George W. Bush all used the *hierarchical* approach, in which the president establishes tight control over who does what in making decisions. Presidents who use this approach usually rely on a "gatekeeper," or trusted adviser such as the chief of staff, to monitor the flow of information to and from the White House. Barack Obama's first chief of staff was Rahm Emanuel, a former member of Congress from Chicago who played a very powerful role in limiting access to his president. Emanuel left the post in early 2009

chief of staff
The head of the White House staff.

Executive Office of the President (EOP)
The cluster of presidential staff agencies that help the president carry out his or her responsibilities. Currently, the office includes the Office of Management and Budget, the Council of Economic Advisers, and several other units.

Office of Management and Budget (OMB)
A presidential staff agency that serves as a clearinghouse for budgetary requests and management improvements for government agencies.

to mount a successful campaign for mayor of Chicago and was replaced by Clinton's former Secretary of Commerce, Bill Daley, who resigned in early 2012. He was replaced by another former Clinton appointee, Jack Lew, who had been Obama's director of the Office of Management and Budget immediately before his move to the White House.

THE WHITE HOUSE BUREAUCRACY The White House staff grew steadily from the early 1900s through the early 1990s, then stabilized at the roughly 400 persons it maintains today. The **chief of staff**, the president's most loyal assistant, heads the staff, which also includes the president's chief lawyer, speechwriters, legislative liaison staff, and press secretary.

There are at least two kinds of White House offices. *Political* offices are designed to help the president run for reelection, control the national party, and shape the president's image through press conferences, television and radio addresses, polling, and travel. *Policy* offices are designed to shape the president's foreign and domestic program. Like congressional committees, these offices collect information and often write legislation. The list of policy offices includes the National Economic Council, which coordinates the president's economic agenda; the National Security Council, which helps set foreign policy; and the Office of Faith-Based and Community Initiatives, which encourages the use of religious institutions to help address community problems.[26]

☐ The Executive Office of the President

The **Executive Office of the President (EOP)** was created in 1939 to give the president enough staff to oversee the growing federal government. It was created after a national commission wrote that "the president needs help."

The EOP consists of the Office of Management and Budget, the Council of Economic Advisers, and several other staff units. It also includes the White House staff, which is a distinct organization of staff who report solely to the president and are not ordinarily subject to Senate confirmation.

No one is quite sure how many people work in the EOP—although many staffers are on the White House budget, the EOP staff also includes between 2,000 and 6,000 staffers who are *detailed*, or loaned to the White House by departments and agencies of government. Because they are paid by their departments and agencies, these staffers do not show up on the traditional head-counts of EOP staff.[27] (See Figure 11.2.)

The **Office of Management and Budget (OMB)** is the central EOP agency for making decisions about the budget. Its director advises the president in detail about

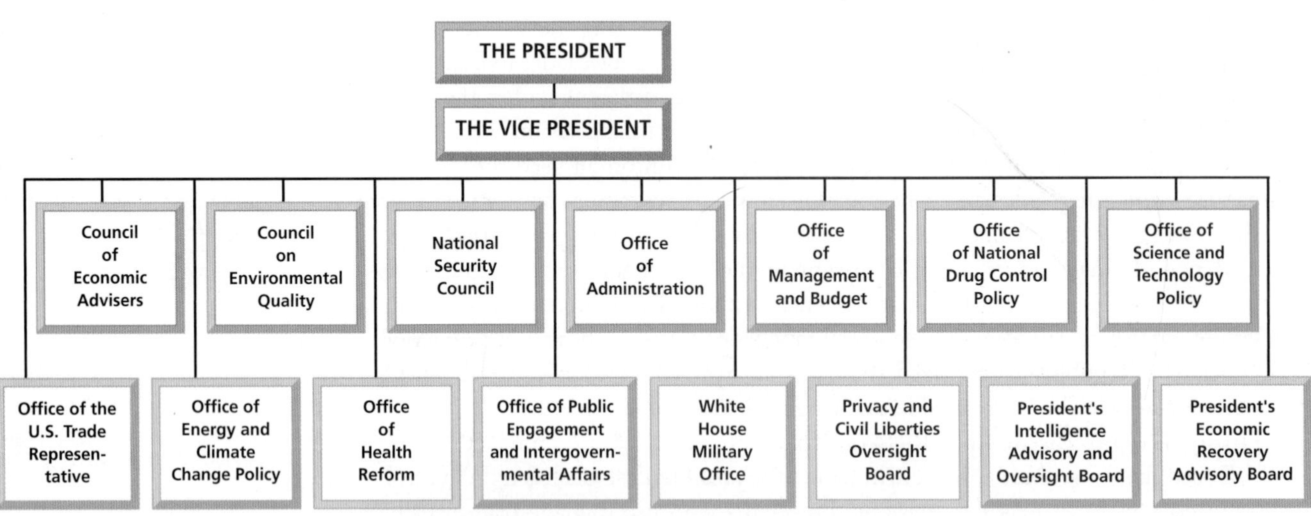

FIGURE 11.2 EXECUTIVE OFFICE OF THE PRESIDENT, 2012

Why are there so many separate offices under the president's direct command? And what do the kinds of offices President Obama includes in his Executive Office indicate about his policy priorities?

SOURCE: www.whitehouse.gov

OF the People Diversity in America

The President's Cabinet

During the past 50 years, the president's cabinet has steadily become more diverse, and will almost certainly continue in the future under Democratic and Republican presidents alike.

Obama's first 20 cabinet appointees were the most diverse team in history but built on the gains made by women and minorities under Presidents Clinton and George W. Bush. The chart shows the increasing diversity among the first round of cabinet appointments each president made.

This increasing diversity brings great assets to the White House. It provides greater creativity and life histories to the discussion of key issues such as economic growth, climate change, and health care reform. It also sends the message that a government of the people involves more than white males. With his appointments, Obama created the first cabinet with a majority of women and minorities.

QUESTIONS

1. **Does partisanship predict the level of diversity in the cabinet? Why or why not?**
2. **Does diversity matter to presidential decisions? Should it?**
3. **How does diversity in the cabinet affect the president's ability to lead the federal government's diverse workforce?**

DIVERSITY IN THE PRESIDENT'S CABINET AT THE START OF THE FIRST TERM IN OFFICE

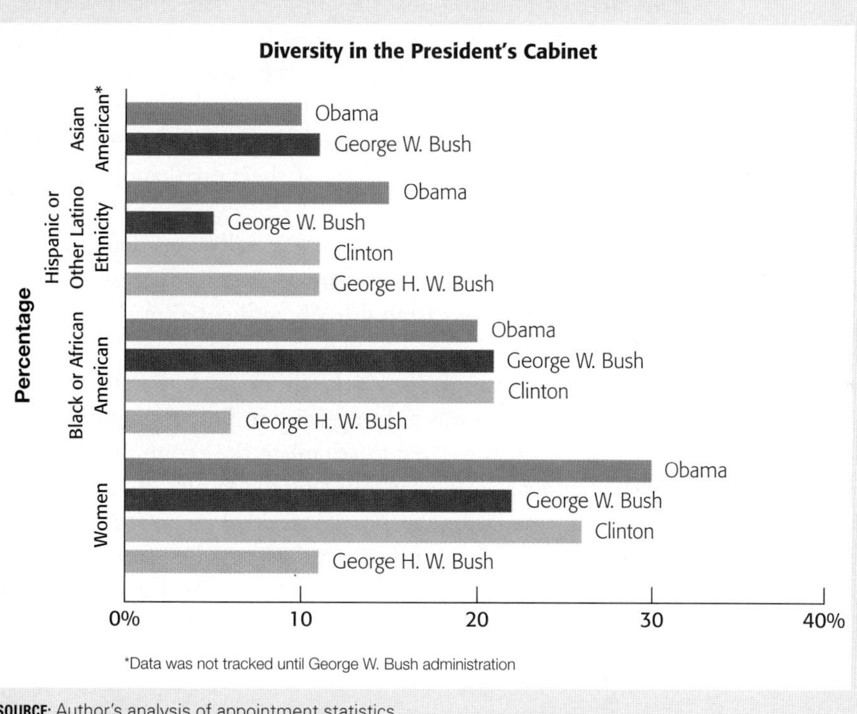

SOURCE: Author's analysis of appointment statistics.

the hundreds of government agencies—how much money they should be allotted in the budget and what kind of job they are doing. The OMB seeks to improve the planning, management, and statistical work of the agencies. It makes a special effort to see that each agency conforms to presidential policies in its dealings with Congress; each agency has to clear its policy recommendations to Congress through the OMB first.[28]

cabinet
The advisory council for the president, consisting of the heads of the executive departments, the vice president, and a few other officials selected by the president.

☐ The Cabinet

It is hard to find a more unusual institution than the president's **cabinet**. The cabinet is not specifically mentioned in the Constitution, yet every president since 1789 has

11.1

11.2

11.3

11.4

11.5

11.6

had one. Washington's consisted of his secretaries of state, treasury, and war, plus his attorney general.

Appointing the cabinet is the first major job for the president-elect. Today, the cabinet consists of the president, the vice president, the heads of the 15 executive departments, and several others a president considers essential for making national decisions. During the Obama administration, for example, the cabinet had 21 members, including the 15 department secretaries, the vice president, White House chief of staff, the head of the Environmental Protection Agency, Office of Management and Budget, U.S. Trade Representative, Ambassador to the United Nations, chairman of the Council of Economic Advisers, and, on occasion, the White House National Security Advisor.

The cabinet has always been a loosely designated body, and it is not always clear whether the group as a whole makes a difference. Because the cabinet is so large, presidents often reserve cabinet meetings for general announcements, not broad debates.

□ The Vice Presidency

The vice presidency has not always been an important job. For most of U.S. history, the vice president was an insignificant officer at best and, at worst, a political rival who sometimes connived against the president. The office was often dismissed as a joke.

No matter how influential they become, vice presidents have only one major responsibility: to be ready to take the oath of office in case the president cannot discharge his duties. Nevertheless, vice presidents enter office with substantial access, including an office just down the hall from the president in the West Wing of the White House, a substantial staff of their own, and access to all of the information flowing into the Oval Office.

Vice President Dick Cheney is generally considered the most influential vice president in modern times. He had more than just access to President George W. Bush, however. He was also extraordinarily influential in shaping the president's decision to go to war.

Joe Biden was given a very different, but still powerful, role in the Obama Administration. He was a strong voice in the president's Afghanistan decision, and he was in charge of the effort to stimulate the economy. He also met regularly with the president and was often consulted by the White House before the president made his decisions. He had a regular, private weekly lunch with Obama to discuss current issues, and had a White House office just down the hall from the president that gave him the opportunity for spontaneous conversation. As a result of these perquisites of office, Biden had the power to persuade, and was deeply involved in important decisions such as the decision to kill bin Laden.

TABLE 11.1 WHAT CAN PRESIDENTS CHANGE?

Percentage of Americans Who Said the President Has a Great Deal of Influence over Each of the Following Issues

Issue	Percentage
International opinions	60%
Federal budget deficit	48%
Taxes	48%
Health care costs	38%
Gas prices	31%
Inflation	30%
Interest rates	23%
Housing prices	20%

SOURCE: Associated Press–Yahoo Poll, January 31, 2008.

The President's Job

11.4 Characterize the various roles that presidents play.

Citizens of the United States want the chief executive to be an international peacemaker as well as a national morale builder, a politician in chief as well as a commander in chief. They want the president to provide leadership on foreign, economic, and domestic policy. They also want presidents to be crisis managers and role models. They want them to be able to connect with ordinary people, yet be smarter, tougher, and more honest than the rest of us. (See Table 11.1 for what U.S. adults thought presidents could change about the world in 2008. The question has not been asked again during the Obama administration.) Alongside the formal powers discussed earlier in this chapter, presidents have a number of informal jobs.

Presidents as Morale Builders

As chief of state, the president must project a sense of national unity and authority as the country's morale-builder-in-chief. The Framers of the Constitution did not fully anticipate the symbolic and morale-building functions a president must perform. But over time, presidents have become national celebrities and command media attention merely by jogging, fishing, golfing, or going to church. By their actions, presidents can arouse a sense of hope or despair, honor, or dishonor.

Morale building means much more than just ceremonies or prayers. At its finest, presidential leadership radiates national self-confidence and helps unlock the possibility for good that exists in the nation. That is certainly what Franklin Delano Roosevelt did early in his first term in calming the nation during the Great Depression that followed the stock market crash in 1929. Using "fireside" radio chats, Roosevelt repeatedly reassured

Barack Obama addresses his supporters at a 2012 election night rally in Chicago. Obama became the 14th president to be reelected to a second term in U.S. history. The other 30 presidents were either defeated for reelection, died in office, returned to the presidency four years after being defeated for reelection, or had been vice presidents who served for the rest of one term only.

The Global Community

Opinions of Barack Obama

Presidents usually start their first terms in office with a burst of public support, both inside the United States and throughout the globe. Once they start making foreign policy decisions, their support tends to erode, especially if those decisions involve unpopular interventions such as the war in Iraq. Almost without exception, they end their terms in office less popular than they were at the beginning.

The pattern is clear in the Pew Research Center's spring 2011 Global Attitudes Survey, which took a snapshot of Obama's popularity throughout the world. Respondents were asked, "How much confidence do you have in Barack Obama to do the right thing regarding world affairs—a lot of confidence, some confidence, not too much confidence, or no confidence at all?"

Obama's extraordinary popularity in Kenya reflects both his personal ties to Africa as the son of a Kenyan citizen and his commitment to improved diplomatic ties with the region. Eighty-six percent of Kenyans reported a lot or some confidence in Obama.

Obama's popularity in the middle of his third year of his first term was in sharp contrast to George W. Bush's popularity in the third year of his second term. Only 16 percent of British citizens had a lot or some confidence in Bush in the middle of his sixth year, compared with 30 percent of the Chinese, 25 percent of Japanese, 16 percent of Mexicans, 55 percent of Nigerians (not Kenyans in this survey), and only 37 percent of Americans.

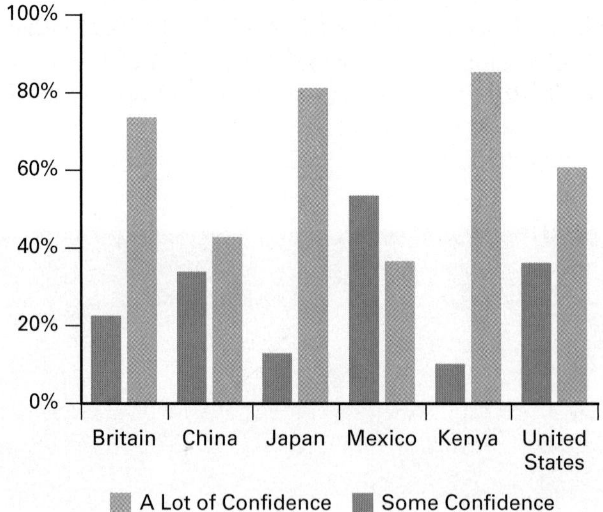

SOURCE: Pew Research Center, *U.S. Favorability Ratings Remain Positive: China Seen Overtaking U.S. as Global Superpower* (Pew Research Center, 2011).

CRITICAL THINKING QUESTIONS

1. Why was most of the world so enthusiastic about Barack Obama's presidency?
2. How does Obama's popularity translate into more effective foreign policy?
3. How will the increase in the U.S. troops in Afghanistan affect Obama's popularity both at home and abroad?

the country that the depression would come to an end. He also used his chats to discuss major national issues such as the growing international conflict that led to World War II.

Presidents as Agenda Setters

By custom and circumstance, presidents are now responsible for proposing initiatives in foreign policy and economic growth and stability. Presidents act as agenda-setters-in-chief when they ask Congress to act on important legislation through special messages such as the annual State of the Union Address.[29] In recent years, however, the number of presidential proposals to Congress has declined steadily, in part because the amount of congressional legislation has declined, and in part because the sagging economy has limited the public's appetite for new programs.

The president's agenda-setting role has also weakened in recent years with growing public anger toward big government. Although Obama was able to convince Congress to enact sweeping health care legislation in 2009, he was soon mired in conflict with the new Republican House over even small-scale legislation such as a temporary freeze on payroll taxes for Social Security and Medicare in 2010 and 2011.

ECONOMIC POLICY Ever since the New Deal, presidents have been expected to promote policies to keep unemployment low, fight inflation, keep taxes down, and promote economic growth and prosperity. The Constitution does not specify these, but presidents know they will be held accountable for economic problems such as inflation and unemployment. Presidents can try to blame their predecessor for bad decisions, but must eventually accept blame if they fail to repair the damage quickly.

SOCIAL POLICY Leadership is often defined as the art of knowing what followers want. John Kennedy and Lyndon Johnson did not launch the civil rights movement, for example. Nor did Bill Clinton or George W. Bush create public pressure for national health insurance or prescription drug coverage. But they all responded to the public demand by supporting legislation on each issue.

NATIONAL SECURITY POLICY The Framers foresaw a special need for speed and unity in dealing with other nations. The Supreme Court has upheld strong presidential authority in this area. In *United States* v. *Curtiss-Wright* (1936), the Court referred to the "exclusive power of the president as the sole organ of the federal government in the field of international relations—a power which does not require as a basis for its exercise an act of Congress, but which, of course, like every other governmental power, must be exercised in subordination to the applicable provisions of the Constitution."[30]

Presidents as Persuaders

Despite their formal powers, presidents spend most of their time *persuading* people. As Richard Neustadt argues, the power to persuade is the president's chief resource.[31] This power to persuade is based on the president's ability to communicate directly with members of Congress and the public through the skillful use of press conferences, speeches, and public events.

Press conferences are the most example of the presidents role as persuader-in-chief. However, the number of solo press conferences has declined sharply over the years. Whereas Franklin Roosevelt averaged nearly seven press conferences a month during his dozen years in office, the past five presidents have averaged just one per month. Barack Obama held three press conferences in his first six months, but from January 2009 to April 2012, he averaged nearly two conferences per month. "Going public" often means carefully staging events before friendly audiences that show strong support for the president.

11.1

11.2

11.3

11.4

11.5

11.6

Going public clearly fits with changes in the electoral process. Presidents now have the staff, the technology, and the public opinion research to tell them how to target their message, and they have nearly instant media access to speak to the public easily. And, as elections have become more image oriented and candidate centered, presidents have the incentive to use these tools to operate a permanent White House campaign.

□ An Impossible Job?

The president's job seems to be getting more difficult as the federal government has grown and conflict between Republicans and Democrats in Congress has increased. With budget deficits increasing in recent years and public support for new programs declining, presidents have faced greater resistance in all their roles.

Although Americans still give presidents higher approval ratings than Congress, they are also less trusting toward government as a whole, and more likely to believe that the "politicians in Washington," as pollsters often describe the nation's leaders, do not have the nation's best interests in mind as they make key decisions. At the same time, campaigns for national office have become more negative with the rise of independent spending by outside groups, while conflict in Congress has escalated.

These trends have added to the public's continued anger and frustration with the federal government. Interviewed in March 2011, for example, 14 percent of Americans said they were angry toward the government in Washington, another 59 percent were frustrated, and just 22 percent said they were basically content.[32] The percentage of Americans expressing anger and frustration has remained about the same since the mid-1990s when the question was first asked in a national poll. The result is a persistent sense that politicians can do nothing right, which constrains the president's ability to lead, and weakens the president's credibility in all aspects of the job.

Congress and the Presidency

11.5 Identify the sources of presidential–congressional conflict and the tools presidents use to influence Congress.

Congress and the presidency have a contentious relationship. They often work closely to address critically important problems but at other times are unable to reach agreement on equally difficult issues. They are most likely to agree in the first year of a president's first term and when one party controls both the White House and Congress, and they are more likely to fight late in the president's first term and off and on throughout the entire second term.

Given the separation of powers, it is a wonder that Congress and the president ever agree at all, which is exactly what the Framers intended. The Framers did not want the legislative process to work like an assembly line. Rather, they wanted ambition to counteract ambition as a way to prevent tyranny.

To the extent that they designed the legislative process to work inefficiently, the Framers succeeded beyond their initial hopes. Presidents work hard to win passage of their top priorities and they often complain that Congress is not listening. However, Congress listens more closely to its constituents, especially when the president's public approval is low. That is why so many of the Obama administration's priorities never reached the floor of the House or Senate. Frustrated with the lack of congressional support, Obama used executive memoranda to address the high unemployment rates that still plagued the nation in 2011 and 2012. Although his actions were relatively minor, they showed his readiness to act regardless of congressional resistance. From 2009 to 2012, he issued a total of 222 memoranda.

☐ Why Presidents and Congress Disagree

Congress and the president disagree for many reasons, not the least of which is the natural tendency of members of Congress to think about elections far into the future.

COMPETING CONSTITUENCIES The Framers guaranteed that members of Congress and the president would represent different constituencies, which often leads to conflict over major legislation. Members of Congress represent either states or local districts, whereas the president represents the nation as a whole. Although these constituencies often overlap, particularly in states that strongly support the president's election, members of Congress often worry most about how the laws and presidential actions will affect their home districts.

COMPETING CALENDARS The Constitution also ensures that Congress and the president will not share the same terms of office. Presidents can serve a maximum of eight years before leaving office, whereas senators and members of the House can serve for decades. Presidents enter office wanting everything passed at once, whereas members of Congress have plenty of time to wait.

COMPETING CAMPAIGNS Finally, the Constitution ensures that Congress and the president will run different kinds of election campaigns. Most members of Congress finance their election campaigns with only minimal assistance from their national

President Jimmy Carter addresses the U.S. public in his first televised address to talk about energy policy. He made a deliberate choice to give the address sitting down near the fireplace dressed in a cardigan sweater as a way to calm the public's concern about increasing gasoline prices.

Explore on MyPoliSciLab

What Influences a President's Public Approval?

Political scientists watch a president's approval because it shows how much political capital is available to him, indicates how the public endorses the executive's performance, and helps us relate popular support to policy success, such as dealing with foreign crises or managing the economy. Gallup approval ratings of two recent presidents are shown below alongside changes in the Gross Domestic Product, which measures the nation's economic growth.

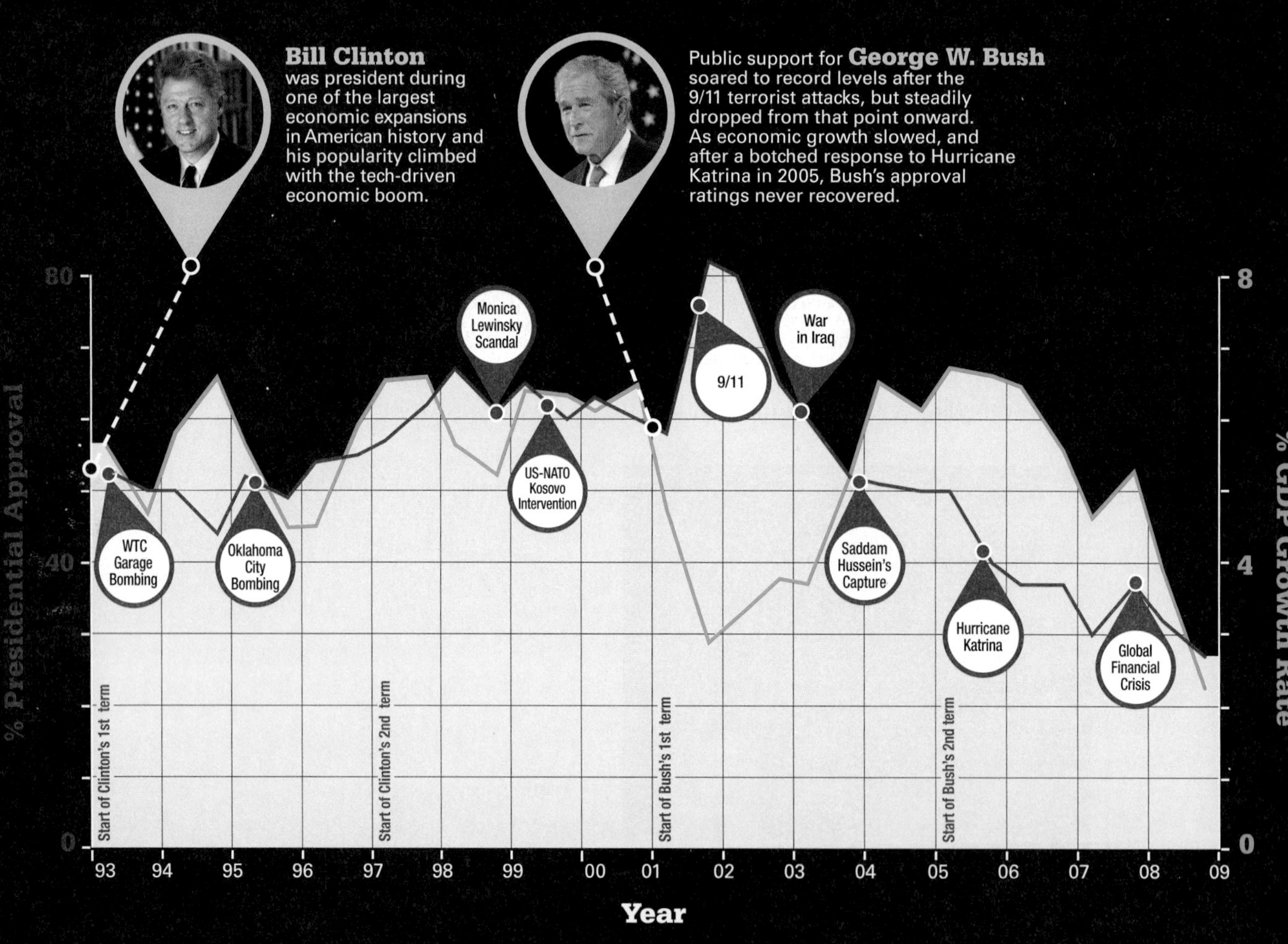

SOURCE: Data from the Gallup Presidential Job Approval Center.

Investigate Further

Concept Do presidents gain or lose popularity over the course of their term? President Clinton's public approval rose as the economy grew, while President Bush's fell and never wrecovered even though the economy grew during most of his term. To see what happened to President Obama's approval, click on MyPoliSciLab.

Connection Is popularity tied to economic performance? Clearly Bill Clinton's popularity moved with the economy. As it grew, so too did Clinton's job approval. For President Bush, there may be correlation between economic approval and popularity, but it is masked for much of his term by the effects of war on public opinion.

Cause How do events shape the popularity of President Bush? The 9/11 terrorist attacks led to a rally-round-the-flag effect which defined George W. Bush's presidency. For a brief period, success in the Iraq war boosted Bush's popularity until war fatigue and failure to manage other crises pulled his approval ratings to record low levels.

political party. They usually run independently of the president or national party platform. Even members of the president's own party have been known to ask the president not to visit their districts in particularly tight elections or when the president's public approval is falling. Whenever possible, members try to make elections about local, not national issues, which means the president is often ignored during the campaign.

☐ Influencing Congress

Presidents have long had a substantial, if not always dominant, role in shaping what Congress does. Their primary vehicle for doing so is the president's agenda, an informal list of top legislative priorities. Whether through the State of the Union Address or through other messages and signals, presidents make clear what they think Congress should do.

It is one thing to proclaim a presidential priority, however, and quite another to actually influence congressional action. As Richard Neustadt argued in *Presidential Power,* a president's constitutional powers add up to little more than a job as the country's most distinguished office clerk. It is a president's ability to persuade others that spells the difference between being a clerk and being a national leader.[33]

The power to persuade on Capitol Hill is often measured through the **presidential support score**, calculated by counting the times the president wins key votes in Congress. Recent presidents have been less effective in persuading Congress on key votes. The Johnson administration won 60 percent of the votes in 1965, compared with Obama at just 16 percent in 2011.[34]

PRESIDENTIAL MANDATES Presidents who enter office with a large electoral margin, high public approval, and a party majority in Congress often claim a **mandate**, or public support, to govern. The winner-take-all nature of the Electoral College system tends to make the president's popular vote look larger than it truly is.

Obama decided to spend his relatively modest 2008 presidential election mandate on just two priorities: an economic stimulus package and health care reform. Although he did win an overwhelming share of the electoral vote, his popular vote total was only 53 percent, which limited his ability to claim a sweeping mandate for change. Moreover, the economic calamity that started in 2008 reduced public support for most new programs.

PUBLIC APPROVAL The mandate to govern depends in part on public approval, which generally falls over time. Most presidents start their terms with their highest approval marks based on election support. Bush became the first incumbent president in modern history to win reelection despite starting his campaign with an approval rating below 50 percent. Although he regained ground after his second inauguration, his ratings continued to fall as his second term continued, which helps explain the declining number of congressional votes on which he took a position. He simply did not have enough **political capital** to take more positions.

Presidents also benefit from **rally points**, spikes in public approval following a domestic or international crisis. Rally points do not necessarily last long, however. George W. Bush's ratings jumped dramatically following the September 11, 2001, attacks when he called on the nation to support the war on terrorism but eventually fell back with the continued violence after the first months of the war in Iraq. His approval rating jumped 29 percent after the September 11 attacks and 12 percent after the start of the Iraq War in 2003.

From 2009–2012, Obama did not have a rally point of any great significance. His approval ratings barely changed after bin Laden was killed as the public continued to worry about the economy, unemployment, and rising gasoline prices.

presidential support score
The percentage of times a president wins on key votes in Congress.

mandate
A president's claim of broad public support.

political capital
The amount of overall public approval that a president can use to win support for major decisions and proposals.

rally point
A rise in public approval of the president that follows a crisis as Americans "rally round the flag" and the chief executive.

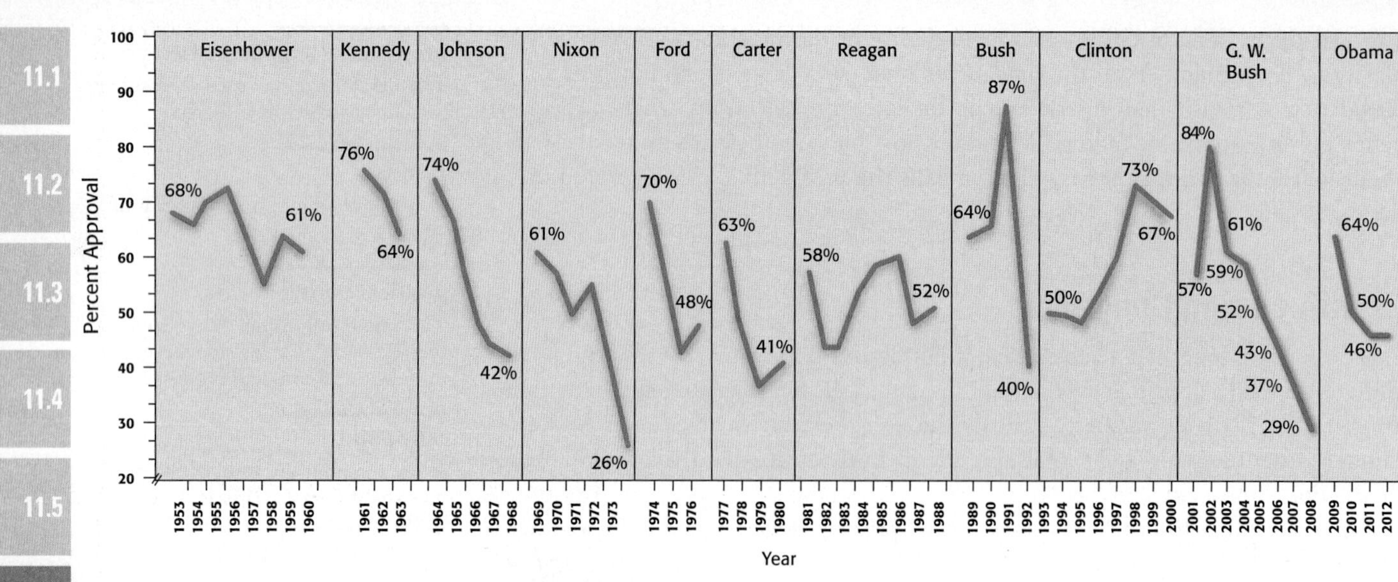

FIGURE 11.3 PRESIDENTIAL APPROVAL RATINGS, 1953–2012

■ *What explains the general decline in presidential popularity over time? How was the economy related to Obama's fall?*

NOTE: Percentage is from the first Gallup/*USA Today* poll taken each calendar year.

SOURCE: Gallup/*USA Today* poll, available at www.pollingreport.com.

REPUTATION The longer presidents stay in office, the better they get at being president. They learn how Washington works, what powers they can use to influence congressional action, and whom they need to convince to win passage of their top priorities. Presidents also learn how to use unilateral powers to accomplish some of their goals.

Nevertheless, presidents pay great attention to the steady erosion of public approval that occurs over time. As a result of this, they have the greatest potential influence at the very point when they know the least about being president, and they know the most about being president when they have the least influence.

Some experts believe the president's reputation has declined in recent years, in part due to political scandals. The controversy over the 2000 election raised questions about the legitimacy of the electoral process, and the war in Iraq led many to doubt President Bush's leadership in the war on terrorism. As a result, Congress may now be quicker to dismiss presidential positions. Nevertheless, presidents still hold many advantages in shaping public opinion, most notably through their role as morale builders during difficult times.

Judging Presidents

11.6 Identify factors that influence judgments about presidents.

Presidents rise and fall in the historical rankings based on a number of factors. Some rise because they led the nation through periods of intense domestic or international crisis; others rise because they had a distinctive vision of where the nation should go on issues such as civil rights, social policy, or the economy. Rankings also include at least some assessment of how presidents fared as political and moral leaders of the nation.

History tends to judge wars and international crises as the most significant test of a president's leadership. Wars that end in stalemate tend to diminish a president's greatness, whereas wars that end in victory raise a president's ranking,

BY the People Making a Difference

Public Service Through the White House Blog

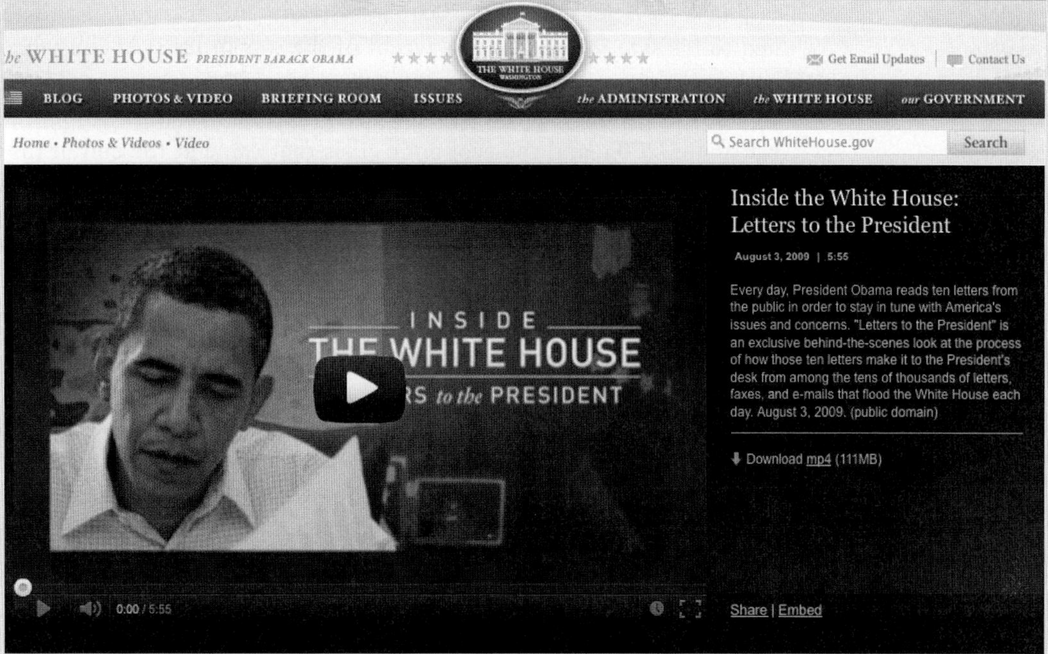

Presidents pay attention to public opinion in many ways. Every president since the 1960s has appointed his own pollster to monitor public opinion. Presidents also travel frequently throughout the country lobbying for their programs, engaging citizens in town hall meetings, raising money for their political party, and campaigning for reelection.

Most of these activities are directed at relatively small numbers of citizens, which puts the burden on citizens to make contact with the president. Citizens are always welcome to send letters and e-mails to the president, but they rarely get a personal response. The White House receives 65,000 letters, 100,000 e-mails, 1,000 faxes, and between 2,500 and 3,500 phone calls per day, but only a handful of these messages end up on the president's desk.

At the start of his administration, however, Obama asked the White House mailroom to give him 10 letters from ordinary Americans every day. Obama has been particularly interested in receiving real stories about the nation's current condition. "These letters, I think, do more to keep me in touch with what's happening around the country than anything else," Obama said in a White House video about the sorting process at http://www.whitehouse.gov/video/Inside-the-White-House-Letters-to-the-President. "Some of them are funny, some of them are angry, a lot of them are sad or frustrated about their current situation."

Under Obama, the White House established a series of forums for receiving public comments. By mid-2012, for example, the president had nearly 20 million Facebook friends.

QUESTIONS

1. What kind of letter makes the most compelling reading in the White House and why?
2. Does a single hit on whitehouse.gov make any difference in the president's opinion?
3. What does the number of friends or followers actually tell the White House about public opinion? Are polls a better way for the president to understand what the country thinks?

especially when the nation's survival is threatened. Abraham Lincoln (the Civil War), Woodrow Wilson (World War I), and Franklin Delano Roosevelt (World War II) rank among the great presidents because of their leadership during just such wars, whereas Lyndon Johnson ranks much lower because of his role in the Vietnam stalemate.

Corruption and inability to deal with economic problems are sure paths to presidential failure. Warren Harding and Richard Nixon both rank as failures because of

11.1

11.2

11.3

11.4

11.5

11.6

scandals that tarnished their presidencies, while Herbert Hoover is ranked a failure because of his lack of leadership at the start of the Great Depression. Although Lyndon Johnson launched a number of great domestic programs such as Medicare for older citizens and helped secure civil rights for African Americans, his role in the Vietnam War continues to cast a shadow on his presidential greatness.

It is too early to guess where George W. Bush will be ranked by history. Bush's response to September 11, 2001, was steady and reassuring, and the nation rallied to his side in the first few weeks of the war in Iraq. At the same time, soaring budget deficits and questions about the war in Iraq undermined both his credibility and his public support. So did the government's weak response to Hurricane Katrina in 2005, and the economic crisis that came at the end of his presidency in 2008. Given these shortcomings, Bush seems destined for no more than an average rating. According to public opinion polls taken in early 2009, only 17 percent of respondents rated Bush outstanding or above average, compared with 45 percent for Clinton, 32 percent for George H. W. Bush, 64 percent for Reagan, 38 percent for Jimmy Carter, and 23 percent for Gerald Ford. (As of 2012, it was still too early to rate Obama in these polls, though Obama hinted that he ranked among the top four presidents in history in terms of early legislative accomplishments.) Of these presidents, only Reagan is likely to emerge as a great or near-great president in future polls.

Ultimately, a president's place in history is determined decades after he or she leaves office and varies over time. Reagan has moved up the charts with each passing survey, for example, as his role in ending the cold war takes on increasing visibility in an uncertain world. By remembering that there is a future accounting, presidents can find some inspiration for making the hard and sometimes unpopular choices that have led to greatness among their predecessors. Thus, the judgment of history may be one of the most important sources of accountability the nation has on its presidents.

Barack Obama's standing in history is still to be determined. He is no doubt one of the most charismatic presidents in modern history, and did engineer passage of health care reform, rescue the U.S. automobile industry, and end the wars in Iraq and Afghanistan. Despite these achievements, his standing will depend in large measure on the state of the economy. After four years in office, unemployment still remained high as the economy struggled to grow.

On MyPoliSciLab

Review the Chapter

 **Listen** to **Chapter 11** on **MyPoliSciLab**

The Structure and Powers of the Presidency

11.1 Describe the constitutional foundations and primary roles of the presidency, p. 347.

The Framers wanted a presidency with enough authority to protect the nation from domestic and foreign threats but not so strong that it would become a threat to liberty. The Framers gave the president three central roles in the new government: commander in chief, diplomat in chief, and administrator in chief. Presidents have expanded their powers in several ways throughout the decades. Crises, both foreign and economic, have enlarged these powers. When there is a need for decisive action, presidents are asked to supply it.

Controversies in Presidential Power

11.2 Evaluate the controversies surrounding presidents' assertion of additional executive powers, p. 357.

The Constitution is not always clear on which branch has what powers, which creates controversies over the president's war power and authority to assert executive privilege, issue executive orders, and control the budget and spending process.

Managing the Presidency

11.3 Outline the functions of the White House staff, Executive Office of the President, cabinet, and vice president, p. 361.

Presidents manage the executive branch with the assistance of an intensely loyal White House staff, a much larger Executive Office of the President (EOP) that is anchored by the Office of Management and Budget (OMB), a cabinet of department secretaries that oversees the federal government's employees, and the vice president. The vice president's authority varies from president to president.

The President's Job

11.4 Characterize the various roles that presidents play, p. 365.

We expect a great deal from our presidents. We want them to be crisis managers, morale builders, and agenda setters, but we also want them to be able to connect with average citizens. Presidents must also act as persuaders, using their staff, technology, and public opinion research to accomplish their agendas.

Congress and the Presidency

11.5 Identify the sources of presidential–congressional conflict and the tools presidents use to influence Congress, p. 368.

The president and Congress often have a tense relationship because of different constitutional expectations and party divisions. Presidents have a variety of tools for influencing Congress, however, and use their political and personal resources to gain support for their policy proposals. Presidents have several powerful tools for influencing Congress. They can create mandates by helping members of Congress win elections, use their public approval to lobby Congress for action, and rely on the reputation of the presidency as a source of prestige.

Judging Presidents

11.6 Identify factors that influence judgments about presidents, p. 373.

Presidential greatness is hard to define. Historians, political scientists, and the American public consider Washington, Jefferson, Lincoln, and Franklin Roosevelt as their greatest presidents. Greatness depends in part on how presidents deal with crisis and war.

Learn the Terms

 **Study** and **Review** the **Flashcards**

parliamentary governments, p. 348
electoral college, p. 349
presidential ticket, p. 350
vesting clause, p. 350
treaty, p. 351
executive agreement, p. 351
congressional–executive agreement, p. 353
recess appointment, p. 353
veto, p. 353
pocket veto, p. 353
take care clause, p. 354
inherent powers, p. 354
State of the Union Address, p. 354
signing statements, p. 354
impeachment, p. 355
War Powers Resolution, p. 357

executive privilege, p. 358
executive orders, p. 359
executive memorandum, p. 359
impoundment, p. 360
line item veto, p. 360
chief of staff, p. 362
Executive Office of the President (EOP), p. 362
Office of Management and Budget (OMB), p. 362
cabinet, p. 363
presidential support score, p. 371
mandate, p. 371
political capital, p. 371
rally point, p. 371

Test Yourself

 **Study** and **Review** the **Practice Tests**

MULTIPLE CHOICE QUESTIONS

11.1 Describe the constitutional foundations and primary roles of the presidency.

All of the following are presidential roles except
- **a.** Senate party leader in chief.
- **b.** federalist in chief.
- **c.** administrator in chief.
- **d.** legislator in chief.
- **e.** economist in chief.

11. 2 Evaluate the controversies surrounding presidents' assertion of additional executive powers.

Which of these are additional executive powers?
- **a.** the power to conduct secret military missions.
- **b.** the power to invoke executive priviledge.
- **c.** the power to issue executive orders.
- **d.** the power to submit a budget to Congress.
- **e.** all of the above.

11. 3 Outline the functions of the White House staff, Executive Office of the President, cabinet, and vice president.

Which of the following is NOT a part of the president's staff?
- **a.** the White House staff.
- **b.** the Cabinet.
- **c.** the Government Accountability Office.
- **d.** the Executive Office of the President.
- **e.** The Office of Management and Budget.

11.4 Characterize the various roles that presidents play.

Which of the following are not presidential roles?
- **a.** persuader.
- **b.** agenda setter.
- **c.** morale builder.
- **d.** legislator.
- **e.** decision maker.

11.5 Identify the sources of presidential-congressional conflict and the tools presidents use to influence Congress.

Which of the following is a main source of conflict between the president and Congress?
- **a.** economic policy.
- **b.** the budget.
- **c.** executive agreements with foreign nations.
- **d.** the electoral calendar.
- **e.** all of the above.

11.6 Identify factors that influence judgments about presidents.

What is the most significant test of presidential leadership?
- **a.** a balanced budget.
- **b.** ethical conduct.
- **c.** economic growth.
- **d.** wars and international crises.
- **e.** public approval.

ESSAY QUESTION

In a short essay, discuss factors other than winning wars that you think make a president "great." How would the two most recent presidents rank in your determination of presidential greatness?

Explore Further

IN THE LIBRARY

Thomas E. Cronin and Michael A. Genovese, *The Paradoxes of the American Presidency*, 3rd ed. (Oxford University Press, 2009).

Terry Eastland, *Energy in the Executive* (Free Press, 1992).

Fred Greenstein, *The Presidential Difference: Leadership Style from FDR to George W. Bush,* 2nd ed. (Princeton University Press, 2004).

Fred Greenstein, *Inventing the Job of the* President: Leadership Style from George Washington to Andrew Jackson, (Princeton University Press, 2009).

Gene Healy, *The Cult of the Presidency: America's Dangerous Devotion to Presidential Power* (Cato Institute, 2008).

Charles O. Jones, *The Presidency in a Separated System*, 2nd ed. (Brookings Institution Press, 2005).

Samuel Kernell, *Going Public: New Strategies of Presidential Leadership*, 4th ed. (CQ Press, 2006).

Gary King Andlyn Ragsdale, *The Elusive Executive: Discovering Statistical Patterns in the Presidency*, 2nd ed. (CQ Press, 2002).

Sidney M. Milkis, *The President and the Parties: The Transformation of the American Party System Since the New Deal* (Oxford University Press, 1993).

Michael Nelson, Ed., *The Presidency and the Political System*, 9th ed. (CQ Press, 2009).

Richard E. Neustadt, *Presidential Power and the Modern Presidents* (Free Press, 1991).
Bradley H. Patterson Jr., *The White House Staff: Inside the West Wing and Beyond* (Brookings Institution Press, 2002).
James Pfiffner, *The Modern Presidency,* 5th ed. (Wadsworth, 2008).
Stephen Skowronek, *Presidential Leadership in Political Time: Reprise and Reappraisal* (University of Kansas Press, 2008).

ON THE WEB

www.whitehouse.gov
Every fact possible on the sitting president, including speeches, blogs, videos, and links to all major executive departments, agencies, and White House offices.

www.loc.gov
The Library of Congress Web site. Click on the presidential history link for portraits and details on each presidency dating back to 1789.

www.thepresidency.org
The Web site of the Center for the Presidency. Loaded with papers and facts.

www.presidency.ucsb.edu
The largest inventory of information on what presidents do. The Web site contains every State of the Union Address, executive orders, press conference transcripts, veto messages, and selected research papers in history. An invaluable resource for research papers.

12

Listen to Chapter 12 on MyPoliSciLab

The Federal Bureaucracy and the Public Policy Process

Creating and Executing the Laws

Early in the morning on April 20, 2010, British Petroleum was almost done drilling one of the deepest oil wells in the Gulf of Mexico. The well was connected to a floating oil rig called the Deepwater Horizon, which was considered one of the safest in the industry. However, on that morning, only days before the Deepwater Horizon was to start pumping oil, methane gas surged up the pipeline and exploded on the rig. Eleven oil workers were killed in the fire and the Deepwater Horizon began sinking. The result was the largest oil spill in U.S. history.

The spill was caused by a number of failures, including the the rush to start pumping oil. However, the disaster was rooted in what President Barack Obama later called the "cozy relationship" between the federal government's Minerals Management Service (MMS) and the oil industry. Located within the Department of the Interior, the MMS was responsible for implementing federal laws regulating oil and gas drilling. It set safety standards for offshore oil drilling even as it granted permits that

12.1 Outline the constitutional roots of the federal bureaucracy, its organizations, and its employees, p. 381.

12.2 Analyze the bureaucracy's implementation options and its effectiveness, p. 388.

12.3 Assess presidential and congressional tools for controlling the federal bureaucracy, p. 391.

12.4 Relate politics and public policy, and differentiate the three types of public policy, p. 395.

12.5 Outline the key steps in making public policy, and assess the different types of policy, p. 396.

12.6 Assess ways in which citizens can influence the public policy process, p. 404.

Oil from the Deepwater Horizon failed drilling project burns during the early hours following the explosion that killed 11 workers. The disaster caused the largest oil spill in U.S. history and affected every state along the Gulf Coast.

MyPoliSciLab Video Series

Watch on MyPoliSciLab

The Big Picture Bureaucracy is a dirty word—but should it be? Author Paul C. Light explains why bureaucrats are necessary for carrying out legislation and public policy in the United States, and he reveals why you may want to thank the TSA employee screening you and other passengers at the airport.

The Basics What does the bureaucracy do? What is its role in our democracy? In this video, you will listen to what people think about bureaucrats and the job they do. You will also learn why the bureaucracy can have such a big impact on your life.

In Context Why is the bureaucracy important in the policymaking process? In this video, University of North Texas political scientist Matthew Eshbaugh-Soha talks about not only the bureaucracy and its importance at the federal level, but also the role the federal bureaucracy plays in cooperation with state and local bureaucracies.

Thinking Like a Political Scientist Are bureaucracies democratic? And if so, how are they democratic? University of North Texas political scientist Matthew Eshbaugh-Soha tackles this question and also looks at political appointments and other important research topics associated with bureaucracies.

In the Real World Is the federal bureaucracy too big and too powerful? Real people weigh in on this question and discuss whether they feel reducing the size of the bureaucracy is worth losing the protections that those agencies provide.

So What? Discover what the bureaucracy can—and cannot—do. Author Paul C. Light discusses why bureaucracy works so slowly that it appears to be doing nothing, and he highlights ways to keep an eye on government and make sure it is working properly.

allowed the industry to extract as much oil as possible. As the spill showed, even the most carefully written laws have little effect if the federal bureaucracy does not do its job in helping the president obey the Constitution's requirement to execute the laws faithfully.

Confronted with these failures, Obama immediately decided to overhaul the MMS by breaking it into two new agencies, one for assuring safety and the other for granting permits. He accepted the resignation of the political appointee heading the agency and gave the U.S. Coast Guard absolute authority to supervise British Petroleum's efforts to stop the spill. He also appointed a special commission to investigate the disaster. Finally, Obama promised a new era of accountability in government oversight of the industry.

Under the reorganization, MMS was split into a new Bureau of Safety and Environmental Enforcement and a Bureau of Ocean Energy Management. The first agency was designed to regulate all laws governing deepwater drilling, while the latter was given responsibility to promote oil drilling. By dividing these responsibilities, Congress and the president hoped to avoid the conflicts of interest that encouraged British Petroleum and its partners to move as fast as possible to drill new wells even if that sometimes caused shortcuts in safety.

In this chapter, we examine the origins, functions, and realities of the federal bureaucracy as it works to implement the laws. Strengthening workplace safety, environmental protection, and economic development are all tasks that require government bureaucracy. All were important endeavors when they emerged from Congress and were signed into law by the president as public policies, but they could not become achievements without the bureaucracy. We also explore how governmental departments, agencies, and employees are held accountable to the president, Congress, and the U.S. public. Finally, we examine the overall process for making public policies and the key questions Congress and the president must answer when they decide to create new programs.

bureaucracy
A form of organization that operates through impersonal, uniform regulations and procedures.

bureaucrat
A negative term for describing a career government employee.

Understanding the Federal Bureaucracy: Constitutional Origins, Organizations, and Employees

12.1 Outline the constitutional roots of the federal bureaucracy, its organizations, and its employees.

he Framers clearly understood that the new national government would need an administrative system to protect the young Republic from foreign and domestic threats. They also understood that the new departments of government would need talented employees if they were to succeed.

This chapter uses the words **bureaucracy** and **bureaucrats** to describe the federal government's organizations and employees. Although these words are often used as a way to criticize government, a bureaucracy is simply a form of organization that delivers goods and services at the lowest cost through specialization of jobs, close supervision of employees, and clear rules for making decisions. Therefore, we will use the word *bureaucracy* as a familiar way to describe the federal government's administrative organizations and employees, but will also refer to government departments and agencies and federal employees whenever possible to make clear that many federal employees and their departments and agencies work hard to meet public expectations for efficient, effective government.

□ Building the Federal Bureaucracy

Under the Constitution, the federal bureaucracy is responsible for faithfully executing the laws on behalf of the president, Congress, and the judiciary. The Framers gave the president the authority to determine how the bureaucracy would look, although Congress had to approve the actual structure of the departments and agencies through

Alexander Hamilton helped set many of the precedents that govern the federal bureaucracy today. He was a strong advocate of what he called "execution in detail," which involved detailed regulations that federal employees must follow, and he argued for an expansion in the number of federal employees as the federal government's mission expanded.

department
Usually the largest organization in government with the largest mission; also the highest rank in the federal hierarchy.

laws. The Framers believed that federal departments and agencies would be relatively small, and they expected Congress to establish the same departments that had existed under the Articles of Confederation, including the departments of war, state, and treasury, and the postal service.[1] Nevertheless, the Framers made three key decisions about executing the laws that continue to shape federal administration to this day.

First, they prohibited members of the House and Senate from holding executive branch positions in Article I, Section 6, of the Constitution: Under this provision, Congress cannot create executive branch jobs for its members.[2]

Second, the Framers decided to give the president authority to nominate the senior officers of government. At the same time, they gave the Senate authority to confirm or reject the president's appointees under the Constitution's "advice and consent" function. They also gave Congress the power to create new departments and agencies through legislation signed by the president, and the power to determine the number of federal employees, the budgets they administer, and the taxes they collect. Nevertheless, the Constitution clearly designates the president as the federal government's *administrator in chief.* Once the laws are passed, employees are hired, and budgets and taxes set, the president is responsible for making sure the laws are implemented and obeyed.

As the federal government's mission grew, so did its bureaucracy. By 2012, the federal bureaucracy was composed of 15 departments, 50 lesser agencies, the U.S. Postal Service, and the three branches of the armed services (Air Force, Army, and Navy). It also employs one of the largest workforces in the world. Nearly 4.5 million people worked for the federal government in 2012, including 700,000 postal workers, more than 2.2 million full-time federal employees, and 1.4 million military personnel. In addition, by the mid-2000s an estimated 7.6 million employees worked indirectly for the bureaucracy under contracts to private firms such as Lockheed Martin and Boeing, while another 3 million also worked indirectly under federal grants to colleges, universities, and state and local governments.[3] (See Figure 12.1 for estimates of the number of contractors and grantees who worked for the federal government from 1990 to 2005, which is the last year that the contractor and grantee estimates were collected.)

☐ Types of Federal Organizations

Federal employees work for departments and agencies, which are classified into four broad types: (1) *departments,* (2) *independent stand-alone agencies,* (3) *independent regulatory commissions,* and (4) *government corporations.*

Departments tend to be the most familiar and largest federal organizations. They also generally have the most extensive missions and biggest budgets.

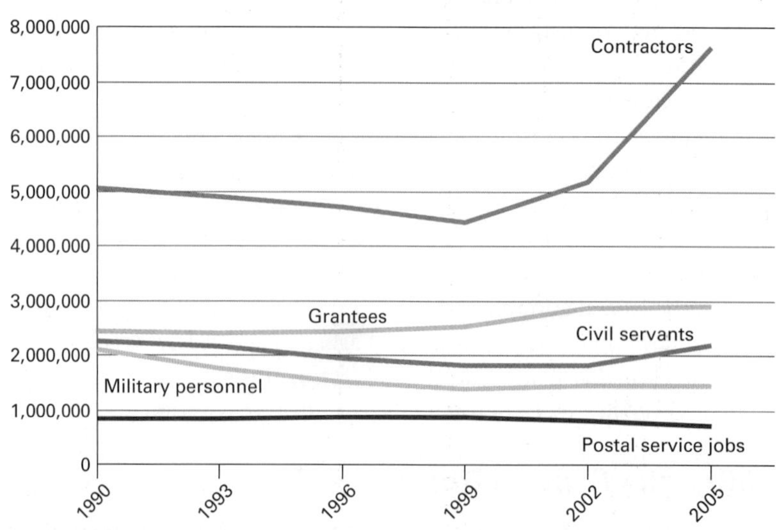

FIGURE 12.1 MEASURING THE ESTIMATED TOTAL NUMBER OF FEDERAL EMPLOYEES

Why has there been such a dramatic increase in the number of contracted employees?

SOURCE: Paul C. Light, *A Government Ill Executed* (Harvard University Press, 2008).

Independent stand-alone agencies are also under the president's control but tend to have fewer federal employees and may have more focused missions than departments. In general, the word "independent" is used to distinguish agencies that exist outside a department from those that operate within a department.

Independent regulatory commissions are a special kind of independent agency. They are created to insulate the agency from congressional and presidential control through the appointment of a board of commissioners who serve for a fixed term of office.

Finally, **government corporations** are designed to operate much like private businesses and have special authority to set the prices of their services. They are supposed to make money.

We will discuss each of the four types of federal organizations next.

independent stand-alone agency
A government agency that operates outside a traditional government department, but under the president's direct control.

independent regulatory commission
A government agency or commission with regulatory power whose independence is protected by Congress.

government corporation
A government agency that is designed like a business corporation, and is created to secure greater freedom of action and flexibility for a particular program.

12.1

12.2

12.3

12.4

12.5

12.6

DEPARTMENTS Departments are the most visible organizations in the federal bureaucracy. Today's 15 departments employ more than 70 percent of all federal civil servants and spend 93 percent of all federal dollars. Secretaries head 14 of the departments, while the attorney general heads the Department of Justice.

Measured by the total number of employees, the five largest departments are the Defense Department, which governs the armed services; the Department of Veterans Affairs, which helps veterans return to civilian life after military service; the Department of Homeland Security, which helps protect the nation from terrorism, runs the airport screening lines, and manages the response to natural disasters such as hurricanes; the Department of the Treasury, which oversees expenditures and raises revenues through the Internal Revenue Service; and the Department of Justice, which enforces the laws by representing the nation in court cases and investigates crime through the Federal Bureau of Investigation.

Defense, Health and Human Services, Justice, State, and Treasury are considered part of the *inner cabinet* that is the most important, while the *outer* cabinet composed of the other ten departments is considered to be less important to the president. Presidents meet with the secretaries of the inner cabinet frequently, but rarely meet with the secretaries of the outer cabinet, and then only when an emergency arises or a key policy issue is under review by Congress or the judiciary.

The 15 federal departments were created using one of three different approaches.

- The first involves a merger of already-existing agencies into a new organization. In 2003, for example, the Congress merged 22 separate agencies and their 170,000 employees into the Department of Homeland Security. (Figure 12.2 shows the department's organization chart as of January 1, 2012.)
- The second approach involves the break-up of an existing department into two or more new departments. In 1979, for example, Congress split the Department of Health, Education, and Welfare into the new departments of Education and Health and Human Services.
- The third approach involves the elevation of an independent stand-alone agency to department-level status. In 1988, for example, Congress elevated the Veterans Administration to cabinet status as the new Department of Veterans Affairs.

INDEPENDENT STAND-ALONE AGENCIES The word *independent* means at least two things in the federal bureaucracy. Applied to a regulatory commission, it means the agency is outside the president's control. Applied to an agency of government, it merely means separate from a traditional department. Whereas independent regulatory commissions do not report to the president, independent agencies do.

As a general rule, independent stand-alone agencies work on specific problems. Becoming an agency is often the first step toward becoming a department. The Veterans Administration was created in 1930 as an agency, for example, and became a department in 1989. Independent stand-alone agencies are usually headed by an administrator or director, the second most senior title in the federal bureaucracy behind secretary or attorney general. There are more than 50 such agencies today.

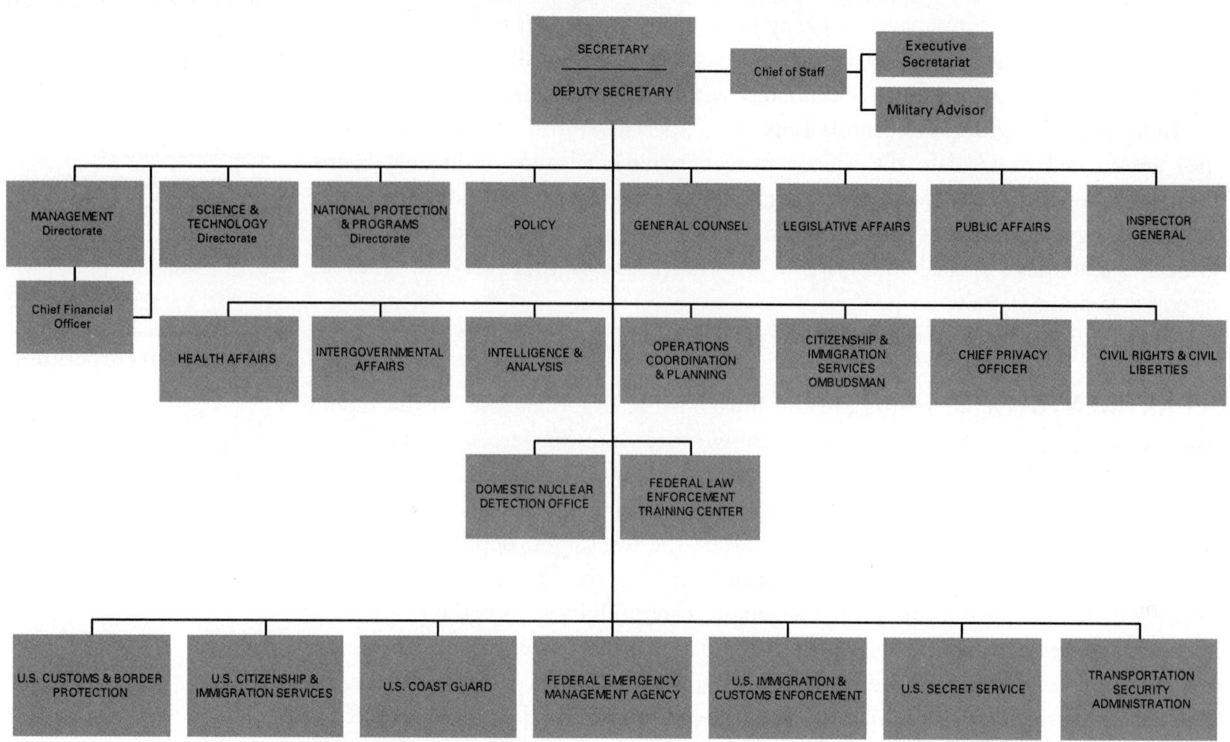

FIGURE 12.2 THE DEPARTMENT OF HOMELAND SECURITY

What are the benefits and drawbacks of having all of these organizations housed within one department?

The spread of independent stand-alone agencies can add to confusion about who is responsible for what in the federal government. For example, the federal government has more than 15 different intelligence agencies, which include the CIA, the Defense Intelligence Agency, the FBI, and the National Security Agency. These agencies had a history of keeping secrets not only from the people but also from each other, which contributed to the intelligence failures leading up to the war in Iraq. In late 2004, Congress created an Office of the Director of National Intelligence to oversee the intelligence community.

INDEPENDENT REGULATORY COMMISSIONS Independent regulatory commissions have a measure of independence from both Congress and the president. By definition, these commissions are headed not by a single executive but by a small number of commissioners appointed by the president, with Senate confirmation, for fixed terms of office. Although the president appoints all independent regulatory commissioners and the Senate confirms each one separately, they have fixed terms of office and are sworn to uphold the Constitution. Unlike other presidential appointees, however, commissioners cannot be removed from office without cause, which is defined by law to mean inefficiency, neglect of duty, or unethical behavior. As a result, independent regulatory commissions are generally insulated from political pressure.

Congress has created dozens of independent regulatory commissions with the power to protect consumers (the Consumer Product Safety Commission), regulate stock markets (the Securities and Exchange Commission), oversee federal election laws (the Federal Election Commission), monitor television and radio (the Federal Communications Commission), regulate business (the Federal Trade Commission), control the supply of money (the Federal Reserve Board), and watch over nuclear power plants (the Nuclear Regulatory Commission). Independent regulatory commissions are not completely independent, however. The president and Congress must approve their annual budgets, and their decisions are subject to judicial review. Moreover, presidents often nominate commissioners on the basis of party loyalty, which means that commissions can be highly political.

Independent regulatory commissions tend to be much less visible than departments until a crisis occurs. The Securities and Exchange Commission (SEC) was on the front pages for three years, for example, as one corporation after another disclosed accounting fraud in

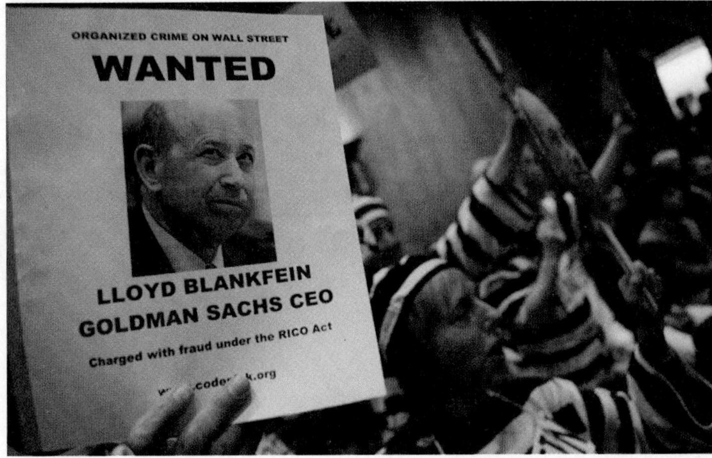

The giant investment firm Goldman Sachs came under fire for its behavior in the 2008 economic collapse. It was accused of betting against investment packages that it sold to clients, which allowed the firm to make money even as its clients lost. Congress began investigating the lack of federal oversight of the action in 2010, but the firm had not been punished for its behavior by 2012.

Senior Executive Service
Established by Congress in 1978 as a flexible, mobile corps of senior career executives who work closely with presidential appointees to manage government.

their annual reports to investors. The SEC was created in the 1930s to restore investor confidence in the stock market after the Great Depression, but it was accused of being negligent in monitoring accounting practices at big companies such as Enron and WorldCom in the early 2000s, and not discovering the financial scandals that led to the 2008 financial collapse.

GOVERNMENT CORPORATIONS Government corporations are the least understood organizations in the federal bureaucracy. Because they are intended to act more like businesses than like traditional government departments and agencies, they generally have more freedom from the internal regulations that control traditional agencies. They often have greater authority to hire and fire employees quickly and are allowed to make money through the sale of services such as train tickets, stamps, or home loans.[4]

Government corporations cover a wide range of policy issues such as public radio and television (the Corporation for Public Broadcasting), mail delivery (the U.S. Postal Service), train travel (the National Railroad Passenger Corporation, which is better known as Amtrak), and national service (the Corporation for National and Community Service), and a host of financial enterprises that make loans to banks and other institutions (the Federal National Mortgage Association, or Fannie Mae).

☐ Types of Federal Employees

The federal civilian workforce is composed of three different types of employees: (1) presidential appointees who run the bureaucracy and make major policy recommendations to the president and Congress; (2) members of the Senior Executive Service who help translate policy into action; and (3) members of the civil service who implement policy under the direction of presidential appointees and senior executives. (A full picture of the federal workforce would also include military personnel, but we will focus on civilian employees here.)

PRESIDENTIAL APPOINTEES Roughly 3,000 presidential appointees head federal departments and agencies, including 600 administrative officers subject to Senate confirmation and another 2,400 who serve "at the pleasure of the president," which means they are appointed by the president without Senate confirmation. As the president's hand-picked team, presidential appointees generally leave their posts at the end of that president's term in office. The president also appoints another 1,000 U.S. marshals, U.S. attorneys, and ambassadors to foreign nations, all confirmed by the Senate, but makes roughly two-thirds of these appointments on a nonpolitical basis.

THE SENIOR EXECUTIVE SERVICE Presidential appointees work closely with the 7,000 members of the **Senior Executive Service**, which includes roughly 6,400 career executives appointed through a rigorous review process and another 600 presidential

12.1

12.2

12.3

12.4

12.5

12.6

OF the People Diversity in America

The Federal Workforce

The federal bureaucracy is more representative of the public now than it was in the 1950s, when most of its employees were white and most female employees were clerk-typists. Women held 44 percent of all federal jobs at the end of 2011, whereas minorities held slightly more than one-third at 34 percent.

Even though the number of women and minorities in the federal workforce is at an all-time high, both groups still face barriers in rising to the top. First, women and minorities are not equally represented in all departments and agencies. They tend to be concentrated in departments with strong social service missions such as Education, Health and Human Services, Housing and Urban Development, and Veterans Affairs. Military and technical departments such as Defense, Energy, and Transportation have far fewer women employees.

Second, women and minorities are not represented at all levels of the federal bureaucracy. Women held two-thirds of lower-paying technical and clerical positions in 2011, and minorities were also heavily represented at the bottom of government. Together, women and minorities held barely 15 percent of the top jobs. Nevertheless, they are moving into the top jobs at a fast rate. Between 1994 and 2011, the number of women and minorities in professional and managerial jobs increased considerably.

QUESTIONS

1. Why should the federal bureaucracy try to recruit more women and minorities to its top jobs?
2. Does increasing diversity improve the bureaucracy's ability to implement policy?
3. Why is the percentage of women in the federal workforce below the percentage of women in the rest of the economy? How can the bureaucracy enhance diversity in scientific and technical fields?

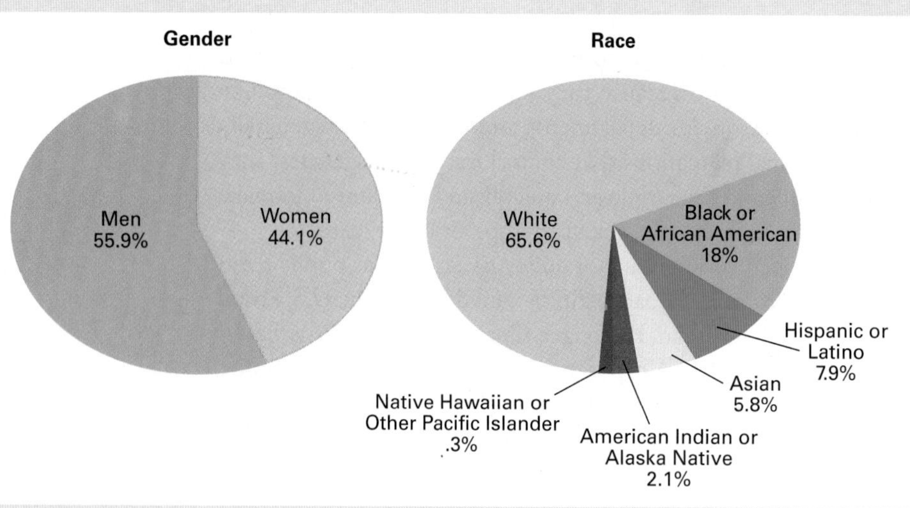

SOURCE: U.S. Office of Personnel Management, "A Message from the Director of the U.S. Office of Personnel Management," June 25, 2013, available at http://www.opm.gov/About_OPM/reports/feorp/2011/feorp2011.pdf

civil service
Federal employees who work for government through a competitive, not political selection process.

spoils system
A system of public employment based on rewarding party loyalists and friends.

patronage
The process of awarding favors to the party in power.

appointees who serve at the pleasure of the president. Except for the 600 political executives who are appointed for a limited time on the basis of their loyalty to the president, members of the Senior Executive Service are selected through a highly competitive process that emphasizes their skills as managers.

THE CIVIL SERVICE The Framers understood that the new federal government would need employees, and that many of these employees would select government for their career. The Framers believed that this **civil service** would outlast each administration, thereby maintaining the "institutional memory" of government.

For the first 100 years, however, members of the federal civil service were selected largely because of their party loyalty. President Andrew Jackson substantially expanded this "to-the-victor-belong-the spoils" system after his election in 1829. Jackson believed that every job in government was a potential opportunity for employing his political allies.

Jackson's **spoils system** gave the president's party complete control over almost every government job, from cabinet secretaries down to post office clerks. Under this method of **patronage**, presidents would patronize, or support, their allies by providing jobs and other benefits after an election. In 1883, Congress abolished the spoils system in favor of today's **merit system**. Under the merit system, employees are selected on the basis of their qualifications for the position, not their political connections.[5]

Ninety percent of federal employees are now selected on the basis of merit. Nearly all the rest are selected through hiring systems that emphasize a special skill such as medicine. The **Office of Personnel Management (OPM)** administers civil service laws and regulations, whereas the independent **Merit Systems Protection Board** is charged with protecting the integrity of the federal merit system and the rights of federal employees.

Under Office of Personnel Management regulations, most prospective government employees apply for jobs by identifying a job through the USA jobs Web site, submitting a formal application, and taking a civil service test. Some also must also be reviewed for a security clearance if their jobs involve access to secret information.

Federal organizations must keep careful records about each candidate and justify their decisions when challenged. Federal organizations must also give veterans special consideration for most jobs and ensure that all jobs are filled through a truly competitive process. Many federal jobs also involve a test of some kind to prove the merit of their choice.

Since 1962, federal civilian employees have had the right to form unions or associations that represent them in seeking to improve government personnel policies, and approximately one-third of them has joined such unions. Some of the most important unions representing federal employees today are the American Federation of Government Employees, the National Treasury Employees Union, the National Association of Government Employees, and the National Federation of Federal Employees.

Unlike unions in the private sector, federal employee unions lack the right to strike and are not able to bargain over pay and benefits. But they can attempt to negotiate better personnel policies and practices for federal workers, they can represent federal employees at grievance and disciplinary proceedings, and they can lobby Congress on measures affecting personnel changes. They can also vote in elections. This is why members of Congress from districts with large numbers of federal workers often sit on the House and Senate civil service subcommittees.

merit system
A system of public employment in which selection and promotion depend on demonstrated performance rather than political patronage.

Office of Personnel Management (OPM)
An agency that administers civil service laws, and regulations.

Merit Systems Protection Board
An independent agency that oversees and protects merit in the federal government personnel system.

Hatch Act
A federal statute barring federal employees from active participation in certain kinds of politics and protecting them from being fired on partisan grounds.

☐ Regulating Employee Conduct

Because federal employees administer so many laws that can affect election outcomes, they are subject to tight regulation regarding most forms of political participation. In 1939, Congress passed the Act to Prevent Pernicious Political Activities, otherwise known as the **Hatch Act**. Under the original act, federal civil servants were prohibited from raising money for candidates, wearing campaign buttons, and even putting "vote-for" signs on their lawns. They were also prohibited from running for political office.[6]

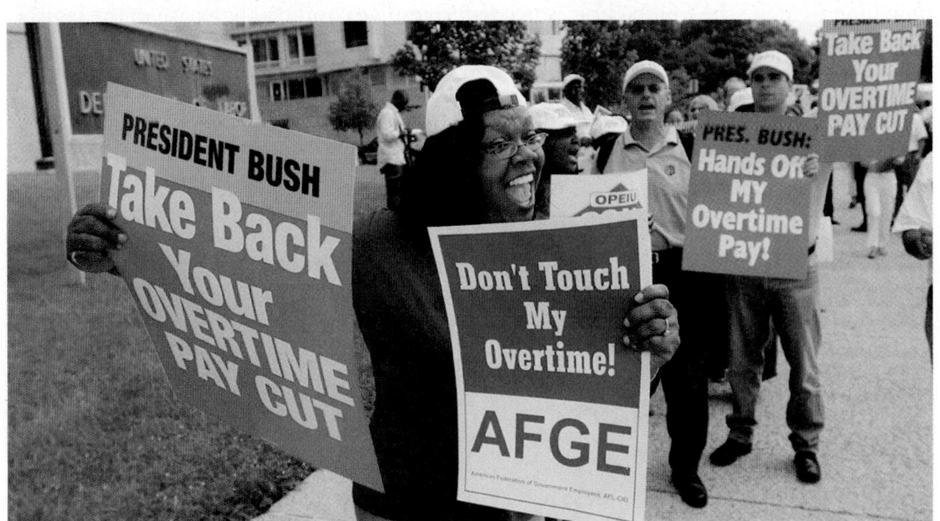

The National Treasury Employees Union represents thousands of federal employees who work within government. Although it started out as a union for Treasury Department employees, it has expanded throughout the years.

implementation
The process of putting a law into practice through bureaucratic regulations or spending.

administrative discretion
Authority given by Congress to the federal bureaucracy to use reasonable judgment in implementing the laws.

regulation
A precise statement of how a law is implemented.

rule-making process
The detailed process for drafting a regulation.

Under pressure from federal employee unions, Congress overhauled the Hatch Act in 1993 to permit greater political participation. The revised act still bars federal officials from running for political offices at the federal, state, or local level, but does permit most federal civil servants to hold party positions and involve themselves in party fund-raising and campaigning. Many advocates of this policy change argued that the old act discouraged political participation by two million people who might otherwise be vigorous political activists.[7]

But the new Hatch Act also contained many restrictions on federal employees: they still cannot raise money for candidates when they are at work, and those employed in highly sensitive federal agencies such as the Central Intelligence Agency, the Federal Bureau of Investigation, and certain divisions of the Internal Revenue Service are specifically barred from nearly all political activity on behalf of a candidate or party. In August 2012, for example, two senior managers at the Federal Aviation Administration were disciplined for telling their employees that Mitt Romney would cut their jobs, while Obama would not. These messages clearly violated the Hatch Act's rules against campaign activity.

The Job of the Federal Bureaucracy

12.2 Analyze the bureaucracy's implementation options and its effectiveness.

Whatever their size or specialty, all federal organizations share one constitutionally mandated job: to faithfully execute, or implement, the laws, which is part of the overall process for implementing the public policies discussed later in this chapter.

Implementation is the act of converting a policy into action. It covers a broad range of activities, such as writing checks at the Social Security Administration, inspecting job sites for the Occupational Safety and Health Administration, swearing in new citizens at the Immigration and Naturalization Service, or monitoring airline traffic for the Federal Aviation Administration.

Because Congress and the president could never pass laws detailed enough to deal with every aspect of their administration, they give federal departments and agencies **administrative discretion** to implement the laws in the most efficient and effective manner possible. This freedom varies from agency to agency, depending on both past performance and congressional politics. Political scientist Theodore Lowi believes that Congress often gives the federal bureaucracy vague directions because it is unable or unwilling to make the tough choices needed to resolve conflicts that arise in the legislative process. Congress gets the credit for passing a law, but the federal workforce gets the challenge of implementing it.

Whether a law is clear or ambiguous, most agencies implement its provisions through three means: (1) writing administrative **regulations** for enforcing the laws, which are produced through the **rule-making process**, (2) collecting revenues from individuals and corporations through taxes and achieving national goals by rewarding specific activities such as giving to charity and buying a home, and (3) spending money for specific programs such as benefits to individuals through Social Security and Medicare, and hiring employees such as military personnel.

□ Making Regulations

Regulations are designed to convert policies into action by providing detailed instructions to government and the nation. These regulations tell citizens, corporations, and government itself what they can and cannot do, as well as what they must or must not do. An Agriculture Department rule tells meat and poultry processors how to handle food; an Environmental Protection Agency rule tells automobile makers how much gasoline mileage their cars must

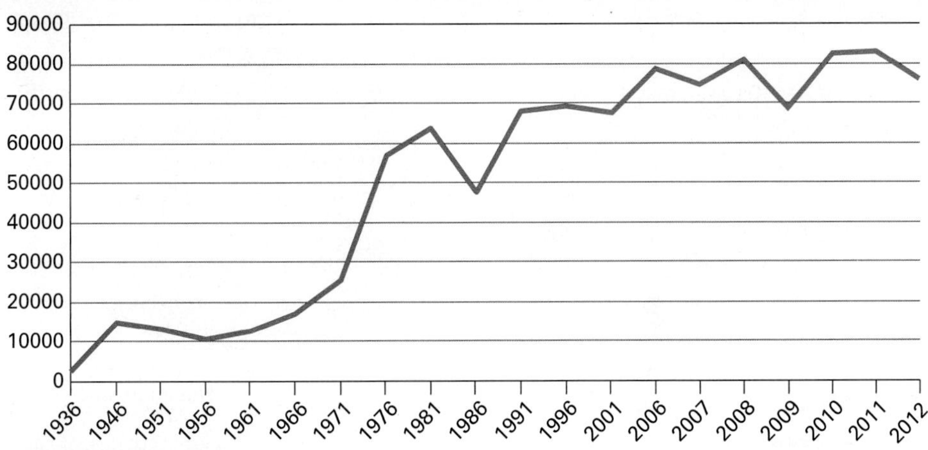

FIGURE 12.3 PAGES IN THE *FEDERAL REGISTER*

Why does the Federal Register grow over time?

SOURCE: U.S. Office of the Federal Register, "Annual Federal Register Pages Published." The 2012 number is based on the length of the federal register on October 10, 2012.

Federal Register
The official record of what the federal bureaucracy does.

get; a Social Security Administration rule tells workers how long they must work before they are eligible for a federal retirement check; a Citizenship and Immigration Service rule tells citizens of other nations how long they can stay on a student visa; and a Justice Department rule tells states what they must do to ensure that every eligible citizen can vote.

Regulations are drafted and reviewed under the Administrative Procedure Act of 1946, which is widely considered to be one of the most important laws regulating the bureaucracy in U.S. history. The act requires that all proposed regulations be published in the ***Federal Register***. Publication marks the beginning of the "notice and comment" period, during which all parties affected by the proposed regulation are encouraged to make their opinions known to the agency. As we will discuss later in the public policy section of the chapter, the process can take years from start to finish and consume thousands of pages of records. Some agencies even hold hearings and take testimony from witnesses in the effort to build a strong case for a particularly controversial rule.

The rule-making process does not end with final publication and enforcement. All regulations are subject to the same judicial review that governs formal laws, thereby creating a check against potential abuse of power when agencies exceed their authority to faithfully execute the laws. As Figure 12.3 shows, the number of pages in the Federal Register has increased dramatically since the 1930s.

□ Raising Revenue

The federal bureaucracy is responsible for collecting all revenue, including individual and corporate income taxes, payroll taxes for Social Security, Medicare, disability programs, and unemployment insurance, leases on federal lands, fees on exports and imports, and even camping permits at national parks and forests. The vast majority of federal tax revenues are collected by the Internal Revenue Service, which is housed within the Treasury Department. The federal government uses four major taxes to collect its revenue:

1. *Individual income taxes.* Taxes on individuals account for the largest share of the federal government's tax revenue. The income tax was prohibited under the Constitution until the Sixteenth Amendment was ratified in 1913.

2. *Payroll taxes.* Payroll taxes to pay for social insurance (Social Security and Medicare) are the second-largest and fastest-rising source of federal revenue. Most workers pay more in Social Security taxes than in federal income taxes.

3. *Corporate income taxes.* Corporate income taxes have fallen steadily from their historic high of two-fifths of all federal revenues during World War II. Due to tax cuts and special deductions, today they account for one-tenth of federal revenues, only one-fourth as much as the individual income tax.

12.1
12.2
12.3
12.4
12.5
12.6

uncontrollable spending
The portion of the federal budget that is spent on previously enacted programs, such as Social Security, that the president and Congress are unwilling to cut.

entitlement program
Program such as unemployment insurance, disaster relief, or disability payments that provides benefits to all eligible citizens.

Federal Reserve Board
A variation of an independent regulatory agency with a chairman and board that controls the supply of money that flows through the U.S. economy.

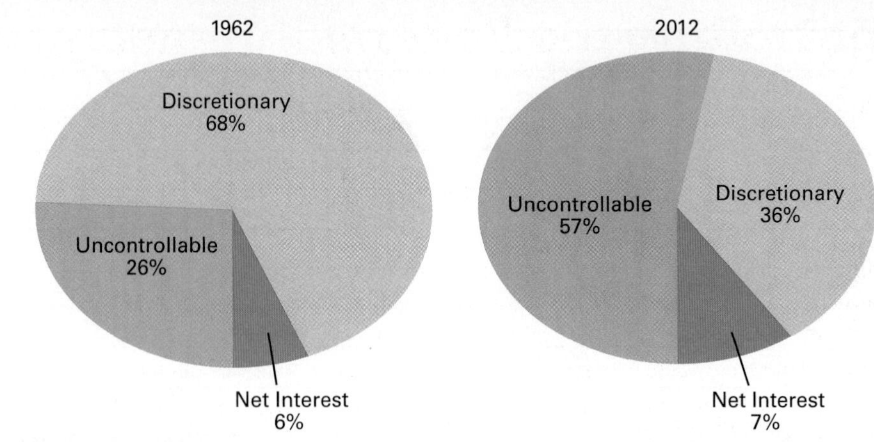

FIGURE 12.4 UNCONTROLLABLE SPENDING IN 1962 AND 2012

■ *Why do you think there are so many federal programs today with uncontrollable spending?*

SOURCE: Office of Management and Budget, *Budget of the U.S. Government, Fiscal Year 2012,* Historical Tables, (U.S. Government Printing Office, February 2011).

4. *Excise taxes.* Federal excise taxes on the sale of liquor, tobacco, gasoline, telephones, air travel, and other so-called luxury items account for a very small percentage of the federal budget.

The federal government can also borrow money by selling Treasury notes, or T-bills, that provide relatively small amounts of interest to the citizens, investment companies, banks, and even foreign nations such as China that buy them. Foreign nations currently own about half of the federal government's debt. Treasury notes are best viewed as an "I-Owe-You" revenue source—the federal government borrows money in the short term, but must repay the buyer when the notes come due. Interest rates on these notes are set by the **Federal Reserve Board,** an independent regulatory agency often called the Fed.

□ Spending Money

The federal bureaucracy also implements policy by spending money, whether by writing checks to millions of Social Security recipients, buying billions of dollars' worth of military equipment, or making grants to state governments and research universities.

Most government spending is uncontrollable, or *nondiscretionary,* which means it is not subject to congressional or presidential control without substantial and often unpopular changes in the law. The bulk of mandatory, **uncontrollable spending** goes to **entitlement programs** such as Social Security and Medicare for older citizens, college loans, and help for the victims of natural disasters such as floods and hurricanes. Everyone eligible for these programs is *entitled* to benefits—hence, spending often rises automatically. (The amount of this *uncontrollable spending* in the 1962 and 2012 federal budgets is shown in Figure 12.4.) The president's Office of Management and Budget estimates that the net interest on the national debt will rise to 13 percent by 2016 unless Congress and the president agree to deep cuts in federal spending to reduce borrowing.

Social Security and Medicare spending shows dramatic increases between 1962 and 2012 as the federal government increased benefits for older Americans. The two programs are already the largest in the federal budget and will eventually account for more than half of all federal spending. The past four years of economic stagnation have also increased mandatory spending for unemployment insurance and other income support programs.

The discretionary budget includes spending for programs such as health research, highway construction, student loans, and defense, all of which are subject to yearly increases or cuts by Congress and the president.

Controlling the Federal Bureaucracy

12.3 Assess presidential and congressional tools for controlling the federal bureaucracy.

oversight
Legislative or executive review of a particular government program or organization that can be in response to a crisis of some kind or part of routine review.

central clearance
Review of all executive branch testimony, reports, and draft legislation by the Office of Management and Budget (OMB) to ensure that each communication to Congress is in accordance with the president's program.

Every president enters office promising to make federal agencies work better. Jimmy Carter, Ronald Reagan, Bill Clinton, George W. Bush, and Barack Obama all made bureaucratic reform a central part of their presidential campaigns. Carter promised to create a government as good as the U.S. people, Reagan promised to reduce waste in government, Clinton promised to reinvent government, Bush promised to make government friendlier to citizens, and Obama promised to reduce duplication and overlap across dozens of federal programs that serve the same purpose. As Obama said in his 2011 State of the Union Address, two federal departments are responsible for regulating the salmon industry—Commerce oversees salmon caught in salt water, while Interior regulates salmon caught in fresh water.

Separate Controls

Modern presidents invariably contend that they should be firmly in charge of federal employees because the chief executive is responsive to the broadest constituency. The Constitution clearly states that presidents are responsible for faithfully executing the laws, which presidents interpret as full control over the basic decisions of government organizations.

However, under the system of checks and balances, the party that wins the presidency does not acquire total control of the national government. The president is not even the undisputed master of the executive structure. Presidents come into an ongoing system over which they have little control and in which they have little leeway to make the bureaucracy responsive.

Nevertheless, presidents have significant control over the bureaucracy through the powers of appointment, reorganization, and budgeting. Presidents can attempt to control the federal system by appointing or promoting sympathetic personnel, mobilizing public opinion and congressional pressure, changing the administrative apparatus, influencing budget decisions, using extensive personal persuasion, and if all else fails, shifting an agency's assignment to another department or agency (although such a shift requires tacit if not explicit congressional approval).[8]

Congress also has strong control over the bureaucracy, whether by establishing agencies, formulating budgets, appropriating funds, confirming personnel, authorizing new programs or new shifts in direction, conducting investigations and hearings, or even terminating agencies. Much of this authority is used to help constituents as they battle federal red tape. Members of Congress earn political credit by influencing federal agencies on behalf of their constituents.

Shared Oversight

Congress and the president spend a great deal of time and energy monitoring the federal bureaucracy through **oversight**, the technical term for their ongoing efforts to assure faithful execution of the laws.

PRESIDENTIAL CONTROLS Presidents use a number of tools for creating what political scientist Joel Aberbach calls the "watchful eye." They can put loyal appointees into the top jobs at key agencies; they can direct White House aides to oversee the work of certain agencies; and they can always call cabinet meetings to learn more about what is happening in the various departments.[9]

However, presidents tend to use the Office of Management and Budget (OMB) for most routine oversight. Departments and agencies must get the president's approval before testifying before Congress on pending legislation, making legislative proposals, or answering congressional inquiries about their activities. Under this **central clearance**

12.1

12.2

12.3

12.4

12.5

12.6

system, OMB tells Congress whether the bureaucracy's requests for legislation are "in accordance" with the president's program (indicating the highest presidential support), "consistent with" the president's program (indicating at least moderate presidential support), or without objection (indicating little or no presidential interest).

CONGRESSIONAL CONTROLS Congress also has a number of tools for overseeing the federal bureaucracy, not least of which are the individual members of Congress themselves, who are free to ask agencies for detailed information on just about any issue. However, most members and committees tend to use the Government Accountability Office or the Congressional Budget Office to conduct a study or investigation of a particular program.

Together, Congress and the president conduct two basic types of oversight.[10] One is "police patrol" oversight, in which the two branches watch the bureaucracy through a routine pattern. They read key reports, monitor the budget, and generally pay attention to the way the departments and agencies are running. The goal is to deter problems before they arise.

The other form of oversight is "fire alarm" oversight, in which the two branches wait for citizens, interest groups, or the press to find a major problem and pull the alarm. The media play a particularly important role in such oversight; using the Freedom of Information Act to gain access to documents the federal bureaucracy keeps secret, they often uncover a scandal before a routine "police patrol" reveals an urgent problem.

☐ Does the Federal Bureaucracy Work?

Despite their complaints about big government today, most Americans are reluctant to support cutbacks in what government does. At the same time, they wonder what can be done to improve the bureaucracy's performance, especially in the wake of recent breakdowns in important programs involving events such as Hurricane Katrina, the Gulf Oil spill, and the failure to detect the 2009 Christmas Day bombing plot.

This is not to argue that the federal bureaucracy is a wasteland of failure. To the contrary, the federal government accomplishes the impossible every day. And over time, the federal bureaucracy has accomplished much for betterment of society, including reducing diseases, building a strong national defense, and increasing access to education.

Nevertheless, there is cause for complaint. The bureaucracy's missions are critically important, but its organizations are dense with layer upon layer of management and red tape; its personnel systems are out of date; the presidential appointments process is needlessly complex and slow; many civil servants believe their pay and promotions are based more on favoritism than performance; and duplication and overlap among

In his 2011 State of the Union address, President Obama argued that the federal bureaucracy is filled with duplication and overlap among its many programs. He mentioned salmon as an example: the Interior Department is responsible for regulating salmon when they swim in fresh water, while the Commerce Department is responsible for salmon when they are in salt water. "I hear it gets even more complicated once they're smoked," Obama said.

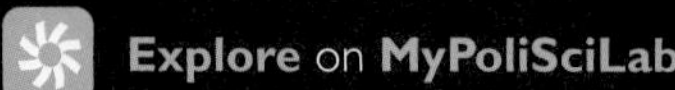

What Puts the "Big" in Big Government?

The national government is actually not as big as it once was. Since 1962, the total number of government employees has fallen due to a reduction in the number of military personnel after Vietnam and the Cold War. The number of civilians employed by the government has also declined since the 1980s. However, even as the size of government has grown smaller, its spending has increased to the point that one-fourth of the U.S. economy comes from government funded programs, contracts, and benefits.

Size of the Government Workforce*

* In Thousands

	EXECUTIVE	MILITARY	LEGISLATIVE AND JUDICIAL	TOTAL
1962	2,485	2,840	30	5,355
1972	2,823	2,360	42	5,225
1982	2,770	2,147	55	4,972
1992	3,017	1,848	66	4,931
2002	2,630	1,456	66	4,152
2012	2,500	1,602	64	4,166

Government as Percent of GDP

1962

Government consumed just under one-fifth of the total economy and paid for that consumption with income such as taxes

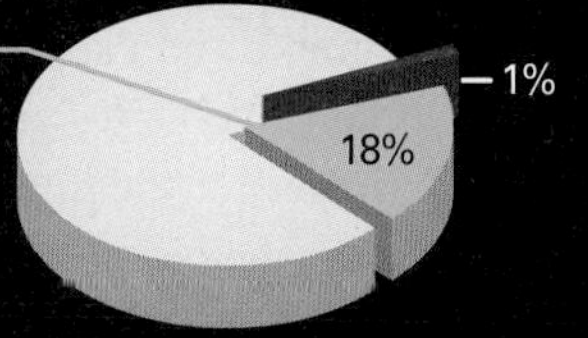

2012

Government consumed one-fourth of the total economy and paid a larger portion of it by borrowing instead of by taxing.

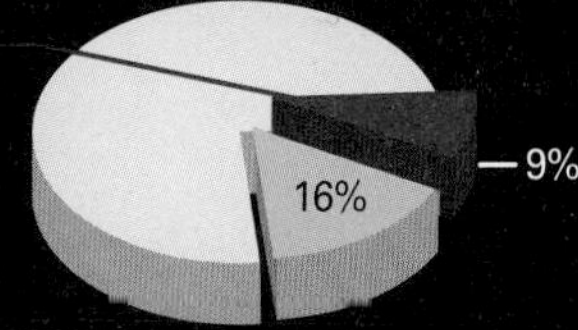

■ Government Spending Through Taxing
■ Government Spending Through Borrowing

SOURCE: Data from Voteview and U.S. Office of Management and Budget.

Investigate Further

Concept Is the federal government growing larger? The number of federal employees has actually decreased by over one million in a half-century. Since the late 1960s, the main difference in the size of its workforce is due to a smaller military.

Connection Do fewer federal employees mean smaller government? While the number of employees may be smaller, the federal government's share of the country's gross domestic product has grown every decade since the 1960s.

Cause If the government employs fewer people, how is it "bigger" than it was in 1962? Even with fewer people, the government implements more expensive programs that contribute to the total U.S. economy. Higher salaries, more expensive defense programs, larger entitlement programs, and increased spending to pay for past debt drive up costs.

12.1

12.2

12.3

12.4

12.5

12.6

public policy
A specific course of action that government takes to address a problem.

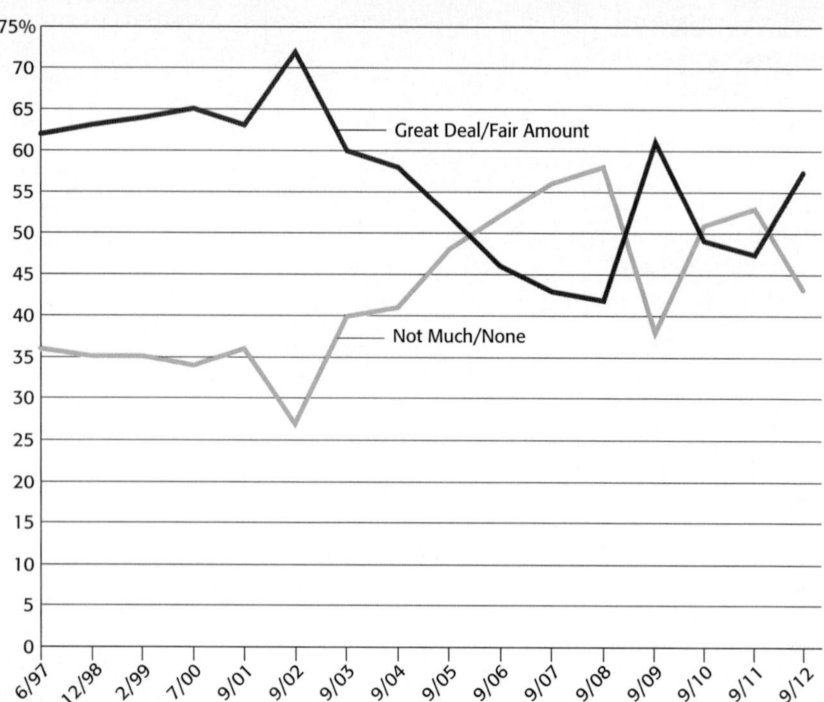

FIGURE 12.5 TRUST IN THE EXECUTIVE BRANCH

How much trust and confidence do you have at this time in the executive branch, headed by the president: a great deal, a fair amount, not very much, or none at all?

■ *What might explain the long-term decline in confidence in the federal bureaucracy? Why did confidence rebound in 2012?*

SOURCE: The Gallup Poll, available at http://pollingreport.com/institut.htm.

programs strangle citizen satisfaction.[11] Moreover, as of 2012 the Obama administration has yet to produce its promised overhaul of the bureaucracy.

It is not surprising, therefore, that the public has serious doubts about the federal bureaucracy's performance, too. As Figure 12.5 shows, public confidence in the executive branch of government has been generally declining throughout the past 10 years, although it did jump after Obama's inauguration in 2009 and again in 2012.

Improving public confidence in the bureaucracy depends in large part on the public itself. Citizens can make a great difference in shaping regulations, monitoring bureaucratic performance, and prompting Congress and the president to adopt needed reforms to prevent government breakdowns. Citizens can also support the many interest groups that lobby for good government and can now keep their own watchful eye over government by visiting government Web sites and collecting information. There is an old saying in politics that Americans get the government they deserve. The more that citizens demand better government, the better government they get.

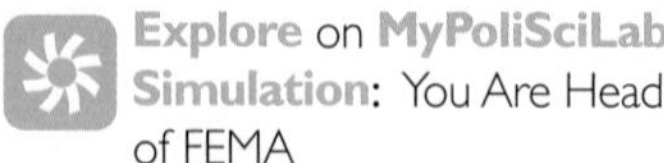
Explore on MyPoliSciLab Simulation: You Are Head of FEMA

Defining Public Policy

12.4 Relate politics and public policy, and differentiate the three types of public policy.

When government decides to solve a problem, it does so through a **public policy**, a specific course of action that government takes to address a challenge such as global warming, health care, or unemployment. Government sets public policy through laws, judicial decisions, and more detailed regulations issued by the bureaucracy. Congress and the president enact the laws, while the bureaucracy puts the laws into effect through implementation.

BY the People Making a Difference

Join the "Distributed Reporting Network"

Under pressure from leading interest groups such as the Project on Government Oversight (www.pogo.org), OMB Watch (ombwatch.org), and the Sunlight Foundation (sunlightfoundation.com), the federal bureaucracy is releasing massive amounts of information to citizens. As the list of sources at www.data.gov shows, citizens can inspect virtually every corner of the bureaucracy except for national security and defense, which have tightly guarded Web sites.

There is also an enormous amount of information at company and interest group Web sites, including detailed information on congressional lobbying and fund-raising at the Center for Responsive Politics (www.opensecrets.org), lists of wasteful government programs at Citizens Against Government Waste (www.cagw.org), and detailed biographies of every Obama administration appointee at the *Washington Post's* dot-com Web site (www.whorunsgov.com)

The problem in monitoring the bureaucracy and public policy is no longer too little public information, however, but perhaps too much. There is so much information that citizens simply cannot put it together. ProPublica is trying to solve the problem by asking ordinary citizens to join its Distributed Report Network. As contributors to ProPublica's news stream, ordinary citizens have the chance to tell their own stories about the real impact of urgent problems such as home foreclosures and student loan debt. ProPublica views the stories as a form of "crowd-sourcing" that enrich its stories. Its reporters use the stories to build award-winning articles that end up in the *New York Times* and on the CBS news program, *60 Minutes.*

The ProPublica network is only one way citizens can monitor government. The more they do to make sense of government information, the more they can contribute to the information that experts read for input to major policy debates.

QUESTIONS

1. **Is there too much information now flowing from Washington?**
2. **Why does the concept of the Distributed Reporting Network give citizens a voice in shaping the news?**
3. **Which citizens are most likely to share their stories, and how might crowd-sourcing improve the quality of reporting?**

This rest of this chapter will explore the various ways in which citizens and government both work to design, enact, and implement public policy. We will start with some simple definitions of public policy. We will then examine the process for making public policy. Laws do not implement themselves: they must be converted into action. The public policy process is the method for making laws a reality in American life.

But whatever its form, a public policy tells the nation and the world who is about to get what, when, and how from the federal government. As Table 12.1 shows, we can define **politics** as the interaction of the people and their government, whereas public policy is the product of that give and take. If politics is a question of who gets what, when, where, and how from government, then policy is a formal statement of who has the greater power and what compromises have been reached. We define **policy makers** as the individuals and groups that make the actual choices to create a public policy—some policy makers are elected officials or government employees, whereas others are lobbyists and interest groups. Citizens are rarely considered to be policy makers.

politics
The interaction of the people and their government, including citizens, interest groups, political parties, and the institutions of government at all levels. Politics is concerned with who gets what, when, where, and how from government.

policy makers
Individuals and groups that make the actual choices to create a public policy.

TABLE 12.1 POLITICS AND POLICY

The People ⟶	Political Action ⟶	Policy Decisions ⟶	Impact
Older Americans	Voting, joining the American Association of Retired People	Creating prescription drug coverage	Lower prescription drug costs
College students	Protesting, tweeting	Reducing college loan costs	Lower debt
Businesses	Contributing money to campaigns	Lower taxes	Higher profits
Environmental groups	Filing lawsuits	Enforcing smokestack regulations	Cleaner air
Community	Holding town-hall meetings	Increasing police patrols	Safer neighborhoods

distributive policy
A public policy such as Social Security that provides benefits to all groups in society.

redistributive policy
A policy that provides to one group of society while taking away benefits from another through policy solutions such as tax increases to pay for job training.

zero-sum games
A policy that takes away benefits or money from one group to give to another.

reverse distributive policy
A policy that reduces benefits for all groups, often by imposing regulations or taxes that govern everyone, rich or poor.

nondecision
A decision not to move ahead with the policy process. In short, it is a decision not to decide.

☐ Types of Public Policy

Public policies do not all have the same impact on society. Some public policies benefit all groups of citizens, others benefit one group of citizens by taking something away from another, and still others take resources from all groups in an effort to create a better society for everyone. These choices create three specific types of public policy.[12]

Federal policies that offer new benefits to all citizens are called **distributive policy**. National parks, air traffic control, the interstate highway system, education funding, national defense, and Social Security are all distributive. They help all groups at some level, whether rich or poor. Although some may get more benefit than others from a particular program such as Social Security, which reduces poverty among low-income beneficiaries, every group receives at least something through distributive policy.

In contrast, federal policies that take resources away from one or more groups in society (usually through taxes) so that another group can benefit (usually through an entitlement program) are **redistributive policy**. Such programs benefit the less fortunate. Welfare, poverty programs, Head Start for poor preschool children, and special programs to help minority groups are redistributive. Some political scientists call them **zero-sum games**, meaning one group's gain (the program's benefits) is another's loss (the program's cost in taxes).

Finally, federal policies that take resources from every group to solve a common problem by reducing benefits such as Social Security or raising taxes on all income levels are a form of what Paul C. Light calls **reverse distributive policy**.[13] When Social Security benefits are increased through annual cost-of-living adjustments, it is a form of distributive policy, but when benefits are cut it becomes a reverse distributive policy by taking away something from all citizens.

Rule makers often use tools such *cost/benefit analysis* to compare and contrast policy proposals. For example, electric cars reduce the nation's need for oil (benefit) but increase the demand for the electricity produced by coal-fired plants (cost). Similarly, new restrictions on carbon emissions from power plants approved in 2012 reduce global warming (benefit) but also increase the cost of electricity (cost) and may even weaken the economy (another cost).

The Public Policy Process

12.5 Outline the key steps in making public policy, and assess the different types of policy.

Every public policy reflects a series of separate decisions leading to its creation. The process can be viewed as a staircase that moves upward toward final implementation. But like any very long staircase, there are times when policy makers simply run out of energy to keep going. The process can even go back down the staircase in reverse as new ideas are introduced and Congress and the president go back down to revisit their earlier decisions. When the Obama administration entered office in 2009, for example, it reversed direction on many of the Bush administration's policies on issues such as global warming. Whereas the Bush administration had long argued that global warming was not a national threat, the Obama administration moved quickly to push for stricter limits on carbon emissions by automobiles and power plants.

The public policy process has eight steps: (1) making assumptions about the problem at the beginning, (2) setting the agenda of problems to be addressed, (3) deciding to act, (4) deciding how much to do, (5) choosing a solution to the problem, (6) deciding who will deliver the goods or services, (7) passing a law and making regulations for implementation, and (8) final implementation as an ongoing policy. Figure 12.6 presents the process.

We will discuss each step, but note that by its very nature, the choice to move forward (in step 3) is the most difficult, largely because of the complexity of passing a bill, issuing an executive order, or making a Supreme Court decision. It is often far easier to make what political scientists call a **nondecision**, which means the policy process stops before final action. A nondecision can take place at any step.

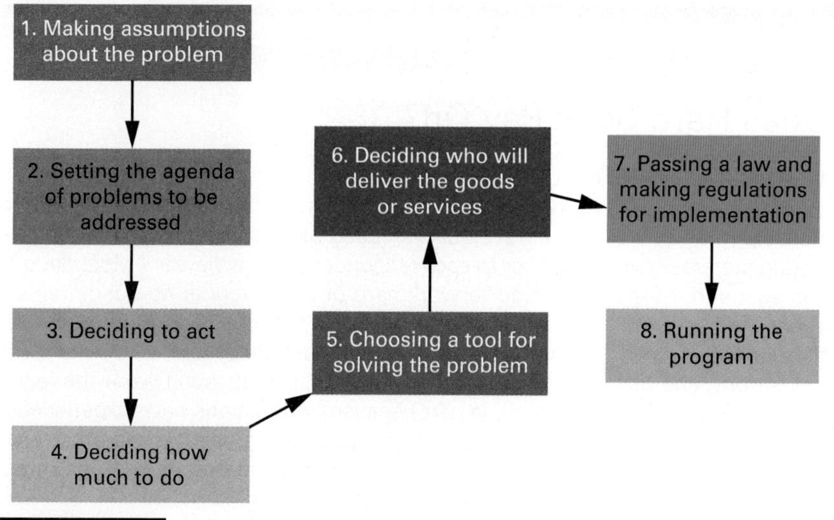

FIGURE 12.6 THE EIGHT STEPS IN MAKING PUBLIC POLICY

Why is step three the most difficult step?

policy agenda
The list of issues that the federal government pays attention to.

It is useful to note that the policy process does not vary greatly throughout the world. Virtually all policies are the product of making assumptions, setting the agenda, deciding to act, and so forth. However, other nations give their citizens different levels of influence in making policy decisions. In Great Britain, policy decisions are shaped by a tight bond between the administrative agencies of government and Parliament. Indeed, it is said that the agenda is never set until a decision has already been made. "It's carrying democracy too far if you don't know the result of the vote before the meeting."[14] Even in nondemocratic countries the bureaucracy is involved in proposing and implementing policy. What is missing in such nations is any meaningful role for the people.

☐ Making Assumptions About the Problem

Every government decision starts with assumptions about the future. Is the economy going to get stronger? If so, perhaps employment will go up and the costs of supporting the unemployed will go down. Is terrorism going to increase? If so, perhaps the federal government needs to inspect more cargo ships in search of bombs and other threats. Answers to questions about the future shape decisions about what the federal government might do.

Making even short-term assumptions about how the world will change is difficult, however. As one senior Reagan administration official once remarked, "I'm beginning to believe that history is a lot shakier than I thought it was. In other words, I think there are random elements, less determinism, and more discretion in the course of history that I ever believed before."[15] For example, the economy can change very quickly, which can increase joblessness overnight, which can put more pressure on the social safety net, which can demand higher taxes, and so on. Many experts were completely surprised in 2007–2008 when the mortgage market collapsed in the wake of billions of dollars of bad loans. They simply had not predicted it could happen.

☐ Setting the Agenda

Choosing the problem to be solved is the essential decision in setting the **policy agenda**. The policy agenda, as political scientist John W. Kingdon defines it, "is the list of subjects or problems to which governmental officials, and people outside of government closely associated with those officials, are paying some serious attention at any given time."[16]

Defined this way, the agenda is a direct product of politics and reflects broad social goals embraced by the people and their government, such as liberty, equality, individualism, and respect for the common person. These values are core to the ideology that shapes the policy agenda, but they often conflict with each other as ideas move toward

The Global Community

Does Hard Work Pay Off?

Views about the individual's ability to determine life's success have an important role in shaping public policies designed to help the poor. The Pew Research Center's Spring 2012 Global Attitudes Survey asked which of the following statements came closer to each respondent's own views: "Most people can succeed if they are willing to work hard or hard work is no guarantee of success for most people." According to the survey, there is enormous variation throughout the world regarding the belief that hard work pays off.

At one end of the spectrum, citizens of Russia and Japan were the least hopeful that hard work pays off, in part because both nations have experienced long periods of economic distress that continue to this day. At the other end of the spectrum, citizens of the United States, India, and Britain were the most confident that people can succeed if they just work hard.

These views affect government policy in many ways, including support for education, job training, and help for the poor. If citizens believe that hard work pays off, they may be less willing to help fellow citizens who cannot find work; if they believe that hard work is not a enough to create success, they may be more willing to endorse programs that even the economic playing field. These views also shape how citizens view the role of government in regulating the economy. Citizens who have faith in hard work are also more likely to believe that people are better off in a free market economy that allows individuals to rise and fall on their own, even if some citizens are very rich and others poor.

Most people can succeed if they are willing to work hard, OR Hard work is no guarantee of success

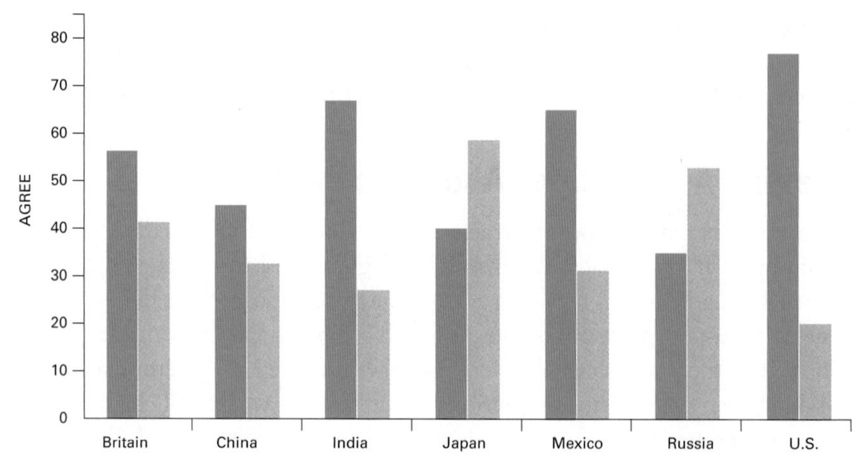

SOURCE: Pew Research Center, *Pervasive Gloom About the World Economy: Faith in Hard Work, Capitalism Falter But Emerging Markets Upbeat* (Pew Research Center, 2012).

CRITICAL THINKING QUESTIONS

1. What factors might contribute to beliefs that hard work does not pay off?
2. Why does faith in hard work create support for a free-market economy?
3. How does faith in hard work affect what government does to help poor people?

public policies. Everyone wants the American dream, for example, but we often disagree on how to get it. Politics affects the rise and fall of these ideologies through elections, party identification, interest group pressure, and a variety of other political expressions.

Problems are distinct from politics and reach the list of possible agenda items from a variety of sources. Some arise from events such as the September 11, 2001, terrorist attacks or Hurricane Katrina. Others become prominent through newspaper or television stories about a controversial issue such as gay marriage, and still others because of interest group pressure for benefits such as prescription drug coverage for older citizens. Some emerge from congressional investigations of issues such as cigarette smoking, drilling accidents, hurricane damage, car safety, or government fraud.

Other possible problems are the subject of ongoing government monitoring. For example, the government regularly reports data on the state of the economy as measured by unemployment, inflation, or new housing starts. These markers can show the beginnings of an economic slowdown or of an improving economy. Readers need only visit a government Web site (see the list at the end of the chapter) to see the range of information government provides to policy makers, investors, and the public. Through these different venues, policy makers latch on to particular problems or solutions depending on the readiness for action.

Nevertheless, the public's attention span can be very short. Problems identified through scientific research such as global warming may be the easiest to ignore, partly because there always seem to be numbers to refute a given analysis. Even as former Vice President Al Gore was accepting the Nobel Peace Prize in 2007 for his work on global warming, a group of scientists challenged much of the evidence on which his work was based. Once the economy collapsed and Americans were faced with a trade-off between jobs and environmental protection, the global warming debate cooled off and has yet to be reenergized.

Policy makers set the agenda using many of the same criteria they apply to other political decisions—public opinion, interest group pressure, their own beliefs, ideology, party affiliation, and loyalty to their institution. In recent years, they have also come to rely on a small number of think tanks to help them sort through the stream of possible problems. A **think tank** is an organization composed of scholars who study public policy. Many are located in Washington, D.C., so that they can be closer to the national political process. Unlike a college or university, which also produces policy research, a think tank exists almost entirely to influence the immediate agenda. Thus, many are described as either liberal or conservative.

think tank
A nongovernmental organization that seeks to influence public policy through research and education.

issue-attention cycle
The movement of public opinion toward public policy from initial enthusiasm for action to realization of costs and a decline in interest.

12.1

12.2

12.3

12.4

12.5

12.6

☐ Deciding to Act

The fact that a problem exists does not automatically mean that Congress, the president, or the courts will try to solve it. Some problems help policy makers achieve their personal or political goals, such as reelection or a place in history, in which case they decide to act, whereas others do not, in which case they pick other problems to solve. Although these decisions are largely hidden from view and therefore difficult to influence, they are the most important step in the policy process.

Policy makers also clearly understand that public pressure for action ebbs and flows over time. In fact, writes political scientist Anthony Downs, "American public attention rarely remains sharply focused upon any one domestic issue for very long—even if it involves a continuing problem of crucial importance to society." According to Downs, the public follows an **issue-attention cycle** in which each problem "suddenly leaps into prominence, remains there for a short time, and then—although still largely unresolved—gradually fades from the center of public attention."[17]

Think about global warming again. Public concern about the issue has gone up and down throughout the years, reflecting competing concerns about the economy and doubt about specific solutions. Figure 12.7 shows the trends according to a variety of polls. As the polls show, the issue-attention cycle varies with a number of factors, most notably the economy. Citizens want government to act even when policy affects economic growth but not when the economy is in trouble. Although global warming is still an important issue for most Americans, it has been sliding somewhat throughout the past few years, suggesting that the issue-attention cycle is at work.

- This cycle starts with what Downs described as the "pre-problem stage," the rise of some "highly undesirable social condition" such as global warming that has yet to capture public attention.

incremental policy
Small adjustments to existing public policies.

punctuating policy
Radical changes to public policy that occur only after the mobilization of large segments of society to demand action.

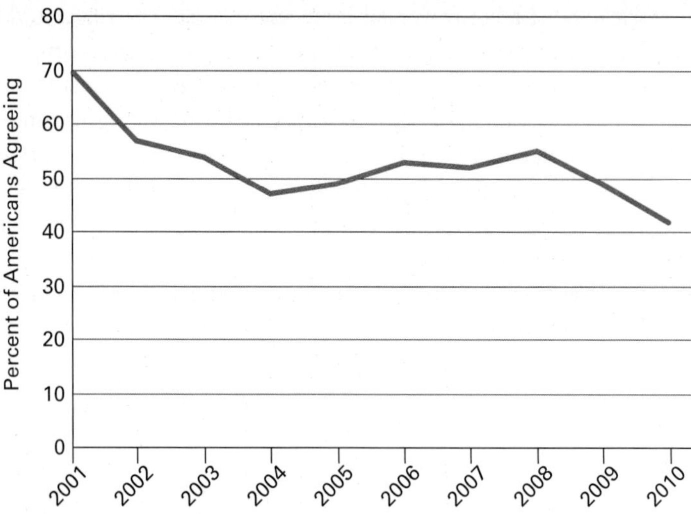

FIGURE 12.7 CONCERNS ABOUT THE ENVIRONMENT, 2000–2010

Agreement with the statement: "Protection of the environment should be given priority, even at the risk of curbing economic growth."

What is one important reason why support for environmental action started to fall in 2008?

SOURCE: Polls on environmental protection are available using the search engine at http://www.polling-report.com.

- The issue-attention cycle continues with "alarmed discovery and euphoric enthusiasm," the sudden emergence of an issue as a topic for public debate. Books are written, documentaries made, speeches retooled, and campaigns rebuilt, all based on the sudden passion that generates public concern.
- The cycle moves onward with the realization that change will incur significant cost. It is one thing to worry about greenhouse gases and quite another to pay more for clean electricity or buy smaller, more efficient cars. The greater the cost of solving a problem, especially if it means tax increases or benefit cuts, the more strongly people pull back from their euphoric view of change.
- The cycle continues with the "gradual decline of intense public interest." Having pressed hard for action on an issue such as universal health insurance, the public may begin to realize that change is nearly impossible given the array of political forces fighting for a nondecision.
- The cycle ends with what Downs calls the "post-problem stage." The problem moves into "prolonged limbo—a twilight realm of lesser attention or spasmodic recurrences of interest."

The ultimate decline of public interest is not inevitable. But if citizens expect big problems to be solved immediately, they will only be disappointed. Although issues such as global warming seem to demand that we take immediate action before the damage is beyond repair, we must acquire enough understanding of the problem, and of the policy process, to stay actively engaged for the long term.

☐ Deciding How Much to Do

Once the federal government decides it *wants* to do something about a problem, the next difficult decision is *how much* to do. Government can launch a comprehensive program such as Social Security or Medicare, or it can expand a smaller program bit by bit over time.

INCREMENTAL OR COMPREHENSIVE POLICY An **incremental policy** makes a small-scale adjustment in an existing program, whereas a **punctuating policy** creates a dramatic change in the government's role. Incremental policies are generally the easiest to create, if only because they build on past decisions in very small ways, such as increasing the amount of federal support for colleges by a few hundred dollars. Punctuating policies, such as providing national prescription drug coverage for older adults, often require citizens, interest groups, political parties, and policy makers to mobilize in a broad movement for change.

Incremental policy is the most frequent response to calls for change. According to James L. True, Bryan D. Jones, and Frank R. Baumgartner, "American political institutions were conservatively designed to resist many efforts at change and thus to make mobilization necessary if established interests are to be overcome."[18] Because of constitutional protections such as separation of powers and checks and balances, incremental policy often becomes the easiest way to advance an idea.

Punctuating policy often depends on alliances of citizens, interest groups, political parties, private businesses, government agencies, congressional committees, and others who come together to place an issue on the agenda and push for or against change. Alliances called **iron triangles** exist for decades; **issue networks** cooperate for a specific cause and then disband.

iron triangle
A policy-making instrument composed of a tightly related alliance of a congressional committee, interest groups, and a federal department or agency.

issue network
A policy-making instrument composed of loosely related interest groups, congressional committee, presidential aides, and other parties.

An iron triangle has three sides that hold together for long periods of time: (1) a federal department or agency, (2) a set of loyal interest groups, and (3) a House and/or Senate committee. Each side supports the other two. Loyal members of Congress work to protect or increase the agency's budget, allowing the agency to flourish, and pass legislation to support the interest groups, providing benefits for its members. Agencies give special services to the interest groups, keeping their members happy, and ensure the constituencies of members of Congress are provided for, aiding in congressional approval ratings. Interest groups give contributions and endorsements to loyal members of Congress, aiding in their reelection, and support the activities and requests of the agency, enhancing their legitimacy. Policy making for veterans, for example, is achieved through an iron triangle composed of the Department of Veterans Affairs, the House and Senate Veterans Committees, and a long list of interest groups that represent veterans, such as the American Legion and Veterans of Foreign Wars.

Iron triangles have been largely replaced by much looser collections of participants in issue networks. As political scientist Hugh Heclo has argued, the notion that iron triangles make all policy was "not so much wrong as it was disastrously incomplete" in today's complicated policy environment.[19] The increasing number of small, highly specialized interest groups makes an iron triangle nearly impossible to create, if only because Congress and federal agencies can no longer identify a steady occupant for the third corner of the triangle. They have to find temporary allies, depending on the issue. There is nothing "iron" about such coalitions: they last only as long as an issue is hot.

Issue networks concentrate power in the relatively small number of individuals who organize and maintain them as the issue-attention cycle moves forward. These networks are composed of interest groups, members of Congress, and outside lobbyists, pollsters, and organizers. Some political scientists thus refer to the rise of well-financed issue networks—such as those that promote prescription drug coverage for older consumers or tax cuts for business—as a form of elitism, not pluralism, in which a very small number of actors accelerate or delay action. Medicare prescription drug coverage, for example, engaged an issue network of drug companies, the AARP, and hospitals.

□ Choosing a Solution

As noted, the federal government generally uses three tools to solve most public problems: (1) making regulations to encourage or prohibit behavior through standards, incentives, or penalties, (2) using taxes both to raise money and encourage certain behaviors, and (3) spending money to purchase goods and services or provide benefits to the public as a whole or specific populations such as the elderly or children.[20]

These three solutions are designed to produce *material* benefits for society. Some benefits are tangible, such as new roads, bridges, schools, and hospitals; others, such as higher pay, greater safety, better education, and cleaner air and water, can only be felt. In theory, action to increase education loans should produce more educated workers who can fill the jobs created in the growing technology sector.

Other solutions produce *symbolic* benefits, such as efforts to educate the public, study an issue, appoint a blue-ribbon commission, or highlight the need for future action. In theory, symbolic benefits highlight an emerging issue and create citizen action. In reality, they are sometimes a way to make a nondecision as policy makers merely express their concern and

Private firms provided most security services to protect U.S. diplomats during the Iraq War. In 2007, employees of Blackwater, Inc., were accused of allegedly killing innocent Iraqi citizens during a patrol. Blackwater later changed its name first to Xe Services then to Academi in an effort to improve its reputation.

move to other tangible policies. It is not yet clear, for example, just how much global warming is caused by sources beyond government's control, but action to reduce global warming through international treaties can give the public a sense that the world is getting better.

☐ Deciding Who Will Deliver the Solution

Part of selecting a solution to implement a policy is deciding who will actually implement the program. The answer is not always a federal employee.[21] Although federal employment has been steady at roughly 2 million workers since the early 1990s, the federal agenda has continued to grow. As a result, in addition to the work of departments and agencies discussed earlier in the chapter, the government often depends on a largely hidden workforce of contractors, institutions of higher education, state and local employees, and charities to achieve its policy goals.

☐ Passing a Law and Making Regulations

Once Congress and the president have decided to act and constructed a policy proposal, they must pass the proposal into law. Although presidents are also allowed to create some policies through executive order, those decisions are easy for the next president to overturn. Therefore, the best way to pass a policy is through legislation. Rule-making, the process for creating regulations, comes near the end of the policy-making process and is virtually invisible to most citizens. Nevertheless, it is the essential step in converting the abstract ideas and language of laws, presidential orders, and court rulings into precise regulations governing what individual members of the public, companies, government, states, and localities must do to achieve the goals of a specific policy.

Regulations can be extraordinarily detailed and are sometimes difficult for even regulated parties to understand. Because they are so complicated, interest groups have much greater influence over their construction than citizens and even members of Congress.

Although the federal government has been issuing regulations since 1789, the number of pages of regulations jumped dramatically during World War II and again in the 1970s.[22] We can see the growth of regulations in the number of pages in the *Federal Register*, which provides a daily record of all new and proposed regulations (See Figure 12.3).

The process starts when a bill is passed and signed into law, which is sent to the appropriate department or agency for "faithful execution" of a policy. With the legislative history as a guide to what Congress and the president want, the department or agency then drafts a proposed rule. The rule itself generally consists of a statement of purpose, the actual rule, and a review of any research or legislative language that shaped it. (The rule-making process is discussed in the first section of this chapter.)

A large solar array atop the Department of Energy building. As the federal government has tightened its regulations on the use of dirty fuels in electric plants, it has increased grants and loans for the development of solar power. The effort reflects a blend of regulation and spending as solutions to global climate change and air pollution.

Although this process seems straightforward, it includes a number of leverage points for lobbying. The process can also be delayed—nothing in the Constitution or the laws regulating the rule-making process says that a department or agency must propose a rule within a specific amount of time. Moreover, the department or agency retains great discretion to interpret information generated during the notice-and-comment period.

Regulations are particularly important because Congress often leaves the details to the federal bureaucracy. Passing legislation requires many compromises, some of which are so vague that the bureaucracy can only act if it provides the details. In this regard, the bureaucracy has enormous *administrative discretion.*

☐ Running the Program Day to Day

Implementation does not end with release of a final rule. It continues with the day-to-day tasks of actually running a federal department or agency, making regulations, supervising contractors, and evaluating impact. And as assumptions change and the issue-attention cycle takes hold, the policy-making process can begin again. Public interest in global warming faded with the onset of the economic crisis, but it is likely to rebound once the economy recovers.

☐ The Order of Action

Making public policy is an often-unpredictable process. It can start with any step and skip back and forth as politics shapes everything from the decision to act to running the program. The result is a policy-making process that is almost always in flux.

Some political scientists such as Kingdon even think of this process as taking place in a "primordial swamp" of competing problems, solutions, political actors, citizens, pressure, and resources such as dollars, public support, and administrative energy.

These policy "streams" are shaped by citizens, interest groups, presidents, and members of Congress and move through the institutions in search of each other. Thus, an idea for solving a problem such as a new weapons system or an increase in the minimum wage may linger in waiting for a specific problem such as terrorism or an increase in unemployment. Politics ties these various streams together into a public policy. According to this view, one reason immigration reform has not yet passed is

12.1

12.2

12.3

12.4

12.5

12.6

FOR the People Government's Greatest Endeavors

Reducing Disease

Protecting the nation from foreign and domestic threats involves more than fighting wars and enforcing laws. It also involves protecting Americans from hidden threats such as disease, pollution, and unsafe foods. As we have learned more about preventing disease, the federal government's role has grown, whether through funding for advanced scientific research or programs to make sure all Americans are vaccinated against life-threatening disease.

Much of the federal government's progress against disease has been through incremental programs that have added up to very significant impacts. Much of the progress has occurred at colleges and universities like yours, which have mapped the human genome, created new vaccines, and developed treatments for life-threatening diseases such as cancer.

The federal government's most impressive successes over the past seventy years have involved vaccinations against diseases such as polio, diphtheria, whooping cough, and tetanus by the age of five.

As the inventory of infectious diseases has grown, so has the federal government's involvement in health care research. Congress created the National Institute of Health (NIH) in 1930; added the National Cancer Institute in 1937; created a division of research grants to promote university research in 1946; added new institutes for dental research, experimental biology, health disease, mental health, and microbiology in 1948; and expanded the federal government's health budget. Congress continued to create new research programs year after year. By 2001, the NIH had 27 separate institutes housed in its 75 buildings on a 300-acre campus in Bethesda, Maryland.

This investment has made a dramatic difference in the quality of life for most Americans. Deaths from heart disease is down by more than a third since the mid-1970s, five-year cancer survival rates are up by 60 percent, schizophrenia and depression are much more treatable, and dental sealants now prevent nearly 100 percent of cavities in children. Although there are still significant differences in disease rates between the rich and poor and among African Americans, Native Americans, and whites, Americans are living longer, healthier lives because of the federal effort to reduce disease.

QUESTIONS

1. How does a longer lifespan affect federal policy? What are the costs and benefits?
2. Why hasn't the number of deaths among infants decreased at the same time life span has increased?
3. Who do you think live the longest? Poor people? Whites? People with health care coverage?

that the streams of problems, solutions, and interests have yet to come together, in part because the political stream is so divided.

Some policies are efforts to terminate a program. As opposed to a nondecision, which stops a policy before it can be made, termination stops a policy that is already running. Because members of Congress, interest groups, citizens and agencies often benefit from a program's existence, even one that is no longer necessary, termination is typically very difficult. The federal government once maintained a helium reserve in Texas to ensure a reliable supply of the gas for its military blimps. Even through the military stopped using blimps after World War II ended in 1945, it took 50 years for Congress and the president to halt the helium reserve program.

Citizens and Public Policy

12.6 Assess ways in which citizens can influence the public policy process.

Public policy is not made in a vacuum. Rather, it takes place in a complicated political process that engages citizens, interest groups, political parties, legislators, judges, and government institutions.

Citizens are often anxious about participating in this process, not only because it can be complex, but also because they have many levers that give them influence. They can certainly vote—the higher the participation, the more the process will heed their voice.

Ralph Nader was a major force in creating pressure for consumer protection. He created many of the tactics used to achieve public policy impact during his 40 years of public service.

But voting is not enough. Citizens cannot vote on the basis of their policy positions if they do not have an opinion or if candidates do not tell the electorate where they stand. And because voting is a blunt instrument of participation that does not convey precise information about what they want, citizens must also find other pathways to influence, including joining interest groups, writing letters, sending e-mails, confronting legislators at community meetings, and even running for office themselves.

They can also join public interest groups that support or oppose government policy action. In this regard, Ralph Nader may have done more than any other person to influence the policy process on behalf of consumers.

Nader started his journey in 1965 with the publication of *Unsafe at Any Speed,* a damning attack on the poor state of automobile safety in the United States. Targeting General Motors and its Chevrolet Corvair, Nader demanded congressional action and got it. Today's airbags are directly traceable to Nader's early pressure for mandatory seat belts and crash-resistant passenger compartments. "You've got to keep the pressure on, even if you lose," he says about representing the public interest. "The essence of the citizen's movement is persistence." Nader went on to create the Center for Study of Responsive Law, the Freedom of Information Clearinghouse, and dozens of other Public Interest Research Groups (PIRGs).

There is no question that citizens want action on the big problems highlighted in this chapter. They know that safeguarding Social Security, reducing global warming, and fixing the economy so that everyone rises on the basis of merit will not happen without pressure. No citizen gets what he or she does not ask for. And asking is part of the politics that leads to ultimate action.

Citizen action is more successful when it involves clear ideas for an alternative policy. It is rarely enough to merely demand that government act. It is also important to tell government what to do. This means thinking through the options and making a clear, well-developed argument for change and pursuing it aggressively through our complicated policy process.

You Will Decide

Should You Join AmeriCorps after You Graduate?

Americans help shape and carry out public policy in many ways, but one of the most meaningful ways they can help influence and implement public policy is by volunteering. More than 60 million Americans volunteered in 2011. They served soup to the hungry, tutored children, worked for advocacy organizations such as the American Civil Liberties Union (ACLU) and Americans for Tax Justice, and organized campus meetings on big issues such as health care reform.

The Serve America Act, which was a top Obama administration priority in 2009, has encouraged more volunteerism at just the right time in the economic downfall. Following unanimous passage in Congress, the Act, which was signed by President Barack Obama on April 21, 2009, Americans were given a variety of new ways to volunteer. For example, the Act designated September 11th as a day of service to commemorate the heroism of those who gave their lives in response to the terrorist acts on New York City and the Pentagon in Washington, D.C. Students on every campus will be asked to participate in this annual event, from cleaning up parks to repainting schools.

In signing the law, Obama emphasized the importance of volunteering to the quality of life in the United States: "I've met countless people of all ages and walks of life who want nothing more than to do their part. I've seen a rising generation of young people work and volunteer and turn out in record numbers. They're a generation that came of age amidst the horrors of 9/11 and Katrina; the wars in Iraq and Afghanistan; an economic crisis without precedent. And yet despite all this, or more likely because of it, they have become a generation of activists possessed with that most American of ideas—that people who love their country can change it."*

What do you think? Is AmeriCorps an option for you after graduation?

Thinking It Through

Volunteering is a form of civic engagement. The more that citizens give, the more they get. And their work is essential to public policy. The federal government often provides grants to charitable organizations such as Habitat for Humanity, Youth Build, and Teach for America to further its goals.

The Serve America Act also expanded AmeriCorps, the national program created in 1993 to provide volunteer opportunities for students both before and immediately after college. The number of AmeriCorps volunteers will rise from 75,000 per year in 2009 to 250,000 by 2015. The pay is very low—only $14,000 or so per year depending on local costs—but the rewards are enormous. Participants report that their two years as volunteers were the most important of their lives.

Most AmeriCorps volunteers serve for one or two years, often in poor communities. Many work in tough schools with few resources, while others provide desperately needed services to the homeless, hungry, and unemployed.

AmeriCorps is not an option for many graduates, however. It pays very little, and involves at least one year of service. Some graduates simply do not have the resources to delay their job searches. Equally important, AmeriCorps members may not have the expertise to do their jobs, and often need extensive training that may not be useful for their future careers.

CRITICAL THINKING QUESTIONS

1. **How do AmeriCorps volunteers help make public policy? Which step of the policymaking process do they affect most?**
2. **Is a volunteer program that pays people for their time a form of volunteering or a job?**
3. **What are the negatives of sending recent college graduates into community organizations? What happens when an AmeriCorps volunteer finishes his or her service?**

Credit: FPO

*Remarks by President Obama on signing the Serve America Act, April 21, 2009, http://www.whitehouse.gov/the_press_office/Remarks-by-the-President-at-Signing-of-the-Edward-M-Kennedy-Serve-America-Act

**These questions can be found at www.americcrps.com

Review the Chapter

 Listen to Chapter 12 on MyPoliSciLab

Understanding the Federal Bureaucracy: Constitutional Origins, Organizations, and Employees

12.1 Outline the constitutional roots of the federal bureaucracy, and its types of federal organizations and employees, p. 381.

The Framers assumed there would be a federal bureaucracy but that it would be small. Therefore, they left many of the details of the bureaucracy to the responsibility of future presidents. Over time, Congress and the president created four types of government organizations: (1) departments, (2) independent stand-alone agencies, (3) independent regulatory commissions, and (4) government corporations. Congress and the president also created three different types of federal employees: (1) presidential appointees usually selected for their loyalty to the president, (2) senior executives selected for their expertise, and (3) civil servants selected on the basis of merit.

The Job of the Federal Bureaucracy

12.2 Analyze the bureaucracy's tools of implementation and their effectiveness, p. 388.

The federal bureaucracy generally makes regulations, raises revenues, or spends money to implement the laws. Regulations tell citizens what they can and cannot do and are enforced by the federal bureaucracy, taxes generate revenues and reward certain activities such as home ownership, while spending supports the purchase of goods and services or provides benefits to the citizenry. Most of the federal budget is uncontrollable, meaning that anyone who qualifies for programs such as Social Security, unemployment insurance, health care for the poor, and Medicare must be given benefits regardless of the impact on the federal budget.

Controlling the Federal Bureaucracy

12.3 Assess presidential and congressional efforts to control the federal bureaucracy, p. 391.

The federal bureaucracy has at least two immediate supervisors: Congress and the president. It must pay considerable attention as well to the courts and their rulings and to well-organized interest groups and public opinion. Despite their efforts to ensure accountability, Congress and the president often give vague instructions to the administrative system, which gives the system significant discretion in implementing the laws.

Defining Public Policy

12.4 Relate politics and public policy, and differentiate the three types of public policy, p. 395.

Public policy is the product of politics, which resolves the question of who gets what, when, where, and how from government. Politics involves the interaction of the people and their government.

There are three types of policy: distributive (which provides benefits to all groups in society), redistributive (which provides benefits to one group in society at the expense of another), and reverse distributive (which eliminates benefits to all groups in society).

The Public Policy Process

12.5 Outline eight steps in making public policy, and assess the types of policy solutions, p. 396.

Every public policy emerges from a process that includes eight steps: (1) making assumptions about the problem, (2) setting the agenda, (3) deciding to act, which can involve nondecisions, (4) deciding how much to do, (5) choosing a solution to the problem, (6) deciding who will deliver the goods or services, (7) passing a law and making regulations for implementation, and (8) running the program itself. The steps do not always occur in order. Some political scientists see problems, solutions, political actors, and so forth as "streams" that flow through the institutions of government and only occasionally come together.

Citizens and Public Policy

12.6 Assess ways in which citizens can influence the public policy process, p. 404.

Citizens face significant obstacles to being heard in the policy process. But they may have more influence at certain stages of the process, and they can make their voices heard through both traditional and nontraditional means, including voting, joining interest groups, writing letters, sending e-mails, confronting legislators at community meetings, and even running for office themselves.

Learn the Terms

Study and **Review** the **Flashcards**

bureaucracy, p. 381
bureaucrat, p. 381
department, p. 383
independent stand-alone agency, p. 383
independent regulatory commission, p. 383
government corporation, p. 383
Senior Executive Service, p. 385
civil service, p. 386
spoils system, p. 386
patronage, p. 386
merit system, p. 387
Office of Personnel Management (OPM), p. 388
Merit Systems Protection Board, p. 387
Hatch Act, p. 387
implementation, p. 388
administrative discretion, p. 388
regulation, p. 388
rule-making, p. 388
Federal Register, p. 389
Federal Reserve Board, p. 390
uncontrollable spending, p. 390
entitlement program, p. 390
oversight, p. 391
central clearance, p. 391
public policy, p. 395
politics, p. 395
policy makers, p. 395
distributive policy, p. 396
redistributive policy, p. 396
zero-sum games, p. 396
reverse distributive policy, p. 396
nondecision, p. 396
policy agenda, p. 397
think tank, p. 399
issue-attention cycle, p. 399
incremental policy, p. 400
punctuating policy, p. 400
iron triangle, p. 401
issue network, p. 401

Test Yourself

Study and **Review** the **Practice Tests**

MULTIPLE CHOICE QUESTIONS

12.1 Outline the constitutional roots of the federal bureaucracy, its different types of federal organizations, and its employees.

Which of the following describes the spoils system?

a. Applicants must fill out an application and demonstrate their ability.
b. Federal jobs are often filled on the basis of a test.
c. Ninety percent of federal employees are selected through this system.
d. The president's party has nearly complete control over almost every government job.
e. Federal jobs are filled on the basis of ability.

12.2 Analyze the bureaucracy's implementation options and its effectiveness.

What is the basic job shared by all federal organizations regardless of their type?

a. to faithfully execute the laws
b. to protect the president from harm
c. to cooperate with Congress in all legal matters
d. to aid the president in electing members of his or her party to political office
e. to make regulations

12.3 Assess presidential and congressional tools for controlling the federal bureaucracy.

Why do many members of Congress prefer the current, complicated federal bureaucracy to a more efficient alternative?

a. It gives members of Congress less control over their favorite programs.
b. It creates more opportunities to claim credit for programs.
c. It gives members opportunities to use their time to fix bureaucratic problems.
d. It provides fewer opportunities to create pet projects for their districts.
e. It makes constituents less dependent on their members to solve problems.

12.4 Relate politics and public policy, and differentiate the three types of public policy.

Which of the following are not examples of redistributive policy?

a. A tax cut for wealthy Americans, funded by benefit cuts in the Food Stamp program.
b. An increase in highway construction funding.
c. A tax increase on wealthy Americans, and benefit increases for low-income Americans.
d. A tax deduction for the purchase of vacation homes, funded by cuts in health care funding for low-income Americans.
e. A tax increase on all Americans.

12.5 Outline the key steps in making public policy, and assess the types of policy.

Which of the following is not a key step in making policy?

a. setting the agenda
b. deciding to act
c. holding a congressional hearing
d. choosing a tool for solving the problem
e. making regulations for implementation

12.6 Assess ways in which citizens can influence the public policy process.

Which of the following is *not* a common way in which citizens seek action on public policy?

a. run for public office
b. join an interest group
c. e-mail or tweet Congress
d. refuse to pay taxes
e. become an activist

ESSAY QUESTION

Write a short essay explaining why bureaucracy and the public policy process belong in the same chapter of an American government book. Think about the role of the bureaucracy at the various steps in making policy decisions, and its eventual role in implementing the laws.

Further Resources

IN THE LIBRARY

James E. Anderson, *Public Policymaking: An Introduction* (Wadsworth, 2010).

Barry Bozeman, *Bureaucracy and Red Tape* (Prentice Hall, 2000).

Steven Conn, ed., *To Promote the General Welfare: The Case for Big Government* (Oxford University Press, 2012).

M. Margaret Conway, David W. Ahern, and Gertrude A. Steurnagel, *Women and Public Policy: A Revolution in Progress* (CQ Press, 2004).

Shelley L. Davis, *Unbridled Power: Inside the Secret Culture of the IRS* (Harper Business, 1997).

Jane Fountain, *Building the Virtual State: Information Technology and Institutional Change* (Brookings Institution Press, 2001).

Al Gore, *Creating a Government That Works Better and Costs Less: The Report of the National Performance Review* (Plume-Penguin, 1993).

William T. Gormley and Steven J. Balla, *Bureaucracy and Democracy: Accountability and Performance*, 2nd ed. (CQ Press, 2007).

Charles T. Goodsell, *The Case for Bureaucracy*, 4th ed. (CQ Press, 2003).

Philip K. Howard, *The Death of Common Sense: How Law Is Suffocating America* (Random House, 1994).

Cornelius Kerwin, R*ulemaking: How Government Agencies Write Law and Make Policy* (CQ Press, 2003).

John W. Kingdon, *Agendas, Alternatives, and Public Policies* (Longman, 2002).

Paul C. Light, *A Government Ill Executed: The Decline of the Federal Service and How to Reverse It* (Harvard University Press, 2008).

G. Calvin Mackenzie and Michael Hafken, *Scandal Proof: Do Ethics Laws Make Government Ethical?* (Brookings Institution Press, 2002).

Kenneth J. Meier and Laurence J. O'toole, Jr., *Bureaucracy in a Democratic State: A Governance Perspective* (Johns Hopkins University Press, 2006).

James Q. Wilson, *Bureaucracy: What Government Agencies Do and Why They Do It* (Basic Books, 1989).

B. Guy Peters, American Public Policy: Promise and Performance (CQ Press, 2009).

Andrew Rich, *Think Tanks, Public Policy, and the Politics of Expertise* (Cambridge University Press, 2005).

Paul A. Sabatier, Ed., *Theories of the Public Policy Process* (Westview Press, 2007).

Joe Soss, Jacob S. Hacker, And Suzanne Mettler, eds., *Remaking America: Democracy and Public Policy in an Age of Inequality* (Russell Sage Foundation, 2007).

ON THE WEB

www.omb.gov
The source of information on the federal budget.

www.USAJobs.gov
Where federal agencies post federal jobs.

www.regulations.gov
The place to go for basic information on the rule-making process.

www.volunteeringinamerica.gov
The government's central Web site on volunteering opportunities.

13

Listen to Chapter 13 on MyPoliSciLab

The Judiciary

The Balancing Branch

On January 21, 2010, the U.S. Supreme Court announced its decision in a much-anticipated case dealing with federal campaign finance laws. The case, *Citizens United* v. *Federal Election Commission,*[1] focused on whether a documentary movie critical of Hillary Clinton, who was then running for the Democratic presidential nomination, violated the 2002 Bipartisan Campaign Reform Act's ban on corporation (and union) expenditures from their general funds—including profits—to advocate for the election or defeat of a candidate. In its 5-to-4 decision, the Court ruled that these expenditures could not be limited under the First Amendment. The decision overturned long-standing restrictions on corporate and union spending and the Supreme Court's own precedent. The Court had previously allowed spending restrictions due to the government's interest in preventing corruption, or the appearance of corruption, that could result from the potential for huge corporate general treasuries to disproportionately influence election outcomes.[2] As we discuss in other chapters, in *Citizens United,* the Supreme Court reaffirmed the free speech rights of corporations and ruled that the government had no right to limit that speech.

The Court's ruling was met with a firestorm of criticism from commentators and politicians alike decrying the harm to the democratic process that would result from this decision. Many members of Congress who had voted for the campaign reform legislation only eight years earlier disparaged the Court's opinion, arguing that the pro-business Roberts Court had struck yet another blow against the average citizen. The debate was amplified when, only six days later, President Obama openly criticized the Court's decision in his 2010 State of the Union Address, saying that the Court had "reversed a century of law to open the floodgates for special interests . . . to spend without limits in our elections."[3] Six of the Court's nine justices attended the address and, as is their tradition, they sat mostly expressionless in the audience. That is, except for Justice Samuel Alito, who was caught by television cameras scowling and appearing to say "not true" in response to the president's remarks.

13.1

Determine characteristics of the federal judiciary and implications of the adversarial process, p. 413.

13.2

Outline the structure of the federal court system, p. 416.

13.3

Analyze the factors that play an important role in selecting judicial nominees, p. 419.

13.4

Trace the process by which Supreme Court decisions are reached, and assess influences on this process, p. 425.

13.5

Assess the limits on judicial action and the role of the judiciary in a constitutional democracy, p. 434.

Stephen Colbert, of *The Colbert Report*, highlighted changes in campaign spending as a result of the Supreme Court's decision in *Citizens United* v. *FEC* by forming his own political action committee. Here he collects contributions outside the Federal Election Commission.

The Big Picture Find out which Supreme Court case judicial scholars agree is the most significant and why. Author Christine L. Nemacheck explains the controversy surrounding the role of the Supreme Court, and she breaks down the powers that it does—and does not—have.

The Basics Do you have confidence in the U.S. court system? Watch this video to discover what the founders did to make sure the federal judiciary would be independent of political influence. You'll also learn about an important check the Supreme Court has on the other two branches of U.S. government.

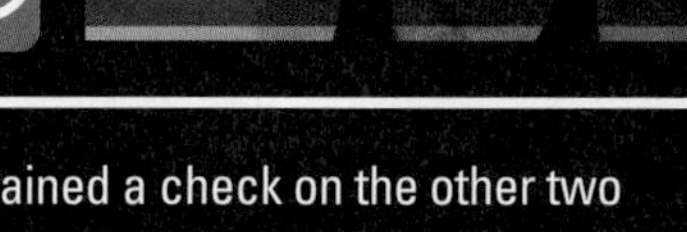

In Context Discover how the Supreme Court gained a check on the other two branches after the U.S. Constitution was written. East Central University political scientist Christine Pappas discusses *Marbury* v. *Madison* and analyzes how the power of judicial review has impacted campaign finance law.

Thinking Like a Political Scientist Why do legal scholars and political scientists disagree over how judges make decisions? East Central University political scientist Christine Pappas analyzes this and other questions scholars study. She explains how the other branches of government limit the role of the judiciary in public policy-making, and discusses research on how public opinion influences the courts.

In the Real World Should the Supreme Court have the power to knock down popular laws? This segment uses the Supreme Court's decision in *U.S.* v. *Arizona* (2012) to illustrate the tension between protecting the law and having a government that's run by the people.

So What? Does the Supreme Court have too much power? Author Christine L. Nemacheck weighs in on this central debate in judicial activism, and she evaluates the opposing claims that the court is both the weakest and the strongest branch of government.

The unusual exchange between the president and a justice provided extensive fodder for commentators and politicians, and further criticism of both the president's comments in the State of the Union Address and Justice Alito's response. Debate over the exchange heated up again in early March when Chief Justice Roberts spoke about the event during a meeting with law students at the University of Alabama. Responding to a student's question, Roberts said he found the president's criticism of the Court at the State of the Union Address "very troubling" and suggested that the event had turned into a "political pep rally" that perhaps the justices should not attend.[4]

The chief justice's remarks and the president's comments highlight a long-standing debate about the appropriate role of the Court in a separation-of-powers system. Is the Court part of the political process, or is it an apolitical institution operating outside the bounds of the political arena? In either case, it is clear that politics shape the courts, especially through the federal judicial appointment process, and the courts shape politics through the reach of their decisions.

In this chapter, we explore how the federal judiciary operates in a system of separated powers and examine the nomination process through which we staff the judiciary. The judicial branch is unlike the elected branches of government in several ways. We will first look at the way the Framers envisioned the judiciary and discuss several of its important characteristics. After exploring the appointment process, we will discuss the Supreme Court in particular. Given that it is the court of last resort in the United States and has the final say on what the Constitution means, it is crucial to our understanding of the federal judiciary.

Understanding the Federal Judiciary

13.1 Determine characteristics of the federal judiciary and implications of the adversarial process.

The Framers viewed the federal judiciary as an important check against both Congress and the president. But the judiciary lacked the institutional resources of the elected branches. As Alexander Hamilton wrote, "The Executive not only dispenses the honors, but holds the sword of the community. The legislature not only commands the purse, but prescribes the rules by which the duties and rights of every citizen are to be regulated. The judiciary, on the contrary, has no influence over either the sword or the purse."[5] So, in order to ensure the judicial check, the Framers insulated the judiciary against both public opinion and the rest of government.

To protect the judiciary from shifts in public opinion, the Framers rejected direct election. That was the method used to select many judges in the colonies, and it is still used today to choose some state and local judges. The Framers also excluded the House, the more representative of the two bodies of Congress, from any role in either selecting or confirming federal judges. To protect the judiciary from Congress as a whole, no limits were allowed on judicial terms. Federal judges serve during good behavior, which typically means for life. And finally, to prevent Congress from assessing a financial penalty against the judiciary, judges' salaries cannot be reduced once confirmed.

These early decisions were essential to protect the judiciary's independence. Because it has no army or police force to enforce its will or make people obey its decisions, the judiciary must often rely on the public's respect to implement its decisions. This is sometimes a challenge, particularly when resolving controversial issues such as abortion rights or the rights of prisoners of war. Even in the face of these challenges, it is crucial that the judiciary maintain its independence.

However, in states where judges are chosen through popular elections, they are presumed to be accountable to the public. Although judicial elections arguably add accountability, some contend that because business, labor and other interests often

13.1

13.2

13.3

13.4

13.5

judicial review
The power of a court to determine whether a law or government regulation is consistent with the U.S. Constitution or, in a state court, the state constitution.

adversary system
A judicial system in which the court of law is a neutral arena where two parties argue their differences.

criminal law
A law that defines crimes against the public order.

civil law
A law that governs relationships between individuals and defines their legal rights.

prosecutor
Government lawyer who tries criminal cases, often referred to as a district attorney or a U.S. Attorney.

defendant
In a criminal action, the person or party accused of an offense.

plea bargain
An agreement between a prosecutor and a defendant that the defendant will plead guilty to a lesser offense to avoid having to stand trial for a more serious offense.

justiciable dispute
A dispute growing out of an actual case or controversy that is capable of settlement by legal methods.

spend millions of dollars to elect or defeat judges that the real accountability is to the groups and corporations that contribute money to the judges' election campaigns, not to average citizens. This is only one of the potential problems in systems that provide for greater accountability at the expense of judicial independence.

The appropriate balance between judicial independence and accountability typically frames the debate about the best way to staff the judiciary. Some countries structure their appointment process so as to ensure independence. For example, in Japan, Great Britain, Germany, and France, individuals interested in the judiciary take a variety of competitive exams and go through specialized judicial training to become eligible for appointment to their country's courts. In other countries, like China, judicial independence is less evident; many judges were simply transferred to the judiciary from military posts in the Communist Party. Since 1995, there have been efforts to improve the quality of the judiciary—judges must now have some basic legal education—but judicial independence is still not assured.

□ Characteristics of the Federal Judiciary

CIVIL AND CRIMINAL LAW Federal judges play a central role in U.S. life. They rule on controversial issues such as partial-birth abortion and affirmative action, and they often decide whether laws are constitutional. Many of these decisions are based on Chief Justice John Marshall's successful claim of **judicial review**—the power to interpret the Constitution. Only a constitutional amendment or a later Supreme Court can modify the Court's decisions.

Several important characteristics distinguish the judiciary from Congress, the presidency, and the administrative system. First, the federal judiciary is an **adversary system**, based on the theory that arguing over law and evidence guarantees fairness.[6] The courts provide a neutral arena in which two parties argue their differences and present evidence supporting those views before an impartial judge. Because the two parties in a case must bring their arguments before the judge, judges may not go looking for cases to decide. The adversary system thus imposes restraints on judicial power.

The courts handle many kinds of legal disputes that fall into one of two broad categories: **criminal law**, which defines crimes against the public order and provides for punishment, and **civil law**, which governs relations between individuals and defines their legal rights. Here are several important distinctions between the criminal and civil law:

- In a criminal trial, a person's liberty is at stake (those judged guilty can be imprisoned); in a civil case, penalties are predominantly monetary.
- Criminal defendants who cannot afford attorneys are provided counsel by the government, but there is no right to a government-provided attorney in civil cases.
- Defendants generally have the right to a jury in criminal trials, but there is no constitutional right to a jury in state civil trials.

The federal government, not the judiciary, brings all federal criminal cases and can also be a party to a civil action, and the federal judiciary decides the cases. For example, when Martha Stewart was tried for securities fraud and obstruction of justice, the U.S. government brought the case. Government **prosecutors**, acting on behalf of the public, choose whether and how to pursue a case against criminal **defendants** who may have violated the law. In some cases, they may decide to offer a **plea bargain**, an arrangement in which a defendant agrees to plead guilty to a lesser offense than he or she was charged with, to avoid having to face trial for a more serious offense and a lengthier sentence.

CASES AND CONTROVERSIES Unlike the legislature and the executive, the federal judiciary is a *passive* and *reactive* branch. It does not instigate cases or conduct its own investigations, nor can it resolve every issue that comes before it. Federal judges decide only **justiciable disputes**—according to the Constitution, they are to decide *cases and controversies.* It is not enough that a judge believes a particular law to be

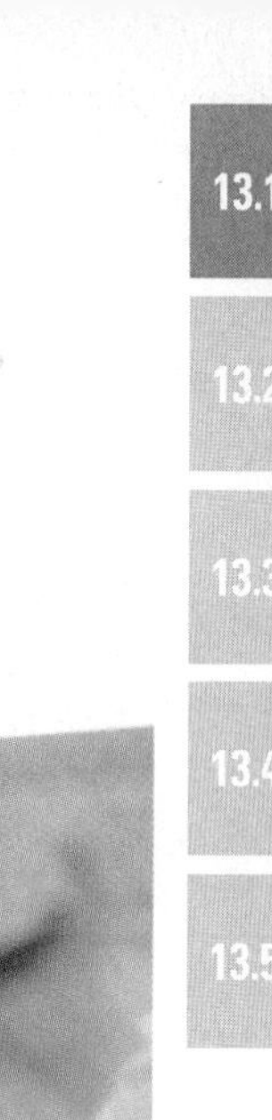

A physician shows her support for the Affordable Care Act outside the U.S. Supreme Court as it hears oral arguments in *National Federation of Independent Business* v. *Sebelius* (2012).

unconstitutional; a real case must be litigated for a judge to reach that decision. In addition, the parties that raise a civil case must have *standing to sue.* That is, the **plaintiff**, the person who begins a civil suit, must have experienced or be in immediate danger of experiencing direct and personal injury. Hypothetical harm is not enough to warrant court review. In an adversary system like ours, it is essential that each side bring forth the best possible arguments before the judge or jury. Because the decision makers depend on the adversaries to bring all the relevant information before them, if one side does not truly have a stake in the outcome, the adversarial process breaks down.

The federal judiciary has also been reluctant to hear disputes on powers the Constitution explicitly assigns to Congress or the president. It resists intervening in foreign policy questions, respecting the power to declare war or economic questions such as the fairness of the federal tax system. The federal judiciary does decide questions about whether the federal government followed the laws, but it generally allows Congress and the president to resolve their differences through the normal legislative process.

plaintiff
The party instigating a civil lawsuit.

U.S. attorney general
The chief law enforcement officer in the United States and the head of the Department of Justice.

solicitor general
The third-ranking official in the Department of Justice who is responsible for representing the United States in cases before the U.S. Supreme Court.

□ Prosecuting Cases

The U.S. Department of Justice is responsible for prosecuting federal criminal and civil cases. The department is led by the **U.S. attorney general**, assisted by the **solicitor general**, 93 U.S. Attorneys, and approximately 1,200 assistant U.S. Attorneys. The solicitor general represents the federal government whenever it has a case before the Supreme Court, whereas U.S. Attorneys represent the government whenever it is party to a case in a lower federal court. U.S. Attorneys are appointed by the president with the advice and consent of the Senate, whereas the attorney general appoints each of the assistant U.S. Attorneys after consulting with the U.S. Attorneys in each district. Some districts have as few as 16 assistant U.S. Attorneys, as does the U.S. Attorney's Office for the

public defender system
An arrangement whereby public officials are hired to provide legal assistance to people accused of crimes who are unable to hire their own attorneys.

district courts
Courts in which criminal and civil cases are originally tried in the federal judicial system.

circuit courts of appeals
Courts with appellate jurisdiction that hear appeals from the decisions of lower courts.

Supreme Court
The court of last resort in the United States. It can hear appeals from federal circuit courts or state high courts.

original jurisdiction
The authority of a court to hear a case "in the first instance."

appellate jurisdiction
The authority of a court to review decisions made by lower courts.

precedent
A decision made by a higher court such as a circuit court of appeals or the Supreme Court that is binding on all other federal courts.

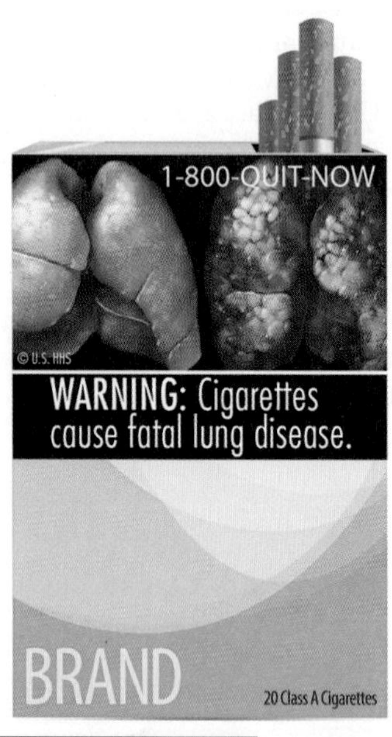

In 2012, First Amendment challenges to the graphic labels the Food and Drug Administration mandated that tobacco companies put on cigarette packaging were successful in the DC Circuit Court of Appeals but failed in the Sixth Circuit. The cases could be appealed to the U.S. Supreme Court.

district of North Dakota; the largest, the U.S. Attorney's Office for the District of Columbia, has more than 330.

The federal judiciary also provides help to defendants who cannot afford their own attorneys in criminal trials. Traditionally, private attorneys have been appointed to provide assistance, but many state and federal courts employ a **public defender system**. This system provides lawyers to any defendant who needs one and is supervised by the federal judiciary to ensure that public defenders are qualified for their jobs.

The Three Types of Federal Courts

13.2 Outline the structure of the federal court system.

rticle III of the Constitution is the shortest of the three articles establishing the institutions of government. Yet as brief as it is, it instructs the judiciary to resolve several kinds of cases, including those to which the United States is a party in enforcing the laws, for example, and disputes between citizens of two or more states.

Article III is not the only part of the Constitution dealing with the federal judiciary, however. The Framers also gave Congress the power to establish "all tribunals inferior to the Supreme Court," which meant that Congress could establish the lower courts we discuss next.

The first Congress used this power to create a hierarchy of federal courts. Under the Judiciary Act of 1789, which was the very first law Congress passed, the federal judiciary was divided into a three-tiered system that exists to this day. The first tier consists of **district courts**, the middle tier of **circuit courts of appeals**, and the highest tier of only one court, the **Supreme Court**. The Supreme Court has **original jurisdiction**, the authority to hear a case essentially as a trial court would, only in cases involving ambassadors and other consuls, and cases in which a state or states are a party.

In all other cases, the Supreme Court has **appellate jurisdiction** and reviews decisions of other federal courts and agencies and appeals from state supreme court decisions that raise questions of federal law. In general, federal courts may decide only cases or controversies arising under the Constitution, a federal law, a treaty, or admiralty and maritime law; cases brought by a foreign nation against a state or the federal government; and diversity suits—lawsuits between citizens of different states—if the amount of the controversy exceeds $75,000.

☐ Level One: District Courts

Although the Supreme Court and its justices receive most of the attention, the workhorses of the federal judiciary are the district courts operating in the states, the District of Columbia, and U.S. territories. In 2011, they heard nearly 290,000 civil cases and more than 75,000 criminal cases.[7] There are 678 judgeships in the 94 district courts across the country, at least one in every state.

District courts are the trial courts where nearly all federal cases begin. They make decisions on the death penalty, drug crimes, and other criminal violations. District court judges normally hold trials and decide cases individually. However, because reapportionment of congressional districts and voting rights are so important to the nation, they hear cases concerned with these issues in three-judge panels.

☐ Level Two: Circuit Courts of Appeals

All district court decisions can be *appealed*, or taken to a higher court for further review. Nearly all of these cases are reviewed by federal courts of appeals. Judges in these courts are bound by **precedent**, or decisions previously made by courts of appeals and the Supreme

BY the People Making a Difference

Create a Space of Her Own: A Partnership Between Courts and the Arts

In addition to dealing with crime through the general criminal justice system, courts in the United States must also deal with crime committed by juvenile offenders. However, the juvenile justice system typically concerns itself more seriously with rehabilitative efforts than does the adult criminal justice system. And, both systems are aimed at deterring criminal activity. There are a number of ways citizens can make a difference in the lives of children who might be at risk of committing a criminal offense.

The research on risk factors associated with juvenile criminal activity is largely in agreement that children living in neighborhoods with high levels of poverty and criminal activity are at an increased risk for involvement in serious crime.* One program aimed at reducing the risk for young girls' involvement in criminal activity is SOHO—a program developed through a partnership between the Alexandria Virginia Court Services Unit and The Art League of Alexandria, a nonprofit arts organization. The Space of Her Own (SOHO) program pairs girls with female mentors in a year-long arts program that culminates in creating a designated space for each of the participants in their homes—similar to the kinds of makeovers often portrayed on networks like HGTV.

By fostering long-term relationships with committed mentors trained by the National Mentoring Partnerships model program, SOHO provides a means by which women can directly make a difference in the lives of at-risk girls. The program includes a variety of art projects that the girls and mentors work on together, a focus on healthy eating with contributions by local chefs, and developing life skills and building self-esteem through one-on-one and group activities during weekly meetings. SOHO now operates three programs, two in Alexandria and one in Richmond, Virginia. Over 90% of the girls who have been a part of the program have remained outside of the juvenile court system.†

QUESTIONS

1. **How could working on arts projects help to reduce juvenile criminal activity?**
2. **Should courts be more focused on deterrence through programs like SOHO or deterrence through more traditional means including harsh sentencing?**
3. **What drawbacks might exist in court involvement in partnerships with youth programs like SOHO?**

*McCord, Joan, Cathy Spatz Widom, and Nancy A. Crowell, eds. 2001. *Juvenile Crime, Juvenile Justice. Panel on Juvenile Crime, Treatment, and Control.* Washington DC: National Academy Press.

†SOHO: Space of Her Own, http://spaceofherown.org. Accessed January 25, 2012.

Court, but they have considerable discretion in applying these earlier decisions to new cases. Although most of their cases come up from federal district courts, federal regulatory commissions bring their cases to the courts of appeals directly. For example, appeals of the Federal Energy Regulatory Commission's decisions may be heard by the U.S. Court of Appeals for the District of Columbia Circuit and by the U.S. Supreme Court.

Courts of appeals are located geographically in 11 *judicial circuits* that include all of the states and U.S. territories (see Figure 13.1 for a map of the states included in each of the 11 geographic circuits). A 12th is located in the District of Columbia and hears the largest number of cases challenging federal statutes, regulations, and administrative decisions. Circuit courts normally operate as panels of three judges; in 2011, they decided more than 55,000 cases.

Except in unusual circumstances, courts of appeals can resolve only cases that have been decided by district courts. Nevertheless, their decisions are usually final. Less than 1 percent of their decisions are appealed to the Supreme Court.[8]

☐ Level Three: The Supreme Court

The Constitution established only one court of appeals for the entire nation: the Supreme Court, or the "court of last resort." Once the Supreme Court decides, the dispute or case is over.

Compared with Congress and the presidency, the Supreme Court has changed the least since its creation. There are nine Supreme Court justices today, compared with six in

writ of *habeas corpus*
A court order requiring explanation to a judge why a prisoner is being held in custody.

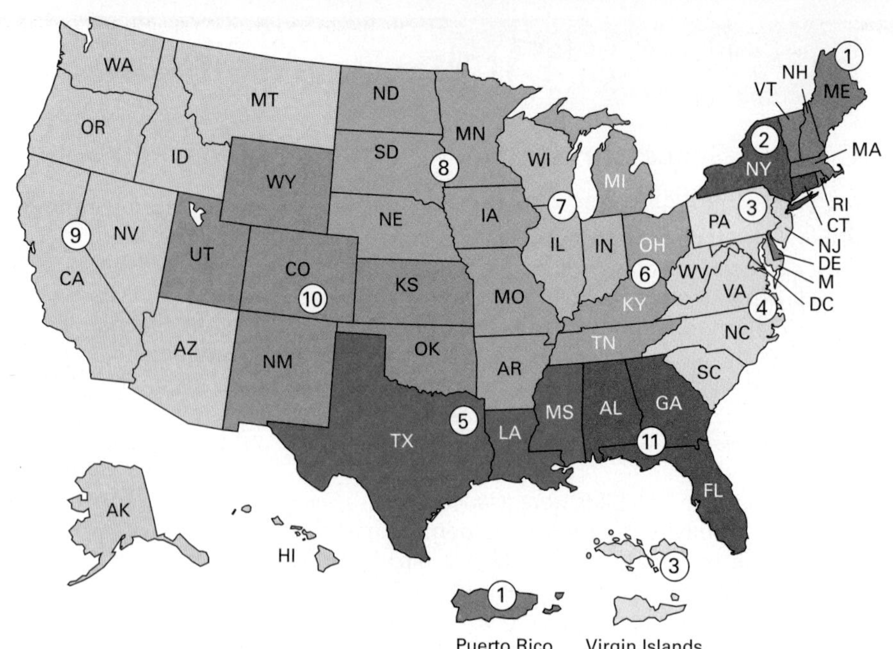

FIGURE 13.1 STATES COVERED BY THE 11 U.S. CIRCUIT COURTS OF APPEALS

Why are some circuits so much larger, geographically, than others? In what circuit do you reside?

1789, and the Court moved into its own building only in 1935. Before then it had shared space with the House and Senate in the U.S. Capitol building. Unlike the current practice in both houses of Congress, oral arguments before the Court about individual cases are not televised, and the justices still appear in robes. Many of the Court's unique characteristics persist due to the constitutional protections the Framers put in place. Given its importance, we will turn to a more in-depth discussion of the Supreme Court later in this chapter.

Judicial Federalism: State and Federal Courts

Unlike most countries, which have a single national judicial system that makes all decisions on criminal and civil laws, the United States has both federal and state courts. Each state maintains a judiciary of its own, and many large cities and counties have judicial systems as complex as those of the states. As in the federal system, state judicial power is divided between trial courts (and other special courts such as traffic courts) and one or more levels of appellate courts. State courts hear the overwhelming majority of cases in the U.S. legal system—since 2000, about 100 million civil and criminal cases annually.[9]

State courts primarily interpret and apply their state constitutions and law. When their decisions are based solely on state law, their rulings may not be appealed to or reviewed by federal courts. Only when decisions raise a federal question that requires the application of the Bill of Rights or other federal law are federal courts able to review them. Federal courts have **writ of *habeas corpus*** jurisdiction, or the power to release persons from custody if a judge determines they are not being detained constitutionally, and may review criminal convictions in state courts if they believe that an accused person's federal constitutional and legal rights have been violated (see the chapter on civil liberties). Except for *habeas corpus* jurisdiction, the Supreme Court is the only federal court that may review state court decisions, and only in cases presenting a conflict with federal law.

Other than the original jurisdiction the Constitution grants to the Supreme Court, no federal court has any jurisdiction except that granted to it by an act of Congress. Congress controls the Supreme Court's appellate jurisdiction (as we discuss later in the chapter) and also established the three-tiered structure of the federal court system through legislation, beginning with the Judiciary Act of 1789. Congress could technically eliminate the lower federal courts, but that is entirely unlikely given their heavy caseloads.

FOR the People Government's Greatest Endeavors

Reducing Crime

State and local governments are responsible for enforcing most laws against criminal activities such as murder, rape, and theft. However, the federal government provides money to help them do so, and it also enforces federal drug laws and gun controls. The federal government has also helped fund larger police forces and imposed tougher sentences against federal crimes such as kidnapping and terrorism.

The federal government's biggest investment has been in providing money to help states control both street crimes and organized crime by the Mafia and other criminal organizations. In 1968, for example, Congress passed the Crime Control and Safe Streets Act, which gave millions of dollars to the states to increase their police forces and patrol the streets. The law also raised the minimum age for purchasing a handgun to 21 years of age.

The 1968 law set an important precedent for federal involvement in state and local crime control, which led to further controls on handguns and a new Crime Control and Safe Streets Act in 1994. Under the new law, the federal government gave states even more money to hire 100,000 new police officers and banned 19 types of assault weapons, such as the M-16 and AK-47, which are rapid-firing rifles often used by the military. The law also banned hate crimes such as painting Nazi slogans and swastikas on Jewish synagogues.

In part because of increased state and local action, national crime rates have fallen dramatically throughout the past quarter-century, particularly in large urban settings such as New York City. Crime fell through the 1990s and early 2000s, but there was an uptick in the number of violent crimes in 2005–2007. However, the rates since then have dropped below levels seen at the end of the 1990s. In fact, the figures for 2009 are the lowest on record since 1984.

QUESTIONS

1. Should the federal government be involved with state and local crime control?
2. What factors might drive the crime rate up or down?
3. How might criminal sentencing affect the crime rate?

**Crime in the United States*, an annual publication of the Federal Bureau of Investigation, http://www.fbi.gov/ucr/ucr.htm#cius. Accessed on February 6, 2012.

The Politics of Appointing Federal Judges

13.3 Analyze the factors that play an important role in selecting judicial nominees.

The Constitution sets absolutely no requirements for serving on the Supreme Court, nor did the first Congress create any requirements for the lower courts. Because judges were to be appointed by the president with the advice and consent of the Senate, the Framers assumed that judges would be experienced in the law. As Alexander Hamilton explained, "there can be but few men in the society who will have sufficient skill in the laws to qualify them for the stations of judges. And making the proper deductions for the ordinary depravity of human nature, the number must be still smaller of those who unite the requisite integrity with the requisite knowledge."[10]

Much as the Framers believed that the judiciary should be independent, the appointment process gives presidents and the Senate ample opportunity to influence the direction of the courts. Indeed, George Washington established two precedents in judicial appointments. First, his appointees were his political and ideological allies—all of Washington's appointees belonged to his Federalist Party. Second, every state was represented on some court somewhere, thereby ensuring at least some representation across the nation.

Presidents have continued to follow Washington's lead on these two points. They nominate judges who are likely to agree with them on the key issues before the courts and tend to nominate judges from their own party. Presidents see these nominations as

13.1

13.2

13.3

13.4

13.5

senatorial courtesy
The presidential custom of submitting the names of prospective appointees for approval to senators from the states in which the appointees are to work.

TABLE 13.1 MOVING UP TO THE SUPREME COURT

Job Experience	Number	Most Recent Example
Federal Judges	33	Sonia Sotomayor, 2009
Practicing Lawyers	22	Lewis F. Powell, 1971
State Court Judges	18	Sandra Day O'Connor, 1981
Cabinet Members	8	Labor Secretary Arthur Goldberg, 1962
Senators	7	Harold H. Burton (R-Ohio), 1945
Attorneys General	6	Tom C. Clark, 1949
Governors	3	Earl Warren (D-Calif.), 1953
Other	15	Solicitor General Elena Kagan, 2010

SOURCE: *CQ Weekly*, October 10, 2005, p. 2701, updated by authors.

■ *How might a justice's experience affect his or her work on the Court? Why do you think so many federal judges have won appointment to the U.S. Supreme Court?*

one of the most important legacies of their time in office. Indeed, if a president is able to appoint a 50-year-old justice, that person could continue to affect law in the United States, perhaps for 30 years or more beyond the president's term.

Presidents also routinely rely on the senators in a given state to make recommendations, especially for district court appointments. Because judges serve for life, presidents see judicial appointments as an opportunity to shape the courts for decades to come. As Table 13.1 shows, federal court experience is the most common preparation for Supreme Court justices—in fact, 10 of the last 16 Supreme Court justices were federal lower-court judges at the time of their nomination. All of the current U.S. Supreme Court justices, with the exception of the most recently appointed justice, Elena Kagan, have federal appeals court experience in particular.

□ Making the Initial Choices

Article II of the Constitution gives the president the power to appoint federal judges with the advice and consent of the Senate. Although that language may seem straightforward, it has caused great controversy over the Senate's appropriate role. The result is a judicial selection process in which presidents are likely to consult with members of Congress, and particularly senators, especially if they want a smooth confirmation.

The process through which the president consults with members of Congress is complex and may differ from one appointment to the next, but one particularly important norm is **senatorial courtesy**—the custom of submitting the names of prospective judges for approval to the senators from the states in which the appointees are to work. The home-state senators, particularly if they are of the president's party, may also develop a list of candidates for the president's consideration. If the senators approve the nomination, all is well. But if negotiations are deadlocked between them, or between the senators and the Department of Justice, a seat may stay vacant for years.[11] For example, Senator Jesse Helms (R-NC) consistently blocked President Bill Clinton's nominees to the Fourth Circuit Court of Appeals because Clinton, upon taking office in 1992, had failed to nominate a former aide to the Senator.[12]

The custom of senatorial courtesy is not observed with Supreme Court appointments, but presidents do strategically consult with members of Congress, as President Clinton did on his 1993 and 1994 appointments of Justices Ruth Bader Ginsburg and Stephen Breyer. Clinton was especially willing to consult with Republican senator Orrin Hatch, then the Senate Judiciary Committee chair, because the Senate was controlled by Republicans and he needed their support. Before selecting Solicitor General Elena Kagan as his candidate to replace Justice Stevens on the Supreme

For the first time in the Supreme Court's history, three of the court's nine justices are women: Justices Ginsburg, Sotomayor, and Kagan.

Court, President Obama met with Senate leaders and consulted with every member of the Senate Judiciary Committee.

Presidents are also advised by their own White House staffs and the Justice Department in compiling a list of potential nominees. Especially in more recent administrations, the Justice Department's Office of Legal Policy and the White House Counsel's Office begin formulating lists of potential court appointees as soon as the president assumes office.

In addition to this process within the government, nongovernmental actors try to influence the selection process. The American Bar Association (ABA) has historically rated candidates being considered for appointment, but conservative groups' concern that the ABA rankings were biased in favor of more liberal judges led the Bush administration to end its preappointment involvement in favor of consulting with The Federalist Society, a conservative legal group.

Liberal and conservative interest groups also provide their own views of nominees' qualifications for appointment. People for the American Way and the Alliance for Justice often support liberal nominees and oppose conservatives, whereas the Heritage Foundation and a coalition of 260 conservative organizations called the Judicial Selection Monitoring Project often support conservative judges and oppose liberals. These organizations once waited to express their opinions until after the president had sent the name of a nominee to the Senate, but now they are active before the choice is known, informing the media of their support or opposition to potential nominees.

☐ Senate Advice and Consent

The normal presumption is that the president should be allowed considerable discretion in the selection of federal judges. Despite this presumption, the Senate takes seriously its responsibility in confirming nominations, especially when the party controlling the Senate is different from that of the president. However, because individual senators can always threaten or actually mount a filibuster, even party control of the Senate is no guarantee that a nomination will succeed.

All judicial nominations are referred to the Senate Judiciary Committee for a hearing and a committee vote before consideration by the entire Senate. Like laws, judges are confirmed with a majority vote. Even before they receive a hearing, however, all district court nominees must survive a preliminary vote by the nominee's two home-state senators. Each senator receives a letter on blue paper, called a *blue slip,* from the committee asking for approval. If either senator declines to return the slip, the nomination is dead and no hearing will be held.

There are other ways to delay or defeat a judicial nominee, including the threat of a filibuster. Just as the Republican Senate majority had stalled Clinton nominations in the late 1990s, the Democratic majority stalled many of the Bush administration's nominees after it took control of the Senate in mid-2001. Democrats also

OF the People Diversity in America

Diversity in the Federal Courts

The federal judiciary has long been dominated by white males. But diversity on the federal bench has been increasing during the last several decades, largely because of the judicial appointments of Presidents Jimmy Carter, George H. W. Bush, Bill Clinton, and George W. Bush. As of January 1, 2012, the Senate had confirmed 71% of President Obama's judicial nominees. Among those appointments were two new U.S. Supreme Court Justices: Sonia Sotomayor, who is also the first Hispanic justice on the Supreme Court, and Elena Kagan, only the fourth woman ever to serve on the Court. He also appointed diverse candidates to the district and appellate courts. At the same point in his presidency, President Obama had appointed 176 federal court judges. Of those appointees, 17% are African American, 12% are Hispanic, and nearly 8% are Asian American. Approximately 46% are women.* Additionally, President Obama's judicial nominees tend to be older than those nominated by recent presidents. His nominees to the circuit courts of appeals are four to five years older than those appointed by Presidents Bush (43), Clinton, Bush (41), Reagan, and Carter.

Ruth Bader Ginsburg

Although the number of women and minorities appointed to the federal courts has only recently increased significantly, the first female judge, Florence Allen, was appointed in 1934 by President Franklin D. Roosevelt. President Harry Truman named the first African American judge, William Henry Hastie, in 1950. President John F. Kennedy appointed the first Hispanic judge, Reynaldo G. Garza, in 1961, and President Richard M. Nixon in 1971 appointed the first Asian American judge, Herbert Choy. The first Native American judge, Billy Michael Burrage, was appointed in 1994 by President Clinton.

There are several arguments for diversifying the federal judiciary. First, some scholars have argued that a diverse federal judiciary may reach decisions that more accurately reflect the views of our diverse populations. But research has not provided much support for the contention that female or minority judges decide

Sonia Sotomayor

Clarence Thomas

cases differently than do white male judges, with the exception of discrimination suits. Even if there are no differences in outcomes, others argue that simply having a federal judiciary that reflects the citizenry is important to maintaining the courts' legitimacy. In short, citizens place value in seeing someone like themselves on the federal judiciary.

Demographic Characteristics of Federal District Court Judges by Appointing President

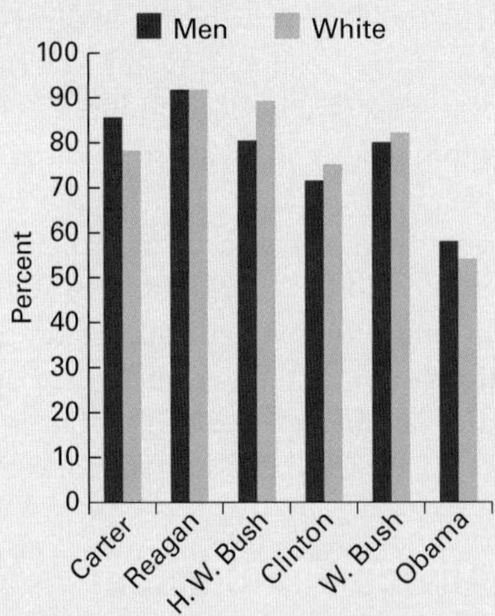

SOURCE: Sheldon Goldman, Elliot Slotnick, Genard Gryski, and Sara Schiavoni, "Picking Judges in Time of Turmoil: W. Bush's Judiciary During the 109th Congress," *Judicature* (May–June 2007). Data updated by authors.

QUESTIONS

1. How might a judge's race or gender affect decisions on the courts?
2. Should presidents consider judicial candidates' race or gender when making appointments to the federal courts?
3. What advantages or disadvantages might there be to having a diverse federal judiciary?

*Alliance for Justice, "The State of the Judiciary: Judicial Selection During the Remainder of President Obama's First Term," May 7, 2012.

stalled many of the Bush nominees even after Republicans regained control of the Senate following the 2002 midterm elections with both the threat and actual use of filibusters.[13] During his first 18 months in office, President Obama's judicial nominees experienced historically low confirmation rates; for example, only 37% of his district court nominees were confirmed. But, by the three-year mark, 73% of his district court nominees and 67% of his appeals court nominees had been confirmed. Still, these figures lag substantially below even the most recent presidents' success in getting their nominees confirmed. Compare those figures with the 91% success rate of President George W. Bush's district court nominees and 71% confirmation rate for appeals court nominees.[14] Even if the Senate delays or rejects a nomination, however, presidents always have the option of making *recess appointments* after the Senate adjourns at the end of a session. Presidents have made more than 300 recess appointments to the federal courts since 1789, including 15 Supreme Court justices who were initially seated as recess appointments.[15]

Before the mid-1950s, the Senate confirmation process was relatively simple and nonpartisan. Until then, the Senate Judiciary Committee did not even hold hearings to ask potential judges questions about their personal history and philosophy. However, as judges became more important in deciding civil rights and other controversial cases, the committee began interviewing candidates on various questions, sometimes imposing a *litmus test* by asking nominees about their positions on specific issues such as abortion. Nominees almost always refuse to answer such questions, to protect themselves from attack and reserve their judgment for actual future cases.

In 1987, however, Supreme Court nominee Robert Bork adopted a different and ultimately unsuccessful strategy. Because he had written so many law articles, made so many speeches, and decided so many cases as a circuit court judge, Bork sought to clarify his constitutional views in defending himself before the Judiciary Committee. His candor may well have contributed to the Senate's rejecting him, and that has made subsequent nominees even more reluctant to respond to similar questions.

Until recently, most judicial appointments, especially those for the district and circuit courts, were processed without much controversy. However, "now that lower-court judges are more commonly viewed as political actors, there is increasing Senate scrutiny of these nominees."[16] The battle over judicial confirmations ordinarily takes place in hearings before the Senate Judiciary Committee, although debates can also occur on the Senate floor after the committee has acted.[17] Supreme Court nominees have typically faced more scrutiny in the confirmation process than have lower federal court judges. Indeed, the Senate has refused to confirm 31 of the 154 presidential nominations for Supreme Court justices since the first justice was nominated in 1789.

□ The Role of Ideology

Presidents so seldom nominate judges from the opposing party (only 10 percent of judicial appointments since the time of Franklin Roosevelt have gone to candidates from the opposition party) that partisan considerations are taken for granted. Today, more attention is paid to other characteristics, such as ideology, race, and gender.[18] (See *Of the People* box for more on the role of race and gender.)

Finding a party member is not enough; presidents want to pick the "right" kind of Republican or "our" kind of Democrat to serve as a judge. Thus judges picked by Republican presidents tend to be judicial conservatives, and judges picked by Democratic presidents are more likely to be liberals. Both orientations are tempered by the need for judges to go through a senatorial confirmation process that requires bipartisan support.

Just as President George W. Bush chose to appoint Chief Justice John Roberts and Justice Samuel Alito, who reflect a more conservative ideology, President Barack Obama selected Justices Sonia Sotomayor and Elena Kagan, who are each reflective of his more liberal ideology. The appointments of these four new justices

13.1 13.2 13.3 13.4 13.5

You Will Decide

Should the Federal Courts Be Active?

Given that a judicially active judge will be more willing to strike down the actions of the elected branches of government, it should not be surprising that legislators are interested to know how federal judicial candidates view judicial activism.

Throughout most of our history, federal courts have been more conservative than Congress, the White House, or state legislatures. Before 1937, judicial restraint was the battle cry of liberals who objected to judges' decisions to strike down many laws, such as state laws limiting the number of hours a person could work each week, that were passed to protect labor and women. These judges broadly construed the words of the Constitution to prevent what they thought were unreasonable regulations of property.

With Presidents Richard Nixon, Ronald Reagan, George H. W. Bush, and George W. Bush, however, these positions changed dramatically, and it was conservatives who advocated judicial restraint. What is needed, they argued, are judges who will step back and let Congress, the president, and the state legislatures regulate or forbid abortions, permit prayer in public schools, and not hinder law enforcement. Even though these presidents argued for restrained judges, many of the Supreme Court justices they appointed were quite active in overturning congressional legislation.

What do you think? Should the federal courts be judicially active? What arguments would you make for and against such a position?

Thinking It Through

Chief Justice John Marshall stated in 1803, "It is emphatically the province and duty of the judicial department to say what the law is."* The Court's decision in *Marbury* v. *Madison* established the use of judicial review to strike down congressional acts. Marshall saw this authority as essential to the Court's ability to check the other branches of government. Justices since Marshall have often been active in striking down legislation that infringes on the rights of minority groups. For example, the Supreme Court's decision in *Brown* v. *Board of Education of Topeka* (1954)† was an active one in that it struck down the state law requiring racial segregation in the public schools. The court's ability to take such action is often seen as an important check on the tyranny of the majority.

The courts have sometimes drawn criticism for too frequently striking down popularly supported legislation. The Roberts' Court decision to strike down restrictions on corporate and union spending from their general treasuries in *Citizens United* v. *Federal Election Commission*‡ resulted in substantial criticism by those who supported such limitations. One school of thought holds that the federal judiciary, composed of unelected judges secure from public pressure, has a responsibility to use restraint in reaching its decisions.

Many critics of judicial activism argue that although the Supreme Court has the authority of judicial review, the Court must also respect the elected branches' interpretations of the constitutionality of their own actions. These critics assert that Congress is especially well situated to determine whether it is acting under the appropriate grant of authority in Article I, and the executive branch is in a similarly good position to evaluate its power under Article II. According to this perspective, the Court's view on the constitutionality of executive or legislative action is that of only one coequal branch of government.

CRITICAL THINKING QUESTIONS

1. **Under what circumstances do you think the Supreme Court should be active and strike down state or federal legislation?**
2. **Might it be preferable to have an unelected body decide whether legislation is constitutional? Why or why not?**
3. **Why do you think most people associate judicial activism with a liberal court?**

* *Marbury* v. *Madison*, 5 U.S. 137 (1803).

† *Brown* v. *Board of Education of Topeka*, 347 U.S. 483 (1954).

‡ *Citizens United* v. *Federal Election Commission*, 558 U.S. 50 (2010).

have shaped the Supreme Court in important ways over the last decade. Justice Alito's appointment to fill the seat left vacant by Justice O'Connor's retirement has had the most significant effect on the Court's opinions, since Justice O'Connor was often the swing vote in closely divided cases. The current Court is one that is substantially more favorable to businesses and corporations, and less receptive to affirmative action policies aimed at diversifying educational institutions than its predecessors.

☐ The Role of Judicial Philosophy

A candidate's judicial philosophy also influences the selection process. Does a candidate believe that judges should interpret the Constitution to reflect what the Framers intended and what its words literally say? Or does the candidate believe that the Constitution should be adapted to reflect current conditions and philosophies? Differences in constitutional interpretation can produce vastly different outcomes on the same legal question.

Presidents and senators also want to know how candidates see the appropriate role of the courts. Does the candidate believe that the courts should strike down acts of the elected branches if they violate broad norms and values that might not be explicitly stated in the Constitution? That is, does the candidate espouse the view of **judicial activism**? Or does the candidate believe in **judicial restraint**, which deems it appropriate for the courts to strike down popularly enacted legislation only when it clearly violates the letter of the Constitution? At the heart of this debate are competing conceptions of the proper balance between government authority and individual rights, and between the power of democratically accountable legislatures and that of courts and unelected judges.

The politics of judicial selection may shock those who like to think judges are picked strictly on the basis of legal merit and without regard for ideology, party, gender, or race. But as a former Justice Department official observed, "When courts cease being an instrument for political change, then maybe the judges will stop being politically selected."[19]

judicial activism
A philosophy proposing that judges should freely strike down laws enacted by the democratically elected branches.

judicial restraint
A philosophy proposing that judges should strike down the actions of the elected branches only if they clearly violate the Constitution.

writ of *certiorari*
A formal writ used to bring a case before the Supreme Court.

How the Supreme Court Decides

13.4 Trace the process by which Supreme Court decisions are reached, and assess influences on this process.

The Supreme Court is a unique institution. Its term runs from the first Monday in October through the end of June. The justices listen to oral arguments for two weeks each month from October to April and then adjourn for two weeks to consider the cases and to write opinions. By agreement, at least six justices must participate in each decision. Cases are decided by a majority vote. In the event of a tie, the decision of the lower court is sustained, although on rare occasions, the case may be reargued.

Explore on **MyPoliSciLab Simulation:** You Are a Supreme Court Clerk

☐ The Eight Steps to Judgment

When citizens vow to take their cases to the highest court of the land even if it costs their last penny, they underestimate the difficulty of securing Supreme Court review and misunderstand the Court's role. The rules for appealing a case are established by the Supreme Court and Congress. Since 1988, when Congress passed the Act to Improve the Administration of Justice, the Supreme Court has not been obligated to grant review of most cases that come to it on appeal. Its *appellate jurisdiction* is almost entirely up to its own discretion; the overwhelming majority of cases appealed to the Court will be denied review.

The process of deciding cases at the U.S. Supreme Court is substantially different than at other federal courts. The Court's first decision is to choose which of the thousands of appeals it will hear each year. Once it has decided to review a case, the Court must then decide the legal question at issue. Next, we discuss, step by step, the Court's process of accepting and deciding a case.

1. REVIEWING APPEALS Many appeals come to the Court by means of a petition for a **writ of *certiorari***, a formal petition seeking the Court's review, or through

Who Are the Activist Judges?

In practice, an activist judge—liberal or conservative—is one who overturns a law as unconstitutional. Even though the current Supreme Court hands down fewer decisions, 19 out of 408 decisions declared laws unconstitutional between 2005 and 2010. The data below shows which justices are most responsible for these controversial decisions.

Supreme Court Decisions

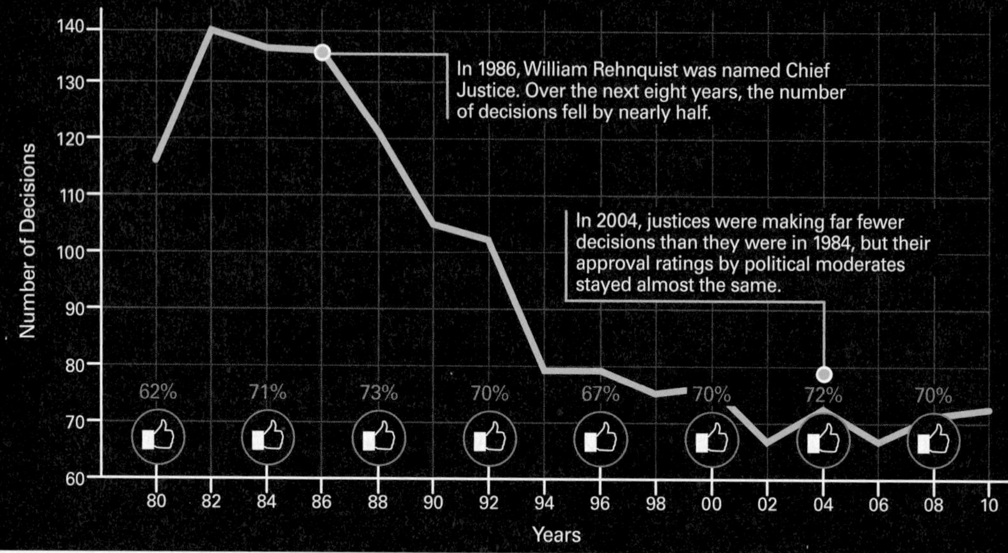

Supreme Court Approval Rating by Moderates

Judicial Activism on the Roberts Court

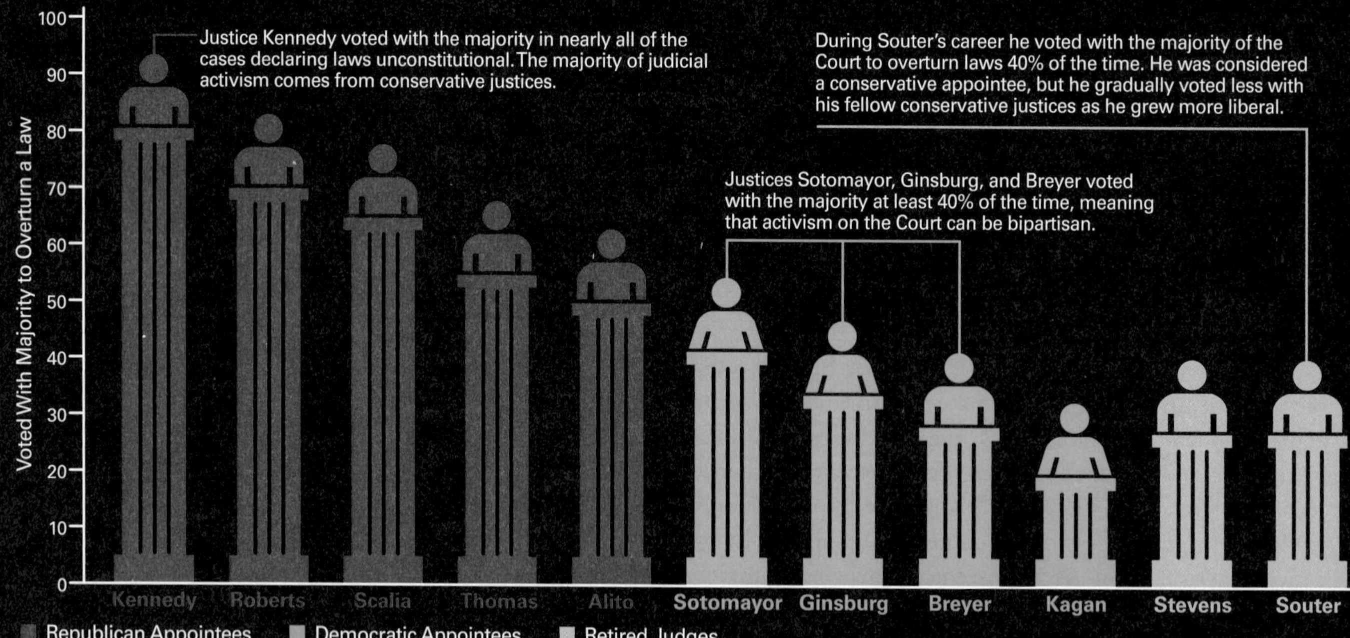

Republican Appointees ■ Democratic Appointees ■ Retired Judges

SOURCE: Data from the United States Supreme Court and the General Social Survey, 1980–2010.

Investigate Further

Concept Why is judicial activism controversial? By declaring a law unconstitutional, judicial activism overturns legislation that is a product of the democratic process. It sets precedent for controversial or divisive issues, and it limits future legislation.

Connection Does judicial activism affect public confidence in the Court? Over two-thirds of American moderates continued to express confidence in the Court, even as it became less active and more conservative in the 2000s.

Cause Is judicial activism conservative or liberal? Both, or neither. On the Roberts Court, the decisions that overturn laws can be bipartisan, but they are usually decided by the conservative justices.

an ***in forma pauperis*** ("as a pauper") petition, which avoids the payment of Court fees. The great majority of *in forma pauperis* petitions come from prisoners. In either case, the appeals may arise from any state supreme court or from the federal court system (see Figure 13.2 for a simplified description of the two paths to the Supreme Court).

in forma pauperis
A petition that allows a party to file "as a pauper" and avoid paying Court fees.

docket
The list of potential cases that reach the Supreme Court.

2. GRANTING THE APPEAL The writs, which the Court can grant or deny, produce its agenda, or **docket**. The docket has grown significantly since the 1970s as citizens have brought more lawsuits, states have imposed more death sentences (which are often appealed), federal regulation has increased, and federal punishment for crimes has become more severe. However, as the number of appeals has grown, the Supreme Court's discretion to decide which cases it will review has allowed it to hear fewer and fewer cases (see Figure 13.3 representing the size of the Supreme Court's docket over time).[20]

The Supreme Court will review a case only if the claim raises a substantial question of federal or constitutional law with broad public significance—what kinds of affirmative action programs are permissible, whether individuals have a right to doctor-assisted suicide, or under what conditions women may have abortions. The Court also tends to review cases in which the courts of appeals disagree. Or a case may raise a constitutional issue on which a state supreme court has presented an interpretation with which the Court disagrees.

The Court decides whether to move forward based on the *rule of four.* If four justices are sufficiently interested in a petition, it will be granted and the case brought up for review. The justices' law clerks work as a group, in what is known as the *cert pool,* to read the petitions and write a memorandum on each, recommending whether a review should be granted. These memos circulate to all the justices except Justice Samuel Alito, who opted out of the cert pool in September 2008.

Denying a writ of *certiorari* does not mean the justices agree with the decision of the lower court, nor does it establish precedent. Refusal to grant a review can indicate all kinds of possibilities. The justices may wish to avoid a political "hot potato," or they may be so divided on an issue that they are not yet prepared to take a stand, or they may want to let an issue "percolate" in the federal courts so that the Court may benefit from their rulings before it decides.

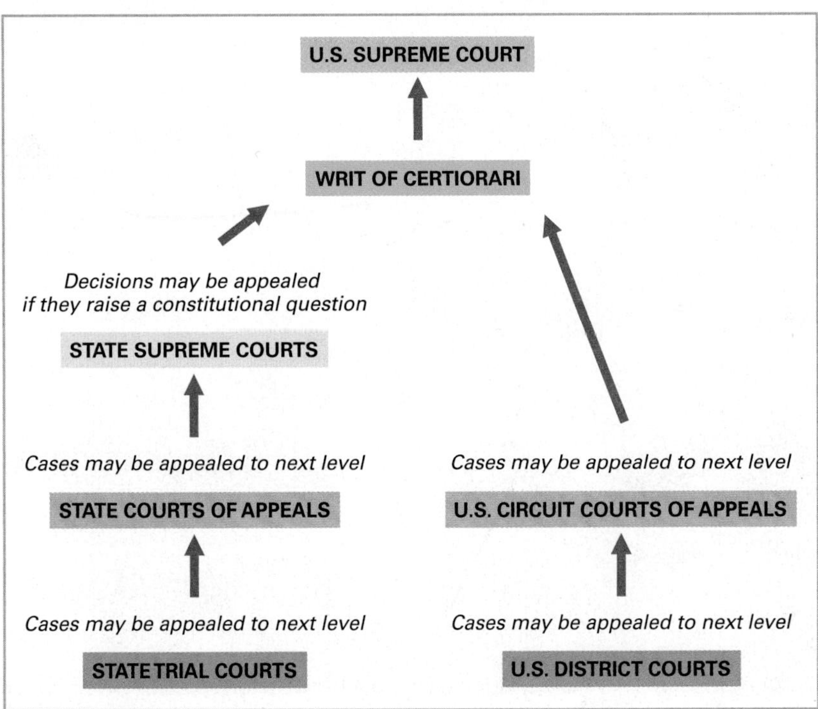

FIGURE 13.2 HOW MOST CASES RISE TO THE SUPREME COURT

■ *Under what conditions can a case that starts off in the state courts be appealed to the U.S. Supreme Court?*

13.1

13.2

13.3

13.4

13.5

***amicus curiae* brief**
Literally, a "friend of the court" brief, filed by an individual or organization to present arguments in addition to those presented by the immediate parties to a case.

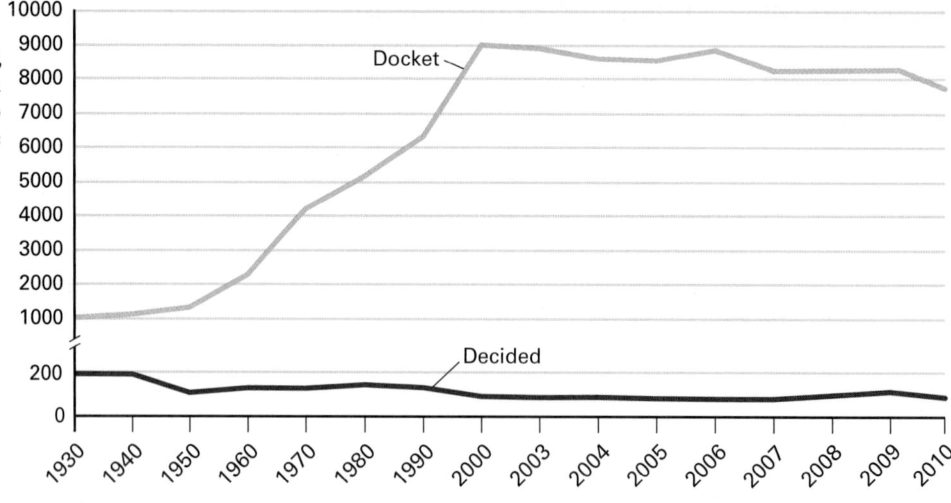

FIGURE 13.3 THE SUPREME COURT CASELOAD

Why do you think the Supreme Court's docket has gotten so much larger over time? Why has the number of cases decided declined at the same time?

SOURCE: Lee Epstein, Jeffrey A. Segal, Harold J. Spaeth, and Thomas G. Walker, *The Supreme Court Compendium: Data, Decisions, and Developments* (CQ Press, 2007). Figures updated by the authors.

3. BRIEFING THE CASE After a case is granted review, each side prepares written *briefs* presenting legal arguments, relevant precedents, and historical background for the justices and their law clerks to study and on which to base their decisions. Prior decisions by the U.S. Supreme Court itself are most highly desirable as precedent; however, the Court may also consider cases decided by the lower federal courts as well as state supreme courts in reaching its decision, depending on the issue presented.

In writing these briefs, the appellants are often aware of the justices' views or concerns about their case, and they attempt to address those concerns. Indeed, attorneys readily admit that they sometimes frame their briefs to appeal to a particular justice on the Court, one they suspect may be the swing, or deciding, vote in the case. Often, outside groups interested in the case file ***amicus curiae* briefs** (Latin for "friend of the court"), through which they can make arguments specific to their members and of interest to the justices.

Because no cameras are allowed in the U.S. Supreme Court during oral arguments, artists provide the only visual record of the arguments. This rendering shows attorney Paul Clement making his arguments before the U.S. Supreme Court on the question of Congress's power to enact health care reform in March 2012.

4. HOLDING THE ORAL ARGUMENT After the Court grants review, a case is set for oral arguments—these arguments are usually heard within three to four months. Lengthy oratory before the Supreme Court, once lasting for several days, is a thing of the past. As a rule, counsel for each side is now allowed only 30 minutes. In order to ensure compliance with this rule, lawyers use a lectern with two lights: A white light flashes five minutes before time is up. When the red light goes on, the lawyer must stop, even in the middle of a sentence.

The entire procedure is informally formal. Sometimes, to the annoyance of attorneys, justices talk among themselves or consult briefs or books during oral arguments. Other times, if justices find a presentation particularly bad, they will tell the attorneys so. Justices freely interrupt the lawyers to ask questions and request additional information. In recent years, "the justices seem barely able to contain themselves, often interrupting the answer to one question with another query."[21] Hence the 30-minute limit can be a problem, especially when the solicitor general participates, because his or her time usually comes out of the 30 minutes of the party he or she is supporting.

If a lawyer is having a difficult time, the justices may try to help out with a question. Occasionally, justices bounce arguments off an attorney and at one another. Justice Antonin Scalia is a harsh questioner. "When Scalia prepares to ask a question, he doesn't just adjust himself in his chair to get closer to the microphone like the others; he looks like a vulture, zooming in for the kill. He strains way forward, pinches his eyebrows, and poses the question, like '... do you want us to believe?'"[22] Justice Ruth Bader Ginsburg is a particularly persistent questioner, frequently rivaling Scalia, whereas Justice Clarence Thomas almost never asks a question at all.[23]

opinion of the Court
An explanation of a decision of the Supreme Court or any other appellate court.

dissenting opinion
An opinion disagreeing with the majority in a Supreme Court ruling.

concurring opinion
An opinion that agrees with the majority in a Supreme Court ruling but differs on the reasoning.

5. MEETING IN CONFERENCE When in session, the justices meet on Friday mornings to discuss the cases they heard that week. These conference meetings are private; no one is allowed in the room except the justices themselves. As a result, much of what we know about the justices' conferences comes from their own notes taken during the meetings.

The conferences are typically a collegial but vigorous give-and-take. The chief justice presides, usually opening the discussion by stating the facts, summarizing the questions of law, and suggesting how to dispose of each case. Each justice, in order of seniority, then gives his or her views and conclusions. The justices do not typically view this as a time to convince others of their views on the case; that will come later as drafts of the opinion are circulated between chambers. After each justice has given his or her view of the case, the writing of the majority opinion is assigned. By practice, if the chief justice is in the majority, he can either assign the opinion to a justice also in the majority or choose to write the opinion himself. If he is not in the majority, the most senior justice in the majority makes that determination.

6. EXPLAINING THE DECISION The Supreme Court announces and explains its decisions in **opinions of the Court**. These opinions are the Court's principal method of expressing its views and reasoning to the world. Their primary function is to instruct judges of state and federal courts how to decide similar cases in the future.

Although the writing is assigned to one justice, the opinion must explain the reasoning of the majority. Consequently, opinions are negotiated documents that require the author to compromise and at times bargain with other justices to attain agreement.[24]

A justice is free to write a **dissenting opinion**. Dissenting opinions are, in Chief Justice Charles Evans Hughes's words, "an appeal to the brooding spirit of the law, to the intelligence of a future day."[25] Dissenting opinions are quite common, as justices hope that someday they will command a majority of the Court. If a justice agrees with the majority on how the case should be decided but differs on the reasoning, that justice may write a **concurring opinion**.

Judicial opinions may also be directed at Congress or at the president. If the Court regrets that "in the absence of action by Congress, we have no choice but to..." or insists that "relief of the sort that petitioner demands can come only from the political branches of government," it is asking Congress to act.[26] Justices also use opinions to communicate with the public. A well-crafted opinion may increase support for a policy the Court favors.[27]

13.1
13.2
13.3
13.4
13.5

7. WRITING THE OPINION Writing the opinion of the Court is an exacting task. The document must win the support of at least four—and more, if possible—intelligent, strong-willed persons. Assisted by the law clerks, the assigned justice writes a draft and sends it to colleagues for comments. If the justice is lucky, the majority will accept the draft, perhaps with only minor changes. If the draft is not satisfactory to the other justices, the author must rewrite and recirculate it until a majority reaches agreement.

The two weapons that justices can use against their colleagues are their votes and the threat of dissenting opinions attacking the majority's opinion. Especially if the Court is closely divided, one justice may be in a position to demand that a certain point or argument be included in, or removed from, the opinion of the Court as the price of his or her vote. Sometimes such bargaining occurs even though the Court is not closely divided. An opinion writer who anticipates that a decision will invite critical public reaction may want a unanimous Court and compromise to achieve unanimity. For this reason, the Court delayed declaring school segregation unconstitutional, in *Brown* v. *Board of Education* (1954), until unanimity was secured.[28] The justices understood that any sign of dissension on this major social issue would be an invitation to evade the Court's ruling.

RELEASING THE OPINION In the past, justices read their entire opinions from the bench on "opinion days." Now, they generally give only brief summaries of the decision and their opinions. Occasionally, when they are unusually unhappy with an opinion, justices read portions of their dissenting opinions from the bench, as Justice Stevens did in *Citizens United* v. *Federal Election Commission*.[29] Copies of the Court's opinions are immediately made available to reporters and the public and published in the official *United States Supreme Court Reports*.[30]

☐ Influences on Supreme Court Decisions

Given the importance of cases that reach the U.S. Supreme Court, the complexity of the Court's decision-making process is not surprising. Supreme Court precedent is a primary influence, but if it were the only one, the lower courts could resolve the question themselves. Typically, there are conflicting precedents, and justices must decide which applies most closely to the legal question at hand.

Outside groups and other legal actors can also influence the Court's decisions. Interest groups' *amicus curiae* briefs may influence a justice's view of the case or the implications of a particular outcome. The chief justice can also affect decision making by the way he frames a case at the conference as well as by his choice of the justice to write the opinion based on the conference vote. Law clerks can affect the Court's decisions by the advice they give their justices, as well as by their role in reviewing the cases appealed to the Court.

THE CHIEF JUSTICE The chief justice of the United States is appointed by the president and confirmed by the Senate, like other federal judges. Yet the chief justice heads the entire federal judiciary; as a result, he (so far in our history, all have been men) has greater visibility than if selected by rotation of fellow justices, as in the state supreme courts, or by seniority, as in the federal courts of appeals. The chief justice has special administrative responsibilities in overseeing the operation of the judiciary, such as assigning judges to committees, responding to proposed legislation that affects the judiciary, and delivering the Annual Report on the State of the Judiciary.

But within the Supreme Court, the chief justice is only "first among equals," even though periods in Court history (such as the Warren Court) are often named after the chief justice. As Rehnquist said when he was still an associate justice, the chief deals not with "eight subordinates whom he may direct or instruct, but eight associates who,

The Global Community

Importance of an Impartial Judiciary

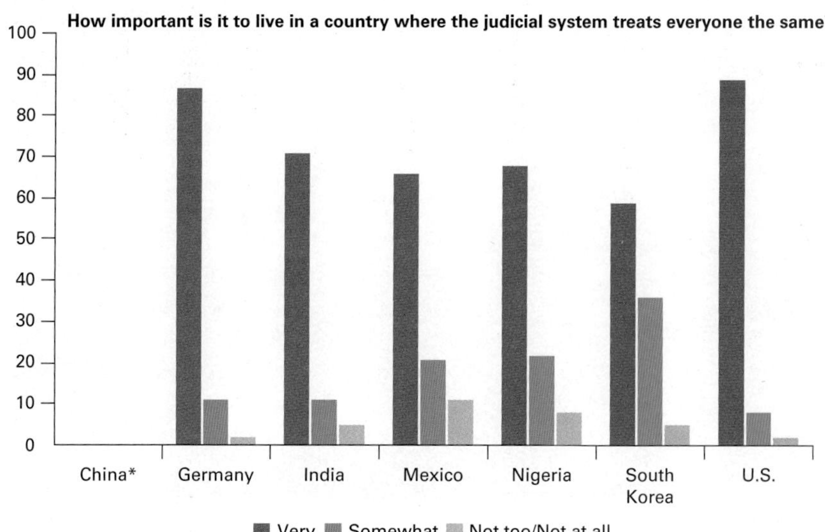

SOURCE: Pew Research Center, *What the World Thinks in 2002: How Global Publics View Their Lives, Their Countries, The World, America* (Pew Research Center, 2002).

In the United States, as in most Western democracies, an independent judiciary serves a crucial role in maintaining democracy and protecting individual rights. In a separation-of-powers system like the United States, the judiciary maintains checks on the other branches of government and has the power to invalidate their actions when they violate the Constitution. It also ensures that the government treats all citizens fairly and impartially; no person is above the law. A Pew Global Attitudes Project survey asked respondents from around the world how important it was to live in a country where the judicial system treats everyone the same.

Even if it is not a present reality, most countries see an impartial judiciary where the judicial system treats everyone the same as an important goal. Nearly 90 percent of respondents in the United States indicated that it is very important that the judicial system treat everyone equally, and support in Germany nearly mirrors that in the United States. However, in other countries such as India, Mexico, Nigeria, and South Korea, there are fewer respondents who agree that an impartial judiciary is very important. It is, perhaps, not surprising that in countries where impartial justice is less assured that respondents value it less than in countries such as the United States and Germany where impartiality is expected in the court systems.

CRITICAL THINKING QUESTIONS

1. In what ways could a judicial system show favoritism toward particular groups or individuals?
2. How do you think judicial elections might affect impartiality?
3. Would you expect greater or lesser impartiality of judges who gain their seats through popular elections?

*Data was not collected in China, in part because they do not have an impartial judiciary.

like him, have tenure during good behavior, and who are as independent as hogs on ice."[31] As political scientist David Danelski observes, "The Chief Justiceship does not guarantee leadership. It only offers its incumbent an opportunity to lead." Yet the chief justice "sets the tone, controls the conference, assigns the most opinions, and usually, takes the most important, nation-changing decisions for himself."[32]

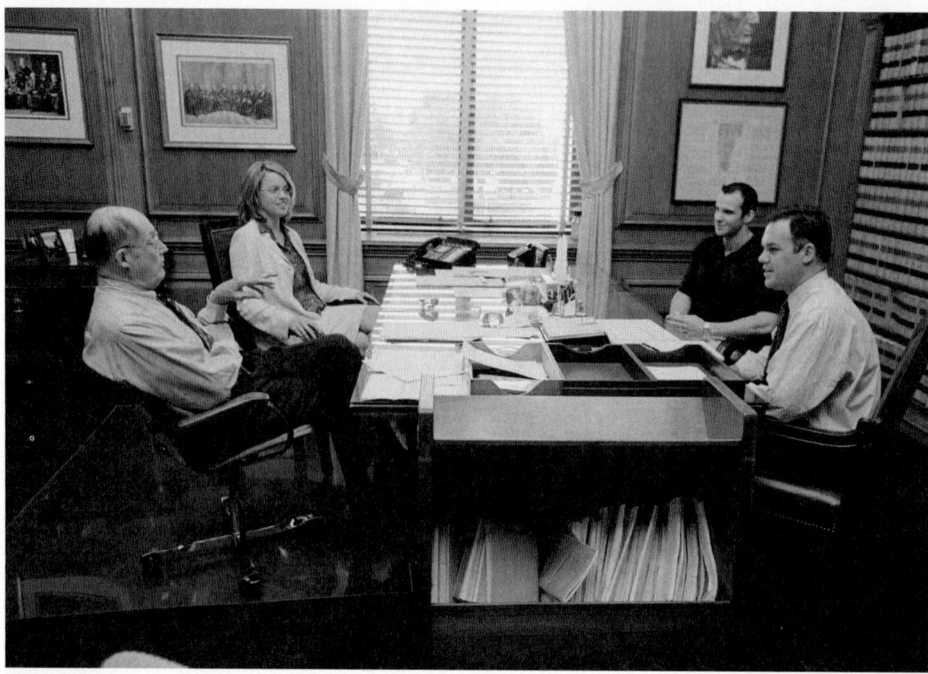

Chief Justice William Rehnquist (on the left) was very popular among his colleagues, both liberal and conservative. He was known for his general efficiency in running the Court and his fairness in assigning opinions. Here he meets with law clerks in his chambers.

LAW CLERKS Beginning in the 1920s and 1930s, federal judges began hiring the best recent graduates of law schools to serve as clerks for a year or two. As the judicial workload increased, more law clerks were appointed, and today, each Supreme Court justice is entitled to four. These are young people who have graduated from a leading law school and have previously clerked for a federal or state court.

Each justice picks his or her own clerks and works closely with them throughout the term. In addition to screening writs of *certiorari* clerks prepare draft opinions for the justices. As the number of law clerks and computers has increased, so has the number of concurring and dissenting opinions. Today's opinions are longer and have more footnotes and elaborate citations of cases and law review articles. This is the result of the greater number of law clerks and the operation of justices' chambers like "nine little law firms," often practicing against each other.[33]

Debate swirls about the degree to which law clerks influence the Court's decisions.[34] Some scholars contend that law clerks have had too much influence, especially as they help write early drafts of their justices' opinions. Others contend that justices select clerks with views very similar to their own, so to the extent law clerks are able to advance their views, they reflect those of the justice they serve. Regardless of this disagreement, however, there is widespread acceptance of law clerks' influence in the decision to grant *certiorari*. Law clerks' influence at this stage of the decision-making process surely provides them with an opportunity at least to influence the Court's docket.

THE SOLICITOR GENERAL Attorneys in the Department of Justice and other federal agencies participate in more than half of the cases the Supreme Court agrees to decide and therefore play a crucial role in setting its agenda. As we noted earlier in this chapter, the solicitor general is responsible for representing the federal government before the Supreme Court and is sometimes called the "tenth justice." Because the U.S. government may not appeal any case upward without the solicitor general's approval, the solicitor general has significant influence over the kinds of cases the Supreme Court eventually sees.[35]

The solicitor general also files *amicus curiae* briefs in cases in which the federal government is not a party. The practice of filing *amicus curiae* briefs guarantees that the

Department of Justice is represented if a suit questions the constitutionality of an act of Congress or the executive branch. The solicitor general may also use these briefs to bring to the Court's attention the views of the current administration.

CITIZENS AND INTERESTED PARTIES Citizens, interest groups, and organizations may also file *amicus curiae* briefs if they claim to have an interest in the case and information of value to the Court.[36] An *amicus* brief may help the justices by presenting arguments or facts the parties to the case have not raised. In recent decades, interest groups have increasingly filed such briefs in an effort to influence the Court and to counter the positions of the solicitor general and the government. For example, in *National Federation of Independent Business* v. *Sebelius* (2012), the case concerning the constitutionality of health care reform, a record 136 *amicus* briefs were filed.[37] Although this case is an outlier, *amicus* briefs are regularly filed in cases before the U.S. Supreme Court. Between 1990 and 2001, at least one *amicus* brief was filed in nearly 90 percent of the cases. Cases involving civil liberties are particularly likely to result in *amicus* participation.[38] Interest groups may also file *amicus curiae* briefs to encourage the Supreme Court to review a case, although this strategy has almost no influence on how the case is decided.[39]

stare decisis
The rule of precedent, whereby a rule or law contained in a judicial decision is commonly viewed as binding on judges whenever the same question is presented.

☐ After the Court Decides

Victory in the Supreme Court does not necessarily mean that winning parties get what they want. Although the Court resolves many issues, it also sometimes *remands* the case, sending it back to the lower court with instructions to act in accordance with its opinion. The lower court often has considerable leeway in interpreting the Court's mandate as it disposes of the case.

The impact of a particular Supreme Court ruling on the behavior of individuals who are not immediate parties to a lawsuit is more uncertain. The most important rulings

The U.S. Solicitor General, Donald Verrilli, represents the United States government in cases before the U.S. Supreme Court. Here he speaks about the 2012 challenge to the Affordable Care Act.

require a change in the behavior of thousands of administrative and elected officials. Sometimes, Supreme Court pronouncements are simply ignored. For example, despite the Court's holding that it is unconstitutional for school boards to require students to pray within a school, some schools continue this practice.[40] And for years after the Supreme Court held public school segregation unconstitutional, many school districts refused to integrate or even closed their public school system, as in Prince Edward County, Virginia, so as to avoid integration.[41]

Judicial Power and Its Limits

13.5 Assess the limits on judicial action and the role of the judiciary in a constitutional democracy.

lthough the Framers worked hard to create an independent federal judiciary, judges are limited in that they cannot ignore earlier decisions unless they have a clear reason to break with the past.

□ Adherence to Precedent

Just because judges make independent decisions does not mean they are free to do whatever they wish. They are subject to a variety of limits on what they decide—some imposed by the political system of which they are a part and some imposed by higher courts and the legal profession. Among these constraints is the policy of ***stare decisis***, the rule of precedent.

Stare decisis pervades our judicial system and promotes certainty, uniformity, and stability in the law. Drawn from the Latin phrase "to stand by that which is decided," the term means that judges are expected to abide by previous decisions of their own courts and by rulings of superior courts. However, the doctrine is not very restrictive.[42] Indeed, lower-court judges sometimes apply precedent selectively, to raise additional questions about an earlier higher-court decision or to give the higher courts a chance to change a precedent entirely.

Stare decisis is even less controlling in the field of constitutional law. Because the Constitution itself, rather than any one interpretation of it, is binding, the Court can *reverse* a previous decision it no longer wishes to follow, as it has done hundreds of times. Supreme Court justices are therefore not seriously restricted by *stare decisis*. Justice William O. Douglas, for one, maintained that *stare decisis* "was really no sure guideline because what did the judges who sat there in 1875 know about, say, electronic surveillance? They didn't know anything about it."[43] Anticipating Justice Stevens' strong dissent in *Citizens United* v. *Federal Election Commission* in which the Court overturned two of its previously decided cases, Chief Justice Roberts wrote that if *stare decisis* were an "inexorable command" or "mechanical formula of adherence to the latest decision... segregation would still be legal, minimum wage laws would be unconstitutional, and the Government could wiretap ordinary suspects without first obtaining warrants."[44] Since 1789, the Supreme Court has reversed nearly 200 of its own decisions and overturned more than 170 acts of Congress, as well as nearly 1,300 state constitutional and legislative provisions and municipal ordinances.[45]

Many Court observers expect the more conservative justices appointed during both Bush administrations to continue to move the law away from the right to abortion established in *Roe* v. *Wade* in 1973. Although they do not expect the Court to overturn the decision in a single, sweeping case, they do expect it to chip away at the precedent as more limited opportunities come before it.[46] The Court did just that when it upheld the federal Partial-Birth Abortion Ban Act in 2007. Although the act affected only late-term abortion procedures, the Court for the first time upheld an abortion restriction that did not provide an exception for the woman's health.[47]

☐ Congressional and Presidential Action

Individual judges are protected from Congress and the president by their life tenure, but the judiciary as a whole can be affected by legislative decisions that alter both the number and the composition of the courts. Because the district and circuit courts are both created through legislation, they can be expanded or altered through legislation.

"PACKING" THE COURT When a political party takes control of both the White House and Congress, it may see an opportunity to increase the number of federal judgeships. With divided government, however, when one party controls Congress and the other holds the White House, a stalemate is likely to occur, and the possibility for new judicial positions is greatly diminished. During Andrew Johnson's administration, Congress went so far as to reduce the size of the Supreme Court to prevent the president from filling two vacancies. After Johnson left the White House, Congress returned the Court to its former size to permit Ulysses S. Grant to fill the vacancies.

In 1937, President Franklin Roosevelt proposed an increase in the size of the Supreme Court by one additional justice for every member of the Court over the age of 70, up to a total of 15 members. Ostensibly, his proposal to "pack" the court with new supporters was aimed at making the Court more efficient. In fact, Roosevelt and his advisers were frustrated because the Court had declared much of the early New Deal legislation unconstitutional. Despite Roosevelt's popularity, his "court-packing scheme" aroused intense opposition and his proposal failed. Although he lost the battle, the Court began to sustain some important New Deal legislation, and subsequent retirements from the bench enabled him to make eight appointments to the Court.

CHANGING THE JURISDICTION Congressional control over the structure and jurisdiction of federal courts has been used to influence the course of judicial policy making. Although unable to get rid of Federalist judges by impeachment, in 1802 Jefferson's Republican Party abolished the circuit courts created by the Federalist Congress just before it lost control of Congress. In 1869, radical Republicans in Congress altered the Supreme Court's appellate jurisdiction in order to remove a case it was about to review weighing the constitutionality of some Reconstruction legislation.[48]

Each year, a number of bills are introduced in Congress to eliminate the jurisdiction of federal courts over cases relating to abortion, school prayer, and school busing, or to eliminate the appellate jurisdiction of the Supreme Court over such matters. These attacks on federal court jurisdiction spark debate about whether the Constitution gives Congress authority to take such actions. Congress has not yet decided to do so because it would amount to a fundamental shift in the relationship between Congress and the Supreme Court.

☐ Judicial Power in a Constitutional Democracy

An independent judiciary is one of the hallmarks of a constitutional democracy and a free society. As impartial dispensers of equal justice under the law, judges should not depend on the executive, the legislature, parties to a case, or the electorate. But judicial independence is often criticized when judges make unpopular decisions. Perhaps in no other society do the people resort to litigation as a means of making public policy as much as they do in the United States. For example, the National Association for the Advancement of Colored People (NAACP) turned to litigation to get relief from segregation practices in the 1930s, 1940s, and 1950s. More recently, an increasing number of women's organizations, environmental groups, and religious and conservative organizations have also turned to the courts.[49]

Whether judges are liberal or conservative, defer to legislatures or not, try to apply the Constitution as they think the Framers intended or interpret it to conform to current values, there are links between what judges do and what the people want. The people never speak with one mind and the links are not direct, but they are the heart of the matter.[50] In the first place, the president and the Senate are likely to appoint justices whose decisions reflect their values. Therefore, elections matter because the views of the people who nominate and confirm the judges are reflected in the composition and decisions of the courts. For instance, in *Planned Parenthood* v. *Casey* in 1992, the Supreme Court refused, by a 5-to-4 vote, to overturn *Roe* v. *Wade* and upheld its core ruling—that the Constitution protects the right of a woman to an abortion—although it also upheld state regulations that do not "unduly burden" that right.[51] This close vote made it clear that presidential elections could determine whether the right to abortion would continue to be protected.

If we as citizens oppose the Court's decisions, we have several avenues through which we can make our opposition known. By communicating with members of Congress, we can pressure them to pass legislation that limits the Court's ruling, as President Obama did when he encouraged Congress to pare back the effects of the Court's decision in *Citizens United* during his 2010 State of the Union Address. We can organize to oppose a particular nomination to the federal judiciary, as many citizens did in response to Judge Robert Bork's nomination to the Supreme Court in 1986. When making our voting decisions, we can also consider the kinds of judges a presidential candidate is likely to appoint to the federal judiciary. In these ways and others, we can affect our federal courts. The Court's power rests, as former Chief Justice Edward White observed, "solely upon the approval of a free people."[52] No better standard for determining the legitimacy of a governmental institution has been discovered.

Review the Chapter

Listen to **Chapter 13** on **MyPoliSciLab**

Understanding the Federal Judiciary

13.1 Determine characteristics of the federal judiciary and implications of the adversarial process, p. 413.

The courts provide a neutral arena in which two parties argue their differences and present evidence supporting those views before an impartial judge. As a result, the courts are largely *reactive;* judges have to wait for parties to a case to bring issues before the courts.

The Three Types of Federal Courts

13.2 Outline the structure of the federal court system, p. 416.

There are three levels of federal courts: (1) district courts, which hear original trials, (2) circuit courts of appeals, which can only review the process by which district courts made their decisions, and (3) the Supreme Court, which makes the final decision.

The Politics of Appointing Federal Judges

13.3 Analyze the factors that play an important role in selecting judicial nominees, p. 419.

Partisanship and ideology are important factors in the selection of all federal judges. In making appointments to the federal courts, presidents must also consider the confirmation environment. They act strategically in selecting a candidate and consulting with Congress. In recent decades, candidates for the presidency and the Senate have made judicial appointments an issue in their election campaigns.

How the Supreme Court Decides

13.4 Trace the process by which Supreme Court decisions are reached, and assess influences on this process, p. 425.

The Supreme Court has almost complete control over the cases it chooses to review as they come up from the state courts, the courts of appeals, and district courts. Law clerks and the solicitor general play important roles in determining the kinds of cases the Supreme Court agrees to decide. Its nine justices dispose of thousands of cases, but most of their time is concentrated on the fewer than 90 cases per year they accept for review. The Court's decisions and opinions establish guidelines for lower courts and the country.

In addition to Supreme Court precedent and justices' own preferences, a number of actors may influence the decision-making process. Law clerks often write early drafts of justices' opinions. *Amicus curiae* participants and the solicitor general's office sometimes affect the opinion-writing process through the briefs they file, as well as through points made during oral argument before the Court.

Judicial Power and Its Limits

13.5 Assess the limits on judicial action and the role of the judiciary in a constitutional democracy, p. 434.

Although the federal judiciary is largely independent, factors such as *stare decisis*, the appointment process, congressional control over its structure and jurisdiction, and the need for the other branches of government to implement its decisions limit the degree to which the courts can or are likely to act without the support of the other branches. As impartial dispensers of equal justice under the law, judges should not depend on the executive, the legislature, the parties to a case, or the electorate. But judicial independence is often criticized when judges make unpopular decisions.

Learn the Terms

Study and **Review** the **Flashcards**

judicial review, p. 414
adversary system, p. 414
criminal law, p. 414
civil law, p. 414
prosecutor, p. 414
defendant, p. 414
plea bargain, p. 414
justiciable dispute, p. 415
plaintiff, p. 415
U.S. attorney general, p. 415
solicitor general, p. 415
public defender system, p. 415
district courts, p. 416
circuit courts of appeals, p. 416
Supreme Court, p. 416
original jurisdiction, p. 416
appellate jurisdiction, p. 416
precedent, p. 416
writ of *habeas corpus*, p. 418
senatorial courtesy, p. 420
judicial activism, p. 425
judicial restraint, p. 425
writ of *certiorari*, p. 425
in forma pauperis, p. 427
docket, p. 427
amicus curiae brief, p. 428
opinion of the Court, p. 429
dissenting opinion, p. 429
concurring opinion, p. 429
stare decisis, p. 433

Test Yourself

Study and **Review** the **Practice Tests**

MULTIPLE CHOICE QUESTIONS

13.1 Determine characteristics of the federal judiciary and implications of the adversarial process.

In a criminal action, the ________ is the person or party accused of an offense.

a. plaintiff
b. defendant
c. public defender
d. judge magistrate
e. petitioner

13.2 Outline the structure of the federal court system.

When the U.S. Supreme Court agrees to hear a case appealed to it from the lower courts, it is exercising

a. original jurisdiction.
b. *stare decisis.*
c. appellate jurisdiction.
d. mandatory jurisdiction.
e. *habeas corpus.*

13.3 Analyze the factors that play an important role in selecting judicial nominees.

According to the norm of senatorial courtesy

a. presidents nominate senators for appointment to the federal courts.
b. senators give the president courtesy in making nominations.
c. same-party home-state senators make recommendations for federal court judges.
d. all senators respond to presidents' nominees with a blue-slip.
e. judicial nominees receive speedy nomination hearings.

13.4 Trace the process by which Supreme Court decisions are reached, and assess influences on this process.

An *amicus curiae* brief is one in which

a. the solicitor general makes his or her case to the Court.
b. a party interested in the case outcome, makes arguments to the Court.
c. a party who cannot afford an attorney petitions the Court for a hearing.
d. the petitioner details his argument in the case.
e. the respondent details the precedent relevant to her case.

13.5 Assess the limits on judicial action and the role of the judiciary in a constitutional democracy.

The norm that the Court should not overturn precedent cases unless absolutely necessary is known as

a. *stare decisis.*
b. *in forma pauperis.*
c. *amicus curiae.*
d. *sui generis.*
e. *habeas corpus.*

ESSAY QUESTION

What is the appropriate role of the judiciary in a separation of powers system? Should federal court judges be active or restrained when evaluating legislation passed by Congress and signed by the president? Would your answer differ in evaluating elected state court judges? Why or why not?

Explore Further

IN THE LIBRARY

Henry J. Abraham, *Justices, Presidents, and Senators: A History of U.S. Supreme Court Appointments from Washington to Bush II,* 5th ed. (Rowman & Littlefield, 2008).

Robert A. Carp and Ronald Stidham, *The Federal Courts* 5th ed. (CQ Press, 2010).

Cornell Clayton and Howard Gilman, eds., *Supreme Court Decision Making: New Institutionalist Approaches* (University of Chicago Press, 1999).

Lee Epstein and Jeffrey A. Segal, *Advice and Consent: The Politics of Judicial Appointments* (Oxford University Press, 2005).

Lee Epstein, Jeffrey A. Segal, Harold Spaeth, and Thomas Walker, eds., *The Supreme Court Compendium,* 5th ed. (CQ Press, 2011).

Sheldon Goldman, *Picking Federal Judges: Lower Court Selection from Roosevelt Through Reagan* (Yale University Press, 1997).

Kermit L. Hall and Kevin T. Mcguire, eds., *Institutions of American Democracy: The Judicial Branch* (Oxford University Press, 2005).

Randolph Jonakait, *The American Jury System* (Yale University Press, 2003).

David Klein, *Making Law in the U.S. Courts of Appeals* (Cambridge University Press, 2002).

Forest Maltzman, James F. Spriggs Ii, and Paul J. Wahlbeck, *Crafting Law on the Supreme Court: The Collegial Game* (Cambridge University Press, 2000).

Kevin Mcguire, ed., *New Directions in Judicial Politics* (Routledge, 2012).

Christine Nemacheck, *Strategic Selection: Presidential Nomination of Supreme Court Justices from Herbert Hoover Through George W. Bush* (University of Virginia Press, 2007).

David M. O'brien, *Storm Center: The Supreme Court in American Politics,* 9th ed. (Norton, 2011).

J. W. Peltason, *Federal Courts in the Political Process* (Doubleday, 1955).

Todd C. Peppers, *Courtiers of the Marble Palace: The Rise and Influence of the Supreme Court Law Clerk* (Stanford University Press, 2006).

Terri Jennings Peretti, *In Defense of a Political Court* (Princeton University Press, 1999).

Gerald N. Rosenberg, *The Hollow Hope: Can Courts Bring About Social Change?* (University of Chicago Press, 1991).

Donald R. Songer, Reginald S. Sheehan, and Susan B. Haire, *Continuity and Change on the United States Courts of Appeals* (University of Michigan Press, 2000).

Artemus Ward and David L. Weiden, *Sorcerers' Apprentices: 100 Years of Law Clerks at the United States Supreme Court* (New York University Press, 2006).

ON THE WEB

www.oyez.org
Oyez is a Web site that contains links to audio recordings of Supreme Court oral arguments. It also provides an overview of the Court's decisions in many cases and links to other interesting Web sites on the judiciary.

www.supremecourt.gov
This is a new Web site released by the Court in 2010. You can obtain oral argument transcripts, read the justices' biographies, and keep up to date with the Court's docket.

www.ncsconline.org
The National Center for State Courts is an independent, nonprofit organization aimed at gathering data on state courts and improving the states' judicial administration.

14

Listen to Chapter 14 on MyPoliSciLab

Civil Liberties

Protections Under the Bill of Rights

In March 2006, Marine Lance Corporal Matthew Snyder was killed while serving in Iraq. Soon after, his family gathered at St. John's Catholic Church in Westminster, Maryland, for his funeral. Not far from St. John's Church, Reverend Fred Phelps Sr., of the Westboro Baptist Church of Topeka, Kansas, was joined by his daughters and grandchildren in protesting Snyder's funeral. The Phelps' did not know Lance Corporal Snyder or his family, but their protest included signs asserting that "God Hates Fags," "Pope in Hell," and "Thank God for Dead Soldiers." The Westboro Baptist Church did not contend that Matthew Snyder himself was gay, and reports indicate that he was not. The Church regularly picketed the funerals of soldiers killed in Iraq and Afghanistan to protest the toleration of homosexuality in the United States. Since 1991, the Church reports that it has engaged in 47,949 protests across 858 cities. This includes protests at over 400 military funerals for soldiers killed in Iraq and Afghanistan.[1] The protest did not violate any law and the Snyders were not aware of it until Albert Snyder, the soldier's father, saw the protest on the Internet.

Mr. Snyder sued Reverend Phelps and the Westboro Baptist Church for, among other things, intentional infliction of emotional distress. A federal District Court in Maryland ruled for Mr. Snyder and awarded him $5 million. But, the U.S. Court of Appeals for the Fourth Circuit overturned the District Court's decision and set aside the award. It ruled that the First Amendment protected Phelps' speech because it involved matters of public concern, such as homosexuality in the military.[2]

The protests angered many Americans who view military funerals as private events to honor soldiers who died defending the United States. The protesters' speech was seen as hateful and ugly, directed at a soldier they did not know. Was such speech protected by the First Amendment?

14.1 Trace the roots of civil liberties in the original Constitution and their subsequent development in the Bill of Rights, p. 443.

14.2 Describe the First Amendment freedoms and the limitations on them, p. 446.

14.3 Explain how the Constitution protects property rights, p. 455.

14.4 Distinguish between procedural and substantive due process, p. 456.

14.5 Assess the kinds of behavior that may be covered by a constitutional right to privacy, p. 456.

14.6 Analyze the constitutional rights of criminal suspects, p. 458.

14.7 Evaluate the roles of institutions and the people in protecting civil liberties, p. 465.

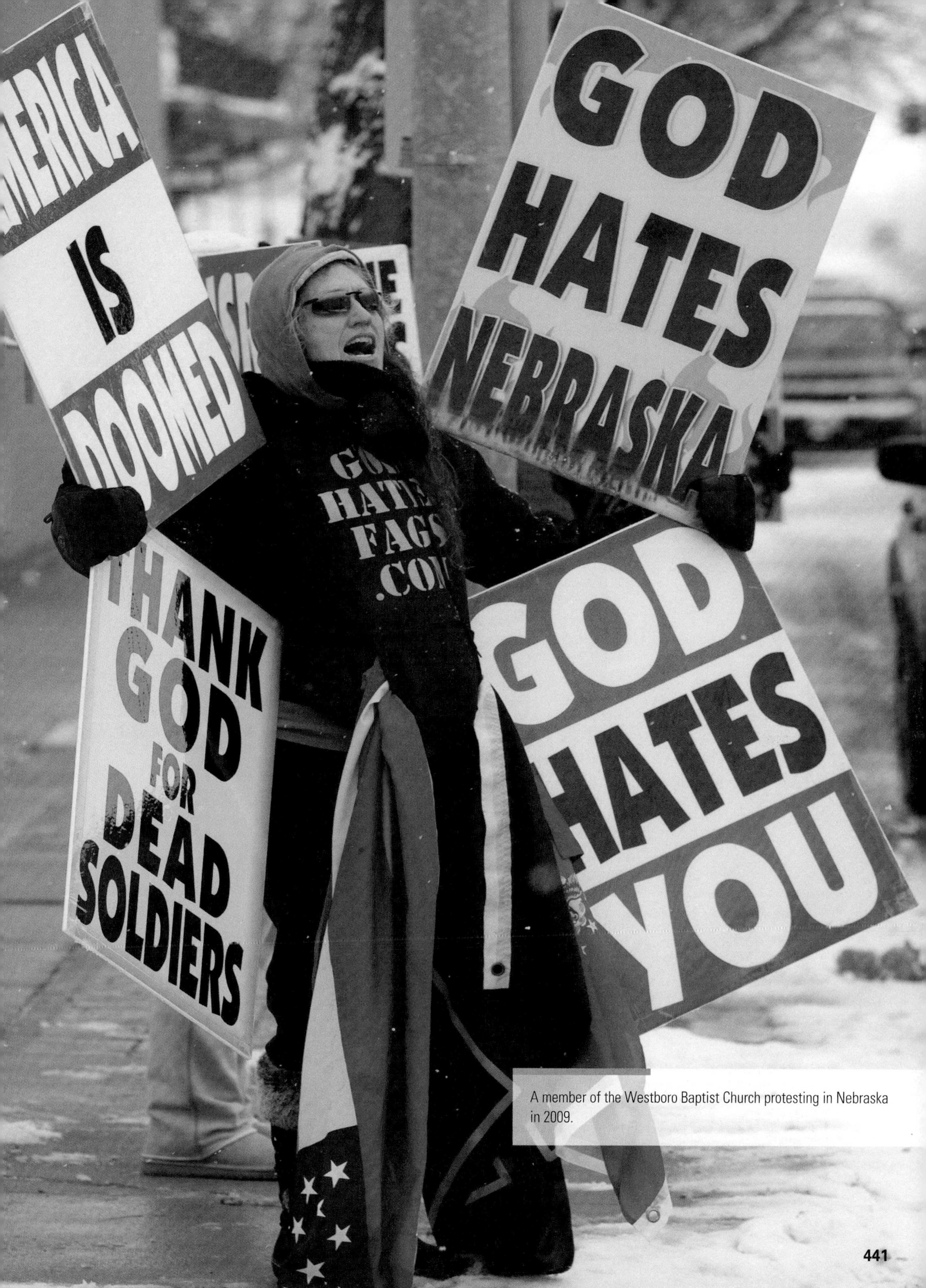

A member of the Westboro Baptist Church protesting in Nebraska in 2009.

The Basics What are civil liberties and where do they come from? In this video, you will learn about our First Amendment guarantees and about protections the Bill of Rights provides those accused of crimes. In the process, you'll discover how our liberties have changed over time to reflect our changing values and needs.

In Context Uncover the importance of civil liberties in a changing American society. University of Massachusetts at Boston political scientist Maurice T. Cunningham identifies the origins of our civil liberties and evaluates the clash between national security and civil liberties in a post 9/11 age.

Thinking Like a Political Scientist What are some of the challenges facing political scientists in regards to civil liberties? In this video, University of Massachusetts at Boston political scientist Maurice T. Cunningham raises some of the thought-provoking questions regarding civil liberties that have arisen during the last decade.

In the Real World The American legal system and the American people have both struggled over whether the death penalty should be imposed in this country. In this segment, we'll hear what citizens have to say about the death penalty.

So What? Know your rights. Author Christine L. Nemacheck discusses what would happen today if the government tried to intern a group of citizens without any real cause—the way it did to the Japanese during World War II—and she explains why we become more aware of our rights as we age.

In March 2011, the Supreme Court upheld the Fourth Circuit Court of Appeals and ruled that it was.

The First Amendment protects unpopular speech. It is when speech is unpopular or offensive, of course, that protection is most needed. Speech that meets with widespread agreement is unlikely to be restricted. However, a majority of citizens may well wish to limit unpopular speech. In an 8-1 decision, the Supreme Court determined that even particularly offensive speech, such as that used in the Westboro Baptist Church's funeral protests, is constitutionally protected when it concerns important public issues.[3]

In this chapter, we examine the fundamental liberties protected in a free society. These include freedom of speech and assembly, issues the Court addressed in *Snyder* v. *Phelps* (2011). We will also discuss the right to practice one's religion without government interference, the right to bear arms, the right to be free from unreasonable searches and seizures, the right to be free from self-incrimination and double jeopardy, and the right to be represented by an attorney in a criminal proceeding. These freedoms are essential to self-determination and self-governance—to government by the people. Yet they have also been vulnerable during times of war and, many would argue, are now threatened because of security measures put into place to combat international terrorism.[4] Regardless of the times, however, these liberties mean nothing if citizens do not challenge the government when they think it has impermissibly limited those freedoms. Unless we act as caretakers of our liberties, we lose them.

writ of *habeas corpus*
A court order requiring explanation to a judge as to why a prisoner is being held in custody.

The Basis for Our Civil Liberties

14.1 Trace the roots of civil liberties in the original Constitution and their subsequent development in the Bill of Rights.

Before we delve into a discussion of freedoms, we need to clarify several terms—*civil liberties, civil rights,* and *legal privileges*—often used interchangeably when discussing rights and freedoms.

Civil liberties are the constitutional protections of all persons against governmental restrictions on the freedoms of conscience, religion, and expression. Civil liberties are secured by the First Amendment and the due process clauses of the Fifth and Fourteenth Amendments, among others.

Civil rights are the constitutional rights of all persons to due process and the equal protection of the laws: the constitutional right not to be discriminated against by the government because of race, ethnic background, religion, or sex. These civil rights are protected by the due process and equal protection clauses of the Fifth and Fourteenth Amendments and by the civil rights laws of national and state governments. *Legal privileges,* like the right to welfare benefits or to have a driver's license, are granted by governments and may be subject to conditions or restrictions.

Rights in the Original Constitution

Even though most of the Framers did not think a bill of rights was necessary, they considered certain rights important enough to spell them out in the Constitution (see Table 14.1).

Foremost among constitutional rights, and deserving of particular mention here, is the **writ of *habeas corpus*.** Literally meaning "you have the body" in Latin, this writ is a court order directing any official holding a person in custody to produce the prisoner in court and explain why the prisoner is being held. Throughout the years, it developed into a remedy for any illegal confinement. People who are incarcerated have the right to appeal to a judge, usually through an attorney, stating why they believe they are being held unlawfully and should be released. The judge then orders the jailer or a lower

14.1
14.2
14.3
14.4
14.5
14.6
14.7

TABLE 14.1 RIGHTS IN THE ORIGINAL CONSTITUTION

1. *Habeas corpus*
2. No bills of attainder (legislative act that sentences a person or group to punishment without a trial)
3. No ex post facto laws
4. No titles of nobility (aristocratic titles that had also been barred by the Articles of Confederation)
5. Trial by jury in national courts
6. Protection for citizens as they move from one state to another, including the right to travel
7. Protection against using the crime of treason to restrict other activities; limitation on punishment for treason
8. Guarantee that each state has a republican form of government
9. No religious test oaths as a condition for holding a federal office
10. Protection against the impairment of contracts (forbids states from passing laws that effectively invalidate contracts)

■ *Why might some rights be mentioned both in the original Constitution and the Bill of Rights?*

court to justify why the writ should not be issued. If a judge finds that a petitioner is detained unlawfully, the judge may order the prisoner's immediate release.

Habeas corpus has become an especially prominent issue during the War on Terror as the United States has captured, detained, and tried alleged terrorists. The Supreme Court has underscored the fundamental nature of the right to a writ of *habeas corpus* in several decisions. The Court rejected the Bush administration's position that it could indefinitely hold foreign nationals and U.S. citizens deemed "enemy combatants," refused to allow them to be tried by military commissions, rather than in civilian courts,

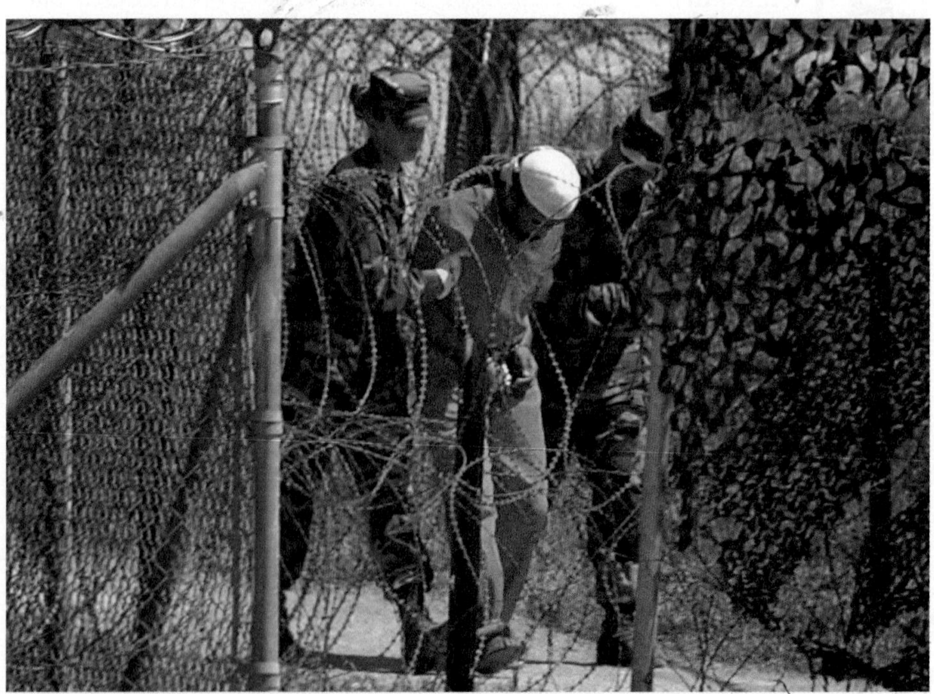

A detainee is escorted by guards at the U.S. military prison at Guantanamo Bay, Cuba. Shortly after he took office, President Obama signed an executive order to close the facility in order to "restore the standards of due process and the core constitutional values that have made this country great even in the midst of war, even in dealing with terrorism."* However, as of 2012, the prison remains open.

*Susan Candiotti, Ed Hornick, and Jeanne Meserve, "What's Next for Guantanamo Bay Detainees?" CNN, *The First 100 Days*, January 26, 2009, http://www.cnn.com/2009/POLITICS/01/26/gitmo.next/index.html.

and ruled that the accused has a right to see and hear the evidence for alleged crimes.[5] In the wake of the Court's decision, Congress passed the Military Commissions Act of 2006, explicitly providing for enemy combatants' trial before military commissions.

In its 2008 decision in *Boumediene* v. *Bush,* the Supreme Court stood firm in its holding that Guantanamo Bay detainees have the right to pursue *habeas* review in the federal courts. In doing so, the Court struck down as unconstitutional the section of the Military Commissions Act barring the federal courts from hearing enemy combatants' *habeas corpus* petitions.[6]

Although the Court has emphasized the importance of *habeas corpus* generally, it has restricted its use, particularly for *habeas* appeals made by prisoners in the state criminal justice system. In these cases, the number of appeals has been restricted and the federal courts must defer to state judges unless their decisions were clearly "unreasonable."[7]

The Constitution also bars **ex post facto laws**, any law that defines an act as a crime after it was committed, increases the punishment for a crime after it was committed, or reduces the proof necessary to convict someone of a crime after it was committed. However, the prohibition does not restrict retroactive application of a law that benefits an accused person, such as decreasing the punishment for a particular crime; nor does it apply to civil laws.

ex post facto law
A retroactive criminal law that works to the disadvantage of a person.

due process clause
A clause in the Fifth Amendment limiting the power of the national government; a similar clause in the Fourteenth Amendment prohibits state governments from depriving any person of life, liberty, or property without due process of law.

selective incorporation
The process by which provisions of the Bill of Rights are brought within the scope of the Fourteenth Amendment and so applied to state and local governments.

☐ The Bill of Rights and the States

Most of the liberties we address in this chapter did not appear in the original Constitution. The Constitution drawn up in Philadelphia included guarantees of a few basic rights discussed previously, but it lacked a specific bill of rights similar to those in most state constitutions. Our civil liberties are found in the Bill of Rights, which is composed of the first 10 amendments to the Constitution, all of which were added in 1791.

The Bill of Rights originally applied *only to the national government,* not to state governments.[8] Why not to the states? The Framers were confident that citizens could control their own state officials, and most state constitutions already had bills of rights. Furthermore, it would not have been politically feasible for the new Constitution to restrict state governments in this way. It was the new and distant central government the people feared. As it turned out, those fears were largely misdirected.

It was not until the Fourteenth Amendment was adopted in 1868 that there became a way for the limits on government action found in the Bill of Rights to be applied to the states. Because the Fourteenth Amendment applies explicitly to the states, supporters contended that its **due process clause**—declaring that no person shall be deprived by a state of life, liberty, or property without due process of law—limits states in precisely the same way the Bill of Rights limits the national government. But for decades, the Supreme Court refused to interpret the Fourteenth Amendment in this way. Then, in *Gitlow* v. *New York* (1925), the Court reversed this trend and decided that when fundamental liberties, such as the "freedom of speech and of the press—which are protected by the First Amendment from abridgment by Congress"—are at stake, the due process clause of the Fourteenth Amendment prohibits the state from infringing on those liberties, just as the First Amendment prohibits Congress.[9]

Gitlow v. *New York* was a revolutionary decision. For the first time, the U.S. Constitution was interpreted to protect freedom of speech from abridgment by state and local governments. This landmark decision changed the balance of federalism in the United States. State action that deprived citizens of fundamental liberties could now be challenged as a constitutional violation. In the 1930s and continuing at an accelerated pace during the 1960s, through the **selective incorporation** of provision after provision of the Bill of Rights into the due process clause, the Supreme Court applied the most important of these rights to the states.[10]

Today, the Fourteenth Amendment imposes on the states all the provisions of the Bill of Rights the Court has deemed essential to ordered liberty (see Figure 14.1). Although the Court had not incorporated a right since 1969, in 2010 it incorporated

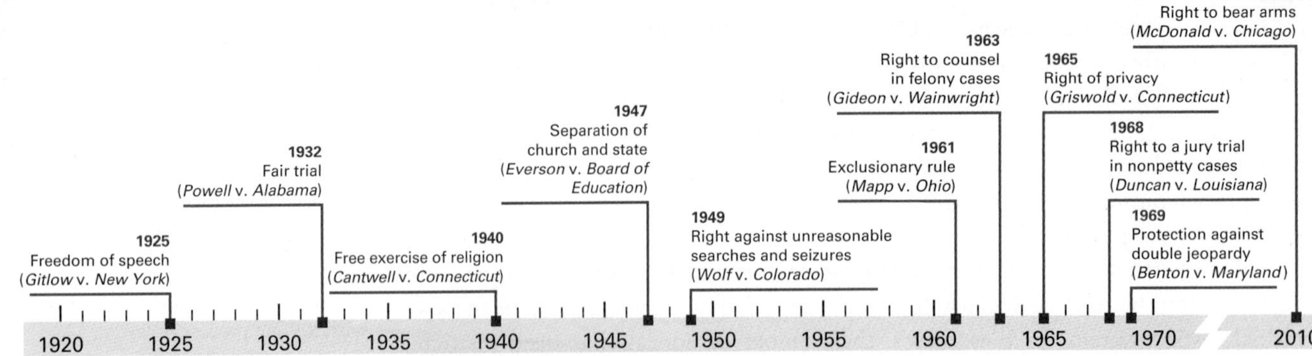

FIGURE 14.1 TIMELINE OF SELECTIVE INCORPORATION

Examine the kinds of rights that the Court first began to incorporate. How are those different than the rights incorporated later, particularly in the 1960s?

establishment clause
A clause in the First Amendment stating that Congress shall make no law respecting an establishment of religion. The Supreme Court has interpreted this to forbid direct governmental support to any or all religions.

the Second Amendment protection of the right to bear arms to the states (*McDonald* v. *Chicago,* 561 U.S. 3025 [2010]). As a result, state restrictions on handguns and other arms are now subject to strict constitutional review. Although the Supreme Court ruled that states have to abide by the Second Amendment, it did not spell out whether and what type of gun control regulation might survive that review.

Selective incorporation of most provisions of the Bill of Rights into the Fourteenth Amendment is arguably the most significant constitutional development that has occurred since the Constitution was written. It has profoundly altered the relationship between the national government and the states, giving greater power to the national government. It has made the federal courts, under the guidance of the Supreme Court, the most important protectors of our liberties—not the individual states. It has created a consistent national standard for interpreting the rights and liberties found in the Bill of Rights.

First Amendment Freedoms

14.2 Describe the First Amendment freedoms and the limitations on them.

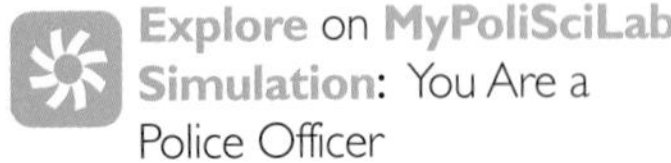

Freedom of Religion

The first words of the First Amendment are emphatic and brief: "Congress shall make no law respecting an establishment of religion, or prohibiting the free exercise thereof." Though terse, it contains two important clauses: the *establishment* clause and the *free exercise* clause. Part of what makes religious liberties questions so interesting and difficult is that there is often tension between these clauses. Does a state scholarship provided to a student who decides to attend a college to become a clergy member violate the establishment clause by indirectly aiding religion? Or would denying the scholarship violate the student's free exercise of religion? In dealing with the questions posed here, the Supreme Court ruled that providing such scholarship benefits does not go so far as to violate the establishment clause, but neither does the free exercise clause *require* that states provide the benefits.[11]

THE ESTABLISHMENT CLAUSE In writing what has come to be called the **establishment clause**, the Framers were reacting to the English system, wherein the Crown was (and still is) the head not only of the government but also of the established church—the Church of England—and public officials were required to take an oath to support the established church as a condition of holding office. At least

The Global Community

Separating Government from Religion

Throughout the world, there is substantial consensus that there ought to be some separation between religious beliefs and government policy. However, there are important differences between countries in which citizens believe more fully in such separation versus those in which citizens tend to agree with the idea. The Pew Research Center's 2007 Global Attitudes Survey asked respondents for their level of agreement with the statement: "Religion is a matter of personal faith and should be kept separate from government policy." According to the survey, a majority of respondents in Great Britain, India, Nigeria, and the United States completely agreed that government ought to be kept separate from religion.

Although most countries' constitutions or laws provide for protections for religious liberties, enforcement of these rights vary, as does the degree to which government and religion are separate. For example, in Nigeria, where tensions between Christians and Muslims have been on the rise, a separate court system exists for each group. Many Nigerian states use Shari'a courts in criminal and civil matters involving Muslims but common law courts for non-Muslims.* In other countries, such as India, there are differences between the national and state governments' involvement in religion. There, the national government has generally remained outside the religious sphere, but some state governments have enforced and enacted "anticonversion" laws.

The percentage of respondents completely agreeing that government policy and religion should be kept separate was significantly lower in China (21 percent), Japan (33 percent), and Mexico (38 percent). In China, the government sanctions only five religions known as "patriotic religious associations" (PRAs): Buddhist, Taoist, Muslim, Catholic, and Protestant. Only these PRAs can legally operate places of worship.

In Japan and Mexico, religious freedoms are constitutionally protected and the Mexican Constitution provides for a separation between church and state. However, particularly in Mexico, there is a great degree of religious homogeneity (88% of Mexicans identify themselves as Catholic) that might diminish the importance of separating government policy from religion in the eyes of many citizens.

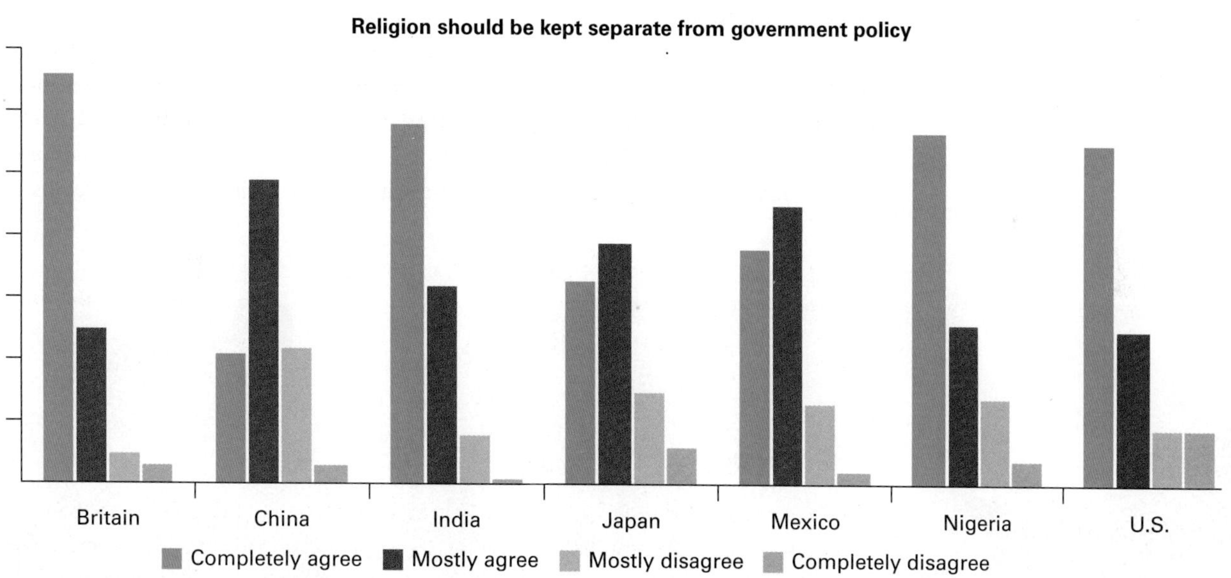

SOURCE: Pew Research Center, *Global Views on Life Satisfaction, National Conditions, and the Global Economy: Highlights from the 2007 Pew Global Attitudes 47-Nation Survey* (Pew Research Center, 2007).

CRITICAL THINKING QUESTIONS

1. Why might it be problematic to have the government involved in sanctioning religious groups as it does in China?
2. Do you think beliefs about separating government and religion depend on whether a person belongs to a religious minority? Should it?
3. How might religious homogeneity affect citizens' views of whether their government ought to be separate from the religion?

*U.S. State Department, Bureau of Democracy, Human Rights, and Labor. "International Religious Freedom Report 2009," October 26, 2009, http://www.state.gov/g/drl/rls/irf/2009/index.htm.

partly because of the brevity of the establishment clause, there is much debate as to its meaning. Some, such as the late Chief Justice William Rehnquist, contend it means *only* that the government cannot establish an official national religion nor prefer one sect or denomination to another.[12] Others argue that it requires the government to maintain neutrality, not only among religious denominations but also between religion and nonreligion.

Those who favor government neutrality regarding religion use the metaphor, coined by Thomas Jefferson, a "wall of separation" to explain the strict separation between government and religion the clause requires. The metaphor was the basis for the Supreme Court's opinion in *Everson* v. *Board of Education of Ewing Township* (1947). The Court's 5-to-4 decision in the case, allowing government funds to reimburse parents for transporting children to private religious schools, is indicative of the confusion over the establishment clause. All nine justices agreed that the wall of separation was the appropriate interpretation of the clause, yet they were divided five to four on whether the township's action violated that test.[13]

The Court's use of the "wall of separation" was hardly its last attempt at resolving debate over interpretation of the establishment clause. In *Lemon* v. *Kurtzman* (1971), the Court laid down the three-part *Lemon* test. To pass constitutional muster, (1) a law must have a secular legislative purpose, (2) it must neither advance nor inhibit religion, and (3) it must avoid "excessive government entanglement with religion."[14] Because the *Lemon* test has not been consistently used, however, the justices remain divided over how much separation between government and religion the First Amendment requires.

In addition to the *Lemon* test, former Justice Sandra Day O'Connor championed what is known as the *endorsement* test. She believed that the establishment clause forbids governmental practices that a reasonable observer would view as endorsing religion.[15] For example, if a reasonable person would understand a crèche (nativity scene) displayed at the entrance to a county courthouse to be government endorsement of religion, Justice O'Connor would vote to strike down the practice.[16] Justices Antonin Scalia and Clarence Thomas joined Chief Justice Rehnquist in supporting a *nonpreferentialist* test.[17] As mentioned previously, they believed that the Constitution

The presence of nativity scenes on public property have led to constitutional challenges by those arguing that a reasonable observer might understand it to be government sponsorship of religion. Here, Christian activists, who believe such scenes are consistent with the First Amendment, portray a living nativity scene in front of the U.S. Supreme Court. The Court has generally upheld holiday displays that include representations of a variety of religious traditions along with secular holiday symbols, such as a Christmas tree or Santa Claus.

prohibits favoritism toward any particular religion but does not prohibit government aid to *all* religions. In their view, government may accommodate religious activities and even support religious organizations so long as government does not coerce individuals to participate in religious activities or show preference for certain religious activities by treating them favorably.[18]

By contrast, the more liberal justices—including Ruth Bader Ginsburg and Stephen Breyer—usually maintained that there should be *strict separation* between religion and the state.[19] They generally have held that even indirect aid for religion, such as scholarships or teaching materials and aids for students attending private religious schools, crosses the line that should separate the government from religion. But today, this view is not able to command a majority on the Court.

free exercise clause
A clause in the First Amendment stating that Congress shall make no law prohibiting the free exercise of religion.

OF the People Diversity in America

Religious Diversity in the United States

From the beginning, religious freedom has been an important tenet of government in the United States. This was largely due to the fact that many of those who settled in the American colonies had experienced religious persecution in their former countries. Even so, many of those early immigrants were not so tolerant of others whose beliefs differed from their own. Respecting religious differences was difficult, even though those differences were largely between sects of Christianity.

Differences among religious beliefs today are substantially greater than when the United States was founded. A report by the Pew Forum on Religion & Public Life provides evidence on religious affiliation in the United States.* Today, approximately 79 percent of adults identify themselves as Christian. However, that label masks substantial differences in beliefs among Protestants, Catholic, and other Christian groups. Other religious groups, including Jewish, Buddhist, Muslim, and Hindu, make up nearly 5 percent of the U.S. adult population. Approximately 16 percent of the adult population does not profess affiliation with any religious group.

Indications are that the United States is likely to become more religiously diverse in the coming years. Protestants, who currently make up a bare majority of the population, are more prevalent among the older population than among younger Americans. And immigrants to the United States tend to bring religious diversity with them. Approximately two-thirds of Muslims and more than 80 percent of those identifying themselves as Hindu are immigrants to the United States.

Religious Diversity in the United States†

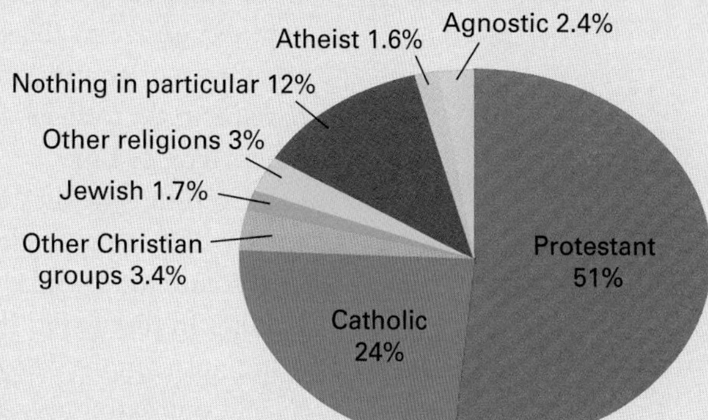

† Rounded percentages do not total 100.

As the country becomes more religiously diverse, protecting Americans' right to exercise their religious beliefs takes on greater importance and, in some cases, means greater controversy.

QUESTIONS

1. **How might religious diversity in the United States affect the Supreme Court's decisions on religious liberties? Should it?**
2. **Do you think religious beliefs affect voting decisions? Why or why not?**

* The Pew Forum on Religion & Public Life, *U.S. Religious Landscape Survey Religious Affiliation: Diverse and Dynamic,* February 2008, http://religions.pewforum.org/pdf/report-religious-landscape-study-full.pdf.

THE FREE EXERCISE CLAUSE The right to hold any or no religious belief is one of our few absolute rights because it occurs solely within each person. The **free exercise clause** affirms that no government can compel us to accept any creed or to deny us any right because of what we do or do not believe. Requiring religious oaths as a condition of public employment or as a prerequisite for running for public office is unconstitutional. In fact, the original Constitution states, "No religious Test shall ever be required as a Qualification to any Office or public Trust under the United States" (Article VI).

Although carefully protected, the right to practice a religion, which typically requires some action such as proselytizing or participating in a religious ritual, is more likely to be restricted than the right to hold particular beliefs. Before 1990, the Supreme Court carefully scrutinized laws allegedly infringing on religious practices and insisted that the government provide some compelling interest to justify actions that might infringe on someone's religion. Then, in *Employment Division* v. *Smith* (1990), the Court significantly altered the interpretation of the free exercise clause when it determined that the government does not always need to show a compelling interest if its laws infringe on religious exercise.[20] As long as a general law is not targeted at particular religious groups or practices, the law may be applied to conduct even if it burdens a particular religious practice.[21]

☐ Free Speech and Free People

Government by the people is based on every person's right to speak freely, to organize in groups, to question the decisions of the government, and to campaign openly against them. Only through free and uncensored expression of opinion can government be kept responsive to the electorate and political power transferred peacefully. Elections, separation of powers, and constitutional guarantees are meaningless unless all persons have the right to speak frankly and to hear and judge for themselves the worth of what others have to say.

Even though the First Amendment explicitly denies Congress the power to pass any law abridging freedom of speech, the courts have never interpreted the amendment in absolute terms. Like almost all rights, the freedoms of speech and of the press are limited. In discussing the constitutional power of government to regulate speech, we distinguish among *belief, speech,* and *action.*

At one extreme is the right to *believe* as we wish. Despite occasional deviations in practice, the traditional view is that government should not punish a person for beliefs or interfere in any way with freedom of conscience. At the other extreme is *action,* which the government may restrain. As the old saying goes, "Your right to swing your fist ends where my nose begins."

Speech stands somewhere between belief and action. It is not an absolute right, like belief, but it is not as easily restricted as is action. Some kinds of speech—libel and fighting words, for example—are not entitled to constitutional protection. But many problems arise in distinguishing between what does and does not fit into the categories of unprotected speech. It usually falls to the courts to decide what free speech means and to defend the right of individual and minority dissenters to exercise it.

Judges must answer a variety of questions when they confront a free speech case: What was said? If it is considered obscene, the government may restrict it. In what context and how was it said? General "time, place, and manner" restrictions typically meet constitutional muster, meaning the government can determine the times, places and modes of speech, though it may not deny speech because leaders dislike the message. How is the government attempting to regulate the speech—by prior restraint (censorship) or by punishment after the speech? If the restriction is made to preempt publication (prior restraint), it is likely to fail. Why is the government regulating the speech—to preserve the public peace or to prevent criticism of the people in power? Although the courts tend to be receptive to restrictions that are a genuine threat to public safety, restrictions on criticism are likely to fail.

Today, the Supreme Court generally holds that speech is protected unless it falls into one of three narrow categories—*libel, obscenity,* or *fighting words.* We discuss each of these later in the chapter. However, the Court has recognized that different kinds of speech are subject to different levels of protection. For example, political speech is strictly protected. Indeed, impermissible restrictions on speech (as paid for through campaign spending) have typically been the downfall of attempts at campaign finance reform.[22] However, the Court has allowed greater governmental restriction on **commercial speech**, particularly that which is misleading, though its willingness to allow these restrictions seems to be waning.[23] This is a change from the Court's position at the beginning of the twentieth century, when it variously relied on one of three tests: the bad tendency test, the clear and present danger test, and the preferred position doctrine.

The **bad tendency test** presumed it was reasonable to forbid speech that tends to corrupt society or cause people to engage in crime. Because the test too broadly restricted speech and ran "contrary to the fundamental premises underlying the First Amendment as the guardian of our democracy,"[24] it was abandoned in the 1920s. The **clear and present danger test** provided that government could restrict speech *only* if it presented an immediate danger—for example, a false shout of "Fire!" in a crowded theater or speech leading to a riot, the destruction of property, or the corruption of an election. This clear and present danger test, which was used through the 1950s, required the government to show the imminent danger of the speech in order to restrict it.

The last of the three historic tests, the **preferred position doctrine**, was advanced in the 1940s when the Court applied all the guarantees of the First Amendment to the states. It comes close to the position that freedom of expression—the use of words and pictures—should rarely, if ever, be curtailed. This interpretation gives these freedoms, especially freedom of speech and of conscience, a preferred position in our constitutional hierarchy.

Although these tests are no longer applied, they provide a background for the current judicial approach to government regulation of speech, which represents an expansion of these more narrow constraints. Today, there is no one single test that is applied to speech cases; however, the Court's reluctance to allow restrictions on speech persists as it evaluates the government's interest in limiting speech along lines similar to the clear and present danger test and the preferred position doctrine.

☐ Protected Speech

Of all the forms of governmental interference with expression, judges are most suspicious of those that impose **prior restraint**—censorship before publication. Prior restraints include governmental review and approval before a speech can be made, before a motion picture can be shown, or before a newspaper can be published. Most prior restraints are unconstitutional, as the Court has said, "Any system of prior restraints of expression comes to this Court bearing a heavy presumption against its constitutional validity."[25] About the only prior restraints the Court has approved relate to military and national security matters—such as the disclosure of troop movements[26]—and to high school authorities' control over student newspapers.[27]

Even for an important purpose, a legislature may not pass a law that impinges on First Amendment freedoms if other, less drastic means are available. For example, a state may protect the public from unscrupulous lawyers not by forbidding attorneys from advertising their fees for simple services, but, for example, by disbarring lawyers who mislead their clients.

Laws that regulate some kinds of speech but not others, or that regulate speech expressing some views but not others, are likely to be struck down. But those that are **content neutral or viewpoint neutral**—that is, laws that apply to *all* kinds of speech and to *all* views—are more likely to be safe. For example, laws may prohibit posting handbills on telephone poles. However, laws prohibiting only religious handbills or only handbills advocating racism or sexism would probably be declared unconstitutional because they would limit the content of handbills rather than restrict all handbills regardless of what they say.

commercial speech
Advertisements and commercials for products and services; they receive less First Amendment protection, primarily to discourage false and misleading ads.

bad tendency test
An interpretation of the First Amendment that would permit legislatures to forbid speech encouraging people to engage in illegal action.

clear and present danger test
An interpretation of the First Amendment holding that the government cannot interfere with speech unless the speech presents a clear and present danger that it will lead to evil or illegal acts.

preferred position doctrine
An interpretation of the First Amendment that holds that freedom of expression is so essential to democracy that governments should not punish persons for what they say, only for what they do.

prior restraint
Censorship imposed before a speech is made or a newspaper is published; usually presumed to be unconstitutional.

content or viewpoint neutrality
Laws that apply to all kinds of speech and to all views, not only that which is unpopular or divisive.

14.1

14.2

14.3

14.4

14.5

14.6

14.7

Police arrested Scott Tyler of Chicago after he set fire to an American flag on the steps of the Capitol building in Washington, D.C. The Supreme Court afterward ruled that free speech covers even "symbolic speech" such as burning the U.S. flag.

☐ Unprotected Speech

Unprotected speech lacks redeeming social value and is not essential to democratic deliberations and self-governance. As noted, the Supreme Court holds that all speech is protected unless it falls into one of three narrow categories: *libel, obscenity,* or *fighting words.* This does not mean that the constitutional issues relating to these kinds of speech are simple. How we prove *libel,* how we define *obscenity,* and how we determine which words are *fighting words* remain hotly contested issues.

LIBEL At one time, newspaper publishers and editors had to take considerable care about what they wrote to avoid prosecution by the government or lawsuits by individuals for **libel**—published defamation or false statements. Today, as a result of gradually rising constitutional standards, it has become more difficult to win a libel suit against a newspaper or magazine.

In *New York Times* v. *Sullivan* (1964) and subsequent cases, the Court established guidelines for libel cases and severely limited state power to award monetary damages in libel suits brought by public officials against critics of official conduct. Neither public officials nor public figures can collect damages unless comments made about them were made with *actual malice,* meaning that the "statements were made with a knowing or reckless disregard for the truth."[28] Nor can they collect damages even when subject to outrageous, clearly inaccurate parodies and cartoons. Such was the case when *Hustler* magazine printed a parody of the Reverend Jerry Falwell; the Court held that parodies and cartoons cannot reasonably be understood as describing actual facts or events.[29]

unprotected speech
Libel, obscenity, and fighting words, which are not entitled to constitutional protection in all circumstances.

libel
Written defamation of another person. For public officials and public figures, the constitutional tests designed to restrict libel actions are especially rigid.

obscenity
The quality or state of a work that, taken as a whole, appeals to a prurient interest in sex by depicting sexual conduct in a patently offensive way and that lacks serious literary, artistic, political, or scientific value.

fighting words
Words that by their very nature inflict injury on those to whom they are addressed or incite them to acts of violence.

OBSCENITY Publications deemed to be obscene are not entitled to constitutional protection, but members of the Supreme Court, like everyone else, have difficulty defining obscenity. As Justice Potter Stewart put it, "I know it when I see it."[30]

In *Miller* v. *California* (1973), the Court finally agreed on a constitutional definition of **obscenity**. A work may be considered legally obscene if (1) the average person, applying contemporary standards of the particular community, would find that the work, taken as a whole, appeals to a prurient interest in sex; (2) the work depicts or describes in a patently offensive way sexual conduct specifically defined by the applicable law or authoritatively construed (meaning that the legislature must carefully and explicitly define by law each obscene act); and (3) the work, taken as a whole, lacks serious literary, artistic, political, or scientific value.[31] Relying on this standard, cities such as New York City use zoning laws to regulate where adult theaters and bookstores may be located,[32] and they may ban totally nude dancing in adult nightclubs.[33]

FIGHTING WORDS **Fighting words** were held to be outside the scope of constitutional protection because "their very utterance may inflict injury or tend to incite an immediate breach of peace."[34] That the words are abusive, offensive, and insulting or that they create anger, alarm, or resentment is not sufficient. Thus, a four-letter word worn on a sweatshirt was not judged to be a fighting word in the constitutional sense, even though it was offensive and angered some people. The word was not aimed at any individual, and those who were offended could look away.[35] However, the Court has struck down statutes criminalizing fighting words or "hate speech" due to vagueness. But, hate crime statutes, which do not limit a person's expression but instead allow courts to consider motive in criminal sentencing, have been broadly upheld.[36]

☐ Freedom of the Press

We have seen that courts are immediately skeptical of prior restraints and have carefully protected the right to publish information, no matter how journalists get it. However, they have not recognized additional protections to allow journalists to withhold information from grand juries or legislative investigating committees. Without this right to withhold information, reporters insist they cannot assure their sources of confidentiality, and they will not be able to get the information they need to keep the public informed.

The Supreme Court, however, has refused to acknowledge that reporters, and presumably scholars, have a constitutional right to ignore legal requests such as subpoenas and to withhold information from governmental bodies.[37] In 2005, *New York Times* reporter Judith Miller was jailed for two months for refusing to disclose her sources to a grand jury. Many states have passed *reporter shield laws* providing some protection for reporters from state court subpoenas, but similar legislation has failed to succeed in the U.S. Congress. Despite its previous difficulties, supporters continue to lobby for a federal shield law.

When the First Amendment was written, freedom of the press referred to leaflets, newspapers, and books. Today, the amendment protects other media as well, and much debate centers on the degree of protection that should be afforded to broadcast media and the Internet.

BROADCAST AND CABLE COMMUNICATIONS Despite the rise of the Internet, television remains an important means of distributing news and appealing for votes. Yet of all the mass media, broadcasting receives the least First Amendment protection. Congress has established a system of commercial broadcasting, supplemented by the Corporation for Public Broadcasting, which provides funds for public radio and television. The Federal Communications Commission (FCC) regulates the entire system by granting licenses, regulating their use, and imposing fines for indecent broadcasts.

The First Amendment would prevent censorship if the FCC tried to impose it. It does not, however, prevent the FCC from refusing to renew a license if, in its opinion, a broadcaster does not serve the public interest. However, stricter enforcement of revitalized FCC regulations in the last 10 years have led to disputes over whether the FCC can regulate indecent material that is "fleeting" such as Bono's use of a four-letter word in an award show acceptance speech or Nicole Richie's ad-libbed remarks

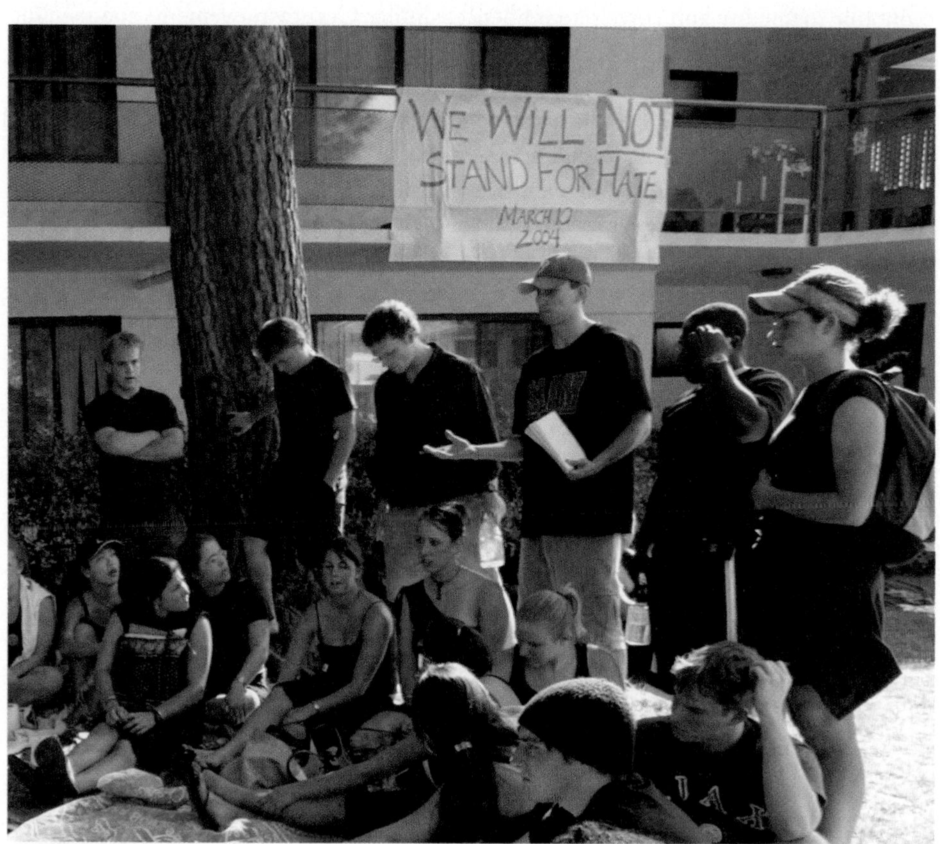

Although government may impose reasonable restrictions on the place and manner in which leaflets are posted, many college "hate speech" restrictions have been struck down because they unlawfully single out a certain kind of speech.

14.1

14.2

14.3

14.4

14.5

14.6

14.7

civil disobedience
Deliberate refusal to obey a law or comply with the orders of public officials as a means of expressing opposition.

as a presenter at the Billboard Music Awards. Although it accepted cases challenging the FCC policy, the Court has not decided whether the FCC can constitutionally restrict fleeting expletives. Instead, in 2012, it ruled narrowly that the FCC failed to give broadcasters adequate notice of its tougher indecency standards and left the First Amendment question for future litigation.[38] And, even though the Court has continued to uphold restrictions on the broadcast media, cable operators are given greater latitude in their programming.[39]

THE INTERNET The Internet presents an interesting problem in determining the appropriate level of First Amendment protection. In many ways, it functions as a newspaper—providing news and information critical to an informed citizenry. But it is also a commercial marketplace where millions of U.S. consumers buy books, clothing, jewelry, airplane tickets, stocks, and bonds.

In general, attempts to regulate Internet content have been unsuccessful. In its major ruling on First Amendment protection for the Internet, *Reno* v. *American Civil Liberties Union* (1997), the Court struck down provisions of the Communications Decency Act of 1996. In doing so, the Court emphasized the unique character of the Internet, holding that it is less intrusive than radio and broadcast television.[40] Although Congress passed additional restrictions aimed at protecting children from sexually explicit material on the Internet, the Supreme Court has continued to strike down such legislation. The majority has reasoned that rather than assessing criminal penalties, Congress could achieve its goal of blocking minors' access to sexually explicit sites through less drastic means such as the use of Internet filters or adult oversight.[41]

Freedom of Assembly

The Occupy Wall Street movement began in mid-September 2011 with protestors gathering in Manhattan's Zuccotti Park. Those involved in the movement protested economic inequality and corporate influence; similar Occupy movements soon sprang up across the United States.[42] The First Amendment protection of peaceable assembly was essential to Occupy groups' ability to march, and those involved that September evening were soon joined by thousands of others. However, by mid-November, New York's Mayor Bloomberg, and other leaders in cities across the United States, began to crack down on Occupy protestors who had been camping in parks and downtowns for several months. Courts typically uphold these actions, citing city regulations against camping in parks.[43] The First Amendment protected the protestors' right to peaceably protest in the parks, but did not allow the Occupy groups to essentially set up residence in these public areas.

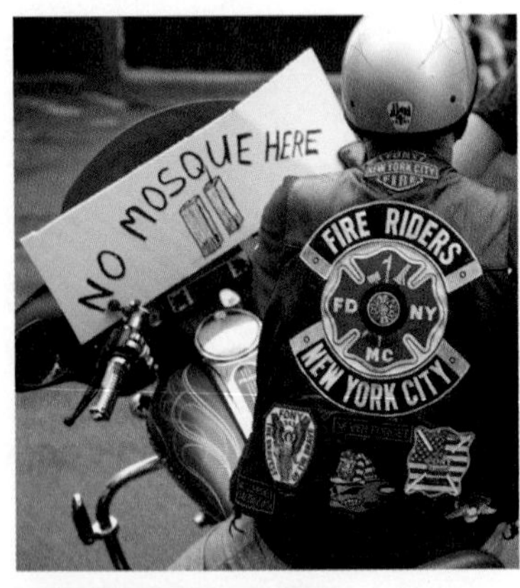

People who want to express their views, like this person protesting the construction of an Islamic community center near Ground Zero in New York City, must obtain the proper permits or paperwork. They must abide by neutral regulations as to the appropriate time and location of their protest. But the government may not deny their permit requests because it disagrees with the group's message.

TIME, PLACE, AND MANNER REGULATIONS The Constitution protects the right to speak, but it does not give people the right to communicate their views to everyone, in every place, at every time they wish. As the evictions of Occupy protestors made clear, no one has the right to block traffic or to hold parades or make speeches in public streets or on public sidewalks whenever he or she wishes. Governments may not censor what can be said, but they can make "reasonable" *time, place,* and *manner* regulations for protests or parades.

Depending on the place where the expressive activities are to occur, such as public parks, public school buildings, or government offices, the Court has been more or less willing to permit speech activities subject to reasonable time, place, and manner restrictions. It is essential, however, that any restriction be applied evenhandedly and that the government not act because of *what* is being said, but how or where it is being said.

Does the right of peaceful assembly include the right to violate a law nonviolently but deliberately? In general, the answer is no. **Civil disobedience**, even if peaceful, is not a protected right. When Martin Luther King Jr. and his followers refused to comply with a state court's injunction forbidding them to parade in Birmingham, Alabama, without first securing a permit, the Supreme Court sustained their conviction, even though there was serious doubt about the constitutionality of the injunction and the ordinance on which it was based.[44] And, as discussed previously, evictions of Occupy groups have also been upheld by the courts.

First Amendment freedoms are crucial for the survival of our republican form of democracy. It is of utmost importance that individuals be able to make their voices heard regardless of the political views they wish to express. However, these freedoms alone do not provide full protection from arbitrary or impermissible government infringements on our liberties more generally. Historically, U.S. political thinking and political institutions have emphasized the close connection between liberty and owning property, and between property and power. One of the Framers' central goals was to establish a government strong enough to protect people's rights to use and enjoy their property. Next, we turn our attention to amendments in the Bill of Rights protecting property, due process, privacy, and the rights of criminal suspects.

property rights
The rights of an individual to own, use, rent, invest in, buy, and sell property.

eminent domain
The power of a government to take private property for public use; the U.S. Constitution gives national and state governments this power and requires them to provide just compensation for property so taken.

regulatory taking
A government regulation that effectively takes land by restricting its use, even if it remains in the owner's name.

Property Rights

14.3 Explain how the Constitution protects property rights.

Property does not have rights; people do. People have the right to own, use, rent, invest in, buy, and sell property. The Framers wanted to limit government so that it could not endanger that right. As a result, the Constitution has a variety of clauses protecting **property rights**.

Although the right of property ownership is highly regarded, both the national and state governments have the power of **eminent domain**—the power to take private property for public use—but the owner must be fairly compensated. What constitutes "taking" for purposes of eminent domain? Ordinarily, but not always, the taking must be direct, and a person must lose title and control over the property. Sometimes, especially in recent years, the courts have found that a governmental taking has gone "too far," and the government must compensate its owners even when the title is left in the owner's name.[45] These are called **regulatory takings**, meaning the regulation has effectively taken the land by restricting its use. Thus, compensation is required when government creates landing and takeoff paths for airplanes over property adjacent to an airport, which makes the land unsuitable for its original use (say, raising chickens).[46] The government may, however, impose land use and environmental regulations, temporarily prohibiting the development of a property, without compensating the owners.[47]

In a controversial ruling with wide-ranging ramifications for urban planners and homeowners, a bare majority of the Court upheld the use of the government's power of eminent domain to condemn and take private property, with just compensation, for the purpose of advancing the economic development of a community. *Kelo* v. *City of New London* (2005) held that "public use" was not limited to eminent domain to build a road or a bridge but includes "promoting economic development," even if the property was taken and sold for development to private developers.[48] Public reaction to the Court's decision in *Kelo* was extremely negative. In a clear reminder that the Court is only one instrument of government, many states and localities acted swiftly to pass laws that barred authorities from taking private property for such purposes.

"Just compensation" is not always easy to define. When there is a dispute over compensation, the courts make the final resolution based on the rule that "the owner is entitled to receive what a willing buyer would pay in cash to a willing seller at the time of the taking."[49] An owner is not entitled to compensation for the personal value of an old, broken-down, dearly loved house—just the value of the old, broken-down house.

14.1

14.2

14.3

14.4

14.5

14.6

14.7

due process
Established rules and regulations that restrain government officials.

procedural due process
A constitutional requirement that governments proceed by proper methods; limits how government may exercise power.

substantive due process
A constitutional requirement that governments act reasonably and that the substance of the laws themselves be fair and reasonable; limits what a government may do.

Due Process Rights

14.4 Distinguish between procedural and substantive due process.

Perhaps the most difficult parts of the Constitution to understand are the clauses in the Fifth and Fourteenth Amendments forbidding the national and state governments to deny any person life, liberty, or property without "due process of law." Cases involving these guarantees have resulted in hundreds of Supreme Court decisions. Even so, it is impossible to explain *due process* precisely. In fact, the Supreme Court has refused to do so and has emphasized that "due process, unlike some legal rules, is not a technical conception with a fixed content unrelated to time, place, and circumstances."[50] We define **due process** as rules and regulations that restrain those in government who exercise power. There are, however, basically two kinds of due process: procedural and substantive.

Procedural Due Process

Traditionally, **procedural due process** refers not to the law itself but to *how a law is applied.* To paraphrase Daniel Webster's famous definition, the due process of law requires a procedure that hears before it condemns, proceeds upon inquiry, and renders judgment only after a trial or some kind of hearing. Originally, procedural due process was limited to criminal prosecutions, but it now applies to most kinds of governmental proceedings.

The liberties that due process protects include "the right of the individual to contract, to engage in any of the common occupations of life, to acquire useful knowledge, to marry, to establish a home and bring up children, to worship God according to the dictates of his own conscience, and generally to enjoy those common law privileges long recognized as essential to the orderly pursuit of happiness by free men."[51]

Substantive Due Process

Procedural due process limits *how* governmental power may be exercised; **substantive due process** limits *what* a government may do. Procedural due process mainly limits the executive and judicial branches because they apply the law and review its application; substantive due process mainly limits the legislative branch because it enacts laws. Substantive due process means that an "unreasonable" law, even if properly passed and properly applied, is unconstitutional. It means that governments *should not be allowed to do certain things.*

Substantive due process has deep roots in concepts of natural law and a long history in U.S. constitutional tradition. For most citizens most of the time, it is not enough merely to say that a law reflects the wishes of the popular or legislative majority. We also want our laws to be just, and we rely heavily on judges to decide what is just.

Privacy Rights

14.5 Assess the kinds of behavior that may be covered by a constitutional right to privacy.

The most important extension of substantive due process in recent decades has protected the right of privacy, especially marital privacy. Although the Constitution does not mention the right to privacy, in *Griswold* v. *Connecticut* (1965), the Supreme Court pulled together elements of the First, Third, Fourth, Fifth, Ninth, and Fourteenth Amendments to recognize that personal privacy is one of the rights the Constitution protects.[52] The decision remains highly controversial because the Bill of Rights does not specifically enumerate a right to privacy. Instead, the Court ruled that the right to privacy was implied by the rights listed above.

This right has three aspects: (1) the right to be free from governmental surveillance and intrusion, especially with respect to intimate decisions on sexuality; (2) the right not to have the government make private affairs public; and (3) the right to be free in thought and belief from governmental regulations.[53] Thus, the right underlies our discussion later in this chapter of unreasonable searches and seizures, government surveillance, and self-incrimination. The right to privacy also encompasses two controversial issues: state regulation of abortion and private, adult consensual sexual conduct.

☐ Abortion Rights

In *Roe* v. *Wade* (1973), the Supreme Court ruled that the right to privacy extended to a woman's decision, in consultation with her physician, to terminate her pregnancy. According to *Roe*'s "trimester framework," (1) during the first trimester of a woman's pregnancy, it is an unreasonable and therefore unconstitutional interference with her liberty and privacy rights for a state to set any limits on her choice to have an abortion or on her doctor's medical judgments about how to carry it out; (2) during the second trimester, the state's interest in protecting the health of women becomes compelling, and a state may make a reasonable regulation about how, where, and when abortions may be performed; and (3) during the third trimester, when the fetus becomes capable of surviving outside the womb, which the Court called "viability," the state's interest in protecting the unborn child is so important that the state can prohibit abortions altogether, except when necessary to preserve the life or health of the mother.[54]

The *Roe* decision led to decades of heated public debate and attempts by Presidents Ronald Reagan and George H. W. Bush to select Supreme Court justices who might reverse it. Nonetheless, *Roe* v. *Wade* was reaffirmed in *Planned Parenthood* v. *Casey* (1992). A bitterly divided Court upheld by a five-person majority the view that the due process clause of the Constitution protects a woman's liberty to choose an abortion prior to viability. The Court, however, held that the right may be subject to state regulation that does not "unduly burden" the woman's liberty. In other words, the Court threw out the trimester framework and permitted states to make "reasonable regulations" on how a woman exercises her right to an abortion, so long as they do not prohibit any woman from making the ultimate decision on whether to terminate a pregnancy before viability.[55] (See Figure 14.2 for U.S. public opinion on abortion.)

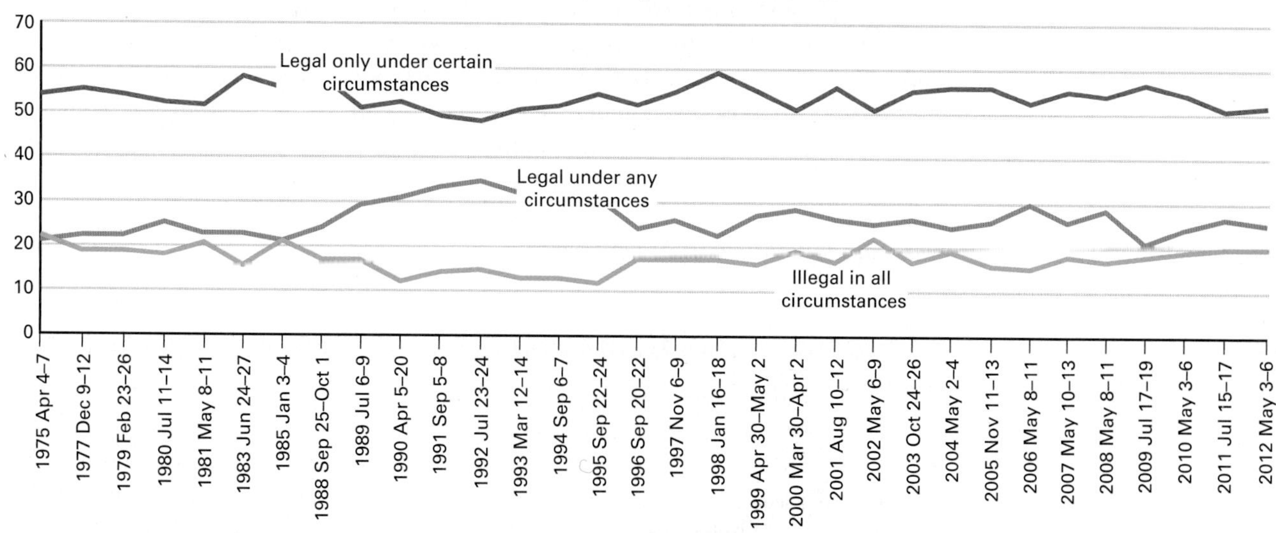

FIGURE 14.2 PUBLIC OPINION ON ABORTION ACCESS

Although there is great controversy over the issue of abortion, a majority of Americans has consistently agreed that abortion access should be "legal only under certain circumstances."

■ *Are the Supreme Court's rulings on abortion access generally in line with public opinion?*

SOURCE: Gallup Poll Social Series: Values and Beliefs, Gallup News Service. May 3–6, 2012.

search warrant

A writ issued by a magistrate that authorizes the police to search a particular place or person, specifying the place to be searched and the objects to be seized.

14.1

14.2

14.3

14.4

14.5

14.6

14.7

Applying the undue burden test, the Court has held, on the one hand, that states can prohibit the use of state funds and facilities for performing abortions; states may make a minor's right to an abortion conditional on her first notifying at least one parent or a judge; and states may require women to sign an informed-consent form and wait 24 hours before having an abortion. On the other hand, a state may not condition a woman's right to an abortion on her first notifying her husband. But, in 2007, the Court upheld (by a 5-to-4 vote) a federal ban on "partial-birth" abortion procedures that, for the first time, did not include an exception for cases where the woman's health was at risk. It reasoned that because of "medical uncertainty" about the banned procedure's necessity, Congress was not required to include a health exception.[56]

□ Sexual Orientation Rights

Although there is general agreement on how much constitutional protection is provided for marital privacy, in *Bowers* v. *Hardwick* (1986), the Supreme Court refused to extend such protection to private relations between homosexual couples.[57] By a 5-to-4 vote in *Bowers,* the Court upheld a Georgia law prohibiting consensual sodomy, determining that the law did not violate privacy rights.

But several state supreme courts, including Georgia's, upheld privacy rights for homosexual couples based on their own state constitutions rather than relying on the U.S. Constitution. Nearly two decades later, in *Lawrence* v. *Texas* (2003),[58] the Court struck down Texas's law making consensual homosexual sodomy a crime. Writing for the Court and noting the trend in state court decisions refusing to follow *Bowers,* Justice Kennedy held the law to violate personal autonomy and the right of privacy. Dissenting, Justice Scalia, along with Chief Justice Rehnquist and Justice Thomas, warned that the decision might lead to overturning laws barring same-sex marriages, as some state courts had already done.

Rights of Criminal Suspects

14.6 Analyze the constitutional rights of criminal suspects.

Despite what you see in police dramas on television and in the movies, law enforcement officers have no general right to break down doors and invade homes. They are not supposed to search people except under certain conditions, and they have no right to arrest them except under certain circumstances. They also may not compel confessions, and they must respect other procedural guarantees aimed at ensuring fairness and the rights of the accused. Persons accused of crimes are guaranteed these and other rights under the Fourth, Fifth, Sixth, Eighth, and Fourteenth Amendments.

□ Freedom from Unreasonable Searches and Seizures

According to the Fourth Amendment, "The right of the people to be secure in their persons, houses, papers, and effects, against unreasonable searches and seizures, shall not be violated, and no Warrants shall issue, but upon probable cause, supported by Oath or affirmation, and particularly describing the place to be searched, and the persons or things to be seized."

Protection from unreasonable searches and seizures requires police, if they have time, to obtain a valid **search warrant**, issued by a magistrate after the police indicate under oath that they have *probable cause* to justify it. Magistrates must perform this function in a neutral and detached manner and not serve merely as rubber stamps for the police. The warrant must specify the place to be searched and the things to be

New full-body scanners used at airports led to concerns that travelers were being subject to unreasonable searches under the Fourth Amendment. Courts have ruled that the scanners do not violate the Amendment.

seized. *General search warrants*—warrants that authorize police to search a particular place or person without limitation—are unconstitutional. A search warrant is usually needed to search a person in any place he or she has an "expectation of privacy that society is prepared to recognize as reasonable," including, for example, in a hotel room, a rented home, or a friend's apartment.[59] In short, the Fourth Amendment protects people, not places, from unreasonable governmental intrusions.[60]

The Fourth Amendment presents a complex area of the law that includes many possible exceptions to the warrant requirement. Beyond obtaining a search warrant, there are several other conditions in which a search might be considered "reasonable" according to the language of the Fourth Amendment. Key to determining whether a *warrantless search* is permissible are factors such as whether a person's consent to a search is coerced or whether an officer's or the public's safety is at risk. The Fourth Amendment does not apply to every encounter between individuals and law enforcement officials, however.

If the police only ask questions or even seek consent to search an individual's person or possessions in a noncoercive atmosphere, and there is no detention, the person's physical liberty has not been limited and the Fourth Amendment does not apply. But if the person refuses to answer questions or consent to a search, and the police, by either physical force or a show of authority, restrain the movement of the person, even though there is no arrest, the Fourth Amendment comes into play.[61] For example, if police approach people in airports and request identification, this act by itself does not constitute a detention.[62]

The Supreme Court also upheld, in *Terry* v. *Ohio* (1968), a *stop and frisk* exception to the warrant requirement when officers have reason to believe someone is armed and dangerous, has committed, or is about to commit a criminal offense. The *Terry* search is limited to a quick pat-down to check for weapons that may be used to assault the arresting officer, to check for contraband, to determine identity, or to maintain the status quo while obtaining more information.[63] If individuals who are stopped for questioning refuse to identify themselves, they may be arrested, although police must have a reasonable suspicion that they are engaged in criminal activities.[64] If an officer stops and frisks a suspect to look for weapons and finds criminal evidence that may justify an arrest, the officer can make a full search.[65]

14.1

14.2

14.3

14.4

14.5

14.6

14.7

exclusionary rule
A requirement that evidence unconstitutionally or illegally obtained be excluded from a criminal trial.

Technological advances have further complicated the Court's Fourth Amendment rulings. Even as the Supreme Court has increasingly allowed exceptions to warrant requirements, it has been reluctant to allow advancing technology to subvert the purposes of the Fourth Amendment. For example, without a warrant, law enforcement officials cannot use thermal imaging devices to gather evidence that a suspect is growing marijuana in his enclosed garage.[66] Nor may they use GPS tracking devices on a suspect's vehicle absent a warrant.[67] However, given that these decisions often turn on a person's reasonable expectation of privacy, as these technological advances continue, the Court will have to revisit the matter to redefine whether electronic intrusions are reasonable and what, if any, limits should be imposed.[68]

THE EXCLUSIONARY RULE Before the development of the *exclusionary rule*, evidence obtained in violation of the Fourth Amendment could still be used at trial against a defendant. The remedy in such cases was the opportunity for the defendant to sue law enforcement. However, suing afterward did not resolve the denial of Fourth Amendment protection in the criminal action.

This changed in the federal courts in 1911 and was applied to the states in 1961. In *Mapp* v. *Ohio* (1961), the Supreme Court adopted a rule excluding from criminal trial evidence that the police obtained unconstitutionally or illegally.[69] This **exclusionary rule** was adopted to prevent police misconduct. Critics question why criminals should go free just because of police misconduct or ineptness,[70] but the Supreme Court has refused to abandon the rule. It has made some exceptions to it, however, such as cases in which police relied in "good faith" on a search warrant that subsequently turned out to be defective or granted improperly.[71]

FOR the People — Government's Greatest Endeavors

Protecting Sixth Amendment Rights of Indigent Defendants

Until 1963, defendants who could not afford an attorney to represent them in state criminal trials were left to defend themselves against charges brought by state prosecutors. Although the Sixth Amendment to the United States Constitution provided for an attorney in federal trials, it had not been incorporated against state infringement. However, all that changed when Clarence Earl Gideon appealed his conviction in the Florida state courts on the grounds that he was not provided with an attorney to fight charges that he had broken into a pool hall and stolen money from the cash register.

In *Gideon* v. *Wainwright*, the U.S. Supreme Court ruled that because of the complexities of the legal system and the potential for being deprived of one's basic liberty, the government must provide an attorney to a criminal defendant who cannot afford one.* This is particularly important in an adversarial legal system such as we have in the United States, where the judge or jury, as a neutral decision maker, depends on the attorneys to bring forth all of the relevant evidence in a case. The Court's decision in *Gideon* v. *Wainwright* resulted in public defender services being provided throughout the United States. Each state has its own method to provide counsel to indigent defendants. For example, in some states, they have a statewide public defender service, and, in others, they use a combination of state-employed defense attorneys and private attorneys whom the state pays by the case to represent indigent defendants.

Providing a defense for indigent persons accused of a crime is essential to fulfilling the requirements of the Sixth Amendment. In 2007, the most recent year for which comprehensive data is available, more than 17,000 attorneys throughout some 964 public defender offices represented nearly 6 million cases involving indigent clients.** Although there are many concerns about the quality of representation provided to indigent defendants, including large caseloads and insufficient funding, indigent clients today are far better represented than they were some 50 years ago.

QUESTIONS

1. Why is it particularly important for indigent defendants to be represented by an attorney in an adversarial legal system?
2. Why might the Supreme Court have allowed the states to develop their own systems for providing indigent defendants with legal counsel?

*Gideon v. Wainwright, 372 U.S. 335 (1963)
** Public Defender Offices, 2007, Bureau of Justice Statistics, http://bjs.ojp.usdoj.gov/index.cfm?ty=pbdetail&iid=1758.

THE RIGHT TO REMAIN SILENT During the seventeenth century, special courts in England forced confessions from religious dissenters by torture and intimidation. The British privilege against self-incrimination developed in response to these practices. Because they were familiar with this history, the Framers of our Bill of Rights included in the Fifth Amendment the provision that persons shall not be compelled to testify against themselves in criminal prosecutions. This protection against self-incrimination is designed to strengthen the fundamental principle that no person has an obligation to prove innocence. Rather, the burden is on the government to prove guilt.

THE MIRANDA WARNING Police questioning of suspects is a key procedure in solving crimes. Approximately 90 percent of all criminal convictions result from guilty pleas and never reach a full trial. Police questioning, however, can easily be abused. Police officers sometimes forget or ignore the constitutional rights of suspects, especially those who are frightened and ignorant. Unauthorized detentions and lengthy interrogations to wring confessions from suspects, common practice in police states, have also occurred in the United States.

To put an end to such practices, the Supreme Court, in *Miranda* v. *Arizona* (1966), announced that no conviction could stand if evidence introduced at the trial had been obtained by the police during "custodial interrogation" unless suspects were notified that they have a right to remain silent and that anything they say can and will be used against them; to terminate questioning at any point; to have an attorney present during questioning by police; and to have a lawyer appointed to represent them if they cannot afford to hire their own attorney.[72] If suspects answer questions in the absence of an attorney, the burden is on prosecutors to demonstrate that suspects knowingly and intelligently gave up their right to remain silent. Failure to comply with these requirements usually leads to reversal of a conviction, even if other evidence is sufficient to establish guilt.

Critics of the *Miranda* decision believe the Supreme Court severely limited the ability of the police to bring criminals to justice. Throughout the years, the Court has modified the original ruling by allowing evidence obtained contrary to the *Miranda* guidelines to be used to attack the credibility of defendants who offer testimony at trial that conflicts with their statements to the police. But, as recently as 2000, the Court has reaffirmed *Miranda*'s constitutional necessity.[73]

The case of Ernesto Miranda (right) led to the Supreme Court decision in 1966 requiring suspects in police custody to be advised of their constitutional right to remain silent and to have an attorney present during questioning.

14.1
14.2
14.3
14.4
14.5
14.6
14.7

grand jury
A jury of 12 to 23 persons, depending on state and local requirements, who privately hear evidence presented by the government to determine whether persons shall be required to stand trial. If the jury believes there is sufficient evidence that a crime was committed, it issues an indictment.

petit jury
A jury of 6 to 12 persons that determines whether a defendant is found guilty in a civil or criminal action.

indictment
A formal written statement from a grand jury charging an individual with an offense; also called a *true bill.*

plea bargain
An agreement between a prosecutor and a defendant that the defendant will plead guilty to a lesser offense to avoid having to stand trial for a more serious offense.

□ Fair Trial Procedures

Many people, perhaps believing that they will never find themselves accused of criminal wrongdoing, consider the rights of the criminally accused to be less important than other rights. Nonetheless, these rights guarantee that all persons accused of crimes will have the right to representation by counsel and to a fair trial by an impartial jury. Procedural protections are guaranteed at each of the stages in the criminal process: (1) pretrial, (2) trial, (3) sentencing, and (4) appeal.

Before a person can be forced to stand trial for a criminal offense (except for members of the armed forces or foreign terrorists), they must be *indicted* by a grand jury, or before a judge in what is called an *information* proceeding. A **grand jury** is concerned not with a person's guilt or innocence, as a **petit jury** would be, but merely with whether there is enough evidence to warrant a trial. The grand jury has wide-ranging investigatory powers and "is to inquire into all information that might bear on its investigations until it is satisfied that it has identified an offense or satisfied itself that none has occurred."[74] The strict rules that govern trial proceedings, and the exclusionary rule to enforce the Fourth Amendment, do not apply, and the grand jury may consider hearsay evidence. If a majority of the grand jurors agree that a trial is justified, they return a *true bill,* or **indictment**. During this stage of the criminal process and throughout the remaining stages, suspects have the right to an attorney, even if they cannot afford one on their own. Communication between the accused and counsel is privileged and cannot be revealed to a jury.

The Constitution guarantees the accused the right to be informed of the nature and cause of the accusation so that he or she can prepare a defense. After indictment, prosecutors and the defense attorney usually discuss the possibility of a **plea bargain** whereby the defendant often pleads guilty to a lesser offense that carries a lesser penalty. Prosecutors, facing more cases than they can handle, like plea bargains because they save the expense and time of going to trial and they result in a conviction. Likewise, defendants are often willing to "cop a plea" for a lesser offense to avoid the risk of more serious punishment for the original indictment.

After indictment and preliminary hearings that determine bail and what evidence will be used against the accused, the Constitution guarantees a *speedy and public trial.* Do not, however, take the word *speedy* too literally. Defendants are given time to prepare their defense and often ask for delays because time works to their advantage. In contrast, if the government denies the accused a speedy trial, not only is the conviction reversed, but the case must also be dismissed outright.

An *impartial jury,* one that meets the requirements of due process and equal protection, consists of persons who represent a fair cross section of the community. Although defendants are not entitled to juries that reflect their own race, sex, religion, or national origin, government prosecutors cannot strike people from juries because of race or sex, and neither can defense attorneys use what are called *peremptory challenges* to keep people off juries because of race, ethnic origin, or sex.[75]

During the trial, the defendant has a right to obtain witnesses in his or her favor and to have the judge subpoena, or order, witnesses to appear at the trial and testify. Both the accused and witnesses may refuse to testify on the grounds that their testimony would tend to incriminate themselves. If witnesses testify, both the prosecution and the defense have the right to confront and cross-examine them.

The sentencing phase begins with the conclusion of the trial. Here, the jury recommends a verdict of guilty or not guilty. If the accused is found guilty, the judge usually hands down the sentence, although in some cases, juries impose the sentence according to the judge's instructions. The Eighth Amendment forbids levying excessive fines and inflicting cruel and unusual punishment.

Although the crime rate has generally declined in the past few years, public concern about crime remains high. At the national and state levels, presidents, governors, and legislators vie with one another to show their toughness on crime. California,

Virginia, Washington, and other states have "three strikes and you're out" laws, requiring a lifetime sentence without the possibility of parole for anyone convicted of a third felony, even if it is a minor offense. In some states, the felonies must be for violent crimes; in others, any three felonies will do. For example, the Supreme Court in *Ewing* v. *California* (2003) upheld California's tough law for committing three felonies, ruling that a 25-years-to-life sentence for a nonviolent third felony conviction for stealing three golf clubs did not violate the prohibition against cruel and unusual punishment.[76]

In the final stage of the criminal process, defendants may *appeal* their convictions if they claim they have been denied some constitutional right or the due process and equal protection of the law. The Fifth Amendment also provides that no person shall be "subject for the same offense to be twice put in jeopardy of life or limb." **Double jeopardy** does not prevent punishment by the national and the state governments for the same offense or for successive prosecutions for the same crime by two states. Nor does the double jeopardy clause forbid a civil suit, where a party could sue another for damages resulting from some action, even after a person has been acquitted in a criminal trial for the same alleged wrongdoing.[77] For example, after O.J. Simpson was acquitted of the 1994 murder of his ex-wife and her friend, he was found civilly liable for their deaths in 1997 and ordered to pay their families $8.5 million in damages.

double jeopardy
Trial or punishment for the same crime by the same government; forbidden by the Constitution.

☐ The Death Penalty

After a 10-year moratorium on executions in the late 1960s and early 1970s, the U.S. Supreme Court ruled that the death penalty does not violate the Eighth Amendment if it is imposed for crimes that resulted in a victim's death, if the courts "ensure that death sentences are not meted out wantonly or freakishly," and if these processes "confer on the sentencer sufficient discretion to take account of the character and record of the individual offender and the circumstances of the particular offense to ensure that death is the appropriate punishment in a specific case."[78]

In the wake of the Supreme Court's 1976 decision upholding Georgia's revised death penalty statute,[79] many states followed Georgia's lead and revised their own statutes, and the federal government increased the number of crimes for which the death penalty could be imposed. As a result, the number of persons on death row increased dramatically. Since capital punishment was reinstated in 1976, more than 1,300 people have been executed nationwide, and nearly 3,200 are on death row.[80] (See Figure 14.3.) Concerns have grown

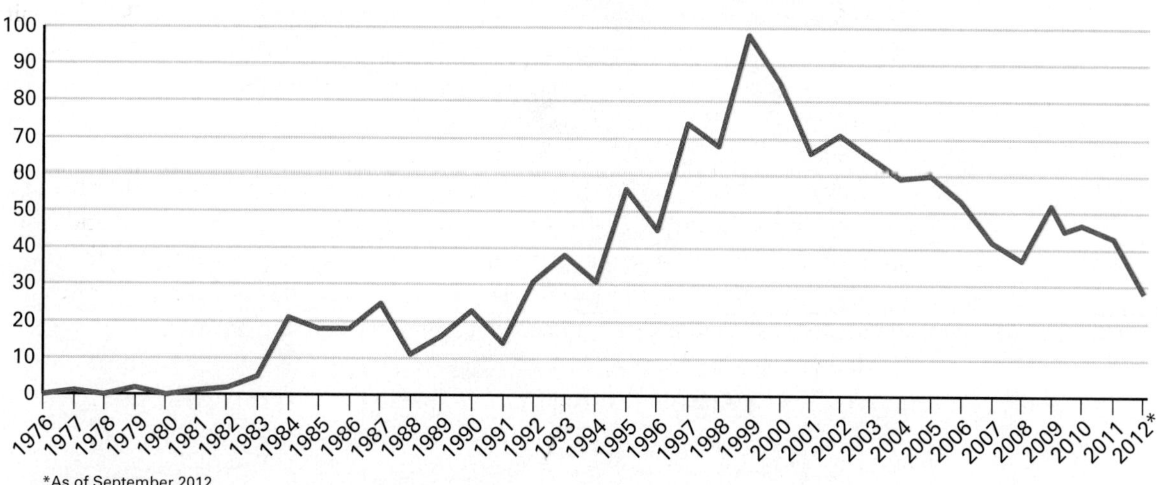

FIGURE 14.3 NUMBER OF EXECUTIONS BY YEAR, 1976–2012

What factors might explain the decline in the number of executions beginning in 2000?

SOURCE: "Death Penalty Information Center: Facts about the Death Penalty," Death Penalty Information Center, http://www.deathpenaltyinfo.org/.

Explore on MyPoliSciLab

Should the Government Apply the Death Penalty?

The United States is the only advanced democracy that practices capital punishment. Proponents argue that the death penalty is a deterrent to violent crimes, but since 1992, public support for it has declined. A majority of Americans still believe the death penalty should exist, but there are racial differences among supporters.

Death Penalty Supporters by Race

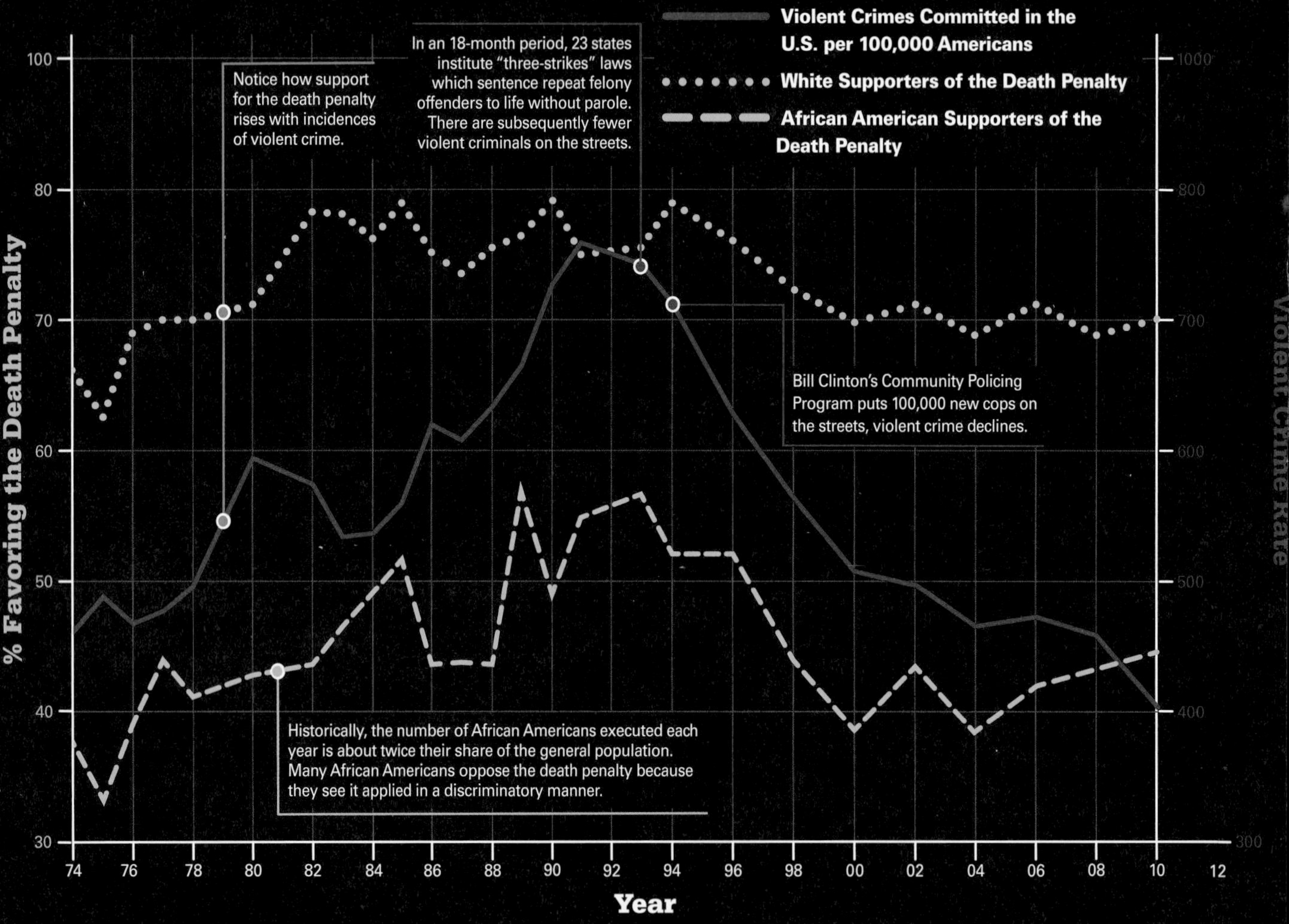

Violent Crimes Committed in the U.S. per 100,000 Americans

White Supporters of the Death Penalty

African American Supporters of the Death Penalty

Notice how support for the death penalty rises with incidences of violent crime.

In an 18-month period, 23 states institute "three-strikes" laws which sentence repeat felony offenders to life without parole. There are subsequently fewer violent criminals on the streets.

Bill Clinton's Community Policing Program puts 100,000 new cops on the streets, violent crime declines.

Historically, the number of African Americans executed each year is about twice their share of the general population. Many African Americans oppose the death penalty because they see it applied in a discriminatory manner.

% Favoring the Death Penalty

100 80 70 60 50 40 30

Violent Crime Rate

1000 800 700 600 500 400 300

74 76 78 80 82 84 86 88 90 92 94 96 98 00 02 04 06 08 10 12

Year

SOURCE: Data from General Social Survey, 1972-2010; Bureau of Justice Statistics, U.S. Department of Justice.

Investigate Further

Concept How widespread is American support for using the death penalty? A majority of Americans endorse capital punishment, but support is stronger among whites than African Americans. The racial disparities are due in part to the fact that African Americans are more likely to be on death row than whites.

Connection Is support for the death penalty related to lower crime rates? When violent crime goes up nationally, so does support for the death penalty because supporters believe it will decrease the crime rate. However, this effect is contested by death penalty opponents and those who see other explanations for less crime.

Cause Are there any competing explanations for the decline of violent crime, besides the death penalty? There are at least two non-death penalty related reasons for the decline of crime: increased federal spending to put more cops on the street, and states using stiffer sentencing for repeat felony offenders.

about the fairness with which capital punishment is imposed. DNA tests that have established the innocence of a sizable number of those convicted of murder have increased these concerns.[81] Since 1973, 140 people who were convicted of murder and sentenced to death have been exonerated.[82] Much of this work has been done by the Innocence Project, a non-profit legal clinic that works to exonerate those who are wrongly convicted.[83]

The prohibition against cruel and unusual punishment also forbids punishments grossly disproportionate to the severity of the crime. In 2002, the Supreme Court overruled an earlier decision and held that it is excessive and disproportionate to execute mentally retarded convicted murderers because they cannot understand the seriousness of their offense.[84] Using similar reasoning four years later, the Court ruled that executing minors also violated the Eighth Amendment.[85]

The Court continued its trend in limiting the use of the death penalty by deciding in *Kennedy* v. *Louisiana* (2008) that death could not be used when the defendant was convicted of child rape in which a death did not result, nor was it intended (the Court had previously ruled that the death penalty violated the Eighth Amendment in the case of adult rape).[86] In March 2008, however, the Court, in a 7-to-2 vote, upheld lethal injections as a constitutionally permissible means of carrying out executions.[87]

Protecting Our Civil Liberties in an Age of Terror: Whose Responsibility?

14.7 Evaluate the roles of institutions and the people in protecting civil liberties.

lthough the courts have resolved many challenges to restrictions on Americans' civil liberties, debate over adequate protections for individual liberties is ongoing. Today, there is particular concern about how to protect those liberties in the face of terrorist threats. As Justice Oliver Wendell Holmes wrote in his famous free speech decision (*Schenck* v. *United States* [1919]), "when a nation is at war, many things that might be said in a time of peace" will not be permissible "so long as men fight."[88] How do we find the correct balance between security and protecting civil liberties?

Ensuring against another terrorist attack would be much easier if the government had open access to listen in on our conversations, search our possessions, and detain or question suspects without having to show cause for doing so. The need to protect national security and gather foreign intelligence presents a special problem for Fourth Amendment protections. Endorsing President George W. Bush's claim that he could authorize warrantless wiretaps and physical searches of agents of foreign countries, Congress created the Foreign Intelligence Surveillance Court to review requests for warrantless wiretaps. The court consists of federal district judges and meets in secret. The USA PATRIOT Act, of 2001 (Uniting and Strengthening America by Providing Appropriate Tools Required to Intercept and Obstruct Terrorism) expanded the size of the court, lowered the requirement to approve warrants in cases involving terrorism, and permits searches for foreign intelligence and evidence of terrorist activities. Congress overwhelmingly voted to extend the PATRIOT Act, and in May 2011, President Obama signed a four-year extension of the Act into law. The extension continued to authorize "roving wiretaps" to monitor one individual's use of multiple communication devices.[89]

You Will Decide

Should We End the Death Penalty in the United States?

The United States is unusual among industrialized nations in its retention and use of the death penalty. In December 2007, the United Nations General Assembly adopted a resolution calling for a worldwide moratorium on the death penalty. More than two-thirds of the countries throughout the world have abolished capital punishment for all or most crimes, and the trend has been growing. The United States and Japan are the only two industrialized countries that retain the death penalty. Most of the 57 countries that still impose capital punishment are in Africa, the Middle East, the Caribbean, and Central America.* Although there is a growing consensus among other nations that the death penalty ought to be abolished, among the American public there is continued support for its use. Since 1972, a majority of Americans have supported the death penalty as a punishment for the crime of murder.† Many proponents of the death penalty argue that it has significant deterrent effects. Opponents often contend that deterrent effects are overstated and express equity concerns over the way the penalty is implemented.

What do you think? Should the death penalty continue to be implemented in the United States? What argument would you make for or against either proposition?

Thinking It Through

The Eighth Amendment's prohibition of cruel and unusual punishment has never been interpreted by a majority of the Supreme Court to bar the death penalty. Death was an available punishment when the Constitution was ratified and the language of the Fifth Amendment's due process clause indicating that a person not be denied of "*life*, liberty, or property, without due process of law" (emphasis added) provides further evidence that those voting to ratify the document understood that a person's life could be taken as long as the government adhered to procedural safeguards.

There is debate about the deterrent effects of the death penalty, but some academic research has found that the death penalty results in fewer murders. Studies have shown that each execution deters anywhere between 3 and 18 murders. Other work indicates that there is a stronger deterrent effect when executions are carried out more quickly.**

Although the Court has understood the "cruel and unusual" provision of the Eighth Amendment to change as society's understanding of the concept evolves (*Trop* v. *Dulles* [1958]), proponents of the death penalty contend that the public continues to support its use as evinced in public opinion polls such as the Gallup Poll mentioned previously. Furthermore, some argue that the appropriate indicator of an evolving understanding of cruel and unusual punishment is whether state legislatures continue to allow death as an available penalty; since 34 states continue to do so, proponents argue that the death penalty does not constitute cruel and unusual punishment.

Opponents of the death penalty argue that at best, studies of its deterrent effects are inconclusive. Indeed, in April 2012, the National Research Council's Committee of Deterrence and the Death Penalty concluded that studies aimed at assessing the death penalty's deterrent effects are flawed in that they have not considered the effects of other forms of punishment, such as sentences to life in prison without the possibility of parole.‡

Furthermore, opponents often argue that the risk of executing an innocent person is too great to continue to use the death penalty. Such arguments have been augmented by the exoneration of 140 people on death row since 1973. Concerns over racial inequities in the implementation of death strengthen the opposition to its use. Not only do black defendants make up a disproportionate percentage of defendants executed, the death penalty is also disproportionately carried out when murder victims are white.§

CRITICAL THINKING QUESTIONS

1. What is the appropriate way to determine whether society's understanding of cruel and unusual punishment has evolved?
2. Why is deterrence such an important consideration in death penalty debates?
3. In determining whether the death penalty is permissible in the United States, should courts consider the conclusions drawn in other countries?

*Amnesty International, "Abolitionist and Retentionist Countries," updated 2012, http://www.amnesty.org/en/death-penalty/abolitionist-and-retentionist-countries#retentionist.

†http://www.gallup.com/poll/1606/death-penalty.aspx.

**Robert Tanner, "Studies Say Death Penalty Deters Crime," *The Washington Post*, June 11, 2007.

‡Dalina Castellanos, "Death Penalty a Deterrent to Murder? Study Says Evidence Unclear," *The Los Angeles Times*, April 18, 2012.

§http://www.deathpenaltyinfo.org/documents/FactSheet.pdf.

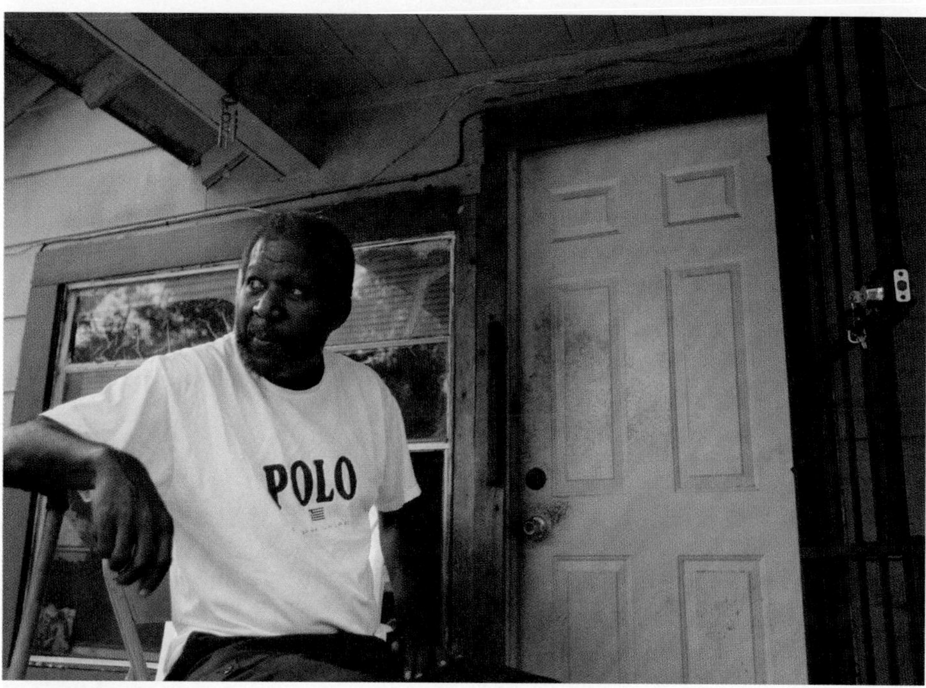

Clarence Brandley spent ten years on Texas' death row before he was exonerated in 1990. Along with other exonerated ex-death row prisoners, Brandley has lobbied for a moratorium on the death penalty in Texas.

Although the U.S. Supreme Court is often seen as the guardian of our civil liberties and minority rights in the United States, the actions of the legislature and executive in fighting the war on terror make clear that the judiciary is not the only branch of government concerned with protecting liberties, and it cannot do this work alone. In fact, some scholars contend that through the legislation it passes, Congress is as important as the Court in protecting individual liberties.[90] And the judiciary relies on the executive and legislative branches to enforce and provide funding to carry out its decisions. What does that imply for the role you play in protecting our civil liberties?

It is essential for citizens to be active in protecting our civil liberties. If we do not elect representatives who will uphold our civil liberties, enforce the Court's decisions, and appoint judges who will respect the individual guarantees in the Constitution, we cannot expect that they will be protected. Furthermore, if we do not act when we know civil liberties are being violated, the courts cannot make rulings. The judiciary is a reactive institution. It depends on individual citizens, or individuals working in cooperation through interest groups, to challenge government restrictions on civil liberties.

BY the People Making a Difference

Students for Liberty

In the summer of 2007, a small group of college students and recent college graduates participated in a round-table discussion at the Institute for Humane Studies at George Mason University. The students were interested in promoting libertarian interests and mobilizing like-minded students on college campuses. Two of the students, Alexander McCobbin and Sloane Frost, spearheaded an effort to hold a conference for students the following year. In February 2008, the first Students for Liberty Conference was held at Columbia University. The conference was attended by 100 students from 42 college campuses.* What began as a single conference has now developed into a nonprofit, student-led organization focused on providing support for students and student groups dedicated to liberty.

According to its most recent annual report, Students for Liberty now includes over 500 student groups. The organization is run by libertarian students who provide leadership training on college campuses and facilitate relationships between students and other libertarian groups such as The Liberty Fund, the Foundation for Individual Rights in Education, and the Koch Charitable Foundation.†

Students with different ideological views could apply a similar approach to bring together students from different institutions as happened with the Students for Liberty Conference. In the 1960s liberal student groups formed on campuses and gathered at national meetings to organize their opposition to the Vietnam War and support for extending civil rights.

QUESTIONS

1. With what kinds of campus issues might Students for Liberty be concerned?
2. How can students affect change on college campuses?
3. What are some advantages of student-led organizations? Are there disadvantages?

*http://studentsforliberty.org/about/

†http://studentsforliberty.org/about/reports/2010-2011-annual-report/

On MyPoliSciLab

Review the Chapter

Listen to Chapter 14 on MyPoliSciLab

The Basis for Our Civil Liberties

14.1 Trace the roots of civil liberties in the original Constitution and their subsequent development in the Bill of Rights, p. 443.

Antifederalists were concerned that the new national government would infringe on individual rights. Although many state constitutions already protected civil liberties, the Bill of Rights was to prevent the national government from infringing on civil liberties.

First Amendment Freedoms

14.2 Describe the First Amendment freedoms and the limitations on them, p. 446.

The First Amendment forbids the establishment of religion and also guarantees its free exercise. These two freedoms, however, are often in conflict with each other and represent conflicting notions of what is in the public interest. The Amendment also includes protections for speech, the press, and the right of assembly. However, each of these are limited: not all speech is protected, members of the press have no greater rights than do ordinary citizens, and the right to peaceably assemble is subject to reasonable time, place, and manner restrictions.

Property Rights

14.3 Explain how the Constitution protects property rights, p. 455.

The Framers saw private property rights as essential for maintaining a republican system of government. Although the government may take private property for public use, it must provide adequate compensation. And, even when the Constitution might allow such a "taking," the political process may prevent it.

Due Process Rights

14.4 Distinguish between procedural and substantive due process, p. 456.

The Constitution imposes limits not only on the procedures government must follow but also on the ends it may pursue. Some actions are out of bounds no matter what procedures are followed. Legislatures have the primary role in determining what is reasonable and what is unreasonable. However, the Supreme Court exercises its own independent and final review of legislative determinations of reasonableness, especially on matters affecting civil liberties and civil rights.

Privacy Rights

14.5 Assess the kinds of behavior that may be covered by a constitutional right to privacy, p. 456.

The right to privacy is implied by a number of the protections in the Bill of Rights, including protections against unreasonable searches and seizures, the protection against self-incrimination, and the right to associate (and not associate) with those you choose. It also protects a woman's right to terminate pregnancy and intimate relationships between consenting adults, regardless of sexual orientation.

Rights of Criminal Suspects

14.6 Analyze the constitutional rights of criminal suspects, p. 458.

The Framers knew from their own experiences that in their zeal to maintain power and to enforce the laws, especially in wartime, public officials are often tempted to infringe on the rights of persons accused of crimes. To prevent such abuse, the Bill of Rights requires federal officials to follow detailed procedures in making searches and arrests and in bringing people to trial.

Protecting Our Civil Liberties in an Age of Terror: Whose Responsibility?

14.7 Evaluate the roles of institutions and the people in protecting civil liberties, p. 465.

Although the judiciary is often seen as the guardian of civil liberties, it cannot carry out this function alone. Congress and the president also play an important role in protecting civil liberties through the laws they make and enforce. In addition, the judiciary is a reactive institution; without citizens who are willing to challenge improper restrictions on liberties, the courts are unable to act.

Learn the Terms

 **Study** and **Review** the **Flashcards**

writ of *habeas corpus*, p. 443
ex post facto law, p. 445
due process clause, p. 445
selective incorporation, p. 445
establishment clause, p. 446
free exercise clause, p. 449
commercial speech, p. 451
bad tendency test, p. 451
clear and present danger test, p. 451
preferred position doctrine, p. 451
prior restraint, p. 451
content or viewpoint neutrality, p. 451
unprotected speech, p. 452
libel, p. 452
obscenity, p. 452
fighting words, p. 452
civil disobedience, p. 454
property rights, p. 455
eminent domain, p. 455
regulatory taking, p. 455
due process, p. 456
procedural due process, p. 456
substantive due process, p. 456
search warrant, p. 458
exclusionary rule, p. 460
grand jury, p. 462
petit jury, p. 462
indictment, p. 462
plea bargain, p. 462
double jeopardy, p. 463

Test Yourself

 **Study** and **Review** the **Practice Tests**

MULTIPLE CHOICE QUESTIONS

14.1 Trace the roots of civil liberties in the original Constitution and their subsequent development in the Bill of Rights.

The state of New York cannot deprive its citizens of their right to practice their religious beliefs due to the

a. First Amendment's protection of religious exercise.
b. application of the First Amendment's protections through the privileges or immunities clause.
c. Fourteenth Amendment's due process clause.
d. incorporation of the First Amendment's protections through the Fourteenth Amendment's due process clause.
e. First Amendment's establishment clause.

14.2 Outline the First Amendment freedoms and the limitations on them.

The Supreme Court has ruled that the government may not censor newspapers by prohibiting publication of articles critical of Congress. Doing so would amount to

a. libel.
b. a prior restraint.
c. incorporation.
d. religious establishment.
e. violation of privacy.

14.3 Explain how the Constitution protects property rights.

After the Supreme Court's decision in *Kelo* v. *City of New London*, many local governments reacted by

a. seizing citizens' property.
b. refusing to provide just compensation to homeowners.
c. barring local authorities from taking property to promote economic development.
d. expanding their eminent domain policies.
e. restricting regulatory takings.

14.4 Distinguish between procedural and substantive due process.

Which of the following is an example of substantive due process?

a. Ensuring that law enforcement officials properly read a suspect her rights prior to interrogating her
b. Requiring that an indigent defendant be provided with an attorney at trial
c. Reviewing the state's reason for restricting privacy by mandating 24-hour waiting periods prior to obtaining an abortion
d. Establishing a grand jury to review evidence prior to pursuing a criminal trial
e. Requiring that a warrant be obtained prior to searching a suspect's home

14.5 Assess the kinds of behavior that may be covered by a constitutional right to privacy.

Which of the following is *not* an aspect of the right to privacy?

a. The right to be free from government surveillance and intrusion
b. The right to engage in adult consensual intimate relationships
c. The right to be free in thought and belief from governmental regulations
d. The right to perform religious acts as dictated by conscience on private property
e. The right not to have the government make private affairs public

14.6 Analyze the constitutional rights of criminal suspects.

If police officers obtain evidence in violation of the Fourth Amendment,

a. the criminal defendant can sue the police officers for redress.
b. it is typically allowed to be used against the accused at trial.
c. it is barred from the trial under the exclusionary rule.
d. it can still be used against the accused in state courts, but not in federal.
e. the accused has an obligation to rebut it at trial.

14.7 Evaluate the roles of institutions and the people in protecting civil liberties.

All of the following are limits on the Supreme Court's ability to protect civil liberties EXCEPT

a. the Court lacks the ability to enforce its decisions.
b. the Bill of Rights applies only to the federal government, not the states.
c. Congress must provide funds to enforce the Court's decisions.
d. to protect civil liberties, the Court must wait for a case to come before it.
e. at least four justices must agree to hear a case.

ESSAY QUESTION

Explain the debate over including a Bill of Rights in the Constitution. Why were many Federalists concerned over its inclusion? What arguments did Antifederalists make that it should be included? Explain the limitations on the judiciary's ability to protect Americans' civil liberties.

Explore Further

IN THE LIBRARY

Jeffrey Abramson, *We, the Jury: The Jury System and the Ideal of Democracy* (Harvard University Press, 2000).

James Macgregor Burns and Stewart Burns, *A People's Charter: The Pursuit of Rights in America* (Knopf, 1991).

David Cole and James X. Dempsey, *Terrorism and the Constitution*, 3rd ed. (New Press, 2006).

Sue Davis, *Corwin and Peltason's Understanding the Constitution*, 17th ed. (Wadsworth, 2008).

Lee Epstein and Thomas Walker, *Constitutional Law for a Changing America: Rights, Liberties, and Justice*, 8th ed. (CQ Press, 2012).

Louis Fisher, *The Constitution and 9/11: Recurring Threats to America's Freedoms* (University Press of Kansas, 2008).

Louis Fisher, *Religious Liberty in America: Political Safeguards* (University Press of Kansas, 2002).

Barry Friedman, *The Will of the People: How Public Opinion has Influenced the Supreme Court and Shaped the Meaning of the Constitution.* (Farrar, Straus and Giroux, 2009).

Robert Justin Goldstein, *Flag Burning and Free Speech: The Case of Texas v. Johnson* (University Press of Kansas, 2002).

Leonard W. Levy, *Emergence of a Free Press* (Oxford University Press, 1985).

Anthony Lewis, *Gideon's Trumpet* (Random House, 1964).

Alexander Meiklejohn, *Political Freedom: The Constitutional Powers of the People* (Harper & Row, 1965).

Shawn Francis Peters, *Judging Jehovah's Witnesses: Religious Persecution and the Dawn of the Rights Revolution* (University Press of Kansas, 2002).

William H. Rehnquist, *All the Laws but One: Civil Liberties in Wartime* (Knopf, 1998).

Barry Scheck, Peter Neufeld, and Jim Dwyer, *Actual Innocence: Five Days to Execution, and Other Dispatches from the Wrongly Convicted* (Doubleday, 2000).

Melvin Urofsky, ed., *100 Americans Making Constitutional History* (CQ Press, 2005).

Mary E. Vogel, *Coercion to Compromise: Plea Bargaining, the Courts, and the Making of Political Authority* (Oxford University Press, 2001).

Thomas G. Walker, *Eligible for Execution: the Daryl Atkins Story* (Washington DC: CQ Press, 2008).

ON THE WEB

www.law.cornell.edu/anncon/index.html
Congressional Research Service's Annotated U.S. Constitution. For each of the constitutional clauses, it describes the convention and/or ratification debate as well as court decisions dealing with the clause.

www.oyez.org
Web site containing MP3 files of oral arguments before the U.S. Supreme Court in both current and historical cases. There also are links to other great Supreme Court resources.

www.deathpenaltyinfo.org
The Death Penalty Information Center Web site. Up-to-date information on death penalty statistics in the United States, changing state laws concerning the death penalty, and data on its use internationally.

www.firstamendmentcenter.org
The First Amendment Center is affiliated with Vanderbilt University and the Freedom Forum, a nonpartisan foundation supporting the First Amendment. Its Web site contains research and analysis on a multitude of First Amendment questions and cases.

15

Listen to Chapter 15 on MyPoliSciLab

Civil Rights

Equal Rights Under the Law

In a 1996 decision, the Court of Appeals for the Fifth Circuit declared that affirmative action in Texas college admissions was unconstitutional. Although the state appealed the decision, the Supreme Court refused to decide the case, so the Court of Appeals decision was the law in the 5th Circuit, which includes Texas, Louisiana, and Mississippi. It was the first time that affirmative action in college admissions had been struck down in nearly 20 years. In reaction to the court's decision, the Texas legislature, in 1997, adopted the Ten Percent Plan; according to the plan, any student in the state, regardless of race, who finished in the top 10 percent of his or her high school class was guaranteed admission into any one of the state's public universities. Many high schools in Texas remain highly segregated by race and socioeconomic status.[1] Thus, the program meant that even without an explicit affirmative action plan, enrollment at Texas universities was nearly guaranteed to remain diverse. Typically, about 70% of the first year class at the University of Texas at Austin (UT) was admitted through the Ten Percent Plan.[2]

Although the Ten Percent Plan increased overall diversity in enrollment, UT subsequently changed its policy in an attempt to increase diversity at the classroom and program level. To do so, the University included race as a factor in its admission and school placement program for all students, consistent with the Supreme Court's later decision allowing race to be considered as one aspect of a holistic admission program (*Grutter* v. *Bollinger* [2003]).

Abigail Fisher, a senior at Stephen F. Austin High School located in a Houston suburb, applied for admission to the University of Texas at Austin in 2008. Fisher, who did not qualify for admission under the Ten Percent Plan, applied in a year in which students guaranteed admission through the Plan accounted for 81% of the admitted class at UT. Fisher sued UT, arguing that her academic

15.1 Explain the concept of equality and assess the rights of citizens, p. 475.

15.2 Compare and contrast the efforts of various groups to obtain equal protection of the law, p. 479.

15.3 Analyze the Supreme Court's three-tiered approach used to evaluate discriminatory laws, p. 487.

15.4 Trace the evolution of voting rights and analyze the protections provided by the 1965 Voting Rights Act, p. 491.

15.5 Describe congressional legislation against discrimination in housing, employment, and accommodations, p. 493.

15.6 Evaluate the historical process of school integration and the current state of affirmative action, p. 496.

15.7 Assess the status of civil rights in the United States today, p. 499.

The undergraduate admission policy at The University of Texas at Austin, which uses race as a factor in admissions' decisions, was reviewed by the U.S. Supreme Court during its October 2012 term.

MyPoliSciLab Video Series

The Big Picture Will the civil rights movement ever really be over? Author Christine L. Nemacheck argues that even though many important events in the civil rights movement happened in the 1960s, it is still an ongoing issue today—especially in regard to same-sex marriage.

The Basics Discover whether we have always had civil rights and whether all American citizens have them. Watch as ordinary people answer questions about where our civil rights come from and how we won them. Consider what equal treatment and protection under the law means today.

In Context Discover how civil rights issues have permeated our society since the United States was founded. In the video, University of Oklahoma political scientist Alisa H. Fryar talks about how civil rights has expanded in scope since the Civil Rights Movement of the twentieth century.

Thinking Like a Political Scientist Where are we headed in terms of civil rights research in the United States? University of Oklahoma political scientist Alisa H. Fryar discusses how current research on voting rights, municipal election methods, and education address civil rights issues.

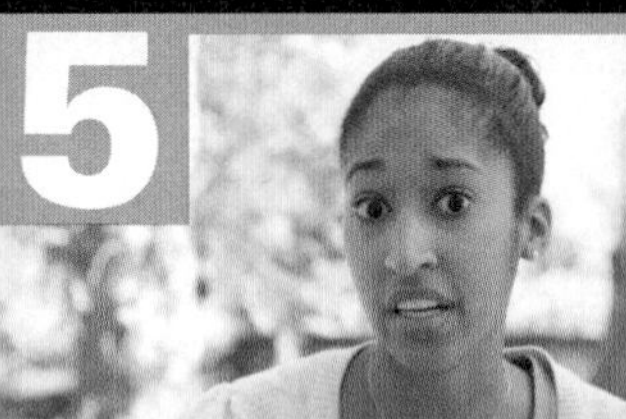

In the Real World The Defense of Marriage Act declares that the federal government does not recognize same-sex marriage. Is that constitutional? Hear real people argue both sides as they discuss their beliefs about same-sex marriage, and find out how public opinion has changed dramatically over the years.

So What? Learn the difference between civil rights and civil liberties. Author Christine L. Nemacheck provides examples of civil rights that the courts have ruled on in recent years, and she demonstrates how civil rights suits over affirmative action can get tricky.

record exceeded that of many admitted minority students. The Supreme Court granted *certiorari* and heard the case in its October 2012 term.

The case presents the first opportunity the Court has taken to rule on affirmative action in university admissions since its 2003 decisions in *Gratz* v. *Bollinger* and *Grutter* v. *Bollinger*, which we discuss later in this chapter. Given the Court's decision to strike down other affirmative action plans in public schools (*Parents Involved in Community Schools* v. *Seattle School District* [2007]), opponents of affirmative action are hopeful that the Court will strike down UT's admission program. Those opponents argue that Chief Justice Roberts had it exactly correct in that decision when he wrote, "The way to stop discrimination on the basis of race is to stop discriminating on the basis of race."[3]

The issues before the Supreme Court in *Fisher* v. *Texas* highlight the United States' continuing dilemma of how to best ensure equality without violating the Constitution's protection from discrimination based on race. In this case, Abigail Fisher's **civil rights** are at issue—her right not to be discriminated against because of race, religion, gender, or ethnic origin. The Constitution protects civil rights in two ways. First, it ensures that government officials do not impermissibly discriminate against us; second, it grants national and state governments the power to protect these civil rights against interference by private individuals.

The Constitution does not make any reference to "equality": the Declaration of Independence proclaims "that all men are created equal," but equality is not mentioned in the Constitution or in the original Bill of Rights. We know, however, that the Framers believed all men—at least all white adult men—were equally entitled to life, liberty, and the pursuit of happiness. Although it took many years for the concept of equality to be extended to all people, the Framers did create a system of government designed to protect what they called *natural rights*. (Today, we speak of *human rights*, but the idea is basically the same.) By **natural rights**, the Framers meant that every person, by virtue of being a human being, has an equal right to protection against arbitrary treatment and an equal right to the liberties the Bill of Rights guarantees.

These rights do not depend on citizenship; governments do not grant them. They are the rights of *all people*. In this chapter, we examine the protection of our rights from abuse *by government*, and the protection *through government* of our right to be free from abuse by our fellow citizens. Of course in many cases, protecting one person's rights may involve restricting another's, and the courts must balance the government's interest in doing so.

We begin this chapter by discussing citizenship rights in general. Although natural rights do not depend on citizenship, the kinds of protections that can be denied based on citizenship have become increasingly important. We then discuss several groups' efforts to secure their civil rights and examine what we mean by "equal protection of the law." In doing so, we will pay particular attention to two laws essential to securing civil rights protections: the Civil Rights Act of 1964 and the Voting Rights Act of 1965. Finally, we further examine the controversy over affirmative action. The debate over civil rights is not finished, and how we resolve it today will establish the boundaries of civil rights in the future.

civil rights
The rights of all people to be free from irrational discrimination such as that based on race, religion, sex, or ethnic origin.

natural rights
The rights of all people to dignity and worth; also called *human rights*.

Equality and Equal Rights

15.1 Explain the concept of equality and assess the rights of citizens.

Citizens of the United States are committed to equality. "Equality," however, is an elusive term. The understanding of equality on which we have the greatest consensus is that everyone should have *equality of opportunity* regardless of race, ethnic origin, religion, and, in recent years, sex and sexual orientation.

There is not much equal opportunity if one person is born into a well-to-do family, lives in a safe suburb, and receives a good education, while another is born into a poor, broken family, lives in a run-down inner-city neighborhood, and attends inferior

15.1

15.2

15.3

15.4

15.5

15.6

15.7

affirmative action
Remedial action designed to overcome the effects of discrimination against minorities and women.

naturalization
A legal action conferring citizenship on an alien.

dual citizenship
Citizenship in more than one nation.

right of expatriation
The right to renounce one's citizenship.

schools. Some argue that providing equalizing opportunities for the disadvantaged through federal programs such as Head Start, which helps prepare preschool children from poor families for elementary school, is necessary to bridge this gap.

Traditionally, Americans focus on *individual* achievement, but in recent decades, some politicians and civil rights leaders have focused attention on the concept of *equality between groups*. When large disparities in wealth and advantage exist between groups—as between black and white people or between women and men—equality becomes a highly divisive political issue. Those who are disadvantaged emphasize economic and social factors that exclude them from the mainstream. They champion programs like **affirmative action** that are designed to provide opportunities for those who have been disadvantaged due to their membership in a certain group, especially when that group has been discriminated against, as with women and minorities. Programs that take these group factors into account, as with affirmative action, have been and continue to be controversial.

Finally, equality can also mean *equality of results*. A perennial debate is whether social justice and genuine equality can exist in a nation in which people of one class have so much and others have so little, and in which the gap between them is growing wider.[4] There is considerable support for guaranteeing a minimum floor below which no one should be allowed to fall, but American adults generally do not support an equality of results.

☐ How Citizenship Is Acquired and Lost

Although natural rights do not depend on citizenship, important legal rights come with citizenship. Citizenship determines nationality and defines who is a member of, owes allegiance to, and is a subject of the nation. But in a constitutional democracy, citizenship is an *office*, and like other offices, it carries with it certain powers and responsibilities. How citizenship is acquired and retained is therefore important.

The basic right of citizenship was not given constitutional protection until 1868, when the Fourteenth Amendment was adopted; before that, each state determined citizenship. The Fourteenth Amendment states, "All persons born or naturalized in the United States, and subject to the jurisdiction thereof, are citizens of the United States and of the State wherein they reside." This means that all persons born in the United States, except children born to foreign ambassadors and ministers, are citizens of this country regardless of the citizenship of their parents.

NATURALIZATION People can also acquire citizenship by **naturalization**, a legal act conferring citizenship on an alien—someone who is living in the United States but is not a citizen. Congress determines naturalization requirements (see Table 15.1 for the list of requirements). Today, with minor exceptions, nonenemy aliens over the age of 18 who have been lawfully admitted for permanent residence and who have resided in the United States for at least five years and in the state for at least six months are eligible for naturalization. Any state or federal court in the United States or the U.S. Citizenship and Immigration Services (USCIS) (formerly Immigration and Naturalization Services) can grant citizenship. USCIS, with the help of the FBI, makes the necessary investigations. Any person denied citizenship after a hearing before an immigration officer may appeal to a federal district judge.

DUAL CITIZENSHIP Because each nation has complete authority to define nationality for itself, two or more nations may consider a person a citizen. **Dual citizenship** is not unusual, especially for people from nations that do not recognize the right of individuals to renounce their citizenship, called the **right of expatriation**. Children born abroad to U.S. citizens may also be citizens of the nation in which they were born. Children born in the United States of parents from a foreign nation may also be citizens of their parents' country.

TABLE 15.1 REQUIREMENTS FOR NATURALIZATION

An applicant for naturalization must:
1. Be over the age of 18.
2. Be lawfully admitted to the United States for permanent residence and have resided in the United States for at least five years and in the state for at least six months.
3. File a petition of naturalization with a clerk of a court of record (federal or state) verified by two witnesses.
4. Be able to read, write, and speak English.
5. Possess a good moral character.
6. Understand and demonstrate an attachment to the history, principles, and form of government of the United States.
7. Demonstrate that he or she is well-disposed toward the good order and happiness of the country.
8. Demonstrate that he or she does not now believe in, nor within the last ten years has ever believed in, advocated, or belonged to an organization that supports opposition to organized government, overthrow of government by violence, or the doctrines of world communism or any other form of totalitarianism.

For more information about immigration and naturalization, go to the Web site of the Federation for American Immigration Reform at www.fairus.org.

How might the United States determine whether a potential citizen is of a "good moral character"?

15.1
15.2
15.3
15.4
15.5
15.6
15.7

Rights of U.S. Citizens

A person becomes a citizen of one of the 50 states merely by residing in that state. *Residence* as understood in the Fourteenth Amendment means the place a person calls home. The legal status of residence is not the same as physical presence. A person may be living in Washington, D.C., but be a citizen of California—that is, consider California home and vote in that state.

Most of our most important rights flow from *state* citizenship. In the *Slaughter-House Cases* (1873), the Supreme Court carefully distinguished between the privileges of U.S. citizens and those of state citizens.[5] It held that the only privileges of national citizenship are those that "owe their existence to the Federal Government, its National Character, its Constitution, or its laws." These privileges have never been completely specified, but they include the right to use the navigable waters of the United States and to protection on the high seas, to assemble peacefully and petition for redress of grievances, to vote if qualified to do so under state laws and have your vote counted properly, and to travel throughout the United States.

In times of war, the rights and liberties of citizenship are tested and have been curbed. The Supreme Court overruled President Abraham Lincoln's use of military courts to try civilians during the Civil War,[6] but it upheld the World War II internment of Japanese Americans in "relocation camps"[7] and has approved the use of military tribunals to try captured foreign saboteurs[8] who were held abroad. However, it also ruled that citizens may not be subject to courts-martial or denied the guarantees of the Bill of Rights.[9]

In the war against international terrorism, President George W. Bush issued orders declaring U.S. citizens "enemy combatants" for plotting with the Al-Qaeda network and authorized their detention, along with that of other captured foreign nationals, in military compounds without counsel or access to a court of law. However, even in these cases, prisoners have a right to have their detention reviewed, and the Court's decision in *Boumediene* v. *Bush* (2008) reinforced this right.[10] The tension over protecting citizens' rights while fighting the war on terror has continued in the Obama Administration. Faisal Shahzad, a naturalized U.S. citizen, was arrested for attempting to detonate a car bomb in Times Square in May 2010. Under the Court's ruling in *Boumediene*, Shahzad's case was heard in the federal court system where Shahzad pled guilty to ten terror related charges. On October 5, 2010, Shahzad was sentenced to life in prison without the possibility of parole.

Although the Court upheld the internment of Japanese American citizens during World War II, it was later determined that the government had misrepresented information to the Court about the potential threat they posed. It was not until 1988 that the U.S. government officially apologized for its actions, and Congress awarded reparations to those interned during the war.

Rights of Resident Aliens

During periods of suspicion and hostility toward aliens, the protections of citizenship are even more precious. Congress enacted the Enemy Alien Act of 1798, which remains in effect, authorizing the president to detain and expel citizens of a country with which we are at war. U.S. citizens may not be expelled from the country, but aliens may be expelled for even minor infractions.[11] The Supreme Court also upheld the 1996 amendments to the Immigration and Nationality Act, which require mandatory detention during deportation hearings of aliens accused of certain crimes,[12] though they may not be held longer than six months.[13]

Still, the Constitution protects many rights of *all persons,* not only of American citizens. Only citizens may run for elective office, and their right to vote may not be denied, but all other rights are not so literally restricted. Neither Congress nor the states can deny to aliens the rights of freedom of religion or freedom of speech. Nor can any government deprive any person of the due process of the law or equal protection under the laws.[14]

However, Congress and the states may deny or limit welfare and many other kinds of benefits to aliens. Congress has denied most federally assisted benefits to illegal immigrants and has permitted states to deny them many other benefits, making an exception only for emergency medical care, disaster relief, and some nutrition programs. The Court has also upheld laws barring the employment of aliens as police officers, schoolteachers, and probation officers.[15] Although states have considerable discretion over what benefits they give to aliens, the Supreme Court has held that states cannot constitutionally exclude children of illegal immigrants from the public schools or charge their parents tuition.[16] In a 2012 challenge to a controversial Arizona law requiring law enforcement officers to check the immigration status of individuals they stop or detain, the Supreme Court struck down most provisions of the law because it violated the federal government's "broad, undoubted power over immigration . . . ."[17] But, it did uphold the immigration check provision as long as state law enforcement had a legitimate basis for making the stop or detention.

The Quest for Equal Justice

15.2 Compare and contrast the efforts of various groups to obtain equal protection of the law.

The rights of citizenship have been prominent throughout our country's history, but not all people in the United States were originally granted full rights of citizenship. Here, we review the political history and social contexts in which constitutional challenges to laws and other government actions relating to civil rights for women and minorities arose. This history involves more than court decisions, laws, and constitutional amendments, however. It encompasses the entire social, economic, and political system. And although the struggles of all groups are interwoven, they are not identical, so we deal briefly and separately with each.

Racial Equality

U.S. citizens had a painful confrontation with the problem of race during the Civil War (1861–1865). As a result of the northern victory, the Thirteenth, Fourteenth, and Fifteenth Amendments became part of the Constitution. The Thirteenth Amendment ended slavery, the Fourteenth ensures that all people are treated equally and establishes citizenship, and the Fifteenth Amendment protects citizens' voting rights. During Reconstruction in the late 1860s and 1870s, Congress passed civil rights laws to implement these amendments and established programs to provide educational and social services for the freed slaves. But the Supreme Court struck down many of these laws, and it was not until the 1950s and 1960s that legal progress was again made toward ensuring African Americans their civil rights.

SEGREGATION AND WHITE SUPREMACY Before Reconstruction programs could have any significant effect, the white southern political leadership regained power, and by 1877, Reconstruction was ended. Northern political leaders abandoned African Americans to their fate at the hands of their former white masters; presidents no longer concerned themselves with enforcing civil rights laws, and Congress enacted no new ones. The Supreme Court either declared old laws unconstitutional or interpreted them so narrowly that they were ineffective. The Court also gave such limited construction to the Thirteenth, Fourteenth, and Fifteenth Amendments that they failed to accomplish their intended purpose of protecting the rights of African Americans.[18]

For nearly a century after the Civil War, white supremacy went unchallenged in the South, where most African Americans then lived. They were kept from voting; they were forced to accept menial jobs; they were denied educational opportunities; they were segregated in public and private facilities.[19] Lynchings of African Americans occurred on an average of once every four days, and few white people raised a voice in protest.

During World War I (1914–1918), African Americans began to migrate to northern cities to seek jobs in war factories. The Great Depression of the 1930s and World War II in the 1940s accelerated their relocation. Although discrimination continued, more jobs became available, and African Americans made social gains. As their migration from the rural South shifted the racial composition of cities across much of the United States, the African American vote became important in national elections. These changes created an African American middle class opposed to segregation as a symbol of servitude and a cause of inequality. There was a growing demand to abolish color barriers, and by the mid-twentieth century, urban African Americans were active and gaining political clout.

SLOW GOVERNMENT RESPONSE By the 1930s, African Americans were challenging the doctrine of segregation in the courts, and after World War II, civil rights litigation began to have a major impact. Beginning with the landmark 1954 ruling in *Brown* v. *Board of Education of Topeka,* the Supreme Court prohibited racially segregated public schools[20] and subsequently struck down most of the devices that state and local

Explore on MyPoliSciLab

Are All Forms of Discrimination the Same?

In the 1967 *Loving v. Virginia* decision, the Supreme Court ruled unconstitutional all laws that restricted marriage based solely on race. Today, a similar debate revolves around marriage for same-sex couples. Public opposition to interracial marriage declined dramatically after the federal government gave its ruling — as shown in the 1972 and 1988 data. Has opinion about same-sex marriage changed in a similar way?

"Should Interracial Marriage Be Legal?"

1972

REGION	YES	NO
Northeast	71%	26%
Midwest	61%	35%
South	43%	53%
Rocky Mountains	54%	41%
Pacifc Coast	74%	24%

1988

REGION	YES	NO
Northeast	85%	11%
Midwest	76%	21%
South	62%	35%
Rocky Mountains	89%	11%
Pacifc Coast	87%	12%

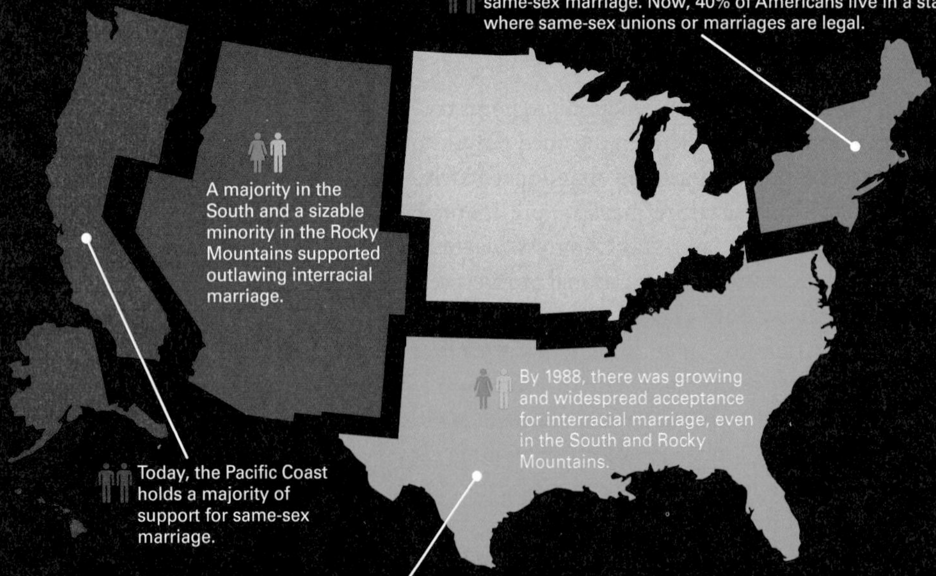

"Should Same-Sex Marriage Be Legal?"

1988

REGION	YES	NO
Northeast	12%	63%
Midwest	12%	66%
South	8%	78%
Rocky Mountains	12%	63%
Pacifc Coast	16%	62%

2010

REGION	YES	NO
Northeast	54%	30%
Midwest	50%	41%
South	38%	46%
Rocky Mountains	46%	44%
Pacifc Coast	52%	33%

SOURCE: General Social Survey data from 1972, 1988, and 2010.

Investigate Further

Concept How do we measure public opinion regarding marriage discrimination based on race and sexual orientation? Pollsters ask if a person agrees or disagrees with policy proposals, such as laws that recognize same-sex or interracial marriage. By watching the responses over time, we are able to determine change across the country.

Connection How does geography help predict public opinion on interracial marriage and same-sex marriage? The American South and Rocky Mountains are historically more conservative regions, and more resistant to changing definitions of marriage. But, even in these regions, opinion on marriage became more liberal over time.

Cause Does opinion about marriage influence policy or vice versa? After the Supreme Court settled the matter of interracial marriage in 1967, majority opinions followed suit across the country. Support for same-sex marriage has also changed over time, but policies vary by state. Legalization is more common where public opinion is most favorable, and bans are most common where support lags.

authorities had used to keep African Americans from voting.[21] We discuss *Brown* and voting rights in detail later in the chapter. Although the Court struck down segregation, achieving a significant level of desegregation required the other branches of government to act.

In the late 1940s and 1950s, Presidents Harry S. Truman and Dwight D. Eisenhower used their executive authority to fight segregation in the armed services and the federal bureaucracy. They directed the Department of Justice to enforce whatever civil rights laws were on the books, but Congress still held back. In the late 1950s, an emerging national consensus in favor of governmental action to protect civil rights, plus the political clout of African Americans in the northern states, began to influence Congress. In 1957, northern and western members of Congress from both parties overrode a southern filibuster in the Senate and enacted the first federal civil rights laws since Reconstruction, the Federal Civil Rights Act of 1957, which made it a crime to intimidate or threaten African Americans exercising their right to vote.

A TURNING POINT Even after the Court's decisions and congressional action, there was widespread resistance to integration in the South. As we discuss in detail later in the chapter, many legal barriers to equal rights had fallen, yet most African Americans still could not buy houses where they wanted, compete fairly for the jobs they needed, send their children to well-equipped schools, eat in "white's only" restaurants, or walk freely on the streets of "white neighborhoods."

Change came by way of a massive social, economic, and political movement. It began in Montgomery, Alabama, on December 1, 1955, when Rosa Parks, an African American seamstress, refused to give up her seat to a white man on a bus as the law required her to do. She was removed from the bus, arrested, and fined. The black community responded by boycotting city buses.

The boycott worked and also produced a charismatic national civil rights leader, the Reverend Martin Luther King Jr. Through his doctrine of nonviolent resistance, King gave a new dimension to the struggle. Following a peaceful 1963 demonstration in Birmingham, Alabama, that was met with fire hoses, police dogs, and mass arrests, more than a quarter of a million people converged on Washington, D.C., to hear King and other civil rights leaders speak. By the time the summer was over, hardly a city, North or South, had not had demonstrations, protests, or sit-ins; some cities erupted in violence.

This direct action had an effect. Many cities enacted civil rights ordinances, more schools were desegregated, and President John F. Kennedy urged Congress to enact a comprehensive civil rights bill. Late in 1963, the nation's grief over the assassination of President Kennedy, who had become identified with civil rights goals, added political fuel to the drive for decisive federal action to protect civil rights.[22] President Lyndon B. Johnson made civil rights legislation his highest priority. On July 2, 1964, after months of divisive debate, he signed into law the Civil Rights Act of 1964, which forbids discrimination on the basis of race, color, religion, sex, or nationality.[23]

The 1964 Civil Rights Act was a monumental legal change, but it was not the end of the struggle for civil rights. However, combined with the Twenty-Fourth Amendment ratified in January 1964, the Voting Rights Act of 1965, and Supreme Court decisions barring the use of gerrymandering and literacy tests as a means to deprive African Americans of the right to vote, the 1964 Civil Rights Act was a major step forward in providing equal protection under the law. We turn to a more thorough discussion of these concepts in the section on Equal Protection of the Laws.

AT THE END OF THE EDMUND PETTUS BRIDGE On November 4, 2008, American voters elected Barack Obama president of the United States, the first time an African American candidate has been elected to the office. The historic election was one where the candidates, more so than at any time in the past, represented the diversity of the United States electorate. That diversity was a direct result of the hard-won successes in our country's long battle over race and sex equality. Indeed, Congressman John Lewis, a longtime civil rights activist who was beaten by Alabama state police as he marched across Selma's Edmund Pettus Bridge in 1965, remarked that "Barack Obama is what comes at the end of that bridge in Selma."[24]

15.1

15.2

15.3

15.4

15.5

15.6

15.7

women's suffrage
The right of women to vote.

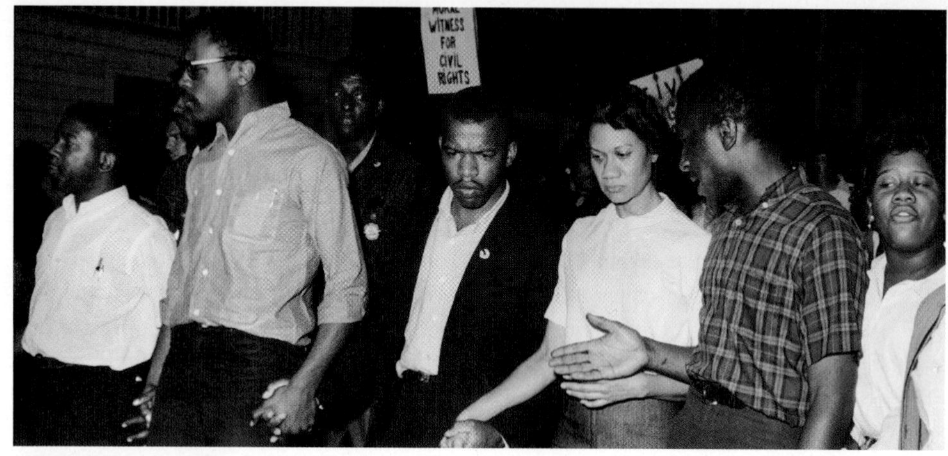

Congressman John Lewis (D-GA), then the chair of the Student Nonviolent Coordinating Committee, led civil rights activists in a 1965 march across the Edmund Pettus Bridge in Selma, Alabama. Lewis was elected to the U.S. Congress in 1977.

☐ Women's Rights

The 2008 election broke other barriers besides race. The Democrats' other major contender for the presidential nomination was Hillary Clinton, who would have been the first woman nominated by a major party for the presidency. Because of the historic nature of the Obama candidacy, less attention was paid to the fact that Senator Clinton was herself breaking barriers in her string of primary election victories and near majority of elected delegates. In the same election, Alaska governor Sarah Palin became the first woman nominated by the Republican party for the vice presidency. In 1984 Geraldine Ferraro broke this gender barrier in the Democratic party.

These developments came 160 years after the Seneca Falls Women's Rights Convention (1848), which launched the women's movement. That convention attracted men and women who actively campaigned to abolish slavery and to secure the rights of African Americans and women. But as the Civil War approached, women were urged to abandon their own cause and devote their energies to ending slavery.[25] The Civil War brought the women's movement to a halt.

By the turn of the twentieth century, however, a vigorous campaign was under way for **women's suffrage**—the right of women to vote. The first victories came in western states, where Wyoming led the way. But many suffragists were dissatisfied with this state-by-state approach. They wanted a decisive victory—a constitutional amendment that would force all states to allow qualified women to vote. Finally, in 1919, Congress proposed the Nineteenth Amendment. Many southerners opposed the amendment because it gave Congress enforcement power, which might bring federal officials to investigate elections and ensure that it was being obeyed—an interference that could call attention to how blacks were being kept from voting.

Women won the right to vote with the ratification of the Nineteenth Amendment in 1920, but they were still denied equal pay and equal rights, and national and state laws imposed many legal disabilities on them, such as the lack of comparable pay and health benefits. In the 1970s and 1980s, the unsuccessful struggle to secure the adoption of the Equal Rights Amendment occupied much of the attention of the women's movement. Since then women have mobilized their political clout behind issues that range from equal pay to world peace, an end to sexual harassment, abortion rights, and the election of more women to office.[26]

The Supreme Court has been reluctant to expand the level of Fourteenth Amendment protection against sex discrimination as it has against racial discrimination. Even so, it has struck down many state laws that discriminate based on sex. For example, it held that Virginia could not create a separate military academy for women instead of admitting them into the all-male Virginia Military Institute, a 150-year-old state-run institution.[27]

And the courts have increasingly enforced the prohibition against sex discrimination found in the 1964 Civil Rights Act and expanded it to forbid sexual harassment in the

The Global Community

Educating Boys and Girls

Education is often seen as a necessary precondition to ensure equal opportunities for all members of society. A Pew Global Attitudes Survey asked respondents, "Which of the following statements comes closest to your opinion about educating children? It is more important for boys than girls, it is more important for girls than boys, or it is equally important for boys and girls."

Throughout the world, there is widespread consensus that it is important to provide educational opportunities for both boys and girls. In Western democracies such as Britain and the United States, this is particularly the case. In each country, 98 percent of respondents indicated that education was equally important for both boys and girls. Japanese respondents also indicated a very high level of support for equal educational opportunities; 95 percent of respondents believed education to be equally important for both boys and girls.

Although there is general consensus on providing education to both boys and girls, there is some variation in the degree of that support. In China and India, 89 and 86 percent of respondents, respectively, indicated that education was important to both boys and girls. Even in regions of the world where there have not traditionally been educational opportunities for girls, such as in Nigeria, a full 84 percent of respondents indicated that it was equally important to provide these opportunities for both boys and girls, although there is still a fair number of respondents who indicate that it is more important to educate boys (14 percent).

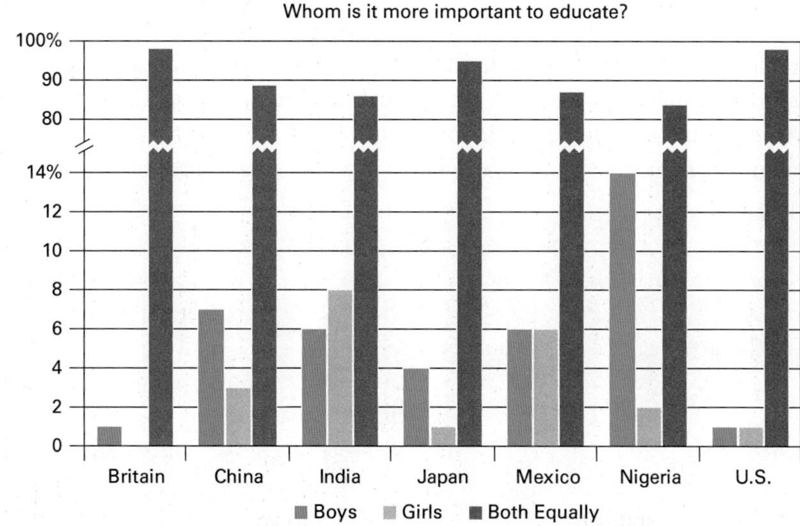

SOURCE: Pew Research Center, *Global Views on Life Satisfaction, National Conditions, and the Global Economy: Highlights from the 2007 Pew Global Attitudes 47-Nation Survey* (Pew Research Center, 2007).

CRITICAL THINKING QUESTIONS

1. Why do you think some respondents indicated that it was more important to educate girls than boys?
2. Is it equally important that boys and girls should be educated together? Or, are separate educational facilities for boys and girls just as valuable as integrated facilities?
3. Is political equality possible without equal educational opportunities?

workplace. In 1986, the Court applied the Act to "quid pro quo" sexual harassment, in which an employer requires sexual favors from a person as a condition of employment (in hiring, promotions, and continued employment).[28] It has since ruled that the Act also forbids a "hostile environment," defined as a workplace "permeated" with intimidation, ridicule, and insult that is severe and pervasive, and this includes same-sex harassment.[29]

Even with these advancements, there is evidence of a "glass ceiling" that prevents women's advancement in large corporations.[30] But major progress has been made, with more and more women going to graduate and professional schools and into the media and business. Indeed, during the past three decades, more women have graduated from colleges and universities than men (see Figure 15.1).

☐ Hispanics

The struggle for civil rights has not been limited to women and African Americans. Throughout U.S. history, many native-born citizens have considered new waves of immigrants suspect, especially if the newcomers were not white or English speaking. Formal barriers of law and informal barriers of custom combined to deny these groups equal rights. But as they established themselves—first economically and then politically—most barriers were swept away, and the newcomers or their children enjoyed the same constitutionally guaranteed rights as other citizens.

In many parts of the United States today, Hispanic immigrants have been met with suspicion. And although there is substantial debate over immigration from Mexico, the issue is not new. In 1954, the Immigration and Naturalization Service began a program known as "Operation Wetback" through which hundreds of thousands of Mexican immigrants were forcibly deported, sometimes with their U.S. born children.[31] As mentioned previously, most of Arizona's 2010 immigration legislation was struck down, including the provision making it a crime to fail to carry immigration documentation. But, in 2012, the Supreme Court did uphold the so-called "show me your papers" provision requiring state law enforcement officers to check the immigration status of individuals they stop or detain for a legitimate purpose.[32] Opponents of the legislation argue that the law will result in unconstitutionally targeting Hispanics.

Hispanics have not always been able to translate their numbers into comparable political clout because of political differences among them and because many are not citizens or registered to vote. However, after California adopted Proposition 187 in 1994, which denied medical, educational, and social services to illegal immigrants, and Congress amended the federal welfare laws to curtail benefits to noncitizens,

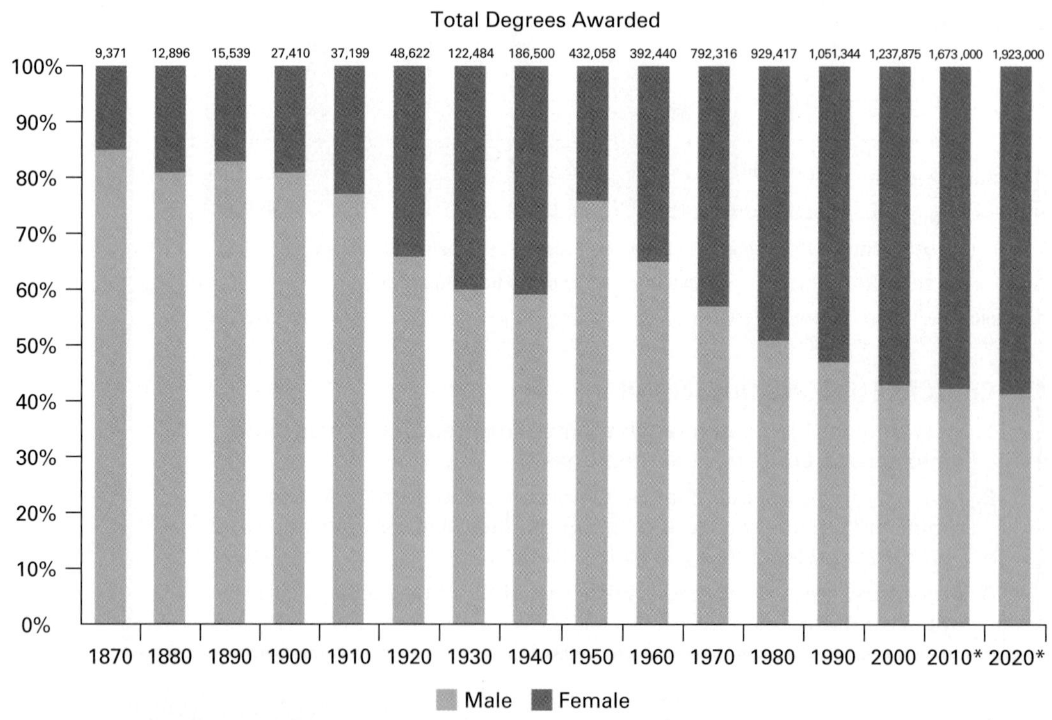

FIGURE 15.1 PERCENTAGE OF BACHELOR'S DEGREES AWARDED, BY SEX

■ *What factors might affect the variation in men's college attendance from the 1920s through the 1950s?*

*Projected Data.

SOURCE: U.S. Department of Education, National Center for Education Statistics, *Earned Degrees Conferred,* 1869–1870 through 1964–1965; *Projections of Education Statistics to 2020;* Higher Education General Information Survey (HEGIS), "Degrees and Other Formal Awards Conferred" surveys, 1965–1966 through 1985–1986; and 1986–1987 through 2005–2006; Integrated Postsecondary Education Data System, "Completions Survey" (IPEDS-C:96–99), and Fall 2000 through Fall 2009; and Degrees Conferred Model, 1975–76 through 2008–09; March 2011.

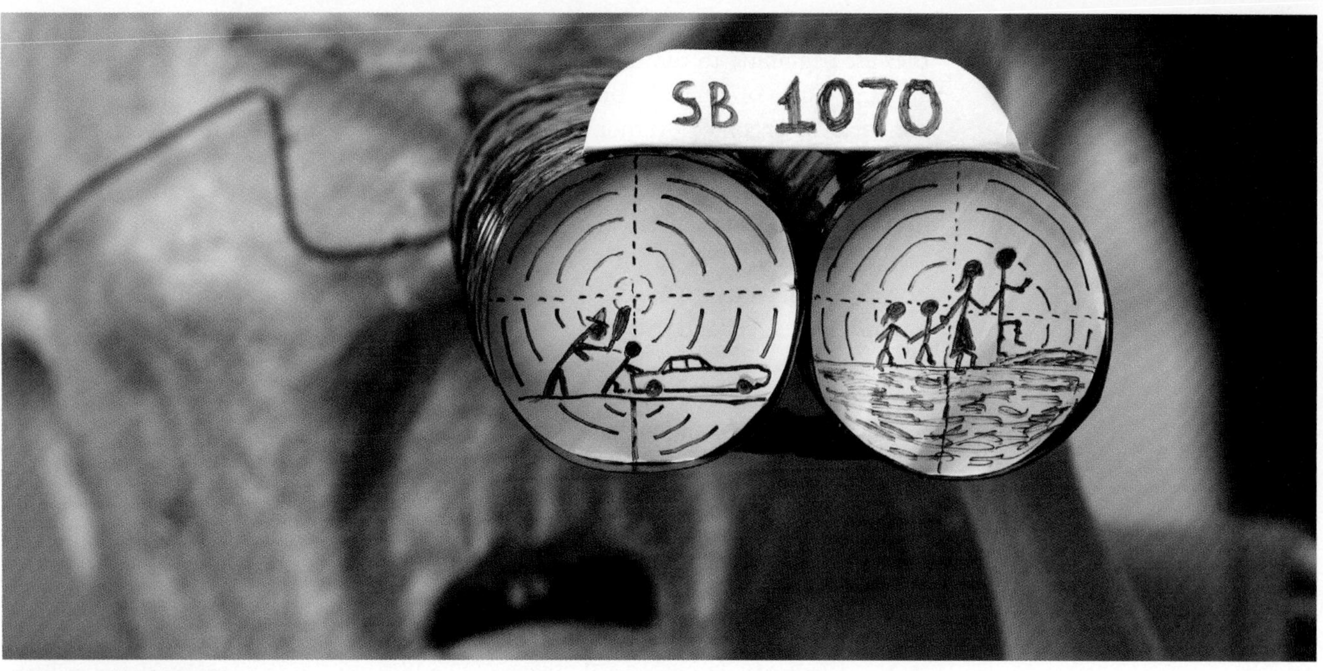

An opponent of Arizona's immigration legislation, known as SB 1070, holds papier-mache binoculars and depicts Maricopa County Sheriff Joe Arpaio in a protest outside the U.S. District Court in Phoenix, Arizona.

many immigrants rushed to become naturalized. Half of all Hispanic Americans live in two states: California and Texas. In 2001, California became the first big state in which white people are in the minority, and Texas followed in 2005; a majority of the population is made up of racial minorities (majority-minority) in Hawaii, New Mexico, and the District of Columbia as well.[33]

☐ Asian Americans

The term "Asian American" describes approximately 10 million people from many different countries and ethnic backgrounds. Most do not think of themselves as Asians but as U.S. citizens of Chinese, Japanese, Indian, Vietnamese, Cambodian, Korean, or other specific ancestry. Although Asian Americans are often considered a "model minority" because of their successes in education and business, the U.S. Civil Rights Commission found in 1992 that "Asian Americans do face widespread prejudice, discrimination, and barriers to equal opportunity" and that racially motivated violence against them "occurs with disturbing frequency."[34] Discrimination against Asian Americans is, unfortunately, nothing new. The Naturalization Act of 1906, for example, made it impossible for any Asian American to become a U.S. citizen. Although the Act was challenged, the Supreme Court upheld its provision that only white persons and aliens of African nativity or descent were eligible for citizenship.[35]

CHINESE AMERICANS The Chinese were the first Asians to come to the United States. Beginning in 1847, when young male Chinese peasants came to the American West to escape poverty and to work in mines, on railroads, and on farms, the Chinese encountered economic and cultural fears by the white majority, who did not understand their language or their culture. Chinese Americans were recruited by the Central Pacific Railroad to work on the transcontinental railroad, but anti-Chinese sentiment grew. By the 1870s, attacks on "Chinatowns" began in cities throughout the United States. The Chinese Exclusion Act of 1882 restricted Chinese immigration and excluded Chinese immigrants already in the United States from the possibility of citizenship. It was not until 1943 that Congress repealed the Chinese Exclusion Act and opened the door to citizenship for Chinese Americans.

The 1965 amendments to the Immigration and Nationality Act went further to end the nationality criteria and thus equalize immigration criteria across race and ethnicity.

Since that time, the Chinese have moved into the mainstream of U.S. society, and they are beginning to run for and win local political offices. Gary Locke, a Democrat and a graduate of Yale and Boston University Law School, became the first Chinese American to become governor of a continental state (Washington in 1996) and later was the American Ambassador to China.

JAPANESE AMERICANS The Japanese migrated first to Hawaii in the 1860s and then to California in the 1880s. By the beginning of the twentieth century, they faced overt hostility. In 1905, white labor leaders organized the Japanese and Korean Exclusion League, and in 1906, the San Francisco Board of Education excluded all Chinese, Japanese, and Korean children from neighborhood schools. Some western states passed laws denying the right to own land to aliens who were ineligible to become citizens—meaning aliens of Asian ancestry.

During World War II, anti-Japanese hysteria provoked the internment of West Coast Japanese—most of whom were loyal U.S. citizens guilty of no crimes—in prison camps in California, Colorado, and other states. Their property was often sold at below market rates, and many of them lost their businesses, jobs, and incomes. Although Japanese Americans challenged the internment policies, the U.S. Supreme Court upheld the government's actions. In *Korematsu* v. *United States* (1944), the Court ruled that under the threat to national security, it could not reject congressional and military judgment that disloyalty existed and must be segregated.[36] Following the war, the exclusionary acts were repealed, though discrimination against Japanese Americans persisted, such as the limits placed on Japanese American student enrollment at many colleges and universities. In 1988, President Ronald Reagan signed a law providing $20,000 restitution to each of the approximately 60,000 surviving World War II internees.

☐ Native Americans

Approximately 20% of the nearly 3 million Native Americans in the United States live on or near a *reservation*—a tract of land given to tribal nations through treaties with the federal government.[37] The history of discrimination against Native Americans in the United States is a great stain on our human rights record. Although discrimination against African Americans often gets more attention in civil rights discussions, legally sanctioned discrimination against Native Americans followed a similar path. Efforts to forcibly move Native American tribes off their land and farther west as more whites migrated to the Midwest and western states are well known. The Indian Removal Act, passed in 1830, required that all Native American tribes be moved from the East and Southeast. The Act also authorized the use of force to meet its goals. It is estimated that 4,000 of the 18,000 Cherokee Indians forced to move west into what became eastern Oklahoma in the late 1830s died on the "Trail of Tears."[38]

Native American rights organizations, including the American Indian Movement, protested discrimination against Native Americans in housing, employment, and health care. Over time, other civil rights groups, such as the American Civil Liberties Union (ACLU), have joined the fight to protect Native American civil rights. In recent years the federal courts have approved settlements in class-action lawsuits regarding the equal treatment of Native American students in the public schools[39] and discrimination against Native American farmers by the U.S. Department of Agriculture, the latter of which required the USDA to pay $680 million in damages to thousands of Native Americans and to forgive another $80 million in outstanding farm loans.[40]

As a result of these efforts and of a greater national consciousness, most citizens are now aware that many Native Americans continue to face discrimination and live in poverty. Unemployment on many reservations continues to be 50 to 60 percent. Some reservations lack adequate health care facilities, schools, housing, and jobs. Congress has started to compensate Native Americans for past injustices and to provide more opportunities to develop tribal economic independence, and judges are showing greater vigilance in enforcing Indian treaty rights.

Equal Protection of the Laws: What Does It Mean?

15.3 Analyze the Supreme Court's three-tiered approach used to evaluate discriminatory laws.

The **equal protection clause** of the Fourteenth Amendment declares that no state (including any subdivision thereof) shall "deny to any person within its jurisdiction the equal protection of the laws." Although no parallel clause explicitly applies to the national government, courts have interpreted the Fifth Amendment's **due process clause**, which states that no person shall "be deprived of life, liberty, or property, without due process of law," to impose the same restraints on the national government as the equal protection clause imposes on the states.

Note that the clause applies only to the actions of *governments,* not to those of private individuals. If a private person performs a discriminatory action, that action does not violate the Constitution. Instead, it may violate federal and state laws passed to protect people from unjust discrimination by private parties.

The equal protection clause does not, however, prevent governments from discriminating in all cases. What the Constitution forbids is *unreasonable* classifications. In general, a classification is unreasonable when there is no relationship between the classes it creates and permissible governmental goals. A law prohibiting redheads from voting, for example, would be unreasonable. In contrast, laws denying persons under the age of 18 the right to vote, to marry without the permission of their parents, or to apply for a driver's license appear to be reasonable (at least to most persons over the age of 18).

☐ Constitutional Classifications and Tests

One of the most troublesome constitutional questions is how to distinguish between constitutional and unconstitutional classifications. The Supreme Court uses three tests for this purpose: the *rational basis* test, the *strict scrutiny* test, and the *heightened scrutiny* test.

THE RATIONAL BASIS TEST The traditional test to determine whether a law complies with the equal protection requirement—the **rational basis test**—places the burden of proof on the parties attacking the law. They must show that the law has no rational or legitimate governmental goals. When a court reviews the government's reason for legislating, it engages in substantive due process. Traditionally, the rational basis test applied only to legislation affecting economic interests and, with two exceptions in the last 70 years, the Court has upheld the legislation and deferred to legislative judgments.[41] But recently, the Court has applied the test when noneconomic interests are challenged.[42] Overwhelmingly in those cases, the legislation is upheld, though there are exceptions. For example, when the Court struck down an amendment to the Colorado state constitution barring sexual orientation as a protected category in antidiscrimination laws in *Romer* v. *Evans* (1996), it did so using the rational basis test. We will discuss laws discriminating based on sexual orientation later in this chapter.

SUSPECT CLASSIFICATIONS AND STRICT SCRUTINY When a law is subject to the **strict scrutiny test**, the burden is on the government to show that there is both a "compelling governmental interest" to justify such a classification and no less restrictive way to accomplish this compelling purpose. The Court applies the strict scrutiny test to suspect classifications. A *suspect classification* is one through which people have been deliberately subjected to severely unequal treatment or that society has used to render people politically powerless.[43] When a law classifies based on race or national origin, it immediately raises a red flag regardless of whether it is intended to aid or inhibit a particular race or nationality. For example, the Supreme Court has held that laws that give preference for public employment based on race are subject to strict scrutiny.

equal protection clause
A clause in the Fourteenth Amendment that forbids any state to deny to any person within its jurisdiction the equal protection of the laws. By interpretation, the Fifth Amendment imposes the same limitation on the national government. This clause is the major constitutional restraint on the power of governments to discriminate against persons because of race, national origin, or sex.

due process clause
A clause in the Fifth Amendment limiting the power of the national government; a similar clause in the Fourteenth Amendment prohibits state governments from depriving any person of life, liberty, or property without due process of law.

rational basis test
A standard developed by the courts to test the constitutionality of a law; when applied, a law is constitutional as long as it meets a reasonable government interest.

strict scrutiny test
A test applied by the court when a classification is based on race; the government must show that there is a compelling reason for the law and no other less restrictive way to meet the interest.

15.1

15.2

15.3

15.4

15.5

15.6

15.7

heightened scrutiny test
This test has been applied when a law classifies based on sex; to be upheld, the law must meet an important government interest.

TABLE 15.2 MAJOR CIVIL RIGHTS LAWS

Civil Rights Act, 1957	Makes it a federal crime to prevent persons from voting in federal elections
Civil Rights Act, 1964	Bars discrimination in employment or in public accommodations on the basis of race, color, religion, sex, or national origin; created the Equal Employment Opportunity Commission
Voting Rights Act, 1965	Authorizes the appointment of federal examiners to register voters in areas with a history of discrimination
Age Discrimination in Employment Act, 1967	Prohibits job discrimination against workers or job applicants aged 40 through 65 and prohibits mandatory retirement
Fair Housing Act, 1968	Prohibits discrimination on the basis of race, color, religion, or national origin in the sale or rental of most housing
Title IX, Education Amendment of 1972	Prohibits discrimination on the basis of sex in any education program receiving federal financial assistance
Rehabilitation Act, 1973	Requires that recipients of federal grants greater than $2,500 hire and promote qualified handicapped individuals
Fair Housing Act Amendments, 1988	Gave the Department of Housing and Urban Development authority to prohibit housing bias against the handicapped and families with children
Americans with Disabilities Act, 1990	Prohibits discrimination based on disability and requires that facilities be made accessible to those with disabilities
Civil Rights Act, 1991	Requires that employers justify practices that negatively affect the working conditions of women and minorities or show that no alternative practices would have a lesser impact; also established a commission to examine the "glass ceiling" that keeps women from becoming executives and to recommend how to increase the number of women and minorities in management positions.

QUASI-SUSPECT CLASSIFICATIONS AND HEIGHTENED SCRUTINY To sustain a law under the **heightened scrutiny test**, the government must show that its classification serves "important governmental objectives." Heightened scrutiny is a standard first used by the Supreme Court in 1971 to declare classifications based on sex unconstitutional. As Justice William J. Brennan Jr. wrote for the Court: "There can be no doubt that our nation has had a long and unfortunate history of sex discrimination. Traditionally, such discrimination was rationalized by an attitude of 'romantic paternalism,' which in practical effect put women, not on a pedestal, but in a cage."[44] In recent years, the Supreme Court has struck down most laws brought before it that were alleged to discriminate against women but has tended to do so on the basis of federal statutes like the 1964 Civil Rights Act (for other legislation, see Table 15.2).

POVERTY AND AGE Just as race and sex classifications receive elevated scrutiny, some argue that economic and age classification ought to be subject to some heightened review. The Supreme Court rejected the argument "that financial need alone identifies a suspect class for purposes of equal protection analysis."[45] However, some state supreme courts (Texas, Ohio, and Connecticut among others) have ruled that unequal funding for public schools, as a result of "rich" districts spending more per pupil than "poor" districts, violates their state constitutional provisions for free and equal education.[46] More recently, the focus of such litigation has centered on requirements to provide an "adequate" or "suitable" education, based on state constitutions' education clauses.[47]

Age is not a suspect classification. Many laws make distinctions based on age to obtain a driver's license, to marry without parental consent, to attend schools, to buy alcohol or tobacco, and so on. Many governmental institutions have age-specific programs: for senior citizens, for adult students, and for people in mid-career. As Justice Sandra Day O'Connor observed: "States may discriminate on the basis of age without offending the Fourteenth Amendment if the age classification in question is rationally related to a legitimate state interest."[48]

Although the Court has been unwilling to extend heightened protection to individuals who have experienced age discrimination, Congress has acted to provide statutory protection, particularly with the Age Discrimination in Employment Act (1967). In 1974, Congress attempted to extend the protections against age

Shelly Bailes and Ellen Pontac, who in 2008 had been together for 34 years, were the first same-sex couple to marry in Yolo County, California, on June 16, 2008, after the California Supreme Court overturned a state statute banning same-sex marriage. On November 4 of that year, California voters passed Proposition 8, which amended the state constitution to bar same-sex marriage. However, the constitutionality of Proposition 8 is being challenged in the federal courts. A federal district court ruled that the proposition violated the Fourteenth Amendment to the U.S. Constitution, a decision upheld by the Ninth Circuit Court of Appeals (*Perry* v. *Brown*).

discrimination to cover state employees, but the Supreme Court ruled that Congress lacks the constitutional authority to open the federal courts to suits by state employees for alleged age discrimination. State employees are limited to recovering monetary damages under state laws in state courts.[49]

SEXUAL ORIENTATION In 1996, the U.S. Supreme Court struck down an initiative amending the Colorado Constitution that prohibited state and local governments from protecting homosexuals from discrimination.[50] The Court ruled in *Romer* v. *Evans* that this provision violated the equal protection clause because it lacked any rational basis and simply represented prejudice toward a particular group. Although in cases like *Romer* (1996) and *Lawrence* v. *Texas* (2003), a case in which the Court struck down a Texas ban on homosexual sodomy, the Court found that state laws based on sexual orientation violated the U.S. Constitution, it has not elevated the level of scrutiny with which it reviews such classifications. However, as we discuss in the *You Will Decide* box, several state courts have ruled that their own state constitutions require at least the right to legal recognition of same-sex civil unions. The supreme courts of Massachusetts, California, Connecticut, and Iowa have gone even further to determine that their state constitutions require that marriage be open to same-sex as well as different-sex couples. Although the California Supreme Court's decision was negated by California voters in the 2008 election, the federal District Court of the Northern District of CA struck down the initiative (Proposition 8) as a violation of the U.S. Constitution's equal protection clause. A panel of the United States Court of Appeals for the Ninth Circuit upheld the District Court's ruling, but on substantially more narrow grounds, making it less likely that the U.S. Supreme Court would agree to hear the case.[51] On July 31, 2012, supporters of Proposition 8 filed an appeal of the Ninth Circuit's decision with the U.S. Supreme Court. Other states (Vermont, New Hampshire, New York, Maryland, Maine and Washington) and the District of Columbia have legalized same-sex marriage through legislative action or referenda.

15.1

15.2

15.3

15.4

15.5

15.6

15.7

You Will Decide

Should Marriage Be Limited to Heterosexual Couples?

On May 15, 2008, the California Supreme Court ruled that denying same-sex couples the opportunity to marry violated the state's constitutional guarantee of equal protection. The state supreme court's decision was immediately challenged by opponents who placed a constitutional amendment banning same-sex marriage on the 2008 ballot. The measure was narrowly approved by voters. However, that did not end the legal battle. Citizens challenged the amendment, and the Federal District Court in the Northern District of California struck down the ballot measure, ruling that it violates the U.S. Constitution's Fourteenth Amendment guarantee of equal protection under the law. The Court of Appeals for the Ninth Circuit upheld the District Court's decision, albeit on narrow grounds. The case is pending appeal.

Proponents of same-sex marriage cite Supreme Court rulings that have upheld marriage as a fundamental right under the U.S. Constitution.* Under these rulings, supporters contend, depriving same-sex couples of the right to marry violates the basic concept of liberty. Others argue that same-sex marriage will provide the same sort of benefits to the community—having stable, caring families and children with two parents—as does heterosexual marriage.

Opponents of same-sex marriage feel equally strongly that such unions should be prohibited by law. They argue that allowing same-sex marriage will lessen the value of marriage and result in fewer heterosexual marriages. Furthermore, they argue that while heterosexual marriage furthers the state's legitimate interest in procreation, same-sex marriage does not and thus it need not be sanctioned by the state.

California was only the second state to allow same-sex marriage. In November 2003, the Massachusetts Supreme Court held that the state constitution's guarantees of equality and due process were violated by a ban on same-sex marriage. In 2008, Connecticut's Supreme Court invalidated that state's civil union law to become the third state to legalize same-sex marriage. Iowa followed suit in 2009 and in the same year, Vermont became the first state to legalize same-sex marriage through the legislative process. New Hampshire and the District of Columbia did the same later in 2009. New York followed suit two years later, and in the 2012 election, voters in Maryland, Maine, and Washington approved same-sex marriage in their states. In other states and localities, propositions and constitutional amendments providing for same-sex civil unions or barring any legal recognition of same-sex unions have been strongly debated.

What do you think? Should marriage be limited to heterosexual couples? What are the arguments for or against it?

Thinking It Through

The rights of homosexuals in the United States have never received the heightened protection against discrimination applied to classifications made on the basis of race or sex. The Supreme Court has ruled that government needs only a reasonable basis for legislating in order to permissibly classify individuals based on sexual orientation. Traditionally, legislation meant to uphold basic values and morals would pass such a test, and those opposed to same-sex marriage contend that it endangers the traditional notion of marriage and the value of the family unit. However, the Court, in *Romer* v. *Evans* (1996), struck down a Colorado constitutional amendment that made a distinction based on sexual orientation by ruling that it did not pass the test of rationality or reasonableness.

Opponents of same-sex marriage also object to state supreme courts' rulings as examples of judicial activism, with courts overturning votes in legislatures and referendums. Many opponents of state court decisions argue that same-sex marriage is not an issue for the courts to decide; instead, they contend, it should be decided through the democratic process. But as state legislatures legalize same-sex marriage, this argument is less credible.

Echoing arguments heard in the civil rights era, many who favor the right of same-sex couples to marry say that just as laws barring interracial marriage violated the U.S. Constitution's Fourteenth Amendment equal protection clause (in *Loving* v. *Virginia*, 1967), so do laws barring same-sex marriage. Supporters argue that once states provide an opportunity for legal recognition of marriage, they must do so equally. Although civil unions, an option provided for in five states (New Jersey, Illinois, Rhode Island, Delaware, and Hawaii), and broad domestic partnerships, allowed in another four states, typically offer many of the benefits afforded to married couples, they do not provide the equal recognition and legal rights of marriage.

CRITICAL THINKING QUESTIONS

1. Why are state courts such an important part of the debate on same-sex marriage?
2. Why is the issue of same-sex marriage so hotly debated? What makes this issue such a difficult one?
3. When voters and courts disagree over a topic such as same-sex marriage, who should prevail?

*_Loving_ v. _Virginia_, 388 U.S. 1 (1967); and _Zablocki_ v. _Redhail_, 434 U.S. 374 (1978).

FUNDAMENTAL RIGHTS AND STRICT SCRUTINY The Court also strictly scrutinizes laws impinging on *fundamental rights.* What makes a right fundamental in the constitutional sense? It is not the importance or the significance of the right but whether it is explicitly or implicitly *guaranteed by the Constitution.* Under this test, the rights to travel and to vote have been held to be fundamental. Rights to education, to housing, or to welfare benefits have not been deemed fundamental. Important as they may be, no constitutional provisions specifically protect them from governmental regulation.

As mentioned previously, the Constitution and particularly the Fourteenth Amendment's equal protection clause is only one of the legal bases for civil rights protections in the United States. Although we often think of court decisions when we think of the civil rights movement, many of the courts' rulings that upheld the civil rights of racial minorities and women were based on congressional legislation. Two pieces of legislation were particularly important to the civil rights movement: the Voting Rights Act of 1965 and the Civil Rights Act of 1964. We turn to these next.

literacy test
A literacy requirement some states imposed as a condition of voting, generally used to disqualify black voters in the South; now illegal.

white primary
A Democratic Party primary in the old "one-party South" that was limited to white people and essentially constituted an election; ruled unconstitutional in *Smith* v. *Allwright* (1944).

Voting Rights

15.4 Trace the evolution of voting rights and analyze the protections provided by the 1965 Voting Rights Act.

Under our Constitution, the states, not the federal government, regulate elections and voting qualifications. However, Article I, Section 4, gives Congress the power to supersede state regulations as to the "Times, Places, and Manner" of elections for representatives and senators. Congress has used this authority, along with its authority under Article II, Section 2, to set the date for selecting electors, to set age qualifications and residency requirements to vote in national elections, to establish a uniform day for all states to hold elections for members of Congress and presidential electors, and to give citizens who live outside the United States the right to vote for members of Congress and presidential electors in the states in which they are legal residents.

In spite of these protections, officials seeking to deny African Americans the right to vote enacted poll taxes, required literacy tests, developed biased registration requirements and even turned to intimidation and violence. Reports of violence and intimidation against black voters were frighteningly prevalent. One representative from Alabama described the efforts to deprive blacks of the right to vote this way: "At first, we used to kill them to keep them from voting; when we got sick of doing that, we began to steal their ballots; and when stealing their ballots got to troubling our consciences, we decided to handle the matter legally, fixing it so they couldn't vote."[52]

In many southern areas, **literacy tests** were used to discriminate against African Americans and poor whites. Although poor white people often avoided registering out of fear of embarrassment from failing a literacy test, the tests were more often used to discriminate against African Americans.[53] White people were often asked simple questions; black people were asked questions that would baffle the college educated. "In the 1960s, southern registrars were observed testing black applicants on such matters as the number of bubbles in a soap bar, the news contained in a copy of the Peking Daily, the meaning of obscure passages in state constitutions, and the definition of terms such as habeas corpus."[54] In Louisiana, 49,603 illiterate white voters were able to persuade election officials that they could understand the Constitution, but only two illiterate black voters were able to do so.

Local officials were also able to keep black voters from participating through the use of the **white primary**. In the one-party South of the early twentieth century, the Democratic Party would hold whites-only primaries, effectively disenfranchising black voters because, in the absence of viable Republican candidates, the winner of the Democratic primary was guaranteed to win the general election.

15.1

15.2

15.3

15.4

15.5

15.6

15.7

BY the People Making a Difference

Protecting Student Voting Rights

Concern over student voting rights dates back to the 1940s and 1950s, when some states such as Kentucky and Georgia granted voting rights to 18-year-olds.* The Twenty-Sixth Amendment, which was ratified in 1971, grants all 18- to 21-year-old citizens the right to vote. There was substantial interest in increasing turnout among young voters in the 2012 presidential election, and much of this effort was focused on college students. Throughout the United States, college students were urged to register to vote, and many sought to do so from their college campuses.

However, some states have strict residency and identification requirements that make it difficult for students to vote. Leading up to the 2008 election, congressional hearings were held to investigate reports that college students had been told they could not vote in the state in which they were attending college if their parents had claimed them as a dependent in another state.† Other reports included a local election official misleading students that registering to vote in their college town might result in losing their residency-based scholarships.‡

What efforts are made to encourage student voter registration on your college campus? In 2012 The Fair Elections Legal Network launched the Campus Vote Project to work with students, college administrators and local election officials to overcome barriers that make it more difficult for college students to vote.§ Is the Campus Vote Project active on your campus? Check your school's Web site and find out what you need to do to vote in the next election and help to protect students' voting rights. If you have more time, you might even become involved in the Campus Vote Project or a student voting registration campaign. Rock the Vote has volunteer Street Teams and Student Public Interest Research Groups (PIRGs) organize efforts to encourage student voting throughout the United States. You could get involved in PIRG's New Voters Project** or start up a group of your own.

QUESTIONS

1. **Why might some local political leaders prefer it if college students did not vote in their local elections?**
2. **Why might you prefer to vote where you go to college instead of in your hometown?**
3. **Should voting rights be extended to 16-year-olds? Why or why not?**

*Thomas H. Heale, "The Eighteen-Year-Old Vote: The Twenty-Sixth Amendment and Subsequent Voting Rates of Newly Enfranchised Age Groups" *Congressional Research Service,* May 20, 1983.

†"Members of Congress Worry That Students Are Being Misled About Voting Rights," *Chronicle of Higher Education,* September 24, 2008.

‡Nikki Schwab, "Confusing Voter Registration Laws Could Affect Presidential Election," *US News and World Report,* September 24, 2008.

§http://www.campusvoteproject.org/.

**http://www.studentpirgs.org/campaigns/sp/new-voters-project.

racial gerrymandering
Drawing election districts so as to ensure that members of a certain race are a minority in the district; ruled unconstitutional in *Gomillion* v. *Lightfoot* (1960).

poll tax
Tax required to vote; prohibited for national elections by the Twenty-Fourth Amendment (1964) and ruled unconstitutional for all elections in *Harper* v. *Board of Elections* (1966).

☐ Protecting Voting Rights

After years of refusing to overturn racially discriminatory voting requirements, the Supreme Court in the 1940s began to strike down one after another of the devices that states and localities had used to keep African Americans from voting. In *Smith* v. *Allwright* (1944), the Court declared the white primary unconstitutional.[55] Later, it struck down other methods. In 1960, the Court held that **racial gerrymandering**—drawing election districts to ensure that African Americans would be a minority in all districts—was contrary to the Fifteenth Amendment.[56] In 1964, the Twenty-Fourth Amendment eliminated the **poll tax**—payment required as a condition for voting—in presidential and congressional elections. In 1966, the Court held that the Fourteenth Amendment forbade the poll tax as a condition in any election.[57]

☐ The Voting Rights Act of 1965

For two decades after World War II, under the leadership of the Supreme Court, many limitations on voting were declared unconstitutional, but as has often been the case, the Court acting alone was unable to open the voting booth to African Americans. Finally, Congress acted in passing the Voting Rights Act of 1965. It was renewed in 1982, and in 2006 it was extended for another 25 years.

The Voting Rights Act prohibits voting qualifications or standards that result in a denial of the right of any citizen to vote on account of race or color. The law also bars any form of threats or intimidation aimed at preventing citizens from voting. Under the Act, the Department of Justice must also review changes in voting practices or laws that may

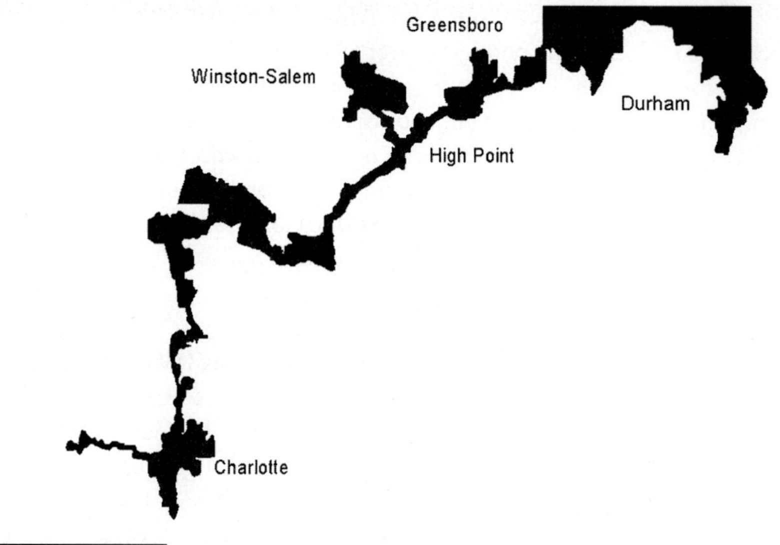

North Carolina's challenged "I-85 district" stretched more than 160 miles through the central region of the state.

majority–minority district
A congressional district created to include a majority of minority voters; ruled constitutional so long as race is not the main factor in redistricting.

Jim Crow laws
State laws formerly pervasive throughout the South requiring public facilities and accommodations to be segregated by race; ruled unconstitutional.

dilute the voting power of these groups,[58] such as changes in candidacy requirements and qualifications or boundary lines of voting districts.[59] The requirement that states obtain Justice Department clearance was recently challenged in the federal courts; in June 2009, the U.S. Supreme Court upheld the requirement.[60] But, in 2012, no fewer than five new lawsuits were filed in the federal courts to overturn the pre-clearance provision of the Act.[61]

In a series of cases beginning with *Shaw* v. *Reno* (1993), the Supreme Court announced that state legislatures could consider race when they drew electoral districts to increase the voting strength of minorities. However, the Court ruled that states could not make race the sole or predominant reason for drawing district lines. A test case examined the North Carolina legislature's creation of a **majority–minority district** that was 160 miles long and in some places only an interstate highway wide. The Supreme Court ruled that it was wrong to force states to create as many majority-minority districts as possible. To comply with the Voting Rights Act, the Court explained, states must provide for districts roughly proportional to the minority voters' respective shares in the voting-age population.[62]

Rights to Equal Access: Accommodations, Jobs, and Homes

15.5 Describe congressional legislation against discrimination in housing, employment, and accommodations.

In 1883, the Supreme Court declared unconstitutional an act of Congress that made it a federal offense for any operator of a public conveyance (such as a train or bus), hotel, or theater to deny accommodations to any person because of race or color, on the grounds that the Fourteenth Amendment does not give Congress such authority.[63] Until the Supreme Court finally moved to strike down such laws in the 1950s, southern states had made it illegal for white and black people to ride in the same train cars, attend the same theaters, go to the same schools, be born in the same hospitals, drink from the same water fountains, or be buried in the same cemeteries. **Jim Crow laws**, as they came to be called, blanketed southern life.

The Court reinforced legalized segregation under the Fourteenth Amendment's equal protection clause in *Plessy* v. *Ferguson* (1896). In *Plessy*, the Supreme Court endorsed the view that government-imposed racial segregation in public transportation, and presumably in public education, did not necessarily constitute discrimination if "equal" accommodations were provided for the members of both races.[64] But the

15.1

15.2

15.3

15.4

15.5

15.6

15.7

commerce clause
The clause of the Constitution (Article I, Section 8, Clause 3) that gives Congress the power to regulate all business activities that cross state lines or affect more than one state or other nations.

"equal" part of the formula was meaningless. African Americans were segregated in unequal facilities and lacked the political power to protest effectively.

Beginning in the 1960s, Congress began to act to prevent such segregation. Its constitutional authority to legislate against discrimination by private individuals is no longer an issue because the Court has broadly construed the **commerce clause**—which gives Congress the power to regulate interstate and foreign commerce—to justify action against discriminatory conduct by individuals. Congress has also used its power to tax and spend to prevent not only racial discrimination but also discrimination based on ethnic origin, sex, disability, and age.

CIVIL RIGHTS ACT OF 1964 AND PLACES OF PUBLIC ACCOMMODATION The key step in establishing rights of equal access was the Civil Rights Act of 1964. Title II of the Act makes it a federal offense to discriminate against any customer or patron in a place of public accommodation because of race, color, religion, or national origin. It applies to any inn, hotel, motel, or lodging establishment (except those with fewer than five rooms and where the proprietor also lives—in other words, small boardinghouses); to any restaurant or gasoline station that serves interstate travelers or sells food or products that are moved in interstate commerce; and to any movie house, theater, concert hall, sports arena, or other place of entertainment that customarily hosts films, performances, athletic teams, or other sources of entertainment that are moved in interstate commerce. Within a few months after its adoption, the Supreme

FOR the People Government's Greatest Endeavors

Reducing Workplace Discrimination

The United States has one of the most diverse workforces in the world. As diversity has grown, so have calls for protection against workplace discrimination. Many of these calls have been answered by the federal judiciary, where women, older Americans, and the disabled have won a series of victories ensuring their basic rights. But the courts did not act alone. These victories also involved congressional action through the 1964 Civil Rights Act, the 1967 Age Discrimination Act, and the 1990 Americans with Disabilities Act. Together, these three acts have created protections that have made reducing workplace discrimination one of the federal government's greatest achievements.

A worker at Delaware's Industries for the Blind sewing scarves for the U.S. military.

The 1964 Civil Rights Act was particularly important for guaranteeing equal rights for women. Under the original bill, women were not included in the law. Ironically, it was a conservative Democrat who added the word "sex" to the prohibition against discrimination on the basis of "race, color, religion, or national origin" in the Act. He did so in the belief that Congress would not pass a bill guaranteeing equality of the sexes. However, the bill did pass, and women had the legislation that would provide the opportunity to take employers to court for sex discrimination.

Disabled Americans won similar protection under the 1990 Americans with Disabilities Act. Senator Bob Dole (R-KS), who had lost the use of his right arm in World War II, led the fight for passage. In addition to providing protection from discrimination, this Act also mandates that all public buildings and transportation be handicap accessible.

QUESTIONS

1. Are there other forms of workplace discrimination that should be protected but currently are not?
2. Might some victims of workplace discrimination be hesitant to bring a suit against their employers?
3. Sexual orientation is not listed in the Civil Rights Act. Should it be illegal to discriminate on the basis of sexual orientation?

Court sustained the constitutionality of Title II.[65] As a result, public establishments, including those in the South, opened their doors to all customers.

class action suit
A lawsuit brought by an individual or a group of people on behalf of all those similarly situated.

restrictive covenant
A provision in a deed to real property prohibiting its sale to a person of a particular race or religion. Judicial enforcement of such deeds is unconstitutional.

15.1

15.2

15.3

15.4

15.5

15.6

15.7

CIVIL RIGHTS ACT OF 1964 AND EMPLOYMENT In addition to dealing with equal access in public accommodations, the Civil Rights Act also barred discrimination in employment. Title VII of the 1964 Act made it illegal for any employer or trade union in any industry affecting interstate commerce and employing 15 or more people (and, since 1972, any state or local agency such as a school or university) to discriminate in employment practices against any person because of race, color, national origin, religion, or sex. Employers must create workplaces that avoid abusive environments. Related legislation made it illegal to discriminate against persons with physical handicaps, veterans, or persons over the age of 40.

There are a few exceptions. Religious institutions such as parochial schools may use religious standards. Employers may take into account the age, sex, or handicap of prospective employees when occupational qualifications are absolutely necessary to the normal operation of a particular business or enterprise—for example, hiring only women to work in women's locker rooms.

The Equal Employment Opportunity Commission (EEOC) was created under the Act to enforce Title VII. The commission works together with state authorities to try to ensure compliance with the Act and may seek judicial enforcement of complaints against private employers. The attorney general prosecutes Title VII violations by public agencies. Not only can aggrieved persons sue for damages for themselves, but they can also sue for other persons similarly situated in a **class action suit**. The courts decide whether the persons in the class are similar enough that they may appropriately file a class action claim. For example, in 2011, the Supreme Court ruled a class action lawsuit alleging sex discrimination against Wal-Mart could not go forward because the plaintiffs had not established that their cases were similar enough to proceed as a single class.[66] However, in October 2011, the plaintiffs again filed suit against Wal-Mart, but in direct response to the Supreme Court's concerns, they limited their claim to the chain's California stores.[67] The vigor with which the EEOC and the attorney general have acted has varied throughout the years, depending on the commitment of the president and the willingness of Congress to provide an adequate budget for the EEOC.[68]

THE FAIR HOUSING ACT AND AMENDMENTS Housing is the last frontier of the civil rights crusade, the area in which progress is slowest and genuine change most remote. Even after legal restrictions on segregated housing have been removed, housing patterns continue to be segregated. The degree to which housing also affects segregation in employment and the public schools makes it a particularly important issue. In 1948, the Supreme Court made racial or religious **restrictive covenants** (a provision in a deed to real property that restricts to whom it can be sold) legally unenforceable.[69] The 1968 Fair Housing Act forbids discrimination in housing, with a few exceptions similar to those mentioned in public accommodations. Owners may not refuse to sell or rent to any person because of race, color, religion, national origin, sex, or physical handicap or because a person has children. Discrimination in housing also covers efforts to deny mortgage loans to minorities. In addition to the federal prohibitions on discrimination, 21 states also have laws that bar discrimination in housing based on sexual orientation.[70]

The Department of Justice has filed hundreds of cases, especially against large apartment complexes, yet African Americans and Hispanics still face discrimination in housing. Some real estate agents steer African Americans and Hispanics toward neighborhoods that are not predominantly white and require minority renters to pay larger deposits than white renters. Yet victims complain about less than 1 percent of these actions because discrimination is so subtle that they are often unaware they are being discriminated against. However, more aggressive enforcement has increased the number of discrimination complaints the Department of Housing and Urban Development and local and state agencies receive.

Education Rights

15.6 Evaluate the historical process of school integration and the current state of affirmative action.

Since the Court's decision in *Plessy,* segregated public as well as private facilities had become the norm. Separate public schools, buses, and bathrooms were commonplace. However, in the late 1930s, African Americans started to file lawsuits challenging *Plessy*'s "separate but equal" doctrine. The National Association for the Advancement of Colored People's (NAACP) Legal Defense Fund (LDF) was active in challenging segregated educational facilities. The LDF cited facts to show that in practice separate was anything but equal and generally resulted in discrimination against African Americans.

Initially, the LDF showed that so-called equal facilities were in fact not equal, or simply not provided. Many of their early successes addressed inequality in higher education. States were forced to either provide separate graduate and law schools for African American students, or integrate those they already had. A major success that laid the groundwork for the LDF's challenge in public secondary and elementary schools came when the Court ruled that, not only did segregated facilities themselves have to be equal, but they also had to provide the same quality of benefits to black students as their white counterparts.[71]

☐ The End of "Separate but Equal": *Brown* v. *Board of Education*

Once the LDF had adequately established that segregated facilities were far from equal, it challenged the *Plessy* doctrine of "separate but equal" head on. And, in *Brown* v. *Board of Education of Topeka* (1954), the Court finally agreed, ruling that "separate but equal" is a contradiction in terms. *Segregation is itself discrimination.*[72]

The question before the Court in *Brown* was whether separate public schools for black and white students violated the Fourteenth Amendment's equal protection clause. Relying heavily on arguments addressing the harm to all schoolchildren, black and white, caused by racial segregation, the Court struck down segregation in the public schools and, in so doing, overturned *Plessy* v. *Ferguson* (1896). A year later, the Court ordered school boards to proceed with "all deliberate speed to desegregate public schools at the earliest practical date."[73]

But many school districts moved slowly or not at all, and in the 1960s, Congress and the president joined even more directly to fight school segregation. Title VI of the Civil Rights Act of 1964, as subsequently amended, stipulated that federal dollars under any grant program or project must be withdrawn from an entire school or institution of higher education (including private schools) that discriminates "on the ground of race, color, or national origin," sex, age, or disability, in "any program or activity receiving federal financial assistance."

☐ From Segregation to Desegregation—But Not yet Integration

School districts that had operated separate schools for white children and black children now had to develop plans and programs to move from segregation to integration. Schools failing to do so were placed under court supervision to ensure that they were doing what was necessary and proper to overcome the evils of segregation. Simply doing away with laws mandating segregation would not be enough; school districts needed to actively integrate their schools.

But because most white people and most African Americans continued to live in separate neighborhoods, merely removing legal barriers to school integration did not by itself integrate the schools. To overcome this residential clustering by race, some

Thurgood Marshall (center), George C. E. Hayes (left), and James Nabrit Jr. (right) argued and won *Brown* v. *Board of Education of Topeka* before the Supreme Court in 1954.

federal courts mandated busing across neighborhoods, moving white students to once predominantly black schools and vice versa.[74] Busing students was unpopular and triggered protests in many cities.

The Supreme Court sustained busing only if it was undertaken to remedy the consequences of *officially* sanctioned segregation, **de jure segregation.** The Court refused to permit federal judges to order busing to overcome the effects of **de facto segregation**, segregation that arises as a result of social and economic conditions such as housing patterns.

de jure segregation
Segregation imposed by law.

de facto segregation
Segregation resulting from economic or social conditions or personal choice.

After a period of vigorous federal court supervision of school desegregation programs, the Supreme Court in the 1990s restricted the role of federal judges.[75] It instructed some of them to restore control of a school system to the state and local authorities and to release districts from any busing obligations once a judge concludes that the authorities "have done everything practicable to overcome the past consequences of segregation."[76]

Political support for busing and for other efforts to integrate the schools also faded.[77] Many school districts eliminated mandatory busing, with the result that *Brown*'s era of court-ordered desegregation drew to a close. As a result, the percentage of southern black students attending white-majority schools fell from a high of 44 percent in 1988 to 30 percent in 2001, or approximately the same level it had been in 1969.[78] In the wake of such resegregation, some school districts have attempted to increase integration through race-conscious school assignment plans. However, in 2007, the Supreme Court ruled that such plans in Seattle, Washington, and Louisville, Kentucky, violated the Fourteenth Amendment's Equal Protection Clause.[79] Another method some schools have pursued, which is presumably constitutional based on court decisions, is integration based on socioeconomic factors rather than race.[80]

□ The Affirmative Action Controversy

When white majorities were using government power to discriminate against African Americans, civil rights advocates cited with approval the famous words of Justice John Marshall Harlan when he dissented from the *Plessy* decision: "Our Constitution is color-blind and neither knows nor tolerates class among citizens."[81] But by the 1960s, a new set of constitutional and national policy debates raged. Many people began to assert that government neutrality is not enough. If governments, universities, and employers simply stopped discriminating but nothing else changed, individuals previously discriminated against would still be kept from equal participation in U.S. life. Furthermore, when barriers to equality in education and employment advancement exist, we all suffer from a lack of diversity in society. Because discrimination had so disadvantaged some people and groups, they suffered disabilities that white males did not share in competing for openings in medical schools, for skilled jobs, or for their share of government grants and contracts.

Supporters call remedies to overcome the consequences of discrimination against African Americans, Hispanics, Native Americans, and women *affirmative action;* opponents call these efforts *reverse discrimination.* The Supreme Court's first major statement on the constitutionality of these programs came in a celebrated case relating to university admissions. Allan Bakke—a white male, a top student at the University of Minnesota and at Stanford, and a Vietnam War veteran—applied in 1973 and again in 1974 to the medical school of the University of California at Davis. In each of those years, the school admitted 100 new students, 84 in a general admissions program and 16 in a special admissions program created for minorities who had previously been underrepresented. Bakke was rejected in both years, while applicants with lower grade-point averages, test scores, and interview ratings were admitted through the special admissions program. Bakke brought suit in federal court, claiming he had been excluded because of his race, contrary to requirements of the Constitution and Title VI of the Civil Rights Act of 1964.

In *University of California Regents* v. *Bakke* (1978), the Supreme Court ruled the California plan unconstitutional[82] because it created a *quota*—a set number of admissions from which whites were excluded solely because of race. But the Court also declared that affirmative action programs are not necessarily unconstitutional. A state university may properly take race and ethnic background into account as "a plus," as one of several factors in choosing students, because of its compelling interest in achieving a diverse student body.

☐ Reaffirming the Importance of Diversity

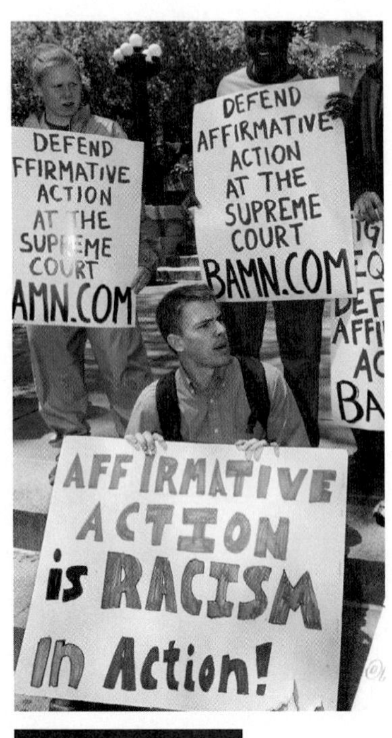

Americans debate whether affirmative action is the best way to address the issue of past racial and ethnic quotas.

For many years following the *Bakke* decision, the Court refused to hear challenges to affirmative action in higher education, despite conflicting lower-court decisions leading to uncertainty about how colleges and universities could pursue diverse student bodies. But, in 2003 the Supreme Court reaffirmed *Bakke* in two cases that challenged the admission policies for undergraduates and law students at the University of Michigan. Both policies sought to achieve diverse student bodies but in different ways.

The University of Michigan's undergraduate admissions program was based on a 150-point "selection index" that ranked applicants' test scores and grades for up to 100 points and allocated 40 points for other factors, including 4 points for children of alumni, 16 points for residents of rural areas, and 20 points for students from underrepresented minority groups or socially and economically disadvantaged families. Jennifer Gratz, a white high school student with a 3.8 GPA who was denied admission, challenged the program.

In *Gratz* v. *Bollinger* (2003), the Court struck down the undergraduate policy as too mechanical and not narrowly tailored to give applicants "individualized consideration" as *Bakke* required.[83] However, a bare majority of the Court upheld the University's law school admissions program that was also challenged. In *Grutter* v. *Bollinger* (2003), the Court ruled that the law school made "special efforts" to achieve racial and ethnic diversity, but unlike the undergraduate program, it did not use a point system based in part on race.[84] Writing for the Court, Justice O'Connor held that law school admissions were based on a "highly individualized, holistic review of each applicant's file" and did not use race as a factor in a "mechanical way." For that reason, it was consistent with *Bakke*'s holding that race may be used as a "plus factor" to achieve a diverse student body.

Although the Court further clarified the requirements to render an affirmative action program permissible, its ruling did not end the debate. The Court does not always have the final word on such questions. Motivated groups have spurred consideration of affirmative action programs at the polls, and several states have abolished affirmative action. Michigan is one example. In the aftermath of the Court's ruling in *Gratz* and *Grutter*, Jennifer Gratz formed the Michigan Civil Rights Initiative to place on the state's 2006 election ballot an initiative banning affirmative action in public colleges and government contracting. The initiative won approval with 58 percent of the vote.[85] In addition to effectively nullifying the Supreme Court's decision as it applied to the University of Michigan, the initiative's success also highlights a motivated group of citizens' success in mobilizing the electorate. But supporters of the ban on affirmative action are not the only citizens who have mobilized on the issue. A different coalition challenged the Michigan ban in federal court, and in July 2011, the U.S. Court of Appeals for the Sixth Circuit struck it down as "impermissibly burdening racial minorities."[86]

State policies and court rulings on the use of affirmative action in university admissions are in a state of flux. There are a number of affirmative action lawsuits making their way through the federal courts and, as discussed at the beginning of the chapter, the Supreme Court has agreed to hear *Fisher* v. *Texas* during its October 2012 term. Although the Court speculated in its 2003 decisions that affirmative action would not be necessary to achieve racial diversity in universities 25 years down the road, the fact that the Court is revisiting the issue fewer than 10 years later seems to indicate that change may be looming in its jurisprudence.

Equal Rights Today

15.7 Assess the status of civil rights in the United States today.

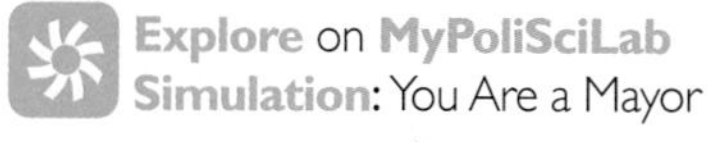
Explore on MyPoliSciLab Simulation: You Are a Mayor

Today, civil rights legislation, executive orders, and judicial decisions have lowered, if not fully removed, legal barriers to full and equal participation in society. Important as these victories are, according to civil rights leader James Farmer, "They were victories largely for the middle class—those who could travel, entertain in restaurants, and stay in hotels. Those victories did not change life conditions for the mass of blacks who are still poor."[87]

Although court rulings and legislation prohibit legal segregation, segregation by race in housing and education persist in the United States. Since 1980, segregation for blacks has slowly declined, but has risen among Hispanics and Asians. A 2011 study found that income alone does not explain this segregation. Indeed, affluent African Americans and Hispanics tend to live in poorer neighborhoods than do low-income whites.[88] Furthermore, the wealth gap between whites and minorities hit an all-time high in 2009 when the median net worth of a white family was 20 times that of a black family and 18 times that of a Hispanic family, the highest disparity since the data was first collected in 1984.[89]

Some contend that we should pay more attention to this economic inequality, and that instead of focusing on issues of race, we need to focus on class differences and support policies that provide jobs and improve education.[90] Others say there has to be a revival of the civil rights crusade, a restoration of vigorous civil rights enforcement, more jobs training, and, above all, an attack on residential segregation.[91] In any event, questions about how best to provide equal opportunities for all citizens remain high on the national agenda.

One of the many important lessons of the civil rights movement is that individuals can affect our government process. Without people like Rosa Parks, one woman sitting on a bus who refused to give up her seat, or Abigail Fisher, who fought for admission to the University of Texas without consideration of her race, we would not

15.1
15.2
15.3
15.4
15.5
15.6
15.7

OF the People Diversity in America

Affirmative Action and Minority Student Enrollment

Affirmative action plans are highly controversial. Some argue that they are essential for ensuring a diverse educational environment, improving all students' learning opportunities. Others argue that such plans are discriminatory and thus impermissible. Despite that controversy, most agree that student enrollment would look significantly different if the U.S. Supreme Court were to end affirmative action in college admissions.*

Levels of minority student enrollment at the University of Texas between 1996 and 2009 provide a snapshot of minority enrollment under different admission plans. Prior to the Fifth Circuit Court of Appeals' decision in *Hopwood* (1996), the University used race as a factor in its admissions program. However, in the years after that decision until the U.S. Supreme Court's decision in *Grutter* v. *Bollinger* (2003), the University operated under a race-neutral policy, the Top Ten Percent program described at the beginning of the chapter. With the Supreme Court's decision that it was permissible to consider race as *a* factor in admissions *(Grutter)*, the University altered its policy once again to include affirmative action while keeping the Ten Percent Plan.

The figure below‡ illustrates the decline in minority student enrollment in the wake of *Hopwood*, and the fluctuations before and after *Grutter*. Although these statistics pertain to Texas in particular, there is evidence of similar patterns more broadly. For example, recent research examining the implications of banning affirmative action at the top 50 public universities (as rated by *U.S. News and World Report*) suggests that subject to such a ban, enrollment among African American students would drop by 1.74 percentage points and Hispanic student enrollment would drop 2.03 percentage points. These declines may seem small, but relative to the current overall percentages of African American and Hispanic students at these universities (5.79% and 7.38%, respectively) they amount to a significant decline in minority student enrollment.†

QUESTIONS

1. How is the Top Ten Percent Plan implemented in Texas race neutral?
2. Are the declines in the University of Texas' minority student enrollment in the wake of *Hopwood* significant?
3. Should it be permissible to distinguish between applicants based on race?

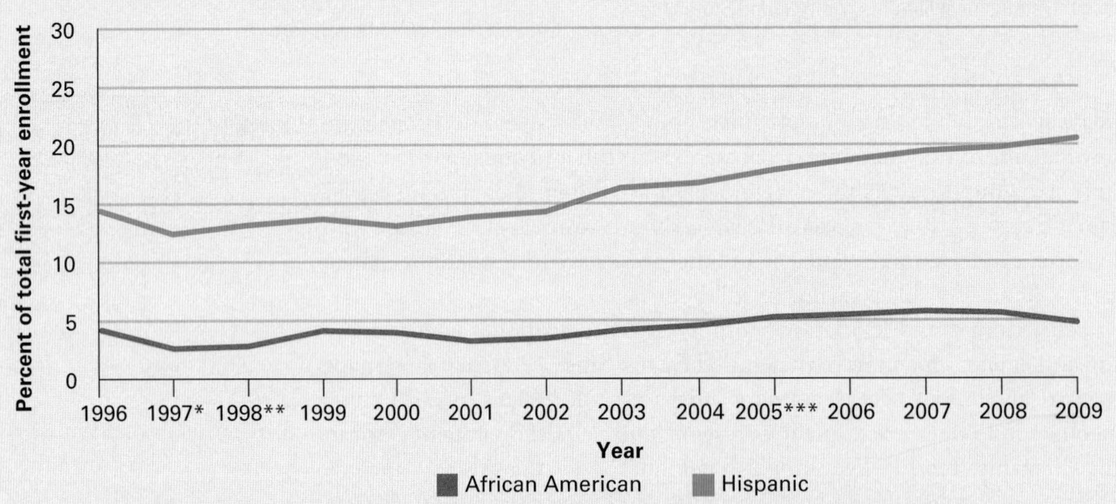

*1997 was the first year in which the *Hopwood* decision was applied to the admissions process.
**Beginning in 1998, the Texas legislature mandated the Top Ten Percent plan.
***2005 was the first year in which affirmative action was reinstated (following *Grutter*)

**Fisher* v. *University of Texas at Austin,* 631 F.3d. 213 (5th Cir. 2011).

†Peter Henrichs, "The Effect of Affirmative Action Bans on College Enrollment, Educational Attainment, and the Demographic Composition of Universities," Forthcoming *Review of Economics and Statistics.*

‡University of Texas at Austin, Office of Admissions, *2007 Top Ten Percent Report;* of *2011 Top Ten Percent Report.*

have experienced the monumental changes in our country's protection of all citizens' rights that we have seen during the last 100 years. By participating in our democratic system and challenging the status quo, we each play a part in promoting equal rights for all citizens.

Review the Chapter

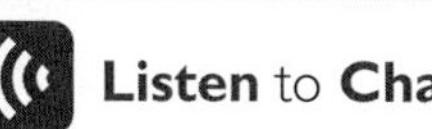

Listen to Chapter 15 on MyPoliSciLab

Equality and Equal Rights

15.1 Explain the concept of equality and assess the rights of citizens, p. 475.

Although there is no single agreed-upon definition of equality in the United States, there is general consensus that everyone should have an equal opportunity to succeed. The Constitution protects the acquisition and retention of citizenship. It protects the basic liberties of citizens as well as aliens, although in times of war, foreign terrorists may be detained and tried without the rights accorded to citizens and other aliens.

The Quest for Equal Justice

15.2 Compare and contrast the efforts of various groups to obtain equal protection of the law, p. 479.

Although African Americans' rights were finally recognized under the Thirteenth, Fourteenth, and Fifteenth Amendments, the government failed to act to prevent racial discrimination for nearly a century thereafter. The women's rights movement was born partly out of the struggle to abolish slavery, and the women's movement learned and gained power from the civil rights movements of the 1950s and early 1960s. Concern for equal rights under the law continues today for African Americans and women as well as other groups, including Hispanics, Asian Americans, and Native Americans.

Equal Protection of the Laws: What Does It Mean?

15.3 Analyze the Supreme Court's three-tiered approach used to evaluate discriminatory laws, p. 487.

The Supreme Court uses a three-tiered approach to evaluate the constitutionality of laws that may violate the equal protection clause. The Court upholds most laws if they simply help accomplish a legitimate government goal. It sustains laws that classify people based on sex only if they serve important government objectives. It subjects laws that touch fundamental rights or classify people because of race or ethnic origin to strict scrutiny and sustains them only if the government can show that they serve a compelling public purpose.

Voting Rights

15.4 Trace the evolution of voting rights and analyze the protections provided by the 1965 Voting Rights Act, p. 491.

A series of constitutional amendments, Supreme Court decisions, and laws passed by Congress have now secured the right to vote to all citizens age 18 and older. As a result of the Voting Rights Act of 1965, the Justice Department oversees practices in locales with a history of discrimination. Recent Supreme Court decisions have refined the lengths to which legislatures can go, or are obliged to go, in creating majority–minority districts.

Rights to Equal Access: Accommodations, Jobs, and Homes

15.5 Describe congressional legislation against discrimination in housing, employment, and accommodations, p. 493.

By its authority under the interstate commerce clause (Article 1, Section 8), Congress has passed important legislation barring discrimination in housing and accommodations. The Civil Rights Act of 1964 outlawed discrimination in public accommodations. This Act also provided for equal employment opportunity. The Fair Housing Act of 1968 and its 1988 amendments prohibited discrimination in housing.

Education Rights

15.6 Evaluate the historical process of school integration and the current state of affirmative action, p. 496.

Brown v. *Board of Education of Topeka* (1954) struck down the "separate but equal" doctrine that had justified segregated schools, but school districts responded slowly. Full integration has proven elusive, as housing patterns and schools continue to be segregated. Affirmative action programs remain controversial and subject to judicial scrutiny. After upholding the University of Michigan Law School's consideration of race in the admission process (2003), the Supreme Court struck down race-conscious school assignment plans in Seattle and Louisville (2007). Programs that individualize assessment of applicants are more likely to pass constitutional muster.

Equal Rights Today

15.7 Assess the status of civil rights in the United States today, p. 499.

Legal barriers to full and equal participation in American society have been largely eliminated. However, the fight to protect civil rights of women and minority groups continues. Some argue that in continuing to meet the challenges of inequality, we should focus on economic integration, job training, and better education opportunities.

Learn the Terms

 **Study** and **Review** the **Flashcards**

civil rights, p. 475
natural rights, p. 475
affirmative action, p. 476
naturalization, p. 476
dual citizenship, p. 476
right of expatriation, p. 476
women's suffrage, p. 482
equal protection clause, p. 487
due process clause, p. 487
rational basis test, p. 487
strict scrutiny test, p. 487
heightened scrutiny test, p. 488
literacy test, p. 491
white primary, p. 491
racial gerrymandering, p. 492
poll tax, p. 492
majority–minority district, p. 493
Jim Crow laws, p. 493
commerce clause, p. 494
class action suit, p. 495
restrictive covenant, p. 495
de jure segregation, p. 497
de facto segregation, p. 497

Test Yourself

 **Study** and **Review** the **Practice Tests**

MULTIPLE CHOICE QUESTIONS

15.1 Explain the concept of equality and assess the rights of citizens.

Naturalization requires new citizens to do all the following *except*

a. be able to read, write, and speak English.
b. agree never to renounce their new citizenship.
c. understand and have an attachment to the history and principles of the government of the United States.
d. demonstrate they do not believe in, advocate, or belong to an organization that advocates violent overthrow of the government.
e. file a naturalization petition.

15.2 Compare and contrast the efforts of various groups to obtain equal protection of the law.

A major turning point in the civil rights movement occurred when

a. *Brown* v. *Board of Education* led to immediate integration of the public schools.
b. the Federal Civil Rights Act of 1957 ended the intimidation of African American voters.
c. Rosa Parks's refusal to give up her bus seat led to the Montgomery bus boycott.
d. the Fourteenth Amendment was ratified in 1868.
e. Reconstruction was implemented after the Civil War.

15.3 Analyze the Supreme Court's three-tiered approach used to evaluate discriminatory laws.

If the state of New York passed a law limiting the elected offices for which women were allowed to run, which of the following would the courts consider in deciding if the state's action was constitutional?

a. whether the reason for the law was legitimate and the legislation was aimed at achieving that goal
b. whether the state had a compelling reason for the law and met it in the least restrictive manner possible
c. whether the state had an important governmental interest and the law was substantially related to achieving that objective
d. whether the state had a rational reason for passing the legislation
e. whether the law was passed by a legislature that included both men and women

15.4 Trace the evolution of voting rights and analyze the protections provided by the 1965 Voting Rights Act.

Which of the following is *not* a provision of the Voting Rights Act?

a. Threats or intimidation in any form to prevent citizens from voting are barred.
b. The Justice Department must review changes in candidacy requirements and qualifications.
c. Voting criteria that result in a denial of the right to vote based on race or color are barred.
d. Political parties must make a "reasonable effort" to nominate minority candidates for public office.
e. The Justice Department must review changes in voting laws that may dilute the voting power of racial minority groups.

15.5 Describe congressional legislation against discrimination in housing, employment, and accommodations.

Which of the following is *not* prohibited by the Fair Housing Act?

a. A bank denies an African American man a mortgage because he has poor credit and no savings.
b. A landlord denies a woman an apartment because he is concerned that her two young children will bother the other tenants.
c. The owner of several apartment complexes charges handicapped tenants an extra $10 rent to help pay for the buildings' wheelchair lifts.
d. A real estate agent shows a Hispanic family mostly Hispanic neighborhoods because, she assumes, they are most likely to feel comfortable with people of their own race.
e. A landlord refuses to rent an apartment to a family because they are atheists.

15.6 Evaluate the historical process of school integration and the current state of affirmative action.

Which of the following has the Supreme Court found acceptable as a compelling state interest in using affirmative action in university admissions?

a. awarding university admissions to compensate for past discrimination
b. creating a diverse educational environment
c. reducing historical racial imbalance
d. improving economic opportunities for all students
e. obtaining an equal number of minority and nonminority students

15.7 Assess the status of civil rights in the United States today.

Rather than focusing on race, which of the following is a proposal some scholars make for addressing civil rights issues today and in the future?

a. focusing on socioeconomic integration
b. alleviating *de jure* segregation
c. mandating affirmative action in employment
d. integrating schools through the use of mandatory busing programs
e. using racial gerrymandering to increase minority representation

ESSAY QUESTION

When evaluating a claim of discrimination, the Supreme Court uses one of three approaches. Explain each of the approaches. Which is used when race is the basis of the alleged discrimination? Sex? Age? Sexual orientation? Is each of these applications appropriate for the type of discrimination? Why or why not?

Explore Further

IN THE LIBRARY

Raymond Arsenault, *Freedom Riders: 1961 and the Struggle for Racial Justice* (Oxford University Press, 2006).

Taylor Branch, *At Canaan's Edge: America in the King Years, 1965–1968* (Simon & Schuster, 2006).

Taylor Branch, *Parting the Waters: America in the King Years, 1954–1963* (Simon & Schuster, 1988).

Taylor Branch, *Pillar of Fire: America in the King Years, 1963–1965* (Simon & Schuster, 1998).

Gordon H. Chang, ed., *Asian Americans and Politics* (Stanford University Press, 2001).

Charles Clotfelter, *After Brown: The Rise and Retreat of School Desegregation* (Princeton University Press, 2004).

Clare Cushman, ed., *Supreme Court Decisions and Women's Rights* (CQ Press, 2000).

Arlene M. Davila, *Latinos, Inc.: The Marketing and Making of a People* (University of California Press, 2001).

William N. Eskridge Jr., *Gaylaw: Challenging the Apartheid of the Closet* (Harvard University Press, 2000).

Richard Kahlenberg, *All Together Now: Creating Middle-Class Schools Through Public School Choice* (Brookings Institution Press, 2001).

Michael J. Klarman, *From Jim Crow to Civil Rights: The Supreme Court and the Struggle for Racial Equality* (Oxford University Press, 2006).

Philip A. Klinker and Roger M. Smith, *The Unsteady March: The Rise and Decline of Racial Equality in America* (University of Chicago Press, 2000).

Peter Kwong and Dusanka Miscevic, *Chinese America: The Untold Story of America's Oldest New Community* (New Press, 2006).

Nancy McGlen, Karen O'Connor, Laura Van Assendelft, and Wendy Gunther-Canada, *Women, Politics, and American Society*, 5th ed. (Pearson, 2011).

Gary Orfield and Chungmei Lee, *Brown at 50: King's Dream or Plessy's Nightmare* (Civil Rights Project, Harvard University, 2004).

J. W. Peltason, *Fifty-Eight Lonely Men: Southern Federal Judges and School Desegregation* (University of Illinois Press, 1971).

Barbara Perry, *The Michigan Affirmative Action Cases* (University Press of Kansas, 2007).

Dan Pinello, *America's Struggle for Same-Sex Marriage* (Cambridge University Press, 2006).

Ruth Rosen, *The World Split Open: How the Modern Women's Movement Changed America* (Viking Press, 2000).

Susan F. Van Burkleo, *"Belonging to the World": Women's Rights and Constitutional Culture* (Oxford University Press, 2001).

ON THE WEB

www.brennancenter.org/studentvoting
This Web site for the Brennan Center for Justice, Student Voting Rights, contains state-by-state information on registration and voting requirements for students.

www.justice.gov/crt/
The Web site for the U.S. Department of Justice, Civil Rights Division; provides information on a variety of civil rights issues such as fair housing, hate crimes, and protecting voting rights.

www.uscis.gov
The U.S. Citizenship and Immigration Services Web site provides an opportunity to test yourself on questions that could appear on a citizenship test. Click on the link to the "Naturalization Test" and see how well you do.

Listen to Chapter 16 on MyPoliSciLab

16

Making Economic Policy

Economic policy is designed to keep the economy from either growing too fast, which usually increases prices, or too slowly, which usually increases unemployment. This effort to forge a steady economic climate often requires tough decisions between how much the federal government should spend, when to borrow more money to get the economy afloat, and where it should get its revenues.

Democrats and Republicans faced just these kinds of choices in 2012 as growth continued to sag across the economy and the national debt ballooned to $16 trillion. Democrats wanted more government spending to support the poor and stimulate the economy, while Republicans wanted tax cuts to free up money that consumers could spend for new products and services.

This debate was at the center of President Barack Obama's reelection campaign. Having been in office a full term after the great economic collapse of 2008, Obama repeatedly argued that the economy's troubles were caused by his predecessor, George W. Bush. He also argued that the economic woes had hurt middle-income Americans the most, and he asked voters to embrace his plans for giving all citizens a chance to reach the top of the economic ladder. Obama never used the word "inequality" in his campaign. Instead, he often spoke about "fairness," and the need for every American, rich or poor, to sacrifice for the good of the nation.[1]

The U.S. public seemed to agree with Obama's philosophy, if not his proposals for more federal spending and higher taxes on people earning more than $250,000 a year. According to a 2012 survey by the Pew Research Center, about three-fourths of Americans believed that the rich were getting richer and the poor were getting poorer. However, more than half of the Pew respondents also said that income inequality is an acceptable part of the economic system. Most citizens wanted a fair shot at the top, and they wanted government to do something about leveling the playing field. For example, almost 60 percent of Pew's respondents said the wealthy did not pay their fair share of taxes. [2]

At the same time, many Americans also said they wanted government to reward hard work, and they said that most needy Americans were in trouble because of their own failure to find jobs.

16.1 Describe the federal government's role in making economic policy and how the economy's performance is measured, p. 507.

16.2 Outline the tools and impact of fiscal policy on the economy, p. 511.

16.3 Outline the tools and impact of monetary policy on the economy, p. 515.

16.4 Identify ways in which the federal government seeks to promote economic growth, p. 519.

16.5 Categorize ways in which the federal government seeks to regulate the economy, p. 522.

16.6 Evaluate the advantages and disadvantages of the deregulation movement, p. 528.

The contrast between poverty and wealth was at the center of the 2012 campaign, although rarely talked about in stark terms.

The Big Picture The United States owes the world trillions of dollars right now, but the size of the national debt after the Revolutionary War was also tremendous. Author Paul C. Light explains how the Framers created economic policies that allow the economy to grow despite having a large debt.

The Basics Watch this video to learn why economic policy is so complicated in the United States. Find out how policies developed to solve new challenges that arose from industrialization. Then, consider whether you should be worried about the national debt.

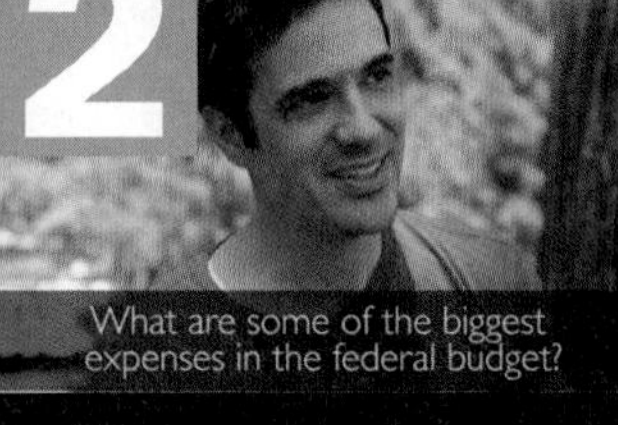

In Context Is your personal budget like the federal budget? If not, how is it different? University of Oklahoma political scientist Alisa H. Fryar breaks down the complexities of the federal budget and explains how the study of economic policy is changing in a more globalized society.

Thinking Like a Political Scientist Was the federal government wise to provide tax cuts during the most recent economic recession? University of Oklahoma political scientist Alisa H. Fryar examines how researchers determine the answer to these and other economic policy questions. She also explores the challenges state and local governments face in achieving their economic goals.

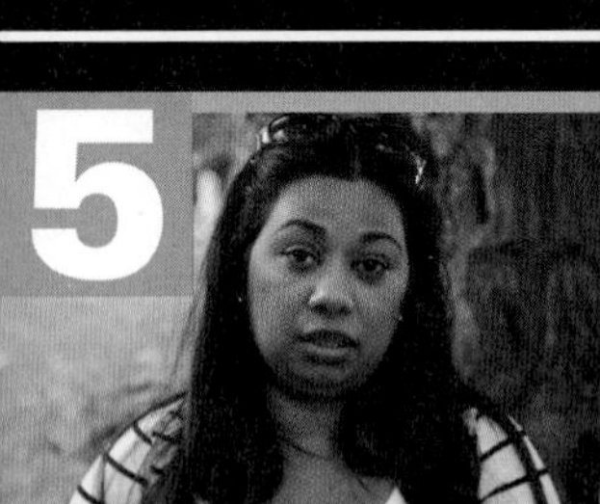

In the Real World Should the wealthy pay a larger percentage of their income in taxes than people with lower incomes? Real people tackle this central question, and they weigh in on what they believe is the fairest system of taxation and what tax reforms need to be made in the United States.

So What? What is the best way to measure the health of the economy? Author Paul C. Light discusses the rates that economists have traditionally looked at to determine the strength of the economy—such as unemployment and inflation—and he explains why the income-inequality rate has become a major topic of discussion in recent years.

Although most Americans understood that the economy was producing fewer jobs, they still argued that the needy could pull themselves out of poverty on their own. Moreover, most Americans supported the general idea that individuals should keep as much of their paychecks as possible. They had concerns about the very rich, and wanted to know more about how much in taxes wealthy Republican candidate Mitt Romney had paid over the years, but were not angry toward people who earned reasonably large salaries.

Given these opinions, it is not surprising that Republicans and Democrats do not agree on the need for more government involvement in economic policy. Rather, many Republicans believe that the biggest barrier to a stronger economy is government itself. They maintain that government spends too much money, imposes too much regulation, and does too little to promote innovation. They also argue that high taxes discourage businesses from creating more jobs, investing in U.S. plants, and hiring new workers.

This debate shows just how complex economic policy can be, especially during periods of great turmoil. With the economy still mired in slow growth and high unemployment, Democrats and Republicans offered two very different visions of the future, one marked by increased government support for economic growth, and the other by a demand for less intervention. The two visions provided a stark choice of how to protect the nation's capitalist system, which is built on free markets and innovation.

However, as the recent economic crisis suggests, there are times when government must play a strong role, whether by increasing its role in protecting free markets, or by reducing its size and spending. Although candidates often frame the choice as all-or-nothing, the federal government will always play a role in supporting a strong economy. It is up to citizens to decide how much the government should do, which is why the 2012 election was such an important referendum on the immediate future of economic policy.

This chapter will examine the many choices involved in supporting the economy through fiscal and monetary policy. We will also examine the government's role in keeping the economy healthy and honest by promoting growth and regulating industries. We will end the chapter with a discussion of the recent deregulation movement.

An Introduction to Economic Policy

16.1 Describe the federal government's role in making economic policy and how the economy's performance is measured.

The federal government has been active in economic policy since the end of the Revolutionary War. The Framers wanted a government strong enough to promote free trade, protect patents and trademarks, and enforce contracts between individuals and businesses. And they wanted a government with enough funding to build the postal roads, bridges, railroads, and canals that would allow the young economy to grow.

In part because the economy is so important, the Framers did not concentrate economic policy in any one branch. Instead, they divided economic policy-making control between the legislative and executive branches and even between the House and the Senate.

This separation of economic powers can be found in the first two articles of the Constitution. Article I, Section 8, of the Constitution gives Congress the power to borrow, coin, and print money, while Article II, Section 2, gives the president the power to appoint the officers of government who administer economic policy.

Article I also gives Congress the power to regulate commerce among the states and with foreign nations, the power to "to lay and collect Taxes, Duties, Imposts, and Excises," and the power to appropriate money and audit government spending, while Article II gives the president the power to negotiate treaties with other nations, which past presidents have used to create trade agreements to increase U.S. exports to other nations.

fiscal policy
Government policy that attempts to manage the economy by controlling taxing and spending, which affect inflation through lower taxes and less government spending, and unemployment through more government spending.

monetary policy
Government policy that attempts to manage the economy by controlling the amount of money in circulation through interest rates.

Finally, Article I gives Congress the power to establish post offices and build postal roads, which were just as important to commerce in the late 1700s as the Internet is today, while Article II gives the president significant discretion to execute economic policy as administrator-in-chief.

Moreover, the Framers were so concerned about taxation without representation, which was the rallying cry of the Revolutionary War, that they even divided the power to lay and collect taxes within Congress by giving the House sole authority to initiate all revenue legislation.

By creating a national government of limited powers and providing constitutional guarantees to protect property from excessive regulation, the Framers succeeded in protecting the nation's capitalist economic system, which allows for free markets and private ownership of property, inventions, and wealth. At the same time, the Constitution is absolutely clear in its preamble that the government's economic policy must be designed to "provide for the common Defense and promote the general welfare of the United States."

As a result, the federal government has a dual role in making economic policy. It must give individuals and businesses the freedom to create and own wealth through new ideas and hard work, but must protect the nation from economic chaos through **fiscal policy**, which uses federal spending and taxation to stimulate or slow the economy, and **monetary policy**, which manipulates the supply of money and access to credit that individuals and businesses have in their hands to buy new houses, use their credit cards, and invest in their retirement accounts.

Congress and the president use fiscal and monetary policy to address problems in what economists call the normal *business cycle* as it moves through four stages: (1) *expansion,* (2) *contraction,* (3) *recession*, which is often called *contraction*, and (4) *recovery*. The goal of effective economic policy today is to make sure the peaks of expansion and recovery are not too high and the troughs of contraction and recession are not too low.

In an ideal world, the economy would always be expanding at a reasonable pace—not too fast, but not too slow either. But in the real world, the economy periodically enters slow-downs called recessions in which growth plummets and unemployment rises, then rebounds through recoveries, settles into periods of stability, and then enters recessions again. And in the worst of economic worlds, the economy can collapse into a depression, which is a particularly deep form of collapse that lasts much longer than the normal one-to-two-year recession and creates much greater unemployment. The U.S. economy entered what is now known as the Great Depression

Fiscal and monetary policies are designed to make sure the cycle is relatively stable. Here, unemployed workers during the Great Depression of the 1930s stand in line to apply for jobs and other assistance.

following the stock market crash on October 29, 1929, a day that is still remembered as *Black Friday*, and only began to rebound 10 years later at the start of World War II, which generated millions of war-time jobs.

The recent economic turmoil is not considered a depression, but is often referred to as the "Great Recession" because of its length and very high levels of unemployment. The current recession began in 2008 with the collapse of the U.S. housing market, which supports local government and is the source of wealth for many Americans. Although economic activity began to increase in 2011, the U.S. economy was still struggling in 2012 because the economic cycle was stuck in the recession phase.

Congress and the president generally focus on two highly visible measures of economic performance to guide their economic decisions. The first is **inflation**, which measures the rising price of goods and services such as gasoline, food, and housing over time. Increased inflation is the primary risk during expansion and recovery. The second measure is **unemployment**, or the number of people looking for work at any given time. Unemployment among the employable is the greatest problem during contraction and recession, and has hovered around 9 percent since 2008. (The end-of-year unemployment rate from 1970–2012 can be found in Figure 16.1.)

In theory, inflation increases when unemployment drops as consumers begin to compete to buy more products and services, which raises prices. In theory again, inflation drops when unemployment increases as consumers pull back on demand for goods and services, which lowers prices. This balance between the demand and supply of goods and services drives the business cycle: When supply is low and demand is high, prices rise; when supply is high and demand is low, prices fall. In reality, inflation and unemployment can rise or fall at the same time, as they did at the start of 2008.

Economists measure inflation with the *consumer price index (CPI)*, which shows how much more or how much less consumers are paying for the same "basket of goods" over time. The major components of the CPI basket are food, shelter, fuel, clothing, transportation, and medical care. In turn, economists measure unemployment by the percentage of able-bodied workers who are looking for jobs but cannot find them. This *unemployment rate* does not include able-bodied workers who have given up looking for work or taken jobs below their skill levels with lower pay. Recent estimates suggest that there are about as many people who have given up as the number who are listed in the unemployment figures.

inflation
A rise in the general price level (and decrease in dollar value) owing to an increase in the volume of money and credit in relation to available goods.

unemployment
The number of Americans who are out of work but actively looking for a job. The number does not usually include those who have given up searching for a job.

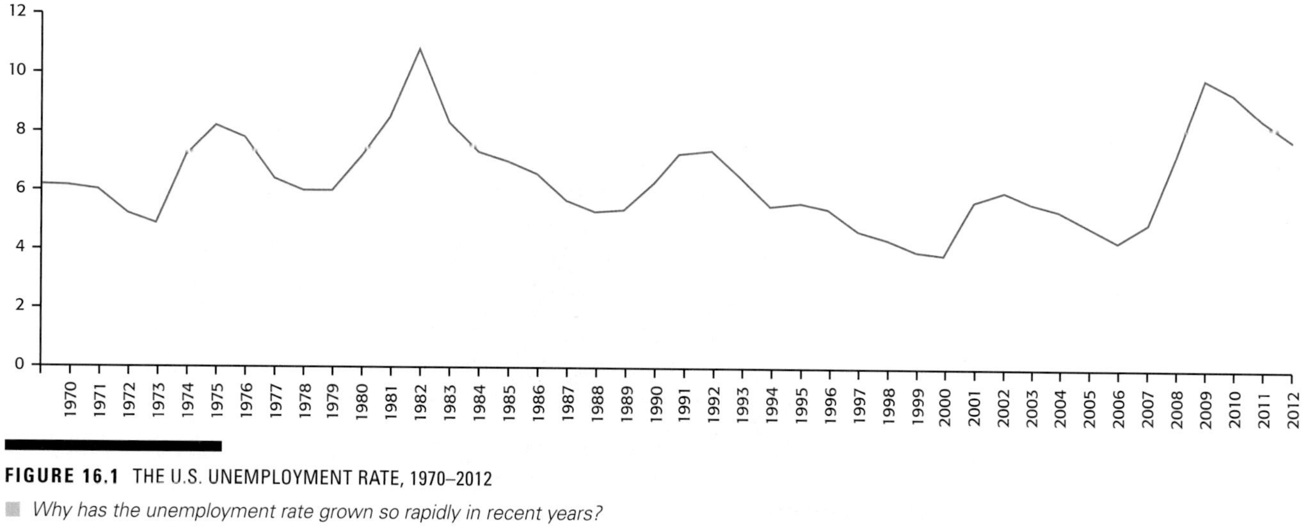

FIGURE 16.1 THE U.S. UNEMPLOYMENT RATE, 1970–2012

Why has the unemployment rate grown so rapidly in recent years?

SOURCE: Bureau of Labor Statistics, January 12 2012, available at http://data.bls.gov/timeseries/LNS14000000.

16.1

16.2

16.3

16.4

16.5

16.6

income inequality
The amount of after-tax income that the richest individuals and families control when compared to the amount that the poorest control; often measured by growth in the gap between the two classes.

wealth
The total amount of economic assets such as income, property, and investments that individuals and families control.

gross domestic product (GDP)
The value of all goods and services produced by an economy during a specific period of time such as a year.

More recently, economists have also used **income inequality** as a key measure of how an economy distributes good and services to different groups in society. Income inequality is one measure of **wealth**, or amount of economic power that individuals, corporations, or segments of society control. Income inequality is often measured by the amount of after-tax income that a family receives. The top 1 percent of U.S. families gained nearly 300 percent in income from 1979 to 2007, while the middle 60 percent reaped a much smaller increase of 40 percent. Speaking in early 2012, the president's top economic adviser summarized the current state of income distribution in simple terms: "The magnitude of these shifts is mindboggling. The share of all income accruing to the top 1 percent increased by 13.5 percent. This is the equivalent of shifting $1.1 trillion of annual income to the top 1 percent of families."[3] The trends also suggest that the middle class is drifing downward.

There are many explanations for this shift, including the decline in the number of manufacturing jobs in the country, which were generally jobs with good pay, lower taxes for higher-income families following the 2001 tax cuts, basic changes in how money gets made in the United States through stock investments, and the deep impact of the 2008 financial collapse on lower-income Americans. But whatever the cause, economists agreed that the U.S. economy is producing more wealth for the richest families, and more poverty at the bottom of the income ladder.[4]

Experts also use a set of measures to show how much the federal government is spending and borrowing (as measured by the federal budget deficit and national debt), the amount of goods and services the U.S. economy is exporting or importing from other nations (as measured by the balance of trade), and how much the economy is growing in terms of goods and services produced from year to year (as measured by year-to-year comparisons of the **gross domestic product**, which is often abbreviated as **GDP**).

The Global Community

Who Has the World's Strongest Economy?

Nations compete against each other for economic growth and strength. Their overall reputations affect investment by other nations, the value of their currencies, the quality of the debt they sell, and their influence in international trade negotiations.

The United States was once perceived as the world's leading economic power, in large part because it had the world's highest gross domestic product. But other nations have moved up in the international ratings as having the most powerful economies during this period of slow growth across the world.

According to a spring 2011 survey by the Pew Global survey, global citizens still believe that the United States is the world's leading economic power. However, China has been gaining ground since 2008 in many countries, and is now rated number one among 7 of the 23 nations surveyed. Japan and the countries that belong to the European Union are tied for third and fourth.

Citizens in Europe express the strongest confidence in China, while citizens in the Middle East and Southeast Asia show the strongest confidence in the United States.

China has steadily gained ground among U.S. citizens since 2008, while the United States has steadily gained ground among the Chinese. The percentage of Chinese who rated the United States as the world's leading economy rose 17 points between 2009 and 2011, while the percentage of Americans who rated the Chinese economy number one rose 10 percent during the same period. Neither group of citizens underrates the quality of their global competition, and may be imagining good economic times for other nations, but not their own.

This battle for international bragging rights may almost be over in the two nations. When asked whether China will replace the United States as the world's leading economic power, 56 percent of Americans and 63 percent of Chinese say, "yes." This competition can affect where individual investors put their money, which affects the amount of economic growth.

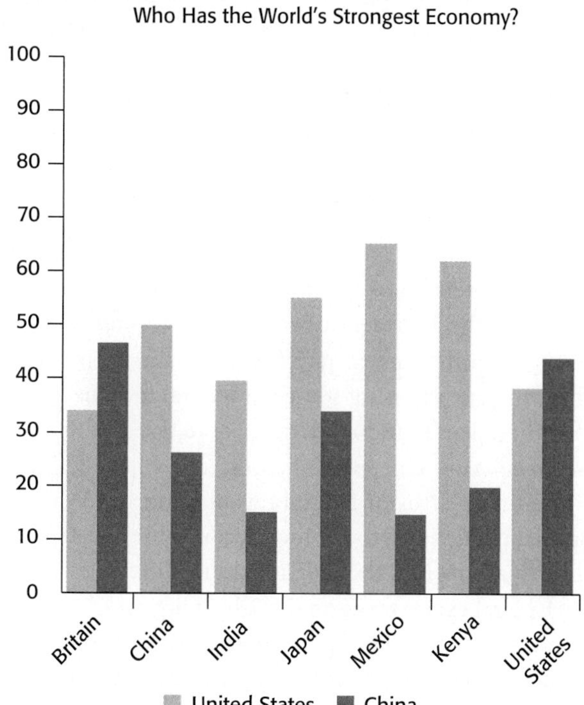

SOURCE: Pew Research Center, *China Seen Overtaking U.S. as Global Superpower: U.S. Favorability Ratings Remain Positive* (Pew Research Center, 2011)

CRITICAL THINKING QUESTIONS

1. Why do Americans believe the Chinese economy is stronger than their own? Why do the Chinese believe the U.S. economy is stronger than their own?
2. Do these ratings make any difference in the performance of an economy? If so, why?
3. Why do Americans and Chinese see China as eventually winning this competition?

Fiscal Policy

16.2 Outline the tools and impact of fiscal policy on the economy.

Congress and the president make fiscal policy by taxing, borrowing, and spending money. In general, lower taxes, higher borrowing, and increased spending are considered ways to stimulate employment during periods of sluggish economic performance, while higher taxes, lower borrowing, and decreased spending are considered ways to reduce inflation during periods of rapid economic growth. Lower taxes and more spending put more money in the pockets of consumers, which increases demand for goods and services, which in turn increases inflation and reduces unemployment. Conversely, higher taxes and lower spending take money away from consumers, which reduces demand for goods and services, which in turn reduces inflation and increases unemployment.

☐ The Federal Budget

Today, federal, state, and local governments spend an amount equal to approximately one-third of the nation's GDP. The federal government is the biggest spender of all—it spends more than all state and local governments combined. More importantly for raising revenue and borrowing money, federal spending has increased dramatically

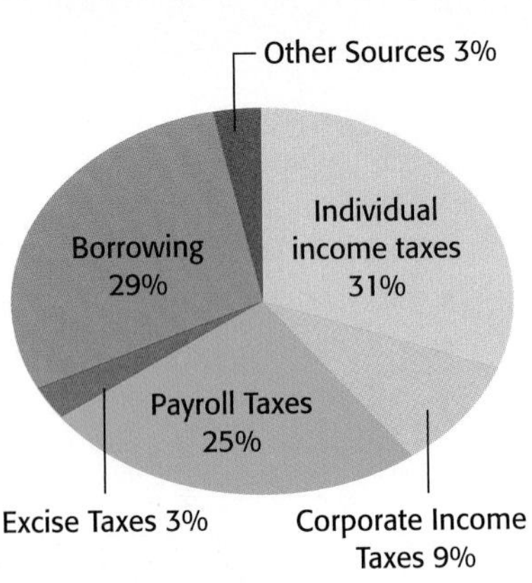

FIGURE 16.2 WHERE THE MONEY CAME FROM, 2012

Are the majority of taxes collected by the government progressive or regressive?

SOURCE: Summary Tables, *Budget of the United States, Fiscal Year 2012* (U.S. Government Printing Office, 2012).

excise tax
A consumer tax on a specific kind of merchandise, such as tobacco.

tariff
A tax levied on imports to help protect a nation's industries, labor, or farmers from foreign competition. It can also be used to raise additional revenue.

budget deficit
The condition that exists when the federal government raises less revenue than it spends.

national debt
The total amount of money the federal government has borrowed to finance deficit spending throughout the years.

progressive tax
A tax graduated so that people with higher incomes pay a larger fraction of their income than people with lower incomes.

regressive tax
A tax whereby people with lower incomes pay a higher fraction of their income than people with higher incomes.

mandatory spending
Required spending under the federal budget.

since the 1930s. Measured as a percent of GDP, the federal budget now accounts for 25 percent of all U.S. economic activity, up from just 4 percent in 1930.[5]

WHERE THE MONEY COMES FROM Although the Framers clearly understood that their new government would need revenues to succeed, they might be surprised at the range of taxes and other revenue sources that Congress and the president now use to fund federal programs (see Figure 16.2 for the percentages from each source).

1. *Individual income taxes.* Taxes on individuals account for the largest share of the federal government's tax revenue. The income tax was prohibited under the Constitution until the Thirteenth Amendment was ratified in 1913.
2. *Payroll taxes.* Payroll taxes to pay for social insurance (Social Security and Medicare) are the fastest-rising source of federal revenue. Most workers pay more in Social Security taxes than in federal income taxes.
3. *Corporate income taxes.* Corporate income taxes have fallen steadily from their historic high of two-fifths of federal revenues during World War II. Due to tax cuts and special deductions, today they account for one-tenth of federal revenues, only one-fourth as much as the individual income tax.
4. *Excise taxes.* Federal **excise taxes** on the sale of liquor, tobacco, gasoline, telephones, air travel, and other so-called luxury items account for a very small percentage of the federal budget, and are often restricted to specific uses such as building highways and airports.
5. *Other sources.* Smaller taxes and fees include admission to national parks and camping fees in national forests, taxes on large estates left behind after death, and interest payments on government loans to college students. The federal government also collects revenues from taxes called **tariffs** that are placed on imports such as cars, food, steel, raw minerals, and other products from other countries, which raise the price of these goods when they reach stores.
6. *Borrowing.* When the federal government cannot raise enough revenue to cover all its services, the only way to cover the resulting **budget deficit** is to borrow money by selling Treasury notes and savings bonds to individual citizens, investment firms, banks, and even foreign governments. Borrowing adds to the **national debt**, which is the total amount of money the federal government owes at any given point in time. As of early autumn 2012, the federal government owed its borrowers more than $16 trillion.

Congress and the president often mix and match revenue sources to achieve specific economic goals. Higher tariffs on specific imports can protect young industries from foreign competition long enough to gain a share of the international market, for example, while increased borrowing and lower taxes can push more money into the economy during slowdowns.

Congress and the president can also mix and match revenue sources to make sure all citizens and corporations pay a reasonable share of government costs. The federal income tax is considered a **progressive tax** that weighs more heavily on individuals with higher incomes, for example, while the federal payroll tax is considered a **regressive tax** that collects the same percentage on all individuals and corporations regardless of income.

As of 2012, 54 percent of Americans were paying federal income tax (a progressive tax), while another 28 percent were paying only payroll taxes (a regressive tax). The rest of Americans did not pay any taxes because they were unemployed, college students, elderly, had incomes under $20,000 per year, or had enough tax breaks to avoid taxes entirely.[6]

WHERE THE MONEY GOES Much of the money the federal government takes in is spent on benefit payments to individuals and on national defense. Nearly half of federal spending in 2012 went to required benefit payments for individuals, such as Social Security, Medicare, Medicaid, and other major social programs (see Figure 16.3 for the figures on where federal revenues were spent in 2012). About two-thirds of all federal spending in 2012 was **mandatory**, or *uncontrollable*, meaning that Congress and the president cannot use their discretion to change the spending rates. Mandatory programs include Social

Security and Medicare for older people and other programs that pay any citizen who qualifies for support. The rest of the 2012 spending was **discretionary**, or *controllable*, meaning that Congress and the president can change the spending rates. In 2011, Congress and the president agreed to cut the 2012 budget entirely with cuts in spending.

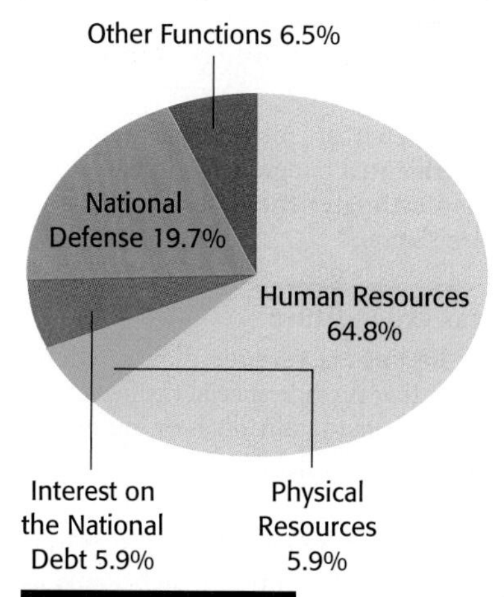

FIGURE 16.3 WHERE THE MONEY WENT, 2012

SOURCE: Summary Tables, *Budget of the United States, Fiscal Year 2012* (U.S. Government Printing Office, 2012).

discretionary spending
Spending that can be altered by congressional and presidential action.

Office of Management and Budget (OMB)
The presidential staff agency that serves as a clearinghouse for budgetary requests and management improvements for government agencies.

☐ The Budget Process

Before Congress enacted the Budget and Accounting Act of 1921, each executive agency dealt with Congress on its own, requesting that the legislature appropriate funds for its activities with little or no presidential coordination. Today, the president is required by law to submit an annual budget proposal for all agencies together.

THE EXECUTIVE BRANCH The federal government's fiscal year (FY) begins every October 1, meaning that the FY 2014 budget covers all spending from October 1, 2013, through September 31, 2014. But the budget process begins nearly two years before it is presented for debate, when the various departments and agencies estimate their needs and propose their budgets to the president.[7] (See Table 16.1 for the budget deadlines in designing the budget for FY 2015.) Agencies develop their specific requests based on federal laws, the president's priorities, and congressional demands, and provide detailed figures for every cost.

The **Office of Management and Budget (OMB)** is responsible for overseeing the budget process on behalf of the president as part of the Executive Office of the President. Once the OMB receives each agency's budget request, its examiners review each agency's budget and reconcile it with the president's overall plans. The OMB then holds informal hearings with every department and agency to give each one a chance to clarify and defend its estimates.

Once this give-and-take is over, the OMB director gives the president a single document that shows where the federal government's money will come from and where it will go. The president reviews these figures and makes adjustments. The president must submit the budget recommendations and accompanying message to Congress between the first Monday in January and the first Monday in February.

THE LEGISLATIVE BRANCH The president's budget proposal is only the beginning of formal approval of the budget. Under the Constitution, Congress must appropriate the funds and raise the taxes. However, the White House also plays a role in all decisions, if only because all appropriations and tax proposals are subject to a presidential veto. Presidents often threaten to veto these bills as a way of winning passage of their priorities.

Congress acts on the budget in several steps. It starts its process by approving an initial budget resolution that sets the broad spending and revenue goals for the process. It then moves forward with hearings on the budget proposal.

TABLE 16.1 STEPS IN BUILDING THE 2015 FISCAL YEAR BUDGET

February–December 2013	Executive branch agencies develop requests for funds, which are reviewed by the Office of Management and Budget and forwarded to the president for final decision.
December 2013	The formal budget documents are prepared.
January–February 2014	The budget is transmitted to Congress as a formal message from the president.
March–September 2014	Congress reviews the president's proposed budget, develops its own budget, and approves spending and revenue bills.
October 1, 2014	Fiscal year 2015 begins (fiscal year is identified by the year that it ends).
October 1, 2013–September 30, 2015	Executive branch agencies execute the budget provided in law.
October–November 2015	Figures on actual spending and receipts for the completed fiscal year become available.

■ *Which step of the process is the most likely to produce budget cuts or increases? What conflicts would you anticipate at each of the steps?*

Congressional Budget Office (CBO)
An agency of Congress that analyzes presidential budget recommendations and estimates the costs of proposed legislation.

tax expenditure
A loss of tax revenue due to federal laws that provide special tax incentives or benefits to individuals or businesses.

sales tax
A general tax on sales transactions, sometimes exempting such items as food and drugs.

value-added tax (VAT)
A tax on increased value of a product at each stage of production and distribution rather than just at the point of sale.

Congress adopted the Budget and Impoundment Control Act of 1974 to strengthen its role in the budget process. This Act requires the president to include proposed changes in tax laws, estimates of amounts of revenue lost through existing preferential tax treatments, and five-year estimates of the costs of new and continuing federal programs. The Act also calls on the president to seek authorizing legislation for a program a year before asking Congress to fund it.

The 1974 Budget Act also created the **Congressional Budget Office (CBO)**, an independent agency that prepares budget data on behalf of Congress, but the information is widely shared with the president and the public and is considered nonpartisan. By February 15 of each year, the CBO director presents an analysis of the president's budget proposal to the House and Senate budget committees. The CBO director also provides Congress with biannual forecasts of the economy, analyzes alternative fiscal policies, prepares five-year cost estimates for bills proposed by congressional committees, and undertakes studies requested by committees.

□ Tax Expenditures

Tax expenditures are a final type of fiscal policy that uses the tax code to provide special tax incentives or benefits to individuals and businesses for economic goals such as homeownership, retirement savings, and college education. The federal government spent more than $1 trillion in 2012 by giving individuals and corporation's tax deductions, credits, and other exemptions that reduced their total taxes. Deductions for medical insurance premiums and health care accounted for an estimated $184 billion in lost revenues in 2012, while deductions for home mortgage interest cost another $98 billion.[8]

Tax expenditures are one means by which the national government carries out public policy objectives. For example, instead of giving out federal grants for research and development (R&D), the government encourages investment in R&D by giving companies tax breaks to invest in innovation and expansion.

However, tax expenditures such as the home mortgage deduction do not help all levels of society, and may divert individuals and corporations toward investments with little yield for economic growth. In 2012, for example, the Obama administration charged that too many U.S. corporations were using a little-known federal tax break to purchase private airplanes for executive travel. Although the break helped U.S. airplane companies sell more planes, it became a symbol of the administration's charge that corporations were not doing their fair share to create jobs.

□ The Politics of Taxing and Spending

In addition to raising funds to run the government, taxes also promote economic growth and reward certain types of behavior, such as contributing to charities. Critics suggest that tax legislation helps individual members of Congress raise campaign funds—laws permitting several of the most popular corporate deductions must be renewed every year. This gives Congress a chance to show support for corporations regularly, and corporations a chance to show their support for Congress, too.[9]

As much as taxpayers complain about taxes, most want more of virtually everything the federal government provides. However, there is considerable disagreement about the best type of tax. Some experts argue that a progressive income tax (also called a *graduated income tax*) is best because it is relatively easy to collect, takes most from those who are most able to pay, and hardly touches those with little income.

The **sales tax**, which is used only at the state and local levels in the United States, is widely used in Europe in a slightly different version. Called the **value-added tax (VAT)**, it applies to the increased value of a product *at each stage of production and distribution* rather than just at the point where it is sold to a customer. A loaf of bread would thus have added value at several steps along the way to the grocery store: The farmer would pay a value-added tax on the grain before selling to the flour maker, who would be taxed before selling the flower to the baker, who would be taxed before selling the bread to consumers, who would be taxed when they bought the bread to eat.

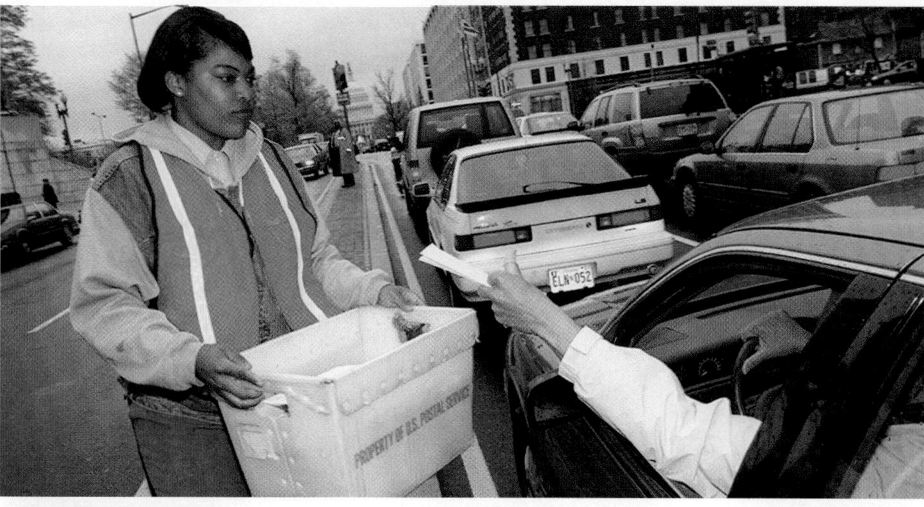

All individual income taxes are due on April 15 of each year. Here, cars line up as taxpayers drop their tax returns at the U.S. Postal Service to make sure they are postmarked on April 15. Failure to pay income taxes on time can result in a fine.

Federal Reserve System
The system created by Congress in 1913 to establish banking practices and regulate currency in circulation and the amount of credit available. It consists of 12 regional banks supervised by the Board of Governors. Often simply called "the Fed."

Some see the value-added tax as a way to infuse a large amount of new revenue into the federal government. The idea has strong support from many economists, but has yet to gain much momentum as a way to increase revenues. However, it is very much under consideration as part of the broad debate about how to lower the national debt.

Monetary Policy

16.3 Outline the tools and impact of monetary policy on the economy.

Monetary policy is the second way the federal government manages the economy. The core element of monetary policy is the idea that prices, incomes, and economic stability reflect growth in the amount of money that circulates through the economy at any one time. More money in the economy means more credit available for investment at a lower cost—a greater supply of low-cost money eventually creates demand. Advocates of aggressive monetary policy contend that the money supply is the key factor affecting the economy's performance. In theory, accelerating the circulation of money increases access to credit for creating jobs, buying homes, and saving for the future. In turn, slowing the circulation has the opposite effect.

Explore on MyPoliSciLab Simulation: You are a Federal Reserve Chair

Before turning to the specific tools of monetary policy, it is important to note that the United States is part of a much larger international economy in which the cost of money and the value of currencies such as the dollar, yen, euro, or pound is set by other governments and markets. Events in distant countries such as Greece, Ireland, Italy, Portugal, and Spain can have as much impact, if not more, on the U.S. economy today as decisions by Congress and the president. In 2012, for example, the threatened collapse of the Greek, Italian, Portuguese, and Spanish economies rocked the global finance markets, sending stock markets across the world falling, and raising the specter of an international depression. Working with its allies across the world, the United States helped strengthen the three economies, which were forced to cut their government spending in return for international loans.

☐ The Federal Reserve System

U.S. monetary policy is made by the Board of Governors of the **Federal Reserve System** (often simply called "the Fed"). As leaders of the nation's, and perhaps the world's, most important central bank, the Fed's chair and six members of the Fed's Board of Governors are appointed by the president with Senate consent to 14-year terms; a different member's

Starting in 2010, Greek citizens began protesting their government's multi-year plan for deep budget cuts, which is sometimes called fiscal austerity. The plan included caps on government wages, vacation days, and spending for social programs. Nevertheless, Greek leaders moved ahead on the cuts, and the protest continued into 2013.

federal funds rate
The amount of interest banks charge for loans to each other.

term expires every two years. As an independent regulatory commission, the Fed is effectively insulated from politics. The governors supervise 12 regional Federal Reserve banks located across the country, each headed by a president and run by a nine-member board of directors chosen from the private financial institutions in each region.

The current Fed chair is Ben S. Bernanke, who is thus one of the most powerful economic leaders in the world and may have more say over economic performance than either the president or Congress. Although Bernanke is protected from politics and is not a visible national figure, he is nonetheless under constant scrutiny by Congress and the president. His support for increasing the nation's debt ceiling in 2011 led some Republicans to call for his resignation, and prompted congressional investigations of the Fed's role in keeping too many banks alive during the recession.

The Fed's most important tool for monetary policy is its **federal funds rate**. The rate establishes the amount of interest the Fed charges banks to borrow money, which eventually determines the amount of interest banks charge their customers to borrow money for automobiles, homes, credit card balances, and that helps businesses hire new employees. Increasing the rate slows down the economy by increasing the cost of borrowing, while lowering the rate stimulates the economy by making more money available for investment and growth.

The cost of borrowing money is linked to the interest rate a bank's best customers receive on their short-term loans. In turn, this *prime rate* determines how much the federal government charges for many of its loans to new industries and college student loans, and flows down to bank home mortgages, car loans, and credit card debt. As Figure 16.4 shows, during the last several years, the Fed has swung between trying to stimulate the economy, slow the economy, and stimulate the economy again. In 2012, the Fed promised not to raise these interest rates until the U.S. economy emerged from the recession.

The rate goes up and down through decisions by the Federal Reserve Board and is based on the current economic situation. In mid-2012, the Federal Reserve Board announced that it would continue to keep interest rates low until at least 2015 as a way to reassure investors and stimulate the weakened U.S. economy. The decision was designed to reassure corporations and markets that the United States would continue to support the borrowing needed to stimulate economic growth and create jobs.

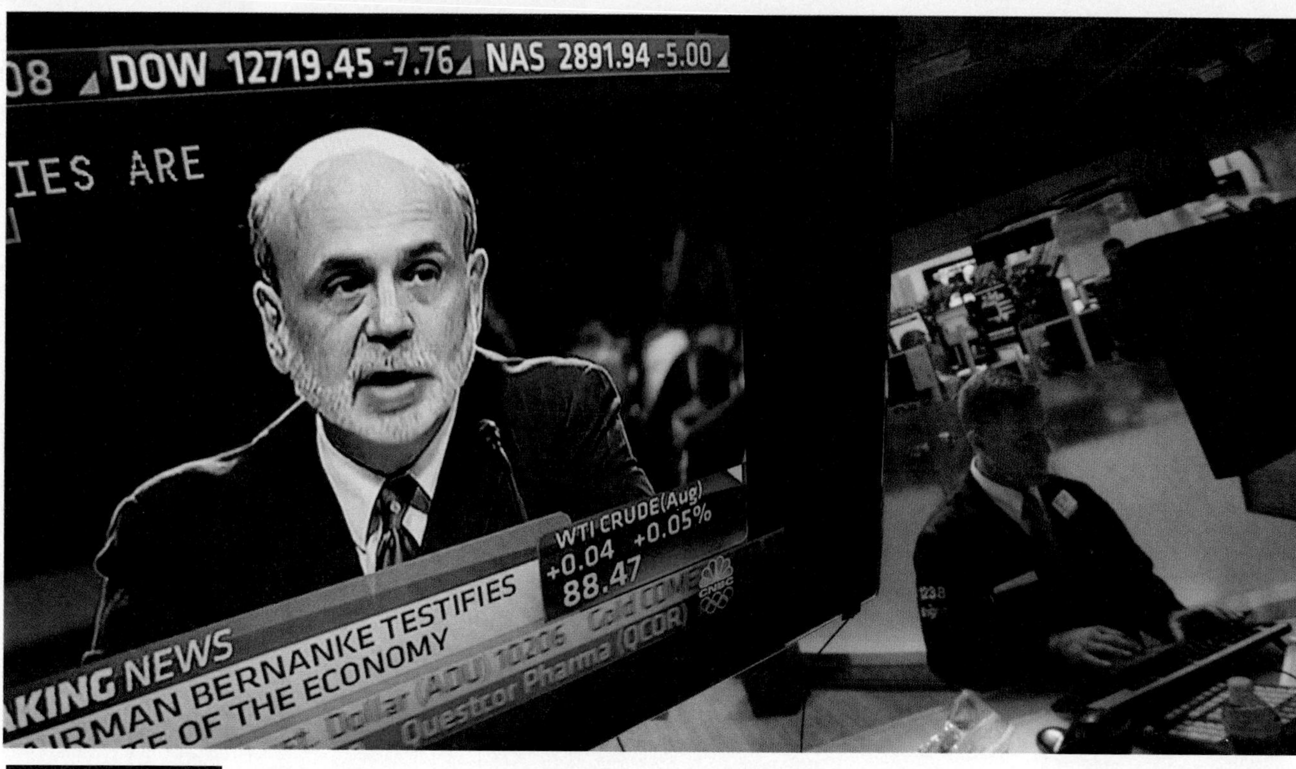

Ben Bernanke, Chairman of the Fed, talks about continued high unemployment and the need for growth in a talk at George Washington University in 2012.

Government and Economic Policy

The Great Depression pitted two groups of economists against each other in the effort to help the economy recover from its collapse. The first group urged the government to reduce spending, cut taxes, reduce regulation, and generally let the normal business cycle takes its course. These economists favored what is called **laissez-faire economics**. Republicans generally support this "light-hand" approach.

The second group urged government to do the opposite. Influenced by English economist John Maynard Keynes,[10] this group recommended that government must take a much more active role in stimulating the economy during desperate times. These economists favored what is called **Keynesian economics**. Democrats generally support this "aggressive-hand" approach.

laissez-faire economics
A theory that opposes governmental interference in economic affairs beyond what is necessary to protect life and property.

Keynesian economics
An economic theory based on the principles of John Maynard Keynes stating that government spending should increase during business slumps and be curbed during booms.

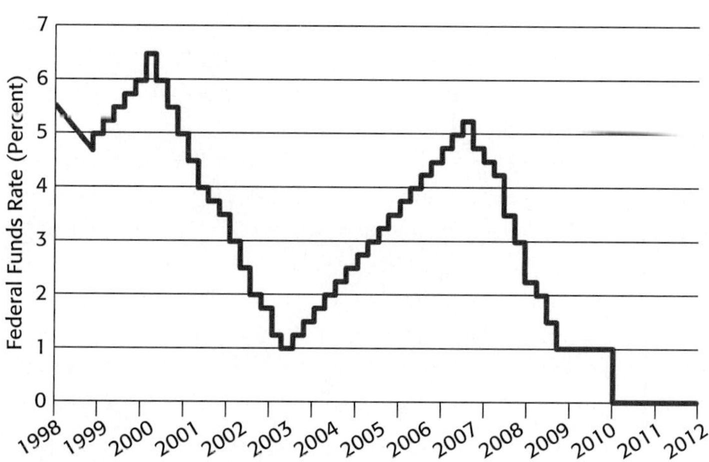

FIGURE 16.4 EFFECTIVE FEDERAL FUNDS RATE, 1998–2012

Why did the Federal Reserve Board reduce interest rates so drastically in 2007?

U.S. companies have offshored thousands of jobs, including service call centers, to India and other low-wage nations.

SOURCE: The Federal Reserve Board, Open Market Operations, federalreserve.gov/monetarypolicy/fomc.htm, December, 2012.

Explore on MyPoliSciLab

Who Broke the Economy?

When Americans ask who "broke" the economy in 2008, there is a practical answer and a political answer. The practical answer involves a chain of events that began with the collapse of the real estate market and resulted in millions of newly unemployed Americans. The political answer usually comes down to the presidents who responded to the events. President Barack Obama has spent more time coping with the recession and increasingly bears more responsibility for the economy, but as of late 2012, more Americans still blamed President George W. Bush—particularly Democrats.

Who Do Americans Blame?

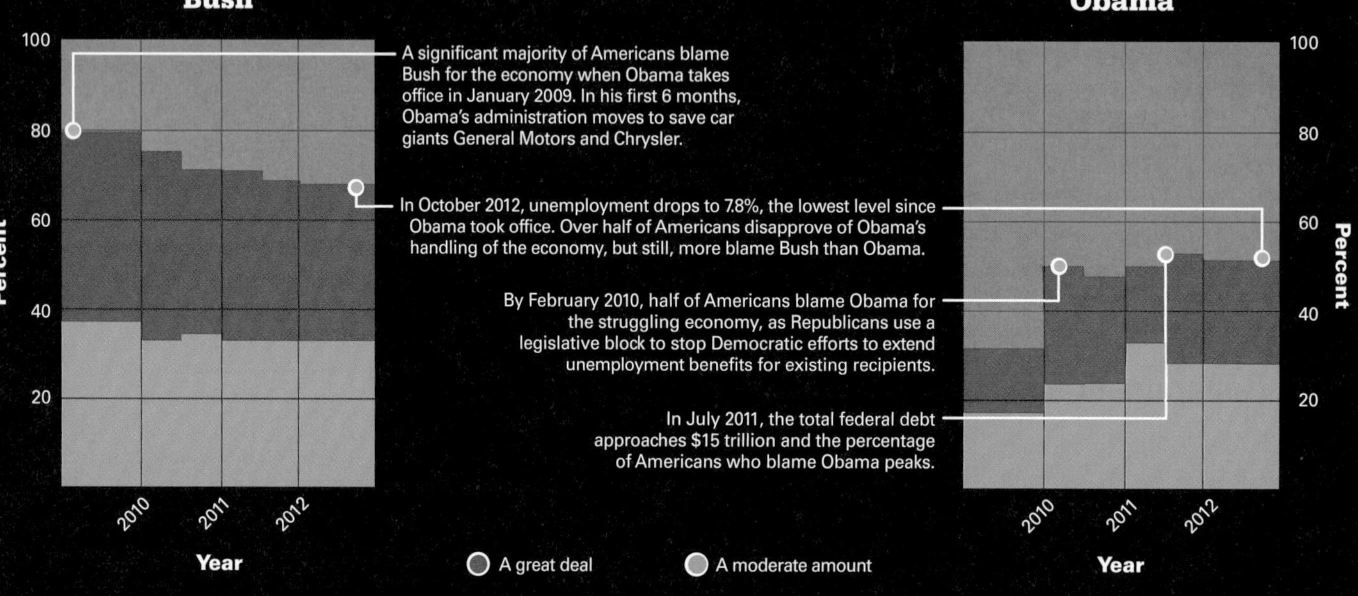

Partisanship Influences the Answer

Republicans | Independents | Democrats

Obama Bears the Majority of the Blame for U.S. Economic Problems.

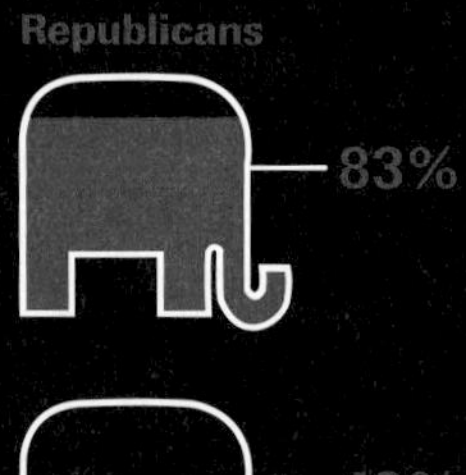

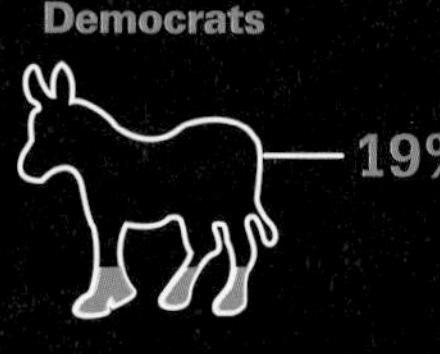

Bush Bears the Majority of the Blame for U.S. Economic Problems.

SOURCE: Data from Gallup.

Investigate Further

Concept Who gets more blame for the broken economy—Bush or Obama? Four years later, Bush is still blamed by the majority of Americans. Obama avoided much of this spotlight until February 2010. The longer a president is in office, the more public attention shifts towards him and away from his predecessor.

Connection Does improvement in the economy shift the blame to or from Obama? Despite the drop in unemployment since Obama took office, half the public still blames him for the bad economy.

Cause Does partisanship influence "blame"? After four years, Democrats overwhelming hold Bush responsible for the economy, instead of Obama. More Republicans hold Obama responsible, but half of them still think Bush is to blame. Though the public has shifted responsibility for the economy to Obama, partisanship largely determines where people place the blame for the recession.

As the growth in the federal budget suggests, Keynesians won the battle. The federal government injected vast amounts of money into the economy during the 1930s, created hundreds of new programs for creating new jobs, introduced new regulations to control the financial markets, and raised the national debt accordingly. Although there have been Democrats such as Bill Clinton who have worked with Republicans to balance the budget through budget cuts and tax increases, the United States has become accustomed to strong interventions during economic downturns, which is exactly what Congress and the Obama administration did by enacting the $800 billion American Recovery and Reinvestment Act in 2009. Between 2009 and 2012 when the program ended, the federal government spent almost $825 billion on a large number of relatively small projects spread out over every state in the Union.[11]

Although the Obama administration claimed that its stimulus package generated millions of jobs, the actual impacts are debatable. According to the Congressional Budget Office, the effect of the stimulus act peaked in late 2010, and has been diminishing ever since. Overall, the CBO estimates that the stimulus helped create between 3 and 6 million jobs between 2009 and 2012, but at a cost of nearly $290,000 per job. Moreover, there is no way of knowing whether the jobs were temporary and part time or turned into lasting employment.[12]

The Recovery Act may have been another victory for Keynesians, but has not gone unchallenged. As noted earlier, Republicans have become increasingly effective in challenging the role of government in economic life, and made the national debt and big government major issues in the 2010 and 2012 elections. Although it is unlikely that the United States will abandon Keynesian economics entirely, the nation is asking hard questions about whether government intervention works and at what cost. It is also asking just how much government should do in both promoting and regulating the economy.

Promoting the Economy

16.4 Identify ways in which the federal government seeks to promote economic growth.

ederal economic policy is designed to do more than smooth the ups and downs of the business cycle. It also tries to promote economic growth, often measured by the number of new jobs or businesses created. This effort involves two different strategies: (1) to support U.S. industries, and (2) to encourage international trade.

□ Supporting U.S. Industry

The Framers knew that building a strong economy was essential for securing the "blessings of liberty" for the nation, and paying off the debt created by the Revolutionary War. They created the navy in part to protect cargo ships from piracy, and built the postal roads to assure the easy movement of goods across the nation. They also gave Congress the power to impose taxes, and exercise control of interstate commerce.

During the decades that followed, Congress and the president created dozens of new departments and agencies to support specific industries such as mining, airlines, small business, energy, and science. These organizations promote the economy through loans, grants, special payments, and advice on how to start new businesses.

For example, the Department of Agriculture is a powerful advocate of the farming industry, supporting higher prices for basic products such as corn, barley, oats, wheat, soybeans, cotton, and rice. In 2012 alone, it spent more than $20 billion in *subsidies* for certain crops such as corn by either guaranteeing a minimum price for crops or paying fees to farmers for not planting fields. By altering the supply and price of crops while promoting new products such as "biofuels" made from corn, sugar cane, and other crops, these subsidies increase the cost of items such as bread, eggs, and soy milk.

Not all U.S. industries receive this kind of support, however, and many business experts argue that government involvement in promoting specific industries gets in

16.1

16.2

16.3

16.4

16.5

16.6

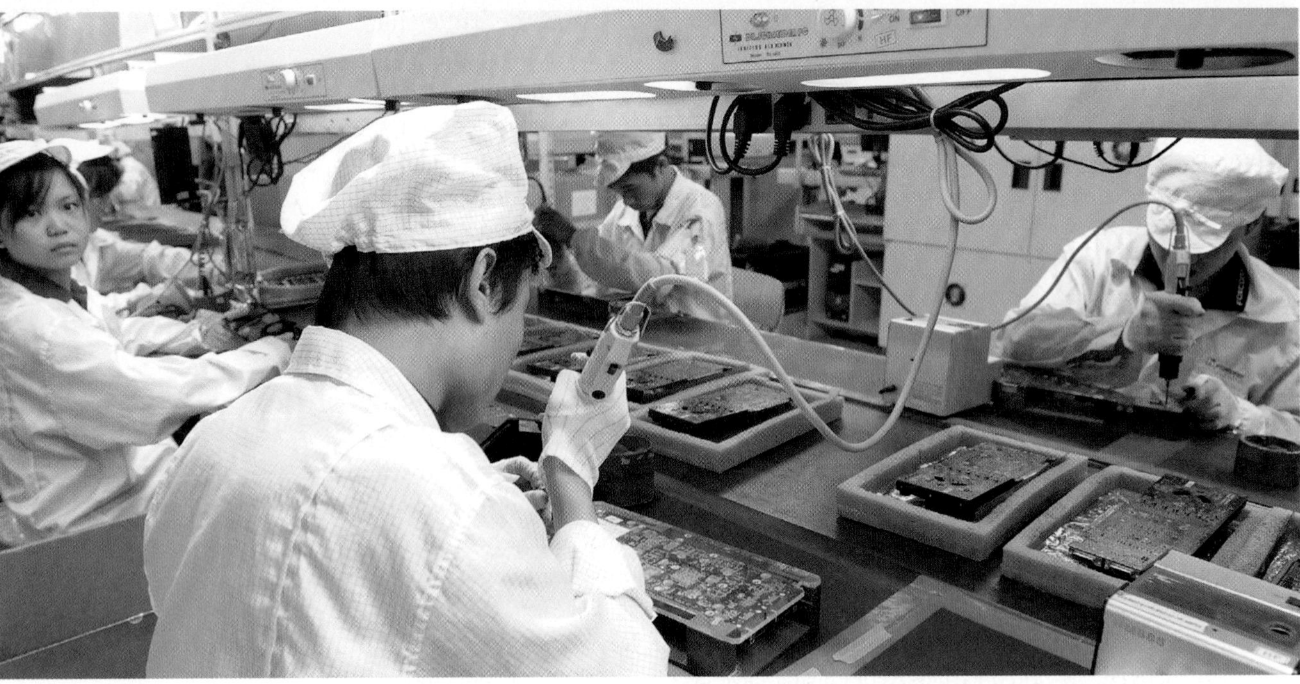

Many of the world's leading technology companies buy computer components such as chips, screens, and cases for their phones and computers from foreign companies that pay very low wages. In 2012, Apple came under pressure for its iPad and iPhone 4S and iPhone contracts with a large Chinese firm called Foxconn. Under pressure from Apple, Foxconn promised to improve working conditions at its factories and raise wages.

protectionism
A policy of erecting trade barriers to protect domestic industry.

trade deficit
An imbalance in international trade in which the value of imports exceeds the value of exports.

the way of the natural market forces that would help lower prices or produce jobs. The high-tech industry does not have its own agency or department, for example, nor does the nation's charitable sector, which employs 11 million workers.

However, the federal government does protect all new inventions through its U.S. Patent and Trademark Office. The office reviews applications for patents and trademarks to make sure that all new ideas are original. Once granted, a patent or trademark is protected by the federal courts. In September 2012, Apple won a $1 billion federal court judgment against Samsung Corporation for patent infringement. Apple argued that Samsung had copied many features of the iPhone in designing its Fascinate, Epic, and Galaxy products.

□ Promoting International Trade

Worries about international competition often lead domestic producers to call for **protectionism**, which can take the form of special taxes, or tariffs, placed on imported goods to make them more expensive. Most economists oppose protectionism because it prevents efficient use of resources and because consumers pay much more for protected products than they otherwise would in the world economy. Tariffs merely divert attention from real solutions such as increased productivity and capital investments, and they inevitably invite retaliation from foreign countries.

Trade barriers are less severe today than they were in the 1930s. But restrictions still exist. Certain tariffs, limits on imported goods, and import regulations limit U.S. consumption of foreign products. Most exist to protect U.S. farmers, businesses, or workers in certain industries, but they often do more harm than good by leading other countries to put tariffs and other restrictions on U.S. goods. The result has been a persistent **trade deficit** in which the United States imports far more than it exports. The trade deficit is also caused by the low wages many foreign companies pay their workers.

The United States experienced its first trade deficit in more than a century when the amount of imports exceeded the value of exports in 1971. In the 40 years since then, the nation has faced billions of dollars in ever-growing trade deficits. Congress and the president are under continuing pressure from industry, unions, and regional political leaders to protect U.S. jobs, companies, and communities from foreign competition. These pressures come from the textile and auto industries as well as from glass, steel,

You Will Decide

Should Government Limit Offshoring?

In search of lower costs, many U.S. corporations have moved hundreds of thousands of jobs from inside the U.S. to other nations such as China, India, and the Philippines, and appear to be ready to move millions more.* This process, called *offshoring* or *offshore outsourcing,* creates wide swaths of unemployment in heavy industries such as steelmaking and customer service industries such as computer support. Most technology manufacturing jobs have been offshored to China, while many customer service telephone lines are staffed in India, the Philippines, and Indonesia. As Apple founder Steven Jobs told Obama at a White House dinner in late January, 2012, "those jobs are not coming back."** Jobs died just before release of another version of the iPhone, leaving Apple in new hands.

Although no one is certain how many jobs have left the United States, some estimates suggest more than one million U.S. jobs have been exported to Mexico, other Central American countries, and China. The number may seem high, but it amounts to a fraction of the U.S. workforce of more than 140 million. Nevertheless, opposition to job migration remains a highly divisive issue between labor and management.

This migration has been driven in part by the U.S. government's economic policies, most notably in setting minimum wages and protecting workers from economic harm. Nevertheless, President Obama made an end to offshoring a major theme in his 2012 State of the Union Address by arguing that the United States should police the migration of jobs to other countries through tax breaks and other incentives for keeping the jobs home.

What do you think? Should the federal government do more to protect U.S. jobs? What arguments would you make for and against such an idea?

Thinking It Through

Most economists agree that efforts to stop the movement of jobs to other nations would hurt the U.S. economy in the longer term. U.S. jobs pay much higher wages than jobs in other countries such as China and India, for example, which lowers the price of U.S. goods that are made with foreign components.

However, Democrats and Republicans disagree on what might be done to keep jobs home. Democrats tend to argue that the United States should negotiate strong trade agreements that require better working conditions and pay for workers everywhere, which would make offshoring less attractive to U.S. companies. They also argue that the federal government should provide greater help for workers who lose their jobs to foreign nations. "The answer is not to try to stop outsourcing," says former Clinton administration Secretary of Labor Robert Reich, using a popular term for offshoring, "but we do have to get serious about job retraining, lifetime learning, extended unemployment insurance, and wage insurance."†

In contrast, Republicans tend to argue that the United States should make job creation its top priority and allow offshoring to occur as a natural product of a free market. They also argue that lower corporate taxes and less regulation would make doing business inside the United States more attractive, and, therefore, would keep more jobs home. As of 2012, there has been no movement to reconcile these two positions, although Obama repeatedly charged that Romney's greatest achievement during his earlier business career was sending American jobs abroad.

Offshoring may be the inevitable long-term cost of doing global business, but it has very visible consequences in the short term. Workers whose jobs move abroad often face years of unemployment, which is why the issue has been so controversial.

The United States' economic policy in the future will continue to combine free trade and selective protectionism. Although it shields highly visible industries from competition at home or abroad, protectionism often favors one industry over another, which reduces competition among those industries. In the short run, it helps protect U.S. jobs but may delay economic growth as companies spend more on pay than research and development.

CRITICAL THINKING QUESTIONS

1. Why should the United States protect its workers from offshoring?
2. Should workers be protected even if doing so results in higher prices for products such as clothing?
3. Do you know of any jobs that have been outsourced? Have you had any contact with a company that uses employees in other nations to deliver basic services?

*For a recent analysis of offshoring, see Linda Levine, "Offshoring (or Offshore Outsourcing) and Job Loss Among U.S. Workers" (Congressional Research Service, January 21, 2011), available at http://forbes.house.gov/UploadedFiles/CRS_-Offshoring_and_Job_Loss_Among_U_S__Workers.pdf.

**Charles Duhigg and Keith Bradsher, "How the U.S. Lost Out on iPhone Work," *New York Times*, January 21, 2012. From http://www.nytimes.com/2012/01/22/business/apple-america-and-a-squeezedmiddle-class.html?pagewanted=all.

†Thottam, Jyoti, Barbara Kiviat, Sara Rajan, Cathy Thomas, and Karen Tumulty. 2004. '04 The Issues: Is Your Job Going Abroad? *Time* March 1, 2004. From http://www.time.com/time/magazine/article/0,9171,993464,00.html.

General Agreement on Tariffs and Trade (GATT)
An international trade agreement that seeks to lower the barriers to free trade.

World Trade Organization (WTO)
An international organization with more than 130 members that seeks to encourage free trade by setting rules for fair competition.

North American Free Trade Agreement (NAFTA)
An agreement signed by the United States, Canada, and Mexico in 1992 to form the largest free trade zone in the world.

shoes, lumber, electronics, book publishing, aluminum, farming, and domestic wine and spirit coalitions, to name only a few. Their leaders claim that the trade deficit justifies the imposition of trade sanctions.

Another unfair trade practice is *dumping*—selling products below the cost of manufacturing or below their domestic price with the intention of driving other producers out of the market and then raising prices to profitable levels. Governments might also *subsidize* certain industries. Some countries, for example, subsidize steel for export. Others require lengthy inspection procedures for imported goods. Japan has protected several of its industries—producers of automobiles, baseball bats, and even chopsticks, for example—by setting standards that are virtually impossible for U.S. manufacturers to meet. Japan also sets limits on rice imports. China has become the United States' largest competitor by subsidizing key industries in the computer industry, prompting Obama to argue for tougher rules against such tactics in 2012.

THE WORLD TRADE ORGANIZATION Recognizing the emergence of the international economy, in 1947 a group of countries began negotiating the pieces of what became known as the **General Agreement on Tariffs and Trade (GATT)**. GATT was amended through seven rounds of intense negotiations over the decades that set the rules of free trade among what are now 155 member nations, which include China, India, Indonesia, Russia, the United States, and all economies in Western Europe, Latin America, South America, and most of Africa.

GATT was replaced by the **World Trade Organization (WTO)** on January 1, 1995. WTO provides a powerful international forum for reaching trade agreements and resolving disputes among its members. The United States has been particularly active in recent years in bringing complaints against China for restricting free trade, and has won a series of rulings penalizing the Chinese for protecting its own automobile, computer, and even motion picture industries from international competition. Despite these victories, China remains an aggressive defender of its young and growing economy.

In the latest case, which began in 2012, the United States, Japan, and the members of the European Union filed a challenge, or case, against China alleging that it was setting unfairly low prices on precious metals such as scandium that are used in the manufacturing of computer chips, television monitors, and other high-tech products. As of 2013, the WTO was still considering the case. If it rules in favor of the United States and its partners in the challenge, China would be punished for price fixing.

Not everyone believes free trade should be unlimited, however. Labor unions, environmentalists, and human rights advocates argue that U.S. trade policies spur the creation of low-wage jobs abroad and encourage child labor, pollution, and worker abuse in countries such as China and India that export large quantities of goods to the United States.

THE NORTH AMERICAN FREE TRADE AGREEMENT In 1992, the United States, Canada, and Mexico signed the **North American Free Trade Agreement (NAFTA)**, which formed the largest geographical free trade zone in the world. Although President George H. W. Bush signed NAFTA near the end of his presidency, the agreement could not become law until ratified by Congress. President Bill Clinton promoted NAFTA, even though many members of his own party were its most vigorous opponents. Congress passed it by a thin margin in a bipartisan vote with Democrats in the minority.

Though trade among the United States, Canada, and Mexico is not absolutely "free" or unimpeded, the agreement has had a tremendous impact on the economies of all three countries. Today, Mexico is the United States' third most important trading partner, and the United States is Mexico's most important. Critics remain concerned because Mexican antipollution laws are significantly less stringent than those in the United States, and Mexican workers receive considerably lower wages. Both these factors make relocation to Mexico attractive to many U.S. companies seeking to reduce labor and pollution control costs.

Regulating the Economy

16.5 Categorize ways in which the federal government seeks to regulate the economy.

Even as U.S. economic policy promotes growth, it also regulates business activities that may create unfair advantages for certain industries that try to gain control of their sector of the market. U.S. citizens believe in competition among businesses, but they also want a level playing field, meaning no industry or company cheats its way to the top or abuses its employees or the environment along the way.

The Constitution explicitly authorizes Congress to regulate commerce among the states and with foreign nations. In our earliest years, Congress used this regulatory power to impose or suspend tariffs on imports from other nations. In the nineteenth century, the federal government created a number of agencies to regulate the conduct of citizens and commercial enterprises with an eye toward promoting economic development. Among these were the Army Corps of Engineers (1824), the Patent and Trademark Office (1836), the Steamboat Inspection Service (1837), and the Copyright Office of the Library of Congress (1870). In 1887, Congress created the Interstate Commerce Commission to deal with widespread dissatisfaction over the practices of railroads.

All governments regulate their economies, but the amount of government regulation varies greatly across the world. Compared to other nations such as Russia and Sweden, the United States actually has fewer rules than many of its competitors. It generally allows wages, prices, and the allocation of goods and services to follow the laws of supply and demand, even when doing so angers environmentalists, labor unions, and public interest groups. The nation relies on private enterprise and market incentives to carry out most production and distribution.

Nevertheless, even opponents of regulation recognize that the market does not always solve every problem. Both political parties say regulatory overkill threatens to overwhelm entrepreneurs and divert them from building vital, innovative companies. The question is not whether there are both costs and benefits from regulation, however,

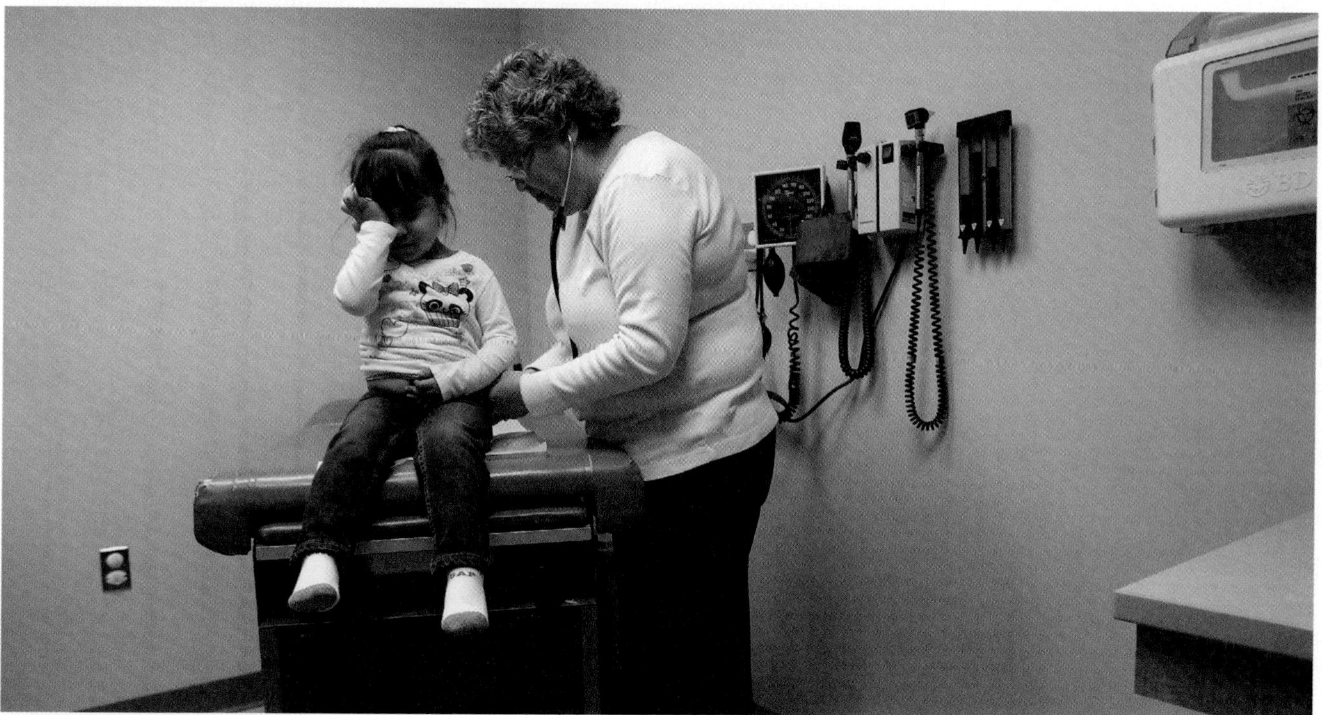

In 2012, the Supreme Court decided that Congress and the president had acted within constitutional boundaries in creating a mandate, which the Court redefined as a tax, requiring citizens to purchase health insurance. This law is an example of regulating the insurance industry to make sure citizens have certain rights when they buy health care coverage.

monopoly
Domination of an industry by a single company; also the company that dominates the industry.

antitrust legislation
Federal laws (starting with the Sherman Antitrust Act of 1890) that try to prevent a monopoly from dominating an industry and restraining trade.

trust
A monopoly that controls goods and services, often in combinations that reduce competition.

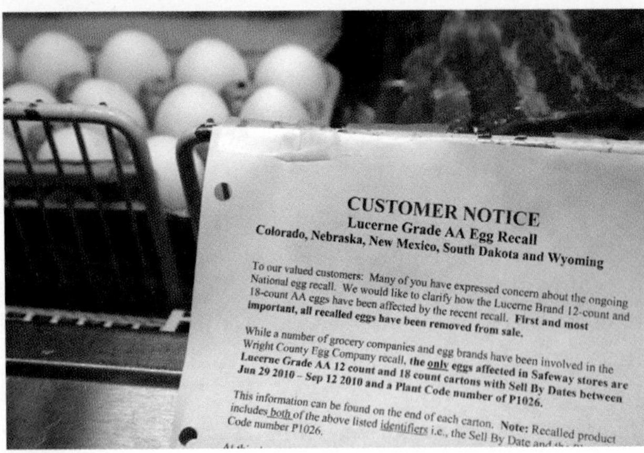

In August 2010, the Food and Drug Administration ordered grocery stores to remove almost 25 million eggs from their shelves due to an outbreak of salmonella, a deadly disease.

but whether the balance is right. Conservatives tend to overstate the costs of many regulations and understate the benefits, whereas liberals tend to overstate the benefits and understate the costs.

☐ Regulating Competition

Business regulation increased in three major waves during the past century. The first came in the 1910s, the second in the 1930s, and the third in the late 1960s through 1980. In each case, changing circumstances gave rise to the legislation.

Perhaps the most important responsibility of government regulation in a free market system is to maintain competition. When one company gains a **monopoly**, or several create an *oligopoly,* the market system operates ineffectively. The aim of **antitrust legislation** is to prevent monopolies, break up those that exist, and ensure competition. In the past, so-called natural monopolies, such as electric utilities and telephone companies, were protected by the government because it was assumed that in these fields, competition would be grossly inefficient.

In the late nineteenth century, social critics and populist reformers believed that the oil, sugar, whiskey, and steel industries were deceiving consumers, in large part because of the rise of large monopolies called **trusts**. Once they became aware of abuses in these industries, citizens began to call for more government regulation. In 1890, Congress responded by passing the Sherman Antitrust Act, designed "to protect trade and commerce against unlawful restraints and monopolies." However, the Sherman Antitrust Act had little immediate impact; presidents made few attempts to enforce it, and the Supreme Court's early interpretation of the Act limited its scope.[13]

Congress added the Clayton Act to the antitrust arsenal in 1914. This Act outlawed such specific abuses as charging different prices to different buyers in order to destroy a weaker competitor, granting rebates, making false statements about competitors and their products, buying up supplies to suppress competition, and bribing competitors' employees. In addition, *interlocking directorates* (in which an officer or director in one corporation served on the board of a competitor) were banned, and corporations were prohibited from acquiring stock in competing companies if such acquisitions substantially lessened interstate competition. That same year, Congress established the Federal Trade Commission (FTC), run by a five-person board, to enforce the Clayton Act and prevent unfair competitive practices. The FTC was to be the "traffic cop" for competition.[14] The FTC's record has been mixed in large part because Congress has created so many exemptions protecting favored industries.

☐ Regulating the Use of Labor

Most laws and rules curb business practices and steer private enterprise into socially useful channels. But regulation cuts two ways. In the case of U.S. workers, most laws in recent decades have tended not to restrict labor but to confer rights and opportunities on it. Actually, many labor laws do not touch labor directly; instead, they regulate labor's relationship with employers.

Federal regulations protect workers in the following important areas, among others:

1. *Public contracts.* The Walsh-Healey Act of 1936, as amended, requires that most workers employed under contracts with the federal government be paid at least the average or prevailing wage for that job, and that they be paid overtime for all work in excess of 8 hours per day or 40 hours per week.
2. *Wages and hours.* The Fair Labor Standards Act of 1938 set a maximum workweek of 40 hours for all employees engaged in interstate commerce or in the production of goods for interstate commerce (with certain exemptions). Work beyond that amount must be paid for at one and a half times the regular rate.
3. *Child labor.* The Fair Labor Standards Act of 1938 prohibits children from working in any industry that engages in interstate commerce, which essentially means that all child labor is illegal.
4. *Industrial safety and occupational health.* The Occupational Safety and Health Act of 1970 created the first comprehensive federal industrial safety program. It gave the secretary of labor broad authority to set safety and health standards for companies engaged in interstate commerce.

closed shop
A company with a labor agreement under which union membership is a condition of employment.

union shop
A company in which new employees must join a union within a stated time period.

labor injunction
A court order forbidding specific individuals or groups from performing certain acts (such as striking) that the court considers harmful to the rights and property of an employer or a community.

collective bargaining
A method whereby representatives of the union and employer determine wages, hours, and other conditions of employment through direct negotiation.

Federal regulations also protect employees' right to organize unions. Under the 1935 National Labor Relations Act (usually called the Wagner Act), for example, the federal government gave workers significant new rights to organize unions, while prohibiting businesses from discriminating against union members or refusing to bargain in good faith with union representatives.

Congress passed a major modification of the labor laws in 1947. Under the Labor-Management Relations Act, commonly called the Taft-Hartley Act, government outlawed the **closed shop**, which restricts the hiring of non-union employees; permitted the **union shop**, which allows unions to require new employees to join their unions within a stated period of time; prohibits businesses from refusing to bargain with employees; allowed courts to issue **labor injunctions**, which forbid specific individuals or groups from performing acts considered harmful to the rights or property of an employer or community; and structures **collective bargaining**, the process between unions and employers that sets wages, benefits, and working conditions.

All of these rules still stand, but the percentage of labor union members in the United States has steadily declined over the past 100 years as the manufacturing industry has shrunk. Membership reached its 100-year peak at 35 percent during the Great Depression in the 1930s, but fell to just 11 percent in 2010, the last year such figures are available.[15]

□ Regulating the Stock Markets

The stock market crash of 1929 did more than devastate the U.S. economy and usher in the Great Depression. It also revealed deep problems in the way companies sold their stock to investors. Millions of new investors entered the stock market in the 1920s, only to find that the companies in which they had invested were virtually worthless.

Before 1934, investors themselves had to determine whether a company was telling the truth about its stock. Since 1934, that responsibility has fallen to the Securities and Exchange Commission (SEC). Under the Securities Exchange Act of 1934, which established the SEC, and a long list of later laws, companies that offer their stock for sale to the public must tell the truth about their businesses, which means full disclosure of their financial condition.

The Act also required that anyone in the business of selling stocks, including brokers, dealers, and stock exchanges such as the New York Stock Exchange and NASDAQ, must treat investors fairly and honestly, putting investors' interests first. That means, for example, that individuals who know about a new stock offering in advance, or who

OF the People Diversity in America

Diversity in the Workforce

The United States has one of the most diverse workforces in the world, with large percentages of men and women, African Americans, and Asian Americans employed either full or part time. Although high unemployment has hit women and minorities hardest, large percentages still remain in the workforce.

Employment and unemployment are only part of the picture, however. According to 2010 information from the U.S. Bureau of Labor Statistics, white men earn about $1,300 a week, compared with white women at about $900, African American men earn about $1,000 a week, compared with African American women at about $800 a week.

Percentage of Employed Americans, January 2012

Percentage of Unemployed Americans, January 2012

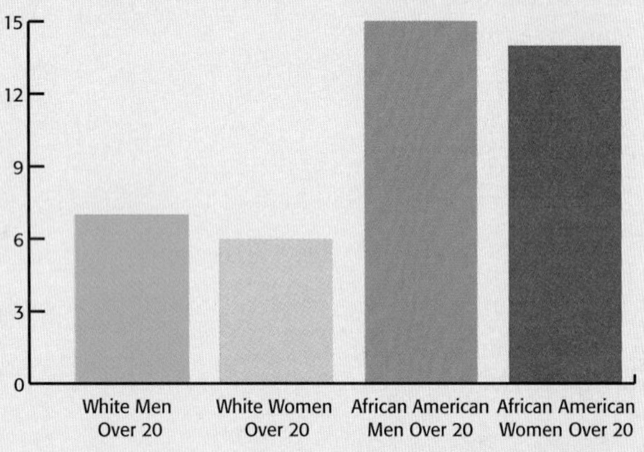

One reason for these differences is that men and women work in different occupations. Women are much more likely to work in sales, office, and service occupations than men, while men are more likely to work in construction and manufacturing jobs, which are more highly paid.

Some experts argue that women of all races work in the "pink ghetto," meaning that their occupations have a very high ratio of women to men. As a result, women may face hidden sex discrimination in service industries such as nursing, childcare, social work, and administrative support, which offer more opportunities for advancement than industries such as banking. Although women and minorities have made progress moving into management and professional occupations, they are still highly unlikely to reach the top of their organizations.

According to the Alliance for Board Diversity, which is a public interest group located in Washington, D.C., women led only 2 percent of the 500 largest companies in the world, while minority women held even fewer at just 0.6 percent.* Minority men were also far behind white men at just 4 percent. Diversity is considered good for corporate profits, but not necessarily essential for high-level leadership posts as board chairman, board member, or chief executive officer.

QUESTIONS

1. What is your theory regarding the unemployment differences across sex and race?
2. Why do women and minorities receive less pay on average than men? What might the federal government do to even the pay rates, and should it act at all?
3. What can your college or university do to change these figures?

*Alliance for Board Diversity Report, *Missing Pieces: Women and Minorities on Fortune 500 Boards—2010 Alliance for Board Diversity Census* (Alliance for Board Diversity, July 21, 2011), available at http://theabd.org/Missing_Pieces_Women_and_Minorities_on_Fortune_500_Boards.pdf.

have other insider information on events that might increase or decrease the value of a given stock, are prohibited from using that information to benefit themselves. The SEC came under fire during a series of investigations of the 2008 financial collapse. Congress charged that the SEC had missed many of the key warning signals of the catastrophe, and passed legislation to strengthen the beleaguered agency.

☐ Protecting the Environment

Until the 1960s, the United States did little to protect the environment, and the little that was done was by state and local governments. In the early 1970s, the federal government took on new responsibilities, starting with passage of the Clean Air and Water Acts. These put

Bernie Madoff pled guilty in 2009 to stealing billions of dollars through his stock market investment fund. Madoff was sentenced to 150 years in prison, which was the maximum sentence allowable under federal law and was effectively a life sentence.

environmental impact statement
A statement required by federal law from all agencies for any project using federal funds to assess the potential effect of the new construction or development on the environment.

corporate social responsibility
Efforts by corporations to improve their reputations by paying attention to their contributions to the social good.

new limits on the amount of pollution companies could release into the environment and launched a long list of laws regulating environmental dangers, such as leaking underground storage tanks and garbage, and encouraging energy conservation and recycling. Congress also created the Environmental Protection Agency (EPA) to enforce the new laws.

Perhaps the most controversial environmental regulations are **environmental impact statements**, which assess the potential effects of new construction or development on the environment. Most projects using federal funds must prepare such statements, and since 1970, thousands have been filed. Supporters contend that the statements reveal major environmental risks in new construction projects and can lead to cost savings and greater environmental awareness. Critics claim that they represent more government interference, paperwork, and delays in the public and private sectors.

Environmental impact statements are only one form of environmental regulation, however. In 1990, Congress amended the Clean Air Act to tighten controls on automobiles and the fuel they use. Building on earlier mileage regulation, the 1990 amendments required automakers to install pollution controls to reduce emissions of hydrocarbons and nitrogen oxides and set stiff standards for the kinds of gasoline that can be sold. The 1990 Act also required power companies to cut pollution from coal-burning power plants, phased out the use of certain chemicals that harm the earth's protective ozone layer and may contribute to global warming, and set new limits on a long list of cancer-causing pollutants. In 2005, the Bush administration implemented a new set of relatively loose regulations supporting its Clear Skies initiative, but most of these regulations were repealed and replaced by more stringent limits by the Obama administration. Despite its track record in improving air and water quality, Republicans have argued that the EPA impedes innovation and weakens U.S. competitiveness. Republican presidential candidate Mitt Romney promised that he would drastically cut EPA regulations if he became president.

☐ Encouraging Corporate Social Responsibility

Many corporations have been dealing with the increased pressure to be more responsible by creating programs to give money and volunteer time to their communities. The Gap has pledged to provide a portion of every sale to charities through "Product Red," and other corporations have promised to be more environmentally conscious. These efforts at **corporate social responsibility** have increased public confidence in big business.

There are three forms of corporate social responsibility. The first is corporate giving to charities. Many corporations have foundations that give 1 or 2 percent of their annual profits to specific causes. The second is free consulting and advertising to help charities become more effective in making their voices heard. The third pairs corporations and charities in partnership activities such as annual walks for cancer. Many

16.1

16.2

16.3

16.4

16.5

16.6

FOR the People Government's Greatest Endeavors

Protecting the Air and Water

One of the most visible forms of economic regulation involves the federal government's effort to protect the nation's air and water from pollution. Although early laws such as the 1948 Water Pollution Act and the 1963 Clean Air Act established a federal role in protecting the environment, the 1970 Clean Air and 1972 Clean Water Acts provided much of the legal power to make progress in both areas.

During the past 30 years, the levels of most air pollution covered by the Clean Air Act have fallen dramatically as the U.S. Environmental Protection Agency has established ever-tighter rules promoting more efficient automobiles and cleaner-burning fuels. Although it is hard to find a single American city where the air quality has not improved, air pollution continues to spread to rural areas such as national parks where automobile pollution is concentrated as tourists arrive in record numbers.

Similarly, it is hard to find a single body of water or river that is not significantly cleaner because of the Clean Water Act. However, as the nation has learned more about pollutants such as arsenic, the pressure to improve water quality has increased. The Obama administration has been moving to expand both acts to cover new pollutants, while tightening limits on acceptable levels of exposure. It is also pushing for legislation to address the rising global temperature.

Despite these successes, there are many challenges ahead in keeping the air and water clean. The 2010 Gulf oil spill is a good example. As technology has become more sophisticated, the oil industry has been drilling at much greater depths below the water and in much more fragile environments. The Gulf oil spill shows how risky such drilling is, especially since the federal rules governing oil exploration were more than 30 years old when the spill occurred.

QUESTIONS

1. How clean should the air and water be in order to be declared "clean"?
2. How can the federal government protect the environment without hurting industry and creating unemployment when dirty factories must close?
3. What can citizens do to improve the environment through their own actions?

corporations also encourage their employees to volunteer by giving them a day or two a month of paid leave.

compliance costs
The cost of meeting regulatory reporting requirements.

The Deregulation Movement

16.6 Evaluate the advantages and disadvantages of the deregulation movement.

There are two reasons that government regulation of the economy is often criticized.

First, government regulations impose heavy paperwork and reporting burdens on the economy. Corporations often complain that they have to fill out too many lengthy reports, hire too many lawyers to interpret the rules, conduct too many studies proving they are obeying the law, and spend too much time monitoring their actions. These tasks help reassure government that they comply with the laws, but cost money that could be used to create jobs, build plants, or develop new ideas for economic growth.

Second, the regulations themselves can raise the cost of economic activity, which are described as **compliance costs**. It costs money to build clean and safe power plants, for example, or manufacture high-mileage automobiles. It also costs money to pay workers a minimum wage, provide family leave for the birth of a child or care for an aging parent, prevent workplace accidents, provide benefits such as health care coverage for employees with preexisting medical conditions, and seek federal approval for mergers with other corporations.

The U.S. government often helps business meet these requirements by providing tax breaks for new equipment, loans for specific activities such as the development of the solar power industry or creation of a small business, direct payments

BY the People Making a Difference

Join (PRODUCT)[RED]

Citizens can affect corporate behavior in many ways. They can boycott products that they think are dangerous to the environment, organize protests against companies that treat their employees unfairly, or purchase products such as a cup of fair-trade coffee that help citizens in other countries.

(PRODUCT)[RED] was launched in 2006 as a partnership between a group of artists, celebrities, and companies. With The GAP clothing stores in the lead, RED promised to give a portion of every purchase of a RED product such as a sweater, cell phone, laptop, or even a car (all colored red, of course) to the Global Fund to Fight AIDS, Tuberculosis, and Malaria. Thus far, more than 20 companies have joined the campaign, including The GAP, Converse Shoes, Motorola, Starbucks, and Apple. In late December 2011, Apple added its iPad Smart Cover Red Special Edition to the list of RED products.

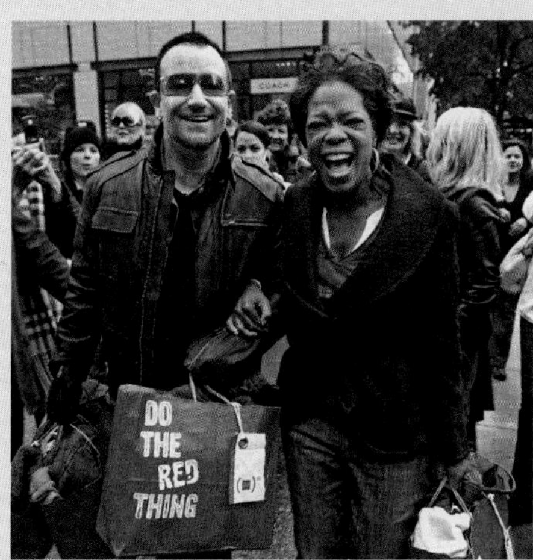

Bono and Oprah Winfrey were the most visible celebrities leading (PRODUCT)[RED].

Corporations clearly had ample incentives to participate, if only because it created greater consumer demand for their products. But they also participated because of a commitment to corporate social responsibility, which is a term that refers to the role that corporations play in improving the quality of life through their own behavior.

Citizens can be involved in RED in many ways. They can join the RED information stream for updates on the fight against AIDS, tuberculosis, and malaria; "brand" their own Web sites by adopting the free RED logo and color scheme; buy RED products; and give money directly to RED. The list of products can be found at http://www.joinred.com. All contributions to RED can be deducted from individual and corporate income taxes.

Although RED was designed as a way to raise money for the Global Fund, it has expanded throughout the past five years to make sure that corporations honor the commitments they make in adopting the RED logo. It also works to make sure the money raised is actually transferred to the Global Fund.

RED has its critics, however. Some argue that the effort is more about selling products and making money than addressing AIDS. Others suggest that RED spends more on advertising its products than needed.

Nevertheless, joining RED, buying TOMS shoes (which gives away a pair of shoes for every pair purchased), or even boycotting products is a tangible, and often successful way to influence the economy and spur corporate social responsibility.

QUESTIONS

1. Is RED a form of economic policy and, if so, why? Does it stimulate purchasing that would not have taken place otherwise?
2. Does it matter that corporations make profits by joining RED? Why would a corporation want to participate in the program, and does its motivation matter as long as it contributes its share to RED?
3. Is RED the best way that citizens can help the world fight AIDS, tuberculosis, and malaria?

and subsidies for certain kinds of goods and services such as land conservation, and even insurance against failure, but many regulations still require significant investments that reduce profit and may increase the cost of developing the new products that create jobs. Even with this support, more than half of small businesses fail within the first five years of their lives, while many new ideas never reach the market.[16]

More troubling, some loans, subsidies, and insurance reward the wrong goals, and are sometimes squandered. In late 2011, for example, the Solyndra Corporation defaulted on a $500 million federal loan after promising a great breakthrough in developing much less expensive power cells. Despite acclaim for its new technology, the corporation closed its doors and fired 1,100 workers. Congress began investigating the loan based on allegations that the Obama administration had asked the corporation to

16.1

16.2

16.3

16.4

16.5

16.6

deregulation
A policy promoting cutbacks in the amount of federal regulation in specific areas of economic activity.

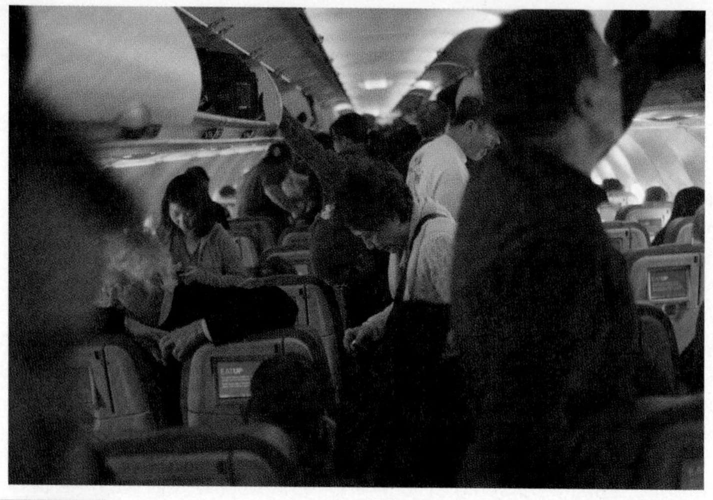

Airline deregulation was the first major breakthrough in the deregulation movement. It sparked the rise of a number of low-cost airlines such as Southwest, but also produced mergers of giant airlines such as Delta and Northwest, and United and Continental, which raised prices in certain "hubs" dominated by a single airline.

continue operations through the 2010 and 2012 elections before making its politically embarrassing decision.

These regulatory impacts have led to persistent calls for **deregulation**, which is a term that encompasses efforts to reduce or abolish federal regulation in either a particular sector of the economy or the economy as a whole. The deregulation movement has always existed to some extent, but achieved its greatest success in the late 1970s with deregulation of the airline, trucking, and railroad industries.

Even as the movement succeeded in deregulating certain industries, it has put pressure on government to limit its regulation on economic activity as a whole. In 1993, for example, President Clinton issued an executive order prohibiting agencies from issuing regulations unless the benefits of the regulations (in lives saved, for example) outweighed the costs. In 2001, President Bush followed suit by imposing a 60-day hold on all regulations published by the Clinton administration until his administration could ensure that they passed the benefit/cost test. And in 2012, President Obama called for further deregulation and a reduction in compliance costs.

☐ Deregulating Transportation

No industry has undergone more extensive deregulation than the transportation industry. During the past generation, airlines, trucking, and railroads have been granted considerable freedom to conduct their businesses with minimal federal regulation.

Airline deregulation was the first major victory in the deregulation movement, and remains one of its most visible successes. The federal government began regulating aviation when it established the Civil Aeronautics Board (CAB) in 1938 to control rates and fares, and protect airlines from what it deemed as unreasonable competition. Critics charged that government regulation reduced the competition that leads to lower fares as airlines built the hub-and-spokes system that gives individual companies almost complete control of airport landing gates.

After years of debate, Congress abolished the CAB in 1978, allowing the market to set fares through competition. The end of airline regulation has created problems but has resulted in generally lower fares, greater choice of routes and fares in most markets, and more efficient use of assets by the industry.[17] If an airline is overcharging passengers, or so the theory of deregulation argues, a competitor will win those travelers to their airline. Carriers have thus had to streamline their operations in order to survive in a competitive market. Southwest and JetBlue

Airlines are examples of discount airlines that took advantage of deregulation to take on larger airlines.[18]

But recent mergers of major airlines have worsened the problems that deregulation and cancellation of service brought to small and medium-sized cities. Facing higher fuel costs and declining passenger loads, most airlines now charge baggage fees and no longer serve free meals. Some have also limited service to smaller markets, while raising fares during peak travel times. Although these are all examples of a free market at work, some of the changes have reduced passenger loyalty and may have compromised required safety checks. Moreover, deregulation has actually encouraged further expansion of the hub-and-spokes system as airlines have merged together to control certain airports and routes. Delta Airlines has most of the landing gates in Atlanta, United holds most of the gates in Chicago, and American controls most of the gates in Dallas. As a result, passengers often pay higher fares to fly in and out of those cities.

☐ Deregulating Banking

Banking deregulation was also a great victory for the movement. Enacted in the 1990s when Congress repealed a long list of regulations that governed the amount of money banks could make and their use of sophisticated products such as mortgage-backed securities, the effort invited industry consolidation and the creation of banks that are still called "too big to fail."[19] Although the deregulation gave consumers new access to home loans, ATMs, and credit cards, it also exposed the economy to greater risk. Specifically, the increased access to home loans stimulated large increases in home values, which fueled more housing construction and a growing inventory of unsold properties.

Eventually, the "housing bubble" popped, and the industry collapsed like a row of dominoes. Many homeowners soon found that their houses were worth less than the amount of their loans, and stopped paying their mortgages. In turn, banks stopped making loans to hopeful home buyers and began foreclosing on homeowners who could not make their monthly payments. As a result, banks moved closer to failure because deregulation had loosened the rules on how much money they needed to keep in reserve to cover bad loans. Then the construction industry stopped building homes, state property tax revenues fell with home prices, and huge investment firms such as Lehman Brothers discovered that the packages of mortgages they had purchased as safe investments were now worthless. Although many factors led to the 2008 collapse, deregulation is often blamed for the spark that led the United States and the rest of the world into a long recession and prolonged high unemployment. Although Congress began reregulating the banking industry in 2010, the industry has fought hard to prevent tough new rules, and spent much of 2012 weakening the proposals for eliminating the risky behavior that led to the 2008 collapse.

A Continued Federal Role

Despite campaign promises to reduce the federal government's economic role and give more money back to citizens and corporations, members of Congress and the president understand the federal government must be active in the economic life of the nation. It will continue to collect taxes, regulate the money supply, prevent monopolies that would hurt consumers, and promote free trade. It will do all this while trying to let the market, not government regulators, shape the demand for and the price of products and services. Nevertheless, regulation is making a comeback in the wake of the banking collapse and continued concerns about breakdowns in regulatory oversight of food and drugs, the airline industry, and oil drilling.

Most U.S. citizens want their government to play only a limited role in the economy, but competing values such as fairness, equality, protection of workers and the environment, and support of healthy competition inevitably encourage elected officials to take on referee responsibilities in order to promote the common good.

At the same time, many citizens blame their government for being too big to fail itself. As much as they want government to do something to create jobs and stimulate growth during difficult times, they also want it to let the free market work. Citizens exert a great deal of influence on economic policy, if only by purchasing goods and services. But they can also influence policy through pressure on their representatives, and by telling their own stories of economic success and frustration.

On MyPoliSciLab

Review the Chapter

Listen to **Chapter 16** on **MyPoliSciLab**

An Introduction to Economic Policy

16.1 Describe the federal government's role in making economic policy and how the economy's performance is measured, p. 507.

Inflation and unemployment are considered the two most important measures of economic performance. However, economists also monitor the size of the federal budget deficit, the balance of trade, income inequality, and gross domestic product (GDP). Inflation and unemployment tend to move together in opposite directions—inflation rises as unemployment drops, and it falls as unemployment rises.

Fiscal Policy

16.2 Outline the tools and impact of fiscal policy on the economy, p. 511.

Fiscal policy consists of economic policies made by Congress and the president. There are two basic tools of fiscal policy—collecting revenues through taxes and fees and spending money through the federal budget. Increasing government spending stimulates the economy, thereby reducing unemployment, whereas increasing taxes generally slows economic growth, thereby curtailing inflation. The federal government also spends money through tax expenditures hidden from public view.

Monetary Policy

16.3 Outline the tools and impact of fiscal policy on the economy, p. 515.

Monetary policy is used by the Federal Reserve Board (the Fed) to affect the supply of money circulating through the economy. The federal funds rate is the Fed's most important tool for making monetary policy. The rate establishes the amount of interest the Fed charges banks to borrow money, which eventually determines the amount of interest banks charge their customers to borrow money for automobiles, homes, and credit card balances. Raising the cost of money is generally a way to slow down the economy and reduce inflation; lowering the cost of money ignites the economy and reduces unemployment.

Promoting the Economy

16.4 Identify ways in which the federal government seeks to promote economic growth, p. 519.

The federal government has long promoted the economy and specific industries. It also promotes trade and commerce with other nations, including efforts to reduce barriers to imports and exports, stabilize prices of certain goods and services, and encourage innovation through patents and other protections.

Regulating the Economy

16.5 Categorize ways in which the federal government seeks to regulate the economy, p. 522.

Economic regulation is designed to control the behavior of the economy in a variety of ways such as preventing monopolies, reducing environmental pollution, and protecting workers. Many regulations were designed to curb specific abuses and promote competition.

The Deregulation Movement

16.6 Evaluate the advantages and disadvantages of the deregulation movement, p. 528.

The deregulation movement centers on the belief that the government's economic regulations are too costly and often fail to achieve their desired ends. Democrats and Republicans have both supported deregulation of key industries during the past four decades, but it sometimes produces new problems that create a backlash in favor of reregulation.

Learn the Terms

Study and **Review** the **Flashcards**

fiscal policy, p. 508
monetary policy, p. 508
inflation, p. 509
unemployment, p. 509
gross domestic product (GDP), p. 510
income inequality, p. 510
wealth, p. 510
excise tax, p. 512
budget deficit, p. 512
tariff, p. 512
progressive tax, p. 512
regressive tax, p. 512
national debt, p. 512
mandatory spending, p. 512
discretionary spending, p. 513
Office of Management and Budget (OMB), p. 513
Congressional Budget Office (CBO), p. 514
tax expenditure, p. 514
sales tax, p. 514

value-added tax (VAT), p. 514
Federal Reserve System, p. 515
federal funds rate, p. 516
laissez-faire economics, p. 517
Keynesian economics, p. 517
protectionism, p. 520
trade deficit, p. 520
General Agreement on Tariffs and Trade (GATT), p. 522
World Trade Organization (WTO), p. 522
North American Free Trade Agreement (NAFTA), p. 522
monopoly, p. 524
antitrust legislation, p. 524
trust, p. 524
closed shop, p. 525
union shop, p. 525
labor injunction, p. 525
collective bargaining, p. 525
environmental impact statement, p. 527
corporate social responsibility, p. 527
compliance costs, p. 528
deregulation, p. 530

Test Yourself

Study and **Review** the **Practice Tests**

MULTIPLE CHOICE QUESTIONS

16.1 Describe the federal government's role in making economic policy and how the economy's performance is measured.

The federal government uses which of these policies in regulating the economy?

a. fiscal policies
b. monetary policies
c. regulation of business, labor, and environmental practices
d. promoting economic growth
e. all of the above

16.2 Outline the tools and impact of fiscal policy on the economy.

The following are all tools of fiscal policy *except*

a. spending money.
b. collecting taxes.
c. imposing tariffs.
d. creating tax expenditures.
e. reducing the supply of money circulating through the economy.

16.3 Outline the tools and impact of monetary policy on the economy.

Which economic theory is central to monetary policy?

a. supply and demand theory
b. the theory of business cycles
c. laissez-faire economics
d. Keynesian economics
e. employment control theory

16.4 Identify ways in which the federal government seeks to promote economic growth.

What is one way Congress and the president promote the economy?

a. raising taxes
b. balancing the budget
c. borrowing money
d. making trade agreements with other nations
e. lowering discretionary spending

16.5 Categorize ways in which the federal government seeks to regulate the economy.

Which of the following are important effects of government regulation?

a. maintaining competition
b. controlling interstate commerce
c. preventing environmental pollution
d. preventing discrimination in employment
e. all of the above

16.6 Evaluate the advantages and disadvantages of the deregulation movement.

The industry that was the first major success in the deregulation movement *was*

a. banking.
b. telecommunications.
c. transportation.
d. publishing.
e. agriculture.

ESSAY QUESTION

Describe the federal government's economic policy making role and how economic performance is measured, then distinguish between fiscal and monetary policy as ways to deal with economic crises such as inflation and unemployment.

Explore Further

IN THE LIBRARY

Stephen G. Breyer, *Breaking the Vicious Circle: Toward Effective Risk Regulation* (Harvard University Press, 1993).

Gary Bryner, *Blue Skies, Green Politics: The Clean Air Act of 1990 and Its Interpretation,* 2d ed. (CQ Press, 1995).

Gary Burtless, Robert J. Lawrence, Robert E. Litan, and Robert J. Shapiro, *Globaphobia: Confronting Fears About Open Trade* (Brookings Institution Press, 1998).

Robert M. Entman, *Competition, Innovation, and Investment in Telecommunications* (Aspen Institute, 1998).

Thomas L. Friedman, *The World Is Flat: A Brief History of the Twenty-First Century* (Farrar, Straus, & Giroux, 2005).

Philip K. Howard, *The Death of Common Sense: How Law Is Suffocating America* (Random House, 1994).

Paul Krugman, *The Return of Depression Economics and the Crisis of 2008* (W.W. Norton, 2009).

Robert Kuttner, *Everything for Sale: The Virtues and Limits of Markets* (Knopf, 1997).

Michael Lewis, *The Big Short: Inside the Doomsday Machine* (W.W. Norton, 2010).

Peter G. Peterson, *Facing Up: Paying Our Nation's Debt and Saving Our Children's Future* (Simon & Schuster, 1994).

Andrew Ross Sorkin, *Too Big to Fail: The Inside Story of How Wall Street and Washington Fought to Save the Financial System and Themselves* (Viking, 2010).

Allen Schick, *The Federal Budget: Politics, Policy, Process,* rev. ed. (Brookings Institution Press, 2007).

Joseph E. Stiglitz, *Globalization and Its Discontents* (Norton, 2002).

U.S. Senate Permanent Subcommittee On Investigations, *Wall Street and the Financial Crisis: Anatomy of a Financial Collapse* (U.S. Government Printing Office, 2011).

Daniel Yergin And Joseph Stanislaw, *The Commanding Heights: The Battle Between Government and the Marketplace That Is Remaking the Modern World* (Simon & Schuster, 1998).

ON THE WEB

OMB.gov
All the information on what the federal government has spent in the past and will spend in the future. Specific information on historical trends can be found in the historical tables section of the federal budget.

Federalreserve.gov
The key Web site for information on monetary policy.

usaspending.gov
An easily accessible source of information on where the federal dollars go.

CBO.gov
A source of detailed budget analysis from the Congressional Budget Office, which provides analysis to Congress.

17

Listen to Chapter 17 on MyPoliSciLab

Making Social Policy

Social policy involves efforts to promote the general welfare of U.S. citizens through domestic programs. It is mostly composed of a long list of programs to help citizens during tough economic times, but contains many other programs that benefit specific groups of citizens such as older Americans. The list of social policy programs has expanded greatly since the Great Depression, and accounted for almost $2.5 trillion of the federal government's $3.7 trillion 2012 budget.[1]

President Barack Obama added his own share of that spending to the budget with one of the largest domestic policy agendas since Lyndon Johnson in the 1960s. None of his priorities was more controversial than health insurance for the millions of Americans without coverage for either hospital or physician care. Obama started the policy process immediately after his inauguration in 2009 with a dramatic proposal to establish a new government insurance plan called the "public option" that would give all Americans, insured or not, the chance to participate in a new national insurance program modeled on the Medicare program discussed later in this chapter.

After months of negotiations, Obama and congressional Democrats reluctantly agreed to drop the public option. In its place, the final bill required every American to purchase health insurance or face a stiff federal penalty. The bill also included new taxes on "Cadillac" private insurance plans that give higher-income Americans almost complete coverage for nearly every medical, dental, and home-health care service. Last-minute bargaining produced just enough votes for passage, and the $1 trillion program became law with the president's signature in March 2010. As enacted, the Patient Protection and Affordable Health Care for America Act included most of Obama's original requests. Although the law provided insurance coverage for nearly 32 million citizens, it still left 5 percent of the population uncovered. The legislation passed with little Republican support, and was immediately challenged. In July 2012, the Supreme Court upheld the law.

Known as "Obamacare," once it was signed, the new legislation was turned over to the Centers for Medicare and Medicaid Services (CMS) for implementation. With 4,000 employees, CMS is an agency within the Department of Health and Human Services and reports directly

17.1

Outline the goals of the federal government's social policy and the forms of protection it provides, p. 539.

17.2

Outline the evolution of social policy throughout the twentieth century, p. 543.

17.3

Evaluate the current status of and challenges for federal government policy in the areas of health care, education, and crime, p. 551.

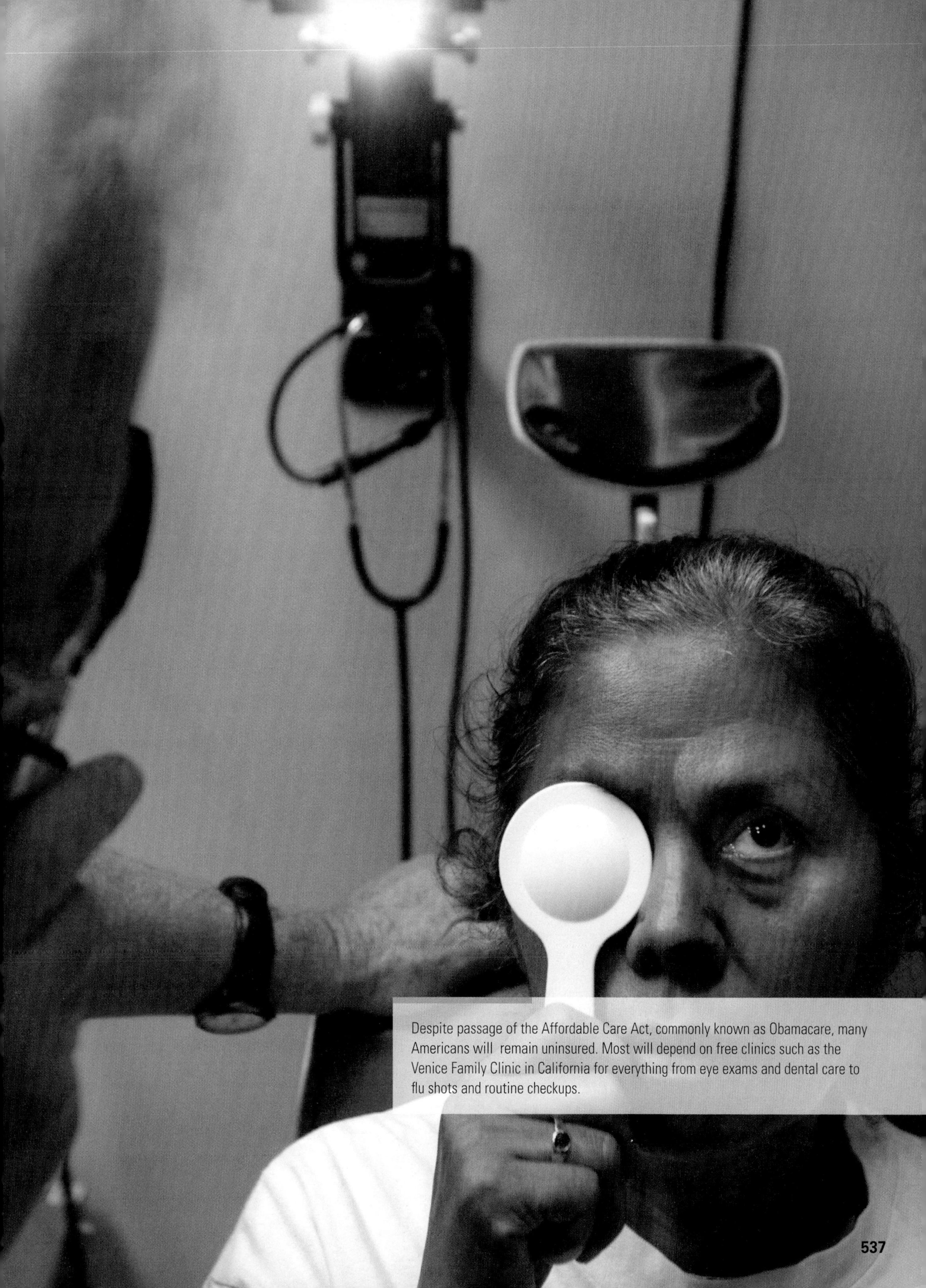

Despite passage of the Affordable Care Act, commonly known as Obamacare, many Americans will remain uninsured. Most will depend on free clinics such as the Venice Family Clinic in California for everything from eye exams and dental care to flu shots and routine checkups.

MyPoliSciLab Video Series

 Watch on MyPoliSciLab

The Big Picture How responsible is the government for your social welfare? Author Paul C. Light traces the government's involvement in welfare from the Revolutionary War to the present, and he explains why charities and corporations are not capable of performing the same role.

The Basics Find out what public policy is, who makes public policy, and how they make it. In this video, you will also explore the major social policy issues we face and consider the role of the federal and state governments in specific areas such as education.

In Context Discover the history of social policy in the United States. In this video, Columbia University political scientist Ester Fuchs discusses why social policy emerged and how the focus of social policy has changed over time.

Thinking Like a Political Scientist What role do political scientists play in policy-making? Columbia University political scientist Ester Fuchs examines not only the research of political scientist on public policy, but the impact of this research on the policy-making process.

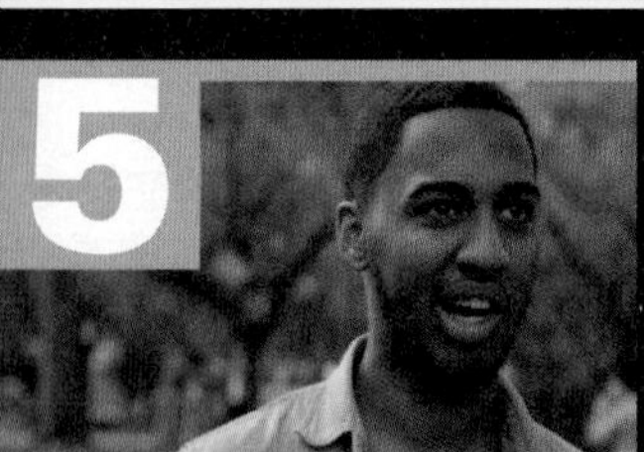

In the Real World In order to reduce unemployment among younger people, the federal government allows companies to pay workers under the age of 20 less than the minimum wage. Real people discuss the larger implications of this law, and whether or not it is beneficial or harmful to young people.

So What? Find out what will happen when the baby boom generation starts to retire. Author Paul C. Light breaks down government spending, and he explains why younger people are going to have to start paying more taxes to support Social Security and other programs for retired people.

to the department's secretary. Reorganized in 1996, it has primary responsibility for making the rules on all health care legislation, including Medicare, Medicaid, and Obamacare. Although Obamacare was still working its way through the federal courts in 2012, CMS had no choice but to issue rules and proceed with faithfully executing the laws. In 2010, it had 26 provisions to implement, and made all the deadlines; it had another 20 in 2011, and made 17; it had 11 in 2012, and made 9, with another 13 due by the end of 2013.[2]

With many states resisting the rules, however, CMS was required under law to create a new federal program that would give citizens a choice of insurance plans. Although implementation of the original bill was anything but easy, implementation of the new insurance program pool, as it is called, would be one of the most difficult tasks in recent history. "They have a Herculean task," one health expert outside CMS told the *Washington Post*, "even if everyone was cooperating."[3]

Obamacare illustrates the difficulties in designing, enacting, and eventually implementing a new federal social program. No matter how well intentioned new legislation may be, new programs require time to take hold and do not always work as intended.

Citizens have a clear interest in social policy, if only because the federal government and its state and local partners are there to protect them in crisis. And, as members of interest groups large and small, such as the Children's Defense Fund, the American Medical Association, or the American Association of Retired Persons (AARP), with nearly 40 million dues-paying members, all over the age of 50, they can make their voices heard on major issues such as health care reform.

The Role of the Federal Government in Social Policy

17.1 Outline the goals of the federal government's social policy and the forms of protection it provides.

Most Western governments expanded their social programs long before the United States did. American adults generally believed that people who could not succeed in a nation as big, rich, and open as the United States simply weren't working hard enough. This commitment to rugged individualism meant that government, whether local, state, or federal, played only a limited role in people's lives. Governments began expanding aid in the early twentieth century, starting with state programs to help older citizens and orphaned children. But government aid was limited, and most low-income people relied on charity for help, as many still do.[4]

This is not to suggest that the new federal government did not embrace at least some forms of social policy, however. From its founding, the government took care of its military veterans. Indeed, with the Revolutionary War barely over, the Continental Congress established the nation's first programs to help soldiers disabled in battle and to provide retirement pensions for officers.

The financial security system for veterans expanded slowly but steadily as the soldiers aged into disability and poverty.[5] In 1818, for example, Congress expanded retirement benefits to cover all veterans of the Revolutionary War, whether officers or not, and created the first old soldiers' homes for poor veterans. In 1840, Congress expanded the veterans program again to provide financial relief to the widows of soldiers killed in battle.

These early programs set two important precedents for contemporary domestic policy. First, they established the notion that some people would be automatically entitled to certain government benefits on the basis of an eligibility requirement such as service in the nation's armed forces. Thus, veterans' relief was the nation's first

The Global Community

The Social Safety Net

The social safety net comprises all government responses to continuing problems such as hunger, disease, and poverty. Although countries vary greatly in the amount of need, the Pew Research Center's 2009 Global Attitudes Survey shows that significant percentages of citizens go without access to basic human needs every year.

The survey asked respondents, "Have there been times during the last year when you did not have enough money to (a) buy food your family needed, (b) pay for medical care your family needed, (c) and buy clothing your family needed?"

These answers provide a barometer of economic and social progress. Most of the world was hard hit by the 2008 recession, but citizens of Britain, China, India, and Japan said the safety nets in their nations were stronger than their fellow citizens in Mexico, Nigeria, and the United States.

Even stronger nations showed weaknesses in some parts of their safety nets than others. In China, for example, citizens reported fewer problems buying food and clothing, but a third said they had problems with access to health care. The problem lies in the rapid expansion of the Chinese population, which is putting pressure on the health system. Although the Chinese economy is growing rapidly too, the country has faced difficulty converting its growth into health care access.

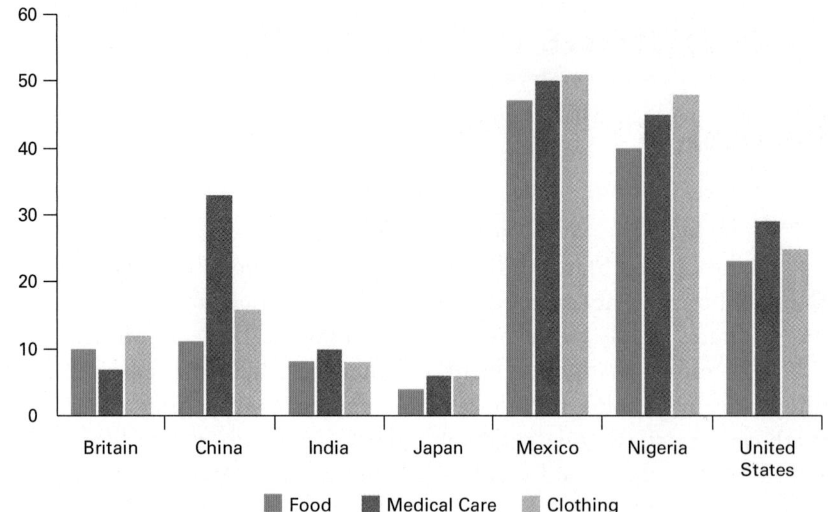

SOURCE: Pew Research Center, *The Global Middle Class: Views on Democracy, Religion, Values, and Life Satisfaction in Emerging Nations* (Pew Research Center, 2009).

CRITICAL THINKING QUESTIONS

1. Besides the economy, why might citizens in some countries have greater problems getting access to basic necessities such as food, health care, and clothing?
2. Does this lack of access have an impact on trust in government and other measures of citizen participation? What is the effect of hunger and poverty on how citizens think of other freedoms?
3. Why do so many Americans lack access to basic necessities? Are you surprised?

entitlement program. An entitlement program provides benefits to any citizen who is eligible for support regardless of need, and is considered an uncontrollable part of the federal budget. In the following 230 years, Congress and the president have created dozens of entitlement programs, including Social Security and Medicare.

Second, as discussed later in this chapter, these early programs also established government's right to restrict some benefits to only those citizens who could actually prove their need for help. These were early examples of what we now call **means-tested entitlements**, which are programs that require individual citizens to prove that they do not exceed certain income and asset levels before they can receive benefits. In most cases, entitlements are available only to low-income citizens, the unemployed, or groups such as older Americans. During and after the Great Depression of the 1930s, Congress and the president created dozens of means-tested entitlement programs, including food stamps for individuals and families that do not make enough money to buy nutritious food. Although the food stamp program was renamed as the Supplemental Nutrition Assistance Program (SNAP) in 2009, is still called food stamps by many beneficiaries. The program only provides benefits to individuals with less than $1,200 in monthly income, and families with less than $2,500. The program also requires individuals and families to count other resources such as bank accounts and the values of their cars in making the eligibility assessment.

Having entered the twentieth century with only a handful of domestic programs, most of which were built around helping veterans, the federal government left the century with a deep inventory of such programs. According to the 2012 *Catalog of Federal Domestic Assistance,* which lists every one of the federal government's approximately 2,220 domestic funding programs in a searchable database (www.cfda.gov), the Department of Health and Human Services had 464 programs, followed by the Department of the Interior at 264, Agriculture at 21, Education at 154, and Housing and Urban Development at 122.[6]

entitlements
Programs such as unemployment insurance, disaster relief, or disability payments that provide benefits to all eligible citizens.

means-tested entitlements
Programs such as Medicaid and welfare under which applicants must meet eligibility requirements based on need.

social safety net
The many programs that the federal government provides to protect Americans against economic and social misfortune.

☐ The Goals of Social Policy

Because most of these programs are restricted to one group of citizens only, they are often described as *categorical* aid. Simply typing a search term online such as "students," "elderly," "children," "disabled," "workers," "farmers," "women," or "veterans" reveals just how much help the federal government provides in each category. But regardless of category, federal domestic policy focuses on two broad goals.

The first is to protect citizens against social and economic problems by creating a **social safety net**, whether through relief for unemployed workers, health care for the elderly, emergency shelter for the homeless, or school lunches for poor children, most of which are available to citizens only on the basis of a means test. Although almost all citizens are covered by federal unemployment insurance through a payroll tax, only workers who have been laid off from their jobs through no fault of their own can qualify for benefits, and then only for a relatively brief period of time.

The second goal of federal social policy is to raise the quality of life for all citizens, whether by improving air and water quality, building roads and bridges, regulating air traffic, fighting crime, or strengthening local schools through federal aid. Nearly all federal aid to the states for these purposes is distributed by formula on the basis of population, not need.

☐ Types of Protection

Most scholars trace the federal government's effort to protect citizens against economic and personal hard times to the Great Depression and the Social Security Act of 1935. Although Franklin Roosevelt's New Deal agenda stimulated a remarkable expansion in the federal government's domestic policy role, federal, state, and local governments were helping citizens long before the Depression hit. However, as the nation sank deeper into economic distress, Congress and the president invented two

17.1

17.2

17.3

public assistance
Aid to the poor; "welfare."

The collapse of the economy in 2008 meant that millions of people lost their homes because they could not pay their mortgages. Here, members of a public interest group called ACORN called on Congress to enact legislation to cap foreclosures by banks. ACORN was disbanded in 2010 after a scandal involving misconduct by several of its employees.

very different types of federal programs to protect citizens against hardship, both of which continue today.

PUBLIC ASSISTANCE One type of help for the poor is called **public assistance**, commonly known as *welfare*. The first public assistance programs were actually created in the late 1800s, when states established aid programs to help poor single mothers and their children. Although these programs were often described as "mothers' pensions" to create the impression that the beneficiaries had earned the benefits through some contribution, they created a precedent for many of the federal government's later antipoverty programs.

Most of these programs are means-tested entitlement programs. Such programs require applicants to disclose all financial assets and income to prove they fall below the poverty line, generally calculated as three times the amount of money an individual or family needs to purchase the food for a nutritious diet. This poverty level changes with the size of the family and the cost of living. In 2012, a family of four with an annual income of $23,050 or less was eligible for most means-tested assistance.[7]

Public assistance in the United States today incorporates elements of job training, transportation subsidies, housing subsidies, free school lunches, food aid for poor families and pregnant mothers with young children, and tax credits for low-income people. The federal government also provides what some critics label "corporate welfare" to favored industries such as agriculture and corporate bailouts to the financial industry, as well as "middle-class welfare" to college students, home buyers, and the citizenry as a whole in the form of college loans, tax deductions for home mortgages, and access to national parks and forests (supported by taxpayers but rarely used by poor people). However, the term "welfare" is generally reserved for public assistance to the low-income Americans.

In absolute numbers, most poor people are white. As a percentage within their own group, however, a larger proportion of African Americans and Hispanics are poor. Moreover, in both absolute and proportional terms, more women than men are poor. Indeed, some scholars refer to the relatively recent rise in poverty among women as the "feminization of poverty."[8]

SOCIAL INSURANCE The second type of protection against hardship is **social insurance**, government programs that provide benefits to anyone who is eligible because of either past service (veterans, miners, merchant marines) or prepayments of some kind (payroll taxes for Social Security and Medicare or insurance premiums).

social insurance
Programs in which eligibility is based on prior contributions to government, usually in the form of payroll taxes.

Many federal assistance programs are partnerships with state governments. There are two reasons for the connection. First, except for veterans' policy, states have been responsible for protecting their citizens against hardship since the United States was formed. Second, state and local governments have the administrative agencies to stay in touch with recipients of aid, whether to make sure they are actually eligible for support or to provide services such as job training or school lunches.

Because states vary greatly in their generosity and resources, most federal assistance is designed to set a minimum floor of support that individual states can raise on their own. The most generous states in the country tend to be located in the Northeast and West, where living costs tend to be higher and legislatures more liberal, whereas the least generous tend to be found in the South. In this way, states act as a check on the federal government's ability to raise benefits too far, frustrating those who believe that the federal government should set a uniform level of benefits for all citizens. (Table 17.1 shows the amount of federal payments to individuals in 2012.)

TABLE 17.1 FEDERAL PAYMENTS TO INDIVIDUALS, 2012 (IN BILLIONS)

Major Public Assistance Programs
Medicaid: $269
Food Stamps (SNAP): $80
Earned Income Tax Credit: $46
Student Loans and Assistance: $45
Supplemental Security Income: $43
Family Support Payments to States: $21
Child Nutrition and Milk Programs: $18
Social Insurance
Social Security: $624
Medicare: $571
Federal Employee and Military Retirement: $175
Disability Insurance: $135
Veterans Programs: $100
Unemployment Insurance: $94
State Children's Health Insurance Program (CHIP): $9

■ *Why is social security so expensive, and why is its cost increasing rapidly?*

SOURCE: *Budget of the U.S. Government, Fiscal Year 2013*, Historical Tables, (U.S. Government Printing Office, February 2012) available at http://www.whitehouse.gov/omb/budget/Historicals

The Expansion of Social Policy in the Twentieth Century

17.2 Outline the evolution of social policy throughout the twentieth century.

he federal government's commitment to helping the poor and improving the quality of life expanded rapidly during the Great Depression, which followed the stock market crash of 1929. The social safety net built by state and local governments and private charities at that time simply could not meet the needs of the huge increase in the homeless, unemployed, and poor.

Social Security
A combination of entitlement programs, paid for by employer and employee taxes, that includes retirement benefits, health insurance, and support for disabled workers and the children of deceased or disabled workers.

☐ The New Deal

Franklin Roosevelt was responsible for the expansion of social programs during the 1930s. As part of his New Deal agenda, the federal government began making loans to states and localities to help the poor, and soon it launched a long list of programs to help older workers (Social Security), the jobless (unemployment insurance), and the poor (Aid to Families with Dependent Children).

THE FIRST 100 DAYS Before creating these signature New Deal programs, however, the Roosevelt administration moved quickly to help low-income Americans. The first 100 days of 1933 produced the most significant list of legislation ever passed in U.S. history, including the Federal Emergency Relief Administration (FERA), which was established to give unemployed workers cash grants to get them through the summer.

The list of "alphabet agencies" grew longer as the administration created a host of new programs to help the poor, including the Works Progress Administration (WPA), which was created in 1935 to provide work for millions of unemployed, and the Civilian Conservation Corps (CCC), which put millions of young people to work clearing trails and building roads in the national forests and parks. Between 1933 and 1945, for example, the WPA put 8.5 million people to work at a cost of $10 billion. All told, the WPA built 650,000 miles of roads, 125,000 public buildings, 8,200 parks, and 850 airports. Though the wages were hardly generous, these and other New Deal programs created a national safety net to catch those in need. It is little wonder that scholars describe the New Deal as the "big bang" of social policy.[9] Although the distinction between the worthy and unworthy poor still remained, joblessness was no longer defined as merely a problem of individual idleness or the unwillingness to work.

HELP FOR OLDER CITIZENS Once past the immediate crisis, the Roosevelt administration began designing the flagship programs of the New Deal. First on the list was **Social Security**, enacted in 1935 and still the federal government's most popular social program. Social Security was designed to meet two goals: (1) provide a

The Civilian Conservation Corps employed young, unmarried men in conservation projects across the United States. More than 2 million young men participated in the program from 1933–1943, and many of their projects can still be seen in U.S. national parks and forests.

minimum income for poor beneficiaries, and (2) ensure that benefits bear a relationship to the amount of payroll taxes a beneficiary actually paid. Supported by equal contributions from employers and employees, the program now covers more than 90 percent of the U.S. workforce.[10] Employees pay half of the annual Social Security tax, which applies to income up to $102,000 per year. The tax is identified on pay stubs as FICA, which stands for the Federal Insurance Contribution Act, and also covers disability insurance for injuries on the job.

Social Security was expanded in 1939 to include financial support for survivors of workers covered by Social Security when the retired worker died, and in 1954, it was expanded again to include support for disabled workers and the children of deceased or disabled workers. Benefit levels were raised repeatedly during the first 40 years of the program, often just before an election. The increases became so frequent and so costly that in 1975, Congress indexed benefits to rise only with inflation. Under legislation enacted in 1983, the Social Security retirement age started to rise in 2003 and will reach 67 by the year 2027.

Until the 1970s, steady growth in Social Security benefits was relatively uncontroversial, largely because "the costs were initially deceptively low," making the system politically painless.[11] It is now the world's largest insurance program for retirees, survivors, and people with disabilities. In 2008, Social Security and Medicare expenditures totaled $966 billion.

Employees now pay more in annual Social Security payroll taxes than in income tax. Employees paid a 6.2 percent FICA tax on all wages up to $102,000 in 2010, and an additional 1.45 percent on all of their wages, both above and below $94,200, for Medicare health coverage. All employee taxes are matched dollar for dollar by employers. People who are self-employed pay both the employee and employer taxes.

As an entitlement program, the expected aging of the U.S. population will not affect Social Security and Medicare even if the payroll taxes used for the two programs falls below costs. However, Social Security and Medicare are both "pay-as-you-go" programs, which means that payments to individuals are generally funded by available taxes. When payroll taxes exceed benefits, the federal government holds the revenues in trust funds that can be used in the future; when payroll taxes fall below benefits, the federal government draws down the trust funds. And when the trust funds are gone, Congress and the president must raise taxes or reduce benefits to cover the pay-as-you-go costs.

At least for now, however, Social Security has a large trust fund collected during the years when payroll taxes exceeded benefits. Medicare has a much smaller trust fund that will run out of money sometime in the next three-to-five years. Both programs have suffered during the economic downturn because unemployed workers do not have the income to pay any taxes at all.[12]

HELP FOR THE POOR The federal government began protecting women and children against poverty when Congress passed the Infancy and Maternity Protection Act of 1921. Supported by many of the same women's groups that had just won ratification of the Nineteenth Amendment, which gave women the right to vote, the Act gave the newly created federal Children's Bureau funds to encourage states to create new maternal, infant, and early childhood health programs.

This precedent eventually produced the Aid to Families with Dependent Children (AFDC) program in 1935.[13] As its name suggests, AFDC tried to reduce public opposition to expanded benefits by shifting the focus away from what the mother had done or not done to deserve poverty, and onto the children, who suffered whatever the cause. Under the program, states were given federal money to establish cash grants for poor families under two conditions: states had to (1) match the federal funds with some contribution of their own and (2) establish a means-test for all families receiving benefits.

Congress also established the school lunch program during the New Deal as a way to both feed the hungry and strengthen the ailing farm economy. The Federal Surplus

17.1

17.2

17.3

FOR the People Government's Greatest Endeavors

Helping the Working Poor

The federal government has passed many laws to help low-income workers make ends meet, including increasing the minimum wage, providing help for day care centers, and creating job-training programs.

Between the end of World War II and today, the federal government has increased the minimum wage from 40 cents an hour in 1945 to $4.25 in 1989 and $5.15 in 1997. Although the federal minimum wage was increased to $7.25 an hour in 2007, many states have raised the amount even higher on their own. Connecticut's minimum wage is $8.25 an hour, while Oregon's is $8.40. States are free to pay more than the federal minimum wage, but not less.

The federal government's greatest contribution to helping low-income workers came in 1975 with the creation of the Earned Income Tax Credit (EITC), which reduces or completely eliminates all taxes for the working poor. Under the EITC, low-income workers also receive money back from the federal government to help raise their income. Because the money comes in the form of a tax refund, not a welfare check, many experts believe that low-income workers are less embarrassed to take the federal support.

The EITC has clearly reduced poverty rates among low-income workers. By 2012, for example, about 25 million low-income workers received more than $50 billion through the program, which lifted more than 5 million Americans above the poverty line. The program has been particularly effective in helping unmarried working mothers, who often take minimum-wage jobs in the service industry (fast-food restaurants, dry cleaners, day care centers, grocery stores, and so forth). The maximum credit for the 2012 tax year, which can be used to pay taxes owed or cashed in as a refund, was $5,891 for a family with three or more children, $5,236 for a family with two children, $3,169 for a family with one child, and $457 for a family with no children.

QUESTIONS

1. **Besides raising the minimum wage and increasing the EITC, what other ways might the federal government help low-income workers?**
2. **Have you ever held a minimum-wage job? Was it enough to live on? Would it be enough for you in the future?**
3. **What would Americans think about the EITC if they knew how much it paid?**

Relief Corporation began purchasing surplus agriculture products for low-income families in 1935 and launched the nation's first school lunch programs for poor children shortly thereafter. By 1941, more than 5 million children were receiving free school lunches, consuming more than 450 million pounds of surplus pork, dairy products, and bread. By 2012, more than 30 million children were participating in the program.

Although the program was disbanded during World War II because of food shortages, it was restored under the 1946 National School Lunch Act. As President Harry Truman said at the signing ceremony, "No nation is any healthier than its children." He could have added that many draftees had been rejected for service in World War II because of malnutrition. As noted later in this chapter, Congress and the president reformed AFDC in 1996 to limit the amount of time individuals could receive benefits.

HELP FOR THE DISABLED AND UNEMPLOYED The New Deal created two new federal programs to help disabled workers and the unemployed. Both were established under the Social Security Act in 1935.

Under the Disability Insurance program, workers can apply for government benefits if they have been injured on the job. They must have been disabled for at least five months and be unable to continue on the job. The process for earning a disability payment, which covers part of a worker's monthly salary, is very strict. Only 20 percent of applications are approved. The worker has to present detailed evidence that the disability was work, not age, related, for example, and must prove that the disability is long term. Approximately 9 million disabled Americans received disability support in 2012 with an average monthly benefit of $1,111.

Unemployment insurance is available to workers who have lost their jobs because of economic conditions. Workers cannot receive benefits if they quit their jobs by their own choice—for example, if they have children, get married, move to another part of

The federal government has several programs to make sure that women, children, and infants receive nutritious food. School lunch programs sometimes provide the only full meal of the day for the nation's poorest children.

the country—or are fired for poor performance. Federal unemployment insurance is jointly administered by the federal government and the 50 states and is covered by monthly premiums that are automatically deducted from paychecks. Employers also pay monthly premiums for their employees. Unemployed workers cannot receive more than half their monthly pay, up to specific limits—in New York, for example, the maximum payment is approximately $500 a month, but it is less than half that amount in Arizona. During normal economic times, the benefit is paid for 26 weeks, although this period was extended several times between 2010 and 2012 to help unemployed workers during the deep economic turndown. By March 2012, more than 17 million Americans received unemployment insurance benefits.

There are exceptions to the length of coverage, however. Coverage was extended as unemployment began to rise in 2008. As of June 2012, nearly 25 million Americans were either unemployed or had stopped looking for work. Most received at least some unemployment coverage, which was eventually extended to longer periods of unemployment. Between January 2000 and July 2012, the unemployment rate increased from 4 percent of employable adults to 8.2 percent.

Although these programs sound generous, and are sometimes abused by employees who invent disabilities, they provide the bare minimum for survival. They are often the only sources of income that stand between a family and homelessness, hunger, and the loss of health care.

☐ The Great Society

The second major expansion of social policy came in the 1960s with what became known as the Great Society. At a commencement speech at the University of Michigan in May 1964, President Lyndon Johnson described his vision of the Great Society:

> The Great Society rests on abundance and liberty for all. It demands an end to poverty and racial injustice.... But that is just the beginning. The Great Society is a place where every child can find knowledge to enrich his mind and to enlarge his talents.... It is a challenge constantly renewed, beckoning us toward a destiny where the meaning of our lives matches the marvelous products of our labors.[14]

 Explore on MyPoliSciLab

Is Health Care a Public Good?

A public good is a material item or service provided by the government to all members of society without competition or exclusion. Before Obama's presidency, most Americans believed the government should guarantee healthcare coverage to all citizens, but after 2009, the debate on healthcare reform divided public opinion. Since the signing of The Patient Protection and Affordable Care Act (PPACA), Americans remained dissatisfied with the cost of healthcare and the number of of people who disagree with government provided healthcare increased.

Should the Government Provide Americans with Healthcare Coverage?

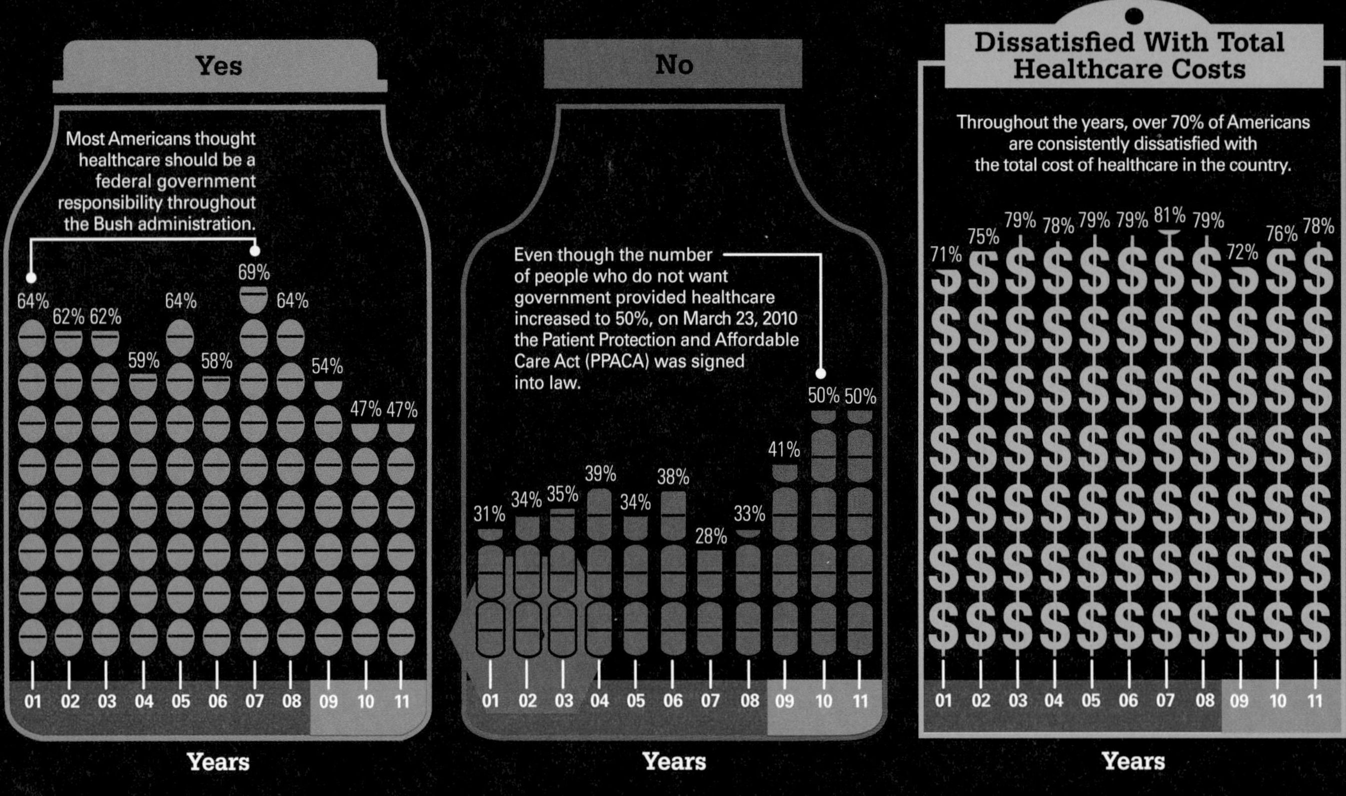

SOURCE: Data from Gallup

Investigate Further

Concept Do Americans think health care is a public good? During Bush's presidency, most Americans wanted government provided healthcare. However, in recent years, support has declined and more people believe private insurers should provide healthcare.

Connection Is the public unhappy with their healthcare costs? Yes, most Americans are dissatisfied with healthcare costs. Concern about healthcare is driven more by the perception that healthcare costs are too high, than by personal dissatisfaction. People are upset with healthcare because of broad circumstances, rather than individual circumstances.

Cause Why did public support for guaranteed government healthcare decline? After Obama took office, support and opposition for reform became a party issue. In a heavily polarized political environment, support for government funded healthcare declined and the public split evenly on issue. After the Obama administration passed the Patient Protection and Affordable Care Act, a majority of the public remained dissatisfied with the costs of healthcare.

Johnson's agenda was as broad as his rhetoric, and Congress enacted much of it in a fairly short period of time. Great Society programs dramatically increased the role of the federal government in health, education, and welfare through a number of programs that continue to exist today:

- *Food Stamps.* The food stamp program gives poor families coupons to purchase the basics of a healthy, nutritious diet. The average benefit is approximately $90 per person per month. Recall that the program was renamed SNAP in 2009.
- *Head Start.* Head Start is a preschool program designed to help poor children get ready for kindergarten. The program served more than 900,000 children each year at a cost of approximately $7,000 per child in 2012. Nearly 30 percent of Head Start teachers and staff are parents of Head Start children or were Head Start children themselves.
- *Medicare.* As noted earlier, **Medicare** was created in 1965 to provide health care to older citizens. It provides all reasonable hospital, medical, and prescription drug insurance. The hospital insurance is funded by a 1.42 percent tax on employees and employers. Medicare pays for inpatient hospital care, skilled nursing care, and other services. Individuals can purchase additional Medicare insurance to cover some expenses not traditionally covered by Medicare. By 2012, almost 50 million Americans received Medicare benefits.
- *Medicaid.* **Medicaid** was also created in 1965 to provide basic health services for poor families. The program is administered and partially funded by state governments and covers items such as hospital care and family planning. Obama's health care plan expanded Medicaid dramatically as a way to provide more coverage for the poor. By 2012, more than 60 million Americans received Medicaid benefits with the number set to rise as Obama's health care plan went into full effect.
- *Supplemental Security Income.* The SSI program was created in 1972 to provide an extra measure of support for the elderly, the poor, and the blind or disabled. Levels of SSI support vary by state to reflect cost-of-living differences, so the program provides monthly benefit checks ranging from only $1 to approximately $800. SSI benefits are financed by general tax revenues and administered by the Social Security Administration. Over 5.5 million Americans received SSI benefits in 2012.
- *Housing Assistance.* The Department of Housing and Urban Development, which was created in 1965, administers a number of programs such as rental assistance designed to help low-income families find affordable, safe housing, in part by giving property owners subsidies to make up the difference between what tenants can pay and what the local housing market will bear. Because of the vast number of housing support programs at the federal and state level, it is difficult to calculate the total number of beneficiaries at any point in time.

Medicare
A national health insurance program for the elderly and disabled.

Medicaid
A federal program that provides medical benefits for low-income people.

☐ Reforming Welfare

Republicans have not been the only critics of the New Deal and Great Society welfare programs. President Bill Clinton made welfare reform a centerpiece of his reelection agenda in 1996, promising to "end welfare as we know it."[15]

Working with the new Republican congressional majority, Clinton won passage of the Personal Responsibility and Work Opportunity Reconciliation Act in 1996, which replaced the New Deal's AFDC with Temporary Assistance for Needy Families (TANF).

Under the new rules, federally funded public assistance is limited to five years during a person's lifetime, and all recipients must enter some kind of work training program within two months of receiving initial benefits. Although states can exempt up to 20 percent of cases from the work requirements and time limits—an exemption intended for blind and disabled persons—the message to recipients is clear: find work soon.

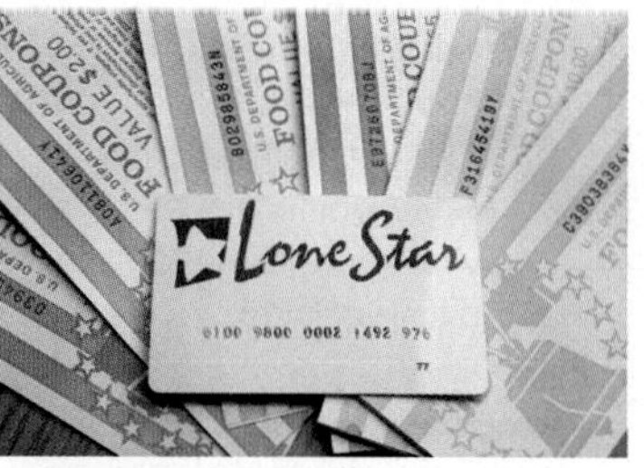

Food stamps (now called SNAP) are often distributed through debit cards for use in grocery stores, thereby allowing needy families to purchase nutritious food without having to reveal that they are receiving government assistance. One out of seven Americans received Food Stamps in 2012.

The law originally excluded legal immigrants from many welfare programs, but at the strong urging of the governors, most welfare benefits were later restored to legal immigrants. To discourage people on welfare from moving to states with more generous assistance payments, the law gave states the option of limiting welfare to newcomers from other states. This provision was declared unconstitutional by a federal district court judge, however, who said it "denies 'equal protection of the laws' to indigent families moving from one state to another."[16] The decision was not appealed.

You Will Decide

Should the Federal Government Promote Marriage?

Although the 1996 welfare reform legislation focused on replacing welfare with work, it also ordered the federal government to promote marriage. Advocates argue that marriage improves the lives of both children and parents. Married adults, whether women or men, are happier, healthier, and wealthier than their unmarried peers and are more likely to give their children a healthier start in life. Some advocates even argue that more marriages would reduce health costs by reducing depression and crime.*

This issue was in the news during the 2012 presidential campaign as Republicans reassured their voters that they would continue to support a Constitutional amendment defining marriage as a union between a man and woman, and promote marriage as a requirement for many federal programs such as aid to the poor. While Democrats also argued that marriage is a source of strength for families, they did not support the Constitutional amendment.

The federal government can promote marriage in two ways. First, it can reduce the penalties it imposes on welfare recipients who get married. Under current law, for example, a single mother working full time at a minimum-wage job who marries stands to lose as much as $8,000 per year in cash and noncash benefits. Second, it can promote marriage through advertising, counseling, or even providing cash grants for getting married.

What do you think? Should the federal government enact policies that promote marriage? What are the arguments for both sides of the issue?

Thinking It Through

Although the federal government has long engaged in activities designed to promote vaccinating children, quitting smoking, wearing seat belts, and driving under 55 miles per hour, not everyone believes that promoting marriage is the answer to reducing the welfare rolls.

Critics note, for example, that domestic violence and child abuse occur almost as frequently in married as in unmarried households. They also worry that government grants for marriage would promote a rash of false marriages designed to get the cash. Most important, opponents believe that the best way to improve conditions for welfare recipients is to find them good-paying jobs. They look to states such as Minnesota and Wisconsin that have created strong welfare-to-work programs that do not punish married women for getting a job.

Nevertheless, marriage appears to affect income. Two paychecks are better than one, and married couples may be more likely to save money for the future. Marital stability also positively influences child well-being on several measures, and marriage fosters healthier living habits as the marriage partners help monitor each other in such areas as smoking, weight gain, and drug use. These effects can be benefits to society in general.

The question, however, is whether they are a consequence of marriage or simply a product of adults living together. Absent a solid answer, support for marriage may be more an indicator of a person's ideology and religion than a position based on careful research.

CRITICAL THINKING QUESTIONS

1. Should the federal government promote social values such as marriage?
2. How is promoting marriage similar to and different from other federal programs such as its campaign to stop smoking?
3. Why is marriage considered a way to reduce poverty? Are there other or better ways to achieve the same goal?

Social Policy Challenges for the Future: Health, Education, and Crime

17.3 Evaluate the current status of and challenges for federal government policy in the areas of health care, education, and crime.

Even if states take on a greater social policy role, the federal government is sure to remain the greatest source of funding for the safety net. As Figure 17.1 shows, spending for human resource programs such as Social Security, Medicare, Medicaid, and child nutrition has doubled since 1950. The figure also shows a very slight increase in spending on physical resources, such as roads and bridges, due to the large, one-time infusion of money through the economic stimulus package. However, the figure does not show the projected interest on the national debt beyond 2012—according to the federal budget presented in 2012, estimated interest payments will swell to $551 billion by 2015, which will make interest one of the largest costs in the total expenditure totals.

Explore on **MyPoliSciLab** **Simulation:** You Are an OMB Staffer

The Federal Role in Health Care

Medicare is only one of the federal government's many health programs. The federal government has been instrumental in reducing disease since 1887, when it opened a one-room laboratory on Staten Island, New York, to study infectious diseases carried to the United States on passenger ships. That one-room laboratory expanded into the National Institutes of Health (NIH), a conglomeration of 37 separate institutes on a 300-acre campus in Bethesda, Maryland.

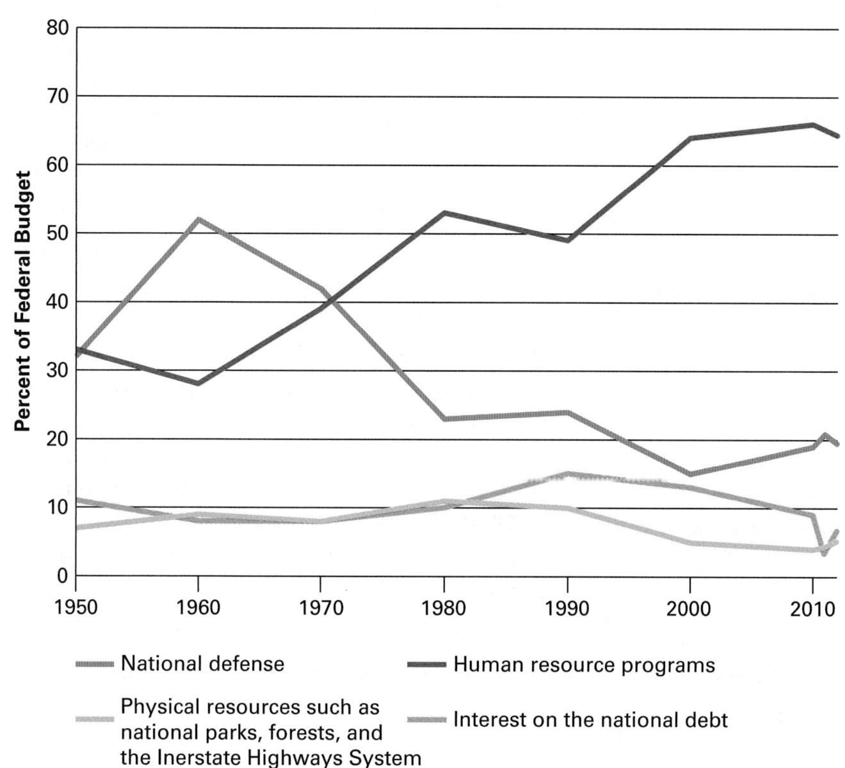

FIGURE 17.1 CHANGING PRIORITIES IN THE FEDERAL BUDGET

What parts of the federal government have seen the greatest change over the last 50 years? What explains these changes in spending priorities?

SOURCE: *Budget of the United States, Fiscal Year 2013,* Historical Tables *(U.S. Government Printing Office, February 2013).*

The Department of Veterans Affairs provides health care to millions of veterans every year. The Iraq and Afghanistan wars have tested the health care system as thousands of soldiers with difficult-to-treat traumatic brain injuries and post-traumatic stress order enter the system.

The surgeon general of the United States is arguably the most visible health care official in government. As head of the Public Health Service (PHS), the surgeon general oversees a diverse array of health care researchers at NIH and elsewhere. Federally funded researchers study causes and seek cures for serious diseases. The PHS also grants fellowships for health research to scientists and physicians and administers grants to states and local communities to help improve public health. Another federal agency promoting health is the Food and Drug Administration (FDA), which oversees the development of new drugs and ensures food safety through inspections of the nation's food supply.

Dozens of other federal agencies work to improve public health. The Centers for Disease Control and Prevention (CDC) in Atlanta is also actively engaged in preventing disease. The CDC and its 7,800 "disease detectives" have been at the forefront of identifying a host of mystery illnesses, including the respiratory disease that attacked attendees at an American Legion convention in 1976 (Legionnaire's disease), toxic shock syndrome in 1980, and hepatitis C in 1989, as well as tracking down the causes of major health disasters, including the outbreak of swine flu in 2009. The swine flu outbreak produced a massive effort to vaccinate Americans against the virus, which was especially threatening to young adults.

Despite its success in improving the nation's health, the federal government faces two major health care challenges in the future: containing costs and expanding coverage as the federal government's new health care program moves toward full implementation over the coming years.

THE RISING COST OF HEALTH CARE Health care costs in the United States have nearly quadrupled, after controlling for inflation, since 1970.[17] Although costs slowed with the rest of the economy in 2001, they are expected to escalate rapidly as the nation ages throughout the next two decades. It's too early to know if the Patient Protection and Affordable Health Care Act will reduce these increases. Extending the recent trends reported by the federal government, annual per person medical costs are likely to increase beyond $10,000 by 2015. (See Table 17.1 for federal payments to individuals, and Figure 17.2 for the trend in health care spending by individual Americans.)

All citizens pay for increasing health care costs. Although employers provide insurance to three of five working adults, they have steadily increased the share of insurance that employees must pay, including increased premiums, higher deductibles, and partial

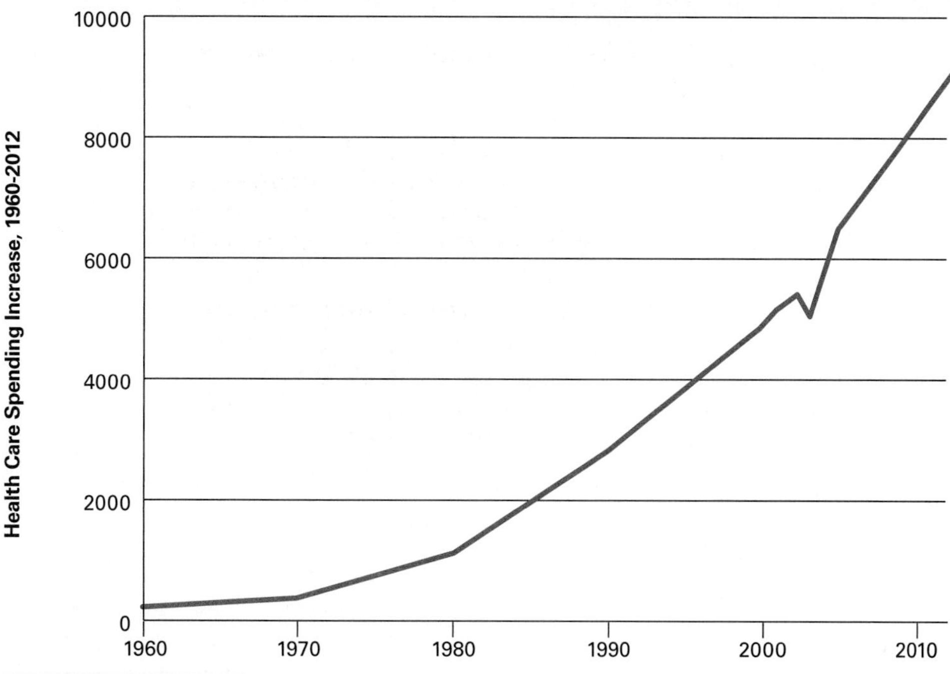

FIGURE 17.2 HEALTH CARE COSTS PER PERSON, 1960–2012

■ *What might explain the continuing rise in individual health care costs?*

SOURCE: The Henry J. Kaiser Family Foundation, *Health Care Costs: A Primer*, May 2012, available at http://www.kff.org/insurance/upload/7670-03.pdf

payments for services (co-pays). Taxpayers also pay for these increases through federal dollars that might otherwise go to other programs such as homeland security, college loans, or highway construction. (Figure 17.3 shows where health care dollars are spent.)

The good news is that costs have risen in part because people are living longer. Average life expectancy increased by more than five years between 1970 and 1995. In 1900, only 1 of every 25 American adults was over the age of 65. By 1950, the number was 1 in 12, and by 1985, 1 in 9. According to experts, the number will rise to 1 in 5 by 2030. In 1900, the average American adult lived to age 47; by 2000, the average had increased to 79. Again according to experts, the number will rise into the mid-80s by 2030.

As people live longer, of course, they place greater demands on the health care system, as well as on the Social Security program. New and advanced medical technology—life-support systems, ultrasound, sophisticated x-ray equipment, and genetic counseling—have all increased the costs of health care. Nuclear magnetic imaging, or as it is more commonly known, magnetic resonance imaging (MRI), is now routinely used to diagnose a host of diseases not easily detected through more traditional tests. Once a medical center purchases this kind of expensive technology, its physicians are given incentives to use it, which increases patients' health care costs. Longer life expectancies also place greater demands on other social policies, subtracting from funding for public assistance and other forms of social insurance.

At least part of the cost crisis is avoidable. Medicare alone spends billions of dollars each year treating smoking-related diseases, and throughout the next 20 years, the costs to treat such diseases will continue to rise. Other illnesses at least partly related to lifestyle choices include heart disease, liver disease, HIV/AIDS, and the epidemic of health disorders caused or made worse by obesity, such as diabetes.

COVERING THE UNINSURED Despite passage of the Medicare program in 1965, the United States did not provide comprehensive insurance to the rest of the uninsured until 2010. Until then, most uninsured Americans either relied on public clinics, emergency room care, or simply lived without health or dental care.[18]

The Patient Protection and Affordable Health Care Act, commonly known as Obamacare, was designed to cover as many of these Americans as possible but was one of the most complicated laws passed in recent history. The bill was more than

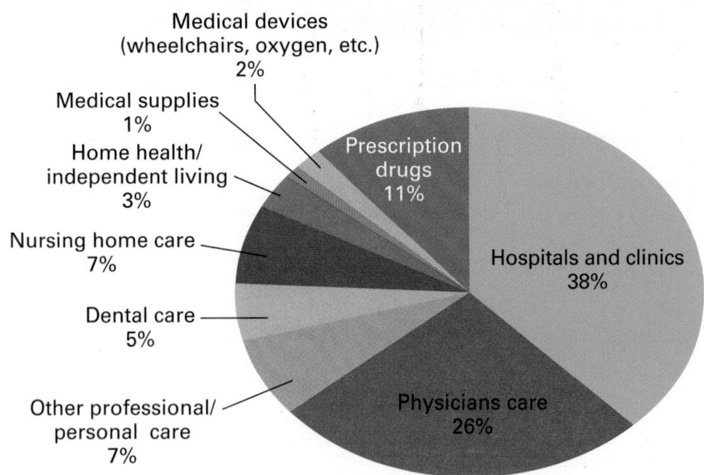

FIGURE 17.3 WHERE THE HEALTH CARE DOLLAR WAS SPENT, 2012

- *On what aspect of health care is the most money spent? How might you expect the new health care program to change where Americans go for preventive medical care?*

SOURCE: The Henry J. Kaiser Family Foundation, *Health Care Costs: A Primer*, May 2012, available at http://www.kff.org/insurance/upload/7670-03.pdf

1,200 pages long and contained a long list of changes in how health care is delivered and to whom. Its key provisions involved expansions of existing health care programs such as Medicaid for the poor and the creation of new health insurance "exchanges" in each state as a source of insurance for Americans who could not buy insurance from private companies. It also contained tax increases and benefit cuts for Medicare. The main provisions of the Act are as follows:

- Most Americans will be required to buy health insurance starting in 2014 and will be fined by the federal government if they do not do so.
- Individuals who cannot buy affordable insurance will be able to purchase insurance from a state insurance exchange.
- Insurance companies will be prevented from denying coverage to people for any reason, including preexisting conditions, such as high blood pressure, cancer, or mental illness.
- Insurance companies will have to extend coverage for young Americans up to 26 years of age under their parents' insurance.
- The Medicaid program will be expanded to all poor Americans under the age of 65, including the unemployed and unmarried individuals.
- General Medicare benefits will not be cut, and all older Americans will qualify for free preventive care, but the special Medicare Advantage program for higher-income beneficiaries will be frozen, and some benefits will be abolished.
- Individual Americans will pay a tax on "Cadillac" insurance plans that offer broader coverage at a much higher cost.
- The Medicare payroll tax will rise 0.9 percent for Americans who make more than $200,000 per year.

Because these changes will be phased in throughout the next decade, it is not clear just how much the new program will cost on a yearly basis. Moreover, it is not clear that older Americans will accept the changes in Medicare, or that states will form the new insurance exchanges on their own.

Nevertheless, the program reflects a 50-year effort to expand the social safety net. However, even with full implementation, there will still be a small number of Americans who will not qualify for any coverage because they already receive benefits through other federal programs such as Supplemental Security Income and veterans hospitals. The reform stands alongside the prescription drug coverage that was passed in 2003 as the latest contributors to health safety for the aged.

□ The Federal Role in Education

The federal government has been a partner in education at least since the Northwest Ordinance of 1785, in which Congress set aside land in every township for a public school. In 1862, the Morrill Land-Grant Colleges Act provided grants of land to states for universities specializing in the mechanical or agricultural arts. The U.S. Office of Education was established in 1867 to oversee these programs, but the scope of federal involvement was modest by today's standards. Even the G.I. Bill, which helped provide a college education for approximately 20 million World War II veterans, was seen more as an employment program than an educational one.

During the Cold War, however, education became one part of the national defense. When the Soviet Union launched *Sputnik*—the first human-made satellite to orbit the earth—Congress responded to the need for more scientists in 1958 by passing the National Defense Education Act to upgrade the quality of engineering, physics, language, and mathematics courses.

BY the People Making a Difference

Improving Health One Playground at a Time

Citizens can make an immediate difference in public policy by simply changing the way they behave. They can stop smoking, change their diets, and get more exercise every day. They can also lobby their local governments to build more sidewalks and bike paths so that other citizens can exercise safely. They can push school boards to remove sugary drinks and junk food from school vending machines and cafeterias, support efforts to bring full-service grocery stores such as Whole Foods, Walmart, and Walgreens to low-income neighborhoods, and even plant community gardens. In 2012, for example, Walmart began to open "small box" stores, as opposed to its well-known "super stores" in poor neighborhoods to provide easy access to nutritious food.

Playgrounds are also an easy place to start. Sixty minutes of exercise a day can reduce health care costs dramatically in the future. Yet, there are thousands of "play deserts" across the country, often in dense urban areas, in which there is no space for children to play. One charitable organization started by Darell Hammond, KaBOOM!, has set out to change that. In 2012, KaBOOM! built more playgrounds across the United States than any state or city in America. You can see play deserts in your community by visiting maps at kaboom.org.*

You can easily find a "play-space" where a new playground would improve the opportunity for healthy exercise for low-income children. Consider joining the KaBOOM! building team as a volunteer.

QUESTIONS

1. What can you do today to reduce health care costs in the future?
2. Why are playgrounds so important to communities? And why are there so few playgrounds in low-income communities?
3. What other resources do low-income communities need to be healthier places to live?

*See Darell Hammond, *KaBOOM! How One Man Built a Movement to Say Play* (Rodale Press, 2011).

ELEMENTARY AND SECONDARY EDUCATION Kindergarten through high school education is generally seen as a state and local responsibility. Most children go to public schools run by local school boards and funded, at least partly, by property taxes. Because school districts vary greatly in the wealth of their residents, children from poor districts are much more likely to have lower-quality public schools than those from wealthier districts. As a result, public schools vary in the quality of teacher preparation, student performance, dropout rates, and educational opportunities provided to minority students.

Although the federal government has been reluctant to make direct investments in poor school districts, it has tried to help the children those districts serve. For example, in 1964, Congress created the Head Start program to help low-income children learn to read and understand numbers. Head Start centers also provide healthy meals and snacks and monitor child health care. Many also work with parents to encourage greater involvement and literacy.

Recent evaluations suggest that Head Start does increase learning but needs improvement. In 2012, Head Start provided funding to more than 20,000 child care centers and almost 1 million children. The student–teacher ratio also varied significantly across centers. Moreover, the program is not an entitlement, meaning funding covers only approximately a third of eligible children. When the dollars run out, Head Start centers stop enrolling participants.

Head Start is not the federal government's only education program, however. In 1965, Congress passed the Elementary and Secondary Education Act (ESEA), which supplied educational materials for underprivileged public school students and provided funding for research on how to help children from disadvantaged backgrounds.

As concerns about the quality of public education increased during the 1990s, however, the federal government became more engaged in local education, first by setting national goals for student achievement, then by passing the No Child Left Behind Act in 2002. Under the Act, in return for federal funding, states were required to annually test at least 95 percent of all third and eighth graders in reading and mathematics. In addition, states were required to grade schools as passing or failing, to set higher standards for teachers, and to give students in failing schools the option to move to higher-performing schools. Schools must either improve test scores each year or risk

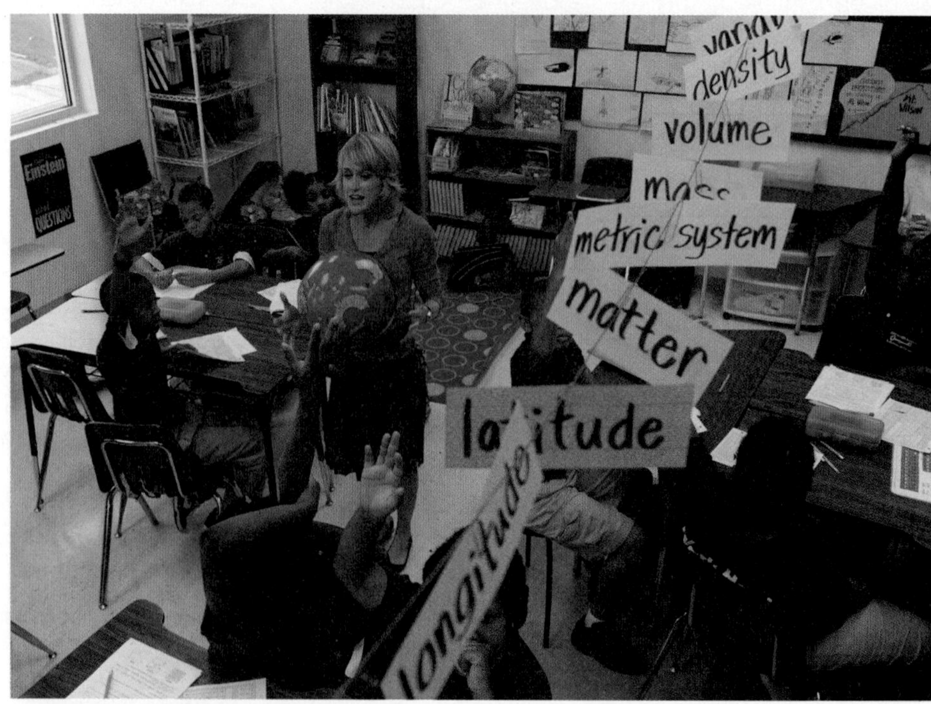

There have been many efforts to improve the performance of public schools. Here, a teacher for the nongovernmental Knowledge is Power Program (KIPP) works with poor children.

being labeled "in need of improvement." Under the Act, all students are supposed to be proficient in reading and mathematics by 2014.

Although the No Child Left Behind Act set higher standards, it increased federal spending for education by only a tiny percentage. Under great pressure during the economic downturn, many states complained that they did not have enough funding to test every student every year or to meet the law's requirement for teacher training and certification. In addition, schools with many disabled or special-needs students were being unfairly categorized as "failing" because they could not meet the test-score requirement. As of 2013, Congress and the Obama administration were still debating changes in the Act to put a greater emphasis on teacher performance. The debate may be irrelevant, however. By 2012, the Obama administration had already let half of the states out of the program.

Parents ask more of their schools than just to educate their children. Schools are now a major means of providing basic nutrition to millions of poor children. They screen at-risk children and attempt to get them medical and psychological assistance; they seek to socialize students into acceptable behaviors, often in the face of increasing violence in the surrounding neighborhoods; and they often reach out to families to provide basic help in parenting.

HIGHER EDUCATION The federal government also provides help to colleges and universities. In 2012, the federal government provided loans and subsidies to more than 20 million students. Pell grants for low-income students and low-interest guaranteed student loans continue to be the biggest source of college aid for low-income students.

In 1998, Congress added three new programs to improve the odds that low-income children will make it to college: (1) GEAR UP, which supports early interventions to help students complete high school; (2) the Learning Anytime Anywhere Partnerships (LAAP), which provide federal funding for distance learning through the Internet; and (3) a new initiative designed to improve teacher quality in primary and elementary schools. Although the three programs account for less than 1 percent of federal spending for education, they acknowledge the link between the quality of primary and elementary education and college success, as well as the need to act early to increase the odds of success for low-income students. All of these programs are means-tested entitlements only to a point—all applicants who qualify for loans are entitled to seek a loan, but the total amount of money available is considered discretionary, not uncontrollable spending. Moreover, the interest rate on student loans is set by Congress and the president, and varies over time. Interest rates were cut in half to 3.7 percent for all student loans in 2007, but the rate may rise to its old level in 2013 as Congress and the president look for ways to cut federal spending. Although the interest rates will continue to change from time to time, Congress and the president seem likely to continue the special loan forgiveness program for students who take public service jobs working for schools, government, or charitable organizations and stay in their jobs for 10 years and make their scheduled repayments during that time.

□ The Federal Role in Crime Control

Crime control is not generally seen as a form of social policy, but neither is it a foreign, defense, or economic policy. As such, crime control is best viewed as a way to promote the general welfare by protecting all citizens from harm.

Like education policy, policing crime is primarily a state and local matter. The federal government has passed sweeping legislation helping state and local governments pay for crime control. Often, the federal government acts more as a banker than a police officer, providing grants to states and local governments to hire their own police officers, build more prisons, improve drug enforcement, and prosecute organized crime. The federal government must also enforce its own laws against activities such as counterfeiting and pollution, while protecting the borders and preventing drugs from flowing into the country.

The federal government enforces its laws primarily through the Department of Justice, which contains the Federal Bureau of Investigation (FBI). The FBI was created in 1908 and charged with gathering and reporting evidence in matters relating to federal criminal laws. In addition, the FBI provides fingerprint identification and laboratory services to local law enforcement on a cooperative basis and has new responsibilities in the war on terrorism. Other law enforcement agencies of the federal government include the Drug Enforcement Agency (DEA), which is responsible for preventing the flow of illegal narcotics and other illegal drugs into the United States, patrolling U.S. borders, and conducting joint operations with countries where drugs are produced. The Bureau of Alcohol, Tobacco, Firearms, and Explosives monitors the sale of destructive

OF the People Diversity in America

Access to College

Federal aid to education has increased access to college for all American students, but it has had a particularly significant effect on women and people of color at both the community college and four-year levels. Women now earn the majority of both associate and bachelor degrees. Between 2008 and 2010, the number of women enrolled in college rose from 52 percent to 58 percent, while the number of black and African American students rose from 10 percent to 15 percent, and the number of Hispanic students rose from just 4 percent to 12 percent.

The number of minority students has more than doubled throughout the decades at both community colleges and four-year colleges and universities. Under the 1998 Higher Education Act, the number of students of color should increase even faster as the federal government puts more dollars into preparing students for college. Although two-year and four-year colleges have seen an increase in enrollments by both women and minority students, growth has been fastest at two-year colleges, which tend to have lower tuition. They are increasingly the destination of choice for many students unable to afford four-year colleges, or who start at two-year colleges to save money, then transfer to four-year institutions.

QUESTIONS

1. Why has the percentage of women attending college increased over the past three decades?
2. Has diversity increased at your college or university? Why or why not?
3. Thinking back to Chapter 5 of this book, what do changes in education mean for U.S. government and politics?

weapons and guns inside the United States, regulates alcoholic beverage production, and oversees the collection of taxes on alcohol and tobacco.

Terrorism is clearly the federal government's top crime priority today. Only weeks after the September 11, 2001, terrorist attacks on New York City and Washington, D.C., Congress passed a massive antiterrorism law, and it created the new Department of Homeland Security the following summer. For his part, President Bush created the Office of Homeland Security within the White House in October 2001, merging 22 agencies and 180,000 federal employees, and ordered a complete reorganization of the Federal Bureau of Investigation in early 2002 to create a stronger focus on preventing terrorism.

Under the USA PATRIOT Act of 2001 (the letters stand for Uniting and Strengthening America by Providing Appropriate Tools Required to Intercept and Obstruct Terrorism), the federal government was given sweeping authority to conduct secret investigations of suspected terrorists. Those investigations may use "roving wiretaps" to intercept conversations on any phones a suspect may use and detain any noncitizens believed to be a national security risk for up to seven days without charging them with a crime. Although the PATRIOT Act expired on December 31, 2005, the Bush administration made its renewal a centerpiece of the president's second-term agenda. The administration also asked Congress to expand the government's authority to investigate what it called "lone-wolf" terrorists who are not affiliated with a foreign government or known terrorist organization such as Al-Qaeda, which planned the September 11 attacks. Congress reauthorized the act as Bush requested. President Obama also signed a four-year authorization of the main provisions in the act in 2011, leaving it in place until 2015.

☐ The Politics of Social Policy

Social policy is a major focus of American politics. Welfare, health care, education, and crime—and their costs—are important political battlegrounds between the parties and between contending interest groups, second only to the economy and national security. The nation long ago answered questions about whether the national government has a role in providing decent housing, adequate health care, and a solid education for all citizens. The question is not whether the nation will provide a safety net for its low-income citizens but how strong the net will be and whether state governments or the federal government will be responsible for providing it. There is obvious politics involved in the question. Although most American adults support Social Security and Medicare, for example, they are sharply divided over how much the nation should do for its poorest citizens. They are also increasingly divided about reforms such as the No Child Left Behind Act and its mandatory testing, which have prompted some states to sue the federal government to recover some of the costs of implementing the unfunded mandate portions of the Act.

Nevertheless, social policy will be part of the federal agenda far into the future. Although presidents and Congress cannot always know what voters will support and how much they are willing to pay, they can be sure that most want government to take care of citizens who are low-income through no fault of their own. As the earlier figures on payments to individuals show, the economic recession has cost the federal government billions in payments to unemployed Americans.

Citizens can influence social policy in several ways. One is to join interest groups that represent low-income Americans or taxpayers. Another is to write letters to their members of Congress when significant legislation such as prescription drug coverage comes to a vote. They can also volunteer for specific programs that are designed to help the needy such as Teach for America or AmeriCorps. Although the federal government has created dozens of programs to help the needy, the nation still relies heavily on charities to fill gaps in coverage, whether through food pantries and soup kitchens or early childhood programs. In turn, these programs rely on volunteers.

Review the Chapter

Listen to **Chapter 17** on **MyPoliSciLab**

The Role of the Federal Government in Social Policy

17.1 Outline the goals of the federal government's social policy and the forms of protection it provides, p. 539.

The goals of social policy are to create a safety net to protect citizens against social and economic problems and to raise the quality of life for all. The two types of social policy are public assistance (usually means-tested) and social insurance. Public assistance takes many forms, including direct payments to the poor, the unemployed, and the disabled; food stamps; job training; housing subsidies; free school lunches; tax credits; and subsidized medical care. Social insurance (usually an entitlement), such as Social Security, is provided to anyone who has paid enough in contributions to receive support after meeting certain requirements, such as reaching retirement age.

The Expansion of Social Policy in the Twentieth Century

17.2 Outline the evolution of social policy throughout the twentieth century, p. 543.

The greatest expansion in the federal government's social programs occurred in two eras: (1) Franklin Roosevelt's New Deal from 1933 to 1945, and (2) Lyndon Johnson's Great Society from 1964 to 1969. The New Deal created a number of public assistance and social insurance programs such as job training for the unemployed, Social Security, and Aid to Families with Dependent Children (now called Temporary Assistance to Needy Families); the Great Society produced help for the homeless, more job training, and Medicare.

Social Policy Challenges for the Future: Health, Education, and Crime

17.3 Evaluate the current status of and challenges for federal government policy in the areas of health care, education, and crime, p. 551.

Health care is well on track to becoming the federal government's largest social program, in part because health care costs are rising rapidly with the increasing lifespan, new technologies, and access to promising new treatments for life-threatening diseases such as cancer. In 2010, Congress passed a new health insurance program to provide greater access for millions of uninsured Americans.

Education and crime continue to be primarily state and local government functions in the United States. However, the federal government plays an important role in funding public schools and pushing national goals for better education and is also heavily engaged in helping finance college and university education. Crime control has also been part of the national agenda for decades, especially related to drugs, but has become much more visible as part of the war on terrorism.

Learn the Terms

Study and **Review** the **Flashcards**

entitlements, p. 541
means-tested entitlements, p. 541
social safety net, p. 541
public assistance, p. 542
social insurance, p. 543
Social Security, p. 544
Medicare, p. 549
Medicaid, p. 549

Test Yourself

 **Study** and **Review** the **Practice Tests**

MULTIPLE CHOICE QUESTIONS

17.1 Outline the goals of the federal government's social policy and the forms of protection it provides.

Which are means-tested entitlement programs?

- **a.** programs that provide guaranteed benefits to anyone who applies
- **b.** programs that are only available to certain groups of people such as older Americans
- **c.** programs that provide guaranteed benefits to anyone who meets a specific requirement based on income and other financial assets
- **d.** programs that are only guaranteed on a first-come, first-served basis
- **e.** all of the above

17.2 Outline the evolution of social policy throughout the twentieth century.

Which of the following was a major goal of Social Security when it was created in 1935?

- **a.** to provide access to health care for older Americans
- **b.** to help veterans transition financially after active duty
- **c.** to provide all older Americans with the same amount of income each month
- **d.** to provide a minimum income floor for poor beneficiaries
- **e.** to help mothers with dependent children

17.3 Evaluate the current status of and challenges for federal government policy in the areas of health care, education, and crime.

What was the largest category of health care spending in 2012?

- **a.** hospital and clinic care
- **b.** prescription drugs
- **c.** nursing home care
- **d.** unnecessary surgery
- **e.** home health aides

ESSAY QUESTION

Outline the goals of the federal government's social policy and the forms of protection it provides, then describe the advantages and disadvantages of using entitlement programs for protecting citizens against hardship, and the reasons why some entitlements are means-tested and others not.

Explore Further

IN THE LIBARY

John Baldock, Nicholas Manning, and Sarah Vickerstaff, eds., *Social Policy* (Oxford University Press, 2007).

Donald L. Barlett and James B. Steele, *Critical Condition: How Health Care in America Became Big Business—and Bad Medicine* (Broadway Books, 2005).

Barbara Ehrenreich, *Nickel and Dimed: On (Not) Getting By in America* (Metropolitan Books, 2001).

George Gilder, *Wealth and Poverty*, (Regnery, 2012).

Michael Hill, *Social Policy in the Modern World: A Comparative Perspective* (Wiley, 2006).

Christopher Jencks, *The Homeless* (Harvard University Press, 1994).

Paul C. Light, *Still Artful Work: The Continuing Politics of Social Security Reform* (McGraw-Hill, 1995).

Paul Mosley, *The Politics of Poverty Reduction* (Oxford, 2012).

Daniel Patrick Moynihan, *Miles to Go: A Personal History of Social Policy* (Harvard University Press, 1996).

Charles Murray, *Losing Ground: American Social Policy, 1950–1980* (Basic Books, 1984).

Paul E. Peterson and Martin R. West, eds., *No Child Left Behind: The Politics and Practice of School Accountability* (Brookings Institution Press, 2004).

Mark Robert Rank, *One Nation Underprivileged: Why American Poverty Affects Us All* (Oxford University Press, 2005).

David K. Shipler, *The Working Poor: Invisible in America* (Vintage Books, 2005).

R. Kent Weaver, *Ending Welfare as We Know It* (Brookings Institution Press, 2001).

Margaret Weir, ed., *The Social Divide: Political Parties and the Future of Activist Government* (Brookings Institution Press, 1998).

Bob Woodward, *Agenda: Inside the Clinton White House* (Simon & Schuster, 1994).

ON THE WEB

healthiergeneration.org
The Web site for the Alliance for a Healthier Generation, an organization founded to promote healthier lives and sponsored by First Lady Michelle Obama.

CMS.gov
The Web site for the Centers for Medicare and Medicaid Services, which administer the largest health programs in the federal government.

health.gov
A portal to every federal program that deals with health care.

www2.ed.gov/about/offices/list/fsa/index.html
The Web site for the federal government's student loan programs.

FBI.gov
The destination for finding details on crime, including statistics on major crimes (http://www.fbi.gov/ucr/cius2008/index.html).

18

Listen to Chapter 18 on MyPoliSciLab

Making Foreign and Defense Policy

Eight years after it began with a "shock and awe" bombing campaign of Iraq's capital city of Baghdad, the Iraq war ended on December 15, 2011, in a heavily guarded courtyard at the Baghdad airport. Standing in that courtyard, Defense Secretary Leon Panetta thanked the U.S. combat troops who were about to go home for their service, and then warned the U.S. that "Iraq will be tested in the days ahead—by terrorism, and by those would seek to divide, by economic and social issues, by the demands of democracy itself."[1]

The nation was more relieved by the end of the war than ready for a victory parade. Even President Obama avoided any hint of celebration. Instead, he went to Fort Bragg in North Carolina to greet the returning soldiers with a simple message: "As your Commander-in-Chief, and on behalf of a grateful nation, I'm proud to finally say these two words, and I know your families agree: Welcome home. Welcome home. Welcome home. Welcome home."[2]

Iraq had been a controversial and expensive war from its very beginning. The war was launched with congressional approval largely based on the Bush administration's claim that Iraq's brutal dictator Saddam Hussein had helped the terrorists who planned the September 11, 2011, attacks, and was also armed with a vast inventory of chemical, biological, and even nuclear weapons that could be used against the United States and its allies, especially Israel. Despite the administration's claim that the war would be quickly won, it eventually claimed the lives of 4,500 U.S. troops, left another 32,000 wounded, and cost more than $1 trillion that was added to the growing national debt. The cost will continue to climb as U.S. military advisers help train the new Iraq Army, and the Department of Veterans Affairs continues to care for wounded soldiers, including many who suffered a traumatic brain injury from hidden road-side bombs.

18.1

Analyze the questions and responses that shape approaches to U.S. foreign policy and defense, p. 565.

18.2

Assess the status of each of the issues that currently dominate the foreign policy and defense agenda, p. 569.

18.3

Outline the structure of the foreign policy and defense bureaucracy, p. 574.

18.4

Evaluate the options for achieving foreign policy and defense goals, p. 580.

U.S. Army soldier Zane Miller is greeted by his wife, Chelsea, and son, Jaxon, 8, during a homecoming ceremony at Fort Carson in Colorado Springs, Colorado. He was one of the soldiers who returned to the U.S. after the army ended its combat mission in Iraq.

The Big Picture What did President Bill Clinton mean when he said he missed the days of the Cold War? Author Paul C. Light remembers the time when the United States had one clear enemy, and he describes how U.S. foreign policy has become much more complicated in the age of globalization.

The Basics Who develops America's foreign policy? How has America emerged as a world leader and what challenges does this present? In this video, you will learn about the actors in the foreign policy arena and consider the United States' role in international affairs.

In Context Explore the history of American foreign policy. In this video, Boston University political scientist Neta C. Crawford explains the international challenges the Unites States has faced during three stages of development. She also reveals who is chiefly responsible for deciding foreign policy.

Thinking Like a Political Scientist Learn what foreign policy scholars are researching. Boston University political scientist Neta C. Crawford reveals how scholars use levels of analysis and advances in cognitive psychology to assess decision-making.

In the Real World The United States has intervened in many countries in order to promote democracy, including Iraq, Germany, Japan, and most recently, Libya. Is this the right thing to do? Learn what real people have to say about this divisive issue, and about the consequences brought on by U.S. involvement abroad.

So What? How is the United States going to compete in this more complicated, globalized world? Author Paul C. Light confronts some of the major issues that Americans will face in the coming years—such as environmental changes and outsourced jobs—and he explains why it is important for younger Americans to start caring about these problems now.

18.1

18.2

18.3

18.4

Was the war a success? On the one hand, the alleged weapons of mass destruction were never found. Nor was the United States ever able to prove a link between Iraq's brutal dictator Saddam Hussein and the September 11 terrorist attacks. Moreover, even as U.S. troops came home from Iraq, the parallel war against terrorism in Afghanistan began to heat up in 2012, assuring that it would become the longest war in U.S. history to date.

On the other hand, Hussein was removed from power, tried for crimes against his own people, and executed in 2006. More important as measures of success, Iraq elected its first democratic government in January 2005, mostly ended a bloody civil war by 2010, and continues to rebuild its oil-based economy at a steady pace.

This chapter will ask how we make choices in planning and executing foreign and defense policy. We will first examine key debates in making policy, look at basic terms and concepts, and examine some of today's greatest foreign policy challenges, such as the continued threats of nuclear war and the growing role of Iran in the Middle East. Then, the chapter will turn to a discussion of the key actors in making U.S. foreign policy and appraise the range of tools the United States uses to accomplish its international goals. The chapter concludes with a more detailed assessment of defense policy.

Citizens clearly play a role in foreign and defense policy, whether through their advocacy and pressure or through their decisions to petition government or join the armed forces. They can also create change through voting, especially if a foreign policy such as the war in Iraq becomes a national issue, as it did in the 2006 congressional elections. That said, citizens often feel that supporting the nation's foreign and defense policy is a patriotic duty, and believe that the president should have the authority to protect the nation from international threats even if that means Congress is excluded from making the central decisions.

Understanding Foreign Policy and Defense

18.1 Analyze the questions and responses that shape approaches to U.S. foreign policy and defense.

In the broadest sense, the primary goal of U.S. foreign and defense policy is to protect the nation and world from international threats such as terrorism, poverty, dictatorships, piracy, and attacks against its own people. Doing so requires more than building strong borders, however, and isolating itself from the rest of the world. The United States tried that prior to World War I and II, and failed to prevent the call to war. As one of the world's great superpowers, the United States still has a wide range of obligations, including promoting democracy abroad in nations such as Iraq, providing help to victims of disaster such as the 2010 earthquake in Haiti, promoting greater economic ties across all nations, and fighting terrorism.

Explore on **MyPoliSciLab Simulation**: You Are a President During a Foreign Policy Crisis

Although the United States supports greater freedom in the world, it has long been divided about its own role in international affairs. Some believe that the United States should defend itself against its enemies but remain isolated from the rest of the world; others question whether it should assume that other nations will act in their own self-interest, or if it should maintain a more hopeful vision of a peaceful world; still others debate whether the United States should use its substantial military strength to force other nations to support its positions, versus using its own history of civil liberties and rights to lead the world through example.

In general, these debates start with five basic questions: (1) Should the United States view the world realistically or idealistically? (2) Should it isolate itself from the world or accept a role in the international community? (3) Should it act on its own or only with the help of other nations? (4) Should it act first against threats to its safety or wait until it is attacked? (5) Should it use its military and economic hard power or its diplomatic soft power? We will discuss each of these issues next.

18.1

18.2

18.3

18.4

realism
A theory of international relations that focuses on the tendency of nations to operate from self-interest.

idealism
A theory of international relations that focuses on the hope that nations will act together to solve international problems and promote peace.

☐ Realism Versus Idealism

Historically, U.S. foreign and defense policy has been built on two very different views of the world. The first relies on **realism**, a belief that other nations are interested first and foremost in their own advancement, whether economic, political, or social, and in strengthening their own power.

Critics of realism argue that nations seek cooperation and stability, not power. This view invokes **idealism**, a belief that nations can work together to solve common problems such as global hunger and poverty with peace, not war, as the ultimate aim. Idealists view national power as a tool for good and for promoting democracy in other nations, not merely as a way to amass more military and economic resources.

Although realism and idealism represent two competing views of the world, they can become part of a broader, more integrated foreign and defense policy. Thus, the United States could be realistic about the need to work with dictators (realism) yet still believe that democracy is the best form of government (idealism). As President Bush often argued in the months leading to the war in Iraq, the United States had to be realistic about Iraq's interest in building biological, chemical, and nuclear weapons, even as he also argued that democracy would lead nations such as Iran and North Korea toward international cooperation and peace. Thus far, the Obama administration has taken a more idealistic approach to nuclear weapons, arguing that it is in the world's best interests to limit access to nuclear materials.

BY the People Making a Difference

Promoting Ethical Investments by Colleges and Universities

Students who care about the continued starvation in the Darfur region of Sudan have many options for making their voices heard. They can certainly join organizations that are campaigning against the human rights abuses and can contribute time and money to organizations such as Save Darfur (savedarfur.org). Save Darfur is an alliance of more than 100 organizations that are working to stop the violence.

Students can also put pressure on their own colleges and universities to stop investing in businesses that operate in Sudan. Colleges and universities have endowment funds, which they invest to generate income for everything from faculty to financial aid. Some of these investments might be with businesses that have ties to or interests with the Sudanese government. Products bought by universities could be made by businesses that do business with Sudan. Because these purchases and investments are helping these businesses, even indirectly, opponents of the Sudanese government argue that colleges and universities should cut off these sources so that they do not support the Darfur oppression in any way.

The University of California system prohibited all such investments in Sudan in 2006, and many colleges and universities have followed suit. Much of the effort has come from students who have worked hard to understand how their colleges and universities invest their endowment money.

The first step in stopping such investments is to know which companies actually operate in Sudan, which is sometimes very difficult. Multinational corporations often operate through subsidiaries that might do business with a specific country. The only way to know is to get a list of all companies in an endowment portfolio or sponsor a general resolution ordering the endowment's investment managers to sell all investments that support Sudan in the war.

The Darfur crisis was still simmering despite efforts to broker a peace agreement in 2011, and other nations continue to abuse their citizens. Students must first decide which crisis demands action, and then turn to their universities to force divestment.

QUESTIONS

1. Should colleges divest unethical investments even if doing so costs money that could support students?
2. How can a college know when it is making an unethical investment? Are broad policies that prohibit such investments enforceable?
3. How can students make sure that their colleges take action on issues such as Darfur? What kinds of political participation might work on your campus?

☐ Isolationism Versus Internationalism

Whether it is based on realism or idealism, U.S. foreign policy has reflected very different views of how it should respond to the rest of the world. Some back an approach based on **isolationism**, a belief that the United States should stay out of international affairs unless other nations constitute a direct threat to its existence. The term was first used during the years leading up to World War I, when many Americans believed that the United States should stay out of the global conflict.

But isolationism is alive and well in the debate about whether the United States should continue fighting in Afghanistan. Isolationists argue that the United States should follow George Washington's advice to avoid international "entanglements," lest those entanglements lead the United States into wars that either cannot be won, put its troops in harm's way, and burden the nation with great costs. Simply put, isolationists argue that the United States should always focus first on its own interests, and leave the rest of the world alone.

Other citizens, including most foreign and defense policy experts, believe in **internationalism**, which says the United States must be engaged in international affairs to protect its own interests. Realists and idealists can disagree on the goals of U.S. foreign and defense policy, but they can still agree that the United States should engage the world on economic, political, and social issues such as human rights for oppressed people, global hunger, and the war on terrorism. Internationalists tend to view themselves as citizens of the world, not only the United States. They feel there are times when the United States should intervene, even when not directly threatened by another nation.

isolationism
The desire to avoid international engagement altogether.

internationalism
The belief that nations must engage in international problem solving.

unilateralism
A philosophy that encourages individual nations to act on their own when facing threats from other nations.

☐ Unilateralism Versus Multilateralism

Although internationalists agree that the United States might have occasional reasons to participate in world affairs, they have two very different views about how. Supporters of **unilateralism** believe that the United States has the right to act alone in response to threats, even if other nations are unwilling to help. They argue that it should never give other nations (or the United Nations) a veto over its actions, even if that means it acts alone in using its great military power.

Hunger remains a serious problem in many less developed countries. Here, Africans stand in line in Southern Sudan waiting for U.S. food aid. Note that the food comes in bags that are marked with the U.S. flag.

Bush Doctrine
A policy adopted by the Bush administration in 2001 that asserts America's right to attack any nation that has weapons of mass destruction that may be used against U.S. interests at home or abroad.

multilateralism
A philosophy that encourages individual nations to act together to solve international problems.

preemption
A policy of taking action before the United States is attacked rather than waiting for provocation.

weapons of mass destruction
Biological, chemical, or nuclear weapons that can cause a massive number of deaths in a single use.

In fact, President Bush announced a new unilateral policy immediately after the September 11 attacks. Under the **Bush Doctrine**, any nation that threatened the United States was automatically a potential target for unilateral action. The Bush Doctrine was built on three basic concepts:

1. The United States reserves the right to attack any nation that either harbors terrorists or constitutes a serious threat to the United States.
2. The United States reserves the right to act unilaterally against other nations even if it does not have the support of its allies.
3. The United States reserves the right to use massive force against its enemies, including nuclear weapons if needed.

Opponents of the Bush Doctrine support **multilateralism**, a belief that the United States should act only with the active support of other nations. According to its advocates, multilateralism not only increases the odds that other nations will share the burdens of war with the United States, but it also increases the potential that other nations will support the U.S. position once a war is over. At least partly because of the advantages of multilateralism, the Bush administration began backing away from the Bush Doctrine only three years after announcing it. Faced with mounting costs of rebuilding Iraq and reducing international tension with other Middle Eastern nations, the administration began working to bring other nations such as Russia, France, and Germany into the debate.

Having rejected the Bush Doctrine in all but very rare cases when an attack is imminent, the Obama administration has generally operated under the multilateralist philosophy, promoting cooperation among U.S. allies in using military force against Libya, for example. The administration also decided early on that it would not use nuclear weapons against Iran's nuclear program, even though those weapons could be used against the United States. However, it continues the long-standing U.S. practice of promising retaliation for attacks on U.S. citizens in other countries. It is particularly concerned about terrorist attacks around the world and inside the United States and is ready to respond immediately with strong military force.

☐ Preemption Versus Provocation

For most of its history, the United States has waited to be provoked before going to war. Although there is considerable debate about what constitutes a provocation to war, **preemption** assumes the United States can attack first when it believes another nation constitutes a very serious threat. This approach was a centerpiece of the Bush Doctrine discussed above, based on the notion that the proliferation of **weapons of mass destruction** such as chemical, biological, or nuclear arms makes waiting for provocation much more dangerous than it once was. However, because Iraq's weapons of mass destruction were never found, U.S. intelligence agencies were widely blamed for providing misleading intelligence, under alleged pressure from the Bush administration and Vice President Dick Cheney.

The war in Iraq is an example of preemption, which some experts call the nation's first "war of choice." Prior to Iraq, the United States engaged in war only in direct response to a first attack by an adversary. Believing that Iraq continued to hold weapons of mass destruction, the Bush administration decided to force Saddam Hussein from his dictatorship before he could use those weapons against the United States. The president's national security adviser Condoleezza Rice also argued that the United States had a moral obligation to remove Hussein from power, even if doing so meant war. "This is an evil man who, left to his own devices, will wreak havoc again on his own population, his neighbors, and, if he gets weapons of mass destruction and the means to deliver them, on all of us," Rice told the British Broadcasting Corporation in August 2002. "There is a very powerful moral case for regime change. We certainly do not have the luxury of doing nothing."[3]

□ Hard Power Versus Soft Power

Internationalists have different views of just how the United States should influence other nations in protecting itself. Some favor the use of **hard power**, or military and economic strength, whereas others favor **soft power**, or negotiation and diplomacy. These two forms of power will be discussed later in this chapter as we look at different options for accomplishing foreign and defense goals.[4]

Hard power depends almost entirely on a nation's ability to threaten or force another nation to act a certain way to avoid an attack. It relies on military strength as measured by the number of soldiers in uniform, their preparation for war, the quality of their equipment, and their nation's willingness to put them in harm's way.

We often associate hard power with the **theory of deterrence**, under which a nation creates enough military strength to ensure a massive response to any attack. During the Cold War, the United States maintained more than enough nuclear weapons to deter the Soviet Union from using its nuclear weapons first and argued that sufficient bombs would survive any Soviet attack to ensure the destruction of the Soviet Union. This notion of *mutual assured destruction*, sometimes called MAD, was enough to keep both nations from using their nuclear weapons, but it kept each on constant alert just in case the other dared to act first.

Soft power is based on more traditional diplomacy and a nation's reputation for keeping its word in honoring treaties, its readiness to provide financial aid, and its ability to find consensus by bargaining with allies and adversaries alike. The Obama administration has been a strong supporter of more diplomacy in international affairs, although it has shown a willingness to use hard power in Afghanistan. Obama's strategy is evidence that nations can use hard and soft power at the same time to resolve disputes. In fact, the threat of military force is often enough to produce a negotiated settlement, as was the case throughout the Cold War.

hard power
Reliance on economic and military strength to solve international problems.

soft power
Reliance on diplomacy and negotiation to solve international problems.

theory of deterrence
A theory that is based on creating enough military strength to persuade other nations not to attack first.

The Foreign Policy and Defense Agenda

18.2 Assess the status of each of the issues that currently dominate the foreign policy and defense agenda.

The United States does not always have a choice about whether to act in world affairs. Many unavoidable issues reach its borders. These issues often dominate the foreign and defense policy agenda, which currently put on six major issues at the top of a long list of concerns. The six issues are presented in the following pages in alphabetical order: (1) addressing global climate change, (2) controlling weapons of mass destruction such the nuclear weapons allegedly being built by Iran and North Korea, (3) fighting terrorism, (4) negotiating peace in the Middle East, (5) promoting free trade abroad, and (6) strengthening democracy and international understanding. Just because an issue such as global health and poverty is not on the list does not mean it is off the agenda. Rather, we focus here on the issues that appear to be at the top of the agenda today.

President Jimmy Carter, Egyptian President Anwar El Sadat, and Israeli Prime Minister Menanchem Begin share a famous handshake in 1978 agreeing to negotiate for peace in the Middle East. The three met at the U.S. president's retreat at Camp David, Maryland.

□ Addressing Global Climate Change

The United States has a mixed record in efforts to control the global climate change often associated with greenhouse gases that trap heat in the environment and raise the world's temperature. Much of the recent increase in greenhouse gases is related to the release of carbon dioxide from the burning of fossil fuels such as gasoline and coal by automobiles and power plants.

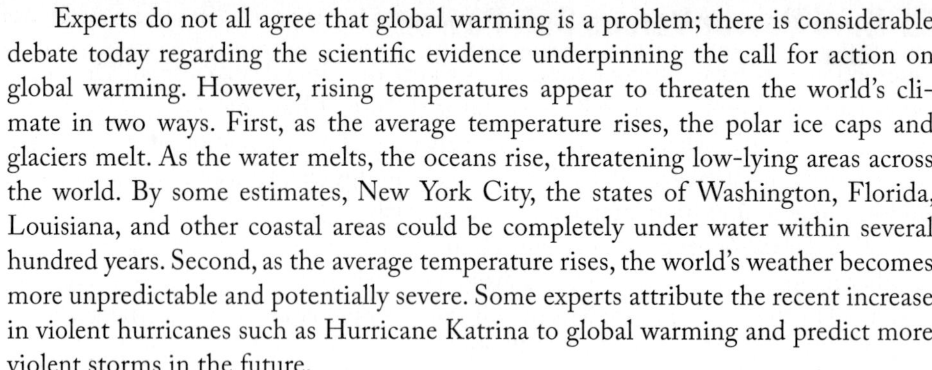

Experts do not all agree that global warming is a problem; there is considerable debate today regarding the scientific evidence underpinning the call for action on global warming. However, rising temperatures appear to threaten the world's climate in two ways. First, as the average temperature rises, the polar ice caps and glaciers melt. As the water melts, the oceans rise, threatening low-lying areas across the world. By some estimates, New York City, the states of Washington, Florida, Louisiana, and other coastal areas could be completely under water within several hundred years. Second, as the average temperature rises, the world's weather becomes more unpredictable and potentially severe. Some experts attribute the recent increase in violent hurricanes such as Hurricane Katrina to global warming and predict more violent storms in the future.

The world acknowledged these problems when it adopted an international treaty called the Kyoto Protocol in 1997. Under the treaty, all participating nations agreed to reduce their emission of greenhouse gases by set amounts during the coming decades. Although 85 nations signed the agreement and 190 have ratified it, the United States has never ratified the treaty and has yet to embrace limits on burning fossil fuels, even though it produces a significant amount of the world's greenhouse gases. The United States has argued that the limits imposed by the Kyoto Protocol would weaken its economy. Efforts continued as many of the world's largest carbon producers met in Copenhagen in early 2010, but they were unable to reach an agreement in setting targets.

☐ Controlling Weapons of Mass Destruction

The international community has been working for decades to reduce the threat of weapons of mass destruction. Although the world is particularly concerned about the development of such weapons in North Korea and Iran, the effort to reduce the spread of nuclear weapons actually started with nuclear disarmament talks between the United States and the Soviet Union in the 1970s.

With the end of the Cold War in 1989, the United States and Russia began to look for new ways of reducing their nuclear arsenals. In 2010, they agreed to reduce the number of nuclear warheads dramatically. Meeting in Prague on April 8, Russia and the United States agreed that each would reduce the number of nuclear warheads to 1,550, a cut of almost 50 percent. In early 2012, the Obama administration began a new round of conversations about reducing the total number of weapons by another 1,500.[5] By late 2012, however, the negotiations were still on hold as Russia backed away from the limits.

The world is also threatened by biological and chemical weapons that can kill millions in a single release. Although chemical weapons were outlawed by international agreement after World War I, at least nine countries say they have developed chemical weapons, such as nerve gases, that kill on contact. Other nations such as Iran and North Korea continue to develop biological weapons that spread disease or poisons, and still others already have or intend to develop nuclear weapons.

The United States has been particularly concerned in recent years about Iran and North Korea's recent efforts to develop nuclear weapons, which the United States and many other nations believe they may use against Israel. By 2012, Iran appeared well on its way to producing the enriched uranium needed for a nuclear weapon. There is also concern about the possibility that terrorists could build and explode some kind of nuclear weapon in the United States.

In early 2009, the United States received satellite photos of Iran's nuclear development program. The United States responded by demanding more international penalties against Iran in an effort to strangle the country's economy. Iran continues to develop nuclear capabilities and shows no readiness to negotiate.

☐ Fighting Terrorism

The war on terrorism is a broad term used to describe efforts to control terrorist acts sponsored by other nations, such as Afghanistan, Iran, Syria, Yemen, and even Iraq, or acts undertaken by independent groups that operate without any connection to a government.

Although the war is most often associated with Osama bin Laden and his Al-Qaeda terrorist organization, dozens of other terrorist organizations exist. These groups have executed bombings in London, Madrid, Moscow, the Middle East, and throughout Southeast Asia, including Thailand, Malaysia, the Philippines, and Indonesia, where terrorists have carried out several bombings at or near popular tourist hotels. For example, in November 2008, terrorists conducted a coordinated attack on major hotels in Mumbai, India, that killed 172 people. The attack was followed in December with the attempted Christmas Day bombing of a Northwest Airlines flight from Amsterdam to Detroit. These attacks showed the power of violence as a tool of terrorism, and the media's widespread coverage of terrorist incidents like these also (unwittingly or not) spreads this fear. Groups that were once small and unknown can achieve widespread notoriety, which helps with fund raising and recruiting.

☐ Negotiating Peace in the Middle East

Long before the September 11 attacks, the United States was working to secure peace between Israel and its neighbors, in part because the Middle East is such an important source of the world's oil and in part because the United States has long considered Israel an ally. However, despite decades of U.S. efforts to promote peace in the region, the Middle East remains locked in a violent struggle over Israel's right to exist. Progress toward peace has been threatened by ongoing conflict with Arab nations and terrorist groups.

In 2002, however, the United States, Israel, and most Arab nations embraced "The Road Map to Peace." Under this agreement, signed in April 2003, Israel and its adversaries agreed to two broad steps toward peace. The Palestinian Authority, which represents citizens in territories captured by Israel in past wars and still claimed as part of Israeli territory, agreed to arrest, disrupt, and restrain individuals and groups that plan and conduct violent attacks on Israel. Israel in turn agreed to start dismantling settlements of Israeli citizens in the occupied territories to its south and east. Israel honored part of its end of the agreement starting in 2005 by beginning to dismantle settlements and turn over control of these territories to the Palestinian Authority.

Osama bin Laden became America's number one public enemy after his Al-Qaeda organization took credit for destroying the World Trade Center on 9/11. He was killed by U.S. commandos in 2011.

18.1

18.2

18.3

18.4

normal trade relations
Trade status granted as part of an international trade policy that gives a nation the same favorable trade concessions and tariffs that the best trading partners receive.

However, the dismantling of settlements happened in Gaza only; the settlements in East Jerusalem and the West Bank continue to expand. The dispute continued into 2012 under the Obama administration, which was still working toward a "soft power" resolution that would create a separate Palestinian nation and restore territorial lines to the pre-1967 war boundaries. The effort was soon complicated, however, by Iran's suspected development of a nuclear weapon that could be used against Israel. Despite repeated efforts to stop the development, Iran was allegedly still at work on the weapon and the rockets to carry it to a target in 2012.

☐ Promoting Free Trade

As the world economy has grown, so has international competition over access to global markets. The United States has generally responded with a basic policy of free trade, meaning a commitment to the free movement of goods across international borders. But it does not allow the unrestricted export of technologies that can be used to build weapons of mass destruction, and it has long protected certain defense industries that are essential for U.S. military strength. The United States has also used trade as a tool to promote human rights and democratic reform.

Conflicting goals have characterized the U.S. debate over free trade with China. On the one hand, China has a long history of violating basic human and democratic rights. But it also has one of the fastest-growing economies in the world. U.S. exports to China have tripled during the past decade, and imports from China have grown rapidly. The conflict between concern for human rights and a desire to benefit from China's growing economy became especially prominent when the Clinton administration asked Congress to grant **normal trade relations** status to China. Despite strong opposition from advocates of strong restrictions on labor, environmental, and human rights abuses, China was granted permanent normal trade status in 2000.

Typically, Congress grants normal trade relations under a "fast-track," or accelerated, basis by limiting its own debate to a simple up-or-down vote with no amendments. Although Congress initially refused to use this process for China, it eventually approved the status and extended the president's authority to negotiate such trade agreements in 2002. Obama used that authority in late 2011 to create proposed agreements with South Korea, Columbia, and Panama, but Congress tabled the proposals until after the 2012 election. He also continued to pressure China to abide by the trade agreements.

☐ Strengthening Democracy and International Understanding

The United States has long engaged in promoting democracy and its freedoms. It does so mostly through economic sanctions to increase the pain that might bring its adversaries to negotiations. However, some efforts conflict with other U.S. goals such as promoting international trade and fighting the war on terrorism. For example, the United States continues to promote international trade with China, one of the world's fastest-growing economies, even though China continues to deny its citizens basic rights such as a free press. In addition, the United States still provides aid to many Middle Eastern nations ruled by dictatorships in order to gain their help in the war on terrorism.

The United States also provides humanitarian aid to nations affected by natural disasters such as the 2010 earthquakes in Chile, Haiti, and China. Although dictators led many of the countries affected, the United States has long believed that citizens should not suffer during crises even though their governments are not free.

Finally, the United States uses programs such as the Peace Corps to promote international understanding. Peace Corps volunteers are expected to serve in another nation for two years and become part of the community they are serving. They work on a variety of projects, such as teaching mathematics and science, doing community development work, and improving water and sanitation systems. Most have a college degree, specific international experience, or both. Approximately 10 percent of the

The Global Community

International Support for Ties with International Business

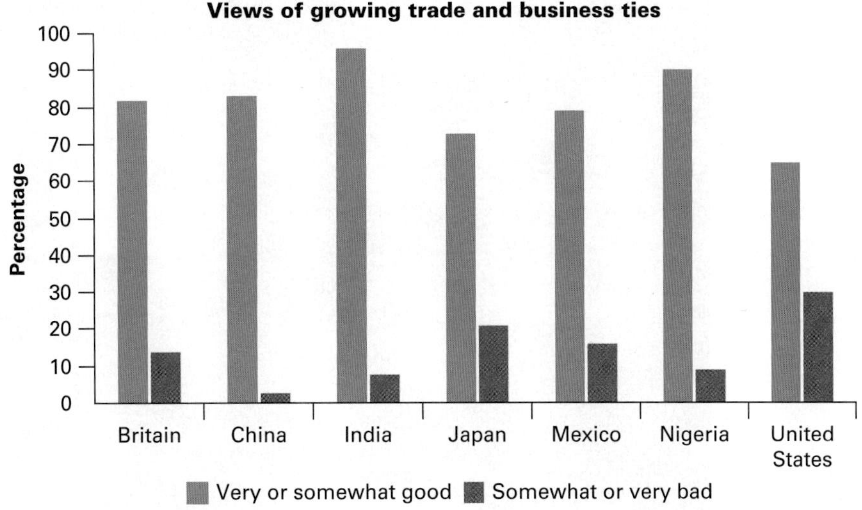

SOURCE: Pew Research Center, *Some Positive Signs for U.S. Image: Global Economic Gloom—China and India Notable Exceptions* (Pew Research Center, 2008).

Global citizens have very different views of ties between business and their countries. Some see the ties as essential for economic growth, whereas others worry that business is only interested in profits. In addition, some global citizens appear to worry about corruption in business dealings with their countries. Many even view business as too involved in local affairs.

Nevertheless, international trade is usually seen as a way to help nations reduce poverty. The Pew Research Center's Spring 2008 Global Attitudes Survey strongly suggests that the world's citizens believe that global trade is very or somewhat good for their nation.

Respondents were asked: What do you think about the growing trade and business ties between your country and other countries—do you think it is a very good thing, somewhat good, somewhat bad, or a very bad thing for your country?

Favorability toward global trade has fallen in most countries during the past three years, in part because of the economic recession. Although Indians have become more supportive of trade as their economy grows, Americans remain skeptical about business ties. Worries about the recession have driven these concerns higher within the nation as Americans blame business and trade for the high unemployment that has followed the economic collapse. However, most Americans understand that trade is one way to rebuild the economy as long as it flows both ways. They want more free trade between all nations.

In general, support for trade varies by the economic conditions of the world's nations. Poorer nations tend to see trade as a way out of poverty, but it is not always clear that trade has benefited them.

CRITICAL THINKING QUESTIONS

1. Why are less developed countries more supportive of international trade, and should they be so favorable?
2. What are the advantages of international trade in creating peaceful relations around the world?
3. How can trade damage a developing nation?

7,300 current volunteers are over the age of 50. The Peace Corps covers travel and a minimum salary and typically trains volunteers in language and job skills for approximately three months before their service abroad.[6]

Although promoting democracy involves persuasion and even global advertising, it is often backed up by the threat and use of military power. For example, the U.S. was deeply involved in the "Arab Spring" uprisings that began in 2011 with the uprising in Tunsia, and quickly spread to Egypt, Syria, and Yemen. The U.S. also participated with the North Atlantic Treaty Organization (NATO) in the air war over Libya, which began in March 2011 after the Libyan public rose up against another brutal dictator, Muammar Gaddafi. The U.S. provided key intelligence the civil war sparked by the protests, supplied arms to anti-Gaddafi forces, and launched Tomahawk missiles

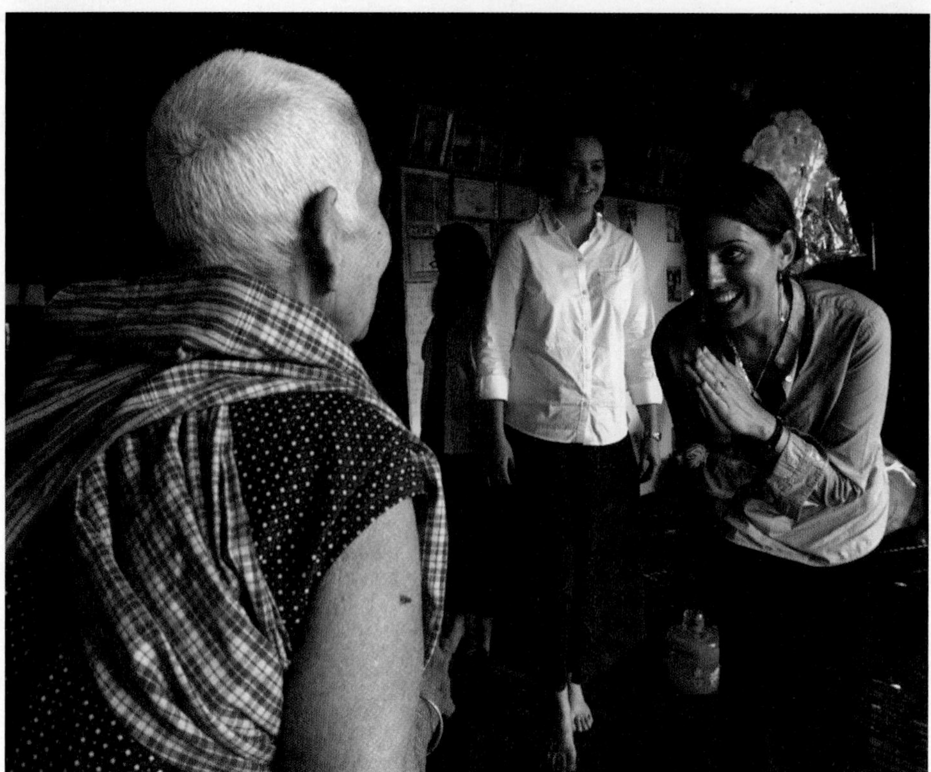

A new Peace Corps volunteer greets a villager in a small village east of Phnom Penh, Cambodia. Almost 200,000 Americans have served in the Peace Corps since its creation in 1961. More than 8,000 served in more than 150 countries in 2012.

against Libyan military targets from its ships and aircraft. But the United States and NATO never committed troops to the battle.

Gaddafi's forces fought hard against the uprising, but eventually surrendered after Gaddafi was caught and killed on October 20, 2011. Many experts heralded the United States and NATO action as a combination of soft and hard power in resolving international conflicts.

The Foreign Policy and Defense Bureaucracy

18.3 Outline the structure of the foreign policy and defense bureaucracy.

Even in troubled times, the president does not have absolute authority to act. Congress has the power to declare war, to appropriate funds for the armed forces, and to make rules that govern them. But the president is commander in chief and is authorized to negotiate treaties and receive and send ambassadors—that is, to recognize or refuse to recognize other governments. The Senate confirms U.S. ambassadorial appointments and gives consent (by a two-thirds vote) to treaty ratification.

Officially, the president's principal foreign policy adviser is the secretary of state, although others, such as the national security adviser or the vice president, are sometimes equally influential. In practice, the secretary of state delegates the day-to-day responsibilities for running the State Department and spends most of the time negotiating with the leaders of other countries.

However, foreign policy requires more than one adviser. The application of hard and soft power is the responsibility of several major departments and agencies, including State, Defense, Treasury, Agriculture, Commerce, Labor, Energy, the Central Intelligence Agency (CIA), and the Department of Homeland Security.

□ The National Security Council

The president's National Security Council (NSC) is the most important White House agency involved in coordinating foreign policy. Created by Congress in 1947, it serves directly under the president and is intended to help integrate foreign, military, and economic policies that affect national security. By law, it consists of the president, vice president, secretary of state, and secretary of defense. Recent presidents have sometimes also included the director of the CIA, the White House chief of staff, and the national security adviser as assistants to the NSC.

The national security adviser, appointed by the president, has emerged as one of the most influential foreign policy makers, sometimes rivaling the secretary of state in influence. Presidents come to rely on these White House aides both because of their proximity (down the hall in the West Wing of the White House) and because they owe their primary loyalties to the president, not to any department or program. Each president has shaped the NSC structure and adapted its staff procedures to suit his personal preferences. Throughout the years, however, the NSC, as both a committee and a staff, has taken on a major role in making and implementing foreign policy.

□ The State Department

The State Department is responsible for the diplomatic realm of foreign and defense policy. It is organized around a series of "desks" representing different parts of the world and foreign policy missions.

DUTIES The State Department is responsible for negotiating treaties with other nations and international organizations, protecting U.S. citizens abroad, promoting U.S. commercial interests in other nations, and granting visas to foreign visitors. The State Department also staffs and protects all U.S. embassies and consulates abroad. Embassies provide full diplomatic services on behalf of the United States and its citizens; consulates are smaller branch offices of embassies that help foreign citizens enter the United States through visas, or entry papers.

The State Department also plays a significant role in homeland security, often in cooperation with the Department of Homeland Security, which was created in 2002 and oversees the Transportation Security Administration that conducts passenger and baggage screening at the nation's airports. Many of the September 11 terrorists had entered the United States on student visas granted by the State Department's Bureau of Consular Affairs. Although their movements once in the United States were supposed to be monitored by the Justice Department's Immigration and Naturalization Service, the State Department was criticized for granting the visas without conducting deep background checks on individuals who might cause harm to the country.

THE FOREIGN SERVICE U.S. embassies are staffed largely by members of the U.S. Foreign Service. Although part of the State Department, the service represents the entire government and performs jobs for many other agencies. Its main duties are to carry out foreign policy as expressed in the directives of the secretary of state; gather political, economic, and intelligence data for U.S. policy makers; protect U.S. citizens and interests in foreign countries; and cultivate friendly relations with host governments and foreign peoples.

The Foreign Service is a select group of approximately 4,000 highly trained civil servants, comparable to army officers in the military and expected to take assignments anywhere in the world on short notice. Approximately two-thirds of U.S. ambassadors to approximately 160 nations come from the ranks of the Foreign Service. The others are usually presidential appointees confirmed by the Senate.

The Foreign Service is one of the most prestigious, and most criticized, career services of the national government. Criticism sometimes comes as much from within as from outside. Critics claim that the organizational culture of the Foreign Service stifles

The spirit of bipartisanship is reflected in the report of the 9/11 Commission, issued on July 22, 2004. The commission was made up of both Democrats and Republicans who managed to put their ideological differences aside and issue a report that is critical of both the Clinton and Bush administrations in their handling of terrorism. Shown here are 9/11 Commission co-chairs Thomas Kean and Lee Hamilton.

creativity; attracts officers who are, or at least become, more concerned about their status than their responsibilities; and requires new recruits to wait 15 years or more before being considered for positions of responsibility. Like other federal agencies, most notably the Central Intelligence Agency (CIA) and the Justice Department's Federal Bureau of Investigation (FBI), the Foreign Service has had great difficulty recruiting officers with Arabic-language skills, which clearly weakens each agency's ability to interpret, let alone collect, intelligence about the terrorist networks that have emerged in the Middle East and Asia.

Despite these criticisms, few would question the courage and commitment of the Foreign Service. Many serve in the most dangerous countries across the world, and often take great risks in their jobs. In September 2012, for example, Ambassador J. Christopher Stevens was killed in a terrorist attack on the U.S. mission in Benghazi, Libya. He had joined the Foreign Service in 1991.

☐ Intelligence Agencies

Accurate, timely information about foreign nations is essential for making wise decisions. As the Senate Intelligence Committee and the national commission created to investigate the September 11, 2001, attacks both noted, the intelligence community failed to provide that information in time to prevent the attacks or change the course of the Iraq War.[7]

THE CENTRAL INTELLIGENCE AGENCY The most important intelligence agency is the Central Intelligence Agency, created in 1947 to gather and analyze information that flows into various parts of the U.S. government from all around the world. In recent years, the CIA has had approximately 20,000 employees, who both collect information and shape the intelligence estimates that policy makers use to set priorities.

Although most of the information the CIA gathers comes from open sources such as the Internet, the CIA does use spies and undercover agents to monitor foreign threats. This secret intelligence occasionally supplies crucial data. But it is not all glamour; much is routine. Intelligence work consists of three basic operations: reporting, analysis, and dissemination. *Reporting* is based on close and rigorous observation of developments around the world; *analysis* is the attempt to detect meaningful patterns in what was observed in the past and to understand what appears to be going on now; *dissemination* means getting the right information to the right people at the right time.

THE BROADER INTELLIGENCE COMMUNITY The CIA is one of almost two dozen intelligence agencies in the federal government, most notably the State Department's Bureau of Intelligence and Research; the Defense Department's Defense Intelligence Agency (which combines the intelligence operations of the Army, Navy, Air Force, and Marine Corps); the Federal Bureau of Investigation; the Treasury Department's Office of Terrorism and Finance Intelligence; the Energy Department's Office of Intelligence; the Homeland Security Department's Directorate of Information Analysis and Infrastructure Protection and Directorate of Coast Guard Intelligence; the National Security Agency (which specializes in electronic reconnaissance and code breaking); the National Reconnaissance Office (which runs the U.S. satellite surveillance programs); and the National Geospatial-Intelligence Agency (which collects and analyzes photographic imagery). Together, these agencies are the heart of the U.S. intelligence community.

Because each of these agencies was created to collect unique information (imagery, electronic intelligence, and so forth) for a unique client (the president, the secretary of defense, or others), the agencies rarely shared information. The lack of cooperation clearly affected the government's ability to prevent the September 11, 2001, attacks. "Many dedicated officers worked day and night for years to piece together the growing body of evidence on Al-Qaeda and to understand the threats," the 9/11 Commission concluded. "Yet, while there were many reports on bin Laden and his growing Al-Qaeda organization, there was no comprehensive review of what the intelligence community knew and what it did not know, and what that meant."[8]

Congress responded by creating the Office of the Director of National Intelligence in 2004 to coordinate the movement of information within the intelligence community. Under its legislation, the new director was responsible for providing the primary advice to the president on intelligence issues and was given the authority to make recommendations regarding the annual budgets of each intelligence agency. The director also oversees a new federal counterterrorism center, responsible for making sense of all national intelligence on potential terrorist threats to the United States. Despite the promise of more coordination, however, congressional critics in both parties complained that the new director merely added a layer of bureaucracy to an already cumbersome system.

The intelligence community has been criticized in recent years for failing to detect several potential attacks, notably the December 2009 "Christmas Day" bombing plot mentioned previously. The bombing plot was thwarted by passengers on Northwest Airlines Flight 253 from Amsterdam to Detroit in the few minutes before the airplane landed as the bomber tried to mix explosive chemicals hidden in his pants. Although several intelligence agencies had information about a terrorist attack coming from Yemen, and had even been given the name of the bomber, they failed to coordinate the information in time to prevent the attempt.

☐ The Department of Defense

The president, Congress, the National Security Council, the State Department, and the Defense Department all make overall defense policy and attempt to integrate U.S. national security programs, but the day-to-day work of organizing for defense is the job of the Defense Department. Its headquarters, the Pentagon, houses within its 17.5 miles of corridors 23,000 top military and civilian personnel. The offices of several hundred generals and admirals are there, as is the office of the secretary of defense. As of 2012, the secretary was former CIA director and member of Congress Leon Panetta. Panetta provides civilian control of the armed services, and was in charge of the armed forces at the end of the Iraq War.

THE JOINT CHIEFS OF STAFF The committee known as the Joint Chiefs of Staff serves as the principal military adviser to the president, the National Security Council, and the secretary of defense. It includes the heads of the Air Force, Army, Navy, and Marine Corps, and the chair and vice chair of the Joint Chiefs. The president, with the consent of the Senate, appoints all the service chiefs to four-year nonrenewable

Explore on MyPoliSciLab

How Much Does America Spend on Defense?

The United States has the largest defense budget in the world, but many observers still ask "Do we spend enough?" At the end of the Vietnam War, Americans all agreed that defense spending should be increased. Since then, Democrats and Independents became more "dovish" (anti-defense spending), while Republicans became far more "hawkish" (pro-defense spending). These differences became most pronounced in the years following the Iraq War and after George W. Bush's reelection in 2004.

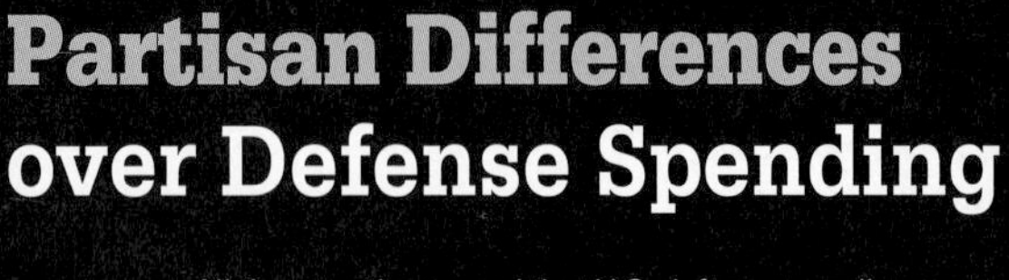

Partisan Differences over Defense Spending

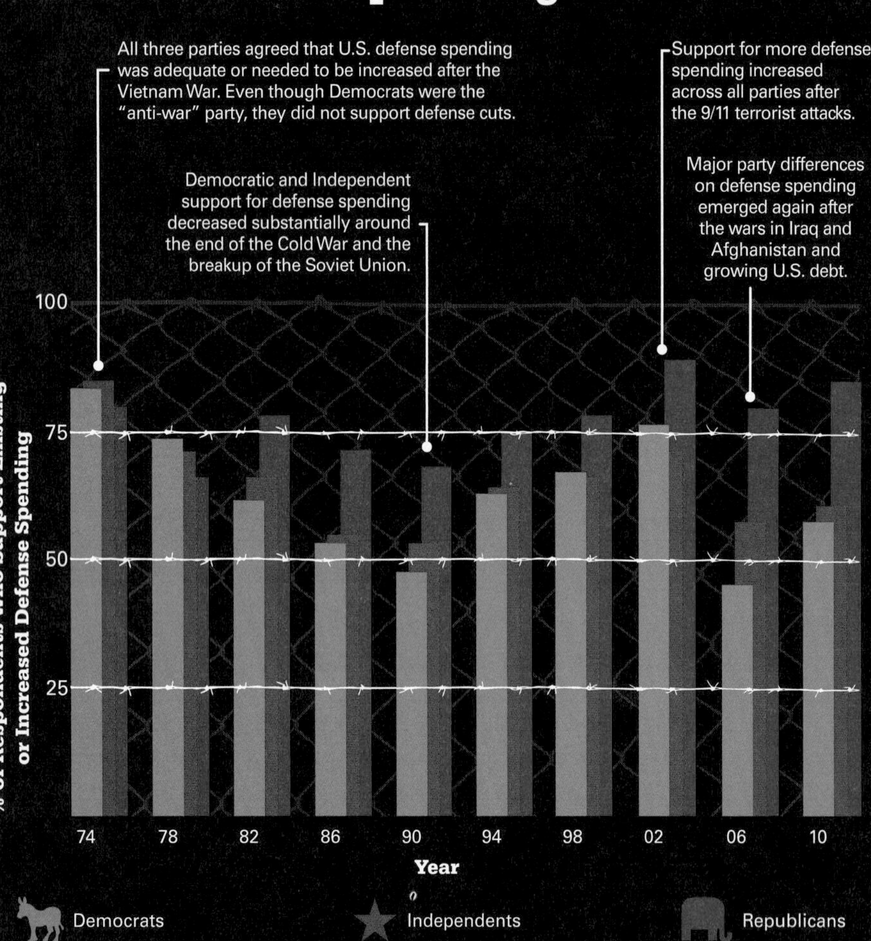

The United States Spends the Most on Defense

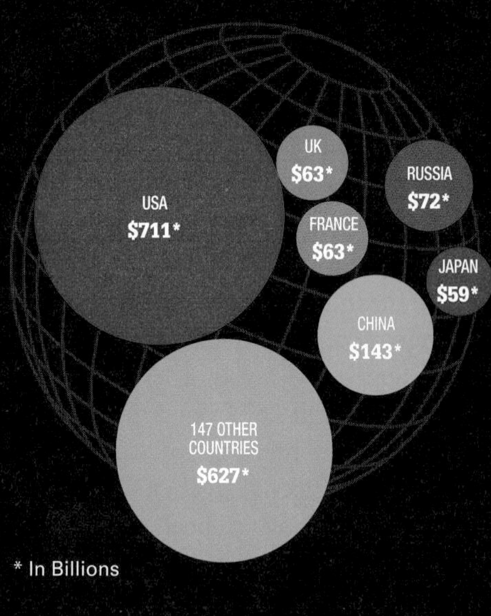

SOURCE: Data from Stockholm International Peace Research Institute (SIPRI) Yearbook, www.sipri.org; and the General Social Survey, 1982–2010.

Investigate Further

Concept Do Americans view defense spending as excessive? The United States currently has the largest defense budget in the world—twice the amount of China, the U.K., France, Japan, and Russia combined. But most Americans think the U.S. spends enough or should spend even more on defense.

Connection How do events relate to changes in support for defense spending? Wars, terrorist attacks, and recessions all influence public opinion of government spending. After the Cold War, both parties agreed not to maintain or increase the defense budget. After the 9/11 attacks, both parties supported increased spending.

Cause How does partisanship shape perceptions of defense spending? Democrats and Independents are more likely than Republicans to say that we spend too much on defense. These differences have become more pronounced in the last decade as the global war on terrorism became increasingly politicized.

terms. Note that the twice-renewable two-year term of the chair of the Joint Chiefs is part of the process of ensuring civilian control over the military.

The Department of Defense Reorganization Act of 1986 shifted considerable power to the chair of the Joint Chiefs. Reporting through the secretary of defense, the chair now advises the president on military matters, exercises authority over the forces in the field, and is responsible for overall military planning. In theory, the chair of the Joint Chiefs can even make a military decision that the chiefs of the other services oppose.

Note, however, that the chair of the Joint Chiefs is *not* the head of the military. The chair and the Joint Chiefs are advisers to the secretary of defense and the president, but the president can disregard their advice and on occasion has done so. A president must weigh military action or inaction against the larger foreign and security interests of the nation.

all-volunteer force
The replacement for the draft (conscription) for recruiting members of the armed services.

THE ALL-VOLUNTEER FORCE The Constitution authorizes Congress to do what is "necessary and proper" in order to "raise and support Armies," "to provide and maintain a Navy," and "to provide for calling forth the Militia." The Joint Chiefs and the presidential appointees who serve as secretaries of the Air Force, Army, Navy, and Marine Corps oversee the 1.5 million soldiers who currently serve in what the founders might call the national militia.

During most of its history, the United States has used military conscription to raise and support its armed services. The draft, as it is called, was first used in 1862, during the Civil War, and again during World War I, World War II, and Vietnam. Shortly before the Vietnam War ended, Congress replaced the draft with an **all-volunteer force**, composed entirely of citizens who choose to serve.

As of 2012, the armed services had almost 1.5 million active-duty personnel, but was scheduled to cut 100,000 positions between 2013 and 2017 with most the cuts scheduled to hit the U.S. Army and Marine Corps. Although the proposal was driven in part by the effort to reduce federal spending, it also reflected the changing nature of war over the past 100 years. Whereas World War I, World War II, and the Korean and Iraq wars were fought by massive armies in face-to-face combat, future wars are likely to involve more precise engagements and the use of sophisticated technologies such as unmanned drones and even the kind of computer viruses used to disable Iranian nuclear centrifuges in 2009. Hence, the Defense Department argues that there will be less need for infantry soldiers, and more need for stealth bomber and fighter pilots, technology experts, and naval ships that act as offshore military bases.

CONTRACTORS The tools of war include contracts with private businesses. The U.S. defense budget reached $555 billion in 2008, not counting the costs of the wars in Afghanistan and Iraq. More than $400 billion of that total is for private business contracts, such as military equipment, computer programming, and housing for troops.

Defense spending fell dramatically at the end of the Cold War as weapons systems were canceled or postponed, bases closed, ships retired, and large numbers of troops brought home from Germany, the Philippines, and elsewhere. The army was cut by more than 30 percent, and the National Guard and the military reserve were cut back by approximately 25 percent. As a result, defense spending also fell, dropping from 25 percent of total federal spending at the height of the Cold War in the mid-1980s to 15 percent in 2000. In part because of the war against terrorism and the wars in Iraq and Afghanistan, the defense budget has been rising ever since and stood at $707 billion by the end of 2012.

Weapons are, in fact, a major U.S. industry, one that members of Congress work hard to promote and protect. As former World War II hero Dwight Eisenhower warned in his presidential Farewell Address in 1960, the United States must be wary

OF the People Diversity in America

Diversity in the Military

The U.S. military has become much more diverse during the past three decades, in part because of much more aggressive recruiting of women and minorities. In 1990, for example, only 11 percent of all military active-duty personnel were women, and 28 percent were minorities. By 2011, 18 percent of military personnel were women, while the percentage of minorities had not changed. However, white males are still heavily represented in the military office corps.*

The four armed services—the army, navy, marine corps, and air force—vary greatly in terms of diversity, however. Looking at new recruits in 2007, which is the latest information available today, 24 percent of the air force, 19 percent of the navy, 17 percent of the army, and only 7 percent of the marine corps were women while 34 percent of the navy, 25 percent of the army, 23 percent of the air force, and 15 percent of the marine corps were minorities.**

Several reasons explain why the armed services have done better recruiting minorities than recruiting women.

First, there have been a series of recent sexual harassment scandals in the armed services, and few women have advanced to senior posts over the decades.

Second, the armed services have worked particularly hard at improving their appeal to minority enlistees. Colin Powell's rise to the highest post in the armed services has often been used to show recruits of color that anything is possible in the military. Powell entered the military as a second lieutenant in 1958, served two tours of duty in Vietnam, and eventually became the first African American officer to chair the Joint Chiefs of Staff.

Third, the military has long focused on recruiting high school graduates who are not college bound, which is a group that contains more minorities. More recently, however, the military has tried to extend its reach to recruits who intend to go to college, and has launched several programs that set aside substantial amounts of funding for future college tuition, which has also been effective in recruiting minorities.

QUESTIONS

1. **What may explain the large percentages of minority soldiers in the military?**
2. **What may explain the much smaller percentages of women in the military?**
3. **Should the military represent all groups in society? Should combat soldiers be equally representative?**

* Military Leadership Diversity Commission, From Representation to Inclusion, U.S. Government Printing Office, March 15, 2011.

** Defense Department, Under Secretary of Personnel and Readiness, available at http://prhome.defense.gov/MPP/ACCESSION%20POLICY/poprep98/intro98.pdf.

of the *military-industrial complex* that supports increased defense spending as a way to protect jobs. Eisenhower's words are well worth rereading today:

> This conjunction of an immense military establishment and a large arms industry is new in the American experience. The total influence—economic, political, and even spiritual—is felt in every city, every State house, and every office of the Federal government. We recognize the imperative need for this development. Yet we must not fail to comprehend its grave implications. Our toil, resources, and livelihood are all involved; so is the very structure of our society.
>
> In the councils of government, we must guard against the acquisition of unwarranted influence, whether sought or unsought, by the military industrial complex. The potential for the disastrous rise of misplaced power exists and will persist.[9]

Despite Eisenhower's warning, the military-industrial complex has grown dramatically since the 1950s. Contractors are now involved in military operations in Afghanistan as the war winds down. In 2011, about 430 contractors were killed in the war as they fought side-by-side with U.S. troops.[10]

Foreign Policy and Defense Options

18.4 Evaluate the options for achieving foreign policy and defense goals.

The United States has a number of tools for achieving foreign policy success, not the least of which is military might. But military might, or hard power as we discussed earlier, is no longer enough to ensure success, or even deter foreign threats. There are also a number of other forms of hard and soft

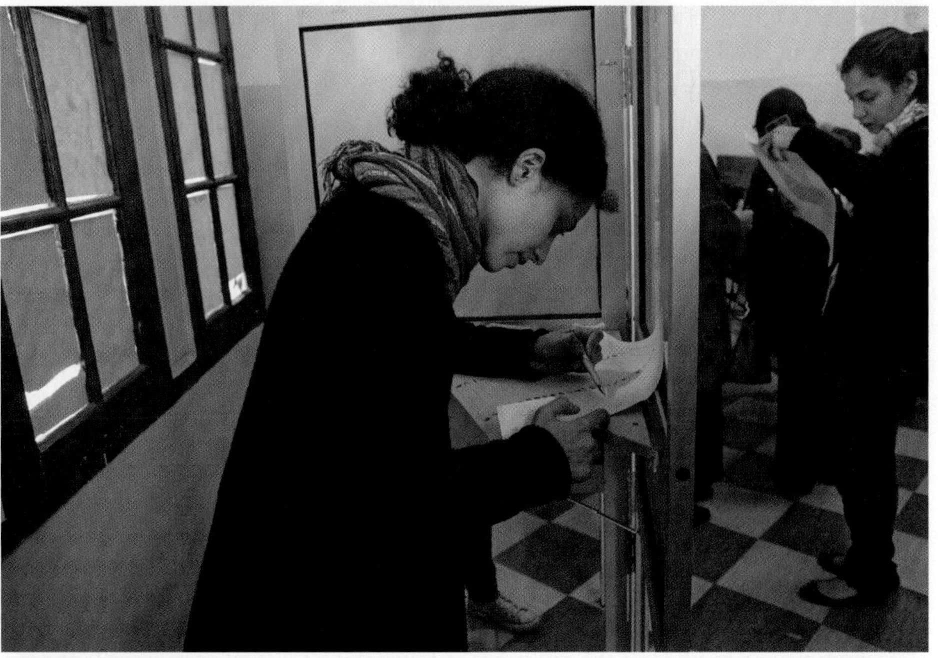

An Egyptian citizen casts a ballot in her nation's first democratic election following the Arab spring uprising that unseated the dictatorship. The United States did not use hard power to support the Egyptian uprising, but applied soft power through quiet diplomacy designed to support the transition to democratic government.

power, such as conventional diplomacy to send its message clearly, foreign aid to help nations in need, economic sanctions to isolate its adversaries, and public diplomacy to help other nations understand its agenda, the nation will not succeed in reaching its foreign policy goals. After reviewing the various forms of soft power below, this section will turn to the ultimate form of hard power, war.

☐ Conventional Diplomacy (Soft Power)

Much of U.S. foreign policy is conducted by the Foreign Service and ambassadors in face-to-face discussions across the world. International summit meetings, with their high-profile pomp and drama, are another form of conventional diplomacy. Even though traditional diplomacy appears more subdued and somewhat less vital in this era of personal leader-to-leader communication by telephone, fax, and teleconferencing, it is still an important, if slow, process by which nations can gain information, talk about mutual interests, and try to resolve disputes.

Conventional diplomacy can become hard power when the United States breaks diplomatic relations with another nation. Doing so greatly restricts tourist and business travel to a country and in effect curbs economic as well as political relations with the nation. Breaking diplomatic relations is a next-to-last resort (force is the last resort), for it undermines the ability to reason with a nation's leaders or use other diplomatic strategies to resolve conflicts. It also hampers our ability to get valuable information about what is going on in a nation and to have a presence there.

The United Nations is one of the most important arenas for traditional diplomacy. Established in 1945 by the victors of World War II, it now has 189 nation members. Despite its promise as a forum for world peace, the United Nations has been frustrated in achieving progress during past decades. Critics contend that the UN has either avoided crucial global issues or has been politically unable to tackle them. During much of that time, the U.N. General Assembly, dominated by a combination of Third World and communist nations, was hostile to many U.S. interests.

More recently, the five permanent members of the U.N. Security Council—the United States, China, Russia, Britain, and France—have usually worked in harmony to resolve pressing global crises. Moreover, the United Nations' assumption of responsibilities in the Persian Gulf War and its extensive peacekeeping missions in Cyprus and Lebanon have been notable examples of the effort to build respect for the United Nations.

Several of the United Nations' specialized agencies—including the World Health Organization, the United Nations High Commission for Refugees, and the World Food Program—are considered major successes in fighting poverty and diseases. But the review is much more mixed with respect to the United Nations' 63 peacekeeping efforts throughout its history. As of early 2012, the United Nations was engaged in 15 different peacekeeping missions around the world, including the continuing effort to help Haiti recover from a 2010 hurricane.

Moreover, some members of Congress steadfastly oppose further U.S. funding of the United Nations, arguing that the U.N. is corrupt and wasteful, and that other nations do not fulfill their financial obligations. And even strong supporters of the United Nations argue that the Security Council gives its five members too much power to veto action by the larger membership. In 2012, for example, Russia vetoed strong U.N. resolutions to curb the humanitarian crisis in Syria following several bloody attacks against civilians. Russia argued that rebels were just as responsible for the crisis as Syrian government troops.

□ Public Diplomacy (Soft Power)

In July 2002, President George W. Bush created the White House Office of Global Communications to address the question he asked before a joint session of Congress only a week after the terrorist attacks on New York City and Washington, D.C.: "Why do they hate us?" The Office of Global Communications is designed to enhance the United States' reputation abroad, countering its image as the "Great Satan," as some of its enemies describe it.[11]

Bush was not the first president to worry about the U.S. image abroad. President Franklin Roosevelt created the Office of War Information early in World War II, which in turn established the Voice of America program to broadcast pro-U.S. information into Nazi Germany. President Harry Truman followed suit early in the Cold War with the Soviet Union by launching the Campaign of Truth, which eventually led to the creation of the U.S. Information Agency under President Dwight Eisenhower. Both agencies exist today and are being strengthened as part of the "new public diplomacy."

Public diplomacy is a blend of age-old propaganda techniques and modern information warfare. It has three basic goals: (1) to cast the enemy in a less favorable light among its supporters, (2) to mold the image of a conflict such as the war in Afghanistan, and (3) to clarify the ultimate goals of U.S. foreign policy. For example, the United States has tried to convince the people of Iran that its leader is moving the nation toward war with further development of a nuclear weapon.

□ Foreign Aid (Soft Power)

The United States offers aid to more than 100 countries directly and to other nations through contributions to various U.N. development funds. Since 1945, the United States has provided approximately $400 billion in economic assistance to foreign countries. In recent years, however, its foreign aid spending has amounted to approximately $15 billion per year, or less than 50 percent of what it spent in inflation-adjusted dollars back in 1985.[12]

Most foreign aid goes to a few countries the United States deems to be of strategic importance to national security: Israel, Egypt, Ukraine, Jordan, India, Russia, South Africa, and Haiti. That list is sure to change in the future as the nation reallocates its budget to nations central to the war on terrorism. However, regardless of which nation receives the aid, most foreign aid is actually spent in the United States, where it pays for the purchase of U.S. services and products being sent to those countries. It thus amounts to a hefty subsidy for U.S. companies and their employees.

The American public thinks the United States spends much more on foreign aid than it actually does and therefore opposes increased spending. Although the United States is one of the largest foreign aid contributors in terms of total dollars, it ranks low among developed countries when aid is measured as a percentage of gross national

FOR the People Government's Greatest Endeavors

Supporting New Democracies Abroad

Approximately 60 years after the United States completed its effort to rebuild Europe after World War II, it continues to engage in what experts call "nation building." Nation building is generally defined as the effort to convert dictatorships into democracies.

This exercise of both soft and hard power has been particularly visible in recent years. It was part of the stated reason for going to war in Iraq and Afghanistan in 2003, and engaging in the effort to overthrow dictatorships in Tunisia, Egypt, Libya, Syria, and Yemen in 2011–2012.

Nation building is a very difficult task. After all, it took 15 years for the United States to declare its independence and remove the British from power during the Revolutionary War. Today's efforts often take longer, in part because of deep divisions within countries led by dictators. Dictators often use their power while in office to build strong support within their countries, and often use heavy military force to suppress calls for democracy from their citizens.

Facing just such an uprising from his own people, Syrian president Bashar al-Assad used every military means at his disposal to fight the rebellion. He deployed heavy tanks and snipers to kill hundreds of protestors in full view of the international community, assassinated opponents, shut off water and electricity to cities and villages that opposed his reign, and opened fire on defenseless civilians engaged in peaceful protests. He even ordered the execution of his own soldiers who refused to fire on the protestors. As of November 2012, the rebels were still fighting with no end of the war in sight.

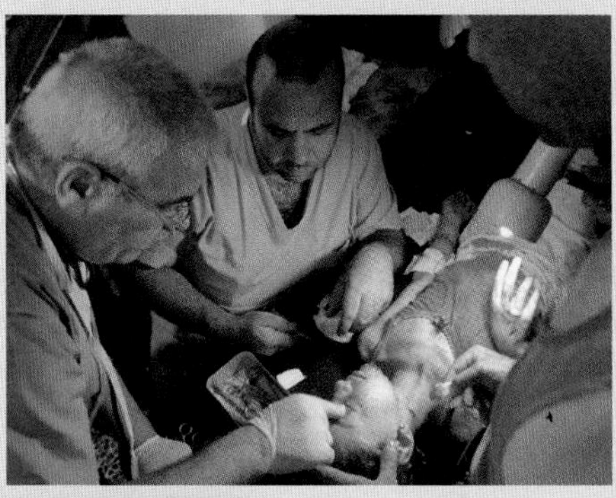

A Syrian child wounded by shelling is treated at a makeshift hospital in Homs, July 2012.

Nation building involves much more than removing a dictator from control, however. Once a nation is free from tyranny, it must create new democratic institutions such as a legislature, presidency, and judiciary. It must also write a constitution, hold free and fair elections, create a free press, and allow peaceful protests. The U.S. often provides aid in the form of health care, education, and food, some of which is provided by volunteers from charitable organizations such as Doctors without Borders.

The U.S. has long played a prominent role in these efforts, usually through large injections of foreign aid. In doing so, it is still applying the lessons it learned at the end of World War II when it helped rebuild the roads, railroads, bridges, and factories that had been bombed into rubble during the war. It also helped to rekindle the economies that had been devastated by labor shortages and address the unemployment, hunger, and homelessness that were pervasive in war-torn Europe. These efforts were part of a program called the Marshall Plan in honor of World War II Gen. George C. Marshall.

The Marshall Plan was a stunning foreign policy success, particularly in helping the United States contain communism. But it was also a great moral victory for America, prompting British Prime Minister Winston Churchill to call it "the most unsordid act in history."

Nation building today is arguably much more difficult. The countries that participated in the Marshall Plan already had the basic institutions of democracy and were ready to return to well-established practices of self-governance after Germany and Italy's defeat. But it is still a noble, if very difficult, goal.

QUESTIONS

1. Why was rebuilding Europe so important to the United States?
2. How is this kind of soft power being used today around the world?
3. Should the United States spend money helping other nations free themselves from tyranny even if their new governments are hostile to U.S. allies such as Israel?

income. A recent poll of U.S. citizens found that few supported increased foreign aid, and approximately half favored reducing it. The rest favor keeping foreign aid at the same level. But these views are often based on a lack of information regarding actual U.S. spending. According to a recent CNN survey, 20 percent of Americans estimated that foreign aid accounts for 30 percent of the federal budget. In reality, the total is barely 1 percent.[13]

State Department officials are invariably the most vocal advocates of foreign aid. Presidents also recognize the vital role foreign aid plays in advancing U.S. interests and have wanted to maintain the leverage with key countries that economic and military assistance provides. One major debate today is how much debt relief to provide for the world's poorest nations, especially ones that are hard hit by war and natural disasters

18.1
18.2
18.3
18.4

economic sanctions
Denial of export, import, or financial relations with a target country in an effort to change that nation's policies.

such as Haiti. Despite these arguments, Congress invariably trims the foreign aid budget, at least in partly in response to Americans misconceptions about the extent of that aid. Critics also note that U.S. foreign aid has subsidized the most autocratic and most corrupt of dictators. And there are plenty of instances in which foreign aid money has been stolen or misspent. Defenders counter that some corruption is inevitable.

☐ Economic Sanctions (Soft Power)

The United States has frequently used economic pressure to punish other nations for opposing its interests. Indeed, it has employed economic sanctions more than any other nation—more than 100 times in the past 50 years. **Economic sanctions** deny export, import, or financial relations with a target country in an effort to change that country's policies. Those imposed on South Africa doubtless helped end apartheid and encourage democracy in that nation; sanctions on Libya helped end its nuclear weapons program. But sanctions imposed on Cuba have not had much effect in dislodging that nation's dictatorial regime. Similarly, recent sanctions against Iran have had little effect in controlling its effort to develop a nuclear weapon.

The use of economic sanctions has varied throughout the years. They are especially unpopular among farmers and corporations that have to sacrifice part of their overseas markets to comply with government controls, and they rarely work as effectively as intended. They can also be costly to U.S. businesses and workers while intensifying anti-U.S. sentiment.

☐ Military Action (Hard Power)

War is the ultimate form of hard power, and reflects the breakdown of soft power. The United States has used military force in other nations on the average of almost once a year since 1789, although usually in short-term initiatives such as NATO's military activities in Bosnia and Kosovo. Although presidential candidate John Kerry argued that the Iraq War was the first time in history the United States had gone to war because it chose to, not because it had to, the country has actually sent forces into combat many times without a clear threat. It did not have to go to war against Spain in 1898 or send troops to Cuba, Haiti, the Dominican Republic, Lebanon, Mexico, Nicaragua, Somalia, South Vietnam, or even Europe in World War I. [14] (See Table 18.1 for the number of troops killed in the nation's major wars.)

Experts tend to agree that the use of force is most successful in small and even medium-sized countries for short engagements (Grenada, Panama, Kuwait, Kosovo, and Afghanistan). They also agree that it "often proves ineffective in the context of national civil wars (the United States in Vietnam; Israel in Lebanon)."[15]

TABLE 18.1 COSTS OF WAR

War	Number Killed
Revolutionary War	4,435
War of 1812	2,260
Civil War	214,939
Spanish-American War	385
World War I	53,402
World War II	291,557
Korean War	35,516
Vietnam War	58,516
Persian Gulf War	382
Iraq War	4,500
Afghanistan War	2,007*

*As of October 9, 2012

SOURCE: *The Washington Post*, May 26, 2003; figures updated by authors.

Military action is not always visible to the public, nor are the intended targets always clear. Covert, or secret activities such as attacks on terrorist leaders are often planned and executed without any notice at all until the operation is over, if they are ever announced at all. The United States repeatedly engaged in covert operations during the Cold War, including early intervention in Vietnam, Central America, and Afghanistan. But covert activities in Cuba, Chile, and elsewhere were quickly discovered, leading to public opposition and new congressional controls once the interventions were discovered and reported by the media. Ironically, U.S. covert aid to the Afghan rebels who fought against the Soviet Union in the late 1970s eventually led to the rise of the Taliban government that gave Osama bin Laden and his followers the freedom to establish the training bases where the September 11 terrorist attacks were planned.

You Will Decide

Should Women Engage in Combat?

As the number of women in the armed forces has increased, so has the number of women who serve near combat zones. Whereas women constituted 6 percent of U.S. forces who served during the first Iraq War in 1991, they made up 15 percent of military personnel who served during the in the second Iraq War from 2003–2011.

Although their jobs were in noncombat positions, Iraq and Afghanistan have been very dangerous places to serve—by December 2012, 113 female soldiers had been killed. Technically, the women killed in Iraq and Afghanistan did not die in combat operations. Under a 1994 Defense Department order, women can fly combat aircraft to and from airfields, protect convoys, guard prisoners of war, and rescue wounded soldiers, but may not participate in any "direct combat on the ground." Although the military is redesigning assignments to ensure that women have an equal opportunity to participate in noncombat operations, women are allowed to serve only in support units.

In February 2012, the Defense Department announced that women would be allowed to take even more dangerous jobs closer to the battlefield. Although some advocates applauded the decision, others expressed strong concern.

The military has changed dramatically in recent years—combat uses high technology weapons and requires tight coordination of air, land, and sea operations, which can blur the lines between support and combat units. As war has become more complicated, experts are asking whether women should be given the order to engage in combat.

What do you think? Should women be engaged in direct ground combat? What are some of the arguments for or against this?

Thinking It Through

Opponents argue that men are physically superior to women—although there are many high-tech jobs in combat, there is nothing high-tech about a face-to-face encounter with a deadly enemy. These opponents believe that men are better suited to win these encounters. There is also concern that men and women would form personal relationships in combat units that might distract them as they enter battle, or that female soldiers might be in the early stages of pregnancy when called for combat.

Moreover, opponents feel women would be much more vulnerable to sexual harassment in combat units, which is harder to police during battle. Nevertheless, recent studies suggest that women in the military face discrimination and harassment.

Advocates of a combat role for women argue that physical differences are mostly irrelevant. All soldiers must meet certain physical qualifications such as height, weight, and conditioning. If women meet these criteria, they argue, they should be allowed to fight. After all, they go through the same boot camps as men and learn how to use the same weapons. With the armed services struggling to recruit new soldiers, advocates also argue, women constitute an important source of future volunteers.

CRITICAL THINKING QUESTIONS

1. What are the political barriers against allowing women in combat?
2. Are women just as able as men to win the face-to-face battles that often arise in combat?
3. How can the military ensure that personal relationships do not affect combat decisions on the battlefield?

18.1
18.2
18.3
18.4

Prospects for the Future

The world has become a much more uncertain place since the end of the Cold War, if only because the United States now faces many potential "hot spots" where individual nations and groups can challenge its views. Moreover, the Internet has increased access to information around the world, the global economy has increased competition for jobs and markets, and the war on terrorism has increased anti-U.S. sentiment in many nations.

The United States is clearly struggling to address this uncertainty without frustrating the public or compromising basic democratic principles. On the one hand, for example, citizens favor open borders, easy movement of imports and exports, short lines at airports, quick access to information, and protection of their privacy. On the other hand, they want government to monitor terrorists, detect dangerous cargo, ensure airport security, keep secrets from the enemy, and make sure no one slips through the border to bring harm to the nation.

Although these goals are not necessarily contradictory, they do require a careful balance of individual liberty and national interest. They also call for an effort to prevent the spread of terrorism by promoting global peace and understanding. The war on terrorism will not be won in a single battle with a single adversary, nor will weapons of mass destruction disappear without a broad international commitment to action. As the United States has learned during the hard months of combat in Iraq, coalition building may be difficult, frustrating, and most certainly time consuming, but, ultimately, it may be the only option available. Having fought the Iraq War largely on its own, the United States has come to realize that it needs help to accomplish its goals.

Citizens can help the United States achieve its goals in many ways, whether by contributing or volunteering to provide humanitarian aid, serving in the military, or trying to improve the nation's reputation by addressing problems at home. At the same time, citizens can help change the foreign policy and defense agenda through active engagement in the political process. Their voices can be and have been heard on many issues. By putting pressure on the federal government, citizens can influence the priorities given to our foreign policy goals, while holding the nation's elected leaders accountable for what they do.

Review the Chapter

 **Listen** to **Chapter 18** on **MyPoliSciLab**

Understanding Foreign Policy and Defense

18.1 Analyze the questions and responses that shape approaches to U.S. foreign policy and defense, p. 565.

Views of foreign policy address five basic questions: Should the United States view the world realistically or idealistically? Should the United States isolate itself from the world or accept a role in the international community? Should the United States act on its own or only with the help of other nations? Should the United States act first against threats to its safety or wait until it is attacked? And should the United States use its military and economic hard power or its diplomatic soft power? Hard power relies on military and economic strength, whereas soft power uses diplomacy.

The Foreign Policy and Defense Agenda

18.2 Assess the status of each of the issues that currently dominate the foreign policy and defense agenda, p. 569.

The foreign policy and defense agenda contains a long list of issues, but seven are currently at the top of the list: controlling weapons of mass destruction such as nuclear missiles, fighting terrorism, negotiating peace in the Middle East, promoting free trade abroad, reducing global warming, ending the war in Afghanistan, and strengthening democracy and international understanding. Congress and the president do not always agree on the specific issues but tend to spend most of their time and the federal budget on them.

The Foreign Policy and Defense Bureaucracy

18.3 Outline the structure of the foreign policy and defense bureaucracy, p. 574.

The defense bureaucracy involves a set of interlocking agencies that engage in many of the same issues. The National Security Council, State Department, intelligence agencies, and Defense Department all play a role in setting and administering foreign policy and defense. The Defense Department is designed to ensure civilian control of the U.S. military but seeks advice from the military through the Joint Chiefs of Staff, who oversee the all-volunteer force. Contractors deliver a large amount of goods and services to the department and are part of what President Eisenhower in the 1950s called the military-industrial complex.

Foreign Policy and Defense Options

18.4 Evaluate the options for achieving foreign policy and defense goals, p. 580.

Foreign policy and defense options involve a mix of hard and soft power, including conventional diplomacy and foreign aid, economic sanctions, and military intervention.

Learn the Terms

 **Study** and **Review** the **Flashcards**

realism, p. 566
idealism, p. 566
isolationism, p. 567
internationalism, p. 567
unilateralism, p. 567
Bush Doctrine, p. 568
multilateralism, p. 568
preemption, p. 568
weapons of mass destruction, p. 568
hard power, p. 569
soft power, p. 569
theory of deterrence, p. 569
normal trade relations, p. 572
all-volunteer force, p. 579
economic sanctions, p. 583

Test Yourself

Study and **Review** the **Practice Tests**

MULTIPLE CHOICE QUESTIONS

18.1 Analyze the questions and responses that shape approaches to U.S. foreign policy and defense.

Which of the following are aspects of soft power?

- **a.** build more nuclear weapons
- **b.** providing aid to developing countries
- **c.** maintaining powerful military forces
- **d.** using drones to kill terrorists
- **e.** using the Air Force to support the overthrow of dictators

18.2 Assess the status of each of the issues that currently dominate the foreign policy and defense agenda.

Which of these issues is not among the very top priorities on the U.S. international agenda?

- **a.** fighting terrorism
- **b.** global climate change
- **c.** controlling weapons of mass destruction
- **d.** global health and poverty
- **e.** negotiating peace in the Middle East

18.3 Outline the structure of the foreign policy and defense bureaucracy.

The State Department's major task is

- **a.** to gather information from around the world.
- **b.** to develop and manufacture technology for the military.
- **c.** to negotiate treaties, protect U.S. citizens abroad, and staff embassies and consulates.
- **d.** to meet with the president, vice president, and others who make foreign policy.
- **e.** to be part of a council consisting of the heads of the army, navy, air force, and marine corps.

18.4 Evaluate the options for achieving foreign policy and defense goals.

Which of the following is an example of public diplomacy?

- **a.** diplomats from Japan, China, and the United States negotiate with North Korea over ending its nuclear weapons program
- **b.** Secretary of Defense Leon Panetta travels to Iraq to announce the end of the Iraq War
- **c.** The Commerce Departments hosts trade negotiations between U.S. and Japanese automobile makers to create fuel-efficient cars
- **d.** The State Department creates a new social media program to strengthen the image of the United States as a nation of freedom and opportunity

ESSAY QUESTION

Analyze the questions and responses that shape approaches to U.S. foreign policy and defense. Write a short essay on the differences between realism and idealism, isolationism and internationalism, unilateralism and multilateralism, preemption and provocation, and hard power and soft power.

Explore Further

IN THE LIBRARY

Kimberly Ann Elliott, Gary Clyde Hufbauer, and Jeffrey J. Schott, *Economic Sanctions Reconsidered,* 3rd ed. (Peterson Institute, 2008).

Dexter Filkins, *The Forever War* (Vintage, 2009).

Louis Fisher, *Presidential War Power,* 2nd ed. (University Press of Kansas, 2004).

John Lewis Gaddis, *The Cold War: A New History* (Penguin, 2005).

Ole Holsti, *Public Opinion and American Foreign Policy,* rev. ed. (University of Michigan Press, 2004).

Steven W. Hook and John Spannier, *U.S. Foreign Policy Since World War II, 18th ed.* (CQ Press, 2010).

Loch K. Johnson, *Secret Agencies: U.S. Intelligence in a Hostile World* (Yale University Press, 1996).

Joyce P. Kaufman, *A Concise History of U.S. Foreign Policy,* 2nd ed. (Rowman & Littlefield, 2010).

Steven Kull and I. M. Destler, *Misreading the Public: The Myth of a New Isolationism* (Brookings Institution Press, 1999).

Robert S. Litwak, *Rogue States and U.S. Foreign Policy: Containment After the Cold War* (Johns Hopkins University Press, 2000).

National Commission On Terrorist Attacks On The United States, *The 9/11 Commission Report* (Norton, 2004).

Joseph Nye, *Soft Power: The Means to Success in World Politics* (Public Affairs, 2005).

Michael E. O'hanlon, *How to Be a Cheap Defense Hawk* (Brookings Institution Press, 2002).

Paul R. Pillar, *Terrorism and U.S. Foreign Policy* (Brookings Institution Press, 2004).

George C. Wilson, *This War Really Matters: Inside the Fight for Defense Dollars* (CQ Press, 2000).

ON THE WEB

state.gov
The State Department's Web site.

defense.gov
The Defense Department's Web site.

foreignaffairs.com
A leading magazine about foreign policy. Many articles are free.

freedomhouse.org
Freedom House is a charitable organization that follows threats to freedom around the world. It also provides news feeds on specific events.

foreignpolicy.com
Another leading magazine about foreign policy. Many articles are also free.

careers.state.gov/officer/index.html
The place to go to apply to the foreign service.

Listen to MyPolisciLab

Conclusion

Sustaining Constitutional Democracy

The United States is rapidly approaching the 250th anniversary of its Declaration of Independence. But independence was just the beginning of our long effort to create a government by, for, and of the people. The Framers began the hard work at the Constitutional Convention in 1787 and later in the first Congress as they confronted the challenges of creating a government, writing a Constitution, and drafting a bill of rights that would protect rights to life, liberty, and self-government for themselves and subsequent generations. However, they always knew, as we also know, that passive allegiance to ideals and rights is never enough. Every generation must become responsible for nurturing these ideals by actively renewing the community and nation of which it is a part.

The Framers knew about the rise and decline of ancient Athens. They were familiar with Pericles's funeral oration, which states that those who take no part in public affairs fail themselves and their community.[1] According to Pericles and many Athenians, the city's business was everyone's business. Though a standard of what a civilized city might be, Athens eventually collapsed in the face of greed, self-centeredness, and complacency. As time went on, the Athenians wanted security more than they wanted liberty; comfort more than freedom. In the end, they lost it all—security, comfort, and freedom. "Responsibility was the price every man must pay for freedom. It was to be had on no other terms."[2]

If we are to be responsible citizens, we must be actively engaged in civic life and speak out about particular policies such as same-sex marriage, health care reform, and the reduction of government debt through tax increases and spending cuts. The exchange of ideas contributes to more representative policy and informed citizens. Our country needs citizens who understand that our well-being is tied to the well-being of our neighbors, community, and country.

More people today live under conditions of greater political freedom than at any previous time. The transition from living under authoritarian rule to shouldering political freedom is often difficult, as evidenced by the efforts to form democratic governments in Russia, Egypt, and Honduras. Our recent involvement in Iraq and Afghanistan is evidence that imposing democracy on societies without supporting values and institutions is problematic.

Throughout history, most people have lived in societies in which a small group at the top imposed its will on others. Neither in Castro's Cuba nor in the military regime of North Korea, neither in the People's Republic of China nor in Saudi Arabia, do ordinary people have a voice in the type of decisions we routinely make in the United States: Should we attend college? What kind of employment should we seek? Who should be allowed to enter or leave the country? How much money should be spent for schools, economic development initiatives, health care, or environmental protection? We take for granted the freedom to make such decisions.

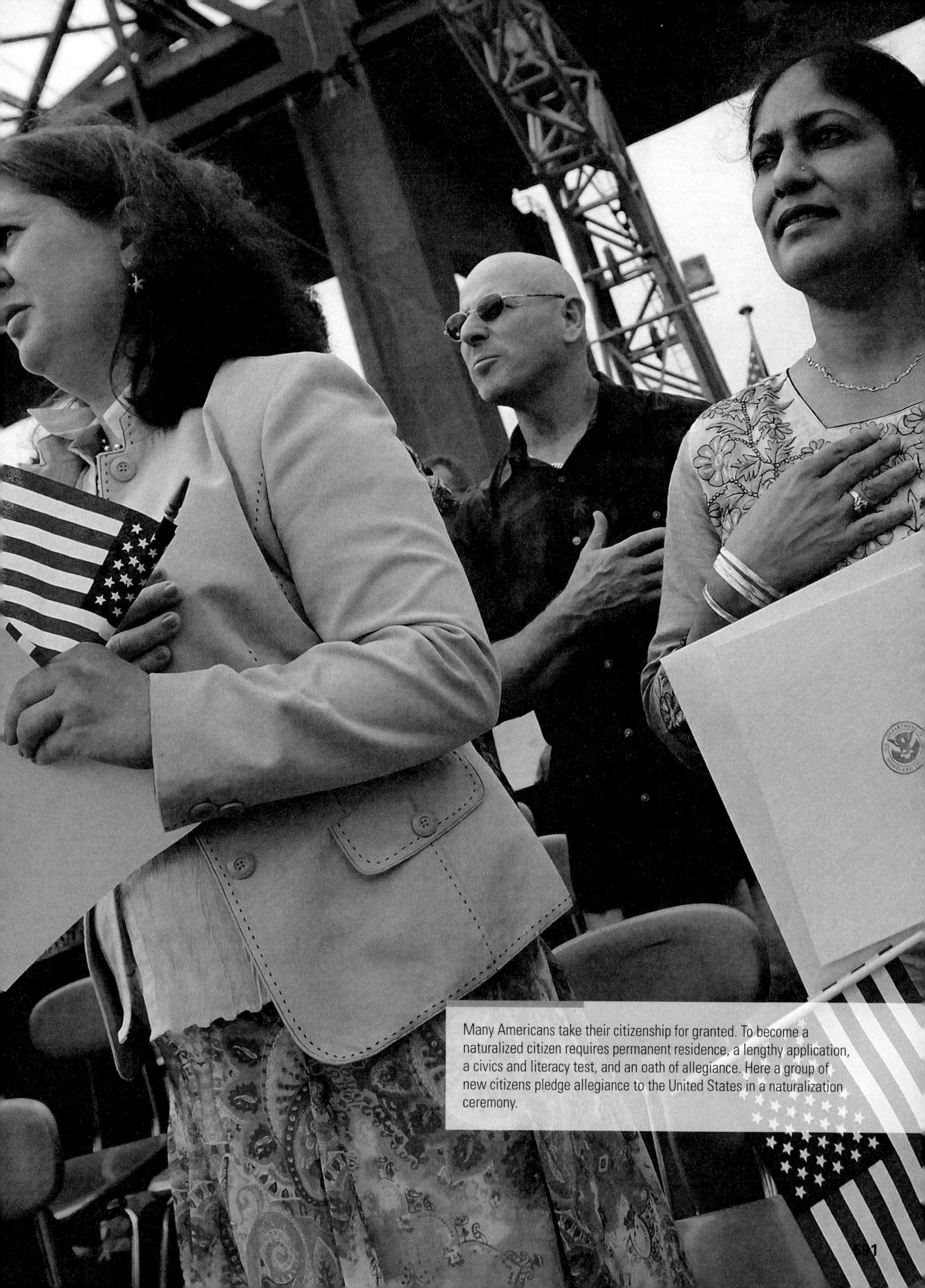

Many Americans take their citizenship for granted. To become a naturalized citizen requires permanent residence, a lengthy application, a civics and literacy test, and an oath of allegiance. Here a group of new citizens pledge allegiance to the United States in a naturalization ceremony.

Elected leadership and constitutional structures and protections are important, but they require an active, committed citizenry. Freedom and obligation go together. Liberty and duty go together. The answers to a nation's problems lie not in producing a perfect constitution or a few larger-than-life leaders. The answers lie in encouraging a nation of attentive and active citizens who will set aside their professional and private ambitions, care about the common concerns of the Republic, and strive to make democracy work.

The Case for Government by the People

The essence of our Constitution is that it both grants and withholds governmental power. Fearing a weak national government and popular disorder, the Framers wanted to strengthen the powers of the national government so that it could carry out its responsibilities, such as ensuring domestic order and maintaining national defense. They also wanted to limit state governments to keep them from interfering with interstate commerce and property rights. Valuing above all the principle of individual liberty, the Framers wanted to protect the people from too much government. They wanted a limited government—yet one that could accomplish essential tasks. The solution was to divide up the power of the national government and to make it ultimately responsive, if only indirectly, to the voters.

Most citizens want an efficient and effective government that also promotes social justice. We want to maintain our commitment to liberty and freedom. We want a government that acts for the majority yet protects minorities. We want to safeguard our nation and our streets in a world full of change and violence. We want to protect the rights of the poor and the elderly. Do we expect too much from our elected officials and public servants? Of course we do!

Our constitutional democracy is a system of checks and balances. Government must balance individual liberties against the collective security needs of society. The questions always are which rights of which people are to be protected, and by what means and at what price to individuals and to the whole society? These questions have arisen again and again in the war on terrorism. The USA PATRIOT Act became law, allowing greater government surveillance and, arguably, national security, but at the expense of individual liberty. Criticized by both conservatives and liberals, the Act was renewed in 2006 but included some new limitations on government investigations. More recent efforts to repeal such provisions as indefinite detainment of suspected terrorists and that such individuals be tried in civilian courts have failed.[3]

Participation and Representation

No political problem is more complicated than working out the proper relationship between voters and elected officials. It is not simply a matter of ensuring that elected officials do what voters want them to do, since every individual has a host of conflicting desires, fears, hopes, and expectations, and no government can represent the conflicting desires and expectations of each individual, let alone those of many people.

Participation

Some propose to bypass this thorny problem of representation by vastly increasing the role of direct popular participation in decision making, through greater use of tools such as the initiative, referendum, or recall.[4] What some regard as the most perfect form of democracy would exist when every person has a full and equal opportunity to participate in all decisions and in all processes of influence, persuasion, and discussion that bear on those decisions. Direct participation in decision making, its advocates contend, will serve two major purposes: First, it will enhance the dignity, self-respect, and understanding of individuals by giving them responsibility for the decisions that shape their lives. Second, direct participation will act as a safeguard against undemocratic and antidemocratic forms of government and prevent the replacement of democracy by a dictatorship or tyranny. Interests can be represented, furthered, and defended best by the people they directly concern.

New technologies have opened up more and more venues for public officials and voters to interact. We now have voting by mail in Oregon and other places, and some people advocate voting online. Digital town halls may be next. In the 2008 and 2012 elections, large numbers of voters, especially younger voters, communicated with each other and with the candidates via the Internet. The Internet has become an important fund-raising tool and will likely grow in importance over time. The Internet is also now an important source of news and political advertising. Throughout the course of its history, the United States has shifted toward greater direct democracy, and this trend is likely to continue.

Since the nation's founding, the right to vote has expanded from only white male property owners to include all citizens over 18 years of age. The Framers designed a system that limited the use of direct representation to the House of Representatives. Today, both the House and Senate are directly elected. Moreover, with the advent of direct primaries, voters decide the nominees for federal office. The initiative and referendum process provides a direct way for citizens to enact or overturn laws and even recall those in government.

However, these legal and technological advances allow for more direct participation from average citizens, but they do not and cannot replace the elected government. We still need elected officials to manage factions, build coalitions, and make the compromises necessary for producing policy and action. We also need institutions such as elected legislatures to digest complicated information and conduct impartial hearings to air competing points of view. The size of our country and the complexity of the problems we face mean we of necessity must delegate decision making to elected officials whom we hold accountable in regularly scheduled elections. As a practical matter, people simply cannot spend hours taking part in every decision that affects their lives. Thus, much of the work of government, at all levels, requires people willing to seek and hold public office.

The United States holds more elections for more offices than any other democracy.

□ Representation

Because we must have representatives, we must struggle with the question of who shall represent whom? By electing representatives in a multitude of districts, we can incorporate most minority interests and attitudes into our representative institutions. In the United States, we generally have election processes in which only the candidate receiving the greatest number of votes wins, but there are other ways of choosing representatives. For example, countries like Austria and Denmark use proportional representation—a system in which each party running receives the proportion of legislative seats corresponding to its proportion of votes.[5]

Representation can also be influenced by the number of competitive political parties. Ours is a strong two-party system that knits local constituencies into coalitions that can elect and sustain national majorities. Parties play a critical role in organizing democracy and helping people participate effectively. Our parties are permeable organizations that respond to people who invest in them. If you don't like the parties today, become active and help change the positions and leadership of the party closest to your perspective on government. A major factor in maintaining our two-party system is that single-member legislative districts, such as those for the U.S. Congress and state legislatures, tend to foster a two-party system. This regularity, called *Duverger's law*, is generally seen as helping to moderate our politics.[6] In contrast, when countries adopt proportional representation, minor parties have greater influence.

The question in the U.S. system is whether elected officials should accurately represent coalitions of minorities or a relatively clear-cut majority. The answer depends on what you expect from government. A system that represents coalitions of minorities usually reflects the trading, competition, and compromising that must take place in order to reach agreement among the various groups. Instead of acting for a united popular majority with a fairly definite program, either liberal or conservative, the government tries to satisfy all major interests by giving them a voice in decisions and sometimes a veto over actions.

Proponents of this form of representation argue that minority interests must be taken into consideration because the United States has not yet achieved equality in political access and representation. The U.S. Congress and many state legislatures, for example, are still composed of relatively few women and minorities. Critics also point to the extent of nonvoting and other forms of nonparticipation. Low-income individuals are politically less well organized and aware than upper-income individuals; strong organized groups are biased toward the status quo; a few corporations dominate television and the press; and the two major parties hold a virtual monopoly on party politics, which does not always offer the voters meaningful alternatives.

Critics of this philosophy of representation are concerned that our system of government is catering too much to minority interests with built-in procedures designed to curtail legislative majorities. For example, a Senate rule allows a minority to filibuster and block the will of the majority of senators. More broadly, rulings by only a bare majority of the Supreme Court can overturn the will of the majority and prior court decisions.[7]

These critics, who believe that governments should be more directly responsive to political majorities, can point to steady improvement in recent years in opening up access to the political system. Election laws have been changed to simplify voter registration, expand and improve voting procedures, and enforce one-person, one-vote standards. Efforts to limit the ability of rich donors and well-financed interests to influence elections were cited by Congress as a motivation for passage of campaign finance reform in 2002, and by the Supreme Court in upholding most of that legislation in 2003.[8]

However, the debate over campaign finance is far from over. Who pays for elections and what, if any, limits can be placed on donors is in dispute. In 2003, the Court upheld new limits and new definitions of what is election activity, only to reverse itself in 2010. As a direct result of that decision, we saw the increased influence of wealthy activists funding campaigns through Super PACs and other organizations in the 2012 elections.

Elections and democracy require money, and the debate continues as to how to balance liberty, equality, and the need for legitimacy in elections. By this point, you undoubtedly appreciate that democracy has to mean much more than popular government and unchecked majority rule. A democracy needs competing politicians with differing views about the public interest. A vital democracy, living and growing, places its faith in the participation of citizens as voters, faith that they will elect not only people who mirror their views but leaders who will exercise their best judgment—"faith that the people will not condemn those whose devotion to principle leads them to unpopular courses, but will reward courage, respect honor, and ultimately recognize right."[9]

The Role of the Politician

oters today have decidedly mixed views about elected officials. We realize that at their best, politicians are skilled at compromising, mediating, negotiating, and brokering—and that governing often requires these qualities. But we also suspect politicians of being ambitious, conniving, unprincipled, opportunistic, and corrupt.

Still, we often find that individual officeholders are bright, hardworking, and friendly (even though we may suspect they are only trying to win our vote), and our liking sometimes turns into reverence after these same politicians die. George Washington, Abraham Lincoln, Dwight D. Eisenhower, and Ronald Reagan are widely acclaimed today. Harry Truman joked that "a statesman is a politician who has been dead for about ten or fifteen years."[10] Of course, we must put the problem in perspective. In all democracies, people probably expect too much from politicians and, at the same time, distrust those who wield power. Public officeholders tax us, regulate us, and conscript us, after all. Some today condemn those who compromise, assuming incorrectly that their point of view enjoys broad support and overlooking the reality that to govern, our representatives often need to find mutually acceptable compromises.[11] At the same time, individuals can and do make a difference in shaping policy on the local, state, national, and international levels, whether the policy be about drunk driving, early childhood medical care, land mines, or using the courts to influence a policy agenda.

Politics and politicians, including those who work in Washington, are necessary and important to our freedom, security, and prosperity. Although many people will disagree about particular policies and processes, there is no disputing the need for government. Political leaders translate the fundamental needs of the people into practical demands on government.

We are fond of saying "it's all politics as usual" when government fails to address pressing problems such as the national debt, unemployment, and health care access. This greatly oversimplified observation implies that things would somehow improve if we did not have politics and politicians. But politics is the lifeblood of democracy, and without politics, there is no freedom. A nation of subservient followers can never be a democratic one. A democratic nation requires educated, skeptical, caring, engaged, and conscientious citizens who will recognize when change is needed and have the courage to bring about necessary reforms.[12] No matter how brilliant our Constitution or strong our economy, ultimately our system depends on individuals willing to study and speak out on issues, become involved in political parties, and run for and serve in office.

Experience teaches that power wielded justly today may be wielded corruptly tomorrow. It is right and necessary to protest when a policy is wrong or when the rights of other citizens are diminished. Democracy rests solidly on a realistic view of human nature. Criticism of official error is not unpatriotic. Our capacity for justice, as theologian and philosopher Reinhold Niebuhr observed, makes democracy possible. But our "inclination to injustice makes democracy necessary."[13] Democratic politics is the forum where, by acting together, citizens become and remain free.[14]

The ultimate test of a democratic system is the legal existence of an officially recognized opposition. A cardinal characteristic of a constitutional democracy is that it not only recognizes the need for the free organization of opposing views, but also encourages this organization. Freedom for political expression and dissent is basic—freedom to speak nonsense allows good sense not yet recognized a chance to be heard.[15]

The Importance of Active Citizenship

Crucial to democracy is belief in the free play of ideas. Only when the safety valve of public discussion is available, and when almost any policy is subject to perpetual questioning and challenge, can we be assured that both minority and majority rights will be served. To be afraid of public debate is to be afraid of self-government.

Thomas Jefferson once said, "Were it left to me to decide whether we should have a government without newspapers or newspapers without a government, I should not hesitate for a moment to prefer the latter."[16] Jefferson greatly valued an informed citizenry and had boundless faith in education. He believed that people are endowed with an innate sense of justice; the average person has only to be informed to act wisely. In the long run, said Jefferson, only an educated and enlightened democracy can hope to endure.

Education is one of the best predictors of voting, participation in politics, and knowledge of public affairs. People may not be equally invested or equally willing to invest in democracy, but those who are most attentive—frequently people like you who have gone to college—are more likely to have the willingness and self-confidence to see government and politics as necessary and important.

You now better understand how to influence public policy and the political process. You have gained an appreciation for the ways individuals and groups can either push or block an agenda. You know that many people choose not to participate in elections or politics, enhancing the power of those who do. Finally, you should also recognize that when individuals combine knowledge with political activity, they expand their influence.

Does political participation by committed individuals bring about constructive change? Remember that in the last half-century, restaurants, motels, and landlords once openly discriminated on the basis of race. Racial segregation in education existed in several states; segregated neighborhoods were a fact of life. Discriminatory practices denied blacks and poor whites access to voting. Women were discriminated against in the workplace and in government. Civil rights legislation and court cases have wrought remarkable changes. This is not to say that we have erased the legacies of racism and other kinds of discrimination from our national life, but as historian Arthur M. Schlesinger Jr. writes, "The genius of America lies in its capacity to forge a single nation from peoples of remarkably diverse racial, religious, and ethnic origins." Schlesinger acknowledges that our government and society have been more open to some than to others, "but it is more open to all today than it was yesterday and it is likely to be even more open tomorrow than today."[17]

Our political system is far from perfect, but it still is an open system and has become more and more democratic over time. People *can* fight city hall. People who disagree with policies in the nation can band together and be heard. We know only too well that the American dream is never fully attained. It must always be pursued.

Millions of citizens visit the great monuments in our nation's capital each year. They are always impressed by the memorials to Washington, Jefferson, Lincoln, Franklin D. Roosevelt, and the Vietnam, Korean, and World War II veterans. They are awed by the beauty of the Capitol, the Supreme Court, and the White House. The strength of the nation, however, resides not in these official buildings and monuments but in the hearts, minds, and behavior of citizens. If we lose faith, stop caring, stop participating, and stop believing in the possibilities of self-government, the monuments "will be meaningless piles of stone, and the venture that began with the Declaration of Independence, the venture familiarly known as America will be as lifeless as the stone."[18]

The future of our democracy will be shaped by citizens who care about preserving and extending our political rights and freedoms. Our individual liberties will never be assured unless we are willing to take responsibility for the progress of the whole community, to exercise our determination and belief in democracy. In the words of U.S. poet Archibald MacLeish, "How shall freedom be defended? By arms when it is attacked by arms, by truth when it is attacked by lies, by democratic faith when it is attacked by authoritarian dogma. Always, in the final act, by determination and faith."[19]

On MyPoliSciLab

Explore Further

IN THE LIBRARY

Derek Bok, *The Trouble with Government* (Harvard University Press, 2001).

Richard D. Brown, *The Strength of a People: The Idea of an Informed Citizenry in America, 1650–1870* (University of North Carolina Press, 1996).

Robert A. Dahl, *On Democracy* (Yale University Press, 1998).

Bob Graham and Chris Hand, *America the Owner's Manual: Making Government Work for You* (CQ Press, 2009).

Amy Gutmann and Dennis Thomson, *Democracy and Discontent: Why Moral Conflict Cannot Be Avoided in Politics, and What Should Be Done About It* (Belknap Press, 1996).

Jane J. Mansbridge, *Beyond Adversary Democracy* (Basic Book, Inc., 1980).

ON THE WEB

www.usa.gov/Contact/Elected.shtml

This Web site provides links to contact information for the president and vice president, U.S. senators, U.S. representatives, state governors, and state legislators.

www.constitutionday.us/link_frameset.asp?url=http://www.constitutioncenter.org/constitution/

This is an "interactive Constitution" Web site, where you can search the Constitution by keywords or phrases, topics, or court cases.

www.dosomething.org/actnow/actionguide/how-get-involved-local-politics

This Web site provides examples of how to get involved in community politics and includes a link to register to vote in your state.

www.rockthevote.com/

This Web site helps young people register to vote and get involved in politics.

GLOSSARY

24/7 news cycle News is now constantly updated and presented via Internet sites like the *New York Times* or *Wall Street Journal* and cable news sources like CNN, Fox News, and MSNBC.

527 organization A political group organized under section 527 of the IRS Code that may accept and spend unlimited amounts of money on election activities so long as they are not spent on broadcast ads run in the last 30 days before a primary or 60 days before a general election in which a clearly identified candidate is referred to and a relevant electorate is targeted.

A

adaptive approach A method used to interpret the Constitution that understands the document to be flexible and responsive to the changing needs of the times.

administrative discretion Authority given by Congress to the federal bureaucracy to use reasonable judgment in implementing the laws.

adversary system A judicial system in which the court of law is a neutral arena where two parties argue their differences.

affirmative action Remedial action designed to overcome the effects of discrimination against minorities and women.

all-volunteer force The replacement for the draft (conscription) for recruiting members of the armed services.

American dream A complex set of ideas that holds that the United States is a land of opportunity where individual initiative and hard work can bring economic success.

American exceptionalism The view that due to circumstances of history, the Constitution, and liberty, the United States is different from other nations.

***amicus curiae* brief** Literally, a "friend of the court" brief, filed by an individual or organization urging the Supreme Court to hear a case (or discouraging it from doing so) or, at the merits stage, to present arguments in addition to those presented by the immediate parties to a case.

Annapolis Convention A convention held in September 1786 to consider problems of trade and navigation, attended by five states and important because it issued the call to Congress and the states for what became the Constitutional Convention.

Antifederalists Opponents of ratification of the Constitution and of a strong central government generally.

antitrust legislation Federal laws (starting with the Sherman Antitrust Act of 1890) that try to prevent a monopoly from dominating an industry and restraining trade.

appellate jurisdiction The authority of a court to review decisions made by lower courts.

Articles of Confederation The first governing document of the confederated states, drafted in 1777, ratified in 1781, and replaced by the present Constitution in 1789.

attentive public Citizens who follow public affairs carefully.

attitudes An individual's propensity to perceive, interpret, or act toward a particular object in a particular way.

autocracy A type of government in which one person with unlimited power rules.

B

bad tendency test An interpretation of the First Amendment that would permit legislatures to forbid speech encouraging people to engage in illegal action.

Bible Belt The region of states in the South and states bordering the South with a large number of strongly committed Protestants who see a public role for religion.

bicameralism The principle of a two-house legislature.

Bipartisan Campaign Reform Act (BCRA) Largely banned party soft money, restored a long-standing prohibition on corporations and labor unions for using general treasury funds for electoral purposes, and narrowed the definition of issue advocacy.

budget deficit The condition that exists when the federal government raises less revenue than it spends.

bundling A tactic in which PACs collect contributions from like-minded individuals (each limited to $2,000) and present them to a candidate or political party as a "bundle," thus increasing the PAC's influence.

bureaucracy A form of organization that operates through impersonal, uniform regulations and procedures.

bureaucrat A negative term for describing a career government employee.

Bush Doctrine A policy adopted by the Bush administration in 2001 that asserts America's right to attack any nation that has weapons of mass destruction that may be used against U.S. interests at home or abroad.

C

cabinet The advisory council for the president, consisting of the heads of the executive departments, the vice president, and a few other officials selected by the president.

candidate appeal How voters feel about a candidate's background, personality, leadership ability, and other personal qualities.

capitalism An economic system based on private property, competitive markets, economic incentives, and limited government involvement in the production, pricing, and distribution of goods and services.

caucus A meeting of local party members to choose party officials or candidates for public office and to decide the platform.

central clearance Review of all executive branch testimony, reports, and draft legislation by the Office of Management and Budget (OMB) to ensure that each communication to Congress is in accordance with the president's program.

centralists People who favor national action over action at the state and local levels.

checks and balances A constitutional grant of powers that enables each of the three branches of government to check some acts of the others and therefore ensures that no branch can dominate.

chief of staff The head of the White House staff.

circuit courts of appeals Courts with appellate jurisdiction that hear appeals from the decisions of lower courts.

civil disobedience Deliberate refusal to obey a law or comply with the orders of public officials as a means of expressing opposition.

civil law A law that governs relationships between individuals and defines their legal rights.

civil rights The rights of all people to be free from irrational discrimination such as that based on race, religion, gender, or ethnic origin.

civil service Federal employees who work for government through a competitive, not political selection process.

class action suit A lawsuit brought by an individual or a group of people on behalf of all those similarly situated.

clear and present danger test An interpretation of the First Amendment, which holds that the government cannot interfere with speech unless the speech presents a clear and present danger that it will lead to evil or illegal acts.

closed primary A primary election in which only persons registered in the party holding the primary may vote.

closed rule A procedural rule in the House of Representatives that prohibits any amendments to bills or provides that only members of the committee reporting the bill may offer amendments.

closed shop A company with a labor agreement under which union membership can be a condition of employment.

cloture A procedure for terminating debate, especially filibusters, in the Senate.

coattail effect The boost that candidates may get in an election because of the popularity of candidates above them on the ballot, especially the president.

collective action How groups form and organize to pursue their goals or objectives, including how to get individuals and groups to participate and cooperate. The term has many applications in the various social sciences such as political science, sociology, and economics.

collective bargaining The process in which a union represents a group of employees in negotiations with the employer about wages, benefits, and workplace safety.

commerce clause The clause in the Constitution (Article I, Section 8, Clause 1) that gives Congress the power to regulate all business activities that cross state lines or affect more than one state or other nations.

commercial speech Advertisements and commercials for products and services; they receive less First Amendment protection, primarily to discourage false and misleading ads.

communism A belief that the state owns property in common for all people and a single political party that represents the working classes controls the government.

compliance costs The cost of meeting regulatory reporting requirements.

concurrent powers Powers that the Constitution gives to both the national and state governments, such as the power to levy taxes.

concurring opinion An opinion that agrees with the majority in a Supreme Court ruling but differs on the reasoning.

confederation A constitutional arrangement in which sovereign nations or states, by compact, create a central government but carefully limit its power and do not give it direct authority over individuals.

conference committee A committee appointed by the presiding officers of each chamber to adjust differences on a particular bill passed by each in different form.

Congressional Budget Office (CBO) An agency of Congress that analyzes presidential budget recommendations and estimates the costs of proposed legislation.

congressional elaboration Congressional legislation that gives further meaning to the Constitution based on sometimes vague constitutional authority, such as the necessary and proper clause.

congressional–executive agreement A formal agreement between the U.S. president and the leaders of other nations that requires approval by both houses of Congress.

Connecticut Compromise The compromise agreement by states at the Constitutional Convention for a bicameral legislature with a lower house in which representation would be based on population and an upper house in which each state would have two senators.

conservatism A belief in private property rights and free enterprise.

constituents The residents of a congressional district or state.

Constitutional Convention The convention in Philadelphia, from May 25 to September 17, 1787, that debated and agreed on the Constitution of the United States.

constitutional democracy Government that enforces recognized limits on those who govern and allows the voice of the people to be heard through free, fair, and relatively frequent elections.

constitutionalism The set of arrangements, including checks and balances, federalism, separation of powers, rule of law, due process, and a bill of rights, that requires our leaders to listen, think, bargain, and explain before they act or make laws. We then hold them politically and legally accountable for how they exercise their powers.

content or viewpoint neutrality Laws that apply to all kinds of speech and to all views, not only that which is unpopular or divisive.

corporate social responsibility Efforts by corporations to improve their reputations by paying attention to their contributions to the social good.

criminal law A law that defines crimes against the public order.

cross-cutting cleavages Divisions within society that cut across demographic categories to produce groups that are more heterogeneous or different.

crossover voting Voting by a member of one party for a candidate of another party.

D

de facto segregation Segregation resulting from economic or social conditions or personal choice.

de jure segregation Segregation imposed by law.

dealignment Weakening of partisan preferences that point to a rejection of both major parties and a rise in the number of Independents.

decentralists People who favor state or local action rather than national action.

defendant In a criminal action, the person or party accused of an offense.

delegate An official who is expected to represent the views of his or her constituents even when personally holding different views; one interpretation of the role of the legislator.

delegated (express) powers Powers given explicitly to the national government and listed in the Constitution.

deliberation The idea of people coming together, listening to each other, exchanging ideas, learning to appreciate each other's differences, and defending their opinions.

democracy Government by the people, both directly or indirectly, with free and frequent elections.

democratic consensus A condition for democracy is that the people widely share a set of attitudes and beliefs about governmental procedures, institutions, core documents and fundamental values.

demography The study of the characteristics of populations.

department Usually the largest organization in government with the largest mission; also the highest rank in the federal hierarchy.

deregulation A policy promoting cutbacks in the amount of federal regulation in specific areas of economic activity.

devolution revolution The effort to slow the growth of the national government by returning many functions to the states.

direct democracy Government in which citizens vote on laws and select officials directly.

direct primary An election in which voters choose party nominees.

discharge petition A petition that, if signed by a majority of the members of the House of Representatives, will pry a bill from committee and bring it to the floor for consideration.

discretionary spending Spending that can be altered by congressional and presidential action.

dissenting opinion An opinion disagreeing with the majority in a Supreme Court ruling.

distributive policy A public policy such as Social Security that provides benefits to all groups in society.

district courts Courts in which criminal and civil cases are originally tried in the federal judicial system.

divided government Governance divided between the parties, as when one holds the presidency and the other controls one or both houses of Congress.

docket The list of potential cases that reach the Supreme Court.

double jeopardy Trial or punishment for the same crime by the same government; forbidden by the Constitution.

dual citizenship Citizenship in more than one nation.

due process Established rules and regulations that restrain government officials.

due process clause A clause in the Fifth Amendment limiting the power of the national government; a similar clause in the Fourteenth Amendment prohibits state governments from depriving any person of life, liberty, or property without due process of law.

E

earmarks Special spending projects that are set aside on behalf of individual members of Congress for their constituents.

economic liberty The belief that individuals should be allowed to pursue their economic self-interest without government restrictions.

economic sanctions Denial of export, import, or financial relations with a target country in an effort to change that nation's policies.

Electoral College The electoral system used in electing the president and vice president, in which voters vote for electors pledged to cast their ballots for a particular party's candidates.

eminent domain The power of a government to take private property for public use; the U.S. Constitution gives national and state governments this power and requires them to provide just compensation for property so taken.

entitlements Programs such as unemployment insurance, disaster relief, or disability payments that provide benefits to all eligible citizens.

enumerated powers The powers explicitly given to Congress in the Constitution.

environmental impact statement A statement required by federal law from all agencies for any project using federal funds to assess the potential effect of the new construction or development on the environment.

equal protection clause A clause in the Fourteenth Amendment that forbids any state to deny to any person within its jurisdiction the equal protection of the laws. By interpretation, the Fifth Amendment imposes the same limitation on the national government. This clause is the major constitutional restraint on the power of governments to discriminate against persons because of race, national origin, or sex.

equality of opportunity All individuals, regardless of race, gender, or circumstance, have the opportunity to participate in politics, self-government, and the economy.

establishment clause A clause in the First Amendment stating that Congress shall make no law respecting an establishment of religion. The Supreme Court has interpreted this to forbid direct governmental support to any or all religions.

ethnicity A social division based on national origin, religion, language, and often race.

ethnocentrism Belief in the superiority of one's nation or ethnic group.

ex post facto law A retroactive criminal law that works to the disadvantage of a person.

excise tax A consumer tax on a specific kind of merchandise, such as tobacco.

exclusionary rule A requirement that evidence unconstitutionally or illegally obtained be excluded from a criminal trial.

executive agreement A formal agreement between the U.S. president and the leaders of other nations that does not require Senate approval.

executive memorandum A less powerful formal order to an agency or agencies, that does not carry the force of law, to undertake a particular course of action.

Executive Office of the President (EOP) The cluster of presidential staff agencies that help the president carry out his or her responsibilities. Currently, the office includes the Office of Management and Budget, the Council of Economic Advisers, and several other units.

executive orders Formal orders to government or an agency or agencies as a whole that carry the force of law issued by the president to direct action by the federal bureaucracy, or by a governor to direct a state bureaucracy.

executive privilege The power to keep executive communications confidential, especially if they relate to national security.

extradition The legal process whereby an alleged criminal offender is surrendered by the officials of one state to officials of the state in which the crime is alleged to have been committed.

F

faction A term the founders used to refer to political parties and special interests or interest groups.

Federal Election Commission (FEC) A commission created by the 1974 amendments to the Federal Election Campaign Act to administer election reform laws. It consists of six commissioners appointed by the president and confirmed by the Senate. Its duties include overseeing disclosure of campaign finance information, public funding of presidential elections, and enforcing contribution limits.

federal funds rate The amount of interest banks charge for loans to each other.

Federal Reserve Board A variation of an independent regulatory agency with a chairman and board that controls the supply of money that flows through the U.S. economy.

Federal Reserve System The system created by Congress in 1913 to establish banking practices and regulate currency in circulation and the amount of credit available. It consists of 12 regional banks supervised by the Board of Governors. Often simply called "the Fed."

federal mandate A requirement the national government imposes as a condition for receiving federal funds.

Federal Register An official document, published every weekday, that lists the new and proposed regulations of executive departments and regulatory agencies.

federalism A constitutional arrangement in which power is distributed between a central government and states, which are sometimes called provinces in other nations.

Federalists A group that argued for ratification of the Constitution, including a stronger national government at the expense of states' power. They controlled the new federal government until Thomas Jefferson's election in 1800.

fighting words Words that by their very nature inflict injury on those to whom they are addressed or incite them to acts of violence.

filibuster A procedural practice in the Senate whereby a senator refuses to relinquish the floor and thereby delays proceedings and prevents a vote on a controversial issue.

fiscal policy Government policy that attempts to manage the economy by controlling taxing and spending, which affect inflation through lower taxes and less government spending, and unemployment through more government spending.

free exercise clause A clause in the First Amendment stating that Congress shall make no law prohibiting the free exercise of religion.

free rider An individual who does not join a group representing his or her interests yet receives the benefit of the group's influence.

freedom of religion The belief that individuals living in a society should be free to exercise their personal religious convictions without government restrictions.

full faith and credit clause The clause in the Constitution (Article IV, Section 1) requiring each state to recognize the civil judgments rendered by the courts of the other states and to accept their public records and acts as valid.

fundamentalists Conservative Christians who, as a group, have become more active in politics in the last two decades and were especially influential in the 2000 and 2004 presidential elections.

gender gap The difference between the political opinions or political behavior of men and of women.

General Agreement on Tariffs and Trade (GATT) An international trade agreement that seeks to lower the barriers to free trade.

general election Election in which voters elect officeholders.

gerrymandering The drawing of legislative district boundaries to benefit a party, group, or incumbent. There are two types of gerrymandering—*cracking*, which the majority party uses to break a strong minority party district into pieces to be merged with other districts, thereby reducing the minority party's strength in that one district, and *packing*, which merges pieces of the majority party in its weak districts into a single, strong district.

government corporation A government agency that is designed like a business corporation, and is created to secure greater freedom of action and flexibility for a particular program.

government The processes and institutions through which binding decisions are made for a society.

grand jury A jury of 12 to 23 persons, depending on state and local requirements, who privately hear evidence presented by the government to determine whether persons shall be required to stand trial. If the jury believes there is sufficient evidence that a crime was committed, it issues an indictment.

gross domestic product (GDP) The value of all goods and services produced by an economy during a specific period of time such as a year.

H

hard money Political contributions given to a party, candidate, or interest group that are limited in amount and fully disclosed. Raising such limited funds was harder than raising unlimited soft money, hence the term *hard money*.

hard power Reliance on economic and military strength to solve international problems.

Hatch Act A federal statute barring federal employees from active participation in certain kinds of politics and protecting them from being fired on partisan grounds.

heightened scrutiny test This test has been applied when a law classifies based on sex; to be upheld, the law must meet an important government interest.

honeymoon The period at the beginning of a new president's term during which the president enjoys generally positive relations with the press and Congress, usually lasting about six months.

horse race A close contest; by extension, any contest in which the focus is on who is ahead and by how much rather than on substantive differences between the candidates.

I

idealism A theory of international relations that focuses on the hope that nations will act together to solve international problems and promote peace.

impeachment A formal accusation by the lower house of a legislature against a public official; the first step in removal from office.

implementation The process of putting a law into practice through bureaucratic regulations or spending.

implied powers Powers inferred from the express powers that allow Congress to carry out its functions.

impoundment A decision by the president not to spend money appropriated by Congress, now prohibited under federal law.

in forma pauperis A petition that allows a party to file "as a pauper" and avoid paying Court fees.

income inequality The amount of after-tax income that the richest individuals and families control when compared to the amount that the poorest control; often measured by growth in the gap between the two classes.

incremental policy Small adjustments to existing public policies.

incumbent The current holder of elected office.

independent expenditures Money spent by individuals or groups not associated with candidates to elect or defeat candidates for office.

independent regulatory commission A government agency or commission with regulatory power whose independence is protected by Congress.

independent stand-alone agency A government agency that operates outside a traditional government department, but under the president's direct control.

indictment A formal written statement from a grand jury charging an individual with an offense; also called a *true bill*.

individualism The moral, political, and ethical philosophy of life that emphasizes individual rights, effort, and independence.

inflation A rise in the general price level (and decrease in dollar value) owing to an increase in the volume of money and credit in relation to available goods.

inherent powers The powers of the national government in foreign affairs that the Supreme Court has declared do not depend on constitutional grants but rather grow out of the national government's obligation to protect the nation from domestic and foreign threats.

initiative A procedure whereby a certain number of voters may, by petition, propose a law or constitutional amendment and have it submitted to the voters.

intensity A measure of how strongly an individual holds a particular opinion.

interest group A collection of people who share a common interest or attitude and seek to influence government for specific ends. Interest groups usually work within the framework of government and try to achieve their goals through tactics such as lobbying.

internationalism The belief that nations must engage in international problem solving.

interstate compact An agreement among two or more states. Congress must approve most such agreements.

iron triangle A policy-making instrument composed of a tightly related alliance of a congressional committee, interest groups, and a federal department or agency.

isolationism The desire to avoid international engagement altogether.

issue advocacy Promoting a particular position or an issue paid for by interest groups or individuals but not candidates. Much issue advocacy is often electioneering for or against a candidate, avoiding words like "vote for," and until 2004 had not been subject to any regulation.

issue network A policy-making instrument composed of loosely related interest groups, congressional committee, presidential aides, and other parties.

issue-attention cycle The movement of public opinion toward public policy from initial enthusiasm for action to realization of costs and a decline in interest.

J

Jim Crow laws State laws formerly pervasive throughout the South requiring public facilities and accommodations to be segregated by race; ruled unconstitutional.

joint committee A committee composed of members of both the House of Representatives and the Senate; such committees oversee the Library of Congress and conduct investigations.

judicial activism A philosophy proposing that judges should freely strike down laws enacted by the democratically elected branches.

judicial restraint A philosophy proposing that judges should strike down the actions of the elected branches only if they clearly violate the Constitution.

judicial review The power of a court to review laws or governmental regulations to determine whether they are consistent with the U.S. Constitution, or in a state court, the state constitution.

justiciable dispute A dispute growing out of an actual case or controversy that is capable of settlement by legal methods.

K

Keynesian economics An economic theory based on the principles of John Maynard Keynes stating that government spending should increase during business slumps and be curbed during booms.

L

labor injunction A court order forbidding specific individuals or groups from performing certain acts (such as striking) that the court considers harmful to the rights and property of an employer or a community.

laissez-faire economics A theory that opposes governmental interference in economic affairs beyond what is necessary to protect life and property.

latency Political opinions that are held but not yet expressed.

leadership PAC A PAC formed by an officeholder that collects contributions from individuals and other PACs and then makes contributions to other candidates and political parties.

libel Written defamation of another person. For public officials and public figures, the constitutional tests designed to restrict libel actions are especially rigid.

liberalism A belief that government can bring about justice and equality of opportunity.

libertarianism Would limit government to such vital activities as national defense while fostering individual liberty. Unlike conservatives, libertarians oppose all government regulation, even of personal morality.

line item veto Presidential power to strike, or remove, specific items from a spending bill without vetoing the entire package; declared unconstitutional by the Supreme Court.

literacy test A literacy requirement some states imposed as a condition of voting, generally used to disqualify black voters in the South; now illegal.

lobbying Engaging in activities aimed at influencing public officials, especially legislators, and the policies they enact.

lobbyist A person who is employed by and acts for an organized interest group or corporation to try to influence policy decisions and positions in the executive and legislative branches.

logrolling Mutual aid and vote trading among legislators.

M

majority The candidate or party that wins more than half the votes cast in an election.

majority leader The legislative leader selected by the majority party who helps plan party strategy, confers with other party leaders, and tries to keep members of the party in line.

majority–minority district A congressional district created to include a majority of minority voters; ruled constitutional so long as race is not the main factor in redistricting.

majority rule Governance according to the expressed preferences of the majority.

mandate A president's claim of broad public support.

mandatory spending Required spending under the federal budget.

manifest destiny A notion held by nineteenth-century Americans that the United States was destined to rule the continent, from the Atlantic to the Pacific.

manifest opinion A widely shared and consciously held view, such as support for abortion rights or for homeland security.

margin of error The range of percentage points in which the sample accurately reflects the population.

mass media Means of communication that reach the public, including newspapers and magazines, radio, television (broadcast, cable, and satellite), films, recordings, books, and electronic communication.

Mayflower Compact A governing document created by the members of the *Mayflower* to temporarily establish self-government in the Plymouth Colonies in America.

means-tested entitlements Programs such as Medicaid and welfare under which applicants must meet eligibility requirements based on need.

Medicaid A federal program that provides medical benefits for low-income people.

Medicare A national health insurance program for the elderly and disabled.

merit system A system of public employment in which selection and promotion depend on demonstrated performance rather than political patronage.

Merit Systems Protection Board An independent agency that oversees and protects merit in the federal government personnel system.

midterm election Election held midway between presidential elections.

minor party A small political party that persists over time that is often composed of ideologies on the right or left, or centered on a charismatic candidate. Such a party is also called a *third party*.

minority leader The legislative leader selected by the minority party as spokesperson for the opposition.

monetary policy Government policy that attempts to manage the economy by controlling the amount of money in circulation through interest rates.

monopoly Domination of an industry by a single company; also the company that dominates the industry.

multilateralism A philosophy that encourages individual nations to act together to solve international problems.

N

name recognition Incumbents have an advantage over challengers in election campaigns because voters are more familiar with them, and incumbents are more recognizable.

national debt The total amount of money the federal government has borrowed to finance deficit spending throughout the years.

national party convention A national meeting of delegates elected in primaries, caucuses, or state conventions who assemble once every four years to nominate candidates for president and vice president, ratify the party platform, elect officers, and adopt rules.

national tide The inclination to focus on national issues, rather than local issues, in an election campaign. The impact of a national tide can be reduced by the nature of the candidates on the ballot who may have differentiated themselves from their party or its leader if the tide is negative, as well as competition in the election.

national supremacy A constitutional doctrine that whenever conflict occurs between the constitutionally authorized actions of the national government and those of a state or local government, the actions of the national government prevail.

natural law God's or nature's law that defines right from wrong and is higher than human law.

natural rights The rights of all people to dignity and worth; also called *human rights*.

naturalization A legal action conferring citizenship on an alien.

necessary and proper clause The clause in the Constitution (Article I, Section 8, Clause 3) setting forth the implied powers of Congress. It states that Congress, in addition to its express powers, has the right to make all laws necessary and proper to carry out all powers the Constitution vests in the national government.

New Jersey Plan The proposal at the Constitutional Convention made by William Paterson of New Jersey for a central government with a single-house legislature in which each state would be represented equally.

news media Media that emphasize the news.

nondecision A decision not to move ahead with the policy process. In short, it is a decision not to decide.

Nongovernmental organization (NGO) A nonprofit association or group operating outside government that advocates and pursues policy objectives.

nonpartisan election An election in which candidates are not selected or endorsed by political parties, and party affiliation is not listed on ballots.

normal trade relations Trade status granted as part of an international trade policy that gives a nation the same favorable trade concessions and tariffs that the best trading partners receive.

North American Free Trade Agreement (NAFTA) An agreement signed by the United States, Canada, and Mexico in 1992 to form the largest free trade zone in the world.

O

obscenity The quality or state of a work that, taken as a whole, appeals to a prurient interest in sex by depicting sexual conduct in a patently offensive way and that lacks serious literary, artistic, political, or scientific value.

Office of Management and Budget (OMB) The presidential staff agency that serves as a clearinghouse for budgetary requests and management improvements for government agencies.

Office of Personnel Management (OPM) An agency that administers civil service laws, and regulations.

open primary A primary election in which any voter, regardless of party, may vote.

open rule A procedural rule in the House of Representatives that permits floor amendments within the overall time allocated to the bill.

open shop A company with a labor agreement under which union membership cannot be required as a condition of employment.

opinion of the Court An explanation of a decision of the Supreme Court or any other appellate court.

original jurisdiction The authority of a court to hear a case "in the first instance."

originalist approach An approach to constitutional interpretation that envisions the document as having a fixed meaning that might be determined by a strict reading of the text or the Framers' intent.

override An action taken by Congress to reverse a presidential veto, requiring a two-thirds majority in each chamber.

oversight Legislative or executive review of a particular government program or organization that can be in response to a crisis of some kind or part of routine review.

P

parliamentary government A form of government in which the chief executive is the leader of the majority party in the legislature.

partisanship Strong allegiance to one's own political party, often leading to unwillingness to compromise with members of the opposing party.

party caucus A meeting of the members of a party in a legislative chamber to select party leaders and to develop party policy.

party convention A meeting of party delegates to vote on matters of policy and, in some cases, to select party candidates for public office.

party identification An informal and subjective affiliation with a political party that most people acquire in childhood.

party registration The act of declaring party affiliation; required by some states when one registers to vote.

party-independent expenditures Spending by political party committees that is independent of the candidate. The spending occurs in relatively few competitive contests and is often substantial.

patronage The dispensing of government jobs to persons who belong to the winning political party.

petit jury A jury of 6 to 12 persons that determines whether a defendant is found guilty in a civil or criminal action.

plaintiff The party instigating a civil lawsuit.

platform Every four years the political parties draft a document stating the policy positions of the party. This party platform details general party-wide issue stances. The process sometimes engenders disputes among fellow partisans but is rarely an election issue and often is written to avoid controversy.

plea bargain An agreement between a prosecutor and a defendant that the defendant will plead guilty to a lesser offense to avoid having to stand trial for a more serious offense.

pluralism A theory of government that holds that open, multiple, and competing groups can check the asserted power by any one group.

plurality The candidate or party with the most votes cast in an election, not necessarily more than half.

pocket veto A formal decision to reject a bill passed by Congress after it adjourns—if Congress adjourns during the ten days that the president is allowed to sign or veto a law, the president can reject the law by taking no action at all.

polarization The extent to which liberals and conservatives occupy the more extreme positions on the liberal–conservative ideological spectrum.

policy agenda The list of issues that the federal government pays attention to.

policy makers Individuals and groups that make the actual choices to create a public policy.

political action committee (PAC) The political arm of an interest group that is legally entitled to raise funds on a voluntary basis from members, stockholders, or employees to contribute funds to candidates or political parties.

political capital The amount of overall public approval that a president can use to win support for major decisions and proposals.

political culture The widely shared beliefs, values, and norms citizens hold about their relationship to government and to one another.

political ideology A constant pattern of ideas or beliefs about political values and the role of government, including how it should work and how it actually does work.

political party An organization that seeks political power by electing people to office so that its positions and philosophy become public policy.

political science An academic discipline that studies the theory and practice of politics and government. It is one of the social sciences that use data and methods that overlap with anthropology, economics, geography, history, psychology, and sociology.

political socialization The process by which we develop our political attitudes, values, and beliefs.

politician An individual who participates in politics and government, often in the service of a group or political community.

politics The interaction of the people and their government, including citizens, interest groups, political parties, and the institutions of government at all levels. Politics is concerned with who gets what, when, where, and how from government.

poll tax Tax required to vote; prohibited for national elections by the Twenty-Fourth Amendment (1964) and ruled unconstitutional for all elections in *Harper* v. *Board of Elections* (1966).

popular consent The idea that a just government must derive its powers from the consent of the people it governs.

popular sovereignty The belief that the authority and legitimacy of government is based in the consent and authority of the individuals living within its boundaries.

precedent A decision made by a higher court such as a circuit court of appeals or the Supreme Court that is binding on all other federal courts.

preemption A policy of taking action before the United States is attacked rather than waiting for provocation (in foreign and defense policy).

preemption The right of a national law or regulation to preclude enforcement of a state or local law or regulation (in federalism).

preferred position doctrine An interpretation of the First Amendment that holds that freedom of expression is so essential to democracy that governments should not punish persons for what they say, only for what they do.

president pro tempore An officer of the Senate selected by the majority party to act as chair in the absence of the vice president.

presidential election Election held in year when the president is on the ballot.

presidential support score The percentage of times a president wins on key votes in Congress.

presidential ticket The joint listing of the presidential and vice presidential candidates on the same ballot, as required by the Twelfth Amendment.

primary election Election in which voters determine party nominees.

prior restraint Censorship imposed before a speech is made or a newspaper is published; usually presumed to be unconstitutional.

procedural due process A constitutional requirement that governments proceed by proper methods; limits how government may exercise power.

professional associations Groups of individuals who share a common profession and are often organized for common political purposes related to that profession.

progressive tax A tax graduated so that people with higher incomes pay a larger fraction of their income than people with lower incomes.

property rights The rights of an individual to own, use, rent, invest in, buy, and sell property.

proportional representation An election system in which each party running receives the proportion of legislative seats corresponding to its proportion of the vote.

prosecutor Government lawyer who tries criminal cases, often referred to as a district attorney or a U.S. Attorney.

prospective issue voting Voting based on what a candidate pledges to do in the future about an issue if elected.

protectionism A policy of erecting trade barriers to protect domestic industry.

public assistance Aid to the poor; "welfare."

public choice Synonymous with "collective action," specifically studies how government officials, politicians, and voters respond to positive and negative incentives.

public defender system An arrangement whereby public officials are hired to provide legal assistance to people accused of crimes who are unable to hire their own attorneys.

public opinion The distribution of individual preferences for or evaluations of a given issue, candidate, or institution within a specific population.

public policy A specific course of action that government takes to address a problem.

punctuating policy Radical changes to public policy that occur only after the mobilization of large segments of society to demand action.

R

race A grouping of human beings with distinctive characteristics determined by genetic inheritance.

racial gerrymandering The drawing of election districts so as to ensure that members of a certain race are a minority in the district; ruled unconstitutional in *Gomillion* v. *Lightfoot* (1960).

rally point A rise in public approval of the president that follows a crisis as Americans "rally round the flag" and the chief executive.

random sample In this type of sample, every individual has a known and equal chance of being selected.

rational basis test A standard developed by the courts to test the constitutionality of a law; when applied, a law is constitutional as long as it meets a reasonable government interest.

realigning election An election during periods of expanded suffrage and change in the economy and society that proves to be a turning point, redefining the agenda of politics and the alignment of voters within parties.

realism A theory of international relations that focuses on the tendency of nations to operate from self-interest.

reapportionment The assigning by Congress of congressional seats after each census. State legislatures reapportion state legislative districts.

recall A procedure for submitting to popular vote the removal of officials from office before the end of their term.

recess appointment Presidential appointment made without Senate confirmation during Senate recess.

redistributive policy A policy that provides to one group of society while taking away benefits from another through policy solutions such as tax increases to pay for job training.

redistricting The redrawing of congressional and other legislative district lines following the census to accommodate population shifts and keep districts as equal as possible in population.

referendum procedure for submitting to popular vote measures passed by the legislature or proposed amendments to a state constitution.

regressive tax A tax whereby people with lower incomes pay a higher fraction of their income than people with higher incomes.

regulation A precise statement of how a law is implemented.

regulatory taking A government regulation that effectively takes land by restricting its use, even if it remains in the owner's name.

reinforcing cleavages Divisions within society that reinforce one another, making groups more homogeneous or similar.

representative democracy Government in which the people elect those who govern and pass laws; also called a *republic.*

reserve powers All powers not specifically delegated to the national government by the Constitution. The reserve power can be found in the Tenth Amendment to the Constitution.

restrictive covenant A provision in a deed to real property prohibiting its sale to a person of a particular race or religion. Judicial enforcement of such deeds is unconstitutional.

retrospective issue voting Holding incumbents, usually the president's party, responsible for their records on issues, such as the economy or foreign policy.

reverse distributive policy A policy that reduces benefits for all groups, often by imposing regulations or taxes that govern everyone, rich or poor.

revolving door An employment cycle in which individuals who work for government agencies that regulate interests eventually end up working for interest groups or businesses with the same policy concern.

rider A provision attached to a bill—to which it may or may not be related—in order to secure its passage or defeat.

right of expatriation The right to renounce one's citizenship.

rule-making process The detailed process for drafting a regulation.

rural Sparsely populated territory and small towns, often associated with farming.

Rust Belt States in the Midwest once known for their industrial output, which have seen factories close and have experienced relatively high unemployment.

S

safe seat An elected office that is predictably won by one party or the other, so the success of that party's candidate is almost taken for granted.

sales tax A general tax on sales transactions, sometimes exempting such items as food and drugs.

salience An individual's belief that an issue is important or relevant to him or her.

search warrant A writ issued by a magistrate that authorizes the police to search a particular place or person, specifying the place to be searched and the objects to be seized.

selective exposure The process by which individuals screen out messages that do not conform to their own biases.

selective incorporation The process by which provisions of the Bill of Rights are brought within the scope of the Fourteenth Amendment and so applied to state and local governments.

selective perception The process by which individuals perceive what they want in media messages.

senatorial courtesy The presidential custom of submitting the names of prospective appointees for approval to senators from the states in which the appointees are to work.

Senior Executive Service Established by Congress in 1978 as a flexible, mobile corps of senior career executives who work closely with presidential appointees to manage government.

seniority rule A legislative practice that assigns the chair of a committee or subcommittee to the member of the majority party with the longest continuous service on the committee.

separation of powers Constitutional division of powers among the legislative, executive, and judicial branches, with the legislative branch making law, the executive applying and enforcing the law, and the judiciary interpreting the law.

Shays' Rebellion A rebellion led by Daniel Shays of farmers in western Massachusetts in 1786–1787 protesting mortgage foreclosures. It highlighted the need for a strong national government just as the call for the Constitutional Convention went out.

signing statements A formal document that explains why a president is signing a particular bill into law. These statements may contain objections to the bill and promises not to implement key sections.

single-member district An electoral district in which voters choose one representative or official.

social capital The value of social contacts, associations, and networks individuals form which can foster trust, coordination, and cooperation.

social conservatives Focus less on economics and more on morality and lifestyle.

social contract An agreement whereby individuals voluntarily commit to establish a government that will protect the common interests of all.

social insurance Programs in which eligibility is based on prior contributions to government, usually in the form of payroll taxes.

social movement A large body of people interested in a common issue, idea, or concern that is of continuing significance and who are willing to take action. Movements seek to change attitudes or institutions, not just policies.

social safety net The many programs that the federal government provides to protect Americans against economic and social misfortune.

Social Security A combination of entitlement programs, paid for by employer and employee taxes, that includes retirement benefits, health insurance, and support for disabled workers and the children of deceased or disabled workers.

socialism A governmental system where some of the means of production are controlled by the state and where the state provides key human welfare services like health care and old age assistance. Allows for free markets in other activities.

socioeconomic status (SES) A division of population based on occupation, income, and education.

soft money Money raised in unlimited amounts by political parties for party-building purposes. Now largely illegal except for limited contributions to state or local parties for voter registration and get-out-the-vote efforts.

soft power Reliance on diplomacy and negotiation to solve international problems.

solicitor general The third-ranking official in the Department of Justice who is responsible for representing the United States in cases before the U.S. Supreme Court.

Speaker The presiding officer in the House of Representatives, formally elected by the House but selected by the majority party.

special or select committee A congressional committee created for a specific purpose, sometimes to conduct an investigation.

spoils system A system of public employment based on rewarding party loyalists and friends.

standing committee A permanent committee established in a legislature, usually focusing on a policy area.

stare decisis The rule of precedent, whereby a rule or law contained in a judicial decision is commonly viewed as binding on judges whenever the same question is presented.

State of the Union Address The president's annual statement to Congress and the nation.

states' rights Powers expressly or implicitly reserved to the states.

statism The idea that the rights of the nation are supreme over the rights of the individuals who make up the nation.

strict scrutiny test A test applied by the court when a classification is based on race; the government must show that there is a compelling reason for the law and no other less restrictive way to meet the interest.

substantive due process A constitutional requirement that governments act reasonably and that the substance of the laws themselves be fair and reasonable; limits what a government may do.

suburban An area that typically surrounds the central city, is often residential, and is not as densely populated.

Sun Belt The region of the United States in the South and Southwest that has seen population growth relative to the rest of the country and which, because of its climate, has attracted retirees.

Super PACs An independent expenditure only committee first allowed in 2010 after court decisions allowing unlimited contributions to such PACs. Super PACs were important in the 2010 and 2012 elections.

supremacy clause Contained in Article IV of the Constitution, the clause gives national laws the absolute power even when states have enacted a competing law.

Supreme Court The court of last resort in the United States. It can hear appeals from federal circuit courts or state high courts.

T

take care clause The constitutional requirement (in Article II, Section 3) that presidents take care that the laws are faithfully executed, even if they disagree with the purpose of those laws.

tariff A tax levied on imports to help protect a nation's industries, labor, or farmers from foreign competition. It can also be used to raise additional revenue.

tax expenditure A loss of tax revenue due to federal laws that provide special tax incentives or benefits to individuals or businesses.

The Federalist Essays promoting ratification of the Constitution, published anonymously by Alexander Hamilton, John Jay, and James Madison in 1787 and 1788.

theocracy Government by religious leaders, who claim divine guidance.

theory of deterrence A theory that is based on creating enough military strength to persuade other nations not to attack first.

think tank A nongovernmental organization that seeks to influence public policy through research and education.

three-fifths compromise The compromise between northern and southern states at the Constitutional Convention that three-fifths of the slave population would be counted for determining direct taxation and representation in the House of Representatives.

trade deficit An imbalance in international trade in which the value of imports exceeds the value of exports.

treaty A formal, public agreement between the United States and one or more nations that must be approved by two-thirds of the Senate.

trust A monopoly that controls goods and services, often in combinations that reduce competition.

trustee An official who is expected to vote independently based on his or her judgment of the circumstances; one interpretation of the role of the legislator.

turnout The proportion of the voting-age public that votes, sometimes defined as the number of registered voters that vote.

U

U.S. attorney general The chief law enforcement officer in the United States and the head of the Department of Justice.

uncontrollable spending The portion of the federal budget that is spent on previously enacted programs, such as Social Security, that the president and Congress are unwilling to cut.

unemployment The number of Americans who are out of work but actively looking for a job. The number does not usually include those who have given up searching for a job.

unified government Governance in which one party controls both the White House and both houses of Congress.

unilateralism A philosophy that encourages individual nations to act on their own when facing threats from other nations.

union shop A company in which new employees must join a union within a stated time period.

unitary system A constitutional arrangement that concentrates power in a central government.

universe The group of people whose preferences we try to measure by taking a sample; also called population.

unprotected speech Libel, obscenity, and fighting words, which are not entitled to constitutional protection in all circumstances.

urban A densely settled territory that is often the central part of a city of metropolitan area.

V

value-added tax (VAT) A tax on increased value of a product at each stage of production and distribution rather than just at the point of sale.

vesting clause The president's constitutional authority to control most executive functions.

veto A formal decision to reject a bill passed by Congress.

Virginia Plan The initial proposal at the Constitutional Convention made by the Virginia delegation for a strong central government with a bicameral legislature dominated by the big states.

voter registration A system designed to reduce voter fraud by limiting voting to those who have established eligibility to vote by submitting the proper documents, including proof of residency.

W

War Power Resolution A resolution passed in 1973 requiring the president to give advance warning of a military attack or ask Congress for a declaration of war or specific legislation.

wealth The total amount of economic assets such as income, property, and investments that individuals and families control.

weapons of mass destruction Biological, chemical, or nuclear weapons that can cause a massive number of deaths in a single use.

whip The party leader who is the liaison between the leadership and the rank-and-file in the legislature.

white primary A Democratic Party primary in the old "one-party South" that was limited to white people and essentially constituted an election; ruled unconstitutional in *Smith* v. *Allwright* (1944).

winner-take-all system An election system in which the candidate with the most votes wins.

women's suffrage The right of women to vote.

World Trade Organization (WTO) An international organization with more than 130 members that seeks to encourage free trade by setting rules for fair competition.

writ of *certiorari* A formal writ used to bring a case before the Supreme Court.

writ of *habeas corpus* A court order requiring explanation to a judge why a prisoner is being held in custody.

writ of mandamus A court order directing an official to perform an official duty.

Z

zero-sum games A policy that takes away benefits or money from one group to give to another.

NOTES

Introduction

1. Dwight B. Heath, ed., *Mourt's Relation: A Journal of the Pilgrims at Plymouth* (Bedford, MA: Applewood Books, 1963), p. 17.
2. November 11, 1620 on the Julian calendar would be on our present-day Gregorian calendar November 21, 1620.
3. Donald McQuade, Robert Atwan, Martha Banta, Justin Kaplan, David Minter, and Robert Stepto, *The Harper American Literature* (New York: Longman, 1998); John T. Wheelwright, *The* Mayflower *Pilgrims: Being a Condescension in the Original Wording and Spelling of the Story Written by Gov. William Bradford* (Boston: McGrath-Sherrill Press, 1930).
4. Nathaniel Philbrick, Mayflower*: A Story of Courage, Community, and War* (New York: Penguin Group, 2006), p. 42.
5. Ibid, p. 352.
6. Michael Kammen, *Mystic Chords of Memory: The Transformation of Tradition in American Culture* (New York: Vintage Books, 1993).
7. Louis Hartz, *The Liberal Tradition in America* (New York: Harcourt, Brace, and World, Inc., 1955), pp. 48-49.
8. Crispin Gill, Mayflower *Remembered: A History of the Plymouth Pilgrims* (New York: Taplinger Publishing, 1970), p. 155; Michael Kammen, *Mystic Chords of Memory: The Transformation of Tradition in American Culture* (New York: Vintage Books, 1993), p. 64.
9. Michael Kammen, *Mystic Chords of Memory: The Transformation of Tradition in American Culture* (New York: Vintage Books, 1993).
10. Mayflower Compact (1620), http://avalon.law.yale.edu/17th_century/mayflower.asp (accessed February 9, 2010).
11. Louis Hartz, *The Liberal Tradition in America* (New York: Harcourt, Brace, and World, Inc., 1955), p. 63; see also Jack Citrin, "Political Culture," in Peter H. Schuck and James Q. Wilson, eds., *Understanding America: The Anatomy of an Exceptional Nation* (New York City, NY: Public Affairs, 2008), pp. 147-148.
12. Jack Citrin, "Political Culture," p. 162.
13. Ibid, p. 170.
14. Nathaniel Philbrick, Mayflower*: A Story of Courage, Community, and War* (New York: Penguin Group, 2006) p. 29.
15. Benjamin M. Friedman, "The Economic System," in Peter H. Shuck and James Q. Wilson, eds., *Understanding America: The Anatomy of an Exceptional Nation* (New York: Public Affairs, 2008), p. 87.
16. See Roger Smith, *Civic Ideals: Conflicting Visions of Citizenship in U.S. History* (Michigan: Book Crafters, 1997).
17. Carl J. Richard, *The Founders and the Classics: Greece, Rome, and the American Enlightenment* (Harvard University Press, 1995).
18. "Essex Result," *The Founders' Constitution,* April 29, 1778, http://press-pubs.uchicago.edu/founders/documents/v1ch4s8.html (accessed December 1, 2009).
19. John Locke, "The Second Treatise of Civil Government," http://www.constitution.org/jl/2ndtreat.htm (accessed May 20, 2010) (Chapter 7, Section 87, 2nd Treatise).
20. "Locke's Political Philosophy," *Stanford Encyclopedia of Philosophy,* November 9, 2005, http://plato.stanford.edu/entries/locke-political/ (accessed December 1, 2009).
21. Louis Hartz, *The Liberal Tradition in America*, pp. 60-61.
22. John Locke, "The Second Treatise of Civil Government," http://www.constitution.org/jl/2ndtreat.htm (accessed May 20, 2010) (Chapter 7, section 87, 2nd Treatise).
23. Frederick G. Whelan, *Hume and Machiavelli: Political Realism and Liberal Thought* (Lanham: Lexington Books, 2005), p. 43.
24. Jean-Jacques Rousseau, "The Social Contract," http://www.constitution.org/jjr/socon_03.htm (accessed May 20, 2010).
25. Peter H. Shuck and James Q. Wilson, eds., *Understanding America: The Anatomy of an Exceptional Nation* (New York, NY: Public Affairs, 2008), p. x.
26. Gary Rosen, "James Madison and the Problem of Founding." *The Review of Politics* 58 (3) (Summer, 1996): pp. 561-595.
27. The Declaration of Independence (1776).
28. James Madison, "The Federalist #10," in *The Federalist Papers* (New York: Penguin Books, 1987), p. 3.
29. James Madison, "The Federalist #51," in *The Federalist Papers* (New York: Penguin Books, 1987), p. 1.
30. Ari Shapiro "Panel Blasts Government on Gulf Oil Spill Response," Oct. 7, 2010. http://www.npr.org/templates/story/story.php?storyId=130390111
31. Ed O'Keefe, "Hurricane Irene: FEMA, Federal Agencies Ramp Up," Federal Eye blog, *Washington Post*, August 27, 2011.
32. We do not enter here into the famous debate in the philosophy of science about "normal science," "paradigm shifts," etc. Rather, we aspire to produce a text that details the foundation of what we do and do not know about the subject. See Thomas Kuhn, *The Structure of Scientific Revolutions*, 2nd ed. (Chicago: University of Chicago Press, 1970), p. 1.
33. Robert Post, 2009, "Debating Disciplinarity," *Critical Inquiry,* 35 (Summer): 749-770.
34. Horace Mann, quoted in Gregory J. Fritzburg, "Schools Can't Do It Alone: A Broader Conception of Equality of Education," www.newhorizons.org/strategies/multicultural/fritzberg.htm (accessed October 30, 2009). This quote is from Mann's Twelfth Annual Report as Secretary of Massachusetts State Board of Education, http://www.tncrimlaw.com/civil_bible/horace_mann.htm (accessed May 20, 2010).

1

1. Mona El-Naggar, "Former Tunisian Leader Faces Legal Charges," *New York Times*, April 14, 2011, http://www.nytimes.com/2011/04/15/world/africa/15tunisia.html?scp=3&sq=Tunisian%20President%20Zine%20El%20Abidine%20Ben%20Ali%20forced%20to%20flee%20the%20country&st=cse (accessed November 17, 2011).
2. Anthony Shadid, "Egypt Officials Widen Crackdown but Officials Offer Concessions," *New York Times,* February 3, 2011, http://www.nytimes.com/2011/02/04/world/middleeast/04egypt.html?scp=1&sq=Egypt%20Officials%20Widen%20Crackdown;%20U.S.%20in%20Talks%20for%20Mubarak%20to%20Quit&st=cse (accessed October 12, 2011).
3. Kira Salak, "Rediscovering Libya," *National Geographic Adventure Magazine*, April 2005, http://www.nationalgeographic.com/adventure/0504/excerpt1.html (accessed October 10, 2011).
4. Jillian Schwedler and Laryssa Chomiak, "And the Winner Is…: Authoritarian Elections in the Arab World," *Middle East Report* no. 238 (Spring 2006): 12-9)
5. Yoram Meital, "The Struggle over Political Order in Egypt: The 2005 Elections," *Middle East Journal* 60, no. 2 (Spring 2006): 257–79
6. Yoram Meital, "The Struggle over Political Order in Egypt: The 2005 Elections," *Middle East Journal* 60, no. 2 (Spring 2006): 257–79
7. Raymond A. Hinnebusch, "Charisma, Revolution, and State Formation: Qaddafi and Libya," *Third World Quarterly* 6, no. 1 (January 1984): 59–73.
8. David Boaz, "The Man Who Would Not Be King," *CATO Institute,* February 20, 2006, www.cato.org/pub_display.php?pub_id=5593 (accessed November 30, 2009).
9. Al Gore, speech delivered on December 13, 2000, http://transcripts.cnn.com/TRANSCRIPTS/0012/13/bn.24.html (accessed June 23, 2011).
10. *Strauss v. Horton*, 46 Cal. 4th 364, 93 Cal. Rptr.3d 591, 207 P.3d 48
11. *Perry v. Schwarzenegger*, 704 F. Supp. 2d 921 (N.D. Cal. 2010)
12. *Reitman* v. *Mulkey*, 387 U.S. 369 (1967).
13. Aristotle, *Politics* (Oxford University Press, 1998); and George Huxley, "On Aristotle's Best State," *History of Political Thought,* 6 (Summer 1985), pp. 139–149.
14. John Locke, *Two Treatises of Government and a Letter Concerning Toleration* (Yale University Press, 2003); and Virginia McDonald, "A Guide to the Interpretation of Locke the Political Theorist," *Canadian Journal of Political Science,* 6 (December 1973), pp. 602–623.
15. Thomas Hobbes, *Leviathan* (Oxford University Press, 1998); and Frank M. Coleman, "The Hobbesian Basis of American Constitutionalism," *Polity,* 7 (Autumn 1974), pp. 57–89.
16. Charles de Montesquieu, *The Spirit of the Laws* (Cambridge University Press, 1989); and E. P. Panagopoulos, *Essays on the History and Meaning of Checks and Balances* (University Press of America, 1986).
17. Clinton Rossiter, *Conservatism in America* (Vintage Books, 1962), p. 72.
18. Bernard Bailyn, *The Ideological Origins of the American Revolution* (Belknap Press, 1967); Gordon S. Wood, *The Creation of the American Republic, 1776–1787* (University of North Carolina Press, 1969); and Jack Citrin, "Political Culture," in *Understanding America: The Anatomy of an Exceptional Nation*, ed. Peter H. Schuck and James Q. Wilson (New York: Public Affairs, 2008), pp. 160–161.

19. Peter H. Shuck and James Q. Wilson, eds. *Understanding America: The Anatomy of an Exceptional Nation* (New York: Public Affairs, 2008), 629.
20. Jeremy Rifkin, *The European Dream* (Penguin, 2005).
21. James Madison, "The Federalist #10" in the *Federalist Papers* (New York: Penguin Books, 1987), p. 124.
22. Alberto Alesina and Edward Glaeser, *Fighting Poverty in the U.S. and Europe: A World of Difference* (Oxford University Press, 2004).
23. When adjusted using the consumer price index (CPI1), the percentage of households earning more than $75,000 a year has risen from 10.1 percent in 1970 to 22.6 percent in 1999. U.S. Bureau of the Census, Statistical Abstracts of the United States, 2001 (U.S. Government Printing Office, 2001), table 661; see also Julia Isaac, "Economic Mobility of Black and White Families," Brookings Institution, Economic Mobility Project, November 2007.
24. See Michael B. Katz, The "Underclass" Debate (Princeton University Press, 1993); Theodore Dalrymple, Life at the Bottom: The Worldview That Makes the Underclass (Dee, 2001); and Charles A. Murray, The Underclass Revisited (AEI Press, 1999).
25. *Marbury* v. *Madison*, 5 U.S. 137 (1803).
26. David B. Magleby, *Direct Legislation: Voting on Ballot Propositions in the United States* (Johns Hopkins University Press, 1984), p. 119.
27. Sheri Berman, "Civil Society and the Collapse of the Weimar Republic," *World Politics,* 49, No. 3 (April 1997), pp. 410–429.
28. Seymour Martin Lipset, "The Social Requisites of Democracy Revisited," *American Sociological Review,* 59 (1994), pp. 1–22.
29. For a discussion of the importance for democracy of such overlapping group memberships, see David Truman's seminal work, *The Governmental Process,* 2nd ed. (Knopf, 1971).
30. Lesli J. Favor, *The Iroquois Constitution: A Primary Source Investigation of the Law of the Iroquois* (Rosen, 2003), p. 60.
31. Joyce Appleby, "The American Heritage: The Heirs and the Disinherited," *Journal of American History,* 74 (December 1987), p. 808.
32. Kevin Butterfield, "What You Should Know About the Declaration of Independence," *St. Louis Post-Dispatch,* July 4, 2000, p. F1.
33. Richard L. Hillard, "Liberalism, Civic Humanism, and the American Revolutionary Bill of Rights, 1775–1790," paper presented at the annual meeting of the Organization of American Historians, Reno, NV, March 26, 1988.
34. Robert W. Hoffert, *A Politics of Tensions: The Articles of Confederation and American Political Ideas* (University Press of Colorado, 1992); see also Merrill Jensen, *The Articles of Confederation: An Interpretation of the Social-Constitutional History of the American Revolution, 1774–1781* (University of Wisconsin Press, 1970).
35. *The Federalist,* No. 40.
36. Quoted in Charles L. Mee Jr., *The Genius of the People* (Harper & Row, 1987), p. 51.
37. Charles A. Beard, *An Economic Interpretation of the Constitution of the United States* (Macmillan, 1913).
38. Robert Brown, *Charles Beard and the Constitution: A Critical Analysis of "An Economic Interpretation of the Constitution"* (Princeton University Press, 1956).
39. Declaration of Congress, February 21, 1787; and Worthington C. Ford et al., eds., *Journals of the Continental Congress, 1774–1789,* 32 (Washington, DC, 1904–1937), p. 74.
40. Seymour Martin Lipset, "George Washington and the Founding of Democracy," *Journal of Democracy,* 9 (October 1998), p. 31.
41. Michael P. Zuckert,. "Federalism and the Founding: Toward a Reinterpretation of the Constitutional Convention." *The Review of Politics* 48 (2) (Spring, 1986) pp. 166–210.
42. David O. Stewart, *The Men Who Invented the Constitution: The Summer of 1787* (Simon & Schuster: NY, 2007).
43. See the essays in Thomas E. Cronin, ed., *Inventing the American Presidency* (University Press of Kansas, 1989); see also Richard J. Ellis, ed., *Founding the American Presidency* (Rowman & Littlefield, 1999).
44. David McKay, *American Politics and Society* (Wiley-Blackwell: Malden, MA, 2009); see also Saul Cornell "Aristocracy Assailed: The Ideology of Backcountry Anti-Federalism," *Journal of American History,* 76 (March), p. 1156, www.jstor.org/stable/pdfplus/2936593.pdf.
45. Charles A. Beard and Mary R. Beard, *A Basic History of the United States* (New Home Library, 1944), p. 136.
46. W. B. Allen and Gordon Lloyd, eds., *The Essential Antifederalist* (University Press of America, 1985), pp. xi–xiii.
47. See Herbert J. Storing, ed., abridgment by Murray Dry, *The Anti-Federalist: Writings by the Opponents of the Constitution* (University of Chicago Press, 1985).
48. On the role of the promised Bill of Rights amendments in the ratification of the Constitution, see Leonard W. Levy, *Constitutional Opinions* (Oxford University Press, 1986), Chapter 6.

2

1. *District of Columbia* v. *Heller,* 554 U.S. 570 (2008).
2. *McDonald* v. *Chicago,* 561 U.S. 3025 (2010).
3. Whaley, Monte, "Colorado Supreme Court Affirms that Licensed Guns Allowed on CU Campus," *The Denver Post* (March 6, 2012).
4. Allie Grasgreen, "Guns Come to Campuses," *Inside Higher Ed.* October 3, 2011.
5. Sanford Levinson, *Constitutional Faith* (Princeton University Press, 1988), pp. 9–52.
6. Richard Morin, "We Love It—What We Know of It," *The Washington Post National Weekly Edition* (September 22, 1997), p. 35.
7. Alexander Hamilton, James Madison, and John Jay, in Clinton Rossiter, ed., *The Federalist Papers* (New American Library, 1961).
8. Quoted in Alpheus T. Mason, *The Supreme Court: Palladium of Freedom* (University of Michigan Press, 1962), p. 10.
9. Hamilton, Madison, and Jay, *The Federalist Papers.*
10. Ibid.
11. Ibid.
12. Justice Brandeis dissenting in *Myers* v. *United States,* 272 U.S. 52 (1926).
13. Charles O. Jones, "The Separate Presidency," in Anthony King, ed., *The New American Political System,* 2nd ed. (AEI Press, 1990), p. 3.
14. Morris P. Fiorina, "An Era of Divided Government," *Political Science Quarterly* 107 (1992), p. 407.
15. David R. Mayhew, *Divided We Govern: Party Control, Lawmaking, and Investigations,* 1946–1990 (Yale University Press, 1991), p. 4; see also James A. Thurber, ed., *Divided Democracy: Presidents and Congress in Cooperation and Conflict* (CQ Press, 1991).
16. Paul C. Light, *Government's Greatest Investigations,* 1945–2012 (Brookings, 2012).
17. Charles O. Jones, *Separate but Equal Branches: Congress and the Presidency* (Chatham House, 1995).
18. Judith A. Best, *The Choice of the People? Debating the Electoral College* (Rowman & Littlefield, 1996).
19. Seema Mehta and Maeve Reston, "Jerry Brown Nearly Matched Meg Whitman's Campaign Spending on TV in Final Weeks of Race," *Los Angeles Times,* February 1, 2011.
20. James Risen and Eric Lichtblau. "Bush Lets U.S. Spy on Callers Without Courts," *New York Times,* December 16, 2005.
21. Hamilton, Madison, and Jay, *The Federalist Papers.*
22. See Alec Stone Sweet, Wayne Sandholtz, and Neil Fligstein, *The Institutionalization of Europe* (Oxford University Press, 2001); Alec Stone Sweet, *Governing with Judges: Constitutional Politics in Europe* (Oxford University Press, 2000); and Anne-Marie Slaughter, Alec Stone Sweet, and J.H.H. Weiler, *The European Court and National Courts—Doctrine, Jurisprudence: Legal Change in Its Social Context* (Hart, 1998).
23. *Marbury* v. *Madison,* 5 U. S. 137 (1803).
24. Dumas Malone, *Jefferson the President: First Term, 1801–1805* (Little, Brown, 1970), p. 145.
25. J. W. Peltason, *Federal Courts in the Political Process* (Random House, 1955).
26. Lyle Denniston, "Analysis: Health Care's Mandate—Part I," December 1, 2011. SCOTUSblog. http://www.scotusblog.com/2011/12/analysis-health-cares-mandate-part-i/.
27. *National Federation of Independent Business v. Sebelius,* 567 U.S. _____ (2012).
28. Executive Order 13577—SelectUSA Initiative. June 15, 2011.
29. Richard E. Neustadt, *Presidential Power* (Free Press, 1990), pp. 180–181.
30. *Marbury* v. *Madison,* 5 U.S. 137 (1803).
31. *Brown* v. *Board of Education,* 347 U.S. 483 (1954).
32. *Griswold* v. *Connecticut,* 381 U.S. 479 (1965).
33. *Texas* v. *Johnson,* 491 U.S. 397 (1989).
34. *United States* v. *Eichman,* 496 U.S. 310 (1990).
35. John A. Clark and Kevin T. McGuire, "Congress, the Supreme Court, and the Flag," *Political Research Quarterly* 49 (1996), pp. 771–781.
36. Senate Joint Resolution 12, 109th Congress, 2d session.
37. Ann Stuart Diamond, "A Convention for Proposing Amendments: The Constitution's Other Method," *Publius* 11 (Summer 1981), pp. 113–146; and Wilbur Edel, "Amending the Constitution by Convention: Myths and Realities," *State Government* 55 (1982), pp. 51–56.
38. Russell L. Caplan, *Constitutional Brinksmanship: Amending the Constitution by National Convention* (Oxford University Press, 1988), p. x; see also David E. Kyvig, *Explicit and Authentic Acts: Amending the U.S. Constitution,* 1776–1995 (University Press of Kansas, 1996), p. 440.
39. Samuel S. Freedman and Pamela J. Naughton, *ERA: May a State Change Its Vote?* (Wayne State University Press, 1979).
40. Kyvig, *Explicit and Authentic Acts,* p. 286; and *Dillon* v. *Gloss,* 256 U.S. 368 (1921).

41. Mark R. Daniels, Robert Darcy, and Joseph W. Westphal, "The ERA Won—at Least in the Opinion Polls," *P.S.: Political Science and Politics* (Fall 1982), p. 583.
42. National Organization for Women, www.now.org/issues/economic/eratext.html.
43. Janet K. Boles, *The Politics of the Equal Rights Amendment: Conflict and Decision-Making Powers* (Longman, 1979), p. 4.

3

1. For further historical background, see Samuel J. Beer, *To Make a Nation: The Rediscovery of American Federalism* (Harvard University Press, 1993).
2. Immigration Policy Center, *Q & A Guide to State Immigration Laws: What You Need to Need to Know if Your State is Considering Arizona SB1070-Type Legislation,* Immigration Policy Center, April, 2011.
3. Campell Robertson, "Critics See 'Chilling Effect' in Alabama Immigration Law," *New York Times*, October 27, 2011, p. A1.
4. For a summary of these cases and state laws on immigration, see the National Conference of State Legislatures' Immigrant Policy Project at http://www.ncsl.org/default.aspx?tabid=22529
5. William H. Stewart, *Concepts of Federalism* (Center for the Study of Federalism/University Press of America, 1984); see also Preston King, *Federalism and Federation*, 2nd ed. (Cass, 2001).
6. *United States* v. *Wheeler,* 435 U. S. 313 (1978)
7. Morton Grodzins, "The Federal System," in *Goals for Americans: The Report of the President's Commission on National Goals* (Columbia University Press, 1960).
8. Thomas R. Dye, *American Federalism: Competition Among Governments* (Lexington Books, 1990), pp. 13–17.
9. Michael D. Reagan and John G. Sanzone, *The New Federalism* (Oxford University Press, 1981), p. 175.
10. For a deeper discussion of federations, see Michael Burgess, "Introduction: Federalism and Building the European Union, *Publius* (Autumn 1996): pp. 1–15.
11. William H. Riker, *The Development of American Federalism* (Academic Press, 1987), pp. 14–15. Riker contends not only that federalism does not guarantee freedom but also that the framers of our federal system, as well as those of other nations, were animated not by considerations of safeguarding freedom but by practical considerations of preserving unity.
12. U.S. Census Bureau, *Statistical Abstract of the United States* (Government Printing Office, 2007), p. 487.
13. *New State Ice Company* v. *Liebmann*, 285 U.S. 262 (1932), Brandeis Dissenting.
14. Charles Evans Hughes, "War Powers Under the Constitution," *ABA Reports,* 62 (1917), p. 238.
15. *Gibbons* v. *Ogden,* 22 U.S. 1 (1824).
16. *Reno* v. *Condon,* 528 U.S. 141 (2000).
17. *Champion* v. *Ames,* 188 U.S. 321 (1907).
18. *Caminetti* v. *United States,* 242 U.S. 470 (1917).
19. *Federal Radio Commission* v. *Nelson Brothers,* 289 U.S. 266 (1933).
20. See Jesse Choper, *Judicial Review and the National Political Process* (University of Chicago Press, 1980); and John T. Noonan Jr., *Narrowing the Nation's Power: The Supreme Court Sides with the States* (University of California Press, 2002).
21. See Michael S. Greve, *Real Federalism: Why It Matters, How It Could Happen* (American Enterprise Institute, 1999).
22. *Printz* v. *United States,* 521 U.S. 898 (1997); see also *New York* v. *United States,* 505 U.S. 144 (1992).
23. See *Franchise Tax Board of California* v. *Hyatt,* 538 U.S. 488 (2003).
24. *California* v. *Superior Courts of California,* 482 U.S. 400 (1987).
25. David C. Nice, "State Participation in Interstate Compacts," *Publius,* 17 (Spring 1987), p. 70; see also *Interstate Compacts and Agencies,* Council of State Governments (Author, 1995), for a list of compacts by subject and by state with brief descriptions.
26. *McCulloch* v. *Maryland,* 4 Wheaton 316 (1819).
27. Joseph F. Zimmerman, "Federal Preemption Under Reagan's New Federalism," *Publius,* 21 (Winter 1991), pp. 7–28.
28. Oliver Wendell Holmes Jr., *Collected Legal Papers* (Harcourt, 1920), pp. 295–296.
29. See, for example, *United States* v. *Lopez,* 514 U.S. 549 (1995).
30. *Seminole Tribe of Florida* v. *Florida,* 517 U.S. 44 (1996).
31. *Alden* v. *Maine,* 527 U.S. 706 (1999); *Kimel* v. *Florida Board of Regents,* 528 U.S. 62 (2000); *Vermont Agency of Natural Resources* v. *United States ex rel. Stevens,* 529 U.S. 765 (2000).
32. George Will, "A Revival of Federalism?" *Newsweek* (May 29, 2000), p. 78.
33. *United States* v. *Morrison,* 529 U.S. 598 (2000).
34. The term "devolution revolution" was coined by Richard P. Nathan in testimony before the Senate Finance Committee, quoted in Daniel Patrick Moynihan, "The Devolution Revolution," *New York Times* (August 6, 1995), p. B15.
35. These figures come from the U.S. Census Bureau's Federal Assistance Award Databse for 2010, at http://www.census.gov/govs/www/faadsmain.html
36. These figures come from the President's Budget for Fiscal Year 2012, and can be found in Table 12.2 at http://www.whitehouse.gov/sites/default/files/omb/budget/fy2012/assets/hist.pdf starting at p. 256.
37. John E. Chubb, "The Political Economy of Federalism," *American Political Science Review,* 79 (December 1985), p. 1005.
38. Donald F. Kettl, *The Regulation of American Federalism* (Johns Hopkins University Press, 1987), pp. 154–155.
39. See Paul J. Posner, *The Politics of Unfunded Mandates: Whither Federalism?* (Georgetown University Press, 1998).
40. See National Conference of State Legislatures, Mandate Monitor, at http:/ncsl.org/StateFederalCommittees/BudgetsRevenue/MandateMonitorOverview/tabid/15850/Default.aspx
41. *Restoring Confidence and Competence,* Advisory Commission on Intergovernmental Relations (Author, 1981), p. 30.
42. Aaron Wildavsky, "Bare Bones: Putting Flesh on the Skeleton of American Federalism," in *The Future of Federalism in the 1980s* (Advisory Commission on Intergovernmental Relations, 1981), p. 79.
43. Peterson, *Price of Federalism,* p. 182.
44. Dye, *American Federalism,* p. 199.

4

1. Congressional Budget Office, "Trends in the Distribution of Household Income Between 1979 and 2007," October 2011, http://www.cbo.gov/ftpdocs/124xx/doc12485/10-25-HouseholdIncome.pdf, ix (accessed January 20, 2012).
2. Conn Carroll, "Morning Examiner: Romney Stump Speech Rattles Left," Beltway Confidential blog, *The Washington Examiner*, December 22, 2011, http://campaign2012.washingtonexaminer.com/blogs/beltway-confidential/morning-examiner-romney-stump-speech-rattles-left/271171 (accessed January 20, 2012).
3. CNN Wire Staff, "Obama Says Economic 'Inequality' Hurts Everyone," CNN, December 6, 2011, http://politicalticker.blogs.cnn.com/2011/12/06/obama-compares-current-economy-to-great-depression/ (accessed January 20, 2012).
4. Larry M. Bartels, *Unequal Democracy: The Political Economy of the New Gilded Age* (Princeton: Princeton University Press, 2008), p. 3.
5. Larry M. Bartels, *Unequal Democracy: The Political Economy of the New Gilded Age* (Princeton: Princeton University Press, 2008), p. 2, 15.
6. Arthur M. Okun, *Equality and Efficiency: The Big Tradeoff* (Washington, D.C.: Brookings Institution, 1975)
7. Albert Einstein, quoted in Laurence J. Peter, *Peter's Quotations* (Morrow, 1977), p. 358.
8. Harold Hongju Koh, "On American Exceptionalism," *Stanford Law Review* 55 (May 2003), p. 1481.
9. Richard Cohen, "The Myth of American Exceptionalism," *The Washington Post,* May 9, 2011, http://www.washingtonpost.com/opinions/the-myth-of-american-exceptionalism/2011/05/09/AF2rm0bG_story.html (accessed January 20, 2012).
10. Mitt Romney, *No Apology: Believe in America, the Case for American Greatness*, New York: St. Martin's Press, 2010) p. 47
11. See David Nakamura, "Obama Touts American Exceptionalism, End of Wars in Air Force Graduation Speech," *Washington Post,* May 23, 2012, http://www.washingtonpost.com/politics/obama-touts-american-exceptionalism-end-of-wars-in-air-force-graduation-speech/2012/05/23/gJQANN2zkU_story.html (accessed June 11, 2012).
12. Alexis de Tocqueville, *Democracy in America,* ed. J. P. Mayer, trans. George Lawrence (Doubleday, 1969), p. 278. Originally published 1835 (Vol. 1) and 1840 (Vol. 2).
13. John Lewis Gaddis, *Surprise, Security, and the American Experience* (Harvard University Press, 2005).
14. This excludes the Japanese attack on the U.S. territory of Hawaii in 1941 and other attacks on U.S. embassies or territories.
15. Food and Agriculture Organization of the United Nations, "Statistical Appendix," *Food Outlook* 1 (June 2007), www.fao.org/docrep/010/ah864e/ah864e14.htm (accessed January 20, 2012).
16. National Conference of State Legislatures, "2011 Post-Election State and Legislative Partisan Composition," December 14, 2011, www.ncsl.org/documents/statevote/2011_Legis_and_State_post.pdf (accessed January 27, 2012).

17. The term was coined by H.L. Mencken, who included it in an article in the *Chicago Daily Tribune* and then reported in a letter to a friend that he was proud of this phrase. See: http://www.aaa.si.edu/collections/viewer/h-l-mencken-letter-to-charles-green-shaw-9819 (accessed January 23, 2012).
18. Robert S. Erikson, Gerald C. Wright, and John P. McIver, *Statehouse Democracy: Public Opinion and Policy in the American States* (Cambridge University Press, 1993).
19. *Statistical Abstract, 2011,* p. 18.
20. *Statistical Abstract, 2011,* p. 36.
21. Ibid.
22. Nadia Abu El-Haj, "The Genetic Reinscription of Race." *Annual Review of Anthropology*, 36 (2007) pp. 283–300.
23. David R. Harris and Jeremiah Joseph Sim, "Who is Multiracial? Assessing the Complexity of Lived Race," *American Sociological Review* (August 2002), p. 615.
24. U.S. Census Bureau, "Race," State and County QuickFacts, http://quickfacts.census.gov/qfd/meta/long_RHI105210.htm (accessed October 24, 2011)
25. *Statistical Abstract, 2011,* p. 25.
26. Ibid.
27. U.S. Census Bureau News, "More Diversity, Slower Growth," U.S. Department of Commerce, December 16, 2009, http://www.imdiversity.com/villages/asian/reference/census_2050_asian_projections.asp
28. On South Dakota see James Meader and John Bart, "The More You Spend, the Less They Listen: The South Dakota U.S. Senate Race," in David B. Magleby and J. Quin Monson, eds., *The Last Hurrah? Soft Money and Issue Advocacy in the 2002 Congressional Elections* (Brookings Institution Press, 2004), p. 173; and Elizabeth Theiss Smith and Richard Braunstein, "The Nationalization of Local Politics in South Dakota," in David B. Magleby and J. Quin Monson, eds., *Dancing Without Partners: How Candidates, Parties, and Interest Groups Interact in the New Campaign Finance Environment* (Center for the Study of Elections and Democracy, 2005), pp. 241–242; on Alaska see Kim Murphy, "Lisa Murkowski Claims Victory in Alaska Senate Election," *Los Angeles Times*, November 18, 2010, http://articles.latimes.com/2010/nov/18/nation/la-na-alaska-senate-20101118 (accessed October 24, 2010), and Yereth Rosen, "Lisa Murkowski Ahead in Alaska, But Long Count of Write-ins Looms," *Christian Science Monitor*, November 4, 2010, http://www.csmonitor.com/USA/Elections/Senate/2010/1104/Lisa-Murkowski-ahead-in-Alaska-but-long-count-of-write-ins-looms (accessed January 25, 2012).
29. Henry J. Kaiser Family Foundation, "Race, Ethnicity, and Healthcare Issue Brief," September 2009, http://www.kff.org/minorityhealth/upload/7977.pdf (accessed January 25, 2012).
30. James, I. Schaap, "The Growth of the Native American Gaming Industry: What Has the Past Provided, and What Does the Future Hold?" *American Indian Quarterly*, (Summer 2010) Vol. 34, Issue 3, pp. 365-389.
31. Robert D. Ballard, "Introduction: Lure of the New South," in Robert D. Ballard, ed., *In Search of the New South: The Black Urban Experience in the 1970s and 1980s* (University of Alabama Press, 1989), p. 5; *Statistical Abstract, 2008,* p. 449.
32. Sonya Rastogi, Tallese D. Johnson, Elizabeth M. Hoeffel, and Malcolm P. Drewery, Jr., "The Black Population: 2010; 2010 Census Briefs," US Census Bureau, September 2011, http://www.census.gov/prod/cen2010/briefs/c2010br-06.pdf (accessed October 25, 2011).
33. *Statistical Abstract, 2012,* p. 177.
34. *Statistical Abstract, 2012,* p. 151.
35. *Statistical Abstract, 2012,* p. 455. Constant 2008 dollars.
36. Ibid., p. 466.
37. *Statistical Abstract, 2012,* p. 454.
38. *Statistical Abstract, 2012,* p. 16.
39. Jeremy D. Mayer, *Running on Race* (Random House, 2002), pp. 4, 297. See also Mark R. Levy and Michael S. Kramer, *The Ethnic Factor: How America's Minorities Decide Elections* (Simon & Schuster, 1973); and Mark Stern, "Democratic Presidency and Voting Rights," in Lawrence W. Mooreland, Robert P. Steed, and Todd A. Baker, eds., *Blacks in Southern Politics* (Praeger, 1987), pp. 50–51.
40. For 1984–2000, see Harold W. Stanley and Richard G. Niemi, *Vital Statistics on American Politics, 2000–2001* (CQ Press, 2001), p. 122; for 2004, see Harold W. Stanley and Richard G. Niemi, *Vital Statistics on American Politics, 2005–2006* (CQ Press, 2006), p. 124.
41. BBC News, "The U.S. Election in Figures" at http://news.bbc.co.uk/2/hi/americas/us_elections_2008/7715914.stm (accessed November 7, 2008).
42. Howard W. Stanley and Richard G. Niemi, *Vital Statistics on American Politics, 2011–2012,* (CQ Press, 2011), pp. 53–54.
43. Ibid.
44. Matt Barreto, Rodolfo O. de la Garza, Jongho Lee, Jaesung Ryu, and Harry P. Pachon, "Latino Voter Mobilization in 2000," Tomás Rivera Policy Institute (2000), pp. 4–5, www.trpi.org/PDFs/Voter_mobiliz_2.pdf (accessed January 25, 2012). See also Richard E. Cohen, "Hispanic Hopes Fade," *National Journal* (February 2, 2002).
45. *Statistical Abstract, 2012,* p. 23.
46. *Statistical Abstract, 2012,* p. 45.
47. Michael Hoefer, Nancy Rytina, and Bryan C. Baker, "Estimates of the Unauthorized Immigrant Population Residing in the United States: January 2010," Department of Homeland Security http://www.dhs.gov/xlibrary/assets/statistics/publications/ois_ill_pe_2010.pdf (accessed November 9, 2011).
48. *Statistical Abstract 2012*, p. 16.
49. Janelle Wong, S. Karthick Ramakrishnan, Taeku Lee, and Jane Junn, *Asian American Political Participation: Emerging Constituents and Their Political Identities* (Russell Sage Foundation: 2011).
50. Zoltan L. Hajnal and Taeku Lee, *Why Americans Don't Join the Party: Race, Immigration, and the Failure (of Political Parties) to Engage the Electorate* (Princeton, NJ: Princeton University Press, 2011).
51. *Statistical Abstract, 2012,* p. 151.
52. Ibid., p. 46.
53. Leni Yahil, *The Holocaust: The Fate of European Jewry* (Oxford University Press, 1990).
54. Stephen C. LeSuer, *The 1838 Mormon War in Missouri* (University of Missouri Press, 1987), pp. 151–153.
55. Nicholas Jay Demerath, *Crossing the Gods: World Religions and Worldly Politics* (Rutgers University Press: 2001).
56. Ronald Inglehart and Wayne E. Baker, "Looking Forward, Looking Back: Continuity and Change at the Turn of the Millennium," *American Sociological Review* (February 2000), pp. 29, 31.
57. Kenneth D. Wald and Allison Calhoun-Brown, *Religion and Politics in the United States,* 5th ed. (New York: Rowman and Littlefield, 2006), p. 9.
58. Pew Forum on Religious and Public Life, "Eastern, New Age Beliefs Widespread Many Americans Mix Multiple Faiths" December 2009, http://pewforum.org/newassets/images/reports/multiplefaiths/multiplefaiths.pdf (accessed February 18, 2010).
59. *Statistical Abstract,* 2012, p. 61.
60. Ibid.
61. Ibid.
62. *Statistical Abstract, 2010,* pp. 18, 59; see also the Association of Religion Data Archives, "U.S. Congregational Membership: State Reports," www.thearda.com/mapsReports/reports/selectState.asp (accessed January 25, 2012).
63. The Association of Religion Data Archives, "Southern Baptist Convention," 2000, http://www.thearda.com/Denoms/D_1087_d.asp (accessed February 22, 2010).
64. Ibid.
65. Association of Religion Data Archives, "Jewish Estimate—Number of Adherents," www.thearda.com/mapsReports/maps/map.asp?state=101&variable=20 (accessed January 25, 2012); ARDA, "Metro Area Membership Report," www.thearda.com/mapsReports/reports/metro/5602_2000.asp (accessed January 25, 2012).
66. *2000 American National Election Study* (Center for Political Studies, 2000); *2004 American National Election Study* (Center for Political Studies, 2004). *2008 American National Election Study* (Center for Political Studies, 2008). Post-election surveys often overestimate the vote, and that appeared to be especially the case in the 2004 National Election Study. See Morris Fiorina and Jon Krosnick, "*Economist/YouGov Internet Presidential Poll*," www.economist.com/media/pdf/Paper.pdf; and Michael P. McDonald and Samuel Popkin, "The Myth of the Vanishing Voter," *American Political Science Review* 95 (2001), pp. 963–974.
67. CNN, "Exit Polls: Results," www.cnn.com/ELECTION/2000/results, www.pollingreport.com/2000.htm, June 9, 2012.
68. Pew Forum on Religion and Public Life, "Voting Religiously," 5 November 2008 http://pewresearch.org/pubs/1022/exit-poll-analysis-religion (accessed February 19, 2010).
69. James West Davidson, William E. Gienapp, Christine Leigh Heyrman, Mark H. Lytle, and Michael B. Stoff, *Nation of Nations* (McGraw-Hill, 1990), pp. 833–834.
70. Margaret C. Trevor, "Political Socialization, Party Identification, and the Gender Gap," *Public Opinion Quarterly* 63 (Spring 1999), p. 62.
71. *Statistical Abstract, 2006*, p. 263; Sue Tolleson-Rinehard and Jyl J. Josephson, eds., *Gender and American Politics* (Sharpe, 2000), pp. 77–78; Center for American Women and Politics, "Gender Differences in Voter Turnout," 2011, http://www.cawp.rutgers.edu/fast_facts/voters/documents/genderdiff.pdf (accessed January 9, 2012).
72. Tolleson-Rinehard and Josephson, *Gender and American Politics,* pp. 232–233. See also Cindy Simon Rosenthal, ed., *Women Transforming Congress* (University of Oklahoma Press, 2002), pp. 128–139.
73. Paul Steinhauser, "Men's Support Gives Palin Edge in Latest Poll," *CNN*, September 9, 2008, http://www.cnn.com/2008/POLITICS/09/09/palin.poll (accessed March 1, 2010).
74. Office of the Clerk, "Women in Congress: Historical Data, Women Representatives and Senators by Congress," 2011, http://womenincongress.house.gov/historical-data/representatives-senators-by-congress.html?congress=111 (accessed January 25, 2012).

75. National Conference of State Legislatures, "Women in State Legislatures: 2010 Legislative Session," 2011, http://www.ncsl.org/default.aspx?tabid=19481 (accessed January 25, 2012).
76. Marjorie Connelly, "The Election; Who Voted: A Portrait of American Politics, 1976–2000," *New York Times,* November 12, 2000, p. D4.
77. *Statistical Abstract, 2006,* p. 247; CNN, "U.S. President National Exit Poll," 2004, http://www.cnn.com/ELECTION/2004/pages/results/states/US/P/00/epolls.0.html (accessed February 18, 2010).
78. CNN, "Obama's Election Redraws America's Electoral Divide," November 5, 2008, http://www.cnn.com/2008/POLITICS/11/05/election.president/index.html (accessed February 18, 2010).
79. Diane L. Fowlkes, "Feminist Theory: Reconstructing Research and Teaching About American Politics and Government," *News for Teachers of Political Science* (Winter 1987), pp. 6–9. See also Sally Helgesen, *Everyday Revolutionaries: Working Women and the Transformation of American Life* (Doubleday, 1998); Karen Lehrman, *The Lipstick Proviso: Women, Sex, and Power in the Real World* (Anchor/Doubleday, 1997); Tanya Melich, *The Republican War Against Women: An Insider's Report from Behind the Lines* (Bantam Books, 1998); and Virginia Valian, *Why So Slow? The Advancement of Women* (MIT Press, 1998).
80. Arlie Russell Hochschild, "There's No Place Like Work," *New York Times,* April 20, 1997, p. 51.
81. The Pew Research Center, *Gay Marriage a Voting Issue, but Mostly for Opponents,* February 27, 2004, www.people-press.org/reports/display.php3?ReportID=204 (accessed January 25, 2012); and Alexis Simendinger, "Why Issues Matter," *National Journal,* April 1, 2000, based on data from a Pew Center Poll conducted March 15–19, 2000.
82. *Statistical Abstract, 2012,* p. 458.
83. U.S. Census Bureau, "Men's and Women's Earnings by State: 2008 American Community Survey," http://www.census.gov/prod/2009pubs/acsbr08-3.pdf (accessed February 22, 2010).
84. Catherine Rampell, "As Layoffs Surge, Women May Pass Men in Job Force," *NY Times*, February 5, 2009 http://www.nytimes.com/2009/02/06/business/06women.html (accessed January 25, 2012).
85. Catherine Rampell, "Women Now a Majority in American Workplaces," *New York Times*, February 5, 2010, p. A10, http://www.nytimes.com/2010/02/06/business/economy/06women.html (accessed January 25, 2012); Kiplinger Washington Editors, "10 Developments That May Surprise You in 2012," *Kiplinger*, December 30, 2011, http://www.kiplinger.com/businessresource/forecast/archive/10-developments-that-may-surprise-you-in-2012.html (accessed January 25, 2012).
86. Anna Quindlen, "Some Struggles Never Seem to End," *New York Times,* November 14, 2001, p. H24.
87. Gay and Lesbian Families in the U.S., Urban Institute, http://www.urban.org/publications/1000491.html (accessed January 25, 2012).
88. Elisabeth Bumiller, "Obama Ends 'Don't Ask, Don't Tell' Policy," *The New York Times,* July 22, 2011, www.nytimes.com/2011/07/23/us/23military.html (accessed June 7, 2012).
89. Jackie Calmes and Peter Baker, "Obama Says Same-Sex Marriage Should Be Legal," *The New York Times,* May 9, 2012, www.nytimes.com/2012/05/10/us/politics/obama-says-same-sex-marriage-should-be-legal.html?pagewanted=all (accessed June 11, 2012).
90. *Statistical Abstract 2012*, p. 55.
91. U.S. Census Bureau, "Table MS-2. Estimated Median Age at First Marriage, by Sex: 1890 to the Present," January 2009, http://www.census.gov/population/socdemo/hh-fam/ms2.csv (accessed February 23, 2010).
92. CIA World Factbook data for 2011. https://www.cia.gov/library/publications/the-world-factbook/geos/us.html
93. CIA World Factbook, "Country Comparison: Total Fertility Rate," 2009, https://www.cia.gov/library/publications/the-world-factbook/rankorder/2127rank.html (accessed February 23, 2010).
94. The census stopped releasing divorce data in 1998, possibly because several states stopped providing it.
95. *Statistical Abstract, 2010,* p. 94.
96. Thomas Jefferson to P. S. du Pont de Nemours, April 24, 1816, in Paul L. Ford, ed. *The Writings of Thomas Jefferson* (Putnam, 1899), vol. 10, p. 25.
97. *Statistical Abstract, 2012,* p. 146.
98. *Statistical Abstract, 2012,* p. 152.
99. *Statistical Abstract, 2012,* p. 152.
100. Herbert McClosky and John Zaller, *The American Ethos: Public Attitudes Toward Capitalism and Democracy* (Harvard University Press, 1984), p. 261.
101. National Center for Education Statistics, *Adult Literacy in America* (April 2002) http://nces.ed.gov/pubs93/93275.pdf (accessed March 8, 2010).
102. National Center for Education Statistics, *A First Look at the Literacy of America's Adults in the 21st Century,* (2006) http://nces.ed.gov/NAAL/PDF/2006470.PDF (accessed March 8, 2010).
103. Ibid.
104. CIRCLE, "Youth Turnout Rate Rises to at Least 52%," Center for Information and Research on Civic Learning and Engagement, November 7, 2008, http://www.civicyouth.org/?p=323.
105. Nicholas L. Danigelis, Stephen J. Cutler, and Melissa Hardy, "Population Aging, Intracohort Aging, and Sociopolitical Attitudes," *American Sociological Review* 72 (October 2007), p. 816.
106. Raymond E. Wolfinger, Fred I. Greenstein, and Martin Shapiro, *Dynamics of American Politics,* 2d ed. (Prentice Hall, 1980), p. 19.
107. Harold W. Stanley and Richard G. Niemi, *Vital Statistics on American Politics, 2007–2008* (CQ Press, 2008), p. 374–375.
108. *Statistical Abstract, 2012,* p. 464.
109. U.S. Bureau of the Census, http://www.census.gov/hhes/www/poverty/data/threshld/ (accessed June 7, 2012).
110. *Statistical Abstract, 2012,* p. 467.
111. Statistical Abstract, 2012, p. 465.
112. *Statistical Abstract*, 2012, p. 465.
113. David Leonhardt, "Income Inequality," *New York Times*, January 18, 2011, http://topics.nytimes.com/top/reference/timestopics/subjects/i/income/income_inequality/index.html (accessed January 28, 2012).
114. Congressional Budget Office, "Trends in the Distribution of Household Income Between 1979 and 2007," October 2011, http://www.cbo.gov/doc.cfm?index=12485 (accessed January 28, 2012).
115. Robert A. Dahl, *Dilemmas of Pluralist Democracy: Autonomy vs. Control* (New Haven, CT: Yale University Press, 1982), 175.
116. David Leonhardt, "Income Inequality." *The New York Times,* http://topics.nytimes.com/top/reference/timestopics/subjects/i/income/income_inequality/index.html (accessed December 2, 2011).
117. David Brooks, "The Populist Myths on Income Inequality," *New York Times*, September 7, 2006, http://www.nytimes.com/2006/09/07/opinion/07brooks.html?hp.
118. Larry M. Bartels, *Unequal Democracy: The Political Economy of the New Gilded Age* (Princeton: Princeton University Press, 2008), p. 54.
119. Larry M. Bartels, *Unequal Democracy: The Political Economy of the New Gilded Age* (Princeton: Princeton University Press, 2008), p. 34.
120. U.S. Department of Commerce, Bureau of Economic Analysis, "Real Gross Domestic Product, 1 Decimal," November 22, 2011, http://research.stlouisfed.org/fred2/data/GDPC1.txt.
121. Daniel Bell, *The Coming of Post-Industrial Society: A Venture in Social Forecasting* (Basic Books, 1973), p. xviii.
122. BLS, News Release, Department of Labor, http://www.bls.gov/news.release/pdf/empsit.pdf, December 2, 2011.
123. BLS, News Release, Department of Labor, http://www.bls.gov/news.release/pdf/empsit.pdf, December 2, 2011; Bureau of Economic Analysis, "National Income and Product Accounts Table," http://www.bea.gov/national/nipaweb/TableView.asp?SelectedTable=6&ViewSeries=NO&Java=no&Request3Place=N&3Place=N&FromView=YES&Freq=Qtr&FirstYear=2010&LastYear=2011&3Place=N&Update=Update&JavaBox=no#Mid, U.S. Department of Commerce, December 22, 2011.
124. Gabriel A. Almond, G. Bingham Powell, Jr., Russell J. Dalton, and Kaare Strøm, eds., *Comparative Politics Today: A World View,* 9th ed. (Pearson Longman, 2008), p. 54.

5

1. Federal Labor Relations Authority, "50th Anniversary: Executive Order 10988," http://www.flra.gov/50th_Anniversary_EO10988 (accessed February 29, 2012).
2. American Federation of Government Employees, "About AFGE," http://www.afge.org/Index.cfm?Page=AboutAFGE (accessed April 26, 2012).
3. American Federation of State, County, and Municipal Employees, "Celebrating 75 Years of Solidarity with America's Working Families," Press Release, October 28, 2011, http://www.afscme.org/news/press-room/press-releases/2011/celebrating-75-years-of-solidarity-with-americas-working-families (accessed February 29, 2012).
4. The criteria for unemployment compensation insurance payments often include the worker having been recently laid-off from work, and the worker being ready, able, and willing to work. The unemployed worker must register with the state office administering the program.See http://workforcesecurity.doleta.gov/unemploy/uifactsheet.asp.
5. Ballotpedia, "State Legislative Elections Results, 2010," under heading "Wisconsin," http://ballotpedia.org/wiki/index.php/State_legislative_elections_results,_2010 (accessed April 26, 2012).
6. Michael Cooper and Katharine Q. Seelye, "Wisconsin Leads Way as Workers Fight State Cuts," *New York Times*, February 18, 2011, http://www.nytimes.com/2011/02/19/us/politics/19states.html?pagewanted=all (accessed April 26, 2012).
7. Monica Davey and Jeff Zeleny, "Walker Survives Wisconsin Recall Vote," *The New York Times*, June 5, 2012, www.nytimes.com/2012/06/06/us/politics/walker-survives-wisconsin-recall-effort.html?pagewanted=all (accessed June 18, 2010).

8. David Ariosto, "Ohio Voters Repeal Law Limiting Union Rights, CNN Projects," *CNN*, November 8, 2011, http://articles.cnn.com/2011-11-08/us/us_ohio-collective-bargaining-vote_1_wisconsin-workers-ohio-voters-philneuenfeldt?_s=PM:US (accessed March 9, 2012).
9. Annie Lowrey, "Obama to Sign Dodd-Frank Financial Regulatory Reform Bill Into Law Today," *The Washington Independent*, July 21, 2010, http://washingtonindependent.com/92161/obama-to-sign-dodd-frank-financial-regulatory-reform-bill-into-law-today (accessed March 1, 2012).
10. James Madison, *The Federalist*, No. 10, November 23, 1787, in Isaac Kramnick, ed., *The Federalist Papers* (Penguin, 1987), pp. 122–128.
11. See Robert Dahl, *Who Governs?* (Yale University Press, 1961).
12. Center for Responsive Politics, "Microsoft Corp: Donor Profile," http://www.opensecrets.org/orgs/summary.asp?ID=D000000115&Name=Microsoft+Corp (accessed May 21, 2010).
13. Gabriel A. Almond, G. Bingham Powell, Jr., Russell J. Dalton, and Kaare Strøm, *Comparative Politics Today*, 9th ed. (Pearson Longman, 2008), p. 70.
14. Bureau of Labor Statistics, "Table 3. Union affiliation of employed wage and salary workers by occupation and industry," Economic News Release, January 27, 2012, available at http://www.bls.gov/news.release/union2.t03.htm (accessed March 12, 2012).
15. Change to Win, "About Us," 2010, http://www.changetowin.org/about (accessed March 15, 2010).
16. Office of Labor Management Standards, Union Reports, and Constitutions, http://www.dol.gov/olms/regs/compliance/rrlo/lmrda.htm (accessed May 21, 2010).
17. http://www.bls.gov/news.release/union2.nr0.htm (accessed June 26, 2012). See also, AFL-CIO, "About Us: Union Facts," www.aflcio.org/aboutus/faq/ (accessed May 21, 2010).
18. U.S. Bureau of Labor Statistics, www.bls.gov/cps/cpsaat40.pdf (accessed May 21, 2010).
19. Douglas Belkin and Kris Maher, "Wisconsin Unions See Ranks Drop Ahead of Recall Vote." *The Wall Street Journal*, May 30, 2012, p. A1.
20. Service Employees International Union, "Fast Facts," (accessed March 12, 2012).
21. Brian C. Mooney, "Nation's Two Biggest Unions to Wait on Presidential Endorsement," *Boston Globe* (September 11, 2003), p. A3.
22. Rachel Weiner, "Issue 2 falls, Ohio Collective Bargaining Law Repealed." *The Washington Post,* November 8, 2011. http://www.washingtonpost.com/blogs/the-fix/post/issue-2-falls-ohio-collective-bargaining-law-repealed/2011/11/08/gIQAyZ0U3M_blog.html (accessed June 27, 2012).
23. Monica Davey and Jeff Zeleny, "Walker Survives Wisconsin Recall Vote," *The New York Times*, June 5, 2012, www.nytimes.com/2012/06/06/us/politics/walker-survives-wisconsin-recall-effort.html?pagewanted=all.
24. Alison Grant, "Labor Chief Sees Anti-Union Efforts Growing Bolder," (Cleveland) *Plain Dealer* (November 22, 2005), p. C1.
25. James MacGregor Burns and Stewart Burns, *A People's Charter: The Pursuit of Rights in America* (Knopf, 1991).
26. Chris W. Cox, "Who We Are, and What We Do," National Rifle Association, 2011, www.nraila.org/About/ (accessed January 12, 2012).
27. Laura Longhine, "Display Cases," *Legal Affairs*, November 2005, http://www.legalaffairs.org/issues/November-December-2005/scene_longhine_novdec05.msp (accessed March 15, 2010).
28. The American Israel Public Affairs Committee, "What is AIPAC?" http://www.aipac.org/en/About%20AIPAC (accessed February 22, 2010).
29. National Education Association, "Our History," 2012, http://www.nea.org/home/1704.htm (accessed January 12, 2012).
30. See Mancur Olson, *The Logic of Collective Action* (Harvard University Press, 1971).
31. Kenneth J. Arrow, "A Difficulty in the Concept of Social Welfare," *Journal of Political Economy,* 58 (August), pp. 328–346; see also David Austen-Smith and Jeffrey S. Banks, "Social Choice Theory, Game Theory, and Positive Political Theory," *Annual Review of Political Science,* 1 (June), pp. 259–287.
32. BIPAC, "Our Model for Political Success," http://bipac.net/bipac_public/initial.asp (accessed May 21, 2010); see also David B. Magleby, Anthony Corrado, and Kelly D. Patterson, *Financing the 2004 Election* (Brookings Institute Press, 2006); and David B. Magleby, J. Quin Monson, and Kelly Patterson, *Electing Congress: New Rules for an Old Game* (Pearson Prentice Hall, 2007).
33. Andrew Chadwick, "Digital Network Repertoires and Organizational Hybridity," *Political Communication,* 24 (July–September 2007), p. 284.
34. R. Kenneth Godwin, *One Billion New Rules for an Old Game* (Prentice Hall, 2006); see also David B. Magleby, J. Quin Monson, and Kelly D. Patterson, *Dancing Without Partners: How Candidates, Parties, and Interest Groups Interact in the Presidential Campaign* (Rowman & Littlefield, 2007); and David B. Magleby and Kelly D. Patterson, eds., *The Battle for Congress: Iraq, Scandal, and Campaign Finance in the 2006 Election* (Paradigm, 2008).
35. See Jose Antonio Vargas, "Obama Raised Half a Billion Online," *Washington Post*, November 20, 2008, http://voices.washingtonpost.com/44/2008/11/obama-raised-half-a-billion-on.html (accessed February 24, 2012).
36. The *Federal Register* is published every weekday. You can find it at the library or on the Internet at www.gpoaccess.gov.
37. Lucius J. Barker, "Third Parties in Litigation: A Systemic View of the Judicial Function," *Journal of Politics,* 29 (February 1967), pp. 41–69; and Jethro K. Lieberman, *Litigious Society,* rev. ed. (Basic Books, 1983).
38. Gregory A. Caldeira and John R. Wright, "Organized Interests and Agenda Setting in the U.S. Supreme Court," *American Political Science Review,* 82 (December 1988), pp. 1109–1127; see also Gregory A. Caldeira and John R. Wright, "*Amici Curiae* Before the Supreme Court: Who Participates, When, and How Much?" *Journal of Politics,* 52 (August 1990), pp. 782–806.
39. National Public Radio, "Understanding the Impact of Citizens United," February 23, 2012; Federal Election Committee, "Ongoing Legislation: Speechnow.org v. FEC"; *Federal Election Commission v. Wisconsin Right to Life, Inc.*, 551 U.S. 449 (2007).
40. Gregory A. Caldeira and John R. Wright, "Amici Curiae before the Supreme Court: Who Participates, When and How Much?" *The Journal of Politics* (August 1990).
41. Terry Baynes, "'Friends' Line up for Obamacare Supreme Court Challenge," *Reuters*, March 18, 2012, http://www.reuters.com/article/2012/03/18/us-usa-supremecourt-friends-idUSBRE82H09F20120318 (accessed April 25, 2012).
42. Robert D. McFadden, "Across the U.S., Protests for Immigrants Draw Thousands," *New York Times* (April 10, 2006), p. A14; and Anna Gorman and J. Michael Kennedy, "The Immigration Debate," *Los Angeles Times* (April 11, 2006), p. A11.
43. Sarah Maslin Nir and Matt Flegenheimer, "Hundreds Held in Oakland Occupy Protest," *New York Times*, January 29, 2012, http://www.nytimes.com/2012/01/30/us/occupy-oakland-protest-leads-to-hundreds-of-arrests.html (accessed April 26, 2012).
44. See Kenneth Klee, "The Siege of Seattle," *Newsweek* (December 13, 1999), p. 30.
45. Theresa Clift, "Two Texas Billionaires Are Nation's Top Super PAC Donors." *San Antonio Express-News*, 27 June 2012, http://blog.chron.com/txpotomac/2012/06/two-texas-billionaires-are-nations-top-super-pac-donors/, www.publicintegrity.org/politics/consider-source/super-donors (accessed June 27, 2012).
46. Ethan Bronner, *Battle for Justice: How the Bork Nomination Shook America* (Norton, 1989), pp. 50–55.
47. David B. Magleby, ed., *The Change Election: Money, Mobilization, and Persuasion in the 2008 Federal Elections* (Temple University Press, 2011), p. 47.
48. http://www.opensecrets.org/revolving/departing.php (accessed June 26, 2012).
49. Hugh Heclo, "Issue Networks and the Executive Establishment," in Anthony King, ed., *The New American Political System* (American Enterprise Institute, 1978).
50. David Mayhew, *Congress: The Electoral Connection* (Yale University Press, 1974), p. 45.
51. John R. Wright, "Contributions, Lobbying, and Committee Voting in the U.S. House of Representatives," *American Political Science Review,* 84 (June 1990), pp. 417–438.
52. http://thinkprogress.org/romm/2011/07/21/275206/koch-exxon-state-legislation-climate-change-laws/.
53. Dan Eggen, "Expecting Final Push on Health Care Reform, Interest Groups Rally for Big Finish," *Washington Post*, February 28, 2010, http://www.washingtonpost.com/wp-dyn/content/article/2010/02/27/AR2010022703253.html (accessed April 29, 2010).
54. *McConnell* v. *Federal Elections Commission,* 124 S. Ct. 621 (2003).
55. For evidence of the impact of PAC expenditures on legislative committee behavior and legislative involvement generally, see Richard L. Hall and Frank W. Wayman, "Buying Time: Moneyed Interests and the Mobilization of Bias in Congressional Committees," *American Political Science Review,* 84 (September 1990), pp. 797–820.
56. Federal Election Commission, "Number of Federal PACs Increases," Press Release, March 9, 2009, http://www.fec.gov/press/press2009/20090309PACcount.shtml (accessed May 21, 2010).
57. Ibid.
58. Open Secrets, "Business Associations," April 25, 2011, http://www.opensecrets.org/pacs/industry.php?txt=N00&cycle=2010 (accessed March 13, 2012).
59. *Citizens United* v. *Federal Election Commission*, 130 S. Ct. 866 (2010).
60. David Carr, "Comic's PAC Is More Than a Gag," *New York Times*, August 21, 2011, http://www.nytimes.ture Summary," http://www.opensecrets.org/pacs/lookup2.php?strID=C00344234 (accessed May 21, 2010).
61. *SpeechNow.org*. v. *Federal Election Commission*, 599 F. (3d Cir.2010).
62. Center for Responsive Politics, "Political Parties: Boehner for Speaker Cmte," http://www.opensecrets.org/parties/affiliatesdetail.php?pacid=C00478354&cycle=2012 (accessed April 27, 2012).

63. SOURCE: Federal Election Commission, "Financial Activity of All Congressional Candidates from 1992 to 2010," includes activity through 12/31/10, www.fec.gov/press/2010_Full_summary_Data.shtml (accessed June 26, 2012).
64. Federal Election Commission, Table 2: PAC Contributions 2009–2010 Through December 31, 2010, http://www.fec.gov/press/bkgnd/cf_summary_info/2010pac_fullsum/36pac%20contributions_2010%20final%20table.pdf]. (accessed June 26, 2012).
65. Federal Election Commission, Table 2: PAC Contributions 2009–2010 Through December 31, 2010, http://www.fec.gov/press/bkgnd/cf_summary_info/2010pac_fullsum/36pac%20contributions_2010%20final%20table.pdf]. (accessed June 26, 2012).
66. J. Quin Monson, "Get On TeleVision vs. Get On the Van: GOTV and the Ground War in 2002," in David B. Magleby and J. Quin Monson, eds., *The Last Hurrah* (Brookings Institution Press, 2004), p. 108.
67. David B. Magleby and Nicole Carlisle Smith, "Party Money in the 2002 Congressional Elections," in David B. Magleby and J. Quin Monson, eds., *The Last Hurrah* (Brookings Institution Press, 2004), p. 54; David B. Magleby and Eric A. Smith, "Party Soft Money in the 2000 Congressional Elections," in David B. Magleby, ed., *The Other Campaign* (Rowman & Littlefield, 2003), pp. 34–35; Marianne Holt, "The Surge in Party Money," in David B. Magleby, ed., *Outside Money* (Rowman & Littlefield, 2000), p. 36; and David B. Magleby, "Conclusions and Implications," in David B. Magleby, ed., *Outside Money* (Rowman & Littlefield, 2000), p. 214.
68. *Federal Election Commission* v. *Wisconsin Right to Life Inc.,* 551 U.S. 449 (2007).
69. *Citizens United* v. *Federal Election Commission*, 130 S. Ct. 876 (2010).
70. http://articles.chicagotribune.com/2010-10-30/news/ct-met-campaign-cash-flood-20101030_1_senate-race-republican-mark-kirk-democrat-alexi-giannoulias (accessed June 26, 2012).
71. Federal Election Commission, "2009-2010 Independent Expenditures", includes activity through 12/31/10, www.fec.gov/press/2010_Full_summary_Data.shtml.
72. *Buckley v. Valeo*, 424 U.S. 1 (1976).
73. Ruth Marcus, "Labor Spent $119 Million for '96 Politics, Study Says; Almost All Contributions Went to Democrats," *Washington Post* (September 10, 1997), p. A19.
74. David B. Magleby, ed., *Outside Money: Soft Money and Issue Advocacy in the 1998 Congressional Elections* (Rowman and Littlefield, 2000), p. 3; David B. Magleby, ed., *The Other Campaign: Soft Money and Issue Advocacy in the 2000 Congressional Elections* (Rowman and Littlefield, 2003), p. 1; David B. Magleby and J. Quin Monson, eds., *The Last Hurrah? Soft Money and Issue Advocacy in the 2002 Congressional Elections* (Brookings Institution Press, 2004), pp. 1–3.
75. Kate Zernike, "Kerry Pressing Swift Boat Case Long After Loss," *New York Times* (May 28, 2006), p. A1.
76. E. J. Dionne, Jr., "Fear of McCain-Feingold," *Washington Post* (December 3, 2002), p. A25.
77. The Campaign Legal Center, "August 7, 2003—Democracy 21: Excerpts of Congressional Sponsors Supreme Court Brief," http://www.campaignlegalcenter.org/index.php?option=com_content&view=article&id=352%3Apr814&catid=36&Itemid=60 (accessed May 21, 2010).
78. David B. Magleby and Kelly D. Patterson, "Campaign Consultants and Direct Democracy: Politics of Citizen Control," in James E. Thurber and Candice J. Nelson, eds., *Campaign Warriors: The Role of Political Consultants in Elections* (Brookings Institution Press, 2000).
79. Ronald Reagan, "Remarks to Administration Officials on Domestic Policy," December 13, 1988, *Weekly Compilation of Presidential Documents,* 24 (December 1988), pp. 1615–1620.
80. Sylvia Tesh, "In Support of Single-Interest Politics," *Political Science Quarterly*, 99 (Spring 1984), pp. 27–44.
81. http://www.fec.gov/info/appfour.htm (accessed, June 26, 2012).
82. Legislative Resource Center's Lobbying Section, telephone interview, April 7, 2004.
83. Matthew Ericson, Haeyoun Park, Alicia Parlapiano, and Derek Willis, "Who's Financing the 'Super PACs,'" *New York Times,* May 7, 2012, www.nytimes.com/interactive/2012/01/31/us/politics/super-pac-donors.html (accessed June 19, 2012); and Michael D. Shear, "Conservative Group Rolls Out Major Ad Campaign," *New York Times*, June 24, http://thecaucus.blogs.nytimes.com/2011/06/24/conservative-group-rolls-out-major-ad-campaign/2011 (accessed June 19, 2012).

6

1. E. E. Schattschneider, *Party Government* (Holt, Rinehart and Winston, 1942), p. 1.
2. See Scott Mainwaring, "Party Systems in the Third Wave," *Journal of Democracy* (July 1998), pp. 67-81.
3. Joseph A. Schlesinger, *Political Parties and the Winning of Office* (University of Michigan Press, 1994).
4. Robert R. Alford and Eugene C. Lee, "Voting Turnout in American Cities," *American Political Science Review* 62 (September), pp. 809–810.
5. Gary W. Cox and Mathew D. McCubbins, *Legislative Leviathan: Party Government in the House* (University of California Press, 1993).
6. David W. Brady and Craig Volden, *Revolving Gridlock: Politics and Policy from Carter to Clinton* (Westview Press, 1998); James A. Thurber, ed., *Divided Democracy: Cooperation and Conflict Between the President and Congress* (CQ Press, 1991); James A. Thurber, ed., *Rivals for Power: Presidential–Congressional Relations* (CQ Press, 1996); Charles O. Jones, *Separate but Equal Branches: Congress and the Presidency* (Chatham House, 1995), Chapters 5 and 6; and Jon R. Bond and Richard Fleisher, *The President in the Legislative Arena* (University of Chicago Press, 1990).
7. *California Democratic Party v. Jones*, 530 U.S. 567 (2000).
8. George Skelton, "California Open Primaries? Give Them a Chance," *Los Angeles Times*, February 11, 2010, http://articles.latimes.com/2010/feb/11/local/la-me-cap11-2010feb11 (accessed March 29, 2010).
9. Judy Treible and Tim Goheen, "Graphic: State caucuses and primaries," *Chicago Tribune*, 2011, available at http://www.chicagotribune.com/news/nationworld/sns-graphics-state-caucuses-and-primaries-gx,0,2199890.graphic (accessed March 23, 2012).
10. "County-Level Map: Republican Primary and Caucus Turnout Down 9%" *Daily Kos*, March 2, 2012. http://www.dailykos.com/story/2012/03/02/107214/county-level-map-republican-primary-caucus-turnout-down-9. (accessed 4.6.12).
11. For an analysis of the potential effects of different electoral rules in the United States, see Todd Donovan and Shawn Bowler, *Reforming the Republic: Democratic Institutions for the New America* (Prentice Hall, 2004).
12. William H. Riker, "The Two-Party System and Duverger's Law: An Essay on the History of Political Science," *American Political Science Review* 76 (December 1982), pp. 753–766. For a classic analysis, see E. E. Schattschneider, *Party Government* (Holt, Rinehart and Winston, 1942).
13. Maurice Duverger, *Party Politics and Pressure Groups* (Nelson, 1972), pp. 23–32.
14. Steven J. Rosenstone, Roy L. Behr, and Edward H. Lazarus, *Third Parties in America: Citizen Response to Major Party Failure,* 2d ed. (Princeton University Press, 1996); see also Xandra Kayden and Eddie Mahe, Jr., *The Party Goes On: The Persistence of the Two-Party System in the United States* (Basic Books, 1985), pp. 143–144. The Republican Party, which started as a third party, was one of the two major parties by 1860, the year Republican Abraham Lincoln won the Presidency; see Lewis L. Gould, *Grand Old Party: A History of the Republicans* (Random House, 2003), pp. 3–17.
15. Dean Lacy and Quin Monson, "The Origins and Impact of Voter Support for Third-Party Candidates: A Case Study of the 1998 Minnesota Gubernatorial Election," *Political Research Quarterly* 55(2), pp. 409–437.
16. On the impact of third parties, see Howard R. Penniman, "Presidential Third Parties and the Modern American Two-Party System," in William J. Crotty, ed., *The Party Symbol* (Freeman, 1980), pp. 101–117; see also Frank Smallwood, *The Other Candidates: Third Parties in Presidential Elections* (University Press of New England, 1983).
17. Benjamin Franklin, George Washington, and Thomas Jefferson, quoted in Richard Hofstadter, *The Idea of a Party System* (University of California Press, 1969), pp. 2, 123.
18. For concise histories of the two parties, see Jules Witcover, *Party of the People: A History of the Democrats* (Random House, 2003); and Gould, *Grand Old Party.*
19. See V. O. Key, Jr., "A Theory of Critical Elections," *Journal of Politics* 17 (February 1955), pp. 3–18; Walter Dean Burnham, *Critical Elections and the Mainsprings of American Politics* (Norton, 1970), pp. 1–10; and E. E. Schattschneider, *The Semisovereign People: A Realist's View of Democracy in America* (Holt, Rinehart and Winston, 1975), pp. 78–80.
20. See Walter Dean Burnham, Critical Elections and the Mainsprings of American Politics (New York: W. W. Norton, 1970), pp. 131–34, and Gerald M. Pomper, "The Decline of the Party in American Elections," Political Science Quarterly 92 (Spring 1977), p. 41.
21. Gould, *Grand Old Party,* p. 88.
22. Ibid.
23. David W. Brady, "Election, Congress, and Public Policy Changes, 1886–1960," in Bruce A. Campbell and Richard Trilling, eds., *Realignment in American Politics: Toward a Theory* (University of Texas Press, 1980), p. 188.
24. L. Sandy Maisel, *Parties and Elections in America: The Electoral Process* (Rowman & Littlefield, 2002), pp. 48–49.
25. Gerald Pomper, "Classification of Presidential Elections," *Journal of Politics* 29 (August 1967), p. 538.
26. During periods of one-party dominance the other party occasionally wins as happened with the election of Woodrow Wilson in 1912 and 1916. See, Gerald Pomper, "Classification of presidential elections," *Journal of Politics* 29, no. 3 (August 1976): 535–566, 549.

27. http://www.u-s-history.com/pages/h1528.html, see also, U.S. Bureau of the Census, *Historical Statistics of the United States, Colonial Times to 1957* (Washington, D.C., 1960), p.70.
28. Earl Black and Merle Black, *The Rise of Southern Republicans* (Belknap Press, 2003).
29. See Byron E. Shafer, *The End of Realignment: Interpreting American Electoral Eras* (University of Wisconsin Press, 1991).
30. See http://www.teaparty.org/about.php.
31. CBS News/New York Times, "The Tea Party Movement: Who They Are," *CBS News*, April 14, 2010, available at http://www.cbsnews.com/htdocs/pdf/poll_tea_party_who_they_are_041410.pdf (accessed August 6, 2012).
32. Michael Cooper, "G.O.P Senate Victory Stuns Democrats," *New York Times*, January 19, 2010, available at http://www.nytimes.com/2010/01/20/us/politics/20election.html (accessed August 6, 2012).
33. Kirk Johnson, "Utah Delegates Oust Three-Term G.O.P Senator From Race," *New York Times*, May 8, 2010, available at http://www.nytimes.com/2010/05/09/us/politics/09utah.html?gwh=39CB142B47CF80B3242559CF135BFBCE
34. Charles S. Bullock, III, "Conclusion: Evaluating Palin, the Tea Party and DeMint Influences," in Charles S. Bullock, III, ed. *Key States, High Stakes: Sarah Palin, the Tea Party and the 2010 Elections.* (Rowman & Littlefield, 2012) p. 217.
35. Charles S. Bullock, III, "Conclusion: Evaluating Palin, the Tea Party and DeMint Influences," in Charles S. Bullock, III, ed. *Key States, High Stakes: Sarah Palin, the Tea Party and the 2010 Elections.*(Rowman & Littlefield, 2012) p. 217.
36. V. O. Key, Jr., *Political Parties and Pressure Groups,* 5th ed. (International, 1964); see also Marjorie Randon Hershey, *Party Politics in America,* 12th ed. (Longman, 2006).
37. Federal Election Commission, "National Party Activity Summarized," press release, October 30, 2006, www.fec.gov/press/press2006/20061030party/20061030party.html.
38. Hershey, *Party Politics in America.*
39. David B. Magleby, J. Quin Monson, and Kelly D. Patterson, "The Lingering Effects of a Night Spent Dancing," in David B. Magleby, J. Quin Monson, and Kelly D. Patterson, eds., *Dancing Without Partners: How Candidates, Parties, and Interest Groups Interact in the Presidential Campaign* (Lanham, MD: Rowman & Littlefield, 2007), pp. 163–167; and David B. Magleby, ed., *The Change Election: Money, Mobilization, and Persuasion in the 2008 Federal Election* (Temple University Press, 2011).
40. The early Republican efforts and advantages over the Democrats are well documented in Thomas B. Edsall, *The New Politics of Inequality* (Norton, 1984); and Gary C. Jacobson, "The Republican Advantage in Campaign Finances," in John E. Chubb and Paul E. Peterson, eds., *New Direction in American Politics* (Brookings Institution Press, 1985), p. 6; see also David B. Magleby and Kelly D. Patterson, "Rules of Engagement: BCRA and Unanswered Questions," in David B. Magleby and Kelly D. Patterson, eds., *The Battle for Congress: Iraq, Scandal, and Campaign Finance in the 2006 Election* (Paradigm, 2008), pp. 33–36.
41. David C. King, "The Polarization of American Political Parties and Mistrust of Government," in Joseph S. Nye, Philip Zelikow, and David C. King, eds., *Why People Don't Trust Government* (Harvard University Press, 1997); and National Election Study, "Important Difference in What Democratic and Republican Parties Stand For, 1952–2000," http://www.electionstudies.org/nesguide/toptable/tab2b_4.htm.
42. Kelly D. Patterson, *Political Parties and the Maintenance of Liberal Democracy* (Columbia University Press, 1996), pp. 30–31.
43. Tom Shales, "Bush, Bringing the Party to Life; From the New Nominee, a Splendid Acceptance Speech," *The Washington Post,* August 19, 1988, p. C1.
44. See James L. Gibson, Cornelius P. Cotter, John F. Bibby, and Robert J. Huckshorn, "Assessing Party Organizational Strength," *American Journal of Political Science* 27 (May 1983), pp. 193–222; see also Cornelius P. Cotter, James L. Gibson, John F. Bibby, and Robert Huckshorn, *Party Organizations in American Politics* (University of Pittsburg Press, 1989).
45. Paul S. Herrnson, *Party Campaigning in the 1980s: Have the National Parties Made a Comeback as Key Players in Congressional Elections?* (Harvard University Press, 1988), p. 122.
46. *Marbury* v. *Madison,* 1 Cranch 137 (1803).
47. See Angus Campbell, Philip E. Converse, Warren E. Miller, and Donald E. Stokes, *The American Voter* (University of Chicago Press, 1960); Norman A. Nie, Sidney Verba, and John R. Petrocik, *The Changing American Voter,* enlarged ed. (Harvard University Press, 1979); and Warren E. Miller and J. Merrill Shanks, *The New American Voter* (Harvard University Press, 1996).
48. Campbell et al., *The American Voter,* pp. 121–128.
49. Ibid.
50. Bruce E. Keith et al., *The Myth of the Independent Voter* (University of California Press, 1992).
51. Nine percent of all voters were Pure Independents in 1956 and 1960; Keith et al., *The Myth of the Independent Voter*, p. 51. In 1992, the figure was also 9 percent; *1992 National Election Study* (Center for Political Studies, University of Michigan, 1992).
52. Jonathan S. Krasno and Daniel E. Seltz, *Buying Time: Television Advertising in the 1998 Congressional Elections,* report of a grant funded by the Pew Charitable Trusts (1998).
53. *Colorado Republican Federal Campaign Committee* v. *Federal Election Commission,* 518 U.S. 604 (1996).
54. "Comparative Data," in the Ace Electoral Knowledge Network Database, http://aceproject.org/epic-en (accessed March 30, 2010).
55. Ndubisi Obiorah, *Political Finance and Democracy in Nigeria* (Center for Law and Social Action, 2004).
56. See, http://www.nationalreview.com/corner/292971/gop-s-superdelegates-brian-bolduc
57. Paul S. Herrnson, *Party Campaigning in the 1980s* (Harvard University Press, 1988), pp. 80–81.

7

1. Brennan Center for Justice, "Citizens Without Proof: A Survey of Americans' Possession of Documentary Proof of Citizenship and Photo Identification," New York University School of Law, November 2006, available at http://www.brennancenter.org/page/-/d/download_file_39242.pdf (accessed March 29, 2012).
2. National Conference of State Legislatures, "2003-2010 Legislative Action," http://www.ncsl.org/legislatures-elections/elections/voter-id.aspx#Legislation
3. Marjorie Randon Hershey, "What We Know about Voter-ID Law, Registration and Turnout." *PS: Political Science and Politics* 42, no. 1 (January 2009), pp. 87-91.
4. *Crawford et al. v. Marion County Election Board et al.,* April 28, 2008. http://www.supremecourt/gov/opinion/07pdf/07-21.pdf
5. John Cornyn, "Voter ID Laws are Reasonable, Constitutional, Necessary," *Statesman.com*, December 17, 2011, http://www.statesman.com/opinion/voter-id-laws-are-reasonable-constitutional-necessary-2038448.html (accessed March 30, 2012).
6. http://www.ncsl.org/legislatures-elections/elections/voter-id-2011-legislation.aspx
7. Matt Laslo, "Virginia Voter ID Law Passes State Senate," American University Radio, March 1, 2012, http://wamu.org/news/12/03/01/virginia_voter_id_law_passes_state_senate (accessed March 29, 2012).
8. David Schultz, "Less than Fundamental: The Myth of Voter Fraud and the Coming of the Second Great Disenfranchisement," *William Mitchell Law Review* 34, no. 2 (2007): 483–532, p. 501.
9. R. Michael Alvarez, Lonna Rae Atkeson and Thad E. Hall, "The New Mexico Election Administration Report: The 2006 November General Election." 2007. Caltech and MIT.
10. Charlie Savage, "Justice Department Blocks Texas on Photo ID for Voting," *The New York Times*, March 12, 2012. http://www.nytimes.com/2012/03/13/us/justice-dept-blocks-texas-photo-id-law.html
11. Robert Coles, *The Political Life of Children* (Atlantic Monthly Press, 2000), pp. 24–25; see also Stephen M. Caliendo, *Teachers Matter: The Trouble with Leaving Political Education to the Coaches* (Greenwood Press, 2000).
12. Caliendo, *Teachers Matter,* pp. 16–17.
13. James Garbarino, *Raising Children in a Socially Toxic Environment* (Jossey-Bass, 1995).
14. Gabriel A. Almond and Sidney Verba, eds. *The Civic Culture Revisited* (Little Brown, 1980), p. 13.
15. J. L. Glanville, "Political Socialization or Selection? Adolescent Extracurricular Participation and Political Activity in Early Adulthood," *Social Science Quarterly* 80 (1999), p. 279.
16. National Association of Secretaries of State, *New Millennium Project, Part I: American Youth Attitudes on Policies, Citizenship, Government, and Voting* (Author, 1999); and "Political Interest on the Rebound Among the Nation's Freshmen," Higher Education Research Institute, Fall 2003, www.gseis.ucla.edu/heri/03_press_release.pdf.
17. Margaret Stimmann Branson, "Making the Case for Civic Education: Educating Young People for Responsible Citizenship," paper presented at the Conference for Professional Development for Program Trainers, Manhattan Beach, Calif., February 25, 2001.
18. Russell J. Dalton, *The Good Citizen: How a Younger Generation is Reshaping American Politics* (Washington, D.C.: CQ Press, 2008), 36, 66, 73, 162.
19. B. Bradford Brown, Sue Ann Eicher, and Sandra Petrie, "The Importance of Peer Group ("Crowd") Affiliation in Adolescence," *Journal of Adolescence* 9 (March 1986), pp. 73–96.
20. Kenneth Feldman and Theodore M. Newcomb, *The Impact of College on Students,* Vol. 2 (Jossey-Bass, 1969), pp. 16–24, 49–56; see also David O.

Sears and Nicholas A. Valentino, "Politics Matters: Political Events as Catalysts for Preadult Socialization," *American Political Science Review* 91 (March 1997), pp. 45–65.

21. Jody C. Baumgartner and Jonathan S. Morris, "MyFaceTube Politics: Social Networking Web Sites and Political Engagement of Young Adults," *Social Science Computer Review* 28 (2010): 24–44.
22. Larry D. Rosen, "Poke Me: How Social Networks Can Both Help and Harm Our Kids" paper presented at the American Psychological Association 119th Convention, Washington, D.C., (August 2011).
23. Daniel B. German, "The Role of the Media in Political Socialization and Attitude Formation Toward Racial/Ethnic Minorities in the U.S.," in Robert F. Farnen, ed., *Nationalism, Ethnicity, and Identity: Cross National and Comparative Perspective* (Transaction, 2004), p. 287.
24. James G. Gimpel, J. Celeste Lay, and Jason E. Schuknecht, *Cultivating Democracy: Civic Environments and Political Socialization in America* (Brookings Institution Press, 2003), p. 127 (see Chapter 5).
25. Robert D. Putnam, "The Rebirth of American Civic Life," *Boston Globe,* March 2, 2008, p. D9.
26. Robert D. Putnam, "Bowling Alone: America's Declining Social Capital," Journal of Democracy 6 (January 1995), pp. 65–78; see also Robert D. Putnam, Bowling Alone: The Collapse and Revival of American Community (Simon & Schuster, 2000); and Robert D. Putnam, "Bowling Together," The American Prospect 13 (February 2002), p. 20.
27. For a general discussion of political knowledge, see Michael Delli Carpini and Scott Keeter, *What Americans Know About Politics and Why It Matters* (Yale University Press, 1996).
28. *The 2000 National Election Study,* Center for Political Studies, University of Michigan; see also the NES Guide to Public Opinion and Electoral Behavior, www.umich.edu/nes/nesguide/nesguide.htm.
29. Erikson and Tedin, *American Public Opinion,* p. 304.
30. http://pewresearch.org/databank/dailynumber/?NumberID=1056
31. http://www.electionstudies.org/nesguide/toptable/tab6d_5.htm (accessed 3.17.12).
32. *The 2004 National Election Study* (Center for Political Studies, University of Michigan, 2004).
33. http://www.gallup.com/poll/111664/Gallup-Daily-Obama-Continues-Outpace-McCain.aspx (accessed November 7, 2008. Note: We removed the "no opinion" and percentaged the other categories to sum to 100 percent.
34. Thomas D. Snyder, Sally A. Dillow, and Charlene M. Hoffman, "Number of Persons Age 18 and Over, by Highest Level of Education Attained, Age, Sex, and Race/Ethnicity: 2005," *Digest of Education Statistics 2007* (U.S. Government Printing Office, 2008), p. 24.
35. Quoted in Hadley Cantril, *Gauging Public Opinion* (Princeton University Press, 1944), p. viii.
36. John G. Geer, *From Tea Leaves to Opinion Polls: A Theory of Democratic Leadership* (Columbia University Press, 1996).
37. Norman J. Ornstein and Amy S. Mitchell, "The Permanent Campaign: The Trend Toward Continuous Campaigning Stems from Advances in Technology and the Proliferation of Public Opinion Polls," *World and I* 12 (January 1997): 48–55.
38. "Do You Approve or Disapprove of the Way George W. Bush Is Handling the Situation with Iraq?" CBS News and *New York Times* Poll, May 3, 2003; and May 20, 2004, www.pollingreport.com/iraq2.htm.
39. CBS News and *New York Times,* "Looking Ahead to the General Election," www.cbsnews .com/htdocs/pdf/apr08b_genelec.pdf.
40. Gallup, "Gallup Daily: Obama Job Approval," http://www.gallup.com/poll/113980/gallup-daily-obama-job-approval.aspx (accessed April 16, 2010).
41. http://www.gallup.com/poll/116500/presidential-approval-ratings-george-bush.aspx.
42. Lawrence R. Jacobs and Robert R. Shapiro, *Politicians Don't Pander* (University of Chicago Press, 2000), p. 3.
43. Robert S. Erikson and Kent L. Tedin, *American Public Opinion: Its Origins, Content, and Impact,* 6th ed. (Longman, 2001), pp. 272–273. On the centrality of the reelection motive, see David R. Mayhew, *Congress: The Electoral Connection* (Yale University Press, 1974).
44. ANES Guide to Public Opinion and Electoral Behavior, "Liberal-Conservative Self-Identification 1972-2008," available at http://www.electionstudies.org/nesguide/toptable/tab3_1.htm (accessed April 12, 2012).
45. See Samuel G. Freedman, Santorum's Catholicism Proves a Draw to Evangelicals, *The New York Times*, March 23, 2012, http://www.nytimes.com/2012/03/24/us/santorums-catholicism-draws-evangelicals.html (accessed April 27, 2012)
46. Jonathan Rauch, "The Accidental Radical," National Journal, July 26, 2003, pp. 2404–2410.
47. Kathleen Day, *S&L Hell: The People and the Politics Behind the $1 Trillion Savings and Loan Scandal* (Norton, 1993).
48. Yuluya Demyanyk and Otto Van Hemert, "Understanding the Subprime Mortgage Crisis," *Review of Financial Studies* 24 (2011):1846-1880.
49. Sylvia Nasar, "Even Among the Well-Off, the Rich Get Richer," New York Times, March 5, 1992, p. A1.
50. Robert Pear and Jennifer Steinhauer, "Tax Cut Extension Passes; Everyone Claims a Win," *New York Times,* February 17, 2012, http://www.nytimes.com/2012/02/18/us/politics/congress-acts-to-extend-payroll-tax-cut-and-aid-to-jobless.html?_r=1 (accessed April 27, 2012).
51. Jackie Calmes, Obama Goes on Offensive Over Taxes on Wealthy, *New York Times,* April 10, 2012, http://www.nytimes.com/2012/04/11/us/politics/obama-to-make-case-for-buffett-rule.html?hp (accessed April 27, 2012).
52. Irving Howe, Socialism and America (Harcourt, 1985); and Michael Harrington, Socialism: Past and Future (Arcade, 1989).
53. Daniel Yergin and Joseph Stanislaw, The Commanding Heights: The Battle Between Government and the Marketplace That Is Remaking the Modern World (Simon & Schuster, 1998).
54. John Zogby, "Ron Paul and the Libertarians Can't Be Discounted," *Forbes*, November 9, 2011, http://www.forbes.com/sites/johnzogby/2011/11/09/paul-libertarians-cant-be-discounted/ (accessed April 27, 2012).
55. Nicole B. Ellison, Charles Steinfield, and Cliff Lampe, "The Benefits of Facebook 'Friends': Social Capital and College Students' Use of Online Social Network Sites," *Journal of Computer-Mediated Communication* 12 (2007), Art. 1.
56. Data from the American National Election Studies, Center for Political Studies, University of Michigan, 1948-2004, www.electionstudies.org/studypages/download/datacenter_all.htm.
57. http://www.electionstudies.org/nesguide/toptable/tab6b_1.htm
58. *The 2008 National Election Study.*
59. Frank R. Parker, *Black Votes Count: Political Empowerment in Mississippi After 1965* (University of North Carolina Press, 1990), p. 3.
60. Bernard Grofman and Lisa Handley, "The Impact of the Voting Rights Act on Black Representation in Southern State Legislatures," *Legislative Studies Quarterly* 16 (February 1991), pp. 111–128.
61. http://www.senate.gov/reference/resources/pdf/R41647.pdf
62. Raymond E. Wolfinger and Steven J. Rosenstone, "The Effect of Registration Laws on Voter Turnout," *American Political Science Review* 72 (March 1978), p. 41.
63. International Institute for Democracy and Electoral Assistance, "Voter Turnout from 1945 to Date: A Global Report on Political Participation," www.idea.int/voter_turnout/index.html.
64. Ibid., p. 24.
65. Raymond E. Wolfinger and Steven J. Rosenstone, *Who Votes?* (Yale University Press, 1980), pp. 78, 88.
66. Federal Election Commission, "The Impact of the National Voter Registration Act on Federal Elections 1999–2000," www.fec.gov.
67. See Raymond E. Wolfinger and Ben Highton, "Estimating the Effects of the National Voter Registration Act of 1993," *Political Behavior* (June 1998), pp. 79–104; and Raymond E. Wolfinger and Jonathan Hoffman, "Registering and Voting with Motor Voter," *PS: Political Science & Politics* (March 2001), pp. 85–92.
68. Marjorie Randon Hershey, "What We Know about Voter-ID Laws, Registration, and Turnout," *PS: Political Science and Politics* 42 (2009) 87-91, http://journals.cambridge.org/action/displayFulltext?type=6&fid=3260784&jid=PSC&volumeId=42&issueId=01&aid=3260780&bodyId=&membershipNumber=&societyETOCSession=&fulltextType=BT&fileId=S1049096509090234
69. Quin Monson and Lindsay Nielson, "Mobilizing the Early Voter," paper presented at the annual meeting of the Midwest Political Science Association, Chicago, Ill., April 3–6, 2008; and Michael P. McDonald and Thomas Schaller, "Voter Mobilization in the 2008 Presidential Election," in David B. Magleby, ed., *The Change Election: Money, Mobilization, and Persuasion in the 2008 Federal Elections* (Temple University Press, 2011).
70. U.S. Census Bureau, "Voting and Registration in the Election of November 2004," www .census.gov/prod/2006pubs/p20–556.pdf.
71. David B. Magleby, "Participation in Mail Ballot Elections," *Political Research Quarterly* 40 (1987), p. 81.
72. Paul Gronke, Eva Galanes-Rosenbaum, and Peter A. Miller, "Early Voting and Turnout," *PS: Political Science & Politics* 40 (2007), pp. 639–645.
73. Fredreka Schouten, "Civil rights groups, Democrats fight early-voting limits," *USA Today*, December 11, 2011, http://www.usatoday.com/news/politics/story/2011-12-11/early-voting-laws-minority/51816886/1 (accessed April 27, 2012).
74. Fredreka Schouten, Civil rights groups, Democrats fight early-voting limits, *USA Today*, December 11, 2011, http://www.usatoday.com/news/politics/story/2011-12-11/early-voting-laws-minority/51816886/1 (accessed April 27, 2012).
75. For a discussion of the differences in the turnout between presidential and midterm elections, see James E. Campbell, "The Presidential Surge and

Its Midterm Decline in Congressional Elections, 1868-1988," *Journal of Politics* 53 (May 1991), pp. 477–487.

76. David E. Rosenbaum, "Democrats Keep Solid Hold on Congress," *New York Times,* November 9, 1988, p. A24; Louis V. Gerstner, "Next Time, Let Us Boldly Vote as No Democracy Has Before," *USA Today,* November 16, 1998, p. A15; and Michael P. McDonald and Thomas Schaller, "Voter Mobilization in the 2008 Presidential Election," in David B. Magleby, ed., *The Change Election: Money, Mobilization, and Persuasion in the 2008 Federal Elections* (Temple University Press, 2011), p. 89.
77. Data from Curtis Gans, "President Bush, Mobilization Drives Propel Turnout to Post-1968 High; Kerry, Democratic Weakness Shown," *Center for Voting and Democracy,* November 4, 2004, www.fairvote.org/reports/csae2004electionreport.pdf.
78. http://www.idea.int/vt/compulsory_voting.cfm
79. Wolfinger and Rosenstone, *Who Votes?,* p. 102.
80. For a discussion of mobilization efforts and race, see Jan Leighley, *Strength in Numbers? The Political Mobilization of Racial and Ethnic Minorities* (Princeton University Press, 2001).
81. New York Times, Portrait of the Electorate: Table of Detailed Results, *New York Times,* November 6, 2010, and http://www.nytimes.com/interactive/2010/11/07/weekinreview/20101107-detailed-exitpolls.html (accessed April 27, 2012).http://www.cnn.com/ELECTION/2008/results/polls (accessed November 6, 2008).
82. U.S. Census Bureau, "Reported Voting and Registration by Race, Hispanic Origin, Sex, and Age Groups: November 1964 to 2008," *Voting and Registration,* July 2009, http://www.census .gov/hhes/www/socdemo/voting/publications/historical/index.html (accessed April 29, 2010).
83. Ibid.
84. http://pewresearch.org/pubs/1790/2010-midterm-elections-exit-poll-hispanic-vote
85. Howard W. Stanley and Richard G. Niemi, *Vital Statistics on Politics, 1999–2000* (CQ Press, 2000), pp. 120–121; and Harold W. Stanley and Richard G. Niemi, *Vital Statistics on Politics, 2011–2012* (CQ Press, 2011), pp. 116-17, 126–127.
86. http://www.cnn.com/ELECTIONS/2008/results/polls (accessed November 6, 2008).
87. http://www.cnn.com/ELECTIONS/2008/results/polls (accessed November 6, 2008).
88. http://www.time.com/time/politics/article/0,8599,1708570,00.html (accessed April 16, 2010); and Heather Smith, Rock the Vote Executive Director, interview with David B. Magleby (March 25, 2009).
89. The Center for Information & Research on Civic Learning and Engagement, "Turnout by Education, Race, and Gender and Other 2008 Youth Voting Statistics," November 2008, http://www.civicyouth.org/?p=324 (accessed April 21, 2010).
90. http://www.cnn.com/election results – 2012 Election Center (accessed November 8, 2012).
91. David B. Magleby, ed., *The Change Election: Money, Mobilization, and Persuasion in the 2008 Federal Elections* (Temple University Press, 2011).
92. http://www.cnn.com/ELECTIONS/2008/results/polls (accessed November 6, 2008).
93. U.S. Census Bureau, "Voting and Registration in the Election of November 2000," www .census.gov/prod/2002pubs/p20–542.pdf.
94. Christopher R. Ellis, Joseph Daniel Ura, and Jenna Ashley-Robinson, "The Dynamic Consequences of Nonvoting in American National Elections," *Political Research Quarterly* 59 (June 2006), pp. 232–233.
95. Austin Ranney, "Nonvoting Is Not a Social Disease," *Public Opinion* (October–November 1983), pp. 16–19.
96. Sidney Verba, "Would the Dream of Political Equality Turn Out to Be a Nightmare?" *Perspectives on Politics* 4 (December 2003), pp. 667–672.
97. E. E. Schattschneider, *The Semisovereign People* (Dryden Press, 1975), p. 96.
98. Stephen Earl Bennett and David Resnick, "The Implications of Nonvoting for Democracy in the United States," *American Journal of Political Science* 84 (August 1990), pp. 771–802.
99. David B. Magleby, Candice J. Nelson, and Mark C. Westlye, "The Myth of the Independent Voter Revisited" Working Paper 10-01, Center for the Study of Elections and Democracy, Brigham Young University, January 2010. http://csed.byu.edu/Assets/Magleby%20Nelson%20Westlye%202010.pdf].
100. Ibid
101. http://www.whitehouse.gov/history/presidents/ (accessed November 8, 2008).
102. David Menefee-Libey, *The Triumph of Campaign-Centered Politics* (Chatham House/Seven Bridges Press, 2000).
103. J. Merrill Shanks and Warren E. Miller, "Policy Direction and Performance Evaluation: Complementary Explanations of the Reagan Elections," *British Journal of Political Science* 20 (1990), pp. 143-235; and Warren E. Miller and J. Merrill Shanks, "Policy Direction and Performance Evaluation: Comparing George Bush's Victory with Those of Ronald Reagan in 1980-1984," paper presented at the annual meeting of the American Political Science Association, Atlanta, Ga., August 31-September 2, 1989.
104. Amihai Glazer, "The Strategy of Candidate Ambiguity," *American Political Science Review* 84 (March 1990), pp. 237-241.
105. Robert S. Erikson and David W. Romero, "Candidate Equilibrium and the Behavioral Model of the Vote," *American Political Science Review* 84 (December 1990), p. 1122.
106. Morris P. Fiorina, *Retrospective Voting in American National Elections* (Yale University Press, 1981).
107. Cable News Network, "Exit Polls Election 2000," www.cnn.com/ELECTION/2000/results/index.epolls.html (last accessed July 12, 2008).
108. Gerald H. Kramer, "Short-Term Fluctuations in U.S. Voting Behavior, 1896-1964," American Political Science Review 65 (March 1971), pp. 131-143; see also Edward R. Tufte, "Determinants of the Outcomes of Midterm Congressional Elections," *American Political Science Review* (September 1975), pp. 812-826; and Andrew E. Busch, *Horses in Midstream: U.S. Midterm Elections and Their Consequences* (University of Pittsburgh Press, 1999).
109. John R. Hibbing and John R. Alford, "The Educational Impact of Economic Conditions: Who Is Held Responsible?" *American Journal of Political Science* 25 (August 1981), pp. 423-439; and Morris P. Fiorina, "Who Is Held Responsible? Further Evidence on the Hibbing-Alford Thesis," *American Journal of Political Science* (February 1983), pp. 158-164.
111. David B. Magleby, "Electoral Politics as Team Sport: Advantage to the Democrats," in John C. Green and Daniel J. Coffey, eds., *The State of the Parties: The Changing Role of Contemporary American Parties* (Rowman & Littlefield, 2011).

8

1. James Meikle, "Foster Friess: The Man atop the Horse Bankrolling Rick Santorum." The Guardian, 08 Feb 2012. http://www.guardian.co.uk/world/2012/feb/08/foster-friess-rick-santorum. Accessed 3 April 2012, see also Jim Rutenberg, "Santorum Upsets G.O.P. Race With Three Victories," *New York Times*, February 7, 2012), Accessed April 3, 2012.
2. Campaign Finance Institute, "Obama's Small-Dollar Percentage Down Slightly in February, Santorum's Stayed High; Romney's Stayed Low." Campaign Finance Institute 22 March 2012. http://cfinst.org/Press/PReleases/12-03-22/Obama%E2%80%99s_Small-Dollar_Percentage_Down_Slightly_in_February_Santorum%E2%80%99s_Stayed_High_Romney%E2%80%99s_Stayed_Low.aspx Accessed 3 May 2012.
3. Legal Information Institute. Citizens United v. Federal Election Commission. Cornell University Law School. http://www.law.cornell.edu/supct/html/08-205.ZS.html>. Accessed 3 May 2012.
4. SCOTUS Blog. SpeechNow.org v. FEC. Bloomberg Law. http://www.scotusblog.com/case-files/cases/speechnow-org-v-fcc/Accessed 3 May 2012.
5. Nicholas Confessore, "New G.O.P. Help from Casino Mogul," *New York Times,* June 6, 2012, http://www.nytimes.com/2012/06/7/us/politics/sheldon-adelson-injects-more-cash-into-gop-groups.html (accessed Oct. 12, 2012).
6. Campaign Finance Institute, "Obama's Small-Dollar Percentage Down Slightly in February, Santorum's Stayed High; Romney's Stayed Low." Campaign Finance Institute 22 March 2012. http://cfinst.org/Press/PReleases/12-03-22/Obama%E2%80%99s_Small-Dollar_Percentage_Down_Slightly_in_February_Santorum%E2%80%99s_Stayed_High_Romney%E2%80%99s_Stayed_Low.aspx Accessed 3 May 2012.
7. T.W. Farnam, Study: Negative campaign ads much more frequent, vicious than in primaries past, *Washington Post*, February 20, 2012, http://www.washingtonpost.com/politics/study-negative-campaign-ads-much-more-frequent-vicious-than-in-primaries-past/2012/02/14/gIQAR7ifPR_story.html (accessed May 7, 2012).
8. U.S. Census Bureau, "Number of Elected Officials Exceeds Half Million—Almost All Are with Local Governments," press release, January 30, 1995.
9. U.S. Senate, www.senate.gov/general/contact_information/senators_cfm.cfm.
10. Associated Press, "Voters Retain State Term Limits," November 4, 2008, http://www.kxmb.com/News/293253.asp (accessed November 6, 2008).
11. *U.S. Term Limits Inc.* v. *Thornton,* 514 U.S. 799 (1995).
12. For an insightful examination of electoral rules, see Bernard Grofman and Arend Lijphart, eds., *Electoral Laws and Their Political Consequences* (Agathon Press, 1986).
13. New York State Board of Elections, "2009 Election Results: 23rd Congressional District," December 15, 2009, http://www.elections .state.ny.us/NYSBOE/Elections/2009/Special/23rdCDSpecial VoteResults.pdf (accessed May 19, 2010).
14. Arend Lijphart, "The Political Consequences of Electoral Laws, 1945–85," *American Political Science Review* 84 (June 1990), pp. 481–495; see also David M. Farrell, *Electoral Systems: A Comparative Introduction* (Macmillan, 2001).

15. There was one faithless elector in 2000 from the District of Columbia who abstained rather than cast her vote for Al Gore in order to protest the lack of congressional representation for Washington, D.C. See www.cnn.com/2001/ALLPOLITICS/stories/01/06/electoral.vote/index.html. The Electoral College vote in 2004 had one faithless elector, an elector from Minnesota who voted for John Edwards instead of John Kerry.
16. As noted, one of Gore's electors abstained, reducing his vote from 267 to 266; www.cnn.com/2001/ALLPOLITICS/stories/01/06/electoral.vote/index.html.
17. Paul D. Schumaker and Burdett A. Loomis, *Choosing a President: The Electoral College and Beyond* (Seven Bridges Press, 2002), p. 60; see also George Rabinowitz and Stuart Elaine MacDonald, "The Power of the States in U.S. Presidential Elections," *American Political Science Review* 80 (March 1986), pp. 65–87 and Dany M. Adkison and Christopher Elliott, "The Electoral College: A Misunderstood Institution," *PS: Political Science and Politics* 30 (March 1997), pp. 77–80.
18. Ryan L. Claasen, David B. Magleby, J. Quin Monson, and Kelly D. Patterson, "At Your Service: Voter Evaluations of Poll Worker Performance," *American Politics Research* 36 (July 2008): 612–634.
19. See, for example, David R. Mayhew, *Congress: The Electoral Connection* (Yale University Press, 1974); Richard F. Fenno, Jr., *Home Style: House Members in Their Districts* (Little, Brown, 1978); and James E. Campbell, "The Return of Incumbents: The Nature of Incumbency Advantage," *Western Political Quarterly* 36 (September 1983), pp. 434–444.
20. Gary King and Andrew Gelman, "Systemic Consequences of Incumbency Advantage in U.S. House Elections," *American Journal of Political Science* 35 (February 1991), pp. 110–137.
21. Alan I. Abramowitz, "Economic Conditions, Presidential Popularity, and Voting Behavior in Midterm Congressional Elections," *Journal of Politics* 47 (February 1985), pp. 31–43 see also Gary C. Jacobson, *The Politics of Congressional Elections,* 5th ed. (Addison-Wesley, 2001), pp. 146–153.
22. See Edward R. Tufte, *Political Control of the Economy* (Princeton University Press, 1978); see also his "Determinants of the Outcomes of Midterm Congressional Elections," *American Political Science Review* 69 (September 1975), pp. 812–826. For a more recent discussion of the same subject, see Jacobson, *Politics of Congressional Elections,* pp. 123–178.
23. Alan I. Abramowitz and Jeffrey A. Segal, "Determinants of the Outcomes of U.S. Senate Elections," *Journal of Politics* 48 (1986), pp. 433–439.
24. David B. Magleby and Kelly D. Patterson, eds., *The Battle for Congress: Iraq, Scandal, and Campaign Finance in the 2006 Election* (Paradigm, 2008).
25. Rhodes Cook, "Congress and Primaries: Looking for Clues to a Tidal Wave," *The Wall Street Journal,* July 24, 2008, http://blogs.wsj.com/politicalperceptions/2008/07/24/Congressional-Primaries-looking-for-clues-to-tidal-wave/.
26. Linda L. Fowler and Robert D. McClure, *Political Ambition: Who Decides to Run for Congress* (Yale University Press, 1989); and Paul S. Herrnson, *Congressional Elections: Campaigning at Home and in Washington,* 5th ed. (CQ Press, 2007), p. 45.
27. David McKay, *American Politics and Society*, 7th ed., Riley-Blackwell, 2009, p. 147; see also, . Kathleen Hall Jamieson, *Everything You Think You Know About Politics...and Why You're Wrong* (Basic Books, 2000), p. 38.
28. For a discussion of different explanations of the impact of incumbency, see Keith Krehbiel and John R. Wright, "The Incumbency Effect in Congressional Elections: A Test of Two Explanations," *American Journal of Political Science* 27 (February 1983), p. 140.
29. Harold W. Stanley and Richard G. Niemi, *Vital Statistics on American Politics 2011–2012* (CQ Press, 2011), pp. 46–47.
30. Federal Election Commission, "Financial Activity of General Election Congressional Candidates from 1992 to 2010," includes activity through 12/31/10, www.fec.gov/press/2010_Full_summary_Data.shtml.
31. For an account of the tone of outside money advertising see David B. Magleby and J. Quin Monson, eds. *The Last Hurrah" Soft Money and Issue Advocacy in the 2002 Congressional Elections.* (Brookings Institution Press, 2004) p. 6.
32. Alex Isenstadt, "Anti-incumbent PAC winds down for now," *Politico,* July 25, 2012, (accessed November 6, 2012). http://www.politico.com/news/stories/0712/89i94.html; "Campaign for Primary Accountability," OpenSecrets.org, November 5, 2012, (accessed November 6, 2012), http://www.opensecrets.org/paces/lookup2.pohp?strID=C00502849.
33. Candice J. Nelson, "Spending in the 2000 Elections," in David B. Magleby, ed., *Financing the 2000 Election* (Brookings Institution Press, 2002), pp. 28–30.
34. Jonathan S. Krasno, *Challengers, Competition, and Reelection: Comparing Senate and House Elections* (Yale University Press, 1994), p. 2.
35. Alan I. Abramowitz, "Explaining Senate Election Outcomes," *American Political Science Review* 82 (June 1988), pp. 385–403.
36. Joseph Morton, "Kerrey, Reid Talked Committee Spots," *Omaha World-Herald*, March 8, 2012, http://www.omaha.com/article/20120308/NEWS01/703089907 (accessed on April 24, 2012).
37. David B. Magleby, "More Bang for the Buck: Campaign Spending in Small State U.S. Senate Elections," paper presented at the annual meeting of the Western Political Science Association, Salt Lake City, Utah (March 30–April 1, 1989).
38. Scott Shepard, "Politicians Already Looking to 2008 Election," *Austin (Texas) American-Statesman,* February 6, 2005; and Associated Press, "Former Bush Aide: 2008 Democratic Nomination Belongs to Hillary," April 30, 2005.
39. Alexander Burns and Jonathan Martin, Rick Perry Fundraising Haul Signals Long GOP Slog, *Politico*, October 5, 2011, http://www.politico.com/news/stories/1011/65261.html (accessed April 25, 2012).
40. Arthur Hadley, *Invisible Primary* (Prentice Hall, 1976).
41. Zachary A. Goldfarb, Gingrich fails to win spot on Virginia primary ballot, *Washington Post*, December 24, 2011, http://www.washingtonpost.com/politics/gingrich-fails-to-win-spot-on-virginia-primary-ballot/2011/12/24/gIQAnErBGP_story.html (accessed April 25, 2012).
42. Joe Hallett, "Santorum loses 9 Ohio delegates," *Columbus Dispatch*, February 16, 2012, http://www.dispatch.com/content/stories/local/2012/02/16/santorum-loses-9-ohio-delegates.html (accessed April 25, 2012).
43. http://www.fec.gov/press/press2012/20120330RoemerCertif.shtml.
44. The Green Papers Presidential Primaries 2012 Democratic Delegate Vote Allocation. The Green Papers. Last modified 3 May 2012. http://www.thegreenpapers.com/P12/D-Del.phtml. Accessed 4 May 2012; See also 2012 Republican Delegates. Real Clear Politics. http://www.realclearpolitics.com/epolls/2012/president/republican_delegate_count.html. Accessed 4 May 2012.
45. The descriptions of these types of primaries are drawn from James W. Davis, *Presidential Primaries,* rev. ed. (Greenwood Press, 1984), Chapter 3. See pp. 56–63 for specifics on each state (and Puerto Rico). This material is used with the permission of the publisher.
46. Paul T. David and James W. Caesar, *Proportional Representation in Presidential Nominating Politics* (University Press of Virginia, 1980), pp. 9–11.
47. See Rhodes Cook, *Race for the Presidency: Winning the 2004 Nomination* (CQ Press, 2004), p. 5; see also the Republican National Committee, www.rnc.org.
48. Staff Report, Details of GOP delegate allocation, *Washington Post*, January 13, 2012, http://www.washingtonpost.com/wp-srv/special/politics/primary-tracker/delegate-allocation/ (accessed April 25, 2012).
49. The Green Papers Republican Detailed Delegate Allocation - 2012. http://www.thegreenpapers.com/P12/R-Alloc.phtml).
50. By combining the presidential primary vote with the regularly scheduled June 2012 primary the state saved approximately $100 million. See Jeff Zeleny, Primary Calendar Stirs Republican Anxiety, *New York Times*, July 25, 2011, http://www.nytimes.com/2011/07/26/us/politics/26primary.html?pagewanted=all (accessed May 30, 2012).
51. Lesley Clark, "DNC Votes to Strip Florida of Delegates: Florida's Status as a Key Presidential Prize Is in Doubt, with National Democratic Party Leaders Rejecting a State Plan to Hold an Early Primary," *Miami Herald,* August 26, 2007; see also "Campaign Briefing: On the Trail," *Newsday*, December 2, 2007, p. A3.
52. Rosalind S. Helderman, Florida takes blame for nasty GOP race, *The Washington Post*, February 5, 2012, Suburban Edition.
53. Federal Election Commission, "2012 Presidential Primary Dates and Candidates Filing Deadlines for Ballot Access," March 30, 2012, http://www.fec.gov/pubrec/fe2012/2012pdates.pdf.
54. *California Democratic Party et al., Petitioners* v. *Bill Jones, Secretary of State of California et al.*, 530 U.S. 567 (2000).
55. David Redlawsk and Arthur Sanders, "Groups and Grassroots in the Iowa Caucuses," in David B. Magleby, ed., *Outside Money in the 2000. Presidential Primaries and Congressional Elections,* in *PS: Political Science and Politics* (June 2001), p. 270; see also Iowa Caucus Project 2004, www.iowacaucus.org.
56. Senator Clinton said that her campaign had "been less successful in caucuses because it brings out the activist base of the Democratic Party." Of these activists, she said, "I don't agree with them. They know I don't agree with them. So they flood into these caucuses and dominate them and really intimidate people who actually show up to support me." See, Perry Bacon, Jr., "Clinton Blames MoveOn for Caucus Losses," *The Washington Post,* blog.washingtonpost.com/the-trail/2008/04/19/clinton_blames_moveon_for_cauc.html.
57. CNN Exit Polls, http://www.cnn.com/election/2012/primaries/state.
58. Jennifer Jacobs, 2012 GOP caucus count unresolved, *Des Moines Register and Tribune*, January 19, 2012, http://caucuses.desmoinesregister.com/2012/01/19/register-exclusive-2012-gop-caucus-count-unresolved/ (accessed April 26, 2012).
59. The viewership of conventions has declined as the amount of time devoted to conventions dropped. In 1988, Democrats averaged 27.1 million viewers and Republicans 24.5 million. By 1996, viewership for the Democrats was 18 million viewers on average; for the Republicans, it was 16.6 million. See John Carmody, "The TV Column," *The Washington Post,* September 2, 1996, p. D4. Viewership figures improved somewhat in 2000: Democrats

averaged 20.6 million viewers and Republicans 19.2 million. See Don Aucoin, "Democrats Hold TV Ratings Edge," *The Boston Globe,* August 19, 2000, p. F3; and Jim Rutenberg and Brain Stelter, "Conventions, Anything but Dull, Are a TV Hit," *New York Times,* September 6, 2008.

60. David Bauder, "Obama Speech Gets 35.7 Million Viewers," ABC News, September 7, 2012, http://abcnews.go.com/Entertainment/wierStory/democratic-convention-beats-football-ratings-17176611#.UE5Xro11TYg
61. Barry Goldwater, speech to the Republican National Convention accepting the Republican nomination for president, July 16, 1964, www.washingtonpost.com/wp-srv/politics/daily/may98/goldwaterspeech.htm.
62. Acceptance speech at the 1980 Convention, July 17, 1980, http://www.nationalcenter .org/ReaganConvention1980.html.
63. Jeff Fishel, *Presidents and Promises* (CQ Press, 1984), pp. 26–28.
64. Joe Von Kanel and Hal Quinley, "Exit Polls: Obama Wins Big Among Young, Minority Voters," *CNN Politics.com,* November 4, 2008, http://www.cnn.com/2008/POLITICS/11/04/exit.polls/ (accessed April 28, 2010).
65. http://www.sos.wa.gov/_assets/elections/Appearing-on-the-Presidential-ballot.pdf (accessed April 26, 2012).
66. See Colorado Secretary of State, Statement of Intent for: President & Vice President, http://www.sos.state.co.us/pubs/elections/Candidates/PresidentStmtOfIntent.html (accessed April 26, 2012)]; however candidates can also qualify with 5,000 signatures instead of the $500 fee [See Colorado Secretary of State, Petition Nomination for: President & Vice President, http://www.sos.state.co.us/pubs/elections/Candidates/PresidentPetition.html (accessed April 26, 2012)].
    Louisiana charges a $500 fee for independent candidates; as with Colorado, candidates need to either pay the fee or get nominating signatures [See Louisiana Secretary of State, Qualifying Fees/Nominating Petitions to Qualify for Office, http://www.sos.la.gov/tabid/160/Default.aspx (accessed April 26, 2012)].
67. North Carolina State Board of Elections, "Fact Sheet: Running for President of the United States of America," http://www.sboe.stak .nc.us/GetDocument.aspx?id=308.
68. Americans Elect, A Statement from Americans Elect, May 17, 2012, http://www.americanselect.org/news/5-2012/release (accessed May 30, 2012).
69. 2012 Primary Debate Schedule. 2012 Presidential Election News. http://www.2012presidentialelectionnews.com/2012-debate-schedule/2011-2012-primary-debate-schedule?wpmp_switcher=mobile Accessed 15 May 2012.
70. http://www.debates.org/index.php?page=candidate-selection-process. Accessed April 27, 2012.
71. Commission on Presidential Debates, www.debates.org/pages/news_040617_p.html.
72. "The Great Ad Wars of 2004," *New York Times,* November 11, 2004, www.polisci.wisc.edu/tvadvertising/Press_Clippings/Press_Clipping_PDFs/110104% 20NYTIMES_AD_GRAPHIC.pdf.
73. http://wiscadproject.wisc.edu/wiscads_report_031710.pdf
74. University of Wisconsin–Madison and the Brennan Center for Justice at NYU School of Law, "Political Advertising Nearly Tripled in 2000 with Half-a-Million More TV Ads," press release, March 14, 2001; David B. Magleby, "Elections as Team Sports: Spending by Candidates, Political Parties, and Interest Groups in the 2008 Election Cycle," in David B. Magleby, ed., *The Change Election: Money, Mobilization, and Persuasion in the 2008 Federal Elections* (Temple University Press, 2011).
75. Robert S. Erikson, "Economic Conditions and the Presidential Vote," *American Political Science Review* 83 (June 1989), pp. 567–575. Class-based voting has also become more important. See Robert S. Erikson, Thomas O. Lancaster, and David W. Romers, "Group Components of the Presidential Vote, 1952–1984," *Journal of Politics* 51 (May 1989), pp. 337–346.
76. John C. Fortier and Norman J. Ornstein, "The Absentee Ballot and the Secret Ballot: Challenges for Election Reform," *University of Michigan Journal of Law Reform* 36 (Spring 2003), pp. 483–517.
77. Jerrold G. Rusk, "The Effect of the Australian Ballot Reform on Split Ticket Voting: 1876–1908," *American Political Science Review* 64 (December 1970), pp. 1220–1238.
78. Fortier and Ornstein, "The Absentee Ballot and the Secret Ballot."
79. Lewis L. Gould, *Grand Old Party: A History of the Republicans* (Random House, 2003), p. 236.
80. David B. Magleby and Candice J. Nelson, *The Money Chase: Congressional Campaign Finance Reform* (Brookings Institution Press, 1990), pp. 13–14.
81. Anthony Corrado, Thomas E. Mann, Daniel R. Ortiz, and Trevor Potter, eds., *The New Campaign Finance Sourcebook* (Brookings Institution Press, 2005).
82. *Davis* v. *FEC.* 128 S.Ct. 2759. (2008).
83. Elizabeth Drew, *The Corruption of American Politics: What Went Wrong and Why* (Carol, 1999), pp. 7–8 Robert Longley, "Campaign Contribution Laws for Individuals," About.com, http://usgovinfo.about.com/od/thepoliticalsystem/a/contriblaws.htm (accessed May 15, 2012); Federal Election Commission, "Contribution Limits for 2011-2012," http://www.fec.gov/info/contriblimits1112.pdf (accessed May 15, 2012); Federal Election Commission, "How Much can I Contribute?" http://www.fec.gov/ans/answers_general.shtml#How_much_can_I_contribute (accessed May 15, 2012).
84. Gould, *Grand Old Party,* pp. 389–391 and Jules Witcover, *Party of the People: A History of the Democrats* (Random House, 2003), pp. 589–590.
85. Anthony Corrado, "Money and Politics: A History of Campaign Finance Law," in *Campaign Finance Reform: A Sourcebook* (Brookings Institution Press, 1997), p. 32.
86. See Senate Committee on Governmental Affairs, "1997 Special Investigation in Connection with the 1996 Federal Election Campaigns," http://hsgac.senate.gov/sireport.htm.
87. *Buckley* v. *Valeo,* 424 U.S. 1 (1976).
88. David B. Magleby and Nicole Carlisle Squires, "Party Money in the 2002 Congressional Elections," in *The Last Hurrah?* p. 45, Figure 2–2.
89. David B. Magleby and Eric A. Smith, "Party Soft Money in the 2000 Congressional Elections," in David B. Magleby, ed., *The Other Campaign: Soft Money and Issue Advocacy in the 2000 Congressional Elections,* p. 29, 38; and David B. Magleby and Nicole Carlisle Squires, "Party Money in the 2002 Congressional Elections," in David B. Magleby and J. Quin Monson, eds., *The Last Hurrah? Soft Money and Issue Advocacy in the 2002 Congressional Elections* (Brookings Institution Press, 2004), pp. 44–5, Figure 2–2. http://hsgac.senate.gov/sireport.htm.
90. *McConnell* v. *Federal Election Commission,* 540 U.S. 93 (2003).
91. Corrado, Mann, Ortiz, and Potter, *The New Campaign Finance Sourcebook,* p. 79.
92. David B. Magleby, ed., *The Last Hurrah* (Brookings Institution Press, 2004), pp. 44–45.
93. Ibid., p. 46.
94. David B. Magleby, "Change and Continuity in the Financing of Federal Elections," in David B. Magleby, Anthony J. Corrado, and Kelly D. Patterson, eds., *Financing the 2004 Elections* (Brookings Institution Press, 2006), p. 15.
95. See, Eric S. Heberlig, Peter L Francia, and Steven H. Greene, "The Conditional Party Teams of the 2008 North Carolina Federal Elections." in David B. Magleby, ed. *The Change Election: Money, Mobilization and Persuasion in the 2008 Federal Elections.* (Philadelphia, Temple University Press, 2011, p. 114.
96. http://www.opensecrets.org/outsidespending/summ.php?cycle=2012&disp+kR&pty=pty=A&type=A.
97. Bipartisan Campaign Reform Act of 2002, 107th Cong., 1st sess., H.R. 2356.
98. *Citizen's United* v. *Federal Election Commission, 558 U.S.* (2010).
99. Fredereka Schouten. Obama now urges donations to super PAC backing him. USA Today. 07 Feb 2012. http://www.usatoday.com/news/politics/story/2012-02-07/obama-super-pac-reversal/53002966/1
100. Corrado, Mann, Ortiz, and Potter, *The New Campaign Finance Sourcebook,* pp. 74–76.
101. David B. Magleby, ed., *Dancing Without Partners Monograph,* csed.byu.edu/Publications/DancingwithoutPartners.pdf, p. 53.
102. Federal Election Commission, "FEC Reports on Congressional Financial Activity for 2000," press release, May 15, 2001; Federal Election Commission, "Congressional Candidates Spend $1.16 Billion During 2003–2004," press release, June 9, 2005; and Federal Election Commission, "Congressional Candidates Raised $1.42 Billion in 2007–2008," press release, December 29, 2009.
103. *Colorado Republican Federal Campaign Committee* v. *Federal Election Commission,* 518 U.S. 604 (1996).
104. New Jersey Election Law Enforcement Commission, "Candidate Disclosure Report," http://www.elec.state.nj.us/ELECReport/StandardSearch.aspx.
105. David B. Magleby, ed., The Change Election (Philadelphia: Temple University Press), 13.
106. Jose Antonia Vargas, "Campaign.USA: With the Internet Comes a New Political 'Clickocracy,'" *The Washington Post,* April 1, 2008, p. C01.
107. Federal Election Commission, herndon1 .sdrdc.com/fecimg/srssea.html; see also FEC, "Congressional Candidates Spend $1.16 Billion During 2003–2004," press release, June 9, 2005, www.fec.gov/press/press2005/20050609candidate/20050609candidate.html.
108. John Avion, "*Why has GOP turnout taken a dive?*". CNN Opinion. 08 Feb 2012. http://articles.cnn.com/2012-02-08/opinion/opinion_avlon-gop-turnout-down_1_gop-turnout-turnout-numbers-republican-rank?_s=PM:OPINION
109. Rick Hampson, "Former Banker Was Big Spender," *USA Today,* November 9, 2000, p. A9.
110. See Todd Donovan and Shawn Bowler, *Reforming the Republic: Democratic Institutions for a New America* (Prentice Hall, 2004).
111. Curtis B. Gans, director, Committee for the Study of the American Electorate, personal communication, September 22, 2004.
112. The President's Commission for a National Agenda for the Eighties, in *A National Agenda for the Eighties* (U.S. Government Printing Office, 1980), p. 97, proposed holding four presidential primaries, scheduled approximately one month apart.

9

1. Ashley Parker, "For Campaigns, Twitter is Both an Early-Warning System and a Weapon." *New York Times*, January 29, 2011, p. A15.
2. David Plouffe, *The Audacity to Win* (Penguin Group, 2009), p. 237.
3. Seema Mehta, "The Rise of the Internet Electorate." *Los Angeles Times*, April 18, 2011. Accessed January 24, 2012.
4. Lee Rainie and Aaron Smith, "The Internet and the 2008 Election," Pew Internet and American Life Project, June 15, 2008, http://pewinternet.org/Reports/2008/The-Internet-and-the-2008-Election/01-Summary-of-Findings.aspx (accessed January 26, 2012).
5. Aaron Smith, "The Internet and Campaign 2010," Pew Internet and American Life Project, March 17, 2011, http://pewinternet.org/Reports/2011/The-Internet-and-Campaign-2010.aspx (accessed January 26, 2012).
6. Perry Bacon Jr., "Obama Starts 2012 Campaign Before Potential Rivals," *The Washington Post*, April 3, 2011, http://www.washingtonpost.com/politics/crisis-in-the-mideast/2010/08/25/AFR9ROXC_story.html
7. William Rivers, *The Other Government* (Universe Books, 1982); Douglas Cater, *The Fourth Branch of Government* (Houghton Mifflin, 1959); Dom Bonafede, "The Washington Press: An Interpreter or a Participant in Policy Making?" *National Journal*, April 24, 1982, pp. 716–721; and Michael Ledeen, "Learning to Say 'No' to the Press," *Public Interest* 73 (Fall 1983), p. 113.
8. Leslie G. Moeller, "The Big Four: Mass Media Actualities and Expectations," in Richard W. Budd and Brent D. Ruben, eds., *Beyond Media: New Approaches to Mass Communication* (Transaction Books, 1988), p. 15.
9. Pew Research Center for the People & the Press, "Far More Voters Believe Election Outcome Matters," questionnaire, May 9, 2006, http://people-press.org/reports/print.php3?PageID=802. One service that e-mails customized news and reminders to subscribers is infobeat.com.
10. Peter Apps, "Social Media—A Political Tool for good or evil?" Reuters, September 29, 2011, http://www.reuters.com/article/2011/09/29/us-technology-risk-idUSTRE78R3CM20110929 (accessed January 26, 2012).
11. http://www.ntia.doc.gov/files/ntia/publications/ntia_internet_use_report_feb2010.pdf
12. http://mashable.com/2011/07/29/obama-compromise-twitter-2/
13. See Doris A. Graber, "Say It with Pictures: The Impact of Audiovisual News on Public Opinion Formation," paper presented at the annual meeting of the Midwest Political Science Association, April 1987, Chicago; and Benjamin I. Page, Robert Y. Shapiro, and Glenn R. Dempsey, "What Moves Public Opinion?" *American Political Science Review* 76 (March 1987), pp. 23–43.
14. U.S. Census Bureau, *Statistical Abstract of the United States: 2011* (U.S. Government Printing Office, 2010), pp. 711–12.
15. Pew Research Center's Project for Excellence in Journalism, "Key Findings," *The State of the News Media: 2011* http://stateofthemedia.org/2011/overview-2/key-findings/ (accessed January 25, 2012).
16. Ibid.
17. Andrew Kohut, Internet's Broader Role in Campaign 2008, Pew Internet and the American Life Project, January 11, 2008, http://www.pewinternet.org/Reports/2008/The-Internet-Gains-in-Politics/Summary-of-Findings.aspx, p. 2.
18. Jesse Holcomb, Amy Mitchell, and Tom Rosenstiel, "Cable: Audience vs. Economics," *The State of the News Media: An Annual Report on American Journalism*, 2011, http://stateofthemedia.org/2011/cable-essay/ (accessed January 26, 2012).
19. Sara Bibel, "Over 6 days of the RNC and DNC, FOX News Channel had the most watched convention coverage," *TV by the Numbers*, September 7, 2012, accessed Oct 12, 2012, htt://tvbythenumbers.zap2it.com/2012/09/07/over-6-days-of-the-rnc-and-dnc-fox-news-channel-delivers-the-most-watched-convention-coverage/147873/
20. Jeffrey W. Koch, "Campaign Ads' Impact on Voter Certainty and Knowledge of Candidates' Ideological Positions," 2003, *American Political Science Association*, http://www.allacademic .com//meta/p_mla_apa_research_citation/0/6/2/4/8/pages62486/p62486-1.php (accessed March 30, 2010).
21. David B. Magleby, "Adaptation and Innovation in the Financing of the 2008 Elections," in David B. Magleby and Anthony Corrado, eds., *Financing the 2008 Election* (Brookings, 2011).
22. Journalism.org, "Local TV," March 15, 2004, http://www.stateofthemedia.org/2004/narrative_localtv_contentanalysis.asp?cat=2&media=6 (accessed May 26, 2010); see also, Marc Fisher, "TV Stations Offer a Clear Picture of Indifference," the *Washington Post*, September 26, 2000, p. B1.
23. *Statistical Abstract of the United States: 2012,* p. 712.
24. Television Bureau of Advertising, "TV Basics: A Report on the Growth and Scope of Television," December 2011, available at http://www.tvb.org/media/file/TV_Basics.pdf (accessed January 25, 2012).
25. *Statistical Abstract of the United States: 2012*, p. 712.
26. Robert J. Duffy, Kyle L. Saunders, and Joshua Dunn, "Colorado: Democrats Expand Their Base and Win Unaffiliated Voters," in David B. Magleby, ed., *The Change Election: Money, Mobilization, and Persuasion in the 2008 Federal Elections* (Temple University Press, 2011).
27. National Public Radio, "Morning Edition: About the Program," *NPR*, 2010, http://www.npr.org/templates/story/story.php?storyId=5003 (accessed April 23, 2010).
28. http://www.npr.org/blogs/gofigure/2011/09/29/140919441/more-steady-broadcast-ratings-for-npr (accessed February 1, 2012); http://www.politicususa.com/en/npr-fox-news-rush, see also, Paul Farhi, "Limbaugh's Audience Size? It's Largely Up in the Air," *The Washington Post,* March 7, 2009, http://www.washingtonpost.com/wp-dyn/content/article/2009/03/06/AR2009030603435.html (accessed April 30, 2010).
29. *Statistical Abstract of the United States: 2012,* p. 714.
30. Newspaper Association of America, "Readership Archives," http://www.naa.org/Trends-and-Numbers/Readership/Readership-Archives.aspx (accessed January 30, 2012).
31. Nat Ives, "Publishers: Why Count Only People Who Pay?" *Advertising Age*, November 12, 2007, p. 8.
32. http://www.naa.org/Trends-and-Numbers/Advertising-Expenditures/Annual-Classified.aspx (accessed January 26, 2012).
33. National Public Radio, "Extra! Extra! We Still Want News," *On the Media* (transcript), March 28, 2008, at http://www.onthemedia.org/transcripts/2008/03/28/05, accessed April 3, 2008; and Noam Cohen, "Craig (of the List) Looks Beyond the Web," *New York Times*, May 12, 2008, C1.
34. *The Huffington Post*, "Newspaper Circulation Figures: 25 Biggest Papers in the United States," May 3, 2011, http://www.huffingtonpost.com/2011/05/03/newspaper-circulation-top-25_n_856910.html#s273415&title=Wall_Street_Journal (accessed January 26, 2012).
35. David Kaplan, "WaPo Sells Newsweek to Harman; Announcement Coming This Afternoon," paidContent.org, August 2, 2010, http://paidcontent.org/article/419-wapo-sells-newsweek-to-harman-announcement-coming-this-afternoon/ (accessed January 26, 2012).
36. Stephanie Clifford, "Newsweek on Block as Era of the Newsweekly Fades" *New York Times*, May 5, 2010, http://www.nytimes.com/2010/05/06/business/media/06newsweek.htm (accessed May 14, 2010).
37. Arthur L. Norberg and Judy E. O'Neill, *Transforming Computer Technology: Information Processing for the Pentagon, 1962–1986* (Johns Hopkins University Press, 1996).
38. Boutell.com, "WWW FAQS: How Many Web Sites Are There?," http://www.boutell.com/newfaq/misc/sizeofweb.html (accessed May 26, 2010).
39. Domain Tools, "Domain Counts & Internet Statistics," http://www.domaintools.com/internet-statistics/ (accessed January 26, 2012); The Official Google Blog, "We Knew the Web Was Big…" July 25, 2008, http://googleblog.blogspot.com/2008/07/we-knew-web-was-big.html (accessed January 26, 2012).
40. http://pewinternet.org/Press-Releasees/2011/How-People-Learn-About-Their-Local-Community.aspx. (Accessed 2.7.12).
41. Alex Mindlin, "Web Passes Papers as a News Source," *New York Times*, January 4, 2009, http://www.nytimes.com/2009/01/05/business/media/05drill.html (accessed March 30, 2010).
42. Pew Internet & American Life Project, *Teens and Technology*, July 27, 2005, www .pewinternet.org/pdfs/PIP_Teens_Tech_July2005web.pdf (accessed May 12, 2006).
43. Amanda Lenhart, Susan Arafeh, Aaron Smith, and Alexandra McGill, "Writing, Technology, and Teens," *Pew Internet & American Life Project*, April 2008, http://www.pewinternet.org/Reports/2008/Writing-Technology-and-Teens/04-The-Lives-of-Teens-and-Their-Technology/05 Many teens go online daily .aspx?r=1 (accessed May 26, 2010); and Amanda Lenhart, "Teens and Social Media: An Overview," *Pew Internet & American Life Project*, April 10, 2009, http://isites.harvard.edu/fs/docs/icb.topic603902.files/Teens%20Social%20Media%20and%20Health%20-%20NYPH%20Dept %20Pew% 20Internet.pdf (accessed May 26, 2010).
44. Cass Sunstein, *Republic.com* (Princeton University Press, 2001), pp. 73–75; See also, Philippe J. Maarek, *Campaign Communication and Political Marketing*, Wiley-Blackwell, 2011.
45. Tom Webster, "Facebook Achieves Majority," Edison Research, March 24th, 2011, http://www.edisonresearch.com/home/archives/2011/03/facebook_achieves_majority.php (accessed January 26, 2012). http://www.edisonreserach.com/twiter_usage_2010.php (accessed June 10, 2010)
46. Time.com, "How Facebook Is Redefining Privacy," (accessed June 10, 2010).
47. http://blog.nielsen.com/nielsenwire/global/facebook-and-twitter-post-large-year-over-year-gains-in-unique-users/ and http://blog.nielsen.com/nielsenwire/global/led-by-facebook-twitter-global-time-spent-on-social-media-sites-up-82-year-over-year/ (accessed June 10, 2010).

48. Michael P. McDonald and Thomas F. Schaller, "Voter Mobilization in the 2008 Presidential Election," in *The Change Election: Money, Mobilizations, and Persuasion in the 2008 Federal Elections*, ed. David B. Magleby, p. 96.
49. Pew Research Center for the People & the Press, "Americans Spending More Time Following the News," September 12, 2010, http://www.people-press.org/2010/09/12/americans-spending-more-time-following-the-news/ (accessed January 30, 2012).
50. Pew Research Center for the People & the Press, Survey Reports, "Bottom-Line Pressures Now Hurting Coverage, Say Journalists" May 23, 2004, http://people-press.org/reports/display.php3?PageID=826 (accessed May 26, 2010).
51. See Robert A. Rutland, *Newsmongers: Journalism in the Life of the Nation, 1690–1972* (Dial Press, 1973).
52. David Paul Nord, *Communities of Journalism* (University of Illinois Press, 2001), pp. 80–89.
53. Quoted in Frank Luther Mott, *American Journalism*, 3d ed. (Macmillan, 1962), p. 412.
54. During the 1930s, members of Congress on one network alone made more than 1,000 speeches. See Edward W. Chester, *Radio, Television, and American Politics* (Sheed & Ward, 1969), p. 62.
55. Frances Perkins, quoted in James MacGregor Burns, *Roosevelt: The Lion and the Fox* (Harcourt, 1956), p. 205.
56. Kathleen Hall Jamieson and Joseph N Cappella, *Echo Chamber: Rush Limbaugh and the Conservative Media Establishment.* (Oxford University Press, 2008.
57. CBS News, "Abuse of Iraqi POWs by GIs Probed: 60 Minutes II Has Exclusive Report on Alleged Mistreatment," April 28, 2004, http://www .cbsnews.com/stories/2004/04/27/60II/main614063.shtml (accessed April 23, 2008).
58. Dana Priest, "CIA Holds Terror Suspects in Secret Prisons," *The Washington Post*, November 2, 2005, p. A01.
59. http://topics.nytimes.com/top/reference/timestopics/organizations/w/wikileaks/index.html?scp=1-spot&sq=WikiLeaks&st=cse (accessed 2.7.12).
60. Fred Emery, *Watergate: The Corruption of American Politics and the Fall of Richard Nixon* (Touchstone, 1995).
61. Bob Woodward and Carl Bernstein, *All the President's Men* (Simon & Schuster, 1994).
62. Mark Felt, John D. O'Connor, and W. Mark Felt, *A G-Man's Life: The FBI, Being 'Deep Throat' and the Struggle for Honor in Washington* (Public Affairs Press, 2006).
63. Martin Peers, "Murdoch Wins His Bid for Dow Jones," *The Wall Street Journal*, August 1, 2007, p. A1.
64. News Corporation, home page, http://www .newscorp.com/index.html (accessed April 3, 2008).
65. Merissa Marr and Christopher S Stewart, "Insider Murdoch's Decision" *The Wall Street Journal,* June 29, 2012, p. B1.
66. John F. Burns, "Murdoch, Center Stage, Plays Powerless Broker." *The New York Times,* April 25, 2012. p. A1. http://www.nytimes.com/2012/04/26/world/europe/ruptert-murdoch-testimony-leveson-inquiry.html?_r=&hb.
67. Cassell Bryan-Low, "Murdoch Contends He Was Misled." *The Wall Street Journal,* 26 April 2012. http://online.wsj.com/article/SB100014240527023047233045773674315668439l6.html. Accessed 22 May 2012.
68. Gannett Company, "Company Profile," www.gannett.com/about/company_profile.htm (accessed April 22, 2010); and "Gannett Company, Inc: Company Information," *New York Times*, http://topics.nytimes.com/topics/news/business/companies/gannett_company/index.html (accessed April 22, 2010).
69. Tribune Company, "About Tribune," http://www.tribune.com/ (accessed April 22, 2010).
70. Television Bureau of Advertising, "TV Basics," December 2011, http://www.tvb.org/media/file/TV_Basics.pdf, p. 10 (accessed January 30, 2012); and "FCC Issues 12th Annual Report to Congress on Video Competition," press release, February 10, 2006, hraunfoss.fcc.gov/edocs_public/attachmatch/DOC-263763A1.pdf (accessed May 11, 2006).
71. Seth Schiesel, "FCC Rules on Ownership Under Review," *New York Times*, April 3, 2002, p. C1.
72. http://www.nytimes.com/2009/03/12/business/media/12papers.html?pagewanted=all (accessed 2.7.12).
73. Donna Britt, "Janet's 'Reveal' Lays Bare an Insidious Trend," *The Washington Post*, February 4, 2004, p. B1.
74. *FCC* v. *Fox Television Stations*, 567 U.S. ______ (2012).
75. Shanto Iyengar, Mark D. Peters, and Donald R. Kinder, "Experimental Demonstrations of the 'Not-So-Minimal' Consequences of Television News Programs," *American Political Science Review* 76 (December 1982), pp. 848–858.
76. Ibid.; Maxwell E. McCombs and Donald L. Shaw, "The Agenda-Setting Function of the Mass Media," *Public Opinion Quarterly* 36 (1972), pp. 176–187; Maxwell E. McCombs and Sheldon Gilbert, "News Influence on Our Pictures of the World," in Jennings Bryant and Dolf Gillman, eds., *Perspectives on Media Effects* (Erlbaum, 1986), pp. 1–15; and Iyengar and Kinder, *News That Matters.*
77. Quoted in Michael J. Robinson and Margaret A. Sheehan, *Over the Wire and on TV: CBS and UPI in Campaign '80* (Russell Sage Foundation, 1983), p. xiii.
78. ABC News, http://abcnews.go.com/US/story? id=92498&page=1 (accessed May 26, 2010).
79. For the Paul Begala response to the Frank Luntz memo see, http://www.politico.com/static/PPM104_090522_luntzresponse.html (accessed 2.7.12.
80. David B. Magleby, *Direct Legislation: Voting on Ballot Propositions in the United States* (Johns Hopkins University Press, 1984).
81. The Rush Limbaugh Show, "This Show Forced Liberal Media to Drop the Pretense of Objectivity," April 19, 2010, http://webtest1.rushlimbaugh.com/home/daily/site_041910/content/01125111.member.html (accessed January 31, 2012).
82. Rick Lyman, "Multimedia Deal: The History; 2 Commanding Publishers, 2 Powerful Empires," *New York Times*, March 14, 2000, p. C16.
83. David Broder, "Beware of the 'Insider' Syndrome: Why Newsmakers and News Reporters Shouldn't Get Too Cozy," *The Washington Post*, December 4, 1988, p. A21; see also Broder, "Thin-Skinned Journalists," *The Washington Post*, January 11, 1989, p. A21.
84. For two perspectives on this see Bernard Goldberg, *Bias* (Regnery Publishing, Inc. 2002); and David Halberstam, *The Powers That Be* (University of Illinois Press, 2000).
85. http://www.fair.org/index.php?page=121.
86. See, for example, Jack Dennis, "Preadult Learning of Political Independence: Media and Family Communications Effects," *Communication Research* 13 (July 1987), pp. 401–433; and Olive Stevens, *Children Talking Politics* (Robertson, 1982).
87. Elihu Katz and Paul Lazarsfeld, *Personal Influence: The Part Played by People in the Flow of Mass Communications* (Free Press, 1955).
88. See Angus Campbell, Philip E. Converse, Warren E. Miller, and Donald E. Stokes, *The American Voter* (Wiley, 1960).
89. Pew Research Center for the People & the Press, Survey Reports, "News Audiences Increasingly Politicized," June 8, 2004, http://people-press.org/reports/display. php3?ReportID=215 (accessed May 26, 2010).
90. Paul Lazarsfeld, Bernard Berelson, and Hazel Gaudet, *The People's Choice: How the Voter Makes Up His Mind in a Presidential Campaign*, 3d ed. (Columbia University Press, 1968); and Bernard Berelson, Paul Lazarsfeld, and William McPhee, *Voting: A Study of Opinion Formation in a Presidential Campaign* (University of Chicago Press, 1954).
91. Stuart Oskamp, ed., *Television as a Social Issue* (Sage, 1988); James W. Carey, ed., *Media, Myths, and Narratives: Television and the Press* (Sage, 1988).
92. Times Mirror Center for the People and the Press, "Times Mirror News Interest Index," press releases, January 16 and February 28, 1992.
93. opensecrets.org, "Swift Boat Veterans for Truth, 2004 Election Cycle," http://www.opensecrets .org/527s/527events.php?id=61 (accessed May 26, 2010).
94. David B. Magleby, J. Quin Monson, and Kelly D. Patterson, *Dancing Without Partners: How Parties, Candidates, and Interest Groups Interact in the 2004 Presidential Campaign* (Rowman & Littlefield, 2007), pp. 24–25.
95. Paul T. David, Ralph M. Goldman, and Richard C. Bain, *The Politics of the National Party Conventions* (Brookings Institution Press, 1960), pp. 300–301.
96. Frank I. Lutz, *Candidates, Consultants, and Campaigns* (Blackwell, 1988), Chapter 7.
97. Michael D. Shear and Michael Barbaro, "In video clip, Romney calls 47% 'Dependent' and feeling entitled," *New York Times,* Sept. 17, 2012, accessed Oct. 9, 2012, http://the caucus.blogs.nytimes.com/2012/09/17/romney-faults-those-dependent-on-government/
98. Larry J. Sabato, "Gerald Ford's 'Free Poland' Gaffe—1976," *The Washington Post*, www.washingtonpost.com/wp-srv/politics/special/clinton/frenzy/ford.htm (accessed May 9, 2006).
99. Arlette Saenz, "Rick Perry's Debate Lapse: 'Oops' – Can't Remember Department of Energy," *ABC News*, November 9, 2011, http://abcnews.go.com/blogs/politics/2011/11/rick-perrys-debate-lapse-oops-cant-remember-department-of-energy/ (accessed February 3, 2012).
100. Larry J. Sabato, *The Rise of Political Consultants* (Basic Books, 1981); Alexis Rice, "Campaigns Online: The Profound Impact of the Internet, Blogs, and E-Technologies in Presidential Political Campaigning," Center for the Study of American Government at Johns Hopkins University, January 2004, http://www.campaignsonline.org/reports/online.pdf (accessed January 31, 2012).
101. See Thurber and Nelson, *Campaign Warriors: Political Consultants in Elections* (Brookings, 2000).
102. Quoted in Sabato, *Rise of Political Consultants*, p. 144.
103. John R. Zaller, *The Nature and Origins of Mass Opinion* (Cambridge University Press, 1992); Jennings Bryant and Mary Beth Oliver, eds., *Media Effects: Advances in Theory and Research*, 3rd ed. (Routledge, 2009).

104. Shanto Iyengar and Donald R. Kinder, *News that Matters: Television and American Opinion* (University of Chicago Press, 1987), p. 2.
105. Thomas E. Patterson, *The Mass Media Election: How Americans Choose Their President* (Praeger, 1980), Chapter 12.
106. John H. Aldrich, *Before the Convention* (University of Chicago Press, 1980), p. 65; see also Patterson, *Mass Media Election.*
107. John Foley et al., *Nominating a President: The Process and the Press* (Praeger, 1980), p. 39. For the press's treatment of incumbents, see James Glen Stovall, "Incumbency and News Coverage of the 1980 Presidential Election Campaign," *Western Political Quarterly* 37 (December 1984), p. 621.
108. Stephen Ansolabehere and Shanto Iyengar, *Going Negative: How Political Advertisements Shrink and Polarize the Electorate* (Free Press, 1995).
109. John G. Geer, *In Defense of Negativity: Attack Ads in Presidential Campaigns* (University of Chicago Press, 2006); and Richard R. Lau, Lee Sigelman, and Ivy Brown Rovner, "The Effects of Negative Political Campaigns: A Meta-Analytic Reassessment," *Journal of Politics* 69 (November 2007), pp. 1176–1209.
110. Kevin Collins, "Who Gives? Political Messages, Activist Motivations, and Campaign Contribution Behavior." Paper presented at the annual meeting of the American Political Science Association, Seattle, WA, September 1-4, 2011. Revised version of paper provided by author, May, 23, 2012.
111. Patterson, *Mass Media Election,* pp. 115–117.
112. Michael Traugott, Benjamin Highton, and Henry E. Brady, *A Review of Recent Controversies Concerning the 2004 Presidential Election Exit Polls*, March 10, 2005, http://elections.ssrc.org/research/ExitPollReport031005.pdf; see also Michael Traugott, "The Accuracy of the National Preelection Polls in the 2004 Presidential Election," *Public Opinion Quarterly* 69 (Special Issue 2005), pp. 642–654.
113. Lewis Wolfson, *The Untapped Power of the Press* (Praeger, 1985), p. 79.
114. Lloyd Cutler, "Foreign Policy on Deadline," *Foreign Policy* 56 (Fall 1984), p. 114.
115. Stephen Hess, *Live from Capitol Hill!* (Brookings Institution, 1991), pp. 62–76; and Timothy E. Cook, *Making Laws and Making News* (Brookings Institution, 1989), pp. 81–86; Congress.org, "Congressional Staff Roles," 2012, http://www.congress.org/congressorg/issues/basics/?style=staff (accessed February 3, 2012).
116. Susan Heilmann Miller, "News Coverage of Congress: The Search for the Ultimate Spokesperson," *Journalism Quarterly* 54 (Autumn 1977), pp. 459–465.
117. See Stephen Hess, *Live from Capitol Hill: Studies of Congress and the Media* (Brookings Institution Press, 1991), pp. 102–110; and Jonathan S. Morris and Rosalee A. Clawson, "Media Coverage of Congress in the 1990s: Scandals, Personalities, and the Prevalence of Policy and Process." *Political Communication.* 22:3, 297–313. http://www.tandfonline.com/doi/pdf/10.1080/10584600591006546 (Accessed 2.7.12)
118. Jonathan S. Morris and Rosalee A. Clawson, "Media Coverage of Congress in the 1990s: Scandals, Personalities and the Prevalence of Policy and Process." *Political Communication* 22 (2005) pp. 297–313.
119. For a discussion of the Supreme Court and public opinion, see Thomas R. Marshall, *Public Opinion and the Supreme Court* (Unwin Hyman, 1989); and Gregory Caldiera, "Neither the Purse nor the Sword: Dynamics of Public Confidence in the Supreme Court," *American Political Science Review* 80 (December 1986), pp. 1209–1228.
120. For a discussion of the relationship between the Supreme Court and the press, see Richard Davis, "Lifting the Shroud: News Media Portrayal of the U.S. Supreme Court," *Communications and the Law* 9 (October 1987), pp. 43–58; and Elliot E. Slotnick, "Media Coverage of Supreme Court Decision Making: Problems and Prospects," *Judicature* (October–November 1991), pp. 128–142.
121. http://www.ajr.org/article.asp?id=3909
122. Quoted in Herbert Schmertz, "The Making of the Presidency," *Presidential Studies Quarterly* 16 (Winter 1986), p. 25.

10

1. The totals can be found at http://www.treasurydirect.gov/govt/reports/pd/histdebt/histdebt_histo5.htm.
2. Joseph J. Schatz, "Debt Bill Brings Relief, Frustration," *CQ Weekly*, August 8, 2001, 1758.
3. Charles Warren, *The Making of the Constitution* (Little, Brown, 1928), p. 195.
4. *Bush* v. *Vera*, 517 U.S. 952 (1996).
5. See David B. Magleby, *Last Hurrah? Soft Money and Issue Advocacy in the 2002 Elections* (Brookings Institution Press, 2004).
6. For a summary of congressional retirement plans, see Katelin P. Isaacs, " Retirement Benefits for Members of Congress," Congressional Research Service, January 7, 2011.
7. See Citizens Against Government Waste at www.cagw.org for the latest information on earmarks.
8. http://www.washingtonpost.com/blogs/2chambers/post/toomey-mccaskill-to-call-for-permanent-earmark-ban/2011/11/29/gIQAlZAu8N_blog.html.
9. R. P. Fairfield, *The Federalist Papers* (Doubleday, 1961), p. 160.
10. See Roger H. Davidson and Walter J. Oleszek, *Congress and Its Members*, 10th ed. (CQ Press, 2005).
11. For discussion of the modern Speakership, see Barbara Sinclair, "House Majority Party Leadership in an Era of Legislative Constraint," in Roger H. Davidson, ed., *The Postreform Congress* (St. Martin's Press, 1992), pp. 91–111; and Ronald M. Peters, Jr., ed., *The Speaker: Leadership in the U.S. House of Representatives* (CQ Press, 1995).
12. For an insightful set of essays on Senate leadership, see Richard A. Baker and Roger H. Davidson, eds., *First Among Equals: Outstanding Senate Leaders of the Twentieth Century* (CQ Press, 1991).
13. Sarah A. Binder and Steven S. Smith, *Politics or Principles? Filibustering in the United States Senate* (Brookings Institution Press, 1997).
14. United States Senate, "Senate Action on Cloture Motions," available at http://www.senate.gov/pagelayout/reference/cloture_motions/clotureCounts.htm
15. Joel D. Aberbach, *Keeping a Watchful Eye: The Politics of Congressional Oversight* (Brookings, 1991).
16. "Résumé of Congressional Activity, 105th Congress," *Congressional Record*, Daily Digest, January 19, 1999, p. D29.
17. The complete list of member caucuses as of April, 2012, can be found at http://cha.house.gov/sites/republicans.cha.house.gov/files/documents/cmo_cso_docs/cmo_112th_congress.pdf
18. Date to November 7, 2012, available at http://www.senate.gov/reference/resources/pdf/Resumes/current.pdf
19. Date to November 7, 2012, available at http://www.senate.gov/reference/resources/pdf/Resumes/current.pdf
20. For a history of the early Congresses, see James Sterling Young, *The Washington Community, 1800–1828* (Columbia University Press, 1966).
21. Davidson and Oleszek, *Congress and Its Members*, p. 30.
22. Nelson Polsby, "The Institutionalization of the U.S. House of Representatives," *American Political Science Association* (March 1968), pp. 144–168.
23. Herbert Asher, "The Learning of Legislative Norms," *American Political Science Review* 67 (June 1973), pp. 499–513.
24. See the case studies in Richard F. Fenno, Jr., *Senators on the Campaign Trail: The Politics of Representation* (University of Oklahoma Press, 1996), p. 331; see also Benjamin Bishin, "Constituency Influence in Congress: Does Subconstituency Matter?" *Legislative Studies Quarterly* (August 2000), pp. 389–415.
25. Statistics from congressional Web sites (www.senate.gov; www.house.gov); see also the Library of Congress Web site (thomas.loc.gov).
26. Bill Bradley, *Time Present, Time Past: A Memoir* (Knopf, 1996), Chapter 4.
27. From a 1999 CBS survey reported in "Poll Readings," *National Journal*, October 9, 1999, p. 2917.
28. Richard E. Cohen, "Vote Ratings," *National Journal*, February 21, 2005, p. 426.
29. Joseph I. Lieberman, *In Praise of Public Life* (Simon & Schuster, 2000), p. 109.
30. Catherine Richert, "Party Unity: United We Stand Opposed," *Congressional Quarterly Weekly*, January 14, 2008, p. 143.
31. Senate S. 1, *Honest Leadership and Open Government Act of 2007*, passed September 14, 2007.
32. See Kimberly Kindy, Scott Higham, David S. Falls, and Dan Keating, "Lawmakers Reworked Financial Portfolios After Talks with Fed, Treasury Officials," *Washington Post*, June 24, 2012, available at http://www.washingtonpost.com/politics/lawmakers-reworked-financial-portfolios-after-talks-with-fed-treasury-officials/2012/06/24/gJQAnQPg0V_story.html?hpid=z11. The story contains detailed information on each of the 34 senators and representatives who moved their money in advance of public knowledge.
33. Pollster Patrick Caddell may have been the first to use this term in work he did for Jimmy Carter in 1976, see Joe Klein, "The Perils of the Permanent Campaign," *Time*, October 5, 2005. Journalist and later advisor to President Bill Clinton used the term as title of his 1982 book. See Sidney Blumenthal, *The Permanent Campaign*, (New York: Simon and Schuster, 1982).

11

1. There are hundreds of stories detailing the raid. For an ABC documentary of the raid and its impacts on the children of the September 11, 2001, attacks, see http://topdocumentaryfilms.com/kill-shot-the-story-behind-osama-bin-ladens-death/.

2. Mark Lander, "THE CAUCUS; Behind the Scenes: Biden Recounts Back-and-Forth on Bin Laden Raid," *New York Times*, January 30, 2012, available at http://query.nytimes.com/gst/fullpage.html?res=9905E1D7143BF932A05752C0A9649D8B63&ref=marklandler.
3. Alexander Hamilton, James Madison, and John Jay, *The Federalist Papers* (Bantam Classic, 2003), pp. 426–427.
4. See Paul C. Light, *Vice Presidential Power* (Johns Hopkins University Press, 1984).
5. Richard Pious, *The American Presidency* (Basic Books, 1978).
6. This history of presidential powers draws heavily on Sidney M. Milkis and Michael Nelson, *The American Presidency: Origins and Development, 1976–2000*, 4th ed. (CQ Press, 2003).
7. For further reading, see Louis Fisher, *Presidential War Power*, (University of Kansas Press, 2004).
8. See Al Kamen, "For Bush, the Fun Begins at Recess," *Washington Post*, June 29, 2007, p. A19; for a scholarly argument about this power, see the paper by Michael B. Rappaport, "The Original Meaning of the Recess Appointments Clause," October 6, 2004, at http://ssrn.com/abstract=601563.
9. For the latest updates, on the stem cell issue, see http://topics.nytimes.com/top/news/health/diseasesconditionsand healthtopics/stemcells/index.html
10. See Margaret Love, *Final Report Card on Pardoning by George W. Bush*, March 13, 2009, available at http://www.pardonlaw.com/materials/FinalReportCard.3.13.09.pdf.
11. For a history of signing statements, see Congressional Research Service, "Presidential Signing Statements: Constitutional and Institutional Implications," Washington, D.C.: Congressional Research Service, September 17, 2007.
12. See http://www.coherentbabble.com/listGWBall.htm for the George W. Bush and Barack Obama lists.
13. White House Office of the Press Secretary, "Statement by the President on H.R. 1473," April 11, 2011, p. 2.
14. Letter from Abraham Lincoln to his Illinois law partner W. H. Herndon, February 15, 1848, *in Abraham Lincoln, Speeches and Writings, 1832–1858* (Library of America, 1989), p. 175.
15. Miles A. Pomper, "Bush Hopes to Avoid Battle with Congress over Iraq," *CQ Weekly*, August 31, 2002, p. 2251.
16. Louis Fisher, *Congressional Abdication on War and Spending* (Texas A&M University Press, 2000), p. 184.
17. Raoul Berger, Executive Privilege: *A Constitutional Myth* (Harvard University Press, 1974).
18. Mark J. Rozell, "The Law: Executive Privilege—Definition and Standards of Application," *Presidential Studies Quarterly* (December 1999), p. 924.
19. *United States* v. *Nixon*, 418 U.S. 683 (1974).
20. An indexed list of all executive orders dating back to 1933 can be found at http://www.archives.gov/federal-register/executive-orders/disposition.html.
21. See http://www.whitehouse.gov/briefing-room/presidential-actions/presidential-memoranda for Obama's list.
22. A detailed look at current federal spending can be found at www.USAspending.gov.
23. *Clinton et al.* v. *New York City et al.*, 524 U.S. 417 (1998).
24. See Bradley H. Patterson Jr., *The White House Staff: Inside the West Wing and Beyond* (Brookings Institution Press, 2000).
25. See Irving Janis, *Groupthink* (Houghton Mifflin, 1982).
26. For the views on presidents and the White House staff of a highly placed White House aide in several administrations, see David Gergen, *Eyewitness to Power: The Essence of Leadership*, Nixon to Clinton (Touchstone, 2000).
27. Biographies of all White House staff can be found at http://www.whorunsgov.com/Departments/White_House_Organizational_Chart.
28. See Shelley Lynne Tomkins, *Inside OMB: Politics and Process in the President's Budget Office* (Sharpe, 1998).
29. See Paul C. Light, *The President's Agenda: Domestic Policy Choice from Kennedy Through Clinton* (Johns Hopkins University Press, 1999).
30. *United States* v. *Curtiss-Wright Export Corp.*, 299 U.S. 304 (1936).
31. Richard E. Neustadt, *Presidential Power and the Modern Presidents* (Free Press, 1991).
32. Pew Research Center, "Fewer are Angry at Government, But Discontent Remains High," March 3, 2001, p. 1.
33. The phrase "power to persuade" is from Richard Neustadt, *Presidential Power and the Modern Presidents: The Politics of Leadership from Roosevelt to Reagan* (Free Press, 1990), p. 7.
34. *CQ.com, "Vote Studies 2011, in Graphics," available at* http://media.cq.com/media/2011/votestudy_2011/graphics/

12

1. See Stanley Elkins and Eric McKitrick, *The Age of Federalism* (Oxford University Press, 1993), pp. 50–51.
2. See John A. Rohr, *To Run a Constitution: The Legitimacy of the Administrative State* (University of Kansas Press, 1986).
3. Paul C. Light, *A Government Ill Executed: The Decline of the Federal Service and How to Reverse It* (Harvard University Press, 2008), Chapter 7.
4. James Fesler and Donald Kettl, *The Politics of the Administrative Process* (Chatham House, 1991).
5. For an analysis of the use and abuse of the civil service system in the early twentieth century, see Stephen Skowronek, *Building a New American State* (Cambridge University Press, 1982).
6. See Jeanne Ponessa, "The Hatch Act Rewrite," *CQ Weekly*, November 13, 1993, pp. 3146–3147.
7. Theodore J. Lowi, Jr., *The End of Liberalism*, 2nd ed. (Norton, 1979).
8. Morris P. Fiorina, "Flagellating the Federal Bureaucracy," *Society* (March–April 1983), p. 73.
9. Joel D. Aberbach, *Keeping a Watchful Eye: The Politics of Congressional Oversight* (Brookings Institution, 1990).
10. Mathew D. McCubbins and Thomas Schwartz, "Congressional Oversight Overlooked: Police Patrols versus Fire Alarms," *American Journal of Political Science*, vol. 28, no. 1, pp. 165–179.
11. See Paul C. Light, *A Government Ill Executed: The Decline of the Federal Service and How to Reverse It* (Harvard University Press, 2008).
12. The original types of public policy were developed by Theodore J. Lowi, "American Business, Public Policy, Case Studies, and Political Theory," *World Politics* 16 (1964), pp. 677–715.
13. See Paul C. Light, *Artful Work: The Politics of Social Security Reform* (Random House, 1985), for a discussion of redistributive policy.
14. Quoted in Gabriel Almond, G. Bingham Powell, Jr., Russell J. Dalton, and Kaare Strom, *Comparative Politics Today: A World View* (Longman, 2008), p. 171.
15. William Greider, "The Education of David Stockman," *Atlantic* (1981), p. 296.
16. John Kingdon, *Agendas, Alternatives, and Public Policies* (Little, Brown, 1984), p. 3.
17. Anthony Downs, "The 'Issue-Attention Cycle," *Public Interest* 28 (Summer 1972), p. 38.
18. James L. True, Bryan D. Jones, and Frank R. Baumgartner, "Punctuated-Equilibrium Theory: Explaining Stability and Change in Public Policy-making," in Paul A. Sabatier, ed., *Theories of the Policy Process* (Westview Press, 2007), p. 157.
19. Hugh Heclo, "Issue Networks and the Executive Establishment," in A. King, ed., *The New American Political System* (American Enterprise Institute, 1978), pp. 87–124.
20. Lester Salamon and Michael Lund, "The Tools Approach: Basic Analytics," in L. Salamon, ed., *Beyond Privatization: The Tools of Government Action* (Urban Institute Press, 1989).
21. See Paul C. Light, *A Government Ill Executed: The Decline of the Federal Service and How to Reverse It* (Harvard University Press, 2008).
22. See Cornelius Kerwin, *Rulemaking: How Government Agencies Write Law and Make Policy* (CQ Press, 2003).

13

1. *Citizens United* v. *Federal Election Commission*, 558 U.S. 50 (2010).
2. *Austin* v. *Michigan Chamber of Commerce*, 494 U.S. 652 (1990).
3. Barack H. Obama, "State of the Union Address." 2010 State of the Union. Capitol Building. Washington, D.C. January 27, 2010.
4. Robert Barnes and Anne Kornblut, "It's Obama vs. the Supreme Court, Round 2, Over Campaign Finance Ruling," *The Washington Post*, March 11, 2010.
5. Roy P. Fairfield, ed., *The Federalist Papers* (Johns Hopkins University Press, 1981), p. 227.
6. Jerome Frank, *Courts on Trial: Myth and Reality in American Justice* (Princeton University Press, 1949), pp. 80–103; see also Martin Shapiro, *Courts* (University of Chicago Press, 1981); and Robert P. Burns, *A Theory of the Trial* (Princeton University Press, 1999).
7. Many of these workload statistics can be found in the Supreme Court's 2011, *Year-End Report on the Federal Judiciary* (U.S. Government Printing Office, December 31, 2011).
8. For more information about the federal judiciary, go to the Web site of the Administrative Office of the U.S. Courts at www.uscourts.gov.

9. Court Statistics Project, National Center for State Courts, http://www.courtstatistics.org/Overview/OverviewUnchanged.aspx.
10. Fairfield, *The Federalist Papers,* p. 228.
11. Harold W. Chase, *Federal Judges: The Appointing Process* (University of Minnesota Press, 1972); and Sheldon Goldman, *Picking Federal Judges: Lower Court Selection from Roosevelt Through Reagan* (Yale University Press, 1997).
12. Sarah Wilson, "Appellate Judicial Appointments During the Clinton Presidency: An Inside Perspective," *The Journal of Appellate Practice and Process* 5:1(Spring 2003), pp. 36-39.
13. See David M. O'Brien, "Ironies and Disappointments: Bush and Federal Judgeships," in Colin Campbell and Bert A. Rockman, eds., *The George W. Bush Presidency* (CQ Press, 2004), pp. 133–157; and Brannon P. Denning, "The Judicial Confirmation Process and the Blue Slip," *Judicature* (March–April 2002), pp. 218–226.
14. Russell Wheeler, "Judicial Nominations and Confirmations after Three Years—Where do Things Stand?" *Governance Studies at Brookings.* The Brookings Institution, January 13, 2012.
15. Scott E. Graves and Robert M. Howard, *Justice Takes a Recess: Judicial Appointments from George Washington to George W. Bush* (Lexington Books, 2009).
16. Lisa M. Holmes and Roger E. Hartley, "Increasing Senate Scrutiny of Lower Federal Court Nominees," *Judicature* (May–June 1997), p. 275.
17. George Watson and John Stookey, "Supreme Court Confirmation Hearings: A View from the Senate," *Judicature* (December 1987–January 1988), p. 193; see also John Massaro, *Supremely Political: The Role of Ideology and Presidential Management in Unsuccessful Supreme Court Nominations* (State University of New York Press, 1990).
18. Barbara A. Perry and Henry J. Abraham, "A 'Representative' Supreme Court? The Thomas, Ginsburg, and Breyer Appointments," *Judicature* (January–February 1998), pp. 158–165.
19. Donald Santarelli, quoted in Jerry Landauer, "Shaping the Bench," *The Wall Street Journal,* December 10, 1970, p. 1.
20. Lee Epstein, Jeffrey A. Segal, Harold J. Spaeth, and Thomas G. Walker. *The Supreme Court Compendium: Data, Decisions, and Developments* (CQ Press, 2007), figures updated by the authors.
21. Tony Mauro, "The Supreme Court as Quiz Show," *Recorder* (December 8, 1993), p. 10.
22. Joyce O'Connor, "Selections from Notes Kept on an Internship at the U.S. Supreme Court" (Fall 1988), *Law, Courts, and Judicial Process* 6 (Spring 1989), p. 44.
23. You can listen to oral arguments [www.oyez.org] and argument transcripts are now made available on the Court's Web site on the same day as the case is heard [www.supremecourt.gov].
24. Forrest Maltzman, James F. Spriggs III, and Paul Wahlbeck, *Crafting Law on the Supreme Court: The Collegial Game* (Cambridge University Press, 2000).
25. Charles Evans Hughes, *The Supreme Court of the United States* (Columbia University Press, 1966), p. 68.
26. Daniel M. Berman, *It Is So Ordered: The Supreme Court Rules on School Segregation* (Norton, 1986), p. 114; and David M. O'Brien, *Storm Center: The Supreme Court in American Politics,* 7th ed. (Norton, 2005), pp. 262–272.
27. Charles H. Franklin and Liane C. Kosaki, "The U.S. Supreme Court, Public Opinion, and Abortion," *The American Political Science Review* (September 1989): 751-771.
28. *Brown* v. *Board of Education of Topeka,* 347 U.S. 483 (1954).
29. *Citizens United* v. *Federal Election Commission,* 558 U.S. 50 (2010).
30. Since April 2000, the Court has made its opinions immediately available on its Web site (www.supremecourt.gov).
31. William H. Rehnquist, quoted in John R. Vile, "The Selection and Tenure of Chief Justices," *Judicature* (September–October 1994), p. 98.
32. David Danelski, "The Influence of the Chief Justice in the Decisional Process of the Supreme Court," in Thomas P. Jahnige and Sheldon Goldman, eds., *The Federal Judicial System: Readings in Process and Behavior* (Holt, Rinehart and Winston, 1968), p. 148.
33. O'Brien, *Storm Center,* Chapter 3.
34. Artemus Ward and David L. Weiden, *Sorcerers' Apprentices: 100 Years of Law Clerks at the United States Supreme Court* (New York University Press, 2006); and Todd C. Peppers, *Courtiers of the Marble Palace: The Rise and Influence of the Supreme Court Law Clerk* (Stanford University Press, 2006).
35. Lincoln Caplan, *The Tenth Justice: The Solicitor General and the Rule of Law* (Knopf, 1987); and Rebecca Mae Salokar, *The Solicitor General: The Politics of Law* (Temple University Press, 1992).
36. Gregory A. Caldeira and John R. Wright, "Organized Interest and Agenda Setting in the U.S. Supreme Court," *American Political Science Review* 82 (December 1988), p. 1110; and Donald R. Songer and Reginald S. Sheehan, "Interest Group Success in the Courts: *Amicus* Participation in the Supreme Court," *Political Research Quarterly* 46 (June 1993), pp. 339–354.
37. *National Federation of Independent Business v. Sebelius,* 567 U.S. (2012); Lichtblau, Eric, "Groups Blanket Supreme Court on Health Care," *The New York Times,* March 24, 2012.
38. Paul M. Collins, Jr., *Friends of the Supreme Court: Interest Groups and Judicial Decision Making* (Oxford University Press, 2008).
39. Caldeira and Wright, "Organized Interest and Agenda Setting," *American Political Science Review* 82 (December 1988), p. 1118; and Songer and Sheehan, "Interest Group Success in the Courts," *Political Research Quarterly* 46 (June 1993).
40. Gerald N. Rosenberg, *Hollow Hope: Can Courts Bring About Sound Change?* (University of Chicago Press, 1991).
41. J. W. Peltason, *Fifty-Eight Lonely Men: Southern Federal Judges and School Desegregation* (University of Illinois Press, 1971); and Gary Orfield and Chungmei Lee, *Brown at 50: King's Dream or Plessy's Nightmare* (Civil Rights Project, Harvard University, 2004).
42. See Benjamin N. Cardozo, *The Nature of the Judicial Process* (Yale University Press, 1921)—a classic.
43. William O. Douglas, quoted in O'Brien, *Storm Center,* p. 184.
44. *Citizens United* v. *Federal Election Commission,* 558 U.S. 50 (2010), C. J. Roberts concurring.
45. Lee Epstein, Jeffrey A. Segal, Harold J. Spaeth, and Thomas G. Walker, *The Supreme Court Compendium: Data, Decisions, and Developments,* 4th ed. (CQ Press, 2007). Data through 2005–2006 Supreme Court term.
46. See Keith Perine, "Precedent Heeded, but Not Revered on High Court," *CQ Weekly,* November 28, 2005, pp. 3180–3184.
47. *Gonzales* v. *Carhart,* 550 U.S. 124 (2007).
48. Ex parte *McCardle,* 74 U.S. 506 (1869).
49. See Shawn Francis Peters, *Judging the Jehovah's Witnesses* (University of Kansas Press, 2002); Clyde Wilcox, *Onward, Christian Soldiers? The Religious Right in American Politics* (Westview Press, 1996); Mark Tushnet, *The NAACP's Legal Strategy Against Segregated Education, 1925–1950* (University of North Carolina Press, 1987); and Karen O'Connor, *Women's Organizations' Use of the Court* (Lexington Books, 1980).
50. J. W. Peltason, "The Supreme Court: Transactional or Transformational Leadership," in Michael R. Beschloss and Thomas E. Cronin, eds., *Essays in Honor of James MacGregor Burns* (Prentice Hall, 1988), pp. 165–180; and Valerie Hoekstra, *Public Reactions to Supreme Court Decisions* (Cambridge University Press, 2003).
51. *Planned Parenthood* v. *Casey,* 505 U.S. 833 (1992).
52. Edward White, "The Supreme Court of the United States," *American Bar Association Journal* 7 (1921), p. 341.

14

1. Web site of the Westboro Baptist Church, http://www.godhatesfags.com/wbcinfo/aboutwbc.html. Last accessed on May 7, 2012.
2. Lyle Denniston, "Court to Rule on Funeral Pickets," *SCOTUSBlog,* March 8, 2010. http://www.scotusblog.com/?p=17263.
3. *Snyder* v. *Phelps,* 562 U.S. ____ (2011)
4. Jeffrey Smith, *War and Press Freedom* (Oxford University Press, 1999); and David Cole, *Enemy Aliens: Double Standards and Constitutional Freedoms in the War on Terrorism* (New Press, 2003).
5. *Hamdan* v. *Rumsfeld,* 548 U.S. 557 (2006).
6. *Boumediene* v. *Bush,* 553 U.S. 723 (2008).
7. *Felker* v. *Turpin,* 518 U.S. 651 (1996); *Winthrow* v. *Williams,* 507 U.S. 680 (1993); *McCleskey* v. *Zant,* 499 U.S. 467 (1991); and *Stone* v. *Powell,* 428 U.S. 465 (1976).
8. *Barron* v. *Baltimore,* 7 Peters 243 (1833).
9. *Gitlow* v. *New York,* 268 U.S. 652 (1925).
10. Richard C. Cortner, *The Supreme Court and the Second Bill of Rights: The Fourteenth Amendment and the Nationalization of Civil Liberties* (University of Wisconsin Press, 1981).
11. *Witters* v. *Washington Department of Services for the Blind,* 474 U.S. 481 (1986); and *Locke* v. *Davey,* 540 U.S. 712 (2004).
12. *Wallace* v. *Jaffree,* 472 U.S. 38 (1985).
13. *Everson* v. *Board of Education of Ewing Township,* 333 U.S. 203 (1947).
14. *Lemon* v. *Kurtzman,* 403 U.S. 602 (1971).
15. *Capital Square Review Board* v. *Pinette,* 515 U.S. 753 (1995).
16. *Allegheny* v. *ACLU,* 492 U.S. 573 (1989).
17. *Bowen* v. *Kendrick,* 487 U.S. 589 (1988); *Lee* v. *Weisman,* 505 U.S. 577 (1992); *Board of Education of Kiryas Joel Village School District* v. *Grumet,* 512 U.S. 687 (1994); and *Zelman* v. *Simmons-Harris,* 536 U.S. 629 (2002).
18. *Mitchell* v. *Helms,* 530 U.S. 793 (2000).
19. *Agostini* v. *Felton,* 521 U.S. 74 (1997).
20. *Employment Division of Human Resources of Oregon* v. *Smith,* 494 U.S. 872 (1990).
21. *Church of Lukumi Babalu Aye* v. *City of Hialeah,* 508 U.S. 520 (1993).

22. *Buckley* v. *Valeo*, 424 U.S. 1 (1976), *McConnell* v. *FEC*, 540 U.S. 93 (2003), *Citizens United* v. *FEC*, 558 U.S. 50 (2010).
23. *44 Liquormart* v. *Rhode Island*, 517 U.S. 484 (1996).
24. *Brown* v. *Hartlage*, 456 U.S. 45 (1982).
25. *New York Times Company* v. *United States*, 403 U.S. 670 (1971).
26. Ibid., *Near* v. *Minnesota*, 283 U.S. 697 (1930).
27. *Hazelwood School District* v. *Kuhlmeier*, 484 U.S. 260 (1988).
28. *New York Times* v. *Sullivan*, 376 U.S. 254 (1964).
29. *Hustler Magazine* v. *Falwell*, 485 U.S. 46 (1988).
30. Potter Stewart, concurring in *Jacobellis* v. *Ohio*, 378 U.S. 184 (1964).
31. *Miller* v. *California*, 413 U.S. 15 (1973).
32. *Young* v. *American Mini Theatres*, 427 U.S. 51 (1976); *Renton* v. *Playtime Theatres, Inc.*, 475 U.S. 41 (1986); and *City of Los Angeles* v. *Alameda Books, Inc.*, 535 U.S. 425 (2002).
33. *Barnes* v. *Glen Theatre, Inc.*, 501 U.S. 560 (1991); and *City of Erie* v. *Pap's A.M.*, 529 U.S. 277 (2000).
34. *Chaplinsky* v. *New Hampshire*, 315 U.S. 568 (1942).
35. *Cohen* v. *California*, 403 U.S. 115 (1971).
36. *Wisconsin* v. *Mitchell*, 508 U.S. 476 (1993).
37. *Branzburg* v. *Hayes*, 408 U.S. 665 (1972).
38. *Federal Communications Commission* v. *Fox Television Stations, Inc.*, 567 U.S. ____ (2012).
39. *United States* v. *Playboy Entertainment Group*, 529 U.S. 803 (2000); and *Denver Area Educational Television* v. *Federal Communications Commission*, 518 U.S. 727 (1996).
40. *Reno* v. *American Civil Liberties Union*, 521 U.S. 844 (1997).
41. *Ashcroft* v. *ACLU*, 542 U.S. 656 (2004).
42. Heather Gautney. "What is Occupy Wall Street? This History of Leaderless Movements," *The Washington Post*, October 10, 2011.
43. Andrew Grossman, Alison Fox and Sean Gardiner. "Wall Street Protestors Evicted From Camp," *The Wall Street Journal*. November 16, 2011.
44. *Walker* v. *Birmingham*, 388 U.S. 307 (1967).
45. *First English Evangelical* v. *Los Angeles County*, 482 U.S. 304 (1987); see Richard A. Epstein, *Taking: Private Property and the Power of Eminent Domain* (Harvard University Press, 1985).
46. *Lucas* v. *South Carolina Coastal Commission*, 505 U.S. 647 (1992).
47. *Tahoe-Sierra Council, Inc.* v. *Tahoe Regional Planning Agency*, 535 U.S. 302 (2002).
48. *Kelo* v. *City of New London*, 545 U.S. 469 (2005).
49. *United States* v. *554 Acres of Land*, 441 U.S. 506 (1979).
50. *Mathews* v. *Eldridge*, 424 U.S. 319 (1976), restated in *Connecticut* v. *Doeher*, 501 U.S. 1 (1991).
51. *Meyer* v. *Nebraska*, 262 U.S. 390 (1923).
52. *Griswold* v. *Connecticut*, 381 U.S. 479 (1965).
53. Philip B. Kurland, *Some Reflections on Privacy and the Constitution* (University of Chicago Center for Policy Study, 1976), p. 9. A classic and influential article about privacy is Samuel D. Warren and Louis D. Brandeis, "The Right to Privacy," *Harvard Law Review* (December 15, 1890), pp. 193–220.
54. *Roe* v. *Wade*, 410 U.S. 113 (1973).
55. *Planned Parenthood of Southeastern Pennsylvania* v. *Casey*, 505 U.S. 833 (1992).
56. *Gonzales* v. *Carhart*, 550 U.S. 124 (2007).
57. *Bowers* v. *Hardwick*, 478 U.S. 186 (1986).
58. *Lawrence* v. *Texas*, 539 U.S. 558 (2003).
59. But see *Washington* v. *Chrisman*, 445 U.S. 1 (1982); and compare *Georgia* v. *Randolph*, 126 547 U.S. 103 (2006).
60. *Katz* v. *United States*, 389 U.S. 347 (1967).
61. *California* v. *Hodari D.*, 499 U.S. 621 (1991).
62. *Bond* v. *United States*, 529 U.S. 334 (2000).
63. *Terry* v. *Ohio*, 392 U.S. 1 (1968).
64. *Hiibel* v. *Sixth Judicial District of Nevada*, 542 U.S. 177 (2004).
65. *Minnesota* v. *Dickerson*, 508 U.S. 366 (1993).
66. *Kyllo* v. *United States*, 533 U.S. 27 (2001).
67. *United States* v. *Jones*, 565 U.S. ____ (2012).
68. Barry Friedman, "Privacy, Technology and the Law," *The New York Times*, January 28, 2012.
69. *Mapp* v. *Ohio*, 367 U.S. 643 (1961).
70. Senate Committee on the Judiciary, the Jury, and the Search for Truth: The Case Against Excluding Relevant Evidence at Trial, Hearing Before the Committee, 104th Cong., 1st sess. (U.S. Government Printing Office, 1997).
71. *United States* v. *Leon*, 468 U.S. 897 (1984); and *Arizona* v. *Evans*, 514 U.S. 1 (1995).
72. *Miranda* v. *Arizona*, 384 U.S. 436 (1966); but see *Yarborough* v. *Alvarado*, 541 U.S. 652 (2004).
73. *Dickerson* v. *United States*, 530 U.S. 428 (2000).
74. *United States* v. *Enterprises, Inc.*, 498 U.S. 292 (1991).
75. *J. E. B.* v. *Alabama ex rel T. B.*, 511 U.S. 127 (1994); *Batson* v. *Kentucky*, 476 U.S. 79 (1986); *Powers* v. *Ohio*, 499 U.S. 400 (1991); *Hernandez* v. *New York*, 500 U.S. 352 (1991); and *Georgia* v. *McCollum*, 505 U.S. 42 (1990).
76. *Ewing* v. *California*, 538 U.S. 11 (2003).
77. *Benton* v. *Maryland*, 395 U.S. 784 (1969); see also *Kansas* v. *Hendricks*, 521 U.S. 346 (1997).
78. *Graham* v. *Collins*, 506 U.S. 461 (1993).
79. *Gregg* v. *Georgia*, 428 U.S. 153 (1976).
80. Death Penalty Information Center, "Facts About the Death Penalty," Updated September 20, 2012, www.death penaltyinfo.org/documents/FactSheet.pdf.
81. Barry Scheck, Peter Neufeld, and Jim Dwyer, *Actual Innocence: Five Days to Execution and Other Dispatches from the Wrongly Convicted* (Doubleday, 2000); and Timothy Kaufman-Osborn, *From Noose to Needle: Capital Punishment and the Late Liberal State* (University of Michigan Press, 2002).
82. Death Penalty Information Center, "Innocence and the Death Penalty," April 23, 2012, http://www.deathpenaltyinfo.org/documents/FactSheet.pdf.
83. Visit the Innocence Project at innocenceproject.org.
84. *Atkins* v. *Virginia*, 536 U.S. 304 (2002).
85. *Roper* v. *Simmons*, 543 U.S. 551 (2006).
86. *Kennedy* v. *Louisiana*, 554 U.S. 407 (2008).
87. *Baze* v. *Rees*, 553 U.S. 35 (2008).
88. *Schenck* v. *United States*, 249 U.S. 47 (1919).
89. Charlie Savage, "Deal Reached on Extension of Patriot Act," *The New York Times*. May 19, 2011.
90. Louis Fisher, *Religious Liberties in America: Political Safeguards* (University Press of Kansas, 2002).

15

1. Christopher B. Swanson, "High School Graduation in Texas," Editorial Projects in Education Research Center, October 2006.
2. Scott Jaschik, "10 Percent Plan Survives in Texas," *Inside Higher Ed*. May 29, 2007.
3. *Parents Involved in Community Schools v. Seattle*, 551 U.S. 701 (2007).
4. Andrew Hacker, *Two Nations: Black and White, Separate, Hostile, Unequal* (Scribner, 1992). Lane Kenworthy, *Jobs With Equality* (Oxford University Press, 2008).
5. *Slaughter-House Cases*, 83 U.S. 36 (1873).
6. Ex Parte *Milligan*, 71 U.S. 2 (1866).
7. *Korematsu* v. *United States*, 323 U.S. 214 (1944).
8. Ex Parte *Quirin*, 317 U.S. 1 (1942).
9. *Reid* v. *Covert*, 354 U.S. 1 (1957).
10. *Boumediene* v. *Bush*, 553 U.S. 723 (2008)
11. *Matxhews* v. *Diaz*, 426 U.S. 67 (1976); and *Shaughnessy* v. *United States ex rel. Mezei*, 345 U.S. 206 (1953).
12. *Demore* v. *Kim*, 538 U.S. 510 (2003).
13. *Zadvydas* v. *Davis*, 533 U.S. 678 (2001).
14. *Yick Wo* v. *Hopkins*, 118 U.S. 356 (1886); *Kwong Hai Chew* v. *Colding*, 344 U.S. 590 (1953); *Zadvydas* v. *Davis*, 533 U.S. 678 (2001); *Rasul* v. *Bush*, 542 U.S. 466 (2004); and *Hamdi* v. *Rumsfeld*, 542 U.S. 507 (2004).
15. *Foley* v. *Connelie*, 435 U.S. 291 (1978); *Ambach* v. *Norwick*, 441 U.S. 68 (1979); *Cabell* v. *Chavez-Salido*, 454 U.S. 432 (1982).
16. *Plyler* v. *Doe*, 457 U.S. 202 (1982).
17. *Arizona* v. *United States*, 567 U.S. ____ (2012).
18. *Slaughter-House Cases*, 83 U.S. 36 (1873); and *Civil Rights Cases*, 109 U.S. 3 (1883).
19. *Plessy* v. *Ferguson*, 163 U.S. 537 (1896).
20. *Brown* v. *Board of Education of Topeka*, 347 U.S. 483 (1954); and *Brown* v. *Board of Education of Topeka*, 349 U.S. 294 (1955).
21. *Gomillion* v. *Lightfoot*, 364 U.S. 339 (1960).
22. Taylor Branch, *Parting the Waters: America in the King Years, 1954–1963* (Simon & Schuster, 1988); see also Harris Wofford, *Of Kennedys and Kings: Making Sense of the Sixties* (Farrar, Straus, & Giroux, 1980).
23. See Charles Whalen and Barbara Whalen, *The Longest Debate: A Legislative History of the 1964 Civil Rights Act* (Mentor, 1985); and Hugh Davis Graham, *The Civil Rights Era* (Oxford University Press, 1990).
24. David Remnick, *The Bridge: The Life and Rise of Barack Obama* (Knopf, 2010).
25. Ellen Carol Du Bois, *Feminism and Suffrage: The Emergence of an Independent Women's Movement in America, 1848–1869* (Cornell University Press, 1978); and Joan Hoff-Wilson, "Women and the Constitution," *News for Teachers of Political Science* (Summer 1985), pp. 10–15.
26. Susan M. Hartmann, *From Margin to Mainstream: American Women and Politics Since 1960* (Temple University Press, 1989); and Susan Gluck Mezey, *In Pursuit of Equality: Women, Public Policy, and the Federal Courts* (St. Martin's Press, 1992).

27. *United States* v. *Virginia,* 518 U.S. 515 (1996); see also Philippa Strum, *Women in the Barracks: The VMI Case and Equal Rights* (University Press of Kansas, 2002).
28. *Meritor Savings Bank, FBD* v. *Vinson,* 477 U.S. 57 (1986).
29. *Oncale* v. *Sundowner Offshore Services,* 523 U.S. 75 (1998); *Faragher* v. *City of Boca Raton,* 524 U.S. 775 (1998); and *Burlington Industries* v. *Ellerth,* 524 U.S. 742 (1998).
30. David A. Cotter, Joan M. Hermsen, Seth Ovadia and Reeve Vanneman, 2001. "The Glass Ceiling Effect," *Social Forces,* 80(2): 655–681.
31. Avi Astor, 2009. "Unauthorized Immigration, Securitization, and the Making of Operation Wetback," *Latino Studies* 7:5-29.
32. *Arizona* v. *United States,* 567 U.S. _____ (2012).
33. U.S. Census Bureau, "Census Bureau Releases State and County Data Depicting Nation's Population Ahead of 2010 Census," May 14, 2009, http://www.census.gov/newsroom/releases/archives/population/cb09-76.html
34. Celia W. Dugger, "U.S. Study Says Asian Americans Face Widespread Discrimination," *New York Times,* February 29, 1992, p. 1, reporting on U.S. Civil Rights Commission, *Civil Rights Issues Facing Asian Americans in the 1990s* (U.S. Government Printing Office, 1992).
35. *Takao Ozawa* v. *United States,* 260 U.S. 178 (1922).
36. *Korematsu* v. *United States,* 323 U.S. 214 (1944).
37. "The American Indian and the Alaska Native Population: 2010," *2010 Census Briefs.* Issued January 2012.
38. "Assimilation, Relocation, Genocide: The Trail of Tears," *Indian Country Diaries,* PBS, November 2006, www.pbs.org/indiancountry/history/trail.html.
39. *Antoine et al* v. *Winner School District,* (D.S.D. 2006).
40. *Keepseagle* v. *Vilsack* (D.D.C. 2011).
41. *Morey* v. *Doud,* 354 U.S. 459 (1957); and *Allegheny Pittsburgh Coal Co.* v. *County Commission,* 488 U.S. 336 (1989).
42. *City of Cleburne, Texas* v. *Cleburne Living Center,* 473 U.S. 432 (1985); *Heller* v. *Doe,* 509 U.S. 312 (1993); and *Romer* v. *Evans,* 517 U.S. 620 (1996).
43. *San Antonio School District* v. *Rodriguez,* 411 U.S. 1 (1973).
44. *Frontiero* v. *Richardson,* 411 U.S. 677 (1973).
45. *San Antonio School District* v. *Rodriguez,* 411 U.S. 1 (1973); and Douglas Reed, *On Equal Terms: The Constitutional Politics of Educational Opportunity* (Princeton University Press, 2001).
46. Matthew Bosworth, *Courts as Catalysts: State Supreme Courts and Public School Finance Equity* (State University of New York Press, 2001).
47. Molly A. Hunter, "Requiring States to Offer a Quality Education to All Students," *Human Rights* (Fall 2005) pp. 10–12.
48. Sandra Day O'Connor, in *Kimel* v. *Florida Board of Regents,* 528 U.S. 62 (2000).
49. Ibid.
50. *Romer* v. *Evans,* 517 U.S. 620 (1996).
51. *Perry* v. *Brown,* 10-16696 (2012).
52. Leon F. Litwack, *Trouble in Mind: Black Southerners in the Age of Jim Crow* (1998), p. 227, as cited in James W. Fox, Jr., "Intimations of Citizenship: Repressions and Expressions of Equal Citizenship in the Era of Jim Crow," *Howard University Law Journal* (Fall 2006).
53. Harold W. Stanley, *Voter Mobilization and the Politics of Race: The South and Universal Suffrage,* 1952–1984 (Praeger, 1987).
54. Abigail M. Thernstrom, *Whose Votes Count? Affirmative Action and Minority Voting Rights* (Harvard University Press, 1987), p. 15.
55. *Smith* v. *Allwright,* 321 U.S. 64 9 (1944).
56. *Gomillion* v. *Lightfoot,* 364 U.S. 339 (1960).
57. *Harper* v. *Virginia Board of Elections,* 383 U.S. 663 (1966).
58. Thernstrom, *Whose Votes Count?* For a contrary view, see Bernard Grofman, Lisa Handley, and Richard G. Niemi, *Minority Representation and the Quest for Voting Equality* (Cambridge University Press, 1992).
59. *Morse* v. *Republican Party of Virginia,* 517 U.S. 116 (1996).
60. *Northwest Austin Municipal Utility District Number One* v. *Holder,* 557 U.S. 193 (2009)
61. Corey Dade, "New Target in Voter ID Battle: 1965 Voting Rights Act," National Public Radio, August 2, 2012.
62. *Shaw* v. *Reno,* 509 U.S. 630 (1993).
63. *Civil Rights Cases,* 109 U.S. 3 (1883).
64. *Plessy* v. *Ferguson,* 163 U.S. 537 (1896).
65. *Heart of Atlanta Motel* v. *United States,* 379 U.S. 421 (1964).
66. *Wal-Mart Stores, Inc.* v. *Dukes,* 564 U.S. _____ (2011).
67. Andrew Martin, "Female Wal-Mart Employees File New Bias Case," *The New York Times* (October 27, 2011).
68. Darryl Van Duch, "Plagued by Politics, EEOC Backlog Grows," *Recorder* (August 18, 1998), p. 1; and David Rovella, "EEOC Chairman Casellas: 'We Are Being Selective,'" *National Law Journal* (November 20, 1995), p. 1.
69. *Shelley* v. *Kraemer,* 334 U.S. 1 (1948).
70. Mapping Advancement Project, "Housing Non-Discrimination Laws," May 12, 2012. www.lgbtmap.org. Last accessed by the authors May 24, 2012.
71. *Sweat* v. *Painter,* 339 U.S. 629 (1950).
72. *Brown* v. *Board of Education of Topeka,* 347 U.S. 483 (1954); see also J. W. Peltason, *Fifty-Eight Lonely Men: Southern Federal Judges and School Desegregation* (University of Illinois Press, 1971), p. 248.
73. *Brown* v. *Board of Education of Topeka,* 349 U.S. 294 (1955).
74. *Swann* v. *Charlotte-Mecklenburg Board of Education,* 402 U.S. 1 (1971)
75. *Freeman* v. *Pitts,* 503 U.S. 467 (1992); and *Missouri* v. *Jenkins,* 515 U.S. 70 (1995).
76. See Gary Orfield, Susan E. Eaton, and the Harvard Project on School Desegregation, *Dismantling Desegregation: The Quiet Reversal of Brown* v. *Board of Education* (New Press, 1996).
77. Raymond Hernandez, "NAACP Suspends Yonkers Leader After Criticism of Usefulness of School Busing," *New York Times,* November 1, 1995, p. A13.
78. Gary Orfield and Chungmei Lee, *Brown at 50: King's Dream or Plessy's Nightmare?* (Civil Rights Project, January 1, 2004), http://civilrightsproject.ucla.edu/research/k-12-education/integration-and-diversity/brown-at-50-king2019s-dream-or-plessy2019s-nightmare/?searchterm=brown%20at%2050; see also Charles Clotfelter, *After Brown: The Rise and Retreat of School Desegregation* (Princeton University Press, 2004).
79. *Parents Involved in Community Schools v. Seattle School District No. 1,* 551 U.S. 701 (2007).
80. Richard Kahlenberg, *All Together Now: Creating Middle-Class Schools Through Public School Choice* (Brookings Institution Press, 2003).
81. John Marshall Harlan, dissenting in *Plessy* v. *Ferguson,* 163 U.S. 537 (1896).
82. *University of California Regents* v. *Bakke,* 438 U.S. 265 (1978); see also Howard Ball, *The Bakke Case* (University Press of Kansas, 2000).
83. *Gratz* v. *Bollinger,* 539 U.S. 244 (2003).
84. *Grutter* v. *Bollinger,* 539 U.S. 306 (2003).
85. Scott Jaschik, "Michigan Votes Down Affirmative Action," *Inside Higher Education* (November 8, 2006), www.insidehighered.com/news/2006/11/08/Michigan.
86. Tamar Lewin, "Court Overturns Michigan Affirmative Action Ban," *The New York Times,* July 1, 2011.
87. James Farmer, quoted in Rochelle L. Stanfield, "Black Complaints Haven't Translated into Political Organization and Power," *National Journal* (June 14, 1980), p. 465.
88. John Logan, "Separate and Unequal: The Neighborhood Gap for Blacks, Hispanics and Asians in Metropolitan America," US2010 Project, July 2011. http://www.s4.brown.edu/us2010/Data/Report/report0727.pdf, accessed by the authors May 24, 2012.
89. Peter Whoriskey, "Wealth Gap Widens Between Whites, Minorities, Report Says," *The Washington Post.* July 26, 2011.
90. William J. Wilson, *The Truly Disadvantaged: The Inner City, the Underclass, and Public Policy* (University of Chicago Press, 1987), esp. Chapter 5; and Kevin Phillips, *The Politics of Rich and Poor* (Random House, 1995).
91. Gary Orfield and Carole Ashkinaze, *The Closing Door: Conservative Policy and Black Opportunity* (University of Chicago Press, 1991), pp. 221–234.

16

1. The White House, Office of the Press Secretary, "Remarks of the President in the State of the Union Address," January 23, 2012, available at http://www.whitehouse.gov/the-press-office/2012/01/24/remarks-president-state-union-address.
2. Andrew Kohut, "Don't Mind the Gap," *New York Times,* January 26, 2012, available at http://campaignstops.blogs.nytimes.com/2012/01/26/dont-mind-the-gap/?ref=opinion.
3. The quote is from Alan Krueger, chairman of the president's Council of Economic Advisers. His speech was delivered was delivered on January 12, 2012, and is available at http://cbo.gov/ftpdocs/124xx/doc12485/10-25-Householdincome.pdf.
4. See Congressional Budget Office, *Trends in the Distribution of Household Income Between 1979 and 2007* (Congressional Budget Office, October 2011, available at http://cbo.gov/ftpdocs/124xx/doc12485/10-25-Householdincome.pdf.
5. See *Budget of the U.S. Government, Fiscal Year 2012* (Government Printing Office, 2011), Historical Tables, Table 1.2, available at http://www.whitehouse.gov/sites/default/files/omb/budget/fy2012/assets/hist.pdf.
6. Brad Plummer, "Mitt Romney versus the 47 percent," Washington Post, September 17, 2012, available at http://www.washingtonpost.com/blogs/ezra-klein/wp/2012/09/17/romney-my-job-is-not-to-worry-about-those-people/?hpid=z2.

7. For a discussion of the budgetary cycle, see Allen Schick, *The Federal Budget: Politics, Policy,* Process, rev. ed. (Brookings Institution Press, 2000).
8. See *Budget of the U.S. Government, Fiscal Year 2012* (U.S. Government Printing Office, 2011), Analytical Tables, Table 17.1, available at http://www.whitehouse.gov/sites/default/files/omb/budget/fy2012/assets/spec.pdf.
9. Efforts at corporate tax refrom in the past are described in Jeffrey H. Birnbaum and Alan S. Murray, *Showdown at Gucci Gulch: Lawmakers, Lobbyists, and the Unlikely Triumph of Tax Reform* (Vintage Books, 1988); see also Timothy J. Conlan, Margaret T. Wrightson, and David R. Beam, *Taxing Choices: The Politics of Tax Reform* (CQ Press, 1990).
10. The debate over Keynes and his economic theories is still alive in the United States. See Donald E. Moggridge, *Maynard Keynes: An Economist's Biography* (Routledge, 1992).
11. Visit www.recovery.gov for a list of Recovery Act projects in your zip code.
12. See Congressional Budget Office, *Estimated Impact of the American Recovery and Reinvestment Act on Employment and Economic Output from October 2010 Through December 2010* (Congressional Budget Office, February, 2011), available at http://www.cbo.gov/ftpdocs/120xx/doc12074/02-23-ARRA.pdf. CBO's estimates of employment for 2011 and 2012 were based on an economic model of how stimulus dollars are converted into employment.
13. *United States* v. *E. C. Knight Co.*, 156 U.S. 1 (1895).
14. On the Origins of the Federal Trade Commission and the role of Louis D. Brandeis, see Thomas K. McCraw, *Prophets of Regulation* (Belknap Press, 1984), Chapter 3.
15. Steven Greenhouse, "Union Membership in U.S. Fell to 70-Year Low Last Year, *New York Times*, January 21, 2011, available at http://www.nytimes.com/2011/01/22/business/22union.html.
16. Scott Shane, *The Illusions of Entrepreneurship: The Costly Myths That Entrepreneurs, Investors, and Policy Makers Live By* (Yale University Press, 2008), p. 99.
17. For a useful history of airline deregulation, see Steven A. Morrison and Clifford Winston, *The Evolution of the Airline Industry* (Brookings Institution Press, 1995).
18. On Southwest Airlines and its longtime chief executive Herb Kelleher, see Kevin Freiberg and Jackie Freiberg, *Nuts!* (Bard Press, 1996).
19. The story of the rescue is told in Andrew Ross Sorkin, *Too Big to Fail: The Inside Story of How Wall Street and Washington Fought to Save the Financial System—and Themselves* (Penquin, 2011).

17

1. *Budget of the U.S. Government, Fiscal Year 2012,* Historical Tables, available at http://www.whitehouse.gov/sites/default/files/omb/budget/fy2012/assets/hist.pdf.
2. See Kaiser Family Foundation, Health Reform Source, "Implementation Timeline," available at http://healthreform.kff.org/Timeline.aspx.
3. See July Appleby, "Concern Growing Over Deadlines for Health-Care Exchanges," *Washington Post*, December 11, 2011, available at http://www.washingtonpost.com/politics/concern-growing-over-deadlines-for-health--care-exchanges/2011/12/16/gIQA51cX3O_story.html.
4. Michael B. Katz, *In the Shadow of the Poorhouse: A Social History of Welfare in America* (Basic Books, 1986).
5. This history draws heavily on Theda Skocpol's research on the subject, starting with "America's First Social Security System: The Expansion of Benefits for Civil War Veterans," *Political Science Quarterly* 108 (Winter 1993), pp. 64–87.
6. Catalog of Federal Domestic Assistance, U.S. Government Printing Office, 2012 update, available at www.cfda.gov.
7. These numbers can be found at the Department of Health and Human Services Web site, http://aspe.hhs.gov/poverty/12poverty.shtml.
8. Gertrude Schaffner Goldberg and Eleanor Kremen, eds., *The Feminization of Poverty: Only in America?* (Greenwood Press, 1990).
9. See, for example, Margaret Weir, "Political Parties and Social Policymaking," in Margaret Weir, ed., *The Social Divide: Political Parties and the Future of Activist Government* (Brookings Institution Press, 1998).
10. Self-employed workers must cover both amounts, and many state and local government workers are not required to participate.
11. Martha Derthick, "No More Easy Votes for Social Security," *Brookings Review* 10 (Fall 1992), pp. 50–53.
12. For a pessimistic view of the viability of Social Security, see Neil Howe and Richard Jackson, "The Myth of the 2.2 Percent Solution," www.cato.org/dailys/7-21-98.html. Robert D. Reischauer of the Brookings Institution testified before the House Committee on Ways and Means on November 19, 1998, that Social Security will start running deficits by 2021 and that by 2032, "reserves will be depleted."
13. See Theda Skocpol, *Protecting Soldiers and Mothers: The Political Origins of Social Policy in the United States* (Belknap Press, 1992), Chapter 9, for a history of the Act.
14. Lyndon Johnson, speech at the University of Michigan, May 1964, in *Congress and the Nation, 1965–1968: A Review of Government and Politics During the Johnson Years* (CQ Press, 1969), Vol. 2, p. 650.
15. William J. Clinton, acceptance speech, Democratic National Convention, Chicago, July 6, 1992.
16. Robert Pear, "Judge Rules States Can't Cut Welfare," *New York Times,* October 14, 1997, p. A1.
17. Centers for Medicare and Medicaid Services, "Health Accounts," www.cms.hhs.gov.
18. U.S. Census Bureau, www.census.gov.

18

1. The quote can be found in Tom Shanker, Michael S. Schmidt, and Robert F. Worth, "In Baghdad, Panetta Leads Uneasy Moment of Closure," *New York Times*, December 15, 2011, available at http://www.nytimes.com/2011/12/16/world/middleeast/panetta-in-baghdad-for-iraq-military-handover-ceremony.html?scp=1&sq=Panetta%20end%20of%20Iraq%20war%20ceremony&st=cse.
2. White House.gov, "Remarks by the President and First Lady on the End of the Iraq War," December 14, 2011, available at http://www.whitehouse.gov/the-press-office/2011/12/14/remarks-president-and-first-lady-end-war-iraq.
3. Condoleezza Rice, quoted in Glenn Kessler, "Rice Lays Out Case for War in Iraq," *The Washington Post,* August 16, 2002, p. A1.
4. See Joseph Nye, *Soft Power: The Means to Success in World Politics* (Public Affairs, 2005).
5. For the Republican reaction to the proposal, see "US Weighing Options for Future Cuts in Nuclear Weapons, including 80% Reduction," February 14, 2012, available at http://hosted.ap.org/dynamic/stories/u/us_nuclear_weapons?site=ap§ion=home&template=default.
6. For more information, visit the Peace Corps Web site, www.peacecorps.gov. For a useful study of the Peace Corps, see Elizabeth Cobbs Hoffman, *All You Need Is Love: The Peace Corps and the Spirit of the 1960s* (Harvard University Press, 1998).
7. For a fascinating history of U.S. intelligence operations, see Christopher Andrew, *For the President's Eyes Only: Secret Intelligence and the American Presidency from Washington to Bush* (HarperCollins, 1995). See also Rhodri Jeffreys-Jones, *The CIA and American Democracy,* 2d ed. (Yale University Press, 1998).
8. National Commission on Terrorist Attacks on the United States, *The 9/11 Commission Report* (Norton, 2004), p. 12.
9. *Public Papers of the Presidents, Dwight D. Eisenhower* (U.S. Government Printing Office, 1960), pp. 1035–1040.
10. See Rod Nordland, "Risks of Afghan War Shift From Soldiers to Contactors," *New York Times*, February 11, 2012, available at http://www.nytimes.com/2012/02/12/world/asia/afghan-war-risks-are-shifting-to-contractors.html?scp=1&sq=%22Risks%20of%20Afghan%20War%22&st=cse.
11. P. W. Singer, "Winning the War of Words: Information Warfare in Afghanistan," *Brookings Analysis Paper No. 5,* October 2001.
12. "U.S. Foreign Aid Spending Since World War II," *Public Perspective* 8 (August–September 1997), p. 11.
13. "CNN Poll: Americans Flunk Political IQ Test," available at http://politicalticker.blogs.cnn.com/2011/04/01/cnn-poll-americans-flunk-budget-iq-test/.
14. See Robert Kagan, "The Kerry Doctrine," *The Washington Post,* August 1, 2004, p. B7, for this argument.
15. Gary Hufbauer and Jeffrey J. Schott, "Economic Sanctions and Foreign Policy," *PS: Political Science and Politics* 18 (Fall 1985), p. 278.

Conclusion

1. Thucydides, *History of the Peloponnesian War,* translated by Benjamin Jowett (Prometheus Books, 1998).
2. Edith Hamilton, *The Echo of Greece* (Norton, 1957), p. 47.
3. http://www.nytimes.com/2012/05/18/us/politics/house-may-limit-detention-after-arrests-on-us-soil.html?_r=1 (accessed May 22, 2012).
4. For a book advocating more direct democracy, see Ted Becker and Christa Daryl Slaton, *The Future of Teledemocracy* (Praeger, 2000); for a contrary view, see Richard J. Ellis, *Democratic Delusions: The Initiative Process in America* (University Press of Kansas, 2002).

5. For an extensive list of countries that use some form of proportional representation, see ACE The Electoral Knowledge Network, "Comparative Data: Electoral Systems," aceproject.org/epic-en/es.
6. For more on the relationship between electoral institutions and party systems, see Maurice Duverger, *Political Parties: Their Organization and Activity in the Modern State* (Wiley, 1954).
7. *Lawrence* v. *Texas,* 539 U.S. 558 (2003).
8. The Campaign Legal Center, www.campaignlegalcenter.org/BCRA.html; and *McConnell* v. *FEC,* 124 S. Ct. 619 (2003).
9. John F. Kennedy, *Profiles in Courage* (Pocket Books, 1956), p. 108.
10. Harry S. Truman, impromptu remarks before the Reciprocity Club, Washington, D.C., April 11, 1958, as reported by the *New York World-Telegram,* April 12, 1958, p. 4, www.bartleby .com/73/1405.html.
11. These books will give you insight into the life of public officeholders: Bill Clinton, *My Life* (Knopf, 2004); Harry Reid and Mark Warren, *The Good Fight* (Putnam Adult, 2008); George Tenet, *At the Center of the Storm: My Years at the CIA* (HarperCollins, 2007); and Alan Greenspan, *The Age of Turbulence* (Penguin, 2007).
12. See Kareem Abdul-Jabar and Alan Steinberg, *Black Profiles in Courage* (Morrow, 1996).
13. Reinhold Niebuhr, *The Children of Light and the Children of Darkness* (Scribner, 1944), p. xi.
14. See Bernard Crick, *In Defense of Politics,* rev. ed. (Pelican Books, 1983); and Stimson Bullitt, *To Be a Politician,* rev. ed. (Yale University Press, 1977).
15. See Nat Hentoff, *Free Speech for Me—but Not for Thee: How the American Left and Right Relentlessly Censor Each Other* (Harper Perennial, 1993).
16. Thomas Jefferson, letter to Edward Carrington, January 16, 1787, in Thomas Jefferson Randolph, ed., *Memoir, Correspondence, and Miscellanies, from the Papers of Thomas Jefferson,* 2d ed., Vol. 2 (Carvill, 1830), Letter 43. Available online from Project Gutenberg at www.gutenberg.org/files/16782/16782-h/16782-h.htm.
17. Arthur M. Schlesinger, Jr., *The Disuniting of America* (Norton, 1993), p. 134.
18. John W. Gardner, *Self-Renewal,* rev. ed. (Norton, 1981), p. xiv.
19. In George Field, ed., *Famous Words of Freedom,* (Freedom House, 1955).

CREDITS

Text and Photo

INTRODUCTION Page 3: The Granger Collection, NYC; 7: The Granger Collection, NYC; 12: AP Photo/Mary Altaffer

CHAPTER 1 Page 18: Mona El-Naggar, "Former Tunisian Leader Faces Legal Charges," *New York Times*, April 14, 2011; 18: Anthony Shadid, "Egypt Officials Widen Crackdown but Officials Offer Concessions," New York Times, February 3, 2011; 18: Kira Salak, "Rediscovering Libya," *National Geographic Adventure Magazine*, April 2005; 18: Jillian Schwedler and Laryssa Chomiak, And the Winner Is…: Authoritarian Elections in the Arab World, Middle East Report no. 238 (Spring 2006); 18: Yoram Meital, The Struggle over Political Order in Egypt: The 2005 Elections, Middle East Journal 60, no.2 (Spring 2006): 257-79; 18: Yoram Meital, The Struggle over Political Order in Egypt: The 2005 Elections, Middle East Journal 60, no.2 (Spring 2006): 257-79; 18: Raymond A. Hinnebusch, Charisma, Revolution, and State Formation: Qaddafi and Libya, Third World Quarterly 6, no. 1; 19: Gerald Herbert/AP Images; 21: David Boaz, "The Man Who Would Not Be King," CATO Institute, February 20, 2006; 21: Al Gore, speech delivered on December 13, 2000, http://transcripts.cnn.com/TRANSCRIPTS/0012/13/bn.24.html; 22: Bettmann/Corbis; 23: *Strauss* v. *Horton*, 46 Cal. 4th 364, 93 Cal. Rptr.3d 591, 207 P.3d 48; 23: *Perry* v. *Schwarzenegger*, 704 F. Supp. 2d 921 (N.D. Cal. 2010); 24: *Reitman* v. *Mulkey*, 387 U.S. 369 (1967); 24: Zuma Press/Newscom; 25: Aristotle, Politics (Oxford University Press, 1998); and George Huxley, "On Aristotle's Best State," History of Political Thought, 6 (Summer 1985), pp. 139–149; 25: Thomas Hobbes, Leviathan (Oxford University Press, 1998); and Frank M. Coleman, "The Hobbesian Basis of American Constitutionalism," Polity, 7 (Autumn 1974), pp. 57–89; 25: Frank M. Coleman, "The Hobbesian Basis of American Constitutionalism," Polity, 7 (Autumn 1974), pp. 57–89; 25: Toby Talbot/AP Images; 26: Clinton Rossiter, Conservatism in America (Vintage Books, 1962); 26: Peter H. Shuck and James Q. Wilson, eds. Understanding America: The Anatomy of an Exceptional Nation (New York: Public Affairs, 2008), 629; 27: Sven Creutzmann/Mambo photo/Getty Images; 28: Data From: World Publics Welcome Global Trade-But Not Immigration, Survey 47, 10-4-2007, by Pew Global Attitudes Project, a project of The Pew Research Center; 28: Jeremy Rifkin, The European Dream (Penguin, 2005); 28: James Madison, "The Federalist #10" in The Federalist Papers (New York: Penguin Books, 1987); 29: Alberto Alesina and Edward Glaeser, Fighting Poverty in the U.S. and Europe: A World of Difference (Oxford University Press, 2004); 30: *Marbury* v. *Madison*, 5 U.S. 137 (1803); 31: David B. Magleby, Direct Legislation: Voting on Ballot Propositions in the United States (Johns Hopkins University Press, 1984), p. 119; 32: Rich Pedroncelli/AP Images; 32: Sheri Berman, "Civil Society and the Collapse of the Weimar Republic," World Politics, 49, No. 3 (April 1997); 32: Tsvangirayi Mukwazhi/AP Images; 33: Central Intelligence Agency, The World Factbook, at https://www.cia.gov/library/publications/the-world-factbook/geos/us.html; and Freedom House, Freedom in the World 2011: The Annual Survey of Political Rights and Civil Liberties, at www.freedomhouse.org/template.cfm?page=363&year=2011; 34: Joyce Appleby, "The American Heritage: The Heirs and the Disinherited," Journal of American History, 74 (December 1987), p. 808. Published with permission from Oxford University Press; 34: Kevin Butterfield, "What You Should Know About the Declaration of Independence," St. Louis Post-Dispatch, July 4, 2000; 34: Richard L. Hillard, "Liberalism, Civic Humanism, and the American Revolutionary Bill of Rights, 1775–1790"; 36: The Federalist, No. 40; 36: Charles L. Mee Jr., The Genius of the People (Harper & Row, 1987), p. 51; 36: Charles A. Beard, An Economic Interpretation of the Constitution of the United States (Macmillan, 1913); 36: Worthington C. Ford et al., eds., Journals of the Continental Congress, 1774–1789, 32 (Washington, DC, 1904–1937); 37: Seymour Martin Lipset, "George Washington and the Founding of Democracy," Journal of Democracy, 9 (October 1998), p. 31; 38: MPI/Archive Photos/Getty Images; 40: maps.com; 43: Charles A. Beard and Mary R. Beard, A Basic History of the United States (New Home Library, 1944), p. 136; 44: Bettmann/Corbis

CHAPTER 2 Page 50: Whaley, Monte, "Colorado Supreme Court Affirms that Licensed Guns Allowed on CU Campus," The Denver Post (March 6, 2012); 50: Allie Grasgreen, "Guns Come to Campuses," Inside Higher Ed. October 3, 2011; 53: Massimo Borchi/Terra/Corbis; 51: James Gibbard/The Tulsa World/AP Images; 53: Sanford Levinson, Constitutional Faith (Princeton University Press, 1988), pp. 9–52; 53: Richard Morin, "We Love It—What We Know of It," The Washington Post National Weekly Edition (September 22, 1997); 53: Richard Morin, "We Love It—What We Know of It," The Washington Post National Weekly Edition (September 22, 1997), p. 35; 54: Alexander Hamilton, James Madison, and John Jay, in Clinton Rossiter, ed., The Federalist Papers (New American Library, 1961); 54: Bettmann/Corbis; 57: Alpheus T. Mason, The Supreme Court: Palladium of Freedom (University of Michigan Press, 1962), p. 10; 57: James Madison, The Federalist, No. 51, The Federalist Papers; 57: Hamilton, Madison, and Jay, The Federalist Papers; 57: Hamilton, Madison, and Jay, The Federalist Papers; 57: Hamilton, Madison, and Jay, The Federalist Papers; 58: The American Presidency Project, University of California, Santa Barbara, http://www.presidency.ucsb.edu/data/vetoes.php; 58: Pearson Education; 58: Pearson; 58: Pearson Education; 59: Myers v. United States, 272 U.S. 52 (1926); 59: Charles O. Jones, "The Separate Presidency," in Anthony King, ed., The New American Political System, 2nd ed. (AEI Press, 1990), p. 3; 59: David R. Mayhew, Divided We Govern: Party Control, Lawmaking, and Investigations, 1946–1990 (Yale University Press, 1991), p. 4; 59: Morris P. Fiorina, "An Era of Divided Government," Political Science Quarterly 107 (1992), p. 407; 59: Paul C. Light, Government's Greatest Investigations, 1945-2012 (Brookings, 2012); 60: Charles O. Jones, Separate but Equal Branches: Congress and the Presidency (Chatham House, 1995); 60: Judith A. Best, The Choice of the People? Debating the Electoral College (Rowman & Littlefield, 1996); 60: Ross D. Franklin/AP Images; 61: Jessica Hill/AP Images; 61: Seema Mehta and Maeve Reston, "Jerry Brown Nearly Matched Meg Whitman's Campaign Spending on TV in Final Weeks of Race," Los Angeles Times, February 1, 2011; 62: James Risen and Eric Lichtblau. "Bush Lets U.S. Spy on Callers Without Courts," New York Times, December 16, 2005; 62: Hamilton, Madison, and Jay, The Federalist Papers; 63: The Granger Collection, NYC; 63: Dumas Malone, Jefferson the President: First Term, 1801–1805 (Little, Brown, 1970), p. 145; 64: M. Spencer Green/AP Images; 65: J. W. Peltason, Federal Courts in the Political Process (Random House, 1955); 66: Lyle Denniston, "Analysis: Health Care's Mandate—Part I," December 1, 2011. SCOTUSblog. http://www.scotusblog.com/2011/12/analysis-health-cares-mandate-part-i/; 66: Lyle Denniston, "Analysis: Health Care's Mandate—Part I," December 1, 2011. SCOTUSblog. http://www.scotusblog.com/2011/12/analysis-health-cares-mandate-part-i/; 67: Richard E. Neustadt, Presidential Power (Free Press, 1990), pp. 180–181; 68: Image Works/Time Life Pictures/Getty Images; 69: Author created; 69: John A. Clark and Kevin T. McGuire, "Congress, the Supreme Court, and the Flag," Political Research Quarterly 49 (1996), pp. 771–781; 70: Samuel S. Freedman and Pamela J. Naughton, ERA: May a State Change Its Vote? (Wayne State University Press, 1979); 70: David E. Kyvig, Explicit and Authentic Acts: Amending theU.S. Constitution, 1776–1995 (University Press of Kansas, 1996) p. 286; 72: Mark R. Daniels, Robert Darcy, and Joseph W. Westphal, "The ERA Won—at Least in the Opinion Polls," P.S.: Political Science and Politics (Fall 1982), p. 583; 72: National Organization for Women, www.now.org/issues/economic/eratext.html; 72: Jacquelyn Martin/AP Images

CHAPTER 3 Page 77: Andrew Lichtenstein/Corbis; 79: Q & A Guide to State Immigration Laws: What You Need to Need to Know if Your State is Considering Arizona SB1070-Type Legislation, Immigration Policy Center, April, 2011; 79: Campbell Robertson, "Critics See 'Chilling Effect' in Alabama Immigration Law," New York Times, October 27, 2011, p. A1; 79: William H. Stewart, Concepts of Federalism (Center for the Study of Federalism/University Press of America, 1984); 80: Morton Grodzins, "The Federal System," in Goals for Americans: The Report of the President's Commission on National Goals (Columbia University Press, 1960); 80: Thomas R. Dye, American Federalism: Competition Among Governments (Lexington Books, 1990); 80: AP Photo/Damian Dovarganes; 81: Michael D. Reagan and John G. Sanzone, The New Federalism (Oxford University Press, 1981); 82: "Evenly Divided and Increasingly Polarized: 2004 Political Landscape, Part 4: Success, Poverty and Government Responsibility" November 5, 2003. Pew Research Center for the People & the Press; 82: William H. Riker, The Development of American Federalism (Academic Press, 1987); 83: U.S. Census Bureau, Statistical Abstract of the United States (Government Printing Office, 2007), p. 487; 83: *New State Ice Company* v. *Liebmann*, 285 U.S. 262 (1932), Brandeis Dissenting; 83: U.S. Census Bureau, 2012 Statistical Abstract of the United States. Accessed at www.census.gov/prod/2012/tables/12s428.pdf; 85: Nagelestock/Alamy; 87: Charles Evans Hughes, "War Powers Under the Constitution," ABA Reports, 62 (1917); 88: Carl D. Walsh/Aurora Photos; 89: Joe Raedle/Getty Images News/Getty Images; 91: David C. Nice, "State Participation in Interstate Compacts," Publius, 17 (Spring 1987); 93: Joseph F. Zimmerman, "Federal Preemption Under Reagan's New Federalism," Publius, 21 (Winter 1991); 93: Oliver Wendell Holmes Jr., Collected Legal Papers (Harcourt, 1920), pp. 295–296; 93: Jonathan Nourok/Stone/Getty Images; 94: George Will, "A Revival of Federalism?" Newsweek (May 29, 2000); 95: AP Photo/Matt Rourke; 96: Daniel Patrick Moynihan, "The Devolution Revolution," New York Times (August 6, 1995), p. B15; 96: January 27, 1996 President Clinton's radio address; 96: U.S. Census Bureau's Federal Assistance Award Database for 2010, at http://www.census.gov/govs/www/faadsmain.html; 97: President's Budget for Fiscal Year 2012 http://www.whitehouse.gov/sites/default/files/omb/budget/fy2012/assets/hist.pdf p. 256; 98: AP Photo/Charles Dharapak; 99: Greer/MCT/Newscom; 99: John E. Chubb, "The Political Economy of Federalism," American Political Science Review, 79 (December 1985) 99: Donald F. Kettl, The Regulation of American Federalism (Johns Hopkins University Press, 1987), pp. 154–155; 101: Paul J. Posner, The Politics of Unfunded Mandates: Whither Federalism? (Georgetown University Press, 1998); 101: National Conference of State Legislatures, Mandate Monitor, at http:/ncsl.org/StateFederalCommittees/BudgetsRevenue/MandateMonitorOverview/tabid/15850/Default.aspx; 101: Restoring Confidence and Competence, Advisory Commission on Intergovernmental Relations (Author, 1981), p. 30; 102: DataMasher.org; 103: Aaron Wildavsky, "Bare Bones: Putting Flesh on the Skeleton of American Federalism," in The Future of Federalism in the 1980s (Advisory Commission on Intergovernmental Relations, 1981), p. 79; 103: Paul E. Peterson, Price of Federalism, Brookings Institution p. 182; 104: Thomas R. Dye, American Federalism: Competition Among Governments (Lexington Books, 1990), p. 199

CHAPTER 4 Page 108: Congressional Budget Office; 108: Conn Carroll, "Morning Examiner: Romney Stump Speech Rattles Left," Beltway Confidential blog, The Washington Examiner, December 22, 2011, http://campaign2012.washingtonexaminer.com/blogs/beltway-confidential/morning-examiner-romney-stump-speech-rattles-left/271171 (accessed January 20, 2012); 108: CNN Wire Staff,

"Obama Says Economic 'Inequality' Hurts Everyone," CNN, December 6, 2011, http://politicalticker.blogs.cnn.com/2011/12/06/obama-compares-current-economy-to-great-depression/ (accessed January 20, 2012); 109: Emmanual Dunand/AFP/Getty Images; 111: Larry M. Bartels, Unequal Democracy: The Political Economy of the New Gilded Age (Princeton: Princeton University Press, 2008), p. 2, 15; 111: Arthur M. Okun, Equality and Efficiency: The Big Tradeoff (Washington, D.C.: Brookings Institution, 1975); 111: Albert Einstein, quoted in Laurence J. Peter, Peter's Quotations (Morrow, 1977), p. 358; 112: Harold Hongju Koh, "On American Exceptionalism," Stanford Law Review 55 (May 2003), p. 1481; 112: Richard Cohen, "The Myth of American Exceptionalism," The Washington Post, May 9, 2011; 112: Alexis de Tocqueville, Democracy in America, ed. J. P. Mayer, trans. George Lawrence (Doubleday, 1969), p. 278. Originally published 1835 (Vol. 1) and 1840 (Vol. 2); 112: John Lewis Gaddis, Surprise, Security, and the American Experience (Harvard University Press, 2005); 112: Food and Agriculture Organization of the United Nations; 114: National Conference of State Legislatures, "2011 Post-Election State and Legislative Partisan Composition," December 14, 2011, www.ncsl.org/documents/statevote/2011_Legis_and_State_post.pdf (accessed January 27, 2012); 115: AP Photo; 115: Robert S. Erikson, Gerald C. Wright, and John P. McIver, Statehouse Democracy: Public Opinion and Policy in the American States (Cambridge University Press, 1993); 115: Statistical Abstract, 2011, p. 18; 116: U.S. Census Bureau, Statistical Abstract of the United States: 2010 (U.S. Government Printing Office, 2009), p. 19; 116: Statistical Abstract, 2011, p. 36; 116: Statistical Abstract, 2011, p. 36; 117: David R. Harris and Jeremiah Joseph Sim, "Who is Multiracial? Assessing the Complexity of Lived Race," American Sociological Review (August 2002), p. 615; 117: U.S. Census Bureau, "Race," State and County QuickFacts, http://quickfacts.census.gov/qfd/meta/long_RHI105210.htm (accessed October 24, 2011); 117: Statistical Abstract, 2011, p. 25; 117: U.S. Census Bureau, Statistical Abstract, 2011, p. 25; 117: U.S. Census Bureau News, "More Diversity, Slower Growth," U.S. Department of Commerce, December 16, 2009, http://www.census.gov/Press-Release/www/releases/archives/population/001720.html; 117: U.S. Census Bureau, Statistical Abstract of the United States:Statistical Abstract, 2011, p. 25; 117: Henry J. Kaiser Family Foundation, "Race, Ethnicity, and Healthcare Issue Brief," September 2009, http://www.kff.org/minorityhealth/upload/7977.pdf, accessed January 25, 2012; 118: 1950 figures from U.S. Bureau of the Census, Census of Population: 1950, Volume II Part I (U.S. Government Printing Office, 1950), p. 106; 118: Robert D. Ballard, "Introduction: Lure of the New South," in Robert D. Ballard, ed., In Search of the New South: The Black Urban Experience in the 1970s and 1980s (University of Alabama Press, 1989), p. 5; 118: Sonya Rastogi, Tallese D. Johnson, Elizabeth M. Hoeffel, and Malcolm P. Drewery, Jr., "Majority of the Black Population Lived in the South: 2010; 118: Bureau of the Census, Statistical Abstract, 2012, p. 177., https://www.census.gov/compendia/statab/; 118: U. S. Bureau of the Census, Statistical Abstract, 2012, p. 151; 118: U. S. Bureau of the Census, Statistical Abstract, 2012, p. 455. Constant 2008 dollars; 118: U.S. Bureau of the Census, Statistical Abstract, 2012, p. 456; 119: U. S. Bureau of the Census, Statistical Abstract, 2012, p. 454; 119: U.S. Bureau of the Census, Statistical Abstract, 2012, p. 16; 119: Harold W. Stanley and Richard G. Niemi, Vital Statistics on American Politics, 2005–2006 (CQ Press, 2006), p. 124; 119: BBC News, "The U.S. Election in Figures" at http://news.bbc.co.uk/2/hi/americas/us_elections_2008/7715914.stm. Accessed 7 November 2008; 119: Howard W. Stanley and Richard G. Niemi, Vital Statistics on American Politics, 2011–2012, (CQ Press, 2011), pp. 53–54; 119: Howard W. Stanley and Richard G. Niemi, Vital Statistics on American Politics, 2011–2012, (CQ Press, 2011), pp. 53–54; 119: U.S. Census Bureau, Statistical Abstract, 2012, p. 23.Statistical Abstract, 2012, p. 16; 119: U.S. Bureau of the Census, Statistical Abstract, 2012, p. 45120: AP Photo/Bebeto Matthews; 119: Michael Hoefer, Nancy Rytina, and Bryan C. Baker, "Estimates of the Unauthorized Immigrant Population Residing in the United States: January 2010," Department of Homeland Security, (accessed November 9, 2011); 119: U.S. Census Bureau, Statistical Abstract 2012, p. 16; 120: Janelle Wong, S. Karthick Ramakrishnan, Taeku Lee, and Jane Junn, Asian American Political Participation: Emerging Constituents and Their Political Identities (Russell Sage Foundation: 2011); 120: Janelle Wong, S. Karthick Ramakrishnan, Taeku Lee, and Jane Junn, Asian American Political Participation: Emerging Constituents and Their Political Identities (Russell Sage Foundation: 2011); 120: U.S. Census Bureau, Statistical Abstract, 2012, p. 151; 120: U.S. Census Bureau, Statistical Abstract, 2012, p. 151; 122: Stephen C. LeSuer, The 1838 Mormon War in Missouri (University of Missouri Press, 1987), pp. 151–153; 122: Ronald Inglehart and Wayne E. Baker, "Looking Forward, Looking Back: Continuity and Change at the Turn of the Millennium," American Sociological Review (February 2000); 122: Kenneth D. Wald and Allison Calhoun-Brown, Religion and Politics in the United States, 5th ed. (New York: Rowman and Littlefield, 2006); 122: U.S. Census Bureau, Statistical Abstract, 2012, p. 61; 122: U.S. Census Bureau, Statistical Abstract, 2012, p. 61; 122: U.S. Census Bureau, Statistical Abstract, 2012, p. 61; 122: U.S. Census Bureau, Statistical Abstract, 2012, p. 61; 122: The Association of Religion Data Archives, "Southern Baptist Convention," 2000, http://www.thearda.com/Denoms/D_1087_d.asp (accessed February 22, 2010); 122: The Association of Religion Data Archives, "Southern Baptist Convention," 2000, http://www.thearda.com/Denoms/D_1087_d.asp (accessed February 22, 2010); 122: The Association of Religion Data Archives, "Southern Baptist Convention," 2000, http://www.thearda.com/Denoms/D_1087_d.asp (accessed February 22, 2010); 122: ARDA, "Metro Area Membership Report," www.thearda.com/mapsReports/reports/metro/5602_2000.asp (accessed January 25, 2012); 122: 2000 American National Election Study (Center for Political Studies, 2000); 2004 American National Election Study (Center for Political Studies, 2004). 2008 American National Election Study (Center for Political Studies, 2008); 122: Pew Forum on Religion and Public Life, "Voting Religiously," 5 Fall 2008 http://pewresearch.org/pubs/1022/exit-poll-analysis-religion (accessed February 19, 2010); 122: U.S. Religious Landscape Survey, Pew Forum on Religion & Public Life, http://religions.pewforum.org. 2008 Pew Research Center; 123: James West Davidson, William E. Gienapp, Christine Leigh Heyrman, Mark H. Lytle, and Michael B. Stoff, Nation of Nations (McGraw-Hill, 1990), pp. 833–834; 123: Margaret Trevor, "Political Socialization, Party Identification, and the Gender Gap," Public Opinion Quarterly 63 (Spring 1999); 123: U. S. Census Bureau, Statistical Abstract, 2006, p. 263; 123: Tolleson-Rinehard and Josephson, Gender and American Politics, M.E. Sharpe, pp. 232–233; 123: Paul Steinhauser, "Men's Support Gives Palin Edge in Latest Poll," CNN, September 9, 2008, http://www.cnn.com/2008/POLITICS/09/09/palin.poll (accessed March 1, 2010); 123: Office of the Clerk, "Women in Congress: Historical Data, Women Representatives and Senators by Congress," 2011, http://womenincongress.house.gov/historical-data/representatives-senators-by-congress.html?congress=111 (accessed January 25, 2012); 123: National Conference of State Legislatures, "Women in State Legislatures: 2010 Legislative Session," 2011, http://www.ncsl.org/default.aspx?tabid=19481 (accessed January 25, 2012); 123: Marjorie Connelly, "The Election; Who Voted: A Portrait of American Politics, 1976–2000," New York Times, November 12, 2000, p. D4; 123: CNN Exit Poll: http://www.cnn.com/ELECTION/2004/pages/results/states/US/P/00/epolls.0.html; 123: CNN, "Obama's Election Redraws America's Electoral Divide," November 5, 2008, http://www.cnn.com/2008/POLITICS/11/05/election.president/index.html (accessed February 18, 2010); 123: Arlie Russell Hochschild, "There's No Place Like Work," New York Times, April 20, 1997, p. 51; 123: The Pew Research Center, Gay Marriage a Voting Issue, but Mostly for Opponents, February 27, 2004, www.people-press.org/reports/display.php3?ReportID=204 (accessed January 25, 2012); and Alexis Simendinger, "Why Issues Matter," National Journal, April 1, 2000, based on data from a Pew Center Poll conducted March 15–19, 2000; 123: U.S. Census Bureau, Statistical Abstract, 2012, p. 458; 123: U.S. Census Bureau, "Men's and Women's Earnings by State: 2008 American Community Survey," http://www.census.gov/prod/2009pubs/acsbr08-3.pdf (accessed February 22, 2010); 123: Catherine Rampell, "As Layoffs Surge, Women May Pass Men in Job Force," NY Times, February 5, 2009 http://www.nytimes.com/2009/02/06/business/06women.html (accessed January 25, 2012); 123: Catherine Rampell, "Women Now a Majority in American Workplaces," New York Times, February 5, 2010, p. A10, http://www.nytimes.com/2010/02/06/business/economy/06women.html (accessed January 25, 2012); 123: Anna Quindlen, "Some Struggles Never Seem to End," New York Times, November 14, 2001; 123: Gay and Lesbian Families in the U.S., Urban Institute, http://www.urban.org/publications/1000491.html (accessed January 25, 2012); 123: CNN, "Exit Polls: Results," www.cnn.com/ELECTION/2000/results, September 1, 2006. © 2012 Cable News Network. Turner Broadcasting Systems, Inc.; 124: David J. Phillip/AP Images; 124: U.S. Census Bureau, Statistical Abstract 2012, p. 55; 124: U.S. Census Bureau, "Table MS-2. Estimated Median Age at First Marriage, by Sex: 1890 to the Present," January 2009, http://www.census.gov/population/socdemo/hh-fam/ms2.csv (accessed February 23, 2010); 124: CIA World Factbook data for 2011. https://www.cia.gov/library/publications/the-world-factbook/geos/us.html;124: CIA World Factbook, "Country Comparison: Total Fertility Rate," 2009, https://www.cia.gov/library/publications/the-world-factbook/rankorder/2127rank.html (accessed February 23, 2010); 124: National Center for Education Statistics, Adult Literacy in America (April 2002), March 8, 2010. Accessed at http://nces.ed.gov/pubs93/93275.pdf; 124: National Center for Education Statistics, A First Look at the Literacy of America's Adults in the 21st Century, (2006). March 8, 2010. Accessed at http://nces.ed.gov/NAAL/PDF/2006470.PDF; 125: U.S. Census Bureau, Statistical Abstract, 2010, p. 94; 125: Thomas Jefferson to P. S. du Pont de Nemours, April 24, 1816, in Paul L. Ford, ed. The Writings of Thomas Jefferson (Putnam, 1899), vol. 10; 125: U.S. Census Bureau, Statistical Abstract, 2012, p. 146; 125: U.S. Census Bureau, Statistical Abstract, 2012, p. 152; 125: U. S. Census Bureau, Statistical Abstract, 2012, p. 152; 125: Central Intelligence Agency, The World Factbook, at https://www.cia.gov/library/publications/the-world-factbook/geos/us.html; and Freedom House, Freedom in the World 2011: The Annual Survey of Political Rights and Civil Liberties, at www.freedomhouse.org/template.cfm?page=363&year=2011; 126: Herbert McClosky and John Zaller, The American Ethos: Public Attitudes Toward Capitalism and Democracy (Harvard University Press, 1984); 126: CIRCLE, "Youth Turnout Rate Rises to at Least 52%," Center for Information and Research on Civic Learning and Engagement; 126: Nicholas L. Danigelis, Stephen J. Cutler, and Melissa Hardy, "Population Aging, Intracohort Aging, and Sociopolitical Attitudes," American Sociological Review 72 (October 2007); 126: Seymour Martin Lipset, Continental Divide: The Values and Institutions of the United States and Canada (Routledge, 1990); 126: U.S. Census Bureau; U.S. Census Bureau, http://www.census.gov/compendia/statab/cats/population/estimates_and_projections_by_age_sex_raceethnicity.htm; and U.S. Census Bureau, Statistical Abstract of the United States: 2010 (U.S. Government Printing Office, 2010), p. 12; 127: WOLFINGER & GREENSTEIN, DYNAMICS OF AMERICAN POLITICS., 2nd ed., (copyright symbol) 1980. Reprinted and Electronically reproduced by permission of Pearson Education Inc., Upper Saddle River, New Jersey; 127: ZUMA Press/Newscom; 128: Harold W. Stanley and Richard G. Niemi, Vital Statistics on American Politics, 2007–2008 (CQ Press, 2008), p. 374–375; 128: U.S. Census Bureau, Statistical Abstract, 2012, p. 464; 128: U.S. Census Bureau, Statistical Abstract, 2012, p. 467; 128: U.S. Census Bureau, Statistical Abstract, 2012, p. 465; 128: U.S. Census Bureau, Statistical Abstract, 2012, p. 465; 128: David Leonhardt, "Income Inequality," New York Times, January 18, 2011; 128: U.S. Census Bureau, "Table 3—Poverty Status, by Age, Race, and Hispanic Origin," http://www.census.gov/hhes/www/poverty/histpov/perindex.html (accessed September 29, 2009); and U.S. Census Bureau, "Table 2—Poverty Status by Family Relationships, Race, and Hispanic Origin,"http://www.census.gov/hhes/www/poverty/histpov/perindex.html (accessed September 29, 2009); 130: Congressional Budget Office, "Trends in the Distribution of Household Income Between 1979 and 2007," October 2011, http://www.cbo.gov/doc.cfm?index=12485 (accessed January 28, 2012); 130: Robert A. Dahl, Dilemmas of Pluralist Democracy: Autonomy vs. Control (New Haven, CT: Yale University Press, 1982), 175; 130: David Leonhardt, "Income Inequality." The New York Times, http://topics.nytimes.com/top/reference/timestopics/subjects/i/income/income_inequality/index.html; 130: Larry M. Bartels, Unequal Democracy: The Political Economy of the New Gilded Age (Princeton: Princeton University Press, 2008), p. 54; 130: Larry M. Bartels, Unequal Democracy: The Political Economy of the New Gilded Age (Princeton: Princeton University Press, 2008), p. 34; 130: U.S. Department of Commerce, Bureau of Economic Analysis, "Real Gross Domestic Product, 1 Decimal," November 22, 2011, Accessed athttp://research.stlouisfed.org/fred2/data/GDPC1.txt; 131: Daniel Bell, The Coming of Post-Industrial Society: A Venture in Social Forecasting (Basic Books, 1973), p. xviii; 131: Gabriel A. Almond, G. Bingham Powell, Jr., Russell J. Dalton, and Kaare Strøm, eds., Comparative Politics Today: A World View, 9th ed. (Pearson Longman, 2008; 131: SOURCE: U.S. Census Bureau, Statistical Abstract of the United States: 2010 (U.S. Government Printing Office, 2010), p. 392; 131: Xiaomei Chen/The Washington Post/Getty Images

CHAPTER 5 Page 136: Federal Labor Relations Authority, "50th Anniversary: Executive Order 10988," http://www.flra.gov/50th_Anniversary_EO10988 (accessed February 29, 2012); 136: American Federation of State, County, and Municipal Employees, "Celebrating 75 Years of Solidarity with America's Working Families," Press Release, October 28, 2011, http://www.afscme.org/news/press-room/press-releases/2011/celebrating-75-years-of-solidarity-with-americas-working-families (accessed February 29, 2012); 136: http://ballotpedia.org/wiki/index.php/State_legislative_elections_results,_2010; 136: Michael Cooper and Katharine Q. Seelye, "Wisconsin Leads Way as Workers Fight State Cuts," New York Times, February 18, 2011, http://www.nytimes.com/2011/02/19/us/politics/19states.html?pagewanted=all (accessed April 26, 2012); 137: Scott Olson/Getty Images; 139: David Ariosto, "Ohio Voters Repeal Law Limiting Union Rights, CNN Projects," CNN, November 8, 2011, http://articles.cnn.com/2011-11-08/us/us_ohio-collective-bargaining-vote_1_wisconsin-workers-ohio-voters-phil-neuenfeldt?_s=PM:US:US (accessed March 9, 2012); 139: Annie Lowrey, "Obama to Sign Dodd-Frank Financial Regulatory Reform Bill Into Law Today," The Washington Independent, July 21, 2010, http://washingtonindependent.com/92161/obama-to-sign-dodd-frank-financial-regulatory-reform-bill-into-law-today (accessed March 1, 2012); 140: James Madison, The Federalist, No. 10, November 23, 1787, in Isaac Kramnick, ed., The Federalist Papers (Penguin, 1987), pp. 122–128; 141: REUTERS/Goran Tomasevic; 142: "Microsoft Corp: Donor Profile," http://www.opensecrets.org/orgs/summary.asp?ID=D000000115&Name=Microsoft+Corp (accessed May 21, 2010); 142: "Celebrating 75 Years of Solidarity with America's Working Families," American Federation of State, County, and Municipal Employees; 143: European Foundation for the Improvement of Living and Working Conditions, 2008 (Wyattville Road, Loughlinstown, Dublin 18, Ireland); 143: United States Department of Labor - State Unemployment Insurance Benefits; 143: "By 2007, dues paid to the AFL-CIO exceeded levels before the division. " Accessed at http://workforcesecurity.doleta.gov/unemploy/uifactsheet.asp; 143: http://www.aflcio.org/aboutus/; 143: "State Legislative Elections Results, 2010," http://ballotpedia.org/wiki/index.php/State_legislative_elections_results,_2010; 144: © 2002, 2012 by Barry T. Hirsch and David A. Macpherson; 144: "Angry Demonstrations in Wisconsin as Cuts Loom," New York Times, http://www.nytimes.com/2011/02/17/us/17wisconsin.html, http://thinkprogress.org/politics/2011/07/06/261319/scott-walker-prison-labor/?mobile=nc (accessed April 26, 2012); 144: Alison Grant, "Labor Chief Sees Anti-Union Efforts Growing Bolder," (Cleveland) Plain Dealer (November 22, 2005), p. C1; 145: Emmanuel Dunand/AFP/Getty Images; 145: James MacGregor Burns and Stewart Burns, A People's Charter: The Pursuit of Rights in America (Knopf, 1991); 145: Chris W. Cox, "Who We Are, and What We Do," National Rifle Association, 2011, www.nraila.org/About/ (accessed January 12, 2012); 146: Laura Longhine, "Display Cases," Legal Affairs, November 2005, http://www.legalaffairs.org/issues/November-December-2005/scene_longhine_novdec05.msp (accessed March 15, 2010); 146: The American Israel Public Affairs Committee, "What is AIPAC?" http://www.aipac.org/en/About%20AIPAC (accessed February 22, 2010); 148: Greenpeace USA, www.greenpeaceusa.org, Defenders of Wildlife, e-mail message to author, May 6, 2010; , Reprinted with permission from the Natural Resources Defense Council.; Sierra Club National Headquarters; The Wilderness Society; 150: AARP; 151: AP Photo/Al Grillo; 153: United States Department of Labor - State Unemployment Insurance Benefits; 155: Lewis Burke Associates; 158: Harold Stanley, Richard Niemi, Vital Statistics on American Politics 2005–2006 (CQ Press); 158: "PAC Activity Continues to Climb in 2006," Press Release, October 5, 2007 Federal Election Commission; 158: Federal Election Commission, "Growth in PAC Financial Activity Slows," Press Release, April 24; 161: Compiled from Federal Election Commission Data, "Candidate Financial Summaries," Accessed at www.fec.gov/finance/disclosure/ftpsum.shtml; 163: AP Photo/NBC; 164: Center for Responsive Politics, "Top 50 Federally Focused Organizations," www.opensecrets.org/527s/527cmtes.php?level=C&cycle=2010 (accessed May 4, 2012). 165: AP Photo/Janet Hostetter

CHAPTER 6 Page 172: E. E. Schattschneider, Party Government (Transaction Publishers, 2003), p. 1; 175: Joseph A. Schlesinger, Political Parties and the Winning of Office (University of Michigan Press, 1994); 175: Robert R. Alford and Eugene C. Lee, "Voting Turnout in American Cities," American Political Science Review 62 (September); 176: Billy Suratt/ZUMA Press/Corbis; 177: Gary W. Cox and Mathew D. McCubbins, Legislative Leviathan: Party Government in the House (University of California Press, 1993); 178: *California Democratic Party* v. *Jones*, 530 U.S. 567 (2000); 178: George Skelton, "California Open Primaries? Give Them a Chance," Los Angeles Times, February 11, 2010, http://articles.latimes.com/2010/feb/11/local/la-me-; 178: Judy Treible and Tim Goheen, "Graphic: State caucuses and primaries," Chicago Tribune, 2011, available at http://www.chicagotribune.com; 178: Dave Kettering/Dubuque Telegraph/ZUMA Press/Newscom; 179: 1964 National Election Study (Center for Political Studies, University of Michigan, 1964); and 2008 National Election Study (Center for Political Studies, University of Michigan, 2008); 180: County-Level Map: Republican Primary and Caucus Turnout Down 9%" Daily Kos, March 2, 2012. http://www.dailykos.com/story/2012/03/02/1070214; 180: Maurice Duverger, Party Politics and Pressure Groups (Nelson, 1972), pp. 23–32; 180: Reiner Jensen/CORBIS; 181: C.Q. Press Voting and Elections Collection, 2010, http://library.cqpress.com/elections/search.php; 182: Richard Hofstadter, The Idea of a Party System (University of California Press, 1969), pp. 2, 123; 184: William E. Gienapp, The Origins of the Republican Party, 1852–1856 (Oxford University Press, 1987); 184: Lewis L. Gould, Grand Old Party: A History of the Republicans (Random House, 2003); 184: Lewis L. Gould, Grand Old Party: A History of the Republicans (Random House, 2003); 184: David W. Brady, "Election, Congress, and Public Policy Changes, 1886–1960," in Bruce A. Campbell and Richard Trilling, eds., Realignment in American; 184: L. Sandy Maisel, Parties and Elections in America: The Electoral Process (Rowman & Littlefield, 2002), pp. 48–49; 184: Gerald Pomper, "Classification of Presidential Elections," Journal of Politics 29 (August 1967), p. 538; 184: U.S. Bureau of the Census, Historical Statistics of the United States, Colonial Times to 1957 (Washington, D.C., 1960), p.70. Also accessed at http://www.u-s-history.com/pages/h1528.html; 185: AP Photo; 185: Earl Black and Merle Black, The Rise of Southern Republicans (Belknap Press, 2003); 186: Byron E. Shafer, The End of Realignment: Interpreting American Electoral Eras (University of Wisconsin Press, 1991); 186: Earl Black and Merle Black, The Rise of Southern Republicans (Belknap Press, 2003); 187: Federal Election Commission, "National Party Activity Summarized," press release, October 30, 2006. Accessed at www.fec.gov/press/press2006/20061030party/20061030party.html; 187: Hershey, Marjorie Randon Party Politics in America, 12th ed. (Longman, 2006); 188: David B. Magleby, J. Quin Monson, and Kelly D. Patterson, eds., Dancing Without Partners: How Candidates, Parties, and Interest Groups Interact in the Presidential Campaign (Lanham, MD: Rowman & Littlefield, 2007), pp. 163–167; 188: Kelly D. Patterson, Political Parties and the Maintenance of Liberal Democracy (Columbia University Press, 1996), pp. 30–31; 188: Tom Shales, "Bush, Bringing the Party to Life; From the New Nominee, a Splendid Acceptance Speech," The Washington Post, August 19, 1988, p. C1; 188: Mark Wilson/Getty Images; 189: 2004 National Election Study, "Important Difference in What Democratic and Republican Parties Stand For, 1952–2004" (Center for Political Studies, University of Michigan, 2004); 189: Paul S. Herrnson, Party Campaigning in the 1980s: Have the National Parties Made a Comeback as Key Players in Congressional Elections? (Harvard University Press, 1988), p. 122; 191: *Marbury* v. *Madison*, 1 Cranch 137 (1803); 192: AP Photo/Houston Chronicle, Johnny Hanson; 192: Angus Campbell, Philip E. Converse, Warren E. Miller, and Donald E. Stokes, The American Voter (University of Chicago Press, 1960) pp. 121–128; 194: Bruce E. Keith et al., The Myth of the Independent Voter (University of California Press, 1992); 194: National Election Study (Center for Political Studies, University of Michigan, 2004); 196: Bruce E. Keith et al., The Myth of the Independent Voter (University of California Press, 1992), p. 51; 196: Jonathan S. Krasno and Daniel E. Seltz, Buying Time: Television Advertising in the 1998 Congressional Elections, report of a grant funded by the Pew Charitable Trusts (1998); 197: *Colorado Republican Federal Campaign Committee* v. *Federal Election Commission*, 518 U.S. 604 (1996); 197: "Comparative Data," in the Ace Electoral Knowledge Network Database, http://aceproject.org/epic-en (accessed March 30, 2010); Ndubisi Obiorah, Political Finance and Democracy in Nigeria (Center for Law and Social Action, 2004); 199: Paul S. Herrnson, Party Campaigning in the 1980s (Harvard University Press, 1988), pp. 80–81; 199: APA/Hulton Archives/Getty Images

CHAPTER 7 Page 204: National Conference of State Legislatures, "2003-2010 Legislative Action," http://www.ncsl.org/legislatures-elections/elections/voter-id.aspx#Legislation; 204: John Cornyn, "Voter ID Laws are Reasonable, Constitutional, Necessary," Statesman.com, December 17, 2011, http://www.statesman.com/opinion/voter-id-laws-are-reasonable-constitutional-necessary-2038448.html (accessed March 30, 2012); 205: Travis Morisse/The Hutchinson News/AP Images; 207: "Voter ID: 2011 Legislation" National Conference of State Legislatures, http://www.ncsl.org/legislatures-elections/elections/voter-id-2011-legislation.aspx; 207: Matt Laslo, "Virginia Voter ID Law Passes State Senate," American University Radio, March 1, 2012, http://wamu.org/news/12/03/01/virginia_voter_id_law_passes_state_senate; 207: David Schultz, "Less than Fundamental: The Myth of Voter Fraud and the Coming of the Second Great Disenfranchisement," William Mitchell Law Review 34, no. 2 (2007): 483–532, p. 501; 207: Charlie Savage, "Justice Department Blocks Texas on Photo ID for Voting," The New York Times, March 12, 2012. http://www.nytimes.com/2012/03/13/us/justice-dept-blocks-texas-photo-id-law.html; 208: Gabriel A. Almond and Sidney Verba, eds. The Civic Culture Revisited (Little Brown, 1980), p. 13; 208: J. L. Glanville, "Political Socialization or Selection? Adolescent Extracurricular Participation and Political Activity in Early Adulthood," Social Science Quarterly 80 (1999), p. 279; 208: National Association of Secretaries of State, New Millennium Project, Part I: American Youth Attitudes on Policies, Citizenship, Government, and Voting (Weiss, 1999); 208: Margaret Stimmann Branson, "Making the Case for Civic Education: Educating Young People for Responsible Citizenship," paper presented at the Conference for Professional Development for Program Trainers, Manhattan Beach, Calif., February 25, 2001; 208: Jody C. Baumgartner and Jonathan S. Morris, "MyFaceTube Politics: Social Networking Web Sites and Political Engagement of Young Adults," Social Science Computer Review 28 (2010): 24–44; 209: Larry D. Rosen, "Poke Me: How Social Networks Can Both Help and Harm Our Kids" paper presented at the American Psychological Association 119th Convention, Washington, D.C., (August 2011); 209: Lynn Avedisian/Century of Image Research; 210: Robert S. Erikson and Kent L. Tedin, American Public Opinion: Its Origins, Content, and Impact, 6th ed. (Longman, 2001); 210: "Well Known: Twitter; Little Known: John Roberts", July 15 2010, The Pew Research Center for the People and the Press, a project of the Pew Research Center; 210: Copyright © (2011) Gallup,Inc. All rights reserved. The content is used with permission; However Gallup retains all rights of publication; 211: Gallup Daily: Obama Continues to Outpace McCain, Gallup Politics, 2008; 211: Suzanne Dechillo/Redux Pictures; 212: * Washington Post-ABC News (March 2012) ** Fox News (May 2012) † CBS News/New York Times (May 2012) ‡ Gallup (May 2012); 214: 2008 National Election Study (Center for Political Studies, University of Michigan, 2008); 215: "Do You Approve or Disapprove of the Way George W. Bush Is Handling the Situation with Iraq?" CBS News and New York Times Poll, May 3, 2003; and May 20, 2004, www.pollingreport.com/iraq2.htm; 215: Gallup, "Gallup Daily: Obama Job Approval," http://www.gallup.com/poll/113980/gallup-daily-obama-job-approval.aspx (accessed April 16, 2010); 215: Gallup, "Gallup Daily: Presidential Approval Ratings -- George W. Bush" http://www.gallup.com/poll/116500/presidential-approval-ratings-george-bush.aspx 216: American National Election Studies, (www.electionstudies.org); 217: AP Photo/Topeka Capital-Journal, Anthony S. Bush; 218: AP Photo/Ron Edmonds, File; 219: AP Photo/Jacquelyn Martin; 220: Chris Maddaloni/CQ-Roll Call Group/Getty Images; 221: Center for Political Studies, University of Michigan, 2008 American National Election Study; 222: U.S. Census Bureau, Statistical Abstract of the United States: 2006 (U.S. Government Printing Office, 2006), p. 263; 2008 National Election Study, Center for Political Studies, University of Michigan; NES Guide to Public Opinion and Electoral Behavior, http://www.electionstudies.org/studypages/2008prepost/2008prepost.htm; and Pew Research Center, "Social Networking and Online Videos Take Off," January 11, 2008, www.pewinternet.org/pdfs/Pew_Media; 223: "Susan B. Anthony Timeline," Anthony Center for Women's Leadership at the University of Rochester. www.rochester.edu/sba/suffragetimeline.html; 224: International Institute for Democracy and Electoral Assistance, "Voter Turnout from 1945 to Date: A Global Report on Political Participation," www.idea.int/voter_turnout/index.html;224: International Institute for Democracy and Electoral Assistance, "Voter Turnout from 1945 to Date: A Global Report on Political

Participation," www.idea.int/voter_turnout/index.html p. 24; 224: Curtis Gans Howard W. Stanley, and Richard G. Niemi, Vital Statistics on American Politics, 2011–2012 (CQ Press, 2011), pp. 4–5; 226: Curtis Gans, "President Bush, Mobilization Drives Propel Turnout to Post-1968 High; Kerry, Democratic Weakness Shown," Center for Voting and Democracy, November 4, 2004, www.fairvote.org/reports/csae2004electionreport.pdf; 226: Curtis Gans, Howard W. Stanley, and Richard G. Niemi, Vital Statistics on American Politics, 2011–2012 (CQ Press, 2011), pp. 4–5; 227: MPI/Archive Photos/Getty Images; 227: Raymond E. Wolfinger and Steven J. Rosenstone, Who Votes? (Yale University Press, 1980), p. 102; 229: http://www.time.com/time/politics/article/0,8599,1708570,00.html (accessed April 16, 2010); 229: The Center for Information &Research on Civic Learning and Engagement, "Turnout by Education, Race, and Gender and Other 2008 Youth Voting Statistics," November 2008, http://www.civicyouth.org/?p=324 (accessed April 21, 2010); 230: Christopher R. Ellis, Joseph Daniel Ura, and Jenna Ashley-Robinson, "The Dynamic Consequences of Nonvoting in American National Elections," Political Research Quarterly 59 (June 2006), pp. 232–233; 230: Austin Ranney, "Nonvoting Is Not a Social Disease," Public Opinion (October–November 1983), pp. 16–19; 230: U.S. Census Bureau, "Reasons for Not Voting, by Selected Characteristics: November 2008," www.census.gov/population/www/socdemo/voting/cps2008.html; 231: Sidney Verba, "Would the Dream of Political Equality Turn Out to Be a Nightmare?" Perspectives on Politics 4 (December 2003), pp. 667–672; 231: Stephen Earl Bennett and David Resnick, "The Implications of Nonvoting for Democracy in the United States," American Journal of Political Science 84 (August 1990), pp. 771–802

CHAPTER 8 Page 240: James Meikle, "Foster Friess: The Man Atop the Horse bankrolling Rick Santorum". The Guardian, 08 Feb 2012. http://www.guardian.co.uk/world/2012/feb/08/foster-friess-rick-santorum. Accessed 3 April 2012; 240: Campaign Finance Institute, "Obama's Small-Dollar Percentage Down Slightly in February, Santorum's Stayed High; Romney's Stayed Low."; 240: SCOTUS Blog. *SpeechNow.org* v. *FEC. Bloomberg Law*. 240: Legal Information Institute. Citizens United v. Federal Election Commission. Cornell University Law School. http://www.law.cornell.edu/supct; http://www.scotusblog.com/case-; 240: Campaign Finance Institute, "Obama's Small-Dollar Percentage Down Slightly in February, Santorum's Stayed High; Romney's Stayed Low." Campaign Finance Institute 22 March 2012. < Accessed 3 May 2012. 3.22.12, http://cfinst.org/Press/PReleases/12-03-22/Obama%E2%80%99s_Small-Dollar_Percentage_Down_Slightly_in_February_Santorum%E2%80%99s_Stayed_High_Romney%E2%80; 241: Rich Pedroncelli/AP Images; 243: T.W. Farnam, Study: Negative campaign ads much more frequent, vicious than in primaries past, Washington Post, February 20, 2012, (accessed May 7, 2012); 243: U.S. Census Bureau, "Number of Elected Officials Exceeds Half Million—Almost All Are with Local Governments," press release, January 30, 1995; 243: U.S. Senate, www.senate.gov/general/contact_information/senators_cfm.cfm; 244: Associated Press, "Voters Retain State Term Limits," November 4, 2008, http://www.kxmb.com/News/293253.asp (accessed November 6, 2008); 244: *U.S. Term Limits Inc.* v. *Thornton*, 514 U.S. 799 (1995); 244: New York State Board of Elections, "2009 Election Results: 23rd Congressional District," December 15, 2009, http://www.elections.state.ny.us/NYSBOE/Elections/2009/Special/23rdCDSpecialVoteResults.pdf (accessed May 19, 2010); 244: Arend Lijphart, "The Political Consequences of Electoral Laws, 1945–85," American Political Science Review 84 (June 1990); 245: MPI/Archive Photos/Getty Images; 246: Federal Election Commission, "Election Results," http://www.fec.gov/pubrec/electionresults.shtml (accessed March 23, 2010); 248: Robert King/Getty Images News/Getty Images; 248: Ryan L. Claasen, David B. Magleby, J. Quin Monson, and Kelly D. Patterson, "At Your Service: Voter Evaluations of Poll Worker Performance," American Politics Research 36 (July 2008): 612–634; 249: Gary King and Andrew Gelman, "Systemic Consequences of Incumbency Advantage in U.S. House Elections," American Journal of Political Science 35 (February 1991), pp. 110–137; 250: Charlie Cook, "National Overview," Cook Political Report, October 16, 2008, p. 6; and Charlie Cook, "Competitive House Race Chart," Cook Political Report; 250: Alan I. Abramowitz, "Economic Conditions, Presidential Popularity, and Voting Behavior in Midterm Congressional Elections," Journal of Politics 47 (February 1985), pp. 31–43; 250: Edward R. Tufte, Political Control of the Economy (Princeton University Press, 1978); 250: Alan I. Abramowitz and Jeffrey A. Segal, "Determinants of the Outcomes of U.S. Senate Elections," Journal of Politics 48 (1986), pp. 433–439; 250: David B. Magleby and Kelly D. Patterson, eds., The Battle for Congress: Iraq, Scandal, and Campaign Finance in the 2006 Election (Paradigm, 2008); 250: Rhodes Cook, "Congress and Primaries: Looking for Clues to a Tidal Wave," The Wall Street Journal, July 24, 2008; 250: Linda L. Fowler and Robert D. McClure, Political Ambition: Who Decides to Run for Congress (Yale University Press, 1989); 251: Harold W. Stanley and Richard G. Niemi, Vital Statistics on American Politics 2011–2012, CQ Press, p. 54; 251: David McKay, American Politics and Society, 7th ed., Wiley-Blackwell, 2009, p. 147; 252: Harold W. Stanley and Richard G. Niemi, Vital Statistics on American Politics 2011–2012 (CQ Press, 2011), pp. 46–47; 252: Federal Election Commission, "Financial Activity of General Election Congressional Candidates from 1992 to 2010," includes activity through 12/31/10, www.fec.gov/press/2010_Full_summary_Data.shtml; 252: David B. Magleby and J. Quin Monson, eds. The Last Hurrah" Soft Money and Issue Advocacy in the 2002 Congressional Elections. (Brookings Institution Press, 2004) p. 6; 252: http://www.opensecrets.org/news/2012/04/outside-spending-group-targets-incu.html; 252: AP Photo/David Kohl; 253: Candice J. Nelson, "Spending in the 2000 Elections," in David B. Magleby, ed., Financing the 2000 Election (Brookings Institution Press, 2002), pp. 28–30; 253: Jonathan S. Krasno, Challengers, Competition, and Reelection: Comparing Senate and House Elections (Yale University Press, 1994), p. 2; 253: Alan I. Abramowitz, "Explaining Senate Election Outcomes," American Political Science Review 82 (June 1988), pp. 385–403; 253: Joseph Morton, "Kerrey, Reid Talked Committee Spots," Omaha World-Herald, March 8, 2012, http://www.omaha.com/article/20120308/NEWS01/703089907 (accessed on April 24, 2012); 253: David B. Magleby, "More Bang for the Buck: Campaign Spending in Small State U.S. Senate Elections," paper presented at the annual meeting of the Western Political Science Association, Salt Lake City, Utah (March 30–April 1, 1989); 253: Harold W. Stanley and Richard G. Niemi, Vital Statistics on American Politics 2007-2008 (CQ Press, 2008), p. 101; 253: Data for 2000-2010: Center for Responsive Politics, "Price of Admission: Winners," www.opensecrets.org/bigpicture/stats.php?cycle=2008&display=T&Type=W (accessed 9 April 2012); 255: Scott Shepard, "Politicians Already Looking to 2008 Election," Austin (Texas) American-Statesman, February 6, 2005; 255: Alexander Burns and Jonathan Martin, Rick Perry Fundraising Haul Signals Long GOP Slog, Politico, October 5, 2011, http://www.politico.com/news/stories/1011/65261.html (accessed April 25, 2012); 255: Arthur Hadley, Invisible Primary (Prentice Hall, 1976); 255: Zachary A. Goldfarb, Gingrich fails to win spot on Virginia primary ballot, Washington Post, December 24, 2011, http://www.washingtonpost.com/politics/gingrich-fails-to-win-spot-on-virginia-primary-ballot/2011/12/24/gIQAnErBGP_story.html (accessed April 25, 2012); 255: Joe Hallett, Santorum loses 9 Ohio delegates, Columbus Dispatch, February 16, 2012, (accessed April 25, 2012); 255: http://www.fec.gov/press/press2012/20120330RoemerCertif.shtml; 256: The Green Papers Presidential Primaries 2012 Democratic Delegate Vote Allocation. The Green Papers. Last modified 3 May 2012. http://www.thegreenpapers.com/P12/D-Del.phtml. Accessed 4 May 2012; 256: James W. Davis, Presidential Primaries, rev. ed. (Greenwood Press, 1984), Chapter 3. pp. 56–63; 256: Paul T. David and James W. Caesar, Proportional Representation in Presidential Nominating Politics (University Press of Virginia, 1980), pp. 9–11; 256: Rhodes Cook, Race for the Presidency: Winning the 2004 Nomination (CQ Press, 2004), p. 5; 256: Staff Report, Details of GOP delegate allocation, Washington Post, January 13, 2012, http://www.washingtonpost.com/wp-srv/special/politics/primary-tracker/delegate-allocation/ (accessed April 25, 2012); 258: Kevork Djansezian/Getty Images; 256: The Green Papers Republican Detailed Delegate Allocation - 2012. http://www.thegreenpapers.com/P12/R-Alloc.phtml); 256: Jeff Zeleny, Primary Calendar Stirs Republican Anxiety, New York Times, July 25, 2011, http://www.nytimes.com/2011/07/26/us/politics/26primary.html?pagewanted=all (accessed May 30, 2012); 256: Lesley Clark, "DNC Votes to Strip Florida of Delegates: Florida's Status as a Key Presidential Prize Is in Doubt, with National Democratic Party Leaders Rejecting a State Plan to Hold an Early Primary," Miami Herald, August 26, 2007; 256: Federal Election Commission, "2012 Presidential Primary Dates and Candidates Filing Deadlines for Ballot Access," March 30, 2012, http://www.fec.gov/pubrec/fe2012/2012pdates.pdf; 257: *California Democratic Party et al., Petitioners* v. *Bill Jones, Secretary of State of California et al.*, 530 U.S. 567 (2000); 257: David Redlawsk and Arthur Sanders, "Groups and Grassroots in the Iowa Caucuses," in David B. Magleby, ed., Outside Money in the 2000. Presidential Primaries and Congressional Elections, in PS: Political Science and Politics (June 2001), p. 270; 257: Perry Bacon, Jr., "Clinton Blames MoveOn for Caucus Losses," The Washington Post, blog.washingtonpost.com/the-trail/2008/04/19/clinton_blames_moveon_for_cauc.html; 257: CNN Exit Polls, http://www.cnn.com/election/2012/primariees/state; 258: Jennifer Jacobs, 2012 GOP caucus count unresolved, Des Moines Register and Tribune, January 19, 2012, http://caucuses.desmoinesregister; 259: Chris Maddaloni/CQ Roll Call/Getty Images; 260: Barry Goldwater, speech to the Republican National Convention accepting the Republican nomination for president, July 16, 1964, www.washingtonpost.com/wp-srv/politics/daily/may98/goldwaterspeech.htm.; 260: Acceptance speech at the 1980 Convention, July 17, 1980, http://www.nationalcenter.org/ReaganConvention1980.html; 260: Jeff Fishel, Presidents and Promises (CQ Press, 1984), pp. 26–28; 260: Joe Von Kanel and Hal Quinley, "Exit Polls: Obama Wins Big Among Young, Minority Voters," CNN Politics.com, November 4, 2008, http://www.cnn.com/2008/POLITICS/11/04/exit.polls/ (accessed April 28, 2010); 261: Friedman, Thomas L. Make Way for the Radical Center. The New York Times, 23 July 2011. http://www.nytimes.com/2011/07/24/opinion/sunday/24friedman.html?_r=3. Accessed 30 May 2012; 261: Americans Elect, A Statement from Americans Elect, May 17, 2012, http://www.americanselect.org/news/5-2012/release (accessed May 30, 2012); 262: http://www.debates.org/index.php?page=candidate-selection-process. Accessed April 27, 2012; 262: Commission on Presidential Debates, www.debates.org/pages/news_040617_p.html; 262: "The Great Ad Wars of 2004," New York Times, November 11, 2004, www.polisci.wisc.edu/tvadvertising/Press_Clippings/Press_Clipping_PDFs/110104% 20NYTIMES_AD_GRAPHIC.pdf; 262: David B. Magleby, "Elections as Team Sports: Spending by Candidates, Political Parties, and Interest Groups in the 2008 Election Cycle," in David B. Magleby, ed., The Change Election: Money, Mobilization, and Persuasion in the 2008 Federal Elections (Temple University Press, 2011); 263: Paul J. Richards/AFP/Getty Images/Newscom; 264: John C. Fortier and Norman J. Ornstein, "The Absentee Ballot and the Secret Ballot: Challenges for Election Reform," University of Michigan Journal of Law Reform 36 (Spring 2003), pp. 483–517; 264: Jerrold G. Rusk, "The Effect of the Australian Ballot Reform on Split Ticket Voting: 1876–1908," American Political Science Review 64 (December 1970), pp. 1220–1238; 264: John C. Fortier and Norman J. Ornstein, "The Absentee Ballot and the Secret Ballot: Challenges for Election Reform," University of Michigan Journal of Law Reform 36 (Spring 2003); 264: Lewis L. Gould, Grand Old Party: A History of the Republicans (Random House, 2003), p. 236; 264: David B. Magleby and Candice J. Nelson, The Money Chase: Congressional Campaign Finance Reform (Brookings Institution Press, 1990), pp. 13–14; 265: FEC reports from each campaign at www.fec.gov,http://fec.gov/finance/disclosure/efile_search.shtml; 266: Anthony Corrado, Thomas E. Mann, Daniel R. Ortiz, and Trevor Potter, eds., The New Campaign Finance Sourcebook (Brookings Institution Press, 2005); 266: *Davis* v. *FEC*. 128 S.Ct. 2759. (2008); 266: Elizabeth Drew, The Corruption of American Politics: What Went Wrong and Why (Carol, 1999), pp. 7–8; 266: Anthony Corrado, "Money and Politics: A History of Campaign Finance Law," in Campaign Finance Reform: A Sourcebook (Brookings Institution Press, 1997), p. 32; 266: Senate Committee on Governmental Affairs, "1997 Special Investigation in Connection with the 1996 Federal Election Campaigns," http://hsgac.senate.gov/sireport.htm; 266: *Buckley* v. *Valeo*, 424 U.S. 1 (1976); 266: David B. Magleby and Nicole Carlisle Squires, "Party Money in the 2002 Congressional Elections," in The Last Hurrah? p. 45, Figure 2–2; 266: David B. Magleby and Eric A. Smith, "Party Soft Money in the 2000 Congressional Elections," in David B. Magleby, ed., The Other Campaign: Soft Money and Issue Advocacy in the 2000 Congressional Elections, p. 29, 38; 266: *McConnell* v. *Federal Election Commission*, 540 U.S. 93 (2003); 267: Corrado, Mann, Ortiz, and Potter, The New Campaign Finance Sourcebook, p. 79; 267: David B. Magleby, ed., The Last Hurrah (Brookings Institution Press, 2004), pp. 44–45; 267: David B. Magleby, ed., The Last Hurrah (Brookings Institution Press, 2004), p. 46; David B. Magleby, "Change and Continuity in the Financing of Federal Elections," in David B. Magleby, Anthony J. Corrado, and Kelly D. Patterson, eds., Financing the

2004 Elections (Brookings Institution Press, 2006), p. 15; 268: Bipartisan Campaign Reform Act of 2002, 107th Cong., 1st sess., H.R. 2356; 268: *Citizen's United* v. *Federal Election Commission*, 558 U.S. (2010); 268: Fredereka Schouten. Obama now urges donations to super PAC backing him. USA Today. 07 Feb 2012. http://www.usatoday.com/news/politics/story/2012-02-07/obama-super-pac-reversal/53002966/1; 268: http://www.opensecrets.org/news/2012/02/fourth-quarter-campaign-finance-reports-show.html; 269: Corrado, Mann, Ortiz, and Potter, The New Campaign Finance Sourcebook, pp. 74–76; 269: Federal Election Commission, "FEC Reports on Congressional Financial Activity for 2000," press release, May 15, 2001; Federal Election Commission, " Financial Activity of General Election Congressional Candidates - 1992-2010". Accessed at www.fec.gov/press/2010_Full_summary_Data.shtml; 270: David B. Magleby, ed., Dancing Without Partners Monograph, csed.byu.edu/Publications/DancingwithoutPartners.pdf, p. 53; 270: Federal Election Commission, "FEC Reports on Congressional Financial Activity for 2000," press release, May 15, 2001; 270: Colorado Republican Federal Campaign Committee v. Federal Election Commission, 518 U.S. 604 (1996); 270: Federal Election Commission, "2009-2010 Financial Activity of All Senate and House Campaigns", includes activity through 12/31/10, www.fec.gov/press/2010_Full_summary_Data.shtml; 271: New Jersey Election Law Enforcement Commission, "Candidate Disclosure Report," http://www.elec.state.nj.us/ELECReport/StandardSearch.aspx; 271: David B. Magleby, ed., The Change Election (Philadelphia: Temple University Press), 13; 271: Jose Antonia Vargas, "Campaign.USA: With the Internet Comes a New Political 'Clickocracy,'" The Washington Post, April 1, 2008, p. C01; 273: Michael McDonald, "2008 Presidential Primary Turnout Rates," United States Election Project at George Mason University; 274: John Avion, "Why has GOP turnout taken a dive?". CNN Opinion. 08 Feb 2012. http://articles.cnn.com/2012-02-08/opinion/opinion_avlon-gop-turnout-down_1_gop-turnout-turnout-numbers-republican-rank?_s=PM:OPINION; 274: Rick Hampson, "Former Banker Was Big Spender," USA Today, November 9, 2000, p. A9; 274: Curtis B. Gans, director, Committee for the Study of the American Electorate, personal communication, September 22, 2004; 274: The President's Commission for a National Agenda for the Eighties, in A National Agenda for the Eighties (U.S. Government Printing Office, 1980), p. 97

CHAPTER 9 Page 280: Ashley Parker, "For Campaigns, Twitter is Both an Early-Warning System and a Weapon." New York Times, January 29, 2011, p. A15; 280: David Plouffe, The Audacity to Win (Penguin Group, 2009), p. 237; 281: Justin Sullivan/Getty Images; 283: Seema Mehta, "The Rise of the Internet Electorate." Los Angeles Times, April 18, 2011. Accessed 1.24.12; 283: Lee Rainie and Aaron Smith, "The Internet and the 2008 Election," Pew Internet and American Life Project, June 15, 2008, http://pewinternet.org/Reports/2008/The-Internet-and-the-2008-Election/01-Summary-of-Findings.aspx (accessed January 26, 2012); 283: Pew Research Center for the People & the Press, "Far More Voters Believe Election Outcome Matters," questionnaire, May 9, 2006, http://people-press.org/reports/print.php3?PageID=802; 284: REUTERS/Shannon Stapleton; 286: Pew Research Center's Project for Excellence in Journalism, "Key Findings," The State of the News Media: 2011 http://stateofthemedia.org/2011/overview-2/key-findings/ (accessed January 25, 2012). copyright 2011; 286: Pew Research Center's Project for Excellence in Journalism, "Key Findings," The State of the News Media: 2011 http://stateofthemedia.org/2011/overview-2/key-findings/ (accessed January 25, 2012). copyright 2011; 286: Andrew Kohut, Internet's Broader Role in Campaign 2008, Pew Internet and the American Life Project, January 11, 2008, http://www.pewinternet.org/Reports/2008/The-Internet-Gains-in-Politics/Summary-of-Findings.aspx, p. 2; 288: Bloomberg/Getty Images; 290: Pew Internet & America Project. 2011 Data. Accessed at http://pewinternet.org/Press-Releasees/2011/How-People-Learn-About-Their-Local-Community.aspx on February 7, 2012; 290: Pew Internet & American Life Project, "Teens and Technology." July 27, 2005. Accessed at www .pewinternet.org/pdfs/PIP_Teens_Tech_July2005web.pdf on May 12, 2006; 290: Pew Research Center for the People & the Press, "Americans Spending More Time Following the News," September 12, 2010, http://www.people-press.org/2010/09/12/americans-spending-more-time-following-the-news/ (accessed January 30, 2012); 290: Pew Research Center for the People & the Press, Survey Reports, "Bottom-Line Pressures Now Hurting Coverage, Say Journalists" May 23, 2004; 291: Quoted in Frank Luther Mott, American Journalism, 3rd ed. (Macmillan, 1962), p. 412; 292: Bettmann/Corbis; 292: Frances Perkins, quoted in James MacGregor Burns, Roosevelt: The Lion and the Fox (1956), p. 205. (c) James MacGregor Burns; 293: Bettmann/Corbis; 295: Kat Woronowicz/ZUMA Press/Newscom; 295: "FCC Issues 12th Annual Report to Congress on Video Competition," press release, February 10, 2006, hraunfoss.fcc.gov/edocs_public/attachmatch/DOC-263763A1.pdf (accessed May 11, 2006; 296: REUTERS/Handout; 298: Rick Lyman, "Multimedia Deal: The History; 2 Commanding Publishers, 2 Powerful Empires," New York Times, March 14, 2000, p. C16; 298: David Broder, "Beware of the 'Insider' Syndrome: Why Newsmakers and News Reporters Shouldn't Get Too Cozy," The Washington Post, December 4; 299: The Kaiser Foundation, The Role of Polls in Policy Making, Combined Topline Results, June 2001, p. 27, www.kff.org/kaiserpolls/loader.cfm?url=/commonspot/security/getfile.cfm&PageID=13842; 300: Pew Research Center for the People & the Press, "July 2009 Political-Media Survey" dataset, people-press.org/data archive; 300: Sacred Heart University poll on media and politics, November 2007; data compiled by Jerry Lindsay, April 30, 2008; 303: Jim Watson/AFP/Getty Images; 304: Emmanuel Dunand/AFP/Getty Images; 305: John H. Aldrich, Before the Convention (University of Chicago Press, 1980), p. 65; 306: Adapted from Martha Joynt Kumar, "Presidential Press Conferences: The Importance and Evolution of an Enduring Forum," Presidential Studies Quarterly 35, No. 1 (March 2005); and Kumar 2006, 2007, 2008, and 2010; 308: Quoted in Herbert Schmertz, "The Making of the Presidency," Presidential Studies Quarterly 16 (Winter 1986), p. 25

CHAPTER 10 Page 312: http://www.treasurydirect.gov/govt/reports/pd/histdebt/histdebt_histo5.htm; 313: Andrew Gombert/EPA/Newscom; 315: Joseph J. Schatz, "Debt Bill Brings Relief, Frustration," CQ Weekly, August 8, 2001, 1758; 316: Charles Warren, The Making of the Constitution (Little, Brown, 1928), p. 195; 317: David B. Magleby, Last Hurrah? Soft Money and Issue Advocacy in the 2002 Elections (Brookings Institution Press,2004); 318: Felicia Sonmez, Toomey, McCaskill to call for permanent earmark ban, Washington Post, 2011; 318: AP Photo/Steven Senne; 319: Jennifer E. Manning, "Membership of the 112th Congress: A Profile," Congressional Research Service, March 1, 2011; 320: Jennifer E. Manning, "Membership of the 112th Congress: A Profile," Congressional Research Service, March 1, 2011; 320: R. P. Fairfield, The Federalist Papers (Doubleday, 1961), p. 160; 321: Roger H. Davidson and Walter J. Oleszek, Congress and Its Members, 10th ed. (CQ Press, 2005); 321: Alexander Nemenov/AFP/Getty Images; 324: Obama's Challenge in the Muslim World: Arab Spring Fails to Improve U.S. Image, PEW Research Center, Pew Global Attitudes Project, May 17, 2011, p. 65; 325: United States Senate; 326: Sarah A. Binder and Steven S. Smith, Politics or Principles? Filibustering in the United States Senate (Brookings Institution Press, 1997); 326: Helen Dewar, "Senate Filibuster Ends with Talk of Next Stage in Fight," Washington Post, November 15, 2003, p. A9; 328: AP Photo/Harry Hamburg; 328: Joel D. Aberbach, Keeping a Watchful Eye: The Politics of Congressional Oversight (Brookings, 1991); 328: "Résumé of Congressional Activity, 105th Congress," Congressional Record, Daily Digest, January 19, 1999, p. D29; 328: Davidson and Oleszek, Congress and Its Members, CQ Press, 2003; 329: cZUMA Press/Newscom; 329: Sarah A. Binder, Thomas E. Mann, and Molly Reynolds, One Year Later: Is Congress Still the Broken Branch? (Brookings Institution Press, 2008); 329: "Resume of Congressional Activity," First Session of the 112th Congress, Congressional Record, December 1, 2011, p. D1305; 330: Alex Wong/Getty Images; 332: House panel takes step to force college football playoff, USA Today, 2009, http://www.usatoday.com/sports/college/football/2009-12-09-bcs-congress_N.htm; 332: Edward Bear, Congress Bill To Determine College Football Postseason, Bleacher Report, 2009; 333: Davidson and Oleszek, Congress and Its Members, CQ Press, 2003, p. 30; 333: Nelson Polsby, "The Institutionalization of the U.S. House of Representatives," American Political Science Association (March 1968), pp. 144–168; 333: Herbert Asher, "The Learning of Legislative Norms," American Political Science Review 67 (June 1973), pp. 499–513; 333: Nicol C. Rae, Colton C. Campbell, eds. New Majority or Old Minority?: The Impact of Republicans on Congress. Lanham, Md.: Rowman & Littlefield Publishers, 1999; 335: Statistics from congressional Web sites (www.senate.gov; www.house.gov); see also the Library of Congress Web site (thomas.loc.gov); 335: "Poll Readings," National Journal, October 9, 1999, p. 2917. Vol. 31, No. 41; 336: Richard E. Cohen, "Vote Ratings," National Journal, February 21, 2005, p. 426; 336: Mark Wilson/Getty Images; 337: Joseph I. Lieberman, In Praise of Public Life (Simon & Schuster, 2000), p. 109.; 337: Catherine Richert, "Party Unity: United We Stand Opposed," Congressional Quarterly Weekly, January 14, 2008, p. 143; 337: U.S. Government Printing Office, Senate S. 1, Honest Leadership and Open Government Act of 2007, passed September 14, 2007; 338: Zoe Fox, Study: Half of Facebook Users Post Political Messages, Mashable, 11-21-2011, http://mashable.com/2011/11/21/social-media-politics/; 338: Bill Clark/Roll Call Photos/Newscom; 339: AP Photo/U.S. Attorney's office

CHAPTER 11 Page 344: Mona El-Naggar, "Former Tunisian Leader Faces Legal Charges," New York Times, April 14, 2011; 345: Pete Souza/The White House/AP Inmages; 347: AP Images/J. Scott Applewhite; 348: Leif Skoogfors/Corbis; 348: The Federalist Papers, The Federalist, No.70; 349: Dr. Paul Light, Vice Presidential Power: Advice and Influence in the White House, The Johns Hopkins University Press (November 1, 1983); 350: Richard Pious, The American Presidency (Basic Books, 1978); 350: Cecil Stoughton/Corbis; 352: AP Photo/Yonhap; 353: See Al Kamen, "For Bush, the Fun Begins at Recess," Washington Post, June 29, 2007, p. A19; for a scholarly argument about this power, see the paper by Michael B. Rappaport, "The Original Meaning of the Recess Appointments Clause," October 6, 2004, at http://ssrn.com/abstract=601563; 354: See http://www.coherentbabble.com/listGWBall.htm for the George W. Bush and Barack Obama lists; 355: White House Office of the Press Secretary, "Statement by the President on H.R. 1473," April 11, 2011, p. 2; 356: Cecil Stoughton/Corbis; 357: Miles A. Pomper, "Bush Hopes to Avoid Battle with Congress over Iraq," CQ Weekly, August 31, 2002, p. 2251; 357: Louis Fisher, "Congressional Abdication on War and Spending" (Texas A&M University Press, 2000); 358: AP Images/Kyodo via AP Images; 359: *Obama through January 1, 2012 SOURCE: http://whitehouse.gov; 360: Smithsonian American Art Museum, Washington, DC/Art Resource, NY; 362: The White House Transition Project; 363: http://whitehouse.gov; 365: Pete Souza/White House via Getty Images; 366: U.S. Favorability Ratings Remain Positive: China Seen Overtaking U.S. as Global Superpower, Pew Research Center, 4-13-2011; 367: Presidential Power and the Modern Presidents: The Politics of Leadership from Roosevelt to Reagan, Free Press; Revised edition (March 1, 1991); 368: "Fewer are Angry at Government, But Discontent Remains High," Pew Research Center For the People & the Press, March 3, 2001; 369: Dirck Halstead/Time & Life Pictures/Getty Images; 370: GL Archive/Alamy; 370: Bob Daemmrich/Alamy; 372: Presidential Approval Ratings, 1953–2012, Gallop Research Reports, 2012; 373: Inside the White House: Letters to the President, White House Blog. August 3, 2009. Accessed at http://www.whitehouse.gov/video/nside-the-White-House-Letters-to-the-President

CHAPTER 12 Page 379: Justin Stumberg/AP Images; 382: The Granger Collection, NYC; 382: Stanley Elkins and Eric McKitrick, The Age of Federalism (Oxford University Press, 1993), pp. 50–51; 382: See John A. Rohr, To Run a Constitution: The Legitimacy of the Administrative State (University of Kansas Press, 1986); 382: Paul C. Light, A Government Ill Executed: The Decline of the Federal Service and How to Reverse It (Harvard University Press, 2008), Chapter 7; 382: Paul C. Light, A Government Ill Executed: The Decline of the Federal Service and How to Reverse It, Harvard University Press, 2009; 384: U.S. Department of Homeland Security; 385: AP Photo/Evan Vucci; 385: James Fesler and Donald Kettl, The Politics of the Administrative Process (Chatham House, 1991); 386: Annual Report on the Federal Workforce, Fiscal year 2009, Government Printing Office, 2010; 387: For an analysis of the use and abuse of the civil service system in the early twentieth century, see Stephen Skowronek, Building a New American State (Cambridge University Press, 1982); 387: See Jeanne Ponessa, "The Hatch Act Rewrite," CQ Weekly, November 13, 1993, pp. 3146–3147; 387: AP Photo/Gerald Herbert; 388: Theodore J. Lowi, Jr., The End of Liberalism, 2d ed. (Norton, 1979); 389: U.S. Office of the Federal Register, "Annual Federal Register Pages Published."; 390: Office of Management and Budget, Budget of the U.S. Government, Fiscal Year 2009, Historical Tables (U.S. Government Printing Office, February 2008); 391: Morris P. Fiorina, "Flagellating the Federal Bureaucracy," Society (March–April 1983), p. 73; 391: Joel D. Aberbach, Keeping a Watchful Eye: The Politics of Congressional Oversight (Brookings Institution, 1990); 392: REUTERS/Lucas Jackson; 392: Mathew D. McCubbins and Thomas Schwartz, "Congressional Oversight Overlooked: Police Patrols versus Fire Alarms," American Journal of Political Science, vol. 28, no. 1, pp. 165-179; 392: See Paul C. Light, A Government Ill Executed: The Decline of the Federal Service and How to Reverse It (Harvard University Press, 2008); 394: The Gallup Poll Copyright © 2012 Gallup, Inc.; 396: The original types of public policy were developed by Theodore J. Lowi, "American Business, Public Policy, Case Studies, and Political Theory," World Politics 16 (1964), pp. 677–715; 397: Quoted in Gabriel Almond, G. Bingham Powell, Jr., Russell J. Dalton, and Kaare Strom, Comparative Politics Today: A World View (Longman, 2008), p. 171; 397: William Greider, "The Education of David Stockman," Atlantic (1981), p. 296; 397: John Kingdon, Agendas, Alternatives, and Public Policies (Little, Brown, 1984), p. 3; 399: Anthony Downs, "UP and down with ecology--the 'issue-attention cycle,'" Public Interest 28 (Summer 1972), p. 38. National Affairs. http://www.nationalaffairs.com/public_interest/detail/up-and-down-with-ecologythe-issue-attention-cycle; 400: www.pollingreport.com/; 401: James L. True, Bryan D. Jones, and Frank R. Baumgartner, "Punctuated-Equilibrium Theory: Explaining Stability and Change in Public Policymaking," in Paul A. Sabatier, ed., Theories of the Policy Process (Westview Press, 2007), p. 157; 401: Hugh Heclo, "Issue Networks and the Executive Establishment," in A. King, ed., The New American Political System (American Enterprise Institute, 1978), pp. 87–124; 401: Lester Salamon and Michael Lund, "The Tools Approach: Basic Analytics," in L. Salamon, ed., Beyond Privatization: The Tools of Government Action (Urban Institute Press, 1989); 402: Peter Andrews/Reuters/Landov Media; 402: See Paul C. Light, A Government Ill Executed: The Decline of the Federal Service and How to Reverse It (Harvard University Press, 2008); 402: See Cornelius Kerwin, Rulemaking: How Government Agencies Write Law and Make Policy (CQ Press, 2003); 403: Don Feria/Getty Images; 405: Bettmann/CORBIS; 406: Jason Reed/Reuters/Corbis

CHAPTER 13 Page 411: Yuri Gripas/Reuters; 413: Robert Barnes and Anne Kornblut, "It's Obama vs. the Supreme Court, Round 2, Over Campaign Finance Ruling," The Washington Post, March 11, 2010; 413: Roy P. Fairfield, ed., The Federalist Papers (Johns Hopkins University Press, 1981), p. 227; 414: Jerome Frank, Courts on Trial: Myth and Reality in American Justice (Princeton University Press, 1949); 415: AP Photo/Charles Dharapak; 416: U.S. Government Printing Office, Year-End Report on the Federal Judiciary; 416: REUTERS/Handout; 418: Court Statistics Project, National Center for State Courts, http://www.courtstatistics.org/Overview; 419: Roy P. Fairfield, ed., The Federalist Papers (Johns Hopkins University Press, 1981), p. 228; 420: CQ Weekly, October 10, 2005, p. 2701, updated by authors; 420: Harold W. Chase, Federal Judges: The Appointing Process (University of Minnesota Press, 1972); 420: Sarah Wilson, "Appellate Judicial Appointments During the Clinton Presidency: An Inside Perspective," The Journal of Appellate Practice and Process 5:1(Spring 2003), pp. 36-39; 421: Chip Somodevilla/Getty Images; 421: David M. O'Brien, "Ironies and Disappointments: Bush and Federal Judgeships," in Colin Campbell and Bert A. Rockman, eds., The George W. Bush Presidency (CQ Press, 2004), pp. 133–157; 422: Mark Wilson/Getty Images; 422: Brendan Smialowski/Getty Images; 422: Stefan Zaklin/EPA/Newscom; 422: Sheldon Goldman, Elliot Slotnick, Genard Gryski, and Sara Schiavoni, "Picking Judges in Time of Turmoil: W. Bush's Judiciary During the 109th Congress," American Judicature Society (May–June 2007); 423: Brannon P. Denning, "The Judicial Confirmation Process and the Blue Slip," Judicature (March–April 2002), pp. 218–226; 423: Russell Wheeler, "Judicial Nominations and Confirmations after Three Years—Where do Things Stand?" Governance Studies at Brookings. The Brookings Institution, January 13, 2012; 423: Scott E. Graves and Robert M. Howard, Justice Takes a Recess: Judicial Appointments from George Washington to George W. Bush (Lexington Books, 2009); 423: Reprinted with the permission of the American Judicature Society. Lisa M. Holmes and Roger E. Hartley, "Increasing Senate Scrutiny of Lower Federal Court Nominees," Judicature (May–June 1997), p. 275; 423: George Watson, John Stookey, Supreme Court Confirmation Hearings: A View From the Senate, Judicature (December 1987– January 1988), American Judicature Society; 423: Barbara A. Perry and Henry J. Abraham, "A 'Representative' Supreme Court? The Thomas, Ginsburg, and Breyer Appointments," Judicature (January– February 1998), pp. 158–165; 425: Donald Santarelli, quoted in Jerry Landauer, "Shaping the Bench," The Wall Street Journal, December 10, 1970, p. 1; 28: Lee Epstein, Jeffrey A. Segal, Harold J. Spaeth, and Thomas G. Walker, The Supreme Court Compendium: Data, Decisions, and Developments (CQ Press, 2007); 428: AP Photo/Dana Verkouteren; 429: Tony Mauro, "The Supreme Court as Quiz Show," Recorder (December 8, 1993), p. 10; 429: From NEUBAUER/MEINHOLD Judicial Process, 5E. © 2010 Wadsworth, a part of Cengage Learning, Inc. Reproduced by permission. www.cengage.com/permissions; 429: Forrest Maltzman, James F. Spriggs III, and Paul Wahlbeck, Crafting Law on the Supreme Court: The Collegial Game (Cambridge University Press, 2000); 429: Charles Evans Hughes, The Supreme Court of the United States (Columbia University Press, 1966), p. 68; 429: Daniel M. Berman, It Is So Ordered: The Supreme Court Rules on School Segregation (Norton, 1986), p. 114; 429: David M. O'Brien, Storm Center: The Supreme Court in American Politics, 7th ed. (Norton, 2005), pp. 262–272; 429: The U.S. Supreme Court, Public Opinion, and Abortion, The American Political Science Review; 430: William H. Rehnquist, quoted in John R. Vile, "The Selection and Tenure of Chief Justices," Judicature (September–October 1994), p. 98; 431: Pew Research Center's Global Attitudes Project; 431: David Danelski, "The Influence of the Chief Justice in the Decisional Process of the Supreme Court," in Thomas P. Jahnige and Sheldon Goldman, eds., The Federal Judicial System: Readings in Process and Behavior (Holt, Rinehart and Winston, 1968), p. 148; 432: David Hume Kennerly/Getty Images; 432: David M. O'Brien, Storm Center: The Supreme Court in American Politics, 7th ed. (Norton, 2005), Chapter 3; 432: Todd C. Peppers, Courtiers of the Marble Palace: The Rise and Influence of the Supreme Court Law Clerk (Stanford University Press, 2006); 432: Lincoln Caplan, The Tenth Justice: The Solicitor General and the Rule of Law (Knopf, 1987); 433: Gregory A. Caldeira and John R. Wright, "Organized Interest and Agenda Setting," American Political Science Review 82 (December 1988), p. 1110; 433: Paul M. Collins, Jr., Friends of the Supreme Court: Interest Groups and Judicial Decision Making (Oxford University Press, 2008); 433: *National Federation of Independent Business* v. *Sebelius* 567 U.S. (2012); Lichtbau, Eric, "Groups Blanket Supreme Court on Health Care," *New York Times*, March 14, 2012. 433: AP Photo/Haraz N. Ghanbari; 434: Gerald N. Rosenberg, Hollow Hope: Can Courts Bring About Sound Change? (University of Chicago Press, 1991); 434: J. W. Peltason, Fifty-Eight Lonely Men: Southern Federal Judges and School Desegregation (University of Illinois Press, 1971); 434: William O. Douglas, quoted in O'Brien, Storm Center, p. 184; 434: Lee Epstein, Jeffrey A. Segal, Harold J. Spaeth, and Thomas G. Walker, The Supreme Court Compendium: Data, Decisions, and Developments, 4th ed. (CQ Press, 2007). Data through 2005–2006 Supreme Court term; 434: See Keith Perine, "Precedent Heeded, but Not Revered on High Court," CQ Weekly, November 28, 2005, pp. 3180–3184; 435: See Shawn Francis Peters, Judging the Jehovah's Witnesses (University of Kansas Press, 2002); 435: J. W. Peltason, "The Supreme Court: Transactional or Transformational Leadership," in Michael R. Beschloss and Thomas E. Cronin, eds., Essays in Honor of James MacGregor Burns (Prentice Hall, 1988), pp. 165–180; 436: Edward White, "The Supreme Court of the United States," American Bar Association Journal 7 (1921), p. 341

CHAPTER 14 Page 440: Website of the Westboro Baptist Church, http://www.godhatesfags.com/wbcinfo/aboutwbc.html. Last accessed on May 7, 2012; 440: Lyle Denniston, "Court to Rule on Funeral Pickets," SCOTUSBlog, March 8, 2010. http://www.scotusblog.com/?p=17263; 441: Nati Harnik/AP Images; 443: Jeffrey Smith, War and Press Freedom (Oxford University Press, 1999); 444: AP Photo/Andres Leighton; 445: Richard C. Cortner, The Supreme Court and the Second Bill of Rights: The Fourteenth Amendment and the Nationalization of Civil Liberties (University of Wisconsin Press, 1981); 447: Pew Research Center, "National Global Attitudes Survey," October 4, 2007; 447: U.S. State Department, Bureau of Democracy, Human Rights, and Labor. "International Religious Freedom Report 2009," October 26, 2009; 448: Alex Wong/Getty Images; 452: AP PHOTO/Charles Tasnadi; 449: Reprinted from the U.S. Religious Landscape Survey Religious Affiliation: Diverse and Dynamic. Pew Research Center's Forum on Religion & Public Life, © 2008, Pew Research Center. http://religions.pewforum.org/pdf/report-religious-landscape-study-full.pdf; 453: AP Photo/Nick Ut; 454: Heather Gautney. "What is Occupy Wall Street? This History of Leaderless Movements," The Washington Post, October 10, 2011; 454: Andrew Grossman, Alison Fox and Sean Gardiner. "Wall Street Protestors Evicted From Camp," The Wall Street Journal. November 16, 2011; 454: Don Emmert/AFP/Getty Images; 455: Richard A. Epstein, Taking: Private Property and the Power of Eminent Domain (Harvard University Press, 1985); 457: Philip B. Kurland, Some Reflections on Privacy and the Constitution (University of Chicago Center for Policy Study, 1976); 457: Copyright (c) 2012 Gallup, Inc. All rights reserved. The content is used with permission; however, Gallup retains all rights of republication; 459: Scott Olson/Getty Images; 460: Barry Friedman, "Privacy, Technology and the Law," The New York Times, January 28, 2012; 460: Senate Committee on the Judiciary, the Jury, and the Search for Truth: The Case Against Excluding Relevant Evidence at Trial, Hearing Before the Committee, 104th Cong., 1st sess. (U.S. Government Printing Office, 1997); 461: Bettmann/Corbis; 463: Death Penalty Information Center; 463: Number of Executions by Year, 1976-2010. Death Penalty Information Center, Accessed at http://www.deathpenaltyinfo.org; 465: Barry Scheck, Peter Neufeld, and Jim Dwyer, Actual Innocence: Five Days to Execution and Other Dispatches from the Wrongly Convicted (Doubleday, 2000); 465: Death Penalty Information Center, "Innocence and the Death Penalty," April 23, 2012; 465: Charlie Savage, "Deal Reached on Extension of Patriot Act," The New York Times. May 19, 2011; 467: AP Photo/The Courier, Eric S. Swist; 467: Louis Fisher, Religious Liberties in America: Political Safeguards (University Press of Kansas, 2002)

CHAPTER 15 Page 472: Christopher B. Swanson, "High School Graduation in Texas," Editorial Projects in Education Research Center, October 2006; 472: Scott Jaschik, "10 Percent Plan Survives in Texas," Inside Higher Ed. May 29, 2007; 473: Marsha Miller/AP Images; 475: *Parents Involved in Community Schools* v. *Seattle*, 551 U.S. 701 (2007); 476: Andrew Hacker, Two Nations: Black and White, Separate, Hostile, Unequal (Scribner, 1992); 477: Slaughter-House Cases, 83 U.S. 36 (1873); 477: *Korematsu* v. *United States*, 323 U.S. 214 (1944); 477: *Reid* v. *Covert*, 354 U.S. 1 (1957); 477: *Boumediene* v. *Bush*, 553 U.S. 723 (2008); 478: Carl Mydans/Time & Life Pictures/Getty Images; 478: *Mathews* v. *Diaz*, 426 U.S. 67 (1976); and *Shaughnessy* v. *United States* ex rel. Mezei, 345 U.S. 206 (1953); 478: *Yick Wo* v. *Hopkins*, 118 U.S. 356 (1886); *Kwong Hai Chew* v. *Colding*, 344 U.S. 590 (1953); *Zadvydas* v. *Davis*, 533 U.S. 678 (2001); *Rasul* v. *Bush*, 542 U.S. 466 (2004); and *Hamdi* v. *Rumsfeld*, 542 U.S. 507 (2004); 478: *Foley* v. *Connelie*, 435 U.S. 291 (1978); *Ambach* v. *Norwick*, 441 U.S. 68 (1979); *Cabell* v. *Chavez-Salido*, 454 U.S. 432 (1982); 481: Taylor Branch, Parting the Waters: America in the King Years, 1954–1963 (Simon & Schuster, 1988); 481: David Remnick, The Bridge: The Life and Rise of Barack Obama (Knopf, 2010); 482: Francis Miller/ Time & Life Pictures/Getty Images; 482: Ellen Carol Du Bois, Feminism and Suffrage: The Emergence of an Independent Women's Movement in America, 1848–1869 (Cornell University Press, 1978); 482: Susan M. Hartmann, From Margin to Mainstream: American Women and Politics Since 1960 (Temple University Press, 1989); 483: World Public's Welcome Global Trade - But Not Immigration, Pew Research Center Global Attitudes Project (10-2007); 483: David A. Cotter, Joan M. Hermsen, Seth Ovadia and Reeve Vanneman, 2001. "The Glass Ceiling Effect," Social Forces, 80(2): 655-681; 484: Avi Astor, 2009. "Unauthorized Immigration, Securitization, and the Making of Operation Wetback," Latino Studies 7:5-29; 484: U.S. Department of Education, National Center for Education Statistics, Earned Degrees Conferred, 1869–1870 through 1964–1965; Projections of Education Statistics to 2016; Higher Education General Information Survey (HEGIS), "Degrees and Other Formal Awards Conferred" surveys, 1965–1966 through 1985–1986; and 1986–1987 through 2005–2006, Integrated Postsecondary Education Data System, "Completions Survey" (IPEDS-C:87–99), and Fall 2000 through Fall 2006; 485: AP Photo/Ross D. Franklin; 485: Celia W. Dugger, "U.S. Study Says Asian Americans Face Widespread Discrimination," New York Times, February 29, 1992, p. 1, reporting on U.S. Civil Rights Commission, Civil Rights Issues Facing Asian Americans in the 1990s (U.S. Government Printing Office, 1992); 486: "Assimilation, Relocation, Genocide: The Trail of Tears," Indian Country Diaries, PBS, November 2006, www.pbs.org/indiancountry/history/trail.html; 488: Matthew Bosworth, Courts as Catalysts: State Supreme Courts and Public School Finance Equity (State University of New York Press, 2001); 488: Molly A. Hunter, "Requiring States to Offer a Quality Education to All Students," American Bar Association Human Rights Magazine (Fall 2005) pp. 10-12; 489: AP Photo/Rich Pedroncelli; 491: Leon F. Litwack, Trouble in Mind: Black Southerners in the Age of Jim Crow (1998), p. 227, as cited in James W. Fox, Jr., "Intimations of Citizenship: Repressions and Expressions of Equal Citizenship in the Era of Jim Crow," Howard University Law Journal (Fall 2006); 491: Harold W. Stanley, Voter Mobilization and the Politics of Race: The South and Universal Suffrage, 1952–1984 (Praeger, 1987); 491: Abigail M. Thernstrom, Whose Votes Count? Affirmative Action and Minority Voting Rights (Harvard University Press, 1987), p. 15; 492: Abigail M. Thernstrom, Whose Votes Count? Affirmative Action and Minority Voting Rights (Harvard University Press, 1987); 493: Library of Congress; 494: William Thomas Cain/Getty Images; 495: Andrew Martin, "Female Wal-Mart Employees File New Bias Case," The New York Times (October 27, 2011); 495: Darryl Van Duch, "Plagued by Politics, EEOC Backlog Grows," Recorder (August 18, 1998), p. 1; 497: AP Photo; 497: Gary Orfield, Susan E. Eaton, and the Harvard Project on School Desegregation, Dismantling Desegregation: The Quiet Reversal of Brown v. Board of Education (New Press, 1996); 497: Raymond Hernandez, "NAACP Suspends Yonkers Leader After Criticism of Usefulness of School Busing," New York Times, November 1, 1995, p. A13; 497: Gary Orfield and Chungmei Lee, Brown at 50: King's Dream or Plessy's Nightmare? (Civil Rights Project, Harvard University, 2004), http://www.civilrightsproject.ucla.edu/research/reseg04/brown50.pdf; 497: Richard Kahlenberg, All Together Now: Creating Middle-Class Schools Through Public School Choice (Brookings Institution Press, 2003); 498: Danny Moloshok/AP Images; 500: University of Texas at Austin, Office of Admissions, *2007 Top Ten Percent Report*; of *2011 Top Ten Percent Report*; 499: Scott Jaschik, "Michigan Votes Down Affirmative Action," Inside Higher Education (November 8, 2006), www.insidehighered.com/news/2006/11/08/Michigan; 499: Tamar Lewin, "Court Overturns Michigan Affirmative Action Ban," The New York Times, July 1, 2011; 499: James Farmer, quoted in Rochelle L. Stanfield, "Black Complaints Haven't Translated into Political Organization and Power," National Journal (June 14, 1980), p. 465; 499: John Logan, "Separate and Unequal: The Neighborhood Gap for Blacks, Hispanics and Asians in Metropolitan America," US2010 Project, July 2011. http://www.s4.brown.edu/us2010/Data/Report/report0727.pdf, accessed May 24, 2012; 499: Peter Whoriskey, "Wealth Gap Widens Between Whites, Minorities, Report Says," The Washington Post. July 26, 2011; 499: William J. Wilson, The Truly Disadvantaged: The Inner City, the Underclass, and Public Policy (University of Chicago Press, 1987); 499: Gary Orfield and Carole Ashkinaze, The Closing Door: Conservative Policy and Black Opportunity (University of Chicago Press, 1991), pp. 221–234

CHAPTER 16 Page 505: Don Emmert/AFP/Getty Images; 509: Unemployment in the U.S. Economy 1970-2012, Bureau of Labor Statistics. January 12, 2012. Accessed at http://data.bls.gov/timeseries/LNS14000000; 511: Pew Research Center's Global Attitudes Project, U.S. Favorability Ratings Remain Positive China Seen Overtaking U.S. as Global Superpower, July, 2011; 512: Summary Tables, Budget of the United States, Fiscal Year 2011, (U.S. Government Printing Office, 2010); 513: Summary Tables, Budget of the United States, Fiscal Year 2009 (U.S. Government Printing Office, 2008); 515: William Philpott/AFP/Getty Images; 516: REUTERS/Pascal Rossignol; 517: AP Photo/Richard Drew; 517: Federal Reserve Board, Open Market Operation; 520: AP Photo/Wen Zi/Color China Photo; 523: John Moore/Getty Images; 524: Rick Wilking/Reuters/Landov Media; 526: U. S. Census Bureau; 526: U. S. Census Bureau; 527: Don Emmert/AFP/Getty Images/Newscom; 529: AP Photo/M. Spencer Green, File

CHAPTER 17 Page 536: Budget of the U.S. Government, Fiscal Year 2012, Historical Tables. Accessed at http://www.whitehouse.gov/sites/default/files/omb/budget/fy2012; 537: REUTERS/Lucy Nicholson; 539: Kaiser Family Foundation, Health Reform Source, "Implementation Timeline," available at http://healthreform.kff.org/Timeline.aspx; 539: July Appleby, "Concern Growing Over Deadlines for Health-Care Exchanges," Washington Post, December 11, 2011, available at http://www.washingtonpost.com/politics/concern-growing-over-deadlines-for-health--care-exchanges/2011/12/16/gIQA51cX3O_story.html; 539: Michael B. Katz, In the Shadow of the Poorhouse: A Social History of Welfare in America (Basic Books, 1986); 539: Theda Skocpol "America's First Social Security System: The Expansion of Benefits for Civil War Veterans," Political Science Quarterly 108 (Winter 1993), pp. 64–87; 542: Matthew Cavanaugh/epa/Corbis; 542: U.S. Department of Health and Human Services aspe.hhs.gov/poverty/07poverty.shtml; 542: Gertrude Schaffner Goldberg and Eleanor Kremen, eds., The Feminization of Poverty: Only in America? (Greenwood Press, 1990); 543: U.S. Government Printing Office: Historical Tables; 544: Margaret Weir, "Political Parties and Social Policymaking," in Margaret Weir, ed., The Social Divide: Political Parties and the Future of Activist Government (Brookings Institution Press, 1998); 544: Bettmann/Corbis; 545: Martha Derthick, "No More Easy Votes for Social Security," Brookings Review 10 (Fall 1992), pp. 50–53; 547: David Buffington/Photodisc/Getty Images; 547: Lyndon Johnson, speech at the University of Michigan, May 1964, in Congress and the Nation, 1965–1968: A Review of Government and Politics During the Johnson Years (CQ Press, 1969), Vol. 2, p. 650; 549: William J. Clinton, acceptance speech, Democratic National Convention, Chicago, July 6, 1992; 549: Bob Daemmrich/The Image Works; 550: Robert Pear, "Judge Rules States Can't Cut Welfare," New York Times, October 14, 1997, p. A1; 551: Historical Tables, Budget of the United States, Fiscal Year 2011 (U.S. Government Printing Office, February 2011); 552: Matt McClain/For The Washington Post via Getty Images; 552: Centers for Medicare and Medicaid Services, "Health Accounts," Accessed at www.cms.hhs.gov; 553: http://www.usgovernmentspending.com/; 553: U.S. Census Bureau, www.census.gov; 554: Centers for Medicare and Medicaid Services, Office of the Actuary, National Statistics Group, http://www.cms.hhs.gov/NationalHealthExpendData/downloads/highlights.pdf; 555: AP Photo/Chrysler LLC, Reinhold Matay/PRNewsFoto; 556: Washington Post/Getty Images; 558: Ricky Carioti/The Washington Post/Getty Images

CHAPTER 18 Page 562: Tom Shanker, Michael S. Schmidt, and Robert F. Worth, "In Baghdad, Panetta Leads Uneasy Moment of Closure," New York Times, December 15, 2011; 562: "Remarks by the President and First Lady on the End of the Iraq War." December 14, 2011. Accessed at http://www.whitehouse.gov/the-press-office/2011/12/14/remarks-president-and-first-lady-end-war-iraq; 563: Christian Murdock/The Gazette/AP Images; 565: Brookings Institution; 567: REUTERS/Goran Tomasevic; 568: Glenn Kessler, "Rice Lays Out Case for War in Iraq," The Washington Post, August 16, 2002, p. A1; 569: Joseph Nye, Soft Power: The Means to Success in World Politics (Public Affairs, 2005); 569: AFP/Getty Images; 570: Reuters/DigitalGlobe/Landov Media; 571: Patrick Gely/Imapress/The Image Works; 573: Pew Research Center's Global Attitudes Project, http://www.pewglobal.org/database/?indicator=16; 573: Pew Research Center's Global Attitudes Project; 573: Views on Trade: Pew Global Attitudes Project: Pew Global Research Center; 574: REUTERS/Chor Sokunthea: Key Indicators Database; 576: Shaun Heasley/Reuters/Corbis; 577: National Commission on Terrorist Attacks on the United States, The 9/11 Commission Report (Norton, 2004), p. 12; 580: Military Leadership Diversity Commission, From Representation to Inclusion, U.S. Government Printing Office, March 15, 2011; 580: Defense Department, Under Secretary of Personnel and Readiness, available athttp://prhome.defense.gov/MPP/ACCESSION%20POLICY/poprep98/intro98.pdf; 580: Public Papers of the Presidents, Dwight D. Eisenhower (U.S. Government Printing Office, 1960), pp. 1035–1040; 580: Rod Nordland, "Risks of Afghan War Shift From Soldiers to Contactors," New York Times, February 11, 2012; 581: Etienne De Malglaive/Getty Images; 582: P. W. Singer, "Winning the War of Words: Information Warfare in Afghanistan," Brookings Analysis Paper No. 5, October 2001; 582: "U.S. Foreign Aid Spending Since World War II," Public Perspective 8 (August–September 1997), p. 11; 583: REUTERS/Handout; 583: "CNN Poll: Americans Flunk Political IQ Test," available at http://politicalticker.blogs.cnn.com/2011/04/01/cnn-poll-americans-flunk-budget-iq-test/; 584: Robert Kagan, "The Kerry Doctrine," The Washington Post, August 1, 2004, p. B7; 584: Gary Hufbauer and Jeffrey J. Schott, "Economic Sanctions and Foreign Policy," PS: Political Science and Politics 18 (Fall 1985), p. 278; 584: The Washington Post, May 26, 2003

CONCLUSION Page 591: AP Photo/The Standard Times, Peter Pereira; 593: David R. Frazier/The Image Works

INDEX

Note: Page numbers followed by "t" refer to material in a table; "m" refers to a map; "f" refers to a figure; and "p" refers to a picture or its caption.

A

B

C

D

S

T

U

V

W

Y

Z

ANSWER KEY

1
1. e
2. d
3. d
4. b
5. e

2
1. a
2. c
3. d
4. b
5. c

3
1. b
2. a – shared
   b – shared
   c – delegated
   d – reserved
   e – delegated
3. e
4. b
5. a

4
1. b
2. e
3. b
4. e
5. e
6. a

5
1. e
2. c
3. d
4. b
5. a
6. b

6
1. d
2. b
3. d
4. b
5. c

7
1. a
2. c
3. b
4. a
5. c

8
1. d
2. b
3. c
4. a
5. d
6. b

9
1. b
2. c
3. c
4. b
5. c

10
1. d
2. b
3. b
4. b
5. e
6. e

11
1. c
2. e
3. c
4. d
5. e
6. d

12
1. d
2. a
3. b
4. e
5. c
6. d

13
1. b
2. c
3. c
4. b
5. a

14
1. d
2. b
3. c
4. c
5. d
6. c
7. b

15
1. b
2. c
3. c
4. d
5. a
6. b
7. a

16
1. e
2. e
3. b
4. d
5. e
6. c

17
1. c
2. d
3. a

18
1. b
2. d
3. c
4. d